HYGRADE®

CATALOG & PRICE GUIDE OF
TOPPS, BOWMAN, DONRUSS, FLEER, LEAF, SCORE, SPORTFLICS AND UPPER DECK

BASEBALL CARDS

Features card values of virtually every baseball card issued by these manufacturers:

- TOPPS—years 1951 to 1991
- BOWMAN—years 1989 to 1990
- DONRUSS—years 1981 to 1991
- FLEER—years 1981 to 1991
- LEAF—year 1990
- SCORE—years 1988 to 1991
- SPORTFLICS—years 1986 to 1991
- UPPER DECK—years 1989 to 1991

Published annually in March—
every year since 1986.

Sixth Edition (1)

Publisher: HYGRADE SPORTS CARD CO., 5 East 17th Street, New York, N.Y. 10003

General Information

Card values in this catalog represent approximate retail values as of **February, 1991.** Due to high demand, the values of popular cards (especially rookie cards of star players from the past five years) have been fluctuating every few weeks. Keep up-to-date on the latest market values with a monthly price guide.

Information on card values was compiled from various sources including dealer ads in card magazines, dealer catalogs, card auctions, offers at card conventions, etc. **The card values in this catalog do not represent an offer to buy or sell by the publisher. We are not responsible for typographical errors.**

What Makes a Card Valuable?

The value of a card is determined by *supply* (how many cards are offered for sale at a certain price), and *demand* (how many cards buyers are willing and able to purchase at a certain price). When the demand is greater than the supply, the card's value *increases;* when supply exceeds demand, the card's value *decreases.* However, as with stamps and coins, the *condition* of a card also affects its value. Cards which have been preserved in *mint* condition are much more in demand by collectors, and therefore worth more than the same cards in worn condition. If the card shows *very light wear*, its value is usually about 65% to 80% of the price for the same card in mint condition. The more wear or damage the card shows, the less it is worth. So if you eventually hope to sell your collection for a profit, try to buy cards in the best possible condition.

Rookie Cards

A *rookie* card is a player's first card from the *main* card set of a major card manufacturer. Today the major card manufacturers are Topps, Donruss, Bowman, Fleer, Leaf, Score and Upper Deck. Sometimes several players are shown on one rookie card. Occasionally a rookie card is issued one or more years after the player's actual rookie season. Each of the major manufacturers issues a main card set each year, as well as several special card sets. But in order for a card to qualify as the *rookie* card it must appear in the main card set, which is universally distributed. Sometimes special card sets, like the *Traded Update*, include a player's first card, but this card is not generally considered to be a rookie card. Traded cards are mainly distributed through card hobby dealers, unlike cards from the main set which are sold everywhere. From 1956 to 1980 Topps was the only major card manufacturer, so each player had only one rookie card. Today there are seven major card sets—so each player can have several rookie cards.

Complete Sets

The total cost of the individual cards in a set is always much greater than the complete set price—which makes the complete set an economical purchase. This is because a complete set includes many common cards, and minor-star cards which a dealer will sell at a reduced price when sold as a group. The complete set value usually does not include any error or variety cards. Factory sealed sets generally sell for a premium over hand-collated sets.

Double-Printed Cards

Baseball cards are not printed individually, but are printed on big sheets that have space for up to 132 cards. Once printed, these sheets are cut apart, and the cards are sorted and packaged. If the number of cards on a sheet is the same as the number of cards in a set, or divides evenly into that set number, then each of the cards on the sheet shows a different player. From 1973 to 1977, Topps issued baseball sets of 660 cards. These were printed on five sheets, each with 132 different cards. But beginning in 1978 and continuing until 1981, Topps changed the number of cards in its sets from 660 to 726, an increase of 66 cards. Rather than print a sixth sheet only half filled, Topps decided to *double-printed* (print twice the quantity) 66 cards in each set.

Common Cards

Common cards are the lowest valued cards in a set. They are cards that feature ordinary players, not stars or popular personalities. There is very little demand by collectors for individual common cards. They are often sold in lots and used primarily to assemble card sets. A typical Topps card set includes about 60% *common* cards, 25% *minor star* cards and 15% *star* cards.

High-Numbers

During the period from 1952 to 1973 Topps released their annual cards sets in series, rather than issuing the complete set at one time as they do now. Most Topps sets consisted of six or seven card series, each released a few weeks or months apart. For example, the first series of the 1970 Topps card set had 132 cards, numbers 1 to 132, the second series contained numbers 133 to 263, etc. Since sales of the cards tended to become less and less as the season progressed, Topps usually printed fewer of the later card series, which contained the high number cards. Because the high number cards are scarcer today, they are generally more valuable as a group, than the low number cards of the same set. If the last series is not scarce, compared to other series in the same set, it is not a high number series. Every Topps set issued from 1952 to 1973 has a high number series except years 1954, 1956, 1957, 1958 and 1969.

Several Topps card sets from 1952 to 1973 also have a *semi-high-number* series. This is the next to the last series of a card set in which there is also a high number series, and the semi-high number cards are scarce. Semi-high number cards as a group are generally worth less than high numbers, but more than low numbers. Beginning in 1974 and continuing until today, Topps changed their policy and distributed their card sets all at one time, thus eliminating high numbers.

TOPPS® SPECIAL CARD SETS

ALL STAR GLOSSY "INSERT" (2½" x 3½")

22 card set features the starting players, managers, and captains of the previous year's All-Star Game. One random card was inserted in rack packs.

1984-$5, 1985-$5, 1986-$5, 1987-$4, 1988-$4, $1989-$3

ALL STAR GLOSSY "MAIL-IN" (2½" x 3½")

From 1983 to 1985 the set consisted of 40 cards; 1986 to date—60 cards. The set was offered by Topps directly to the consumer through the mail.

1983-$13, 1984-$14, 1985-$14, 1986-$13, 1987-$13, 1988-$13, 1989-$12

ROOKIES GLOSSY (2½" x 3½")

22 card set features the top rookies from the previous season. One random card was inserted in supermarket jumbo rack packs.

1987-$10, 1988-$8

WAX BOX CARDS

Printed on the bottom of wax boxes of the main card set (except 1987 printed on the side of the box). Printed in panels of four cards per box. All sets include 16 cards (2½" x 3½") except 1987 has 8 cards (2⅛" x 3"). Values are for full panels—cut cards are worth 60% less.

1986-$10, 1987-$4 1988-$5, 1989-$4

MINI LEAGUE LEADERS (2⅛" x 2¹⁵⁄₁₆")

Features the highest rated players statistically from the previous year. All sets include 77 cards except 1986 has 66 cards.

1986-$7, 1987-$6, 1988-$6, 1989-$6

BIG BASEBALL (2⅝" x 3¾")

The design was styled after the Topps 1956 card set. Each set was distributed in wax packs and released in three different series.

1988 (264 cards)-$30, 1989 (330 cards)-$25

CHAIN STORE SETS (2½" x 3½")

Topps sold each card set exclusively to the chain stores listed below. Each set features a high gloss finish and is individually boxed. All sets include 33 cards—unless otherwise noted. Worth about $4. each.

AMES—1989 20/20 club

BOARDWALK & BASEBALL—1987 Run Makers

CIRCLE K—1985 Home Run Kings

CUMBERLAND FARMS—1989 Superstars

HILLS—1989 Team MVP's

K-MART—1982 MVP (44 cards). 1987 Stars of Decade, 1988 Memorable Moments, 1989 Dream Team

KAY BEE—1986 Young Superstars, 1987 to 1989 Superstars

REVCO—1988 League Leaders

RITE AID—1988 Team MVP's

TOYS R US—1987 to 1989 Rookies

WOOLWORTH—1985 All-Time Record Holders (44 cards). 1986 Champion Superstars, 1987 to 1989 Baseball Highlights

MISCELLANEOUS (1984 to 1989)

1989 United Kingdom (88 cards, size 2⅛" x 3")-$7

1989 Double Header All-Star (24 cards)-$18

1989 Heads Up (24 cards)

1988 United Kingdom (88 cards, size 2⅛" x 3")-$8

1986 Three Dimensional (30 cards, size 4½" x 6")-$10

1986 Supers (60 cards, 4⅞" x 6⅞")-$10

1985 Three Dimensional (30 cards, size 4½" x 6")-$15

1985 Supers (60 cards, size 4⅞" x 6⅞")-$15

1984 Supers (30 cards, size 4⅞" x 6⅞")-$10

1987 GLOSSY INSERTS

GLOSSY MAIL-INS

1989 BIG BASEBALL

1987 ROOKIES

1986 KAY-BEE

DONRUSS® SPECIAL SETS

ACTION ALL STARS (3½" x 5")
Each 60 card set features an action shot of an All Star Player. The cards were sold in wax packs.

1983-$7, 1984-$7, 1985-$7

ALL STARS
Issued in conjunction with Donruss Pop-Up cards. Each wax pack includes one Pop-Up and three All Star Cards.

1986 (60 cards, 3½" x 5")—$7
1987 60 cards (3½" x 5")—$7,
1988 (64 cards, 2½" x 3½")—$7
1989 (64 cards, 2½" x 3½")—$7

POP-UPS
Issued in conjunction with Donruss All Star cards. Each wax pack includes one Pop-Up and three All Star Cards. Features the starting lineup of the previous year's All Star Game. The cards are die-cut and fold out to stand up.

1986 (18 cards, 2½" x 5")—$7,
1987 (20 cards, 2½" x 5")—$7,
1988 (20 cards, 2½" x 3½")—$6,
1989 (20 cards, 2½" x 3½")—$6

SUPER DIAMOND KINGS (4¾" x 6¾")
These are enlarged versions of the Diamond King cards of the main card set. All sets include 28 cards. Available through the mail directly from Perez Steele Galleries.

1985-$9, 1986-$9, 1987-$9, 1988-$9, 1989-$7

BONUS MVP's (2½" x 3½")
26 card set features Donruss' selection of MVP for each team. One card was inserted in wax and rack packs.

1988-$9, 1989-$5, 1990-$4

BASEBALLS BEST (2½" x 3½")
Cards look like the main card set except they have a different color border. The 336 card set is packaged in a plastic gift tray.

1988—$20, 1989—$20

HIGHLIGHTS (2½" x 3½")
56 card glossy set features highlights of the season and Player of the Month. Packaged in a printed box.

1985-$20, 1986-$9, 1987-$7

WAX BOX CARDS (2½" x 3½")
Four cards were printed in panels on the bottom of wax and cello boxes of the main card set. All sets include four cards. Values are for panels—cut cards are worth 60% less.

1985-$7, 1986-$2, 1987-$3

"ALL STAR" WAX BOX CARDS (2½" x 3½")
Four cards were printed in panels on the bottom of wax boxes of All Star cards. All sets include four cards. Values are for full panels—cut cards are worth 60% less.

1986-$4, 1987-$3

MISCELLANEOUS (1981 to 1989)
1983 Hall of Fame Heroes (44 cards, 2½" x 3½")—$4
1984 Grand Champions (60 cards, size 3½" x 5")—$6
1987 Opening Day (272 cards, size 2½" x 3½")—$20
1989 Traded (56 cards, size 2½" x 3½")—$6

1988 ALL-STARS

1987 POP-UPS

1989 BONUS MVP's

1987 HIGHLIGHTS

FLEER® SPECIAL SETS

ALL STAR TEAM (2½" x 3½")
12 card set features Fleer's selection of players for an All Star team. One card was inserted in wax and cello packs.

1986-$16, 1987-$15, 1988-$13, 1989-$10

FUTURE HALL OF FAMERS (2½" x 3½")
6 card set features Fleer's selection of players who would probably enter the Hall of Fame. One random card was inserted in three-pack racks.

1986-$8

HEADLINERS (2½" x 3½")
6 card set features players who made news headlines the previous season. One card was inserted in rack packs.

1987-$7, 1988-$7

FOR THE RECORD (2½" x 3½")
6 card set features players who broke records in the previous season. One card was inserted in rack packs.

1989-$5

WORLD SERIES (2½" x 3½")
12 card set features highlights from the previous year's World Series. The complete set was packaged as a bonus with the Fleer factory sealed sets.

1987-$4, 1988-$4, 1989-$3, 1990-$3

WAX BOX CARDS (2½" x 3½")
Printed on the bottom of wax and cello boxes in panels of four cards per box. Values are for full panels—cut cards are worth 60% less.

1986-(8 cards)—$3, 1987—(16 cards)—$6, 1988 (16 cards)—$5, 1989 (28 cards)—$6

LEAGUE STANDOUTS (2½" x 3½")
Six card set features baseball's top players. One card was inserted in rack packs.

1990-$3

CLASSIC MINI (1⅞" x 2⅝")
120 card glossy coated set sold as a complete set and packaged in a printed box.

1986-$10, 1987-$10, 1988-$9

CHAIN STORE SETS (2½" x 3½")
Fleer sold each card set exclusively to the chain stores listed below. Each set features a high gloss finish and is individually boxed. All sets include 44 cards—worth about $4 each

BEN FRANKLIN—1987 to 1989 All Stars
CUMBERLAND FARMS—1987 to 1988 Exciting Stars
ECKERD DRUG—1987 to 1988 Record Setters
KAYBEE—1988 Team Leaders

McCRORY—1985 to 1989 Superstars, 1986 to 1988 Sluggers vs. Pitchers (some store display boxes feature cards printed on the bottom)
McCRORY—1985 to 1989 Superstars (from 1987 to 1989 six cards are printed on store display boxes); 1986 to 1988 Sluggers vs. Pitchers (six cards are printed on store display boxes).
PAY 'N SAVE—1987 Game Winners.
REVCO DRUG—1987 to 1988 Hottest Stars
7-ELEVEN—1987 to 1988 Award Winners
TOYS R US—1988 to 1989 MVP's
WALGREEN—1986 to 1989 League Leaders
WOOLWORTH—1989 Heroes of Baseball

1986 ALL-STAR TEAM

1986 FUTURE HALL OF FAMERS

1987 HEADLINERS

1988 WORLD SERIES

1986 McCRORY

SCORE® SPECIAL SETS

YOUNG SUPERSTARS (2½" x 3½")
Each set features a high gloss finish and is packaged in a printed box.

1988 Series No. 1 (40 cards)—$8, 1988 Series No. 2 (40 cards)—$8, 1989 Series No. 1 (42 cards)—$7, 1989 Series No. 2 (42 cards)—$7.

WAX BOX CARDS (2½" x 3½")
Four cards were printed in panels on the bottom of wax boxes. Values are for panels—cut cards are worth 60% less.

1988 (18 cards)—$7

HOTTEST ROOKIES (2½" x 3½")
100 card set was sold with a 48 page book featuring information about each player.

1989-$10

HOTTEST PLAYERS (2½" x 3½")
100 card set was sold with a 48 page book featuring information about each player.

1989-$8

SPORTFLICS® SPECIAL SETS

ROOKIES (2½ x 3½")
Each set was packaged in a printed box.

1986 (50 cards)-$15, 1987 series 1 (25 cards)-$8, 1987 Series 2 (25 cards)-$5

ROOKIE PROSPECTS (2½" x 3½")
Offered to hobby dealers who purchased Team Preview sets.

1987 (10 cards)-$8

TEAM PREVIEW (2½" x 3½")
Features a card for each team with outlook for the season.

1987 (26 cards)-$7

DECADE GREATS (2½" x 3½")
Features the best players at each position for each decade.

1986 (75 cards)-$15

LEGEND

R—the player's rookie card. Only rookie cards of "star" players are noted.

RR—the manufacturer's first card for that player, which is in the Traded Update or Rookie set.

*—there is a special feature of this card, which can be determined by referring to the headline for the set.

AS—a card featuring a player who was on the previous year's all-star team.

DK—abbreviation for Diamond King, which is a Donruss card with artwork by the Perez-Steele Gallery.

Mgr.—a card featuring the manager of a baseball team.

MVP—Most Valuable Player award

1951 Topps "Red Backs" . . . Complete Set of 52 Cards—Value $375.00 (Exc.); $700.00 (Near Mint)

This set, as well as the 1951 "Blue Backs", was Topps' first baseball card issue. The backs of the 2" x 2⅝" cards can be used to play a baseball card game. Card 36 was issued as either White Sox or Athletics. Card 52 was issued as either Hartford or Braves.

NO. PLAYER	NR. MT.	NO. PLAYER	NR. MT.	NO. PLAYER	NR. MT.	NO. PLAYER	NR. MT.
1 Yogi Berra	80.00	14 Wayne Terwilliger	6.00	27 Wally Westlake	6.00	40 Mike Garcia	8.00
2 Sid Gordon	5.00	15 Ralph Kiner	25.00	28 Elmer Valo	6.00	41 Whitey Lockman	6.00
3 Ferris Fain	8.00	16 Preacher Roe	10.00	29 Bob Kennedy	6.00	42 Ray Scarborough	6.00
4 Verne Stephens	9.00	17 Dave Bell	7.50	30 Warren Spahn	25.00	43 Maurice McDermott	6.00
5 Phil Rizzuto	30.00	18 Gerry Coleman	7.50	31 Gil Hodges	25.00	44 Sid Hudson	6.00
6 Allie Reynolds	11.00	19 Dick Kokos	6.00	32 Henry Thompson	6.00	45 Andy Seminick	6.00
7 Howie Pollet	6.00	20 Dominick DiMaggio	11.00	33 William Werle	6.00	46 Billy Goodman	6.00
8 Early Wynn	25.00	21 Larry Jansen	6.00	34 Grady Hatton	6.00	47 Tom Glaviano	6.00
9 Roy Sievers	10.00	22 Bob Feller	25.00	35 Al Rosen	10.00	48 Ed Stanky	8.00
10 Mel Parnell	10.00	23 Ray Boone	8.00	36 Gus Zernial*	20.00	49 Al Zarilla	6.00
11 Gene Hermanski	6.00	24 Hank Bauer	12.00	37 Wes Westrum	8.00	50 M. Irvin	25.00
12 Jim Hegan	6.00	25 Cliffe Chambers	6.00	38 Duke Snider	65.00	51 Eddie Robinson	6.00
13 Dale Mitchell	6.00	26 Luke Easter	8.00	39 Ted Kluszewski	10.00	52 Tommy Holmes*	22.00

1951 Topps "Blue Backs" . . . Complete Set of 52 Cards—Value $1000.00 (Exc.); $1750.00 (Near Mint)

Similar in format to the 1951 "Red Backs." The backs of the 2" x 2⅝" cards can be used to play a baseball card game.

NO. PLAYER	NR. MT.	NO. PLAYER	NR. MT.	NO. PLAYER	NR. MT.	NO. PLAYER	NR. MT.
1 Eddie Yost	30.00	14 George Munger	30.00	27 Andy Pafko	30.00	40 Vic Wertz	24.00
2 Hank Majeski	30.00	15 Eddie Joost	30.00	28 Harry Brecheen	30.00	41 Johnny Schmitz	30.00
3 Richie Ashburn	50.00	16 Murry Dickson	30.00	29 Granville Hamner	30.00	42 Bruce Edwards	30.00
4 Del Ennis	30.00	17 Roy Smalley	30.00	30 Enos Slaughter	70.00	43 Willie Jones	30.00
5 Johnny Pesky	24.00	18 Ned Garver	30.00	31 Lou Brissie	30.00	44 Johnny Wyrostek	30.00
6 Al Schoendienst	40.00	19 Phil Masi	30.00	32 Bob Elliott	30.00	45 Bill Pierce (R)	30.00
7 Gerald Staley	30.00	20 Ralph Branca	30.00	33 Don Lenhardt	30.00	46 Gerry Priddy	30.00
8 Dick Sisler	30.00	21 Bill Johnson	30.00	34 Earl Torgeson	30.00	47 Herman Wehmeier	30.00
9 Johnny Sain	40.00	22 Bob Kuzava	30.00	35 Tom Byrne (R)	30.00	48 Billy Cox	30.00
10 Joe Page	30.00	23 Dizzy Trout	30.00	36 Cliff Fannin	30.00	49 Hank Sauer	30.00
11 Johnny Groth	25.00	24 Sherman Lollar	30.00	37 Bobby Doerr	60.00	50 John Mize	65.00
12 Sam Jethroe	25.00	25 Sam A. Mele	30.00	38 Irv Noren	30.00	51 Ed Waitkus	30.00
13 Mickey Vernon	25.00	26 Chico Carrasquel	30.00	39 Ed Lopat	35.00	52 Sam Chapman	30.00

1952 Topps . . . Complete Set of 407 Cards—Value $17,000.00 (Exc.); $40,000.00 (Near Mint)

Features the rookie cards of Hoyt Wilhelm, Billy Martin and Eddie Mathews. This is Topps' first *major* baseball card set. Cards 1 to 80 were printed with *black* or *red* backs. The high number series is 311 to 407. Semi-high numbers are 251 to 310. Topps introduced a new card size—2⅝" x 3¾", used until 1956. Cards 48 and 49 exist with each other's backs transposed—worth $275.00 each.

NO.	PLAYER	NR. MT.
1	Andy Pafko (Exc. $100.00)	1100.00
2	James Runnels	70.00
3	Hank Thompson	50.00
4	Donald Lenhardt	50.00
5	Larry Jansen	50.00
6	Grady Hatton	50.00
7	Wayne Terwilliger	50.00
8	Fred Marsh	50.00
9	Bob Hogue	50.00
10	Al Rosen	75.00
11	Phil Rizzuto	160.00
12	Monty Basgall	50.00
13	Johnny Wyrostek	50.00
14	Bob Elliott	50.00
15	Johnny Pesky	50.00
16	Gene Hermanski	50.00
17	Jim Hegan	50.00
18	Merrill Combs	50.00
19	John Bucha	50.00
20	Billy Loes	100.00
21	Ferris Fain	50.00
22	Dom DiMaggio	80.00
23	Billy Goodman	50.00
24	Luke Easter	50.00
25	Johnny Grothe	50.00
26	Monte Irvin	100.00
27	Sam Jethroe	50.00
28	Jerry Priddy	50.00
29	Ted Kluszewski	85.00
30	Mel Parnell	50.00
31	Gus Zernial	50.00
32	Eddie Robinson	50.00
33	Warren Spahn	225.00
34	Elmer Valo	50.00
35	Hank Sauer	50.00
36	Gil Hodges	150.00
37	Duke Snider	260.00
38	Wally Westlake	50.00
39	Dizzy Trout	50.00
40	Irv Noren	50.00
41	Bob Wellman	50.00
42	Lou Kretlow	50.00
43	Ray Scarborough	50.00
44	Con Dempsey	50.00
45	Ed Joost	50.00
46	Gordon Goldsberry	50.00
47	Willie Jones	50.00
48	Joe Page*	75.00
49	Johnny Sain*	90.00
50	Marv Rickert	50.00
51	Jim Russell	50.00
52	Don Mueller	50.00
53	Chris Van Cuyk	50.00
54	Leo Kiely	50.00
55	Ray Boone	50.00
56	Tom Glaviano	50.00
57	Eddie Lopat	100.00
58	Bob Mahoney	50.00
59	Robin Roberts	125.00
60	Sid Hudson	50.00
61	Tookie Gilbert	50.00
62	Chuck Stobbs	50.00
63	Howie Pollett	50.00
64	Roy Sievers	50.00
65	Enos Slaughter	120.00
66	Preacher Roe	90.00
67	Allie Reynolds	90.00
68	Cliff Chambers	50.00
69	Virgil Stallcup	50.00
70	Al Zarilla	50.00
71	Tom Upton	50.00
72	Karl Olson	50.00
73	William Werle	50.00
74	Andy Hansen	50.00
75	Wes Westrum	50.00
76	Eddie Stanky	50.00
77	Bob Kennedy	50.00
78	Ellis Kinder	50.00
79	Gerald Staley	50.00
80	Herman Wehmeier	50.00
81	Vernon Law	20.00
82	Duane Pillette	20.00
83	Billy Johnson	20.00
84	Vern Stephens	20.00
85	Bob Kuzava	20.00
86	Teddy Gray	20.00
87	Dale Coogan	20.00
88	Bob Feller	125.00
89	Johnny Lipon	20.00
90	Mickey Grasso	20.00
91	Al Schoendienst	65.00
92	Dale Mitchell	20.00
93	Al Sima	20.00
94	Sam Mele	20.00
95	Ken Holcombe	20.00
96	Willard Marshall	20.00
97	Earl Torgeson	20.00
98	Bill Pierce	20.00
99	Gene Woodling	40.00
100	Del Rice	20.00
101	Max Lanier	20.00
102	Bill Kennedy	20.00
103	Cliff Mapes	20.00
104	Don Kolloway	20.00
105	John Pramesa	20.00
106	Mickey Vernon	20.00
107	Connie Ryan	20.00
108	Jimmy Konstanty	20.00
109	Ted Wilks	20.00
110	Dutch Leonard	20.00
111	Harry Lowrey	20.00
112	Henry Majeski	20.00
113	Dick Sisler	20.00
114	Willard Ramsdell	20.00
115	George Munger	20.00
116	Carl Scheib	20.00
117	Sherman Lollar	20.00
118	Ken Raffensberger	20.00
119	Maurice McDermott	20.00
120	Bob Chakales	20.00
121	Gus Niarhos	20.00
122	Jack Jensen	60.00
123	Eddie Yost	20.00
124	Monte Kennedy	20.00
125	Bill Rigney	20.00
126	Fred Hutchinson	20.00
127	Paul Minner	20.00
128	Don Bollweg	20.00
129	Johnny Mize	80.00
130	Sheldon Jones	20.00
131	Morris Martin	20.00
132	Clyde Klutz	20.00
133	Al Widmar	20.00
134	Joe Tipton	20.00
135	Dixie Howell	20.00
136	Johnny Schmitz	20.00
137	Roy McMillan	20.00
138	Bill MacDonald	20.00
139	Ken Wood	20.00
140	John Antonelli	20.00
141	Clint Hartung	20.00
142	Harry Perkowski	20.00
143	Les Moss	20.00
144	Edward Blake	20.00
145	Joe Haynes	20.00
146	Frank House	20.00
147	Bob Young	20.00
148	John Klippstein	20.00
149	Dick Kryhoski	20.00
150	Ted Beard	20.00
151	Wally Post	20.00
152	Al Evans	20.00
153	Bob Rush	20.00
154	Joe Muir	20.00
155	Frank Overmire	20.00
156	Frank Hiller	20.00
157	Bob Usher	20.00
158	Eddie Waitkus	20.00
159	Saul Rogovin	20.00
160	Owen Friend	20.00
161	Bud Byerly	20.00
162	Del Crandall	20.00
163	Stan Rojek	20.00
164	Walt Dubiel	20.00
165	Ed Kazak	20.00
166	Paul LaPalme	20.00
167	Bill Howerton	20.00
168	Charlie Silvera	20.00
169	Howie Judson	20.00
170	Gus Bell	20.00
171	Ed Erautt	20.00
172	Eddie Miksis	20.00
173	Roy Smalley	20.00
174	Clarence Marshall	20.00
175	Billy Martin (R)	300.00
176	Hank Edwards	20.00
177	Bill Wight	20.00
178	Cass Michaels	20.00
179	Frank Smith	20.00
180	Charley Maxwell	20.00
181	Bob Swift	20.00
182	Bill Hitchcock	20.00
183	Erv Dusak	20.00
184	Bob Ramazzotti	20.00
185	Bill Nicholson	20.00
186	Walt Masterson	20.00
187	Bob Miller	20.00
188	Clarence Podbielan	20.00
189	Harold Reiser	20.00
190	Don Johnson	20.00
191	Yogi Berra	325.00
192	Myron Ginsberg	20.00
193	Harry Simpson	20.00
194	Joe Hatten	20.00
195	Orestes Minoso (R)	65.00
196	Solly Hemus	20.00
197	George Strickland	20.00
198	Phil Haugstad	20.00
199	George Zuverink	20.00
200	Ralph Houk (R)	60.00
201	Alex Kellner	20.00
202	Joe Collins	20.00
203	Curt Simmons	20.00
204	Ron Northey	20.00
205	Clyde King	20.00
206	Joe Ostrowski	20.00
207	Mickey Harris	20.00
208	Marlin Stuart	20.00
209	Howie Fox	20.00
210	Dick Fowler	20.00
211	Ray Coleman	20.00
212	Ned Garver	20.00
213	Nippy Jones	20.00
214	Johnny Hopp	20.00
215	Hank Bauer	45.00
216	Richie Ashburn	75.00
217	George Stirnweiss	20.00
218	Clyde McCullough	20.00
219	Bobby Shantz	30.00
220	Joe Presko	20.00
221	Granny Hamner	20.00
222	Walter Evers	20.00
223	Del Ennis	20.00
224	Bruce Edwards	20.00
225	Frank Baumholtz	20.00
226	Dave Philley	20.00
227	Joe Garagiola	100.00
228	Al Brazle	20.00
229	Gene Bearden	20.00
230	Matt Batts	20.00
231	Sam Zoldak	20.00
232	Billy Cox	20.00
233	Bob Friend	20.00
234	Steve Souchock	20.00
235	Walt Dropo	20.00
236	Ed Fitzgerald	20.00
237	Jerry Coleman	20.00
238	Art Houtteman	20.00
239	Rocky Bridges	20.00
240	Jack Phillips	20.00
241	Tommy Byrne	20.00
242	Tom Poholsky	20.00
243	Larry Doby	45.00
244	Vic Wertz	20.00
245	Sherry Robertson	20.00
246	George Kell	65.00
247	Randy Gumpert	20.00
248	Frank Shea	20.00
249	Bobby Adams	20.00
250	Carl Erskine	45.00
251	Chico Carrasquel	35.00
252	Vern Bickford	35.00
253	Johnny Berardino	35.00
254	Joe Dobson	35.00
255	Clyde Vollmer	35.00
256	Pete Suder	35.00
257	Bob Avila	35.00
258	Steve Gromek	35.00
259	Bob Addis	35.00
260	Pete Castiglione	35.00
261	Willie Mays	1100.00
262	Virgil Trucks	35.00
263	Harry Brecheen	35.00
264	Roy Hartsfield	35.00
265	Chuck Diering	35.00
266	Murry Dickson	35.00
267	Sid Gordon	35.00
268	Bob Lemon	150.00
269	Willard Nixon	35.00
270	Lou Brissie	35.00
271	Jim Delsing	35.00
272	Mike Garcia	35.00

NO. PLAYER	NR. MT.	NO. PLAYER	NR. MT.	NO. PLAYER	NR. MT.	NO. PLAYER	NR. MT.
273 Erv Palica	35.00	307 Frank Campos	35.00	341 Hal Jeffcoat	150.00	375 Jack Merson	150.00
274 Ralph Branca	75.00	308 Luis Aloma	35.00	342 Clem Labine	150.00	376 Faye Throneberry	150.00
275 Pat Mullin	35.00	309 Jim Busby	35.00	343 Dick Gernert	150.00	377 Chuck Dressen	175.00
276 Jim Wilson	35.00	310 George Metkovich	35.00	344 Ewell Blackwell	150.00	378 Les Fusselman	150.00
277 Early Wynn	175.00	311 M. Mantle (Exc. $3000.00)	7000.00	345 Sammy White	150.00	379 Joe Rossi	150.00
278 Al Clark	35.00	312 Jackie Robinson	900.00	346 George Spencer	150.00	380 Clem Koshorek	150.00
279 Ed Stewart	35.00	313 Bobby Thomson	180.00	347 Joe Adcock	175.00	381 Milton Stock	150.00
280 Cloyd Boyer	35.00	314 Roy Campanella	1500.00	348 Bob Kelly	150.00	382 Samuel Jones	150.00
281 Tom Brown	45.00	315 Leo Durocher (Mgr)	250.00	349 Bob Cain	150.00	383 Del Wilber	150.00
282 Birdie Tebbetts	45.00	316 Dave Williams	150.00	350 Cal Abrams	150.00	384 Frank Crosetti	250.00
283 Phil Masi	45.00	317 Connie Marrerro	150.00	351 Alvin Dark	200.00	385 Herman Franks	150.00
284 Hank Arft	45.00	318 Hal Gregg	150.00	352 Karl Drews	150.00	386 Eddie Yuhas	150.00
285 Cliff Fannin	45.00	319 Al Walker	150.00	353 Robert Del Greco	150.00	387 Bill Meyer	150.00
286 Joe DeMaestri	45.00	320 John Rutherford	150.00	354 Fred Hatfield	150.00	388 Bob Chipman	150.00
287 Steve Bilko	45.00	321 Joe Black (R)	200.00	355 Bobby Morgan	150.00	389 Ben Wade	150.00
288 Chet Nichols	45.00	322 Randy Jackson	150.00	356 Toby Atwell	150.00	390 Glenn Nelson	150.00
289 Tommy Holmes	45.00	323 Bubba Church	150.00	357 Smokey Burgess	175.00	391 Ben Chapman	150.00
290 Joe Astroth	45.00	324 Warren Hacker	150.00	358 John Kucab	150.00	(photo of Sam Chapman)	
291 Gil Coan	45.00	325 Bill Serena	150.00	359 Dee Fondy	150.00	392 Hoyt Wilhelm (R)	550.00
292 Floyd Baker	45.00	326 George Shuba	150.00	360 George Crowe	150.00	393 Ebba St. Claire	150.00
293 Sibby Sisti	45.00	327 Archie Wilson	150.00	361 Bill Posedel	150.00	394 Billy Herman	200.00
294 Walker Cooper	45.00	328 Bob Borkowski	150.00	362 Kenny Heintzelman	150.00	395 Jake Pitler	150.00
295 Phil Cavarretta	45.00	329 Ivan Delock	150.00	363 Dick Rozek	150.00	396 Dick Williams (R)	200.00
296 Red Rolfe	45.00	330 Turk Lown	150.00	364 Clyde Sukeforth	150.00	397 Forrest Main	150.00
297 Andy Seminick	45.00	331 Tom Morgan	150.00	365 Cookie Lavagetto	150.00	398 Hal Rice	150.00
298 Bob Ross	45.00	332 Anthony Bartirome	150.00	366 Dave Madison	150.00	399 Jim Fridley	150.00
299 Ray Murray	45.00	333 Pee Wee Reese	700.00	367 Bob Thorpe	150.00	400 Bill Dickey	500.00
300 Barney McCosky	45.00	334 Wilmer Mizell	150.00	368 Ed Wright	150.00	401 Bob Schultz	150.00
301 Bob Porterfield	35.00	335 Ted Lepcio	150.00	369 Dick Groat (R)	275.00	402 Earl Harrist	150.00
302 Max Surkont	35.00	336 Dave Koslo	150.00	370 Bill Hoeft	150.00	403 Bill Miller	150.00
303 Harry Dorish	35.00	337 Jim Hearn	150.00	371 Bob Hofman	150.00	404 Dick Brodowski	150.00
304 Sam Dente	35.00	338 Sal Yvars	150.00	372 Gil McDougald (R)	250.00	405 Eddie Pellagrini	150.00
305 Paul Richards	35.00	339 Russ Meyer	150.00	373 Jim Turner	150.00	406 Joseph Nuxhall (R)	200.00
306 Lou Sleater	35.00	340 Bob Hooper	150.00	374 Al Benton	150.00	407 E. Mathews (R)	1700.00
						(Exc. $400.00)	

1953 Topps . . . Complete Set of 274 Cards—Value $4500.00 (Exc.); $12,000.00 (Near Mint)

Features the rookie cards of Johnny Padres and Jim Gilliam. Although the cards are numbered up to 280, there are only 274 cards in the set. Six cards were not issued—numbers 253, 261, 267, 268, 271 and 275. The high number series is 221 to 280. Card size 2⅝″ x 3¾″.

NO. PLAYER	NR. MT.	NO. PLAYER	NR. MT.	NO. PLAYER	NR. MT.	NO. PLAYER	NR. MT.
1 J. Robinson (Exc. $150.00)	600.00	23 Toby Atwell	20.00	45 Grady Hatton	20.00	67 Roy Sievers	20.00
2 Luke Easter	20.00	24 Ferris Fain	20.00	46 John Klippstein	20.00	68 Del Rice	20.00
3 George Crowe	20.00	25 R. Boone	20.00	47 Bubba Church	20.00	69 Dick Brodowski	20.00
4 Benjamin Wade	20.00	26 Dale Mitchell	20.00	48 Bob Del Greco	20.00	70 Eddie Yuhas	20.00
5 Joe Dobson	20.00	27 Roy Campanella	175.00	49 Faye Throneberry	20.00	71 Tony Bartirome	20.00
6 Sam Jones	20.00	28 Eddie Pellagrini	20.00	50 Chuck Dressenn	20.00	72 Fred Hutchinson	20.00
7 Bob Borkowski	15.00	29 Hal Jeffcoat	20.00	51 Frank Campos	20.00	73 Eddie Robinson	20.00
8 Clem Koshorek	15.00	30 Willard Nixon	20.00	52 Ted Gray	20.00	74 Joe Rossi	20.00
9 Joe Collins	15.00	31 Ewell Blackwell	30.00	53 Sherman Lollar	20.00	75 Mike Garcia	20.00
10 Smokey Burgess	25.00	32 Clyde Vollmer	20.00	54 Bob Feller	90.00	76 Pee Wee Reese	125.00
11 Sal Yvars	20.00	33 Bob Kennedy	20.00	55 Maurice McDermott	20.00	77 John Mize	60.00
12 Howie Judson	15.00	34 George Shuba	20.00	56 Gerald Staley	20.00	78 Al Schoendienst	50.00
13 Connie Marrero	20.00	35 Irv Noren	20.00	57 Carl Scheib	20.00	79 Johnny Wyrostek	20.00
14 Clem Labine	15.00	36 Johnny Groth	20.00	58 George Metkovich	20.00	80 Jim Hegan	20.00
15 Bobo Newsom	15.00	37 Ed Mathews	100.00	59 Karl Drews	20.00	81 Joe Black	40.00
16 Harry Lowrey	14.00	38 Jim Hearn	20.00	60 Cloyd Boyer	20.00	82 Mickey Mantle	1800.00
17 Billy Hitchcock	18.00	39 Eddie Miksis	20.00	61 Early Wynn	65.00	83 Howie Pollett	20.00
18 Ted Lepcio	15.00	40 Johnny Lipon	20.00	62 Monte Irvin	35.00	84 Bob Hooper	20.00
19 Melvin Parnell	20.00	41 Enos Slaughter	75.00	63 Gus Niarhos	15.00	85 Bobby Morgan	20.00
20 Hank Thompson	20.00	42 Gus Zernial	20.00	64 David Philley	20.00	86 Billy Martin	110.00
21 Billy Johnson	20.00	43 Gil McDougald	35.00	65 Earl Harrist	20.00	87 Ed Lopat	32.00
22 Howie Fox	20.00	44 Ellis Kinder	20.00	66 Orestes Minoso	30.00	88 Willie Jones	15.00

NO. PLAYER	NR. MT.	NO. PLAYER	NR. MT.	NO. PLAYER	NR. MT.	NO. PLAYER	NR. MT.
89 Chuck Stobbs	16.00	136 Ken Heintzelman	20.00	183 Stuart Miller	15.00	229 Rocky Krsnich	70.00
90 Hank Edwards	16.00	137 John Rutherford	20.00	184 Hal Brown	15.00	230 Johnny Lindell	70.00
91 Ebba St. Claire	16.00	138 George Kell	40.00	185 Jim Pendleton	15.00	231 Solly Hemus	70.00
92 Paul Minner	16.00	139 Sammy White	18.00	186 Charles Bishop	15.00	232 Dick Kokos	70.00
93 Hal Rice	16.00	140 Tommy Glaviano	18.00	187 Jim Fridley	15.00	233 Al Aber	70.00
94 William Kennedy	16.00	141 Allie Reynolds	30.00	188 Andy Carey	15.00	234 Ray Murray	70.00
95 Willard Marshall	16.00	142 Vic Wertz	16.00	189 Ray Jablonski	15.00	235 John Hetki	70.00
96 Virgil Trucks	16.00	143 Billy Pierce	16.00	190 Dixie Walker	15.00	236 Harold Perkowski	70.00
97 Don Kolloway	16.00	144 Bob Schultz	16.00	191 Ralph Kiner	50.00	237 Clarence Podbielan	70.00
98 Cal Abrams	16.00	145 Harry Dorish	16.00	192 Wally Westlake	15.00	238 Cal Hogue	70.00
99 Dave Madison	16.00	146 Granville Hamner	16.00	193 Mike Clark	15.00	239 Jim Delsing	70.00
100 Bill Miller	16.00	147 Warren Spahn	120.00	194 Eddie Kazak	15.00	240 Fred Marsh	70.00
101 Ted Wilks	16.00	148 Mickey Grasso	16.00	195 Eddie McGhee	15.00	241 Al Sima	70.00
102 Connie Ryan	16.00	149 Dom DiMaggio	30.00	196 Bob Keegan	15.00	242 Charlie Silvera	70.00
103 Joe Astroth	16.00	150 Harry Simpson	16.00	197 Del Crandall	15.00	243 Carlos Bernier	70.00
104 Yogi Berra	175.00	151 Hoyt Wilhelm	50.00	198 Forrest Main	15.00	244 Willie Mays	1350.00
105 Joe Nuxhall	20.00	152 Bob Adams	16.00	199 Marion Fricano	15.00	245 Bill Norman	70.00
106 John Antonelli	20.00	153 Andy Seminick	16.00	200 Gordon Goldsberry	15.00	246 Roy Face (R)	80.00
107 Danny O'Connell	20.00	154 Dick Groat	25.00	201 Paul LaPalme	15.00	247 Mike Sandlock	70.00
108 Bob Porterfield	20.00	155 Dutch Leonard	16.00	202 Carl Sawatski	15.00	248 Gene Stephens	70.00
109 Alvin Dark	25.00	156 Jim Rivera	16.00	203 Cliff Fannin	15.00	249 Ed O'Brien	70.00
110 Herman Wehmeier	16.00	157 Bob Addis	16.00	204 Dick Bokelmann	15.00	250 Bob Wilson	70.00
111 Hank Sauer	16.00	158 John Logan	16.00	205 Vern Benson	15.00	251 Sid Hudson	70.00
112 Ned Garver	16.00	159 Wayne Terwilliger	16.00	206 Ed Bailey	15.00	252 Henry Foiles	70.00
113 Jerry Priddy	16.00	160 Bob Young	16.00	207 Whitey Ford	125.00	254 Preacher Roe	90.00
114 Phil Rizzuto	90.00	161 Vern Bickford	16.00	208 Jim Wilson	15.00	255 Dixie Howell	70.00
115 George Spencer	20.00	162 Ted Kluszewski	30.00	209 Jim Greengrass	15.00	256 Les Peden	70.00
116 Frank Smith	20.00	163 Fred Hatfield	16.00	210 Bob Cerv	15.00	257 Bob Boyd	70.00
117 Sidney Gordon	20.00	164 Frank Shea	16.00	211 J.W. Porter	15.00	258 Jim Gilliam (R)	260.00
118 Gus Bell	20.00	165 Billy Hoeft	16.00	212 Jack Dittmer	15.00	259 Roy McMillan	70.00
119 Johnny Sain	30.00	166 Bill Hunter	15.00	213 Ray Scarborough	15.00	260 Sam Calderone	70.00
120 Davey Williams	20.00	167 Art Schult	15.00	214 Bill Bruton	15.00	262 Bob Oldis	70.00
121 Walt Dropo	20.00	168 Willard Schmidt	15.00	215 Gene Conley	15.00	263 John Podres (R)	250.00
122 Elmer Valo	20.00	169 Dizzy Trout	15.00	216 Jim Hughes	15.00	264 Gene Woodling	75.00
123 Tommy Byrne	20.00	170 Bill Werle	15.00	217 Murray Wall	15.00	265 Jackie Jensen	100.00
124 Sibby Sisti	20.00	171 Bill Glynn	15.00	218 Les Fusselman	15.00	266 Bob Cain	70.00
125 Dick Williams	18.00	172 Rip Repulski	15.00	219 Pete Runnels	15.00	269 Duane Pillette	70.00
126 Billy Connelly	16.00	173 Preston Ward	15.00	(Photo of Don Johnson)		270 Vern Stephens	70.00
127 Clint Courtney	16.00	174 Billy Loes	15.00	220 Satchell Paige	400.00	272 Bill Antonello	70.00
128 Wilmer Mizell	16.00	175 Ronald Kline	15.00	221 Bob Milliken	70.00	273 Harvey Haddix (R)	95.00
129 Keith Thomas	16.00	176 Don Hoak	15.00	222 Vic Janowicz	70.00	274 John Riddle	70.00
130 Turk Lown	16.00	177 Jim Dyck	15.00	223 John O'Brien	70.00	276 Ken Raffensberger	70.00
131 Harry Byrd	16.00	178 Jim Waugh	15.00	224 Lou Sleater	70.00	277 Don Lund	70.00
132 Tom Morgan	16.00	179 Gene Hermanski	15.00	225 Bobby Shantz	75.00	278 Willie Miranda	70.00
133 Gil Coan	16.00	180 Virgil Stallcup	15.00	226 Edward Erautt	70.00	279 Joe Coleman	70.00
134 Rube Walker	16.00	181 Al Zarilla	15.00	227 Morris Martin	70.00	280 M. Boling (R) (Exc. $45.00)	300.00
135 Al Rosen	30.00	182 Robert Hofman	15.00	228 Hal Newhouser	100.00		

1954 Topps . . . Complete Set of 250 Cards—Value $2750.00 (Exc.); $7000.00 (Near Mint)

Features the rookie cards of Hank Aaron, Al Kaline and Ernie Banks. Card size 2⅝″ x 3¾″. Topps' signed Ted Williams to a special contract for this set, and he appears on two cards.

NO. PLAYER	NR. MT.	NO. PLAYER	NR. MT.	NO. PLAYER	NR. MT.	NO. PLAYER	NR. MT.
1 Ted Williams (Exc. $120.00)	550.00	6 Pete Runnels	9.00	11 Paul Smith	9.00	16 Vic Janowicz	9.00
2 Gus Zernial	10.00	7 Ted Kluszewski	20.00	12 Del Crandall	9.00	17 Phil Rizzuto	60.00
3 Monte Irvin	30.00	8 Bobby Young	9.00	13 Billy Martin	60.00	18 Walt Dropo	9.00
4 Hank Sauer	9.00	9 Harvey Haddix	9.00	14 Preacher Roe	16.00	19 Johnny Lipon	9.00
5 Ed Lopat	20.00	10 Jackie Robinson	225.00	15 Al Rosen	15.00	20 Warren Spahn	85.00

NO. PLAYER	NR. MT.	NO. PLAYER	NR. MT.	NO. PLAYER	NR. MT.	NO. PLAYER	NR. MT.
21 Bobby Shantz	10.00	79 Andy Pafko	9.00	137 Wally Moon	20.00	193 Johnny Hopp	12.00
22 Jim Greengrass	9.00	80 Jackie Jensen	15.00	138 Bob Borkowski	12.00	194 Bill Sarni	12.00
23 Luke Easter	9.00	81 Dave Hoskins	9.00	139 The O'Brien's:	22.00	195 Bill Consolo	12.00
24 Granny Hamner	9.00	82 Milt Bolling	9.00	Johnny O'Brien,		196 Stan Jok	12.00
25 Harv. Kuenn (R)	30.00	83 Joe Collins	9.00	Eddie O'Brien		197 L. Rowe	12.00
26 Ray Jablonski	9.00	84 Dick Cole	9.00	140 Tom Wright	12.00	198 Carl Sawatski	12.00
27 Ferris Fain	9.00	85 Bob Turley (R)	20.00	141 Joe Jay	12.00	199 Glenn Nelson	12.00
28 Paul Minner	9.00	86 Billy Herman	15.00	142 Tom Poholsky	12.00	200 Larry Jansen	12.00
29 Jim Hegan	9.00	87 Roy Face	9.00	143 Rollie Hemsley	12.00	201 Al Kaline (R)	650.00
30 Ed Mathews	75.00	88 Matt Batts	9.00	144 Bill Werle	12.00	202 Bob Purkey	12.00
31 John Klippstein	9.00	89 Howie Pollet	9.00	145 Elmer Valo	12.00	203 Harry Brecheen	12.00
32 Duke Snider	120.00	90 Willie Mays	325.00	146 Don Johnson	12.00	204 Angel Scull	12.00
33 Johnny Schmitz	9.00	91 Bob Oldis	9.00	147 John Riddle	12.00	205 Johnny Sain	20.00
34 Jim Rivera	9.00	92 Wally Westlake	9.00	148 Bob Trice	12.00	206 Ray Crone	12.00
35 Junior Gilliam	17.00	93 Sid Hudson	9.00	149 Jim Robertson	12.00	207 Tom Oliver	12.00
36 Hoyt Wilhelm	30.00	94 Ernie Banks (R)	650.00	150 Dick Kryhoski	12.00	208 Grady Hatton	12.00
37 Whitey Ford	80.00	95 Hal Rice	10.00	151 Alex Grammas	12.00	209 Charlie Thompson	12.00
38 Eddie Stanky	9.00	96 Charlie Silvera	10.00	152 Mike Blyzka	12.00	210 Bob Buhl	12.00
39 Sherm Lollar	9.00	97 Jerry Lane	10.00	153 Albert Walker	12.00	211 Don Hoak	12.00
40 Mel Parnell	9.00	98 Joe Black	12.00	154 Mike Fornieles	12.00	212 Bob Micelotta	12.00
41 Willie Jones	9.00	99 Bob Hofman	10.00	155 Bob Kennedy	12.00	213 John Fitzpatrick	12.00
42 Don Mueller	9.00	100 Bob Keegan	10.00	156 Joe Coleman	12.00	214 A. Portocarrero	12.00
43 Dick Groat	11.00	101 Gene Woodling	12.00	157 Don Lenhardt	12.00	215 Ed McGhee	12.00
44 Ned Garver	9.00	102 Gil Hodges	70.00	158 Peanuts Lowrey	12.00	216 Al Sima	12.00
45 Richie Ashburn	25.00	103 Jim Lemon	10.00	159 Dave Philley	12.00	217 Paul Schreiber	12.00
46 Ken Raffensberger	9.00	104 Mike Sandlock	10.00	160 Red Kress	12.00	218 Fred Marsh	12.00
47 Ellis Kinder	9.00	105 Andy Carey	10.00	161 John Hetki	12.00	219 Charles Kress	12.00
48 Bill Hunter	9.00	106 Dick Kokos	10.00	162 Herman Wehmeier	12.00	220 Ruben Gomez	12.00
49 Ray Murray	9.00	107 Duane Pillette	10.00	163 Frank House	12.00	221 Dick Brodowski	12.00
50 Y. Berra	210.00	108 Thornton Kipper	10.00	164 Stuart Miller	12.00	222 Bill Wilson	12.00
51 Johnny Lindell	22.00	109 Bill Bruton	10.00	165 Jim Pendleton	12.00	223 Joe Haynes	12.00
52 Vic Power	22.00	110 Harry Dorish	10.00	166 Johnny Podres	21.00	224 Dick Weik	12.00
53 Jack Dittmer	22.00	111 Jim Delsing	10.00	167 Don Lund	12.00	225 Don Liddle	12.00
54 Vern Stephens	22.00	112 Bill Renna	10.00	168 Morrie Martin	12.00	226 Jehosie Heard	12.00
55 Phil Cavarretta	22.00	113 Bob Boyd	10.00	169 Jim Hughes	12.00	227 Buster Mills	12.00
56 Willie Miranda	22.00	114 Dean Stone	10.00	170 Jim Rhodes	12.00	228 Gene Hermanski	12.00
57 Luis Aloma	22.00	115 Rip Repulski	10.00	171 Leo Kiely	12.00	229 Bob Talbot	12.00
58 Bob Wilson	22.00	116 Steve Bilko	10.00	172 Hal Brown	12.00	230 Bob Kuzava	12.00
59 Gene Conley	22.00	117 Solly Hemus	10.00	173 Jack Harshman	12.00	231 Roy Smalley	12.00
60 Frank Baumholtz	22.00	118 Carl Scheib	10.00	174 Tom Qualters	12.00	232 Lou Limmer	12.00
61 Bob Cain	22.00	119 John Antonelli	10.00	175 Frank Leja	12.00	233 Augie Galan	12.00
62 Eddie Robinson	22.00	120 Roy McMillan	10.00	176 Robert Kelley	12.00	234 Jerry Lynch	12.00
63 Johnny Pesky	22.00	121 Clem Labine	10.00	177 Bob Milliken	12.00	235 Vernon Law	12.00
64 Hank Thompson	22.00	122 Johnny Logan	10.00	178 Bill Glynn	12.00	236 Paul Penson	12.00
65 Bob Swift	22.00	123 Bobby Adams	10.00	179 Gair Allie	12.00	237 Mike Ryba	12.00
66 Thad Lepcio	22.00	124 Marion Fricano	10.00	180 Wes Westrum	12.00	238 Al Aber	12.00
67 Jim Willis	22.00	125 Harry Perkowski	10.00	181 Mel Roach	12.00	239 Bill Skowron (R)	55.00
68 Sammy Calderone	22.00	126 Ben Wade	12.00	182 Chuck Harmon	12.00	240 Sam Mele	12.00
69 Bud Podbielan	22.00	127 Steve O'Neill	12.00	183 Earle Combs	17.00	241 Bob Miller	12.00
70 Larry Doby	40.00	128 Hank Aaron (R)	1250.00	184 Ed Bailey	12.00	242 Curt Roberts	12.00
71 Frank Smith	22.00	129 Forrest Jacobs	12.00	185 Chuck Stobbs	12.00	243 Ray Blades	12.00
72 Preston Ward	22.00	130 Hank Bauer	20.00	186 Karl Olson	12.00	244 Leroy Wheat	12.00
73 Wayne Terwilliger	22.00	131 Reno Bertoia	12.00	187 Heinie Manush	16.00	245 Roy Sievers	15.00
74 Bill Taylor	22.00	132 Tommy Lasorda (R)	150.00	188 Dave Jolly	12.00	246 Howie Fox	12.00
75 Fred Haney	22.00	133 Del Baker	12.00	189 Bob Ross	12.00	247 Ed Mayo	12.00
76 Bob Scheffing	9.00	134 Cal Hogue	12.00	190 Ray Herbert	12.00	248 Al Smith	12.00
77 Ray Boone	9.00	135 Joe Presko	12.00	191 Dick Schofield	12.00	249 Wilmer Mizell	12.00
78 Ted Kazanski	9.00	136 Connie Ryan	12.00	192 Ellis Deal	12.00	250 Ted Williams (Exc. $120.00)	600.00

1955 Topps . . . Complete Set of 206 Cards—Value $2250.00 (Exc.) $5500.00 (Near Mint)

Features the rookie cards of Roberto Clemente, Sandy Koufax and Harmon Killebrew. Topps' switched to a horizontal format in 1955. Card size 2⅝" x 3¾". Four cards originally intended to be issued—175, 186, 203 and 209 were withdrawn. The high number series is 161 to 210.

NO.	PLAYER	NR. MT.
1	Dusty Rhodes (Exc. $8.00)	40.00
2	Ted Williams	300.00
3	Art Fowler	5.00
4	Al Kaline	160.00
5	Jim Gilliam	9.00
6	Stan Hack	5.00
7	Jim Hegan	5.00
8	Hal Smith	5.00
9	Bob Miller	5.00
10	Bob Keegan	5.00
11	Ferris Fain	5.00
12	Vernon Thies	5.00
13	Fred Marsh	5.00
14	Jim Finigan	5.00
15	Jim Pendleton	5.00
16	Roy Sievers	5.00
17	Bobby Hofman	5.00
18	Russ Kemmerer	5.00
19	Billy Herman	10.00
20	Andy Carey	5.00
21	Alex Grammas	5.00
22	Bill Skowron	11.00
23	Jack Parks	5.00
24	Hal Newhouser	8.00
25	Johnnie Podres	11.00
26	Dick Groat	5.00
27	Billy Gardner	5.00
28	Ernie Banks	140.00
29	Herman Wehmeier	5.00
30	Vic Power	5.00
31	Warren Spahn	70.00
32	Ed McGhee	5.00
33	Tom Qualters	5.00
34	Wayne Terwilliger	5.00
35	Dave Jolly	5.00
36	Leo Kiely	5.00
37	Joe Cunningham	5.00
38	Bob Turley	8.00
39	Billy Glynn	5.00
40	Don Hoak	5.00
41	Chuck Stobbs	5.00
42	John McCall	5.00
43	Harvey Haddix	6.00
44	Harold Valentine	5.00
45	Hank Sauer	5.00
46	Ted Kazanski	5.00
47	Hank Aaron	275.00
48	Bob Kennedy	5.00
49	J.W. Porter	5.00
50	Jack Robinson	175.00
51	Jim Hughes	5.00
52	Bill Tremel	5.00
53	Bill Taylor	5.00
54	Lou Limmer	5.00
55	Eldon Repulski	5.00
56	Ray Jablonski	5.00
57	Bill O'Dell	5.00
58	Manuel Rivera	5.00
59	Gair Allie	5.00
60	Dean Stone	5.00
61	Forrest Jacobs	5.00
62	Thornton Kipper	5.00
63	Joe Collins	6.00
64	Gus Triandos	6.00
65	Ray Boone	5.00
66	Ron Jackson	5.00
67	Wally Moon	5.00
68	Jim Davis	5.00
69	Ed Bailey	5.00
70	Al Rosen	9.00
71	Ruben Gomez	5.00
72	Karl Olson	5.00
73	Jack Shepard	5.00
74	Bob Borkowski	5.00
75	Sandy Amoros (R)	9.00
76	Howie Pollet	5.00
77	Arnold Portocarrero	5.00
78	Gordon Jones	5.00
79	Clyde Schell	5.00
80	Bob Grim (R)	9.00
81	Gene Conley	5.00
82	Chuck Harmon	5.00
83	Thomas Brewer	5.00
84	Camilo Pascual (R)	6.00
85	Don Mossi (R)	7.50
86	Bill Wilson	5.00
87	Frank House	5.00
88	Bob Skinner	5.00
89	Joe Frazier	5.00
90	Karl Spooner	5.00
91	Milton Bolling	5.00
92	Don Zimmer (R)	25.00
93	Steve Bilko	5.00
94	Reno Bertoia	5.00
95	Preston Ward	5.00
96	Charlie Bishop	5.00
97	Carlos Paula	5.00
98	Johnny Riddle	5.00
99	Frank Leja	5.00
100	Monte Irvin	20.00
101	Johnny Gray	5.00
102	Wally Westlake	5.00
103	Charlie White	5.00
104	Jack Harshman	5.00
105	Chuck Diering	5.00
106	Frank Sullivan	5.00
107	Curt Roberts	5.00
108	Rube Walker	5.00
109	Ed Lopat	12.00
110	Gus Zernial	5.00
111	Bob Milliken	5.00
112	Nelson King	5.00
113	Harry Brecheen	5.00
114	Louie Ortiz	5.00
115	Ellis Kinder	5.00
116	Tom Hurd	5.00
117	Mel Roach	5.00
118	Bob Purkey	5.00
119	Bob Lennon	5.00
120	Ted Kluszewski	15.00
121	Bill Renna	4.00
122	Carl Sawatski	4.00
123	Sandy Koufax (R)	750.00
124	Harmon Killebrew (R)	300.00
125	Ken Boyer (R)	35.00
126	Dick Hall	5.00
127	Dale Long	5.00
128	Ted Lepcio	5.00
129	Elvin Tappe	5.00
130	Mayo Smith	5.00
131	Grady Hatton	5.00
132	Bob Trice	5.00
133	Dave Hoskins	5.00
134	Joe Jay	5.00
135	Johnny O'Brien	5.00
136	Bunky Stewart	5.00
137	Harry Elliott	5.00
138	Ray Herbert	5.00
139	Steve Kraly	5.00
140	Mel Parnell	5.00
141	Tom Wright	5.00
142	Jerry Lynch	5.00
143	Dick Schofield	5.00
144	Joe Amalfitano	5.00
145	Elmer Valo	5.00
146	Dick Donovan	5.00
147	Laurin Pepper	5.00
148	Hal Brown	5.00
149	Ray Crone	5.00
150	Michael Higgins	5.00
151	Ralph Kress	12.00
152	Harry Agganis (R)	60.00
153	Bud Podbielan	12.00
154	Willie Miranda	12.00
155	Eddie Mathews	100.00
156	Joe Black	20.00
157	Bob Miller	12.00
158	Tommy Carroll	12.00
159	Johnny Schmitz	12.00
160	Raymond Narleski	12.00
161	Chuck Tanner (R)	25.00
162	Joe Coleman	15.00
163	Faye Throneberry	15.00
164	Roberto Clemente (R)	900.00
165	Don Johnson	15.00
166	Hank Bauer	32.00
167	Tom Casagrande	15.00
168	Duane Pillette	15.00
169	Bob Oldis	15.00
170	Jim Pearce	15.00
171	Dick Brodowski	15.00
172	Frank Baumholtz	15.00
173	Bob Kline	15.00
174	Rudy Minarcin	15.00
176	Norm Zauchin	15.00
177	Jim Robertson	15.00
178	Bobby Adams	15.00
179	Jim Bolger	15.00
180	Clem Labine	15.00
181	Roy McMillan	15.00
182	Humberto Robinson	15.00
183	Anthony Jacobs	15.00
184	Harry Perkowski	15.00
185	Don Ferrarese	15.00
187	Gil Hodges	135.00
188	Charlie Silvera	15.00
189	Phil Rizzuto	135.00
190	Gene Woodling	15.00
191	Eddie Stanky	15.00
192	Jim Delsing	15.00
193	Johnny Sain	27.00
194	Willie Mays	375.00
195	Eddie Roebuck	15.00
196	Gale Wade	15.00
197	Al Smith	15.00
198	Yogi Berra	225.00
199	Bert Hamrick	15.00
200	Jack Jensen	40.00
201	Sherman Lollar	15.00
202	Jim Owens	15.00
204	Frank Smith	15.00
205	Gene Freese	15.00
206	Pete Daley	15.00
207	Bill Consolo	15.00
208	Ray Moore	15.00
210	Duke Snider (Exc. $90.00)	450.00

1956 Topps . . . Complete Set of 340 Cards—Value $2500.00 (Exc.) $5750.00 (Near Mint)

In 1956 Topps bought its competitor—Bowman Card Co., including all of its player contracts. Topps card sets would now be larger and more complete. Card size 2⅝″ x 3¾″. Features the rookie card of Luis Aparicio. Card numbers 1 to 180 were printed with *gray* or *white* backs. The six team cards indicated by an *asterisk* were issued with three different *face* designs. The team card dated *1955* is worth about four times the value of the other team cards. The two checklists are not included in the complete set price.

NO.	PLAYER	NR. MT.
1	W. Harridge (Exc. $10.00) (AL President)	100.00
2	Warren Giles (NL President)	15.00

NO.	PLAYER	NR. MT.
3	Elmer Valo	5.00
4	Carlos Paula	5.00
5	Ted Williams	250.00
6	Ray Boone	5.00

NO.	PLAYER	NR. MT.
7	Ron Negray	5.00
8	Walter Alston (Mgr)	25.00
9	Ruben Gomez	5.00
10	Warren Spahn	60.00

NO.	PLAYER	NR. MT.
11	Chicago Cubs*	16.00
12	Andy Carey	5.00
13	Roy Face	5.00
14	Ken Boyer	12.00

NO.	PLAYER	NR. MT.
15	Ernie Banks	75.00
16	Hector Lopez	5.00
17	Gene Conley	5.00
18	Dick Donovan	5.00
19	Chuck Diering	5.00
20	Al Kaline	65.00
21	Joe Collins	6.00
22	Jim Finigan	5.00
23	Freddie Marsh	5.00
24	Dick Groat	5.00
25	Ted Kluszeski	13.00
26	Grady Hatton	5.00
27	Nelson Burbrink	5.00
28	Bobby Hofman	5.00
29	Jack Harshman	5.00
30	Jackie Robinson	150.00
31	Hank Aaron	210.00
32	Frank House	5.00
33	Roberto Clemente	275.00
34	Tom Brewer	5.00
35	Al Rosen	9.00
36	Rudy Minarcin	5.00
37	Alex Grammas	5.00
38	Bob Kennedy	5.00
39	Don Mossi	5.00
40	Bob Turley	9.00
41	Hank Sauer	5.00
42	Sandy Amoros	6.00
43	Ray Moore	5.00
44	Windy McCall	5.00
45	Gus Zernial	5.00
46	Gene Freese	5.00
47	Art Fowler	5.00
48	Jim Hegan	5.00
49	Pedro Ramos	5.00
50	Dusty Rhode	5.00
51	Ernie Oravetz	5.00
52	Bob Grim	5.00
53	Arnold Portocarrero	5.00
54	Bob Keegan	5.00
55	Wally Moon	5.00
56	Dale Long	5.00
57	Duke Maas	5.00
58	Ed Roebuck	5.00
59	Jose Santiago	5.00
60	Mayo Smith	5.00
61	Bill Skowron	10.00
62	Hal Smith	5.00
63	Roger Craig (R)	18.00
64	Luis Arroyo	5.00
65	Johnny O'Brien	5.00
66	Bob Speake	5.00
67	Vic Power	5.00
68	Chuck Stobbs	5.00
69	Chuck Tanner	5.00
70	Jim Rivera	5.00
71	Frank Sullivan	5.00
72	Philadelphia Phillies*	16.00
73	Wayne Terwilliger	5.00
74	Jim King	5.00
75	Roy Sievers	6.00
76	Ray Crone	5.00
77	Harvey Haddix	6.00
78	Herman Wehmeier	5.00
79	Sandy Koufax	300.00
80	Gus Triandos	6.00
81	Wally Westlake	5.00
82	Bill Renna	5.00
83	Karl Spooner	5.00
84	Babe Birrer	5.00
85	Cleveland Indians*	15.00
86	Ray Jablonski	5.00
87	Dean Stone	5.00
88	Johnny Kucks	5.00
89	Norm Zauchin	5.00
90	Cincinnati Redlegs*	16.00
91	Gail Harris	5.00
92	Red Wilson	5.00
93	George Susce Jr.	5.00
94	Ronald Kline	5.00
95	Milwaukee Braves*	15.00
96	Bill Tremel	5.00

NO.	PLAYER	NR. MT.
97	Jerry Lynch	5.00
98	Camilo Pascual	5.00
99	Don Zimmer	15.00
100	Baltimore Orioles*	15.00
101	Roy Campanella	120.00
102	Jim Davis	7.00
103	Willie Miranda	7.00
104	Bob Lennon	7.00
105	Al Smith	7.00
106	Joe Astroth	7.00
107	Ed Mathews	50.00
108	Laurin Pepper	7.00
109	Enos Slaughter	25.00
110	Yogi Berra	120.00
111	Boston Red Sox	20.00
112	Dee Fondy	7.00
113	Phil Rizzuto	50.00
114	Jim Owens	7.00
115	Jackie Jensen	10.00
116	Eddie O'Brien	7.00
117	Virgil Trucks	7.00
118	Nellie Fox	20.00
119	Larry Jackson	7.00
120	Richie Ashburn	20.00
121	Pittsburgh Pirates	16.00
122	Willard Nixon	7.00
123	Roy McMillan	7.00
124	Don Kaiser	7.00
125	Minnie Minoso	16.00
126	Jim Brady	7.00
127	Willie Jones	7.00
128	Eddie Yost	7.00
129	Jake Martin	7.00
130	Willie Mays	225.00
131	Bob Roselli	7.00
132	Bobby Avila	7.00
133	Ray Narleski	7.00
134	St. Louis Cardinals	16.00
135	Mickey Mantle	750.00
136	Johnny Logan	7.00
137	Al Silvera	7.00
138	Johnny Antonelli	7.00
139	Tommy Carroll	7.00
140	Herb Score (R)	15.00
141	Joe Frazier	7.00
142	Gene Baker	7.00
143	Jimmy Piersall	9.00
144	Leroy Powell	7.00
145	Gil Hodges	45.00
146	Washington Nat'l	15.00
147	Earl Torgeson	7.00
148	Alvin Dark	7.00
149	Dixie Howell	7.00
150	Duke Snider	125.00
151	Spook Jacobs	7.00
152	Billy Hoeft	7.00
153	Frank Thomas	7.00
154	David Pope	7.00
155	Harvey Kuenn	10.00
156	Wes Westrum	7.00
157	Dick Brodowski*	7.00
158	Wally Post	7.00
159	Clint Courtney	7.00
160	Billy Pierce	8.00
161	Joe DeMaestri	7.00
162	Gus Bell	7.00
163	Gene Woodling	7.00
164	Harmon Killebrew	100.00
165	Red Schoendienst	20.00
166	Brooklyn Dodgers	150.00
167	Harry Dorish	7.00
168	Sammy White	7.00
169	Bob Nelson	7.00
170	Bill Virdon	10.00
171	Jim Wilson	7.00
172	Frank Torre	7.00
173	Johnny Podres	15.00
174	Glen Gorbous	7.00
175	Del Crandall	7.00
176	Alex Kellner	7.00
177	Hank Bauer	13.00
178	Joe Black	7.00

NO.	PLAYER	NR. MT.
179	Harry Chiti	7.00
180	Robin Roberts	25.00
181	Billy Martin	75.00
182	Paul Minner	10.00
183	Stan Lopata	10.00
184	Don Bessent	10.00
185	Bill Bruton	10.00
186	Ron Jackson	10.00
187	Early Wynn	25.00
188	Chicago White Sox	20.00
189	Ned Garver	10.00
190	Carl Furillo	16.00
191	Frank Lary	11.00
192	Smokey Burgess	10.00
193	Wilmer Mizell	10.00
194	Monte Irvin	25.00
195	George Kell	24.00
196	Tom Poholsky	10.00
197	Granny Hamner	10.00
198	Ed Fitzgerald	10.00
199	Hank Thompson	10.00
200	Bob Feller	80.00
201	Rip Repulski	10.00
202	Jim Hearn	10.00
203	Bill Tuttle	10.00
204	Arthur Swanson	10.00
205	Whitey Lockman	10.00
206	Erv Palica	10.00
207	Jim Small	10.00
208	Elston Howard	25.00
209	Max Surkont	10.00
210	Mike Garcia	10.00
211	Murry Dickson	10.00
212	Johnny Temple	10.00
213	Detroit Tigers	25.00
214	Bob Rush	10.00
215	Tommy Byrne	10.00
216	Jerry Schoonmaker	10.00
217	Billy Klaus	10.00
218	Joe Nuxhall	10.00
219	Lew Burdette	12.00
220	Del Ennis	10.00
221	Bob Friend	10.00
222	Dave Philley	10.00
223	Randy Jackson	10.00
224	Bud Podbielan	10.00
225	Gil McDougald	20.00
226	New York Giants	50.00
227	Russ Meyer	10.00
228	Mickey Vernon	10.00
229	Harry Brecheen	10.00
230	Chico Carrasquel	10.00
231	Bob Hale	10.00
232	Toby Atwell	10.00
233	Carl Erskine	15.00
234	Pete Runnels	10.00
235	Don Newcombe	25.00
236	Kansas C. Athletics*	17.00
237	Jose Valdivielso	10.00
238	Walt Dropo	10.00
239	Harry Simpson	10.00
240	Whitey Ford	90.00
241	Don Mueller	10.00
242	Hershell Freeman	10.00
243	Sherm Lollar	10.00
244	Bob Buhl	10.00
245	Billy Goodman	10.00
246	Tom Gorman	10.00
247	Bill Sarni	10.00
248	Bob Porterfield	10.00
249	Johnny Klippstein	10.00
250	Larry Doby	15.00
251	New York Yankees	175.00
252	Vernon Law	10.00
253	Irv Noren	10.00
254	George Crowe	10.00
255	Bob Lemon	25.00
256	Tom Hurd	10.00
257	Bobby Thomson	15.00
258	Art Ditmar	10.00
259	Sam Jones	10.00
260	Pee Wee Reese	120.00

NO.	PLAYER	NR. MT.
261	Bobby Shantz	8.00
262	Howie Pollett	8.00
263	Bob Miller	8.00
264	Ray Monzant	8.00
265	Sandy Consuegra	8.00
266	Don Ferrarese	8.00
267	Bob Nieman	8.00
268	Dale Mitchell	8.00
269	Jack Meyer	8.00
270	Billy Loes	8.00
271	Foster Castleman	8.00
272	Danny O'Connell	8.00
273	Walker Cooper	8.00
274	Frank Baumholtz	8.00
275	Jim Greengrass	8.00
276	George Zuverink	8.00
277	Daryl Spencer	8.00
278	Chet Nichols	8.00
279	Johnny Groth	8.00
280	Jim Gilliam	12.00
281	Art Houtteman	8.00
282	Warren Hacker	8.00
283	Hal Smith	8.00
284	Ike Delock	8.00
285	Eddie Miksis	8.00
286	Bill Wight	8.00
287	Bobby Adams	8.00
288	Bob Cerv	10.00
289	Hal Jeffcoat	8.00
290	Curt Simmons	8.00
291	Frank Kellert	8.00
292	Luis Aparicio (R)	125.00
293	Stu Miller	8.00
294	Ernie Johnson	8.00
295	Clem Labine	8.00
296	Andy Seminick	8.00
297	Bob Skinner	8.00
298	Johnny Schmitz	8.00
299	Charley Neal	12.00
300	Vic Wertz	8.00
301	Marv Grissom	8.00
302	Eddie Robinson	8.00
303	Jim Dyck	8.00
304	Frank Malzone	15.00
305	Brooks Lawrence	8.00
306	Curt Roberts	8.00
307	Hoyt Wilhelm	30.00
308	Charles Harmon	8.00
309	Don Blasingame	8.00
310	Steve Gromek	8.00
311	Hal Naragon	8.00
312	Andy Pafko	8.00
313	Gene Stephens	8.00
314	Hobie Landrith	8.00
315	Milt Bolling	8.00
316	Jerry Coleman	8.00
317	Al Aber	8.00
318	Fred Hatfield	8.00
319	Jack Crimian	8.00
320	Joe Adcock	8.00
321	Jim Konstanty	8.00
322	Karl Olson	8.00
323	Willard Schmidt	8.00
324	Rocky Bridges	8.00
325	Don Liddle	8.00
236	Connie Johnson	8.00
327	Bob Wiesler	8.00
328	Preston Ward	8.00
329	Lou Berberet	8.00
330	Jim Busby	8.00
331	Dick Hall	8.00
332	Don Larsen	22.00
333	Rube Walker	8.00
334	Bob Miller	8.00
335	Don Hoak	8.00
336	Ellis Kinder	8.00
337	Bobby Morgan	8.00
338	Jim Delsing	8.00
339	Rance Pless	8.00
340	M. McDermott (Exc. $5.00)	20.00
—	Checklist 1/3	200.00
—	Checklist 2/4	200.00

1957 Topps . . . Complete Set of 407 Cards—Value $2400.00 (Exc.), $6500.00 (Near Mint)

Topps' switched to a 2½" x 3½" card size. The 1957 set features the rookie cards of Don Drysdale, Frank Robinson, Tony Kubek and Brooks Robinson. The four checklists are not included in the complete set price.

NO. PLAYER	NR. MT.
1 Ted Williams (Exc. $75.00)	400.00
2 Yogi Berra	140.00
3 Dale Long	6.00
4 Johnny Logan	6.00
5 Sal Maglie	9.00
6 Hector Lopez	6.00
7 Luis Aparicio	25.00
8 Don Mossi	6.00
9 Johnny Temple	6.00
10 Willie Mays	175.00
11 George Zuverink	6.00
12 Dick Groat	8.00
13 Wally Burnette	6.00
14 Bob Nieman	6.00
15 Robin Roberts	25.00
16 Walt Moryn	6.00
17 Billy Gardner	6.00
18 Don Drysdale (R)	225.00
19 Bob Wilson	6.00
20 Hank Aaron	275.00
(negative reversed)	
21 Frank Sullivan	6.00
22 Jerry Snyder	6.00
(photo of Ed Fitzgerald)	
23 Sherm Lollar	6.00
24 Bill Mazeroski (R)	35.00
25 W. Ford	60.00
26 Bob Boyd	6.00
27 Ted Kazanski	6.00
28 Gene Conley	6.00
29 Whitey Herzog	20.00
30 Pee Wee Reese	50.00
31 Ron Northey	6.00
32 Hersh Freeman	6.00
33 Jim Small	6.00
34 Tom Sturdivant	6.00
35 Frank Robinson (R)	250.00
36 Bob Grim	6.00
37 Frank Torre	6.00
38 Nellie Fox	12.00
39 Al Worthington	6.00
40 Early Wynn	16.00
41 Hal Smith	6.00
42 Dee Fondy	6.00
43 Connie Johnson	6.00
44 Joe DeMaestri	6.00
45 Carl Furillo	10.00
46 Bob Miller	6.00
47 Don Blasingame	6.00
48 Bill Bruton	6.00
49 Daryl Spencer	6.00
50 Herb A. Score	9.00
51 Clint Courtney	6.00
52 Lee Walls	6.00
53 Clem Labine	6.00
54 Elmer Valo	6.00
55 Ernie Banks	80.00
56 Dave Sisler	6.00
57 Jim Lemon	6.00
58 Ruben Gomez	6.00
59 Dick Williams	6.00
60 Billy Hoeft	6.00
61 Dusty Rhodes	6.00
62 Billy Martin	45.00
63 Ike Delock	6.00
64 Pete Runnels	6.00

NO. PLAYER	NR. MT.
65 Wally Moon	6.00
66 Brooks Lawrence	6.00
67 Chico Carrasquel	6.00
68 Ray Crone	6.00
69 Roy McMillan	6.00
70 Richie Ashburn	15.00
71 Murry Dickson	6.00
72 Bill Tuttle	6.00
73 George Crowe	6.00
74 Vito Valentinetti	6.00
75 Jim Piersall	9.00
76 Roberto Clemente	175.00
77 Paul Foytack	6.00
78 Vic Wertz	6.00
79 Lindy McDaniel	6.00
80 Gil Hodges	35.00
81 Herman Wehmeier	6.00
82 Elston Howard	11.00
83 Lou Skizas	6.00
84 Moe Drabowsky	6.00
85 Larry Doby	9.00
86 Bill Sarni	6.00
87 Tom Gorman	6.00
88 Harvey Kuenn	9.00
89 Roy Sievers	6.00
90 Warren Spahn	60.00
91 Mack Burk	4.00
92 Mickey Vernon	4.00
93 Hal Jeffcoat	4.00
94 Bobby Del Greco	4.00
95 Mickey Mantle	750.00
96 Hank Aguirre	4.00
97 New York Yankees	40.00
98 Alvin Dark	6.00
99 Bob Keegan	4.00
100 Giles and Harridge	9.00
(League Presidents)	
101 Chuck Stobbs	4.00
102 Ray Boone	4.00
103 Joe Nuxhall	4.00
104 Hank Foiles	4.00
105 Johnny Antonelli	4.00
106 Ray Moore	4.00
107 Jim Rivera	4.00
108 Tommy Byrne	4.00
109 Hank Thompson	4.00
110 Bill Virdon	6.00
111 Hal Smith	4.00
112 Tom Brewer	4.00
113 Wilmer Mizell	4.00
114 Milwaukee Braves	12.00
115 Jim Gilliam	8.00
116 Mike Fornieles	4.00
117 Joe Adcock	7.00
118 Bob Porterfield	4.00
119 Stan Lopata	4.00
120 Bob Lemon	18.00
121 Cletis Boyer	11.00
122 Ken Boyer	9.00
123 Steve Ridzik	4.00
124 Dave Philley	4.00
125 Al Kaline	65.00
126 Bob Wiesler	4.00
127 Bob Buhl	4.00
128 Ed Bailey	4.00
129 Saul Rogovin	4.00

NO. PLAYER	NR. MT.
130 Don Newcombe	10.00
131 Milt Bolling	4.00
132 Art Ditmar	4.00
133 Del Crandall	4.00
134 Don Kaiser	4.00
135 Bill Skowron	10.00
136 Jim Hegan	4.00
137 Bob Rush	4.00
138 Minnie Minoso	9.00
139 Lou Kretlow	4.00
140 Frank Thomas	4.00
141 Al Aber	4.00
142 Charley Thompson	4.00
143 Andy Pafko	4.00
144 Ray Narleski	4.00
145 Al Smith	4.00
146 Don Ferrarese	4.00
147 Al Walker	4.00
148 Don Mueller	4.00
149 Bob Kennedy	4.00
150 Bob Friend	4.00
151 Willie Miranda	4.00
152 Jack Harshman	4.00
153 Karl Olson	4.00
154 Red Schoendienst	18.00
155 Jim Brosnan	4.00
156 Gus Triandos	4.00
157 Wally Post	4.00
158 Curt Simmons	4.00
159 Solly Drake	4.00
160 Billy Pierce	8.00
161 Pittsburgh Pirates	10.00
162 Jack Meyer	4.00
163 Sammy White	4.00
164 Tommy Carroll	4.00
165 Ted Kluszewski	15.00
166 Roy Face	4.00
167 Vic Power	4.00
168 Frank Lary	4.00
169 Herb Plews	4.00
170 Duke Snider	100.00
171 Boston Red Sox	10.00
172 Gene Woodling	4.00
173 Roger Craig	9.00
174 Willie Jones	4.00
175 Don Larsen	12.00
176 Gene Baker	4.00
177 Eddie Yost	3.00
178 Don Bessent	3.00
179 Ernie Oravetz	3.00
180 Dave Bell	3.00
181 Dick Donovan	3.00
182 Hobie Landrith	3.00
183 Chicago Cubs	9.00
184 Tito Francona	3.00
185 Johnny Kucks	3.00
186 Jim King	3.00
187 Virgil Trucks	3.00
188 Felix Mantilla	3.00
189 Willard Nixon	3.00
190 Randy Jackson	3.00
191 Joe Margoneri	3.00
192 Gerry Coleman	3.00
193 Del Rice	3.00
194 Hal Brown	3.00
195 Bobby Avila	3.00

NO. PLAYER	NR. MT.
196 Larry Jackson	3.00
197 Hank Sauer	3.00
198 Detroit Tigers	10.00
199 Vernon Law	3.00
200 Gil McDougald	11.00
201 Sandy Amoros	3.00
202 Dick Gernert	3.00
203 Hoyt Wilhelm	17.00
204 Kansas C. Athletics	9.00
205 Charlie Maxwell	3.00
206 Willard Schmidt	3.00
207 Bill Hunter	3.00
208 Lew Burdette	8.00
209 Bob Skinner	3.00
210 Roy Campanella	100.00
211 Camilo Pascual	3.00
212 Rocco Colavito (R)	50.00
213 Les Moss	3.00
214 Philadelphia Phillies	9.00
215 Enos Slaughter	18.00
216 Marv Grissom	3.00
217 Gene Stephens	3.00
218 Ray Jablonski	3.00
219 Tom Acker	3.00
220 Jackie Jensen	9.00
221 Dixie Howell	3.00
222 Alex Grammas	3.00
223 Frank House	3.00
224 Marv Blaylock	3.00
225 Harry Simpson	3.00
226 Preston Ward	3.00
227 Jerry Staley	3.00
228 Smokey Burgess	3.00
229 George Susce	3.00
230 George Kell	16.00
231 Solly Hemus	3.00
232 Whitey Lockman	3.00
233 Art Fowler	3.00
234 Dick Cole	3.00
235 Tom Poholsky	3.00
236 Joe Ginsberg	3.00
237 Foster Catleman	3.00
238 Eddie Robinson	3.00
239 Tom Morgan	3.00
240 Hank Bauer	9.00
241 Joe Lonnett	3.00
242 Charlie Neal	3.00
243 St. Louis Cardinals	9.00
244 Billy Loes	3.00
245 Rip Repulski	3.00
246 Jose Valdivielso	3.00
247 Turk Lown	3.00
248 Jim Finigan	3.00
249 Dave Pope	3.00
250 Ed Mathews	30.00
251 Baltimore Orioles	9.00
252 Carl Erskine	8.00
253 Gus Zernial	3.00
254 Ron Negray	3.00
255 Charlie Silvera	3.00
256 Ronnie Kline	3.00
257 Walt Dropo	3.00
258 Steve Gromek	3.00
259 Eddie O'Brien	3.00
260 Del Ennis	3.00
261 Bob Chakales	3.00

NO. PLAYER	NR. MT.	NO. PLAYER	NR. MT.	NO. PLAYER	NR. MT.	NO. PLAYER	NR. MT.
262 Bobby Thomson	9.00	301 Sam Esposito	13.00	339 Bob Speake	13.00	377 Andre Rodgers	4.00
263 George Strickland	3.00	302 Sandy Koufax	325.00	340 Bill Wight	13.00	378 Elmer Singleton	4.00
264 Bob Turley	8.00	303 Billy Goodman	13.00	341 Don Gross	13.00	379 Don Lee	4.00
265 Harvey Haddix	16.00	304 Joe Cunningham	13.00	342 Gene Mauch	17.00	380 Walker Cooper	4.00
266 Kenny Kuhn	13.00	305 Chico Fernandez	13.00	343 Taylor Phillips	13.00	381 Dean Stone	4.00
267 Danny Kravitz	13.00	306 Darrell Johnson	13.00	344 Paul LaPalme	13.00	382 Jim Brideweser	4.00
268 Jackie Collum	13.00	307 Jack Phillips	13.00	345 Paul Smith	13.00	383 Juan Pizarro	4.00
269 Bob Cerv	13.00	308 Dick Hall	13.00	346 Dick Littlefield	13.00	384 Bobby Smith	4.00
270 Washington Senators	25.00	309 Jim Busby	13.00	347 Hal Naragon	13.00	385 Art Houtteman	4.00
271 Danny O'Connell	13.00	310 Max Surkont	13.00	348 Jim Hearn	13.00	386 Lyle Luttrell	4.00
272 Bobby Shantz	25.00	311 Al Pilarcik	13.00	349 Nelson King	13.00	387 Jack Sanford (R)	6.00
273 Jim Davis	13.00	312 Tony Kubek (R)	120.00	350 Eddie Miksis	13.00	388 Pete Daley	4.00
274 Don Hoak	13.00	313 Mel Parnell	13.00	351 Dave Hillman	13.00	389 Dave Jolly	4.00
275 Cleveland Indians	25.00	314 Ed Bouchee	13.00	352 Ellis Kinder	13.00	390 Reno Bertoia	4.00
276 Jim Pyburn	13.00	315 Lou Berberet	13.00	353 Cal Neeman	4.00	391 Ralph Terry (R)	10.00
277 Johnny Podres	55.00	316 Billy O'Dell	13.00	354 Rip Coleman	4.00	392 Chuck Tanner	4.00
278 Fred Hatfield	13.00	317 New York Giants	40.00	355 Frank Malzone	4.00	393 Raul Sanchez	4.00
279 Bob Thurman	13.00	318 Mickey McDermott	13.00	356 Faye Throneberry	4.00	394 Luis Aroyo	4.00
280 Alex Kellner	13.00	319 Gino Cimoli	13.00	357 Earl Torgeson	4.00	395 Bubba Phillips	4.00
281 Gail Harris	13.00	320 Neil Chrisley	13.00	358 Jerry Lynch	4.00	396 Casey Wise	4.00
282 Jack Dittmer	13.00	321 Red Murff	13.00	359 Tom Cheney	4.00	397 Roy Smalley	4.00
283 Wes Covington	13.00	322 Cincinnati Redlegs	50.00	360 Johnny Groth	4.00	398 Al Cicotte	4.00
284 Don Zimmer	25.00	323 Wes Westrum	13.00	361 Curt Barclay	4.00	399 Billy Consolo	4.00
285 Ned Garver	12.00	324 Brooklyn Dodgers	100.00	362 Roman Mejias	4.00	400 Dodgers' Sluggers:	165.00
286 Bobby Richardson (R)	90.00	325 Frank Bolling	13.00	363 Eddie Kasko	4.00	Carl Furillo, Gil Hodges	
287 Sam Jones	13.00	326 Pedro Ramos	13.00	364 Cal McLish	4.00	Duke Snider,	
288 Ted Lepcio	13.00	327 Jim Pendleton	13.00	365 Ossie Virgil	4.00	Roy Campanella	
289 Jim Bolger	13.00	328 Brooks Robinson (R)	350.00	366 Ken Lehman	4.00	401 Earl Battey	4.00
290 Andy Carey	13.00	329 Chicago White Sox	25.00	367 Ed Fitzgerald	4.00	402 Jim Pisani	4.00
291 Windy McCall	13.00	330 Jim Wilson	13.00	368 Bob Purkey	4.00	403 Dick Hyde	4.00
292 Bill Klaus	13.00	331 Ray Katt	13.00	369 Milt Graff	4.00	404 Harry Anderson	4.00
293 Ted Abernathy	13.00	332 Bob Bowman	13.00	370 Warren Hacker	4.00	405 Duke Maas	4.00
294 Rocky Bridges	13.00	333 Ernie Johnson	13.00	371 Bob Lennon	4.00	406 Bob Hale	4.00
295 Joe Collins	13.00	334 Jerry Schoonmaker	13.00	372 Norm Zauchin	4.00	407 Yanks' Power Hitters:	300.00
296 Johnny Klippstein	13.00	335 Granny Hamner	13.00	373 Pete Whisenant	4.00	M. Mantle, Y. Berra (Exc. $60.00)	
297 Jack Crimian	13.00	336 Haywood Sullivan	13.00	374 Don Cardwell	4.00	— Checklist 1/2	100.00
298 Irv Noren	13.00	337 Rene Valdes	13.00	375 Jim Landis	4.00	— Checklist 2/3	225.00
299 Chuck Harmon	13.00	338 Jim Bunning (R)	125.00	376 Don Elston	4.00	— Checklist 3/4	300.00
300 Mike Garcia	13.00					— Checklist 4/5	500.00

1958 Topps . . . Complete Set of 494 Cards—Value $1600.00 (Exc.); $4000.00 (Near Mint)

Features the rookie cards of Roger Maris and Orlando Cepeda. 33 cards exist with the player's name or team in *yellow* type. These cards are worth more than the cards with *white* type. Card 145 was not issued. Prices for team checklists (377, 397, 408 and 428) are with the teams listed in alphabetical order. Team checklists with the teams in numerical order are worth about $12.00 each.

NO. PLAYER	NR. MT.	NO. PLAYER	NR. MT.	NO. PLAYER	NR. MT.	NO. PLAYER	NR. MT.
1 Ted Williams (Exc. $50.00)	300.00	11 Jim Rivera (yellow type)	18.00	21 Curt Barclay	5.00	31 Tex Clevenger	5.00
2 Bob Lemon	16.00	12 George Crowe	5.00	22 Hal Naragon	5.00	32 J.W. Porter	5.00
2 Bob Lemon (yellow type)	32.00	13 Billy Hoeft	5.00	23 Bill Tuttle	5.00	32 J.W. Porter (yellow letters)	20.00
3 Alex Kellner	5.00	13 Billy Hoeft (yellow type)	20.00	23 Bill Tuttle (yellow type)	20.00	33 Cal Neeman	5.00
4 Hank Foiles	5.00	14 Rip Repulski	5.00	24 Hobie Landrith	5.00	33 Cal Neeman (yellow letters)	20.00
5 Willie Mays	150.00	15 Jim Lemon	5.00	24 Hobie Landrith (yellow type)	20.00	34 Bob Thurman	5.00
6 George Zuverink	5.00	16 Charley Neal	5.00	25 Don Drysdal	50.00	35 Don Mossi	5.00
7 Dale Long	6.00	17 Felix Mantilla	5.00	26 Ron Jackson	5.00	35 Don Mossi (yellow letters)	20.00
8 Eddie Kasko	6.00	18 Frank Sullivan	5.00	27 Bud Freeman	5.00	36 Ted Kazanski	5.00
8 Eddie Kasko (yellow type)	22.00	19 New York Giants	15.00	28 Jim Busby	5.00	37 Mike McCormick (photo of Ray Monzant)	8.00
9 Hank Bauer	8.00	20 Gil McDougald	7.00	29 Ted Lepcio	5.00	38 Dick Gernert	5.00
10 Lou Burdette	6.00	20 Gil McDougald (yellow type)	25.00	30 Hank Aaron	150.00		
11 Jim Rivera	5.00			30 Hank Aaron (yellow letters)	300.00		

1958 Topps (Continued)

NO.	PLAYER	NR. MT.
39	Bob Martyn	5.00
40	George Kell	13.00
41	Dave Hillman	5.00
42	John Roseboro (R)	7.00
43	Sal Maglie	8.00
44	Wash Senators	8.00
45	Dick Groat	7.00
46	Lou Sleater	5.00
46	Lou Sleater (yellow letters)	20.00
47	Roger Maris (R)	300.00
48	Chuck Harmon	5.00
49	Smokey Burgess	5.00
50	Billy Pierc	5.00
50	Billy Pierc (yellow letters)	20.00
51	Del Rice	5.00
52	Bob Clemente	100.00
52	Bob Clemente (yellow letters)	200.00
53	Morrie Martin	5.00
53	Morrie Martin (yellow letters)	20.00
54	Norm Siebern	5.00
55	Chico Carrasquel	5.00
56	Bill Fischer	5.00
57	Tim Thompson	5.00
57	Tim Thompson (yellow letters)	20.00
58	Art Schult	5.00
58	Art Schult (yellow letters)	20.00
59	Dave Sisler	5.00
60	Del Ennis	5.00
60	Del Ennis (yellow letters)	20.00
61	Darrell Johnson	5.00
61	Darrell Johnson (yellow letters)	20.00
62	Joe DeMaestri	5.00
63	Joe Nuxhall	5.00
64	Joe Lonnett	5.00
65	Von McDaniel	5.00
65	Von McDaniel (yellow letters)	20.00
66	Lee Walls	5.00
67	Joe Ginsberg	5.00
68	Daryl Spencer	5.00
69	Wally Burnette	5.00
70	Al Kaline	50.00
70	Al Kaline (yellow letters)	100.00
71	Brooklyn Dodgers	20.00
72	Bud Byerly	5.00
73	Pete Daley	5.00
74	Roy Face	5.00
75	Gus Bell	5.00
76	Dick Farrell	5.00
76	Dick Farrell (yellow letters)	20.00
77	Don Zimmer	5.00
77	Don Zimmer (yellow letters)	20.00
78	Ernie Johnson	5.00
78	Ernie Johnson (yellow letters)	20.00
79	Dick Williams	5.00
79	Dick Williams (yellow letters)	20.00
80	Dick Drott	5.00
81	Steve Boros	5.00
81	Steve Boros (yellow letters)	20.00
82	Ronnie Kline	5.00
83	Bob Hazle	5.00
84	Billy O'Dell	5.00
85	Luis Aparicio	20.00
85	Luis Aparicio (yellow letters)	40.00
86	Valmy Thomas	5.00
87	Johnny Kucks	5.00
88	Duke Snider	70.00
89	Bill Klaus	5.00
90	Robin Roberts	15.00
91	Chuck Tanner	5.00
92	Clint Courtney	5.00
92	Clint Courtney (yellow letters)	18.00
93	Sandy Amoros	5.00
94	Bob Skinner	5.00
95	Frank Bolling	5.00
96	Joseph Durham	5.00
97	Larry Jackson	5.00
97	Larry Jackson (yellow letters)	18.00
98	Bill Hunter	5.00
98	Bill Hunter (yellow letters)	18.00
99	Bobby Adams	5.00
100	Early Wynn	15.00
100	Early Wynn (yellow letters)	30.00
101	Bob Richardson	10.00
101	Bob Richardson (yellow letters)	32.00
102	George Strickland	5.00
103	Jerry Lynch	5.00
104	Jim Pendleton	5.00
105	Billy Gardner	5.00
106	Dick Schofield	5.00
107	Ossie Virgil	5.00
108	Jim Landis	5.00
108	Jim Landis (yellow letters)	20.00
109	Herb Plews	5.00
110	Johnny Logan	5.00
111	Stu Miller	4.00
112	Gus Zernial	4.00
113	Jerry Walker	4.00
114	Irv Noren	4.00
115	Jim Bunning	15.00
116	Dave Philley	4.00
117	Frank Torre	4.00
118	Harvey Haddix	4.00
119	Harry Chiti	4.00
120	Johnny Podres	8.00
121	Ed Miksis	4.00
122	Walter Moryn	4.00
123	Dick Tomanek	4.00
124	Bobby Usher	4.00
125	Al Dark	4.00
126	Stan Palys	4.00
127	Tom Sturdivant	4.00
128	Willie Kirkland	4.00
129	Jim Derrington	4.00
130	Jackie Jensen	8.00
131	Bob Henrich	4.00
132	Vernon Law	4.00
133	Russ Nixon	6.00
134	Philadelphia Phillies	9.00
135	Mike Drabowsky	4.00
136	Jim Finigan	4.00
137	Russ Kemmerer	4.00
138	Earl Torgeson	4.00
139	George Brunet	4.00
140	Wes Covington	4.00
141	Ken Lehman	4.00
142	Enos Slaughter	17.00
143	Billy Muffett	4.00
144	Bobby Morgan	4.00
146	Dick Gray	4.00
147	Don McMahon	4.00
148	Billy Consolo	4.00
149	Tom Acker	4.00
150	Mickey Mantle	500.00
151	Buddy Pritchard	4.00
152	Johnny Antonelli	4.00
153	Les Moss	4.00
154	Harry Byrd	4.00
155	Hector Lopez	4.00
156	Dick Hyde	4.00
157	Dee Fondy	4.00
158	Cleveland Indians	9.00
159	Taylor Phillips	4.00
160	Don Hoak	4.00
161	Don Larsen	9.00
162	Gil Hodges	20.00
163	Jim Wilson	4.00
164	Bob Taylor	4.00
165	Bob Nieman	4.00
166	Danny O'Connell	4.00
167	Frank Baumann	4.00
168	Joe Cunningham	4.00
169	Ralph Terry	4.00
170	Vic Wertz	4.00
171	Harry Anderson	4.00
172	Don Gross	4.00
173	Eddie Yost	4.00
174	Kansas C. Athletics	9.00
175	Marv Throneberry (R)	8.00
176	Bob Buhl	4.00
177	Al Smith	4.00
178	Ted Kluszewski	8.00
179	Willy Miranda	4.00
180	Lindy McDaniel	4.00
181	Willie Jones	4.00
182	Joe Caffie	4.00
183	Dave Jolly	4.00
184	Elvin Tappe	4.00
185	Ray Boone	4.00
186	Jack Meyer	4.00
187	Sandy Koufax	130.00
188	Milt Bolling (photo of Lou Berberet)	4.00
189	George Susce	4.00
190	Red Schoendienst	15.00
191	Art Ceccarelli	4.00
192	Milt Graff	4.00
193	Jerry Lumpe	4.00
194	Roger Craig	6.00
195	Whitey Lockman	4.00
196	Mike Garcia	4.00
197	Haywood Sullivan	4.00
198	Bill Virdon	4.00
199	Don Blasingame	3.00
200	Bob Keegan	3.00
201	Jim Bolger	3.00
202	Woody Held	3.00
203	Al Walker	3.00
204	Leo Kiely	3.00
205	Johnny Temple	3.00
206	Bob Shaw	3.00
207	Solly Hemus	3.00
208	Cal McLish	3.00
209	Bob Anderson	3.00
210	Wally Moon	3.00
211	Pete Burnside	3.00
212	Bubba Phillips	3.00
213	Red Wilson	3.00
214	Willard Schmidt	3.00
215	Jim Gilliam	7.50
216	St. Louis Cardinals	9.00
217	Jack Harshman	3.00
218	Dick Rand	3.00
219	Camilo Pascual	3.00
220	Tom Brewer	3.00
221	Jerry Kindall	3.00
222	Bud Daley	3.00
223	Andy Pafko	3.00
224	Bob Grim	3.00
225	Billy Goodman	3.00
226	Bob Smith	3.00
227	Gene Stephens	3.00
228	Duke Maas	3.00
229	Frank Zupo	3.00
230	Richie Ashburn	11.00
231	Lloyd Merritt	3.00
232	Reno Bertoia	3.00
233	Mickey Vernon	3.00
234	Carl Sawatski	3.00
235	Tom Gorman	3.00
236	Ed Fitzgerald	3.00
237	Bill Wight	3.00
238	Bill Mazeroski	10.00
239	Chuck Stobbs	3.00
240	Moose Skowron	8.00
241	Dick Littlefield	3.00
242	Johnny Klippstein	3.00
243	Larry Raines	3.00
244	Don Demeter	3.00
245	Frank Lary	3.00
246	New York Yankees	30.00
247	Casey Wise	3.00
248	Herm Wehmeier	3.00
249	Ray Moore	3.00
250	Roy Sievers	3.00
251	Warren Hacker	3.00
252	Bob Trowbridge	3.00
253	Don Mueller	3.00
254	Alex Grammas	3.00
255	Bob Turley	7.00
256	Chicago White Sox	9.00
257	Hal Smith	3.00
258	Carl Erskine	5.00
259	Alan Pilarcik	3.00
260	Frank Malzone	3.00
261	Turk Lown	3.00
262	John Groth	3.00
263	Ed Bressoud	3.00
264	Jack Sanford	3.00
265	Pete Runnels	3.00
266	Connie Johnson	3.00
267	Sherm Lollar	3.00
268	Granny Hamner	3.00
269	Paul Smith	3.00
270	Warren Spahn	40.00
271	Billy Martin	16.00
272	Ray Crone	3.00
273	Hal Smith	3.00
274	Rocky Bridges	3.00
275	Elston Howard	8.00
276	Bobby Avila	3.00
277	Virgil Trucks	3.00
278	Mack Burk	3.00
279	Bob Boyd	3.00
280	Jim Piersall	6.00
281	Sam Taylor	3.00
282	Paul Foytack	3.00
283	Ray Shearer	3.00
284	Ray Katt	3.00
285	Frank Robinson	65.00
286	Gino Cimoli	3.00
287	Sam Jones	3.00
288	Harmon Killebrew	65.00
289	Hurling Rivals: Lou Burdette, Bobby Shantz	7.00
290	Dick Donovan	3.00
291	Don Landrum	3.00
292	Ned Garver	3.00
293	Gene Freese	3.00
294	Hal Jeffcoat	3.00
295	Minnie Minoso	6.00
296	Ryne Duren	7.00
297	Don Buddin	3.00
298	Jim Hearn	3.00
299	Harry Simpson	3.00
300	Harridge and Giles League Presidents	7.00
301	Randy Jackson	3.00
302	Mike Baxes	3.00
303	Neil Chrisley	3.00
304	Tigers' Big Bats: Harvey Kuenn, Al Kaline	10.00
305	Clem Labine	3.00
306	Whammy Douglas	3.00
307	Brooks Robinson	75.00
308	Paul Giel	3.00
309	Gail Harris	3.00
310	Ernie Banks	65.00
311	Bob Purkey	3.00
312	Boston Red Sox	11.00
313	Bob Rush	3.00
314	Boss and Power Duke Snider, Walt Alston	15.00
315	Bob Friend	3.00
316	Tito Francona	3.00
317	Albie Pearson	3.00
318	Frank House	3.00

NO.	PLAYER	NR. MT.
319	Lou Skizas	3.00
320	Whitey Ford	40.00
321	Sluggers Supreme:	25.00
	Ted Kluszewski,	
	Ted Williams	
322	Harding Peterson	3.00
323	Elmer Valo	3.00
324	Hoyt Wilhelm	15.00
325	Joe Adcock	4.00
326	Bob Miller	3.00
327	Chicago Cubs	9.00
328	Ike Delock	3.00
329	Bob Cerv	3.00
330	Ed Bailey	3.00
331	Pedro Ramos	3.00
332	Jim King	3.00
333	Andy Carey	3.00
334	Mound Aces:	4.00
	Bob Friend, Billy Pierce	
335	Ruben Gomez	2.50
336	Bert Hamric	2.50
337	Hank Aguirre	2.50
338	Walter Dropo	2.50
339	Fred Hatfield	2.50
340	Don Newcombe	7.00
341	Pittsburgh Pirates	9.00
342	Jim Brosnan	2.50
343	Orlando Cepeda (R)	50.00
344	Bob Porterfield	3.00
345	Jim Hegan	3.00
346	Steve Bilko	3.00
347	Don Rudolph	3.00
348	Chico Fernandez	3.00
349	Murry Dickson	3.00
350	Ken Boyer	6.00
351	Braves Fence Busters:	20.00
	Del Crandall, Eddie Mathews,	
	Hank Aaron, Joe Adcock	
352	Herb Score	4.00
353	Stan Lopata	2.00
354	Art Ditmar	2.00
355	Billy Bruton	2.00
356	Bob Malkmus	2.00
357	Danny McDevitt	2.00
358	Gene Baker	2.00
359	Billy Loes	2.00
360	Roy McMillan	2.00
361	Mike Fornieles	2.00

NO.	PLAYER	NR. MT.
362	Ray Jablonski	2.00
363	Don Elston	2.00
364	Earl Battey	2.00
365	Tom Morgan	2.00
366	Gene Green	2.00
367	Jack Urban	2.00
368	Rocky Colavito	13.00
369	Ralph Lumenti	2.00
370	Yogi Berra	70.00
371	Marty Keough	2.00
372	Don Cardwell	2.00
373	Joe Pignatano	2.00
374	Brooks Lawrence	2.00
375	Pee Wee Reese	45.00
376	Charley Rabe	2.00
377	Milwaukee Braves*	7.00
378	Hank Sauer	2.00
379	Ray Herbert	2.00
380	Charley Maxwell	2.00
381	Hal Brown	2.00
382	Al Cicotte	2.00
383	Lou Berberet	2.00
384	John Goryl	2.00
385	Wilmer Mizell	2.00
386	Young Sluggers:	7.00
	Ed Bailey, Birdie Tebbetts,	
	Frank Robinson	
387	Wally Post	2.00
388	Billy Moran	2.00
389	Bill Taylor	2.00
390	Del Crandall	2.00
391	Dave Melton	2.00
392	Bennie Daniels	2.00
393	Tony Kubek	15.00
394	Jim Grant	2.00
395	Willard Nixon	2.00
396	Dutch Dotterer	2.00
397	Detroit Tigers*	7.00
398	Gene Woodling	2.00
399	Marv Grissom	2.00
400	Nellie Fox	10.00
401	Don Bessent	2.00
402	Bobby Gene Smith	2.00
403	Steve Korcheck	2.00
404	Curt Simmons	2.00
405	Ken Aspromonte	2.00
406	Vic Power	2.00

NO.	PLAYER	NR. MT.
407	Carlton Willey	2.00
408	Baltimore Orioles*	9.00
409	Frank Thomas	2.00
410	Murray Wall	2.00
411	Tony Taylor	2.00
412	Jerry Staley	2.00
413	Jim Davenport	2.00
414	Sammy White	2.00
415	Bob Bowman	2.00
416	Foster Castleman	2.00
417	Carl Furillo	7.00
418	W. Series Batting Foes:	125.00
	Mickey Mantle, Hank Aaron	
419	Bobby Shantz	2.50
420	Vada Pinson	15.00
421	Dixie Howell	2.00
422	Norm Zauchin	2.00
423	Phil Clark	2.00
424	Larry Doby	5.00
425	Sam Esposito	2.00
426	Johnny O'Brien	2.00
427	Al Worthington	2.00
428	Cincinnati Redlegs*	10.00
429	Gus Triandos	2.00
430	Bobby Thomson	5.00
431	Gene Conley	2.00
432	John Powers	2.00
433	Pancho Herrera	4.00
433	Pancho Herrer	200.00
	(name spelled wrong)	
434	Harvey Kuenn	6.00
435	Ed Roebuck	6.00
436	Rival Fence Busters:	50.00
	Willie Mays, Duke Snider	
437	Bob Speake	2.00
438	Whitey Herzog	2.00
439	Ray Narleski	2.00
440	Eddie Mathews	28.00
441	Jim Marshall	2.00
442	Phil Paine	2.00
443	Billy Harrell	7.00
444	Danny Kravitz	2.00
445	Bob Smith	2.00
446	Carroll Hardy	5.00
447	Ray Monzant	2.00
448	Charlie Lau	5.00
449	Gene Fodge	2.00

NO.	PLAYER	NR. MT.
450	Preston Ward	7.00
451	Joe Taylor	2.00
452	Roman Mejias	2.00
453	Tom Qualters	2.00
454	Harry Hanebrink	2.00
455	Hal Griggs	2.00
456	Dick Brown	2.00
457	Milt Pappas (R)	6.00
458	Julio Becquer	2.00
459	Ron Blackburn	2.00
460	Chuck Essegian	2.00
461	Ed Mayer	2.00
462	Gary Geiger	6.00
463	Vito Valentinetti	2.00
464	Curt Flood (R)	12.00
465	Arnie Portocarrero	2.00
466	Pete Whisenant	2.00
467	Glen Hobbie	2.00
468	Bob Schmidt	2.00
469	Don Ferrarese	2.00
470	R.C. Stevens	2.00
471	Lenny Green	2.00
172	Joe Jay	2.00
473	Bill Renna	2.00
474	Roman Semproch	2.00
475	All-Star Managers:	15.00
	Stengel, Haney	
476	Stan Musial (AS)	30.00
477	Bill Skowron (AS)	3.00
478	Johnny Temple (AS)	3.00
479	Nellie Fox (AS)	5.00
480	Eddie Mathews (AS)	12.00
481	Frank Malzone (AS)	3.00
482	Ernie Banks (AS)	15.00
483	Luis Aparicio (AS)	9.00
484	Frank Robinson (AS)	13.00
485	Ted Williams (AS)	45.00
486	Willie Mays (AS)	30.00
487	Mickey Mantle (AS)	70.00
488	Hank Aaron (AS)	30.00
489	Jackie Jensen (AS)	4.00
490	Ed Bailey (AS)	3.00
491	Sherm Lollar (AS)	3.00
492	Bob Friend (AS)	3.00
493	Bob Turley (AS)	3.00
494	Warren Spahn (AS)	15.00
495	H. Score (AS) (Exc. $1.50)	7.00

1959 Topps . . . Complete Set of 572 Cards—Value $1600.00 (Exc.); $4000.00 (Near Mint)

Includes Bob Gibson's rookie card. The high numbers are 507 to 572. Cards 199 to 286 were issued with *white* or *gray* backs. Cards 316, 321, 322, 336 and 362 exist without the *option* or *traded* line—worth $75.00 each.

NO.	PLAYER	NR. MT.
1	BB Commissioner	50.00
	Ford Frick (Exc. $7.50)	
2	Eddie Yost	3.50
3	Don McMahon	3.50
4	Albie Pearson	3.50
5	Dick Donovan	3.50
6	Alex Grammas	3.50
7	Al Pilarcik	3.50
8	Philadelphia Phillies	6.00
9	Paul Giel	3.50

NO.	PLAYER	NR. MT.
10	Mickey Mantle	350.00
11	Billy Hunter	3.50
12	Vern Law	4.00
13	Dick Gernert	3.50
14	Pete Whisenant	3.50
15	Dick Drott	3.50
16	Joe Pignatano	3.50
17	Danny's All-Stars:	5.00
	Frank Thomas, Danny	
	Murtaugh, Ted Kluszewski	

NO.	PLAYER	NR. MT.
18	Jack Urban	3.50
19	Ed Bressoud	3.50
20	Duke Snider	50.00
21	Connie Johnson	3.50
22	Al Smith	3.50
23	Murry Dickson	3.50
24	Red Wilson	3.50
25	Dan Hoak	3.50
26	Chuck Stobbs	3.50
27	Andy Pafko	3.50

NO.	PLAYER	NR. MT.
28	Red Worthington	3.50
29	Jim Bolger	3.50
30	Nellie Fox	9.00
31	Ken Lehman	3.50
32	Don Buddin	3.50
33	Ed Fizgerald	3.50
34	Pitchers Beware:	8.00
	Al Kaline, Charley Maxwell	
35	Ted Kluszewski	6.00
36	Hank Aguirre	3.00

NO. PLAYER	NR. MT.
37 Gene Green	3.50
38 Morrie Martin	3.50
39 Ed Bouchee	3.50
40 Warren Spahn	40.00
41 Bob Martyn	3.50
42 Murray Wall	3.50
43 Steven Bilko	3.50
44 Vito Valentinetti	3.50
45 Andy Carey	3.50
46 Bill Henry	3.50
47 Jim Finigan	3.50
48 Baltimore Orioles	7.00
49 Bill Hall	3.50
50 Willie May	110.00
51 Rip Coleman	3.50
52 Coot Veal	3.50
53 Stan Williams	3.50
54 Mel Roach	3.50
55 Tom Brewer	3.50
56 Carl Sawatski	3.50
57 Al Cicotte	3.50
58 Eddie Miksis	3.50
59 Irv Noren	3.50
60 Bob Turley	6.00
61 Dick Brown	3.50
62 Tony Taylor	3.50
63 Jim Hearn	3.50
64 Joe DeMaestri	3.50
65 Frank Torre	3.50
66 Joe Ginsberg	3.50
67 Brooks Lawrence	3.50
68 Dick Schofield	3.50
69 San F. Giants	9.00
70 Harvey Kuenn	5.00
71 Don Bessent	3.50
72 Bill Renna	3.50
73 Ron Jackson	3.50
74 Directing the Power: Jim Lemon, Cookie Lavagetto, Roy Sievers	4.00
75 Sam Jones	3.50
76 Bobby Richardson	8.00
77 John Goryl	3.50
78 Pedro Ramos	3.50
79 Harry Chiti	3.50
80 Minnie Minoso	6.00
81 Hal Jeffcoat	3.50
82 Bob Boyd	3.50
83 Bob Smith	3.50
84 Reno Bertoia	3.50
85 Harry Anderson	3.50
86 Bob Keegan	3.50
87 Danny O'Connell	3.50
88 Herb Score	4.00
89 Billy Gardner	3.50
90 Bill Skowron	7.00
91 Herb Moford	3.50
92 David Philley	3.50
93 Julio Becquer	3.50
94 Chicago White Sox	7.00
95 Carl Willey	3.50
96 Lou Berberet	3.50
97 Jerry Lynch	3.50
98 Arnie Portocarrero	3.50
99 Ted Kazanski	3.50
100 Bob Cerv	3.50
101 Alex Kellner	3.50
102 Felipe Alou (R)	8.00
103 Billy Goodman	3.50
104 Del Rice	3.50
105 Lee Walls	3.50
106 Hal Woodeshick	3.50
107 Norm Larker	3.50
108 Zack Monroe	3.50
109 Bob Schmidt	3.50
110 George Witt	3.50
111 Cincinnati Redlegs	9.00
112 Billy Consolo	2.00
113 Taylor Phillips	2.00
114 Earl Battey	2.00
115 Mickey Vernon	2.00

No. 116 to 146 Rookie Stars

NO. PLAYER	NR. MT.
116 Bob Allison	5.00
117 John Blanchard	2.00
118 John Buzhardt	2.00
119 John Callison	4.00
120 Chuck Coles	2.00
121 Bob Conley	2.00
122 Bennie Daniels	2.00
123 Donald Dillard	2.00
124 Dan Dobbek	2.00
125 Ron Fairly	4.00
126 Eddie Haas	2.00
127 Kent Hadley	2.00
128 Bob Hartman	2.00
129 Frank Herrera	2.00
130 Lou Jackson	2.00
131 Deron Johnson	2.00
132 Don Lee	2.00
133 Bob Lillis	2.00
134 Jim McDaniel	2.00
135 Gene Oliver	2.00
136 Jim O'Toole	2.00
137 Dick Ricketts	2.00
138 John Romano	2.00
139 Ed Sadowski	2.00
140 Charlie Secrest	2.00
141 Joe Shipley	2.00
142 Dick Stigman	2.00
143 Willie Tasby	2.00
144 Jerry Walker	2.00
145 Dom Zanni	2.00
146 Jerry Zimmerman	2.00
147 Cubs' Clubbers: Dale Long, Ernie Banks, Walt Moryn	7.00
148 Mike McCormick	2.00
149 Jim Bunning	9.00
150 Stan Musial	120.00
151 Bob Malkmus	2.00
152 Johnny Klippstein	2.00
153 Jim Marshall	2.00
154 Ray Herbert	2.00
155 Enos Slaughter	15.00
156 Ace Hurlers: Billy Pierce, Robin Roberts	5.00
157 Felix Mantilla	2.00
158 Walt Dropo	2.00
159 Bob Shaw	2.00
160 Dick Groat	5.00
161 Frank Baumann	2.00
162 Bobby Smith	2.00
163 Sandy Koufax	125.00
164 Johnny Groth	2.00
165 Bill Bruton	2.00
166 Destruction Crew: Minnie Minoso, Rocky Colavito, Larry Doby	4.00
167 Duke Maas	2.00
168 Carroll Hardy	2.00
169 Ted Abernathy	2.00
170 Gene Woodling	2.00
171 Willard Schmidt	2.00
172 Kansas C. Athletics	7.00
173 Bill Monbouquette	2.00
174 Jim Pendleton	2.00
175 Dick Farrell	2.00
176 Preston Ward	2.00
177 John Briggs	2.00
178 Ruben Amaro	2.00
179 Don Rudolph	2.00
180 Yogi Berra	60.00
181 Bob Porterfield	2.00
182 Milt Graff	2.00
183 Stu Miller	2.00
184 Harvey Haddix	3.00
185 Jim Busby	2.00
186 Mudcat Grant	2.00
187 Bubba Phillips	2.00
188 Juan Pizarro	2.00
189 Neil Chrisley	2.00
190 Bill Virdon	5.00

NO. PLAYER	NR. MT.
191 Russ Kemmerer	2.00
192 Charley Beamon	2.00
193 Sammy Taylor	2.00
194 Jim Brosnan	2.00
195 Rip Repulski	2.00
196 Billy Moran	2.00
197 Ray Semproch	2.00
198 Jim Davenport	2.00
199 Leo Kiely	2.00
200 NL President: Warren Giles	4.00
201 Tom Acker	2.00
202 Roger Maris	125.00
203 Ozzie Virgil	2.00
204 Casey Wise	2.00
205 Don Larsen	5.00
206 Carl Furillo	5.00
207 George Strickland	2.00
208 Willie Jones	2.00
209 Lenny Green	2.00
210 Ed Bailey	2.00
211 Bob Blaylock	2.00
212 Fence Busters: Hank Aaron, Eddie Mathews	30.00
213 Jim Rivera	2.00
214 Marcelino Solis	2.00
215 Jim Lemon	2.00
216 Andre Rodgers	2.00
217 Carl Erskine	4.00
218 Roman Mejias	2.00
219 George Zuverink	2.00
220 Frank Malzone	2.00
221 Bob Bowman	2.00
222 Bobby Shantz	2.00
223 St. Louis Cardinals	9.00
224 Claude Osteen (R)	4.00
225 Johnny Logan	2.00
226 Art Ceccarelli	2.00
227 Hal Smith	2.00
228 Don Gross	2.00
229 Vic Power	2.00
230 Bill Fischer	2.00
231 Ellis Burton	2.00
232 Eddie Kasko	2.00
233 Paul Foytack	2.00
234 Chuck Tanner	4.00
235 Valmy Thomas	2.00
236 Ted Bowsfield	2.00
237 Run Preventers: Gil McDougald, Bob Turley, Bobby Richardson	4.00
238 Gene Baker	2.00
239 Bob Trowbridge	2.00
240 Hank Bauer	5.00
241 Billy Muffett	2.00
242 Ron Samford	2.00
243 Marv Grissom	2.00
244 Dick Gray	2.00
245 Ned Garver	2.00
246 J.W. Porter	2.00
247 Don Ferrarese	2.00
248 Boston Red Sox	9.00
249 Bobby Adams	2.00
250 Billy O'Dell	2.00
251 Cletis Boyer	4.00
252 Ray Boone	2.00
253 Seth Morehead	2.00
254 Zeke Bella	2.00
255 Del Ennis	2.00
256 Jerry Davie	2.00
257 Leon Wagner	2.00
258 Fred Kipp	2.00
259 Jim Pisoni	2.00
260 Early Wynn	12.00
261 Gene Stephens	2.00
262 Hitters' Foes: Johnny Podres, Clem Labine, Don Drysdale	4.00
263 Buddy Daley	2.00
264 Chico Carrasquel	2.00
265 Ron Kline	2.00

NO. PLAYER	NR. MT.
266 Woody Held	2.00
267 John Romonosky	2.00
268 Tito Francona	2.00
269 Jack Mayer	2.00
270 Gil Hodges	15.00
271 Orlando Pena	2.00
272 Jerry Lumpe	2.00
273 Joey Jay	2.00
274 Jerry Kindall	2.00
275 Jack Sanford	2.00
276 Pete Daley	2.00
277 Turk Lown	2.00
278 Chuck Essegian	2.00
279 Ernie Johnson	2.00
280 Frank Bolling	2.00
281 Walt Craddock	2.00
282 R.C. Stevens	2.00
283 Russ Heman	2.00
284 Steve Korcheck	2.00
285 Joe Cunningham	2.00
286 Dean Stone	2.00
287 Don Zimmer	2.00
288 Dutch Dotterer	2.00
289 Johnny Kucks	2.00
290 Wes Covington	2.00
291 Pitching Partners: Pedro Ramos, Camilo Pascual	3.00
292 Dick Williams	2.00
293 Ray Moore	2.00
294 Hank Foiles	2.00
295 Billy Martin	13.00
296 Ernie Broglio	2.00
297 Jackie Brandt	2.00
298 Tex Clevenger	2.00
299 Billy Klaus	2.00
300 Richie Ashburn	10.00
301 Earl Averill	2.00
302 Don Mossi	2.00
303 Marty Keough	2.00
304 Chicago Cubs	9.00
305 Curt Raydon	2.00
306 Jim Gilliam	5.00
307 Curt Barclay	2.00
308 Norm Siebern	2.00
309 Sal Maglie	4.00
310 Luis Aparicio	15.00
311 Norm Zauchin	2.00
312 Don Newcombe	4.00
313 Frank House	2.00
314 Don Cardwell	2.00
315 Joe Adcock	2.50
316 Ralph Lumenti* (photo of Camilo Pascual)	2.00
317 Hitting Kings: Willie Mays, Richie Ashburn	15.00
318 Rocky Bridges	2.00
319 Dave Hillmann	2.00
320 Bob Skinner	2.00
321 Bob Giallombardo*	2.00
322 Harry Hanebrink*	2.00
323 Frank Sullivan	2.00
324 Donald Demeter	2.00
325 Ken Boyer	5.00
326 Marv Throneberry	3.00
327 Gary Bell	2.00
328 Lou Skizas	2.00
329 Detroit Tigers	9.00
330 Gus Triandos	2.00
331 Steve Boros	2.00
332 Ray Monzant	2.00
333 Harry Simpson	2.00
334 Glen Hobbie	2.00
335 Johnny Temple	2.00
336 Billy Loes*	2.00
337 George Crowe	1.25
338 Sparky Anderson (R)	20.00
339 Roy Face	3.00
340 Roy Sievers	4.00
341 Tom Qualters	2.00
342 Ray Jablonski	2.00

NO. PLAYER	NR. MT.	NO. PLAYER	NR. MT.	NO. PLAYER	NR. MT.	NO. PLAYER	NR. MT.
343 Billy Hoeft	2.00	401 Ron Blackburn	2.00	458 Gordon Jones	2.00	518 Mike Cueller (R)	16.00
344 Russ Nixon	2.00	402 Hector Lopez	2.00	459 Bill Tuttle	2.00	519 Infield Power:	10.00
345 Gil McDougald	5.00	403 Clem Labine	2.00	460 Bob Friend	2.00	Pete Runnels, Dick	
346 Batter Bafflers:	2.00	404 Hank Sauer	2.00	461 Mantle Hits 42nd HR	35.00	Gernert, Frank Malzone	
Tom Brewer, Dave Sisler		405 Roy McMillan	2.00	462 Colavito's Catch	3.50	520 Don Elston	10.00
347 Bob Buhl	2.00	406 Solly Drake	2.00	463 Kaline Bat Champ	10.00	521 Gary Geiger	10.00
348 Ted Lepcio	2.00	407 Moe Drabowsky	2.00	464 Mays' Series Catch	15.00	522 Gene Snyder	10.00
349 Hoyt Wilhelm	12.00	408 Keystone Combo:	6.00	465 Sievers HR Mark	3.00	523 Harry Bright	10.00
350 Ernie Banks	55.00	Nellie Fox, Luis Aparicio		466 Pierce All-Star	3.00	524 Larry Osborne	10.00
351 Earl Torgeson	2.00	409 Gus Zernial	2.00	467 Aaron Clubs Homer	15.00	525 Jim Coates	10.00
352 Robin Roberts	15.00	410 Billy Pierce	2.00	468 Snider's Play	10.00	526 Bob Speake	10.00
353 Curt Flood	4.00	411 Whitey Lockman	2.00	469 Banks MVP	9.00	527 Solly Hemus	10.00
354 Pete Burnside	2.00	412 Stan Lopata	2.00	470 Musial's 3000 Hits	13.00	528 Pittsburgh Pirates	27.00
355 Jim Piersall	4.00	413 Camillo Pascual	2.00	471 Tom Sturdivant	2.00	529 George Bamberger (R)	10.00
356 Bob Mabe	2.00	414 Dale Long	2.00	472 Gene Freese	2.00	530 Wally Moon	10.00
357 Dick Stuart (R)	3.00	415 Bill Mazeroski	5.00	473 Mike Fornieles	2.00	531 Ray Webster	10.00
358 Ralph Terry	2.00	416 Haywood Sullivan	2.00	474 Moe Thacker	2.00	532 Mark Freeman	10.00
359 Bill White (R)	15.00	417 Virgil Trucks	2.00	475 Jack Harshman	2.00	533 Darrell Johnson	10.00
360 Al Kaline	45.00	418 Gino Cimoli	2.00	476 Cleveland Indians	6.00	534 Faye Throneberry	10.00
361 Willard Nixon	2.00	419 Milwaukee Braves	4.00	477 Barry Latman	2.00	535 Ruben Gomez	10.00
362 Dolan Nichols*	2.00	420 Rocky Colavito	6.00	478 Bob Clemente	85.00	536 Dan Kravitz	10.00
363 Bobby Avila	2.00	421 Herm Wehmeier	2.00	479 Lindy McDaniel	2.00	537 Rudolph Arias	10.00
364 Danny McDevitt	2.00	422 Hobie Landrith	2.00	480 Red Schoendienst	11.00	538 Chick King	10.00
365 Gus Bell	2.00	423 Bob Grim	2.00	481 Charlie Maxwell	2.00	539 Gary Blaylock	10.00
366 Humberto Robinson	2.00	424 Ken Aspromonte	2.00	482 Russ Meyer	2.00	540 Willie Miranda	10.00
367 Cal Neeman	2.00	425 Del Crandall	2.00	483 Clint Courtney	2.00	541 Bob Thurman	10.00
368 Don Mueller	2.00	426 Jerry Staley	2.00	484 Willie Kirkland	2.00	542 Jim Perry (R)	15.00
369 Dick Tomanek	2.00	427 Charlie Neal	2.00	485 Ryne Duren	2.00	543 Corsair Outfield Trio:	50.00
370 Pete Runnels	2.00	428 Buc Hill Aces:	4.00	486 Sammy White	2.00	Bob Skinner, Bll Virdon,	
371 Dick Brodowski	2.00	Ron Kline, Bob Friend,		487 Hal Brown	2.00	Roberto Clemente	
372 Jim Hegan	2.00	Vernon Law, Roy Face		488 Walt Moryn	2.00	544 Lee Tate	10.00
373 Herb Plews	2.00	429 Bobby Thomson	2.50	489 John Powers	2.00	545 Tom Morgan	10.00
374 Art Ditmar	2.00	430 Whitey Ford	35.00	490 Frank Thomas	2.00	546 Al Schroll	10.00
375 Bob Nieman	2.00	431 Whammy Douglas	2.00	491 Don Blasingame	2.00	547 Jim Baxes	10.00
376 Hal Naragon	2.00	432 Smokey Burgess	2.00	492 Gene Conley	2.00	548 Elmer Singleton	10.00
377 Johnny Antonelli	2.00	433 Billy Harrell	2.00	493 Jim Landis	2.00	549 Howie Nunn	10.00
378 Gail Harris	2.00	434 Hal Griggs	2.00	494 Don Pavletich	2.00	550 Symbol of Courage:	120.00
379 Bob Miller	2.00	435 Frank Robinson	35.00	495 Johnny Podres	4.00	Roy Campanella	
380 Hank Aaron	100.00	436 Granny Hamner	2.00	496 Wayne Terwilliger	2.00	551 F. Haney—Mgr.(AS)	10.00
381 Mike Baxes	2.00	437 Ike Delock	2.00	497 Hal R. Smith	2.00	552 C. Stengel—Mgr. (AS)	25.00
382 Curt Simmons	2.00	438 Sam Esposito	2.00	498 Dick Hyde	2.00	553 Orlando Cepeda (AS)	15.00
383 Words of Wisdom:	6.00	439 Brooks Robinson	45.00	499 Johnny O'Brien	2.00	554 Bll Skowron (AS)	10.00
Don Larsen, Casey Stengel		440 Lou Burdette	6.00	500 Vic Wertz	2.00	555 Bill Mazeroski (AS)	11.00
384 Dave Sisler	2.00	441 John Roseboro	2.00	501 Bobby Tiefenauer	2.00	556 Nellie Fox (AS)	15.00
385 Sherm Lollar	2.00	442 Ray Narleski	2.00	502 Al Dark	2.00	557 Ken Boyer (AS)	10.00
386 Jim Delsing	2.00	443 Daryl Spencer	2.00	503 Jim Owens	2.00	558 Frank Malzone (AS)	10.00
387 Don Drysdale	35.00	444 Ronnie Hansen	2.00	504 Ossie Alvarez	2.00	559 Ernie Banks (AS)	35.00
388 Bob Will	2.00	445 Cal McLish	2.00	505 Tony Kubek	7.50	560 Luis Aparicio (AS)	17.00
389 Joe Nuxhall	2.00	446 Rocky Nelson	2.00	506 Bob Purkey	2.00	561 Hank Aaron (AS)	90.00
390 Orlando Cepeda	12.00	447 Bob Anderson	2.00	507 Bob Hale	7.50	562 Al Kaline (AS)	30.00
391 Milt Pappas	2.00	448 Vada Pinson	5.00	508 Art Fowler	7.50	563 Willie Mays (AS)	90.00
392 Whitey Herzog	3.00	449 Tom Gorman	2.00	509 Norm Cash (R)	30.00	564 Mickey Mantle (AS)	200.00
393 Frank Lary	2.00	450 Ed Mathews	25.00	510 New York Yankees	50.00	565 Wes Covington (AS)	10.00
394 Randy Jackson	2.00	451 Jimmy Constable	2.00	511 George Susce	10.00	566 Roy Sievers (AS)	10.00
395 Elston Howard	6.00	452 Chico Fernandez	2.00	512 George Altman	10.00	567 Del Crandall (AS)	10.00
396 Bob Rush	2.00	453 Les Moss	2.00	513 Tommy Carroll	10.00	568 Gus Triandos (AS)	10.00
397 Washington Senators	8.00	454 Phil Clark	2.00	514 Bob Gibson (R)	375.00	569 Bob Friend (AS)	10.00
398 Wally Post	2.00	455 Larry Doby	4.00	515 Harmon Killebrew	100.00	570 Bob Turley (AS)	10.00
399 Larry Jackson	2.00	456 Jerry Casale	2.00	516 Mike Garcia	10.00	571 Warren Spahn (AS)	35.00
400 Jackie Jensen	3.00	457 Los Angeles Dodgers	15.00	517 Joe Koppe	10.00	572 B. Pierce (AS) (Exc. $5.00)	20.00

1960 Topps . . . Complete Set of 572 Cards—Value $1500.00 (Exc.); $3500.00 (Near Mint)

This set features the rookie cards of Willie McCovey and Carl Yastrzemski. The high numbers are 507 to 572. Semi-high numbers are 441 to 506. Topps' switched to a predominately horizontal format, and used it for the last time. Cards 375 to 440 exist with *gray* or *white* backs.

NO.	PLAYER	NR. MT.
1	E. Wynn (Exc. $6.00)	30.00
2	Roman Mejias	1.50
3	Joe Adcock	3.00
4	Bob Purkey	1.50
5	Wally Moon	1.50
6	Lou Berberet	1.50
7	Master & Mentor: Willie Mays, Bill Rigney	10.00
8	Bud Daley	1.50
9	Faye Throneberry	1.50
10	Ernie Banks	35.00
11	Norm Siebern	1.50
12	Milt Pappas	1.50
13	Wally Post	1.50
14	Jim Grant	1.50
15	Pete Runnels	1.50
16	Ernie Broglio	1.50
17	John Callison	1.50
18	Los Angeles Dodgers	9.00
19	Felix Mantilla	1.50
20	Roy Face	2.25
21	Dutch Dotterer	1.50
22	Rocky Bridges	1.50
23	Eddie Fisher	1.50
24	Dick Gray	1.50
25	Ray Sievers	1.50
26	Wayne Terwilliger	1.50
27	Dick Drott	1.50
28	Brooks Robinson	30.00
29	Clem Labine	1.50
30	Tito Francona	1.50
31	Sammy Esposito	1.50
32	Sophomore Stalwarts: Jim O'Toole, Vada Pinson	2.00
33	Tom Morgan	1.50
34	Sparky Anderson	5.00
35	Whitey Ford	30.00
36	Russ Nixon	1.50
37	Bill Bruton	1.50
38	Jerry Casale	1.50
39	Earl Averill	1.50
40	Joe Cunningham	1.50
41	Barry Latman	1.50
42	Hobie Landrith	1.50
43	Washington Senators	5.00
44	Bobby Locke	1.50
45	Roy McMillan	1.50
46	Jack Fisher	1.50
47	Don Zimmer	5.00
48	Hal Smith	1.50
49	Curt Raydon	1.50
50	Al Kaline	30.00
51	Jim Coates	1.50
52	Dave Philley	1.50
53	Jackie Brandt	1.50
54	Mike Fornieles	1.50
55	Bill Mazeroski	4.00
56	Steve Korcheck	1.50
57	Win Savers: Turk Lown, Jerry Staley	2.00
58	Gino Cimoli	1.50
59	Juan Pizarro	1.50
60	Gus Triandos	1.50
61	Eddie Kasko	1.50
62	Roger Craig	3.00
63	George Strickland	1.50
64	Jack Meyer	1.50
65	Elston Howard	4.00
66	Bob Trowbridge	1.50
67	Jose Pagan	1.50
68	Dave Hillman	1.50
69	Billy Goodman	1.50
70	Lou Burdette	3.00
71	Marty Keough	1.50
72	Detroit Tigers	4.00
73	Bob Gibson	35.00
74	Walt Moryn	1.50
75	Vic Power	1.50
76	Bill Fischer	1.50
77	Hank Foiles	1.50
78	Bob Grim	1.50
79	Walt Dropo	1.50
80	Johnny Antonelli	1.50
81	Russ Snyder	1.50
82	Ruben Gomez	1.50
83	Tony Kubek	5.00
84	Hal Smith	1.50
85	Frank Lary	1.50
86	Dick Gernert	1.50
87	John Romonosky	1.50
88	John Roseboro	1.50
89	Hal Brown	1.50
90	Bobby Avila	1.50
91	Bennie Daniels	1.50
92	Whitey Herzog	2.50
93	Art Schult	1.50
94	Leo Kiely	1.50
95	Frank Thomas	1.50
96	Ralph Terry	1.50
97	Ted Lepcio	1.50
98	Gordon Jones	1.50
99	Lenny Green	1.50
100	Nellie Fox	6.00
101	Bob Miller	1.50
102	Kent Hadley	1.50
103	Dick Farrell	1.50
104	Dick Schofield	1.50
105	Larry Sherry (R)	2.00
106	Billy Gardner	1.50
107	Carl Willey	1.50
108	Pete Daley	1.50
109	Cletis Boyer	2.00
110	Cal McLish	1.50
111	Vic Wertz	1.50
112	Jack Harshman	1.50
113	Bob Skinner	1.50
114	Ken Apromonte	1.50
115	Fork & Knuckler: Roy Face, Hoyt Wilhelm	4.00
116	Jim Rivera	1.50

No. 117 to 148—ROOKIE STARS

NO.	PLAYER	NR. MT.
117	Tom Borland	1.50
118	Bob Bruce	1.50
119	Chico Cardenas	1.50
120	Duke Carmel	1.50
121	Camilo Carreon	1.50
122	Don Dillard	1.50
123	Dan Dobbek	1.50
124	Jim Donohue	1.50
125	Dick Ellsworth	1.50
126	Chuck Estrada (R)	2.00
127	Ronnie Hansen	1.50
128	Bill Harris	1.50
129	Bob Hartman	1.50
130	Frank Herrera	1.50
131	Ed Hobaugh	1.50
132	Frank Howard (R)	10.00
133	Manuel Javier	1.50
134	Deron Johnson	1.50
135	Ken Johnson	1.50
136	Jim Kaat (R)	22.00
137	Lou Klimchock	1.50
138	Art Mahaffey	1.50
139	Carl Mathias	1.50
140	Julio Navarro	1.50
141	Jim Proctor	1.50
142	Bill Short	1.50
143	Al Spangler	1.50
144	Al Stieglitz	1.50
145	Jim Umbricht	1.50
146	Ted Wieand	1.50
147	Bob Will	1.50
148	Carl Yastrzemski (R)	300.00
149	Bob Nieman	1.50
150	Billy Pierce	2.00
151	San F. Giants	6.00
152	Gail Harris	1.00
153	Bobby Thomson	2.00
154	Jim Davenport	1.50
155	Charlie Neal	1.50
156	Art Ceccarelli	1.50
157	Rocky Nelson	1.50
158	Wes Covington	1.50
159	Jim Piersall	2.50
160	Rival All-Stars: Mickey Mantle, Ken Boyer	30.00
161	Ray Narleski	1.50
162	Sammy Taylor	1.50
163	Hector Lopez	1.50
164	Cincinnati Reds	5.00
165	Jack Sanford	1.50
166	Chuck Essegian	1.50
167	Valmy Thomas	1.50
168	Alex Grammas	1.50
169	Jake Striker	1.50
170	Del Crandall	1.50
171	Johnny Groth	1.50
172	Willie Kirkland	1.50
173	Billy Martin	10.00
174	Cleveland Indians	5.00
175	Pedro Ramos	1.50
176	Vada Pinson	3.00
177	Johnny Kucks	1.50
178	Woody Held	1.50
179	Rip Coleman	1.50
180	Harry Simpson	1.50
181	Billy Loes	1.50
182	Glen Hobbie	1.50
183	Eli Grba	1.50
184	Gary Geiger	1.50
185	Jim Owens	1.50
186	Dave Sisler	1.50
187	Jay Hook	1.50
188	Dick Williams	1.50
189	Don McMahon	1.50
190	Gene Woodling	1.50
191	Johnny Klippstein	1.50
192	Danny O'Connell	1.50
193	Dick Hyde	1.50
194	Bobby Gene Smith	1.50
195	Lindy McDaniel	1.50
196	Andy Carey	1.50
197	Ron Kline	1.50
198	Jerry Lynch	1.50
199	Dick Donovan	1.50
200	Willie Mays	90.00
201	Larry Osborne	1.50
202	Fred Kipp	1.50
203	Sammy White	1.50
204	Ryne Duren	1.50
205	Johnny Logan	1.50
206	Claude Osteen	1.50
207	Bob Boyd	1.50
208	Chicago White Sox	5.00
209	Ron Blackburn	1.50
210	Harmon Killebrew	27.00
211	Taylor Phillips	1.50
212	Walt Alston (Mgr.)	9.00
213	Chuck Dressen (Mgr.)	2.00
214	Jim Dykes (Mgr.)	2.00
215	Bob Elliott (Mgr.)	2.00
216	Joe Gordon (Mgr.)	2.00
217	Charley Grimm (Mgr.)	2.00
218	Solly Hemus (Mgr.)	2.00
219	Fred Hutchinson (Mgr.)	2.00
220	Billy Jurges (Mgr.)	2.00
221	Cookie Lavagetto (Mgr.)	2.00
222	Al Lopez (Mgr.)	6.00
223	Danny Murtaugh (Mgr.)	2.00
224	Paul Richards (Mgr.)	2.00
225	Bill Rigney (Mgr.)	2.00
226	Eddie Sawyer (Mgr.)	2.00
227	Casey Stengel (Mgr.)	15.00
228	Ernie Johnson	2.00
229	Joe Morgan	5.00
230	Mound Magicians: Lou Burdette, Warren Spahn, Bob Buhl	7.00
231	Hal Naragon	1.50
232	Jim Busby	1.50
233	Don Elston	1.50
234	Don Demeter	1.50
235	Gus Bell	1.50
236	Dick Ricketts	1.50
237	Elmer Valo	1.50
238	Danny Kravitz	1.50
239	Joe Shipley	1.50
240	Luis Aparicio	11.00
241	Albie Pearson	1.50
242	St. Louis Cardinals	4.00
243	Bubba Phillips	1.50
244	Hal Griggs	1.50
245	Eddie Yost	1.50
246	Lee Maye	1.50
247	Gil McDougald	4.00
248	Del Rice	1.50
249	Earl Wilson	1.50
250	Stan Musial	100.00
251	Bobby Malkmus	1.50
252	Ray Herbert	1.50
253	Eddie Bressoud	1.50
254	Arnie Portocarrero	1.50
255	Jim Gilliam	3.00
256	Dick Brown	1.50
257	Gordy Coleman	1.50
258	Dick Groat	4.00
259	George Altman	1.50
260	Power Plus: Rocky Colavito, Tito Francona	2.00
261	Pete Burnside	1.50
262	Hank Bauer	1.50
263	Darrell Johnson	1.50
264	Robin Roberts	10.00
265	Rip Repulski	1.50
266	Joe Jay	1.50
267	Jim Marshall	1.50
268	Al Worthington	1.50
269	Gene Green	1.50
270	Bob Turley	2.00
271	Julio Bequer	1.50
272	Fred Green	1.50
273	Neil Chrisley	1.50
274	Tom Acker	1.50
275	Curt Flood	3.00
276	Ken McBride	1.50
277	Harry Bright	1.50
278	Stan Williams	1.50
279	Chuck Tanner	1.50
280	Frank Sullivan	1.50
281	Ray Boone	1.50
282	Joe Nuxhall	1.50
283	John Blanchard	1.50
284	Don Gross	1.50
285	Harry Anderson	1.50
286	Ray Semproch	1.50
287	Felipe Alou	3.00
288	Bob Mabe	2.00
289	Willie Jones	2.00
290	Jerry Lumpe	2.00
291	Bob Keegan	2.00
292	Dodger Backstops: Joe Pignatano, John Roseboro	3.00
293	Gene Conley	2.00
294	Tony Taylor	2.00
295	Gil Hodges	15.00
296	Nelson Chittum	2.00
297	Reno Bertoia	2.00
298	George Witt	2.00
299	Earl Torgeson	2.00
300	Hank Aaron	100.00
301	Jerry Davie	2.00
302	Philadelphia Phillies	5.00
303	Billy O'Dell	2.00
304	Joe Ginsberg	2.00
305	Richie Ashburn	8.00
306	Frank Baumann	2.00
307	Gene Oliver	2.00
308	Dick Hall	2.00
309	Bob Hale	2.00
310	Frank Malzone	2.00
311	Raul Sanchez	2.00
312	Charlie Lau	2.00
313	Turk Lown	2.00
314	Chico Fernandez	2.00
315	Bobby Shantz	3.00

NO. PLAYER	NR. MT.
316 Willie McCovey (R) ...	200.00
317 Pumpsie Green	2.00
318 Jim Baxes	2.00
319 Joe Koppe	2.00
320 Bob Allison	2.00
321 Ron Fairly	2.00
322 Willie Tasby	2.00
323 Johnny Romano	2.00
324 Jim Perry	3.00
325 Jim O'Toole	2.00
326 Bob Clemente.......	90.00
327 Ray Sadecki	2.00
328 Earl Battey	2.00
329 Zack Monroe.........	2.00
330 Harvey Kuenn........	4.00
331 Henry Mason	2.00
332 New York Yankees ...	20.00
333 Danny McDevitt	2.00
334 Ted Abernathy	2.00
335 Red Schoendienst	10.00
336 Ike Delock	2.00
337 Cal Neeman	2.00
338 Ray Monzant	2.00
339 Harry Chiti	2.00
340 Harvey Haddix	4.00
341 Carroll Hardy	2.00
342 Casey Wise	2.00
343 Sandy Koufax	100.00
344 Clint Courtney	2.00
345 Don Newcombe	2.50
346 J.C. Martin.........	2.00
(photo of Gary Peters)	
347 Ed Bouchee..........	2.00
348 Barry Shetrone	2.00
349 Moe Drabowsky	2.00
350 Mickey Mantle	350.00
351 Don Nottebart......	2.00
352 Cincy Clouters:	4.00
Gus Bell, Frank	
Robinson, Jerry Lynch	
353 Don Larsen	3.00
354 Bob Lillis	2.00
355 Bill White	4.00
356 Joe Amalfitano	2.00
357 Al Schroll	2.00
358 Joe DeMaestri	2.00
359 Buddy Gilbert	2.00
360 Herb Score	3.00
361 Bob Oldis	2.00
362 Russ Kemmerer	2.00
363 Gene Stephens......	2.00
364 Paul Foytack	2.00
365 Minnie Minoso	4.00
366 Dallas Green (R)	8.00
367 Bill Tuttle	2.00
368 Daryl Spencer	2.00
369 Billy Hoeft	2.00
370 Bill Skowron	5.00
371 Bud Byerly.........	2.00
372 Frank House	2.00
373 Don Hoak	2.00
374 Bob Buhl	2.00
375 Dale Long	2.00
376 Johnny Briggs	2.00
377 Roger Maris..........	100.00
378 Stu Miller	2.00
379 Red Wilson	2.00
380 Bob Shaw	2.00
381 Milwakee Braves	5.00
382 Ted Bowsfield.......	2.00
383 Leon Wagner	2.00
384 Don Cardwell	2.00
385 World Series Game 1 .	4.00
Neal Steals Second	

NO. PLAYER	NR. MT
386 World Series Game 2 ...	4.00
Neal Belts 2nd Homer	
387 World Series Game 3 ...	4.00
Furillo Breaks Up Game	
388 World Series Game 4 ..	4.00
Hodges' Winning Homer	
389 World Series Game 5 ...	4.00
Luis Swipes Base	
390 World Series Game 6 ..	4.00
Scrambling After Ball	
391 World Series	4.00
The Champs Celebrate	
392 Tex Clevenger	2.00
393 Smokey Burgess	2.50
394 Norm Larker	2.00
395 Hoyt Wilhelm	10.00
396 Steve Bilko	2.00
397 Don Blasingame	2.00
398 Mike Cuellar	2.00
399 Young Hill Stars:	2.00
Milt Pappas, Jack Fisher,	
Jerry Walker	
400 Rocky Colavito	5.00
401 Bob Duliba	2.00
402 Dick Stuart	2.00
403 Ed Sadowski	2.00
404 Bob Rush	2.00
405 Bobby Richardson	5.00
406 Billy Klaus	2.00
407 Gary Peters	2.00
(photo of J.C. Martin)	
408 Carl Furillo	4.00
409 Ron Samford	2.00
410 Sam Jones	2.00
411 Ed Bailey	2.00
412 Bob Anderson	2.00
413 Kansas C. Athletics	5.00
414 Don Williams	2.00
415 Bob Cerv	2.00
416 Humberto Robinson	2.00
417 Chuck Cottier (R)	2.50
418 Don Mossi	2.00
419 George Crowe	2.00
420 Ed Mathews	25.00
421 Duke Maas..........	2.00
422 Johnny Powers	2.00
423 Ed Fitzgerald	2.00
424 Pete Whisenant	2.00
425 Johnny Podres	3.00
426 Ron Jackson	2.00
427 Al Grunwald	2.00
428 Al Smith	2.00
429 Amer. League Kings: ...	4.00
Nellie Fox, Harvey Kuenn	
430 Art Ditmar	2.00
431 Andre Rodgers	2.00
432 Chuck Stobbs	2.00
433 Irv Noren	2.00
434 Brooks Lawrence.......	2.00
435 Gene Freese	2.00
436 Marv Throneberry	3.00
437 Bob Friend	2.00
438 Jim Coker	2.00
439 Tom Brewer	2.00
440 Jim Lemon	2.00
441 Gary Bell	3.00
442 Joe Pignatano	3.00
443 Charlie Maxwell	3.00
444 Jerry Kindall	3.00
445 Warren Spahn.........	35.00
446 Ellis Burton	3.00
447 Ray Moore	3.00
448 Jim Gentile	5.00

NO. PLAYER	NR. MT.
449 Jim Brosnan	3.00
450 Orlando Cepeda	10.00
451 Curt Simmons	3.50
452 Ray Webster	3.50
453 Vern Law	5.00
454 Hal Woodeschick.......	3.00
455 Orioles Coaches:	4.00
Robinson, Brecheen, Harris	
456 Red Sox Coaches:	4.00
York, Herman, Maglie, Baker	
457 Cubs Coaches:	4.00
Klein, Tappe, Root	
458 White Sox Coaches:	4.00
Cooney, Gutteridge,	
Cuccinello, Berres	
459 Reds Coaches:	4.00
Deal, Moses, Otero	
460 Indians Coaches:	4.00
White, Lemon, Harder, Kress	
461 Tigers Coaches:	4.00
Ferrick, Appling, Hitchcock	
462 Athletics Coaches:	4.00
Cooper, Fitzsimmons,	
Heffner	
463 Dodgers Coaches:......	4.00
Bragan, Reiser,	
Becker, Mulleavy	
464 Braves Coaches:	4.00
Scheffing, Myatt,	
Wyatt, Pafko	
465 Yankees Coaches:......	10.00
Dickey, Houk,	
Lopat, Crosetti	
466 Phillies Coaches:	4.00
Silvestri, Cohen, Carter	
467 Pirates Coaches:	4.00
Vernon, Oceak,	
Narron, Burwell	
468 Cardinals Coaches:......	4.00
Keane, Pollet,	
Katt, Walker	
469 Giants Coaches:	4.00
Westrum, Parker, Posedel	
470 Senators Coaches:	4.00
Swift, Mele, Clary	
471 Ned Garver	3.00
472 Al Dark	4.00
473 Al Cicotte	3.00
474 Haywood Sullivan	3.00
475 Don Drysdale	30.00
476 Lou Johnson	3.00
477 Don Ferrarese	3.00
478 Frank Torre	3.00
479 Georges Maranda	3.00
480 Yogi Berra	60.00
481 Wes Stock	4.00
482 Frank Bolling	3.00
483 Camilo Pascual	3.00
484 Pittsburgh Pirates	15.00
485 Ken Boyer	6.00
486 Bobby Del Greco	3.00
487 Tom Sturdivant	3.00
488 Norm Cash	5.00
489 Steve Ridzik	3.00
490 Frank Robinson	35.00
491 Mel Roach	3.00
492 Larry Jackson	3.00
493 Duke Snider	45.00
494 Baltimore Orioles	8.00
495 Sherm Lollar	3.00
496 Bill Virdon	4.00
497 John Tsitouris	3.00
498 Al Pilarcik	3.00

NO. PLAYER	NR. MT.
499 Johnny James	3.00
500 Johnny Temple	3.00
501 Bob Schmidt	3.00
502 Jim Bunning	9.00
503 Don Lee	3.00
504 Seth Morehead	3.00
505 Ted Kluszewski	5.00
506 Lee Walls	3.00
507 Dick Stigman	8.00
508 Billy Consolo	8.00
509 Tommy Davis (R)	15.00
510 Jerry Staley	8.00
511 Ken Walters	8.00
512 Joe Gibbon	8.00
513 Chicago Cubs	25.00
514 Steve Barber	8.00
515 Stan Lopata	8.00
516 Marty Kutyna	8.00
517 Charley James	8.00
518 Tony Gonzalez	8.00
519 Ed Roebuck..........	8.00
520 Don Buddin	8.00
521 Mike Lee	8.00
522 Ken Hunt	8.00
523 Clay Dalrymple	8.00
524 Bill Henry	8.00
525 Marv Breeding	8.00
526 Paul Giel	8.00
527 Jose Valdivielso	8.00
528 Ben Johnson	8.00
529 Norm Sherry (R)	8.00
530 Mike McCormick	8.00
531 Sandy Amoros	8.00
532 Mike Garcia	8.00
533 L. Clinton	8.00
534 Ken Mackenzie	8.00
535 Whitey Lockman	8.00
536 Wynn Hawkins	8.00
537 Boston Red Sox	30.00
538 Frank Barnes	8.00
539 Gene Baker	8.00
540 Jerry Walker	8.00
541 Tony Curry	8.00
542 Ken Hamlin	8.00
543 Elio Chacon	8.00
544 Bill Monbouquette	8.00
545 Carl Sawatski	8.00
546 Hank Aguirre	8.00
547 Bob Aspromonte	8.00
548 Don Mincher	8.00
549 John Buzhardt	8.00
550 Jim Landis	8.00
551 Ed Rakow	8.00
552 Walt Bond	8.00
553 Bill Skowron (AS)	9.00
554 Willie McCovey (AS)...	45.00
555 Nellie Fox (AS)	15.00
556 Charlie Neal (AS)	9.00
557 Frank Malzone (AS) ..	9.00
558 Eddie Mathews (AS) ..	25.00
559 Luis Aparicio (AS) ...	17.00
560 Ernie Banks (AS)	35.00
561 Al Kaline (AS)	32.00
562 Joe Cunningham (AS) ..	9.00
563 Mickey Mantle (AS) ...	200.00
564 Willie Mays (AS)	90.00
565 Roger Maris (AS)	80.00
566 Hank Aaron (AS)	90.00
567 Sherm Lollar (AS)	9.00
568 Del Crandall (AS)	9.00
569 Camilo Pascual (AS) ..	9.00
570 Don Drysdale (AS)	20.00
571 Billy Pierce (AS).......	9.00
572 J. Antonelli (AS).......	15.00
(Exc. $5.00)	

1961 Topps. . . .Complete Set of 587 Cards—Value $1850.00 (Exc.); $4800.00 (Near Mint)

Juan Marichal and Billy Williams' rookie cards are in this set. The high numbers are 523 to 589. Cards 587 and 588 were not issued. Card 426 (Braves team) was mistakenly numbered 463.

NO.	PLAYER	NR. MT.
1	Dick Groat (Exc. $2.00)	15.00
2	Roger Maris	125.00
3	John Buzhardt	1.00
4	Lenny Green	1.00
5	Johnny Romano	1.00
6	Ed Roebuck	1.00
7	Chicago White Sox	3.00
8	Dick Williams	1.00
9	Bob Purkey	1.00
10	Brooks Robinson	30.00
11	Curt Simmons	1.50
12	Moe Thacker	1.00
13	Chuck Cottier	1.00
14	Don Mossi	1.00
15	Willie Kirkland	1.00
16	Billy Muffett	1.00
17	Checklist No. 1	8.00
18	Jim Grant	1.00
19	Cletis Boyer	3.00
20	Robin Roberts	11.00
21	Zorro Versalles	1.50
22	Clem Labine	1.25
23	Don Demeter	1.00
24	Ken Johnson	1.00
25	Reds' Heavy Artillery: Vada Pinson, Gus Bell, Frank Robinson	5.00
26	Wes Stock	1.00
27	Jerry Kindall	1.00
28	Hector Lopez	1.00
29	Don Nottebart	1.00
30	Nellie Fox	5.00
31	Bob Schmidt	1.00
32	Ray Sadecki	1.00
33	Gary Geiger	1.00
34	Wynn Hawkins	1.00
35	Ron Santo (R)	17.00
36	Jack Kralick	1.00
37	Charlie Maxwell	1.00
38	Bob Lillis	1.00
39	Leo Posada	1.00
40	Bob Turley	1.50
41	NL Batting Leaders: Willie Mays, Dick Gorat, Norm Larker, Roberto Clemente	4.00
42	AL Batting Leaders: Pete Runnels, Minnie Minoso, Al Smith, Bill Skowron	2.00
43	NL Home Run Leaders: Ernie Banks, Ed Mathews, Hank Aaron, Ken Boyer	5.00
44	AL Home Run Leaders: Mickey Mantle, Roger Maris, Jim Lemon, Rocky Colavito	15.00
45	NL ERA Leaders: Mike McCormick, Ernie Broglio, Don Drysdale, Bob Friend, Stan Williams	3.00
46	AL ERA Leaders: Frank Baumann, Jim Bunning, Art Ditmar, Hal Brown	3.00
47	NL Pitching Leaders: E. Broglio, W. Spahn, Vern Law, Lou Burdette	3.00
48	AL Pitching Leaders: Chuck Estrada, Jim Perry, Bud Daley, Art Ditmar, Frank Lary, Milt Pappas	2.50
49	NL Strikeout Leaders: Don Drysdale, Sandy Koufax, Sam Jones, Ernie Broglio	4.00
50	AL Strikeout Leaders: Jim Bunning, Pedro Ramos, Early Wynn, Frank Lary	2.50
51	Detroit Tigers	4.00
52	George Crowe	1.00
53	Russ Nixon	1.00
54	Earl Francis	1.00
55	Jim Davenport	1.00
56	Russ Kemmerer	1.00
57	Marv Throneberry	2.00
58	Joe Schaffernoth	1.00
59	Jim Woods	1.00
60	Woodie Held	1.00
61	Ron Piche	1.00
62	Al Pilarcik	1.00
63	Jim Kaat	7.00
64	Alex Grammas	.90
65	Ted Kluszewski	4.00
66	Bill Henry	1.00
67	Ossie Virgil	1.00
68	Deron Johnson	1.50
69	Earl Wilson	1.00
70	Bill Virdon	2.00
71	Jerry Adair	1.00
72	Stu Miller	1.00
73	Al Spangler	1.00
74	Joe Pignatano	1.00
75	Lindy Shows Larry: Lindy McDaniel, Larry Jackson	2.00
76	Harry Anderson	1.00
77	Dick Stigman	1.00
78	Lee Walls	1.00
79	Joe Ginsberg	1.00
80	Harmon Killebrew	20.00
81	Tracy Stallard	1.00
82	Joe Christopher	1.00
83	Bob Bruce	1.00
84	Lee Maye	1.00
85	Jerry Walker	1.00
86	Los Angeles Dodgers	4.00
87	Joe Amalfitano	1.00
88	Richie Ashburn	6.00
89	Billy Martin	7.00
90	Jerry Staley	1.00
91	Walt Moryn	1.00
92	Hal Naragon	1.00
93	Tony Gonzalez	1.00
94	John Kucks	1.00
95	Norm Cash	3.00
96	Bill O'Dell	1.00
97	Jerry Lynch	1.00
98	Checklist No. 2	8.00
99	Don Buddin	1.00
100	Harvey Haddix	3.00
101	Bubba Phillips	1.00
102	Gene Stephens	1.00
103	Ruben Amaro	1.00
104	John Blanchard	1.50
105	Carl Willey	1.00
106	Whitey Herzog	3.00
107	Seth Morehead	1.00
108	Dan Dobbek	1.00
109	Johnny Podres	3.00
110	Vada Pinson	3.00
111	Jack Meyer	1.50
112	Chico Fernandez	1.50
113	Mike Fornieles	1.50
114	Hobie Landrith	1.50
115	Johnny Antonelli	2.00
116	Joe DeMaestri	1.50
117	Dale Long	1.50
118	Chris Cannizzaro	1.50
119	A's Big Armor: Norm Siebern, Hank Bauer, Jerry Lumpe	2.00
120	Ed Mathews	20.00
121	Eli Grba	1.50
122	Chicago Cubs	3.00
123	Billy Gardner	1.50
124	J.C. Martin	1.50
125	Steve Barber	1.50
126	Dick Stuart	1.50
127	Ron Kline	1.50
128	Rip Repulski	1.50
129	Ed Hobaugh	1.50
130	Norm Larker	1.50
131	Paul Richards (Mgr.)	2.00
132	Al Lopez (Mgr.)	4.00
133	Ralph Houk (Mgr.)	3.00
134	Mickey Vernon (Mgr.)	2.00
135	Fred Hutchinson (Mgr.)	2.00
136	Walt Alston (Mgr.)	4.00
137	Chuck Dressen (Mgr.)	1.50
138	Danny Murtaugh (Mgr.)	1.50
139	Solly Hemus (Mgr.)	1.50
140	Gus Triandos	1.50
141	Billy Williams (R)	100.00
142	Luis Arroyo	1.50
143	Russ Snyder	1.50
144	Jim Coker	1.50
145	Bob Buhl	1.50
146	Marty Keough	1.50
147	Ed Rakow	1.50
148	Julian Javier	1.50
149	Bob Oldis	1.50
150	Willie Mays	90.00
151	Jim Donohue	1.50
152	Earl Torgeson	1.50
153	Don Lee	1.50
154	Bobby Del Greco	1.50
155	Johnny Temple	1.50
156	Ken Hunt	1.50
157	Cal McLish	1.50
158	Pete Daley	1.50
159	Baltimore Orioles	3.00
160	Whitey Ford	30.00
161	Sherman Jones	1.50
162	Jay Hook	1.50
163	Ed Sadowski	1.50
164	Felix Mantilla	1.50
165	Gino Cimoli	1.50
166	Danny Kravitz	1.50
167	San F. Giants	3.00
168	Tommy Davis	3.00
169	Don Elston	1.50
170	Al Smith	1.50
171	Paul Foytack	1.50
172	Don Dillard	1.50
173	Beantown Bombers: Frank Malzone, Vic Wertz, Jackie Jensen	2.00
174	Ray Semproch	1.50
175	Gene Freese	1.50
176	Ken Aspromonte	1.50
177	Don Larsen	2.00
178	Bob Nieman	1.50
179	Joe Koppe	1.50
180	Bobby Richardson	5.00
181	Fred Green	1.50
182	Dave Nicholson	1.50
183	Andre Rodgers	1.50
184	Steve Bilko	1.50
185	Herb Score	2.00
186	Elmer Valo	1.50
187	Billy Klaus	1.50
188	Jim Marshall	1.50
189	Checklist No. 3	8.00
190	Stan Williams	1.50
191	Mike De La Hoz	1.50
192	Dick Brown	1.50
193	Gene Conley	1.50
194	Gordy Coleman	1.50
195	Jerry Casale	1.50
196	Ed Bouchee	1.50
197	Dick Hall	1.50
198	Carl Sawatski	1.50
199	Bob Boyd	1.50
200	Warren Spahn	24.00
201	Pete Whisenant	1.50
202	Al Neiger	1.50
203	Eddie Bressoud	1.50
204	Bob Skinner	1.50
205	Bill Pierce	1.50
206	Gene Green	1.50
207	Dodger Southpaws: Sandy Koufax, J. Podres	15.00
208	Larry Osborne	1.50
209	Ken McBride	1.50
210	Pete Runnels	1.50
211	Bob Gibson	30.00
212	Haywood Sullivan	1.50
213	Bill Stafford	1.50
214	Danny Murphy	1.50
215	Gus Bell	1.50
216	Ted Bowsfield	1.50
217	Mel Roach	1.50
218	Hal Brown	1.50
219	Gene Mauch (Mgr.)	2.50
220	Al Dark (Mgr.)	2.00
221	Mike Higgins (Mgr.)	2.00
222	Jimmie Dykes (Mgr.)	2.00
223	Bob Scheffing (Mgr.)	2.00
224	Joe Gordon (Mgr.)	2.00
225	Bill Rigney (Mgr.)	2.00
226	Harry Lavagetto (Mgr.)	2.00
227	Juan Pizarro	1.50
228	New York Yankees	20.00
229	Rudy Hernandez	1.50
230	Don Hoak	1.50
231	Dick Drott	1.50
232	Bill White	4.00
233	Joe Jay	1.50

NO. PLAYER	NR. MT.
234 Ted Lepcio	1.50
235 Camilo Pascual	1.50
236 Don Gile	1.50
237 Billy Loes	1.50
238 Jim Gilliam	3.00
239 Dave Sisler	1.50
240 Ron Hansen	1.50
241 Al Cicotte	1.50
242 Hal Smith	1.50
243 Frank Lary	1.50
244 Chico Cardenas	1.50
245 Joe Adcock	2.00
246 Bob Davis	1.50
247 Billy Goodman	1.50
248 Ed Keegan	1.50
249 Cincinnati Reds	3.00
250 Buc Hill Aces:	2.00
Vern Law, Roy Face	
251 Bill Bruton	1.50
252 Bill Short	1.50
253 Sammy Taylor	1.50
254 Ted Sadowski	1.50
255 Vic Power	1.50
256 Billy Hoeft	1.50
257 Carroll Hardy	1.50
258 Jack Sanford	1.50
259 John Schaive	1.50
260 Don Drysdale	24.00
261 Charlie Lau	1.50
262 Tony Curry	1.50
263 Ken Hamlin	1.50
264 Glen Hobbie	1.50
265 Tony Kubek	5.00
266 Lindy McDaniel	1.50
267 Norm Siebern	1.50
268 Ike Delock	1.50
269 Harry Chiti	1.50
270 Bob Friend	1.50
271 Jim Landis	1.50
272 Tom Morgan	1.50
273 Checklist No. 4	8.00
274 Gary Bell	1.50
275 Gene Woodling	1.50
276 Ray Rippelmeyer	1.50
277 Hank Foiles	1.50
278 Don McMahon	1.50
279 Jose Pagan	1.50
280 Frank Howard	4.00
281 Frank Sullivan	1.50
282 Faye Throneberry	1.50
283 Bob Anderson	1.50
284 Dick Gernert	1.50
285 Sherm Lollar	1.50
286 George Witt	1.50
287 Carl Yastrzemski	150.00
288 Albie Pearson	1.50
289 Ray Moore	1.50
290 Stan Musial	90.00
291 Tex Clevenger	1.50
292 Jim Baumer	1.50
293 Tom Sturdivant	1.50
294 Don Blasingame	1.50
295 Milt Pappas	1.50
296 Wes Covington	1.50
297 Kansas C. Athletics	3.00
298 Jim Golden	1.50
299 Clay Dalrymple	1.50
300 Mickey Mantle	325.00
301 Chet Nichols	1.50
302 Al Heist	1.50
303 Gary Peters	1.50
304 Rocky Nelson	1.50
305 Mike McCormick	1.50
306 World Series Game 1	4.00
Virdon Saves Game	
307 World Series Game 2	25.00
Mantle Slams 2 Home	
308 World Series Game 3	5.00
Richardson is Hero	
309 World Series Game 4	5.00
Cimoli Safe	

NO. PLAYER	NR. MT.
310 World Series Game 5	5.00
Face Saves the Day	
311 World Series Game 6	5.00
Ford Shutout	
312 World Series Game 7	5.00
Mazeroski's Homer	
313 W.S. Celebration	5.00
314 Bob Miller	1.50
315 Earl Battey	1.50
316 Bobby Gene Smith	1.50
317 Jim Brewer	1.50
318 Danny O'Connell	1.50
319 Valmy Thomas	1.50
320 Lou Burdette	3.00
321 Marv Breeding	1.50
322 Bill Kunkel	1.50
323 Sammy Esposito	1.50
324 Hank Aguirre	1.50
325 Wally Moon	1.50
326 Dave Hillman	1.50
327 Matty Alou (R)	5.00
328 Jim O'Toole	1.50
329 Julio Becquer	1.50
330 Rocky Colavito	4.00
331 Ned Garver	1.50
332 Dutch Dotterer	1.50
(photo of Tommy Dotterer)	
333 Fritz Brickell	1.50
334 Walt Bond	1.50
335 Frank Bolling	1.50
336 Don Mincher	1.50
337 Al's Aces:	4.00
Herb Score, Early Wynn,	
Al Lopez	
338 Don Landrum	1.50
339 Gene Baker	1.50
340 Vic Wertz	1.50
341 Jim Owens	1.50
342 Clint Courtney	1.50
343 Earl Robinson	1.50
344 Sandy Koufax	100.00
345 Jim Piersall	2.00
346 Howie Nunn	1.50
347 St. Louis Cardinals	3.00
348 Steve Boros	1.50
349 Danny McDevitt	1.50
350 Ernie Banks	35.00
351 Jim King	1.50
352 Bob Shaw	1.50
353 Howie Bedell	1.50
354 Billy Harrell	1.50
355 Bob Allison	1.50
356 Ryne Duren	1.50
357 Daryl Spencer	1.50
358 Earl Averill	1.50
359 Dallas Green	4.00
360 Frank Robinson	35.00
361 Checklist No. 5	8.00
362 Frank Funk	1.50
363 John Roseboro	1.50
364 Moe Drabowsky	1.50
365 Jerry Lumpe	1.50
366 Eddie Fisher	1.50
367 Jim Rivera	1.50
368 Bennie Daniels	1.50
369 Dave Philley	1.50
370 Roy Face	2.00
371 Bill Skowron	15.00
372 Bob Hendley	1.50
373 Boston Red Sox	3.00
374 Paul Giel	2.00
375 Ken Boyer	4.00
376 Mike Roarke	2.00
377 Ruben Gomez	2.00
378 Wally Post	2.00
379 Bobby Shantz	2.00
380 Minnie Minoso	4.00
381 Dave Wickersham	2.00
382 Frank Thomas	2.00
383 Frisco First Liners:	2.00
Mike McCormick, Jack	
Sanford, Billy O'Dell	

NO. PLAYER	NR. MT.
384 Chuck Essegian	2.00
385 Jim Perry	2.00
386 Joe Hicks	2.00
387 Duke Maas	2.00
388 Bob Clemente	90.00
389 Ralph Terry	2.00
390 Del Crandall	2.00
391 Winston Brown	2.00
392 Reno Bertoia	2.00
393 Batter Bafflers:	2.00
Don Cardwell, Glen Hobbie	
394 Ken Walters	2.00
395 Chuck Estrada	2.00
396 Bob Aspromonte	2.00
397 Hal Woodeschick	2.00
398 Hank Bauer	2.00
399 Cliff Cook	2.00
400 Vern Law	2.00
401 Ruth 60th Homer	15.00
402 Larsen—Perfect Game	8.00
403 26 Inning Tie	4.00
404 Honsby .424 Average	5.00
405 Gehrig—2,130 Games	11.00
406 Mantle 565 Ft. HR	30.00
407 Chesbro Wins 41	4.00
408 Mathewson 267 SO's	5.00
409 Johnson Shutouts	5.00
410 Haddix Perfect Game	4.00
411 Tony Taylor	2.00
412 Larry Sherry	2.00
413 Dick Yost	2.00
414 Dick Donovan	2.00
415 Hank Aaron	100.00
416 Dick Howser (R)	7.00
417 Juan Marichal (R)	120.00
418 Ed Bailey	2.00
419 Tom Borland	2.00
420 Ernie Broglio	2.00
421 Ty Cline	2.00
422 Bud Daley	2.00
423 Charlie Neal	2.00
424 Turk Lown	2.00
425 Yogi Berra	60.00
426 Milwaukee Braves	6.00
(error—numbered 463)	
427 Dick Ellsworth	2.00
428 Ray Barker	2.00
429 Al Kaline	35.00
430 Bill Mazeroski	12.00
431 Chuck Stobbs	2.00
432 Coot Veal	2.00
433 Art Mahaffey	2.00
434 Tom Brewer	2.00
435 Orlando Cepeda	7.00
436 Jim Maloney (R)	6.00
437 Checklist No. 6	8.00
438 Curt Flood	3.00
439 Phil Regan	2.00
440 Luis Aparicio	10.00
441 Dick Bertell	2.00
442 Gordon Jones	2.00
443 Duke Snider	35.00
444 Joe Nuxhall	2.00
445 Frank Malzone	2.00
446 Bob Taylor	2.00
447 Harry Bright	2.50
448 Del Rice	2.50
449 Bobby Bolin	2.50
450 Jim Lemon	2.50
451 Power for Ernie:	2.50
Daryl Spencer, Bill White,	
Ernie Broglio	
452 Bob Allen	2.50
453 Dick Schofield	2.50
454 Pumpsie Green	2.50
455 Early Wynn	10.00
456 Hal Bevan	2.50
457 Johnny James	2.50
458 Willie Tasby	2.50
459 Terry Fox	2.50
460 Gil Hodges	13.00
461 Smoky Burgess	2.50

NO. PLAYER	NR. MT.
462 Lou Klimchock	2.50
463 Jack Fisher (see #426)	2.50
464 Leroy Thomas	2.50
465 Roy McMillan	2.50
466 Ron Moeller	2.50
467 Cleveland Indians	3.00
468 John Callison	2.50
469 Ralph Lumenti	2.50
470 Roy Sievers	2.50
471 Phil Rizzuto (MVP)	11.00
472 Yogi Berra (MVP)	30.00
473 Bobby Shantz (MVP)	3.00
474 Al Rosen (MVP)	3.00
475 Mickey Mantle (MVP)	90.00
476 Jackie Jensen (MVP)	3.00
477 Nellie Fox (MVP)	3.00
478 Roger Maris (MVP)	30.00
479 Jim Konstanty (MVP)	3.00
480 R. Campanella (MVP)	25.00
481 Hank Sauer (MVP)	3.00
482 Willie Mays (MVP)	30.00
483 Don Newcombe (MVP)	3.00
484 Hank Aaron (MVP)	30.00
485 Ernie Banks (MVP)	18.00
486 Dick Groat (MVP)	3.00
487 Gene Oliver	2.50
488 Joe McClain	2.50
489 Walt Dropo	2.50
490 Jim Bunning	7.00
491 Philadelphia Phillies	3.00
492 Ron Fairly	2.50
493 Don Zimmer	3.00
494 Tom Cheney	2.50
495 Elston Howard	5.00
496 Ken MacKenzie	2.50
497 Willie Jones	2.50
498 Ray Herbert	2.50
499 Chuck Schilling	2.50
500 Harvey Kuenn	4.00
501 John DeMerit	2.50
502 Clarence Coleman	2.50
503 Tito Francona	2.50
504 Billy Consolo	2.50
505 Red Schoendienst	12.00
506 Willie Davis (R)	8.00
507 Pete Burnside	2.50
508 Rocky Bridges	2.50
509 Camilo Carreon	2.50
510 Art Ditmar	2.50
511 Joe Morgan	4.00
512 Bob Will	2.50
513 Jim Brosnan	2.50
514 Jake Wood	2.50
515 Jackie Brandt	2.50
516 Checklist No. 7	8.00
517 Willie McCovey	55.00
518 Andy Carey	2.50
519 Jim Pagliaroni	2.50
520 Joe Cunningham	2.50
521 Brother Battery:	2.50
Norm Sherry, Larry Sherry	
522 Dick Farrell	2.50
523 Joe Gibbon	20.00
524 Johnny Logan	20.00
525 Ron Perranoski	20.00
526 R.C. Stevens	20.00
527 Gene Leek	20.00
528 Pedro Ramos	20.00
529 Bob Roselli	20.00
530 Bobby Malkmus	20.00
531 Jim Coates	20.00
532 Bob Hale	20.00
533 Jack Curtis	20.00
534 Eddie Kasko	20.00
535 Larry Jackson	20.00
536 Bill Tuttle	20.00
537 Bobby Locke	20.00
538 Chuck Hiller	20.00
539 John Klippstein	20.00
540 Jackie Jensen	30.00
541 Roland Sheldon	20.00
542 Minnesota Twins	40.00

NO. PLAYER	NR. MT.	NO. PLAYER	NR. MT.	NO. PLAYER	NR. MT.	NO. PLAYER	NR. MT.
543 Roger Craig	25.00	555 Sam Jones	20.00	566 P. Richards—Mgr. (AS)	20.00	577 Hank Aaron (AS)	150.00
544 George Thomas	20.00	556 Ken R. Hunt	20.00	567 D. Murtaugh—Mgr. (AS)	20.00	578 Mickey Mantle (AS)	350.00
545 Hoyt Wilhelm	50.00	557 Jose Valdivielso	20.00	568 Bill Skowron (AS)	20.00	579 Willie Mays (AS)	120.00
546 Marty Kutyna	20.00	558 Don Ferrarese	20.00	569 Frank Herrera (AS)	20.00	580 Al Kaline (AS)	70.00
547 Leon Wagner	20.00	559 Jim Gentile	20.00	570 Nellie Fox (AS)	30.00	581 Frank Robinson (AS)	75.00
548 Ted Wills	20.00	560 Barry Latman	20.00	571 Bill Mazeroski (AS)	20.00	582 Earl Battey (AS)	20.00
549 Hal R. Smith	20.00	561 Charley James	20.00	572 Brooks Robinson	70.00	583 Del Crandall (AS)	20.00
550 Frank Baumann	20.00	562 Bill Monbouquette	20.00	573 Ken Boyer (AS)	20.00	584 Jim Perry (AS)	20.00
551 George Altman	20.00	563 Bob Cerv	20.00	574 Luis Aparicio (AS)	40.00	585 Bob Friend (AS)	20.00
552 Jim Archer	20.00	564 Don Cardwell	20.00	575 Ernie Banks (AS)	75.00	586 Whitey Ford (AS)	70.00
553 Bill Fischer	20.00	565 Felipe Alou	20.00	576 Roger Maris (AS)	100.00	589 W. Spahn (AS) (Exc. $35.00)	120.00
554 Pittsburgh Pirates	35.00						

1962 Topps . . . Complete Set of 598 Cards—Value $1400.00 (Exc.); $4200.00 (Near Mint)

The rookie cards of Lou Brock, Gaylord Perry and Bob Uecker are in this set. The high numbers are 523 to 598. Nine cards were reprinted with different photos. These are worth a premium. The value of the complete set does not include the *variety* cards.

NO. PLAYER	NR. MT.	NO. PLAYER	NR. MT.	NO. PLAYER	NR. MT.	NO. PLAYER	NR. MT.
1 Roger Maris (Exc. $20.00)	150.00	42 Jim King	.90	62 Steve Boros	.90	104 Ted Savage	.90
2 Jim Brosnan	.90	43 Los Angeles Dodgers	3.00	63 Tony Cloninger	.90	105 Don Mossi	.90
3 Pete Runnels	.90	44 Don Taussig	.90	64 Russ Snyder	.90	106 Carl Sawatski	.90
4 John DeMerit	.90	45 Brooks Robinson	25.00	65 Bobby Richardson	5.00	107 Mike McCormick	.90
5 Sandy Koufax	100.00	46 Jack Baldschun	.90	66 Cuno Barragan	.90	108 Willie Davis	.90
6 Marv Breeding	.90	47 Bob Will	.90	67 Harvey Haddix	.90	109 Bob Shaw	.90
7 Frank Thomas	.90	48 Ralph Terry	.90	68 Ken Hunt	.90	110 Bill Skowron	4.00
8 Ray Herbert	.90	49 Hal Jones	.90	69 Phil Ortega	.90	111 Dallas Green	3.00
9 Jim Davenport	.90	50 Stan Musal	75.00	70 Harmon Killebrew	20.00	112 Hank Foiles	1.50
10 Bob Clemente	80.00	51 AL Batting Leaders:	1.50	71 Dick Le May	.90	113 Chicago White Sox	3.00
11 Tom Morgan	.90	Al Kaline, Norm Cash,		72 Bob's Pupils:	.90	114 Howie Koplitz	1.25
12 Harry Craft (Mgr.)	.90	Jim Piersall, Elston Howard		Steve Boros, Bob		115 Bob Skinner	1.25
13 Dick Howser	1.50	52 NL Batting Leaders:	3.00	Scheffing, Jake Wood		116 Herb Score	2.00
14 Bill White	3.00	Wally Moon, Bob Clemente,		73 Nellie Fox	5.00	117 Gary Geiger	1.25
15 Dick Donovan	.90	Vada Pinson, Ken Boyer		74 Bob Lillis	.90	118 Julian Javier	1.25
16 Darrell Johnson	.90	53 AL Home Run Leaders:	20.00	75 Milt Pappas	.90	119 Danny Murphy	1.25
17 Johnny Callison	.90	Jim Gentile, Roger		76 Howie Bedell	.90	120 Bob Purkey	1.25
18 Managers' Dream:	100.00	Maris, Mickey Mantle,		77 Tony Taylor	.90	121 Billy Hitchcock	1.25
Mickey Mantle, Willie Mays		Harmon Killebrew		78 Gene Green	.90	122 Norm Bass	1.25
19 Ray Washburn	.90	54 NL Home Run Leaders:	4.00	79 Ed Hobaugh	.90	123 Mike De La Hoz	1.25
20 Rocky Colavito	3.00	Orlando Cepeda, Willie		80 Vada Pinson	2.50	124 Bill Pleis	1.25
21 Jim Kaat	4.00	Mays, Frank Robinson		81 Jim Pagliaroni	.90	125 Gene Woodling	1.25
22 Checklist No. 1	5.00	55 AL ERA Leaders:	1.50	82 Deron Johnson	.90	126 Al Cicotte	1.25
23 Norm Larker	.90	Dick Donovan, Bill Stafford,		83 Larry Jackson	.90	127 Pride of A's:	
24 Detroit Tigers	3.00	Don Mossi, Milt Pappas		84 Lenny Green	.90	Norm Siebern, Hank Bauer,	
25 Ernie Bank	30.00	56 NL ERA Leaders:	1.50	85 Gil Hodges	13.00	Jerry Lumpe	
26 Chris Cannizzaro	.90	Warren Spahn, Jim		86 Donn Clendenon	.90	128 Art Fowler	1.25
27 Chuck Cottier	.90	O'Toole, Curt Simmons,		87 Mike Roarke	.90	129 Lee Walls (faces right)	1.50
28 Minnie Minoso	3.00	Mike McCormick		88 Ralph Houk	1.50	129 Lee Walls (faces left)	12.00
29 Casey Stengel (Mgr.)	12.00	57 AL Win Leaders:	1.50	89 Barney Schultz	.90	130 Frank Bolling	1.25
30 Ed Mathews	17.00	Frank Lary, Whitey Ford,		90 Jim Piersall	1.25	131 Pete Richert	1.25
31 Tom Tresh (R)	7.50	Steve Barber, Jim Bunning		91 J.C. Martin	.90	132 Los Angeles Angels*	3.00
32 John Roseboro	.90	58 NL Win Leaders:	1.50	92 Sam Jones	.90	133 Felipe Alou	1.25
33 Don Larsen	.90	Warren Spahn, Joe Jay,		93 John Blanchard	.90	134 Billy Hoeft (faces right)	1.50
34 Johnny Temple	.90	Jim O'Toole		94 Jay Hook	.90	134 Billy Hoeft (faces front)	12.00
35 Don Schwall	.90	59 AL Strikeout Leaders:	1.50	95 Don Hoak	.90	135 Babe Ruth Special:	6.00
36 Don Leppert	.90	Camilo Pascual, Whitey		96 Eli Grba	.90	Babe as a Boy	
37 Tribe Hill Trio:	.90	Ford, Jim Bunning,		97 Tito Francona	.90	136 Babe Ruth Special:	6.00
Barry Latman, Dick		Juan Pizzaro		98 Checklist No. 2	5.00	Babe Joins Yanks	
Stigman, Jim Perry		60 NL Strikeout Leaders:	4.00	99 John Powell (R)	11.00	137 Babe Ruth Special:	6.00
38 Gene Stephens	.90	Sandy Koufax, Stan		100 Warren Spahn	30.00	Babe and Mgr. Huggins	
39 Joe Koppe	.90	Williams, Don Drysdale,		101 Carroll Hardy	.90	138 Babe Ruth Special:	6.00
40 Orlando Cepeda	5.00	Jim O'Toole		102 Al Schroll	.90	Famous Slugger	
41 Cliff Cook	.90	61 St. Louis Cardinals	4.00	103 Don Blasingame	.90		

NO.	PLAYER	NR. MT.
139	Babe Ruth Special...... Babe Hits 60 See Card no. 159	9.00
140	Babe Ruth Special:..... Gehrig and Ruth	6.00
141	Babe Ruth Special:..... Twilight Years	6.00
142	Babe Ruth Special:..... Coaching for Dodgers	6.00
143	Babe Ruth Special:..... Greatest Sports Hero	6.00
144	Babe Ruth Special:..... Farewell Speech	6.00
145	Barry Latman	1.25
146	Don Demeter	1.25
147	Bill Kunkel (head shot)	1.50
147	Bill Kunkel (pitching)	12.00
148	Wally Post	1.25
149	Bob Duliba	1.25
150	Al Kaline	25.00
151	Johnny Klippstein	1.25
152	Mickey Vernon (Mgr.)	1.50
153	Pumpsie Green	1.25
154	Lee Thomas	1.25
155	Stu Miller	1.25
156	Merritt Ranew	1.25
157	Wes Covington	1.25
158	Milwaukee Braves	3.00
159	Hal Reniff	1.50
159	Hal Reniff Error—reads no. 139	12.00
159	Hal Reniff (pitching) Error—reads no. 139	45.00
160	Dick Stuart	1.50
161	Frank Baumann	1.25
162	Sammy Drake	1.25
163	Hot Corner Guardians: Billy Gardner, Cletis Boyer	2.00
164	Hal Naragon	1.25
165	Jackie Brandt	1.25
166	Don Lee	1.25
167	Tim McCarver (R)	22.00
168	Leo Posada	1.25
169	Bob Cerv	1.25
170	Ron Santo	5.00
171	Dave Sisler	1.25
172	Fred Hutchinson (Mgr.)	1.25
173	Chico Fernandez	1.25
174	Carl Willey (no hat)	1.50
174	Carl Willey (with hat)	12.00
175	Frank Howard	2.50
176	Eddie Yost (head shot)	1.50
176	Eddie Yost (with bat)	12.00
177	Bobby Shantz	1.50
178	Camilo Carreon	1.25
179	Tom Sturdivant	1.25
180	Bob Allison	1.25
181	Paul Brown	1.25
182	Bob Nieman	1.25
183	Roger Craig	1.50
184	Haywood Sullivan	1.25
185	Roland Sheldon	1.25
186	Mack Jones	1.25
187	Gene Conley	1.25
188	Chuck Hiller	1.25
189	Dick Hall	1.25
190	Wally Moon (head shot)	1.50
190	Wally Moon (with bat)	12.00
191	Jim Brewer	1.25
192	Checklist No. 3	5.00
193	Eddie Kasko	1.25
194	Dean Chance	2.00
195	Joe Cunningham	1.25
196	Terry Fox	1.25
197	Daryl Spencer	1.25
198	Johnny Keane (Mgr.)	1.25
199	Gaylord Perry (R)	120.00
200	Mickey Mantle	400.00
201	Ike Delock	1.25
202	Carl Warwick	1.25
203	Jack Fisher	1.25
204	Johnny Weekly	1.25
205	Gene Freese	1.25
206	Washington Senators	2.00
207	Pete Burnside	1.25
208	Billy Martin	7.00
209	Jim Fregosi (R)	5.00
210	Roy Face	1.50
211	Midway Masters: Frank Bolling, Roy McMillan	1.50
212	Jim Owens	1.25
213	Richie Ashburn	6.00
214	Dom Zanni	1.25
215	Woody Held	1.25
216	Ron Kline	1.25
217	Walt Alston (Mgr.)	14.00
218	Joe Torre (R)	13.00
219	Al Downing (R)	4.00
220	Roy Sievers	1.50
221	Bill Short	1.25
222	Jerry Zimmerman	1.25
223	Alex Grammas	1.25
224	Don Rudolph	1.25
225	Frank Malzone	1.25
226	San F. Giants	3.00
227	Bobby Tiefenauer	1.25
228	Dale Long	1.25
229	Jesus McFarlane	1.25
230	Camilo Pascual	1.25
231	Ernie Bowman	1.25
232	World Series Game 1: Yanks Win Opener	3.00
233	World Series Game 2: Jay Ties It Up	3.00
234	World Series Game 3: Maris Wins In 9th	8.00
235	World Series Game 4: Ford Sets New Mark	5.00
236	World Series Game 5: Yanks Crush Reds	3.00
237	World Series Winners Celebrate	3.00
238	Norm Sherry	1.50
239	Cecil Butler	1.25
240	George Altman	1.25
241	Johnny Kucks	1.25
242	Mel McGaha (Mgr.)	1.25
243	Robin Roberts	11.00
244	Don Gile	1.25
245	Ron Hansen	1.25
246	Art Ditmar	1.25
247	Joe Pignatano	1.25
248	Bob Aspromonte	1.25
249	Ed Keegan	1.25
250	Norm Cash	3.00
251	New York Yankees	15.00
252	Earl Francis	1.25
253	Harry Chiti	1.25
254	Gordon Windhorn	1.25
255	Joan Pizarro	1.25
256	Elio Chacon	1.25
257	Jack Spring	1.25
258	Marty Keough	1.25
259	Lou Klimchock	1.25
260	Bill Pierce	1.50
261	George Alusik	1.25
262	Bob Schmidt	1.25
263	The Right Pitch: Bob Purkey, Jim Turner, Joe Jay	1.25
264	Dick Ellsworth	1.25
265	Joe Adcock	2.00
266	John Anderson	1.25
267	Dan Dobbek	1.25
268	Ken McBride	1.25
269	Bob Oldis	1.25
270	Dick Groat	2.50
271	Ray Rippelmeyer	1.25
272	Earl Robinson	1.25
273	Gary Bell	1.25
274	Sammy Taylor	1.25
275	Norm Siebern	1.25
276	Hal Kolstad	1.25
277	Checklist No. 4	5.00
278	Ken Johnson	1.25
279	Hobie Landrith	1.25
280	Johnny Podres	3.00
281	Jake Gibbs	1.50
282	Dave Hillman	1.25
283	Charlie Smith	1.25
284	Ruben Amaro	2.00
285	Curt Simmons	2.00
286	Al Lopez (Mgr.)	3.00
287	George Witt	2.00
288	Billy Williams	25.00
289	Mike Krsnich	2.00
290	Jim Gentile	2.50
291	Hal Stowe	2.00
292	Jerry Kindall	2.00
293	Bob Miller	2.00
294	Philadelphia Phillies	3.00
295	Vern Law	2.50
296	Ken Hamlin	2.00
297	Ron Perranoski	2.00
298	Bill Tuttle	2.00
299	Don Wert	2.00
300	Willie Mays	100.00
301	Galen Cisco	2.00
302	John Edwards	2.00
303	Frank Torre	2.00
304	Dick Farrell	2.00
305	Jerry Lumpe	2.00
306	Redbird Rippers: Lindy McDaniel, Larry Jackson	2.00
307	Jim Grant	2.00
308	Neil Chrisley	2.00
309	Moe Morhardt	2.00
310	Whitey Ford	25.00
311	Kubek Double Play	3.00
312	Spahn No-Hit	7.50
313	Maris Blasts 61 HR	12.00
314	Colavito's Power	3.00
315	Ford Curveball	6.00
316	Killebrew's Orbit	6.00
317	Musial's 21st Season	15.00
318	Switch Hitter Mantle	35.00
319	McCormick in Action	3.00
320	Hank Aaron	110.00
321	Lee Stange	2.00
322	Al Dark (Mgr.)	2.50
323	Don Landrum	2.00
324	Joe McClain	2.00
325	Luis Aparicio	10.00
326	Tom Parsons	2.00
327	Ozzie Virgil	2.00
328	Ken Walters	2.00
329	Bob Bolin	2.00
330	Johnny Romano	2.00
331	Moe Drabowsky	2.00
332	Don Buddin	2.00
333	Frank Cipriani	2.00
334	Boston Red Sox	3.00
335	Bill Bruton	2.00
336	Bill Muffett	2.00
337	Jim Marshall	2.50
338	Billy Gardner	2.50
339	Jose Valdivielso	2.00
340	Don Drysdale	25.00
341	Mike Hershberger	2.00
342	Ed Rakow	2.00
343	Albie Pearson	2.00
344	Ed Bauta	2.00
345	Chuck Schilling	2.00
346	Jack Kralick	2.00
347	Chuck Hinton	2.00
348	Larry Burright	2.00
349	Paul Foytack	2.00
350	Frank Robinson	30.00
351	Braves' Backstops: Joe Torre, Del Crandall	2.00
352	Frank Sullivan	2.00
353	Bill Mazeroski	3.00
354	Roman Mejias	2.00
355	Steve Barber	2.00
356	Tom Haller	2.00
357	Jerry Walker	2.00
358	Tommy Davis	3.00
359	Bobby Locke	2.00
360	Yogi Berra	50.00
361	Bob Hendley	2.00
362	Ty Cline	2.00
363	Bob Roselli	2.00
364	Ken Hunt	2.00
365	Charley Neal	2.00
366	Phil Regan	2.00
367	Checklist No. 5	5.00
368	Bob Tillman	2.00
369	Ted Bowsfield	2.00
370	Ken Boyer	4.00
371	Earl Battey	3.00
372	Jack Curtis	3.00
373	Al Heist	3.00
374	Gene Mauch (Mgr.)	3.00
375	Ron Fairly	3.00
376	Bud Daley	3.00
377	Johnny Orsino	3.00
378	Bennie Daniels	3.00
379	Chuck Essegian	3.00
380	Lou Burdette	4.00
381	Chico Cardenas	3.00
382	Dick Williams	5.00
383	Ray Sadecki	3.00
384	K.C. Athletics	7.00
385	Early Wynn	12.00
386	Don Mincher	3.00
387	Lou Brock (R)	150.00
388	Ryne Duren	3.00
389	Smoky Burgess	3.00
390	Orlando Cepeda (AS)	5.00
391	Bill Mazeroski (AS)	4.00
392	Ken Boyer (AS)	4.00
393	Roy McMillan (AS)	4.00
394	Hank Aaron (AS)	30.00
395	Willie Mays (AS)	30.00
396	Frank Robinson (AS)	11.00
397	John Roseboro (AS)	4.00
398	Don Drysdale (AS)	7.00
399	Warren Spahn (AS)	7.00
400	Elston Howard	6.00
401	AL & NL Homer Kings: Roger Maris, O. Cepeda	25.00
402	Gino Cimoli	3.00
403	Chet Nichols	3.00
404	Tim Harkness	3.00
405	Jim Perry	3.00
406	Bob Taylor	3.00
407	Hank Aguirre	3.00
408	Gus Bell	3.00
409	Pittsburgh Pirates	8.00
410	Al Smith	3.00
411	Danny O'Connell	3.00
412	Charlie James	3.00
413	Matty Alou	4.00
414	Joe Gaines	3.00
415	Bill Virdon	4.00
416	Bob Scheffing (Mgr.)	3.00
417	Joe Azcue	3.00
418	Andy Carey	3.00
419	Bob Bruce	3.00
420	Gus Triandos	3.00
421	Ken MacKenzie	3.00
422	Steve Bilko	3.00
423	Rival Relief Aces: Roy Face, Hoyt Wilhelm	4.00
424	Al McBean	3.00
425	Carl Yastrzemski	175.00
426	Bob Farley	3.00
427	Jake Wood	3.00
428	Joe Hicks	3.00
429	Billy O'Dell	3.00
430	Tony Kubek	9.00
431	Bob Rodgers	2.00
432	Jim Pendleton	3.00
433	Jim Archer	3.00
434	Clay Dalrymple	3.00
435	Larry Sherry	3.00
436	Felix Mantilla	3.00

NO.	PLAYER	NR. MT.
437	Ray Moore	3.00
438	Dick Brown	3.00
439	Jerry Buchek	3.00
440	Joe Jay	3.00
441	Checklist No. 6	5.00
442	Wes Stock	3.00
443	Del Crandall	4.00
444	Ted Wills	3.00
445	Vic Power	3.00
446	Don Elston	3.00
447	Willie Kirland	4.00
448	Joe Gibbon	4.00
449	Jerry Adair	4.00
450	Jim O'Toole	4.00
451	Jose Tartabull	4.00
452	Earl Averill	4.00
453	Cal McLish	4.00
454	Floyd Robinson	4.00
455	Luis Arroyo	4.00
456	Joe Amalfitano	4.00
457	Lou Clinton	4.00
458	Bob Buhl ("M" on hat)	5.00
458	Bob Buhl (without "M" on hat)	35.00
459	Ed Bailey	4.00
460	Jim Bunning	8.00
461	Ken Hubbs (R)	9.00
462	Willie Tasby ("W" on hat)	4.00
462	Willie Tasby (without "W" on hat)	35.00
463	Hank Bauer (Mgr.)	5.00
464	Al Jackson	4.00
465	Cincinnati Reds	6.00
466	Norm Cash (AS)	6.00
467	Chuck Schilling (AS)	4.00
468	Brooks Robinson (AS)	12.00
469	Luis Aparicio (AS)	8.00
470	Al Kaline (AS)	13.00
471	Mickey Mantle (AS)	90.00
472	Rocky Colavito (AS)	5.00
473	Elston Howard (AS)	5.00
474	Frank Lary (AS)	4.00
475	Whitey Ford (AS)	11.00
476	Baltimore Orioles	5.00
477	Andre Rodgers	4.00
478	Don Zimmer	6.00
479	Joel Horlen	4.00

NO.	PLAYER	NR. MT.
480	Harvey Kuenn	4.00
481	Vic Wertz	4.00
482	Sam Mele	4.00
483	Don McMahon	4.00
484	Dick Schofield	4.00
485	Pedro Ramos	4.00
486	Jim Gilliam	6.00
487	Jerry Lynch	4.00
488	Hal Brown	4.00
489	Julio Gotay	4.00
490	Clete Boyer	5.00
491	Leon Wagner	4.00
492	Hal Smith	4.00
493	Danny McDevitt	4.00
494	Sammy White	4.00
495	Don Cardwell	4.00
496	Wayne Causey	4.00
497	Ed Bouchee	4.00
498	Jim Donohue	4.00
499	Zoilo Versalles	4.00
500	Duke Snider	45.00
501	Claude Osteen	4.00
502	Hector Lopez	4.00
503	Danny Murtaugh (Mgr.)	4.00
504	Eddie Bressoud	4.00
505	Juan Marichal	35.00
506	Charley Maxwell	4.00
507	Ernie Broglio	4.00
508	Gordy Coleman	4.00
509	Dave Giusti	4.00
510	Jim Lemon	4.00
511	Bubba Phillips	4.00
512	Mike Fornieles	4.00
513	Whitey Herzog	5.00
514	Sherm Lollar	4.00
515	Stan Williams	4.00
516	Checklist No. 7	10.00
517	Dave Wickersham	4.00
518	Lee Maye	4.00
519	Bob Johnson	4.00
520	Bob Friend	4.00
521	Jacke Davis	4.00
522	Lindy McDaniel	4.00
523	Russ Nixon	8.00
524	Howie Nunn	8.00
525	George Thomas	8.00
526	Hal Woodeschick	8.00

NO.	PLAYER	NR. MT.
527	Dick McAuliffe	8.00
528	Turk Lown	8.00
529	John Schaive	8.00
530	Bob Gibson	125.00
531	Bobby G. Smith	8.00
532	Dick Stigman	8.00
533	Charley Lau	8.00
534	Tony Gonzalez	8.00
535	Ed Roebuck	8.00
536	Dick Gernert	8.00
537	Cleveland Indians	25.00
538	Jack Sanford	8.00
539	Billy Moran	8.00
540	Jim Landis	8.00
541	Don Nottebart	8.00
542	Dave Philley	8.00
543	Bob Allen	8.00
544	Willie McCovey	135.00
545	Hoyt Wilhelm	50.00
546	Moe Thacker	8.00
547	Don Ferrarese	8.00
548	Bobby Del Greco	8.00
549	Bill Rigney (Mgr.)	8.00
550	Art Mahaffey	8.00
551	Harry Bright	8.00
552	Chicago Cubs	25.00
553	Jim Coates	9.00
554	Bubba Morton	8.00
555	John Buzhardt	8.00
556	Al Spangler	8.00
557	Bob Anderson	8.00
558	John Goryl	8.00
559	Mike Higgins (Mgr.)	8.00
560	Chuck Estrada	8.00
561	Gene Oliver	8.00
562	Bill Henry	8.00
563	Ken Aspromonte	8.00
564	Bob Grim	8.00
565	Jose Pagan	8.00
566	Marty Kutyna	8.00
567	Tracy Stallard	8.00
568	Jim Golden	8.00
569	Ed Sadowski	8.00
570	Bill Stafford	8.00
571	Billy Klaus	8.00
572	Bob Miller	8.00
573	Johnny Logan	8.00

NO.	PLAYER	NR. MT.
574	Dean Stone	8.00
575	Red Schoendienst	35.00
576	Russ Kemmerer	8.00
577	Dave Nicholson	8.00
578	Jim Duffalo	8.00
579	Jim Schaffer	8.00
580	Bill Monbouquette	8.00
581	Mel Roach	8.00
582	Ron Piche	8.00
583	Larry Osborne	8.00
584	Minnesota Twins	25.00
585	Glen Hobbie	8.00
586	Sammy Esposito	8.00
587	Frank Funk	8.00
588	Birdie Tebbetts (Mgr.)	8.00
589	Bob Turley	12.00
590	Curt Flood	15.00
591	Rookie Pitchers: Sam McDowell, D. Radatz, Ron Taylor, Ron Nischwitz, Art Quirk	35.00
592	Rookie Pitchers: D. Stenhouse, Dan Pfister, Bo Belinsky, Jim Bouton, Joe Bonikowski	45.00
593	Rookie Pitchers: Bob Moorhead, Jack Lamabe, Jack Hamilton, Bob Veale, Craig Anderson	15.00
594	Rookie Catchers: Bob Uecker, Doc Edwards, Ken Retzer, Doug Camilli, Don Pavletich	125.00
595	Rookie Infielders: Bob Sadowski, Marlan Coughtry, Ed Charles, Felix Torres	15.00
596	Rookie Infielders: Bernie Allen, Phil Linz, Rich Rollins, Joe Pepitone	35.00
597	Rookie Infielders: Denis Menke, Jim McKnight, Rod Kanehl, Amado Samuel	15.00
598	Rookie Outfielders: Al Luplow, Danny Jimenez, Ed Olivares, Howie Gross, Jim Hickman	40.00

1963 Topps . . . Complete Set of 576 Cards—Value $1500.00 (Exc.) $4000.00 (Near Mint)

Pete Rose's rookie card is in this set. Cards 507 to 576 are the high numbers. Also includes the rookie cards of Willie Stargell, Tony Oliva, and Rusty Staub. Cards 29 and 54 exist with the error "1962 Rookie Stars" instead of "1963 Rookie Stars"—worth $5.00 each.

NO.	PLAYER	NR. MT.
1	NL Bat Ldrs.: (Exc. $7.50) Frank Robinson, Stan Musial, Tommy Davis, Bill White, Hank Aaron	25.00
2	AL Batting Leaders: Norm Siebern, Pete Runnels, Floyd Robinson, C. Hinton, Mickey Mantle	11.00

NO.	PLAYER	NR. MT.
3	NL Home Run Leaders: O. Cepeda, Hank Aaron, Ernie Banks, Frank Robinson, Willie Mays	9.00
4	AL Home Run Leaders: Roger Maris, R. Colavito, Harmon Killebrew, Norm Cash, J. Gentile, L. Wagner	2.50

NO.	PLAYER	NR. MT.
5	NL ERA Leaders: Bob Purkey, Bob Shaw, Sandy Koufax, Bob Gibson, Don Drysdale	3.50
6	AL ERA Leaders: Whitey Ford, Robin Roberts, Eddie Fisher, Hank Aguirre, Dean Chance	2.50

NO.	PLAYER	NR. MT.
7	NL Pitching Leaders: Don Drysdale, Billy O'Dell, Jack Sanford, Bob Purkey, Art Mahaffey, Joe Jay	2.50
8	AL Pitching Leaders: Dick Donovan, Ray Herbert, Ralph Terry, Jim Bunning, Camilo Pascual	2.50

NO. PLAYER	NR. MT.	NO. PLAYER	NR. MT.	NO. PLAYER	NR. MT.	NO. PLAYER	NR. MT.
9 NL Strikeout Leaders: Sandy Koufax, Bob Gibson, Don Drysdale, Billy O'Dell, Dick Farrell	4.00	77 Al Spangler	.80	150 Johnny Podres	2.00	221 Cookie Rojas	2.00
		78 Marv Throneberry	1.00	151 Pittsburgh Pirates	2.00	222 Chicago Cubs	1.50
		79 Checklist No. 1	4.00	152 Ron Nischwitz	1.00	223 Eddie Fisher	1.50
10 AL Strikeout Leaders: Ralph Terry, Juan Pizarro, Camilo Pascual, Jim Bunning, Jim Kaat	2.00	80 Jim Gilliam	2.00	153 Hal Smith	1.00	224 Mike Roarke	1.50
		81 Jim Schaffer	.80	154 Walt Alston (Mgr.)	4.00	225 Joe Jay	1.50
		82 Ed Rakow	.80	155 Bill Stafford	1.00	226 Julian Javier	1.50
		83 Charley James	.80	156 Roy McMillan	1.00	227 Jim Grant	1.50
11 Lee Walls	.80	84 Ron Kline	.80	157 Diego Segui	1.00	228 Rookie Stars: Max Alvis, Bob Bailey, Pedro Oliva, Ed Kranepool	32.00
12 Steve Barber	.80	85 Tom Haller	.80	158 Rookie Stars: Bob Saverine, Rogelio Alvarez, Dave Roberts, Tommy Harper	1.00		
13 Philadelphia Phillies	2.00	86 Charley Maxwell	.80			229 Willie Davis	1.50
14 Pedro Ramos	.80	87 Bob Veale	.80			230 Pete Runnels	1.50
15 Ken Hubbs	2.00	88 Ron Hansen	.80	159 Jim Pagliaroni	1.00	231 Eli Grba (photo of Ryne Duren)	1.50
16 Al Smith	.80	89 Dick Stigman	.80	160 Juan Pizarro	1.00		
17 Ryne Duren	.80	90 Gordy Coleman	.80	161 Frank Torre	1.00	232 Frank Malzone	1.50
18 Buc Blasters: Smoky Burgess, Dick Stuart, Bob Clemente, Bob Skinner	9.00	91 Dallas Green	2.00	162 Minnesota Twins	2.00	233 Casey Stengel (Mgr.)	15.00
		92 Hector Lopez	.80	163 Don Larsen	1.00	234 Dave Nicholson	1.50
		93 Galen Cisco	.80	164 Bubba Morton	1.00	235 Bill O'Dell	1.50
19 Pete Burnside	.80	94 Bob Schmidt	.80	165 Jim Kaat	4.00	236 Bill Bryan	1.50
20 Tony Kubek	3.00	95 Larry Jackson	.80	166 Johnny Keane (Mgr.)	1.00	237 Jim Coates	1.50
21 Marty Keough	.80	96 Lou Clinton	.80	167 Jim Fregosi	1.50	238 Lou Johnson	1.50
22 Curt Simmons	.80	97 Bob Duliba	.80	168 Russ Nixon	1.00	239 Harvey Haddix	1.50
23 Ed Lopat (Mgr.)	1.00	98 George Thomas	.80	169 Rookie Stars: Gaylord Perry, Dick Egan, Julio Navarro, Tommie Sisk	20.00	240 Rocky Colavito	4.00
24 Bob Bruce	.80	99 Jim Umbricht	.80			241 Billy Smith	1.50
25 A. Kaline	25.00	100 Joe Cunningham	.80			242 Power Plus: Ernie Banks, Hank Aaron	21.00
26 Ray Moore	.80	101 Joe Gibbon	.80	170 Joe Adcock	1.00		
27 Choo Choo Coleman	.80	102 Checklist No. 2	4.00	171 Steve Hamilton	1.00	243 Don Leppert	1.50
28 Mike Fornieles	.80	103 Chuck Essegian	.80	172 Gene Oliver	1.00	244 John Tsitouris	1.50
29 Rookie Stars: Sammy Ellis, Jesse Gonder, Ray Culp, John Boozer	2.00	104 Lew Krausse	.80	173 Bombers' Best: Tom Tresh, Mickey Mantle, Bobby Richardson	40.00	245 Gil Hodges	13.00
		105 Ron Fairly	.80			246 Lee Stange	1.50
30 Harvey Kuenn	1.00	106 Bob Bolin	.80			247 New York Yankees	11.00
31 Cal Koonce	.80	107 Jim Hickman	.80	174 Larry Burright	1.00	248 Tito Francona	1.50
32 Tony Gonzalez	.80	108 Hoyt Wilhelm	9.00	175 Bob Buhl	1.00	249 Leo Burke	1.50
33 Bo Belinsky	.80	109 Lee Maye	.80	176 Jim King	1.00	250 Stan Musial	100.00
34 Dick Schofield	.80	110 Rich Rollins	1.00	177 Bubba Phillips	1.00	251 Jack Lamabe	1.50
35 John Buzhardt	.80	111 Al Jackson	1.00	178 Johnny Edwards	1.00	252 Ron Santo	4.00
36 Jerry Kindall	.80	112 Dick Brown	1.00	179 Ron Pich	1.00	253 Rookie Stars: Len Gabrielson, Pete Jernigan, Deacon Jones, John Wojcik	1.50
37 Jerry Lynch	.80	113 Don Landrum (photo of Ron Santo)	1.00	180 Bill Skowron	1.50		
38 Bud Daley	.80			181 Sammy Esposito	1.00		
39 Los Angeles Angels	2.00	114 Dan Osinski	.65	182 Albie Pearson	1.00	254 Mike Hershberger	1.50
40 Vic Power	.80	115 Carl Yastrzemski	75.00	183 Joe Pepitone	2.00	255 Bob Shaw	1.50
41 Charlie Lau	.80	116 Jim Brosnan	1.00	184 Vern Law	1.00	256 Jerry Lumpe	1.50
42 Stan Williams	.80	117 Jacke Davis	1.00	185 Chuck Hiller	1.00	257 Hank Aguirre	1.50
43 Veteran Masters: C. Stengel, G. Woodling	4.00	118 Sherm Lollar	1.00	186 Jerry Zimmerman	1.00	258 Alvin Dark (Mgr.)	1.50
		119 Bob Lillis	1.00	187 Willie Kirkland	1.00	259 Johnny Logan	1.50
44 Terry Fox	.80	120 Roger Maris	60.00	188 Eddie Bressoud	1.00	260 Jim Gentile	1.50
45 Bob Aspromonte	.80	121 Jim Hannan	1.00	189 Dave Giusti	1.00	261 Bob Miller	1.50
46 Tommie Aaron	.80	122 Julio Gotay	1.00	190 Minnie Minoso	2.00	262 Ellis Burton	1.50
47 Don Lock	.80	123 Frank Howard	2.00	191 Checklist No. 3	4.00	263 Dave Stenhouse	1.50
48 Birdie Tebbetts (Mgr.)	.80	124 Dick Howser	1.00	192 Clay Dalrymple	1.00	264 Phil Linz	1.50
49 Dal Maxvill	.80	125 Robin Roberts	10.00	193 Andre Rodgers	1.00	265 Vada Pinson	3.00
50 Bill Pierc	1.00	126 Bob Uecker	35.00	194 Joe Nuxhall	1.00	266 Bob Allen	1.50
51 George Alusik	.80	127 Bill Tuttle	1.00	195 Manny Jimenez	1.00	267 Carl Sawatski	1.50
52 Chuck Schilling	.80	128 Matty Alou	1.00	196 Doug Camilli	1.00	268 Don Demter	1.50
53 Joe Moeller	.80	129 Gary Bell	1.00	197 Roger Craig	1.50	269 Don Mincher	1.50
54 Rookie Stars: N. Mathews, D. DeBusschere, Harry Fanok, J. Cullen	4.00	130 Dick Groat	1.00	198 Lenny Green	1.50	270 Felipe Alou	1.50
		131 Washington Senators	2.00	199 Joe Amalfitano	1.00	271 Dean Stone	1.50
55 Bill Virdon	1.00	132 Jack Hamilton	1.00	200 Mickey Mantle	350.00	272 Danny Murphy	1.50
56 Dennis Bennett	.80	133 Gene Freese	1.00	201 Cecil Butler	1.50	273 Sammy Taylor	1.50
57 Billy Moran	.80	134 Bob Scheffing (Mgr.)	1.00	202 Boston Red Sox	3.00	274 Checklist No. 4	4.00
58 Bob Will	.80	135 Richie Ashburn	6.00	203 Chico Cardenas	1.50	275 Ed Mathews	17.00
59 Craig Anderson	.80	136 Ike Delock	1.00	204 Don Nottebart	1.50	276 Barry Shetrone	1.50
60 Elston Howard	4.00	137 Mack Jones	1.00	205 Luis Aparicio	11.00	277 Dick Farrell	1.50
61 Ernie Bowman	.80	138 Pride Of N.L.: Willie Mays, Stan Musial	25.00	206 Ray Washburn	1.50	278 Chico Fernandez	1.50
62 Bob Hendley	.80			207 Ken Hunt	1.50	279 Wally Moon	1.50
63 Cincinnati Reds	2.00	139 Earl Averill	1.00	208 Rookie Stars: Ron Herbel, John Miller, Ron Taylor, Wally Wolf	1.50	280 Bob Rodgers	1.50
64 Dick McAuliffe	.80	140 Frank Lary	1.00			281 Tom Sturdivant	1.50
65 Jackie Brandt	.80	141 Manny Mota (R)	6.00			282 Bob Del Greco	1.50
66 Mike Joyce	.80	142 World Series Game 1 Ford Wins Opener	4.00	209 Hobie Landrith	1.50	283 Roy Sievers	1.50
67 Ed Charles	.80			210 Sandy Koufax	120.00	284 Dave Sisler	2.00
68 Friendly Foes: Duke Snider, Gil Hodges	8.00	143 World Series Game 2 Sanford Shutout	3.00	211 Fred Whitfield	1.50	285 Dick Stuart	2.00
				212 Glen Hobbie	1.50	286 Stu Miller	2.00
69 Bud Zipfel	.80	144 World Series Game 3 Maris Sparks Rally	7.00	213 Billy Hitchcock (Mgr.)	1.50	287 Dick Bertell	2.00
70 Jim O'Toole	.80			214 Orlando Pena	1.50	288 Chicago White Sox	3.00
71 Bobby Wine	.80	145 World Series Game 4 Hiller Grand Slam	3.00	215 Bob Skinner	1.50	289 Hal Brown	2.00
72 Johnny Romano	.80			216 Gene Conley	1.50	290 Bill White	4.00
73 Bob Bragan (Mgr.)	.80	146 World Series Game 5 Tresh's Homer	3.00	217 Joe Christopher	1.50	291 Don Rudolph	2.00
74 Denver Lemaster	.80			218 Tiger Twirlers: Frank Lary, Don Mossi, Jim Bunning	2.00	292 Pumpsie Green	2.00
75 Bobby Allison	.80	147 World Series Game 6 Pierce Victory	3.00			293 Bill Pleis	2.00
76 Earl Wilson	.80	148 World Series Game 7 Yanks Celebrate	4.00	219 Chuck Cottier	1.50	294 Bill Rigney (Mgr.)	2.00
		149 Marv Breeding	1.00	220 Camilo Pascual	1.50	295 Ed Roebuck	2.00

NO. PLAYER	NR. MT.
296 Doc Edwards	2.00
297 Jim Golden	2.00
298 Don Dillard	2.00
299 Rookie Stars:	2.00
Dave Morehead, Bob Dustal,	
Dan Schenider, Tom Butters	
300 Willie Mays	10.00
301 Bill Fischer	2.00
302 Whitey Herzog	2.50
303 Earl Francis	2.00
304 Harry Bright	2.00
305 Don Hoak	2.00
306 Star Receivers:	2.50
Earl Battey, Elston Howard	
307 Chet Nichols	2.00
308 Camilo Carreon	2.00
309 Jim Brewer	2.00
310 Tommy Davis	3.00
311 Joe McClain	2.00
312 Houston Colts	7.50
313 Ernie Broglio	2.00
314 John Goryl	2.00
315 Ralph Terry	2.00
316 Norm Sherry	2.00
317 Sam McDowell	2.00
318 Gene Mauch (Mgr.)	2.00
319 Joe Gaines	2.00
320 Warren Spahn	30.00
321 Gino Cimoli	2.00
322 Bob Turley	2.00
323 Bill Mazeroski	3.00
324 Rookie Stars:	3.00
G. Williams, Vic Davalillo,	
P. Ward, Phil Roof	
325 Jack Sanford	2.00
326 Hank Foiles	2.00
327 Paul Foytack	2.00
328 Dick Williams	2.00
329 Lindy McDaniel	2.00
330 Chuck Hinton	2.00
331 Series Foes:	2.00
Bill Stafford, Bill Pierce	
332 Joel Horlen	2.00
333 Carl Warwick	2.00
334 Wynn Hawkins	2.00
335 Leon Wagner	2.00
336 Ed Bauta	2.00
337 Los Angeles Dodgers	8.00
338 Russ Kemmerer	2.00
339 Ted Bowsfield	2.00
340 Yogi Berra	60.00
341 Jack Baldschun	2.00
342 Gene Woodling	2.00
343 Johnny Pesky (Mgr.)	2.00
344 Don Schwall	2.00
345 Brooks Robinson	35.00
346 Billy Hoeft	2.00
347 Joe Torre	4.00
348 Vic Wertz	2.00
349 Zoilo Versalles	2.00
350 Bob Purkey	2.00
351 Al Luplow	2.00
352 Ken Johnson	2.00
353 Billy Williams	20.00
354 Dom Zanni	2.00
355 Dean Chance	2.00
356 John Schaive	2.00
357 George Altman	2.00
358 Milt Pappas	2.00
359 Haywood Sullivan	2.00
360 Don Drysdale	22.00
361 Clete Boyer	2.50
362 Checklist No. 5	4.00
363 Dick Radatz	2.00
364 Howie Goss	2.00
365 Jim Bunning	6.00
366 Tony Taylor	2.00
367 Tony Cloninger	2.00
368 Ed Bailey	2.00
369 Jim Lemon	2.00
370 Dick Donovan	2.00
371 Rod Kanehl	2.00
372 Don Lee	2.00
373 Jim Campbell	2.00
374 Claude Osteen	2.00
375 Ken Boyer	4.00
376 John Wyatt	2.00
377 Baltimore Orioles	3.00
378 Bill Henry	2.00
379 Bob Anderson	2.00
380 Ernie Banks	45.00
381 Frank Baumann	2.00
382 Ralph Houk (Mgr.)	1.50
383 Pete Richert	2.00
384 Bob Tillman	2.00
385 Art Mahaffey	2.00
386 Rookie Stars:	2.50
Ed Kirkpatrick, J. Bateman,	
G. Roggenburk, L. Bearnarth	
387 Al McBean	2.00
388 Jim Davenport	2.00
389 Frank Sullivan	2.00
390 Hank Aaron	110.00
391 Bill Dailey	2.00
392 Tribe Thumpers:	2.00
Johnny Romano,	
Tito Francona	
393 Ken MacKenzie	2.00
394 Tim McCarver	7.00
395 Don McMahon	2.00
396 Joe Koppe	2.00
397 Kansas C. Athletics	3.00
398 Boog Powell	8.00
399 Dick Ellsworth	2.00
400 Frank Robinson	35.00
401 Jim Bouton	4.00
402 Mickey Vernon (Mgr.)	2.00
403 Ron Perranoski	2.00
404 Bob Oldis	2.00
405 Floyd Robinson	2.00
406 Howie Koplitz	2.00
407 Rookie Stars:	2.00
Dick Simpson, Frank Kostro,	
Chico Ruiz, Larry Elliot	
408 Billy Gardner	2.00
409 Roy Face	2.00
410 Earl Battey	2.00
411 Jim Constable	2.00
412 Dodger Big Three:	30.00
Sandy Koufax, Johnny	
Podres, Don Drysdale	
413 Jerry Walker	2.00
414 Ty Cline	2.00
415 Bob Gibson	35.00
416 Alex Grammas	2.00
417 San F. Giants	4.00
418 Johnny Orsino	2.00
419 Tracy Stallard	2.00
420 Bobby Richardson	5.00
421 Tom Morgan	2.00
422 Fred Hutchinson (Mgr.)	2.00
423 Ed Hobaugh	2.00
424 Charley Smith	2.00
425 Smokey Burgess	2.00
426 Barry Latman	2.00
427 Bernie Allen	2.00
428 Carl Boles	2.00
429 Lou Burdette	2.50
430 Norm Siebern	2.00
431 Checklist No. 6	4.00
432 Roman Mejias	2.00
433 Denis Menke	2.00
434 Johnny Callison	2.00
435 Woody Held	2.00
436 Tim Harkness	2.00
437 Bill Bruton	2.00
438 Wes Stock	2.00
439 Don Zimmer	3.00
440 Juan Marichal	20.00
441 Lee Thomas	2.00
442 J.C. Hartman	2.00
443 Jim Piersall	2.50
444 Jim Maloney	2.00
445 Norm Cash	3.00
446 Whitey Ford	35.00
447 Felix Mantilla	9.00
448 Jack Kralick	9.00
449 Jose Tartabull	9.00
450 Bob Friend	9.00
451 Cleveland Indians	9.00
452 Barney Schultz	9.00
453 Jake Wood	9.00
454 Art Fowler	9.00
455 Ruben Amaro	9.00
456 Jim Coker	9.00
457 Tex Clevenger	9.00
458 Al Lopez (Mgr.)	13.00
459 Dick LeMay	10.00
460 Del Crandall	10.00
461 Norm Bass	10.00
462 Wally Post	10.00
463 Joe Schaffernoth	10.00
464 Ken Aspromonte	10.00
465 Chuck Estrada	10.00
466 Rookie Stars:	25.00
Tony Martinez, Bill Freehan,	
Jerry Robinson, Nate Oliver	
467 Phil Ortega	9.00
468 Carroll Hardy	9.00
469 Jay Hook	9.00
470 Tom Tresh	25.00
471 Ken Retzer	9.00
472 Lou Brock	125.00
473 New York Mets	40.00
474 Jack Fisher	9.00
475 Gus Triandos	9.00
476 Frank Funk	9.00
477 Donn Clendenon	9.00
478 Paul Brown	9.00
479 Ed Brinkman	9.00
480 Bill Monbouquette	9.00
481 Bob Taylor	9.00
482 Felix Torres	9.00
483 Jim Owens	9.00
484 Dale Long	9.00
485 Jim Landis	9.00
486 Ray Sadecki	9.00
487 John Roseboro	9.00
488 Jerry Adair	9.00
489 Paul Toth	9.00
490 Willie McCovey	110.00
491 Harry Craft (Mgr.)	9.00
492 Dave Wickersham	9.00
493 Walt Bond	9.00
494 Phil Regan	9.00
495 Frank Thomas	9.00
496 Rookie Stars:	9.00
Steve Dalkowski, Carl	
Bouldin, Fred Newman,	
Jack Smith	
497 Bennie Daniels	9.00
498 Eddie Kasko	9.00
499 J.C. Martin	9.00
500 Harmon Killebrew	80.00
501 Joe Azcue	9.00
502 Daryl Spencer	9.00
503 Milwaukee Braves	12.00
504 Bob Johnson	9.00
505 Curt Flood	15.00
506 Gene Green	9.00
507 Roland Sheldon	9.00
508 Ted Savage	9.00
509 Checklist No. 7	15.00
510 Ken McBride	9.00
511 Charlie Neal	9.00
512 Cal McLish	9.00
513 Gary Geiger	9.00
514 Larry Osborne	9.00
515 Don Elston	9.00
516 Purnal Goldy	9.00
517 Hal Woodeschick	9.00
518 Don Blasingame	9.00
519 Claude Raymond	9.00
520 Orlando Cepeda	15.00
521 Dan Pfister	9.00
522 Rookie Stars:	9.00
Mel Nelson, Gary Peters,	
Art Quirk, Jim Roland	
523 Bill Kunkel	6.00
524 St. Louis Cards	12.00
525 Nellie Fox	12.00
526 Dick Hall	6.00
527 Ed Sadowski	6.00
528 Carl Willey	6.00
529 Wes Covington	6.00
530 Don Mossi	6.00
531 Sam Mele (Mgr.)	6.00
532 Steve Boros	6.00
533 Bobby Shantz	6.00
534 Ken Walters	6.00
535 Jim Perry	6.00
536 Norm Larker	6.00
537 Rookie Stars:	600.00
Pedro Gonzalez, Pete Rose,	
Ken McMullen, Al Weis	
538 George Brunet	6.00
339 Wayne Causey	6.00
540 Bob Clemente	180.00
541 Ron Moeller	6.00
542 Lou Klimchock	6.00
543 Russ Snyder	6.00
544 Rookie Stars:	35.00
Rusty Staub, Duke Carmel,	
Bill Haas, Dick Phillips	
545 Jose Pagan	6.00
546 Hal Reniff	6.00
547 Gus Bell	6.00
548 Tom Satriano	6.00
549 Rookie Stars:	6.00
Paul Ratliff, Marcelino	
Lopez, Pete Lovrich,	
Elmo Plaskett	
550 Duke Snider	75.00
551 Billy Klaus	6.00
552 Detroit Tigers	20.00
553 Rookie Stars:	250.00
Brock Davis, Jim Gosger,	
W. Stargell, J. Herrnstein	
554 Hank Fischer	6.00
555 John Blanchard	6.00
556 Al Worthington	6.00
557 Cuno Barragan	6.00
558 Rookie Stars:	6.00
Bill Faul, Ron Hunt,	
Bob Lipski, Al Moran	
559 Danny Murtaugh (Mgr.)	6.00
560 Ray Herbert	6.00
561 Mike De La Hoz	6.00
562 Rookie Stars:	10.00
Don Rowe, Randy Ca	
Dave McNally, Ken R(	
563 Mike McCormick	6.00
564 George Banks	6.00
565 Larry Sherry	6.00
566 Clif Cook	6.00
567 Jim Duffalo	6.00
568 Bob Sadowski	6.00
569 Luis Arroyo	6.00
570 Frank Bolling	6.00
571 Johnny Klippstein	6.00
572 Jack Spring	6.00
573 Coot Veal	6.00
574 Hal Kolstad	6.00
575 Don Cardwell	6.00
576 Johnny Temple	6.00

1964 Topps. . . . Complete Set of 587 Cards—Value $950.00 (Exc.); $2500.00 (Near Mint)

Phil Niekro's rookie card is in this set. The high numbers are 523 to 587. For the first time a card was issued for a deceased player—Ken Hubbs.

    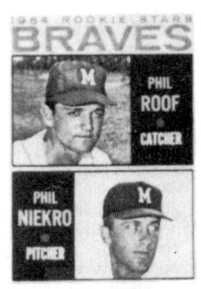

NO. PLAYER	NR. MT.
1 NL ERA Ldrs.. (Exc. $3.00)	13.00
Sandy Koufax, Dick Ellsworth, Bob Friend	
2 AL ERA Leaders:	1.50
Gary Peters, Juan Pizarro, Camilo Pascual	
3 NL Pitching Leaders:	5.00
S. Koufax, Juan Marichal, W. Spahn, Jim Maloney	
4 AL Pitching Leaders:	1.75
Whitey Ford, Camilo Pascual, Jim Bouton	
5 NL Strikeout Leaders:	5.00
Sandy Koufax, Jim Maloney, Don Drysdale	
6 AL Strikeout Leaders:.	1.75
Camilo Pascual, Jim Bunning, Dick Stigman	
7 NL Batting Leaders:	3.00
T. Davis, Bob Clemente, D. Groat, Hank Aaron	
8 AL Batting Leaders:	4.00
Carl Yastrzemski, Al Kaline, Rich Rollins	
9 NL Home Run Leaders:	10.00
Hank Aaron, W. McCovey, W. Mays, Orlando Cepeda	
10 AL Home Run Leaders:	1.75
Harmon Killebrew, Dick Stuart, Bob Allison	
11 NL RBI Leaders:	2.50
Hank Aaron, Ken Boyer, Bill White	
12 AL RBI Leaders:	1.75
Dick Stuart, Al Kaline, Harmon Killebrew	
13 Hoyt Wilhelm	8.00
14 Dodgers Rookies:	.75
Dick Nen, Nick Willhite	
15 Zoilo Versalles	.75
16 John Boozer	.75
17 Willie Kirkland	.75
18 Bill O'Dell	.75
19 Don Wert	.75
20 Bob Friend	.75
21 Yogi Berra (Mgr.)	30.00
22 Jerry Adair	.75
23 Chris Zachary	.75
24 Carl Sawatski	.75
25 Bill Monbouquett	.75
26 Gino Cimoli	.75
27 New York Mets	5.00
28 Claude Osteen	.75
29 Lou Brock	32.00
30 Ron Perranoski	.75
31 Dave Nicholson	.75
32 Dean Chance	1.50
33 Reds Rookies:	.75
Sammy Ellis, Mel Queen	
34 Jim Perry	.75
35 Ed Mathews	15.00
36 Hal Reniff	.75
37 Smoky Burgess	.75
38 Jim Wynn (R)	3.00
39 Hank Aguirre	.75
40 Dick Groat	1.00

NO. PLAYER	NR. MT.
41 Friendly Foes:	4.00
W. McCovey, Leon Wagner	
42 Moe Drabowski	.75
43 Roy Sievers	.75
44 Duke Carmel	.75
45 Milt Pappas	.75
46 Ed Brinkman	.75
47 Giants Rookies:	1.00
Jesus Alou, Ron Herbel	
48 Bob Perry	.75
49 Bill Henry	.75
50 M. Mantle	225.00
51 Pete Richert	.75
52 Chuck Hinton	.75
53 Denis Menke	.75
54 Sam Mele	.75
55 Ernie Banks	25.00
56 Hal Brown	.75
57 Tim Harkness	.75
58 Don Demeter	.75
59 Ernie Broglio	.75
60 Frank Malzone	.75
61 Angel Backstops:	.75
Bob Rodgers, Ed Sadowski	
62 Ted Savage	.75
63 Johnny Orsino	.75
64 Ted Abernathy	.75
65 Felipe Alou	.75
66 Eddie Fisher	.75
67 Detroit Tigers	2.00
68 Willie Davis	.75
69 Clete Boyer	.75
70 Joe Torre	2.50
71 Jack Spring	.75
72 Chico Cardenas	.75
73 Jimmie Hall	.75
74 Pirates Rookies:	.75
Bob Priddy, Tom Butters	
75 Wayne Causey	.75
76 Checklist No. 1	4.00
77 Jerry Walker	.75
78 Merritt Ranew	.75
79 Bob Heffner	.75
80 Vada Pinson	2.50
81 All-Star Vets:	5.00
Nellie Fox, H. Killebrew	
82 Jim Davenport	.75
83 Gus Triandos	.75
84 Carl Willey	.75
85 Pete Ward	.75
86 Al Doning	.75
87 St. Louis Cardinals	2.00
88 John Roseboro	.75
89 Boog Powell	3.00
90 Earl Battey	.75
91 Bob Bailey	.75
92 Steve Ridzik	.75
93 Gary Geiger	.75
94 Braves Rookies:	.75
Jim Britton, Larry Maxie	
95 George Altman	.75
96 Bob Buhl	.75
97 Jim Fregosi	.75
98 Bill Bruton	.75
99 Al Stanek	.75
100 Elston Howard	3.00

NO. PLAYER	NR. MT.
101 Walt Alston (Mgr.)	3.00
102 Checklist No. 2	4.00
103 Curt Flood	2.50
104 Art Mahaffey	.75
105 Woody Held	.75
106 Joe Nuxhall	.75
107 White Sox Rookies:	.75
B. Howard, F. Kreutzer	
108 John Wyatt	.75
109 Rusty Staub	6.00
110 Albie Pearson	.75
111 Don Elston	.75
112 Bob Tillman	.75
113 Grover Powell	.75
114 Don Lock	.75
115 Frank Bolling	.75
116 Twins Rookies:	10.00
Jay Ward, Tony Oliva	
117 Earl Francis	.75
118 John Blanchard	.75
119 Gary Kolb	.75
120 Don Drysdale	15.00
121 Pete Runnels	.75
122 Don McMahon	.75
123 Jose Pagan	.75
124 Orlando Pena	.75
125 Pete Rose	160.00
126 Russ Snyder	.75
127 Angels Rookies:	.75
Dick Simpson, Aubrey Gatewood	
128 Mickey Lolich (R)	10.00
129 Amado Samuel	.75
130 Gary Peters	.75
131 Steve Boros	.75
132 Milwaukee Braves	2.00
133 Jim Grant	.75
134 Don Zimmer	1.25
135 Johnny Callison	.75
136 World Series Game 1	9.00
Koufax Strikes Out 15	
137 World Series Game 2	3.00
Davis Sparks Rally	
138 World Series Game 3	3.00
LA Takes 3 Straight	
139 World Series Game 4	3.00
Sealing Yanks' Doom	
140 World Series	3.00
Dodgers Celebrate	
141 Danny Murtaugh (Mgr.)	.75
142 John Bateman	.75
143 Bubba Phillips	.75
144 Al Worthington	.75
145 Norm Siebern	.75
146 Indians Rookies:	50.00
Tommy John, Bob Chance	
147 Ray Sadecki	.75
148 J.C. Martin	.75
149 Paul Foytack	.75
150 Willie Mays	70.00
151 K.C. Athletics	2.00
152 Denver LeMaster	.75
153 Dick Williams	.75
154 Dick Tracewski	.75
155 Duke Snider	25.00
156 Bill Dailey	.75

NO. PLAYER	NR. MT.
157 Gene Mauch	.75
158 Ken Johnson	.75
159 Charlie Dees	.75
160 Ken Boyer	5.00
161 Dave McNally	.75
162 Hitting Area:	.75
Dick Sisler, Vada Pinson	
163 Donn Clendenon	.75
164 Bud Daley	.75
165 Jerry Lumpe	.75
166 Marty Keough	.75
167 Senators Rookies:	25.00
Mike Brumley, Lou Piniella	
168 Al Weis	.75
169 Del Crandall	.75
170 Dick Radatz	.75
171 Ty Cline	.75
172 Cleveland Indians	2.00
173 Ryne Duren	.75
174 Doc Edwards	.75
175 Billy Williams	12.00
176 Tracy Stallard	.75
177 Harmon Killebrew	15.00
178 Hank Bauer (Mgr.)	.75
179 Carl Warwick	.75
180 Tommy Davis	.75
181 Dave Wickersham	.75
182 Sox Sockers:	10.00
C. Schilling, C. Yastrzemski	
183 Ron Taylor	.75
184 Al Luplow	.75
185 Jim O'Toole	.75
186 Roman Mejias	.75
187 Ed Roebuck	.75
188 Checklist No. 3	4.00
189 Bob Hendley	.75
190 Bobby Richardson	4.00
191 Clay Dalrymple	.75
192 Cubs Rookies:	.75
J. Boccabella, B. Cowan	
193 Jerry Lynch	.75
194 John Goryl	.75
195 Floyd Robinson	.75
196 Jim Gentile	.75
197 Frank Lary	1.00
198 Len Gabrielson	1.00
199 Joe Azcue	1.00
200 Sandy Koufax	75.00
201 Orioles Rookies:	1.00
Wally Bunker, Sam Bowens	
202 Galen Cisco	1.00
203 John Kennedy	1.00
204 Matty Alou	1.00
205 Nellie Fox	4.00
206 Steve Hamilton	1.00
207 Fred Hutchinson (Mgr.)	1.00
208 Wes Covington	1.00
209 Bob Allen	1.00
210 Carl Yastrzemski	75.00
211 Jim Coker	1.00
212 Pete Lovrich	1.00
213 L.A. Angels	2.00
214 Ken McMullen	1.00
215 Ray Herbert	1.00
216 Mike De La Hoz	1.00
217 Jim King	1.00

NO. PLAYER	NR. MT.
218 Hank Fischer	1.00
219 Young Aces:	1.75
Al Downing, Jim Bouton	
220 Dick Ellsworth	1.00
221 Bob Saverine	1.00
222 Bill Pierce	1.25
223 George Banks	1.00
224 Tommie Sisk	1.00
225 Roger Maris	55.00
226 Colts Rookies:	1.00
Gerald Grote, Larry Yellen	
227 Barry Latman	1.00
228 Felix Mantilla	1.00
229 Charley Lau	1.00
230 Brooks Robinson	30.00
231 Dick Calmus	1.00
232 Al Lopez (Mgr.)	2.50
233 Hal Smith	1.00
234 Gary Bell	1.00
235 Ron Hunt	1.00
236 Bill Faul	1.00
237 Chicago Cubs	2.00
238 Roy McMillan	1.00
239 Herm Starrette	1.00
240 Bill White	2.50
241 Jim Owens	1.00
242 Harvey Kuenn	1.25
243 Phillies Rookies (R)	12.00
Richie Allen, J. Herrnstein	
244 Tony LaRussa (R)	10.00
245 Dick Stigman	1.00
246 Manny Mota	1.25
247 Dave DeBusschere	2.50
248 Johnny Pesky	1.00
249 Doug Camilli	1.00
250 Al Kaline	22.00
251 Choo Choo Coleman	1.00
252 Ken Aspromonte	1.00
253 Wally Post	1.00
254 Don Hoak	1.00
255 Lee Thomas	1.00
256 Johnny Weekly	1.00
257 San F. Giants	2.00
258 Garry Roggenburk	1.00
259 Harry Bright	1.00
260 Frank Robinson	20.00
261 Jim Hannan	1.00
262 Cardinals Rookies:	4.00
Harry Fanok, Mike Shannon	
263 Chuck Estrada	1.00
264 Jim Lndis	1.00
265 Jim Bunning	4.00
266 Gene Freese	1.00
267 Wilbur Wood	1.00
268 Bill's Got It:	1.00
Bill Virdon, D. Murtaugh	
269 Ellis Burton	1.00
270 Rich Rollins	1.00
271 Bob Sadowski	1.00
272 Jake Wood	1.00
273 Mel Nelson	1.00
274 Checklist No. 4	4.00
275 John Tsitouris	1.00
276 Jose Tartabull	1.00
277 Ken Retzer	1.00
278 Bobby Shantz	1.00
279 Joe Koppe	1.00
280 Juan Marichal	11.00
281 Yankees Rookies:	1.00
Jake Gibbs, Tom Metcalf	
282 Bob Bruce	1.00
283 Tommy McCraw	1.00
284 Dick Schofield	1.00
285 Robin Roberts	9.00
286 Don Landrum	1.00
287 Red Sox Rookies:	15.00
T. Conigliaro, B. Spanswick	
288 Al Moran	1.00
289 Frank Funk	1.00
290 Bob Allison	1.00
291 Phil Ortega	1.00

NO. PLAYER	NR. MT.
292 Mike Roarke	1.00
293 Philadelphia Phillies	2.00
294 Ken Hunt	1.00
295 Roger Craig	1.00
296 Ed Kirkpatrick	1.00
297 Ken MacKenzie	1.00
298 Harry Craft (Mgr.)	1.00
299 Bill Stafford	1.00
300 Hank Aaron	75.00
301 Larry Brown	1.00
302 Dan Pfister	1.00
303 Jim Campbell	1.00
304 Bob Johnson	1.00
305 Jack Lamabe	1.00
306 Giant Gunners:	16.00
Willie Mays, O. Ceped	
307 Joe Gibbon	1.00
308 Gene Stephens	1.00
309 Paul Toth	1.00
310 Jim Gilliam	2.50
311 Tom Brown	1.00
312 Tigers Rookies:	1.00
Fred Gladding, Fritz F	
313 Chuck Hiller	1.00
314 Jerry Buchek	1.00
315 Bo Belinsky	1.00
316 Gene Oliver	1.00
317 Al Smith	1.00
318 Minnesota Twins	2.00
319 Paul Brown	1.00
320 Rocky Colavito	3.00
321 Bob Lillis	1.00
322 George Brunet	1.00
323 John Buzhardt	1.00
324 Casey Stengel (Mgr.)	11.00
325 Hector Lopez	1.00
326 Ron Brand	1.00
327 Don Blasingame	1.00
328 Bob Shaw	1.00
329 Russ Nixon	1.00
330 Tommy Harper	1.00
331 AL Bombers:	75.00
Mickey Mantle, R. Mar	
Norm Cash, Al Kaline	
332 Ray Washburn	1.00
333 Billy Moran	1.00
334 Lew Krausse	1.00
335 Don Mossi	1.00
336 Andre Rodgers	1.00
337 Dodgers Rookies:	4.00
Al Ferrara, Jeff Torbor	
338 Jack Kralick	1.00
339 Walt Bond	1.00
340 Joe Cunningham	1.00
341 Jim Roland	1.00
342 Willie Stargell	40.00
343 Washington Senators	2.00
344 Phil Linz	1.00
345 Frank Thomas	1.00
346 Joe Jay	1.00
347 Bobby Wine	1.00
348 Ed Lopat	1.25
349 Art Fowler	1.00
350 Willie McCovey	24.00
351 Dan Schneider	1.00
352 Eddie Bressoud	1.00
353 Wally Moon	1.00
354 Dan Giusti	1.00
355 Vic Power	1.00
356 Reds Rookies:	1.00
Bill McCool, Chico Ru	
357 Charley James	1.00
358 Ron Kline	1.00
359 Jim Schaffer	1.00
360 Joe Pepitone	1.50
361 Jay Hook	1.00
362 Checklist No. 5	4.00
363 Dick McAuliffe	1.00
364 Joe Gaines	1.00
365 Cal McLish	1.00
366 Nelson Mathews	1.00

NO. PLAYER	NR. MT.
367 Fred Whitfield	1.00
368 White Sox Rookies:	1.00
Fritz Ackley, Don Buford	
369 Jerry Zimmerman	1.00
370 Hal Woodeschick	1.00
371 Frank Howard	2.00
372 Howie Koplitz	2.00
373 Pittsburgh Pirates	4.00
374 Bobby Bolin	2.00
375 Ron Santo	4.00
376 Dave Morehead	2.00
377 Bob Skinner	2.00
378 Braves Rookies:	2.00
W. Woodward, Jack Smith	
379 Tony Gonzalez	2.00
380 Whitey Ford	25.00
381 Bob Taylor	2.00
382 Wes Stock	2.00
383 Bill Rigney (Mgr.)	2.00
384 Ron Hansen	2.00
385 Curt Simmons	1.50
386 Lenny Green	2.00
387 Terry Fox	2.00
388 A's Rookies:	2.00
G. Williams, J. O'Donoghue	
389 Jim Umbricht	2.00
390 Orlando Cepeda	7.00
391 Sam McDowell	1.25
392 Jim Pagliaroni	2.00
393 Casey Teaches:	5.00
C. Stengel, Ed Kranepool	
394 Bob Miller	2.00
395 Tom Tresh	2.50
396 Dennis Bennett	2.00
397 Chuck Cottier	2.00
398 Mets Rookies:	2.00
Bill Haas, Dick Smith	
399 Jackie Brandt	2.00
400 Warren Spahn	25.00
401 Charlie Maxwell	2.00
402 Tom Sturdivant	2.00
403 Cincinnati Reds	5.00
404 Tony Martinez	2.00
405 Ken McBride	2.00
406 Al Spangler	2.00
407 Bill Freehan	4.00
408 Cubs Rookies:	2.00
Jim Stewart, Fred Burdette	
409 Bill Fischer	2.00
410 Dick Stuart	1.50
411 Lee Walls	2.00
412 Ray Culp	2.00
413 Johnny Keane (Mgr.)	2.00
414 Jack Sanford	2.00
415 Tony Kubek	5.00
416 Lee Maye	2.00
417 Don Cardwell	2.00
418 Orioles Rookies:	2.00
Les Narum, D. Knowles	
419 Ken Harrelson (R)	5.00
420 Jim Maloney	2.00
421 Camilo Carreon	2.00
422 Jack Fisher	2.00
423 Tops in N.L.:	60.00
Hank Aaron, Willie Mays	
424 Dick Bertell	2.00
425 Norm Cash	3.00
426 Bob Rodgers	2.00
427 Don Rudolph	2.00
428 Red Sox Rookies:	2.00
Archie Skeen, Pete Smith	
429 Tim McCarver	5.00
430 Juan Pizarro	2.00
431 George Alusik	2.00
432 Ruben Amaro	2.00
433 New York Yankees	11.00
434 Don Nottebart	2.00
435 Vic Davalillo	2.00
436 Charlie Neal	2.00
437 Ed Bailey	2.00
438 Checklist No. 6	4.00

NO. PLAYER	NR. MT.
439 Harvey Haddix	1.50
440 Bob Clemente	75.00
441 Bob Duliba	2.00
442 Pumpsie Green	2.00
443 Chuck Dressen (Mgr.)	2.00
444 Larry Jackson	2.00
445 Bill Skowron	2.50
446 Julian Javier	2.00
447 Ted Bowsfield	2.00
448 Cookie Rojas	2.00
449 Deron Johnson	2.00
450 Steve Barber	2.00
451 Joe Amalfitano	2.00
452 Giants Rookies:	2.00
Gil Garrido, Jim Hart	
453 Frank Baumann	2.00
454 Tommie Aaron	2.00
455 Bernie Allen	2.00
456 Dodgers Rookies:	3.00
John Werhas, Wes Parker	
457 Jesse Gonder	2.00
458 Ralph Terry	2.00
459 Red Sox Rookies:	2.00
Pete Charton, D. Jone	
460 Bob Gibson	25.00
461 George Thomas	2.00
462 Birdie Tebbetts	2.00
463 Don Leppert	2.00
464 Dallas Green	2.50
465 Mike Hershberger	2.00
466 A's Rookies:	2.00
D. Green, A. Monteagudo	
467 Bob Aspromonte	2.00
468 Gaylord Perry	30.00
469 Cubs Rookies:	2.00
S. Slaughter, Fred Norman	
470 Jim Bouton	3.00
471 Gates Brown (R)	2.50
472 Vern Law	2.50
473 Baltimore Orioles	4.00
474 Larry Sherry	2.00
475 Ed Charles	2.00
476 Braves Rookies:	5.00
Rico Carty, Dick Kelle	
477 Mike Joyce	2.00
478 Dick Howser	2.50
479 Cardinals Rookies:	2.00
D. Bakenhaster, J. Lewis	
480 Bob Purkey	2.00
481 Chuck Schilling	2.00
482 Phillies Rookies:	2.50
John Briggs, Danny Cater	
483 Fred Valentine	2.00
484 Bill Pleis	2.00
485 Tom Haller	2.00
486 Bob Kennedy	2.00
487 Mike McCormick	2.00
488 Yankees Rookies:	2.00
Pete Mikkelsen, Bob Meyer	
489 Julio Navarro	2.00
490 Ron Fairly	2.00
491 Ed Rakow	2.00
492 Colts Rookies:	2.00
Jim Beauchamp, M. White	
493 Don Lee	2.00
494 Al Jackson	2.00
495 Bill Virdon	2.50
496 Chicago White Sox	4.00
497 Jeoff Long	2.00
498 Dave Stenhouse	2.00
499 Indians Rookies:	2.00
Chico Salmon, G. Seyfried	
500 Camilo Pascual	2.00
501 Bob Veale	2.00
502 Angels Rookies:	2.00
Bobby Knoop, Bob Lee	
503 Earl Wilson	2.00
504 Claude Raymond	2.00
505 Stan Williams	2.00
506 Bobby Bragan (Mgr.)	2.00
507 John Edwards	2.00

NO.	PLAYER	NR. MT.
508	Diego Segui	2.00
509	Pirates Rookies:	3.00
	Gene Alley, O. McFarlane	
510	Lindy McDaniel	2.00
511	Lou Jackson	2.00
512	Tigers Rookies:	5.00
	Joe Sparma, Willie Horton	
513	Don Larsen	2.50
514	Jim Hickman	2.00
515	Johnny Romano	2.00
516	Twins Rookies:	2.00
	Dwight Siebler, Jerry Arrigo	
517	Checklist No. 7	8.00
518	Carl Bouldin	2.00
519	Charlie Smith	2.00
520	Jack Baldschun	2.00
521	Tom Satriano	2.00
522	Bobby Tiefenauer	2.00
523	Lou Burdette	7.00
524	Reds Rookies:	5.00
	Jim Dickson, Bobby Klaus	
525	Al McBean	5.00
526	Lou Clinton	5.00
527	Larry Bearnarth	5.00
528	A's Rookies:	5.00
	D. Duncan, Tom Reynolds	

NO.	PLAYER	NR. MT.
529	Al Dark	5.00
530	Leon Wagner	5.00
531	L.A. Dodgers	10.00
532	Twins Rookies:	5.00
	Bud Bloomfield (wrong photo), Joe Nossek	
533	John Klippstein	5.00
534	Gus Bell	5.00
535	Phil Regan	5.00
536	Mets Rookies:	5.00
	Larry Elliot, J. Stephenson	
537	Dan Osinski	5.00
538	Minnie Minoso	8.00
539	Roy Face	6.00
540	Luis Aparicio	20.00
541	Braves Rookies:	150.00
	Phil Niekro, Phil Roof	
542	Don Mincher	5.00
543	Bob Uecker	55.00
544	Colts Rookies:	5.00
	Steve Hertz, Joe Hoerner	
545	Max Alvis	5.00
546	Joe Christopher	5.00
547	Gil Hodges (Mgr.)	11.00
548	NL Rookies:	5.00
	W. Schurr, P. Speckenbach	

NO.	PLAYER	NR. MT.
549	Joe Moeller	5.00
550	Ken Hubbs	12.00
	(In Memoriam)	
551	Billy Hoeft	5.00
552	Indians Rookies:	5.00
	Tom Kelley, Sonny Siebert	
553	Jim Brewer	5.00
554	Hank Foiles	5.00
555	Lee Stange	5.00
556	Mets Rookies:	5.00
	Steve Dillon, Ron Locke	
557	Leo Burke	5.00
558	Don Schwall	5.00
559	Dick Phillips	5.00
560	Dick Farrell	5.00
561	Phillies Rookies:	8.00
	Dave Bennett, Rick Wise	
562	Pedro Ramos	5.00
563	Dal Maxvill	5.00
564	AL Rookies:	5.00
	Joe McCabe, J. McNertney	
565	Stu Miller	5.00
566	Ed Kranepool	5.00
567	Jim Kaat	10.00

NO.	PLAYER	NR. MT.
568	NL Rookies:	5.00
	Phil Gagliano, Cap Peterson	
569	Fred Newman	5.00
570	Bill Mazeroski	7.00
571	Gene Conley	5.00
572	AL Rookies:	5.00
	Dave Gray, Dick Egan	
573	Jim Duffalo	5.00
574	Manny Jimenez	5.00
575	Tony Cloninger	5.00
576	Mets Rookies:	5.00
	J. Hinsley, Bill Wakefield	
577	Gordy Coleman	5.00
578	Glen Hobbie	5.00
579	Boston Red Sox	12.00
580	Johnny Podres	9.00
581	Yankees Rookies:	5.00
	P. Gonzalez, Archie Moore	
582	Rod Kanehl	5.00
583	Tito Francona	5.00
584	Joel Horlen	5.00
585	Tony Taylor	5.00
586	Jim Piersall	7.00
587	Bennie Daniels (Exc. $2.00)	8.00

1965 Topps. . . . Complete Set of 598 Cards—Value $1300.00 (Exc.); $2900.00 (Near Mint)

This set includes the rookie cards of Steve Carlton, Joe Morgan, Tony Perez and "Catfish" Hunter. Cards 523 to 598 are the high numbers. Semi-high numbers are 447 to 522.

NO.	PLAYER	NR. MT.
1	AL Bat Ldrs.: (Exc. $1.00)	10.00
	Elston Howard, Tony Oliva, Brooks Robinson	
2	NL Batting Leaders:	6.00
	Hank Aaron, Bob Clemente, Rico Carty	
3	AL Home Run Leaders:	9.00
	Boog Powell, Harmon Killebrew, Mickey Mantle	
4	NL Home Run Leaders:	5.00
	Willie Mays, Billy Williams, Johnny Callison, Jim Hart, Orlando Cepeda	
5	AL RBI Leaders:	7.50
	Brooks Robinson, Dick Stuart, Harmon Killebrew, Mickey Mantle	
6	NL RBI Leaders:	2.50
	Ken Boyer, Willie Mays, Ron Santo	
7	AL ERA Leaders:	2.00
	Dean Chance, Joel Horlen	
8	NL ERA Leaders:	2.00
	S. Koufax, Don Drysdale	
9	AL Pitching Leaders:	1.50
	D. Chance, G. Peters, J. Pizarro, W. Bunker, D. Wickersham	
10	NL Pitching Leaders:	2.00
	L. Jackson, Juan Marichal, Ray Sadecki	

NO.	PLAYER	NR. MT.
11	AL Strikeout Leaders:	1.50
	A. Downing, D. Chance, C. Pascual	
12	NL Strikeout Leaders:	2.00
	Bob Gibson, B. Veale, Don Drysdale	
13	Pedro Ramos	.75
14	Len Gabrielson	.75
15	Robin Roberts	7.50
16	Houston Rookies:	150.00
	Joe Morgan, Sonny Jackson	
17	John Romano	.75
18	Bill McCool	.75
19	Gates Brown	.75
20	Jim Bunning	4.00
21	Don Blasingame	.75
22	Charlie Smith	.75
23	Bob Tiefenauer	.75
24	Twins—6th Place	2.00
25	Al McBeane	.75
26	Bob Knoop	.75
27	Dick Bertell	.75
28	Barney Schultz	.75
29	Felix Mantilla	.75
30	Jim Bouton	1.50
31	Mike White	.75
32	Herman Franks	.75
33	Jackie Brandt	.75
34	Cal Koonce	.75
35	Ed Charles	.75
36	Bobby Wine	.75

NO.	PLAYER	NR. MT.
37	Fred Gladding	.75
38	Jim King	.75
39	Gerry Arrigo	.75
40	Frank Howard	1.50
41	White Sox Rookies:	.75
	Bruce Howard, Marv Staehle	
42	Earl Wilson	.75
43	Mike Shannon	.90
44	Wade Blasingame	.75
45	Roy McMillan	.75
46	Bob Lee	.75
47	Tommy Harper	.75
48	Claude Raymond	.75
49	Orioles Rookies:	1.50
	John Miller, Curt Blefary	
50	Juan Marical	8.00
51	Billy Bryan	.75
52	Ed Roebuck	.75
53	Dick McAuliffe	.75
54	Joe Gibbon	.75
55	Tony Conigliaro	6.00
56	Ron Kline	.75
57	Cardinals—1st Place	2.00
58	Fred Talbot	.75
59	Nate Oiver	.75
60	Jim O'Toole	.75
61	Chris Cannizzaro	.75
62	Jim Kaat	5.00
63	Ty Cline	.75
64	Lou Burdette	1.50
65	Tony Kubek	3.00

NO.	PLAYER	NR. MT.
66	Bill Rigney	.75
67	Harvey Haddix	.75
68	Del Crandall	.75
69	Bill Virdon	1.25
70	Bill Skowron	1.50
71	John O'Donoghue	.75
72	Tony Gonzalez	.75
73	Dennis Ribant	.75
74	Red Sox Rookies:	4.00
	R. Petrocelli, J. Stephenson	
75	Deron Johnson	.75
76	Sam McDowell	1.00
77	Doug Camilli	.75
78	Dal Maxvill	.75
79	Checklist No. 1	4.00
80	Turk Farrell	.75
81	Don Buford	.75
82	Braves Rookies:	.75
	Santos Alomar, John Braun	
83	George Thomas	.75
84	Ron Herbel	.75
85	Willie Smith	.75
86	Les Narum	.75
87	Nelson Mathews	.75
88	Jack Lamabe	.75
89	Mike Hershberger	.75
90	Rich Rollins	.75
91	Cubs—8th Place	2.00
92	Dick Howser	1.25
93	Jack Fisher	.75
94	Charlie Lau	.75

NO. PLAYER	NR. MT.	NO. PLAYER	NR. MT.	NO. PLAYER	NR. MT.	NO. PLAYER	NR. MT.
95 Bill Mazeroski	2.00	168 Dick Green	.75	248 Gus Triandos	1.00	329 Hawk Taylor	1.50
96 Sonny Siebert	.75	169 Dave Vineyard	.75	249 Dave McNally	1.50	330 Whitey Ford	20.00
97 Pedro Gonzalez	.75	170 Hank Aaron	70.00	250 Willie Mays	90.00	331 Dodgers Rookies:	2.00
98 Bob Miller	.75	171 Jim Roland	.75	251 Billy Herman (Mgr.)	2.00	Al Ferrara, John Purdin	
99 Gil Hodges	6.00	172 Jim Piersall	1.25	252 Pete Richert	1.00	332 Ted Abernathy	1.50
100 Ken Boyer	3.00	173 Tigers—4th Place	2.00	253 Danny Cater	1.00	333 Tommie Reynolds	1.50
101 Fred Newman	.75	174 Joe Jay	.75	254 Roland Sheldon	1.00	334 Vic Roznovsky	1.50
102 Steve Boros	.75	175 Bob Aspromonte	.75	255 Camilo Pascual	1.00	335 Mickey Lolich	3.00
103 Harvey Kuenn	1.00	176 Willie McCovey	15.00	256 Tito Francona	1.00	336 Woody Held	1.50
104 Checklist No. 2	4.00	177 Pete Mikkelsen	.75	257 Jim Wynn	1.25	337 Mike Cuellar	2.00
105 Chico Salmon	.75	178 Dalton Jones	.75	258 Larry Bearnarth	1.00	338 Phillies—2nd Place	3.00
106 Gene Oliver	.75	179 Hal Woodeschick	.75	259 Tigers Rookies:	2.50	339 Ryne Duren	1.50
107 Phillies Rookies:	2.00	180 Bob Allison	1.00	Jim Northrup, Ray Oyler		340 Tony Oliva	6.00
C. Shockley, Pat Corrales		181 Senators Rookies:	.75	260 Don Drysdale	15.00	341 Bobby Bolin	1.50
108 Don Mincher	.75	Don Loun, Joe McCabe		261 Duke Carmel	1.00	342 Bob Rodgers	1.50
109 Walt Bond	.75	182 Mike De La Hoz	.75	262 Bud Daley	1.00	343 Mike McCormick	1.50
110 Ron Santo	2.50	183 Dave Nicholson	.75	263 Marty Keough	1.00	344 Wes Parker	1.50
111 Lee Thomas	.75	184 John Boozer	.75	264 Bob Buhl	1.00	345 Floyd Robinson	1.50
112 Derrell Griffith	.75	185 Max Alvis	.75	265 Jim Pagliaroni	1.00	346 Bob Bragan (Mgr.)	1.50
113 Steve Barber	.75	186 Bill Cowan	.75	266 Bert Campaneris	3.00	347 Roy Face	2.00
114 Jim Hickman	.75	187 Casey Stengel (Mgr.)	10.00	267 Senators—9th Place	3.00	348 George Banks	1.50
115 Bob Richardson	3.00	188 Sam Bowens	.75	268 Ken McBride	1.00	349 Larry Miller	1.50
116 Cardinals Rookies:	1.50	189 Checklist No. 3	4.00	269 Frank Bolling	1.00	350 Mickey Mantle	400.00
Dave Dowling, Bob Tolan		190 Bill White	2.00	270 Milt Pappas	1.00	351 Jim Perry	2.00
117 Wes Stock	.75	191 Phil Regan	.75	271 Don Wert	1.00	352 Alex Johnson	1.50
118 Hal Lanier (R)	1.50	192 Jim Coker	.75	272 Chuck Schilling	1.00	353 Jerry Lumpe	1.50
119 John Kennedy	.75	193 Gaylord Perry	12.00	273 Checklist No. 4	4.00	354 Cubs Rookies:	1.50
120 Frank Robinson	15.00	194 Angels Rookies:	.75	274 Lum Harris (Mgr.)	1.00	Billy Ott, Jack Warner	
121 Gene Alley	.75	Rick Reichardt, Bill Kelso		275 Dick Groat	1.25	355 Vada Pinson	2.00
122 Bill Pleis	.75	195 Bob Veale	.75	276 Hoyt Wilhelm	8.00	356 Bill Spanswick	1.50
123 Frank Thomas	.75	196 Ron Fairly	.75	277 Johnny Lewis	1.00	357 Carl Warwick	1.50
124 Tom Satriano	.75	197 Diego Segui	1.00	278 Ken Retzer	1.00	358 Albie Pearson	1.50
125 Juan Pizarro	.75	198 Smoky Burgess	1.00	279 Dick Tracewski	1.00	359 Ken Johnson	1.50
126 Dodgers—6th Place	4.00	199 Bob Heffner	1.00	280 Dick Stuart	1.00	360 Orlando Cepeda	6.00
127 Frank Lary	.75	200 Joe Torre	2.00	281 Bill Stafford	1.00	361 Checklist No. 5	4.00
128 Vic Davalillo	.75	201 Twins Rookies:	1.50	282 Giants Rookies:	2.00	362 Don Schwall	1.50
129 Bennie Daniels	.75	S. Valdespino, Cesar Tovar		Dick Estelle, M. Murakami		363 Bob Johnson	1.50
130 Al Kaline	20.00	202 Leo Burke	1.00	283 Fred Whitfield	1.00	364 Galen Cisco	1.50
131 Johnny Keane (Mgr.)	.75	203 Dallas Green	2.00	284 Nick Willhite	1.50	365 Jim Gentile	1.50
132 World Series Game 1	2.50	204 Russ Snyder	1.00	285 Ron Hunt	1.50	366 Dan Schneider	1.50
Cards Take Opener		205 Warren Spahn	18.00	286 Athletics Rookies:	1.50	367 Leon Wagner	1.50
133 World Series Game 2	2.50	206 Willie Horton	1.50	J. Dickson, A. Monteagudo		368 White Sox Rookies:	2.00
Stottlemyre Wins		207 Pete Rose	160.00	287 Gary Kolb	1.50	Ken Berry, Joel Gibson	
134 World Series Game 3	25.00	208 Tommy John	10.00	288 Jack Hamilton	1.50	369 Phil Linz	1.50
Mantle's Clutch Homer		209 Pirates—6th Place	3.00	289 Gordy Coleman	1.50	370 Tommy Davis	2.00
135 World Series Game 4	2.50	210 Jim Fregosi	1.50	290 Wally Bunker	1.50	371 Frank Kreutzer	2.00
Boyer's Grand-Slam		211 Steve Ridzik	1.00	291 Jerry Lynch	1.50	372 Clay Dalrymple	2.00
136 World Series Game 5	2.50	212 Ron Brand	1.00	292 Larry Yellen	1.50	373 Curt Simmons	2.00
10th Inning Triumph		213 Jim Davenport	1.00	293 Angels—5th Place	3.00	374 Angels Rookies:	2.50
137 World Series Game 6	2.50	214 Bob Purkey	1.00	294 Tim McCarver	3.00	J. Cardenal, D. Simpson	
Bouton Wins Again		215 Pete Ward	1.00	295 Dick Radatz	1.50	375 Dave Wickersham	2.00
138 World Series Game 7	6.00	216 Al Worthington	1.00	296 Tony Taylor	1.50	376 Jim Landis	2.00
Gibson Wins Finale		217 Walt Alston (Mgr.)	4.00	297 Dave Debusschere	2.50	377 Willie Stargell	25.00
139 World Series	3.00	218 Dick Schofield	1.00	298 Jim Stewart	1.50	378 Chuck Estrada	2.00
The Cards Celebrate		219 Bob Meyer	1.00	299 Jerry Zimmerman	1.50	379 Giants—4th Place	3.00
140 Dean Chance	.75	220 Billy Williams	10.00	300 Sandy Koufax	100.00	380 Rocky Colavito	3.00
141 Charlie James	.75	221 John Tsitouris	1.00	301 Birdie Tebbetts	1.50	381 Al Jackson	2.00
142 Bill Monbouquette	.75	222 Bob Tillman	1.00	302 Al Stanek	1.50	382 J.C. Martin	2.00
143 Pirates Rookies:	.75	223 Dan Osinski	1.00	303 John Orsino	1.50	383 Felipe Alou	3.00
John Gelnar, Jerry May		224 Bob Chance	1.00	304 Dave Stenhouse	1.50	384 Johnny Klippstein	2.00
144 Ed Kranepool	.75	225 Bo Belinsky	1.00	305 Rico Carty	2.00	385 Carl Yastrzemski	90.00
145 Luis Tiant (R)	7.50	226 Yankees Rookies:	2.00	306 Bubba Phillips	1.50	386 Cubs Rookies:	2.50
146 Ron Hansen	.75	Elvio Jimenez, Jake Gibbs		307 Barry Latman	1.50	Paul Jaeckel, Fred Norman	
147 Dennis Bennett	.75	227 Bobby Klaus	1.00	308 Mets Rookies:	1.50	387 Johnny Podres	2.50
148 Willie Kirkland	.75	228 Jack Sanford	1.00	Tom Parsons, Cleon Jones		388 John Blanchard	2.00
149 Wayne Schurr	.75	229 Lou Clinton	1.00	309 Steve Hamilton	1.50	389 Don Larsen	3.00
150 Brooks Robinson	20.00	230 Ray Sadecki	1.00	310 Johnny Callison	1.50	390 Bill Freehan	2.50
151 Athletics—10th Place	2.00	231 Jerry Adair	1.00	311 Orlando Pena	1.50	391 Mel McGaha	2.00
152 Phil Ortega	.75	232 Steve Blass (R)	1.50	312 Joe Nuxhall	1.50	392 Bob Friend	2.00
153 Norm Cash	2.00	233 Don Zimmer	1.50	313 Jim Schaffer	1.50	393 Ed Kirkpatrck	2.00
154 Bob Humphreys	.75	234 White Sox—2nd Place	3.00	314 Sterling Slaughter	1.50	394 Jim Hannan	2.00
155 Roger Maris	50.00	235 Chuck Hinton	1.00	315 Frank Malzone	1.50	395 Jim Hart	2.50
156 Bob Sadowski	.75	236 Dennis McLain (R)	15.00	316 Reds—2nd Place	4.00	396 Frank Bertaina	2.00
157 Zoilo Versalles	1.25	237 Bernie Allen	1.00	317 Don McMahon	1.50	397 Jerry Buchek	2.00
158 Dick Sisler (Mgr.)	.75	238 Joe Moeller	1.00	318 Matty Alou	1.50	398 Reds Rookies:	2.00
159 Jim Duffalo	.75	239 Doc Edwards	1.25	319 Ken McMullen	1.50	Art Shamsky, Dan Neville	
160 Bob Clemente	.75	240 Bob Bruce	1.00	320 Bob Gibson	20.00	399 Ray Herbert	2.00
161 Frank Baumann	.75	241 Mack Jones	1.00	321 Rusty Staub	3.50	400 Harmon Killebrew	21.00
162 Russ Nixon	.75	242 George Brunet	1.00	322 Rick Wise	1.50	401 Carl Willey	2.00
163 John Briggs	.75	243 Reds Rookies:	2.00	323 Hank Bauer (Mgr.)	1.50	402 Joe Amalfitano	2.00
164 Al Spangler	.75	T. Helms, Ted Davidson		324 Bobby Locke	1.50	403 Red Sox—8th Place	3.00
165 Dick Ellsworth	.75	244 Lindy McDaniel	1.00	325 Donn Clendenon	1.50	404 Stan Williams	2.00
166 Indians Rookies:	1.50	245 Joe Pepitone	1.50	326 Dwight Siebler	1.50	405 John Roseboro	2.00
G. Culver, Tommie Agee		246 Tom Butters	1.00	327 Dennis Menke	1.50	406 Ralph Terry	2.00
167 Bill Wakefield	.75	247 Wally Moon	1.00	328 Eddie Fisher	1.50	407 Lee Maye	2.00

NO. PLAYER	NR. MT.	NO. PLAYER	NR. MT.	NO. PLAYER	NR. MT.	NO. PLAYER	NR. MT.
408 Larry Sherry	2.00	461 Braves Rookies: Clay Carroll, Phil Niekro	50.00	510 Ernie Banks	40.00	554 Chico Ruiz	5.00
409 Astros Rookies: Jim Beauchamp, L. Dierker	2.50	462 Lew Krausse (photo of Pete Lovrich)	3.00	511 Ron Locke	3.00	555 Jack Baldschun	5.00
410 Luis Aparicio	10.00	463 Manny Mota	3.00	512 Cap Peterson	3.00	556 Red Schoendienst	15.00
411 Roger Craig	2.00	464 Ron Piche	3.00	513 Yankees—1st Place	10.00	557 Jose Santiago	5.00
412 Bob Bailey	2.00	465 Tom Haller	3.00	514 Joe Azcue	3.00	558 Tommie Sisk	5.00
413 Hal Reniff	2.00	466 Senators Rookies: Pete Craig, Dick Nen	3.00	515 Vern Law	3.00	559 Ed Bailey	5.00
414 Al Lopez	3.00	467 Ray Washburn	3.00	516 Al Weis	3.00	560 Boog Powell	9.00
415 Curt Flood	4.00	468 Larry Brown	3.00	517 Angels Rookies: Paul Schaal, Jack Warner	3.00	561 Dodgers Rookies: D. Daboll, Mike Kekich, H. Valle, Jim Lefebvre	10.00
416 Jim Brewer	2.00	469 Don Nottebart	3.00	518 Ken Rowe	3.00	
417 Ed Brinkman	2.00	470 Yogi Berra	50.00	519 Bob Uecker	45.00	562 Billy Moran	5.00
418 Johnny Edwards	2.00	471 Billy Hoeft	3.00	520 Tony Cloninger	3.00	563 Julio Navarro	5.00
419 Ruben Amaro	2.00	472 Don Pavletich	3.00	521 Phillies Rookies: Dave Bennett, M. Steevens	3.00	564 Mel Nelson	5.00
420 Larry Jackson	2.00	473 Orioles Rookies: Paul Blair, Dave Johnson	10.00		565 Ernie Broglio	5.00
421 Twins Rookies: Gary Dotter, Jay Ward	2.00	474 Cookie Rojas	3.00	522 Hank Aguirre	3.00	566 Yankees Rookies: Art Lopez, Gil Blanco, Ross Moschitto	5.00
422 Aubrey Gatewood	2.00	475 Clete Boyer	4.00	523 Mike Brumley	5.00	
423 Jesse Gonder	2.00	476 Billy O'Dell	3.00	524 Dave Giusti	5.00	567 Tommie Aaron	5.00
424 Gary Bell	2.00	477 Cards Rookies: Fritz Ackley, Steve Carlton	400.00	525 Ed Bressoud	5.00	568 Ron Taylor	5.00
425 Wayne Causey	2.00		526 Athletics Rookies: S. Lockwood, R. Lachemann, Johnny Odom, Jim Hunter	150.00	569 Gino Cimoli	5.00
426 Braves—5th Place	3.00	478 Wilbur Wood	3.00		570 Claude Osteen	5.00
427 Bob Saverine	2.00	479 Ken Harrelson	5.00		571 Ossie Virgil	5.00
428 Bob Shaw	2.00	480 Joel Horlen	3.00	527 Jeff Torborg	5.00	572 Orioles—3rd Place	10.00
429 Don Demeter	2.00	481 Indians—7th Place	8.00	528 George Altman	5.00	573 Red Sox Rookies: Jim Lonborg, Mike Ryan, G. Moses, Bill Schlesinger	15.00
430 Gary Peters	2.00	482 Bob Priddy	3.00	529 Jerry Fosnow	5.00	
431 Cards Rookies: Nelson Briles, W. Spiezio	2.50	483 George Smith	3.00	530 Jim Maloney	5.00	
432 Jim Grant	2.00	484 Ron Perranoski	4.00	531 Chuck Hiller	5.00	574 Roy Sievers	5.00
433 John Bateman	2.00	485 Nellie Fox	7.00	532 Hector Lopez	5.00	575 Jose Pagan	5.00
434 Dave Morehead	2.00	486 Angels Rookies: Pat Rogan, Tom Egan	3.00	533 Mets Rookies: Dan Napoleon, Ron Swoboda, Jim Bethke, Tug McGraw	25.00	576 Terry Fox	5.00
435 Willie Davis	2.50			577 AL Rookie Stars: D. Knowles, R. Scheinblum, Don Buschhorn	5.00
436 Don Elston	2.00	487 Woody Woodward	3.00		
437 Chico Cardenas	2.00	488 Ted Wills	3.00	534 John Herrnstein	5.00	
438 Harry Walker (Mgr.)	2.00	489 Gene Mauch (Mgr.)	3.00	535 Jack Kralick	5.00	578 Camilo Carreon	5.00
439 Moe Drabowsky	2.00	490 Earl Battey	3.00	536 Andre Rodgers	5.00	579 Dick Smith	5.00
440 Tom Tresh	2.50	491 Tracy Stallard	3.00	537 Angels Rookies: Marcelino Lopez, Rudy May, Phil Roof	5.00	580 Jimmie Hall	5.00
441 Denver LeMaster	2.00	492 Gene Freese	3.00		581 NL Rookie Stars: Tony Perez, Dave Ricketts, Kevin Collins	90.00
442 Vic Power	2.00	493 Tigers Rookies: Bill Roman, Bruce Brubaker	3.00		
443 Checklist No. 6	4.00		538 Chuck Dressen (Mgr.)	5.00	
444 Bob Hendley	2.00	494 Jay Ritchie	3.00	539 Herm Starrette	5.00	582 Bob Schmidt	5.00
445 Don Lock	2.00	495 Joe Christopher	3.00	540 Lou Brock	50.00	583 Wes Covington	5.00
446 Art Mahaffey	2.00	496 Joe Cunningham	3.00	541 White Sox Rookies: Bob Locker, Greg Bollo	5.00	584 Harry Bright	5.00
447 Julian Javier	3.00	497 Giants Rookies: Ken Henderson, Jack Hiatt	3.00		585 Hank Fischer	5.00
448 Lee Stange	3.00		542 Lou Klimchock	5.00	586 Tommy McCraw	5.00
449 Mets Rookies: Jerry Hinsley, Gary Kroll	3.00	498 Gene Stephens	3.00	543 Ed Connolly	5.00	587 Joe Sparma	5.00
450 Elston Howard	6.00	499 Stu Miller	3.00	544 Howie Reed	5.00	588 Lenny Green	5.00
451 Jim Owens	3.00	500 Ed Mathews	25.00	545 Jesus Alou	5.00	589 Giants Rookies: Frank Linzy, B. Schroder	5.00
452 Gary Geiger	3.00	501 Indians Rookies: Jim Rittwage, R. Gagliano	3.00	546 Indians Rookies: Floyd Weaver, Bill Davis, Mike Hedlund, Ray Barker	5.00	
453 Dodgers Rookies: W. Crawford, J. Werhas	4.00			590 Johnnie Wyatt	5.00
454 Ed Rakow	3.00	502 Don Cardwell	3.00		591 Bob Skinner	5.00
455 Norm Siebern	3.00	503 Phil Gagliano	3.00	547 Jake Wood	5.00	592 Frank Bork	5.00
456 Bill Henry	3.00	504 Jerry Grote	3.00	548 Dick Stigman	5.00	593 Tigers Rookies: Jackie Moore, John Sullivan	5.00
457 Bob Kennedy—Coach	3.00	505 Ray Culp	3.00	549 Cubs Rookies: R. Pena, Glenn Beckert	10.00	
458 John Buzhardt	3.00	506 Sam Mele	3.00		594 Joe Gaines	5.00
459 Frank Kostro	3.00	507 Sammy Ellis	3.00	550 Mel Stottlemyre (R)	22.00	595 Don Lee	5.00
460 Richie Allen	7.00	508 Checklist No. 7	4.00	551 Mets—10th Place	15.00	596 Don Landrum	5.00
		509 Red Sox Rookies: Bob Guindon, G. Vezendy	3.00	552 Julio Gotay	5.00	597 Twins Rookies: Dick Reese, Joe Nossek, John Sevcik	5.00
				553 Astros Rookies: Gene Ratliff, Dan Coombs, Jack McClure	5.00	
						598 Al Downing (Exc. $3.00)	12.00

1966 Topps. . . . Complete Set of 598 Cards—Value $1250.00 (Exc.); $3500.00 (Near Mint)

Features the rookies cards of Jim Palmer and Don Sutton. The high numbers are 523 to 598. Cards 62, 103 and 104 (worth $30.00) and card 91 (worth $60.00) exist without a *traded* or *sold* line. Card 101 (checklist) exists identifying card 115 as either Bill Henry—worth $4.00 or Warren Spahn—worth $10.00

NO. PLAYER	NR. MT.
1 Willie Mays (Exc. $25.00)	125.00
2 Ted Abernathy	.75
3 Sam Mele (Mgr.)	.75
4 Ray Culp	.75
5 Jim Fregosi	1.50
6 Chuck Schilling	.75
7 Tracy Stallard	.75
8 Floyd Robinson	.75
9 Clete Boyer	1.75
10 Tony Cloninger	.75
11 Senators Rookies:	.75
Brant Alyea, Pete Craig	
12 John Tsitouris	.75
13 Lou Johnson	.75
14 Norm Siebern	.75
15 Vern Law	1.50
16 Larry Brown	.75
17 John Stephenson	.75
18 Roland Sheldon	.75
19 Giants—2nd Place	2.00
20 Willie Horton	1.75
21 Don Nottebart	.75
22 Joe Nossek	.75
23 Jack Sanford	.75
24 Don Kessinger (R)	2.00
25 Joe Ward	.75
26 Ray Sadecki	.75
27 Orioles Rookies:	1.00
D. Knowles, A. Etchebarren	
28 Phil Niekro	14.00
29 Mike Brumley	1.25
30 Pete Rose	60.00
31 Jack Cullen	.75
32 Adolfo Phillips	.75
33 Jim Pagliaroni	.75
34 Checklist No. 1	4.00
35 Ron Swoboda	1.25
36 Jim Hunter	25.00
37 Billy Herman	1.75
38 Ron Nischwitz	.75
39 Ken Henderson	.75
40 Jim Grant	.75
41 Don LeJohn	.75
42 Aubrey Gatewood	.75
43 Don Landrum	.75
44 Indians Rookies:	.75
Bill Davis, Tom Kelley	
45 Jim Gentile	.90
46 Howie Koplitz	.75
47 J.C. Martin	.75
48 Paul Blair	1.25
49 Woody Woodward	.75
50 Mick Mantle	200.00
51 Gordon Richardson	.75
52 Power Plus:	1.00
W. Covington, J. Callison	
53 Bob Duliba	.75
54 Jose Pagan	.75
55 Ken Harrelson	1.25
56 Sandy Valdespino	.75
57 Jim Lefebvre	.75
58 Dave Wickersham	.75
59 Reds—4th Place	2.00
60 Curt Flood	1.50
61 Bob Bolin	.75
62 Merritt Ranew*	.75
63 Jim Stewart	.75
64 Bob Bruce	.75
65 Leon Wagner	.75
66 Al Weis	.75
67 Mets Rookies:	1.50
Cleon Jones, Dick Selma	
68 Hal Reniff	.75
69 Ken Hamlin	.75
70 Carl Yastrzemski	50.00
71 Frank Carpin	.75
72 Tony Perez	13.00
73 Jerry Zimmerman	.75
74 Don Mossi	1.00
75 Tommy Davis	1.25
76 R. Schoendienst (Mgr.)	4.00
77 Johnny Orsino	.75
78 Frank Linzy	.75
79 Joe Pepitone	1.50
80 Richie Allen	3.00

NO. PLAYER	NR. MT.
81 Ray Oyler	.75
82 Bob Hendley	.75
83 Albie Pearson	.75
84 Braves Rookies:	.75
J. Beauchamp, D. Kelley	
85 Eddie Fisher	.75
86 John Bateman	.75
87 Dan Napoleon	.75
88 Fred Whitfield	.75
89 Ted Davidson	.75
90 Luis Aparicio	7.00
91 Bob Uecker*	15.00
92 Yankees—6th Place	3.00
93 Jim Lonborg	1.25
94 Matty Alou	1.25
95 Pete Richert	.75
96 Felipe Alou	1.25
97 Jim Merritt	.75
98 Don Demeter	.75
99 Buc Belters:	3.00
W. Stargell, D. Clendenon	
100 Sandy Koufax	75.00
101 Checklist No. 2*	4.00
102 Ed Kirkpatrick	.75
103 Dick Groat*	1.25
104 Alex Johnson*	1.25
105 Milt Pappas	1.00
106 Rusty Staub	2.00
107 A's Rookies:	.75
L. Stahl, Ron Tompkins	
108 Bobby Klaus	.75
109 Ralph Terry	.75
110 Ernie Banks	17.50
111 Gary Peters	.75
112 Manny Mota	1.00
113 Hank Aguirre	.75
114 Jim Gosger	.75
115 Bill Henry*	.75
116 Walt Alston (Mgr.)	3.00
117 Jake Gibbs	.75
118 Mike McCormick	.75
119 Art Shamsky	.75
120 Harmon Killebrew	15.00
121 Ray Herbert	.75
122 Joe Gaines	.75
123 Pirates Rookies:	.75
Frank Bork, Jerry May	
124 Tug McGraw	3.00
125 Lou Brock	16.00
126 Jim Palmer (R)	200.00
127 Ken Berry	.75
128 Jim Landis	.75
129 Jack Kralick	.75
130 Joe Torre	1.50
131 Angels—7th Place	2.00
132 Orlando Cepeda	4.00
133 Don McMahon	.75
134 Wes Parker	.75
135 Dave Morehead	.75
136 Woody Held	.75
137 Pat Corrales	1.00
138 Roger Repoz	.75
139 Cubs Rookies:	.75
Byron Browne, Don Young	
140 Jim Maloney	1.00
141 Tom McCraw	.75
142 Don Dennis	.75
143 Jose Tartabull	.75
144 Don Schwall	.75
145 Bill Freehan	1.00
146 George Altman	.75
147 Lum Harris (Mgr.)	.75
148 Bob Johnson	.75
149 Dick Nen	.75
150 Rocky Colavito	2.00
151 Gary Wagner	.75
152 Frank Malzone	.75
153 Rico Carty	1.25
154 Chuck Hiller	.75
155 Marcelino Lopez	.75
156 Double Play Combo:	1.00
Dick Schofield, Hal Lanier	
157 Rene Lachemann	.75
158 Jim Brewer	.75
159 Chico Ruiz	.75

NO. PLAYER	NR. MT.
160 Whitey Ford	17.50
161 Jerry Lumpe	.75
162 Lee Maye	.75
163 Tito Francona	.75
164 White Sox Rookies:	1.00
Tommie Agee, M. Staehle	
165 Don Lock	.75
166 Chris Krug	.75
167 Boog Powell	3.00
168 Dan Osinski	.75
169 Duke Sims	.75
170 Cookie Rojas	.75
171 Nick Willhite	.75
172 Mets—10th Place	2.00
173 Al Spangler	.75
174 Ron Taylor	.75
175 Bert Campaneris	1.25
176 Jim Davenport	.75
177 Hector Lopez	.75
178 Bob Tillman	.75
179 Cards Rookies:	1.00
Dennis Aust, Bob Tolan	
180 Vada Pinson	1.50
181 Al Worthington	.75
182 Jerry Lynch	.75
183 Checklist No. 3	4.00
184 Denis Menke	.75
185 Bob Buhl	.75
186 Ruben Amaro	.75
187 Chuck Dressen (Mgr.)	1.00
188 Al Luplow	.75
189 John Roseboro	.75
190 Jimmie Hall	.75
191 Darrell Sutherland	.75
192 Vic Power	.75
193 Dave McNally	1.00
194 Senators—8th Place	2.00
195 Joe Morgan	30.00
196 Don Pavletich	.75
197 Sonny Siebert	.75
198 Mickey Stanley	1.25
199 Chisox Clubbers:	1.00
Bill Skowron, Johnny	
Romano, Floyd Robinson	
200 Ed Mathews	11.00
201 Jim Dickson	.75
202 Clay Dalrymple	.75
203 Jose Santiago	.75
204 Cubs—8th Place	2.00
205 Tom Tresh	1.50
206 Alvin Jackson	.75
207 Frank Quilici	1.00
208 Bob Miller	1.00
209 Tigers Rookies:	1.50
Fritz Fisher, John Hiller	
210 Bill Mazeroski	1.50
211 Frank Kreutzer	.75
212 Ed Kranepool	1.00
213 Fred Newman	.75
214 Tommy Harper	.75
215 NL Batting Leaders:	12.00
Willie Mays, Bob	
Clemente, Hank Aaron	
216 AL Batting Leaders:	3.00
Tony Oliva, Carl	
Yastrzemski, Vic Davalillo	
217 NL Home Run Leaders:	7.00
Willie McCovey, Willie	
Mays, Billy Williams	
218 AL Home Run Leaders:	2.00
Norm Cash, Willie	
Horton, Tony Conigliaro	
219 NL RBI Leaders:	3.00
Frank Robinson, Deron	
Johnson, Willie Mays	
220 AL RBI Leaders:	2.00
Rocky Colavito, Willie	
Horton, Tony Oliva	
221 NL ERA Leaders:	3.00
Sandy Koufax, Vern	
Law, Juan Marichal	
222 AL ERA Leaders:	2.00
Sam McDowell, Sonny	
Siebert, Eddie Fisher	
223 NL Pitching Leaders:	3.00
Sandy Koufax, Tony	
Cloninger, Don Drysdale	

NO. PLAYER	NR. MT.
224 AL Pitching Leaders:	2.00
Mel Stottlemyre,	
Jim Grant, Jim Kaat	
225 NL Strikeout Leaders:	4.00
Bob Gibson, Sandy Koufax,	
Bob Veale	
226 AL Strikeout Leaders:	2.50
Sam McDowell, Mickey	
Lolich, Denny McLain,	
Sonny Siebert	
227 Russ Nixon	.75
228 Larry Dierker	.75
229 Hank Bauer	1.00
230 Johnny Callison	1.00
231 F. Weaver	.75
232 Glenn Beckert	1.00
233 Dom Zanni	.75
234 Yankees Rookies:	4.00
Roy White, Rich Beck	
235 Don Cardwell	.75
236 Mike Hershberger	.75
237 Billy O'Dell	.75
238 Dodgers—1st Place	2.00
239 Orlando Pena	.75
240 Earl Battey	.75
241 Dennis Ribant	.75
242 Jesus Alou	.75
243 Nelson Briles	.75
244 Astros Rookies:	.75
C. Harrison, S. Jackson	
245 John Buzhardt	.75
246 Ed Bailey	.75
247 Carl Warwick	.75
248 Pete Mikkelsen	.75
249 Bill Rigney (Mgr.)	.75
250 Sam Ellis	.75
251 Ed Brinkman	.75
252 Denver Lemaster	.75
253 Don Wert	.75
254 Phillies Rookies:	50.00
Ferguson Jenkins,	
Bill Sorrell	
255 Willie Stargell	17.00
256 Lew Krausse	.75
257 Jeff Torborg	.75
258 Dave Giusti	.75
259 Red Sox—9th Place	2.00
260 Bob Shaw	.75
261 Ron Hansen	.75
262 Jack Hamilton	.75
263 Tom Egan	.75
264 Twins Rookies:	.75
Ted Uhlaender, Andy Kosco	
265 Stu Miller	.75
266 Pedro Gonzalez	.75
267 Joe Sparma	.75
268 John Blanchard	.75
269 Don Heffner (Mgr.)	.75
270 Claude Osteen	1.00
271 Hal Lanier	1.00
272 Jack Baldschun	.75
273 Astro Aces:	1.50
Bob Aspromonte,	
Rusty Staub	
274 Buster Narum	.75
275 Tim McCarver	2.00
276 Jim Bouton	1.50
277 George Thomas	.75
278 Calvin Koonce	.75
279 Checklist No. 4	4.00
280 Bobby Knoop	.75
281 Bruce Howard	.75
282 Johnny Lewis	.75
283 Jim Perry	1.25
284 Bobby Wine	1.00
285 Luis Tiant	2.00
286 Gary Geiger	1.00
287 Jack Aker	1.00
288 Dodgers Rookies:	110.00
Bill Singer, Don Sutton	
289 Larry Sherry	1.00
290 Ron Santo	2.50
291 Moe Drabowsky	1.00
292 Jim Coker	1.00

NO. PLAYER	NR. MT.
293 Mike Shannon	1.00
294 Steve Ridzik	1.00
295 Jim Hart	1.00
296 Johnny Keane (Mgr.)	1.00
297 Jim Owens	1.00
298 Rico Petrocelli	1.25
299 Lou Burdette	1.50
300 Bob Clemente	75.00
301 Greg Bollo	1.00
302 Ernie Bowman	1.00
303 Indians—5th Place	2.00
304 John Herrnstein	1.00
305 Camilo Pascual	1.25
306 Ty Cline	1.00
307 Clay Carroll	1.00
308 Tom Haller	1.00
309 Diego Segui	1.00
310 Frank Robinson	30.00
311 Reds Rookies:	1.25
D. Simpson, T. Helms	
312 Bob Saverine	1.00
313 Chris Zachary	1.00
314 Hector Valle	1.00
315 Norm Cash	2.50
316 Jack Fisher	1.00
317 Dalton Jones	1.00
318 Harry Walker	1.00
319 Gene Freese	1.00
320 Bob Gibson	18.00
321 Rick Reichardt	1.00
322 Bill Faul	1.00
323 Ray Barker	1.00
324 John Boozer	1.00
325 Vic Davalillo	1.25
326 Braves—5th Place	1.50
327 Bernie Allen	1.00
328 Jerry Grote	1.00
329 Pete Charton	1.00
330 Ron Fairly	1.25
331 Ron Herbel	1.00
332 Billy Bryan	1.00
333 Senators Rookies:	1.00
Joe Coleman, Jim French	
334 Marty Keough	1.00
335 Juan Pizarro	1.00
336 Gene Alley	1.00
337 Fred Gladding	1.00
338 Dal Maxvill	1.00
339 Del Crandall	.75
340 Dean Chance	.60
341 Wes Westrum	1.00
342 Bob Humphreys	1.00
343 Joe Christopher	1.00
344 Steve Blass	1.25
345 Bob Allison	1.25
346 Mike De La Hoz	1.00
347 Phil Regan	1.00
348 Orioles—3rd Place	1.00
349 Cap Peterson	1.00
350 Mel Stottlemyre	2.50
351 Fred Valentine	1.00
352 Bob Aspromonte	1.00
353 Al McBean	1.00
354 Smoky Burgess	1.00
355 Wade Blasingame	1.00
356 Red Sox Rookies:	1.00
Owen Johnson, Ken Sanders	
357 Gerry Arrigo	1.00
358 Charlie Smith	1.00
359 Johnny Briggs	1.00
360 Ron Hunt	1.00
361 Tom Satriano	1.00
362 Gates Brown	1.00
363 Checklist No. 5	4.00
364 Nate Oliver	1.00
365 Roger Maris	50.00
366 Wayne Causey	1.00
367 Mel Nelson	1.00
368 Charlie Lau	1.00
369 Jim King	1.00
370 Chico Cardenas	1.00
371 Lee Stange	1.50
372 Harvey Kuenn	2.00
373 Giants Rookies:	1.50
Jack Hiatt, Dick Estelle	

NO. PLAYER	NR. MT.
374 Bob Locker	1.50
375 Donn Clendenon	2.00
376 Paul Schaal	1.50
377 Turk Farrell	1.50
378 Dick Tracewski	1.50
379 Cardinal—7th Place	2.00
380 Tony Conigliaro	5.00
381 Hank Fischer	1.50
382 Phil Roof	1.50
383 Jack Brandt	1.50
384 Al Downing	2.00
385 Ken Boyer	3.00
386 Gil Hodges (Mgr.)	5.00
387 Howie Reed	1.50
388 Don Mincher	1.50
389 Jim O'Toole	1.50
390 Brooks Robinson	20.00
391 Chuck Hinton	1.50
392 Cubs Rookies:	1.50
Bill Hands, Randy Hundley	
393 George Brunet	1.50
394 Ron Brand	1.50
395 Len Gabrielson	1.50
396 Jerry Stephenson	1.50
397 Bill White	2.00
398 Danny Cater	1.50
399 Ray Washburn	1.50
400 Zoilo Versalles	1.50
401 Ken McMullen	1.50
402 Jim Hickman	1.50
403 Fred Talbot	1.50
404 Pirates—3rd Place	2.00
405 Elston Howard	3.00
406 Joe Jay	1.50
407 John Kennedy	1.50
408 Lee Thomas	1.50
409 Billy Hoeft	1.50
410 Al Kaline	20.00
411 Gene Mauch (Mgr.)	2.00
412 Sam Bowens	1.50
413 John Romano	1.50
414 Dan Coombs	1.50
415 Max Alvis	1.50
416 Phil Ortega	1.50
417 Angels Rookies:	1.50
Jim McGlothlin, Ed Sukla	
418 Phil Gagliano	1.50
419 Mike Ryan	1.50
420 Juan Marichal	9.00
421 Roy McMillan	1.50
422 Ed Charles	1.50
423 Ernie Broglio	1.50
424 Reds Rookies:	4.00
Lee May, Darrell Osteen	
425 Bob Veale	1.50
426 White Sox—2nd Place	2.00
427 John Miller	1.50
428 Sandy Alomar	1.50
429 Bill Monbouquette	1.50
430 Don Drysdale	15.00
431 Walt Bond	1.50
432 Bob Heffner	1.50
433 Alvin Dark (Mgr.)	2.00
434 Willie Kirkland	13.00
435 Jim Bunning	5.00
436 Julian Javier	1.50
437 Al Stanek	1.50
438 Willie Smith	1.50
439 Pedro Ramos	1.50
440 Deron Johnson	1.50
441 Tommie Sisk	1.50
442 Orioles Rookies:	1.50
Ed Barnowski, Eddie Watt	
443 Bill Wakefield	1.50
444 Checklist No. 6	4.00
445 Jim Kaat	5.00
446 Mack Jones	1.50
447 Dick Ellsworth	4.50
(photo of Ken Hubbs)	
448 Eddie Stanky	4.50
449 Joe Moeller	4.50
450 Tony Oliva	6.00
451 Barry Latman	4.00
452 Joe Azcue	4.00
453 Ron Kline	4.00
454 Jerry Buchek	4.00

NO. PLAYER	NR. MT.
455 Mickey Lolich	5.00
456 Red Sox Rookies:	4.00
Darrell Brandon, Joe Foy	
457 Joe Gibbon	4.00
458 Manny Jiminez	4.00
459 Bill McCool	4.00
460 Curt Blefary	4.00
461 Roy Face	5.00
462 Bob Rodgers	5.00
463 Phillies—6th Place	7.50
464 Larry Bearnarth	4.00
465 Don Buford	4.00
466 Ken Johnson	4.00
467 Vic Roznovsky	4.00
468 Johnny Podres	5.00
469 Yankees Rookies:	15.00
Bobby Murcer, Dooley Womack	
470 Sam McDowell	5.00
471 Bob Skinner	4.00
472 Terry Fox	4.00
473 Rich Rollins	4.00
474 Dick Schofield	4.00
475 Dick Radatz	4.00
476 Bobby Bragan	4.00
477 Steve Barber	4.00
478 Tony Gonzalez	4.00
479 Jim Hannan	4.00
480 Dick Stuart	4.00
481 Bob Lee	4.00
482 Cubs Rookies:	4.00
J. Boccabella, D. Dowling	
483 Joe Nuxhall	5.00
484 Wes Covington	4.00
485 Bob Bailey	4.00
486 Tommy John	10.00
487 Al Ferrara	4.00
488 George Banks	4.00
489 Curt Simmons	4.00
490 Bobby Richardson	10.00
491 Dennis Bennett	4.00
492 Athletics—10th Place	7.50
493 John Klippstein	4.00
494 Gordon Coleman	4.00
495 Dick McAuliffe	4.00
496 Lindy McDaniel	4.00
497 Chris Cannizzaro	4.00
498 Pirates Rookies:	4.00
Luke Walker, W. Fryman	
499 Wally Bunker	4.00
500 Hank Aaron	85.00
501 John O'Donoghue	4.00
502 Lenny Green	4.00
503 Steve Hamilton	4.00
504 Grady Hatton	4.00
505 Jose Cardenal	4.00
506 Bo Belinsky	4.00
507 John Edwards	4.00
508 Steve Hargan	4.00
509 Jake Wood	4.00
510 Hoyt Wilhelm	12.00
511 Giants Rookies:	4.00
Bob Barton, Tito Fuentes	
512 Dick Stigman	4.00
513 Camilo Carreon	4.00
514 Hal Woodeschick	4.00
515 Frank Howard	5.00
516 Eddie Bressoud	4.00
517 Checklist No. 7	10.00
518 Braves Rookies:	4.00
Arnie Umbach, H. Hippauf	
519 Bob Friend	4.00
520 Jim Wynn	4.00
521 John Wyatt	4.00
522 Phil Linz	4.00
523 Bob Sadowski	13.00
524 Giants Rookies:	13.00
Ollie Brown, Don Mason	
525 Gary Bell	13.00
526 Twins—1st Place	50.00
527 Julio Navarro	13.00
528 Jesse Gonder	13.00
529 White Sox Rookies:	13.00
Dennis Higgins, Lee Elia, Bill Voss	
530 Robin Roberts	37.00

NO. PLAYER	NR. MT.
531 Joe Cunningham	13.00
532 Aurelio Monteagudo	13.00
533 Jerry Adair	13.00
534 Mets Rookies:	13.00
Dave Eilers, Rob Gardner	
535 Willie Davis	25.00
536 Dick Egan	13.00
537 Herman Franks (Mgr.)	13.00
538 Bob Allen	13.00
539 Astros Rookies:	13.00
Bill Heath, Carroll Sembera	
540 Denny McLain	55.00
541 Gene Oliver	13.00
542 George Smith	13.00
543 Roger Craig	30.00
544 Cardinals Rookies:	13.00
J. Williams, J. Hoerner, George Kernek	
545 Dick Green	13.00
546 Dwight Siebler	13.00
547 Horace Clarke (R)	30.00
548 Gary Kroll	13.00
549 Senators Rookies:	13.00
Al Closter, Casey Cox	
550 Willie McCovey	100.00
551 Bob Purkey	13.00
552 Birdie Tebbetts	13.00
553 Rookie Stars:	13.00
Pat Garrett, Jackie Warner	
554 Jim Northrup	13.00
555 Ron Perranoski	13.00
556 Mel Queen	13.00
557 Felix Mantilla	13.00
558 Red Sox Rookies:	25.00
Pete Magrini, Guido Grilli, George Scott	
559 Roberto Pena	13.00
560 Joel Horlen	13.00
561 Choo Choo Coleman	30.00
562 Russ Snyder	13.00
563 Twins Rookies:	13.00
Pete Cimino, Cesar Tovar	
564 Bob Chance	13.00
565 Jimmy Piersall	30.00
566 Mike Cuellar	14.00
567 Dick Howser	15.00
568 Athletics Rookies:	13.00
Paul Lindblad, Ron Stone	
569 Orlando McFarlane	13.00
570 Art Mahaffey	13.00
571 Dave Roberts	13.00
572 Bob Priddy	13.00
573 Derrell Griffith	13.00
574 Mets Rookies:	13.00
Billy Hepler, Bill Murphy	
575 Earl Wilson	13.00
576 Dave Nicholson	13.00
577 Jack Lamabe	13.00
578 Chi Chi Olivo	13.00
579 Orioles Rookies:	20.00
F. Bertaina, G. Brabender, Dave Johnson	
580 Billy Williams	85.00
581 Tony Martinez	13.00
582 Garry Roggenburk	100.00
583 Tigers—3rd Place	65.00
584 Yankees Rookies:	13.00
F. Fernandez, F. Peterson	
585 Tony Taylor	13.00
586 Claude Raymond	13.00
587 Dick Bertell	13.00
588 Athletics Rookies:	13.00
Ken Suarez, Chuck Dobson	
589 Lou Klimchock	13.00
590 Bill Skowron	40.00
591 NL Rookie Stars	13.00
Bart Shirley, Grant Jackson	
592 Andre Rodgers	13.00
593 Doug Camilli	13.00
594 Chico Salmon	13.00
595 Larry Jackson	13.00
596 John Sullivan	13.00
597 Astros Rookies:	13.00
Nate Colbert, Greg Sims	
598 G. Perry (Exc. $40.00)	225.00

1967 Topps.... Complete Set of 609 Cards—Value $1600.00 (Exc.); $4250.00 (Mint)

Features the rookie cards of Tom Seaver and Rod Carew. Cards 534 to 609 are high numbers. Cards 458 to 533 are semi-high numbers. Cards 26 and 86 exist without the *traded* line—worth $12.00 each. Card 191 exists identifying card 214 as either Dick Kelley—worth $5.00 or Tom Kelley—worth $1.50.

NO. PLAYER	NR. MT.
1 The Champs: (Exc. $2.50)	15.00
Frank Robinson, Hank	
Bauer, Brooks Robinson	
2 Jack Hamilton	.75
3 Duke Sims	.75
4 Hal Lanier	1.25
5 Whitey Ford	15.00
6 Dick Simpson	.75
7 Don McMahon	.75
8 Chuck Harrison	.75
9 Ron Hansen	.75
10 Matty Alou	1.25
11 Barry Moore	.75
12 Dodgers Rookies:	1.25
J. Campanis, Bill Singer	
13 Joe Sparma	.75
14 Phil Linz	.75
15 Earl Battey	1.00
16 Bill Hands	.75
17 Jim Gosger	.75
18 Gene Oliver	.75
19 Jim McGlothlin	.75
20 Orlando Cepeda	6.00
21 Dave Bristol (Mgr.)	.75
22 Gene Brabender	.75
23 Larry Elliot	.75
24 Bob Allen	.75
25 Elstan Howard	2.50
26 Bob Priddy*	.75
27 Bob Saverine	.75
28 Barry Latman	.75
29 Tom McCraw	.75
30 Al Kaline	15.00
31 Jim Brewer	.75
32 Bob Bailey	.75
33 Athletic Rookies:	2.00
Sal Bando, R. Schwartz	
34 Pete Cimino	.75
35 Rico Carty	1.50
36 Bob Tillman	.75
37 Rick Wise	1.00
38 Bob Johnson	.75
39 Curt Simmons	1.00
40 Rick Reichardt	.75
41 Joe Hoerner	.75
42 Mets Team	3.00
43 Chico Salmon	.75
44 Joe Nuxhall	1.00
45 Roger Maris	35.00
46 Lindy McDaniel	.75
47 Ken McMullen	.75
48 Bill Freehan	1.25
49 Roy Face	1.50
50 Tony Olava	3.00
51 Astros Rookies:	.75
Dave Adlesh, W. Bales	
52 Dennis Higgins	.75
53 Clay Dalrymple	.75
54 Dick Green	.75
55 Don Drysdale	10.00
56 Jose Tartabull	.75
57 Pat Jarvis	.75
58 Paul Schaal	.75
59 Ralph Terry	.75
60 Luis Aparicio	6.00
61 Gordy Coleman	.75

NO. PLAYER	NR. MT.
62 Checklist No. 1	4.00
63 Cards Clubbers	6.00
Lou Brock, Curt Flood	
64 Fred Valentine	.75
65 Tom Haller	.75
66 Manny Mota	1.50
67 Ken Berry	.75
68 Bob Buhl	.75
69 Vic Davalillo	.75
70 Ron Santo	2.00
71 Camilo Pascual	.75
72 Tigers Rookies:	1.25
George Korince (Photo of	
John Brown), J. Matchick	
73 Rusty Staub	2.00
74 Wes Stock	.75
75 George Scott	1.00
76 Jim Barbieri	.75
77 Dooley Womack	.75
78 Pat Corrales	1.00
79 Bubba Morton	.75
80 Jim Maloney	.75
81 Eddie Stanky (Mgr.)	1.00
82 Steve Barber	.75
83 Ollie Brown	.75
84 Tommie Sisk	.75
85 Johnny Callison	1.00
86 Mike McCormick*	1.00
87 George Altman	.75
88 Mickey Lolich	2.00
89 Felix Millan	.75
90 Jim Nash	.75
91 Johnny Lewis	.75
92 Ray Washburn	.75
93 Yankees Rookies:	3.00
Stan Bahnsen, B. Murcer	
94 Ron Fairly	1.00
95 Sonny Siebert	1.00
96 Art Shamsky	.75
97 Mike Cuellar	1.00
98 Rich Rollins	.75
99 Lee Stange	.75
100 Frank Robinson	15.00
101 Ken Johnson	.75
102 Phillies Team	2.00
103 Checklist No. 2	6.00
104 Minnie Rojas	.75
105 Ken Boyer	1.50
106 Randy Hundley	.75
107 Joel Horlen	.75
108 Alex Johnson	.75
109 Tribe Thumpers:	1.00
R. Colavito, Leon Wagner	
110 Jack Aker	1.00
111 John Kennedy	1.00
112 Dave Wickersham	1.00
113 Dave Nicholson	1.00
114 Jack Baldschun	1.00
115 Paul Casanova	1.00
116 Herman Franks	1.00
117 Darrell Brandon	1.00
118 Bernie Allen	1.00
119 Wade Blasingame	1.00
120 Floyd Robinson	1.00
121 Ed Bressoud	1.00
122 George Brunet	1.00

NO. PLAYER	NR. MT.
123 Pirates Rookies:	1.00
Jim Price, L. Walker	
124 Jim Stewart	1.00
125 Moe Drabowsky	1.00
126 Tony Taylor	1.00
127 John O'Donoghue	1.00
128 Ed Spiezio	1.00
129 Phil Roof	1.00
130 Phil Regan	1.00
131 Yankees Team	5.00
132 Ozzie Virgil	1.00
133 Ron Kline	1.00
134 Gates Brown	1.00
135 Deron Johnson	1.00
136 Carroll Sembera	1.00
137 Twins Rookies:	1.00
Ron Clark, Jim Ollum	
138 Dick Kelley	1.00
139 Dalton Jones	1.00
140 Willie Stargell	17.00
141 John Miller	1.00
142 Jackie Brandt	1.00
143 Sox Sockers:	1.00
Don Buford, Pete Ward	
144 Bill Hepler	1.00
145 Larry Brown	1.00
146 Steve Carlton	80.00
147 Tom Egan	1.00
148 Adolfo Phillips	1.00
149 Joe Moeller	1.00
150 Mickey Mantle	225.00
151 World Series Game 1:	2.00
Moe Mows Down 11	
152 World Series Game 2:	4.00
Palmer Blanks Dodgers	
153 World Series Game 3:	2.00
Blair's Homer Defeats L.A.	
154 World Series Game 4:	2.00
Orioles Win 4 Straight	
155 World Series:	2.00
The Winners Celebrate	
156 Ron Herbel	1.00
157 Danny Cater	1.00
158 Jimmy Coker	1.00
159 Bruce Howard	1.00
160 Willie Davis	1.25
161 Dick Williams (Mgr.)	1.25
162 Billy O'Dell	1.00
163 Vic Roznovsky	1.00
164 Dwight Siebler	1.00
165 Cleon Jones	1.00
166 Ed Mathews	10.00
167 Senators Rookies:	1.00
Joe Coleman, Tim Cullen	
168 Ray Culp	1.00
169 Horace Clarke	1.00
170 Dick McAuliffe	1.00
171 Calvin Koonce	1.00
172 Bill Heath	1.00
173 Cardinals Team	2.00
174 Dick Radatz	1.00
175 Bobby Knoop	1.00
176 Sammy Ellis	1.00
177 Tito Fuentes	1.00
178 John Buzhardt	1.00
179 Braves Rookies:	1.00
C. Vaughan, Cecil Upshaw	

NO. PLAYER	NR. MT.
180 Curt Blefary	1.00
181 Terry Fox	1.00
182 Ed Charles	1.00
183 Jim Pagliaroni	1.00
184 George Thomas	1.00
185 Ken Holtzman (R)	2.00
186 Mets Maulers	1.25
Ed Kranepool, R. Swoboda	
187 Pedro Ramos	1.00
188 Ken Harrelson	1.50
189 Chuck Hinton	1.00
190 Turk Farrell	1.00
191 Checklist No. 3*	4.00
192 Fred Gladding	1.00
193 Jose Cardenal	1.00
194 Bob Allison	1.00
195 Al Jackson	1.00
196 Johnny Romano	1.00
197 Ron Perranoski	1.00
198 Chuck Hiller	1.00
199 Billy Hitchcock	1.00
200 Willie Mays	65.00
201 Hal Reniff	1.00
202 Johnny Edwards	1.00
203 Al McBean	1.00
204 Orioles Rookies:	1.25
Mike Epstein, Tom Phoebus	
205 Dick Groat	1.25
206 Dennis Bennett	1.00
207 John Orsino	1.00
208 Jack Lamabe	1.00
209 Joe Nossek	1.00
210 Bob Gibson	15.00
211 Twins Team	2.00
212 Chris Zachary	1.00
213 Jay Johnstone	1.25
214 Tom Kelley	1.00
215 Ernie Banks	15.00
216 Bengal Belters:	5.00
Norm Cash, Al Kaline	
217 Rob Gardner	1.00
218 Wes Parker	1.00
219 Clay Carroll	1.00
220 Jim Hart	1.00
221 Woody Fryman	1.00
222 Reds Rookies:	1.25
Darrell Osteen, Lee May	
223 Mike Ryan	1.00
224 Walt Bond	1.00
225 Mel Stottlemyre	2.00
226 Julian Javier	1.00
227 Paul Lindblad	1.00
228 Gil Hodges (Mgr.)	5.00
229 Larry Jackson	1.00
230 Boog Powell	2.50
231 John Bateman	1.00
232 Don Buford	1.00
233 AL ERA Leaders:	2.00
Joel Horlen, Gary Peters,	
Steve Hargan	
234 NL ERA Leaders:	5.00
Sandy Koufax, Mike	
Cuellar, Juan Marichal	
235 AL Pitching Leaders:	2.00
Earl Wilson, Jim Kaat,	
Denny McLain	

NO. PLAYER	NR. MT.
236 NL Pitching Leaders: Sandy Koufax, Juan Marichal, Gaylord Perry, Bob Gibson	11.00
237 AL Strikeout Leaders: Jim Kaat, Earl Wilson, Sam McDowell	11.00
238 NL Strikeout Leaders: Sandy Koufax, Jim Bunning, Bob Veale	3.00
239 AL Batting Leaders: Al Kaline, Frank Robinson, Tony Oliva	3.00
240 NL Batting Leaders: Matty Alou, Felipe Alou, Rico Carty	1.50
241 AL RBI Leaders: Frank Robinson, Boog Powell, Harmon Killebrew	3.00
242 NL RBI Leaders: Bob Clemente, Richie Allen, Hank Aaron	4.00
243 AL Home Run Leaders: Frank Robinson, Harmon Killebrew, Boog Powell	2.50
244 NL Home Run Leaders: Hank Aaron, Richie Allen, Willie Mays	6.00
245 Curt Flood	1.50
246 Jim Perry	1.50
247 Jerry Lumpe	1.00
248 Gene Mauch (Mgr.)	1.25
249 Nick Willhite	1.00
250 Hank Aaron	70.00
251 Woody Held	1.00
252 Bob Bolin	1.00
253 Indians Rookies: Bill Davis, Gus Gil	1.00
254 Milt Pappas	1.00
255 Frank Howard	1.50
256 Bob Hendley	1.00
257 Charley Smith	1.00
258 Lee Maye	1.00
259 Don Dennis	1.00
260 Jim Lefebvre	1.25
261 John Wyatt	1.00
262 Athletics Team	2.50
263 Hank Aguirre	1.00
264 Ron Swoboda	1.25
265 Lou Burdette	1.50
266 Pitt Power: W. Stargell, D. Clendenon	4.00
267 Don Schwall	1.00
268 John Briggs	1.00
269 Don Nottebart	1.00
270 Zoilo Versalles	1.00
271 Eddie Watt	1.00
272 Cubs Rookies: Bill Connors, Dave Dowling	1.00
273 Dick Lines	1.00
274 Bob Aspromonte	1.00
275 Fred Whitfield	1.00
276 Bruce Brubaker	1.00
277 Steve Whitaker	1.00
278 Checklist No. 4	4.00
279 Frank Linzy	1.00
280 Tony Conigliaro	3.00
281 Bob Rodgers	1.00
282 Johnny Odom	1.00
283 Gene Alley	1.00
284 Johnny Podres	1.50
285 Lou Brock	15.00
286 Wayne Causey	1.00
287 Mets Rookies: Greg Goossen, Bart Shirley	1.00
288 Denver Lemaster	1.00
289 Tom Tresh	1.50
290 Bill White	2.00
291 Jim Hannan	1.00
292 Don Pavletich	1.00
293 Ed Kirkpatrick	1.00
294 Walt Alston (Mgr.)	2.50
295 Sam McDowell	1.50
296 Glenn Beckert	1.00
297 Dave Morehead	1.00

NO. PLAYER	NR. MT.
298 Ron Davis	1.00
299 Norm Siebern	1.00
300 Jim Kaat	3.00
301 Jesse Gonder	1.00
302 Orioles Team	2.50
303 Gil Blanco	1.00
304 Phil Gagliano	1.00
305 Earl Wilson	1.00
306 Bud Harrelson	1.50
307 Jim Beauchamp	1.00
308 Al Downing	1.25
309 Hurlers Beware: J. Callison, Richie Allen	1.50
310 Gary Peters	1.00
311 Ed Brinkman	1.00
312 Don Mincher	1.00
313 Bob Lee	1.00
314 Red Sox Rookies: Mike Andrews, R. Smith	4.00
315 Billy Williams	10.00
316 Jack Kralick	1.00
317 Cesar Tovar	1.00
318 Dave Giusti	1.00
319 Paul Blair	1.00
320 Gaylord Perry	10.00
321 Mayo Smith (Mgr.)	1.00
322 Jose Pagan	1.00
323 Mike Hershberger	1.00
324 Hal Woodeschick	1.00
325 Chico Cardenas	1.00
326 Bob Uecker	17.00
327 Angels Team	2.50
328 Clete Boyer	1.25
329 Charlie Lau	1.25
330 Claude Osteen	1.00
331 Joe Foy	1.00
332 Jesus Alou	1.00
333 Ferguson Jenkins	10.00
334 Twin Terrors: Bob Allison, H. Killebrew	4.00
335 Bob Veale	1.00
336 Joe Azcue	1.00
337 Joe Morgan	16.00
338 Bob Locker	1.00
339 Chico Ruiz	1.00
340 Joe Pepitone	1.50
341 Giants Rookies: Dick Dietz, Bill Sorrell	1.50
342 Hank Fischer	1.00
343 Tom Satriano	1.00
344 Ossie Chavarria	1.00
345 Stu Miller	1.00
346 Jim Hickman	1.00
347 Grady Hatton (Mgr.)	1.00
348 Tug McGraw	1.50
349 Bob Chance	1.00
350 Joe Torre	2.00
351 Vern Law	1.00
352 Ray Oyler	1.00
353 Bill McCool	1.00
354 Cubs Team	2.50
355 Carl Yastrzemski	100.00
356 Larry Jaster	1.00
357 Bill Skowron	1.50
358 Ruben Amaro	1.00
359 Dick Ellsworth	1.00
360 Leon Wagner	1.00
361 Checklist No. 5	4.00
362 Darold Knowles	1.00
363 Dave Johnson	1.50
364 Claude Raymond	1.00
365 John Roseboro	1.00
366 Andy Kosco	1.00
367 Angels Rookies: Bill Kelso, Don Wallace	1.00
368 Jack Hiatt	1.00
369 Jim Hunter	14.00
370 Tommy Davis	1.00
371 Jim Lonborg	2.50
372 Mike De La Hoz	1.50
373 White Sox Rookies: D. Josephson, F. Klages	1.50
374 Mel Queen	1.50
375 Jake Gibbs	1.50
376 Don Lock	1.50

NO. PLAYER	NR. MT.
377 Luis Tiant	2.50
378 Tigers Team	2.50
379 Jerry May	1.50
380 Dean Chance	1.50
381 Dick Schofield	1.50
382 Dave McNally	2.00
383 Ken Henderson	1.50
384 Cardinals Rookies: Dick Hughes, Jim Cosman	1.50
385 Jim Fregosi	2.00
386 Dick Selma	1.50
387 Cap Peterson	1.50
388 Arnold Earley	1.50
389 Al Dark (Mgr.)	2.00
390 Jim Wynn	1.50
391 Wilbur Wood	1.50
392 Tommy Harper	1.50
393 Jim Bouton	2.50
394 Jake Wood	1.50
395 Chris Short	1.50
396 Atlanta Aces: D. Meke, T. Cloninger	1.50
397 Willie Smith	1.50
398 Jeff Torborg	1.75
399 Al Worthington	1.50
400 Bob Clemente	60.00
401 Jim Coates	1.50
402 Phillies Rookies: Grant Jackson, Billy Wilson	2.00
403 Dick Nen	1.50
404 Nelson Briles	1.50
405 Russ Snyder	1.50
406 Lee Elia	1.50
407 Reds Team	2.50
408 Jim Northrup	1.50
409 Ray Sadecki	1.50
410 Lou Johnson	1.50
411 Dick Howser	2.00
412 Astros Rookies: Norm Miller, Doug Rader	2.50
413 Jerry Grote	1.50
414 Casey Cox	1.50
415 Sonny Jackson	1.50
416 Roger Repoz	1.50
417 Bob Bruce	1.50
418 Sam Mele (Mgr.)	1.50
419 Don Kessinger	1.50
420 Denny McLain	4.00
421 Dal Maxvill	1.50
422 Hoyt Wilhelm	7.00
423 Fence Busters: Willie Mays, Willie McCovey	15.00
424 Pedro Gonzalez	1.50
425 Pete Mikkelsen	1.50
426 Lou Clinton	1.50
427 Ruben Gomez	1.50
428 Dodgers Rookies: Tom Hutton, Gene Michael	2.00
429 Garry Roggenburk	1.50
430 Pete Rose	75.00
431 Ted Uhlaender	1.50
432 Jimmie Hall	1.50
433 Al Luplow	1.50
434 Eddie Fisher	1.50
435 Mack Jones	1.50
436 Pete Ward	1.50
437 Senators Team	2.50
438 Chuck Dobson	1.50
439 Byron Browne	1.50
440 Steve Hargan	1.50
441 Jim Davenport	1.50
442 Yankees Rookies: Bill Robinson, Joe Verbanic	3.00
443 Tito Francona	1.50
444 George Smith	1.50
445 Don Sutton	20.00
446 Russ Nixon	1.50
447 Bo Belinsky	1.50
448 Harry Walker (Mgr.)	1.50
449 Orlando Pena	1.50
450 Richie Allen	3.00
451 Fred Newman	1.50
452 Ed Kranepool	2.00
453 Aurelio Monteagudo	1.50
454 Checklist No. 6	4.00

NO. PLAYER	NR. MT.
455 Tommy Agee	1.50
456 Phil Niekro	10.00
457 Andy Etchebarren	1.50
458 Lee Thomas	5.00
459 Senators Rookies: Dick Bosman, Pete Craig	5.00
460 Harmon Killebrew	40.00
461 Bob Miller	4.00
462 Bob Barton	4.00
463 Hill Aces: Sam McDowell, S. Siel	4.00
464 Dan Coombs	4.00
465 Willie Horton	4.00
466 Bobby Wine	4.00
467 Jim O'Toole	4.00
468 Ralph Houk (Mgr.)	6.00
469 Len Gabrielson	5.00
470 Bob Shaw	5.00
471 Rene Lachemann	5.00
472 Rookies Pirates: John Gelnar, G. Spriggs	5.00
473 Jose Santiago	5.00
474 Bob Tolan	5.00
475 Jim Palmer	80.00
476 Tony Perez	60.00
477 Braves Team	9.00
478 Bob Humphreys	5.00
479 Gary Bell	5.00
480 Willie McCovey	25.00
481 Leo Durocher (Mgr.)	5.00
482 Bill Monbouquette	5.00
483 Jim Landis	5.00
484 Jerry Adair	5.00
485 Tim McCarver	10.00
486 Twins Rookies: Rich Reese, Bill Whitby	5.00
487 Tom Reynolds	5.00
488 Gerry Arrigo	5.00
489 Doug Clemens	5.00
490 Tony Cloninger	5.00
491 Sam Bowens	5.00
492 Pirates Team	10.00
493 Phil Ortega	5.00
494 Bill Rigney (Mgr.)	5.00
495 Fritz Peterson	5.00
496 Orlando McFarlane	5.00
497 Ron Campbell	5.00
498 Larry Dierker	5.00
499 Indians Rookies: George Culver, Jose Vidal	5.00
500 Juan Marichal	16.00
501 Jerry Zimmerman	5.00
502 Derrell Griffith	5.00
503 Dodgers Team	10.00
504 Orlando Martinez	5.00
505 Tommy Helms	5.00
506 Smoky Burgess	5.00
507 Orioles Rookies: Ed Barnowski, Larry Haney	5.00
508 Dick Hall	5.00
509 Jim King	5.00
510 Bill Mazeroski	10.00
511 Don Wert	5.00
512 R. Schoendienst (Mgr.)	10.00
513 Marcelino Lopez	5.00
514 John Werhas	5.00
515 Bert Campaneris	6.00
516 Giants Team	10.00
517 Fred Talbot	5.00
518 Denis Menke	5.00
519 Ted Davidson	5.00
520 Max Alvis	5.00
521 Bird Bombers: Boog Powell, Curt Blefary	6.00
522 John Stephenson	5.00
523 Jim Merritt	5.00
524 Felix Mantilla	5.00
525 Ron Hunt	5.00
526 Tigers Rookies: Pat Dobson, G. Korince	6.00
527 Dennis Ribant	5.00
528 Rico Petrocelli	6.00
529 Gary Wagner	5.00
530 Felipe Alou	6.00
531 Checklist No. 7	10.00

NO. PLAYER	NR. MT.	NO. PLAYER	NR. MT.	NO. PLAYER	NR. MT.	NO. PLAYER	NR. MT.
532 Jim Hicks	5.00	552 Ted Savage	15.00	571 Larry Sherry	15.00	591 Ty Cline	15.00
533 Jack Fisher	5.00	553 Yankees Rookies:	25.00	572 Don Demeter	30.00	592 NL Rookies:	15.00
534 Hank Bauer (Mgr.)	15.00	Mike Hegan, Thad Tillotson		573 White Sox Team	18.00	Jim Shellenback, Ron Wi'	
535 Donn Clendenon	15.00	554 Andre Rodgers	15.00	574 Jerry Buchek	15.00	593 Wes Westrum (Mgr.)	15.00
536 Cubs Rookies:	30.00	555 Don Cardwell	15.00	575 Dave Boswell	15.00	594 Dan Osinski	15.00
Joe Niekro, Paul Popovich		556 Al Weis	15.00	576 NL Rookies:	15.00	595 Cookie Rojas	15.00
537 Chuck Estrada	15.00	557 Al Ferrara	15.00	R. Hernandez, Norm Gigon		596 Galen Cisco	15.00
538 J.C. Martin	15.00	558 Orioles Rookies:	40.00	577 Bill Short	15.00	597 Ted Abernathy	15.00
539 Dick Egan	15.00	Mark Belanger, Bill Dillman		578 John Boccabella	15.00	598 White Sox Rookies:	15.00
540 Norm Cash	28.00	559 Dick Tracewski	15.00	579 Bill Henry	15.00	Ed Stroud, Walt Williams	
541 Joe Gibbon	15.00	560 Jim Bunning	35.00	580 Rocky Colavito	35.00	599 Bob Duliba (Mgr.)	15.00
542 Athletics Rookies:	12.00	561 Sandy Alomar	15.00	581 Mets Rookies:	1100.00	600 Brooks Robinson	200.00
Tony Pierce, Rick Monday		562 Steve Blass	15.00	Bill Denehy, Tom Seaver		601 Bill Bryan	15.00
543 Dan Schneider	15.00	563 Joe Adcock (Mgr.)	20.00	582 Jim Owens	15.00	602 Juan Pizarro	15.00
544 Indians Team	25.00	564 Astros Rookies:	15.00	583 Ray Barker	15.00	603 Athletics Rookies:	15.00
545 Jim Grant	15.00	Alonzo Harris, A. Pointer		584 Jim Piersall	22.00	Tim Talton, Ramon Webster	
546 Woody Woodward	15.00	565 Lew Krausse	15.00	585 Wally Bunker	15.00	604 Red Sox Team	65.00
547 Red Sox Rookies:	15.00	566 Gary Geiger	15.00	586 Manny Jimenez	15.00	605 Mike Shannon	35.00
Russ Gibson, Bill Rohr		567 Steve Hamilton	15.00	587 NL Rookies:	15.00	606 Ron Taylor	15.00
548 Tony Gonzalez	15.00	568 John Sullivan	15.00	Don Shaw, Gary Sutherland		607 Mickey Stanley	30.00
549 Jack Sanford	15.00	569 AL Rookies:	400.00	588 Johnny Klippstein	15.00	608 Cubs Rookies:	15.00
550 Vada Pinson	18.00	Rod Carew, Hank Allen		589 Dave Ricketts	15.00	John Upham, Rich Nye	
551 Doug Camilli	15.00	570 Maury Wills	100.00	590 Pete Richert	15.00	609 Tommy John (Exc. $25.00)	100.00

1968 Topps. . . . Complete Set of 598 Cards—Value $1000.00 (Exc.); $2500.00 (Near Mint)

Features the rookie cards of Johnny Bench and Nolan Ryan. High numbers are 534 to 598. Card 66 exists with "Senators" in *white*—worth $.50 and "Senators" in *yellow*—$35.00. Card 518 (checklist) exists identifying card 539 as "Maj. L. Rookies"—worth $3.00 or "Am. L. Rookies"—worth $8.00.

NO. PLAYER	NR. MT.	NO. PLAYER	NR. MT.	NO. PLAYER	NR. MT.	NO. PLAYER	NR. MT.
1 NL Ldrs.: (Exc. $2.00)	10.00	13 Chuck Hartenstein	.75	47 Ralph Houk (Mgr.)	1.00	81 Larry Jackson	.75
Bob Clemente, Matty Alou, Tony Gonzalez		14 Jerry McNertney	.75	48 Ted Davidson	.75	82 Sam Bowens	.75
2 AL Batting Leaders:	5.00	15 Ron Hunt	.75	49 Ed Brinkman	.75	83 John Stephenson	.75
Frank Robinson, Al Kaline, Carl Yastrzemski		16 Indians Rookies:	3.00	50 Willy Mays	50.00	84 Bob Tolan	.75
3 NL RBI Leaders:	3.00	Lou Piniella, R. Schienblum		51 Bob Locker	.75	85 Gaylord Perry	7.00
Hank Aaron, O. Cepeda, Bob Clemente		17 Dick Hall	.75	52 Hawk Taylor	.75	86 Willie Stargell	11.00
4 AL RBI Leaders:	5.00	18 Mike Hershberger	.75	53 Gene Alley	.75	87 Dick Williams (Mgr.)	1.00
C. Yastrzemski, H. Killebrew, F. Robinson		19 Juan Pizarro	.75	54 Stan Williams	.75	88 Phil Regan	.75
5 NL Home Run Leaders:	4.00	20 Brooks Robinson	15.00	55 Felipe Alou	1.25	89 Jake Gibbs	.75
Ron Santo, Hank Aaron, Jim Wynn, Willie McCovey		21 Ron Davis	.75	56 Orioles Rookies:	1.00	90 Vada Pinson	1.25
6 AL Home Run Leaders:	4.00	22 Pat Dobson	.75	Dave May, Dave Leonhard		91 Jim Ollom	.75
C. Yastrzemski, H. Killebrew, F. Howard		23 Chico Cardenas	.75	57 Dan Schneider	.75	92 Ed Kranepool	.75
7 NL ERA Leaders:	1.50	24 Bobby Locke	.75	58 Ed Mathews	7.50	93 Tony Cloninger	.75
Jim Bunning, Chris Short, Phil Niekro		25 Jan Javier	.75	59 Don Lock	.75	94 Lee Maye	.75
8 AL ERA Leaders:	1.50	26 Darrell Brandon	.75	60 Ken Holtzman	1.00	95 Bob Aspromonte	.75
Joe Horlen, Sonny Siebert, Gary Peters		27 Gil Hodges (Mgr.)	5.00	61 Reggie Smith	1.25	96 Senator Rookies:	.75
9 NL Pitching Leaders:	1.50	28 Ted Uhlaender	.75	62 Chuck Dobson	.75	Frank Coggins, Dick Nold	
C. Osteen, M. McCormick, F. Jenkins, J. Bunning		29 Joe Verbanic	.75	63 Dick Kenworthy	.75	97 Tom Phoebus	.75
10 AL Pitching Leaders:	1.50	30 Joe Torre	1.50	64 Jim Merritt	.75	98 Gary Sutherland	.75
Jim Lonborg, Earl Wilson, Dean Chance		31 Ed Stroud	.75	65 John Roseboro	.75	99 Rocky Colavito	1.50
11 NL Strikeout Leaders:	1.50	32 Joe Gibbon	.75	66 Casey Cox*	.75	100 Bob Gibson	15.00
Ferguson Jenkins, Gaylord Perry, Jim Bunning		33 Pete Ward	.75	67 Checklist No. 1	3.00	101 Glenn Beckert	.75
12 AL Strikeout Leaders:	1.50	34 Al Ferrara	.75	68 Ron Willis	.75	102 Jose Cardenal	.75
Jim Lonborg, Dean Chance, Sam McDowell		35 Steve Hargan	.75	69 Tom Tresh	1.00	103 Don Sutton	8.00
		36 Pirates Rookies:	1.00	70 Bob Veale	1.00	104 Dick Dietz	.75
		Bob Moose, B. Robertson		71 Vern Fuller	.75	105 Al Downing	1.00
		37 Billy Williams	9.00	72 Tommy John	4.00	106 Dalton Jones	.75
		38 Tony Pierce	.75	73 Jim Hart	.75	107 Checklist No. 2	3.00
		39 Cookie Rojas	.75	74 Milt Pappas	1.00	108 Don Pavletich	.75
		40 Denny McLain	5.00	75 Don Mincher	.75	109 Bert Campaneris	.75
		41 Julio Gotay	.75	76 Braves Rookies:	1.25	110 Hank Aaron	50.00
		42 Larry Haney	.75	Jim Britton, Ron Reed		111 Rich Reese	.75
		43 Gary Bell	.75	77 Don Wilson	.75	112 Woody Fryman	.75
		44 Frank Kostro	.75	78 Jim Northrup	1.00	113 Tigers Rookies:	.75
		45 Tom Seaver	160.00	79 Ted Kubiak	.75	T. Matchick, D. Patterson	
		46 Dave Ricketts	.75	80 Rod Carew	110.00	114 Ron Swoboda	1.00

NO. PLAYER	NR. MT.
115 Sam McDowell	1.00
116 Ken McMullen	.75
117 Larry Jaster	.75
118 Mark Belanger	1.25
119 Ted Savage	.75
120 Mel Stottlemyre	1.25
121 Jimmie Hall	.75
122 Gene Mauch (Mgr.)	.60
123 Jose Santiago	.75
124 Nate Oliver	.75
125 Joe Horlen	.75
126 Bobby Etheridge	.75
127 Paul Lindblad	.75
128 Astros Rookies:	.75
Alonzo Harris, Tom Dukes	
129 Mickey Stanley	.75
130 Tony Perez	6.00
131 Frank Bertaina	.75
132 Bud Harrelson	.75
133 Fred Whitfield	.75
134 Pat Jarvis	.75
135 Paul Blair	.75
136 Randy Hundley	.75
137 Minnesota Twins	2.00
138 Ruben Amaro	.75
139 Chris Short	.75
140 Tony Conigliaro	2.50
141 Dal Maxvill	.75
142 White Sox Rookies:	.75
Bill Voss, B. Bradford	
143 Pete Cimino	.75
144 Joe Morgan	12.00
145 Don Drysdale	8.00
146 Sal Bando	1.50
147 Frank Linzy	.75
148 Dave Bristol (Mgr.)	.75
149 Bob Saverine	.75
150 Bob Clemente	45.00
151 World Series Game 1:	5.00
Brock Socks 4 Hits	
152 World Series Game 2:	7.00
Yaz Smashes 2 Homers	
153 World Series Game 3:	2.00
Briles Cools Off Boston	
154 World Series Game 4:	4.00
Gibson Hurls Shutout	
155 World Series Game 5:	2.00
Lonborg Wins Again	
156 World Series Game 6:	2.00
Petrocelli 2 Homers	
157 World Series Game 7:	2.00
St. Louis Wins It	
158 World Series:	2.00
The Cardinal Celebrate	
159 Don Kessinger	1.00
160 Earl Wilson	.75
161 Norm Miller	.75
162 Cardinals Rookies:	1.50
Hal Gilson, Mike Torrez	
163 Gene Brabender	.75
164 Ramon Webster	.75
165 Tony Oliva	3.00
166 Claude Raymond	.75
167 Elston Howard	2.00
168 Los Angeles Dodgers	2.00
169 Bob Bolin	.75
170 Jim Fregosi	1.50
171 Don Nottebart	.75
172 Walt Williams	.75
173 John Boozer	.75
174 Bob Tillman	.75
175 Maury Wills	4.00
176 Bob Allen	.75
177 Mets Rookies:	1250.00
J. Koosman, Nolan Ryan	
178 Don Wert	.75
179 Bill Stoneman	.75
180 Curt Flood	1.00
181 Jerry Zimmerman	.75
182 Dave Guisti	.75
183 Bob Kennedy	.75
184 Lou Johnson	.75
185 Tom Haller	.75
186 Eddie Watt	.75
187 Sonny Jackson	.75

NO. PLAYER	NR. MT.
188 Cap Peterson	.75
189 Bill Landis	.75
190 Bill White	2.50
191 Dan Frisella	.75
192 Checklist No. 3	3.00
193 Jack Hamilton	.75
194 Don Buford	.75
195 Joe Pepitone	1.00
196 Gary Nolan	.75
197 Larry Brown	.75
198 Roy Face	1.50
199 A's Rookies:	.75
R. Rodriguez, D. Osteen	
200 Orlando Cepeda	4.00
201 Mike Marshall (R)	1.25
202 Adolfo Phillips	.75
203 Dick Kelley	.75
204 Andy Etchebarren	.75
205 Juan Marichal	6.00
206 Cal Ermer	.75
207 Carroll Sembera	.75
208 Willie Davis	1.25
209 Tim Cullen	.75
210 Gary Peters	.75
211 J.C. Martin	.75
212 Dave Morehead	.75
213 Chico Ruiz	.75
214 Yankees Rookies:	1.50
S. Bahnsen, F. Fernandez	
215 Jim Bunning	3.00
216 Bubba Morton	.75
217 Turk Farrell	.75
218 Ken Suarez	.75
219 Rob Gardner	.75
220 Harmon Killebrew	11.00
221 Atlanta Braves	1.50
222 Jim Hardin	.75
223 Ollie Brown	.75
224 Jack Aker	.75
225 Richie Allen	2.00
226 Jimmie Price	.75
227 Joe Hoerner	.75
228 Dodgers Rookies:	1.00
Jack Billingham, Jim Fairey	
229 Fred Klages	.75
230 Pete Rose	50.00
231 Dave Baldwin	.75
232 Denis Menke	.75
233 George Scott	1.00
234 Bill Monbouquette	.75
235 Ron Santo	1.50
236 Tug McGraw	1.75
237 Alvin Dark (Mgr.)	1.00
238 Tom Satriano	.75
239 Bill Henry	.75
240 Al Kaline	15.00
241 Felix Millan	.75
242 Moe Drabowsky	.75
243 Rich Rollins	.75
244 John Donaldson	.75
245 Tony Gonzalez	.75
246 Fritz Peterson	.75
247 Reds Rookies:	450.00
Johnny Bench, R. Tompkins	
248 Fred Valentine	.75
249 Bill Singer	.75
250 Carl Yastrzemski	40.00
251 Manny Sanguillen (R)	2.00
252 Angels Team	2.00
253 Dick Hughes	.75
254 Cleon Jones	.75
255 Dean Chance	.75
256 Norm Cash	2.00
257 Phil Niekro	5.00
258 Cubs Rookies:	1.00
J. Arcia, B. Schlesinger	
259 Ken Boyer	1.50
260 Jim Wynn	1.25
261 Dave Duncan	.75
262 Rick Wise	.75
263 Horace Clarke	1.00
264 Ted Abernathy	.75
265 Tommy Davis	1.00
266 Paul Popovich	.75
267 Herman Franks (Mgr.)	.75

NO. PLAYER	NR. MT.
268 Bob Humphreys	.75
269 Bob Tiefenauer	.75
270 Matty Alou	1.50
271 Bobby Knoop	.75
272 Ray Culp	.75
273 Dave Johnson	1.25
274 Mike Cuellar	1.00
275 Tim McCarver	2.00
276 Jim Roland	.75
277 Jerry Buchek	.75
278 Checklist No. 4	3.00
279 Bill Hands	.75
280 Mickey Mantle	200.00
281 Jim Campanis	.75
282 Rick Monday	1.50
283 Mel Queen	.75
284 John Briggs	.75
285 Dick McAuliffe	.75
286 Cecil Upshaw	.75
287 White Sox Rookies:	1.00
Mickey Abarbanel,	
Cisco Carlos	
288 Dave Wickersham	.75
289 Woody Held	.75
290 Willie McCovey	8.00
291 Dick Lines	.75
292 Art Shamsky	.75
293 Bruce Howard	.75
294 Red Schoendienst	3.00
295 Sonny Siebert	.75
296 Byron Browne	.75
297 Russ Gibson	.75
298 Jim Brewer	.75
299 Gene Michael	1.00
300 Rusty Staub	1.25
301 Twins Rookies:	1.00
G. Mitterwald, R. Renick	
302 Gerry Arrigo	.75
303 Dick Green	.75
304 Sandy Valdespino	.75
305 Minnie Rojas	.75
306 Mike Ryan	.75
307 John Hiller	.75
308 Pittsburgh Pirates	2.00
309 Ken Henderson	.75
310 Luis Aparicio	5.00
311 Jack Lamabe	.75
312 Curt Blefary	.75
313 Al Weis	.75
314 Red Sox Rookies:	.75
Bill Rohr, George Spriggs	
315 Zoilo Versalles	.75
316 Steve Barber	.75
317 Ron Brand	.75
318 Chico Salmon	.75
319 George Culver	.75
320 Frank Howard	1.00
321 Leo Durocher (Mgr.)	1.50
322 Dave Boswell	.75
323 Deron Johnson	.75
324 Jim Nash	.75
325 Manny Mota	1.25
326 Denny Ribant	.75
327 Tony Taylor	.75
328 Angels Rookies:	.75
Chuck Vinson, Jim Weaver	
329 Duane Josephson	.75
330 Roger Maris	25.00
331 Dan Osinski	.75
332 Doug Rader	.75
333 Ron Herbel	.75
334 Baltimore Orioles	2.00
335 Bob Allison	.75
336 John Purdin	.75
337 Bill Robinson	.75
338 Bob Johnson	.75
339 Rich Nye	.75
340 Max Alvis	.75
341 Jim Lemon (Mgr.)	.75
342 Ken Johnson	.75
343 Jim Gosger	.75
344 Don Clendenon	1.00
345 Bob Hendley	.75
346 Jerry Adair	.75
347 George Brunet	.75

NO. PLAYER	NR. MT.
348 Phillies Rookies:	.75
Larry Colton, Dick Thoenen	
349 Ed Spiezio	.75
350 Hoyt Wilhelm	5.00
351 Bob Barton	.75
352 Jackie Hernandez	.75
353 Mack Jones	.75
354 Pete Richert	.75
355 Ernie Banks	12.00
356 Checklist No. 5	3.00
357 Len Gabrielson	.75
358 Mike Epstein	.75
359 Joe Moeller	.75
360 Willie Horton	1.25
361 Harmon Killebrew (AS)	5.00
362 Orlando Cepeda (AS)	3.00
363 Rod Carew (AS)	11.00
364 Joe Morgan (AS)	5.00
365 Brooks Robinson (AS)	5.00
366 Ron Santo (AS)	1.50
367 Jim Fregosi (AS)	1.00
368 Gene Alley (AS)	1.00
369 Carl Yastrzemski (AS)	10.00
370 Hank Aaron (AS)	12.00
371 Tony Oliva (AS)	2.00
372 Lou Brock (AS)	5.00
373 Frank Robinson (AS)	500
374 Bob Clemente (AS)	10.00
375 Bill Freehan (AS)	1.00
376 Tim McCarver (AS)	2.00
377 Joe Horlen (AS)	1.00
378 Bob Gibson (AS)	5.00
379 Gary Peters (AS)	1.00
380 Ken Holtzman (AS)	1.00
381 Boog Powell	2.00
382 Ramon Hernandez	.75
383 Steve Whitaker	.75
384 Reds Rookies:	5.00
Bill Henry, Hal McRae	
385 Jim Hunter	9.00
386 Greg Goossen	.75
387 Joe Foy	.75
388 Ray Washburn	.75
389 Jay Johnstone	.75
390 Bill Mazeroski	2.00
391 Bob Priddy	.75
392 Grady Hatton (Mgr.)	.75
393 Jim Perry	1.00
394 Tommie Aaron	1.00
395 Camilo Pascual	1.00
396 Bobby Wine	.75
397 Vic Davalillo	.75
398 Jim Grant	.75
399 Ray Oyler	.75
400 Mike McCormick	.75
401 New York Mets	2.00
402 Mike Hegan	.75
403 John Buzhardt	.75
404 Floyd Robinson	.75
405 Tommy Helms	.75
406 Dick Ellsworth	.75
407 Gary Kolb	.75
408 Steve Carlton	50.00
409 Orioles Rookies:	.75
Frank Peters, Don Stone	
410 Ferguson Jenkins	5.00
411 Ron Hansen	.75
412 Clay Carroll	.75
413 Tommy McCraw	.75
414 Mickey Lolich	2.50
415 Johnny Callison	.75
416 Bill Rigney (Mgr.)	.75
417 Willie Crawford	.75
418 Eddie Fisher	.75
419 Jack Hiatt	.75
420 Cesar Tovar	.75
421 Ron Taylor	.75
422 Rene Lachemann	.75
423 Fred Gladding	.75
424 Chicago White Sox	2.00
425 Jim Maloney	.75
426 Hank Allen	.75
427 Dick Calmus	.75
428 Vic Roznovsky	.75
429 Tommie Sisk	.75

NO. PLAYER	NR. MT.
430 Rico Petrocelli	2.00
431 Dooley Womack	.75
432 Indians Rookies:	.75
Bill Davis, Jose Vidal	
433 Bob Rodgers	.75
434 Ricardo Joseph	.75
435 Ron Perranoski	1.00
436 Hal Lanier	.75
437 Don Cardwell	.75
438 Lee Thomas	.75
439 Luman Harris (Mgr.)	.75
440 Claude Osteen	.75
441 Alex Johnson	.75
442 Dick Bosman	.75
443 Joe Azcue	.75
444 Jack Fisher	.75
445 Mike Shannon	.75
446 Ron Kline	.75
447 Tigers Rookies:	.75
G. Korince, F. Lasher	
448 Gary Wagner	.75
449 Gene Oliver	.75
450 Jim Kaat	3.00
451 Al Spangler	.75
452 Jesus Alou	.75
453 Sammy Ellis	.75
454 Checklist No. 6	3.00
455 Rico Carty	1.50
456 John O'Donoghue	.75
457 Jim Lefebvre	.75
458 Lew Krausse	1.25
459 Dick Simpson	1.25
460 Jim Lonborg	1.25
461 Chuck Hiller	1.25
462 Barry Moore	1.25
463 Jimmie Schaffer	1.25
464 Don McMahon	1.25
465 Tommie Agee	1.25
466 Bill Dillman	1.25
467 Dick Howser	1.25
468 Larry Sherry	1.25
469 Ty Cline	1.25
470 Bill Freehan	1.25
471 Orlando Pena	1.50
472 Walt Alston (Mgr.)	2.00
473 Al Worthington	1.25

NO. PLAYER	NR. MT.
474 Paul Schaal	1.25
475 Joe Niekro	2.00
476 Woody Woodward	1.25
477 Philadelphia Phillies	2.00
478 Dave McNally	1.25
479 Phil Gagliano	1.25
480 Manager's Dream:	16.00
Tony Oliva, Chico Cardenas, Bob Clemente	
481 John Wyatt	1.25
482 Jose Pagan	1.25
483 Darold Knowles	1.25
484 Phil Roof	1.25
485 Ken Berry	1.25
486 Cal Koonce	1.25
487 Lee May	1.50
488 Dick Tracewski	1.25
489 Wally Bunker	1.25
490 Super Stars:	50.00
Harmon Killebrew, Willie Mays, Mickey Mantle	
491 Denny LeMaster	1.25
492 Jeff Torborg	1.25
493 Jim McGlothlin	1.25
494 Ray Sadecki	1.25
495 Leon Wagner	1.25
496 Steve Hamilton	1.25
497 St. Louis Cardinals	2.50
498 Bill Bryan	1.25
499 Steve Blass	1.25
500 Frank Robinson	15.00
501 John Odom	1.25
502 Mike Andrews	1.25
503 Al Jackson	1.25
504 Russ Snyder	1.25
505 Joe Sparma	1.25
506 Clarence Jones	1.25
507 Wade Blasingame	1.25
508 Duke Sims	1.25
509 Dennis Higgins	1.25
510 Ron Fairly	1.25
511 Bill Kelso	1.25
512 Grant Jackson	1.25
513 Hank Bauer (Mgr.)	1.25
514 Al McBean	1.25
515 Russ Nixon	1.25

NO. PLAYER	NR. MT.
516 Pete Mikkelsen	1.25
517 Diego Segui	1.25
518 Checklist No. 7*	3.00
519 Jerry Stephenson	1.25
520 Lou Brock	15.00
521 Don Shaw	1.25
522 Wayne Causey	1.25
523 John Tsitouris	1.25
524 Andy Kosco	1.25
525 Jim Davenport	1.25
526 Bill Denehy	1.25
527 Tito Francona	1.25
528 Detroit Tigers	16.00
529 Bruce Von Hoff	1.25
530 Bird Belters:	6.00
Frank Robinson, Brooks Robinson	
531 Chuck Hinton	1.25
532 Luis Tiant	2.00
533 Wes Parker	1.25
534 Bob Miller	1.25
535 Danny Cater	1.25
536 Bill Short	1.25
537 Norm Siebern	1.25
538 Manny Jimenez	1.25
539 Major League Rookies:	1.50
Jim Ray, Mike Ferraro	
540 Nelson Briles	1.25
541 Sandy Alomar	1.25
542 John Boccabella	1.25
543 Bob Lee	1.25
544 Mayo Smith (Mgr.)	1.25
545 Lindy McDaniel	1.25
546 Roy White	2.00
547 Dan Coombs	1.25
548 Bernie Allen	1.25
549 Orioles Rookies:	1.25
Curt Motton, Roger Nelson	
550 Clete Boyer	1.50
551 Darrell Sutherland	1.25
552 Ed Kirkpatrick	1.25
553 Hank Aguirre	1.25
554 Oakland A's	3.00
555 Jose Tartabull	1.25
556 Dick Selma	1.25
557 Frank Quilici	1.25

NO. PLAYER	NR. MT.
558 John Edwards	1.25
559 Pirates Rookies:	2.00
Carl Taylor, Luke Walker	
560 Paul Casanova	1.25
561 Lee Elia	1.25
562 Jim Bouton	2.00
563 Ed Charles	1.25
564 Eddie Stanky	1.25
565 Larry Dierker	1.25
566 Ken Harrelson	2.00
567 Clay Dalrymple	1.25
568 Willie Smith	1.25
569 NL Rookies:	1.25
Ivan Murrell, Les Rohr	
570 Rick Reichardt	1.25
571 Tony LaRussa	2.00
572 Don Bosch	1.25
573 Joe Coleman	1.25
574 Cincinnati Reds	3.00
575 Jim Palmer	35.00
576 Dave Adlesh	1.25
577 Fred Talbot	1.25
578 Orlando Martinez	1.25
579 NL Rookies:	1.50
Larry Hisle, Mike Lum	
580 Bob Bailey	1.25
581 Garry Roggenburk	1.25
582 Jerry Grote	1.25
583 Gates Brown	1.25
584 Larry Shepard	1.25
585 Wilbur Wood	1.25
586 Jim Pagliaroni	1.25
587 Roger Repoz	1.25
588 Dick Schofield	1.25
589 Twins Rookies:	1.25
Ron Clark, Moe Ogier	
590 Tommy Harper	1.25
591 Dick Nen	1.25
592 John Bateman	1.25
593 Lee Stange	1.25
594 Phil Linz	1.25
595 Phil Ortega	1.25
596 Charlie Smith	1.25
597 Bill McCool	1.25
598 Jerry May (Exc. $1.00)	4.00

1969 Topps.... Complete Set of 664 Cards—Value $900.00 (Exc.); $2000.00 (Near Mint)

Includes the rookie cards of Reggies Jackson, Al Oliver and Rollie Fingers. The high numbers are 513 to 664. The values listed for the 23 cards with an *asterisk* are with the player's entire name in *yellow* letters. These cards also exist with the player's name in *white* letters—worth $12.50 each, except card no. 440—$80.00, no. 485—$50.00 and no. 500—$500.00.

NO. PLAYER	NR. MT.
1 AL Bat Ldrs. (Exc. $1.50)	7.00
Carl Yastrzemski, Tony Oliva, Danny Cater	
2 NL Batting Leaders:	3.00
Matty Alou, Felipe Alou, Pete Rose	
3 AL RBI Leaders:	1.50
Frank Howard, Ken Harrelson, Jim Northrup	

NO. PLAYER	NR. MT.
4 NL RBI Leaders:	2.50
Willie McCovey, Ron Santo, Billy Williams	
5 AL Home Run Leaders:	1.25
Frank Howard, Willie Horton, Ken Harrelson	
6 NL Home Run Leaders:	3.00
Willie McCovey, Richie Allen, Ernie Banks	

NO. PLAYER	NR. MT.
7 AL ERA Leaders:	1.50
Luis Tiant, Sam McDowell, Dave McNally	
8 NL ERA Leaders:	1.50
Bobby Bolin, Bob Gibson, Bob Veale	
9 AL Pitching Leaders:	1.50
Mel Stottlemyre, Denny McLain, Dave McNally, Luis Tiant	

NO. PLAYER	NR. MT.
10 NL Pitching Leaders:	3.00
Juan Marichal, Bob Gibson, Fergie Jenkins	
11 AL Strikeout Leaders:	1.50
Sam McDowell, Denny McLain, Luis Tiant	
12 NL Strikeout Leaders:	2.00
Bob Gibson, Fergie Jenkins, Bill Singer	

NO. PLAYER	NR. MT.
13 Mickey Stanley	.75
14 Al McBean	.50
15 Boog Powell	1.50
16 Giants Rookies:	.75
C. Gutierrez, R. Robertson	
17 Mike Marshall	1.00
18 Dick Schofield	.50
19 Ken Suarez	.50
20 Ernie Banks	12.00
21 Jose Santiago	.50
22 Jesus Alou	.50
23 Lew Krause	.50
24 Walt Alston (Mgr.)	2.00
25 Ray White	.75
26 Clay Carroll	.50
27 Bernie Allen	.50
28 Mike Ryan	.50
29 Dave Morehead	.50
30 Bob Allison	.50
31 Mets Rookies:	1.50
Gary Gentry, Amos Otis	
32 Sammy Ellis	.50
33 Wayne Causey	.50
34 Gary Peters	.50
35 Joe Morgan	10.00
36 Luke Walker	.50
37 Curt Motton	.50
38 Zoilo Versalles	.50
39 Dick Hughes	.50
40 Mayo Smith (Mgr.)	.50
41 Bob Barton	.50
42 Tommy Harper	.50
43 Joe Niekro	1.00
44 Danny Cater	.50
45 Maury Wills	2.00
46 Fritz Peterson	.50
47 Paul Popovich	.50
(without "C" on helmet)	
47 Paul Popovich	15.00
(with "C" on helmet)	
48 Brant Alyea	.50
49 Royals Rookies:	.50
Steve Jones, E. Rodriguez	
49 Royals Rookies:	15.00
Error—name misspelled "Rodriquez"	
50 Bob Clement	35.00
51 Woody Fryman	.50
52 Mike Andrews	.50
53 Sonny Jackson	.50
54 Cisco Carlos	.50
55 Jerry Grote	.50
56 Rich Reese	.50
57 Checklist No. 1	3.00
58 Fred Gladding	.50
59 Jay Johnstone	.50
60 Nelson Briles	.50
61 Jimmie Hall	.50
62 Chico Salmon	.50
63 Jim Hickman	.50
64 Bill Monbouquette	.50
65 Willie Davis	1.00
66 Orioles Rookies:	.75
M. Adamson, M. Rettenmund	
67 Bill Stoneman	.50
68 Dave Duncan	.50
69 Steve Hamilton	.50
70 Tommy Helms	.50
71 Steve Whitaker	.50
72 Ron Taylor	.50
73 Johnny Briggs	.50
74 Preston Gomez (Mgr.)	.50
75 Luis Aparicio	5.00
76 Norm Miller	.50
77 Ron Perranoski	.50
(no team logo on hat)	
77 Ron Perranoski	15.00
(with team logo on hat)	
78 Tom Satriano	.50
79 Milt Pappas	.50
80 Norm Cash	1.50
81 Mel Queen	.50
82 Pirates Rookies:	8.00
Rich Hebner, Al Oliver	
83 Mike Ferraro	.50

NO. PLAYER	NR. MT.
84 Bob Humphreys	.50
85 Lou Brock	12.00
86 Pete Richert	.50
87 Horace Clarke	.50
88 Rich Nye	.50
89 Russ Gibson	.50
90 Jerry Koosman	3.00
91 Al Dark (Mgr.)	.75
92 Jack Billingham	.50
93 Joe Foy	.50
94 Hank Aguirre	.50
95 Johnny Bench	150.00
96 Denver LeMaster	.50
97 Buddy Bradford	.50
98 Dave Giusti	.50
99 Twins Rookies:	15.00
Danny Morris, Graig Nettles	
100 Hank Aaron	45.00
101 Daryl Patterson	.50
102 Jim Davenport	.50
103 Roger Repoz	.50
104 Steve Blass	.50
105 Rick Monday	.50
106 Jim Hannan	.50
107 Checklist No.2	3.00
(error—#161 Jim Purdin)	
107 Checklist No.2	10.00
(correct—#161 John Purdin)	
108 Tony Taylor	.50
109 Jim Lonborg	.50
110 Mike Shannon	.50
111 Johnny Morris	.50
112 J.C. Martin	.50
113 Dave May	.50
114 Yankees Rookies:	.50
A. Closter, J. Cumberland	
115 Bill Hands	.50
116 Chuck Harrison	.50
117 Jim Fairey	.50
118 Stan Williams (Mgr.)	.50
119 Doug Rader	.50
120 Pete Rose	35.00
121 Joe Grzenda	.50
122 Ron Fairly	.50
123 Wilbur Wood	.50
124 Hank Bauer (Mgr.)	.50
125 Ray Sadecki	.50
126 Dick Tracewski	.50
127 Kevin Collins	.50
128 Tommie Aaron	.50
129 Bill McCool	.50
130 Carl Yastrzemski	35.00
131 Chris Cannizzaro	.50
132 Dave Baldwin	.50
133 Johnny Callison	.50
134 Jim Weaver	.50
135 Tommy Davis	1.00
136 Cards Rookies:	.75
Steve Huntz, Mike Torrez	
137 Wally Bunker	.50
138 John Bateman	.50
139 Andy Kosco	.50
140 Jim Lefebvre	.50
141 Bill Dillman	.50
142 Woody Woodward	.50
143 Joe Nossek	.50
144 Bob Hendley	.50
145 Max Alvis	.50
146 Jim Perry	.75
147 Leo Durocher (Mgr.)	1.50
148 Lee Stange	.50
149 Ollie Brown	.50
150 Denny McLain	3.00
151 Clay Dalrymple	.50
(Orioles Team)	
151 Clay Dalrymple	12.00
(Phillies Team)	
152 Tommie Sisk	.50
153 Ed Brinkman	.50
154 Jim Britton	.50
155 Pete Ward	.50
156 Houston Rookies:	.50
Hal Gilson, Leon McFadden	
157 Bob Rodgers	.50
158 Joe Gibbon	.50

NO. PLAYER	NR. MT.
159 Jerry Adair	.50
160 Vada Pinson	1.00
161 John Purdin	.50
162 World Series Game 1:	3.00
Gibson Fans 17	
163 World Series Game 2:	2.00
Tigers Deck Cards	
164 World Series Game 3:	2.00
McCarver's Homer	
165 World Series Game 4:	3.00
Brock Lead-Off HR	
166 World Series Game 5:	4.00
Kaline's Key Hit	
167 World Series Game 6:	2.00
Tigers 10-Run Inning	
168 World Series Game 7:	3.00
Lolich Outduels Gibson	
169 World Series:	2.00
Tigers Celebrate Victory	
170 Frank Howard	1.00
171 Glenn Beckert	.50
172 Jerry Stephenson	.50
173 White Sox Rookies:	.50
B. Christian, G. Nyman	
174 Grant Jackson	.50
175 Jim Bunning	2.50
176 Joe Azcue	.50
177 Ron Reed	.50
178 Ray Oyler	.50
179 Don Pavletich	.50
180 Willie Horton	.75
181 Mel Nelson	.50
182 Bill Rigney (Mgr.)	.50
183 Don Shaw	.50
184 Roberto Pena	.50
185 Tom Phoebus	.50
186 John Edwards	.50
187 Leon Wagner	.50
188 Rick Wise	.50
189 Red Sox Rookies:	.75
J. Lahoud, J. Thibadeau	
190 Willie Mays	45.00
191 Lindy McDaniel	.50
192 Jose Pagan	.50
193 Don Cardwell	.50
194 Ted Uhlaender	.50
195 John Odom	.50
196 Lum Harris (Mgr.)	.50
197 Dick Selma	.50
198 Willie Smith	.50
199 Jim French	.50
200 Bob Gibson	10.00
201 Russ Snyder	.50
202 Don Wilson	.50
203 Dave Johnson	1.00
204 Jack Hiatt	.50
205 Rick Reichardt	.50
206 Phillies Rookies:	.75
Larry Hisle, Barry Lersch	
207 Roy Face	.75
208 Donn Clendenon	.50
(Astros Team)	
208 Donn Clendenon	15.00
(Expos Team)	
209 Larry Haney	.50
(negative reversed)	
210 Felix Millan	.50
211 Galen Cisco	.50
212 Tom Tresh	.75
213 Gerry Arrigo	.50
214 Checklist No. 3	3.00
215 Rico Petrocelli	.50
216 Don Sutton	6.00
217 John Donaldson	.50
218 John Roseboro	.50
219 Freddie Patek	1.00
220 Sam McDowell	1.00
221 Art Shamsky	1.00
222 Duane Josephson	1.00
223 Tom Dukes	1.00
224 Angels Rookies:	1.00
B. Harrelson, S. Kealey	
225 Don Kessinger	1.50
226 Bruce Howard	1.00
227 Frank Johnson	1.00

NO. PLAYER	NR. MT.
228 Dave Leonhard	1.00
229 Don Lock	1.00
230 Rusty Staub	2.50
231 Pat Dobson	1.00
232 Dave Ricketts	1.00
233 Steve Barber	1.00
234 Dave Bristol (Mgr.)	1.00
235 Jim Hunter	11.00
236 Manny Mota	1.50
237 Bobby Cox	1.25
238 Ken Johnson	1.00
239 Bob Taylor	1.00
240 Ken Harrelson	1.25
241 Jim Brewer	1.00
242 Frank Kostro	1.00
243 Ron Kline	1.00
244 Indians Rookies:	1.50
R. Fosse, G. Woodson	
245 Ed Charles	1.00
246 Joe Coleman	1.00
247 Gene Oliver	1.00
248 Bob Priddy	1.00
249 Ed Spiezio	1.00
250 Frank Robinson	18.00
251 Ron Herbel	1.00
252 Chuck Cottier	1.00
253 Jerry Johnson	1.00
254 Joe Schultz (Mgr.)	1.00
255 Steve Carlton	35.00
256 Gates Brown	1.00
257 Jim Ray	1.00
258 Jackie Hernandez	1.00
259 Bill Short	1.00
260 Reggie Jackson (R)	450.00
261 Bob Johnson	1.00
262 Mike Kekich	1.00
263 Jerry May	1.00
264 Bill Landis	1.00
265 Chico Cardenas	1.00
266 Dodger Rookies:	1.25
Tom Hutton, Alan Foster	
267 Vicente Romo	1.00
268 Al Spangler	1.00
269 Al Weis	1.00
270 Mickey Lolich	2.00
271 Larry Stahl	1.00
272 Ed Stroud	1.00
273 Ron Willis	1.00
274 Clyde King (Mgr.)	1.00
275 Vic Davalillo	1.00
276 Gary Wagner	1.00
277 Ron Hendricks	1.00
278 Gary Geiger	1.00
279 Roger Nelson	1.00
280 Alex Johnson	1.00
281 Ted Kubiak	1.00
282 Pat Jarvis	1.00
283 Sandy Alomar	1.00
284 Expos Rookies:	1.00
M. Wegener, J. Robertson	
285 Don Mincher	1.00
286 Dock Ellis	1.25
287 Jose Tartabull	1.00
288 Ken Holtzman	1.25
289 Bart Shirley	1.00
290 Jim Kaat	3.00
291 Vern Fuller	1.00
292 Al Downing	1.25
293 Dick Dietz	1.00
294 Jim Lemon	1.00
295 Tony Perez	7.00
296 Andy Messersmith (R)	1.50
297 Deron Johnson	1.00
298 Dave Nicholson	1.00
299 Mark Belanger	1.25
300 Felipe Alou	1.25
301 Darrell Brandon	1.00
302 Jim Pagliaroni	1.00
303 Cal Koonce	1.00
304 Padres Rookies:	3.00
Bill Davis, Clarence Gaston	
305 Dick McAuliffe	1.00
306 Jim Grant	1.00
307 Gary Kolb	1.00
308 Wade Blasingame	1.00

NO.	PLAYER	NR. MT.
309	Walt Williams	1.00
310	Tom Haller	1.00
311	Sparky Lyle (R)	8.00
312	Lee Elia	1.00
313	Bill Robinson	1.25
314	Checklist No. 4	3.00
315	Eddie Fisher	1.00
316	Hal Lanier	1.25
317	Bruce Look	1.00
318	Jack Fisher	1.00
319	Ken McMullen	1.00
320	Dal Maxvill	1.00
321	Jim McAndrew	1.00
322	Jose Vidal	1.00
323	Larry Miller	1.00
324	Tiger Rookies:	1.50
	Les Cain, Dave Campbell	
325	Jose Cardenal	1.00
326	Gary Sutherland	1.00
327	Willie Crawford	1.00
328	Joe Horlen	.50
329	Rick Joseph	.50
330	Tony Conigliaro	1.50
331	Braves Rookies:	.75
	Tom House, Gil Garrido	
332	Fred Talbot	.50
333	Ivan Murrell	.50
334	Phil Roof	.50
335	Bill Mazeroski	1.50
336	Jim Roland	.50
337	Marty Martinez	.50
338	Del Unser	.50
339	Reds Rookies:	.75
	Steve Mingori, Jose Pena	
340	Dave McNally	.75
341	Dave Adlesh	.50
342	Bubba Morton	.50
343	Dan Frisella	.50
344	Tom Matchick	.50
345	Frank Linzy	.50
346	Wayne Comer	.50
347	Randy Hundley	.50
348	Steve Hargan	.50
349	Dick Williams (Mgr.)	.50
350	Richie Allen	1.50
351	Carroll Sembera	.50
352	Paul Schaal	.50
353	Jeff Torborg	.50
354	Nate Oliver	.50
355	Phil Niekro	4.00
356	Frank Quilici	.50
357	Carl Taylor	.50
358	Athletics Rookies:	.50
	George Lauzerique, Roberto Rodriguez	
359	Dick Kelley	.50
360	Jim Wynn	.50
361	Gary Holman	.50
362	Jim Maloney	.50
363	Russ Nixon	.50
364	Tommie Agee	.50
365	Jim Fregosi	1.00
366	Bo Belinsky	.50
367	Lou Johnson	.50
368	Vic Roznovsky	.50
369	Bob Skinner (Mgr.)	.50
370	Juan Marichal	5.00
371	Sal Bando	.75
372	Adolfo Phillips	.50
373	Fred Lasher	.50
374	Bob Tillman	.50
375	Harmon Killebrew	15.00
376	Royals Rookies:	.75
	Mike Fiore, Jim Rooker	
377	Gary Bell	.50
378	Jose Herrera	.50
379	Ken Boyer	1.00
380	Stan Bahnsen	.50
381	Ed Kranepool	.50
382	Pat Corrales	.50
383	Casey Cox	.50
384	Larry Shepard	.50
385	Orlando Cepeda	2.50
386	Jim McGlothlin	.50

NO.	PLAYER	NR. MT.
387	Bobby Klaus	.50
388	Tom McCraw	.50
389	Dan Coombs	.50
390	Bill Freehan	.50
391	Ray Culp	.50
392	Bob Burda	.50
393	Gene Brabender	.50
394	Pilots Rookies:	3.00
	Lou Piniella, M. Staehle	
395	Chris Short	.50
396	Jim Campanis	.50
397	Chuck Dobson	.50
398	Tito Francona	.50
399	Bob Bailey	.50
400	Don Drysdale	9.00
401	Jake Gibbs	.50
402	Ken Boswell	.50
403	Bob Miller	.50
404	Cubs Rookies:	.75
	Vic LaRose, Gary Ross	
405	Lee May	.75
406	Phil Ortega	.50
407	Tom Egan	.50
408	Nate Colbert	.50
409	Bob Moose	.50
410	Al Kaline	11.00
411	Larry Dierker	.50
412	Checklist No. 5	7.00
413	Roland Sheldon	.50
414	Duke Sims	.50
415	Ray Washburn	.50
416	Willie McCovey (AS)	6.00
417	Ken Harrelson (AS)	1.00
418	Tommy Helms (AS)	1.00
419	Rod Carew (AS)	6.00
420	Ron Santo (AS)	1.00
421	Brooks Robinson (AS)	5.00
422	Don Kessinger (AS)	1.00
423	Bert Campaneris (AS)	1.00
424	Pete Rose (AS)	10.00
425	Carl Yastrzemski (AS)	10.00
426	Curt Flood (AS)	1.00
427	Tony Oliva (AS)	1.25
428	Lou Brock (AS)	5.00
429	Willie Horton (AS)	1.00
430	Johnny Bench (AS)	14.00
431	Bill Freehan (AS)	1.00
432	Bob Gibson (AS)	5.00
433	Denny McLain (AS)	.60
434	Jerry Koosman (AS)	1.00
435	Sam McDowell (AS)	1.00
436	Gene Alley	.50
437	Luis Alcaraz	.50
438	Gary Waslewski	.50
439	White Sox Rookies:	.50
	Ed Herrmann, Dan Lazar	
440	Willie McCovey*	15.00
441	Dennis Higgins*	.50
442	Ty Cline	.50
443	Don Wert	.50
444	Joe Moeller*	.50
445	Bobby Knoop	.50
446	Claude Raymond	.50
447	Ralph Houk (Mgr.)*	.65
448	Bob Tolan	.50
449	Paul Lindblad	.50
450	Billy Williams	7.00
451	Rich Rollins*	.50
452	Al Ferrara*	.50
453	Mike Cuellar	1.25
454	Phillies Rookies:*	.75
	Larry Colton, Don Money	
455	Sonny Siebert	.50
456	Bud Harrelson	.50
457	Dalton Jones	.50
458	Curt Blefary	.50
459	Dave Boswell	.50
460	Joe Torre	1.25
461	Mike Epstein*	.50
462	Red Schoendienst	3.00
463	Dennis Ribant	.50
464	Dave Marshall*	.50
465	Tommy John	4.00
466	John Boccabella	.50

NO.	PLAYER	NR. MT.
467	Tom Reynolds	.50
468	Pirates Rookies:*	.75
	Bruce Del Canton, Bob Robertson	
469	Chico Ruiz	.50
470	Mel Stottlemyre*	1.25
471	Ted Savage*	.50
472	Jim Price	.50
473	Jose Arcia*	.50
474	Tom Murphy	.50
475	Tim McCarver	1.50
476	Boston Rookies:*	.75
	Ken Brett, Gerry Moses	
477	Jeff James	.50
478	Don Buford	.50
479	Richie Scheinblum	.50
480	Tom Seaver	100.00
481	Bill Melton	.50
482	Jim Gosger*	.50
483	Ted Abernathy	.50
484	Joe Gordon	.50
485	Gaylord Perry*	7.00
486	Paul Casanova*	.50
487	Denis Menke	.50
488	Joe Sparma	.50
489	Clete Boyer	.75
490	Matty Alou	.75
491	Twins Rookies:*	.75
	Jerry Crider, George Mitterwald	
492	Tony Cloninger	.50
493	Wes Parker*	.50
494	Ken Berry	.50
495	Bert Campaneris	.75
496	Larry Jaster	.50
497	Julian Javier	.50
498	Juan Pizarro	.50
499	Astro Rookies:	.75
	Don Bryant, Steve Shea	
500	Mickey Mantle*	175.00
501	Tony Gonzalez*	.50
502	Minnie Rojas	.50
503	Larry Brown	.50
504	Checklist No. 6	2.00
505	Bobby Bolin*	.50
506	Paul Blair	.50
507	Cookie Rojas	.50
508	Moe Drabowsky	.50
509	Manny Sanguillen	.50
510	Rod Carew	50.00
511	Diego Segui*	.50
512	Cleon Jones	.50
513	Camilo Pascual	1.00
514	Mike Lum	.75
515	Dick Green	.75
516	Earl Weaver (Mgr.)	5.00
517	Mike McCormick	.75
518	Fred Whitfield	.75
519	Yankees Rookies:	1.00
	G. Kenney, Len Boehmer	
520	Bob Veale	1.00
521	George Thomas	.75
522	Joe Hoerner	.75
523	Bob Chance	.75
524	Expos Rookies:	.75
	Jose Laboy, Floyd Wicker	
525	Earl Wilson	.75
526	Hector Torres	.75
527	Al Lopez (Mgr.)	2.50
528	Claude Osteen	.75
529	Ed Kirkpatrick	.75
530	Cesar Tovar	.75
531	Dick Farrell	.75
532	Bird Hill Aces:	1.00
	D. McNally, T. Phoebus, J. Hardin, M. Cuellar	
533	Nolan Ryan	350.00
534	Jerry McNertney	.75
535	Phil Regan	.75
536	Padres Rookies:	1.00
	D. Breeden, Dave Roberts	
537	Mike Paul	.75
538	Charlie Smith	.75
539	Ted Shows How:	4.00
	Mike Epstein, Ted Williams	

NO.	PLAYER	NR. MT.
540	Curt Flood	1.00
541	Joe Verbanic	.75
542	Bob Aspromonte	.75
543	Fred Newman	.75
544	Tigers Rookies:	1.00
	Mike Kilkenny, Ron Woods	
545	Willie Stargell	12.00
546	Jim Nash	.75
547	Billy Martin (Mgr.)	4.00
548	Bob Locker	.75
549	Ron Brand	.75
550	Brooks Robinson	15.00
551	Wayne Granger	.75
552	Dodgers Rookies:	1.25
	Ted Sizemore, Bill Sudakis	
553	Ron Davis	.75
554	Frank Bertaina	.75
555	Jim Hart	.75
556	A's Stars:	1.00
	Bert Campaneris, Sal Bando, Danny Cater	
557	Frank Fernandez	.75
558	Tom Burgmeier	.75
559	Cardinals Rookies:	.75
	Joe Hague, Jim Hicks	
560	Luis Tiant	1.50
561	Ron Clark	.75
562	Bob Watson (R)	2.50
563	Marty Pattin	.75
564	Gil Hodges (Mgr.)	6.00
565	Hoyt Wilhelm	5.00
566	Ron Hansen	.75
567	Pirates Rookies:	.75
	Elvio Jimenez, Jim Shellenback	
568	Cecil Upshaw	.75
569	Billy Harris	.75
570	Ron Santo	2.00
571	Cap Peterson	.75
572	Giants Heroes:	8.00
	Willie McCovey, Juan Marichal	
573	Jim Palmer	25.00
574	George Scott	.75
575	Bill Singer	.75
576	Phillies Rookies:	.75
	Ron Stone, Bill Wilson	
577	Mike Hegan	.75
578	Don Bosch	.75
579	Dave Nelson	.75
580	Jim Northrup	.75
581	Gary Nolan	.75
582	Checklist No. 7	3.00
583	Clyde Wright	.75
584	Don Mason	.75
585	Ron Swoboda	.75
586	Tim Cullen	.75
587	Joe Rudi (R)	2.50
588	Bill White	2.00
589	Joe Pepitone	1.25
590	Rico Carty	1.00
591	Mike Hedlund	1.00
592	Padres Rookies:	1.00
	R. Robles, Al Santorini	
593	Don Nottebart	1.00
594	Dooley Womack	1.00
595	Lee Maye	1.00
596	Chuck Hartenstein	1.00
597	AL Rookies:	60.00
	Bob Floyd, Larry Burchart, Rollie Fingers	
598	Ruben Amaro	1.00
599	John Boozer	1.00
600	Tony Oliva	3.00
601	Tug McGraw	1.50
602	Cubs Rookies:	1.00
	Alec Distaso, Jim Qualls, Don Young	
603	Joe Keough	1.00
604	Bobby Etheridge	1.00
605	Dick Ellsworth	1.00
606	Gene Mauch (Mgr.)	1.00
607	Dick Bosman	1.00
608	Dick Simpson	1.00

NO.	PLAYER	NR. MT.
609	Phil Gagliano	1.00
610	Jim Hardin	1.00
611	Braves Rookies:	1.00
	Bob Didier, Walt Hriniak,	
	Gary Neibauer	
612	Jack Aker	1.00
613	Jim Beauchamp	1.00
614	Houston Rookies:	1.00
	Tom Griffin, Skip Guinn	
615	Len Gabrielson	1.00
616	Don McMahon	1.00
617	Jesse Gonder	1.00
618	Ramon Webster	1.00
619	Royals Rookies:	1.25
	Pat Kelly, Juan Rios,	
	Bill Butler	
620	Dean Chance	1.00
621	Bill Voss	1.00
622	Dan Osinski	1.00
623	Hank Allen	1.00

NO.	PLAYER	NR. MT.
624	NL Rookies:	1.00
	Darrel Chaney, Duffy Dyer,	
	Terry Harmon	
625	Mack Jones	1.00
626	Gene Michael	1.00
627	George Stone	1.00
628	Red Sox Rookies:	1.50
	Bill Conigliaro, Syd	
	O'Brien, Fred Wenz	
629	Jack Hamilton	1.00
630	Bobby Bonds (R)	15.00
631	John Kennedy	1.00
632	Jon Warden	1.00
633	Harry Walker (Mgr.)	1.00
634	Andy Etchebarren	1.00
635	George Culver	1.00
636	Woodie Held	1.00
637	Padres Rookies:	1.00
	Jerry DaVanon, Frank	
	Reberger, Clay Kirby	

NO.	PLAYER	NR. MT.
638	Ed Sprague	1.00
639	Barry Moore	1.00
640	Fergie Jenkins	5.00
641	NL Rookies:	1.00
	Bobby Darwin, John Miller,	
	Tommy Dean	
642	John Hiller	1.00
643	Billy Cowan	1.00
644	Chuck Hinton	1.00
645	George Brunet	1.00
646	Expos Rookies:	1.00
	Carl Morton, Dan McGinn	
647	Dave Wickersham	1.00
648	Bobby Wine	1.00
649	Al Jackson	1.00
650	Ted Williams (Mgr.)	9.00
651	Gus Gil	1.00
652	Eddie Watt	1.00
653	Aurelio Rodriguez	2.00
	(Photo of Angels Batboy)	

NO.	PLAYER	NR. MT.
654	White Sox Rookies:	1.25
	Carlos May, Don Secrist,	
	Rich Morales	
655	Mike Hershberger	1.00
656	Dan Schneider	1.00
657	Bobby Murcer	2.00
658	AL Rookies:	1.00
	Tom Hall, Bill Burbach,	
	Jim Miles	
659	Johnny Podres	1.25
660	Reggie Smith	2.00
661	Jim Merritt	1.00
662	Royals Rookies:	1.50
	Dick Drago, Bob Oliver,	
	George Spriggs	
663	Dick Radatz	1.00
664	Ron Hunt (Exc. $.50)	2.00

1970 Topps.... Complete Set of 720 Cards—Value $900.00 (Exc.); $1600.00 (Near Mint)

Features the rookie cards of Thurman Munson, Darrell Evans, Vida Blue, and Bill Buckner. The high numbers are 634 to 720. Card 588 (checklist) exists with *Adolpho* misspelled *Adolfo*—worth $7.00

  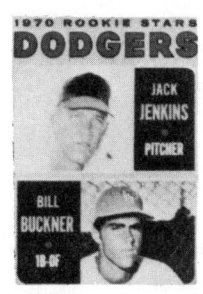  

NO.	PLAYER	NR. MT.
1	Champ Mets (Exc. $2.00)	10.00
2	Diego Segui	.40
3	Darrel Chaney	.40
4	Tom Egan	.40
5	Wes Parker	.40
6	Grant Jackson	.40
7	Indians Rookies:	.40
	Gary Boyd, Russ Nagelson	
8	Jose Martinez	.40
9	Checklist No. 1	2.50
10	Carl Yastrzemski	30.00
11	Nate Colbert	.40
12	John Hiller	.40
13	Jack Hiatt	.40
14	Hank Allen	.40
15	Larry Dierker	.40
16	Charlie Metro	.40
17	Hoyt Wilhelm	4.00
18	Carlos May	.40
19	John Boccabella	.40
20	Dave McNally	.60
21	A's Rookies:	2.50
	Gene Tenace, Vida Blue	
22	Ray Washburn	.40
23	Bill Robinson	.60
24	Dick Selma	.40
25	Cesaer Tovar	.40
26	Tug McGraw	1.25
27	Chuck Hinton	.40
28	Billy Wilson	.40
29	Sandy Alomar	.40
30	Matty Alou	.65
31	Marty Pattin	.40
32	Harry Walker	.40
33	Don Wert	.40
34	Willie Crawford	.40
35	Joe Horlen	.40

NO.	PLAYER	NR. MT.
36	Red Rookies:	.40
	D. Breeden, B. Carbo	
37	Dick Drago	.40
38	Mack Jones	.40
39	Mike Nagy	.40
40	Rich Allen	1.25
41	George Lauzerique	.40
42	Tito Fuentes	.40
43	Jack Aker	.40
44	Roberto Pena	.40
45	Dave Johnson	1.00
46	Ken Rudolph	.40
47	Bob Miller	.40
48	Gil Garrido	.40
49	Tim Cullen	.40
50	Tommy Agee	.60
51	Bob Christian	.40
52	Bruce Dal Canton	.40
53	John Kennedy	.40
54	Jeff Torborg	.50
55	John Odom	.40
56	Phillies Rookies:	.40
	Joe Lis, Scott Reid	
57	Pat Kelly	.40
58	Dave Marshall	.40
59	Dick Ellsworth	.40
60	Jim Wynn	.60
61	NL Batting Leaders:	4.00
	Cleon Jones, Pete Rose,	
	Bob Clemente	
62	AL Batting Leaders:	1.50
	Rod Carew, Reggie Smith,	
	Tony Oliva	
63	NL RBI Leaders:	1.50
	Ron Santo, Tony Perez,	
	Willie McCovey	

NO.	PLAYER	NR. MT.
64	AL RBI Leaders:	2.00
	Harmon Killebrew, Boog	
	Powell, Reggie Jackson	
65	NL Home Run Leaders:	2.50
	Hank Aaron, Willie	
	McCovey, Lee May	
66	AL Home Run Leaders:	3.00
	Harmon Killebrew, Frank	
	Howard, Reggie Jackson	
67	NL ERA Leaders:	4.00
	Bob Gibson, Juan	
	Marichal, Steve Carlton	
68	AL ERA Leaders:	1.50
	Dick Bosman, Jim Palmer,	
	Mike Cuellar	
69	NL Pitching Leaders:	3.00
	Phil Niekro, Tom Seave	
	F. Jenkins, Juan Marich	
70	AL Pitching Leaders:	1.50
	Dennis McLain, Mike	
	Cuellar, Dave McNally,	
	Jim Perry, Dave Boswell,	
	Mel Stottlemyre	
71	NL Strikeout Leaders:	1.50
	Fergie Jenkins, Bob	
	Gibson, Bill Singer	
72	AL Strikeout Leaders:	1.50
	Andy Messersmith, Sam	
	McDowell, Mickey Lolich	
73	Wayne Granger	.40
74	Angels Rookies:	.60
	Greg Washburn, Wally Wolf	
75	Jim Kaat	2.00
76	Carl Taylor	.40
77	Frank Linzy	.40
78	Joe Lahoud	.40
79	Clay Kirby	.40

NO.	PLAYER	NR. MT.
80	Don Kessinger	.40
81	Dave May	.40
82	Frank Fernandez	.40
83	Don Cardwell	.40
84	Paul Casanova	.40
85	Max Alvis	.40
86	Lum Harris (Mgr.)	.40
87	Steve Renko	.40
88	Pilots Rookies:	.40
	Miguel Fuentes, Dick Baney	
89	Juan Rios	.40
90	Tim McCarver	1.50
91	Rich Morales	.40
92	George Culver	.40
93	Rick Renick	.40
94	Fred Patek	.40
95	Earl Wilson	.40
96	Cardinals Rookies:	2.00
	Leron Lee, Jerry Reuss	
97	Joe Moeller	.40
98	Gates Brown	.40
99	Bobby Pfeil	.40
100	Mel Stottlemyre	.75
101	Bobby Floyd	.40
102	Joe Rudi	.75
103	Frank Reberger	.40
104	Gerry Moses	.40
105	Tony Gonzalez	.40
106	Darold Knowles	.40
107	Bobby Etheridge	.40
108	Tom Burgmeier	.40
109	Expos Rookies:	.60
	Garry Jestadt, Carl Morton	
110	Bob Moose	.40
111	Mike Hegan	.40
112	Dave Nelson	.40
113	Jim Ray	.40

NO.	PLAYER	NR. MT.
114	Gene Michael	.40
115	Alex Johnson	.40
116	Sparky Lyle	1.00
117	Don Young	.40
118	George Mitterwald	.40
119	Chuck Taylor	.40
120	Sal Bando	.60
121	Orioles Rookies:	.60
	Fred Beene, Terry Crowley	
122	George Stone	.40
123	Don Gutteridge (Mgr.)	.40
124	Larry Jaster	.40
125	Deron Johnson	.40
126	Marty Martinez	.40
127	Joe Coleman	.40
128	Checklist No. 2	2.50
129	Jimmie Price	.40
130	Ollie Brown	.40
131	Dodgers Rookies:	.60
	Ray Lamb, Bob Stinson	
132	Jim McGlothlin	.40
133	Clay Carroll	.40
134	Danny Walton	.40
135	Dick Dietz	.40
136	Steve Hargan	.40
137	Art Shamsky	.40
138	Joe Foy	.40
139	Rich Nye	.40
140	Reggie Jackson	110.00
141	Pirates Rookies:	.60
	Dave Cash, Johnny Jeter	
142	Fritz Peterson	.40
143	Phil Gagliano	.40
144	Ray Culp	.40
145	Rico Carty	.75
146	Danny Murphy	.40
147	Angel Hermoso	.40
148	Earl Weaver (Mgr.)	1.00
149	Billy Champion	.50
150	Harmon Killebrew	7.00
151	Dave Roberts	.40
152	Ike Brown	.40
153	Gary Gentry	.40
154	Senators Rookies:	.60
	Jim Miles, Jan Dukes	
155	Denis Menke	.40
156	Eddie Fisher	.40
157	Manny Mota	.60
158	Jerry McNertney	.40
159	Tommy Helms	.50
160	Phil Niekro	4.00
161	Richie Scheinblum	.40
162	Jerry Johnson	.40
163	Syd O'Brien	.40
164	Ty Cline	.40
165	Ed Kirkpatrick	.40
166	Al Oliver	2.50
167	Bill Burbach	.40
168	Dave Watkins	.40
169	Tom Hall	.40
170	Billy Williams	5.00
171	Jim Nash	.40
172	Braves Rookies:	1.00
	Garry Hill, Ralph Garr	
173	Jim Hicks	.40
174	Ted Sizemore	.40
175	Dick Bosman	.40
176	Jim Hart	.50
177	Jim Northrup	.40
178	Denny Lemaster	.40
179	Ivan Murrell	.40
180	Tommy John	2.50
181	Sparky Anderson	.75
182	Dick Hall	.40
183	Jerry Grote	.40
184	Ray Fosse	.40
185	Don Mincher	.40
186	Rick Joseph	.40
187	Mike Hedlund	.40
188	Manny Sanguillen	.60
189	Yankees Rookies:	90.00
	Thurman Munson, Dave McDonald	
190	Joe Torre	1.25
191	Vicente Romo	.40
192	Jim Qualls	.40
193	Mike Wegener	.40
194	Chuck Manuel	.40
195	NL Playoff Game 1:	3.50
	Seaver Wins Opener	
196	NL Playoff Game 2:	1.50
	Mets Show Muscle	
197	NL Playoff Game 3:	5.00
	Ryan Saves the Day	
198	We're Number One	1.50
	Mets Celebrate	
199	AL Playoff Game 1:	1.50
	Orioles Win Squeaker	
200	AL Playoff Game 2:	1.50
	Powell Scores Winning Run	
201	AL Playoff Game 3:	1.50
	Birds Wrap it Up	
202	Sweep Twins in Three!.	1.50
	Orioles Celebrate	
203	Rudy May	.40
204	Len Gabrielson	.40
205	Bert Campaneris	.60
206	Clete Boyer	.40
207	Tigers Rookies:	.65
	Norman McRae, Bob Reed	
208	Fred Gladding	.40
209	Ken Suarez	.40
210	Juan Marichal	6.00
211	Ted Williams (Mgr.)	7.00
212	Al Santorini	.40
213	Andy Etchebarren	.40
214	Ken Boswell	.40
215	Reggie Smith	1.00
216	Chuck Hartenstein	.40
217	Ron Hansen	.40
218	Ron Stone	.40
219	Jerry Kenney	.40
220	Steve Carlton	20.00
221	Ron Brand	.40
222	Jim Rooker	.40
223	Nate Oliver	.40
224	Steve Barber	.40
225	Lee May	.60
226	Ron Perranoski	.50
227	Astros Rookies:	1.00
	J. Mayberry, B. Watkins	
228	Aurelio Rodriguez	.40
229	Rich Robertson	.40
230	Brooks Robinson	10.00
231	Luis Tiant	1.00
232	Bob Didier	.40
233	Lew Krausse	.40
234	Tommy Dean	.40
235	Mike Epstein	.40
236	Bob Veale	.40
237	Russ Gibson	.40
238	Jose Laboy	.40
239	Ken Berry	.40
240	Fergie Jenkins	3.00
241	Royals Rookies:	.60
	A. Fitzmorris, S. Northey	
242	Walter Alston (Mgr.)	1.50
243	Joe Sparma	.40
244	Checklist No. 3	2.50
245	Leo Cardenas	.40
246	Jim McAndrew	.40
247	Lou Klimchock	.40
248	Jesus Alou	.40
249	Bob Locker	.40
250	Willie McCovey	8.00
251	Dick Schofield	.40
252	Lowell Palmer	.40
253	Ron Woods	.40
254	Camilo Pascual	.40
255	Jim Spencer	.40
256	Vic Davalillo	.40
257	Dennis Higgins	.40
258	Paul Popovich	.40
259	Tommie Reynolds	.40
260	Claude Osteen	.40
261	Curt Motton	.40
262	Twins Rookies:	.50
	Jerry Morales, Jim Williams	
263	Duane Josephson	.40
264	Rich Hebner	.60
265	Randy Hundley	.50
266	Wally Bunker	.50
267	Twins Rookies:	.60
	Paul Ratliff, Herman Hill	
268	Claude Raymond	.50
269	Cesar Gutierrez	.50
270	Chris Short	.50
271	Greg Goossen	.50
272	Hector Torres	.50
273	Ralph Houk (Mgr.)	.60
274	Gerry Arrigo	.50
275	Duke Sims	.50
276	Ron Hunt	.50
277	Paul Doyle	.50
278	Tommie Aaron	.75
279	Bill Lee	.75
280	Donn Clendenon	.75
281	Casey Cox	.50
282	Steve Huntz	.50
283	Angel Bravo	.50
284	Jack Baldschun	.50
285	Paul Blair	.50
286	Dodgers Rookies:	8.00
	Bill Buckner, Jack Jenkins	
287	Fred Talbot	.50
288	Larry Hisle	.60
289	Gene Brabender	.50
290	Rod Carew	30.00
291	Leo Durocher (Mgr.)	1.00
292	Eddie Leon	.50
293	Bob Bailey	.50
294	Jose Azcue	.50
295	Cecil Upshaw	.50
296	Woody Woodward	.50
297	Curt Blefary	.50
298	Ken Henderson	.50
299	Buddy Bradford	.50
300	Tom Seaver	60.00
301	Chico Salmon	.50
302	Jeff James	.50
303	Brant Alyea	.50
304	Bill Russell (R)	1.50
305	World Series Game 1	1.50
	Buford's Leadoff Homer	
306	World Series Game 2	1.50
	Clendenon's Homer	
307	World Series Game 3	1.50
	Agee's Catch	
308	World Series Game 4	1.50
	Martin's Bunt	
309	World Series Game 5	1.50
	Koosman Shuts Door	
310	World Series Celebration	1.50
	Mets Whoop it Up	
311	Dick Green	.50
312	Mike Torrez	.60
313	Mayo Smith (Mgr.)	.50
314	Bill McCool	.50
315	Luis Aparicio	4.00
316	Skip Guinn	.50
317	Red Sox Rookies:	.75
	B. Conigliaro, L. Alvarado	
318	Willie Smith	.50
319	Clay Dalrymple	.50
320	Jim Maloney	.50
321	Lou Piniella	2.00
322	Luke Walker	.50
323	Wayne Comer	.50
324	Tony Taylor	.50
325	Dave Boswell	.50
326	Bill Voss	.50
327	Hal King	.50
328	George Brunet	.50
329	Chris Cannizzaro	.50
330	Lou Brock	7.00
331	Chuck Dobson	.50
332	Bobby Wine	.50
333	Bobby Murcer	1.00
334	Phil Regan	.50
335	Bill Freehan	.75
336	Del Unser	.50
337	Mike McCormick	.50
338	Paul Schaal	.50
339	Johnny Edwards	.50
340	Tony Conigliaro	.75
341	Bill Sudakis	.50
342	Wilbur Wood	.50
343	Checklist No. 4	2.50
344	Marcelino Lopez	.50
345	Al Ferrara	.50
346	Red Schoendienst	2.50
347	Russ Snyder	.50
348	Mets Rookies:	.60
	M. Jorgensen, J. Hudson	
349	Steve Hamilton	.50
350	Roberto Clemente	35.00
351	Tom Murphy	.50
352	Bob Barton	.50
353	Stan Williams	.50
354	Amos Otis	.60
355	Doug Rader	.50
356	Fred Lasher	.50
357	Bob Burda	.50
358	Pedro Borbon	.50
359	Phil Roof	.50
360	Curt Flood	.75
361	Ray Jarvis	.50
362	Joe Hague	.50
363	Tom Shopay	.50
364	Dan McGinn	.50
365	Zoilo Versalles	.50
366	Barry Moore	.50
367	Mike Lum	.50
368	Ed Herrmann	.50
369	Alan Foster	.50
370	Tommy Harper	.50
371	Rod Gaspar	.50
372	Dave Guisti	.50
373	Roy White	.60
374	Tommie Sisk	.50
375	Johnny Callison	.50
376	Lefty Phillips (Mgr.)	.50
377	Bill Butler	.50
378	Jim Davenport	.50
379	Tom Tischinski	.50
380	Tony Perez	3.00
381	Athletics Rookies:	.60
	Bobby Brooks, Mike Olivo	
382	Jack DiLauro	.50
383	Mickey Stanley	.60
384	Gary Neibauer	.50
385	George Scott	.60
386	Bill Dillman	.50
387	Baltimore Orioles	1.00
388	Byron Browne	.50
389	Jim Shellenback	.50
390	Willie Davis	.75
391	Larry Brown	.50
392	Walt Hriniak	.50
393	John Gelnar	.50
394	Gil Hodges (Mgr.)	3.00
395	Walt Williams	.50
396	Steve Blass	.50
397	Roger Repoz	.50
398	Bill Stoneman	.50
399	New York Yankees	1.50
400	Denny McLain	1.50
401	Giants Rookies:	.60
	John Harrell, B. Williams	
402	Ellie Rodriguez	.50
403	Jim Bunning	2.50
404	Rich Reese	.50
405	Bill Hands	.50
406	Mike Andrews	.50
407	Bob Watson	.60
408	Paul Lindblad	.50
409	Bob Tolan	.50
410	Boog Powell	2.50
411	L.A. Dodgers	1.50
412	Larry Burchart	.50
413	Sonny Jackson	.50
414	Paul Edmondson	.50
415	Julian Javier	.50
416	Joe Verbanic	.50
417	John Bateman	.50
418	John Donaldson	.50
419	Ron Taylor	.50
420	Ken McMullen	.50
421	Pat Dobson	.50
422	Kansas City Royals	.75

NO.	PLAYER	NR. MT.
423	Jerry May	.50
424	Mike Kilkenny	.50
425	Bobby Bonds	4.00
426	Bill Rigney (Mgr.)	.50
427	Fred Norman	.50
428	Don Buford	.50
429	Cubs Rookies:	.60
	Randy Bobb, Jim Cosman	
430	Andy Messersmith	.75
431	Ron Swoboda	.75
432	Checklist No. 5	2.50
433	Ron Bryant	.50
434	Felipe Alou	.60
435	Nelson Briles	.50
436	Philadelphia Phillies	1.50
437	Danny Cater	.50
438	Pat Jarvis	.50
439	Lee Maye	.50
440	Bill Mazeroski	.75
441	John O'Donoghue	.50
442	Gene Mauch (Mgr.)	.60
443	Al Jackson	.50
444	White Sox Rookies:	.60
	Billy Farmer, John Matias	
445	Vada Pinson	1.00
446	B. Grabarkewitz	.50
447	Lee Stange	.50
448	Houston Astros	1.00
449	Jim Palmer	15.00
450	Willie McCovey (AS)	4.00
451	Boog Powell (AS)	1.00
452	Felix Millan (AS)	.75
453	Rod Carew (AS)	5.00
454	Ron Santo (AS)	.75
455	Brooks Robinson (AS)	4.00
456	Don Kessinger (AS)	.75
457	Rico Petrocelli (AS)	.75
458	Pete Rose (AS)	12.00
459	Reggie Jackson (AS)	15.00
460	Matty Alou (AS)	.75
461	Carl Yastrzemski (AS)	10.00
462	Hank Aaron (AS)	11.00
463	Frank Robinson (AS)	5.00
464	Johnny Bench (AS)	10.00
465	Bill Freehan (AS)	.75
466	Juan Marichal (AS)	4.00
467	Denny McLain (AS)	1.00
468	Jerry Koosman (AS)	.75
469	Sam McDowell (AS)	.75
470	Willie Stargell	9.00
471	Chris Zachary	.75
472	Atlanta Braves	1.00
473	Don Bryant	.75
474	Dick Kelley	.75
475	Dick McAuliffe	.75
476	Don Shaw	.75
477	Orioles Rookies:	.90
	Roger Freed, Al Severinsen	
478	Bob Heise	.75
479	Dick Woodson	.75
480	Glen Beckert	.75
481	Jose Tartabull	.75
482	Tom Hilgendorf	.75
483	Gail Hopkins	.75
484	Gary Nolan	.75
485	Jay Johnstone	.90
486	Terry Harmon	.75
487	Cisco Carlos	.75
488	J.C. Martin	.75
489	Eddie Kasko (Mgr.)	.75
490	Bill Singer	.75
491	Graig Nettles	4.00
492	Astros Rookies:	.75
	K. Lampard, S. Spinks	
493	Lindy McDaniel	.75
494	Larry Stahl	.75
495	Dave Morehead	.75
496	Steve Whitaker	.75
497	Eddie Watt	.75
498	Al Weis	.75
499	Skip Lockwood	.75

NO.	PLAYER	NR. MT.
500	Hank Aaron	35.00
501	Chicago White Sox	2.00
502	Rollie Fingers	10.00
503	Dal Maxvill	.75
504	Don Pavletich	.75
505	Ken Holtzman	.75
506	Ed Stroud	.75
507	Pat Corrales	.75
508	Joe Niekro	1.50
509	Montreal Expos	1.50
510	Tony Oliva	2.00
511	Joe Hoerner	.75
512	Billy Harris	.75
513	Preston Gomez (Mgr.)	.75
514	Steve Hovley	.75
515	Don Wilson	.75
516	Yankees Rookies:	1.25
	John Ellis, Jim Lyttle	
517	Joe Gibbon	.75
518	Bill Melton	.75
519	Don McMahon	.75
520	Willie Horton	1.00
521	Cal Koonce	.75
522	California Angels	1.25
523	Jose Pena	.75
524	Alvin Dark (Mgr.)	1.50
525	Jerry Adair	.75
526	Ron Herbel	.75
527	Don Bosch	.75
528	Elrod Hendricks	.75
529	Bob Aspromonte	.75
530	Bob Gibson	8.00
531	Ron Clark	.75
532	Danny Murtaugh (Mgr.)	.75
533	Buzz Stephen	.75
534	Minnesota Twins	1.50
535	Andy Kosco	.75
536	Mike Kekich	.75
537	Joe Morgan	8.00
538	Bob Humphreys	.75
539	Phillies Rookies:	.75
	Larry Bowa, Dennis Doyle	
540	Gary Peters	.75
541	Bill Heath	.75
542	Checklist No. 6	2.50
543	Clyde Wright	.75
544	Cincinnati Reds	2.50
545	Ken Harrelson	1.25
546	Ron Reed	.75
547	Rick Monday	1.50
548	Howie Reed	1.00
549	St. Louis Cardinals	1.50
550	Frank Howard	1.50
551	Dock Ellis	1.00
552	Royals Rookies:	1.00
	Dennis Paepke, Fred Rico, Don O'Riley	
553	Jim LeFebvre	1.00
554	Tom Timmermann	1.00
555	Orlando Cepeda	4.00
556	Dave Bristol	1.00
557	Ed Kranepool	1.00
558	Vern Fuller	1.00
559	Tommy Davis	1.00
560	Gaylord Perry	7.50
561	Tom McCraw	1.00
562	Ted Abernathy	1.00
563	Boston Red Sox	2.50
564	Johnny Briggs	1.00
565	Jim Hunter	8.00
566	Gene Alley	1.00
567	Bob Oliver	1.00
568	Stan Bahnsen	1.00
569	Cookie Rojas	1.00
570	Jim Fregosi	1.50
571	Jim Brewer	1.00
572	Frank Quilici	1.00
573	Padres Rookies:	1.00
	Mike Corkins, Rafael Robles, Ron Slocum	
574	Bobby Bolin	1.00

NO.	PLAYER	NR. MT.
575	Cleon Jones	1.00
576	Milt Pappas	1.00
577	Bernie Allen	1.00
578	Tom Griffin	1.00
579	Detroit Tigers	2.50
580	Pete Rose	75.00
581	Tom Satriano	1.00
582	Mike Paul	1.00
583	Hal Lanier	1.00
584	Al Downing	1.00
585	Rusty Staub	2.00
586	Rickey Clark	1.00
587	Jose Arcia	1.00
588	Checklist No. 7*	3.00
589	Joe Keough	1.00
590	Mike Cuellar	1.25
591	Mike Ryan	1.00
592	Daryl Patterson	1.00
593	Chicago Cubs	1.50
594	Jake Gibbs	1.00
595	Maury Wills	2.50
596	Mike Hershberger	1.00
597	Sonny Siebert	1.00
598	Joe Pepitone	2.00
599	Senators Rookies:	1.00
	Dick Such, Gene Martin, Dick Stelmaszek,	
600	Willie Mays	50.00
601	Pete Richert	1.00
602	Ted Savage	1.00
603	Ray Oyler	1.00
604	Clarence Gaston	1.00
605	Rick Wise	1.00
606	Chico Ruiz	1.00
607	Gary Waslewski	1.00
608	Pittsburgh Pirates	2.00
609	Buck Martinez	1.00
610	Jerry Koosman	2.00
611	Norm Cash	1.50
612	Jim Hickman	1.00
613	Dave Baldwin	1.00
614	Mike Shannon	1.00
615	Mark Belanger	1.00
616	Jim Merritt	1.00
617	Jim French	1.00
618	Billy Wynne	1.00
619	Norm Miller	1.00
620	Jim Perry	1.50
621	Braves Rookies:	15.00
	Darrell Evans, Mike McQueen, Rick Kester	
622	Don Sutton	8.00
623	Horace Clarke	1.00
624	Clyde King	1.00
625	Dean Chance	1.00
626	Dave Ricketts	1.00
627	Gary Wagner	1.00
628	Wayne Garrett	1.00
629	Merv Rettenmund	1.00
630	Ernie Banks	24.00
631	Oakland Athletics	2.00
632	Gary Sutherland	1.00
633	Roger Nelson	1.00
634	Bud Harrelson	4.00
635	Bob Allison	3.00
636	Jim Stewart	3.00
637	Cleveland Indians	6.00
638	Frank Bertaina	3.00
639	Dave Campbell	3.00
640	Al Kaline	35.00
641	Al McBean	3.00
642	Angels Rookies:	3.00
	Greg Garrett, Jarvis Tatum, Gordon Lund	
643	Jose Pagan	3.00
644	Gerry Nyman	3.00
645	Don Money	3.00
646	Jim Britton	3.00
647	Tom Matchick	3.00
648	Larry Haney	3.00
649	Jimmie Hall	3.00

NO.	PLAYER	NR. MT.
650	Sam McDowell	3.00
651	Jim Gosger	3.00
652	Rich Rollins	3.00
653	Moe Drabowsky	3.00
654	NL Rookies:	4.00
	Oscar Gamble, Boots Day, Angel Mangual	
655	John Roseboro	3.00
656	Jim Hardin	3.00
657	San Diego Padres	6.00
658	Ken Tatum	3.00
659	Pete Ward	3.00
660	Johnny Bench	160.00
661	Jerry Robertson	3.00
662	Frank Lucchesi	3.00
663	Tito Francona	3.00
664	Bob Robertson	3.00
665	Jim Lonborg	3.00
666	Adolfo Phillips	3.00
667	Bob Meyer	3.00
668	Bob Tillman	3.00
669	White Sox Rookies:	3.00
	Bart Johnson, Dan Lazar, Mickey Scott	
670	Ron Santo	5.00
671	Jim Campanis	3.00
672	Leon McFadden	3.00
673	Ted Uhlaender	3.00
674	Dave Leonhard	3.00
675	Jose Cardenal	3.00
676	Washington Senators	6.00
677	Woodie Fryman	3.00
678	Dave Duncan	3.00
679	Ray Sadecki	3.00
680	Rico Petrocelli	3.00
681	Bob Garibaldi	3.00
682	Dalton Jones	3.00
683	Reds Rookies:	4.00
	Wayne Simpson, Vern Geishert, Hal McRae	
684	Jack Fisher	3.00
685	Tom Haller	3.00
686	Jackie Hernandez	3.00
687	Bob Priddy	3.00
688	Ted Kubiak	3.00
689	Frank Tepedino	3.00
690	Ron Fairly	3.00
691	Joe Grzenda	3.00
692	Duffy Dyer	3.00
693	Bob Johnson	3.00
694	Gary Ross	3.00
695	Bobby Knoop	3.00
696	S.F. Giants	6.00
697	Jim Hannan	3.00
698	Tom Tresh	4.00
699	Hank Aguirre	3.00
700	Frank Robinson	35.00
701	Jack Billingham	3.00
702	AL Rookies:	3.00
	Bob Johnson, Ron Klimkowski, Bill Zepp	
703	Lou Marone	3.00
704	Frank Baker	3.00
705	Tony Cloninger	3.00
706	John McNamara (R)	6.00
707	Kevin Collins	3.00
708	Jose Santiago	3.00
709	Mike Fiore	3.00
710	Felix Millan	3.00
711	Ed Brinkman	3.00
712	Nolan Ryan	325.00
713	Seattle Pilots	12.00
714	Al Spangler	3.00
715	Mickey Lolich	4.00
716	Cardinals Rookies:	3.00
	Sal Campisi, R. Cleveland, Santiago Guzman	
717	Tom Phoebus	3.00
718	Ed Spiezio	3.00
719	Jim Roland	3.00
720	R. Reichardt (Exc. $1.00)	6.00

1971 Topps.... Complete Set of 752 Cards—Value $750.00 (Exc.); $1750.00 (Near Mint)

Features the rookie cards of Steve Garvey, Don Baylor and George Foster. The high numbers are 644 to 752. Semi-high numbers are 524 to 643. The cards in this set are more difficult to find in *mint* condition because the black border scratches easily.

NO. PLAYER	NR. MT.
1 World Champs (Exc. $2.00)	8.00
2 Dock Ellis	.35
3 Dick McAuliffe	.35
4 Vic Davalillo	.35
5 Thurman Munson	25.00
6 Ed Spiezio	.35
7 Jim Holt	.35
8 Mike McQueen	.35
9 George Scott	.35
10 Claude Osteen	.35
11 Elliott Maddox	.35
12 Johnny Callison	.35
13 White Sox Rookies:	.40
C. Brinkman, D. Moloney	
14 Dave Concepcion (R)	8.00
15 Andy Messersmith	.40
16 Ken Singleton (R)	2.50
17 Billy Sorrell	.35
18 Norm Miller	.35
19 Skip Pitlock	.35
20 Reggie Jackson	50.00
21 Dan McGinn	.35
22 Phil Roof	.35
23 Oscar Gamble	.45
24 Rich Hand	.35
25 Clarence Caston	.35
26 Bert Blyleven (R)	45.00
27 Pirates Rookies	.40
Fred Cambria, Gene Clines	
28 Ron Klimkowski	.35
29 Don Buford	.35
30 Phil Niekro	4.00
31 Eddie Kasko	.35
32 Jerry Da Vanon	.35
33 Del Unser	.35
34 Sandy Vance	.35
35 Lou Piniella	1.00
36 Dean Chance	.35
37 Rich McKinney	.35
38 Jim Colborn	.35
39 Tiger Rookies:	.45
L. LaGrow, Gene Lamont	
40 Lee May	.35
41 Rick Austin	.35
42 Boots Day	.35
43 Steve Kealey	.35
44 Johnny Edwards	.35
45 Jim Hunter	6.00
46 Dave Campbell	.35
47 Johnny Jeter	.35
48 Dave Baldwin	.35
49 Don Money	.35
50 Willy McCovey	7.00
51 Steve Kline	.35
52 Braves Rookies:	.60
Oscar Brown, Earl Williams	
53 Paul Blair	.35
54 Checklist No. 1	2.00
55 Steve Carlton	20.00
56 Duane Josephson	.35
57 Von Joshua	.35
58 Bill Lee	.35
59 Gene Mauch (Mgr.)	.35
60 Dick Bosman	.35
61 AL Batting Leaders:	2.00
Alex Johnson, Carl Yastrzemski, Tony Oliva	

NO. PLAYER	NR. MT.
62 NL Batting Leaders:	1.25
Joe Torre, Rico Carty, Manny Sanguillen	
63 AL RBI Leaders:	1.50
Boog Powell, Frank Robinson, Tony Conigliaro	
64 NL RBI Leaders:	2.00
Johnny Bench, Billy Williams, Tony Perez	
65 AL HR Leaders:	2.00
Frank Howard, Harmon Killebrew, C. Yastrzemski	
66 NL HR Leaders:	2.50
Johnny Bench, Billy Williams, Tony Perez	
67 AL ERA Leaders:	1.25
Clyde Wright, Diego Segui, Jim Palmer	
68 NL ERA Leaders:	1.50
Wayne Simpson, Luke Walker, Tom Seaver	
69 AL Pitching Leaders:	1.25
Mike Cuellar, Dave McNally, Jim Perry	
70 NL Pitching Leaders:	2.00
Gaylord Perry, Bob Gibson, Fergie Jenkins	
71 AL Strikeout Leaders:	1.00
Sam McDowell, Micke Lolich, Bob Johnson	
72 NL Strikeout Leaders:	2.00
Bob Gibson, Tom Seaver, Fergie Jenkins	
73 George Brunet	.35
74 Twins Rookies:	.40
Pete Hamm, Jim Nettles	
75 Gary Nolan	.35
76 Ted Savage	.35
77 Mike Compton	.35
78 Jim Spencer	.35
79 Wade Blasingame	.35
80 Bill Melton	.35
81 Felix Millan	.35
82 Casey Cox	.35
83 Met Rookies:	.45
Tim Foli, Randy Bobb	
84 Marcel Lachemann	.35
85 Bill Grabarkewitz	.35
86 Mike Kilkenny	.35
87 Jack Heidemann	.35
88 Hal King	.35
89 Ken Brett	.35
90 Joe Pepitone	.45
91 Bob Lemon (Mgr.)	1.50
92 Fred Wenz	.45
93 Senators Rookies:	.45
Norm McRae, Denny Riddleberger	
94 Don Hahn	.35
95 Luis Tiant	.75
96 Joe Hague	.35
97 Floyd Wicker	.35
98 Joe Decker	.35
99 Mark Belanger	.50
100 Pete Rose	45.00
101 Les Cain	.35

NO. PLAYER	NR. MT.
102 Astros Rookies:	1.00
Ken Forsch, Larry Howard	
103 Rich Severson	.35
104 Dan Frisella	.35
105 Tony Conigliaro	1.00
106 Tom Dukes	.35
107 Roy Foster	.35
108 John Cumberland	.35
109 Steve Hovley	.35
110 Bill Mazeroski	1.00
111 Yankee Rookies:	.45
L. Colson, B. Mitchell	
112 Manny Mota	.60
113 Jerry Crider	.35
114 Billy Conigliaro	.35
115 Donn Clendenon	.35
116 Ken Sanders	.35
117 Ted Simmons (R)	9.00
118 Cookie Rojas	.35
119 Frank Lucchesi (Mgr.)	.35
120 Willie Horton	.40
121 Cubs Rookies:	.40
J. Dunegan, R. Skidmore	
122 Eddie Watt	.35
123 Checklist No. 2	2.00
124 Don Gullett	.35
125 Ray Fosse	.35
126 Danny Coombs	.35
127 Danny Thompson	.35
128 Frank Johnson	.35
129 Aurelio Monteagudo	.35
130 Denis Menke	.35
131 Curt Blefary	.35
132 Jose Laboy	.35
133 Mickey Lolich	.75
134 Jose Arcia	.35
135 Rick Monday	.60
136 Duffy Dyer	.35
137 Marcelino Lopez	.35
138 Phillies Rookies:	.45
Joe Lis, W. Montanez	
139 Paul Casanova	.40
140 Gaylord Perry	5.00
141 Frank Quilici	.35
142 Mack Jones	.35
143 Steve Blass	.35
144 Jackie Hernandez	.35
145 Bill Singer	.35
146 Ralph Houk (Mgr.)	.40
147 Bob Priddy	.35
148 John Mayberry	.35
149 Mike Hershberger	.35
150 Sam McDowell	.60
151 Tommy Davis	.40
152 Angels Rookies:	.35
Lloyd Allen, Winston Llenas	
153 Gary Ross	.35
154 Cesar Gutierrez	.35
155 Ken Henderson	.35
156 Bart Johnson	.35
157 Bob Bailey	.35
158 Jerry Reuss	.65
159 Jarvis Tatum	.35
160 Tom Seaver	40.00
161 Coins Checklist	1.25
162 Jack Billingham	.35

NO. PLAYER	NR. MT.
163 Buck Martinez	.35
164 Reds Rookies:	.75
Frank Duffy, Milt Wilcox	
165 Cesar Tovar	.35
166 Joe Hoerner	.35
167 Tom Grieve	.75
168 Bruce Dal Canton	.35
169 Ed Herrmann	.35
170 Mike Cuellar	.60
171 Bobby Wine	.35
172 Duke Sims	.35
173 Gil Garrido	.35
174 Dave LaRoche	.35
175 Jim Hickman	.35
176 Red Sox Rookies:	.45
Bob Montgomery, Doug Griffin	
177 Hal McRae	.60
178 Dave Duncan	.35
179 Mike Corkins	.35
180 Al Kaline	12.00
181 Hal Lanier	.60
182 Al Downing	.35
183 Gil Hodges (Mgr.)	3.00
184 Stan Bahnsen	.35
185 Julian Javier	.35
186 Bob Spence	.35
187 Ted Abernathy	.35
188 Dodgers Rookies:	2.50
Mike Strahler, Bob Valentine	
189 George Mitterwald	.35
190 Bob Tolan	.35
191 Mike Andrews	.35
192 Billy Wilson	.35
193 Bob Grich (R)	2.00
194 Mike Lum	.35
195 AL Playoff Game 1	1.50
Powell Muscles Twins	
196 AL Playoff Game 2	1.50
McNally's Two Straight	
197 AL Playoff Game 3	2.00
Palmer Mows 'Em Down	
198 Orioles Celebrate	1.50
A Team Effort	
199 NL Playoff Game 1	1.50
Cline Pinch-Triple	
200 NL Playoff Game 2	1.50
Tolan Scores Third Time	
201 NL Playoff Game 3	1.50
Cline Scores Winning Run	
202 Reds Celebrate	1.50
World Series Bound	
203 Larry Gura (R)	1.00
204 Brewers Rookies:	.40
B. Smith, G. Kopacz	
205 Gerry Moses	.35
206 Checklist No. 3	2.00
207 Alan Foster	.35
208 Billy Martin	3.00
209 Steve Renko	.35
210 Rod Carew	25.00
211 Phil Hennigan	.35
212 Rich Hebner	.35
213 Frank Baker	.35
214 Al Ferrara	.35
215 Diego Segui	.35

NO.	PLAYER	NR. MT.
216	Cards Rookies:	.40
	Reggie Cleveland,	
	Luis Melendez	
217	Ed Stroud	.35
218	Tony Cloninger	.35
219	Elrod Hendricks	.35
220	Ron Santo	1.00
221	Dave Morehead	.35
222	Bob Watson	.50
223	Cecil Upshaw	.35
224	Alan Gallagher	.35
225	Gary Peters	.35
226	Bill Russell	.50
227	Floyd Weaver	.35
228	Wayne Garrett	.35
229	Jim Hannan	.35
230	Willie Stargell	7.50
231	Indians Rookies:	.45
	Vince Colbert,	
	John Lowenstein	
232	John Strohmayer	.35
233	Larry Bowa	2.00
234	Jim Lyttle	.35
235	Nate Colbert	.35
236	Bob Humphreys	.35
237	Cesar Cedeno (R)	2.00
238	Chuck Dobson	.35
239	R. Schoendienst (Mgr.)	1.25
240	Clyde Wright	.35
241	Dave Nelson	.35
242	Jim Ray	.35
243	Carlos May	.35
244	Bob Tillman	.35
245	Jim Kaat	2.00
246	Tony Taylor	.35
247	Royals Rookies:	.75
	Jerry Cram, Paul Splittorff	
248	Hoyt Wilhelm	3.00
249	Chico Salmon	.35
250	Johnny Bench	40.00
251	Frank Reberger	.35
252	Eddie Leon	.35
253	Bill Sudakis	.35
254	Cal Koonce	.35
255	Bob Robertson	.35
256	Tony Gonzalez	.35
257	Nelson Briles	.35
258	Dick Green	.35
259	Dave Marshall	.35
260	Tommy Harper	.35
261	Darold Knowles	.35
262	Padres Rookies:	.40
	D. Robinson, J. Williams	
263	John Ellis	.35
264	Joe Morgan	7.00
265	Jim Northrup	.35
266	Bill Stoneman	.35
267	Rich Morales	.35
268	Philadelphia Phillies	1.50
269	Gail Hopkins	.35
270	Rico Carty	.60
271	Bill Zepp	.35
272	Tommy Helms	.35
273	Pete Richert	.35
274	Ron Slocum	.35
275	Vada Pinson	1.00
276	Giants Rookies:	5.00
	M. Davison, George Foster	
277	Gary Waslewski	.35
278	Jerry Grote	.35
279	Lefty Phillips (Mgr.)	.35
280	Fergie Jenkins	4.00
281	Danny Walton	.35
282	Jose Pagan	.35
283	Dick Such	.35
284	Jim Gosger	.35
285	Sal Bando	.50
286	Jerry McNertney	.35
287	Mike Fiore	.35
288	Joe Moeller	.35
289	Chicago White Sox	1.50
290	Tony Oliva	2.50
291	George Culver	.35
292	Jay Johnstone	.35
293	Pat Corrales	.50
294	Steve Dunning	.35
295	Bobby Bonds	3.00
296	Tom Timmermann	.35
297	Johnny Briggs	.35
298	Jim Nelson	.35
299	Ed Kirkpatrick	.35
300	Brooks Robinson	10.00
301	Earl Wilson	.35
302	Phil Gagliano	.35
303	Lindy McDaniel	.35
304	Ron Brand	.35
305	Reggie Smith	.75
306	Jim Nash	.35
307	Don Wert	.35
308	St. Louis Cardinals	1.00
309	Dick Ellsworth	.35
310	Tommie Agee	.50
311	Lee Stange	.35
312	Harry Walker	.35
313	Tom Hall	.35
314	Jeff Torborg	.35
315	Ron Fairly	.50
316	Fred Scherman	.35
317	Athletic Rookies:	.35
	Angel Mangual, Jim Driscoll	
318	Rudy May	.35
319	Ty Cline	.35
320	Dave McNally	.40
321	Tom Matchick	.35
322	Jim Beauchamp	.35
323	Billy Champion	.35
324	Graig Nettles	2.50
325	Juan Marichal	5.00
326	Richie Scheinblum	.35
327	World Series Game 1	1.50
	Powell Homers	
328	World Series Game 2	1.50
	Buford Goes 2 For 4	
329	World Series Game 3	2.50
	F. Robinson Shows Muscle	
330	World Series Game 4	1.50
	Reds Stay Alive	
331	World Series Game 5	2.50
	B. Robinson Robbery	
332	World Series Celebration	1.50
	Convincing Performance	
333	Clay Kirby	.35
334	Roberto Pena	.35
335	Jerry Koosman	1.00
336	Detroit Tigers	1.00
337	Jesus Alou	.35
338	Gene Tenace	.45
339	Wayne Simpson	.35
340	Rico Petrocelli	.35
341	Steve Garvey (R)	80.00
342	Frank Tepedino	.35
343	Pirates Rookies:	.40
	Ed Acosta, M. May	
344	Ellie Rodriguez	.35
345	Joe Horlen	.35
346	Lum Harris	.35
347	Ted Uhlaender	.35
348	Fred Norman	.35
349	Rich Reese	.35
350	Billy Williams	5.00
351	Jim Shellenback	.35
352	Denny Doyle	.35
353	Carl Taylor	.35
354	Don McMahon	.35
355	Bud Harrelson	.50
356	Bob Locker	.35
357	Cincinnati Reds	1.50
358	Danny Cater	.35
359	Ron Reed	.35
360	Jim Fregosi	.60
361	Don Sutton	4.00
362	Orioles Rookies:	.40
	Mike Adamson, R. Freed	
363	Mike Nagy	.35
364	Tommy Dean	.35
365	Bob Johnson	.35
366	Ron Stone	.35
367	Dalton Jones	.35
368	Bob Veale	.35
369	Checklist No. 4	2.00
370	Joe Torre	2.00
371	Jack Hiatt	.35
372	Lew Krausse	.35
373	Tom McCraw	.35
374	Clete Boyer	.50
375	Steve Hargan	.35
376	Expos Rookies:	.35
	C. Mashore, E. McAnally	
377	Greg Garrett	.35
378	Tito Fuentes	.35
379	Wayne Granger	.35
380	Ted Williams (Mgr.)	4.00
381	Fred Gladding	.35
382	Jake Gibbs	.35
383	Rod Gaspar	.35
384	Rollie Fingers	6.00
385	Maury Wills	2.00
386	Boston Red Sox	1.00
387	Ron Herbel	.35
388	Al Oliver	2.00
389	Ed Brinkman	.35
390	Glenn Beckert	.35
391	Twins Rookies:	.35
	Steve Brye, Cotton Nash	
392	Grant Jackson	.35
393	Merv Rettenmund	.35
394	Clay Carroll	.75
395	Roy White	1.25
396	Dick Schofield	.75
397	Alvin Dark (Mgr.)	1.00
398	Howie Reed	.75
399	Jim French	.75
400	Hank Aaron	30.00
401	Tom Murphy	.75
402	Los Angeles Dodgers	1.50
403	Joe Coleman	.75
404	Astros Rookies:	.75
	B. Harris, R. Metzger	
405	Leo Cardenas	.75
406	Ray Sadecki	.75
407	Joe Rudi	1.00
408	Rafael Robles	.75
409	Don Pavletich	.75
410	Ken Holtzman	1.00
411	George Spriggs	.75
412	Jerry Johnson	.75
413	Pat Kelly	.75
414	Woodie Fryman	.75
415	Mike Hegan	.75
416	Gene Alley	.75
417	Dick Hall	.75
418	Adolfo Phillips	.75
419	Ron Hansen	.75
420	Jim Merritt	.75
421	John Stephenson	.75
422	Frank Bertaina	.75
423	Tigers Rookies:	.75
	T. Marting, D. Saunders	
424	Roberto Rodriguez	.75
425	Doug Rader	1.00
426	Chris Cannizzaro	.75
427	Bernie Allen	.75
428	Jim McAndrew	.75
429	Chuck Hinton	.75
430	Wes Parker	1.00
431	Tom Burgmeier	.75
432	Bob Didier	.75
433	Skip Lockwood	.75
434	Gary Sutherland	.75
435	Jose Cardenal	.75
436	Wilbur Wood	.75
437	Danny Murtaugh (Mgr.)	.75
438	Mike McCormick	.75
439	Phillies Rookies:	2.50
	Greg Luzinski, Scott Reid	
440	Bert Campaneris	1.00
441	Milt Pappas	.75
442	California Angels	1.50
443	Rich Robertson	.75
444	Jimmie Price	.75
445	Art Shamsky	.75
446	Bobby Bolin	.75
447	Cesar Geronimo	.75
448	Dave Roberts	.75
449	Brant Alyea	.75
450	Bob Gibson	9.00
451	Joe Keough	.75
452	John Boccabella	.75
453	Terry Crowley	.75
454	Mike Paul	.75
455	Don Kessinger	1.00
456	Bob Meyer	.75
457	Willie Smith	.75
458	White Sox Rookies:	1.00
	Ron Lolich, Dave Lemonds	
459	Jim LeFebvre	.75
460	Fritz Peterson	.75
461	Jim Hart	1.00
462	Senators Team	1.50
463	Tom Kelley	.75
464	Aurelio Rodriguez	.75
465	Tim McCarver	2.00
466	Ken Berry	.75
467	Al Santorini	.75
468	Frank Fernandez	.75
469	Bob Aspromonte	.75
470	Bob Oliver	.75
471	Tom Griffin	.75
472	Ken Rudolph	.75
473	Gary Wagner	.75
474	Jim Fairey	.75
475	Ron Perranoski	1.00
476	Dal Maxvill	.75
477	Earl Weaver (Mgr.)	1.50
478	Bernie Carbo	.75
479	Dennis Higgins	.75
480	Manny Sanguillen	1.00
481	Daryl Patterson	.75
482	San Diego Padres	1.25
483	Gene Michael	1.00
484	Don Wilson	.75
485	Ken McMullen	.75
486	Steve Huntz	.75
487	Paul Schaal	.75
488	Jerry Stephenson	.75
489	Luis Alvardao	.75
490	Deron Johnson	.75
491	Jim Hardin	.75
492	Ken Boswell	.75
493	Dave May	.75
494	Braves Rookies:	1.00
	Ralph Garr, Rick Kester	
495	Felipe Alou	1.00
496	Woody Woodward	1.00
497	Horacio Pina	.75
498	John Kennedy	.75
499	Checklist No. 5	2.00
500	Jim Perry	1.00
501	Andy Etchebarren	.75
502	Chicago Cubs	1.50
503	Gates Brown	.75
504	Ken Wright	.75
505	Ollie Brown	.75
506	Bobby Knoop	.75
507	George Stone	.75
508	Roger Repoz	.75
509	Jim Grant	.75
510	Ken Harrelson	1.25
511	Chris Short	.75
512	Red Sox Rookies:	1.00
	Dick Mills, Mike Garman	
513	Nolan Ryan	125.00
514	Ron Woods	.75
515	Carl Morton	.75
516	Ted Kubiak	.75
517	Charlie Fox (Mgr.)	.75
518	Joe Grzenda	.75
519	Willie Crawford	.75
520	Tommy John	3.00
521	Leron Lee	.75
522	Minnesota Twins	1.50
523	John Odom	.75
524	Mickey Stanley	1.50
525	Ernie Banks	20.00
526	Ray Jarvis	1.50
527	Cleon Jones	1.50
528	Wally Bunker	1.50
529	NL Rookies:	4.00
	Enzo, Hernandez, Bill	
	Buckner, Marty Perez	

NO. PLAYER	NR. MT.
530 Carl Yastrzemski	40.00
531 Mike Torrez	1.50
532 Bill Rigney (Mgr.)	1.50
533 Mike Ryan	1.50
534 Luke Walker	1.50
535 Curt Flood	2.00
536 Claude Raymond	1.50
537 Tom Egan	1.50
538 Angel Bravo	1.50
539 Larry Brown	1.50
540 Larry Dierker	1.50
541 Bob Burda	1.50
542 Bob Miller	1.50
543 New York Yankees	3.00
544 Vida Blue	3.00
545 Dick Dietz	1.50
546 John Matias	1.50
547 Pat Dobson	1.50
548 Don Mason	1.50
549 Jim Brewer	1.50
550 Harmon Killebrew	16.00
551 Frank Linzy	1.50
552 Buddy Bradford	1.50
553 Kevin Collins	1.50
554 Lowell Palmer	1.50
555 Walt Williams	1.50
556 Jim McGlothlin	1.50
557 Tom Satriano	1.50
558 Hector Torres	1.50
559 AL Rookies:	1.50
Gary Jones, Terry Cox	
Bill Gogolewski	
560 Rusty Staub	3.00
561 Syd O'Brien	1.50
562 Dave Giusti	1.50
563 Giants Team	2.50
564 Al Fitzmorris	1.50
565 Jim Wynn	1.50
566 Tim Cullen	1.50
567 Walt Alston (Mgr.)	2.50
568 Sal Campisi	1.50
569 Ivan Murrell	1.50
570 Jim Palmer	20.00
571 Ted Sizemore	1.50
572 Jerry Kenney	1.50
573 Ed Kranepool	1.50
574 Jim Bunning	3.00
575 Bill Freehan	2.00
576 Cubs Rookies:	1.50
Brock Davis, Adrian	
Garrett, Garry Jestadt	
577 Jim Lonborg	2.00
578 Ron Hunt	1.50
579 Marty Pattin	1.50
580 Tony Perez	4.00
581 Roger Nelson	1.50
582 Dave Cash	1.50
583 Ron Cook	1.50
584 Cleveland Indians	3.00
585 Willie Davis	1.50
586 Dick Woodson	1.50

NO. PLAYER	NR. MT.
587 Sonny Jackson	1.50
588 Tom Bradley	1.50
589 Bob Barton	1.50
590 Alex Johnson	1.50
591 Jackie Brown	1.50
592 Randy Hundley	1.50
593 Jack Aker	1.50
594 Cardinals Rookies:	2.00
Bob Chlupsa, Bob Stir	
Al Hrabosky	
595 Dave Johnson	2.50
596 Mike Jorgensen	1.50
597 Ken Suarez	1.50
598 Rick Wise	1.50
599 Norm Cash	2.50
600 Willie Mays	60.00
601 Ken Tatum	1.50
602 Marty Martinez	1.50
603 Pittsburgh Pirates	3.00
604 John Gelnar	1.50
605 Orlando Cepeda	4.00
606 Chuck Taylor	1.50
607 Paul Ratliff	1.50
608 Mike Wegener	1.50
609 Leo Durocher (Mgr.)	3.00
610 Amos Otis	2.00
611 Tom Phoebus	1.50
612 Indians Rookies:	1.50
Ted Ford, Steve Mingo	
Lou Camilli	
613 Pedro Borbon	1.50
614 Billy Cowan	1.50
615 Mel Stottlemyre	2.00
616 Larry Hisle	1.50
617 Clay Dalrymple	1.50
618 Tug McGraw	1.50
619 Checklist No. 6	2.00
620 Frank Howard	2.00
621 Ron Bryant	1.50
622 Joe LaHoud	1.50
623 Pat Jarvis	1.50
624 Oakland Athletics	3.00
625 Lou Brock	16.00
626 Freddie Patek	1.50
627 Steve Hamilton	1.50
628 John Bateman	1.50
629 John Hiller	1.50
630 Roberto Clemente	40.00
631 Eddie Fisher	1.50
632 Darrel Chaney	1.50
633 AL Rookies:	1.50
Pete Koegel, Bobby Br	
Scott Northey	
634 Phil Regan	1.50
635 Bobby Murcer	2.50
636 Denny LeMaster	1.50
637 Dave Bristol (Mgr.)	1.50
638 Stan Williams	1.50
639 Tom Haller	1.50
640 Frank Robinson	30.00
641 New York Mets	6.00

NO. PLAYER	NR. MT.
642 Jim Roland	1.50
643 Rick Reichardt	1.50
644 Jim Stewart	3.00
645 Jim Maloney	2.50
646 Bobby Floyd	3.00
647 Juan Pizarro	3.00
648 Mets Rookies:	5.00
Rich Folkers, Ted Martin	
John Matlack	
649 Sparky Lyle	4.00
650 Rich Allen	9.00
651 Jerry Robertson	3.00
652 Atlanta Braves	7.00
653 Russ Snyder	3.00
654 Don Shaw	3.00
655 Mike Epstein	3.00
656 Gerry Nyman	3.00
657 Jose Azcue	3.00
658 Paul Lindblad	3.00
659 Byron Browne	3.00
660 Ray Culp	3.00
661 Chuck Tanner (Mgr.)	4.00
662 Mike Hedlund	3.00
663 Marv Staehle	3.00
664 Rookies Pitchers:	3.00
Archie Reynolds, Bob	
Reynolds, K. Reynolds	
665 Ron Swoboda	3.00
666 Gene Brabender	3.00
667 Pete Ward	3.00
668 Gary Neibauer	3.00
669 Ike Brown	3.00
670 Bill Hands	3.00
671 Bill Voss	3.00
672 Ed Crosby	3.00
673 Gerry Janeski	3.00
674 Montreal Expos	7.00
675 Dave Boswell	3.00
676 Tommie Reynolds	3.00
677 Jack DiLauro	3.00
678 George Thomas	3.00
679 Don O'Riley	3.00
680 Don Mincher	3.00
681 Bill Butler	3.00
682 Terry Harmon	3.00
683 Bill Burbach	3.00
684 Curt Motton	3.00
685 Moe Drabowsky	3.00
686 Chico Ruiz	3.00
687 Ron Taylor	3.00
688 S. Anderson (Mgr.)	7.00
689 Frank Baker	3.00
690 Bob Moose	3.00
691 Bob Heise	3.00
692 AL Rookies Pitchers:	3.00
Hal Haydel, Rogelio Mo	
Wayne Twitchell	
693 Jose Pena	3.00
694 Rick Renick	3.00
695 Joe Niekro	4.00
696 Jerry Morales	3.00

NO. PLAYER	NR. MT.
697 Rickey Clark	3.00
698 Milwaukee Brewers	7.00
699 Jim Britton	3.00
700 Boog Powell	7.00
701 Bob Garibaldi	3.00
702 Milt Ramirez	3.00
703 Mike Kekich	3.00
704 J.C. Martin	3.00
705 Dick Selma	3.00
706 Joe Foy	3.00
707 Fred Lasher	3.00
708 Russ Nagelson	3.00
709 Rookie Outfielders:	30.00
Don Baylor, Tom Paci	
Dusty Baker	
710 Sonny Siebert	3.00
711 Larry Stahl	3.00
712 Jose Martinez	3.00
713 Mike Marshall	4.00
714 Dick Williams (Mgr.)	4.00
715 Horace Clarke	3.00
716 Dave Leonhard	3.00
717 Tommie Aaron	3.00
718 Billy Wynne	3.00
719 Jerry May	3.00
720 Matty Alou	3.00
721 John Morris	3.00
722 Houston Astros	7.00
723 Vicente Romo	3.00
724 Tom Tischinski	3.00
725 Gary Gentry	3.00
726 Paul Popovich	3.00
727 Ray Lamb	3.00
728 NL Rookie Outfielders:	3.00
Wayne Redmond, Keit	
Lampard, Bernie Willia	
729 Dick Billings	3.00
730 Jim Rooker	3.00
731 Jim Qualls	3.00
732 Bob Reed	3.00
733 Lee Maye	3.00
734 Rob Gardner	3.00
735 Mike Shannon	3.00
736 Mel Queen	3.00
737 Preston Gomez (Mgr.)	3.00
738 Russ Gibson	3.00
739 Barry Lersch	3.00
740 Luis Aparicio	15.00
741 Skip Guinn	3.00
742 Kansas City Royals	4.00
743 John O'Donoghue	3.00
744 Chuck Manuel	3.00
745 Sandy Alomar	3.00
746 Andy Kosco	3.00
747 NL Rookie Pitchers:	3.00
Al Severinsen, Scipio	
Spinks, Balor Moore	
748 John Purdin	3.00
749 Ken Szotkiewicz	3.00
750 Denny McLain	6.00
751 Al Weis	3.00
752 Dick Drago (Exc. $1.50)	6.00

1972 Topps. . . . Comptele Set of 787 Cards—Value $650.00 (Exc.) $1500.00 (Near Mint)

Features the rookie cards of Carlton Fisk and Ben Oglivie. The high numbers are 657 to 787. Semi-high numbers are 526 to 656.

NO.	PLAYER	NR. MT.
1	Pirates-Champs (Exc. $1.50)	6.00
2	Ray Culp	.25
3	Bob Tolan	.25
4	Checklist No. 1	1.50
5	John Bateman	.25
6	Fred Scherman	.25
7	Enzo Hernandez	.25
8	Ron Swoboda	.25
9	Stan Williams	.25
10	Amos Otis	.35
11	Bobby Valentine	.50
12	Jose Cardenal	.25
13	Joe Grzenda	.25
14	Phillies Rookies:	.30
	Pete Koegel, Mike	
	Anderson, W. Twitchell	
15	Walt Williams	.25
16	Mike Jorgensen	.25
17	Dave Duncan	.25
18	Juan Pizarro	.25
19	Billy Cowan	.25
20	Don Wilson	.25
21	Atlanta Braves	.75
22	Rob Gardner	.25
23	Ted Kubiak	.25
24	Ted Ford	.25
25	Will Singer	.25
26	Andy Etchebarren	.25
27	Bob Johnson	.25
28	Twins Rookies:	.30
	Steve Brye, Bob Gebhard,	
	Hal Haydel	
29	Bill Bonham	.25
30	Rico Petrocelli	.30
31	Cleon Jones	.25
32	C. Jones (In Action)	.25
33	Billy Martin	2.50
34	B. Martin (In Action)	1.25
35	Jerry Johnson	.25
36	J. Johnson (In Action)	.25
37	Carl Yastrzemski	16.00
38	Yastrzemski (In Action)	8.00
39	Bob Barton	.25
40	B. Barton (In Action)	.25
41	Tommy Davis	.60
42	T. Davis (In Action)	.30
43	Rick Wise	.35
44	R. Wise (In Action)	.35
45	Glenn Beckert	.35
46	G. Beckert (In Action)	.35
47	John Ellis	.25
48	J. Ellis (In Action)	.25
49	Willie Mays	25.00
50	W. Mays (All Action)	12.50
51	Harmon Killebrew	5.00
52	H. Killebrew (In Action)	2.50
53	Bud Harrelson	.50
54	B. Harrelson (In Action)	.30
55	Clyde Wright	.25
56	Rich Chiles	.25
57	Bob Oliver	.25
58	Ernie McAnally	.25
59	Fred Stanley	.25
60	Manny Sanguillen	.25
61	Cubs Rookies:	1.00
	Burt Hooton, Gene Hiser,	
	Earl Stephenson	
62	Angel Mangual	.25
63	Duke Sims	.25
64	Pete Broberg	.25
65	Cesar Cedeno	.75
66	Ray Corbin	.25
67	Red Schoendienst	1.25
68	Jim York	.25
69	Roger Freed	.25
70	Mike Cuellar	.40
71	Angels Team	.50
72	Bruce Kison (R)	.50
73	Steve Huntz	.25
74	Cecil Upshaw	.25
75	Bert Campaneris	.50
76	Don Carrithers	.25
77	Ron Theobald	.25
78	Steve Arlin	.25

NO.	PLAYER	NR. MT.
79	Red Sox Rookies:	125.00
	Carlton Fisk, Mike Garman,	
	Cecil Cooper	
80	Tony Perez	2.50
81	Mike Hedlund	.25
82	Ron Woods	.25
83	Dalton Jones	.25
84	Vince Colbert	.25
85	NL Batting Leaders:	1.00
	Ralph Garr, Glenn Beckert,	
	Joe Torre	
86	AL Batting Leaders:	1.00
	Tony Oliva, Bobby Murcer,	
	Merv Rettenmund	
87	NL RBI Leaders:	1.75
	Joe Torre, Willie Stargell,	
	Hank Aaron	
88	AL RBI Leaders:	1.50
	Harmon Killebrew, Frank	
	Robinson, Reggie Smith	
89	NL Home Run Leaders:	1.75
	Willie Stargell, Lee May,	
	Hank Aaron	
90	AL Home Run Leaders:	1.50
	Reggie Jackson, Bill	
	Melton, Norm Cash	
91	NL ERA Leaders:	1.25
	Tom Seaver, Dave Roberts	
	(wrong photo), D. Wilson	
92	AL ERA Leaders:	1.00
	Vida Blue, Wilbur Wood,	
	Jim Palmer	
93	NL Pitching Leaders:	2.00
	Tom Seaver, Fergie	
	Jenkins, Steve Carlton,	
	Al Downing	
94	AL Pitching Leaders:	1.00
	Mickey Lolich, Vida Blue,	
	Wilbur Wood	
95	NL Strikeout Leaders:	1.25
	Bill Stoneman, Tom Seaver,	
	Fergie Jenkins	
96	AL Strikeout Leaders:	1.00
	Mickey Lolich, Vida Blue,	
	Joe Coleman	
97	Tom Kelley	.25
98	Chuck Tanner	.35
99	Ross Grimsley	.25
100	Frank Robinson	5.00
101	Astros Rookies:	1.50
	B. Greif, J.R. Richard,	
	Ray Busse	
102	Lloyd Allen	.25
103	Checklist No. 2	1.50
104	Toby Harrah (R)	1.50
105	Gary Gentry	.25
106	Milwaukee Brewers	.75
107	Jose Cruz (R)	2.00
108	Gary Waslewski	.25
109	Jerry May	.25
110	Ron Hunt	.25
111	Jim Grant	.25
112	Greg Luzinski	1.00
113	Rogelio Moret	.25
114	Bill Buckner	1.50
115	Jim Fregosi	.35
116	Ed Farmer	.25
117	Cleo James	.25
118	Skip Lockwood	.25
119	Marty Perez	.25
120	Bill Freehan	.35
121	Ed Sprague	.25
122	Larry Biittner	.25
123	Ed Acosta	.25
124	Yankees Rookies:	.45
	Alan Closter, Rusty	
	Torres, R. Hambright	
125	Dave Cash	.25
126	Bart Johnson	.25
127	Duffy Dyer	.25
128	Eddie Watt	.25
129	Charlie Fox	.25
130	Bob Gibson	5.00
131	Jim Nettles	.25

NO.	PLAYER	NR. MT.
132	Joe Morgan	4.00
133	Joe Keough	.35
134	Carl Morton	.35
135	Vada Pinson	.50
136	Darrel Chaney	.35
137	Dick Williams	.35
138	Mike Kekich	.35
139	Tim McCarver	.50
140	Pat Dobson	.35
141	Mets Rookies:	.60
	Buzz Capra, Leroy Stanton,	
	Jon Matlack	
142	Chris Chambliss (R)	2.00
143	Garry Jestadt	.35
144	Marty Pattin	.35
145	Don Kessinger	.30
146	Steve Kealey	.35
147	Dave Kingman (R)	5.00
148	Dick Billings	.35
149	Gary Neibauer	.35
150	Norm Cash	.35
151	Jim Brewer	.35
152	Gene Clines	.35
153	Rick Auerbach	.35
154	Ted Simmons	2.00
155	Larry Dierker	.30
156	Minnesota Twins	.50
157	Don Gullett	.35
158	Jerry Kenney	.35
159	John Boccabella	.35
160	Andy Messersmith	.35
161	Brock Davis	.35
162	Brewers Rookies:	1.00
	Darrell Porter, Jerry Bell,	
	Bob Reynolds (Bell and	
	Porter photos switched)	
163	Tug McGraw	.75
164	T. McGraw (In Action)	.40
165	Chris Speier	.50
166	C. Speier (In Action)	.35
167	Deron Johnson	.35
168	D. Johnson (In Action)	.75
169	Vida Blue	.35
170	V. Blue (In Action)	1.25
171	Darrell Evans	1.25
172	D. Evans (In Action)	.65
173	Clay Kirby	.35
174	C. Kirby (In Action)	.35
175	Tom Haller	.35
176	T. Haller (In Action)	.35
177	Paul Schaal	.35
178	P. Schaal (In Action)	.35
179	Dock Ellis	.35
180	D. Ellis (In Action)	.35
181	Ed Kranepool	.30
182	E. Kranepool (In Action)	.35
183	Bill Melton	.35
184	B. Melton (In Action)	.35
185	Ron Bryant	.35
186	R. Bryant (In Action)	.35
187	Gates Brown	.35
188	Frank Lucchesi	.35
189	Gene Tenace	.30
190	Dave Giusti	.35
191	Jeff Burroughs	.75
192	Chicago Cubs	.60
193	Kurt Bevacqua	.35
194	Fred Norman	.35
195	Orlando Cepeda	2.00
196	Mel Queen	.35
197	Johnny Briggs	.35
198	Dodgers Rookies:	2.00
	Charlie Hough, Bob	
	O'Brien, Mike Strahler	
199	Mike Fiore	.35
200	Lou Brock	6.00
201	Phil Roof	.35
202	Scipio Spinks	.35
203	Ron Blomberg	.35
204	Tommy Helms	.35
205	Dick Drago	.35
206	Dal Maxvill	.35
207	Tom Egan	.35
208	Milt Pappas	.35

NO.	PLAYER	NR. MT.
209	Joe Rudi	.30
210	Denny McLain	1.25
211	Gary Sutherland	.35
212	Grant Jackson	.35
213	Angels Rookies:	.30
	Tom Silverio, Billy Parker,	
	Art Kusnyer	
214	Mike McQueen	.35
215	Alex Johnson	.35
216	Joe Niekro	.50
217	Roger Metzger	.35
218	Eddie Kasko	.35
219	Rennie Stennett	.30
220	Jim Perry	.30
221	NL Playoffs:	1.00
	Bucs Champs	
222	AL Playoffs:	1.50
	Orioles Champs	
223	World Series Game 1	1.00
224	World Series Game 2	1.00
225	World Series Game 3	1.00
226	World Series Game 4	2.50
227	World Series Game 5	1.00
228	World Series Game 6	1.00
229	World Series Game 7	1.00
230	World S. Celebration	1.00
231	Casey Cox	.35
232	Giants Rookies:	.30
	Chris Arnold, Jim Barr,	
	Dave Rader	
233	Jay Johnstone	.30
234	Ron Taylor	.35
235	Merv Rettenmund	.35
236	Jim McGlothlin	.35
237	New York Yankees	1.00
238	Leron Lee	.35
239	Tom Timmermann	.35
240	Rich Allen	2.00
241	Rollie Fingers	5.00
242	Don Mincher	.35
243	Frank Linzy	.35
244	Steve Braun	.35
245	Tommie Agee	.40
246	Tom Burgmeier	.35
247	Milt May	.35
248	Tom Bradley	.35
249	Garry Walker	.35
250	Boog Powell	1.00
251	Checklist No. 3	1.50
252	Ken Reynolds	.35
253	Sandy Alomar	.35
254	Boots Day	.35
255	Jim Lonborg	.30
256	George Foster	1.50
257	Tigers Rookies:	.30
	Paul Jata, Jim Foor,	
	Tim Hosley	
258	Randy Hundley	.35
259	Sparky Lyle	.35
260	Ralph Garr	.35
261	Steve Mingori	.35
262	San Diego Padres	.50
263	Felipe Alou	.30
264	Tommy John	2.00
265	Wes Parker	.50
266	Bobby Bolin	.50
267	Dave Concepcion	1.50
268	A's Rookies:	.40
	Dwain Anderson, C. Floethe	
269	Don Hahn	.50
270	Jim Palmer	9.00
271	Ken Rudolph	.50
272	Mickey Rivers	1.00
273	Bobby Floyd	.50
274	Al Severinsen	.50
275	Cesar Tovar	.50
276	Gene Mauch	.50
277	Eliott Maddox	.50
278	Dennis Higgins	.50
279	Larry Brown	.50
280	Willie McCovey	5.00
281	Bill Parsons	.50
282	Houston Astros	.75
283	Darrell Brandon	.50

NO. PLAYER	NR. MT.
284 Ike Brown	.50
285 Gaylord Perry	5.00
286 Gene Alley	.50
287 Jim Hardin	.50
288 Johnny Jeter	.50
289 Syd O'Brien	.50
290 Sonny Siebert	.50
291 Hal McRae	.60
292 H. McRae (In Action)	.50
293 Danny Frisella	.50
294 D. Frisella (In Action)	.50
295 Dick Dietz	.50
296 D. Dietz (In Action)	.50
297 Claude Osteen	.50
298 C. Osteen (In Action)	.50
299 Hank Aaron	24.00
300 H. Aaron (In Action)	12.00
301 George Mitterwald	.50
302 Mitterwald (In Action)	.50
303 Joe Pepitone	.60
304 J. Pepitone (In Action)	.50
305 Ken Boswell	.50
306 K. Boswell (In Action)	.50
307 Steve Renko	.50
308 S. Renko (In Action)	.50
309 Roberto Clemente	24.00
310 Clemente (In Action)	12.00
311 Clay Carroll	.50
312 C. Carroll (In Action)	.50
313 Luis Aparicio	3.00
314 L. Aparicio (In Action)	1.50
315 Paul Splittorff	.40
316 Cardinals Rookies:	.65
Jim Bibby, Jorge Roque,	
Santiago Guzman	
317 Rich Hand	.50
318 Sonny Jackson	.50
319 Aurelio Rodriguez	.50
320 Steve Blass	.50
321 Joe LaHoud	.50
322 Jose Pena	.50
323 Earl Weaver	.75
324 Mike Ryan	.50
325 Mel Stottlemyre	.50
326 Pat Kelly	.50
327 Steve Stone (R)	.75
328 Boston Red Sox	1.00
329 Roy Foster	.50
330 Jim Hunter	5.00
331 Stan Swanson	.50
332 Buck Martinez	.50
333 Steve Barber	.50
334 Rangers Rookies:	.40
Bill Fahey, Jim Mason,	
Tom Ragland	
335 Bill Hands	.50
336 Marty Martinez	.50
337 Mike Kilkenny	.50
338 Bob Grich	.75
339 Ron Cook	.50
340 Roy White	.60
341 Joe Torre (Boyhood)	.75
342 Wilbur Wood (Boyhood)	.75
343 W. Stargell (Boyhood)	1.25
344 D. McNally (Boyhood)	.75
345 Rick Wise (Boyhood)	.75
346 Jim Fregosi (Boyhood)	.75
347 Tom Seaver (Boyhood)	2.00
348 Sal Bando (Boyhood)	.75
349 Al Fitzmorris	.50
350 Frank Howard	.75
351 Braves Rookies:	.40
Tom House, Rick Kester,	
Jimmy Britton	
352 Dave LaRoche	.50
353 Art Shamsky	.50
354 Tom Murphy	.50
355 Bob Watson	.50
356 Gerry Moses	.50
357 Woodie Fryman	.50
358 Sparky Anderson	.50
359 Don Pavletich	.50
360 Dave Roberts	.50
361 Mike Andrews	.50
362 New York Mets	1.25

NO. PLAYER	NR. MT.
363 Ron Klimkowski	.50
364 Johnny Callison	.50
365 Dick Bosman	.50
366 Jimmy Rosario	.50
367 Ron Perranoski	.45
368 Danny Thompson	.50
369 Jim LeFebvre	.50
370 Don Buford	.50
371 Denny LeMaster	.50
372 Royals Rookies:	.50
Lance Clemons,	
Monty Montgomery	
373 John Mayberry	.45
374 Jack Heidemann	.50
375 Reggie Cleveland	.50
376 Andy Kosco	.50
377 Terry Harmon	.50
378 Checklist No. 4	1.50
379 Ken Berry	.50
380 Earl Williams	.50
381 Chicago White Sox	1.00
382 Joe Gibbon	.50
383 Brant Alyea	.50
384 Dave Campbell	.50
385 Mickey Stanley	.50
386 Jim Colborn	.50
387 Horace Clarke	.50
388 Charlie Williams	.50
389 Bill Rigney	.50
390 Willie Davis	.45
391 Kan Sanders	.50
392 Pirates Rookies:	.75
Fred Cambria, Richie Zisk	
393 Curt Motton	.50
394 Ken Forsch	.45
395 Matty Alou	.75
396 Paul Lindblad	.65
397 Philadelphia Phillies	2.00
398 Larry Hisle	.65
399 Milt Wilcox	.65
400 Tony Oliva	1.50
401 Jim Nash	.65
402 Bobby Heise	.65
403 John Cumberland	.65
404 Jeff Torborg	.65
405 Ron Fairly	.65
406 George Hendrick (R)	1.25
407 Chuck Taylor	.65
408 Jim Northrup	.65
409 Frank Baker	.65
410 Fergie Jenkins	2.50
411 Bob Montgomery	.65
412 Dick Kelley	.65
413 White Sox Rookies:	.75
Don Eddy, Dave Lemonds	
414 Bob Miller	.65
415 Cookie Rojas	.65
416 Johnny Edwards	.65
417 Tom Hall	.65
418 Tom Shopay	.65
419 Jim Spencer	.65
420 Steve Carlton	18.00
421 Ellie Rodriguez	.65
422 Ray Lamb	.65
423 Oscar Gamble	.65
424 Bill Gogolewski	.65
425 Ken Singleton	1.00
426 K. Singleton (In Action)	.65
427 Tito Fuentes	.65
428 T. Fuentes (In Action)	.65
429 Bob Robertson	.65
430 B. Robertson (In Action)	.65
431 Clarence Gaston	.65
432 C. Gaston (In Action)	.65
433 Johnny Bench	35.00
434 J. Bench (In Action)	17.00
435 Reggie Jackson	30.00
436 R. Jackson (In Action)	15.00
437 Maury Wills	1.50
438 M. Wills (In Action)	.75
439 Billy Williams	3.50
440 B. Williams (In Action)	1.75
441 Thurman Munson	16.00
442 T. Munson (In Action)	8.00
443 Ken Henderson	.65

NO. PLAYER	NR. MT.
444 Henderson (In Action)	.65
445 Tom Seaver	25.00
446 T. Seaver (In Action)	12.00
447 Willie Stargell	5.00
448 W. Stargell (In Action)	2.50
449 Bob Lemon	1.00
450 Mickey Lolich	1.00
451 Tony LaRussa	1.00
452 Ed Herrmann	.65
453 Barry Lersch	.65
454 Oakland A's	1.50
455 Tommy Harper	.65
456 Mark Belanger	.75
457 Padres Rookies:	.75
Darcy Fast, Derrel Thomas,	
Mike Ivie	
458 Aurelio Monteagudo	.65
459 Rick Renick	.65
460 Al Downing	.65
461 Tim Cullen	.65
462 Rickey Clark	.65
463 Bernie Carbo	.65
464 Jim Roland	.65
465 Gil Hodges	2.50
466 Norm Miller	.65
467 Steve Kline	.65
468 Richie Scheinblum	.65
469 Ron Herbel	.65
470 Ray Fosse	.65
471 Luke Walker	.65
472 Phil Gagliano	.65
473 Dan McGinn	.65
474 Orioles Rookies:	3.00
Johnny Oates, Don Baylor,	
Roric Harrison	
475 Gary Nolan	.65
476 Lee Richard	.65
477 Tom Phoebus	.65
478 Checklist No. 5	1.50
479 Don Shaw	.65
480 Lee May	1.00
481 Billy Conigliaro	.65
482 Joe Hoerner	.65
483 Ken Suarez	.65
484 Lum Harris	.65
485 Phil Regan	.65
486 John Lowenstein	.65
487 Detroit Tigers	2.00
488 Mike Nagy	.65
489 Expos Rookies:	.65
T. Humphrey, K. Lampard	
490 Dave McNally	.65
491 Lou Piniella (Boyhood)	.65
492 M. Stottlemyre (Boyhood)	.65
493 Bob Bailey (Boyhood)	.65
494 Willie Horton (Boyhood)	.65
495 Bill Melton (Boyhood)	.65
496 B. Harrelson (Boyhood)	.65
497 Jim Perry (Boyhood)	.65
498 B. Robinson (Boyhood)	1.50
499 Vicente Romo	.65
500 Joe Torre	1.00
501 Pete Hamm	.65
502 Jackie Hernandez	.65
503 Gary Peters	.65
504 Ed Spiezio	.65
505 Mike Marshall	.65
506 Indians Rookies:	.65
Terry Ley, Dick Tidrow,	
Jim Moyer	
507 Fred Gladding	.65
508 Ellie Hendricks	.65
509 Don McMahon	.65
510 Ted Williams (Mgr.)	5.00
511 Tony Taylor	.65
512 Paul Popovich	.65
513 Lindy McDaniel	.65
514 Ted Sizemore	.65
515 Bert Blyleven	8.00
516 Oscar Brown	.65
517 Ken Brett	.65
518 Wayne Garrett	.65
519 Ted Abernathy	.65
520 Larry Bowa	1.50
521 Alan Foster	.65

NO. PLAYER	NR. MT.
522 Los Angeles Dodgers	2.00
523 Chuck Dobson	.65
524 Reds Rookies:	.75
Ed Armbrister, Mel Behney	
525 Carlos May	.65
526 Bob Bailey	1.00
527 Dave Leonhard	1.00
528 Ron Stone	1.00
529 Dave Nelson	1.00
530 Don Sutton	4.00
531 Freddie Patek	1.00
532 Fred Kendall	1.00
533 Ralph Houk (Mgr.)	1.00
534 Jim Hickman	1.00
535 Ed Brinkman	1.00
536 Doug Rader	1.00
537 Bob Locker	1.00
538 Charlie Sands	1.00
539 Terry Forster (R)	1.50
540 Felix Milan	1.00
541 Roger Repoz	1.00
542 Jack Billingham	1.00
543 Duane Josephson	1.00
544 Ted Martinez	1.00
545 Wayne Granger	1.00
546 Joe Hague	1.00
547 Cleveland Indians	1.50
548 Frank Reberger	1.00
549 Dave May	1.00
550 Brooks Robinson	18.00
551 Ollie Brown	1.00
552 O. Brown (In Action)	1.00
553 Wilbur Wood	1.25
554 W. Wood (In Action)	1.00
555 Ron Santo	2.00
556 R. Santo (In Action)	1.00
557 John Odom	1.00
558 J. Odom (In Action)	1.00
559 Pete Rose	60.00
560 P. Rose (In Action)	30.00
561 Leo Cardenas	1.00
562 L. Cardenas (In Action)	1.00
563 Ray Sadecki	1.00
564 R. Sadecki (In Action)	1.00
565 Reggie Smith	1.25
566 R. Smith (In Action)	1.00
567 Juan Marichal	5.00
568 J. Marichal (In Action)	2.50
569 Ed Kirkpatrick	1.00
570 Kirkpatrick (In Action)	1.00
571 Nate Colbert	1.00
572 N. Colbert (In Action)	1.00
573 Fritz Peterson	1.00
574 F. Peterson (In Action)	1.00
575 Al Oliver	2.00
576 Leo Durocher	1.50
577 Mike Paul	1.00
578 Billy Grabarkewitz	1.00
579 Doyle Alexander (R)	3.00
580 Lou Piniella	2.50
581 Wade Blasingame	1.00
582 Montreal Expos	1.50
583 Darold Knowles	1.00
584 Jerry McNertney	1.00
585 George Scott	1.00
586 Denis Menke	1.00
587 Billy Wilson	1.00
588 Jim Holt	1.00
589 Hal Lanier	1.00
590 Graig Nettles	2.50
591 Paul Casanova	1.00
592 Lew Krausse	1.00
593 Rich Morales	1.00
594 Jim Beauchamp	1.00
595 Nolan Ryan	135.00
596 Manny Mota	1.25
597 Jim Magnuson	1.00
598 Hal King	1.00
599 Billy Champion	1.00
600 Al Kaline	15.00
601 George Stone	1.00
602 Dave Bristol	1.00
603 Jim Ray	1.00
604 Checklist No. 6	4.00
605 Nelson Briles	1.00

NO. PLAYER	NR. MT.
606 Luis Melendez	1.00
607 Frank Duffy	1.00
608 Mike Corkins	1.00
609 Tom Grieve	1.00
610 Bill Stoneman	1.00
611 Rich Reese	1.00
612 Joe Decker	1.00
613 Mike Ferraro	1.00
614 Ted Uhlaender	1.00
615 Steve Hargan	1.00
616 Joe Ferguson (R)	1.00
617 Kansas City Royals	1.50
618 Rich Robertson	1.00
619 Rich McKinney	1.00
620 Phil Niekro	5.00
621 Commissioners Award	2.00
622 MVP Award	2.00
623 Cy Young Award	2.00
624 Minor League Player of the Year	2.00
625 Rookie of the Year	2.00
626 Babe Ruth Award	2.00
627 Moe Drabowsky	1.00
628 Terry Crowley	1.00
629 Paul Doyle	1.00
630 Rich Hebner	1.00
631 John Strohmayer	1.00
632 Mike Hegan	1.00
633 Jack Hiatt	1.00
634 Dick Woodson	1.00
635 Don Money	1.25
636 Bill Lee	1.25
637 Preston Gomez	1.00
638 Ken Wright	1.00
639 J.C. Martin	1.00
640 Joe Coleman	1.00
641 Mike Lum	1.00
642 Dennis Riddleberger	1.00
643 Russ Gibson	1.00
644 Bernie Allen	1.00
645 Jim Maloney	1.25
646 Chico Salmon	1.00
647 Bob Moose	1.00
648 Jim Lyttle	1.00
649 Pete Richert	1.00
650 Sal Bando	1.25
651 Cincinnati Reds	1.50
652 Marcelino Lopez	1.00

NO. PLAYER	NR. MT.
653 Jim Fairey	1.00
654 Horacio Pina	1.00
655 Jerry Grote	1.00
656 Rudy May	1.00
657 Bobby Wine	3.00
658 Steve Dunning	3.00
659 Bob Aspromonte	3.00
660 Paul Blair	3.50
661 Bill Virdon	4.00
662 Stan Bahnsen	3.00
663 Fran Healy	3.00
664 Bobby Knoop	3.00
665 Chris Short	3.00
666 Hector Torres	3.00
667 Ray Newman	3.00
668 Texas Rangers	7.00
669 Willie Crawford	3.00
670 Ken Holtzman	4.00
671 Donn Clendenon	4.00
672 Archie Reynolds	3.00
673 Dave Marshall	3.00
674 John Kennedy	3.00
675 Pat Jarvis	3.00
676 Danny Cater	3.00
677 Ivan Murrell	3.00
678 Steve Luebber	3.00
679 Astros Rookies:	3.00
Bob Fenwick, Bob Stinson	
680 Dave Johnson	5.00
681 Bobby Pfeil	3.00
682 Mike McCormick	3.00
683 Steve Hovley	3.00
684 Hal Breeden	3.00
685 Joe Horlen	3.00
686 Steve Garvey	80.00
687 Del Unser	3.00
688 St. Louis Cardinals	7.00
689 Eddie Fisher	3.00
690 Willie Montanez	3.00
691 Curt Blefary	3.00
692 C. Blefary (In Action)	3.00
693 Alan Gallagher	3.00
694 Gallagher (In Action)	3.00
695 Rod Carew	85.00
696 R. Carew (In Action)	40.00
697 Jerry Koosman	6.00
698 J. Koosman (In Action)	3.00
699 Bobby Murcer	6.00

NO. PLAYER	NR. MT.
700 B. Murcer (In Action)	3.00
701 Jose Pagan	3.00
702 J. Pagan (In Action)	3.00
703 Doug Griffin	3.00
704 D. Griffin (In Action)	3.00
705 Pat Corrales	3.00
706 P. Corrales (In Action)	3.00
707 Tim Foli	3.00
708 T. Foli (In Action)	3.00
709 Jim Kaat	10.00
710 J. Kaat (In Action)	5.00
711 Bobby Bonds	10.00
712 B. Bonds (In Action)	5.00
713 Gene Michael	3.00
714 G. Michael (In Action)	3.00
715 Mike Epstein	3.00
716 Jesus Alou	3.00
717 Bruce Dal Canton	3.00
718 Del Rice	3.00
719 Cesar Geronimo	3.00
720 Sam McDowell	3.00
721 Eddie Leon	3.00
722 Bill Sudakis	3.00
723 Al Santorini	3.00
724 AL Rookie Pitchers:	3.00
John Curtis, Rich Hinton, Mickey Scott	
725 Dick McAuliffe	3.00
726 Dick Selma	3.00
727 Jose LaBoy	3.00
728 Gail Hopkins	3.00
729 Bob Veale	3.00
730 Rick Monday	4.00
731 Baltimore Orioles	4.00
732 George Culver	3.00
733 Jim Hart	3.00
734 Bob Burda	3.00
735 Diego Segui	3.00
736 Bill Russell	5.00
737 Lenny Randle	3.00
738 Jim Merritt	3.00
739 Don Mason	3.00
740 Rico Carty	4.00
741 Rookie Stars:	4.00
Tom Hutton, John Milner, Rick Miller	
742 Jim Rooker	3.00
743 Cesar Gutierrez	3.00

NO. PLAYER	NR. MT.
744 Jim Slaton	3.00
745 Julian Javier	3.00
746 Lowell Palmer	3.00
747 Jim Stewart	3.00
748 Phil Hennigan	3.00
749 Walter Alston (Mgr.)	7.00
750 Willie Horton	3.00
751 S. Carlton (Traded)	45.00
752 Joe Morgan (Traded)	25.00
753 D. McLain (Traded)	6.00
754 F. Robinson (Traded)	25.00
755 Jim Fregosi (Traded)	4.00
756 Rick Wise (Traded)	4.00
757 J. Cardenal (Traded)	4.00
758 Gil Garrido	3.00
759 Chris Cannizzaro	3.00
760 Bill Mazeroski	5.00
761 Rookie Stars:	12.50
Bernie Williams, Ben Oglivie, Ron Cey	
762 Wayne Simpson	3.00
763 Ron Hansen	3.00
764 Dusty Baker	5.00
765 Ken McMullen	3.00
766 Steve Hamilton	3.00
767 Tom McCraw	3.00
768 Denny Doyle	3.00
769 Jack Aker	3.00
770 Jim Wynn	4.00
771 San Francisco Giants	4.00
772 Ken Tatum	3.00
773 Ron Brand	3.00
774 Luis Alvarado	3.00
775 Jerry Reuss	5.00
776 Bill Voss	3.00
777 Hoyt Wilhelm	14.00
778 Twins Rookies:	5.00
Vic Albury, Rick Dempsey, Jim Strickland	
779 Tony Cloninger	3.00
780 Dick Green	3.00
781 Jim McAndrew	3.00
792 Larry Stahl	3.00
783 Les Cain	3.00
784 Ken Aspromonte	3.00
785 Vic Davalillo	3.00
786 Chuck Brinkman	3.00
787 Ron Reed (Exc. $1.25)	5.00

1973 Topps.... Complete Set of 660 Cards—Value $375.00 (Exc.); $900.00 (Near Mint)

Includes the rookie cards of Mike Schmidt, Darrell Evans and Davey Lopes. The high numbers are 529 to 660. This was the last Topps' set to be issued in *series*. Starting in 1974 the entire set was issued at one time.

NO. PLAYER	NR. MT.
1 All-Time HR Leaders	20.00
Babe Ruth, Hank Aaron, Willie Mays (Exc. $6.00)	
2 Rich Hebner	.30
3 Jim Lonborg	.30
4 John Milner	.30
5 Ed Brinkman	.30
6 Mac Scarce	.30
7 Texas Rangers	.30
8 Tom Hall	.30
9 Johnny Oates	.30

NO. PLAYER	NR. MT.
10 Don Sutton	2.50
11 Chris Chambliss	.60
12 Don Zimmer (Mgr.)	.50
13 George Hendrick	.75
14 Sonny Siebert	.30
15 Ralph Garr	.30
16 Steve Braun	.30
17 Fred Gladding	.30
18 Leroy Stanton	.30
19 Tim Foli	.30
20 Stan Bahnsen	.30

NO. PLAYER	NR. MT.
21 Randy Hundley	.30
22 Ted Abernathy	.30
23 Dave Kingman	1.50
24 Al Santorini	.30
25 Ray White	.40
26 Pittsburgh Pirates	.60
27 Bill Gogolewski	.30
28 Hal McRae	.50
29 Tony Taylor	.30
30 Tug McGraw	.75
31 Buddy Bell (R)	4.00

NO. PLAYER	NR. MT.
32 Fred Norman	.30
33 Jim Breazeale	.30
34 Pat Dobson	.30
35 Willie Davis	.40
36 Steve Barber	.30
37 Bill Robinson	.30
38 Mike Epstein	.30
39 Dave Roberts	.30
40 Reggie Smith	.75
41 Tom Walker	.30
42 Mike Andrews	.30

NO. PLAYER	NR. MT.
43 Randy Moffitt	.30
44 Rick Monday	.40
45 Ellie Rodriguez	.30
(wrong photo)	
46 Lindy McDaniel	.30
47 Luis Melendez	.30
48 Paul Splittorff	.35
49 Frank Quilici (Mgr.)	.50
50 Roberto Clement	25.00
51 Chuck Seelbach	.30
52 Denis Menke	.30
53 Steve Dunning	.30
54 Checklist No. 1	1.50
55 Jon Matlack	.45
56 Merv Rettenmund	.30
57 Derrel Thomas	.30
58 Mike Paul	.30
59 Steve Yeager (R)	.60
60 Ken Holtzman	.40
61 Batting Leaders:	2.00
Billy Williams, Rod Carew	
62 Home Run Leaders:	1.50
Johnny Bench, Dick Allen	
63 RBI Leaders:	1.50
Johnny Bench, Dick Allen	
64 Stolen Base Leaders:	1.00
B. Campaneris, L. Brock	
65 ERA Leaders:	1.25
Steve Carlton, Luis Tiant	
66 Victory Leaders:	1.25
Wilbur Wood, Steve	
Carlton, Gaylord Perry	
67 Strikeout Leaders:	5.00
Steve Carlton, Nolan Ryan	
68 Leading Firemen:	1.00
Clay Carroll, Sparky Lyle	
69 Phil Gagliano	.30
70 Milt Pappas	.30
71 Johnny Briggs	.30
72 Ron Reed	.30
73 Ed Herrmann	.30
74 Billy Champion	.30
75 Vada Pinson	.50
76 Doug Rader	.30
77 Mike Torrez	.40
78 Richie Scheinblum	.30
79 Jim Willoughby	.30
80 Tony Oliva	1.25
81 Whitey Lockman (Mgr.)	.45
82 Fritz Peterson	.30
83 Leron Lee	.30
84 Rollie Fingers	4.00
85 Ted Simmons	1.50
86 Tom McCraw	.30
87 Ken Boswell	.30
88 Mickey Stanley	.30
89 Jack Billingham	.30
90 Brooks Robinson	4.00
91 Los Angeles Dodgers	.75
92 Jerry Bell	.30
93 Jesus Alou	.30
94 Dick Billings	.30
95 Steve Blass	.30
96 Doug Griffin	.30
97 Willie Montanez	.30
98 Dick Woodson	.30
99 Carl Taylor	.30
100 Hank Aaron	20.00
101 Ken Henderson	.30
102 Rudy May	.30
103 Celerino Sanchez	.30
104 Reggie Cleveland	.30
105 Carlos May	.30
106 Terry Humphrey	.30
107 Phil Hennigan	.30
108 Bill Russell	.30
109 Doyle Alexander	.50
110 Bob Watson	.40
111 Dave Nelson	.30
112 Gary Ross	.30
113 Jerry Grote	.30
114 Lynn McGlothen	.30
115 Ron Santo	.60
116 Ralph Houk (Mgr.)	.60
117 Ramon Hernandez	.30

NO. PLAYER	NR. MT.
118 John Mayberry	.40
119 Larry Bowa	.75
120 Joe Coleman	.30
121 Dave Rader	.30
122 Jim Strickland	.30
123 Sandy Alomar	.30
124 Jim Hardin	.30
125 Ron Fairly	.30
126 Jim Brewer	.30
127 Milwaukee Brewers	.75
128 Ted Sizemore	.30
129 Terry Forster	.40
130 Pete Rose	18.00
131 Eddie Kasko (Mgr.)	.50
132 Matty Alou	.50
133 Dave Roberts	.30
134 Milt Wilcox	.40
135 Lee May	.40
136 Earl Weaver (Mgr.)	.75
137 Jim Beauchamp	.30
138 Horacio Pina	.30
139 Carmen Fanzone	.30
140 Lou Piniella	.75
141 Bruce Kison	.40
142 Thurman Munson	9.00
143 John Curtis	.30
144 Marty Perez	.30
145 Bobby Bonds	.60
146 Woodie Fryman	.30
147 Mike Anderson	.30
148 Dave Goltz	.30
149 Ron Hunt	.30
150 Wilbur Wood	.30
151 Wes Parker	.30
152 Dave May	.30
153 Al Hrabosky	.40
154 Jeff Torborg	.30
155 Sal Bando	.45
156 Cesar Geronimo	.30
157 Denny Riddleberger	.30
158 Houston Astros	.60
159 Clarence Gaston	.30
160 Jim Palmer	7.00
161 Ted Martinez	.30
162 Pete Broberg	.30
163 Vic Davalillo	.30
164 Monty Montgomery	.30
165 Luis Aparicio	2.50
166 Terry Harmon	.30
167 Steve Stone	.35
168 Jim Northrup	.30
169 Ron Schueler	.30
170 Harmon Killebrew	4.00
171 Bernie Carbo	.30
172 Steve Kline	.30
173 Hal Breeden	.30
174 Rich Gossage (R)	11.00
175 Frank Robinson	4.00
176 Chuck Taylor	.30
177 Bill Plummer	.30
178 Don Rose	.30
179 Dick Williams (Mgr.)	.50
180 Fergie Jenkins	1.50
181 Jack Brohamer	.30
182 Mike Caldwell (R)	.50
183 Don Buford	.30
184 Jerry Koosman	.50
185 Jim Wynn	.35
186 Bill Fahey	.30
187 Luke Walker	.30
188 Cookie Rojas	.30
189 Greg Luzinski	.75
190 Bob Gibson	3.00
191 Detroit Tigers	.75
192 Pat Jarvis	.30
193 Carlton Fisk	16.00
194 Jorge Orta	.30
195 Clay Carroll	.30
196 Ken McMullen	.30
197 Ed Goodson	.30
198 Horace Clarke	.30
199 Bert Blyleven	3.00
200 Billy Williams	3.50
201 AL Playoffs:	.75
Hendrick Scores	

NO. PLAYER	NR. MT.
202 NL Playoffs:	.75
Foster's Run Decides It	
203 World Series Game 1	.75
Tenace the Menace	
204 World Series Game 2	.75
A's Make It Two Straight	
205 World Series Game 3	.75
Reds Win Squeaker	
206 World Series Game 4	.75
Tenace Singles In Ninth	
207 World Series Game 5	.75
Odom Out at Plate	
208 World Series Game 6	.75
Red's Ties Series	
209 World Series Game 7	.75
Campy Stars Rally	
210 World Series	.75
A's— World Champions	
211 Balor Moore	.30
212 Joe LaHoud	.30
213 Steve Garvey	12.00
214 Steve Hamilton	.30
215 Dusty Baker	.75
216 Toby Harrah	.35
217 Don Wilson	.30
218 Aurelio Rodriguez	.30
219 St. Louis Cardinals	.75
220 Nolan Ryan	50.00
221 Fred Kendall	.30
222 Rob Gardner	.30
223 Bud Harrelson	.30
224 Bill Lee	.30
225 Al Oliver	1.25
226 Ray Fosse	.30
227 Wayne Twitchell	.30
228 Bobby Darwin	.30
229 Roric Harrison	.30
230 Joe Morgan	4.00
231 Bill Parsons	.30
232 Ken Singleton	.60
233 Ed Kirkpatrick	.30
234 Bill North	.30
235 Jim Hunter	4.00
236 Tito Fuentes	.30
237 Eddie Mathews (Mgr.)	1.00
238 Tony Muser	.30
239 Pete Richert	.30
240 Bobby Murcer	.75
241 Dwain Anderson	.30
242 George Culver	.30
243 California Angels	.75
244 Ed Acosta	.30
245 Carl Yastrzemski	13.00
246 Ken Sanders	.30
247 Del Unser	.30
248 Jerry Johnson	.30
249 Larry Biittner	.30
250 Manny Sanguillen	.40
251 Roger Nelson	.30
252 Charlie Fox (Mgr.)	.50
253 Mark Belanger	.35
254 Bill Stoneman	.30
255 Reggie Jackson	25.00
256 Chris Zachary	.30
257 Yogi Berra (Mgr.)	1.50
258 Tommy John	1.50
259 Jim Holt	.30
260 Gary Nolan	.30
261 Pat Kelly	.30
262 Jack Aker	.30
263 George Scott	.30
264 Checklist No. 2	1.50
265 Gene Michael	.50
266 Mike Lum	.30
267 Lloyd Allen	.30
268 Jerry Morales	.30
269 Tim McCarver	1.00
270 Luis Tiant	.50
271 Tom Hutton	.30
272 Ed Farmer	.30
273 Chris Speier	.45
274 Darold Knowles	.30
275 Tony Perez	2.00
276 Joe Lovitto	.30
277 Bob Miller	.30

NO. PLAYER	NR. MT.
278 Baltimore Orioles	.75
279 Mike Strahler	.30
280 Al Kaline	5.00
281 Mike Jorgensen	.30
282 Steve Hovley	.30
283 Ray Sadecki	.30
284 Glenn Borgmann	.30
285 Don Kessinger	.40
286 Frank Linzy	.30
287 Eddie Leon	.30
288 Gary Gentry	.30
289 Bob Oliver	.30
290 Cesar Cedeno	.65
291 Rogelio Moret	.30
292 Jose Cruz	1.00
293 Bernie Allen	.30
294 Steve Arlin	.30
295 Bert Campaneris	.45
296 Sparky Anderson (Mgr.)	.50
297 Walt Williams	.30
298 Ron Bryant	.30
299 Ted Ford	.30
300 Steve Carlton	13.00
301 Billy Grabarkewitz	.30
302 Terry Crowley	.30
303 Nelson Briles	.30
304 Duke Sims	.30
305 Willie Mays	22.00
306 Tom Burgmeier	.30
307 Boots Day	.30
308 Skip Lockwood	.30
309 Paul Popovich	.30
310 Dick Allen	.75
311 Joe Decker	.30
312 Oscar Brown	.30
313 Jim Ray	.30
314 Ron Swoboda	.30
315 John Odom	.30
316 San Diego Padres	.50
317 Danny Cater	.30
318 Jim McGlothlin	.30
319 Jim Spencer	.30
320 Lou Brock	5.00
321 Rich Hinton	.30
322 Garry Maddox (R)	.75
323 Billy Martin (Mgr.)	1.00
324 Al Downing	.50
325 Boog Powell	.75
326 Darrell Brandon	.30
327 John Lowenstein	.30
328 Bill Bonham	.30
329 Ed Kranepool	.50
330 Rod Carew	12.00
331 Carl Morton	.30
332 John Felske	.30
333 Gene Clines	.30
334 Freddie Patek	.30
335 Bob Tolan	.30
336 Tom Bradley	.30
337 Dave Duncan	.30
338 Checklist No. 3	1.50
339 Dick Tidrow	.30
340 Nate Colbert	.30
341 Jim Palmer (Boyhood)	1.50
342 S. McDowell (Boyhood)	.60
343 B. Murcer (Boyhood)	.30
344 Jim Hunter (Boyhood)	1.25
345 Chris Speier (Boyhood)	.60
346 G. Perry (Boyhood)	1.25
347 Kansas City Royals	.75
348 Rennie Stennett	.30
349 Dick McAuliffe	.30
350 Tom Seaver	16.00
351 Jimmy Stewart	.30
352 Don Stanhouse	.30
353 Steve Brye	.30
354 Billy Parker	.30
355 Mike Marshall	.50
356 Chuck Tanner (Mgr.)	.60
357 Ross Grimsley	.30
358 Jim Nettles	.30
359 Cecil Upshaw	.30
360 Joe Rudi	.60
(photo of Gene Tenace)	
361 Fran Healy	.30

NO. PLAYER	NR. MT.	NO. PLAYER	NR. MT.	NO. PLAYER	NR. MT.	NO. PLAYER	NR. MT.
362 Eddie Watt	.30	447 Joe Hague	.50	523 Wayne Granger	.50	603 Rookie 3rd Basemen: Billy McNulty, Ken Reitz, Terry Hughes	1.75
363 Jackie Hernandez	.30	448 John Hiller	.50	524 Gene Tenace	.65		
364 Rick Wise	.30	449 Ken Aspromonte (Mgr.)	.65	525 Jim Fregosi	.75	604 Rookie Pitchers: Jesse Jefferson, Dennis O'Toole, Bob Strampe	1.75
365 Rico Petrocelli	.50	450 Joe Torre	1.00	526 Ollie Brown	.50		
366 Brock Davis	.30	451 John Vuckovich	.50	527 Dan McGinn	.50		
367 Burt Hooton	.30	452 Paul Casanova	.50	528 Paul Blair	.50	605 Rookie 1st Basemen: Pat Bourque, Enos Cabell, Gonzalo Marquez	1.75
368 Bill Buckner	1.00	453 Checklist No. 4	1.25	529 Milt May	1.50		
369 Lerrin LaGrow	.30	454 Tom Haller	.50	530 Jim Kaat	3.00		
370 Willie Stargell	4.00	455 Bill Melton	.50	531 Ron Woods	1.50	606 Rookie Outfielders: Jorge Roque, Gary Matthews, T. Paciorek	4.00
371 Mike Kekich	.30	456 Dick Green	.50	532 Steve Mingori	1.50		
372 Oscar Gamble	.40	457 John Strohmayer	.50	533 Larry Stahl	1.50		
373 Clyde Wright	.30	458 Jim Mason	.50	534 Dave Lemonds	1.50	607 Rookie Shortstops: Pepe Frias, Ray Busse, Mario Guerrero	1.50
374 Darrell Evans	.75	459 Jimmy Howarth	.50	535 John Callison	1.50		
375 Larry Dierker	.40	460 Bill Freehan	.65	536 Philadelphia Phillies	3.00		
376 Frank Duffy	.30	461 Mike Corkins	.50	537 Bill Slayback	1.50	608 Rookie Pitchers: S. Busby, G. Medich, Dick Colpaert	1.50
377 Gene Mauch (Mgr.)	.50	462 Ron Blomberg	.50	538 Jim Hart	1.50		
378 Lenny Randle	.30	463 Ken Tatum	.50	539 Tom Murphy	1.50		
379 Cy Acosta	.30	464 Chicago Cubs	1.00	540 Cleon Jones	1.75	609 Rookie 2nd Basemen: Larvell Blanks, P. Garcia, Dave Lopes	4.00
380 Johnny Bench	20.00	465 Dave Giusti	.50	541 Bob Bolin	1.50		
381 Vicente Romo	.30	466 Jose Arcia	.50	542 Pat Corrales	1.75		
382 Mike Hegan	.30	467 Mike Ryan	.50	543 Alan Foster	1.50	610 Rookie Pitchers: Hank Webb, J. Freeman, Charlie Hough	3.00
383 Diego Segui	.30	468 Tom Griffin	.50	544 Von Joshua	1.50		
384 Don Baylor	1.25	469 Dan Monzon	.50	545 Orlando Cepeda	3.00		
385 Jim Perry	.35	470 Mike Cuellar	.60	546 Jim York	1.50	611 Rookie Outfielders: Richie Zisk, Rich Coggins, J. Wohlford	2.00
386 Don Money	.30	471 All-Time Hits Ty Cobb (4,191)	4.00	547 Bobby Heise	1.50		
387 Jim Barr	.30			548 Don Durham	1.50		
388 Ben Oglivie	.50	472 All-Time Grand Slams: Lou Gehrig (23)	4.00	549 Whitey Herzog (Mgr.)	2.00	612 Rookie Pitchers: Steve Lawson, Bob Reynolds, Brent Strom	1.75
389 New York Mets	2.50			550 Dave Johnson	2.50		
390 Mickey Lolich	.60	473 All-Time Total Bases hank Aaron (6,172)	4.00	551 Mike Kilkenny	1.50		
391 Lee Lacy (R)	.75			552 J.C. Martin	1.50	613 Rookie Catchers: Bob Boone, S. Jutze, Mike Ivie	25.00
392 Dick Drago	.30	474 All-Time RBI's Babe Ruth (2,209)	6.00	553 Mickey Scott	1.50		
393 Jose Cardenal	.30			554 Dave Concepcion	3.00		
394 Sparky Lyle	.50	475 All-Time Batting: Ty Cobb (.367)	4.00	555 Bill Hands	1.50	614 Rookie Outfielders: A. Bumbry, Dwight Evans, Charlie Spikes	60.00
395 Roger Metzger	.30			556 New York Yankees	4.00		
396 Grant Jackson	.30	476 All-Time Shutouts: Walter Johnson (113)	1.50	557 Bernie Williams	1.50		
397 Dave Cash	.50			558 Jerry May	1.50	615 Rookie 3rd Basemen: Ron Cey, Mike Schmidt, John Hilton	450.00
398 Rich Hand	.50	477 All-Time Victory Ldrs. Cy Young (511)	1.50	559 Barry Lersch	1.50		
399 George Foster	1.50			560 Frank Howard	2.50		
400 Gaylord Perry	4.00	478 All-Time Strikeouts: Walter Johnson (3,508)	1.50	561 Jim Geddes	1.50	616 Rookie Pitchers: S. Blateric, Norm Angelini, Mike Garman	1.50
401 Clyde Mashore	.50			562 Wayne Garrett	1.50		
402 Jack Hiatt	.50	479 Hal Lanier	.75	563 Larry Haney	1.50		
403 Sonny Jackson	.50	480 Juan Marichal	4.00	564 Mike Thompson	1.50	617 Rich Chiles	1.50
404 Chuck Brinkman	.50	481 Chicago White Sox	.75	565 Jim Hickman	1.50	618 Andy Etchebarren	1.50
405 Cesar Tovar	.50	482 Rick Reuschel (R)	7.00	566 Lew Krausse	1.50	619 Billy Wilson	1.50
406 Paul Lindblad	.5C	483 Dal Maxvill	.50	567 Bob Fenwick	1.50	620 Tommy Harper	1.50
407 Felix Millan	.50	484 Ernie McAnally	.50	568 Ray Newman	1.50	621 Joe Ferguson	1.50
408 Jim Colborn	.50	485 Norm Cash	.60	569 Walt Alston (Mgr.)	3.00	622 Larry Hisle	1.50
409 Ivan Murrell	.50	486 Danny Ozark (Mgr.)	.60	570 Bill Singer	1.50	623 Steve Renko	1.50
410 Willie McCovey	5.00	487 Bruce Dal Canton	.50	571 Rusty Torres	1.50	624 Leo Durocher (Mgr.)	2.50
411 Ray Corbin	.50	488 Dave Campbell	.50	572 Gary Sutherland	1.50	625 Angel Mangual	1.50
412 Manny Mota	.75	489 Jeff Burroughs	.50	573 Fred Beene	1.50	626 Bob Barton	1.50
413 Tom Timmerman	.50	490 Claude Osteen	.60	574 Bob Didier	1.50	627 Luis Alvarado	1.50
414 Ken Rudolph	.50	491 Bob Montgomery	.50	575 Dock Ellis	1.50	628 Jim Slaton	1.50
415 Marty Pattin	.50	492 Pedro Borbon	.50	576 Montreal Expos	3.00	629 Cleveland Indians	2.50
416 Paul Schaal	.50	493 Duffy Dyer	.50	577 Eric Soderholm	1.50	630 Denny McLain	3.00
417 Scipio Spinks	.50	494 Rich Morales	.50	578 Ken Wright	1.50	631 Tom Matchick	1.50
418 Bobby Grich	.65	495 Tommy Helms	.50	579 Tom Grieve	1.50	632 Dick Selma	1.50
419 Casey Cox	.50	496 Ray Lamb	.50	580 Joe Pepitone	2.00	633 Ike Brown	1.50
420 Tommie Agee	.50	497 R. Schoendienst (Mgr.)	.60	581 Steve Kealey	1.50	634 Alan Closter	1.50
421 Bobby Winkles (Mgr.)	.65	498 Graig Nettles	2.50	582 Darrell Porter	1.75	635 Gene Alley	1.50
422 Bob Robertson	.50	499 Bob Moose	.50	583 Bill Grief	1.50	636 Rick Clark	1.50
423 Johnny Jeter	.50	500 Oakland A's	1.25	584 Chris Arnold	1.50	637 Norm Miller	1.50
424 Denny Doyle	.50	501 Larry Gura	.50	585 Joe Niekro	3.00	638 Ken Reynolds	1.50
425 Alex Johnson	.50	502 Bobby Valentine	.65	586 Bill Sudakis	1.50	639 Willie Crawford	1.50
426 Dave LaRoche	.50	503 Phil Niekro	4.00	587 Rich McKinney	1.50	640 Dick Bosman	1.50
427 Rick Auerbach	.50	504 Earl Williams	.50	588 Checklist No. 5	15.00	641 Cincinnati Reds	3.00
428 Wayne Simpson	.50	505 Bob Bailey	.50	589 Ken Forsch	1.75	642 Jose LaBoy	1.50
429 Jim Fairey	.50	506 Bart Johnson	.50	590 Deron Johnson	1.50	643 Al Fitzmorris	1.50
430 Vida Blue	.75	507 Darrel Chaney	.50	591 Mike Hedlund	1.50	644 Jack Heidemann	1.50
431 Gerry Moses	.50	508 Gates Brown	.50	592 John Boccabella	1.50	645 Bob Locker	1.50
432 Dan Frisella	.50	509 Jim Nash	.50	593 Jack McKeon (Mgr.)	1.50	646 Del Crandall (Mgr.)	2.00
433 Willie Horton	.60	510 Amos Otis	.65	594 Vic Harris	1.50	647 George Stone	1.50
434 San F. Giants	.75	511 Sam McDowell	.60	595 Don Gullett	1.75	648 Tom Egan	1.50
435 Rico Carty	.60	512 Dalton Jones	.50	596 Boston Red Sox	3.00	649 Rich Folkers	1.50
436 Jim McAndrew	.50	513 Dave Marshall	.50	597 Mickey Rivers	2.00	650 Felipe Alou	2.00
437 John Kennedy	.50	514 Jerry Kenney	.50	598 Phil Roof	1.50	651 Don Carrithers	1.50
438 Enzo Hernandez	.50	515 Andy Messersmith	.65	599 Ed Crosby	1.50	652 Ted Kubiak	1.50
439 Eddie Fisher	.50	516 Danny Walton	.50	600 Dave McNally	1.50	653 Joe Hoerner	1.50
440 Glenn Beckert	.50	517 Bill Virdon (Mgr.)	.65	601 Rookie Catchers: George Pena, Sergio Robles, R. Stelmaszek	1.75	654 Minnesota Twins	3.00
441 Gail Hopkins	.50	518 Bob Veale	.50			655 Clay Kirby	1.50
442 Dick Dietz	.50	519 John Edwards	.50			656 John Ellis	1.50
443 Danny Thompson	.50	520 Mel Stottlemyre	.50	602 Rookie Pitchers: Doug Rau, Mel Behney, Ralph Garcia	1.75	657 Bob Johnson	1.50
444 Ken Brett	.50	521 Atlanta Braves	.60			658 Elliott Maddox	1.50
445 Ken Berry	.50	522 Leo Cardenas	.50			659 Jose Pagan	1.50
446 Jerry Reuss	.60					660 F. Scherman (Exc. $.60)	3.00

1974 Topps.... Complete Set of 660 Cards—Value $500.00 (Mint)

Features the rookie cards of Dave Parker and Dave Winfield. This was Topps' first card set to be released all at one time. Previous card sets were released in series, several weeks or months apart. Fifteen Padres cards were printed either "San Diego" or "Washington". Because of a false rumor that the Padres were moving, Topps printed "Washington" on the cards, but it was quickly corrected.

NO. PLAYER	NR. MT.
1 Hank Aaron (Exc. $8.00) . .	25.00
Home Run King	
2 Aaron Special (1954-57)	5.00
3 Aaron Special (1958-61)	5.00
4 Aaron Special (1962-65)	5.00
5 Aaron Special (1966-69)	5.00
6 Aaron Special (1970-73)	5.00
7 Jim Hunter	4.00
8 George Theodore	.25
9 Mickey Lolich	.50
10 Johnny Bench	13.00
11 Jim Bibby	.25
12 Dave May	.25
13 Tom Hilgendorf	.25
14 Paul Popovich	.25
15 Joe Torre	.75
16 Baltimore Orioles	.50
17 Doug Bird	.25
18 Gary Thomasson	.25
19 Gerry Moses	.25
20 Nolan Ryan	30.00
21 Bob Gallagher	.25
22 Cy Acosta	.25
23 Craig Robinson	.25
24 John Hiller	.25
25 Len Singleton	.40
26 Bill Campbell (R)	.35
27 George Scott	.25
28 Manny Sanguillen	.25
29 Phil Niekro	2.50
30 Bobby Bonds	.50
31 Preston Gomez (Mgr.)	.25
32 John Grubb (SD)	.50
32 John Grubb (Wash)	3.00
33 Don Newhauser	.25
34 Andy Kosco	.25
35 Gaylord Perry	2.50
36 St. Louis Cardinals	.45
37 Dave Sells	.25
38 Don Kessinger	.25
39 Ken Suarez	.25
40 Jim Palmer	5.00
41 Bobby Floyd	.25
42 Claude Osteen	.25
43 Jim Wynn	.25
44 Mel Stottlemyre	.35
45 Dave Johnson	.60
46 Pat Kelly	.25
47 Dick Ruthven	.25
48 Dick Sharon	.25
49 Steve Renko	.25
50 R. Carew	8.00
51 Bob Heise	.25
52 Al Oliver	1.00
53 Fred Kendall (SD)	.25
53 Fred Kendall (Wash.)	3.00
54 Elias Sosa	.25
55 Frank Robinson	3.00
56 New York Mets	1.00
57 Darold Knowles	.25
58 Charlie Spikes	.25
59 Ross Grimsley	.25
60 Lou Brock	4.00
61 Luis Aparicio	2.00
62 Bob Locker	.25
63 Bill Sudakis	.25

NO. PLAYER	NR. MT.
64 Doug Rau	.25
65 Amos Otis	.35
66 Sparky Lyle	.50
67 Tommy Helms	.25
68 Grant Jackson	.25
69 Del Unser	.25
70 Dick Allen	.50
71 Dan Frisella	.25
72 Aurelio Rodriguez	.25
73 Mike Marshall	.60
74 Minnesota Twins	.50
75 Jim Colborn	.25
76 Mickey Rivers	.25
77 Rich Troedson (SD)	.25
77 Rich Troedson (Wash)	3.00
78 Charlie Fox (Mgr.)	.25
79 Gene Tenace	.25
80 Tom Seaver	10.00
81 Frank Duffy	.25
82 Dave Giusti	.25
83 Orlando Cepeda	1.00
84 Rick Wise	.25
85 Joe Morgan	4.00
86 Joe Ferguson	.25
87 Fergie Jenkins	1.50
88 Freddie Patek	.25
89 Jackie Brown	.25
90 Bobby Murcer	.50
91 Ken Forsch	.25
92 Paul Blair	.25
93 Rod Gilbreath	.25
94 Detroit Tigers	.75
95 Steve Carlton	7.50
96 Jerry Hairston	.25
97 Bob Bailey	.25
98 Bert Blyleven	2.00
99 Del Crandall (Mgr.)	.35
100 Willie Stargell	3.00
101 Bobby Valentine	.35
102 Bill Greif (SD)	.30
102 Bill Greif (Wash.)	3.00
103 Sal Bando	.50
104 Ron Bryant	.25
105 Carlton Fisk	9.00
106 Harry Parker	.25
107 Alex Johnson	.25
108 Al Hrabosky	.35
109 Bob Grich	.35
110 Billy Williams	3.00
111 Clay Carroll	.25
112 Dave Lopes	.50
113 Dick Drago	.25
114 California Angels	.50
115 Willie Horton	.40
116 Jerry Reuss	.35
117 Ron Blomberg	.25
118 Bill Lee	.30
119 Danny Ozark (Mgr.)	.30
120 Wilbur Wood	.25
121 Larry Lintz	.25
122 Jim Holt	.25
123 Nellie Briles	.25
124 Bobby Coluccio	.25
125 Nate Colbert (SD)	.30
125 Nate Colbert (Wash.)	3.00
126 Checklist No. 1	1.50

NO. PLAYER	NR. MT.
127 Tom Paciorek	.25
128 John Ellis	.25
129 Chris Speier	.25
130 Reggie Jackson	16.00
131 Bob Boone	2.00
132 Felix Milan	.25
133 David Clyde	.25
134 Denis Menke	.25
135 Roy White	.30
136 Rick Reuschel	2.00
137 Al Bumbry	.25
138 Ed Brinkman	.25
139 Aurelio Monteagudo	.25
140 Darrell Evans	.50
141 Pat Bourque	.25
142 Pedro Garcia	.25
143 Dick Woodson	.25
144 Walter Alston (Mgr.)	.75
145 Dock Ellis	.25
146 Ron Fairly	.25
147 Bart Johnson	.25
148 Dave Hilton (SD)	.30
148 Dave Hilton (Wash.)	3.00
149 Mac Scarce	.25
150 John Mayberry	.30
151 Diego Segui	.25
152 Oscar Gamble	.30
153 Jon Matlack	.25
154 Houston Astros	.40
155 Bert Campaneris	.35
156 Randy Moffitt	.25
157 Vic Harris	.25
158 Jack Billingham	.25
159 Jim Hart	.25
160 Brooks Robinson	4.00
161 Ray Burris (R)	.60
162 Bill Freehan	.40
163 Ken Berry	.25
164 Tom House	.25
165 Willie Davis	.25
166 Jack McKeon (Mgr.)	.25
167 Luis Tiant	.40
168 Danny Thompson	.25
169 Steve Rogers (R)	.75
170 Bill Melton	.25
171 Eduardo Rodriguez	.25
172 Gene Clines	.25
173 Randy Jones (SD)	.50
173 Randy Jones (Wash.)	3.50
174 Bill Robinson	.25
175 Reggie Cleveland	.25
176 John Lowenstein	.25
177 Dave Roberts	.25
178 Garry Maddox	.25
179 Yogi Berra (Mgr.)	1.25
180 Ken Holtzman	.25
181 Cesar Geronimo	.25
182 Lindy McDaniel	.25
183 Johnny Oates	.25
184 Texas Rangers	.60
185 Jose Cardenal	.25
186 Fred Scherman	.25
187 Don Baylor	1.00
188 Rudy Meoli	.25
189 Jim Brewer	.25
190 Tony Oliva	1.00

NO. PLAYER	NR. MT.
191 Al Fitzmorris	.25
192 Mario Guerrero	.25
193 Tom Walker	.25
194 Darrell Porter	.25
195 Carlos May	.25
196 Jim Fregosi	.35
197 Vicente Romo (SD)	.30
197 Vicente Romo (Wash.)	3.00
198 Dave Cash	.25
199 Mike Kekich	.25
200 Cesar Cedeno	.50
201 Batting Leaders:	3.00
Rod Carew, Pete Rose	
202 Home Run Leaders:	2.00
R. Jackson, Willie Stargell	
203 RBI Leaders:	2.00
R. Jackson, Willie Stargell	
204 Stolen Base Leaders:	.75
Tommy Harper, Lou Brock	
205 Victory Leaders:	.75
Wilbur Wood, Ron Bryant	
206 ERA Leaders:	2.50
Jim Palmer, T. Seaver	
207 Strikeout Leaders:	5.00
Nolan Ryan, Tom Seaver	
208 Leading Firemen:	.75
John Hiller, M. Marshall	
209 Ted Sizemore	.25
210 Bill Singer	.25
211 Chicago Cubs	.50
212 Rollie Fingers	2.50
213 Dave Rader	.25
214 Bill Grabarkewitz	.25
215 Al Kaline	4.00
216 Ray Sadecki	.25
217 Tim Foli	.25
218 Johnny Briggs	.25
219 Doug Griffin	.25
220 Don Sutton	2.00
221 Chuck Tanner (Mgr.)	.35
222 Ramon Hernandez	.25
223 Jeff Burroughs	.50
224 Roger Metzger	.25
225 Paul Splittorff	.30
226 Padres Team (SD)	.75
226 Padres Team (Wash.)	4.00
227 Mike Lum	.25
228 Ted Kubiak	.25
229 Fritz Peterson	.25
230 Tony Perez	1.50
231 Dick Tidrow	.25
232 Steve Brye	.25
233 Jim Barr	.25
234 John Milner	.25
235 Dave McNally	.25
236 R. Schoendienst (Mgr.)	.40
237 Ken Brett	.25
238 Fran Healy	.25
239 Bill Russell	.25
240 Joe Coleman	.25
241 Glenn Beckert (SD)	.25
241 Glenn Beckert (Wash.)	3.00
242 Bill Gogolewski	.25
243 Bob Oliver	.25
244 Carl Morton	.25
245 Cleon Jones	.25

NO.	PLAYER	NR. MT.
246	Oakland Athletics	.40
247	Rick Miller	.25
248	Tom Hall	.25
249	George Mitterwald	.25
250	W. McCovey (SD)	5.00
250	W. McCovey (Wash.)	20.00
251	Graig Nettles	1.25
252	Dave Parker (R)	35.00
253	John Boccabella	.25
254	Stan Bahnsen	.25
255	Larry Bowa	.60
256	Tom Griffin	.25
257	Buddy Bell	1.25
258	Jerry Morales	.25
259	Bob Reynolds	.25
260	Ted Simmons	1.00
261	Jerry Bell	.25
262	Ed Kirkpatrick	.25
263	Checklist No. 2	1.50
264	Joe Rudi	.25
265	Tug McGraw	.50
266	Jim Northrup	.25
267	Andy Messersmith	.35
268	Tom Grieve	.25
269	Bob Johnson	.25
270	Ron Santo	.40
271	Bill Hands	.25
272	Paul Casanova	.25
273	Checklist No. 3	1.50
274	Fred Beene	.25
275	Ron Hunt	.25
276	Bobby Winkles (Mgr.)	.35
277	Gary Nolan	.25
278	Cookie Rojas	.25
279	Jim Crawford	.25
280	Carl Yastrzemski	12.00
281	San F. Giants	.40
282	Doyle Alexander	.25
283	Mike Schmidt	100.00
284	Dave Duncan	.25
285	Reggie Smith	.40
286	Tony Muser	.25
287	Clay Kirby	.25
288	Gorman Thomas (R)	2.00
289	Rick Auerback	.25
290	Vida Blue	.40
291	Don Hahn	.25
292	Chuck Seelbach	.25
293	Milt May	.25
294	Steve Foucault	.25
295	Rick Monday	.35
296	Ray Corbin	.25
297	Hal Breeden	.25
298	Roric Harrison	.25
299	Gene Michael	.30
300	Pete Rose	15.00
301	Bob Montgomery	.25
302	Rudy May	.25
303	George Hendrick	.50
304	Don Wilson	.25
305	Tito Fuentes	.25
306	Earl Weaver (Mgr.)	.60
307	Luis Melendez	.25
308	Bruce Dal Canton	.25
309	Dave Roberts (SD)	.30
309	Dave Roberts (Wash.)	4.00
310	Terry Forster	.25
311	Jerry Grote	.25
312	Deron Johnson	.25
313	Barry Lersch	.25
314	Milwaukee Brewers	.40
315	Ron Cey	1.00
316	Jim Perry	.25
317	Richie Zisk	.25
318	Jim Merritt	.25
319	Randy Hundley	.25
320	Dusty Baker	.50
321	Steve Braun	.25
322	Ernie McAnally	.25
323	Richie Scheinblum	.25
324	Steve Kline	.25
325	Tommy Harper	.25
326	Sparky Anderson (Mgr.)	.50
327	Tom Timmerman	.25
328	Skip Jutze	.25

NO.	PLAYER	NR. MT.
329	Mark Belanger	.25
330	Juan Marichal	2.50
331	All-Star Catchers: Carlton Fisk, Johnny Bench	2.50
332	AS 1st Baseman: Dick Allen, Hank Aaron	2.00
333	AS 2nd Baseman: Rod Carew, Joe Morgan	2.50
334	AS 3rd Baseman: B. Robinson, Ron Santo	1.25
335	AS Shortstops: B. Campaneris, C. Speier	.35
336	AS Left Fielders: Pete Rose, Bobby Mercer	2.50
337	AS Center Fielders: Amos Otis, Cesar Cedeno	.35
338	AS Right Fielders: R. Jackson, B. Williams	3.00
339	AS Pitchers: Jim Hunter, Rick Wise	.75
340	Thurman Munson	6.00
341	Dan Driessen	.75
342	Jim Lonborg	.25
343	Kansas City Royals	.50
344	Mike Caldwell	.25
345	Bill North	.25
346	Ron Reed	.25
347	Sandy Alomar	.25
348	Pete Richert	.25
349	John Vukovich	.25
350	Bob Gibson	3.00
351	Dwight Evans	12.00
352	Bill Stoneman	.25
353	Rich Coggins	1.00
354	Whitey Lockman (Mgr.)	.60
355	Dave Nelson	.25
356	Jerry Koosman	.50
357	Buddy Bradford	.25
358	Dal Maxvill	.25
359	Brent Strom	.25
360	Greg Luzinski	.75
361	Don Carrithers	.25
362	Hal King	.25
363	New York Yankees	1.00
364	C. Gaston (SD)	.30
364	C. Gaston (Wash.)	3.00
365	Steve Busby	.25
366	Larry Hisle	.25
367	Norm Cash	.40
368	Manny Mota	.40
369	Paul Lindblad	.25
370	Bob Watson	.35
371	Jim Slaton	.25
372	Ken Reitz	.25
373	John Curtis	.25
374	Marty Perez	.25
375	Earl Williams	.25
376	Jorge Orta	.25
377	Ron Woods	.25
378	Burt Hooton	.25
379	Billy Martin (Mgr.)	.60
380	Bud Harrelson	.60
381	Charlies Sands	.25
382	Bob Moose	.25
383	Phil. Phillies	.50
384	Chris Chambliss	.35
385	Don Gullett	.35
386	Gary Matthews	.50
387	Rich Morales (SD)	.30
387	Rich Morales (Wash.)	3.00
388	Phil Roof	.25
389	Gates Brown	.25
390	Lou Piniella	.50
391	Billy Champion	.25
392	Dick Green	.25
393	Orlando Pena	.25
394	Ken Henderson	.25
395	Doug Rader	.25
396	Tommy Davis	.35
397	George Stone	.25
398	Duke Sims	.25
399	Mike Paul	.25
400	Harmon Killebrew	3.50
401	Elliott Maddox	.25
402	Jim Rooker	.25

NO.	PLAYER	NR. MT.
403	Darrell Johnson (Mgr.)	.30
404	Jim Howarth	.25
405	Ellie Rodriguez	.25
406	Steve Arlin	.25
407	Jim Wohlford	.25
408	Charlie Hough	.35
409	Ike Brown	.25
410	Pedro Borbon	.25
411	Frank Baker	.25
412	Chuck Taylor	.25
413	Don Money	.35
414	Checklist No. 4	1.50
415	Gary Gentry	.25
416	Chicago White Sox	.60
417	Rich Folkers	.25
418	Walt Williams	.25
419	Wayne Twitchell	.25
420	Ray Fosse	.25
421	Dan Fife	.25
422	Gonzalo Marquez	.25
423	Fred Stanley	.25
424	Jim Beauchamp	.25
425	Pete Broberg	.25
426	Rennie Stennett	.25
427	Bobby Bolin	.25
428	Gary Sutherland	.25
429	Dick Lange	.25
430	Matty Alou	.40
431	Gene Garber	.25
432	Chris Arnold	.25
433	Lerrin LaGrow	.25
434	Ken McMullen	.25
435	Dave Concepcion	.75
436	Don Hood	.25
437	Jim Lyttle	.25
438	Ed Herrmann	.25
439	Norm Miller	.25
440	Jim Kaat	1.00
441	Tom Ragland	.25
442	Alan Foster	.25
443	Tom Hutton	.25
444	Vic Davalillo	.25
445	George Medich	.25
446	Len Randle	.25
447	Frank Quilici (Mgr.)	.30
448	Ron Hodges	.25
449	Tom McCraw	.25
450	Rich Hebner	.25
451	Tommy John	1.50
452	Gene Hiser	.25
453	Balor Moore	.25
454	Kurt Bevacqua	.25
455	Tom Bradley	.25
456	Dave Winfield (R)	50.00
457	Chuck Goggin	.25
458	Jim Ray	.25
459	Cincinnati Reds	.50
460	Boog Powell	.50
461	John Odom	.25
462	Luis Alvarado	.25
463	Pat Dobson	.25
464	Jose Cruz	.50
465	Dick Bosman	.25
466	Dick Billings	.25
467	Winston Llenas	.25
468	Pepe Frias	.25
469	Joe Decker	.25
470	A.L. Playoffs: A's Beat Orioles	3.00
471	N.L. Playoffs: Mets Beat Reds	.75
472	World Series Game 1: Oakland 2, N.Y. 1	.75
473	World Series Game 2: N.Y. 10, Oakland 7	3.00
474	World Series Game 3: Oakland 3, N.Y. 2	.75
475	World Series Game 4: N.Y. 6, Oakland 1	.75
476	World Series Game 5: N.Y. 2, Oakland 0	.75
477	World Series Game 6: Oakland 3, N.Y. 1	3.00
478	World Series Game 7: Oakland 5, N.Y. 2	.75

NO.	PLAYER	NR. MT.
479	World Series: A's Win	.75
480	Willie Crawford	.25
481	Jerry Terrell	.25
482	Bob Didier	.25
483	Atlanta Braves	.50
484	Carmen Fanzone	.25
485	Felipe Alou	.40
486	Steve Stone	.30
487	Ted Martinez	.25
488	Andy Etchebarren	.25
489	Danny Murtaugh (Mgr.)	.25
490	Vada Pinson	.50
491	Roger Nelson	.25
492	Mike Rogodzinski	.25
493	Joe Hoerner	.25
494	Ed Goodson	.25
495	Dick McAuliffe	.25
496	Tom Murphy	.25
497	Bobby Mitchell	.25
498	Pat Corrales	.35
499	Rusty Torres	.25
500	Lee May	.30
501	Eddie Leon	.25
502	Dave LaRoche	.25
503	Eric Soderholm	.25
504	Joe Niekro	.50
505	Bill Buckner	.75
506	Ed Farmer	.25
507	Larry Stahl	.25
508	Montreal Expos	.40
509	Jesse Jefferson	.30
510	Wayne Garrett	.30
511	Toby Harrah	.35
512	Joe Lahoud	.25
513	Jim Campanis	.25
514	Paul Schaal	.25
515	Willie Montanez	.25
516	Horacio Pina	.25
517	Mike Hegan	.25
518	Derrel Thomas	.25
519	Bill Sharp	.25
520	Tim McCarver	.50
521	Ken Aspromonte (Mgr.)	.30
522	J.R. Richard	.40
523	Cecil Cooper	2.00
524	Bill Plummer	.25
525	Clyde Wright	.25
526	Frank Tepedino	.25
527	Bobby Darwin	.25
528	Bill Bonham	.25
529	Horace Clarke	.25
530	Mickey Stanley	.25
531	Gene Mauch (Mgr.)	.35
532	Skip Lockwood	.25
533	Mike Phillips	.25
534	Eddie Watt	.25
535	Bob Tolan	.25
536	Duffy Dyer	.25
537	Steve Mingori	.25
538	Cesar Tovar	.25
539	Lloyd Allen	.25
540	Bob Robertson	.25
541	Cleveland Indians	.60
542	Rich Gossage	2.00
543	Danny Cater	.25
544	Ron Schueler	.25
545	Billy Conigliaro	.25
546	Mike Corkins	.25
547	Glenn Borgmann	.25
548	Sonny Siebert	.25
549	Mike Jorgensen	.25
550	Sam McDowell	.35
551	Von Joshua	.25
552	Denny Doyle	.25
553	Jim Willoughby	.25
554	Tim Johnson	.25
555	Woodie Fryman	.25
556	Dave Campbell	.25
557	Jim McGlothlin	.25
558	Bill Fahey	.25
559	Darrell Chaney	.25
560	Mike Cuellar	.35
561	Ed Kranepool	.35
562	Jack Aker	.25

NO.	PLAYER	NR. MT.
563	Hal McRae	.35
564	Mike Ryan	.25
565	Milt Wilcox	.25
566	Jackie Hernandez	.25
567	Boston Red Sox	.50
568	Mike Torrez	.35
569	Rick Dempsey	.25
570	Ralph Garr	.25
571	Rich Hand	.25
572	Enzo Hernandez	.25
573	Mike Adams	.25
574	Bill Parsons	.25
575	Steve Garvey	12.00
576	Scipio Spinks	.25
577	Mike Sadek	.25
578	Ralph Houk (Mgr.)	.35
579	Cecil Upshaw	.25
580	Jim Spencer	.25
581	Fred Norman	.25
582	Bucky Dent (R)	2.00
583	Marty Pattin	.25
584	Ken Rudolph	.25
585	Merv Rettenmund	.25
586	Jack Brohamer	.25
587	Larry Christenson	.25
588	Hal Lanier	.35
589	Boots Day	.25
590	Roger Moret	.25
591	Sonny Jackson	.25
592	Ed Bane	.25
593	Steve Yeager	.25
594	Leroy Stanton	.25
595	Steve Blass	.25
596	Rookie Pitchers:	.40
	Wayne Garland, Fred Holdsworth, Dick Pole, Mark Littell	

NO.	PLAYER	NR. MT.
597	Rookie Shortstops:	.75
	John Gamble, Pete MacKanin, Dave Chalk, Manny Trillo	
598	Rookie Outfielders:	10.00
	Steve Ontiveros, Dave Augustine, Ken Griffey, Jim Tyrone	
599	Rookie Pitchers	5.00
	"San Diego"—small type	
	Ron Diorio, D. Freisleben, F. Riccelli, G. Shanahan	
599	Rookie Pitchers	2.50
	"San Diego"—large type	
599	Rookie Pitchers	1.00
	"Washington"	
	Ron Diorio, D. Freisleben, F. Riccelli, G. Shanahan	
600	Rookie Infielders:	5.00
	Ron Cash, Jim Cox, Bill Madlock, Reggie Sanders	
601	Rookie Outfielders:	2.50
	Ed Armbrister, Rich Bladt, B. Downing, B. McBride	
602	Rookie Pitchers	.50
	Glenn Abbott, Craig Swan R. Henninger, D. Vossler	
603	Rookie Catchers:	.40
	B. Foote, T. Lundstedt, C. Moore, S. Robles	
604	Rookie Infielders:	4.00
	Terry Hughes, John Knox, A. Thornton, F. White	

NO.	PLAYER	NR. MT.
605	Rookie Pitchers:	2.00
	Vic Albury, Ken Frailing, Kevin Kobel, Frank Tanana	
606	Rookie Outfielders:	.50
	Jim Fuller, Wilbur Howard, Tommy Smith, Otto Velez	
607	Rookie Shortstops:	.50
	Leo Foster, Dave Rosello, T. Heintzelman, F. Taveras	
608	Rookie Pitchers:	2.50
	Bob Apodaca, Mike Wallace D. Baney, J. D'Acquisto	
608	"Apodaca"—error misspelled "Apodoco"	2.00
609	Rico Petrocelli	.25
610	Dave Kingman	1.00
611	Rich Stelmaszek	.25
612	Luke Walker	.25
613	Dan Monzon	.25
614	Adrian Devine	.25
615	John Jeter	.25
616	Larry Gura	.35
617	Ted Ford	.25
618	Jim Mason	.25
619	Mike Anderson	.25
620	Al Downing	.35
621	Bernie Carbo	.25
622	Phil Gagliano	.25
623	Celerino Sanchez	.25
624	Bob Miller	.25
625	Ollie Brown	.25
626	Pittsburgh Pirates	.40
627	Carl Taylor	.25
628	Ivan Murrell	.25

NO.	PLAYER	NR. MT.
629	Rusty Staub	.75
630	Tommie Agee	.40
631	Steve Barber	.25
632	George Foster	.25
633	Dave Hamilton	.25
634	Eddie Mathews (Mgr.)	1.00
635	John Edwards	.25
636	Dave Goltz	.25
637	Checklist No. 5	1.50
638	Ken Sanders	.25
639	Joe Lovitto	.25
640	Milt Pappas	.40
641	Chuck Brinkman	.25
642	Terry Harmon	.25
643	Los Angeles Dodgers	.75
644	Wayne Granger	.25
645	Ken Boswell	.25
646	George Foster	1.25
647	Juan Beniquez	.60
648	Terry Crowley	.25
649	Fernando Gonzalez	.25
650	Mike Epstein	.25
651	Leron Lee	.25
652	Gail Hopkins	.25
653	Bob Stinson	.25
654	Jesus Alou	.40
654	Jesus Alou	5.00
	"outfield" deleted on front	
655	Mike Tyson	.25
656	Adrian Garrett	.25
657	Jim Shellenback	.25
658	Lee Lacy	.25
659	Joe Lis	.25
660	Larry Dierker (Exc. .15)	.50

1974 Topps Traded.... Complete Set of 44 Cards—Value $10.00 (Near Mint)

Topps' first Traded set. Topps issued another in 1976, and beginning in 1981 issued a Traded set every year. The traded set features players who were traded after the main set was printed. This set uses the same numbers as the regular set, followed by a "T".

NO.	PLAYER	NR. MT.
23 T	Craig Robinson	.15
42 T	Claude Osteen	.15
43 T	Jim Wynn	.25
51 T	Bobby Heise	.15
59 T	Ross Grimsley	.15
62 T	Bob Locker	.15
63 T	Bill Sudakis	.15
73 T	Mike Marshall	.25
123 T	Nelson Briles	.15
139 T	Aurelio Monteagudo	.15
151 T	Diego Segui	.15

NO.	PLAYER	NR. MT.
165 T	Willie Davis	.25
175 T	Reggie Cleveland	.15
182 T	Lindy McDaniel	.15
186 T	Fred Scherman	.15
249 T	George Mitterwald	.15
262 T	Ed Kirkpatrick	.15
269 T	Bob Johnson	.15
270 T	Ron Santo	.40
313 T	Barry Lersch	.15
319 T	Randy Hundley	.15
330 T	Juan Marichal	1.25

NO.	PLAYER	NR. MT.
348 T	Pete Richert	.15
373 T	John Curtis	.15
390 T	Lou Piniella	.60
428 T	Gary Sutherland	.15
454 T	Kurt Bevacqua	.15
458 T	Jim Ray	.15
485 T	Felipe Alou	.20
486 T	Steve Stone	.15
496 T	Tom Murphy	.15
516 T	Horacio Pina	.15
534 T	Eddie Watt	.15

NO.	PLAYER	NR. MT.
538 T	Cesar Tovar	.15
544 T	Ron Schueler	.15
579 T	Cecil Upshaw	.15
585 T	Merv Rettenmund	.15
612 T	Luke Walker	.15
616 T	Larry Gura	.20
618 T	Jim Mason	.15
630 T	Tommie Agee	.15
648 T	Terry Crowley	.15
649 T	Fernando Gonzalez	.15
—	Traded Checklist	.75

1975 Topps. . . . Complete Set of 660 Cards—Value $700.00 (Near Mint)

Features the rookie cards of Robin Yount, George Brett, Jim Rice, Gary Carter, Fred Lynn and Keith Hernandez. The set was also issued in a mini-size (2¼" x 3⅛") which was tested in a section of the country. The mini-size cards are worth 2 to 2½ times more than the regular size cards.

NO. PLAYER	NR. MT.	NO. PLAYER	NR. MT.	NO. PLAYER	NR. MT.	NO. PLAYER	NR. MT.
1 Highlights: (Exc. $3.00) ... 20.00 Aaron Sets Homer Mark		59 Ken Henderson	.30	124 Jerry Reuss	.45	188 Tom Griffin	.30
2 Highlights: Brock Steals 118 Bases	3.00	60 Fergie Jenkins	1.25	125 Ken Singleton	.45	189 1951 MVP's: Y. Berra, R. Campanella	1.25
3 Highlights: Gibson's 3000th Strikeout	3.00	61 Dave Winfield	12.00	126 Checklist No.1	1.00	190 1952 MVP': B. Shantz, Hank Bauer	.50
4 Highlights: Kaline's 3000th Hit	3.00	62 Fritz Peterson	.30	127 Glenn Borgmann	.30	191 1953 MVP's: Al Rosen, R. Campanella	.75
5 Highlights: Ryan Fans 300—3rd Year	9.00	63 Steve Swisher	.30	128 Bill Lee	.40	192 1954 MVP's: Yogi Berra, Willie Mays	1.25
6 Highlights: Marshall Hurls 106 Games	.75	64 Dave Chalk	.30	129 Rick Monday	.45	193 1955 MVP's: Y. Berra, R. Campanella	1.25
7 Highlights: No Hitters: Nolan Ryan, Dick Bosman, Steve Busby	1.50	65 Don Gullett	.30	130 Phil Niekro	2.00	194 1956 MVP's: M. Mantle, D. Newcombe	4.00
8 Rogelio Moret	.30	66 Willie Horton	.50	131 Toby Harrah	.35	195 1957 MVP's: Hank Aaron, M. Mantle	5.00
9 Frank Tepedino	.30	67 Tug McGraw	.60	132 Randy Moffitt	.30	196 1958 MVP's: J. Jensen, Ernie Banks	.75
10 Willie Davis	.45	68 Ron Blomberg	.30	133 Dan Driessen	.45	197 1959 MVP's: Nellie Fox, Ernie Banks	1.00
11 Bill Melton	.30	69 John Odom	.30	134 Ron Hodges	.30	198 1960 MVP's: Roger Maris, Dick Groat	.75
12 David Clyde	.30	70 Mike Schmidt	50.00	135 Charlie Spikes	.30	199 1961 MVP's: F. Robinson, Roger Maris	1.25
13 Gene Locklear	.30	71 Charlie Hough	.40	136 Jim Mason	.30	200 1962 MVP's: M. Mantle, Maury Wills	3.50
14 Milt Wilcox	.30	72 Royals/J. McKeon (Mgr.)	.75	137 Terry Forster	.45	201 1963 MVP's: Elston Howard, S. Koufax	.75
15 Jose Cardenal	.30	73 J.R. Richard	.50	138 Del Unser	.30	202 1964 MVP's: Ken Boyer, B. Robinson	.75
16 Frank Tanana	.50	74 Mark Belanger	.50	139 Horacio Pina	.30	203 1965 MVP's: Zoilo Versalles, W. Mays	1.00
17 Dave Concepcion	.65	75 Ted Simmons	1.00	140 Steve Garvey	7.00	204 1966 MVP's: F. Robinson, Bob Clemente	1.00
18 Tigers/R. Houk (Mgr.)	.75	76 Ed Sprague	.30	141 Mickey Stanley	.45	205 1967 MVP's: C. Yastrzemski, O. Cepeda	1.00
19 Jerry Koosman	.60	77 Richie Zisk	.50	142 Bob Reynolds	.30	206 1968 MVP's: D. McLain, Bob Gibson	1.00
20 Thurman Munson	6.00	78 Ray Corbin	.30	143 Cliff Johnson	.30	207 1969 MVP's: W. McCovey, H. Killebrew	1.00
21 Rollie Fingers	2.00	79 Gary Matthews	.50	144 Jim Wohlford	.30	208 1970 MVP's: Boog Powell, J. Bench	.75
22 Dave Cash	.30	80 Carlton Fisk	7.50	145 Ken Holtzman	.40	209 1971 MVP's; Vida Blue, Joe Torre	.60
23 Bill Russell	.40	81 Ron Reed	.30	146 San Diego Padres J. McNamara (Mgr.)	.75	210 1972 MVP's: Richie Allen, J. Bench	.60
24 Al Fitzmorris	.30	82 Pat Kelly	.30	147 Pedro Garcia	.30	211 1973 MVP's: Pete Rose, R. Jackson	3.00
25 Lea May	.50	83 Jim Merritt	.30	148 Jim Rooker	.30	212 1974 MVP's: J. Burroughs, S. Garvey	.75
26 Dave McNally	.50	84 Enzo Hernandez	.30	149 Tim Foli	.30	213 Oscar Gamble	.35
27 Ken Reitz	.30	85 Bill Bonham	.30	150 Bob Gibson	4.00	214 Harry Parker	.30
28 Tom Murphy	.30	86 Joe Lis	.30	151 Steve Brye	.30	215 Bobby Valentine	.45
29 Dave Parker		87 George Foster	1.00	152 Mario Guerrero	.30	216 San Francisco Giants Wes Westrum (Mgr.)	.45
30 Bert Blyleven		88 Tom Egan	.30	153 Rick Reuschel	.75	217 Lou Piniella	.60
31 Dave Rader	.30	89 Jim Ray	.30	154 Mike Lum	.30	218 Jerry Johnson	.30
32 Reggie Cleveland	.30	90 Rusty Staub	.75	155 Jim Bibby	.30	219 Ed Herrmann	.30
33 Dusty Baker	.75	91 Dick Green	.30	156 Dave Kingman	1.00	220 Don Sutton	2.00
34 Steve Renko	.30	92 Cecil Upshaw	.30	157 Pedro Borbon	.30	221 Aurelio Rodriguez	.30
35 Ron Santo	.50	93 Dave Lopes	.50	158 Jerry Grote	.30	222 Dan Spillner	.30
36 Joe Lovitto	.30	94 Jim Lonborg	.30	159 Steve Arlin	.30	223 Robin Yount (R)	120.00
37 Dave Freisleben	.30	95 John Mayberry	.50	160 Graig Nettles	1.00	224 Ramon Hernandez	.30
38 Buddy Bell	1.00	96 Mike Cosgrove	.30	161 Stan Bahnsen	.30	225 Bob Grich	.45
39 Andy Thornton	.50	97 Earl Williams	.30	162 Willie Montanez	.30	226 Bill Campbell	.30
40 Bill Singer	.30	98 Rich Folkers	.30	163 Jim Brewer	.30	227 Bob Watson	.40
41 Cesar Geronimo	.30	99 Mike Hegan	.30	164 Mickey Rivers	.45	228 George Brett (R)	150.00
42 Joe Coleman	.30	100 Willie Stargell	3.00	165 Doug Rader	.30		
43 Cleon Jones	.30	101 Expos/G. Mauch (Mgr.)	.75	166 Woodie Fryman	.30		
44 Pat Dobson	.30	102 Joe Decker	.30	167 Rich Coggins	.30		
45 Joe Rudi	.50	103 Rick Miller	.30	168 Bill Greif	.30		
46 Phillies/D. Ozark (Mgr.)	.75	104 Bill Madlock	1.50	169 Cookie Rojas	.30		
47 Tommy John	1.25	105 Buzz Capra	.30	170 Bert Campaneris	.50		
48 Freddie Patek	.30	106 Mike Hargrove (R)	.75	171 Ed Kirkpatrick	.30		
49 Larry Dierker	.30	107 Jim Barr	.30	172 Boston Red Sox D. Johnson (Mgr.)	1.00		
50 Brook Robinson	5.00	108 Tom Hall	.30	173 Steve Rogers	.40		
51 Bob Forsch	1.00	109 George Hendrick	.50	174 Bake McBride	.30		
52 Darrell Porter	.50	110 Wilbur Wood	.40	175 Don Money	.30		
53 Dave Giusti	.30	111 Wayne Garrett	.30	176 Burt Hooton	.40		
54 Eric Soderholm	.30	112 Larry Hardy	.30	177 Vic Correll	.30		
55 Bobby Bonds	.60	113 Elliot Maddox	.30	178 Cesar Tovar	.30		
56 Rick Wise	.30	114 Dick Lange	.30	179 Tom Bradley	.30		
57 Dave Johnson	.60	115 Joe Ferguson	.30	180 Joe Morgan	5.00		
58 Chuck Taylor	.30	116 Lerrin LaGrow	.30	181 Fred Beene	.30		
		117 Orioles/E. Weaver (Mgr.)	.75	182 Don Hahn	.30		
		118 Mike Anderson	.30	183 Mel Stottlemyre	.45		
		119 Tommy Helms	.30	184 Jorge Orta	.30		
		120 Steve Busby (photo of Fran Healy)	.50	185 Steve Carlton	6.00		
		121 Bill North	.30	186 Willie Crawford	.30		
		122 Al Hrabosky	.40	187 Denny Doyle	.30		
		123 Johnny Briggs	.30				

NO.	PLAYER	NR. MT.
229	Barry Foote	.30
230	Jim Hunter	2.50
231	Mike Tyson	.30
232	Diego Segui	.30
233	Billy Grabarkewitz	.30
234	Tom Grieve	.30
235	Jack Billingham	.30
236	Angels/D. Williams (Mgr.)	.75
237	Carl Morton	.30
238	Dave Duncan	.30
239	George Stone	.30
240	Garry Maddox	.45
241	Dick Tidrow	.30
242	Jay Johnstone	.30
243	Jim Kaat	1.00
244	Bill Buckner	.65
245	Mickey Lolich	.50
246	St. Louis Cardinals Red Schoendienst (Mgr.)	.75
247	Enos Cabell	.30
248	Randy Jones	.30
249	Danny Thompson	.30
250	Ken Brett	.30
251	Fran Healy	.30
252	Fred Scherman	.30
253	Jesus Alou	.30
254	Mike Torrez	.45
255	Dwight Evans	4.00
256	Billy Champion	.30
257	Checklist No. 2	1.00
258	Dave LaRoche	.30
259	Len Randle	.30
260	Johnny Bench	12.00
261	Andy Hassler	.30
262	Rowland Office	.30
263	Jim Perry	.30
264	John Milner	.30
265	Ron Bryant	.30
266	Sandy Alomar	.30
267	Dick Ruthven	.30
268	Hal McRae	.45
269	Doug Rau	.30
270	Ron Fairly	.30
271	Jerry Moses	.30
272	Lynn McGlothen	.30
273	Steve Braun	.30
274	Vincente Romo	.30
275	Paul Blair	.30
276	Chicago White Sox Chuck Tanner (Mgr.)	.75
277	Frank Taveras	.50
278	Paul Lindblad	.30
279	Milt May	.30
280	Carl Yastrzemski	10.00
281	Jim Slaton	.30
282	Jerry Morales	.30
283	Steve Foucault	.30
284	Ken Griffey	1.50
285	Ellie Rodriguez	.30
286	Mike Jorgensen	.30
287	Roric Harrison	.30
288	Bruce Ellingsen	.30
289	Ken Rudolph	.30
290	Jon Matlack	.40
291	Bill Sudakis	.30
292	Ron Schueler	.30
293	Dick Sharon	.30
294	Geoff Zahn	.30
295	Vada Pinson	.50
296	Alan Foster	.30
297	Craig Kusick	.30
298	Johnny Grubb	.30
299	Bucky Dent	.60
300	Reggie Jackson	13.00
301	Dave Roberts	.30
302	Rick Burleson (R)	.60
303	Grant Jackson	.30
304	Pittsburgh Pirates Danny Murtaugh (Mgr.)	.75
305	Jim Colborn	.30
306	Batting Leaders: Rod Carew, Ralph Garr	.75
307	Home Run Leaders: Dick Allen, Mike Schmidt	1.50

NO.	PLAYER	NR. MT.
308	RBI Leaders: J. Burroughs, J. Bench	.75
309	Stolen Base Leaders: Bill North, Lou Brock	.60
310	Victory Leaders: Andy Messersmith, Jim Hunter, Fergie Jenkins, Phil Niekro	.60
311	ERA Leaders: Jim Hunter, Buzz Capra	.50
312	Strikeout Leaders: Nolan Ryan, Steve Carlton	3.00
313	Leading Firemen: Mike Marshall, Terry Forster	.45
314	Buck Martinez	.30
315	Don Kessinger	.40
316	Jackie Brown	.30
317	Joe LaHoud	.30
318	Ernie McAnally	.30
319	Johnny Oates	.30
320	Pete Rose	14.00
321	Rudy May	.30
322	Ed Goodson	.30
323	Fred Holdsworth	.30
324	Ed Kranepool	.45
325	Tony Oliva	.75
326	Wayne Twitchell	.30
327	Jerry Hairston	.30
328	Sonny Siebert	.30
329	Ted Kubiak	.30
330	Mike Marshall	.40
331	Cleveland Indians Frank Robinson (Mgr.)	.75
332	Fred Kendall	.30
333	Dick Drago	.30
334	Greg Gross	.30
335	Jim Palmer	5.00
336	Rennie Stennett	.30
337	Kevin Kobel	.30
338	Rick Stelmaszek	.30
339	Jim Fregosi	.40
340	Paul Splittorff	.30
341	Hal Breeden	.30
342	Leroy Stanton	.30
343	Danny Frisella	.30
344	Ben Oglivie	.40
345	Clay Carroll	.30
346	Bobby Darwin	.30
347	Mike Caldwell	.30
348	Tony Muser	.30
349	Ray Sadecki	.30
350	Bobby Murcer	.65
351	Bob Boone	.75
352	Darold Knowles	.30
353	Luis Melendez	.30
354	Dick Bosman	.30
355	Chris Cannizzaro	.30
356	Rico Petrocelli	.40
357	Ken Frosch	.30
358	Al Bumbry	.30
359	Paul Popovich	.30
360	George Scott	.30
361	Los Angeles Dodgers Walter Alston (Mgr.)	.75
362	Steve Hargan	.30
363	Carmen Fanzone	.30
364	Doug Bird	.30
365	Bob Bailey	.30
366	Ken Sanders	.30
367	Craig Robinson	.30
368	Vic Albury	.30
369	Merv Rettenmund	.30
370	Tom Seaver	9.00
371	Gates Brown	.30
372	John D'Acquisto	.30
373	Bill Sharp	.30
374	Eddie Watt	.30
375	Roy White	.45
376	Steve Yeager	.30
377	Tom Hilgendorf	.30
378	Derrel Thomas	.30
379	Bernie Carbo	.30
380	Sal Bando	.45

NO.	PLAYER	NR. MT.
381	John Curtis	.30
382	Don Baylor	1.00
383	Jim York	.30
384	Milwaukee Brewers Del Crandall (Mgr.)	.60
385	Dock Ellis	.30
386	Checklist: No. 3	1.00
387	Jim Spencer	.30
388	Steve Stone	.30
389	Tony Solaita	.30
390	Ron Cey	1.00
391	Don DeMola	.30
392	Bruce Bochte (R)	.60
393	Gary Gentry	.30
394	Larvell Blanks	.30
395	Bud Harrelson	.50
396	Fred Norman	.30
397	Bill Freehan	.40
398	Elias Sosa	.30
399	Terry Harmon	.30
400	Dick Allen	.45
401	Mike Wallace	.30
402	Bob Tolan	.30
403	Tom Buskey	.30
404	Ted Sizemore	.30
405	John Montague	.30
406	Bob Gallagher	.30
407	Herb Washington	.30
408	Clyde Wright	.30
409	Bob Robertson	.30
410	Mike Cueller	.40
411	George Mitterwald	.30
412	Bill Hands	.30
413	Marty Pattin	.30
414	Manny Mota	.45
415	John Hiller	.30
416	Larry Lintz	.30
417	Skip Lockwood	.30
418	Leo Foster	.30
419	Dave Goltz	.30
420	Larry Bowa	.60
421	Mets/Y. Berra (Mgr.)	.75
422	Brian Downing	.50
423	Clay Kirby	.30
424	John Lowenstein	.30
425	Tito Fuentes	.30
426	Geroge Medich	.30
427	Clarence Gaston	.30
428	Dave Hamilton	.30
429	Jim Dwyer	.30
430	Luis Tiant	.45
431	Rod Gilbreath	.30
432	Ken Berry	.30
433	Larry Demery	.30
434	Bob Locker	.30
435	Dave Nelson	.30
436	Ken Frailing	.30
437	Al Cowens (R)	.65
438	Don Carrithers	.30
439	Ed Brinkman	.30
440	Andy Messersmith	.40
441	Bobby Heise	.30
442	Maximino Leon	.30
443	Twins/F. Quilici (Mgr.)	.60
444	Gene Garber	.30
445	Felix Millan	.30
446	Bart Johnson	.30
447	Terry Crowley	.30
448	Frank Duffy	.30
449	Charlie Williams	.30
450	Willie McCovey	3.00
451	Rick Dempsey	.40
452	Angel Mangual	.30
453	Claude Osteen	.30
454	Doug Griffin	.30
455	Don Wilson	.30
456	Bob Coluccio	.30
457	Mario Mendoza	.30
458	Ross Grimsley	.30
459	1974 AL Champs: A's over Orioles	.50
460	1974 NL Champs: Dodgers over Pirates	.75
461	World Series Game 1: Oakland 3, Los Angeles 2	2.00

NO.	PLAYER	NR. MT.
462	World Series Game 2: Los Angeles 3, Oakland 2	.60
463	World Series Game 3: Oakland 3, Los Angeles 2	.75
464	World Series Game 4: Oakland 5, Los Angeles 2	.50
465	World Series Game 5 Oakland 3, Los Angeles 2	.50
466	A's Win 3rd World Series	.60
467	Ed Halicki	.30
468	Bobby Mitchell	.30
469	Tom Dettore	.30
470	Jeff Burroughs	.40
471	Bob Stinson	.30
472	Bruce Dal Canton	.30
473	Ken McMullen	.30
474	Luke Walker	.30
475	Darrell Evans	.65
476	Eduardo Figueroa	.30
477	Tom Hutton	.30
478	Tom Burgmeier	.30
479	Ken Boswell	.30
480	Carlos May	.30
481	Will McEnaney	.30
482	Tom McCraw	.30
483	Steve Ontiveros	.30
484	Glenn Beckert	.30
485	Sparky Lyle	.45
486	Ray Fosse	.30
487	Astros/P. Gomez (Mgr.)	.75
488	Bill Travers	.30
489	Cecil Cooper	1.50
490	Reggie Smith	.40
491	Doyle Alexander	.30
492	Rich Hebner	.30
493	Don Stanhouse	.30
494	Pete LaCock	.30
495	Nelson Briles	.30
496	Pepe Frias	.30
497	Jim Nettles	.30
498	Al Downing	.30
499	Marty Perez	.30
500	Nolan Ryan	35.00
501	Bill Robinson	.30
502	Pat Bourque	.30
503	Fred Stanley	.30
504	Buddy Bradford	.30
505	Chris Speier	.30
506	Leron Lee	.30
507	Tom Carroll	.30
508	Bob Hansen	.30
509	Dave Hilton	.30
510	Vida Blue	.45
511	Rangers/B. Martin (Mgr.)	.75
512	Larry Milbourne	.30
513	Dick Pole	.30
514	Jose Cruz	.60
515	Manny Sanguillen	.30
516	Don Hood	.30
517	Checklist: No. 4	1.00
518	Leo Cardenas	.30
519	Jim Todd	.30
520	Amos Otis	.50
521	Dennis Blair	.30
522	Gary Sutherland	.30
523	Tom Paciorek	.30
524	John Doherty	.30
525	Tom House	.30
526	Larry Hisle	.30
527	Mac Scarce	.30
528	Eddie Leon	.30
529	Gary Thomasson	.30
530	Gaylord Perry	2.00
531	Cincinnati Reds Sparky Anderson (Mgr.)	.75
532	Gorman Thomas	.75
533	Rudy Meoli	.30
534	Alex Johnson	.30
535	Gene Tenace	.30
536	Bob Moose	.30
537	Tommy Harper	.30
538	Duffy Dyer	.30
539	Jesse Jefferson	.30
540	Lou Brock	3.00

NO.	PLAYER	NR. MT.	NO.	PLAYER	NR. MT.	NO.	PLAYER	NR. MT.	NO.	PLAYER	NR. MT.
541	Roger Metzger	.30	579	Skip Pitlock	.30	615	Rookie Pitchers:	1.00	627	Tom Walker	.30
542	Pete Broberg	.30	580	Frank Robinson	3.00		Dennis Leonard, Tom		628	Ron LeFlore (R)	.60
543	Larry Biittner	.30	581	Darrel Chaney	.30		Underwood, Hank Webb,		629	Joe Hoerner	.30
544	Steve Mingori	.30	582	Eduardo Rodriguez	.30		Pat Darcy		630	Greg Luzinski	.50
545	Billy Williams	3.00	583	Andy Etchebarren	.30	616	Rookie Outfielders	30.00	631	Lee Lacy	.30
546	John Knox	.30	584	Mike Garman	.30		Jim Rice, D. Augustine,		632	Morris Nettles	.30
547	Von Joshua	.30	585	Chris Chambliss	.50		Pepe Mangual, J. Scott		633	Paul Casanova	.30
548	Charlie Sands	.30	586	Tim McCarver	.75	617	Rookie Infielders:	2.00	634	Cy Acosta	.30
549	Bill Butler	.30	587	Chris Ward	.30		Mike Cubbage, Reggie		635	Chuck Dobson	.30
550	Ralph Garr	.30	588	Rick Auerbach	.30		Sanders, Manny Trillo,		636	Charlie Moore	.30
551	Larry Christenson	.30	589	Braves/C. King (Mgr.)	.75		Doug DeCinces		637	Ted Martinez	.30
552	Jack Brohamer	.30	590	Cesar Cedeno	.65	618	Rookie Pitchers:	3.00	638	Cubs/J. Marshall (Mgr.)	.75
553	John Boccabella	.30	591	Glenn Abbott	.30		Tom Johnson, Jamie		639	Steve Kline	.30
554	Rich Gossage	1.50	592	Balor Moore	.30		Easterly, Scott McGregor,		640	Harmon Killebrew	4.00
555	Al Oliver	.75	593	Gene Lamont	.30		Rick Rhoden		641	Jim Northrup	.30
556	Tim Johnson	.30	594	Jim Fuller	.30	619	Rookie Outfielders:	.40	642	Mike Phillips	.30
557	Larry Gura	.30	595	Joe Niekro	.75		Benny Ayala, Nyls Nyman,		643	Brent Strom	.30
558	Dave Roberts	.30	596	Ollie Brown	.30		Tommy Smith, Jerry Turner		644	Bill Fahey	.30
559	Bob Montgomery	.30	597	Winston Llenas	.30	620	Rookie Catchers/OF's	35.00	645	Danny Cater	.30
560	Tony Perez	1.25	598	Bruce Kison	.30		Gary Carter, Marc Hill,		646	Checklist No. 5	1.00
561	A's/Alvin Dark (Mgr.)	.60	599	Nate Colbert	.30		Danny Meyer, Leon Roberts		647	Claudell Washington	2.00
562	Gary Nolan	.30	600	Rod Carew	6.00	621	Rookie Pitchers:	.75	648	Dave Pagan	.30
563	Wilbur Howard	.30	601	Juan Beniquez	.30		John Denny, Rawly		649	Jack Heidemann	.30
564	Tommy Davis	.40	602	John Vukovich	.30		Eastwick, Jim Kern,		650	Dave May	.30
565	Joe Torre	.60	603	Lew Krausse	.30		Juan Veintidos		651	John Morlan	.30
566	Ray Burris	.30	604	Oscar Zamora	.30	622	Rookie Outfielders:	12.00	652	Lindy McDaniel	.30
567	Jim Sundberg (R)	.75	605	John Ellis	.30		Ed Armbrister, Fred Lynn,		653	Lee Richards	.30
568	Dale Murray	.30	606	Bruce Miller	.30		T. Whitfield, Tom Poquette		654	Jerry Terrell	.30
569	Frank White	.75	607	Jim Holt	.30	623	Rookie Infielders:	24.00	655	Rico Carty	.50
570	Jim Wynn	.40	608	Gene Michael	.30		Phil Garner, Bob Sheldon,		656	Bill Plummer	.30
571	Dave Lemanczyk	.30	609	Ellie Hendricks	.30		K. Hernandez, T. Veryzer		657	Bob Oliver	.30
572	Roger Nelson	.30	610	Ron Hunt	.30	624	Rookie Pitchers:	.40	658	Vic Harris	.30
573	Orlando Pena	.30	611	Yankees/B. Virdon (Mgr.)	.75		Doug Konieczny, Gary		659	Bob Apodaca	.30
574	Tony Taylor	.30	612	Terry Hughes	.30		Lavelle, Jim Otten,		660	Hank Aaron	20.00
575	Gene Clines	.30	613	Bill Parsons	.30		Eddie Solomon				
576	Phil Roof	.30	614	Rookie Pitchers:	.45	625	Boog Powell	.50			
577	John Morris	.30		Jack Kucek, Dyar Miller,		626	Larry Haney	.30			
578	Dave Tomlin	.30		Paul Siebert, Vern Ruhle			(Photo of Dave Duncan)				

1976 Topps. . . . Complete Set of 660 Cards—Value $375.00 (Near Mint)

Features the rookie card of Ron Guidry. This set includes the only card ever issued for the Joe Garagiola and Bazooka "Bubble Gum Blowing Champ". Topps added a 44-card Traded set later in the season.

NO.	PLAYER	NR. MT.	NO.	PLAYER	NR. MT.	NO.	PLAYER	NR. MT.	NO.	PLAYER	NR. MT.
1	Record—Aaron (Exc. $3.50)	13.00	9	Paul Lindblad	.20	29	Rick Burleson	.30	49	Dave Duncan	.20
	Most RBI's—2,262		10	Lou Brock	2.50	30	John Montefusco (R)	.35	50	F. Lynn	2.00
2	Record—Bonds	.40	11	Jim Hughes	.20	31	Len Randle	.20	51	Ray Buris	.20
	Most Lead-Off Homers—32;		12	Richie Zisk	.30	32	Danny Frisella	.20	52	Dave Chalk	.20
	Most Seasons of 30 HR's;		13	Johnny Wockenfuss	.20	33	Bill North	.20	53	Mike Beard	.20
	and 30 Stolen Bases		14	Gene Garber	.20	34	Mike Garman	.20	54	Dave Rader	.20
3	Record—Lolich	.40	15	George Scott	.25	35	Tony Oliva	.75	55	Gaylord Perry	2.00
	Most Strikeouts		16	Bob Apodaca	.20	36	Frank Taveras	.20	56	Bob Toaln	.20
	Lefthander—2,679		17	New York Yankees	1.00	37	John Hiller	.20	57	Phil Garner	.25
4	Record—Lopes	.40	18	Dale Murray	.20	38	Garry Maddox	.20	58	Ron Reed	.20
	Most Consecutive Steal		19	George Brett	35.00	39	Pete Broberg	.20	59	Larry Hisle	.20
	Attempts—38		20	Bob Watson	.20	40	Dave Kingman	.75	60	Jerry Reuss	.25
5	Record—Seaver	2.50	21	Dave LaRoche	.20	41	Tippy Martinez (R)	.35	61	Ron LeFlore	.25
	Most Consecutive Seasons		22	Bill Russell	.20	42	Barry Foote	.20	62	Johnny Oates	.20
	of 200 Strikeouts—8		23	Brian Downing	.30	43	Paul Splittorff	.30	63	Bobby Darwin	.20
6	Record—Stennett	.40	24	Cesar Geronimo	.20	44	Doug Rader	.20	64	Jerry Koosman	.30
	Most Hits in a Nine		25	Mick Torrez	.20	45	Boog Powell	.40	65	Chris Chambliss	.30
	Inning Game—7		26	Andy Thornton	.30	46	Los Angeles Dodgers	1.00	66	Father & Son:	.40
7	Jim Umbarger	.20	27	Ed Figueroa	.20	47	Jesse Jefferson	.20		Gus Bell,	
8	Tito Fuentes	.20	28	Dusty Baker	.35	48	Dave Concepcion	.50		Buddy Bell	

NO. PLAYER	NR. MT.
67 Father & Son:	.25
Ray Boone,	
Bob Boone	
68 Father & Son:	.25
Joe Coleman,	
Joe Coleman, Jr.	
69 Father & Son:	.25
Jim Hegan,	
Mike Hegan	
70 Father & Son:	.25
Roy Smalley,	
Roy Smalley Jr.	
71 Steve Rogers	.35
72 Hal McRae	.30
73 Baltimore Orioles	.75
74 Oscar Gamble	.25
75 Larry Dierker	.20
76 Willie Crawford	.20
77 Pedro Borbon	.20
78 Cecil Cooper	1.00
79 Jerry Morales	.20
80 Jim Kaat	.75
81 Darrell Evans	.50
82 Von Joshua	.20
83 Jim Spencer	.20
84 Brent Strom	.20
85 Mickey Rivers	.30
86 Mike Tyson	.20
87 Tom Burgmeier	.20
88 Duffy Dyer	.20
89 Vern Ruhle	.20
90 Sal Bando	.30
91 Tom Hutton	.20
92 Eduardo Rodriguez	.20
93 Mike Phillips	.20
94 Jim Dwyer	.20
95 Brooks Robinson	3.00
96 Doug Bird	.20
97 Wilbur Howard	.20
98 Dennis Eckersley (R)	25.00
99 Lee Lacy	.25
100 Jim Hunter	2.50
101 Pete LaCock	.20
102 Jim Willoughby	.20
103 Biff Pocoroba	.20
104 Cincinnati Reds	.75
105 Gary Lavelle	.20
106 Tom Grieve	.20
107 Dave Roberts	.20
108 Don Kirkwood	.20
109 Larry Lintz	.20
110 Carlos May	.20
111 Danny Thompson	.20
112 Kent Tekulve (R)	.75
113 Gary Sutherland	.20
114 Jay Johstone	.20
115 Ken Holtzman	.20
116 Charlie Moore	.20
117 Mike Jorgensen	.20
118 Boston Red Sox	1.00
119 Checklist No. 1	1.50
120 Rusty Staub	.35
121 Tony Solaita	.20
122 Mike Cosgrove	.20
123 Walt Williams	.20
124 Doug Rau	.20
125 Don Baylor	.75
126 Tom Dettore	.20
127 Larvell Blanks	.20
128 Ken Griffey	.75
129 Andy Etchebarren	.20
130 Luis Tiant	.35
131 Bill Stein	.20
132 Don Hood	.20
133 Gary Matthews	.30
134 Mike Ivie	.20
135 Bake McBride	.20
136 Dave Goltz	.20
137 Bill Robinson	.20
138 Lerrin LaGrow	.20
139 Gorman Thomas	.50
140 Vida Blue	.30
141 Larry Parrish (R)	1.25
142 Dick Drago	.20
143 Jerry Grote	.20

NO. PLAYER	NR. MT.
144 Al Fitzmorris	.20
145 Larry Bowa	.50
146 George Medich	.20
147 Houston Astros	.75
148 Stan Thomas	.20
149 Tommy Davis	.30
150 Steve Garvey	5.00
151 Bill Bonham	.20
152 Leroy Stanton	.20
153 Buzz Capra	.20
154 Bucky Dent	.50
155 Jack Billingham	.20
156 Rico Carty	.30
157 Mike Caldwell	.20
158 Ken Reitz	.20
159 Jerry Terrell	.20
160 Dave Winfield	7.50
161 Bruce Kison	.20
162 Jack Pierce	.20
163 Jim Staton	.20
164 Pepe Mangual	.20
165 Gene Tenace	.20
166 Skip Lockwood	.20
167 Freddie Patek	.20
168 Tom Hilgendorf	.20
169 Graig Nettles	1.00
170 Rick Wise	.30
171 Greg Gross	.20
172 Texas Rangers	.75
173 Steve Swisher	.20
174 Charlie Hough	.30
175 Ken Singleton	.30
176 Dick Lange	.20
177 Marty Perez	.20
178 Tom Buskey	.20
179 George Foster	1.00
180 Rich Gossage	1.25
181 Willie Montanez	.20
182 Harry Rasmussen	.20
183 Steve Braun	.20
184 Bill Greif	.20
185 Dave Parker	6.00
186 Tom Walker	.20
187 Pedro Garcia	.20
188 Fred Scherman	.20
189 Claudell Washington	.50
190 Jon Matlack	.25
191 NL Batting Leaders:	.50
Ted Simmons, Bill Madlock,	
Manny Sanguillen	
192 AL Batting Leaders:	1.50
Fred Lynn, Rod Carew,	
Thurman Munson	
193 NL Home Run Leaders:	1.25
Mike Schmidt, Greg	
Luzinski, Dave Kingman	
194 AL Home Run Leaders:	.75
John Mayberry, Reggie	
Jackson, George Scott	
195 NL RBI Leaders:	1.00
Greg Luzinski, Johnny	
Bench, Tony Perez	
196 AL RBI Leaders:	.60
John Mayberry, George	
Scott, Fred Lynn	
197 NL Stolen Base Leaders:	1.00
Dave Lopes, Lou Brock,	
Joe Morgan	
198 AL Stolen Base Leaders:	.50
Mickey Rivers, Claudell	
Washington, Amos Otis	
199 NL Victory Leaders:	.60
Tom Seaver, Randy Jones,	
Andy Messersmith	
200 AL Victory Leaders:	1.00
Jim Palmer, Jim Hunter,	
Vida Blue	
201 NL ERA Leaders:	.60
Randy Jones, Andy	
Messersmith, Tom Seaver	
202 AL ERA Leaders:	1.50
Jim Hunter, Dennis	
Eckersley, Jim Palmer	
203 NL Strikeout Leaders:	.60
John Montefusco, Andy	
Messersmith, Tom Seaver	

NO. PLAYER	NR. MT.
204 AL Strikeout Leaders:	.60
Frank Tanana, Gaylord	
Perry, Bert Blyleven	
205 Leading Firemen:	.50
Al Hrabosky, Rich Gossage	
206 Manny Trillo	.30
207 Andy Hassler	.20
208 Mike Lum	.20
209 Alan Ashby	.30
210 Lee May	.30
211 Clay Carroll	.20
212 Pat Kelly	.20
213 Dave Heaverlo	.20
214 Eric Soderholm	.20
215 Reggie Smith	.35
216 Montreal Expos	.60
217 Dave Freisleben	.20
218 John Knox	.20
219 Tom Murphy	.20
220 Manny Sanguillen	.30
221 Jim Todd	.20
222 Wayne Garrett	.20
223 Ollie Brown	.20
224 Jim York	.20
225 Roy White	.30
226 Jim Sundberg	.25
227 Oscar Zamora	.20
228 John Hale	.20
229 Jerry Remy (R)	.30
230 Carl Yastrzemski	8.00
231 Tom House	.20
232 Frank Duffy	.20
233 Grant Jackson	.20
234 Mike Sadek	.20
235 Bert Blyleven	1.25
236 Kansas City Royals	.75
237 Dave Hamilton	.20
238 Larry Biittner	.20
239 John Curtis	.20
240 Pete Rose	15.00
241 Hector Torres	.20
242 Dan Meyer	.20
243 Jim Rooker	.20
244 Bill Sharp	.20
245 Felix Millan	.20
246 Cesar Tovar	.20
247 Terry Harmon	.20
248 Dick Tidrow	.20
249 Cliff Johnson	.20
250 Fergie Jenkins	1.00
251 Rick Monday	.30
252 Tim Nordbrook	.20
253 Bill Buckner	.50
254 Rudy Meoli	.20
255 Fritz Peterson	.20
256 Rowland Office	.20
257 Ross Grimsley	.20
258 Nyls Nyman	.20
259 Darrel Chaney	.20
260 Steve Busby	.30
261 Gary Thomasson	.50
262 Checklist No. 2	1.00
263 Lyman Bostock (R)	.50
264 Steve Renko	.20
265 Willie Davis	.30
266 Alan Foster	.20
267 Aurelio Rodriguez	.20
268 Del Unser	.20
269 Rick Austin	.20
270 Willie Stargell	3.00
271 Jim Lonborg	.20
272 Rick Dempsey	.25
273 Joe Niekro	.30
274 Tommy Harper	.20
275 Rick Manning (R)	.30
276 Mickey Scott	.20
277 Chicago Cubs	.75
278 Bernie Carbo	.20
279 Roy Howell	.20
280 Burt Hooton	.30
281 Dave May	.20
282 Dan Osborn	.20
283 Merv Rettenmund	.20
284 Steve Ontiveros	.20
285 Mike Cuellar	.25

NO. PLAYER	NR. MT.
286 Jim Wohlford	.20
287 Pete Mackanin	.20
288 Bill Campbell	.20
289 Enzo Hernandez	.20
290 Ted Simmons	.75
291 Ken Sanders	.20
292 Leon Roberts	.20
293 Bill Castro	.20
294 Ed Kirkpatrick	.20
295 Dave Cash	.20
296 Pat Dobson	.20
297 Roger Metzger	.20
298 Dick Bosman	.20
299 Champ Summers	.20
300 Johnny Bench	10.00
301 Jackie Brown	.20
302 Rick Miller	.20
303 Steve Foucault	.20
304 California Angels	.75
305 Andy Messersmith	.30
306 Rod Gilbreath	.20
307 Al Bumbry	.20
308 Jim Barr	.20
309 Bill Melton	.20
310 Randy Jones	.30
311 Cookie Rojas	.20
312 Don Carrithers	.20
313 Dan Ford (R)	.35
314 Ed Kranepool	.30
315 Al Hrabosky	.20
316 Robin Yount	35.00
317 John Candelaria (R)	3.00
318 Bob Boone	.75
319 Larry Gura	.20
320 Willie Horton	.30
321 Jose Cruz	.40
322 Glenn Abbott	.20
323 Rob Sperring	.20
324 Jim Bibby	.20
325 Tony Perez	1.00
326 Dick Pole	.20
327 Dave Moates	.20
328 Carl Morton	.20
329 Joe Ferguson	.20
330 Nolan Ryan	24.00
331 San Diego Padres	.75
332 Charlie Williams	.20
333 Bob Coluccio	.20
334 Dennis Leonard	.25
335 Bob Grich	.25
336 Vic Albury	.20
337 Bud Harrelson	.20
338 Bob Bailey	.20
339 John Denny	.35
340 Jim Rice	8.00
341 All-Time 1B:	3.00
Lou Gehrig	
342 All-Time 2B:	2.00
Rogers Hornsby	
343 All-Time 3B:	1.00
Pie Traynor	
344 All-Time SS:	2.00
Honus Wagner	
345 All-Time OF:	7.00
Babe Ruth	
346 All-Time OF:	4.00
Ty Cobb	
347 All-Time OF:	4.00
Ted Williams	
348 All-Time Catcher:	1.00
Mickey Cochrane	
349 All-Time Pitcher (Right)	1.50
Walter Johnson	
350 All-Time Pitcher (Left)	.75
Lefty Grove	
351 Randy Hundley	.20
352 Dave Giusti	.20
353 Sixto Lezcano (R)	.40
354 Ron Blomberg	.20
355 Steve Carlton	6.00
356 Ted Martinez	.20
357 Ken Forsch	.20
358 Buddy Bell	.50
359 Rick Reuschel	.75
360 Jeff Burroughs	.20

NO.	PLAYER	NR. MT.
361	Detroit Tigers	.75
362	Will McEnaney	.20
363	Dave Collins (R)	.75
364	Elias Sosa	.20
365	Carlton Fisk	5.00
366	Bobby Valentine	.30
367	Bruce Miller	.20
368	Wilbur Wood	.20
369	Frank White	.35
370	Ron Cey	.50
371	Ellie Hendricks	.20
372	Rick Baldwin	.20
373	Johnny Briggs	.20
374	Dan Warthen	.20
375	Ron Fairly	.20
376	Rich Hebner	.20
377	Mike Hegan	.20
378	Steve Stone	.20
379	Ken Boswell	.20
380	Bobby Bonds	.30
381	Denny Doyle	.20
382	Matt Alexander	.20
383	John Ellis	.20
384	Philadelphia Phillies	.75
385	Mickey Lolich	.35
386	Ed Goodson	.20
387	Mike Miley	.20
388	Stan Perzanowski	.20
389	Glenn Adams	.20
390	Don Gullett	.20
391	Jerry Hariston	.20
392	Checklist No. 3	1.00
393	Paul Mitchell	.20
394	Fran Healy	.20
395	Jim Wynn	.25
396	Bill Lee	.20
397	Tim Foli	.20
398	Dave Tomlin	.20
399	Luis Melendez	.20
400	Rod Carew	5.00
401	Ken Brett	.20
402	Don Money	.20
403	Geoff Zahn	.20
404	Enos Cabell	.20
405	Rollie Fingers	2.00
406	Ed Herrmann	.20
407	Tom Underwood	.20
408	Charlie Spikes	.20
409	Dave Lemanczyk	.20
410	Ralph Garr	.20
411	Bill Singer	.20
412	Toby Harrah	.30
413	Pete Varney	.20
414	Wayne Garland	.20
415	Vada Pinson	.30
416	Tommy John	1.00
417	Gene Clines	.20
418	Jose Morales	.20
419	Reggie Cleveland	.20
420	Joe Morgan	4.00
421	Oakland A's	.40
422	Johnny Grubb	.20
423	Ed Halicki	.20
424	Phil Roof	.20
425	Rennie Stennett	.20
426	Bob Forsch	.30
427	Kurt Bevacqua	.20
428	Jim Crawford	.20
429	Fred Stanley	.20
430	Jose Cardenal	.20
431	Dick Ruthven	.20
432	Tom Veryzer	.20
433	Rick Waits	.20
434	Morris Nettles	.20
435	Phil Niekro	2.00
436	Bill Fahey	.20
437	Terry Forster	.20
438	Doug DeCinces	.60
439	Rick Rhoden	.50
440	John Mayberry	.30
441	Gary Carter	8.00
442	Hank Webb	.20

NO.	PLAYER	NR. MT.
443	S.F. Giants	.75
444	Gary Nolan	.20
445	Rico Petrocelli	.20
446	Larry Haney	.20
447	Gene Locklear	.20
448	Tom Johnson	.20
449	Bob Robertson	.20
450	Jim Palmer	4.00
451	Buddy Bradford	.20
452	Tom Hausman	.20
453	Lou Piniella	.35
454	Tom Griffin	.20
455	Dick Allen	.30
456	Joe Coleman	.20
457	Ed Crosby	.20
458	Earl Williams	.20
459	Jim Brewer	.20
460	Cesar Cedeno	.30
461	Championships:	.50
	Reds Sweep Bucs,	
	Bosox Surprise A's	
462	World Series:	.50
	Reds Champs!	
463	Steve Hargan	.20
464	Ken Henderson	.20
465	Mike Marshall	.30
466	Bob Stinson	.20
467	Woodie Fryman	.20
468	Jesus Alou	.20
469	Rawly Eastwick	.20
470	Bobby Murcer	.40
471	Jim Burton	.20
472	Bob Davis	.20
473	Paul Blair	.20
474	Ray Corbin	.20
475	Joe Rudi	.30
476	Bob Moose	.20
477	Cleveland Indians	.75
478	Lynn McGlothen	.20
479	Bobby Mitchell	.20
480	Mike Schmidt	30.00
481	Rudy May	.20
482	Tim Hosley	.20
483	Mickey Stanley	.20
484	Eric Raich	.20
485	Mike Hargrove	.20
486	Bruce Dal Canton	.20
487	Leron Lee	.20
488	Claude Osteen	.20
489	Skip Jutze	.20
490	Frank Tanana	.30
491	Terry Crowley	.20
492	Marty Pattin	.20
493	Derrel Thomas	.20
494	Craig Swan	.20
495	Nate Colbert	.20
496	Juan Beniquez	.20
497	Joe McIntosh	.20
498	Glenn Borgmann	.20
499	Mario Guerrero	.20
500	Reggie Jackson	12.00
501	Billy Champion	.20
502	Tim McCarver	.40
503	Elliott Maddox	.20
504	Pittsburgh Pirates	.75
505	Mark Belanger	.30
506	George Mitterwald	.20
507	Ray Bare	.20
508	Duane Kuiper	.20
509	Bill Hands	.20
510	Amos Otis	.30
511	Jamie Easterley	.20
512	Ellie Rodriguez	.20
513	Bart Johnson	.20
514	Dan Driessen	.25
515	Steve Yeager	.20
516	Wayne Granger	.20
517	John Milner	.20
518	Doug Flynn	.20
519	Steve Brye	.20
520	Willie McCovey	3.00

NO.	PLAYER	NR. MT.
521	Jim Colborn	.20
522	Ted Sizemore	.20
523	Bob Montgomery	.20
524	Pete Falcone	.20
525	Billy Williams	2.00
526	Checklist No. 4	1.00
527	Mike Anderson	.20
528	Dock Ellis	.20
529	Deron Johnson	.20
530	Don Sutton	1.50
531	New York Mets	1.00
532	Milt May	.20
533	Lee Richard	.20
534	Stan Bahnsen	.20
535	Dave Nelson	.20
536	Mike Thompson	.20
537	Tony Muser	.20
538	Pat Darcy	.20
539	John Balaz	.20
540	Bill Freehan	.30
541	Steve Mingori	.20
542	Keith Hernandez	6.00
543	Wayne Twitchell	.20
544	Pepe Frias	.20
545	Sparky Lyle	.30
546	Dave Rosello	.20
547	Roric Harrison	.20
548	Manny Mota	.30
549	Randy Tate	.20
550	Hank Aaron	12.00
551	Jerry DaVanon	.20
552	Terry Humphrey	.20
553	Randy Moffitt	.20
554	Ray Fosse	.20
555	Dyar Miller	.20
556	Minnesota Twins	.75
557	Dan Spillner	.20
558	Clarence Gaston	.20
559	Clyde Wright	.20
560	Jorge Orta	.20
561	Tom Carroll	.20
562	Adrian Garrett	.20
563	Larry Demery	.20
564	Gum Blowing Champ:	.30
	Kurt Bevacqua	
565	Tug McGraw	.40
566	Ken McMullen	.20
567	George Stone	.20
568	Rob Andrews	.20
569	Nelson Briles	.20
570	George Hendrick	.30
571	Don DeMola	.20
572	Rich Coggins	.20
573	Bill Travers	.20
574	Don Kessinger	.20
575	Dwight Evans	3.00
576	Maximino Leon	.20
577	Marc Hill	.20
578	Ted Kubiak	.20
579	Clay Kirby	.20
580	Bert Campaneris	.30
581	St. Louis Cardinals	.75
582	Mike Kekich	.20
583	Tommy Helms	.20
584	Stan Wall	.20
585	Joe Torre	.40
586	Ron Schueler	.20
587	Leo Cardenas	.20
588	Kevin Kobel	.20
589	Rookie Pitchers:	2.00
	Joe Pactwa, Santo Alcala,	
	Mike Flanagan, P. Torrealba	
590	Rookie Outfielders:	1.25
	Henry Cruz, Ellis Valentine,	
	Chet Lemon, T. Whitfield	
591	Rookie Pitchers:	.30
	Steve Grilli, C. Mitchell,	
	Jose Sosa, George Throop	
592	Rookie Infielders	4.50
	W. Randolph, D. McKay,	
	J. Royster, R. Staiger	

NO.	PLAYER	NR. MT.
593	Rookie Pitchers:	.40
	Larry Anderson, M. Littell,	
	Butch Metzger, Ken Crosby	
594	Rookie Catchers & OF's	.40
	Andy Merchant, Ed Ott,	
	R. Stillman, Jerry White	
595	Rookie Pitchers:	.40
	Art DeFillipis, R. Lerch,	
	Sid Monge, Steve Barr	
596	Rookie Infielders:	.50
	C. Reynolds, L. Johnson,	
	J. LeMaster, J. Manuel	
597	RooKie Pitchers:	.60
	D. Aase, Jack Kucek,	
	Frank LaCorte, Mike Pazik	
598	Rookie Outfielders:	.40
	Hector Cruz, J. Quirk,	
	Jerry Turner, Joe Wallis	
599	Rookie Pitchers:	12.00
	Rob Dressler, Ron Guidry,	
	Bob McClure, Pat Zachry	
600	Tom Seaver	7.00
601	Ken Rudolph	.20
602	Doug Konieczny	.20
603	Jim Holt	.20
604	Joe Lovitto	.20
605	Al Downing	.30
606	Milwaukee Brewers	.75
607	Rich Hinton	.20
608	Vic Correll	.20
609	Fred Norman	.20
610	Greg Luzinski	.50
611	Rich Folkers	.20
612	Joe Lahoud	.20
613	Tim Johnson	.20
614	Fernando Arroyo	.20
615	Mike Cubbage	.20
616	Buck Martinez	.20
617	Darold Knowles	.20
618	Jack Brohamer	.20
619	Bill Butler	.20
620	Al Oliver	.50
621	Tom Hall	.20
622	Rick Auerbach	.20
623	Bob Allietta	.20
624	Tony Taylor	.20
625	J.R. Richard	.25
626	Bob Sheldon	.20
627	Bill Plummer	.20
628	John D'Acquisto	.20
629	Sandy Alomar	.20
630	Chris Speier	.20
631	Atlanta Braves	.75
632	Rogelio Moret	.20
633	John Stearns (R)	.25
634	Larry Christenson	.20
635	Jim Fregosi	.25
636	Joe Decker	.20
637	Bruce Bochte	.20
638	Doyle Alexander	.20
639	Fred Kendall	.20
640	Bill Madlock	1.00
641	Tom Paciorek	.20
642	Dennis Blair	.20
643	Checklist No. 5	1.00
644	Tom Bradley	.20
645	Darrell Porter	.20
646	John Lowenstein	.20
647	Ramon Hernandez	.20
648	Al Cowens	.20
649	Dave Roberts	.20
650	Thurman Munson	7.00
651	John Odom	.20
652	Ed Armbrister	.20
653	Mike Norris (R)	.25
654	Doug Griffin	.20
655	Mike Vail	.20
656	Chicago White Sox	.75
657	Roy Smalley (R)	.50
658	Jerry Johnson	.20
659	Ben Oglivie	.30
660	D. Lopes (Exc. .15)	.75

1976 Topps Traded. . . . Complete Set of 44 Cards—Value $10.00 (Near Mint)

This set features players who were traded after the regular 1976 set was printed. The card numbers are the same as the main set, with the addition of "T" after the number.

NO. PLAYER	NR. MT.	NO. PLAYER	NR. MT.	NO. PLAYER	NR. MT.	NO. PLAYER	NR. MT.
27 T Ed Figueroa	.15	146 T George Medich	.15	380 T Bobby Bonds	.45	527 T Mike Anderson	.15
28 T Dusty Baker	.35	158 T Ken Reitz	.15	383 T John Ellis	.15	528 T Dock Ellis	.15
44 T Doug Rader	.20	208 T Mike Lum	.15	385 T Mickey Lolich	.50	532 T Milt May	.15
58 T Ron Reed	.20	211 T Clay Carroll	.15	401 T Ken Brett	.20	554 T Ray Fosse	.15
74 T Oscar Gamble	.25	231 T Tom House	.15	410 T Ken Brett	.20	579 T Clay Kirby	.15
80 T Jim Kaat	.50	250 T Fergie Jenkins	.60	411 T Bill Singer	.15	583 T Tommy Helms	.15
83 T Jim Spencer	.15	259 T Darrel Chaney	.15	428 T Jim Crawford	.15	592 T Willie Randolph	.75
85 T Mickey Rivers	.25	292 T Leon Roberts	.15	434 T Morris Nettles	.15	618 T Jack Brohamer	.15
99 T Lee Lacy	.25	296 T Pat Dobson	.15	464 T Ken Henderson	.15	632 T Rogelio Moret	.15
120 T Rusty Staub	.75	309 T Bill Melton	.15	497 T Joe McIntosh	.15	649 T Dave Roberts	.15
127 T Larvell Blanks	.15	338 T Bob Bailey	.15	524 T Pete Falcone	.15	— Checklist	.75

1977 Topps. . . . Complete Set of 660 Cards—Value $375.00 (Near Mint)

Dale Murphy, Tony Armas, and Andre Dawson's rookie cards are in this set. There is an error on card 634—the photos are switched.

  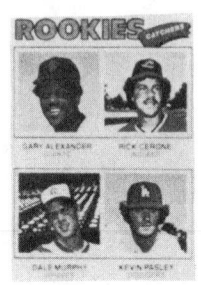  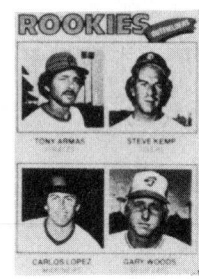

NO. PLAYER	NR. MT.	NO. PLAYER	NR. MT.	NO. PLAYER	NR. MT.	NO. PLAYER	NR. MT.
1 Batting Leaders: George Brett, Bill Madlock	3.50	21 Ken Frosch	.18	50 R. Cey	.50	78 Bob Davis	.18
2 Home Run Leaders: Graig Nettles, Mike Schmidt	1.00	22 Bill Freehan	.18	51 Milwaukee Brewers/ Alex Grammas (Mgr.)	.60	79 Don Money	.18
3 RBI Leaders: Lee May, George Foster	.40	23 Dan Driessen	.18	52 Ellis Valentine	.18	80 Andy Messersmith	.30
4 Stolen Base Leaders: B. North, Dave Lopes	.40	24 Carl Morton	.18	53 Paul Mitchell	.18	81 Juan Beniquez	.20
5 Victory Leaders: Jim Palmer, Randy Jones	.75	25 Dwight Evans	2.50	54 Sandy Alomar	.18	82 Jim Rooker	.18
6 Strikeout Leaders: Nolan Ryan, Tom Seaver	4.00	26 Ray Sadeki	.18	55 Jeff Burroughs	.25	83 Kevin Bell	.18
7 ERA Leaders: Mark Fidrych, J. Denny	.40	27 Bill Buckner	.40	56 Rudy May	.18	84 Ollie Brown	.18
8 Leading Firemen: B. Campbell, R. Eastwick	.40	28 Woodie Fryman	.18	57 Marc Hill	.18	85 Duane Kuiper	.18
9 Doug Rader	.18	29 Bucky Dent	.35	58 Chet Lemon	.40	86 Pat Zachry	.18
10 Reggie Jackson	9.00	30 Greg Luzinski	.35	59 Larry Christenson	.18	87 Glenn Borgmann	.18
11 Rob Dressler	.18	31 Jim Todd	.18	60 Jim Rice	5.00	88 Stan Wall	.18
12 Larry Haney	.18	32 Checklist No. 1	.75	61 Manny Sanguillen	.18	89 Butch Hobson	.18
13 Luis Gomez	.18	33 Wayne Garland	.18	62 Eric Raich	.18	90 Cesar Cedeno	.35
14 Tommy Smith	.18	34 Angels/Norm Sherry (Mgr.)	.50	63 Tito Fuentes	.18	91 John Verhoeven	.18
15 Don Gullett	.18	35 Rennie Stennett	.18	64 Larry Biittner	.18	92 Dave Rosello	.18
16 Bob Jones	.18	36 John Ellis	.18	65 Skip Lockwood	.18	93 Tom Poquette	.18
17 Steve Stone	.18	37 Steve Hargan	.18	66 Roy Smalley	.18	94 Craig Swan	.18
18 Cleveland Indians/ Frank Robinson (Mgr.)	.60	38 Craig Kusick	.18	67 Joaquin Andujar (R)	.75	95 Keith Hernandez	3.00
19 John D'Acquisto	.18	39 Tom Griffin	.18	68 Bruce Bochte	.18	96 Lou Piniella	.45
20 Graig Nettles	.75	40 Bobby Murcer	.50	69 Jim Crawford	.18	97 Dave Heaverlo	.18
		41 Jim Kern	.18	70 Johnny Bench	7.00	98 Milt May	.18
		42 Jose Cruz	.30	71 Dock Ellis	.18	99 Tom Hausman	.18
		43 Ray Bare	.18	72 Mike Anderson	.18	100 Joe Morgan	2.00
		44 Bud Harrelson	.18	73 Charlie Williams	.18	101 Dick Bosman	.18
		45 Rawly Eastwick	.18	74 A's/J. McKeon (Mgr.)	.60	102 Jose Morales	.18
		46 Buck Martinez	.18	75 Dennis Leonard	.18	103 Mike Bacsik	.18
		47 Lynn McGlothen	.18	76 Tim Foli	.18	104 Omar Moreno (R)	.35
		48 Tom Paciorek	.18	77 Dyar Miller	.18	105 Steve Yeager	.18
		49 Grant Jackson	.18			106 Mike Flanagan	.40

NO.	PLAYER	NR. MT.
107	Bill Melton	.18
108	Alan Foster	.18
109	Jorge Orta	.18
110	Steve Carlton	5.00
111	Rico Petrocelli	.25
112	Bill Greif	.18
113	Toronto Blue Jays/ Roy Hartsfield (Mgr.)	.60
114	Bruce Dal Canton	.18
115	Rick Manning	.18
116	Joe Niekro	.40
117	Frank White	.40
118	Rick Jone	.18
119	John Stearns	.18
120	Rod Carew	6.00
121	Gary Nolan	.18
122	Ben Oglivie	.25
123	Fred Stanley	.18
124	George Mitterwald	.18
125	Bill Travers	.18
126	Rod Gilbreath	.18
127	Ron Fairly	.18
128	Tommy John	1.00
129	Jim Sadek	.18
130	Al Oliver	.50
131	Orlando Ramirez	.18
132	Chip Lang	.18
133	Ralph Garr	.18
134	San Diego Padres/ John McNamara (Mgr.)	.60
135	Mark Belanger	.30
136	Jerry Mumphrey (R)	.50
137	Jeff Terpko	.18
138	Bob Stinson	.18
139	Fred Norman	.18
140	Mike Schmidt	20.00
141	Mark Littell	.18
142	Steve Dillard	.18
143	Ed Herrmann	.18
144	Bruce Sutter (R)	3.00
145	Tom Veryzer	.18
146	Dusty Baker	.40
147	Jackie Brown	.18
148	Fran Healy	.18
149	Mike Cubbage	.18
150	Tom Seaver	5.00
151	Johnnie LeMaster	.18
152	Gaylord Perry	2.00
153	Ron Jackson	.18
154	Dave Guisti	.18
155	Joe Rudi	.25
156	Pete Mackanin	.18
157	Ken Brett	.18
158	Ted Kubiak	.18
159	Bernie Carbo	.18
160	Will McEnaney	.18
161	Garry Templeton (R)	1.50
162	Mike Cuellar	.25
163	Dave Hilton	.18
164	Tug McGraw	.35
165	Jim Wynn	.18
166	Bill Campbell	.18
167	Rich Hebner	.18
168	Charlie Spikes	.18
169	Darold Knowles	.18
170	Thurman Munson	4.00
171	Ken Sanders	.18
172	John Milner	.18
173	Chuck Scrivener	.18
174	Nelson Briles	.18
175	Butch Wynegar (R)	.75
176	Bob Robertson	.18
177	Bart Johnson	.18
178	Bombo Rivera	.18
179	Paul Hartzell	.18
180	Dave Lopes	.35
181	Ken McMullen	.18
182	Dan Spillner	.18
183	Cardinals/V. Rapp (Mgr.)	.60
184	Bo McLaughlin	.18
185	Sixto Lezcano	.18
186	Doug Flynn	.18
187	Dick Pole	.18
188	Bob Tolan	.18
189	Rick Dempsey	.20
190	Ray Burris	.18
191	Doug Griffin	.18
192	Clarence Gaston	.18
193	Larry Gura	.18
194	Gary Matthews	.35
195	Ed Figueroa	.18
196	Len Randle	.18
197	Ed Ott	.18
198	Wilbur Wood	.18
199	Pepe Frias	.18
200	Frank Tanana	.25
201	Ed Kranepool	.30
202	Tom Johnson	.18
203	Ed Armbrister	.18
204	Jeff Newman	.18
205	Pete Falcone	.18
206	Boog Powell	.40
207	Glenn Abbott	.18
208	Checklist No. 2	.75
209	Rob Andrews	.18
210	Fred Lynn	1.50
211	San Francisco Giants/ Joe Altobelli (Mgr.)	.60
212	Jim Mason	.18
213	Maximino Leon	.18
214	Darrell Porter	.30
215	Butch Metzger	.30
216	Doug DeCinces	.50
217	Tom Underwood	.18
218	John Wathan	1.25
219	Joe Coleman	.18
220	Chris Chambliss	.25
221	Bob Bailey	.18
222	Francisco Barrios	.18
223	Earl Williams	.18
224	Rusty Torres	.18
225	Bob Apodaca	.18
226	Leroy Stanton	.18
227	Joe Sambito	.40
228	Minnesota Twins/ Gene Mauch (Mgr.)	.60
229	Don Kessinger	.18
230	Vida Blue	.35
231	Record—Brett Most Consecutive Games with 3 or More Hits	3.50
232	Record—Minoso Oldest Player to Hit Safely	.35
233	Record—Morales Most Pinch-Hits for Season	.30
234	Record—Ryan Most Seasons 300 SO's	5.00
235	Cecil Cooper	.60
236	Tom Buskey	.18
237	Gene Clines	.18
238	Tippy Martinez	.18
239	Bill Plummer	.18
240	Ron LeFlore	.20
241	Dave Tomlin	.18
242	Ken Henderson	.18
243	Ron Reed	.18
244	John Mayberry	.35
245	Rick Rhoden	.30
246	Mike Vail	.18
247	Chris Knapp	.18
248	Wilbur Howard	.18
249	Pete Redfern	.18
250	Bill Madlock	.50
251	Tony Muser	.18
252	Dale Murray	.18
253	John Hale	.18
254	Doyle Alexander	.18
255	George Scott	.18
256	Joe Hoerner	.18
257	Mike Miley	.18
258	Luis Tiant	.20
259	Mets/J. Frazier (Mgr.)	.75
260	J.R. Richard	.25
261	Phil Garner	.25
262	Al Cowens	.25
263	Mike Marshall	.25
264	Tom Hutton	.18
265	Mark Fidrych (R)	.50
266	Derrel Thomas	.18
267	Ray Fosse	.18
268	Rick Sawyer	.18
269	Joe Lis	.18
270	Dave Parker	4.00
271	Terry Forster	.25
272	Lee Lacy	.20
273	Eric Soderholm	.18
274	Don Stanhouse	.18
275	Mike Hargrove	.18
276	A.L. Championship: Chambliss' Homer	.50
277	N.L. Championship: Reds Sweep Phillies in 3	.60
278	Danny Frisella	.18
279	Joe Wallis	.18
280	Jim Hunter	2.00
281	Roy Staiger	.18
282	Sid Monge	.18
283	Jerry DaVanon	.18
284	Mike Norris	.18
285	Brooks Robinson	3.00
286	Johnny Grubb	.18
287	Cincinnati Reds Sparky Anderson (Mgr.)	.75
288	Bob Montgomery	.18
289	Gene Garber	.18
290	Amos Otis	.35
291	Jason Thompson (R)	.60
292	Rogelio Moret	.18
293	Jack Brohamer	.18
294	George Medich	.18
295	Gary Carter	5.00
296	Don Hood	.18
297	Ken Reitz	.18
298	Charlie Hough	.18
299	Otto Velez	.18
300	Jerry Koosman	.40
301	Toby Harrah	.20
302	Mike Garman	.18
303	Gene Tenace	.18
304	Jim Hughes	.18
305	Mickey Rivers	.30
306	Rick Waits	.18
307	Gary Sutherland	.18
308	Gene Pentz	.18
309	Boston Red Sox/ Don Zimmer (Mgr.)	.75
310	Larry Bowa	.30
311	Vern Ruhle	.18
312	Rob Belloir	.18
313	Paul Blair	.18
314	Steve Mingori	.18
315	Dave Chalk	.18
316	Steve Rogers	.25
317	Kurt Bevacqua	.18
318	Duffy Dyer	.18
319	Rich Gossage	.75
320	Ken Griffey	.75
321	Dave Goltz	.18
322	Bill Russell	.18
323	Larry Lintz	.18
324	John Curtis	.18
325	Mike Ivie	.18
326	Jesse Jefferson	.18
327	Astros/B. Virdon (Mgr.)	.60
328	Tommy Boggs	.18
329	Ron Hodges	.18
330	George Hendrick	.35
331	Jim Colborn	.18
332	Elliott Maddox	.18
333	Paul Reuschel	.18
334	Bill Stein	.18
335	Bill Robinson	.18
336	Denny Doyle	.18
337	Ron Schueler	.18
338	Dave Duncan	.18
339	Adrian Devine	.18
340	Hal McRae	.25
341	Joe Kerrigan	.18
342	Jerry Remy	.18
343	Ed Halicki	.18
344	Brian Downing	.18
345	Reggie Smith	.30
346	Bill Singer	.18
347	George Foster	1.25
348	Brent Strom	.18
349	Jim Holt	.18
350	Larry Dierker	.18
351	Jim Sundberg	.18
352	Mike Phillips	.18
353	Stan Thomas	.18
354	Pirates/C. Tanner (Mgr.)	.50
355	Lou Brock	2.50
356	Checklist No. 3	.75
357	Tim McCarver	.45
358	Tom House	.18
359	Willie Randolph	1.00
360	Rick Monday	.25
361	Eduardo Rodriguez	.18
362	Tommy Davis	.18
363	Dave Roberts	.18
364	Vic Correll	.18
365	Mike Torrez	.18
366	Ted Sizemore	.18
367	Dave Hamilton	.18
368	Mike Jorgensen	.18
369	Terry Humphrey	.18
370	John Montefusco	.18
371	Royals/W. Herzog (Mgr.)	.60
372	Rich Folkers	.18
373	Bert Campaneris	.25
374	Kent Tekulve	.20
375	Larry Hisle	.20
376	Nino Espinosa	.18
377	Dave McKay	.18
378	Jim Umbarger	.18
379	Larry Cox	.18
380	Lee May	.25
381	Bob Forsch	.25
382	Charlie Moore	.18
383	Stan Bahnsen	.18
384	Darrel Chaney	.18
385	Dave LaRoche	.18
386	Manny Mota	.30
387	New York Yankees/ Billy Martin (Mgr.)	.75
388	Terry Harmon	.30
389	Ken Kravec	.30
390	Dave Winfield	4.00
391	Dan Warthen	.18
392	Phil Roof	.18
393	John Lowenstein	.18
394	Bill Laxton	.18
395	Manny Trillo	.25
396	Tom Murphy	.18
397	Larry Herndon (R)	.50
398	Tom Burgmeier	.18
399	Bruce Boisclair	.18
400	Steve Garvey	3.00
401	Mickey Scott	.18
402	Tommy Helms	.18
403	Tom Grieve	.18
404	Eric Rasmussen	.18
405	Claudell Washington	.25
406	Tim Johnson	.18
407	Dave Freisleben	.18
408	Cesar Tovar	.18
409	Pete Broberg	.18
410	Willie Montanez	.18
411	World Series Morgan Homers, Bench Stars for Reds	.60
412	World Series # 1 & 2 Reds' Defense, Bench's Two Homers	.60
413	World Series # 3 & 4 Cincy Wins	.60
414	Tommy Harper	.18
415	Jay Johnstone	.18
416	Chuck Hartenstein	.18
417	Wayne Garrett	.18
418	Chicago White Sox/ Bob Lemon (Mgr.)	.60
419	Steve Swisher	.18
420	Rusty Staub	.35
421	Doug Rau	.18
422	Freddie Patek	.18
423	Gary Lavelle	.18
424	Steve Brye	.18
425	Joe Torre	.35
426	Dick Drago	.18

NO.	PLAYER	NR. MT.
427	Dave Rader	.18
428	Texas Rangers/	.60
	Frank Lucchesi (Mgr.)	
429	Ken Boswell	.18
430	Fergie Jenkins	.75
431	Dave Collins	.30
	(photo of Bobby Jones)	
432	Buzz Capra	.18
433	Turn Back Clock (1972)	.30
	Colbert Hits 5 Homers	
434	Turn Back Clock (1967)	2.00
	Yaz Wins Triple Crown	
435	Turn Back Clock (1962)	.60
	Wills 104 Steals	
436	Turn Back Clock (1957)	.30
	Keegan No-Hitter	
437	Turn Back Clock (1952)	.60
	Kiner Leads NL	
438	Marty Perez	.18
439	Gorman Thomas	.50
440	Jon Matlack	.18
441	Larvell Blanks	.18
442	Atlanta Braves/	.60
	Dave Bristol (Mgr.)	
443	Lamar Johnson	.18
444	Wayne Twitchell	.18
445	Ken Singleton	.40
446	Bill Bonham	.18
447	Jerry Turner	.18
448	Ellie Rodriguez	.18
449	Al Fitzmorris	.18
450	Pete Rose	7.50
451	Checklist No. 4	.75
452	Mike Caldwell	.18
453	Pedro Garcia	.18
454	Andy Etchebarren	.18
455	Rick Wise	.18
456	Leon Roberts	.18
457	Steve Luebber	.18
458	Leo Foster	.18
459	Steve Foucault	.18
460	Willie Stargell	2.50
461	Dick Tidrow	.18
462	Don Baylor	.60
463	Jamie Quirk	.18
464	Randy Moffitt	.18
465	Rico Carty	.35
466	Fred Holdsworth	.18
467	Philadelphia Phillies/	.60
	Danny Ozark (Mgr.)	
468	Ramon Hernandez	.18
469	Pat Kelly	.18
470	Ted Simmons	.60
471	Del Unser	.18
472	Rookie Pitchers:	.50
	Bob McClure, Don Aase,	
	Gil Patterson, Dave	
	Wehrmeister	
473	Rookie Outfielders:	50.00
	Gene Richards, John Scott,	
	D. Walling, A. Dawson	
474	Rookie Shortstops:	.40
	Bob Bailor, Kiko Garcia,	
	C. Reynolds, A. Taveras	
475	Rookie Pitchers:	.50
	Chris Batton, Rick Camp	
	S. McGregor, M. Sarmiento	
476	Rookie Catchers:	50.00
	Dale Murphy, Rick Cerone,	
	G. Alexander, K. Pasley	
477	Rookie Infielders:	.40
	R. Dauer, O. Gonzalez,	
	D. Ault, P. Mankowski	

NO.	PLAYER	NR. MT.
478	Rookie Pitchers:	.40
	Leon Hooten, Jim Gideon,	
	Mark Lemongello,	
	Dave Johnson,	
479	Rookie Outfielders:	.40
	A. Woods, Wayne Gross,	
	B. Asselstine, S. Mejias	
480	Carl Yastrzemski	5.00
481	Roger Metzger	.18
482	Tony Solaita	.18
483	Richie Zisk	.30
484	Burt Hooton	.30
485	Roy White	.30
486	Ed Bane	.18
487	Rookie Pitchers:	.35
	Joe Henderson, Ed Glynn,	
	L. Anderson, G. Terlecky	
488	Rookie Outfielders:	20.00
	Lee Mazzilli, Jack Clark,	
	R. Jones, D. Thomas	
489	Rookie Pitchers:	.50
	Len Barker, Randy Lerch,	
	Greg Minton, Mike Overy	
490	Rookie Shortstops:	.40
	T. McMillan, B. Almon,	
	M. Klutts, M. Wagner	
491	Rookie Pitchers:	2.00
	Mike Dupree, Bob Sykes,	
	D. Martinez, C. Mitchell	
492	Rookie Outfielders:	1.25
	Tony Armas, Steve Kemp,	
	C. Lopez, Gary Woods	
493	Rookie Pitchers:	1.00
	G. Wheelock, M. Krukow,	
	Jim Otten, Mike Willis	
494	Rookie Infielders:	.60
	Juan Bernhardt, J. Gantner,	
	M. Champion, B. Wills	
495	Al Hrabosky	.18
496	Gary Thomasson	.18
497	Clay Carroll	.18
498	Sal Bando	.30
499	Pablo Torealba	.18
500	Dave Kingman	.50
501	Jim Bibby	.18
502	Randy Hundley	.18
503	Bill Lee	.18
504	Los Angeles Dodgers/	.75
	Tom Lasorda (Mgr.)	
505	Oscar Gamble	.25
506	Steve Grilli	.18
507	Mike Hegan	.18
508	Dave Pagan	.18
509	Cookie Rojas	.18
510	John Candelaria	.75
511	Bill Fahey	.18
512	Jack Billingham	.18
513	Jerry Terrell	.18
514	Cliff Johnson	.18
515	Chris Speier	.18
516	Bake McBride	.20
517	Pete Vuckovich (R)	.50
518	Chicago Cubs/	.60
	Herman Franks (Mgr.)	
519	Don Kirkwood	.18
520	Garry Maddox	.20
521	Bob Grich	.25
522	Enzo Hernandez	.18
523	Rollie Fingers	1.25
524	Rowland Office	.12
525	Dennis Eckersley	5.00
526	Larry Parrish	.30

NO.	PLAYER	NR. MT.
527	Dan Meyer	.18
528	Bill Castro	.18
529	Jim Essian	.18
530	Rick Reuschel	.50
531	Lyman Bostock	.30
532	Jim Willoughby	.18
533	Mickey Stanley	.18
534	Paul Splittorff	.18
535	Cesar Geronimo	.18
536	Vic Albury	.18
537	Dave Roberts	.18
538	Frank Taveras	.18
539	Mike Wallace	.18
540	Bob Watson	.25
541	John Denny	.30
542	Frank Duffy	.18
543	Ron Blomberg	.18
544	Gary Ross	.18
545	Bob Boone	.50
546	Baltimore Orioles/	.60
	Earl Weaver (Mgr.)	
547	Willie McCovey	2.50
548	Joel Youngblood	.18
549	Jerry Royster	.18
550	Randy Jones	.18
551	Bill North	.18
552	Pepe Mangual	.18
553	Jack Heidemann	.18
554	Bruce Kimm	.18
555	Dan Ford	.18
556	Doug Bird	.18
557	Jerry White	.18
558	Elias Sosa	.18
559	Alan Bannister	.18
560	Dave Concepcion	.50
561	Pete LaCock	.18
562	Checklist No. 5	.75
563	Bruce Kison	.18
564	Alan Ashby	.20
565	Mickey Lolich	.25
566	Rick Miller	.18
567	Enos Cabell	.18
568	Carlos May	.18
569	Jim Lonborg	.18
570	Bobby Bonds	.30
571	Darrell Evans	.35
572	Ross Grimsley	.18
573	Joe Ferguson	.18
574	Aurelio Rodriguez	.18
575	Dick Ruthven	.18
576	Fred Kendall	.18
577	Jerry Augustine	.18
578	Bob Randall	.18
579	Don Carrithers	.18
580	George Brett	20.00
581	Pedro Borbon	.18
582	Ed Kirkpatrick	.18
583	Paul Lindblad	.18
584	Ed Goodson	.18
585	Rick Burleson	.18
586	Steve Renko	.18
587	Rick Baldwin	.18
588	Dave Moates	.18
589	Mike Cosgrove	.18
590	Buddy Bell	.40
591	Chris Arnold	.18
592	Dan Briggs	.18
593	Dennis Blair	.18
594	Biff Pocoroba	.18
595	John Hiller	.18
596	Jerry Martin	.18

NO.	PLAYER	NR. MT.
597	Seattle Mariners/	.50
	Darrell Johnson (Mgr.)	
598	Sparky Lyle	.40
599	Mike Tyson	.18
600	Jim Palmer	3.00
601	Mike Lum	.18
602	Andy Hassler	.18
603	Willie Davis	.18
604	Jim Slaton	.18
605	Felix Millan	.18
606	Steve Braun	.18
607	Larry Demery	.18
608	Roy Howell	.18
609	Jim Barr	.18
610	Jose Cardenal	.18
611	Dave Lemanczyk	.18
612	Barry Foote	.18
613	Reggie Cleveland	.18
614	Greg Gross	.18
615	Phil Niekro	1.50
616	Tommy Sandt	.18
617	Bobby Darwin	.18
618	Pat Dobson	.18
619	Johnny Oates	.18
620	Don Sutton	1.25
621	Detroit Tigers/	.60
	Ralph Houk (Mgr.)	
622	Jim Wohlford	.18
623	Jack Kucek	.18
624	Hector Cruz	.18
625	Ken Holtzman	.18
626	Al Bumbry	.18
627	Bob Myrick	.18
628	Mario Guerrero	.18
629	Bobby Valentine	.30
630	Bert Blyleven	1.00
631	Big League Brothers:	2.50
	George Brett, Ken Brett	
632	Big League Brothers:	.30
	Ken Forsch, Bob Forsch	
633	Big League Brothers:	.30
	Lee May, Carlos May	
634	Big League Brothers:	.30
	Paul Reuschel, Rick	
	Reuschel (photos switched)	
635	Robin Yount	16.00
636	Santo Alcala	.18
637	Alex Johnson	.18
638	Jim Kaat	.50
639	Jerry Morales	.18
640	Carlton Fisk	4.00
641	Dan Larson	.18
642	Willie Crawford	.18
643	Mike Pazik	.18
644	Matt Alexander	.18
645	Jerry Reuss	.20
646	Andres Mora	.18
647	Montreal Expos/	.50
	Dick Williams (Mgr.)	
648	Jim Spencer	.18
649	Dave Cash	.18
650	Nolan Ryan	20.00
651	Von Joshua	.18
652	Tom Walker	.18
653	Diego Segui	.18
654	Ron Pruitt	.18
655	Tony Perez	.75
656	Ron Guidry	2.50
657	Mick Kelleher	.18
658	Marty Pattin	.18
659	Merv Rettenmund	.18
660	W. Horton (Exc. .12)	.50

1978 Topps. . . . Complete Set of 726 Cards—Value $300.00 (Near Mint)

After five consecutive years of issuing sets of 660 cards, Topps increased the size of its main set to 726 cards. 66 cards were double printed. Eddie Murray, Paul Molitor, and Lou Whitaker's rookie cards are in this set.

NO. PLAYER	NR. MT.	NO. PLAYER	NR. MT.	NO. PLAYER	NR. MT.	NO. PLAYER	NR. MT.
1 Record — L. Brock	2.00	60 Thurman Munson	3.50	126 Paul Moskau	.15	192 San Diego Padres	.50
Most Career Steals		61 Larvell Blanks	.15	127 Chet Lemon	.20	193 Rich Chiles	.15
2 Record — S. Lyle	.25	62 Jim Barr	.15	128 Bill Russell	.15	194 Derrel Thomas	.15
Most Career Relief		63 Don Zimmer (Mgr.)	.15	129 Jim Colborn	.15	195 Larry Dierker	.15
3 Record — W. McCovey	1.25	64 Gene Pentz	.15	130 Jeff Burroughs	.20	196 Bob Bailor	.15
Most 2 HR's in Inning		65 Ken Singleton	.25	131 Bert Blyleven	1.00	197 Nino Espinosa	.15
4 Record — B. Robinson	1.00	66 Chicago White Sox	.50	132 Enos Cabell	.15	198 Ron Pruitt	.15
Most Seasons — Same Club		67 Claudell Washington	.20	133 Jerry Augustine	.15	199 Craig Reynolds	.15
5 Record — P. Rose	1.75	68 Steve Foucault	.15	134 Steve Henderson	.15	200 Reggie Jackson	6.00
Most Hits — Switch Hitter		69 Mike Vail	.15	135 Ron Guidry	.60	201 Batting Leaders:	1.00
6 Record — N. Ryan	4.00	70 Rich Gossage	1.00	136 Ted Sizemore	.15	Dave Parker, Rod Carew	
Games 10 or More SO's		71 Terry Humphrey	.15	137 Craig Kusick	.15	202 Home Run Leaders:	.25
7 Record — R. Jackson	2.50	72 Andre Dawson	9.00	138 Larry Demery	.15	George Foster, Jim Rice	
Most Homers — W. Series		73 Andy Hassler	.15	139 Wayne Gross	.15	203 RBI Leaders:	.25
8 Mike Sadek	.15	74 Checklist No. 1	.50	140 Rollie Fingers	1.00	George Foster, Larry Hisle	
9 Doug DeCinces	.30	75 Dick Ruthven	.15	141 Ruppert Jones	.15	204 Stolen Base Leaders:	.20
10 Phil Niekro	1.25	76 Steve Ontiveros	.15	142 John Montefusco	.15	F. Taveras, Freddie Patek	
11 Rick Manning	.15	77 Ed Kirpatrick	.15	143 Keith Hernandez	2.00	205 Victory Leaders:	.60
12 Don Aase	.25	78 Pablo Torrealba	.15	144 Jesse Jefferson	.15	Steve Carlton, D. Goltz,	
13 Art Howe	.15	79 Darrell Johnson (Mgr.)	.15	145 Rick Monday	.15	D. Leonard, J. Palmer	
14 Lerrin LaGrow	.15	80 Ken Griffey	.50	146 Doyle Alexander	.15	206 Strikeout Leaders:	.75
15 Tony Perez	.25	81 Pete Redfern	.15	147 Lee Mazzilli	.20	Phil Niekro, Nolan Ryan	
16 Roy White	.25	82 San Fran. Giants	.50	148 Andre Thornton	.25	207 ERA Leaders:	.20
17 Mike Krukow	.30	83 Bob Montgomery	.15	149 Dale Murray	.15	J. Candelaria, F. Tanana	
18 Bob Grich	.25	84 Kent Tekulve	.20	150 Bobby Bonds	.25	208 Leading Firemen:	.30
19 Darrell Porter	.25	85 Ron Fairly	.15	151 Milt Wilcox	.15	R. Fingers, B. Campbell	
20 Pete Rose	3.50	86 Dave Tomlin	.15	152 Ivan DeJesus	.15	209 Dock Ellis	.15
21 Steve Kemp	.30	87 John Lowenstein	.15	153 Steve Stone	.15	210 Jose Cardenal	.15
22 Charlie Hough	.15	88 Mike Phillips	.15	154 Cecil Cooper	.30	211 Earl Weaver (Mgr.)	.50
23 Bump Wills	.15	89 Ken Clay	.15	155 Butch Hobson	.15	212 Mike Caldwell	.15
24 Don Money	.15	90 Larry Bowa	.20	156 Andy Messersmith	.15	213 Alan Bannister	.15
25 Jon Motlack	.15	91 Oscar Zamora	.15	157 Pete LaCock	.15	214 California Angels	.50
26 Rich Hebner	.15	92 Adrian Devine	.15	158 Joaquin Andujar	.25	215 Darrell Evans	.35
27 Geoff Zahn	.15	93 Bobby Cox (Mgr.)	.15	159 Lou Piniella	.40	216 Mike Paxton	.15
28 Ed Ott	.15	94 Chuck Scrivener	.15	160 Jim Palmer	2.50	217 Rod Gilbreath	.15
29 Bob Lacey	.15	95 Jamie Quirk	.15	161 Bob Boone	.35	218 Marty Pattin	.15
30 George Hendrick	.25	96 Baltimore Orioles	.40	162 Paul Thormodsgard	.15	219 Mike Cubbage	.15
31 Glenn Abbott	.15	97 Stan Bahnsen	.15	163 Bill North	.15	220 Pedro Borbon	.15
32 Garry Templeton	.30	98 Jim Essian	.15	164 Bob Owchinko	.15	221 Chris Speier	.15
33 Dave Lemanczyk	.15	99 Willie Hernandez (R)	1.25	165 Rennie Stennett	.15	222 Jerry Martin	.15
34 Willie McCovey	2.00	100 George Brett	10.00	166 Carlos Lopez	.15	223 Bruce Kison	.15
35 Sparky Lyle	.25	101 Sid Monge	.15	167 Tim Foli	.15	224 Jerry Tabb	.15
36 Eddie Murray (R)	45.00	102 Matt Alexander	.15	168 Reggie Smith	.25	225 Don Gullett	.15
37 Rick Waits	.15	103 Tom Murphy	.15	169 Jerry Johnson	.15	226 Joe Ferguson	.15
38 Willie Montanez	.15	104 Lee Lacy	.15	170 Lou Brock	2.25	227 Al Fitzmorris	.15
39 Floyd Bannister (R)	1.00	105 Reggie Cleveland	.15	171 Pat Zachry	.15	228 Manny Mota	.15
40 Carl Yastrzemski	4.00	106 Bill Plummer	.15	172 Mike Hargrove	.15	229 Leo Foster	.15
41 Burt Hooton	.15	107 Ed Halicki	.15	173 Robin Yount	8.00	230 Al Hrabosky	.15
42 Jorge Orta	.15	108 Von Joshua	.15	174 Wayne Garland	.15	231 Wayne Nordhagen	.15
43 Bill Atkinson	.15	109 Joe Torre (Mgr.)	.25	175 Jerry Morales	.15	232 Mickey Stanley	.15
44 Toby Harrah	.15	110 Richie Zisk	.25	176 Milt May	.15	233 Dick Pole	.15
45 Mark Fidrych	.25	111 Mike Tyson	.15	177 Gene Garber	.15	234 Herman Franks (Mgr.)	.15
46 Al Cowens	.20	112 Houston Astros	.50	178 Dave Chalk	.15	235 Tim McCarver	.35
47 Jack Billingham	.15	113 Don Carrithers	.15	179 Dick Tidrow	.15	236 Terry Whitfield	.15
48 Don Baylor	.40	114 Paul Blair	.15	180 Dave Concepcion	.25	237 Rich Dauer	.15
49 Ed Kranepool	.25	115 Gary Nolan	.15	181 Ken Forsch	.15	238 Juan Beniquez	.15
50 Rick Reuschel	.40	116 Tucker Ashford	.15	182 Jim Spencer	.15	239 Dyar Miller	.15
51 Charlie Moore	.15	117 John Montague	.15	183 Doug Bird	.15	240 Gene Tenace	.15
52 Jim Lonborg	.15	118 Terry Harmon	.15	184 Checklist No. 2	.50	241 Pete Vuckovich	.20
53 Phil Garner	.25	119 Denny Martinez	.15	185 Ellis Valentine	.15	242 Barry Bonnell	.15
54 Tom Johnson	.15	120 Gary Carter	3.00	186 Bob Stanley (R)	.35	243 Bob McClure	.15
55 Mitchell Page	.15	121 Alvis Woods	.15	187 Jerry Royster	.15	244 Montreal Expos	.40
56 Randy Jones	.15	122 Dennis Eckersley	3.00	188 Al Bumbry	.15	245 Rick Burleson	.15
57 Dan Meyer	.15	123 Manny Trillo	.20	189 Tom Lasorda (Mgr.)	.20	246 Dan Driessen	.15
58 Bob Forsch	.20	124 Dave Rozema	.15	190 John Candelaria	.20	247 Larry Christenson	.15
59 Otto Velez	.15	125 George Scott	.15	191 Rodney Scott	.15	248 Frank White	.15

NO.	PLAYER	NR. MT.
249	Dave Goltz	.15
250	Graig Nettles	.25
251	Don Kirkwood	.15
252	Steve Swisher	.15
253	Jim Kern	.15
254	Dave Collins	.20
255	Jerry Reuss	.20
256	Joe Altobelli (Mgr.)	.15
257	Hector Cruz	.15
258	John Hiller	.15
259	Los Angeles Dodgers	.50
260	Bert Campaneris	.20
261	Tim Hosely	.15
262	Rudy May	.15
263	Danny Walton	.15
264	Jamie Easterly	.15
265	Sal Bando	.15
266	Bob Shirley	.15
267	Doug Ault	.15
268	Gil Flores	.15
269	Wayne Twitchell	.15
270	Carlton Fisk	3.00
271	Randy Lerch	.15
272	Royle Stillman	.15
273	Fred Norman	.15
274	Freddie Patek	.15
275	Dan Ford	.15
276	Bill Bonham	.15
277	Bruce Boisclair	.15
278	Enrique Romo	.15
279	Bill Virdon (Mgr.)	.20
280	Buddy Bell	.30
281	Eric Rasmussen	.15
282	New York Yankees	.60
283	Omar Moreno	.20
284	Randy Moffitt	.15
285	Steve Yeager	.15
286	Ben Oglivie	.20
287	Kiko Garcia	.15
288	Dave Hamilton	.15
289	Checklist No. 3	.50
290	Willie Horton	.20
291	Gary Ross	.15
292	Gene Richards	.15
293	Mike Willis	.15
294	Larry Parrish	.20
295	Bill Lee	.15
296	Biff Pocoroba	.15
297	Warren Brusstar	.15
298	Tony Armas	.40
299	Whitey Herzog (Mgr.)	.20
300	Joe Morgan	2.00
301	Buddy Schultz	.15
302	Chicago Cubs	.50
303	Sam Hinds	.15
304	John Milner	.15
305	Rico Carty	.25
306	Joe Niekro	.25
307	Glenn Borgmann	.15
308	Jim Rooker	.15
309	Cliff Johnson	.15
310	Don Sutton	1.00
311	Jose Baez	1.25
312	Greg Minton	.15
313	Andy Etchebarren	.15
314	Paul Lindblad	.15
315	Mark Belanger	.15
316	Henry Cruz	.15
317	Dave Johnson	.30
318	Tom Griffin	.15
319	Alan Ashby	.15
320	Fred Lynn	1.00
321	Santo Alcala	.15
322	Tom Paciorek	.15
323	Jim Fregosi	.15
324	Vern Rapp (Mgr.)	.15
325	Bruce Sutter	.75
326	Mike Lum	.15
327	Rick Langford	.15
328	Milwaukee Brewers	.50
329	John Verhoeven	.15
330	Bob Watson	.20
331	Mark Littell	.15
332	Duane Kuiper	.15
333	Jim Todd	.15
334	John Stearns	.15
335	Bucky Dent	.20
336	Steve Busby	.15
337	Tom Grieve	.15
338	Dave Heaverlo	.15
339	Mario Guerrero	.15
340	Bake McBride	.15
341	Mike Flanagan	.25
342	Aurelio Rodriguez	.15
343	John Wathan	.15
344	Sam Ewing	.15
345	Luis Tiant	.25
346	Larry Biittner	.15
347	Terry Forster	.20
348	Del Unser	.15
349	Rick Camp	.15
350	Steve Garvey	2.50
351	Jeff Torborg (Mgr.)	.15
352	Tony Scott	.15
353	Doug Bair	.15
354	Cesar Geronimo	.15
355	Bill Travers	.15
356	New York Mets	.50
357	Tom Poquette	.15
358	Mark Lemongello	.15
359	Marc Hill	.15
360	Mike Schmidt	10.00
361	Chris Knapp	.15
362	Dave May	.15
363	Bob Randall	.15
364	Jerry Turner	.15
365	Ed Figueroa	.15
366	Larry Milbourne	.15
367	Rick Dempsey	.20
368	Balor Moore	.15
369	Tim Nordbrook	.15
370	Rusty Staub	.25
371	Ray Burris	.15
372	Brian Asselstine	.15
373	Jim Willoughby	.15
374	Jose Morales	.15
375	Tommy John	.60
376	Jim Wohlford	.15
377	Manny Sarmiento	.15
378	Bobby Winkles (Mgr.)	.15
379	Skip Lockwood	.15
380	Ted Simmons	.40
381	Philadelphia Phillies	.50
382	Joe Lahoud	.15
383	Mario Mendoza	.15
384	Jack Clark	3.00
385	Tito Fuentes	.15
386	Bob Gorinski	.15
387	Ken Holtzman	.15
388	Bill Fahey	.15
389	Julio Gonzalez	.15
390	Oscar Gamble	.15
391	Larry Haney	.15
392	Billy Almon	.15
393	Tippy Martinez	.15
394	Roy Howell	.15
395	Jim Hughes	.15
396	Bob Stinson	.15
397	Greg Gross	.15
398	Don Hood	.15
399	Pete Mackanin	.15
400	Nolan Ryan	15.00
401	Sparky Anderson (Mgr.)	.20
402	Dave Campbell	.15
403	Bud Harrelson	.15
404	Detroit Tigers	.60
405	Rawly Eastwick	.15
406	Mike Jorgensen	.15
407	Odell Jones	.15
408	Joe Zdeb	.15
409	Ron Schueler	.15
410	Bill Madlock	.50
411	AL Championships: Yankees Defeat Royals	.75
412	NL Championships: Dodgers Defeat Phillies	.75
413	World Series: Yankees Reign Supreme	1.50
414	Darold Knowles	.15
415	Ray Fosse	.15
416	Jack Brohamer	.15
417	Mike Garman	.15
418	Tony Muser	.15
419	Jerry Garvin	.15
420	Greg Luzinski	.30
421	Junior Moore	.15
422	Steve Braun	.15
423	Dave Rosello	.15
424	Boston Red Sox	.50
425	Steve Rogers	.15
426	Fred Kendall	.15
427	Mario Soto (R)	.60
428	Joel Youngblood	.15
429	Mike Barlow	.15
430	Al Oliver	.40
431	Butch Metzger	.15
432	Terry Bulling	.15
433	Fernando Gonzalez	.15
434	Mike Norris	.15
435	Checklist No. 4	.50
436	Vic Harris	.15
437	Bo McLaughlin	.15
438	John Ellis	.15
439	Ken Kravec	.15
440	Dave Lopes	.25
441	Larry Gura	.20
442	Elliott Maddox	.15
443	Darrell Chaney	.15
444	Roy Hartsfield (Mgr.)	.15
445	Mike Ivie	.15
446	Tug McGraw	.25
447	Leroy Stanton	.15
448	Bill Castro	.15
449	Tim Blackwell	.15
450	Tom Seaver	4.00
451	Minnesota Twins	.35
452	Jerry Mumphrey	.15
453	Doug Flynn	.15
454	Dave LaRoche	.15
455	Bill Robinson	.15
456	Vern Ruhle	.15
457	Bob Bailey	.15
458	Jeff Newman	.15
459	Charlie Spikes	.15
460	Jim Hunter	1.50
461	Rob Andrews	.15
462	Rogelio Moret	.15
463	Kevin Bell	.15
464	Jerry Grote	.15
465	Hal McRae	.20
466	Dennis Blair	.15
467	Alvin Dark (Mgr.)	.15
468	Warren Cromartie	.15
469	Rick Cerone	.15
470	J.R. Richard	.20
471	Roy Smalley	.15
472	Ron Reed	.15
473	Bill Buckner	.25
474	Jim Slaton	.15
475	Gary Matthews	.25
476	Bill Stein	.15
477	Doug Capilla	.15
478	Jerry Remy	.15
479	St. Louis Cardinals	.50
480	Ron LeFlore	.20
481	Jackson Todd	.15
482	Rick Miller	.15
483	Ken Macha	.15
484	Jim Norris	.15
485	Chris Chambliss	.20
486	John Curtis	.15
487	Jim Tyrone	.15
488	Dan Spillner	.15
489	Rudy Meoli	.15
490	Amos Otis	.20
491	Scott McGregor	.20
492	Jim Sundberg	.15
493	Steve Renko	.15
494	Chuck Tanner (Mgr.)	.15
495	Dave Cash	.15
496	Jim Clancy	.20
497	Glenn Adams	.15
498	Joe Sambito	.15
499	Seattle Mariners	.40
500	George Foster	.75
501	Dave Roberts	.15
502	Pat Rockett	.15
503	Ike Hampton	.15
504	Roger Freed	.15
505	Felix Millan	.15
506	Ron Blomberg	.15
507	Willie Crawford	.15
508	Johnny Oates	.15
509	Brent Strom	.15
510	Willie Stargell	2.50
511	Frank Duffy	.15
512	Larry Herndon	.20
513	Barry Foote	.15
514	Rob Sperring	.15
515	Tim Corcoran	.15
516	Gary Beare	.15
517	Andres Mora	.15
518	Tommy Boggs	.15
519	Brian Downing	.15
520	Larry Hisle	.15
521	Steve Staggs	.15
522	Dick Williams (Mgr.)	.20
523	Donnie Moore (R)	.40
524	Bernie Carbo	.15
525	Jerry Terrell	.15
526	Cincinnati Reds	.45
527	Vic Correll	.15
528	Rob Picciolo	.15
529	Paul Hartzell	.15
530	Dave Winfield	2.50
531	Tom Underwood	.15
532	Skip Jutze	.15
533	Sandy Alomar	.15
534	Wilbur Howard	.15
535	Checklist No. 5	.50
536	Roric Harrison	.15
537	Bruce Bochte	.15
538	Johnnie LeMaster	.15
539	Vic Davalillo	.15
540	Steve Carlton	3.00
541	Larry Cox	.15
542	Tim Johnson	.15
543	Larry Harlow	.15
544	Len Randle	.15
545	Bill Campbell	.15
546	Ted Martinez	.15
547	John Scott	.15
548	Billy Hunter (Mgr.)	.15
549	Joe Kerrigan	.15
550	John Mayberry	.20
551	Atlanta Braves	.35
552	Francisco Barrios	.15
553	Terry Puhl (R)	.45
554	Joe Coleman	.15
555	Butch Wynegar	.20
556	Ed Armbrister	.15
557	Tony Solaita	.15
558	Paul Mitchell	.15
559	Phil Mankowski	.15
560	Dave Parker	3.00
561	Charlie Williams	.15
562	Glenn Burke	.15
563	Dave Rader	.15
564	Mick Kelleher	.15
565	Jerry Koosman	.25
566	Merv Rettenmund	.15
567	Dick Drago	.15
568	Tom Hutton	.15
569	Lary Sorensen	.15
570	Dave Kingman	.50
571	Buck Martinez	.15
572	Rick Wise	.15
573	Luis Gomez	.15
574	Bob Lemon (Mgr.)	.25
575	Pat Dobson	.15
576	Sam Mejias	.15
577	Oakland A's	.30
578	Buzz Capra	.15
579	Rance Mulliniks	.15
580	Rod Carew	3.00
581	Lynn McGlothen	.15
582	Fran Healy	.15
583	George Medich	.15
584	John Hale	.15
585	Woodie Fryman	.15

NO. PLAYER	NR. MT.	NO. PLAYER	NR. MT.	NO. PLAYER	NR. MT.	NO. PLAYER	NR. MT.
586 Ed Goodson	.15	628 Ralph Garr	.15	669 Pete Falcone	.15	704 Rookie 2nd Basemen:	12.00
587 John Urrea	.15	629 Don Stanhouse	.15	670 Jim Rice	3.50	Garth Iorg, Sam Perlozzo,	
588 Jim Mason	.15	630 Ron Cey	.40	671 Gary Lavelle	.15	Dave Oliver, Lou Whitaker	
589 Bob Knepper (R)	1.00	631 Danny Ozark (Mgr.)	.20	672 Don Kessinger	.15	705 Rookie Outfielders:	.50
590 Bobby Murcer	.30	632 Rowland Office	.15	673 Steve Brye	.15	D. Bergman, W. Norwood,	
591 George Zeber	.15	633 Tom Veryzer	.15	674 Ray Knight (R)	1.00	M. Dilone, C. Hurdle	
592 Bob Apodaca	.15	634 Len Barker	.15	675 Jay Johnstone	.15	706 Rookie 1st Basemen:	.40
593 Dave Skaggs	.15	635 Joe Rudi	.15	676 Bob Myrick	.15	Wayne Cage, Ted Cox,	
594 Dave Freisleben	.15	636 Jim Bibby	.15	677 Ed Herrmann	.15	P. Putnam, D. Revering	
595 Sixto Lezcano	.15	637 Duffy Dyer	.15	678 Tom Burgmeier	.15	707 Rookie Shortstops:	45.00
596 Gary Wheelock	.15	638 Paul Splittorff	.15	679 Wayne Garrett	.15	Mickey Klutts, Paul Molitor,	
597 Steve Dillard	.15	639 Gene Clines	.15	680 Vida Blue	.20	Alan Trammell,	
598 Eddie Solomon	.15	640 Lee May	.15	681 Rob Belloir	.15	U.L. Washington	
599 Gary Woods	.15	641 Doug Rau	.15	682 Ken Brett	.15	708 Rookie Catchers:	24.00
600 Frank Tanana	.25	642 Denny Doyle	.15	683 Mike Champion	.15	Bo Diaz, Dale Murphy,	
601 Gene Mauch (Mgr.)	.20	643 Tom House	.15	684 Ralph Houk (Mgr.)	.20	Ernie Whitt, Lance Parrish	
602 Eric Soderholm	.15	644 Jim Dwyer	.15	685 Frank Taveras	.15	709 Rookie Pitchers:	.40
603 Will McEnaney	.15	645 Mike Torrez	.15	686 Gaylord Perry	1.50	Steve Burke, Lance	
604 Earl Williams	.15	646 Rick Auerbach	.15	687 Julio Cruz (R)	.30	Rautzhan, Matt Keough,	
605 Rick Rhoden	.25	647 Steve Dunning	.15	688 George Mitterwald	.15	Dan Schatzeder	
606 Pittsburgh Pirates	.50	648 Gary Thomasson	.15	689 Cleveland Indians	.50	710 Rookie Outfielders:	.75
607 Fernando Arroyo	.15	649 Moose Haas (R)	.30	690 Mickey Rivers	.20	Dell Alston, Rick Bosetti,	
608 Johnny Grubb	.15	650 Cesar Cedeno	.25	691 Ross Grimsley	.15	Mike Easler, Keith Smith	
609 John Denny	.25	651 Doug Rader	.15	692 Ken Reitz	.15	711 Rookie Pitchers:	.35
610 Garry Maddox	.20	652 Checklist No. 6	.50	693 Lamar Johnson	.15	C. Camper, D. Lamp,	
611 Pat Scanlon	.15	653 Ron Hodges	.15	694 Elias Sosa	.15	R. Thomas, C. Mitchell	
612 Ken Henderson	.15	654 Pepe Frias	.15	695 Dwight Evans	1.50	712 Bobby Valentine	.25
613 Marty Perez	.15	655 Lyman Bostock	.20	696 Steve Mingori	.15	713 Bob Davis	.15
614 Joe Wallis	.15	656 Dave Garcia (Mgr.)	.15	697 Roger Metzger	.15	714 Mike Anderson	.15
615 Clay Carroll	.15	657 Bombo Rivera	.15	698 Juan Bernhardt	.15	715 Jim Kaat	.40
616 Pat Kelly	.15	658 Manny Sanguillen	.15	699 Jackie Brown	.15	716 Clarence Gaston	.15
617 Joe Nolan	.15	659 Texas Rangers	.35	700 Johnny Bench	4.00	717 Nelson Briles	.15
618 Tommy Helms	.15	660 Jason Thompson	.25	701 Rookie Pitchers:	.40	718 Ron Jackson	.15
619 Thad Bosley	.15	661 Grant Jackson	.15	Larry Landreth, Tom Hume,		719 Randy Elliott	.15
620 Willie Randolph	.30	662 Paul Dade	.15	Steve McCatty, B. Taylor		720 Fergie Jenkins	.50
621 Craig Swan	.15	663 Paul Reuschel	.15	702 Rookie Catchers:	.25	721 Billy Martin (Mgr.)	.35
622 Champ Summers	.15	664 Fred Stanley	.15	Rick Sweet, Bill Nahorodny		722 Pete Broberg	.15
623 Eduardo Rodriquez	.15	665 Dennis Leonard	.20	Kevin Pasley, Don Werner		723 John Wockenfuss	.15
624 Gary Alexander	.15	666 Billy Smith	.15	703 Rookie Pitchers:	6.00	724 K.C. Royals	.50
625 Jose Cruz	.35	667 Jeff Byrd	.15	Jack Morris, L. Andersen,		725 Kurt Bevacqua	.15
626 Toronto Blue Jays	.40	668 Dusty Baker	.25	Tim Jones, M. Mahler		726 W. Wood (Exc. .10)	.40
627 Dave Johnson	.15						

1979 Topps. . . . Complete Set of 726 Cards—Value $250.00

Features the rookie cards of Pedro Guerrero and Bob Horner. 66 cards were double printed. Card 369 (Bump Wills) was originally issued in error as a "Blue Jay". A corrected card was issued showing Wills as a "Ranger"

NO. PLAYER	MINT	NO. PLAYER	MINT	NO. PLAYER	MINT	NO. PLAYER	MINT
1 Batting Leaders:	2.00	9 Dave Campbell	.10	25 Steve Carlton	2.50	41 Minnesota Twins/	.40
Rod Carew, Dave Parker		10 Lee May	.10	26 Jamie Quirk	.10	Gene Mauch (Mgr.)	
2 Home Run Leaders:	.50	11 Marc Hill	.10	27 Dave Goltz	.10	42 Ron Blomberg	.10
Jim Rice, George Foster		12 Dick Drago	.10	28 Steve Brye	.10	43 Wayne Twitchell	.10
3 RBI Leaders:	.50	13 Paul Dade	.10	29 Rick Langford	.10	44 Kurt Bevacqua	.10
Jim Rice, George Foster		14 Rafael Landestoy	.10	30 Dave Winfield	2.50	45 Al Hrabosky	.10
4 Stolen Base Leaders:	.35	15 Ross Grimsley	.10	31 Tom House	.10	46 Ron Hodges	.10
Ron LeFlore, Omar Moreno		16 Fred Stanley	.10	32 Jerry Mumphrey	.15	47 Fred Norman	.10
5 Victory Leaders:	.40	17 Donnie Moore	.15	33 Dave Rozema	.10	48 Merv Rettenmund	.10
Ron Guidry, Gaylord Perry		18 Tony Solaita	.10	34 Rob Andrews	.10	49 Vern Ruhle	.10
6 Stikeout Leaders:	.40	19 Larry Gura	.10	35 Ed Figueroa	.10	50 Steve Garvay	1.25
Nolan Ryan, J.R. Richard		20 Joe Morgan	.75	36 Alan Ashby	.10	51 Ray Fosse	.10
7 ERA Leaders:	.35	21 Kevin Kobel	.10	37 Joe Kerrigan	.10	52 Randy Lerch	.10
Ron Guidry, Craig Swan		22 Mike Jorgensen	.10	38 Bernie Carbo	.10	53 Mick Kelleher	.10
8 Leading Firemen:	.45	23 Terry Forster	.15	39 Dale Murphy	8.00	54 Del Alston	.10
R. Gossage, R. Fingers		24 Paul Molitor	3.50	40 Dennis Eckersley	2.00	55 Wllie Stargell	2.50

NO. PLAYER	MINT
56 John Hale	.10
57 Eric Rasmussen	.10
58 Bob Randall	.10
59 John Denny	.10
60 Mickey Rivers	.15
61 Bo Diaz	.25
62 Randy Moffitt	.10
63 Jack Brohamer	.10
64 Tom Underwood	.10
65 Mark Belanger	.10
66 Tigers/L. Moss (Mgr.)	.50
67 Jim Mason	.10
68 Joe Niekro	.10
69 Elliott Maddox	.10
70 John Candelaria	.15
71 Brian Downing	.15
72 Steve Mingori	.10
73 Ken Henderson	.10
74 Shane Rawley (R)	1.00
75 Steve Yeager	.10
76 Warren Cromartie	.10
77 Dan Briggs	.10
78 Elias Sosa	.10
79 Ted Cox	.10
80 Jason Thompson	.15
81 Roger Erickson	.10
82 Mets/J. Torre (Mgr.)	.40
83 Fred Kendall	.10
84 Greg Minton	.10
85 Gary Matthews	.20
86 Rodney Scott	.10
87 Pete Falcone	.10
88 Bob Molinaro	.10
89 Dick Tidrow	.10
90 Bob Boone	.35
91 Terry Crowley	.10
92 Jim Bibby	.10
93 Phil Mankowski	.10
94 Len Barker	.15
95 Robin Yount	7.00
96 Cleveland Indians/ Jeff Torborg (Mgr.)	.25
97 Sam Mejias	.10
98 Ray Burris	.10
99 John Wathan	.10
100 Tom Seaver	2.50
101 Roy Howell	.10
102 Mike Anderson	.10
103 Jim Todd	.10
104 Johnny Oates	.10
105 Rick Camp	.10
106 Frank Duffy	.10
107 Jesus Alou	.10
108 Eduardo Rodriguez	.10
109 Joel Youngblood	.10
110 Vida Blue	.15
111 Roger Freed	.10
112 Philadelphia Phillies/ Danny Ozark (Mgr.)	.35
113 Pete Redfern	.10
114 Cliff Johnson	.10
115 Nolan Ryan	12.00
116 Ozzie Smith (R)	40.00
117 Grant Jackson	.10
118 Bud Harrelson	.10
119 Don Stanhouse	.10
120 Jim Sundberg	.10
121 Checklist No. 1	.20
122 Mike Paxton	.10
123 Lou Whitaker	3.00
124 Dan Schatzeder	.10
125 Rick Burleson	.10
126 Doug Bair	.10
127 Thad Bosley	.10
128 Ted Martinez	.10
129 Marty Pattin	.10
130 Bob Watson	.10
131 Jim Clancy	.10
132 Rowland Office	.10
133 Bill Castro	.10
134 Alan Bannister	.10
135 Bobby Murcer	.25
136 Jim Kaat	.45
137 Larry Wolfe	.10
138 Mark Lee	.10

NO. PLAYER	MINT
139 Luis Pujols	.10
140 Don Gullett	.10
141 Tom Paciorek	.10
142 Charlie Williams	.10
143 Tony Scott	.10
144 Sandy Alomar	.10
145 Rick Rhoden	.20
146 Duane Kuiper	.10
147 Dave Hamilton	.10
148 Bruce Boisclair	.10
149 Manny Sarmiento	.10
150 Wayne Cage	.10
151 John Hiller	.10
152 Rick Cerone	.10
153 Dennis Lamp	.10
154 Jim Gantner	.10
155 Dwight Evans	1.25
156 Buddy Solomon	.10
157 U.L. Washington	.10
158 Joe Sambito	.10
159 Roy White	.10
160 Mike Flanagan	.35
161 Barry Foote	.10
162 Tom Johnson	.10
163 Glenn Burke	.10
164 Mickey Lolich	.15
165 Frank Taveras	.10
166 Leon Roberts	.10
167 Roger Metzger	.10
168 Dave Freisleben	.10
169 Bill Nahorodny	.10
170 Don Sutton	1.25
171 Gene Clines	.10
172 Mike Bruhert	.10
173 John Lowenstein	.10
174 Rick Auerbach	.10
175 George Hendrick	.15
176 Aurelio Rodriguez	.10
177 Ron Reed	.10
178 Alvis Woods	.10
179 Jim Beattie	.10
180 Larry Hisle	.10
181 Mike Garman	.10
182 Tim Johnson	.10
183 Paul Splittorff	.10
184 Darrel Chaney	.10
185 Mike Torrez	.10
186 Eric Soderholm	.10
187 Mark Lemongello	.10
188 Pat Kelly	.10
189 Eddie Whitson (R)	1.50
190 Ron Cey	.40
191 Mike Norris	.10
192 St. Louis Cardinals/ Ken Boyer (Mgr.)	.35
193 Glenn Adams	.10
194 Randy Jones	.10
195 Bill Madlock	.40
196 Steve Kemp	.10
197 Bob Apodaca	.10
198 Johnny Grubb	.10
199 Larry Milbourne	.10
200 Johnny Bench	1.50
201 Record — M. Edwards Most Unassisted DP's by 2nd Baseman	.15
202 Record — R. Guidry Most Strikeouts, Lefthander, 9 Inning Game	.25
203 Record — J.R. Richard Most Season Stikeouts, Righthander	.25
204 Record — P. Rose Most Consecutive Games Batting Safely	1.25
205 Record — J. Stearns Most Steals by Catcher, Season	.20
206 Record — S. Stewart 7 Straight Stikeouts, First Major League Game	.20
207 Dave Lemanczyk	.10
208 Clarence Gaston	.10
209 Reggie Cleveland	.10
210 Larry Bowa	.20

NO. PLAYER	MINT
211 Denny Martinez	.10
212 Carney Lansford (R)	6.00
213 Bill Travers	.10
214 Boston Red Sox/ Don Zimmer (Mgr.)	.45
215 Willie McCovey	1.50
216 Wilbur Wood	.10
217 Steve Dillard	.10
218 Dennis Leonard	.15
219 Roy Smalley	.10
220 Cesar Geronimo	.10
221 Jesse Jefferson	.10
222 Bob Beall	.10
223 Kent Tekulve	.15
224 Dave Revering	.10
225 Rich Gossage	.50
226 Ron Pruitt	.10
227 Steve Stone	.10
228 Vic Davalillo	.10
229 Doug Flynn	.10
230 Bob Forsch	.10
231 Johnny Wockenfuss	.10
232 Jimmy Sexton	.10
233 Paul Mitchell	.10
234 Toby Harrah	.15
235 Steve Rogers	.15
236 Jim Dwyer	.10
237 Billy Smith	.10
238 Balor Moore	.10
239 Willie Horton	.10
240 Rick Reuschel	.30
241 Checklist No. 2	.20
242 Pablo Torrealba	.10
243 Buck Martinez	.10
244 Pittsburgh Pirates/ Chuck Tanner (Mgr.)	.35
245 Jeff Burroughs	.10
246 Darrell Jackson	.10
247 Tucker Ashford	.10
248 Pete LaCock	.10
249 Paul Thormodsgard	.10
250 Willie Randolph	.25
251 Jack Morris	2.50
252 Bob Stinson	.10
253 Rick Wise	.10
254 Luis Gomez	.10
255 Tommy John	.60
256 Mike Sadek	.10
257 Adrian Devine	.10
258 Mike Phillips	.10
259 Cincinnati Reds/ Sparky Anderson (Mgr.)	.40
260 Richie Zisk	.10
261 Mario Guerrero	.10
262 Nelson Briles	.10
263 Oscar Gamble	.10
264 Don Robinson (R)	1.25
265 Don Money	.10
266 Jim Willoughby	.10
267 Joe Rudi	.10
268 Julio Gonzalez	.10
269 Woodie Fryman	.10
270 Butch Hobson	.10
271 Rawly Eastwick	.10
272 Tim Corcoran	.10
273 Jerry Terrell	.10
274 Willie Norwood	.10
275 Junior Moore	.10
276 Jim Colborn	.10
277 Tom Grieve	.10
278 Andy Messersmith	.20
279 Jerry Grote	.10
280 Andre Thornton	.15
281 Vic Correll	.10
282 Toronto Blue Jays/ Roy Hartsfield (Mgr.)	.20
283 Ken Kravec	.10
284 Johnnie LeMaster	.10
285 Bobby Bonds	.20
286 Duffy Dyer	.10
287 Andres Mora	.10
288 Milt Wilcox	.10
289 Jose Cruz	.25
290 Dave Lopes	.20
291 Tom Griffin	.10

NO. PLAYER	MINT
292 Don Reynolds	.10
293 Jerry Garvin	.10
294 Pepe Frias	.10
295 Mitchell Page	.10
296 Preston Hanna	.10
297 Ted Sizemore	.10
298 Rich Gale	.10
299 Steve Ontiveros	.10
300 Rod Carew	2.00
301 Tom Hume	.10
302 Atlanta Braves/ Bobby Cox (Mgr.)	.35
303 Lary Sorensen	.10
304 Steve Swisher	.10
305 Willie Montanez	.10
306 Floyd Bannister	.15
307 Larvell Blanks	.10
308 Bert Blyleven	.75
309 Ralph Garr	.10
310 Thurman Munson	2.25
311 Gary Lavelle	.10
312 Bob Robertson	.10
313 Dyar Miller	.10
314 Larry Harlow	.10
315 John Matlack	.10
316 Milt May	.10
317 Jose Cardenal	.10
318 Bob Welch (R)	12.00
319 Wayne Garrett	.10
320 Carl Yastrzemski	3.00
321 Gaylord Perry	1.50
322 Danny Goodwin	.10
323 Lynn McGlothen	.10
324 Mike Tyson	.10
325 Cecil Cooper	.50
326 Pedro Borbon	.10
327 Art Howe	.10
328 Oakland A's/ Jack McKeon (Mgr.)	.20
329 Joe Coleman	.10
330 George Brett	7.50
331 Mickey Mahler	.10
332 Gary Alexander	.10
333 Chet Lemon	.35
334 Craig Swan	.10
335 Chris Chambliss	.15
336 Bobby Thompson	.10
337 John Montague	.10
338 Vic Harris	.10
339 Ron Jackson	.10
340 Jim Palmer	2.00
341 Willie Upshaw (R)	.60
342 Dave Roberts	.10
343 Ed Glynn	.10
344 Jerry Royster	.10
345 Tug McGraw	.20
346 Bill Buckner	.20
347 Doug Rau	.10
348 Andre Dawson	8.00
349 Jim Wright	.10
350 Garry Templeton	.30
351 Wayne Nordhagen	.10
352 Steve Mura	.10
353 Checklist No. 3	.50
354 Bill Bonham	.10
355 Lee Mazzilli	.15
356 San Francisco Giants/ Joe Altobelli (Mgr.)	.40
357 Jerry Augustine	.10
358 Alan Trammell	8.00
359 Dan Spillner	.15
360 Amos Otis	.15
361 Tom Dixon	.10
362 Mike Cubbage	.10
363 Craig Skok	.10
364 Gene Richards	.10
365 Sparky Lyle	.15
366 Juan Bernhardt	.10
367 Dave Skaggs	.10
368 Don Aase	.10
369 Bump Wills (error) (Blue Jays)	3.00
369 Bump Wills (correct) (Rangers)	4.00
370 Dave Kingman	.40

NO.	PLAYER	MINT
371	Jeff Holly	.10
372	Lamar Johnson	.10
373	Lance Rautzhan	.10
374	Ed Herrmann	.10
375	Bill Campbell	.10
376	Gorman Thomas	.35
377	Paul Moskau	.10
378	Rob Picciolo	.10
379	Dale Murray	.10
380	John Mayberry	.15
381	Houston Astros/ Bill Virdon (Mgr.)	.25
382	Jerry Martin	.10
383	Phil Garner	.10
384	Tommy Boggs	.10
385	Dan Ford	.10
386	Francisco Barrios	.10
387	Gary Thomasson	.10
388	Jack Billingham	.10
389	Joe Zdeb	.10
390	Rollie Fingers	.75
391	Al Oliver	.35
392	Doug Ault	.10
393	Scott McGregor	.15
394	Randy Stein	.10
395	Dave Cash	.10
396	Bill Plummer	.10
397	Sergio Ferrer	.10
398	Ivan DeJesus	.10
399	David Clyde	.10
400	Jim Rice	2.50
401	Ray Knight	.15
402	Paul Hartzell	.10
403	Tim Foli	.10
404	Chicago White Sox/ Don Kessinger (Mgr.)	.25
405	Butch Wynegar	.10
406	Joe Wallis	.10
407	Pete Vuckovich	.10
408	Charlie Moore	.10
409	Willie Wilson (R)	1.75
410	Darrell Evans	.30
411	All-Time Hits: Season — George Sisler, Career — Ty Cobb	.50
412	All-Time RBI's: Season — Hack Wilson Career — Hank Aaron	.50
413	All-Time Home Runs: Season — Roger Maris Career — Hank Aaron	.50
414	All-Time Batting Avg.: Career — Ty Cobb Season — R. Hornsby	.50
415	All-Time Stolen Bases: Career — Lou Brock Season — Lou Brock	.50
416	All-Time Wins: Career — Cy Young Season: J. Chesbro	.25
417	All-Time Strikeouts: Career: Walter Johnson Season: Nolan Ryan	.25
418	All-Time ERA: Career: W. Johnson Season: Dutch Leonard	.25
419	Dick Ruthven	.10
420	Ken Griffey	.50
421	Doug DeCinces	.20
422	Ruppert Jones	.15
423	Bob Montgomery	.10
424	California Angels/ Jim Fregosi (Mgr.)	.30
425	Rick Manning	.10
426	Chris Speier	.10
427	Andy Replogle	.10
428	Bobby Valentine	.10
429	John Urrea	.10
430	Dave Parker	2.00
431	Glenn Borgmann	.10
432	Dave Heaverlo	.10
433	Larry Biittner	.10
434	Ken Clay	.10
435	Gene Tenace	.10
436	Hector Cruz	.10

NO.	PLAYER	MINT
437	Rick Williams	.10
438	Horace Speed	.10
439	Frank White	.15
440	Rusty Staub	.20
441	Lee Lacy	.15
442	Doyle Alexander	.10
443	Bruce Bochte	.10
444	Aurelio Lopez (R)	.25
445	Steve Henderson	.10
446	Jim Lonborg	.10
447	Manny Sanguillen	.10
448	Moose Haas	.10
449	Bombo Rivera	.10
450	Dave Concepcion	.25
451	Kansas City Royals/ Whitey Herzog (Mgr.)	.25
452	Jerry Morales	.10
453	Chris Knapp	.10
454	Len Randle	.10
455	Bill Lee	.10
456	Chuck Baker	.10
457	Bruce Sutter	.75
458	Jim Essian	.10
459	Sid Monge	.10
460	Graig Nettles	.40
461	Jim Barr	.10
462	Otto Velez	.10
463	Steve Comer	.10
464	Joe Nolan	.10
465	Reggie Smith	.20
466	Mark Littell	.10
467	Don Kessinger	.10
468	Stan Bahnsen	.10
469	Lance Parrish	3.00
470	Garry Maddox	.10
471	Joaquin Andujar	.30
472	Craig Kusick	.10
473	Dave Roberts	.10
474	Dick Davis	.10
475	Dan Driessen	.10
476	Tom Poquette	.10
477	Bob Grich	.15
478	Juan Beniquez	.10
479	San Diego Padres/ Roger Craig (Mgr.)	.25
480	Fred Lynn	.75
481	Skip Lockwood	.10
482	Craig Reynolds	.10
483	Checklist No. 4	.20
484	Rick Waits	.10
485	Bucky Dent	.15
486	Bob Knepper	.25
487	Miguel Dilone	.10
488	Bob Owchinko	.10
489	Larry Cox (photo of Dave Rader)	.10
490	Al Cowens	.10
491	Tippy Martinez	.10
492	Bob Bailor	.10
493	Larry Christenson	.10
494	Jerry White	.10
495	Tony Perez	.50
496	Barry Bonnell	.10
497	Glenn Abbott	.10
498	Rich Chiles	.10
499	Texas Rangers/ Pat Corrales (Mgr.)	.25
500	Ron Guidry	1.00
501	Junior Kennedy	.10
502	Steve Braun	.10
503	Terry Humphrey	.10
504	Larry McWilliams (R)	.40
505	Ed Kranepool	.10
506	John D'Acquisto	.10
507	Tony Armas	.35
508	Charlie Hough	.10
509	Mario Mendoza	.10
510	Ted Simmons	.35
511	Paul Reuschel	.10
512	Jack Clark	2.00
513	Dave Johnson	.25
514	Mike Proly	.10
515	Enos Cabell	.10
516	Champ Summers	.10
517	Al Bumbry	.10
518	Jim Umbarger	.10

NO.	PLAYER	MINT
519	Ben Oglivie	.15
520	Gary Carter	2.50
521	Sam Ewing	.10
522	Ken Holtzman	.10
523	John Milner	.10
524	Tom Burgmeier	.10
525	Freddie Patek	.10
526	Los Angeles Dodgers/ Tom Lasorda (Mgr.)	.50
527	Lerrin LaGrow	.10
528	Wayne Gross	.10
529	Brian Asselstine	.10
530	Frank Tanana	.15
531	Fernando Gonazalez	.10
532	Buddy Schultz	.10
533	Leroy Stanton	.10
534	Ken Forsch	.10
535	Ellis Valentine	.10
536	Jerry Reuss	.15
537	Tom Veryzer	.10
538	Mike Ivie	.10
539	John Ellis	.10
540	Greg Luzinski	.25
541	Jim Slaton	.10
542	Rick Bosetti	.10
543	Kiko Garcia	.10
544	Fergie Jenkins	.40
545	John Stearns	.10
546	Bill Russell	.10
547	Clint Hurdle	.10
548	Enrique Romo	.10
549	Bob Bailey	.10
550	Sal Bando	.10
551	Chicago Cubs/ Herman Franks (Mgr.)	.35
552	Jose Morales	.10
553	Denny Walling	.10
554	Matt Keough	.10
555	Biff Pocoroba	.10
556	Mike Lum	.10
557	Ken Brett	.10
558	Jay Johnstone	.10
559	Greg Pryor	.10
560	John Montefusco	.10
561	Ed Ott	.10
562	Dusty Baker	.20
563	Roy Thomas	.10
564	Jerry Turner	.10
565	Rico Carty	.10
566	Nino Espinosa	.10
567	Rich Hebner	.10
568	Carlos Lopez	.10
569	Bob Sykes	.10
570	Cesar Cedeno	.20
571	Darrell Porter	.15
572	Rod Gilbreath	.10
573	Jim Kern	.10
574	Claudell Washington	.15
575	Luis Tiant	.20
576	Mike Parrott	.10
577	Milwaukee Brewers/ George Bamberger (Mgr.)	.30
578	Pete Broberg	.10
579	Greg Gross	.10
580	Ron Fairly	.10
581	Darold Knowles	.10
582	Paul Blair	.10
583	Julio Cruz	.10
584	Jim Rooker	.10
585	Hal McRae	.15
586	Bob Horner (R)	2.00
587	Ken Reitz	.10
588	Tom Murphy	.10
589	Terry Whitfield	.10
590	J.R. Richard	.15
591	Mike Hargrove	.10
592	Mike Krukow	.10
593	Rick Dempsey	.10
594	Bob Shirley	.10
595	Phil Niekro	1.00
596	Jim Wohlford	.10
597	Bob Stanley	.15
598	Mark Wagner	.10
599	Jim Spencer	.10
600	George Foster	.50

NO.	PLAYER	MINT
601	Dave LaRoche	.10
602	Checklist No. 5	.50
603	Rudy May	.10
604	Jeff Newman	.10
605	Rick Monday	.10
606	Montreal Expos/ Dick Williams (Mgr.)	.25
607	Omar Moreno	.10
608	Dave McKay	.10
609	Silvio Martinez	.10
610	Mike Schmidt	7.00
611	Jim Norris	.10
612	Rick Honeycutt (R)	.60
613	Mike Edwards	.10
614	Willie Hernandez	.50
615	Ken Singleton	.15
616	Billy Almon	.10
617	Terry Puhl	.10
618	Jerry Remy	.10
619	Ken Landreaux	.30
620	Bert Campaneris	.15
621	Pat Zachry	.10
622	Dave Collins	.15
623	Bob McClure	.10
624	Larry Herndon	.10
625	Mark Fidrych	.15
626	New York Yankees/ Bob Lemon (Mgr.)	.40
627	Gary Serum	.10
628	Del Unser	.10
629	Gene Garber	.10
630	Bake McBride	.10
631	Jorge Orta	.10
632	Don Kirkwood	.10
633	Rob Wilfong	.10
634	Paul Lindblad	.10
635	Don Baylor	.75
636	Wayne Garland	.10
637	Bill Robinson	.10
638	Al Fitzmorris	.10
639	Manny Trillo	.10
640	Eddie Murray	10.00
641	Bobby Castillo	.10
642	Wilbur Howard	.10
643	Tom Hausman	.10
644	Manny Mota	.10
645	George Scott	.10
646	Rick Sweet	.10
647	Bob Lacey	.10
648	Lou Piniella	.30
649	John Curtis	.10
650	Pete Rose	4.00
651	Mike Caldwell	.10
652	Stan Papi	.10
653	Warren Brusstar	.10
654	Rick Miller	.10
655	Jerry Koosman	.20
656	Hosken Powell	.10
657	George Medich	.10
658	Taylor Duncan	.10
659	Seattle Mariners/ Darrell Johnson (Mgr.)	.20
660	Ron LeFlore	.10
661	Bruce Kison	.10
662	Kevin Bell	.10
663	Mike Vail	.10
664	Doug Bird	.10
665	Lou Brock	1.25
666	Rich Dauer	.10
667	Don Hood	.10
668	Bill North	.10
669	Checklist No. 6	.50
670	Jim Hunter	.50
671	Joe Ferguson	.10
672	Ed Halicki	.10
673	Tom Hutton	.10
674	Dave Tomlin	.10
675	Tim McCarver	.25
676	Johnny Sutton	.10
677	Larry Parrish	.10
678	Geoff Zahn	.10
679	Derrel Thomas	.10
680	Carlton Fisk	2.50
681	John Johnson	.10
682	Dave Chalk	.10

NO. PLAYER	MINT	NO. PLAYER	MINT	NO. PLAYER	MINT	NO. PLAYER	MINT
683 Dan Meyer	.10	703 Angels Prospects:	.15	711 A's Prospects:	.45	719 Dodgers Prospects:	11.00
684 Jamie Easterly	.10	Bob Slater, J. Anderson,		Dwayne Murphy, Bruce		Pedro Guerrero, Rudy Law,	
685 Sixto Lezcano	.10	Dave Frost		Robinson, Alan Wirth		Joe Simpson	
686 Ron Schueler	.10	704 White Sox Prospects:	.15	712 Mariners Prospects:	.15	720 Expos Prospects:	1.25
687 Rennie Stennett	.10	Ross Baumgarten, Mike		Greg Biercevicz,		Jerry Fry, Jerry Pirtle,	
688 Mike Willis	.10	Colbern, Mike Squires		B. McLaughlin, B. Anderson		Scott Sanderson	
689 Baltimore Orioles/	.35	705 Indians Prospects:	1.00	713 Rangers Prospects:	1.00	721 Mets Prospects:	.25
Earl Weaver (Mgr.)		Tim Norrid, D. Oliver,		Danny Darwin, Pat Putnam,		Dwight Bernard, Juan	
690 Buddy Bell	.10	Alfredo Griffin		Billy Sample		Berenguer, Dan Norman	
691 Dock Ellis	.10	706 Tigers Prospects:	.20	714 Blue Jays Prospects:	.15	722 Phillies Prospects:	2.50
692 Mickey Stanley	.10	Dave Stegman, Dave Tobik,		Victor Cruz, Pat Kelly,		Jim Morrison, Lonnie	
693 Dave Rader	.10	Kip Young		Ernie Whitt		Smith, Jim Wright	
694 Burt Hooton	.10	707 Royals Prospects:	.15	715 Braves Prospects:	.40	723 Pirates Prospects:	.35
695 Keith Hernandez	2.00	Randy Bass, Jim Gaudet,		Larry Whisenton, Bruce		Eugenio Cotes,	
696 Andy Hassler	.10	R. McGilberry		Benedict, Glenn Hubbard		B. Wiltbank, Dale Berra	
697 Dave Bergman	.10	708 Brewers Prospects:	1.50	716 Cubs Prospects	.20	724 Cardinals Prospects:	.50
698 Bill Stein	.10	Kevin Bass, Ned Yost,		S. Thompson, Dave Geisel,		Tom Bruno, George	
699 Hal Dues	.10	Eddie Romero		Karl Pagel		Frazier, Terry Kennedy	
700 Reggie Jackson	2.50	709 Twins Prospects:	.15	717 Reds Prospects:	.45	725 Padres Prospects:	.15
701 Orioles Prospects:	.35	R. Sofield, Kevin Stanfield,		M. LaCoss, Ron Oester,		Jim Beswick, Broderick	
Mark Corey, John Flinn,		Sam Perlozzo		Harry Spilman		Perkins, Steve Mura	
Sammy Stewart		710 Yankees Prospects:	.40	718 Astros Prospects:	.15	726 Giants Prospects:	.20
702 Red Sox Prospects:	.20	Mike Heath, D. Rajsich,		Mike Fischlin, Bruce Bochy,		J. Tamargo, Greg	
Garry Hancock, Joel Finch,		Brian Doyle		Don Pisker		Johnston, Joe Strain	
Allen Ripley							

1980 Topps. . . . Complete Set of 726 Cards—Value $275.00

Features the rookie cards of Rickey Henderson, Dan Quisenberry, Mike Scott and Dave Stieb. 66 cards were double printed.

NO. PLAYER	MINT	NO. PLAYER	MINT	NO. PLAYER	MINT	NO. PLAYER	MINT
1 Highlights: Brock and	1.50	30 Vida Blue	.15	64 Joe Nolan	.08	96 Oakland A's/	.35
Yaz Get 3000 Hits (Exc. .30)		31 Jay Johnstone	.08	65 Al Bumbry	.08	Jim Marshall (Mgr.)	
2 Highlights: McCovey	.75	32 Julio Cruz	.08	66 Kansas City Royals/	.35	97 Bill Lee	.15
512 Home Runs		33 Tony Scott	.08	Jim Frey (Mgr.)		98 Jerry Terrell	.08
3 Highlights: Manny Mota	.15	34 Jeff Newman	.08	67 Doyle Alexander	.08	99 Victor Cruz	.08
145 Pinch Hits		35 Luis Tiant	.12	68 Larry Harlow	.08	100 Johnny Bench	3.00
4 Highlights: Pete Rose	2.00	36 Rusty Torres	.08	69 Rick Williams	.08	101 Aurelio Lopez	.08
10th 200 Hit Season		37 Kiko Garcia	.08	70 Gary Carter	2.00	102 Rich Dauer	.08
5 Highlights: G. Templeton	.25	38 Dan Spillner	.08	71 John Milner	.08	103 Bill Caudill (R)	.40
100 Lefty and Righty Hits		39 Rowland Office	.08	72 Fred Howard	.08	104 Manny Mota	.15
6 Highlights: Del Unser	.15	40 Carlton Fisk	2.00	73 Dave Collins	.08	105 Frank Tanana	.15
3rd Consec. Pinch Homer		41 Texas Rangers/	.30	74 Sid Monge	.08	106 Jeff Leonard (R)	1.75
7 Mike Lum	.08	Pat Corrales (Mgr.)		75 Bill Russell	.08	107 Francisco Barrios	.08
8 Craig Swan	.08	42 Dave Palmer (R)	.40	76 John Stearns	.08	108 Bob Horner	.65
9 Steve Braun	.08	43 Bombo Rivera	.08	77 Dave Stieb (R)	9.00	109 Bill Travers	.08
10 Denny Martinez	.12	44 Bill Fahey	.08	78 Ruppert Jones	.08	110 Fred Lynn	.35
11 Jimmy Sexton	.08	45 Frank White	.15	79 Bob Owchinko	.08	111 Bob Knepper	.20
12 John Curtis	.08	46 Rico Carty	.15	80 Ron LeFlore	.12	112 Chicago White Sox/	.35
13 Ron Pruitt	.08	47 Bill Bonham	.08	81 Ted Sizemore	.08	Tony LaRussa (Mgr.)	
14 Dave Cash	.08	48 Rick Miller	.08	82 Houston Astros/	.35	113 Geoff Zahn	.08
15 Bill Campbell	.08	49 Mario Guerrero	.08	Bill Virdon (Mgr.)		114 Juan Beniquez	.12
16 Jerry Narron	.08	50 J. Richard	.12	83 Steve Trout (R)	.30	115 Sparky Lyle	.15
17 Bruce Sutter	.50	51 Joe Ferguson	.08	84 Gary Lavelle	.08	116 Larry Cox	.08
18 Ron Jackson	.08	52 Warren Brusstar	.08	85 Ted Simmons	.30	117 Dock Ellis	.08
19 Balor Moore	.08	53 Ben Oglivie	.12	86 Dave Hamilton	.08	118 Phil Garner	.08
20 Dan Ford	.08	54 Dennis Lamp	.08	87 Pepe Frias	.08	119 Sammy Stewart	.08
21 Manny Sarmiento	.08	55 Bill Madlock	.40	88 Ken Landreaux	.12	120 Greg Luzinski	.25
22 Pat Putnam	.08	56 Bobby Valentine	.12	89 Don Hood	.08	121 Checklist No. 1	.25
23 Derrel Thomas	.08	57 Pete Vuckovich	.12	90 Manny Trillo	.08	122 Dave Rosello	.08
24 Jim Slaton	.08	58 Doug Flynn	.08	91 Rick Dempsey	.08	123 Lynn Jones	.08
25 Lee Mazzilli	.12	59 Eddy Putman	.08	92 Rick Rhoden	.12	124 Dave Lemanczyk	.08
26 Marty Pattin	.08	60 Bucky Dent	.12	93 Dave Roberts	.08	125 Tony Perez	.50
27 Del Unser	.08	61 Gary Serum	.08	94 Neil Allen (R)	.40	126 Dave Tomlin	.08
28 Bruce Kison	.08	62 Mike Ivie	.08	95 Cecil Cooper	.40	127 Gary Thomasson	.08
29 Mark Wagner	.08	63 Bob Stanley	.12			128 Tom Burgmeier	.08

NO. PLAYER	MINT
129 Craig Reynolds	.08
130 Amos Otis	.15
131 Paul Mitchell	.08
132 Biff Pocoroba	.08
133 Jerry Turner	.08
134 Matt Keough	.08
135 Bill Buckner	.20
136 Dick Ruthven	.08
137 John Castino	.20
138 Ross Baumgarten	.08
139 Dane Iorg	.20
140 Rich Gossage	.50
141 Gary Alexander	.08
142 Phil Huffman	.08
143 Bruce Bochte	.08
144 Steve Comer	.08
145 Darrell Evans	.30
146 Bob Welch	2.50
147 Terry Puhl	.08
148 Manny Sanguillen	.15
149 Tom Hume	.08
150 Jason Thompson	.15
151 Tom Hausman	.12
152 John Fulgham	.08
153 Tim Blackwell	.08
154 Lary Sorensen	.08
155 Jerry Remy	.08
156 Tony Brizzolara	.08
157 Willie Wilson	.25
158 Rob Picciolo	.08
159 Ken Clay	.08
160 Eddie Murray	4.00
161 Larry Christenson	.08
162 Bob Randall	.08
163 Steve Swisher	.08
164 Greg Pryor	.08
165 Omar Moreno	.08
166 Glenn Abbott	.08
167 Jack Clark	1.50
168 Rick Waits	.08
169 Luis Gomez	.08
170 Burt Hooton	.08
171 Fernando Gonzalez	.08
172 Ron Hodges	.08
173 John Henry Johnson	.08
174 Ray Knight	.20
175 Rick Reuschel	.30
176 Champ Summers	.08
177 Dave Heaverlo	.08
178 Tim McCarver	.20
179 Ron Davis (R)	.25
180 Warren Cromartie	.08
181 Moose Haas	.08
182 Ken Reitz	.08
183 Jim Anderson	.08
184 Steve Renko	.08
185 Hal McRae	.12
186 Junior Moore	.08
187 Alan Ashby	.08
188 Terry Crowley	.08
189 Kevin Kobel	.08
190 Buddy Bell	.25
191 Ted Martinez	.08
192 Atlanta Braves/	.35
Bobby Cox (Mgr.)	
193 Dave Goltz	.08
194 Mike Easler	.25
195 John Montefusco	.15
196 Lance Parrish	1.50
197 Byron McLaughlin	.08
198 Dell Alston	.08
199 Mike LaCoss	.15
200 Jim Rice	1.50
201 Batting Leaders:	.30
K. Hernandez, Fred Lynn	
202 Home Run Leaders:	.30
Dave Kingman, G. Thomas	
203 RBI Leaders:	.30
Don Baylor, Dave Winfield	
204 Stolen Base Leaders:	.15
Omar Moreno, Willie Wilson	
205 Victory Leaders:	.25
Phil Niekro, Joe Niekro,	
Mike Flanagan	

NO. PLAYER	MINT
206 Strikeout Leaders:	.75
J.R. Richard, Nolan Ryan	
207 ERA Leaders:	.20
J.R. Richard, Ron Guidry	
208 Wayne Cage	.08
209 Von Joshua	.08
210 Steve Carlton	2.00
211 Dave Skaggs	.08
212 Dave Roberts	.08
213 Mike Jorgensen	.08
214 California Angels/	.35
Jim Fregosi (Mgr.)	
215 Sixto Lezcano	.08
216 Phil Mankowski	.08
217 Ed Halicki	.08
218 Jose Morales	.08
219 Steve Mingori	.08
220 Dave Concepcion	.35
221 Joe Cannon	.08
222 Ron Hassey	.25
223 Bob Sykes	.08
224 Willie Montanez	.08
225 Lou Piniella	.25
226 Bill Stein	.08
227 Len Barker	.08
228 Johnny Oates	.08
229 Jim Bibby	.08
230 Dave Winfield	2.00
231 Steve McCatty	.08
232 Alan Trammell	3.00
233 LaRue Washington	.08
234 Vern Ruhle	.08
235 Andre Dawson	3.00
236 Marc Hill	.08
237 Scott McGregor	.12
238 Rob Wilfong	.08
239 Don Aase	.08
240 Dave Kingman	.35
241 Checklist No. 2	.25
242 Lamar Johnson	.08
243 Jerry Augustine	.08
244 St. Louis Cardinals/	.40
Ken Boyer (Mgr.)	
245 Phil Niekro	.75
246 Tim Foli	.08
247 Frank Riccelli	.08
248 Jamie Quirk	.08
249 Jim Clancy	.08
250 Jim Kaat	.40
251 Kip Young	.08
252 Ted Cox	.08
253 John Montague	.08
254 Paul Dade	.08
255 Dusty Baker	.08
256 Roger Erickson	.08
257 Larry Herndon	.08
258 Paul Moskau	.08
259 New York Mets/	.50
Joe Torre (Mgr.)	
260 Al Oliver	.35
261 Dave Chalk	.08
262 Benny Ayala	.08
263 Dave LaRoche	.08
264 Bill Robinson	.08
265 Robin Yount	4.00
266 Bernie Carbo	.08
267 Dan Schatzeder	.08
268 Rafael Landestoy	.08
269 Dave Tobik	.08
270 Mike Schmidt	3.00
271 Dick Drago	.08
272 Ralph Garr	.08
273 Eduardo Rodriguez	.08
274 Dale Murphy	5.00
275 Jerry Koosman	.20
276 Tom Veryzer	.08
277 Rick Bosetti	.08
278 Jim Spencer	.08
279 Rob Andrews	.08
280 Gaylord Perry	.75
281 Paul Blair	.08
282 Seattle Mariners/	.35
Darrell Johnson (Mgr.)	
283 John Ellis	.08

NO. PLAYER	MINT
284 Larry Murray	.08
285 Don Baylor	.50
286 Darold Knowles	.08
287 John Lowenstein	.08
288 Dave Rozema	.08
289 Bruce Bochy	.08
290 Steve Garvey	2.00
291 Randy Scarberry	.08
292 Dale Berra	.08
293 Elias Sosa	.08
294 Charlie Spikes	.08
295 Larry Gura	.08
296 Dave Rader	.08
297 Tim Johnson	.08
298 Ken Holtzman	.08
299 Steve Henderson	.08
300 Ron Guidry	.75
301 Mike Edwards	.08
302 Los Angeles Dodgers/	.50
Tom Lasorda (Mgr.)	
303 Bill Castro	.08
304 Butch Wynegar	.08
305 Randy Jones	.08
306 Denny Walling	.08
307 Rick Honeycutt	.12
308 Mike Hargrove	.08
309 Mike McWilliams	.12
310 Dave Parker	1.25
311 Roger Metzger	.08
312 Mike Barlow	.08
313 Johnny Grubb	.08
314 Tim Stoddard	.20
315 Steve Kemp	.15
316 Bob Lacey	.08
317 Mike Anderson	.08
318 Jerry Reuss	.12
319 Chris Speier	.08
320 Dennis Eckersley	1.50
321 Keith Hernandez	1.25
322 Claudell Washington	.15
323 Mick Kelleher	.08
324 Tom Underwood	.08
325 Dan Driessen	.08
326 Bo McLaughlin	.08
327 Ray Fosse	.08
328 Minnesota Twins/	.35
Gene Mauch (Mgr.)	
329 Bert Roberge	.08
330 Al Cowens	.08
331 Rich Hebner	.08
332 Enrique Romo	.08
333 Jim Norris	.08
334 Jim Beattie	.08
335 Willie McCovey	1.50
336 George Medich	.08
337 Carney Lansford	1.50
338 Johnny Wockenfuss	.08
339 John D'Acquisto	.08
340 Ken Singleton	.15
341 Jim Essian	.08
342 Odell Jones	.08
343 Mike Vail	.08
344 Randy Lerch	.08
345 Larry Parrish	.12
346 Buddy Solomon	.08
347 Harry Chappas	.08
348 Checklist No. 3	.25
349 Jack Brohamer	.08
350 George Hendrick	.15
351 Bob Davis	.08
352 Dan Briggs	.08
353 Andy Hassler	.08
354 Rick Auerbach	.08
355 Gary Matthews	.15
356 San Diego Padres/	.35
Jerry Coleman (Mgr.)	
357 Bob McClure	.08
358 Lou Whitaker	1.50
359 Randy Moffitt	.08
360 Darrell Porter	.08
361 Wayne Garland	.08
362 Danny Goodwin	.08
363 Wayne Gross	.08
364 Ray Burris	.08

NO. PLAYER	MINT
365 Bobby Murcer	.20
366 Rob Dressler	.08
367 Billy Smith	.08
368 Willie Aikens (R)	.25
369 Jim Kern	.08
370 Cesar Cedeno	.15
371 Jack Morris	1.25
372 Joel Youngblood	.08
373 Dan Petry (R)	.50
374 Jim Gantner	.08
375 Ross Grimsley	.08
376 Gary Allenson	.15
377 Junior Kennedy	.08
378 Jerry Mumphrey	.08
379 Kevin Bell	.08
380 Garry Maddox	.09
381 Chicago Cubs/	.35
Preston Gomez (Mgr.)	
382 Dave Freisleben	.08
383 Ed Ott	.08
384 Joey McLaughlin	.08
385 Enos Cabell	.08
386 Darrell Jackson	.08
387 Fred Stanley	.08
388 Mike Paxton	.08
389 Pete LaCock	.08
390 Fergie Jenkins	.40
391 Tony Armas	.12
392 Milt Wilcox	.08
393 Ozzie Smith	6.00
394 Reggie Cleveland	.08
395 Ellis Valentine	.08
396 Dan Meyer	.08
397 Roy Thomas	.08
398 Barry Foote	.08
399 Mike Proly	.08
400 George Foster	.50
401 Pete Falcone	.08
402 Merv Rettenmund	.08
403 Pete Redfern	.08
404 Baltimore Orioles/	.45
Earl Weaver (Mgr.)	
405 Dwight Evans	1.00
406 Paul Molitor	1.25
407 Tony Solaita	.08
408 Bill North	.08
409 Paul Splittorff	.08
410 Bobby Bonds	.12
411 Frank LaCorte	.08
412 Thad Bosley	.08
413 Allen Ripley	.08
414 George Scott	.12
415 Bill Atkinson	.08
416 Tom Brookens	.08
417 Craig Chamberlain	.08
418 Roger Freed	.08
419 Vic Correll	.08
420 Butch Hobson	.08
421 Doug Bird	.08
422 Larry Milbourne	.08
423 Dave Frost	.08
424 New York Yankees/	.60
Dick Howser (Mgr.)	
425 Mark Belanger	.15
426 Grant Jackson	.08
427 Tom Hutton	.08
428 Pat Zachry	.08
429 Duane Kuiper	.08
430 Larry Hisle	.08
431 Mike Krukow	.12
432 Willie Norwood	.08
433 Rich Gale	.08
434 Johnnie LeMaster	.08
435 Don Gullett	.08
436 Billy Almon	.08
437 Joe Niekro	.15
438 Dave Revering	.08
439 Mike Phillips	.08
440 Don Sutton	1.00
441 Eric Soderholm	.08
442 Jorge Orta	.08
443 Mike Parrott	.08
444 Alvis Woods	.08
445 Mark Fidrych	.15

NO.	PLAYER	MINT
446	Duffy Dyer	.08
447	Nino Espinosa	.08
448	Jim Wohlford	.08
449	Doug Bair	.08
450	George Brett	5.00
451	Cleveland Indians/ Dave Garcia (Mgr.)	.35
452	Steve Dillard	.08
453	Mike Bacsik	.08
454	Tom Donohue	.08
455	Mike Torrez	.08
456	Frank Taveras	.08
457	Bert Blyleven	.50
458	Billy Sample	.08
459	Mickey Lolich	.08
460	Willie Randolph	.20
461	Dwayne Murphy	.15
462	Mike Sadek	.08
463	Jerry Royster	.08
464	John Denny	.15
465	Rick Monday	.15
466	Mike Squires	.08
467	Jesse Jefferson	.08
468	Aurelio Rodriquez	.08
469	Randy Niemann	.08
470	Bob Boone	.30
471	Hosken Powell	.08
472	Willie Hernandez	.30
473	Bump Wills	.08
474	Steve Busby	.08
475	Cesar Geronimo	.08
476	Bob Shirley	.08
477	Buck Martinez	.08
478	Gil Flores	.08
479	Montreal Expos/ Dick Williams (Mgr.)	.35
480	Bob Watson	.08
481	Tom Paciorek	.08
482	R. Henderson (R)	175.00
483	Bo Diaz	.08
484	Checklist No. 4	.25
485	Mickey Rivers	.15
486	Mike Tyson	.08
487	Wayne Nordhagen	.08
488	Roy Howell	.08
489	Preston Hanna	.08
490	Lee May	.15
491	Steve Mura	.08
492	Todd Cruz	.08
493	Jerry Martin	.08
494	Craig Minetto	.08
495	Bake McBride	.08
496	Silvio Martinez	.08
497	Jim Mason	.08
498	Danny Darwin	.08
499	San Francisco Giants/ Dave Bristol (Mgr.)	.35
500	Tom Seaver	2.50
501	Rennie Stennett	.08
502	Rich Wortham	.08
503	Mike Cubbage	.08
504	Gene Garber	.08
505	Bert Campaneris	.15
506	Tom Buskey	.08
507	Leon Roberts	.08
508	U.L. Washington	.08
509	Ed Glynn	.08
510	Ron Cey	.35
511	Eric Wilkins	.08
512	Jose Cardenal	.08
513	Tom Dixon	.08
514	Steve Ontiveros	.08
515	Mike Caldwell	.08
516	Hector Cruz	.08
517	Don Stanhouse	.08
518	Nelson Norman	.08
519	Steve Nicosia	.08
520	Steve Rogers	.15
521	Ken Brett	.08
522	Jim Morrison	.08
523	Ken Henderson	.08
524	Jim Wright	.08
525	Clint Hurdle	.08
526	Philadelphia Phillies/ Dallas Green (Mgr.)	.35
527	Doug Rau	.08

NO.	PLAYER	MINT
528	Adrian Devine	.08
529	Jim Barr	.08
530	Jim Sundberg	.08
531	Eric Rasmussen	.08
532	Willie Horton	.12
533	Checklist No. 5	.25
534	Andre Thornton	.15
535	Bob Forsch	.12
536	Lee Lacy	.12
537	Alex Trevino	.12
538	Joe Strain	.08
539	Rudy May	.08
540	Pete Rose	4.00
541	Miguel Dilone	.08
542	Joe Coleman	.08
543	Pat Kelly	.08
544	Rick Sutcliffe (R)	3.50
545	Jeff Burroughs	.08
546	Rick Langford	.08
547	John Wathan	.08
548	Dave Rajsich	.08
549	Larry Wolfe	.08
550	Ken Griffey	.25
551	Pittsburgh Pirates/ Chuck Tanner (Mgr.)	.35
552	Bill Nahorodny	.08
553	Dick Davis	.08
554	Art Howe	.08
555	Ed Figueroa	.08
556	Joe Rudi	.15
557	Mark Lee	.08
558	Alfredo Griffin	.15
559	Dale Murray	.08
560	Dave Lopes	.15
561	Eddie Whitson	.12
562	Joe Wallis	.08
563	Will McEnaney	.08
564	Rick Manning	.08
565	Dennis Leonard	.12
566	Bud Harrelson	.08
567	Skip Lockwood	.08
568	Gary Roenicke (R)	.30
569	Terry Kennedy	.30
570	Roy Smalley	.08
571	Joe Sambito	.08
572	Jerry Morales	.08
573	Kent Tekulve	.12
574	Scot Thompson	.08
575	Ken Kravec	.08
576	Jim Dwyer	.08
577	Toronto Blue Jays/ Bobby Mattick (Mgr.)	.30
578	Scott Sanderson	.08
579	Charlie Moore	.08
580	Nolan Ryan	9.00
581	Bob Bailor	.08
582	Brian Doyle	.08
583	Bob Stinson	.08
584	Kurt Bevacqua	.08
585	Al Hrabosky	.08
586	Mitchell Page	.08
587	Garry Templeton	.25
588	Greg Minton	.08
589	Chet Lemon	.15
590	Jim Palmer	2.00
591	Rick Cerone	.08
592	Jon Matlack	.08
593	Jesus Alou	.08
594	Dick Tidrow	.08
595	Don Money	.08
596	Rick Matula	.08
597	Tom Poquette	.08
598	Fred Kendall	.08
599	Mike Norris	.08
600	Reggie Jackson	3.00
601	Buddy Schultz	.08
602	Brian Downing	.08
603	Jack Billingham	.08
604	Glenn Adams	.08
605	Terry Forster	.12
606	Cincinnati Reds/ John McNamara (Mgr.)	.30
607	Woodie Fryman	.08
608	Alan Bannister	.08
609	Ron Reed	.08
610	Willie Stargell	1.50

NO.	PLAYER	MINT
611	Jerry Garvin	.08
612	Cliff Johnson	.08
613	Randy Stein	.08
614	John Hiller	.08
615	Doug DeCinces	.20
616	Gene Richards	.08
617	Joaquin Andujar	.30
618	Bob Montgomery	.08
619	Sergio Ferrer	.08
620	Richie Zisk	.15
621	Bob Grich	.12
622	Mario Soto	.20
623	Gorman Thomas	.25
624	Lerrin LaGrow	.08
625	Chris Chambliss	.12
626	Detroit Tigers/ S. Anderson (Mgr.)	.50
627	Pedro Borbon	.08
628	Doug Capilla	.08
629	Jim Todd	.08
630	Larry Bowa	.15
631	Mark Littell	.08
632	Barry Bonnell	.08
633	Bob Apodaca	.08
634	Glenn Borgmann	.08
635	John Candelaria	.12
636	Toby Harrah	.08
637	Joe Simpson	.08
638	Mark Clear (R)	.30
639	Larry Biittner	.08
640	Mike Flanagan	.12
641	Ed Kranepool	.15
642	Ken Forsch	.08
643	John Mayberry	.15
644	Charlie Hough	.12
645	Rick Burleson	.12
646	Checklist No. 6	.25
647	Milt May	.08
648	Roy White	.12
649	Tom Griffin	.08
650	Joe Morgan	1.50
651	Rollie Fingers	1.00
652	Mario Mendoza	.08
653	Stan Bahnsen	.08
654	Bruce Boisclair	.08
655	Tug McGraw	.15
656	Larvell Blanks	.08
657	Dave Edwards	.08
658	Chris Knapp	.08
659	Milwaukee Brewers/ George Bamberger (Mgr.)	.25
660	Rusty Staub	.25
661	Orioles Rookies: Wayne Krenchicki, Mark Corey, D. Ford	.15
662	Red Sox Rookies: J. Finch, Mike O'Berry, Chuck Rainey	.15
663	Angels Rookies: Ralph Botting, Bob Clark, Dickey Thon	.50
664	White Sox Rookies: Guy Hoffman, M. Colbern, Dewey Robinson	.15
665	Indians Rookies: Larry Anderson, Bobby Cuellar, Randy Wihtol	.15
666	Tigers Rookies: M. Chris, Bruce Robbins, Al Greene	.25
667	Royals Rookies: R. Martin, Bill Paschall, Dan Quisenberry	1.50
668	Brewers Rookies: Danny Boitano, W. Mueller, Lenn Sakata	.15
669	Twin Rookies: Rick Sofield, Dan Graham, Gary Ward	.50
670	Yankee Rookies: B. Brown, Brad Gulden, Darryl Jones	.25
671	A's Rookies: Derek Bryant, B. Kingman, Mike Morgan	.75

NO.	PLAYER	MINT
672	Mariners Rookies: Rodney Craig, Charlie Beamon, Rafael Vasquez	.15
673	Rangers Rookies: Brian Allard, Jerry Don Gleaton, Greg Mahlberg	.15
674	Blue Jays Rookies: Butch Edge, Pat Kelly, Ted Wilborn	.15
675	Braves Rookies: Bruce Benedict, Eddie Miller, Larry Bradford	.20
676	Cubs Rookies: Steve Macko, Dave Geisel, Karl Pagel	.20
677	Reds Rookies: Art DeFreites, Harry Spilman, Frank Pastore	.15
678	Astros Rookies: Reggie Baldwin, A. Knicely, Pete Ladd	.20
679	Dodgers Rookies: Joe Beckwith, Mickey Hatcher, Dave Patterson	.50
680	Expos Rookies: Randy Miller, Tony Bernazard, John Tamargo	.40
681	Mets Rookies: Dan Norman, J. Orosco, Mike Scott	8.00
682	Phillies Rookies: Kevin Saucier, Ramon Aviles, Dickie Noles	.25
683	Pirates Rookies: D. Boyland, Alberto Lois, Harry Saferight	.15
684	Cardinals Rookies: George Frazier, Tom Herr, Dan O'Brien	1.00
685	Padres Rookies: Brian Greer, Tim Flannery, Jim Wilhelm	.15
686	Giants Rookies: Greg Johnston, D. Littlejohn, Phil Nastu	.15
687	Mike Heath	.08
688	Steve Stone	.15
689	Boston Red Sox/ Don Zimmer (Mgr.)	.40
690	Tommy John	.50
691	Ivan DeJesus	.08
692	Rawly Eastwick	.08
693	Craig Kusick	.08
694	Jim Rooker	.08
695	Reggie Smith	.15
696	Julio Gonzalez	.08
697	David Clyde	.08
698	Oscar Gamble	.15
699	Floyd Bannister	.15
700	Rod Carew	1.00
701	Ken Oberkfell	.30
702	Ed Farmer	.08
703	Otto Velez	.08
704	Gene Tenace	.08
705	Freddie Patek	.08
706	Tippy Martinez	.08
707	Elliott Maddox	.08
708	Bob Tolan	.08
709	Pat Underwood	.08
710	Graig Nettles	.25
711	Bob Galasso	.08
712	Rodney Scott	.08
713	Terry Whitfield	.08
714	Fred Norman	.08
715	Sal Bando	.15
716	Lynn McGlothen	.08
717	Mickey Klutts	.08
718	Greg Gross	.08
719	Don Robinson	.08
720	Carl Yastrzemski	1.50
721	Paul Hartzell	.08
722	Jose Cruz	.25
723	Shane Rawley	.12
724	Jerry White	.08
725	Rick Wise	.08
726	Steve Yeager	.12

1981 Topps.... Complete Set of 726 Cards— Value $125.00

Features the rookie cards of Fernando Valenzuela, Kirk Gibson, Harold Baines and Tim Raines. 66 cards were double printed. In 1981 Topps began getting competition from two other card manufacturers—Donruss and Fleer.

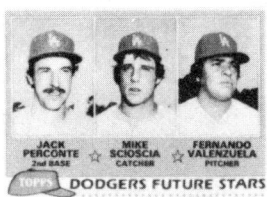

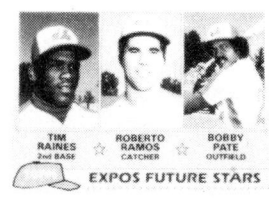

NO. PLAYER	MINT
1 Batting Leaders: Bill Buckner, George Brett	.75
2 Home Run Leaders: Reggie Jackson, Ben Oglivie, M. Schmidt	.30
3 RBI Leaders: Cecil Cooper, Mike Schmidt	.25
4 Stolen Base Leaders: Rickey Henderson, Ron LeFlore	.20
5 Victory Leaders: Steve Carlton, Steve Stone	.15
6 Strikeout Leaders: Len Barker, Steve Carlton	.15
7 ERA Leaders: Don Sutton, Rudy May	.10
8 Leading Firemen: Dan Quisenberry, Tom Hume, Rollie Fingers	.15
9 Pete LaCock	.07
10 Mike Flanagan	.12
11 Jim Wohlford	.07
12 Mark Clear	.07
13 Joe Charboneau	.12
14 John Tudor (R)	1.50
15 Larry Parrish	.10
16 Ron Davis	.10
17 Cliff Johnson	.07
18 Glenn Adams	.07
19 Jim Clancy	.07
20 Jeff Burroughs	.07
21 Ron Oester	.07
22 Danny Darwin	.07
23 Alex Trevino	.07
24 Don Stanhouse	.07
25 Sixto Lezcano	.07
26 U.L. Washington	.07
27 Champ Summers	.07
28 Enrique Romo	.07
29 Gene Tenace	.07
30 Jack Clark	.60
31 Checklist No. 1	.15
32 Ken Oberkfell	.07
33 Rick Honeycutt	.07
34 Aurelio Rodriquez	.07
35 Mitchell Page	.07
36 Ed Farmer	.07
37 Gary Roenicke	.07
38 Win Remmerswaal	.07
39 Tom Veryzer	.07
40 Tug McGraw	.12
41 Ranger Rookies: Bob Babcock, J. Butcher, Jerry Don Gleaton	.20
42 Jerry White	.07
43 Jose Morales	.07
44 Larry McWilliams	.07
45 Enos Cabell	.07
46 Rick Bosetti	.07
47 Ken Brett	.07
48 Dave Skaggs	.07
49 Bob Shirley	.07
50 Dave Lope	.12
51 Bill Robinson	.07
52 Hector Cruz	.07

NO. PLAYER	MINT
53 Kevin Saucier	.07
54 Ivan DeJesus	.07
55 Mike Norris	.07
56 Buck Martinez	.07
57 Dave Roberts	.07
58 Joel Youngblood	.07
59 Dan Petry	.25
60 Willie Randolph	.12
61 Butch Wynegar	.10
62 Joe Pettini	.07
63 Steve Renko	.07
64 Brian Asselstine	.07
65 Scott McGregor	.10
66 Royals Rookies: Tim Ireland, Manny Castillo, Mike Jones	.15
67 Ken Kravec	.07
68 Matt Alexander	.07
69 Ed Halicki	.07
70 Al Oliver	.12
71 Hal Dues	.07
72 Barry Evans	.07
73 Doug Bair	.07
74 Mike Hargrove	.07
75 Reggie Smith	.12
76 Mario Mendoza	.07
77 Mike Barlow	.07
78 Steve Dillard	.07
79 Bruce Robbins	.07
80 Rusty Staub	.15
81 Dave Stapleton	.15
82 Astros Rookies: Bobby Sprowl, Danny Heep, Alan Knicely	.10
83 Mike Proly	.07
84 Johnnie LeMaster	.07
85 Mike Caldwell	.07
86 Wayne Gross	.07
87 Rick Camp	.07
88 Joe LeFebvre	.15
89 Darrell Jackson	.07
90 Bake McBride	.07
91 Tim Stoddard	.07
92 Mike Easler	.12
93 Ed Glynn	.07
94 Harry Spilman	.07
95 Jim Sundberg	.07
96 A's Rookies: Dave Beard, Pat Dempsey, E. Camacho	.12
97 Chris Speier	.07
98 Clint Hurdle	.07
99 Eric Wilkins	.07
100 Rod Carew	1.50
101 Benny Ayala	.07
102 Dave Tobik	.07
103 Jerry Martin	.07
104 Terry Forster	.12
105 Jose Cruz	.20
106 Don Money	.07
107 Rich Wortham	.07
108 Bruce Benedict	.07
109 Mike Scott	1.25
110 Carl Yastrzemski	1.50
111 Greg Minton	.07

NO. PLAYER	MINT
112 White Sox Rookies: Rusty Kuntz, F. Mullin, Leo Sutherland	.15
113 Mike Phillips	.07
114 Tom Underwood	.07
115 Roy Smalley	.07
116 Joe Simpson	.07
117 Pete Falcone	.07
118 Kurt Bevacqua	.07
119 Tippy Martinez	.07
120 Larry Bowa	.12
121 Larry Harlow	.07
122 John Denny	.15
123 Al Cowens	.07
124 Jerry Garvin	.07
125 Andre Dawson	2.00
126 Charlie Leibrandt (R)	.50
127 Rudy Law	.07
128 Garry Allenson	.07
129 Art Howe	.07
130 Larry Gura	.07
131 Keith Moreland (R)	.30
132 Tommy Boggs	.07
133 Jeff Cox	.07
134 Steve Mura	.07
135 Gorman Thomas	.20
136 Doug Capilla	.07
137 Hosken Powell	.07
138 Rich Dotson (R)	.30
139 Oscar Gamble	.07
140 Bob Forsch	.07
141 Miguel Dilone	.07
142 Jackson Todd	.07
143 Dan Meyer	.07
144 Allen Ripley	.07
145 Mickey Rivers	.10
146 Bobby Castillo	.07
147 Dale Berra	.07
148 Randy Niemann	.07
149 Joe Nolan	.07
150 Mark Fidrych	.10
151 Claudell Washington	.10
152 John Urrea	.07
153 Tom Poquette	.07
154 Rick Langford	.07
155 Chris Chambliss	.10
156 Bob McClure	.07
157 John Wathan	.07
158 Fergie Jenkins	.30
159 Brian Doyle	.07
160 Garry Maddox	.07
161 Dan Graham	.07
162 Doug Corbett	.12
163 Billy Almon	.07
164 LaMarr Hoyt (R)	.20
165 Tony Scott	.07
166 Floyd Bannister	.07
167 Terry Whitfield	.07
168 Don Robinson	.07
169 John Mayberry	.07
170 Ross Grimsley	.07
171 Gene Richards	.07
172 Gary Woods	.07
173 Bump Wills	.07
174 Doug Rau	.07
175 Dave Collins	.07

NO. PLAYER	MINT
176 Mike Krukow	.07
177 Rick Peters	.12
178 Jim Essian	.07
179 Rudy May	.07
180 Pete Rose	3.00
181 Elias Sosa	.07
182 Bob Grich	.12
183 Dick Davis	.07
184 Jim Dwyer	.07
185 Dennis Leonard	.07
186 Wayne Nordhagen	.07
187 Mike Parrott	.07
188 Doug DeCinces	.15
189 Craig Swan	.07
190 Cesar Cedeno	.15
191 Rick Sutcliffe	.50
192 Braves Rookies: Terry Harper, Rafael Ramirez, Ed Miller	.35
193 Pete Vuckovich	.12
194 Rod Scurry	.10
195 Rich Murray	.07
196 Duffy Dyer	.07
197 Jim Kern	.07
198 Jerry Dybzinski	.07
199 Chuck Rainey	.07
200 George Foster	.30
201 Record—J. Bench Most HR's, Catcher, Career	.45
202 Record—S. Carlton Strikeouts, Lefty, Career	.35
203 Record—B. Gullickson Strikeouts, Game, Rookie	.12
204 Rec.—LeFlore, Scott SB's, Teammates, Season	.12
205 Record—P. Rose Most Consecutive Seasons, 600 or More At-Bats	.75
206 Record—M. Schmidt Homers, 3B, Season	.45
207 Record—O. Smith Assists, SS, Season	.15
208 Record—W. Wilson Most At-Bats, Season	.15
209 Dickie Thon	.07
210 Jim Palmer	1.25
211 Derrel Thomas	.07
212 Steve Nicosia	.07
213 Al Holland (R)	.20
214 Angels Rookies: John Harris, Ralph Botting, Jim Dorsey	.15
215 Larry Hisle	.07
216 John Henry Johnson	.07
217 Rich Hebner	.07
218 Paul Splittorff	.07
219 Ken Landreaux	.07
220 Tom Seaver	1.50
221 Bob Davis	.07
222 Jorge Orta	.07
223 Roy Lee Jackson	.10
224 Pat Zachry	.07
225 Ruppert Jones	.07
226 Manny Sanguillen	.07
227 Fred Martinez	.07
228 Tom Paciorek	.07

NO.	PLAYER	MINT
229	Rollie Fingers	.50
230	George Hendrick	.12
231	Joe Beckwith	.07
232	Mickey Klutts	.07
233	Skip Lockwood	.07
234	Lou Whitaker	.50
235	Scott Sanderson	.07
236	Mike Ivie	.07
237	Charlie Moore	.07
238	Willie Hernandez	.20
239	Rick Miller	.07
240	Nolan Ryan	5.00
241	Checklist No. 2	.15
242	Chet Lemon	.12
243	Sal Butera	.07
244	Cardinals Rookies:	.20
	Andy Rincon, T. Landrum,	
	Al Olmsted	
245	Ed Figueroa	.07
246	Ed Ott	.07
247	Glenn Hubbard	.07
248	Joey McLaughlin	.07
249	Larry Cox	.07
250	Ron Guidry	.50
251	Tom Brookens	.07
252	Victor Cruz	.07
253	Dave Bergman	.07
254	Ozzie Smith	2.50
255	Mark Littell	.07
256	Bombo Rivera	.07
257	Rennie Stennett	.07
258	Joe Price	.07
259	Mets Rookies:	2.50
	Juan Berenguer, H. Brooks,	
	Mookie Wilson	
260	Ron Cey	.30
261	Ricky Henderson	35.00
262	Sammy Stewart	.07
263	Brian Downing	.07
264	Jim Norris	.07
265	John Candelaria	.10
266	Tom Herr	.20
267	Stan Bahnsen	.07
268	Jerry Royster	.07
269	Ken Forsch	.07
270	Greg Luzinski	.15
271	Bill Castro	.07
272	Bruce Kimm	.07
273	Stan Papi	.07
274	Craig Chamberlain	.07
275	Dwight Evans	.50
276	Dan Spillner	.07
277	Alfredo Griffin	.10
278	Rick Sofield	.07
279	Bob Knepper	.12
280	Ken Griffey	.30
281	Fred Stanley	.07
282	Mariners Rookies:	.15
	Rick Anderson, Rodney	
	Craig, Greg Biercevicz	
283	Billy Sample	.07
284	Brian Kingman	.07
285	Jerry Turner	.07
286	Dave Frost	.07
287	Lenn Sakata	.07
288	Bob Clark	.07
289	Mickey Hatcher	.07
290	Bob Boone	.07
291	Aurelio Lopez	.07
292	Mike Squires	.07
293	Charlie Lea (R)	.20
294	Mike Tyson	.07
295	Hal McRae	.10
296	Bill Nahorodny	.07
297	Bob Bailor	.07
298	Buddy Solomon	.07
299	Elliott Maddox	.07
300	Paul Molitor	.50
301	Matt Keough	.07
302	Dodgers Rookies:	7.50
	Mike Scioscia, Jack	
	Perconte, F. Valenzuela	
303	Johnny Oates	.07
304	John Castino	.07
305	Ken Clay	.07

NO.	PLAYER	MINT
306	Juan Beniquez	.07
307	Gene Garber	.07
308	Rick Manning	.07
309	Luis Salazar	.15
310	Vida Blue	.07
311	Freddie Patek	.07
312	Rick Rhoden	.12
313	Luis Pujols	.07
314	Rich Dauer	.07
315	Kirk Gibson (R)	7.50
316	Craig Minetto	.07
317	Lonnie Smith	.15
318	Steve Yeager	.07
319	Rowland Office	.07
320	Tom Burgmeier	.07
321	Leon Durham (R)	.40
322	Neil Allen	.07
323	Jim Morrison	.07
324	Mike Willis	.07
325	Ray Knight	.15
326	Biff Pocoroba	.07
327	Moose Haas	.07
328	Twins Rookies:	.15
	Dave Engle, G. Johnston,	
	Gary Ward	
329	Joaquin Andujar	.15
330	Frank White	.12
331	Dennis Lamp	.07
332	Lee Lacy	.07
333	Sid Monge	.07
334	Dane Iorg	.07
335	Rick Cerone	.07
336	Eddie Whitson	.10
337	Lynn Jones	.05
338	Checklist No.3	.15
339	John Ellis	.07
340	Bruce Kison	.07
341	Dwayne Murphy	.12
342	Eric Rasmussen	.07
343	Frank Taveras	.07
344	Byron McLaughlin	.07
345	Warren Cromartie	.07
346	Larry Christenson	.07
347	Harold Baines (R)	4.00
348	Bob Sykes	.12
349	Glenn Hoffman	.15
350	J.R. Richard	.12
351	Otto Velez	.07
352	Dick Tidrow	.07
353	Terry Kennedy	.15
354	Mario Soto	.15
355	Bob Horner	.20
356	Padres Rookies:	.15
	George Stablein, C. Stimac,	
	Tom Tellmann	
357	Jim Slaton	.07
358	Mark Wagner	.07
359	Tom Hausman	.07
360	Willie Wilson	.25
361	Joe Strain	.07
362	Bo Diaz	.07
363	Geoff Zahn	.07
364	Mike Davis (R)	.30
365	Graig Nettles	.07
366	Mike Ramsey	.07
367	Denny Martinez	.07
368	Leon Roberts	.07
369	Frank Tanana	.15
370	Dave Winfield	1.25
371	Charlie Hough	.07
372	Jay Johnstone	.07
373	Pat Underwood	.07
374	Tom Hutton	.07
375	Dave Concepcion	.15
376	Ron Reed	.07
377	Jerry Morales	.07
378	Dave Rader	.07
379	Lary Sorensen	.07
380	Willie Stargell	1.00
381	Cubs Rookies:	.20
	Carlos Lezcano, Steve	
	Macko, Randy Martz	
382	Paul Mirabella	.07
383	Eric Soderholm	.07
384	Mike Sadek	.07

NO.	PLAYER	MINT
385	Joe Sambito	.07
386	Dave Edwards	.07
387	Phil Niekro	.65
388	Andre Thornton	.15
389	Marty Pattin	.07
390	Cesar Geronimo	.07
391	Dave Lemanczyk	.07
392	Lance Parrish	.60
393	Broderick Perkins	.07
394	Woodie Fryman	.07
395	Scot Thompson	.07
396	Bill Campbell	.07
397	Julio Cruz	.07
398	Ross Baumgarten	.07
399	Orioles Rookies:	2.00
	Mike Boddicker, Mark	
	Corey, Floyd Rayford	
400	Reggie Jackson	2.00
401	A.L. Championships:	.50
	Royals Sweep Yanks	
402	N.L. Championships:	.25
	Phillies Beat Astros	
403	1980 World Series:	.25
	Phillies Beat Royals	
404	1980 World Series:	.25
	Phillies Win	
405	Nino Espinosa	.07
406	Dickie Noles	.07
407	Ernie Whitt	.07
408	Fernando Arroyo	.07
409	Larry Herndon	.07
410	Bert Campaneris	.07
411	Terry Puhl	.07
412	Britt Burns (R)	.15
413	Tony Bernazard	.07
414	John Pacella	.07
415	Ben Oglivie	.12
416	Gary Alexander	.07
417	Dan Schatzeder	.07
418	Bobby Brown	.07
419	Tom Hume	.07
420	Keith Hernandez	.75
421	Bob Stanley	.07
422	Dan Ford	.07
423	Shane Rawley	.12
424	Yankees Rookies:	.20
	Tim Lollar, Bruce	
	Robinson, Dennis Werth	
425	Al Bumbry	.07
426	Warren Brusstar	.07
427	Jonn D'Acquisto	.07
428	John Stearns	.07
429	Mick Kelleher	.07
430	Jim Bibby	.07
431	Dave Roberts	.07
432	Len Barker	.12
433	Rance Mulliniks	.07
434	Roger Erickson	.07
435	Jim Spencer	.07
436	Gary Lucas	.12
437	Mike Heath	.07
438	John Montefusco	.07
439	Denny Walling	.07
440	Jerry Reuss	.12
441	Ken Reitz	.07
442	Ron Pruitt	.07
443	Jim Beattie	.07
444	Garth Iorg	.07
445	Ellis Valentine	.07
446	Checklist No. 4	.15
447	Junior Kennedy	.07
448	Tim Corcoran	.07
149	Paul Mitchell	.07
450	Dave Kingman	.15
451	Indians Rookies:	.20
	Chris Bando, Tom Brennan,	
	Sandy Wihtol	
452	Renie Martin	.07
453	Rob Wilfong	.07
454	Andy Hassler	.07
455	Rick Burleson	.12
456	Jeff Reardon (R)	1.50
457	Mike Lum	.07
458	Randy Jones	.07
459	Greg Gross	.07

NO.	PLAYER	MINT
460	Rich Gossage	.35
461	Dave McKay	.07
462	Jack Brohamer	.07
463	Milt May	.07
464	Adrian Devine	.07
465	Bill Russell	.07
466	Bob Molinaro	.07
467	Dave Stieb	2.00
468	Johnny Wockenfuss	.07
469	Jeff Leonard	.30
470	Manny Trillo	.07
471	Mike Vail	.07
472	Dyar Miller	.07
473	Jose Cardenal	.07
474	Mike LaCoss	.07
475	Buddy Bell	.20
476	Jerry Koosman	.15
477	Luis Gomez	.07
478	Juan Eichelberger	.07
479	Expos Rookies:	9.00
	B. Pate, Tim Raines,	
	Roberto Ramos	
480	Carlton Fisk	1.00
481	Bob Lacey	.07
482	Jim Gantner	.07
483	Mike Griffin	.07
484	Max Venable	.07
485	Garry Templeton	.20
486	Marc Hill	.07
487	Dewey Robinson	.07
488	Damaso Garcia (R)	.20
489	John Littlefield	.07
490	Eddie Murray	1.50
491	Gordy Pladson	.07
492	Barry Foote	.07
493	Dan Quisenberry	.25
494	Bob Walk	.25
495	Dusty Baker	.12
496	Paul Dade	.07
497	Fred Norman	.07
498	Pat Putnam	.07
499	Frank Pastore	.07
500	Jim Rice	.75
501	Tim Foli	.07
502	Giants Rookies:	.15
	Chris Bourjos, Mike	
	Rowland, A. Hargesheimer	
503	Steve McCatty	.07
504	Dale Murphy	2.50
505	Jason Thompson	.12
506	Phil Huffman	.07
507	Jamie Quirk	.07
508	Rob Dressler	.07
509	Pete Mackanin	.07
510	Lee Mazzilli	.07
511	Wayne Nordhagen	.07
512	Gary Thomasson	.07
513	Frank LaCorte	.07
514	George Riley	.07
515	Robin Yount	2.00
516	Doug Bird	.07
517	Richie Zisk	.07
518	Grant Jackson	.07
519	John Tamargo	.07
520	Steve Stone	.07
521	Sam Mejias	.07
522	Mike Colbern	.07
523	John Fulgham	.07
524	Willie Aikens	.10
525	Mike Torrez	.07
526	Phillies Rookies:	.20
	Marty Bystrom, Jay	
	Loviglio, J. Wright	
527	Danny Goodwin	.07
528	Gary Matthews	.12
529	Dave LaRoche	.07
530	Steve Garvey	1.00
531	John Curtis	.07
532	Bill Stein	.07
533	Jesus Figueroa	.07
534	Dave Smith	.40
535	Omar Moreno	.12
536	Bob Owchinko	.07
537	Ron Hodges	.07
538	Tom Griffin	.07

NO.	PLAYER	MINT
539	Rodney Scott	.07
540	Mike Schmidt	2.00
541	Steve Swisher	.07
542	Larry Bradford	.07
543	Terry Crowley	.07
544	Rich Gale	.07
545	Johnny Grubb	.07
546	Paul Moskau	.07
547	Mario Guerrero	.07
548	Dave Goltz	.07
549	Jerry Remy	.07
550	Tommy John	.30
551	Pirates Rookies:	2.00
	Vance Law, Pascual Perez	
	Tony Pena	
552	Steve Trout	.07
553	Tim Blackwell	.07
554	Bert Blyleven	.40
555	Cecil Cooper	.30
556	Jerry Mumphrey	.07
557	Chris Knapp	.07
558	Barry Bonnell	.07
559	Willie Montanez	.07
560	Joe Morgan	.75
561	Dennis Littlejohn	.07
562	Checklist No. 5	.15
563	Jim Kaat	.25
564	Ron Hassey	.07
565	Burt Hooton	.07
566	Del Unser	.07
567	Mark Bomback	.07
568	Dave Revering	.07
569	Al Williams	.07
570	Ken Singleton	.12
571	Todd Cruz	.07
572	Jack Morris	.50
573	Phil Garner	.07
574	Bill Caudill	.15
575	Tony Perez	.25
576	Reggie Cleveland	.07
577	Blue Jays Rookies:	.20
	Luis Leal, Brian Miller,	
	Ken Schrom	
578	Bill Gullickson (R)	.30
579	Tim Flannery	.07
580	Don Baylor	.30
581	Roy Howell	.07
582	Gaylord Perry	.50
583	Larry Milbourne	.07
584	Randy Lerch	.07

NO.	PLAYER	MINT
585	Amos Otis	.12
586	Silvio Martinez	.07
587	Jeff Newman	.07
588	Gary Lavelle	.07
589	Lamar Johnson	.07
590	Bruce Sutter	.30
591	John Lowenstein	.07
592	Steve Comer	.07
593	Steve Kemp	.15
594	Preston Hanna	.07
595	Butch Hobson	.07
596	Jerry Augustine	.07
597	Rafael Landestoy	.07
598	George Vukovich	.07
599	Dennis Kinney	.07
600	Johnny Bench	2.00
601	Don Aase	.07
602	Bobby Murcer	.15
603	John Verhoeven	.07
604	Rob Picciolo	.07
605	Don Sutton	.50
606	Reds Rookies:	.15
	Bruce Berenyi, Geoff	
	Combe, P. Householder	
607	Dave Palmer	.07
608	Greg Pryor	.07
609	Lynn McGlothen	.07
610	Darrell Porter	.07
611	Rick Matula	.07
612	Duane Kuiper	.07
613	Jim Anderson	.07
614	Dave Rozema	.07
615	Rick Dempsey	.07
616	Rick Wise	.07
617	Craig Reynolds	.07
618	John Milner	.07
619	Steve Henderson	.07
620	Dennis Eckersley	.75
621	Tom Donohue	.07
622	Randy Moffitt	.07
623	Sal Bando	.07
624	Bob Welch	.60
625	Bill Buckner	.15
626	Tigers Rookies:	.20
	D. Steffen, Jerry Ujdur,	
	Roger Weaver	
627	Luis Tiant	.12
628	Vic Correll	.07
629	Tony Armas	.20
630	Steve Carlton	1.50

NO.	PLAYER	MINT
631	Ron Jackson	.07
632	Alan Bannister	.07
633	Bill Lee	.07
634	Doug Flynn	.07
635	Bobby Bonds	.12
636	Al Hrabosky	.07
637	Jerry Narron	.07
638	Checklist No. 6	.15
639	Carney Lansford	.40
640	Dave Parker	.75
641	Mark Belanger	.07
642	Vern Ruhle	.07
643	Lloyd Moseby (R)	1.25
644	Ramon Aviles	.07
645	Rick Reuschel	.15
646	Marvis Foley	.07
647	Dick Drago	.07
648	Darrell Evans	.20
649	Manny Sarmiento	.07
650	Bucky Dent	.12
651	Pedro Guerrero	2.00
652	John Montague	.07
653	Bill Fahey	.07
654	Ray Burris	.07
655	Dan Driessen	.07
656	Jon Matlack	.07
657	Mike Cubbage	.07
658	Milt Wilcox	.07
659	Brewers Rookies:	.07
	Ned Yost, J. Flinn,	
	Ed Romero	
660	Gary Carter	1.25
661	Orioles Team	.20
662	Red Sox Team	.20
663	Angels Team	.20
664	White Sox Team	.20
665	Indians Team	.20
666	Tigers Team	.25
667	Royals Team	.20
668	Brewers Team	.20
669	Twins Team	.20
670	Yankees Team	.25
671	A's Team	.20
672	Mariners Team	.15
673	Rangers Team	.20
674	Blue Jays Team	.20
675	Braves Team	.20
676	Cubs Team	.20
677	Reds Team	.20
678	Astros Team	.20

NO.	PLAYER	MINT
679	Dodgers Team	.25
680	Expos Team	.15
681	Mets Team	.20
682	Phillies Team	.20
683	Pirates Team	.20
684	Cardinals Team	.20
685	Padres Team	.20
686	Giants Team	.20
687	Jeff Jones	.10
688	Kiko Garcia	.07
689	Red Sox Rookies:	2.00
	Bruce Hurst, Reid Nichols,	
	Keith MacWhorter	
690	Bob Watson	.07
691	Dick Ruthven	.07
692	Lenny Randle	.07
693	Steve Howe (R)	.20
694	Bud Harrelson	.07
695	Kent Tekulve	.07
696	Alan Ashby	.07
697	Rick Waits	.07
698	Mike Jorgensen	.07
699	Glenn Abbott	.07
700	George Brett	3.00
701	Joe Rudi	.07
702	George Medich	.07
703	Alvis Woods	.07
704	Bill Travers	.07
705	Ted Simmons	.25
706	Dave Ford	.07
707	Dave Cash	.07
708	Doyle Alexander	.07
709	Alan Trammell	.25
710	Ron LeFlore	.07
711	Joe Ferguson	.07
712	Bill Bonham	.07
713	Bill North	.07
714	Pete Redfern	.07
715	Bill Madlock	.20
716	Glenn Borgmann	.07
717	Jim Barr	.07
718	Larry Biittner	.07
719	Sparky Lyle	.12
720	Fred Lynn	.30
721	Toby Harrah	.07
722	Joe Niekro	.12
723	Bruce Bochte	.07
724	Lou Piniella	.15
725	Steve Rogers	.12
726	Rick Monday	.15

1981 Topps Traded.... Complete Set of 132 Cards—Value $30.00

This was the first Topps "traded" set issued since 1976. It updates the main 1981 card set with players who had changed teams during the season and rookies who joined their teams early in the season. The first card in the traded set is numbered 727. It begins where the main set ends. The complete set was packaged in a printed box and only distributed through card hobby dealers.

NO.	PLAYER	MINT
727	Danny Ainge (RR)	.75
728	Doyle Alexander	.15
729	Gary Alexander	.08
730	Billy Almon	.08
731	Joaquin Andujar	.15
732	Bob Bailor	.08
733	Juan Beniquez	.12

NO.	PLAYER	MINT
734	Dave Bergman	.08
735	Tony Bernazard	.08
736	Larry Biittner	.08
737	Doug Bird	.08
738	Bert Blyleven	1.00
739	Mark Bomback	.08
740	Bobby Bonds	.12

NO.	PLAYER	MINT
741	Rick Bosetti	.08
742	Hubie Brooks	1.50
743	Rick Burleson	.10
744	Ray Burris	.08
745	Jeff Burroughs	.10
746	Enos Cabell	.08
747	Ken Clay	.08

NO.	PLAYER	MINT
748	Mark Clear	.08
749	Larry Cox	.08
750	Hector Cruz	.08
751	Victor Cruz	.08
752	Mike Cubbage	.08
753	Dick Davis	.08
754	Brian Doyle	.08

NO.	PLAYER	MINT
755	Dick Drago	.08
756	Leon Durham	.40
757	Jim Dwyer	.08
758	Dave Edwards	.08
759	Jim Essian	.08
760	Bill Fahey	.08
761	Rollie Ringers	.75
762	Carlton Fisk	3.00
763	Barry Foote	.08
764	Ken Forsch	.12
765	Kiko Garcia	.08
766	Cesar Geronimo	.08
767	Gary Gray	.08
768	Mickey Hatcher	.08
769	Steve Henderson	.12
770	Marc Hill	.08
771	Butch Hobson	.08
772	Rick Honeycutt	.12
773	Roy Howell	.08
774	Mike Ivie	.08
775	Roy Lee Jackson	.08
776	Cliff Johnson	.08
777	Randy Jones	.10
778	Ruppert Jones	.08
779	Mick Kelleher	.08
780	Terry Kennedy	.20

NO.	PLAYER	MINT
781	Dave Kingman	.30
782	Bob Knepper	.12
783	Ken Kravec	.08
784	Bob Lacey	.08
785	Dennis Lamp	.08
786	Rafael Landestoy	.08
787	Ken Landreaux	.12
788	Carney Lansford	1.00
789	Dave LaRoche	.08
790	Joe LeFebvre	.08
791	Ron LeFlore	.12
792	Randy Lerch	.08
793	Sixto Lezcano	.12
794	John Littlefield	.08
795	Mike Lum	.08
796	Greg Luzinski	.25
797	Fred Lynn	.60
798	Jerry Martin	.08
799	Buck Martinez	.08
800	Gary Matthews	.12
801	Mario Mendoza	.08
802	Larry Milbourne	.08
803	Rick Miller	.08
804	John Montefusco	.12
805	Jerry Morales	.08
806	Jose Morales	.08

NO.	PLAYER	MINT
807	Joe Morgan	1.50
808	Jerry Mumphrey	.12
809	Gene Nelson	.35
810	Ed Ott	.08
811	Bob Owchinko	.08
812	Gaylord Perry	1.00
813	Mike Phillips	.08
814	Darrell Porter	.12
815	Mike Proly	.08
816	Tim Raines	8.00
817	Lenny Randle	.08
818	Doug Rau	.08
819	Jeff Reardon	.50
820	Ken Reitz	.08
821	Steve Renko	.08
822	Rick Reuschel	.20
823	Dave Revering	.08
824	Dave Roberts	.08
825	Leon Roberts	.08
826	Joe Rudi	.12
827	Kevin Saucier	.08
828	Tony Scott	.08
829	Bob Shirley	.08
830	Ted Simmons	.40
831	Lary Sorensen	.08
832	Jim Spencer	.08

NO.	PLAYER	MINT
833	Harry Spilman	.08
834	Fred Stanley	.08
835	Rusty Staub	.25
836	Bill Stein	.08
837	Joe Strain	.08
838	Bruce Sutter	.50
839	Don Sutton	1.00
840	Steve Swisher	.08
841	Frank Tanana	.08
842	Gene Tenace	.08
843	Jason Thompson	.15
844	Dickie Thon	.25
845	Bill Travers	.08
846	Tom Underwood	.08
847	John Urrea	.08
848	Mike Vail	.08
849	Ellis Valentine	.12
850	Fernando Valenzuela	5.00
851	Pete Vuckovich	.12
852	Mark Wagner	.08
853	Bob Walk	.08
854	Claudell Washington	.12
855	Dave Winfield	3.00
856	Geoff Zahn	.08
857	Richie Zisk	.12
858	Traded Checklist	.20

1982 Topps.... Complete Set of 792 Cards—Value $110.00

The complete set was increased to 792 cards. Double printed cards were eliminated (66 double prints were in each set from 1978 to 1981). Includes the rookie cards of Cal Ripken, Jesse Barfield, Kent Hrbek and Steve Sax. Card 342 exists with the *autograph* deleted.

NO.	PLAYER	MINT
1	Highlights—Carlton	.50
	Sets NL Strikeout Record	
2	Highlights—Davis	.10
	Fans 8 Straight	
3	Highlights—Raines	.25
	Swipes 71 Bases, Rookie	
4	Highlights—Rose	.60
	Sets NL Career Hit Mark	
5	Highlights—Ryan	1.00
	5th Career No-Hitter	
6	Highlights—Valenzuela	.25
	8 Rookie Shutouts	
7	Scott Sanderson	.07
8	Rich Dauer	.07
9	Ron Guidry	.30
10	Guidry (Action)	.15
11	Gary Alexander	.07
12	Moose Haas	.07
13	Lamar Johnson	.07
14	Steve Howe	.07
15	Ellis Valentine	.07
16	Steve Comer	.07
17	Darrell Evans	.15
18	Fernando Arroyo	.07
19	Ernie Whitt	.07
20	Garry Maddox	.07
21	Orioles Rookies:	25.00
	Bob Bonner, Cal Ripken, Jeff Schneider	
22	Jim Beattie	.07
23	Willie Hernandez	.20
24	Dave Frost	.07
25	Jerry Remy	.07
26	George Orta	.07

NO.	PLAYER	MINT
27	Tom Herr	.15
28	John Urrea	.07
29	Dwayne Murphy	.07
30	Tom Seaver	1.50
31	Seaver (Action)	.25
32	Gene Garber	.07
33	Jerry Morales	.07
34	Joe Sambito	.07
35	Willie Aikens	.10
36	Rangers Leaders:	.15
	Al Oliver, George Medich	
37	Dan Graham	.07
38	Charlie Lea	.07
39	Lou Whitaker	.35
40	Dave Parker	.40
41	Parker (Action)	.20
42	Rick Sofield	.07
43	Mike Cubbage	.07
44	Britt Burns	.10
45	Rick Cerone	.07
46	Jerry Augustine	.07
47	Jeff Leonard	.15
48	Bobby Castillo	.07
49	Alvis Woods	.07
50	Buddy Bell	.15
51	Cubs Rookies:	.40
	Jay Howell, C. Lezcano, Ty Waler	
52	Larry Andersen	.07
53	Greg Gross	.07
54	Ron Hassey	.07
55	Rick Burleson	.07
56	Mark Littell	.07
57	Craig Reynolds	.07

NO.	PLAYER	MINT
58	John D'Acquisto	.07
59	Rich Gedman (R)	.50
60	Tony Armas	.20
61	Tommy Boggs	.07
62	Mike Tyson	.07
63	Mario Soto	.15
64	Lynn Jones	.07
65	Terry Kennedy	.15
66	Astros Leaders:	.15
	Art Howe, Nolan Ryan	
67	Rich Gale	.07
68	Roy Howell	.07
69	Al Williams	.07
70	Tim Raines	2.00
71	Roy Lee Jackson	.07
72	Rick Auerbach	.07
73	Buddy Solomon	.07
74	Bob Clark	.07
75	Tommy John	.25
76	Greg Pryor	.07
77	Miguel Dilone	.07
78	George Medich	.07
79	Bob Bailor	.07
80	Jim Palmer	1.00
81	Palmer (Action)	.15
82	Bob Welch	.50
83	Yankees Rookies:	.50
	S. Balboni, A. Robertson, A. McGaffigan	
84	Rennie Stennett	.07
85	Lynn McGlothen	.07
86	Dane Iorg	.07
87	Matt Keough	.07
88	Biff Pocoroba	.07

NO.	PLAYER	MINT
89	Steve Henderson	.07
90	Nolan Ryan	3.50
91	Carney Lansford	.25
92	Brad Havens	.10
93	Larry Hisle	.07
94	Andy Hassler	.75
95	Ozzie Smith	1.00
96	Royals Leaders:	.20
	G. Brett, L. Gura	
97	Paul Moskau	.07
98	Terry Bulling	.07
99	Barry Bonnell	.07
100	Mike Schmidt	2.00
101	Schmidt (Action)	.60
102	Dan Briggs	.07
103	Bob Lacey	.07
104	Rance Mulliniks	.07
105	Kirk Gibson	1.25
106	Enrique Romo	.07
107	Wayne Krenchicki	.07
108	Bob Sykes	.07
109	Dave Revering	.07
110	Carlton Fisk	1.00
111	Fisk (Action)	.15
112	Billy Sample	.07
113	Steve McCatty	.07
114	Ken Landreaux	.07
115	Gaylord Perry	.40
116	Jim Wohlford	.07
117	Rawly Eastwick	.07
118	Expos Rookies:	.75
	Brad Mills, Terry Francona, Bryn Smith	
119	Joe Pittman	.07

NO.	PLAYER	MINT
120	Gary Lucas	.07
121	Ed Lynch	.12
122	Jamie Easterly	.07
123	Danny Goodwin	.07
124	Reid Nichols	.07
125	Danny Ainge	.25
126	Braves Leaders:	.15
	C. Washington, Rick Mahler	
127	Lonnie Smith	.12
128	Frank Pastore	.07
129	Checklist No. 1	.15
130	Julio Cruz	.07
131	Stan Bahnsen	.07
132	Lee May	.07
133	Pat Underwood	.07
134	Dan Ford	.07
135	Adny Rincon	.07
136	Lenn Sakata	.07
137	George Cappuzzello	.07
138	Tony Pena	.30
139	Jeff Jones	.07
140	Ron Leflore	.07
141	Indians Rookies:	1.50
	Chris Bando, Von Hayes,	
	Tom Brennan	
142	Dave LaRoche	.07
143	Mookie Wilson	.15
144	Fred Breining	.12
145	Bob Horner	.20
146	Mike Griffin	.07
147	Denny Walling	.07
148	Mickey Klutts	.07
149	Pat Putnam	.07
150	Ted Simmons	.15
151	Dave Edwards	.07
152	Ramon Aviles	.07
153	Roger Erickson	.07
154	Dennis Werth	.07
155	Otto Velez	.07
156	A's Leaders:	.15
	Rickey Henderson,	
	Steve McCatty	
157	Steve Crawford	.10
158	Brian Downing	.07
159	Larry Biittner	.07
160	Luis Tiant	.10
161	Batting Leaders:	.15
	B. Madlock, C. Lansford	
162	Home Run Leaders:	.25
	Bobby Grich, Mike	
	Schmidt, T. Armas, Dwight	
	Evans, Eddie Murray	
163	RBI Leaders:	.50
	M. Schmidt, E. Murray	
164	Stolen Base Leaders:	.50
	R. Henderson, T. Raines	
165	Victory Leaders:	.25
	Tom Seaver, D. Martinez,	
	Steve McCatty, Pete	
	Vuckovich, Jack Morris	
166	Strikeout Leaders:	.20
	F. Valenzuela, L. Barker	
167	ERA Leaders:	.50
	Steve McCatty, Nolan Ryan	
168	Leading Relievers:	.25
	Bruce Sutter, Rollie Fingers	
169	Charlie Leibrandt	.10
170	Jim Bibby	.07
171	Giants Rookies:	1.00
	Bob Tufts, Bob Brenly,	
	Chili Davis	
172	Bill Gullickson	.07
173	Jamie Quirk	.07
174	Dave Ford	.07
175	Jerry Mumphrey	.07
176	Dewey Robinson	.07
177	John Ellis	.07
178	Dyar Miller	.07
179	Steve Garvey	.75
180	Garvey (Action)	.35
181	Silvio Martinez	.07
182	Larry Herndon	.07
183	Mike Proly	.07
184	Mick Kelleher	.07
185	Phil Niekro	.50

NO.	PLAYER	MINT
186	Cardinals Leaders:	.15
	K. Hernandez, B. Forsch	
187	Jeff Newman	.07
188	Randy Martz	.07
189	Glenn Hoffman	.07
190	J.R. Richard	.10
191	Tim Wallach (R)	2.00
192	Broderick Perkins	.07
193	Darrell Jackson	.07
194	Mike Vail	.07
195	Paul Molitor	.35
196	Willie Upshaw	.25
197	Shane Rawley	.07
198	Chris Speier	.07
199	Don Aase	.07
200	George Brett	2.00
201	Brett (Action)	.60
202	Rick Manning	.07
203	Blue Jays Rookies:	4.00
	Jesse Barfield, Brian	
	Milner, Boomer Wells	
204	Gray Roenicke	.07
205	Neil Allen	.07
206	Tony Bernazard	.07
207	Rod Scurry	.07
208	Bobby Murcer	.15
209	Gary Lavelle	.07
210	Keith Hernandez	.50
211	Dan Petry	.25
212	Mario Mendoza	.07
213	Dave Steward (R)	10.00
214	Brian Asselstine	.07
215	Mike Krukow	.07
216	White Sox Leaders:	.15
	Chet Lemon, Dennis Lamp	
217	Bo McLaughlin	.07
218	Dave Roberts	.07
219	John Curtis	.07
220	Manny Trillo	.07
221	Jim Slaton	.07
222	Butch Wynegar	.07
223	Lloyd Moseby	.25
224	Bruce Bochte	.07
225	Mike Torrez	.07
226	Checklist No. 2	.15
227	Ray Burris	.07
228	Sam Mejias	.07
229	Geoff Zahn	.07
230	Willie Wilson	.20
231	Phillies Rookies:	1.00
	Ozzie Virgil, Bob Dernier,	
	Mark Davis	
232	Terry Crowley	.07
233	Duane Kuiper	.07
234	Ron Hodges	.07
235	Mike Easler	.10
236	John Martin	.07
237	Rusty Kuntz	.07
238	Kevin Saucier	.07
239	Jon Matlack	.07
240	Bucky Dent	.10
241	Dent (Action)	.07
242	Milt May	.07
243	Bob Owchinko	.07
244	Rufino Linares	.07
245	Ken Reitz	.07
246	Mets Leaders	.20
	Hubie Brooks, Mike Scott	
247	Pedro Guerrero	.75
248	Frank LaCorte	.07
249	Tim Flannery	.07
250	Tug McGraw	.10
251	Fred Lynn	.30
252	Lynn (Action)	.20
253	Chuck Baker	.07
254	Jorge Bell (R)	9.00
255	Tony Perez	.20
256	Perez (Action)	.12
257	Larry Harlow	.07
258	Bo Diaz	.10
259	Rodney Scott	.07
260	Bruce Sutter	.25
261	Tigers Rookies:	.20
	Howard Bailey, M. Castillo,	
	Dave Rucker	

NO.	PLAYER	MINT
262	Doug Bair	.07
263	Victor Cruz	.07
264	Dan Quisenberry	.20
265	Al Bumbry	.07
266	Rick Leach	.12
267	Kurt Bevacqua	.07
268	Rickey Keeton	.07
269	Jim Essian	.07
270	Rusty Staub	.20
271	Larry Bradford	.07
272	Bump Wills	.07
273	Doug Bird	.07
274	Bob Ojeda (R)	.75
275	Bob Watson	.07
276	Angels Leaders:	.20
	Ken Forsch, Rod Carew	
277	Terry Puhl	.07
278	John Littlefield	.07
279	Bill Russell	.07
280	Ben Oglivie	.10
281	John Verhoeven	.07
282	Ken Macha	.07
283	Brian Allard	.07
284	Bob Grich	.10
285	Sparky Lyle	.10
286	Bill Fahey	.07
287	Alan Bannister	.07
288	Garry Templeton	.15
289	Bob Stanley	.07
290	Ken Singleton	.15
291	Pirates Rookies:	1.00
	Vance Law, Bob Long,	
	Johnny Ray	
292	David Palmer	.07
293	Rob Picciolo	.07
294	Mike LaCoss	.07
295	Jason Thompson	.10
296	Bob Walk	.07
297	Clint Hurdle	.07
298	Danny Darwin	.07
299	Steve Trout	.07
300	Reggie Jackson	1.50
301	Jackson (Action)	.75
302	Doug Flynn	.07
303	Bill Caudill	.10
304	Johnnie LeMaster	.07
305	Don Sutton	.40
306	Sutton (Action)	.10
307	Randy Bass	.07
308	Charlie Moore	.07
309	Pete Redfern	.07
310	Mike Hargrove	.10
311	Dodgers Leaders:	.20
	Dusty Baker, Burt Hooton	
312	Lenny Randle	.07
313	John Harris	.07
314	Buck Martinez	.07
315	Burt Hooton	.07
316	Steve Braun	.07
317	Dick Ruthven	.07
318	Mike Heath	.07
319	Dave Rozema	.07
320	Chris Chambliss	.10
321	Chambliss (Action)	.07
322	Garry Hancock	.07
323	Bill Lee	.07
324	Steve Dillard	.07
325	Jose Cruz	.15
326	Pete Falcone	.07
327	Joe Nolan	.07
328	Ed Farmer	.07
329	U.L. Washington	.07
330	Rick Wise	.07
331	Benny Ayala	.07
332	Don Robinson	.07
333	Brewers Rookies:	.20
	Frank DiPino, M. Edwards,	
	Chuck Porter	
334	Aurelio Rodriguez	.07
335	Jim Sundberg	.07
336	Mariners Leaders:	.15
	G. Abbott, T. Paciorek	
337	Pete Rose (AS)	.75
338	Dave Lopes (AS)	.10
339	Mike Schmidt (AS)	.60

NO.	PLAYER	MINT
340	Dave Concepcion (AS)	.15
341	Andre Dawson (AS)	.20
342	George Foster (AS)	.25
342	George Foster	2.00
	(autograph deleted)	
343	Dave Parker (AS)	.25
344	Gary Carter (AS)	.25
345	F. Valenzuela (AS)	.25
346	Tom Seaver (AS)	.25
347	Bruce Sutter (AS)	.15
348	Derrel Thomas	.07
349	George Frazier	.07
350	Thad Bosley	.07
351	Reds Rookies:	.15
	Geoff Coumbe, Scott	
	Brown, P. Householder	
352	Dick Davis	.07
353	Jack O'Connor	.07
354	Roberto Ramos	.07
355	Dwight Evans	.25
356	Denny Lewallyn	.07
357	Butch Hobson	.07
358	Mike Parrott	.07
359	Jim Dwyer	.07
360	Len Barker	.07
361	Rafael Landestoy	.07
362	Jim Wright	.07
	(wrong autograph)	
363	Bob Molinaro	.07
364	Doyle Alexander	.07
365	Bill Madlock	.20
366	Padres Leaders:	.15
	L. Salazar, J. Eichelberger	
367	Jim Kaat	.15
368	Alex Trevino	.07
369	Champ Summers	.07
370	Mike Norris	.07
371	Jerry Don Gleaton	.07
372	Luis Gomez	.07
373	Gene Nelson	.10
374	Tim Blackwell	.07
375	Dusty Baker	.12
376	Chris Welsh	.10
377	Kiko Garcia	.07
378	Mike Caldwell	.07
379	Rob Wilfong	.07
380	Dave Stieb	.75
381	Red Sox Rookies:	.75
	D. Schmidt, Julio Valdez,	
	Bruce Hurst	
382	Joe Simpson	.07
383	Pascual Perez	.20
383	P. Perez (error)	30.00
	No position on front	
384	Keith Moreland	.07
385	Ken Forsch	.07
386	Jerry White	.07
387	Tom Veryzer	.07
388	Joe Rudi	.07
389	George Vukovich	.07
390	Eddie Murray	1.25
391	Dave Tobik	.07
392	Rick Bosetti	.07
393	Al Hrabosky	.07
394	Checklist No. 3	.12
395	Omar Moreno	.10
396	Twins Leaders:	.15
	John Castino, F. Arroyo	
397	Ken Brett	.07
398	Mike Squires	.07
399	Pat Zachry	.07
400	Johnny Bench	1.50
401	Bench (Action)	.50
402	Bill Stein	.07
403	Jim Tracy	.07
404	Dickie Thon	.10
405	Rick Reuschel	.07
406	Al Holland	.07
407	Danny Boone	.07
408	Ed Romero	.07
409	Don Cooper	.07
410	Ron Cey	.15
411	Cey (Action)	.10
412	Luis Leal	.07
413	Dan Meyer	.07
414	Elias Sosa	.07
415	Don Baylor	.15

NO.	PLAYER	MINT
416	Marty Bystrom	.07
417	Pat Kelly	.07
418	Rangers Rookies:	.25
	John Butcher, B. Johnson, Dave Schmidt	
419	Steve Stone	.10
420	George Hendrick	.10
421	Mark Clear	.07
422	Cliff Johnson	.07
423	Stan Papi	.07
424	Bruce Benedict	.07
425	John Candelaria	.10
426	Orioles Leaders:	.15
	Eddie Murray, S. Stewart	
427	Ron Oester	.07
428	LaMarr Hoyt	.15
429	John Wathan	.07
430	Vida Blue	.10
431	Blue (Action)	.07
432	Mike Scott	.75
433	Alan Ashby	.07
434	Joe LeFebvre	.07
435	Robin Yount	1.75
436	Joe Strain	.07
437	Juan Berenguer	.07
438	Pete Mackanin	.07
439	Dave Righetti (R)	2.00
440	Jeff Burroughs	.07
441	Astros Rookies:	.15
	Danny Heep, Billy Smith, Bobby Sprowl	
442	Bruce Kison	.07
443	Mark Wagner	.07
444	Terry Forster	.10
445	Larry Parrish	.10
446	Wayne Garland	.07
447	Darrell Porter	.12
448	Porter (Action)	.07
449	Luis Aguayo	.07
450	Jack Morris	.50
451	Ed Miller	.07
452	Lee Smith (R)	1.00
453	Art Howe	.07
454	Rick Langford	.07
455	Tom Burgmeier	.07
456	Cubs Leaders:	.15
	R. Martz, Bill Buckner	
457	Tim Stoddard	.07
458	Willie Montanez	.07
459	Bruce Berenyi	.07
460	Jack Clark	.50
461	Rich Dotson	.10
462	Dave Chalk	.07
463	Jim Kern	.07
464	Juan Bonilla	.10
465	Lee Mazzilli	.07
466	Randy Lerch	.07
467	Mickey Hatcher	.07
468	Floyd Bannister	.10
469	Ed Ott	.07
470	John Mayberry	.07
471	Royals Rookies:	.25
	Mike Jones, Atlee Hammaker, Darryl Motley	
472	Oscar Gamble	.07
473	Mike Stanton	.07
474	Ken Oberkfell	.07
475	Alan Trammell	.50
476	Brian Kingman	.07
477	Steve Yeager	.10
478	Ray Searage	.10
479	Rowland Office	.07
480	Steve Carlton	1.00
481	Carlton (Action)	.30
482	Glenn Hubbard	.07
483	Gary Woods	.07
484	Ivan DeJesus	.07
485	Kent Tekulve	.10
486	Yankees Leaders:	.20
	J. Mumphrey, Tommy John	
487	Bob McClure	.07
488	Ron Jackson	.07
489	Rick Dempsey	.07
490	Dennis Eckersley	.50
491	Checklist No. 4	.15
492	Joe Price	.07
493	Chet Lemon	.10
494	Hubie Brooks	.30
495	Dennis Leonard	.07
496	Johnny Grubb	.07
497	Jim Anderson	.07
498	Dave Bergman	.07
499	Paul Mirabella	.07
500	Rod Carew	1.00
501	Carew (Action)	.30
502	Braves Rookies:	1.50
	Steve Bedrosian, B. Butler, Larry Owen	
503	Julio Gonzalez	.07
504	Rick Peters	.07
505	Graig Nettles	.20
506	Nettles (Action)	.15
507	Terry Harper	.07
508	Jody Davis (R)	.50
509	Harry Spilman	.07
510	Fernando Valenzuela	1.00
511	Ruppert Jones	.07
512	Jerry Dybzinski	.07
513	Rick Rhoden	.07
514	Joe Ferguson	.07
515	Larry Bowa	.10
516	Bowa (Action)	.07
517	Mark Brouhard	.10
518	Garth Iorg	.07
519	Glenn Adams	.07
520	Mike Flanagan	.10
521	Billy Almon	.07
522	Chuck Rainey	.07
523	Gary Gray	.07
524	Tom Hausman	.07
525	Ray Knight	.07
526	Expos Leaders:	.15
	W. Cromartie, Bill Gullickson	
527	John Henry Johnson	.07
528	Matt Alexander	.07
529	Allen Ripley	.07
530	Dickie Noles	.07
531	A's Rookies:	.12
	Rich Bordi, M. Budaska, Kelvin Moore	
532	Toby Harrah	.07
533	Joaquin Andujar	.15
534	Dave McKay	.07
535	Lance Parrish	.35
536	Rafael Ramirez	.07
537	Doug Capilla	.07
538	Lou Piniella	.15
539	Vern Ruhle	.07
540	Andre Dawson	.75
541	Barry Evans	.07
542	Ned Yost	.07
543	Bill Robinson	.07
544	Larry Christenson	.07
545	Reggie Smith	.10
546	Smith (Action)	.07
547	Rod Carew (AS)	.25
548	Willie Randolph (AS)	.12
549	George Brett (AS)	.40
550	Bucky Dent (AS)	.12
551	Reggie Jackson (AS)	.50
552	Ken Singleton (AS)	.12
553	Dave Winfield (AS)	.35
554	Carlton Fisk (AS)	.20
555	Scott McGregor (AS)	.12
556	Jack Morris (AS)	.15
557	Rich Gossage (AS)	.20
558	John Tudor	.40
559	Indians Leaders:	.15
	M. Hargrove, B. Blyleven	
560	Doug Corbett	.07
561	Cardinals Rookies:	.20
	Glenn Brummer, Luis DeLeon, Gene Roof	
562	Mike O'Berry	.07
563	Ross Baumgarten	.07
564	Doug DeCinces	.15
565	Jackson Todd	.07
566	Mike Jorgensen	.07
567	Bob Babcock	.07
568	Joe Pettini	.07
569	Willie Randolph	.10
570	Randolph (Action)	.07
571	Glenn Abbott	.07
572	Juan Beniquez	.07
573	Rick Waits	.07
574	Mike Ramsey	.07
575	Al Cowens	.07
576	Giants Leaders:	.12
	Milt May, Vida Blue	
577	Rick Monday	.07
578	Shooty Babitt	.07
579	Rick Mahler (R)	.35
580	Bobby Bonds	.10
581	Ron Reed	.07
582	Luis Pujols	.07
583	Tippy Martinez	.07
584	Hosken Powell	.07
585	Rollie Fingers	.35
586	Fingers (Action)	.15
587	Tim Lollar	.07
588	Dale Berra	.07
589	Dave Stapleton	.07
590	Al Oliver	.25
591	Oliver (Action)	.15
592	Craig Swan	.07
593	Billy Smith	.07
594	Renie Martin	.07
595	Dave Collins	.07
596	Damaso Garcia	.12
597	Wayne Nordhagen	.07
598	Bob Galasso	.07
599	White Sox Rookies:	.12
	Jay Loviglio, R. Patterson, Leo Sutherland	
600	Dave Winfield	.75
601	Sid Monge	.07
602	Freddie Patek	.07
603	Rich Hebner	.07
604	Orlando Sanchez	.10
605	Steve Rogers	.10
606	Blue Jays Leaders:	.10
	John Mayberry, Dave Stieb	
607	Leon Durham	.30
608	Jerry Royster	.07
609	Rick Sutcliffe	.25
610	Rickey Henderson	7.50
611	Joe Niekro	.12
612	Gary Ward	.07
613	Jim Gantner	.07
614	Juan Eichelberger	.07
615	Bob Boone	.07
616	Boone (Action)	.07
617	Scott McGregor	.10
618	Tim Foli	.07
619	Bill Campbell	.07
620	Ken Griffey	.30
621	Griffey (Action)	.07
622	Dennis Lamp	.07
623	Mets Rookies:	.75
	Ron Gardenhire, T. Leach, Tim Leary	
624	Fergie Jenkins	.15
625	Hal McRae	.10
626	Randy Jones	.07
627	Enos Cabell	.07
628	Bill Travers	.07
629	Johnny Wockenfuss	.07
630	Joe Charboneau	.07
631	Gene Tenace	.07
632	Bryan Clark	.10
633	Mitchell Page	.07
634	Checklist No. 5	.15
635	Ron Davis	.07
636	Phillies Leaders:	.35
	Pete Rose, Steve Carlton	
637	Rick Camp	.07
638	John Milner	.07
639	Ken Kravec	.07
640	Cesar Cedeno	.10
641	Steve Mura	.07
642	Mike Scioscia	.07
643	Pete Vuckovich	.12
644	John Castino	.07
645	Frank White	.10
646	White (Action)	.07
647	Warren Brusstar	.07
648	Jose Morales	.07
649	Ken Clay	.07
650	Carl Yastrzemski	1.25
651	Yastrzemski (Action)	.50
652	Steve Nicosia	.07
653	Angels Rookies:	3.00
	Luis Sanchez, Tom Brunansky, Daryl Sconiers	
654	Jim Morrison	.07
655	Joel Youngblood	.07
656	Eddie Whitson	.10
657	Tom Poquette	.07
658	Tito Landrum	.07
659	Fred Martinez	.07
660	Dave Concepcion	.12
661	Concepcion (Action)	.07
662	Luis Salazar	.07
663	Hector Cruz	.07
664	Dan Spillner	.07
665	Jim Clancy	.07
666	Tigers Leaders:	.20
	Steve Kemp, Dan Petry	
667	Jeff Reardon	.30
668	Dale Murphy	2.00
669	Larry Milbourne	.07
670	Steve Kemp	.10
671	Mike Davis	.15
672	Bob Knepper	.07
673	Keith Drumright	.07
674	Dave Goltz	.07
675	Cecil Cooper	.25
676	Sal Butera	.07
677	Alfredo Griffin	.10
678	Tom Paciorek	.07
679	Sammy Stewart	.07
680	Gary Matthews	.10
681	Dodgers Rookies:	4.50
	Steve Sax, Mike Marshall, Ron Roenicke	
682	Jesse Jefferson	.07
683	Phil Garner	.07
684	Harold Baines	.75
685	Bert Blyleven	.25
686	Gary Allenson	.07
687	Greg Minton	.07
688	Leon Roberts	.07
689	Lary Sorensen	.07
690	Dave Kingman	.20
691	Dan Schatzeder	.07
692	Wayne Gross	.07
693	Cesar Geronimo	.07
694	Dave Wehrmeister	.07
695	Warren Cromartie	.07
696	Pirates Leaders:	.15
	Bill Madlock, B. Solomon	
697	John Montefusco	.07
698	Tony Scott	.07
699	Dick Tidrow	.07
700	George Foster	.25
701	Foster (Action)	.15
702	Steve Renko	.07
703	Brewers Leaders:	.15
	Cecil Cooper, P. Vuckovich	
704	Mickey Rivers	.07
705	Rivers (Action)	.07
706	Barry Foote	.07
707	Mark Bomback	.07
708	Gene Richards	.07
709	Don Money	.07
710	Jerry Reuss	.10
711	Mariners Rookies:	1.50
	Dave Edler, Reggie Walton, Dave Henderson	
712	Denny Martinez	.07
713	Del Unser	.07
714	Jerry Koosman	.10
715	Willie Stargell	.50
716	Stargell (Action)	.20
717	Rick Miller	.07
718	Charlie Hough	.07
719	Jerry Narron	.07
720	Greg Luzinski	.15
721	Luzinski (Action)	.10

NO.	PLAYER	MINT
722	Jerry Martin	.07
723	Junior Kennedy	.07
724	Dave Rosello	.07
725	Amos Otis	.10
726	Otis (Action)	.07
727	Sixto Lezcano	.07
728	Aurelio Lopez	.07
729	Jim Spencer	.07
730	Gary Carter	.75
731	Padres Rookies:	.15
	Doug Gwosdz, Mike	
	Armstrong, Fred Kuhaulua	
732	Mike Lum	.07
733	Larry McWilliams	.10
734	Mike Ivie	.07
735	Rudy May	.07
736	Jerry Turner	.07
737	Reggie Cleveland	.07
738	Dave Engle	.07
739	Joey McLaughlin	.07

NO.	PLAYER	MINT
740	Dave Lopes	.10
741	Lopes (Action)	.07
742	Dick Drago	.07
743	John Stearns	.07
744	Mike Witt (R)	.75
745	Bake McBride	.07
746	Andre Thornton	.12
747	John Lowenstein	.07
748	Marc Hill	.07
749	Bob Shirley	.07
750	Jim Rice	.60
751	Rick Honeycutt	.07
752	Lee Lacy	.07
753	Tom Brookens	.07
754	Joe Morgan	.50
755	Morgan (Action)	.20
756	Reds Leaders:	.20
	Ken Griffey, Tom Seaver	
757	Tom Underwood	.07

NO.	PLAYER	MINT
758	Claudell Washington	.12
759	Paul Splittorff	.07
760	Bill Buckner	.15
761	Dave Smith	.07
762	Mike Phillips	.07
763	Tom Hume	.07
764	Steve Swisher	.07
765	Gorman Thomas	.12
766	Twins Rookies:	5.00
	Lenny Faedo, Kent Hrbek,	
	Tim Laudner	
767	Roy Smalley	.07
768	Jerry Garvin	.07
769	Richie Zisk	.07
770	Rich Gossage	.25
771	Gossage (Action)	.15
772	Bert Campaneris	.07
773	John Denny	.10
774	Jay Johnstone	.07

NO.	PLAYER	MINT
775	Bob Forsch	.07
776	Mark Belanger	.07
777	Tom Griffin	.07
778	Kevin Hickey	.07
779	Grant Jackson	.07
780	Pete Rose	2.00
781	Rose (Action)	.85
782	Frank Taveras	.07
783	Greg Harris	.30
784	Milt Wilcox	.07
785	Dan Driessen	.07
786	Red Sox Leaders:	.20
	C. Lansford, M. Torrez	
787	Fred Stanley	.07
788	Woodie Fryman	.07
789	Checklist No. 6	.15
790	Larry Gura	.07
791	Bobby Brown	.07
792	Frank Tanana	.15

1982 Topps Traded.... Complete Set of 132 Cards—Value $50.00

Updates the main 1982 card set with players who changed teams during the season and rookies. Unlike the 1981 Traded set, the cards are numbered from 1T to 132T. The complete set was packaged in a printed box and only distributed through card hobby dealers.

NO.	PLAYER	MINT
1 T	Doyle Alexander	.15
2 T	Jesse Barfield	2.00
3 T	Ross Baumgarten	.10
4 T	Steve Bedrosian	.75
5 T	Mark Belanger	.10
6 T	Kurt Bevacqua	.10
7 T	Tim Blackwell	.10
8 T	Vida Blue	.15
9 T	Bob Boone	.10
10 T	Larry Bowa	.20
11 T	Dan Briggs	.10
12 T	Bobby Brown	.10
13 T	Tom Brunansky	1.50
14 T	Jeff Burroughs	.12
15 T	Enos Cabell	.10
16 T	Bill Campbell	.10
17 T	Bobby Castillo	.10
18 T	Bill Caudill	.15
19 T	Cesar Cedeno	.15
20 T	Dave Collins	.12
21 T	Doug Corbett	.10
22 T	Al Cowens	.15
23 T	Chili Davis	1.25
24 T	Dick Davis	.10
25 T	Ron Davis	.10
26 T	Doug DeCince	.25
27 T	Ivan DeJesus	.12
28 T	Bob Dernier	.20
29 T	Bo Diaz	.10
30 T	Roger Erickson	.10
31 T	Jim Essian	.10
32 T	Ed Farmer	.10
33 T	Doug Flynn	.10

NO.	PLAYER	MINT
34 T	Tim Foli	.10
35 T	Dan Ford	.10
36 T	George Foster	.35
37 T	Dave Frost	.10
38 T	Rich Gale	.10
39 T	Ron Gardenhire	.10
40 T	Ken Griffey	.50
41 T	Greg Harris	.10
42 T	Von Hayes	1.50
43 T	Larry Herndon	.10
44 T	Kent Hrbek	5.00
45 T	Mike Ivie	.10
46 T	Grant Jackson	.10
47 T	Reggie Jackson	4.00
48 T	Ron Jackson	.10
49 T	Fergie Jenkins	.40
50 T	Lamar Johnson	.10
51 T	Ray Johnson	.10
52 T	Jay Johnstone	.10
53 T	Mick Kelleher	.10
54 T	Steve Kemp	.12
55 T	Junior Kennedy	.10
56 T	Jim Kern	.10
57 T	Ray Knight	.20
58 T	Wayne Krenchicki	.10
59 T	Mike Krukow	.10
60 T	Duane Kuiper	.10
61 T	Mike LaCoss	.10
62 T	Chet Lemon	.15
63 T	Sixto Lezcano	.10
64 T	Dave Lopes	.15
65 T	Jerry Martin	.10
66 T	Renie Martin	.10

NO.	PLAYER	MINT
67 T	John Mayberry	.10
68 T	Lee Mazzilli	.10
69 T	Bake McBride	.15
70 T	Dan Meyer	.10
71 T	Larry Milbourne	.10
72 T	Eddie Milner	.25
73 T	Sid Monge	.10
74 T	John Montefusco	.10
75 T	Jose Morales	.10
76 T	Keith Moreland	.15
77 T	Jim Morrison	.10
78 T	Rance Mulliniks	.10
79 T	Steve Mura	.10
80 T	Gene Nelson	.10
81 T	Joe Nolan	.10
82 T	Dickie Noles	.10
83 T	Al Oliver	.20
84 T	Jorge Orta	.10
85 T	Tom Paciorek	.10
86 T	Larry Parrish	.20
87 T	Jack Perconte	.10
88 T	Gaylord Perry	1.00
89 T	Rob Picciolo	.10
90 T	Joe Pittman	.10
91 T	Hosken Powell	.10
92 T	Mike Proly	.10
93 T	Greg Pryor	.10
94 T	Charlie Puleo	.10
95 T	Shane Rawley	.12
96 T	Johnny Ray	.75
97 T	Dave Revering	.10
98 T	Cal Ripken	20.00
99 T	Allen Ripley	.10

NO.	PLAYER	MINT
100 T	Bill Robinson	.10
101 T	Aurelio Rodriquez	.10
102 T	Joe Rudi	.10
103 T	Steve Sax	5.00
104 T	Dan Schatzeder	.10
105 T	Bob Shirley	.10
106 T	Eric Show (RR)	.75
107 T	Roy Smalley	.10
108 T	Lonnie Smith	.15
109 T	Ozzie Smith	7.00
110 T	Reggie Smith	.20
111 T	Lary Sorensen	.10
112 T	Elias Sosa	.10
113 T	Mike Stanton	.10
114 T	Steve Stroughter	.10
115 T	Champ Summers	.10
116 T	Rick Sutcliffe	.50
117 T	Frank Tanana	.10
118 T	Frank Taveras	.10
119 T	Garry Templeton	.20
120 T	Alex Trevino	.10
121 T	Jerry Turner	.10
122 T	Ed VandeBerg (RR)	.25
123 T	Tom Veryzer	.10
124 T	Ron Washington	.10
125 T	Bob Watson	.10
126 T	Dennis Werth	.10
127 T	Eddie Whitson	.10
128 T	Rob Wilfong	.10
129 T	Bump Wills	.10
130 T	Gary Woods	.10
131 T	Butch Wynegar	.10
132 T	Traded Checklist	.25

1983 Topps. . . . Complete Set of 792 Cards—Value $140.00

Features the rookie cards of Willie McGee, Ryne Sandberg, Wade Boggs, Tony Gwynn, Frank Viola and Gary Gaetti.

NO. PLAYER	MINT
1 Record—T. Armas	.20
11 Rightfield Putouts	
2 Record—R. Henderson	.75
Stolen Base Record	
3 Record—G. Minton	.08
No HR's in 269⅓ Innings	
4 Record—L. Parrish	.15
Threw Out 3 in AS Game	
5 Record—Trillo	.08
479 Errorless Chances	
6 Record—J. Wathan	.08
31st Stolen Base, Catcher	
7 Gene Richards	.06
8 Steve Balboni	.10
9 Joey McLaughlin	.06
10 Gorman Thomas	.15
11 Billy Gardner (Mgr.)	.06
12 Paul Mirabella	.06
13 Larry Herndon	.08
14 Frank LaCorte	.06
15 Ron Cey	.15
16 George Vukovich	.06
17 Kent Tekulve	.06
18 Tekulve (Veteran)	.06
19 Oscar Gamble	.08
20 Carlton Fisk	.50
21 Orioles Leaders:	.20
Eddie Murray, Jim Palmer	
22 Randy Martz	.06
23 Mike Heath	.06
24 Steve Mura	.06
25 Hal McRae	.06
26 Jerry Roystar	.06
27 Doug Corbett	.06
28 Bruce Bochte	.06
29 Randy Jones	.06
30 Jim Rice	.40
31 Bill Gullickson	.08
32 Dave Bergman	.06
33 Jack O'Connor	.06
34 Paul Householder	.06
35 Rollie Fingers	.30
36 Fingers (Veteran)	.15
37 Darrell Johnson (Mgr.)	.06
38 Tim Flannery	.06
39 Terry Puhl	.06
40 Fernando Valenzuela	.50
41 Jerry Turner	.06
42 Dale Murray	.06
43 Bob Dernier	.08
44 Don Robinson	.06
45 John Mayberry	.06
46 Richard Dotson	.08
47 Dave McKay	.06
48 Lary Sorensen	.06
49 Willie McGee (R)	4.00
50 Bob Horner	.15
51 Cubs Leaders:	.20
Leon Durham, F. Jenkins	
52 Onix Concepcion	.15
53 Mike Witt	.20
54 Jim Maler	.10
55 Mookie Wilson	.08
56 Chuck Rainey	.06
57 Tim Blackwell	.06
58 Al Holland	.06

NO. PLAYER	MINT
59 Benny Ayala	.06
60 Johnny Bench	1.00
61 Bench (Veteran)	.30
62 Bob McClure	.06
63 Rick Monday	.06
64 Bill Stein	.06
65 Jack Morris	.35
66 Bob Lillis (Mgr.)	.06
67 Sal Butera	.06
68 Eric Show (R)	.30
69 Lee Lacy	.08
70 Steve Carlton	.75
71 Carlton (Veteran)	.25
72 Tom Paciorek	.06
73 Allen Ripley	.06
74 Julio Gonzalez	.06
75 Amos Otis	.06
76 Rick Mahler	.06
77 Hosken Powell	.06
78 Bill Caudill	.08
79 Mick Kelleher	.06
80 George Foster	.25
81 Yankees Leaders:	.20
J. Mumphrey, D. Righetti	
82 Bruce Hurst	.06
83 Ryne Sandberg (R)	40.00
84 Milt May	.06
85 Ken Singleton	.08
86 Tom Hume	.06
87 Joe Rudi	.06
88 Jim Gantner	.06
89 Leon Roberts	.06
90 Jerry Reuss	.08
91 Larry Milbourne	.06
92 Mike LaCoss	.06
93 John Castino	.06
94 Dave Edwards	.06
95 Alan Trammell	.40
96 Dick Howser (Mgr.)	.06
97 Ross Baumgarten	.06
98 Vance Law	.06
99 Dickie Noles	.06
100 Pete Rose	2.00
101 Rose (Veteran)	.60
102 Dave Beard	.06
103 Darrell Porter	.08
104 Bob Walk	.06
105 Don Baylor	.20
106 Gene Nelson	.06
107 Mike Jorgensen	.06
108 Glenn Hoffman	.06
109 Luis Leal	.06
110 Ken Griffey	.25
111 Expos Leaders:	.15
Al Oliver, Steve Rogers	
112 Bob Shirley	.06
113 Ron Roenicke	.06
114 Jim Slaton	.06
115 Chili Davis	.15
116 Dave Schmidt	.06
117 Alan Knicely	.06
118 Chris Welsh	.06
119 Tom Brookens	.06
120 Len Barker	.06
121 Mickey Hatcher	.06
122 Jimmy Smith	.10

NO. PLAYER	MINT
123 George Frazier	.06
124 Marc Hill	.06
125 Leon Durham	.25
126 Joe Torre (Mgr.)	.08
127 Preston Hanna	.06
128 Mike Ramsey	.06
129 Checklist No. 1	.12
130 Dave Stieb	.50
131 Ed Ott	.06
132 Todd Cruz	.06
133 Jim Barr	.06
134 Hubie Brooks	.20
135 Dwight Evans	.25
136 Willie Aikens	.06
137 Woodie Fryman	.06
138 Rick Dempsey	.08
139 Bruce Berenyi	.06
140 Willie Randolph	.10
141 Indians Leaders:	.12
Toby Harrah, Rick Sutcliffe	
142 Mike Caldwell	.06
143 Joe Pettini	.06
144 Mark Wagner	.06
145 Don Sutton	.40
146 Don Sutton (Veteran)	.15
147 Rick Leach	.06
148 Dave Roberts	.06
149 Johnny Ray	.15
150 Bruce Sutter	.20
151 B. Sutter (Veteran)	.15
152 Jay Johnstone	.06
153 Jerry Koosman	.06
154 Johnnie LeMaster	.06
155 Dan Quisenberry	.20
156 Billy Martin (Mgr.)	.15
157 Steve Bedrosian	.20
158 Rob Wilfong	.06
159 Mike Stanton	.06
160 Dave Kingman	.15
161 D. Kingman (Veteran)	.10
162 Mark Clear	.06
163 Cal Ripken	4.00
164 David Palmer	.06
165 Dan Driessen	.06
166 John Pacella	.06
167 Mark Brouhard	.06
168 Juan Eichelberger	.06
169 Doug Flynn	.06
170 Steve Howe	.06
171 Giants Leaders:	.12
Bill Laskey, Joe Morgan	
172 Vern Ruhle	.06
173 Jim Morrison	.06
174 Jerry Ujdur	.06
175 Bo Diaz	.06
176 Dave Righetti	.35
177 Harold Baines	.30
178 Luis Tiant	.08
179 Luis Tiant (Veteran)	.06
180 Rickey Henderson	5.00
181 Terry Felton	.12
182 Mike Fischlin	.06
183 Ed VandeBerg (R)	.25
184 Bob Clark	.06
185 Tim Lollar	.06
186 Whitey Herzog (Mgr.)	.06

NO. PLAYER	MINT
187 Terry Leach	.06
188 Rick Miller	.06
189 Dan Schatzeder	.06
190 Cecil Cooper	.20
191 Joe Price	.06
192 Floyd Rayford	.06
193 Harry Spilman	.06
194 Cesar Geronimo	.06
195 Bob Stoddard	.10
196 Bill Fahey	.06
197 Jim Eisenreich	.60
198 Kiko Garcia	.06
199 Marty Bystrom	.06
200 Rod Carew	.75
201 Rod Carew (Veteran)	.25
202 Blue Jays Leaders:	.12
Damaso Garcia, Dave Stieb	
203 Mike Morgan	.06
204 Junior Kennedy	.06
205 Dave Parker	.35
206 Ken Oberkfell	.06
207 Rick Camp	.06
208 Dan Meyer	.06
209 Mike Moore (R)	1.50
210 Jack Clark	.40
211 John Denny	.15
212 John Stearns	.06
213 Tom Burgmeier	.06
214 Jerry White	.06
215 Mario Soto	.10
216 Tony LaRussa (Mgr.)	.08
217 Tim Stoddard	.06
218 Roy Howell	.06
219 Mike Armstrong	.06
220 Dusty Baker	.12
221 Joe Niekro	.08
222 Damaso Garcia	.15
223 John Montefusco	.06
224 Mickey Rivers	.06
225 Enos Cabell	.06
226 Enrique Romo	.06
227 Chris Bando	.06
228 Joaquin Andujar	.12
229 Phillies Leaders:	.12
Bo Diaz, Steve Carlton	
230 Fergie Jenkins	.20
231 F. Jenkins (Veteran)	.08
232 Tom Brunansky	.50
233 Wayne Gross	.06
234 Larry Andersen	.06
235 Claudell Washington	.15
236 Steve Renko	.06
237 Dan Norman	.06
238 Bud Black (R)	.75
239 Dave Stapleton	.06
240 Rich Gossage	.25
241 Gossage (Veteran)	.15
242 Joe Nolan	.06
243 Duane Walker	.12
244 Dwight Bernard	.06
245 Steve Sax	.75
246 G. Bamberger (Mgr.)	.06
247 Dave Smith	.06
248 Bake McBride	.06
249 Checklist No. 2	.12
250 Bill Buckner	.15

NO.	PLAYER	MINT
251	Alan Wiggins (R)	.15
252	Luis Aguayo	.06
253	Larry McWilliams	.06
254	Rick Cerone	.06
255	Gene Garber	.06
256	G. Garber (Veteran)	.06
257	Jesse Barfield	.60
258	Manny Castillo	.06
259	Jeff Jones	.06
260	Steve Kemp	.08
261	Tigers Leaders:	.12
	L. Herndon, Dan Petry	
262	Ron Jackson	.06
263	Renie Martin	.06
264	Jamie Quirk	.06
265	Joel Youngblood	.06
266	Paul Boris	.08
267	Terry Francona	.06
268	Storm Davis (R)	.75
269	Ron Oester	.06
270	Dennis Eckersley	.35
271	Ed Romero	.06
272	Frank Tanana	.06
273	Mark Belanger	.06
274	Terry Kennedy	.10
275	Ray Knight	.06
276	Gene Mauch (Mgr.)	.06
277	Rance Mulliniks	.06
278	Kevin Hickey	.06
279	Greg Gross	.06
280	Bert Blyleven	.25
281	Andre Robertson	.06
282	Reggie Smith	.10
283	R. Smith (Veteran)	.08
284	Jeff Lahti	.15
285	Lance Parrish	.35
286	Rick Langford	.06
287	Bobby Brown	.06
288	Joe Cowley (R)	.30
289	Jerry Dybzinski	.06
290	Jeff Reardon	.08
291	Pirates Leaders:	.12
	B. Madlock, J. Candelaria	
292	Craig Swan	.06
293	Glen Gulliver	.08
294	Dave Engle	.06
295	Jerry Remy	.06
296	Greg Harris	.06
297	Ned Yost	.06
298	Floyd Chiffer	.10
299	George Wright	.15
300	Mike Schmidt	2.00
301	M. Schmidt (Veteran)	.25
302	Ernie Whitt	.06
303	Miguel Dilone	.06
304	Dave Rucker	.06
305	Larry Bowa	.10
306	Tom Lasorda (Mgr.)	.10
307	Lou Piniella	.12
308	Jesus Vega	.08
309	Jeff Leonard	.15
310	Greg Luzinski	.15
311	Glenn Brummer	.06
312	Brian Kingman	.06
313	Gary Gray	.06
314	Ken Dayley	.06
315	Rick Burleson	.06
316	Paul Splittorff	.06
317	Gary Rajsich	.10
318	John Tudor	.30
319	Lenn Sakata	.06
320	Steve Rogers	.08
321	Brewers Leaders:	.15
	P. Vuckovich, R. Yount	
322	Dave Van Gorder	.10
323	Luis DeLeon	.06
324	Mike Marshall	.30
325	Von Hayes	.35
326	Garth Iorg	.06
327	Bobby Castillo	.06
328	Craig Reynolds	.06
329	Randy Niemann	.06
330	Buddy Bell	.15
331	Mike Krukow	.06
332	Glenn Wilson (R)	.35

NO.	PLAYER	MINT
333	Dave LaRoche	.06
334	D. LaRoche (Veteran)	.06
335	Steve Henderson	.06
336	R. Lachemann (Mgr.)	.06
337	Tito Landrum	.06
338	Bob Owchinko	.06
339	Terry Harper	.06
340	Larry Gura	.06
341	Doug DeCinces	.15
342	Atlee Hammaker	.08
343	Bob Bailor	.06
344	Roger LaFrancois	.08
345	Jim Clancy	.06
346	Joe Pittman	.06
347	Sammy Stewart	.06
348	Alan Bannister	.06
349	Checklist No. 3	.12
350	Robin Yount	1.00
351	Reds Leaders:	.12
	Cesar Cedeno, Mario Soto	
352	Mike Scioscia	.06
353	Steve Comer	.06
354	Randy Johnson	.06
355	Jim Bibby	.06
356	Gary Woods	.06
357	Len Matuszek	.15
358	Jerry Garvin	.06
359	Dave Collins	.08
360	Nolan Ryan	3.00
361	N. Ryan (Veteran)	.20
362	Bill Almon	.06
363	John Stuper	.15
364	Bret Butler	.20
365	Dave Lopes	.07
366	Dick Williams (Mgr.)	.06
367	Bud Anderson	.06
368	Richie Zisk	.06
369	Jesse Orosco	.10
370	Gary Carter	.50
371	Mike Richardt	.08
372	Terry Crowley	.06
373	Kevin Saucier	.06
374	Wayne Krenchicki	.06
375	Pete Vuckovich	.06
376	Ken Landreaux	.06
377	Lee May	.06
378	Lee May (Veteran)	.06
379	Guy Sularz	.10
380	Ron Davis	.06
381	Red Sox Leaders:	.15
	Bob Stanley, Jim Rice	
382	Bob Knepper	.06
383	Ozzie Virgil	.06
384	Dave Dravecky (R)	.75
385	Mike Easler	.06
386	Rod Carew	.25
387	Bob Grich (AS)	.08
388	George Brett (AS)	.40
389	Robin Yount (AS)	.35
390	Reggie Jackson (AS)	.40
391	Rickey Henderson (AS)	.60
392	Fred Lynn (AS)	.15
393	Carlton Fisk (AS)	.15
394	Pete Vuckovich (AS)	.08
395	Larry Gura (AS)	.08
396	Dan Quisenberry (AS)	.12
397	Pete Rose (AS)	.60
398	Manny Trillo (AS)	.08
399	Mike Schmidt (AS)	.50
400	Dave Concepcion (AS)	.10
401	Dale Murphy (AS)	.30
402	Andre Dawson (AS)	.20
403	Tim Raines (AS)	.18
404	Gary Carter (AS)	.25
405	Steve Rogers (AS)	.08
406	Steve Carlton (AS)	.25
407	Bruce Sutter (AS)	.20
408	Rudy May	.06
409	Marvis Foley	.06
410	Phil Niekro	.30
411	P. Niekro (Veteran)	.12
412	Rangers Leaders:	.10
	Buddy Bell, Charlie Hough	
413	Matt Keough	.06
414	Julio Cruz	.06

NO.	PLAYER	MINT
415	Bob Forsch	.06
416	Joe Ferguson	.06
417	Tom Hausman	.06
418	Greg Pryor	.06
419	Steve Crawford	.06
420	Al Oliver	.15
421	Al Oliver (Veteran)	.08
422	George Cappuzzello	.06
423	Tom Lawless	.12
424	Jerry Augustine	.06
425	Pedro Guerrero	.50
426	Earl Weaver (Mgr.)	.12
427	Roy Lee Jackson	.06
428	Champ Summers	.06
429	Eddie Whitson	.08
430	Kirk Gibson	.40
431	Gary Gaetti (R)	4.00
432	Porfirio Altamirano	.10
433	Dale Berra	.06
434	Dennis Lamp	.06
435	Tony Armas	.15
436	Bill Campbell	.06
437	Rick Sweet	.06
438	Dave LaPoint (R)	.50
439	Rafael Ramirez	.06
440	Ron Guidry	.25
441	Astros Leaders:	.12
	Joe Niekro, Ray Knight	
442	Brian Downing	.06
443	Don Hood	.06
444	Wally Backman	.20
445	Mike Flanagan	.08
446	Reid Nichols	.06
447	Bryn Smith	.06
448	Darrell Evans	.12
449	Eddie Milner	.12
450	Ted Simmons	.15
451	Ted Simmons (Veteran)	.10
452	Lloyd Moseby	.15
453	Lamar Johnson	.06
454	Bob Welch	.35
455	Sixto Lezcano	.06
456	Lee Elia (Mgr.)	.06
457	Milt Wilcox	.06
458	Ron Washington	.12
459	Ed Farmer	.06
460	Roy Smalley	.06
461	Steve Trout	.06
462	Steve Nicosia	.06
463	Gaylord Perry	.30
464	G. Perry (Veteran)	.12
465	Lonnie Smith	.12
466	Tom Underwood	.06
467	Rufino Linares	.06
468	Dave Goltz	.06
469	Ron Gardenhire	.06
470	Greg Minton	.06
471	Royals Leaders:	.12
	Willie Wilson, Vida Blue	
472	Gary Allenson	.06
473	John Lowenstein	.06
474	Ray Burris	.06
475	Cesar Cedeno	.12
476	Rob Picciolo	.06
477	Tom Niedenfuer	.12
478	Phil Garner	.06
479	Charlie Hough	.06
480	Toby Harrah	.06
481	Scot Thompson	.06
482	Tony Gwynn (R)	20.00
483	Lynn Jones	.06
484	Dick Ruthven	.06
485	Omar Moreno	.06
486	Clyde King (Mgr.)	.06
487	Jerry Hairston	.06
488	Alfredo Griffin	.06
489	Tom Herr	.15
490	Jim Palmer	.60
491	Jim Palmer (Veteran)	.15
492	Paul Serna	.06
493	Steve McCatty	.06
494	Bob Brenly	.08
495	Warren Cromartie	.06
496	Tom Veryzer	.06
497	Rick Sutcliffe	.20

NO.	PLAYER	MINT
498	Wade Boggs (R)	32.00
499	Jeff Little	.10
500	Reggie Jackson	1.00
501	R. Jackson (Veteran)	.25
502	Braves Leaders:	.15
	Dale Murphy, Phil Niekro	
503	Moose Haas	.06
504	Don Werner	.06
505	Garry Templeton	.15
506	Jim Gott	.35
507	Tony Scott	.06
508	Tom Filer (R)	.15
509	Lou Whitaker	.30
510	Tug McGraw	.08
511	Tug McGraw (Veteran)	.06
512	Doyle Alexander	.06
513	Fred Stanley	.06
514	Rudy Law	.06
515	Gene Tenace	.06
516	Bill Virdon (Mgr.)	.06
517	Gary Ward	.06
518	Bill Laskey (R)	.20
519	Terry Bulling	.06
520	Fred Lynn	.25
521	Bruce Benedict	.06
522	Pat Zachry	.06
523	Carney Lansford	.25
524	Tom Brennan	.06
525	Frank White	.06
526	Checklist No. 4	.12
527	Larry Biittner	.06
528	Jamie Easterly	.06
529	Tim Laudner	.06
530	Eddie Murray	1.00
531	A's Leaders:	.12
	R. Henderson, R. Langford	
532	Dave Stewart	2.00
533	Luis Salazar	.06
534	John Butcher	.06
535	Manny Trillo	.08
536	Johnny Wockenfuss	.06
537	Rod Scurry	.06
538	Danny Heep	.06
539	Roger Erickson	.06
540	Ozzie Smith	.75
541	Britt Burns	.08
542	Jody Davis	.10
543	Alan Fowlkes	.10
544	Larry Whisenton	.06
545	Floyd Bannister	.06
546	Dave Garcia (Mgr.)	.06
547	Geoff Zahn	.06
548	Brian Giles	.12
549	Charlie Puleo	.09
550	Carl Yastrzemski	1.25
551	Yastrzemski (Veteran)	.30
552	Tim Wallach	.35
553	Denny Martinez	.06
554	Mike Vail	.06
555	Steve Yeager	.06
556	Willie Upshaw	.15
557	Rick Honeycutt	.06
558	Dickie Thon	.08
559	Peter Redfern	.06
560	Ron LeFlore	.08
561	Cardinals Leaders:	.12
	L. Smith, J. Andujar	
562	Dave Rozema	.06
563	Juan Bonilla	.06
564	Sid Monge	.06
565	Bucky Dent	.06
566	Manny Sarmiento	.06
567	Joe Simpson	.06
568	Willie Hernandez	.20
569	Jack Perconte	.06
570	Vida Blue	.08
571	Mickey Klutts	.06
572	Bob Watson	.06
573	Andy Hassler	.06
574	Glenn Adams	.06
575	Neil Allen	.06
576	Frank Robinson (Mgr.)	.15
577	Luis Aponte	.08
578	David Green	.15
579	Rich Dauer	.06

NO. PLAYER	MINT
580 Tom Seaver	1.00
581 T. Seaver (Veteran)	.25
582 Marshall Edwards	.06
583 Terry Forster	.08
584 Dave Hostetler	.12
585 Jose Cruz	.12
586 Frank Viola (R)	11.00
587 Ivan DeJesus	.06
588 Pat Underwood	.06
589 Alvis Woods	.06
590 Tony Pena	.25
591 White Sox Leaders: Greg Luzinski, LaMarr	.12
592 Shane Rawley	.06
593 Broderick Perkins	.06
594 Eric Rasmussen	.06
595 Tim Raines	.75
596 Randy Johnson	.10
597 Mike Proly	.06
598 Dwayne Murphy	.06
599 Don Aase	.06
600 George Brett	1.50
601 Ed Lynch	.06
602 Rich Gedman	.15
603 Joe Morgan	.40
604 Joe Morgan (Veteran)	.15
605 Gary Roenicke	.06
606 Bobby Cox (Mgr.)	.06
607 Charlie Leibrandt	.08
608 Don Money	.06
609 Danny Darwin	.06
610 Steve Garvey	.60
611 Bert Roberge	.06
612 Steve Swisher	.06
613 Mike Ivie	.06
614 Ed Glynn	.08
615 Garry Maddox	.06
616 Bill Nahorodny	.06
617 Butch Wynegar	.06
618 LaMarr Hoyt	.15
619 Keith Moreland	.08
620 Mike Norris	.06
621 Mets Leaders: Mookie Wilson, Craig Swan	.12
622 Dave Edler	.06
623 Luis Sanchez	.06
624 Glenn Hubbard	.06
625 Ken Forsch	.06
626 Jerry Martin	.06
627 Doug Bair	.06
628 Julio Valdez	.06
629 Charlie Lea	.06
630 Paul Molitor	.30
631 Tippy Martinez	.06
632 Alex Trevino	.06
633 Vicente Romo	.06
634 Max Venable	.06
635 Graig Nettles	.15

NO. PLAYER	MINT
636 G. Nettles (Veteran)	.10
637 Pat Corrales (Mgr.)	.06
638 Dan Petry	.15
639 Art Howe	.06
640 Andre Thornton	.10
641 Billy Sample	.06
642 Checklist: No. 5	.12
643 Bump Wills	.06
644 Joe LeFebvre	.06
645 Bill Madlock	.15
646 Jim Essian	.06
647 Bobby Mitchell	.06
648 Jeff Burroughs	.06
649 Tommy Boggs	.06
650 George Hendrick	.10
651 Angels Leaders: Rod Carew, Mike Witt	.20
652 Butch Hobson	.06
653 Ellis Valentine	.06
654 Bob Ojeda	.12
655 Al Bumbry	.06
656 Dave Frost	.06
657 Mike Gates	.08
658 Frank Pastore	.06
659 Charlie Moore	.06
660 Mike Hargrove	.06
661 Bill Russell	.06
662 Joe Sambito	.06
663 Tom O'Malley (R)	.12
664 Bob Molinaro	.06
665 Jim Sundberg	.06
666 Sparky Anderson (Mgr.)	.06
667 Dick Davis	.06
668 Larry Christenson	.06
669 Mike Squires	.06
670 Jerry Mumphrey	.06
671 Lenny Faedo	.06
672 Jim Kaat	.10
673 Jim Kaat (Veteran)	.06
674 Kurt Bevacqua	.06
675 Jim Beattie	.06
676 Biff Pocoroba	.06
677 Dave Revering	.06
678 Juan Beniquez	.06
679 Mike Scott	.40
680 Andre Dawson	.60
681 Dodgers Leaders: Fernando Valenzuela, Pedro Guerrero	.15
682 Bob Stanley	.06
683 Dan Ford	.06
684 Rafael Landestoy	.06
685 Lee Mazzilli	.06
686 Randy Lerch	.06
687 U.L. Washington	.06
688 Jim Wohlford	.06
689 Ron Hassey	.06
690 Kent Hrbek	.75

NO. PLAYER	MINT
691 Dave Tobik	.06
692 Denny Walling	.06
693 Sparky Lyle	.08
694 S. Lyle (Veteran)	.06
695 Ruppert Jones	.06
696 Chuck Tanner (Mgr.)	.06
697 Barry Foote	.06
698 Tony Bernazard	.06
699 Lee Smith	.10
700 Keith Hernandez	.40
701 Batting Leaders: Willie Wilson, Al Oliver	.15
702 Home Run Leaders: Gorman Thomas, Reggie Jackson, Dave Kingman	.15
703 RBI Leaders: Hal McRae, Al Oliver, Dale Murphy	.15
704 Stolen Base Leaders: R. Henderson, T. Raines	.25
705 Victory Leaders: LaMarr Hoyt, Steve Carlton	.15
706 Strikeout Leaders: F. Bannister, Steve Carlton	.15
707 ERA Leaders: Rick Sutcliffe, Steve Rogers	.12
708 Leading Firemen: D. Quisenberry, B. Sutter	.12
709 Jimmy Sexton	.06
710 Willie Wilson	.20
711 Mariners Leaders: Bruce Bochte, Jim Beattie	.10
712 Bruce Kison	.06
713 Ron Hodges	.06
714 Wayne Nordhagen	.06
715 Tony Perez	.15
716 T. Perez (Veteran)	.10
717 Scott Sanderson	.06
718 Jim Dwyer	.06
719 Rich Gale	.06
720 Dave Concepcion	.12
721 John Martin	.06
722 Jorge Orta	.06
723 Randy Moffitt	.06
724 Johnny Grubb	.06
725 Dan Spillner	.06
726 Harvey Kuenn (Mgr.)	.06
727 Chet Lemon	.10
728 Ron Reed	.06
729 Jerry Morales	.06
730 Jason Thompson	.12
731 Al Williams	.06
732 Dave Henderson	.25
733 Buck Martinez	.06
734 Steve Braun	.06
735 Tommy John	.15
736 T. John (Veteran)	.08
737 Mitchell Page	.06

NO. PLAYER	MINT
738 Tim Foli	.06
739 Rick Ownbey	.08
740 Rusty Staub	.12
741 R. Staub (Veteran)	.08
742 Padres Leaders: Terry Kennedy, Tim Lollar	.10
743 Mike Torrez	.06
744 Brad Mills	.06
745 Scott McGregor	.18
746 John Wathan	.06
747 Fred Breining	.06
748 Derrel Thomas	.06
749 Jon Matlack	.06
750 Ben Oglivie	.10
751 Brad Havens	.06
752 Luis Pujols	.06
753 Elias Sosa	.06
754 Bill Robinson	.06
755 John Candelaria	.06
756 Russ Nixon (Mgr.)	.06
757 Rick Manning	.06
758 Aurelio Rodriguez	.06
759 Doug Bird	.06
760 Dale Murphy	1.50
761 Gary Lucas	.06
762 Cliff Johnson	.06
763 Al Cowens	.06
764 Pete Falcone	.06
765 Bob Boone	.06
766 Barry Bonnell	.06
767 Duane Kuiper	.06
768 Chris Speier	.06
769 Checklist No. 6	.12
770 Dave Winfield	.50
771 Twins Leaders: Kent Hrbek, Bobby Castillo	.10
772 Jim Kern	.06
773 Larry Hisle	.06
774 Alan Ashby	.06
775 Burt Hooton	.06
776 Larry Parrish	.06
777 John Curtis	.06
778 Rich Hebner	.06
779 Rick Waits	.06
780 Gary Matthews	.10
781 Rick Rhoden	.06
782 Bobby Murcer	.08
783 B. Murcer (Veteran)	.06
784 Jeff Newman	.06
785 Dennis Leonard	.06
786 Ralph Houk (Mgr.)	.06
787 Dick Tidrow	.06
788 Dane Iorg	.06
789 Bryan Clark	.06
790 Bob Grich	.06
791 Gary Lavelle	.06
792 Chris Chambliss	.15

1983 Topps Traded.... Complete Set of 132 Cards—Value $100.00

Updates the main 1983 card set with players who changed teams during the season, and rookies. Features the first Topps card of Darryl Strawberry. The complete set was packaged in a printed box and only distributed through card hobby dealers.

1983 Topps Traded (Continued)

NO. PLAYER	MINT	NO. PLAYER	MINT	NO. PLAYER	MINT	NO. PLAYER	MINT
1 T Neil Allen	.12	34 T Julio Franco (RR)	4.00	67 T Lee Mazzilli	.12	100 T Mike Scott	1.00
2 T Bill Almon	.09	35 T Rich Gale	.09	68 T Andy McGaffigan	.09	101 T Tom Seaver	3.00
3 T Joe Altobelli (Mgr.)	.09	36 T Kiko Garcia	.09	69 T Craig McMurtry	.20	102 T John Shelby	.20
4 T Tony Armas	.10	37 T Steve Garvey	1.25	70 T J. McNamara (Mgr.)	.09	103 T Bob Shirley	.08
5 T Doug Bair	.09	38 T Johnny Grubb	.09	71 T Orlando Mercado	.09	104 T Joe Simpson	.08
6 T Steve Baker	.12	39 T Mel Hall	1.25	72 T Larry Milbourne	.09	105 T Doug Sisk	.15
7 T Floyd Bannister	.12	40 T Von Hayes	1.00	73 T Randy Moffitt	.09	106 T Mike Smithson	.15
8 T Don Baylor	.10	41 T Danny Heep	.09	74 T Sid Monge	.09	107 T Elias Sosa	.06
9 T Tony Bernazard	.09	42 T Steve Henderson	.09	75 T Jose Morales	.09	108 T D. Strawberry (RR)	75.00
10 T Larry Biittner	.09	43 T Keith Hernandez	.75	76 T Omar Moreno	.12	109 T Tom Tellmann	.08
11 T Dann Bilardello	.09	44 T Leo Hernandez	.15	77 T Joe Morgan	1.50	110 T Gene Tenace	.08
12 T Doug Bird	.09	45 T Willie Hernandez	.25	78 T Mike Morgan	.09	111 T Gorman Thomas	.20
13 T Steve Boros (Mgr.)	.09	46 T Al Holland	.12	79 T Dale Murray	.09	112 T Dick Tidrow	.08
14 T Greg Brock	.40	47 T F. Howard (Mgr.)	.09	80 T Jeff Newman	.09	113 T Dave Tobik	.08
15 T Mike Brown	.12	48 T Bobby Johnson	.09	81 T Pete O'Brien (RR)	1.50	114 T Wayne Tolleson	.12
16 T Tom Burgmeier	.09	49 T Cliff Johnson	.09	82 T Jorge Orta	.09	115 T Mike Torrez	.10
17 T Randy Bush	.30	50 T Odell Jones	.09	83 T Alejandro Pena	.50	116 T Manny Trillo	.12
18 T Bert Campaneris	.15	51 T Mike Jorgenson	.09	84 T Pascual Perez	.12	117 T Steve Trout	.10
19 T Ron Cey	.20	52 T Bob Kearney	.09	85 T Tony Perez	.50	118 T Lee Tunnell	.12
20 T Chris Codiroli	.12	53 T Steve Kemp	.12	86 T Broderick Perkins	.09	119 T Mike Vail	.08
21 T Dave Collins	.15	54 T Matt Keough	.09	87 T Tony Phillips	.30	120 T Ellis Valentine	.15
22 T Terry Crowley	.09	55 T Ron Kittle (RR)	1.00	88 T Charlie Puleo	.09	121 T Tom Veryzer	.08
23 T Julio Cruz	.09	56 T Mickey Klutts	.09	89 T Pat Putnam	.09	122 T George Vukovich	.08
24 T Mike Davis	.15	57 T Alan Knicely	.09	90 T Jamie Quirk	.09	123 T Rick Waits	.08
25 T Frank DiPino	.12	58 T Mike Krukow	.09	91 T Doug Rader (Mgr.)	.12	124 T Greg Walker	.50
26 T Bill Doron (RR)	2.00	59 T Rafael Landestoy	.09	92 T Chuck Rainey	.09	125 T Chris Welsh	.08
27 T Jerry Dybzinski	.09	60 T Carney Lansford	.50	93 T Bobby Ramos	.09	126 T Len Whitehouse	.08
28 T Jamie Easterly	.09	61 T Joe Lefebvre	.09	94 T Gary Redus	.35	127 T Eddie Whitson	.10
29 T Juan Eichelberger	.09	62 T Bryan Little	.12	95 T Steve Renko	.09	128 T Jim Wohlford	.08
30 T Jim Essian	.09	63 T Aurelio Lopez	.15	96 T Leon Roberts	.09	129 T Matt Young	.20
31 T Pete Falcone	.09	64 T Mike Madden	.20	97 T Aurelio Rodriquez	.09	130 T Joel Youngblood	.08
32 T Mike Ferraro (Mgr.)	.09	65 T Rick Manning	.09	98 T Dick Ruthven	.09	131 T Pat Zachry	.08
33 T Terry Forster	.12	66 T Billy Martin (Mgr.)	.15	99 T Daryl Sconiers	.09	132 T Traded Checklist	.25

1984 Topps.... Complete Set of 792 Cards—Value $120.00

Features the rookie cards of Don Mattingly and Darryl Strawberry. Topps also introduced a "Tiffany" version of the set—printed on white stock, high gloss finish, and production limited to 10,000 sets.

NO. PLAYER	MINT	NO. PLAYER	MINT	NO. PLAYER	MINT	NO. PLAYER	MINT
1 Highlight—S. Carlton 300th Win and SO King	.35	18 Dale Berra	.06	43 Ron Reed	.06	68 Luis Salazar	.06
2 Highlight—Henderson 100 SB's, 3 Seasons	.50	19 Ray Fontenot	.15	44 Jim Morrison	.06	69 Rod Scurry	.06
3 Highlight—Quisenberry Save Record	.15	20 Greg Luzinski	.12	45 Jerry Mumphrey	.06	70 Gary Matthews	.08
4 Highlight—N. Ryan, G. Perry, S. Carlton— Surpass Walter Johnson	.45	21 Joe Altobelli (Mgr.)	.06	46 Ray Smith	.08	71 Leo Hernandez	.15
5 Highlight—D. Righetti, B. Forsch, B. Warren— No Hitters	.15	22 Bryan Clark	.06	47 Rudy Law	.06	72 Mike Squires	.06
6 Highlight—Bench, Yaz, Perry,—All Retire	.35	23 Keith Moreland	.08	48 Julio Franco	1.50	73 Jody Davis	.10
7 Gary Lucas	.06	24 John Martin	.06	49 John Stuper	.06	74 Jerry Martin	.06
8 Don Mattingly (R)	25.00	25 Glenn Hubbard	.08	50 Chris Chambliss	.08	75 Bob Forsch	.06
9 Jim Gott	.06	26 Bill Black	.06	51 Jim Fray (Mgr.)	.06	76 Alfredo Griffin	.06
10 Robin Yount	.75	27 Daryl Sconiers	.06	52 Paul Splittorff	.06	77 Brett Butler	.08
11 Twins Leaders: Kent Hrbek, Ken Schrom	.10	28 Frank Viola	1.25	53 Juan Beniquez	.08	78 Mike Torrez	.06
12 Billy Sample	.06	29 Danny Heep	.06	54 Jesse Orosco	.10	79 Rob Wilfong	.06
13 Scott Holman	.06	30 Wade Boggs	6.00	55 Dave Concepcion	.15	80 Steve Rogers	.08
14 Tom Brookens	.06	31 Andy McGaffigan	.06	56 Gary Allenson	.06	81 Billy Martin (Mgr.)	.15
15 Burt Hooton	.06	32 Bobby Ramos	.06	57 Dan Schatzeder	.06	82 Doug Bird	.06
16 Omar Moreno	.08	33 Tom Burgmeier	.06	58 Max Venable	.06	83 Richie Zisk	.08
17 John Denny	.08	34 Eddie Milner	.06	59 Sammy Stewart	.06	84 Lenny Faedo	.06
		35 Don Sutton	.30	60 Paul Molitor	.15	85 Atlee Hammaker	.06
		36 Denny Walling	.06	61 Chris Codiroli	.15	86 John Shelby	.30
		37 Rangers Leaders: Buddy Bell, Rick Honeycutt	.10	62 Dave Hostetler	.06	87 Frank Pastore	.06
		38 Luis DeLeon	.06	63 Ed VandeBerg	.08	88 Rob Picciolo	.06
		39 Garth Iorg	.06	64 Mike Scioscia	.06	89 Mike Smithson	.15
		40 Dusty Baker	.10	65 Kirk Gibson	.40	90 Pedro Guerrero	.40
		41 Tony Bernazard	.06	66 Astros Leaders: Nolan Ryan, Jose Cruz	.10	91 Dan Spillner	.06
		42 Johnny Grubb	.06	67 Gary Ward	.06	92 Lloyd Moseby	.20
						93 Bob Knepper	.06

NO.	PLAYER	MINT
94	Mario Ramirez	.08
95	Aurelio Lopez	.06
96	Royals Leaders:	.10
	Hal McRae, Larry Gura	
97	LaMarr Hoyt	.15
98	Steve Nicosia	.06
99	Criag Lefferts (R)	.25
100	Reggie Jackson	.75
101	Porfirio Altamirano	.06
102	Ken Oberkfell	.06
103	Dwayne Murphy	.08
104	Ken Dayley	.06
105	Tony Armas	.15
106	Tim Stoddard	.06
107	Ned Yost	.06
108	Randy Moffitt	.06
109	Brad Wellman	.08
110	Ron Guidry	.20
111	Bill Virdon (Mgr.)	.06
112	Tom Niedenfuer	.08
113	Kelly Paris	.12
114	Checklist No. 1	.08
115	Andre Thornton	.08
116	George Bjorkman	.08
117	Tom Veryzer	.06
118	Charlie Hough	.06
119	Johnny Wockenfuss	.06
120	Keith Hernandez	.35
121	Pat Sheridan	.15
122	Cecilio Guante	.06
123	Butch Wynegar	.06
124	Damaso Garcia	.10
125	Britt Burns	.08
126	Braves Leaders:	.10
	Dale Murphy, C. McMurtry	
127	Mike Madden	.15
128	Rick Manning	.06
129	Bill Laskey	.06
130	Ozzie Smith	.50
131	Batting Leaders:	
	Bill Madlock, Wade Boggs	
132	Home Run Leaders:	.30
	Mike Schmidt, Jim Rice	
133	RBI Leaders:	.25
	Dale Murphy, C. Cooper,	
	Jim Rice	
134	Stolen Base Leaders:	.35
	T. Raines, R. Henderson	
135	Victory Leaders:	.15
	John Denny, LaMarr Hoyt	
136	Stikeout Leaders:	.25
	Steve Carlton, Jack Morris	
137	ERA Leaders:	.08
	A. Hammaker, R. Honeycutt	
138	Leading Firemen:	.10
	A. Holland, D. Quisenberry	
139	Bert Campaneris	.06
140	Storm Davis	.12
141	Pat Corrales (Mgr.)	.06
142	Rich Gale	.06
143	Jose Morales	.06
144	Brian Harper	.40
145	Gary Lavelle	.06
146	Ed Romero	.06
147	Dan Petry	.15
148	Joe Lefebvre	.06
149	Jon Matlack	.06
150	Dale Murphy	1.00
151	Steve Trout	.06
152	Glenn Brummer	.06
153	Dick Tidrow	.06
154	Dave Henderson	.15
155	Frank White	.06
156	A's Leaders:	.10
	R. Henderson, T. Conroy	
157	Gary Gaetti	.60
158	John Curtis	.06
159	Darryl Cias	.08
160	Mario Soto	.08
161	Junior Ortiz	.10
162	Bob Ojeda	.06
163	Lorenzo Gray	.08
164	Scott Sanderson	.06
165	Ken Singleton	.08
166	Jamie Nelson	.12

NO.	PLAYER	MINT
167	Marshall Edwards	.06
168	Juan Bonilla	.06
169	Larry Parrish	.06
170	Jerry Reuss	.08
171	Frank Robinson (Mgr.)	.12
172	Frank DiPino	.06
173	Marvell Wynne	.15
174	Juan Berenguer	.06
175	Graig Nettles	.15
176	Lee Smith	.10
177	Jerry Hairston	.06
178	Bill Krueger	.12
179	Buck Martinez	.06
180	Manny Trillo	.08
181	Roy Thomas	.06
182	Darryl Strawberry (R)	17.00
183	Al Williams	.06
184	Mike O'Berry	.06
185	Sixto Lezcano	.06
186	Cardinal Leaders:	.10
	Lonnie Smith, John Stuper	
187	Luis Aponte	.06
188	Bryan Little	.08
189	Tim Conroy	.12
190	Ben Oglivie	.08
191	Mike Boddicker	.15
192	Nick Esasky (R)	.75
193	Darrell Brown	.08
194	Domingo Ramos	.08
195	Jack Morris	.20
196	Don Slaught	.06
197	Garry Hancock	.06
198	Bill Doran (R)	.75
199	Willie Hernandez	.20
200	Andre Dawson	.40
201	Bruce Kison	.06
202	Bobby Cox (Mgr.)	.06
203	Matt Keough	.06
204	Bobby Meacham	.20
205	Greg Minton	.06
206	Andy Van Slyke (R)	2.50
207	Donnie Moore	.08
208	Jose Oquendo (R)	.50
209	Manny Sarmiento	.06
210	Joe Morgan	.35
211	Rick Sweet	.06
212	Broderick Perkins	.06
213	Bruce Hurst	.20
214	Paul Householder	.06
215	Tippy Martinez	.06
216	White Sox Leaders:	.10
	C. Fisk, R. Dotson	
217	Alan Ashby	.06
218	Rick Waits	.06
219	Joe Simpson	.06
220	Fernando Valenzuela	.35
221	Cliff Johnson	.06
222	Rick Honeycutt	.08
223	Wayne Krenchicki	.06
224	Sid Monge	.06
225	Lee Mazzilli	.06
226	Juan Eichelberger	.06
227	Steve Braun	.06
228	John Rabb	.15
229	Paul Owens (Mgr.)	.06
230	Rickey Henderson	4.00
231	Gary Woods	.06
232	Tim Wallach	.20
233	Checklist No. 2	.08
234	Rafael Ramirez	.06
235	Matt Young	.15
236	Ellis Valentine	.06
237	John Castino	.06
238	Reid Nichols	.06
239	Jay Howell	.06
240	Eddie Murray	.75
241	Billy Almon	.06
242	Alex Trevino	.06
243	Pete Ladd	.06
244	Candy Maldonado	.50
245	Rick Sutcliffe	.30
246	Mets Leaders:	.12
	M. Wilson, Tom Seaver	
247	Onix Concepcion	.06
248	Bill Dawley	.20

NO.	PLAYER	MINT
249	Jay Johnstone	.06
250	Bill Madlock	.15
251	Tony Gwynn	3.50
252	Larry Christenson	.06
253	Jim Wohlford	.06
254	Shane Rawley	.06
255	Bruce Benedict	.06
256	Dave Geisel	.06
257	Julio Cruz	.06
258	Luis Sanchez	.06
259	Sparky Anderson (Mgr.)	.08
260	Scott McGregor	.08
261	Bobby Brown	.06
262	Tom Candiotti	.40
263	Jack Fimple	.08
264	Doug Frobel	.12
265	Donnie Hill	.15
266	Steve Lubratich	.08
267	Carmelo Martinez (R)	.25
268	Jack O'Connor	.06
269	Aurelio Rodriguez	.06
270	Jeff Russell (R)	.40
271	Moose Haas	.06
272	Rick Dempsey	.06
273	Charlie Puleo	.06
274	Rick Monday	.06
275	Len Matuszek	.06
276	Angels Leaders:	.10
	Rod Carew, Geoff Zahn	
277	Eddie Whitson	.06
278	Jorge Bell	1.00
279	Ivan DeJesus	.06
280	Floyd Bannister	.10
281	Larry Milbourne	.06
282	Jim Barr	.06
283	Larry Biittner	.06
284	Howard Bailey	.06
285	Darrell Porter	.06
286	Lary Sorensen	.06
287	Warren Cromartie	.06
288	Jim Beattie	.06
289	Randy Johnson	.06
290	Dave Dravecky	.08
291	Chuck Tanner (Mgr.)	.06
292	Tony Scott	.06
293	Ed Lynch	.06
294	U.L. Washington	.06
295	Mike Flanagan	.08
296	Jeff Newman	.06
297	Bruce Berenyi	.06
298	Jim Gantner	.06
299	John Butcher	.06
300	Pete Rose	1.25
301	Frank LaCorte	.06
302	Barry Bonnell	.06
303	Marty Castillo	.06
304	Warren Brusstar	.06
305	Roy Smalley	.06
306	Dodgers Leaders:	.12
	Pedro Guerrero, Bob Welch	
307	Bobby Mitchell	.06
308	Ron Hassey	.06
309	Tony Phillips	.20
310	Willie McGee	.40
311	Jerry Koosman	.06
312	Jorge Orta	.06
313	Mike Jorgensen	.06
314	Orlando Mercado	.08
315	Bob Grich	.06
316	Mark Bradley	.08
317	Greg Pryor	.06
318	Bill Gullickson	.08
319	Al Bumbry	.06
320	Bob Stanley	.06
321	Harvey Kuenn (Mgr.)	.06
322	Ken Schrom	.06
323	Alan Knicely	.06
324	Alejandro Pena (R)	.30
325	Darrell Evans	.12
326	Bob Kearney	.06
327	Ruppert Jones	.06
328	Vern Ruhle	.06
329	Pat Tabler	.20
330	John Candelaria	.06
331	Bucky Dent	.06

NO.	PLAYER	MINT
332	Kevin Gross (R)	.30
333	Larry Herndon	.06
334	Chuck Rainey	.06
335	Don Baylor	.12
336	Mariners Leaders:	.10
	Pat Putnam, M. Young	
337	Kevin Hagen	.08
338	Mike Warren	.12
339	Roy Lee Jackson	.06
340	Hal McRae	.06
341	Dave Tobik	.06
342	Tim Foli	.06
343	Mark Davis	.15
344	Rick Miller	.06
345	Kent Hrbek	.50
346	Kurt Bevacqua	.06
347	Allan Ramirez	.08
348	Toby Harrah	.06
349	Bob Gibson	.12
350	George Foster	.20
351	Russ Nixon (Mgr.)	.06
352	Dave Stewart	1.00
353	Jim Anderson	.06
354	Jeff Burroughs	.06
355	Jason Thompson	.08
356	Glenn Abbott	.06
357	Ron Cey	.15
358	Bob Dernier	.08
359	Jim Acker (R)	.15
360	Willie Randolph	.08
361	Dave Smith	.06
362	David Green	.06
363	Tim Laudner	.06
364	Scott Fletcher	.12
365	Steve Bedrosian	.12
366	Padres Leaders:	.10
	T. Kennedy, D. Dravecky	
367	Jamie Easterly	.06
368	Hubie Brooks	.15
369	Steve McCatty	.06
370	Tim Raines	.50
371	Dave Gumpert	.08
372	Gary Roenicke	.06
373	Bill Scherrer	.08
374	Don Money	.06
375	Dennis Leonard	.06
376	Dave Anderson	.15
377	Danny Darwin	.06
378	Bob Brenly	.06
379	Checklist No.3	.08
380	Steve Garvey	.40
381	Ralph Houk (Mgr.)	.06
382	Chris Nyman	.08
383	Terry Puhl	.06
384	Lee Tunnell	.12
385	Tony Perez	.15
386	George Hendrick (AS)	.10
387	Johnny Ray (AS)	.10
388	Mike Schmidt (AS)	.40
389	Ozzie Smith (AS)	.12
390	Tim Raines (AS)	.20
391	Dale Murphy (AS)	.35
392	Andre Dawson (AS)	.25
393	Gary Carter (AS)	.30
394	Steve Rogers (AS)	.12
395	Steve Carlton (AS)	.30
396	Jesse Orosco (AS)	.08
397	Eddie Murray (AS)	.30
398	Lou Whitaker (AS)	.12
399	George Brett (AS)	.40
400	Cal Ripken (AS)	.30
401	Jim Rice (AS)	.25
402	Dave Winfield (AS)	.25
403	Lloyd Moseby (AS)	.12
404	Ted Simmons (AS)	.12
405	LaMarr Hoyt (AS)	.12
406	Ron Guidry (AS)	.15
407	Dan Quisenberry (AS)	.15
408	Lou Piniella	.10
409	Juan Agosto	.15
410	Claudell Washington	.08
411	Houston Jimenez	.08
412	Doug Rader (Mgr.)	.06
413	Spike Owen (R)	.25
414	Mitchell Page	.06

NO. PLAYER	MINT
415 Tommy John	.15
416 Dane Iorg	.06
417 Mike Armstrong	.06
418 Ron Hodges	.06
419 John Johnson	.06
420 Cecil Cooper	.15
421 Charlie Lea	.06
422 Jose Cruz	.12
423 Mike Morgan	.06
424 Dann Bilardello	.08
425 Steve Howe	.06
426 Orioles Leaders:	.12
M. Boddicker, C. Ripken	
427 Rick Leach	.06
428 Fred Breining	.06
429 Randy Bush	.20
430 Rusty Staub	.10
431 Chris Bando	.06
432 Charlie Hudson (R)	.15
433 Rich Hebner	.06
434 Harold Baines	.25
435 Neil Allen	.06
436 Rick Peters	.06
437 Mike Proly	.06
438 Biff Pocoroba	.06
439 Bob Stoddard	.06
440 Steve Kemp	.06
441 Bob Lillis (Mgr.)	.06
442 Byron McLaughlin	.06
443 Benny Ayala	.06
444 Steve Renko	.06
445 Jerry Remy	.06
446 Luis Pujols	.06
447 Tom Brunansky	.35
448 Ben Hayes	.06
449 Joe Pettini	.06
450 Gary Carter	.45
451 Bob Jones	.06
452 Chuck Porter	.06
453 Willie Upshaw	.15
454 Joe Beckwith	.06
455 Terry Kennedy	.10
456 Cubs Leaders:	.12
F. Jenkins, K. Moreland	
457 Dave Rozema	.06
458 Kiko Garcia	.06
459 Kevin Hickey	.06
460 Dave Winfield	.40
461 Jim Maler	.06
462 Lee Lacy	.06
463 Dave Engle	.06
464 Jeff Jones	.06
465 Mookie Wilson	.08
466 Gene Garber	.06
467 Mike Ramsey	.06
468 Geoff Zahn	.06
469 Tom O'Malley	.06
470 Nolan Ryan	3.00
471 Dick Howser (Mgr.)	.06
472 Mike Brown	.08
473 Jim Dwyer	.06
474 Greg Bargar	.09
475 Gary Redus (R)	.30
476 Tom Tellmann	.06
477 Rafael Landestoy	.06
478 Alan Bannister	.06
479 Frank Tanana	.06
480 Ron Kittle	.30
481 Mark Thurmond	.20
482 Enos Cabell	.06
483 Fergie Jenkins	.15
484 Ozzie Virgil	.06
485 Rick Rhoden	.06
486 Yankees Leaders:	.12
Don Baylor, Ron Guidry	
487 Ricky Adams	.08
488 Jesse Barfield	.30
489 Dave Von Ohlen	.09
490 Cal Ripken	1.50
491 Bobby Castillo	.06
492 Tucker Ashford	.06
493 Mike Norris	.06
494 Chili Davis	.15
495 Rollie Fingers	.20
496 Terry Francona	.06

NO. PLAYER	MINT
497 Bud Anderson	.06
498 Rich Gedman	.06
499 Mike Witt	.20
500 George Brett	1.00
501 Steve Henderson	.06
502 Joe Torre (Mgr.)	.08
503 Elias Sosa	.06
504 Mickey Rivers	.08
505 Pete Vuckovich	.08
506 Ernie Whitt	.06
507 Mike LaCoss	.06
508 Mel Hall	.50
509 Brad Havens	.06
510 Alan Trammell	.35
511 Marty Bystrom	.06
512 Oscar Gamble	.08
513 Dave Beard	.06
514 Floyd Rayford	.06
515 Gorman Thomas	.15
516 Expos Leaders:	.10
Al Oliver, Charlie Lea	
517 John Moses	.12
518 Greg Walker (R)	.30
519 Ron Davis	.06
520 Bob Boone	.06
521 Pete Falcone	.06
522 Dave Bergman	.06
523 Glenn Hoffman	.06
524 Carlos Diaz	.06
525 Willie Wilson	.20
526 Ron Oester	.06
527 Checklist No. 4	.08
528 Mark Brouhard	.06
529 Keith Atherton	.08
530 Dan Ford	.06
531 Steve Boros (Mgr.)	.06
532 Eric Show	.06
533 Ken Landreaux	.06
534 Pete O'Brien (R)	.75
535 Bo Diaz	.06
536 Doug Bair	.06
537 Johnny Ray	.12
538 Kevin Bass	.06
539 George Frazier	.06
540 George Hendrick	.08
541 Dennis Lamp	.06
542 Duane Kuiper	.06
543 Craig McMurtry (R)	.15
544 Cesar Geronimo	.06
545 Bill Buckner	.10
546 Indians Leaders:	.08
Mike Hargrove, L. Sorensen	
547 Mike Moore	.15
548 Ron Jackson	.06
549 Walt Terrell (R)	.20
550 Jim Rice	.35
551 Scott Ullger	.08
552 Ray Burris	.06
553 Joe Nolan	.06
554 Ted Power	.06
555 Greg Brock	.15
556 Joey McLaughlin	.06
557 Wayne Tolleson	.10
558 Mike Davis	.08
559 Mike Scott	.35
560 Carlton Fisk	.35
561 Whitey Herzog (Mgr.)	.08
562 Manny Castillo	.06
563 Glenn Wilson	.12
564 Al Holland	.06
565 Leon Durham	.20
566 Jim Bibby	.06
567 Mike Heath	.06
568 Pete Filson	.10
569 Bake McBride	.06
570 Dan Quisenberry	.20
571 Bruce Bochy	.06
572 Jerry Royster	.06
573 Dave Kingman	.10
574 Brian Downing	.06
575 Jim Clancy	.06
576 Giants Leaders:	.07
J. Leonard, A. Hammaker	
577 Mark Clear	.06
578 Lenn Sakata	.06

NO. PLAYER	MINT
579 Bob James (R)	.15
580 Lonnie Smith	.08
581 Jose DeLeon (R)	.50
582 Bob McClure	.06
583 Derrel Thomas	.06
584 Dave Schmidt	.06
585 Dan Driessen	.06
586 Joe Niekro	.08
587 Von Hayes	.20
588 Milt Wilcox	.06
589 Mike Easler	.08
590 Dave Stieb	.30
591 Tony LaRussa (Mgr.)	.06
592 Andre Robertson	.06
593 Jeff Lahti	.06
594 Gene Richards	.06
595 Jeff Reardon	.06
596 Ryne Sandberg	6.00
597 Rick Camp	.06
598 Rusty Kuntz	.06
599 Doug Sisk	.15
600 Rod Carew	.65
601 John Tudor	.15
602 John Wathan	.06
603 Renie Martin	.06
604 John Lowenstein	.06
605 Mike Caldwell	.06
606 Blue Jays Leaders:	.10
Lloyd Moseby, Dave Stieb	
607 Tom Hume	.06
608 Bobby Johnson	.06
609 Dan Meyer	.06
610 Steve Sax	.30
611 Chet Lemon	.08
612 Harry Spilman	.06
613 Greg Gross	.06
614 Len Barker	.06
615 Garry Templeton	.12
616 Don Robinson	.06
617 Rick Cerone	.06
618 Dickie Noles	.06
619 Jerry Dybzinski	.06
620 Al Oliver	.15
621 Frank Howard (Mgr.)	.06
622 Al Cowens	.06
623 Ron Washington	.06
624 Terry Harper	.06
625 Larry Gura	.06
626 Bob Clark	.06
627 Dave LaPoint	.06
628 Ed Jurak	.12
629 Rick Langford	.06
630 Ted Simmons	.12
631 Denny Martinez	.06
632 Tom Foley	.12
633 Mike Krukow	.06
634 Mike Marshall	.15
635 Dave Righetti	.20
636 Pat Putman	.06
637 Phillies Leaders:	.10
G. Matthews, J. Denny	
638 George Vuckovich	.06
639 Rick Lysander	.08
640 Lance Parrish	.25
641 Mike Richardt	.06
642 Tom Underwood	.06
643 Mike Brown	.15
644 Tim Lollar	.06
645 Tony Pena	.12
646 Checklist No.5	.08
647 Ron Roenicke	.06
648 Len Whitehouse	.08
649 Tom Herr	.12
650 Phil Niekro	.25
651 J. McNamara (Mgr.)	.06
652 Rudy May	.06
653 Dave Stapleton	.06
654 Bob Bailor	.06
655 Amos Otis	.06
656 Bryn Smith	.06
657 Thad Bosley	.06
658 Jerry Augustine	.06
659 Duane Walker	.06
660 Ray Knight	.06
661 Steve Yeager	.06

NO. PLAYER	MINT
662 Tom Brennan	.06
663 Johnnie LeMaster	.06
664 Dave Stegman	.06
665 Buddy Bell	.15
666 Tigers Leaders:	.12
Lou Whitaker, J. Morris	
667 Vance Law	.06
668 Larry McWilliams	.06
669 Dave Lopes	.08
670 Rich Gossage	.20
671 Jamie Quirk	.06
672 Ricky Nelson	.12
673 Mike Walters	.12
674 Tim Flannery	.06
675 Pascual Perez	.08
676 Brian Giles	.06
677 Doyle Alexander	.06
678 Chris Speier	.06
679 Art Howe	.06
680 Fred Lynn	.20
681 Tom Lasorda (Mgr.)	.08
682 Dan Morogiello	.08
683 Marty Barrett (R)	.75
684 Bob Shirley	.06
685 Willie Aikens	.06
686 Joe Price	.06
687 Roy Howell	.06
688 George Wright	.06
689 Mike Fischlin	.06
690 Jack Clark	.30
691 Steve Lake	.12
692 Dickie Thon	.06
693 Alan Wiggins	.08
694 Mike Stanton	.06
695 Lou Whitaker	.30
696 Pirates Leaders:	.08
Bill Madlock, Rick Rhoden	
697 Dale Murray	.06
698 Marc Hill	.06
699 Dave Rucker	.06
700 Mike Schmidt	1.25
701 Batting Leaders:	.25
Bill Madlock, Dave Parker, Pete Rose	
702 Hit Leaders:	.25
Pete Rose, Rusty Staub, Tony Perez	
703 Home Run Leaders:	.25
Mike Schmidt, Tony Perez, D. Kingman	
704 RBI Leaders:	.15
Rusty Staub, Tony Perez, Al Oliver	
705 Stolen Bases Leaders:	.12
Larry Bowa, Joe Morgan, Cesar Cedeno	
706 Victory Leaders:	.15
Steve Carlton, F. Jenkins, Tom Seaver	
707 Strikeout Leaders:	.35
Tom Seaver, Steve Carlton, Nolan Ryan	
708 ERA Leaders:	.15
Tom Seaver, Steve Rogers, Steve Carlton	
709 Save Leaders:	.12
Bruce Sutter, Tug McGraw, G. Garber	
710 Batting Leaders:	.25
Rod Carew, Cecil Cooper, George Brett	
711 Hit Leaders:	.20
Reggie Jackson, Rod Carew, Bert Campaneris	
712 Home Run Leaders:	.20
Graig Nettles, Reggie Jackson, Greg Luzinski	
713 RBI Leaders:	.20
Reggie Jackson, Ted Simmons, Graig Nettles	
714 Stolen Bases Leaders:	.12
Bert Campaneris, D. Lopes, Omar Moreno	
715 Victory Leaders:	.15
Jim Palmer, Don Sutton, Tommy John	

NO.	PLAYER	MINT
716	Strikeouts Leaders: Don Sutton, Jerry Koosman, Bert Blyleven	.12
717	ERA Leaders: Jim Palmer, R. Fingers, Ron Guidry	.15
718	Save Leaders: Rollie Fingers, R. Gossage, Dan Quisenberry	.15
719	Andy Hassler	.06
720	Dwight Evans	.25
721	Del Crandall (Mgr.)	.06
722	Bob Welch	.25
723	Rich Dauer	.06
724	Eric Rasmussen	.06
725	Cesar Cedeno	.08
726	Brewers Leaders: Ted Simmons, Moose Haas	.10
727	Joel Youngblood	.06
728	Tug McGraw	.08
729	Gene Tenace	.06
730	Bruce Sutter	.20

NO.	PLAYER	MINT
731	Lynn Jones	.06
732	Terry Crowley	.06
733	Dave Collins	.06
734	Odell Jones	.06
735	Rick Burleson	.06
736	Dick Ruthven	.06
737	Jim Essian	.06
738	Bill Schroeder (R)	.15
739	Bob Watson	.06
740	Tom Seaver	.60
741	Wayne Gross	.06
742	Dick Williams (Mgr.)	.06
743	Don Hood	.06
744	Jamie Allen	.12
745	Dennis Eckersley	.25
746	Mickey Hatcher	.06
747	Pat Zachry	.06
748	Jeff Leonard	.06
749	Doug Flynn	.06
750	Jim Palmer	.60
751	Charlie Moore	.06

NO.	PLAYER	MINT
752	Phil Garner	.06
753	Doug Gwosdz	.06
754	Kent Tekulve	.06
755	Garry Maddox	.06
756	Reds Leaders: Ron Oester, Mario Soto	.08
757	Larry Bowa	.08
758	Bill Stein	.06
759	Richard Dotson	.08
760	Bob Horner	.25
761	John Montefusco	.06
762	Rance Mulliniks	.06
763	Craig Swan	.06
764	Mike Hargrove	.06
765	Ken Forsch	.06
766	Mike Vail	.06
767	Carney Lansford	.12
768	Champ Summers	.06
769	Bill Caudill	.08
770	Ken Griffey	.08
771	Billy Gardner (Mgr.)	.06

NO.	PLAYER	MINT
772	Jim Slaton	.06
773	Todd Cruz	.06
774	Tom Gorman	.12
775	Dave Parker	.25
776	Craig Reynolds	.06
777	Tom Paciorek	.06
778	Andy Hawkins (R)	.35
779	Jim Sundberg	.06
780	Steve Carlton	.50
781	Checklist No. 6	.08
782	Steve Balboni	.06
783	Luis Leal	.06
784	Leon Roberts	.06
785	Joaquin Andujar	.12
786	Red Sox Leaders: Bob Ojeda, Wade Boggs	.20
787	Bill Campbell	.06
788	Milt May	.06
789	Bert Blyleven	.20
790	Doug DeCinces	.08
791	Terry Forster	.06
792	Bill Russell	.12

1984 Topps Traded.... Complete Set of 132 Cards—Value $100.00

Updates the main 1984 card set with players who changed teams during the season and rookies. Features the first Topps card for Dwight Gooden and Bret Saberhagen. The complete set was packaged in a printed box and only distributed through card hobby dealers.

NO.	PLAYER	MINT
1 T	Willie Aikens	.15
2 T	Luis Aponte	.10
3 T	Mike Armstrong	.10
4 T	Bob Bailor	.10
5 T	Dusty Baker	.12
6 T	Steve Balboni	.15
7 T	Alan Bannister	.10
8 T	Dave Beard	.10
9 T	Joe Beckwith	.10
10 T	Bruce Berenyi	.10
11 T	Dave Bergman	.10
12 T	Tony Bernazard	.10
13 T	Yogi Berra (Mgr.)	.50
14 T	Barry Bonnell	.10
15 T	Phil Bradley (RR)	2.00
16 T	Fred Breining	.10
17 T	Bill Buckner	.25
18 T	Ray Burris	.10
19 T	John Butcher	.10
20 T	Brett Butler	.35
21 T	Enos Cabell	.10
22 T	Bill Campbell	.10
23 T	Bill Caudill	.15
24 T	Bob Clark	.10
25 T	Bryan Clark	.10
26 T	Jaimes Cocanower	.20
27 T	Ron Darling (RR)	4.00
28 T	Alvin Davis (RR)	6.00
29 T	Ken Dayley	.12
30 T	Jeff Dedmon	.20
31 T	Bob Dernier	.10
32 T	Carlos Diaz	.10
33 T	Mike Easler	.12

NO.	PLAYER	MINT
34 T	Dennis Eckersley	.75
35 T	Jim Essian	.08
36 T	Darrell Evans	.25
37 T	Mike Fitzgerald	.15
38 T	Tim Foli	.10
39 T	George Frazier	.10
40 T	Rich Gale	.10
41 T	Barbaro Garbey	.20
42 T	D. Gooden (RR)	40.00
43 T	Rich Gossage	.30
44 T	Wayne Gross	.10
45 T	Mark Gublcza (RR)	4.00
46 T	Jackie Gutierrez	.15
47 T	Mel Hall	.20
48 T	Toby Harrah	.12
49 T	Ron Hassey	.10
50 T	Rich Hebner	.10
51 T	Willie Hernandez	.25
52 T	Ricky Horton	.35
53 T	Art Howe	.10
54 T	Dane Iorg	.10
55 T	Brook Jacoby (RR)	2.00
56 T	Mike Jeffcoat	.15
57 T	D. Johnson (Mgr.)	.20
58 T	Lynn Jones	.10
59 T	Ruppert Jones	.10
60 T	Mike Jorgensen	.10
61 T	Bob Kearney	.10
62 T	Jimmy Key (RR)	2.50
63 T	Dave Kingman	.25
64 T	Jerry Koosman	.40
65 T	Wayne Krenchicki	.10
66 T	Rusty Kuntz	.10

NO.	PLAYER	MINT
67 T	R. Lachemann (Mgr.)	.10
68 T	Frank LaCorte	.10
69 T	Dennis Lamp	.10
70 T	Mark Langston (RR)	12.00
71 T	Rich Leach	.10
72 T	Craig Lefferts	.10
73 T	Gary Lucas	.10
74 T	Jerry Martin	.10
75 T	Carmelo Martinez	.25
76 T	Mike Mason	.20
77 T	Gary Matthews	.15
78 T	Andy McGaffigan	.10
79 T	Larry Milbourne	.10
80 T	Sid Monge	.10
81 T	Jackie Moore (Mgr.)	.10
82 T	Joe Morgan	2.00
83 T	Graig Nettles	.50
84 T	Phil Niekro	1.25
85 T	Ken Oberkfell	.12
86 T	Mike O'Berry	.10
87 T	Al Oliver	.20
88 T	Jorge Orta	.10
89 T	Amos Otis	.15
90 T	Dave Parker	1.25
91 T	Tony Perez	.50
92 T	Gerald Perry	1.25
93 T	Gary Pettis	.35
94 T	Rob Picciolo	.08
95 T	Vern Rapp (Mgr.)	.08
96 T	Floyd Rayford	.08
97 T	Randy Ready	.35
98 T	Ron Reed	.10
99 T	Gene Richards	.10

NO.	PLAYER	MINT
100 T	Jose Rijo (RR)	2.50
101 T	Jeff Robinson	.50
102 T	Ron Romanick	.25
103 T	Pete Rose	7.00
104 T	B. Saberhagen (RR)	20.00
105 T	Juan Samuel (RR)	3.00
106 T	Scott Sanderson	.12
107 T	Dick Schofield	.50
108 T	Tom Seaver	5.00
109 T	Jim Slaton	.08
110 T	Mike Smithson	.08
111 T	Lary Sorensen	.08
112 T	Tim Stoddard	.08
113 T	Champ Summers	.08
114 T	Jim Sundberg	.08
115 T	Rick Sutcliffe	.50
116 T	Craig Swan	.10
117 T	Tim Teufel	.40
118 T	Derrel Thomas	.10
119 T	Gorman Thomas	.15
120 T	Alex Trevino	.08
121 T	Manny Trillo	.12
122 T	John Tudor	.30
123 T	Tom Underwood	.10
124 T	Mike Vail	.10
125 T	Tom Waddell	.20
126 T	Gary Ward	.20
127 T	Curt Wilkerson	.25
128 T	Frank Williams	.20
129 T	Glenn Wilson	.25
130 T	Johnny Wockenfuss	.10
131 T	Ned Yost	.10
132 T	Traded Checklist	.15

1985 Topps.... Complete Set of 792 Cards—Value $120.00

Features the rookie cards of Dwight Gooden, Roger Clemens, Eric Davis, Bret Saberhagen, Mark McGwire, Orel Hershiser, and Kirby Puckett.
Includes players and coaches of the 1984 USA Olympic Baseball Team, "#1 Draft Picks" and a revival of "Father & Son" cards.

NO. PLAYER	MINT
1 Record—C. Fisk	.15
Longest Game, Catcher	
2 Record—S. Garvey	.20
Errorless Games, 18	
3 Record—D. Gooden	.75
Most Strikeouts, Rookie	
4 Record—C. Johnson	.08
Most Pinch Homers	
5 Record—J. Morgan	.15
Most Homers, 2B	
6 Record—P. Rose	.50
Most Singles, Career	
7 Record—N. Ryan	.50
Most Strikeouts, Career	
8 Record—J. Samuel	.15
Stolen Bases, Rookie	
9 Record—B. Sutter	.12
Most Saves, Season	
10 Record—D. Sutton	.12
100 Strikeout Seasons	
11 Ralph Houk (Mgr.)	.05
12 Dave Lopes	.08
13 Tim Lollar	.05
14 Chris Bando	.05
15 Jerry Koosman	.15
16 Bobby Meacham	.05
17 Mike Scott	.30
18 Mickey Hatcher	.05
19 Geroge Frazier	.05
20 Chet Lemon	.08
21 Lee Tunnell	.05
22 Duane Kuiper	.05
23 Bret Saberhagen (R)	5.00
24 Jesse Barfield	.30
25 Steve Bedrosian	.15
26 Ray Smalley	.05
27 Bruce Berenyi	.05
28 Dann Bilardello	.05
29 Odell Jones	.05
30 Cal Ripken	.60
31 Terry Whitfield	.05
32 Chuck Porter	.05
33 Tito Landrum	.05
34 Ed Nunez	.10
35 Graig Nettles	.12
36 Fred Breining	.05
37 Reid Nichols	.05
38 Jackie Moore (Mgr.)	.05
39 Johnny Wockenfuss	.05
40 Phil Niekro	.20
41 Mike Fischlin	.05
42 Luis Sanchez	.05
43 Andre David (R)	.12
44 Dickie Thon	.07
45 Greg Minton	.05
46 Gary Woods	.05
47 Dave Rozema	.05
48 Tony Fernandez	1.25
49 Butch Davis	.08
50 John Candelaria	.08
51 Rob Watson	.05
52 Jerry Dybzinski	.05
53 Tom Gorman	.07
54 Cesar Cedeno	.08
55 Frank Tanana	.05
56 Jim Dwyer	.05

NO. PLAYER	MINT
57 Pat Zachry	.05
58 Orlando Mercado	.05
59 Rick Waits	.05
60 George Hendrick	.08
61 Curt Kaufman (R)	.12
62 Mike Ramsey	.05
63 Steve McCatty	.05
64 Mark Bailey (R)	.12
65 Bill Buckner	.10
66 Dick Williams (Mgr.)	.05
67 Rafael Santana (R)	.12
68 Von Hayes	.15
69 Jim Winn (R)	.12
70 Don Baylor	.10
71 Tim Laudner	.05
72 Rick Sutcliffe	.15
73 Rusty Kuntz	.05
74 Mike Krukow	.05
75 Willie Upshaw	.10
76 Alan Bannister	.05
77 Joe Beckwith	.05
78 Scott Fletcher	.05
79 Rick Mahler	.05
80 Keith Hernandez	.30
81 Lenn Sakata	.05
82 Joe Price	.05
83 Charlie Moore	.05
84 Spike Owen	.05
85 Mike Marshall	.12
86 Don Aase	.05
87 David Green	.05
88 Bryn Smith	.05
89 Jackie Gutierrez (R)	.12
90 Rich Gossage	.15
91 Jeff Burroughs	.05
92 Paul Owens (Mgr.)	.05
93 Don Schulze (R)	.12
94 Toby Harrah	.05
95 Jose Cruz	.08
96 Johnny Ray	.12
97 Pete Filson	.05
98 Steve Lake	.05
99 Milt Wilcox	.05
100 George Brett	.50
101 Jim Acker	.05
102 Tommy Dunbar	.08
103 Randy Lerch	.05
104 Mike Fitzgerald	.07
105 Ron Kittle	.15
106 Pascual Perez	.05
107 Tom Foley	.05
108 Darnell Coles	.15
109 Gary Roenicke	.05
110 Alejandro Pena	.05
111 Doug DeCinces	.10
112 Tom Tellmann	.05
113 Tom Herr	.15
114 Bob James	.05
115 Rickey Henderson	1.50
116 Dennis Boyd	.25
117 Greg Gross	.05
118 Eric Show	.08
119 Pat Corrales (Mgr.)	.05
120 Steve Kemp	.05
121 Checklist No. 1	.08
122 Tom Brunansky	.25

NO. PLAYER	MINT
123 Dave Smith	.05
124 Rich Hebner	.05
125 Ken Tekulve	.05
126 Ruppert Jones	.05
127 Mark Gubicza (R)	1.25
128 Ernie Whitt	.05
129 Gene Garber	.05
130 Al Oliver	.10
131 Father & Son:	.07
Gus and Buddy Bell	
132 Father & Son:	.07
Yogi and Dale Berra	
133 Father & Son:	.07
Ray and Bob Boone	
134 Father & Son:	.07
Tito and Terry Francona	
135 Father & Son:	.07
Bob and Terry Kennedy	
136 Father & Son:	.07
Jim and Jeff Kunkel	
137 Father & Son:	.07
Vern and Vance Law	
138 Father & Son:	.07
Dick and Dick Schofield	
139 Father & Son:	.07
Bob and Joel Skinner	
140 Father & Son:	.07
Roy and Roy Smalley	
141 Father & Son:	.07
Dave and Mike Stenhouse	
142 Father & Son:	.07
Dizzy and Steve Trout	
143 Father & Son:	.07
Ossie and Ozzie Virgil	
144 Ron Gardenhire	.05
145 Alvin Davis (R)	2.00
146 Gary Redus	.08
147 Bill Swaggerty (R)	.12
148 Steve Yeager	.05
149 Dickie Noles	.05
150 Jim Rice	.25
151 Moose Haas	.05
152 Steve Braun	.05
153 Frank LaCorte	.05
154 Argenis Salazar	.08
155 Yogi Berra (Mgr.)	.12
156 Craig Reynolds	.05
157 Tug McGraw	.08
158 Pat Tabler	.05
159 Carlos Diaz	.05
160 Lance Parrish	.20
161 Ken Schrom	.05
162 Benny Distefano (R)	.12
163 Dennis Eckersley	.20
164 Jorge Orta	.05
165 Dusty Baker	.08
166 Keith Atherton	.05
167 Rufino Linares	.05
168 Garth Iorg	.05
169 Dan Spillner	.05
170 George Foster	.15
171 Bill Stein	.05
172 Jack Perconte	.05
173 Mike Young	.10
174 Rick Honeycutt	.05
175 Dave Parker	.25

NO. PLAYER	MINT
176 Bill Schroeder	.05
177 Dave Von Ohlen	.05
178 Miguel Dilone	.05
179 Tommy John	.15
180 Dave Winfield	.40
181 Roger Clemens (R)	12.50
182 Tim Flannery	.05
183 Larry McWilliams	.05
184 Carmen Castillo	.05
185 Al Holland	.05
186 Bob Lillis (Mgr.)	.05
187 Mike Walters	.05
188 Greg Pryor	.05
189 Warren Brusstar	.05
190 Rusty Staub	.12
191 Steve Nicosia	.05
192 Howard Johnson	4.00
193 Jimmy Key (R)	1.00
194 Dave Stegman	.05
195 Glenn Hubbard	.05
196 Pete O'Brien	.10
197 Mike Warren	.05
198 Eddie Milner	.05
199 Denny Martinez	.05
200 Reggie Jackson	.40
201 Burt Hooton	.05
202 Gorman Thomas	.08
203 Bob McClure	.05
204 Art Howe	.05
205 Steve Rogers	.05
206 Phil Garner	.05
207 Mark Clear	.05
208 Champ Summers	.05
209 Bill Campbell	.05
210 Gary Matthews	.08
211 Clay Christiansen (R)	.12
212 George Vukovich	.05
213 Billy Gardner (Mgr.)	.05
214 John Tudor	.15
215 Bob Brenly	.08
216 Jerry Don Gleaton	.05
217 Leon Roberts	.05
218 Doyle Alexander	.05
219 Gerald Perry	.30
220 Fred Lynn	.15
221 Ron Reed	.05
222 Hubie Brooks	.08
223 Tom Hume	.05
224 Al Cowens	.05
225 Mike Boddicker	.10
226 Juan Beniquez	.05
227 Danny Darwin	.05
228 Dion James	.20
229 Dave LaPoint	.05
230 Gary Carter	.35
231 Dwayne Murphy	.08
232 Dave Beard	.05
233 Ed Jurak	.05
234 Jerry Narron	.05
235 Garry Maddox	.05
236 Mark Thurmond	.08
237 Julio Franco	.35
238 Jose Rijo (R)	.50
239 Tim Teufel	.20
240 Dave Stieb	.15
241 Jim Frey (Mgr.)	.05

NO.	PLAYER	MINT
242	Greg Harris	.05
243	Barbaro Garbey (R)	.12
244	Mike Jones	.05
245	Chili Davis	.08
246	Mike Norris	.05
247	Wayne Tolleston	.05
248	Terry Forster	.05
249	Harold Baines	.20
250	Jesse Orosco	.05
251	Brad Gulden	.05
252	Dan Ford	.05
253	Sid Bream (R)	.35
254	Pete Vuckovich	.08
255	Lonnie Smith	.08
256	Mike Stanton	.05
257	Bryan Little	.05
258	Mike Brown	.05
259	Gary Allenson	.05
260	Dave Righetti	.12
261	Checklist No. 2	.08
262	Greg Booker (R)	.12
263	Mel Hall	.10
264	Joe Sambito	.05
265	Juan Samuel	.50
266	Frank Viola	.40
267	Henry Cotto	.12
268	Chuck Tanner (Mgr.)	.05
269	Doug Baker (R)	.12
270	Dan Quisenberry	.15

No. 271 to 282 (# 1 Draft Picks)

NO.	PLAYER	MINT
271	Tim Foli (1968)	.12
272	Jeff Burroughs (1969)	.12
273	Bill Almon (1974)	.12
274	Floyd Bannister (1976)	.12
275	Harold Baines (1977)	.18
276	Bob Horner (1978)	.18
277	Al Chambers (1979)	.12
278	D. Strawberry (1980)	1.00
279	Mike Moore (1981)	.12
280	S. Dunston (R) (1982)	2.50
281	Tim Belcher (R) (1983)	1.00
282	S. Abner (R) (1984)	.35
283	Fran Mullins	.05
284	Marty Bystrom	.05
285	Dan Driessen	.05
286	Rudy Law	.05
287	Walt Terrell	.05
288	Jeff Kunkel (R)	.12
289	Tom Underwood	.05
290	Cecil Cooper	.15
291	Bob Welch	.12
292	Brad Komminsk	.10
293	Curt Young (R)	.30
294	Tom Nieto (R)	.12
295	Joe Niekro	.12
296	Ricky Nelson	.05
297	Gary Lucas	.05
298	Marty Barrett	.12
299	Andy Hawkins	.08
300	Rod Carew	.40
301	John Montefusco	.05
302	Tim Corcoran	.05
303	Mike Jeffcoat	.08
304	Gary Gaetti	.30
305	Dale Berra	.05
306	Rick Reuschel	.10
307	Sparky Anderson (Mgr.)	.05
308	John Wathan	.05
309	Mike Witt	.10
310	Manny Trillo	.05
311	Jim Gott	.05
312	Marc Hill	.05
313	Dave Schmidt	.05
314	Ron Oester	.05
315	Doug Sisk	.05
316	John Lowenstein	.05
317	Jack Lazorko (R)	.12
318	Ted Simmons	.10
319	Jeff Jones	.05
320	Dale Murphy	.60
321	Ricky Horton (R)	.25
322	Dave Stapleton	.05
323	Andy McGaffigan	.05
324	Bruce Bochy	.05
325	John Denny	.05

NO.	PLAYER	MINT
326	Kevin Bass	.15
327	Brook Jacoby	.30
328	Bob Shirley	.05
329	Ron Washington	.05
330	Leon Durham	.15
331	Bill Laskey	.05
332	Brian Harper	.15
333	Willie Hernandez	.15
334	Dick Howser (Mgr.)	.05
335	Bruce Benedict	.05
336	Rance Mulliniks	.05
337	Billy Sample	.05
338	Britt Burns	.05
339	Danny Heep	.05
340	Robin Yount	.50
341	Floyd Rayford	.05
342	Ted Power	.05
343	Bill Russell	.05
344	Dave Henderson	.10
345	Charlie Lea	.05
346	Terry Pendleton (R)	.50
347	Rick Langford	.05
348	Bob Boone	.05
349	Domingo Ramos	.05
350	Wade Boggs	3.00
351	Juan Agosto	.05
352	Joe Morgan	.25
353	Julio Solano (R)	.12
354	Andre Robertson	.05
355	Bert Blyleven	.10
356	Dave Meier (R)	.12
357	Rich Bordi	.05
358	Tony Pena	.12
359	Pat Sheridan	.05
360	Steve Carlton	.35
361	Alfredo Griffin	.05
362	Craig McMurtry	.05
363	Ron Hodges	.05
364	Richard Dotson	.05
365	Danny Ozark (Mgr.)	.05
366	Todd Cruz	.05
367	Keefe Cato (R)	.12
368	Dave Bergman	.05
369	R.J. Reynolds (R)	.25
370	Bruce Sutter	.15
371	Mickey Rivers	.05
372	Roy Howell	.05
373	Mike Moore	.07
374	Brian Downing	.05
375	Jeff Reardon	.15
376	Jeff Newman	.05
377	Checklist No. 3	.08
378	Alan Wiggins	.08
379	Charles Hudson	.05
380	Ken Griffey	.08
381	Roy Smith (R)	.12
382	Denny Walling	.05
383	Rick Lysander	.05
384	Jody Davis	.10
385	Jose DeLeon	.05
386	Dan Gladden (R)	.40
387	Buddy Biancalana	.12
388	Bert Roberge	.05

No. 389 to 404 (U.S. Olympic Team)

NO.	PLAYER	MINT
389	Rod Dedeaux (Coach)	.10
390	Sid Akins	.10
391	Flavio Alfaro	.10
392	Don August	.25
393	Scott Bankhead	.75
394	Bob Caffrey	.10
395	Mike Dunne (R)	.25
396	Gary Green	.10
397	John Hoover	.10
398	Shane Mack	.40
399	John Marzano (R)	.35
400	Oddibe McDowell (R)	.60
401	Mark McGwire (R)	20.00
402	Pat Pacillo (R)	.15
403	Cory Snyder (R)	4.00
404	Billy Swift	.20
405	Tom Veryzer	.05
406	Len Whitehouse	.05
407	Bobby Ramos	.05
408	Sid Monge	.05
409	Brad Wellman	.05

NO.	PLAYER	MINT
410	Bob Horner	.20
411	Bobby Cox (Mgr.)	.05
412	Bud Black	.05
413	Vance Law	.05
414	Gary Ward	.05
415	Ron Darling	1.00
416	Wayne Gross	.05
417	John Franco (R)	1.00
418	Ken Landreaux	.05
419	Mike Caldwell	.05
420	Andre Dawson	.35
421	Dave Rucker	.05
422	Carney Lansford	.10
423	Barry Bonnell	.05
424	Al Nipper (R)	.15
425	Mike Hargrove	.05
426	Vern Ruhle	.05
427	Mario Ramirez	.05
428	Larry Andersen	.05
429	Rick Cerone	.05
430	Ron Davis	.05
431	U.L. Washington	.05
432	Thad Bosley	.05
433	Jim Morrison	.05
434	Gene Richards	.05
435	Dan Petry	.12
436	Willie Aikens	.05
437	Al Jones (R)	.12
438	Joe Torre (Mgr.)	.07
439	Junior Ortiz	.05
440	Fernando Valenzuela	.30
441	Duane Walker	.05
442	Ken Forsch	.05
443	George Wright	.05
444	Tony Phillips	.05
445	Tippy Martinez	.05
446	Jim Sundberg	.05
447	Jeff Lahti	.05
448	Derrel Thomas	.05
449	Phil Bradley	.75
450	Steve Garvey	.40
451	Bruce Hurst	.05
452	John Castino	.05
453	Tom Waddell (R)	.12
454	Glenn Wilson	.10
455	Bob Knepper	.05
456	Tim Foli	.05
457	Cecillio Guante	.05
458	Randy Johnson	.05
459	Charlie Leibrandt	.05
460	Ryne Sandberg	1.50
461	Marty Castillo	.05
462	Gary Lavelle	.05
463	Dave Collins	.05
464	Mike Mason (R)	.12
465	Bob Grich	.07
466	Tony LaRussa (Mgr.)	.05
467	Ed Lynch	.05
468	Wayne Krenchicki	.05
469	Sammy Stewart	.05
470	Steve Sax	.25
471	Pete Ladd	.05
472	Jim Essian	.05
473	Tim Wallach	.12
474	Kurt Kepshire (R)	.12
475	Andre Thornton	.08
476	Jeff Stone (R)	.12
477	Bob Ojeda	.05
478	Kurt Bevacqua	.05
479	Mike Madden	.05
480	Lou Whitaker	.15
481	Dale Murray	.05
482	Harry Spilman	.05
483	Mike Smithson	.05
484	Larry Bowa	.05
485	Matt Young	.06
486	Steve Balboni	.06
487	Frank Williams (R)	.12
488	Joel Skinner	.10
489	Bryan Clark	.05
490	Jason Thompson	.08
491	Rick Camp	.05
492	Dave Johnson (Mgr.)	.20
493	Orel Hershiser (R)	5.00
494	Rich Dauer	.05

NO.	PLAYER	MINT
495	Mario Soto	.08
496	Donnie Scott (R)	.12
497	Gary Pettis (wrong photo—It's his brother—Lynn)	.25
498	Ed Romero	.05
499	Danny Cox	.25
500	Mike Schmidt	.75
501	Dan Schatzeder	.05
502	Rick Miller	.05
503	Tim Conroy	.05
504	Jerry Willard	.08
505	Jim Beattie	.05
506	Franklin Stubbs (R)	.40
507	Ray Fontenot	.05
508	John Shelby	.05
509	Milt May	.05
510	Kent Hrbek	.30
511	Lee Smith	.08
512	Tom Brookens	.05
513	Lynn Jones	.05
514	Jeff Cornell (R)	.12
515	Dave Concepcion	.08
516	Roy Lee Jackson	.05
517	Jerry Martin	.05
518	Chris Chambliss	.05
519	Doug Rader (Mgr.)	.05
520	LaMarr Hoyt	.08
521	Rick Dempsey	.05
522	Paul Molitor	.20
523	Candy Maldonado	.15
524	Rob Wilfong	.05
525	Darrell Porter	.05
526	Dave Palmer	.05
527	Checklist No. 4	.08
528	Bill Krueger	.05
529	Rich Gedman	.08
530	Dave Dravecky	.08
531	Joe Lefebvre	.25
532	Frank DiPino	.05
533	Tony Bernazard	.05
534	Brian Dayett	.08
535	Pat Putnam	.05
536	Kirby Puckett (R)	15.00
537	Don Robinson	.05
538	Keith Moreland	.05
539	Aurelio Lopez	.05
540	Claudell Washington	.08
541	Mark Davis	.10
542	Don Slaught	.05
543	Mike Squires	.05
544	Bruce Kison	.05
545	Lloyd Moseby	.15
546	Brent Gaff	.08
547	Pete Rose (Mgr.)	.50
548	Larry Parrish	.07
549	Mike Scioscia	.05
550	Scott McGregor	.07
551	Andy Van Slyke	.35
552	Chris Codiroli	.05
553	Bob Clark	.05
554	Doug Flynn	.05
555	Bob Stanley	.05
556	Sixto Lezcano	.05
557	Len Barker	.05
558	Carmelo Martinez	.05
559	Jay Howell	.05
560	Bill Madlock	.15
561	Darryl Motley	.05
562	Houston Jimenez	.05
563	Dick Ruthven	.05
564	Alan Ashby	.05
565	Kirk Gibson	.35
566	Ed Vande Berg	.05
567	Joel Youngblood	.05
568	Cliff Johnson	.05
569	Ken Oberkfell	.05
570	Darryl Strawberry	3.00
571	Charlie Hough	.05
572	Tom Paciorek	.05
573	Jay Tibbs (R)	.12
574	Joe Altobelli (Mgr.)	.05
575	Pedro Guerrero	.25
576	Jaime Cocanower (R)	.12
577	Chris Speier	.05

NO.	PLAYER	MINT
578	Terry Francona	.05
579	Ron Romanick (R)	.12
580	Dwight Evans	.12
581	Mark Wagner	.05
582	Ken Phelps	.20
583	Bobby Brown	.05
584	Kevin Gross	.05
585	Butch Wynegar	.05
586	Bill Scherrer	.05
587	Doug Frobel	.05
588	Bobby Castillo	.05
589	Bob Dernier	.05
590	Ray Knight	.05
591	Larry Herndon	.05
592	Jeff Robinson (R)	.30
593	Rick Leach	.05
594	Curt Wilkerson	.08
595	Larry Gura	.05
596	Jerry Hairston	.05
597	Brad Lesley	.05
598	Jose Oquendo	.05
599	Storm Davis	.08
600	Pete Rose	1.00
601	Tom Lasorda (Mgr.)	.08
602	Jeff Dedmon (R)	.12
603	Rick Manning	.05
604	Daryl Sconiers	.05
605	Ozzie Smith	.30
606	Rich Gale	.05
607	Bill Almon	.05
608	Craig Lefferts	.05
609	Broderick Perkins	.05
610	Jack Morris	.25
611	Ozzie Virgil	.05
612	Mike Armstrong	.05
613	Terry Puhl	.05
614	Al Williams	.05
615	Marvell Wynne	.05
616	Scott Sanderson	.05
617	Willie Wilson	.15
618	Pete Falcone	.05
619	Jeff Leonard	.05
620	Dwight Gooden (R)	9.00
621	Marvis Foley	.05
622	Luis Leal	.05
623	Greg Walker	.12
624	Benny Ayala	.05
625	Mark Langston (R)	2.00
626	German Rivera (R)	.15
627	Eric Davis (R)	13.00
628	R. Lachemann (Mgr.)	.05
629	Dick Schofield	.12
630	Tim Raines	.40
631	Bob Forsch	.05

NO.	PLAYER	MINT
632	Bruce Bochte	.05
633	Glenn Hoffman	.05
634	Bill Dawley	.05
635	Terry Kennedy	.08
636	Shane Rawley	.05
637	Brett Butler	.08
638	Mike Pagliarulo (R)	.40
639	Ed Hodge (R)	.12
640	Steve Henderson	.05
641	Rod Scurry	.05
642	Dave Owen (R)	.12
643	Johnny Grubb	.05
644	Mark Huismann	.10
645	Damaso Garcia	.08
646	Scot Thompson	.05
647	Rafael Ramierz	.05
648	Bob Jones	.05
649	Sid Fernandez	1.00
650	Greg Luzinski	.08
651	Jeff Russell	.05
652	Joe Nolan	.05
653	Mark Brouhard	.05
654	Dave Anderson	.05
655	Joaquin Andujar	.08
656	Chuck Cottier (Mgr.)	.05
657	Jim Slaton	.05
658	Mike Stenhouse	.08
659	Checklist No. 5	.08
660	Tony Gwynn	1.00
661	Steve Crawford	.05
662	Mike Heath	.05
663	Luis Aguayo	.05
664	Steve Farr	.20
665	Don Mattingly	8.00
666	Mike LaCoss	.05
667	Dave Engle	.05
668	Steve Trout	.05
669	Lee Lacy	.05
670	Tom Seaver	.35
671	Dane Iorg	.05
372	Juan Berenguer	.05
673	Buck Martinez	.05
674	Atlee Hammaker	.05
675	Tony Perez	.15
676	Albert Hall (R)	.12
677	Wally Backman	.05
678	Joey McLaughlin	.05
679	Bob Kearney	.05
680	Jerry Reuss	.05
681	Ben Oglivie	.05
682	Doug Corbett	.05
683	Whitey Herzog (Mgr.)	.05
684	Bill Doran	.10
685	Bill Caudill	.08

NO.	PLAYER	MINT
686	Mike Easler	.05
687	Bill Gullickson	.05
688	Len Matuszek	.05
689	Luis DeLeon	.05
690	Alan Trammell	.30
691	Dennis Rasmussen	.25
692	Randy Bush	.05
693	Tim Stoddard	.05
694	Joe Carter	3.00
695	Rick Rhoden	.05
696	John Rabb	.05
697	Onix Concepcion	.05
698	Jorge Bell	.50
699	Donnie Moore	.08
700	Eddie Murray	.45
701	Eddie Murray (AS)	.20
702	Damaso Garcia (AS)	.10
703	George Brett (AS)	.30
704	Cal Ripken (AS)	.25
705	Dave Winfield (AS)	.20
706	Rickey Henderson (AS)	.50
707	Tony Armas (AS)	.10
708	Lance Parrish (AS)	.15
709	Mike Boddicker (AS)	.10
710	Frank Viola (AS)	.10
711	Dan Quisenberry (AS)	.15
712	Keith Hernandez (AS)	.20
713	Ryne Sandberg (AS)	.35
714	Mike Schmidt (AS)	.40
715	Ozzie Smith (AS)	.10
716	Dale Murphy (AS)	.30
717	Tony Gwynn (AS)	.25
718	Jeff Leonard (AS)	.10
719	Gary Carter (AS)	.20
720	Rick Sutcliffe (AS)	.15
721	Bob Knepper (AS)	.10
722	Bruce Sutter (AS)	.15
723	Dave Stewart	.35
724	Oscar Gamble	.05
725	Floyd Bannister	.05
726	Al Bumbry	.05
727	Frank Pastore	.05
728	Bob Bailor	.05
729	Don Sutton	.20
730	Dave Kingman	.10
731	Neil Allen	.05
732	John McNamara (Mgr.)	.05
733	Tony Scott	.05
734	John Henry Johnson	.05
735	Garry Templeton	.10
736	Jerry Mumphrey	.05
737	Bo Diaz	.05
738	Omar Moreno	.05
739	Ernie Camacho	.05

NO.	PLAYER	MINT
740	Jack Clark	.30
741	John Butcher	.05
742	Ron Hassey	.05
743	Frank White	.05
744	Doug Bair	.05
745	Buddy Bell	.10
746	Jim Clancy	.05
747	Alex Trevino	.05
748	Lee Mazzilli	.05
749	Julio Cruz	.05
750	Rollie Fingers	.15
751	Kelvin Chapman (R)	.12
752	Bob Owchinko	.05
753	Greg Brock	.08
754	Larry Milbourne	.05
755	Ken Singleton	.08
756	Rob Picciolo	.05
757	Willie McGee	.35
758	Ray Burris	.05
759	Jim Fanning (Mgr.)	.05
760	Nolan Ryan	1.50
761	Jerry Remy	.05
762	Eddie Whitson	.05
763	Kiko Garcia	.05
764	Jamie Easterly	.05
765	Willie Randolph	.05
766	Paul Mirabella	.05
767	Darrell Brown	.05
768	Ron Cey	.10
769	Joe Cowley	.05
770	Carlton Fisk	.25
771	Geoff Zahn	.05
772	Johnnie LeMaster	.05
773	Hal McRae	.05
774	Dennis Lamp	.05
775	Mookie Wilson	.08
776	Jerry Royster	.05
777	Ned Yost	.05
778	Mike Davis	.08
779	Nick Esasky	.15
780	Mike Flanagan	.05
781	Jim Gantner	.05
782	Tom Niedenfuer	.05
783	Mike Jorgensen	.05
784	Checklist No. 6	.08
785	Tony Armas	.12
786	Enos Cabell	.05
787	Jim Wohlford	.05
788	Steve Comer	.05
789	Luis Salazar	.05
790	Ron Guidry	.15
791	Ivan DeJesus	.05
792	Darrell Evans	.12

1985 Topps Traded.... Complete Set of 132 Cards—Value $20.00

Updates the main 1985 card set with players who changed teams during the season and rookies who joined their teams early in the season. Features the first Topps card of Vince Coleman, Tom Browning and Teddy Higuera. The complete set was packaged in a printed box and only distributed through card hobby dealers. Topps also tested a small quantity of wax packs. A "Tiffany" version of the set was also issued.

NO.	PLAYER	MINT
1 T	Don Aase	.08
2 T	Bill Almon	.06
3 T	Benny Ayala	.06
4 T	Dusty Baker	.12

NO.	PLAYER	MINT
5 T	G. Bamberger (Mgr.)	.06
6 T	Dale Berra	.10
7 T	Rich Bordi	.06
8 T	Daryl Boston (RR)	.25

NO.	PLAYER	MINT
9 T	Hubie Brooks	.12
10 T	Chris Brown (RR)	.15
11 T	T. Browning (RR)	1.00
12 T	Al Bumbry	.06

NO.	PLAYER	MINT
13 T	Ray Burris	.06
14 T	Jeff Burroughs	.06
15 T	Bill Campbell	.06
16 T	Don Carman	.25

1985 Topps Traded (Continued)

NO.	PLAYER	MINT
17 T	Gary Carter	.75
18 T	Bobby Castillo	.06
19 T	Bill Caudill	.10
20 T	Rick Cerone	.08
21 T	Bryan Clark	.06
22 T	Jack Clark	.40
23 T	Pat Clements	.15
24 T	V. Coleman (RR)	6.00
25 T	Dave Collins	.08
26 T	Dave Darwin	.06
27 T	J. Davenport (Mgr.)	.06
28 T	Jerry Davis	.12
29 T	Brian Dayett	.06
30 T	Ivan DeJesus	.06
31 T	Ken Dixon	.15
32 T	M. Duncan (RR)	.75
33 T	John Felske (Mgr.)	.06
34 T	Mike Fitzgerald	.06
35 T	Ray Fontenot	.06
36 T	Greg Gagne	.30
37 T	Oscar Gamble	.10
38 T	Scott Garrelts (RR)	.75
39 T	Bob Gibson	.06
40 T	Jim Gott	.06
41 T	David Green	.12
42 T	Alfredo Griffin	.12
43 T	Ozzie Guillen (RR)	2.00
44 T	Eddie Haas (Mgr.)	.06
45 T	Terry Harper	.06

NO.	PLAYER	MINT
46 T	Toby Harrah	.08
47 T	Greg Harris	.06
48 T	Ron Hassey	.06
49 T	Rickey Henderson	3.00
50 T	Steve Henderson	.06
51 T	George Hendrik	.12
52 T	Joe Hesketh (RR)	.15
53 T	T. Higuera (RR)	2.00
54 T	Donnie Hill	.06
55 T	Al Holland	.08
56 T	Burt Hooton	.06
57 T	Jay Howell	.08
58 T	Ken Howell	.20
59 T	LaMarr Hoyt	.12
60 T	Tim Hulett	.12
61 T	Bob James	.06
62 T	Steve Jeltz (RR)	.20
63 T	Cliff Johnson	.06
64 T	Howard Johnson	2.00
65 T	Ruppert Jones	.08
66 T	Steve Kemp	.06
67 T	Bruce Kison	.06
68 T	Alan Knicely	.06
69 T	Mike LaCoss	.06
70 T	Lee Lacy	.08
71 T	Dave LaPoint	.06
72 T	Gary Lavelle	.06
73 T	Vance Law	.06
74 T	Johnnie LeMaster	.06

NO.	PLAYER	MINT
75 T	Sixto Lezcano	.06
76 T	Tim Lollar	.06
77 T	Fred Lynn	.20
78 T	Billy Martin (Mgr.)	.15
79 T	Ron Mathis	.15
80 T	Len Matuszek	.06
81 T	Gene Mauch (Mgr.)	.06
82 T	Oddibe McDowell	.50
83 T	R. McDowell (RR)	1.00
84 T	J. McNamara (Mgr.)	.06
85 T	Donnie Moore	.08
86 T	Gene Nelson	.06
87 T	Steve Nicosia	.06
88 T	Al Oliver	.12
89 T	Joe Orsulak	.25
90 T	Rob Picciolo	.06
91 T	Chris Pittaro	.15
92 T	Jim Presley (RR)	.75
93 T	Rick Reuschel	.15
94 T	Bert Roberge	.06
95 T	Bob Rodgers (Mgr.)	.06
96 T	Jerry Royster	.06
97 T	Dave Rozema	.06
98 T	Dave Rucker	.06
99 T	Vern Ruhle	.06
100 T	Paul Runge	.15
101 T	Mark Salas (R)	.15
102 T	Luis Salazar	.06
103 T	Joe Sambito	.08

NO.	PLAYER	MINT
104 T	Rick Schu	.15
105 T	Donnie Scott	.06
106 T	Larry Sheets	.35
107 T	Don Slaught	.06
108 T	Roy Smalley	.08
109 T	Lonnie Smith	.12
110 T	Nate Snell	.15
111 T	Chris Speier	.06
112 T	Mike Stenhouse	.06
113 T	Tim Stoddard	.06
114 T	Jim Sundberg	.08
115 T	Bruce Sutter	.25
116 T	Don Sutton	.50
117 T	Kent Tekulve	.08
118 T	Tom Tellmann	.06
119 T	Walt Terrell	.15
120 T	Mickey Tettleton (RR)	.75
121 T	Derrel Thomas	.06
122 T	Rich Thompson	.15
123 T	Alex Trevino	.06
124 T	John Tudor	.20
125 T	Jose Uribe	.30
126 T	B. Valentine (Mgr.)	.10
127 T	Dave Von Ohlen	.06
128 T	U.L. Washington	.06
129 T	Earl Weaver (Mgr.)	.12
130 T	Eddie Whitson	.08
131 T	Herm Winningham	.15
132 T	Traded Checklist	.10

1986 Topps.... Complete Set of 792 Cards—Value $50.00

Features the rookie cards of Vince Coleman and Teddy Higuera. There are no card numbers 51 or 171. They were given wrong numbers in error. A "Tiffany" version of the set was also issued.

VINCE COLEMAN

TEDDY HIGUERA

ROGER McDOWELL

LEN DYKSTRA

HAROLD REYNOLDS

NO.	PLAYER	MINT
1	Pete Rose	1.00
2	Rose (Years 1963-66)	.35
3	Rose (Years 1967-70)	.35
4	Rose (Years 1971-74)	.35
5	Rose (Years 1975-78)	.35
6	Rose (Years 1979-82)	.35
7	Rose (Years 1983-85)	.35
8	Dwayne Murphy	.08
9	Roy Smith	.04
10	Tony Gwynn	.50
11	Bob Ojeda	.05
12	Jose Uribe (R)	.30
13	Bob Kearney	.04
14	Julio Cruz	.04
15	Eddie Whitson	.06
16	Rick Schu	.10
17	Mike Stenhouse	.04
18	Brent Gaff	.04
19	Rich Hebner	.04
20	Lou Whitaker	.15
21	G. Bamberger (Mgr.)	.04
	Brewers Checklist	
22	Duane Walker	.08
23	Manny Lee	.15
24	Len Barker	.06
25	Willie Wilson	.20
26	Frank DePino	.04
27	Ray Knight	.06

NO.	PLAYER	MINT
28	Eric Davis	2.50
29	Tony Phillips	.04
30	Eddie Murray	.40
31	Jamie Easterly	.04
32	Steve Yeager	.06
33	Jeff Lahti	.04
34	Ken Phelps	.04
35	Jeff Reardon	.12
36	Tigers Leaders:	.15
	Lance Parrish	
37	Mark Thurmond	.04
38	Glenn Hoffman	.04
39	Dave Rucker	.04
40	Ken Griffey	.10
41	Brad Wellman	.04
42	Geoff Zahn	.04
43	Dave Engle	.04
44	Lance McCullers (R)	.30
45	Damaso Garcia	.12
46	Billy Hatcher	.20
47	Juan Berenguer	.04
48	Bill Almon	.04
49	Rick Manning	.04
50	Dan Quisenberry	.15
51	Rob Wine (Mgr.)	.08
	Braves Checklist	
	Error-reads card no. 57	
52	Chris Welsh	.04

NO.	PLAYER	MINT
53	Len Dykstra (R)	3.00
54	John Franco	.08
55	Fred Lynn	.20
56	Tom Niedenfuer	.08
57	Bill Doran	.08
58	Bill Krueger	.04
59	Andre Thornton	.08
60	Dwight Evans	.12
61	Karl Best	.12
62	Bob Boone	.04
63	Ron Roenicke	.04
64	Floyd Bannister	.04
65	Dan Driessen	.04
66	Cardinals Leaders:	.08
	Bob Forsch	
67	Carmelo Martinez	.04
68	Ed Lynch	.04
69	Luis Aguayo	.04
70	Dave Winfield	.30
71	Ken Schrom	.04
72	Shawon Dunston	.40
73	Randy O'Neal	.08
74	Rance Mulliniks	.04
75	Jose DeLeon	.04
76	Dion James	.04
77	Charlie Leibrandt	.06
78	Bruce Benedict	.04
79	Dave Schmidt	.04

NO.	PLAYER	MINT
80	Darryl Strawberry	1.00
81	Gene Mauch (Mgr.)	.08
	Angels Checklist	
82	Tippy Martinez	.04
83	Phil Garner	.04
84	Curt Young	.04
85	Tony Perez	.25
86	Tom Waddell	.04
87	Candy Maldonado	.04
88	Tom Nieto	.04
89	Randy St. Claire	.08
90	Garry Templeton	.15
91	Steve Crawford	.04
92	Al Cowens	.04
93	Scot Thompson	.04
94	Rich Bordi	.04
95	Ozzie Virgil	.04
96	Blue Jays Leaders:	.06
	Jim Clancy	
97	Gary Gaetti	.15
98	Dick Ruthven	.04
99	Buddy Biancalana	.04
100	Nolan Ryan	1.50
101	Dave Bergman	.04
102	Joe Orsulak (R)	.20
103	Luis Salazar	.04
104	Sid Fernandez	.15
105	Gary Ward	.04

NO.	PLAYER	MINT
106	Ray Burris	.04
107	Rafael Ramirez	.04
108	Ted Power	.04
109	Len Matuszek	.04
110	Scott McGregor	.06
111	Roger Craig (Mgr.)	.08
	Giants Checklist	
112	Bill Campbell	.04
113	U.L. Washington	.04
114	Mike Brown	.04
115	Jay Howell	.04
116	Brook Jacoby	.10
117	Bruce Kison	.04
118	Jerry Royster	.04
119	Barry Bonnell	.04
120	Steve Carlton	.30
121	Nelson Simmons	.15
122	Pete Filson	.04
123	Greg Walker	.10
124	Luis Sanchez	.04
125	Dave Lopes	.06
126	Mets Leaders:	.08
	Mookie Wilson	
127	Jack Howell (R)	.30
128	John Wathan	.04
129	Jeff Dedmon	.04
130	Alan Trammell	.20
131	Checklist No. 1	.08
132	Razor Shines	.08
133	Andy McGaffigan	.04
134	Carney Lansford	.08
135	Joe Niekro	.08
136	Mike Hargrove	.04
137	Charlie Moore	.04
138	Mark Davis	.10
139	Daryl Boston	.20
140	John Candelaria	.08
141	Chuck Cottier (Mgr.)	.08
	Mariners Checklist	
	see card 171	
142	Bob Jones	.04
143	Dave Van Gorder	.04
144	Doug Sisk	.04
145	Pedro Guerrero	.20
146	Jack Perconte	.04
147	Larry Sheets	.15
148	Mike Heath	.04
149	Brett Butler	.10
150	Joaquin Andujar	.08
151	Dave Stapleton	.04
152	Mike Morgan	.04
153	Ricky Adams	.04
154	Bert Roberge	.04
155	Bob Grich	.06
156	White Sox Leaders:	.08
	Richard Dotson	
157	Ron Hassey	.04
158	Derrel Thomas	.04
159	Orel Hershiser	.75
160	Chet Lemon	.06
161	Lee Tunnell	.04
162	Greg Gagne	.12
163	Pete Ladd	.04
164	Steve Balboni	.08
165	Mike Davis	.06
166	Dickie Thon	.04
167	Zane Smith	.30
168	Jeff Burroughs	.04
169	George Wright	.04
170	Gary Carter	.30
171	Bob Rodgers (Mgr.)	.08
	Expo Checklist	
	error—reads #141	
172	Jerry Reed	.15
173	Wayne Gross	.04
174	Brian Snyder	.15
175	Steve Sax	.15
176	Jay Tibbs	.04
177	Joel Youngblood	.04
178	Ivan DeJesus	.04
179	Stu Cliburn	.15
180	Don Mattingly	3.00
181	Al Nipper	.04
182	Bobby Brown	.04
183	Larry Andersen	.04
184	Tim Laudner	.04
185	Rollie Fingers	.15
186	Astros Leaders:	.08
	Jose Cruz	
187	Scott Fletcher	.04
188	Bob Dernier	.04
189	Mike Mason	.04
190	George Hendrick	.08
191	Wally Backman	.04
192	Milt Wilcox	.04
193	Daryl Sconiers	.04
194	Craig McMurtry	.04
195	Dave Concepcion	.08
196	Doyle Alexander	.04
197	Enos Cabell	.04
198	Ken Dixon	.08
199	Dick Howser (Mgr.)	.08
	(Royals Checklist)	
200	Mike Schmidt	.75
201	Record—V. Coleman	.30
	Most Stolen Bases—	
	Season, Rookie	
202	Record—D. Gooden	.40
	Youngest 20-Game Winner	
203	Rec.—K. Hernandez	.15
	Most Game Winning RBI,	
	Season	
204	Record—Phil Niekro	.15
	Oldest Shutout Pitcher	
205	Record—Tony Perez	.12
	Oldest to Hit Grand Slam	
206	Record—Pete Rose	.40
	Most Hits, Career	
207	Record—F. Valenzuela	.15
	Most Consecutive Innings,	
	No Earned Runs	
208	Ramon Romero	.15
209	Randy Ready	.10
210	Calvin Schiraldi	.10
211	Ed Wojna	.15
212	Chris Speier	.04
213	Bob Shirley	.04
214	Randy Bush	.04
215	Frank White	.04
216	A's Leaders:	.08
	Dwayne Murphy	
217	Bill Scherrer	.04
218	Randy Hunt	.12
219	Dennis Lamp	.04
220	Bob Horner	.15
221	Dave Henderson	.15
222	Craig Gerber	.15
223	Atlee Hammaker	.06
224	Cesar Cedeno	.08
225	Ron Darling	.20
226	Lee Lacy	.04
227	Al Jones	.04
228	Tom Lawless	.04
229	Bill Gullickson	.04
230	Terry Kennedy	.06
231	Jim Frey (Mgr.)	.08
	Cubs Checklist	
232	Rick Rhoden	.04
233	Steve Lyons	.10
234	Doug Corbett	.04
235	Butch Wynegar	.06
236	Frank Eufemia	.15
237	Ted Simmons	.15
238	Larry Parrish	.06
239	Joel Skinner	.04
240	Tommy John	.15
241	Tony Fernandez	.20
242	Rich Thompson	.12
243	Johnny Grubb	.04
244	Craig Lefferts	.04
245	Jim Sundberg	.04
246	Phillies Leaders:	.15
	Steve Carlton	
247	Terry Harper	.04
248	Spike Owen	.04
249	Rob Deer	.40
250	Dwight Gooden	1.50
251	Rich Dauer	.04
252	Bobby Castillo	.04
253	Dann Bilardello	.04
254	Ozzie Guillen (R)	.75
255	Tony Armas	.10
256	Kurt Kepshire	.04
257	Doug DeCinces	.08
258	Tim Burke (R)	.25
259	Dan Pasqua	.20
260	Tony Pena	.10
261	Bobby Valentine (Mgr.)	.08
	Rangers Checklist	
262	Mario Ramirez	.04
263	Checklist No. 2	.08
264	Darren Daulton (R)	.30
265	Ron Davis	.04
266	Keith Moreland	.04
267	Paul Molitor	.15
268	Mike Scott	.25
269	Dane Iorg	.04
270	Jack Morris	.15
271	Dave Collins	.04
272	Tim Tolman	.15
273	Jerry Willard	.04
274	Ron Gardenhire	.04
275	Charlie Hough	.04
276	Yankees Leaders:	.10
	Willie Randolph	
277	Jaime Cocanower	.04
278	Sixto Lezcano	.04
279	Al Pardo	.15
280	Tim Raines	.25
281	Steve Mura	.04
282	Jerry Mumphrey	.04
283	Mike Fischlin	.04
284	Brian Dayett	.04
285	Buddy Bell	.10
286	Luis DeLeon	.04
287	John Christensen	.15
288	Don Aase	.04
289	Johnnie LeMaster	.04
290	Carlton Fisk	.35
291	Tom Lasorda (Mgr.)	.12
	Dodgers Checklist	
292	Chuck Porter	.04
293	Chris Chambliss	.06
294	Danny Cox	.10
295	Kirk Gibson	.30
296	Geno Petralli	.08
297	Tim Lollar	.04
298	Craig Reynolds	.04
299	Bryn Smith	.04
300	George Brett	.50
301	Dennis Rasmussen	.04
302	Greg Gross	.04
303	Curt Wardle	.15
304	Mike Gallego	.15
305	Phil Bradley	.15
306	Padres Leaders:	.08
	Terry Kennedy	
307	Dave Sax	.08
308	Ray Fontenot	.04
309	John Shelby	.04
310	Greg Minton	.04
311	Dick Schofield	.04
312	Tom Filer	.04
313	Joe De Sa	.15
314	Frank Pastore	.04
315	Mookie Wilson	.06
316	Sammy Khalifa	.15
317	Ed Romero	.04
318	Terry Whitfield	.04
319	Rick Camp	.04
320	Jim Rice	.25
321	Earl Weaver (Mgr.)	.12
	Orioles Checklist	
322	Bob Forsch	.04
323	Jerry Davis	.08
324	Dan Schatzeder	.04
325	Juan Beniquez	.04
326	Kent Tekulve	.04
327	Mike Pagliarulo	.12
328	Pete O'Brien	.12
329	Kirby Puckett	2.50
330	Rick Sutcliffe	.12
331	Alan Ashby	.04
332	Darryl Motley	.04
333	Tom Henke	.25
334	Ken Oberkfell	.04
335	Don Sutton	.20
336	Indians Leaders:	.08
	Andre Thornton	
337	Darnell Coles	.04
338	Jorge Bell	.30
339	Bruce Berenyi	.04
340	Cal Ripken	.40
341	Frank Williams	.04
342	Gary Redus	.04
343	Carlos Diaz	.04
344	Jim Wohlford	.04
345	Donnie Moore	.04
346	Bryan Little	.04
347	Teddy Higuera (R)	1.00
348	Cliff Johnson	.04
349	Mark Clear	.04
350	Jack Clark	.25
351	Chuck Tanner (Mgr.)	.08
	Pirates Checklist	
352	Harry Spilman	.04
353	Keith Atherton	.04
354	Tony Bernazard	.04
355	Lee Smith	.06
356	Mickey Hatcher	.04
357	Ed VandeBerg	.04
358	Rick Dempsey	.04
359	Mike LaCoss	.04
360	Lloyd Moseby	.15
361	Shane Rawley	.04
362	Tom Paciorek	.04
363	Terry Forster	.06
364	Reid Nichols	.04
365	Mike Flanagan	.06
366	Reds Leaders:	.10
	Dave Concepcion	
367	Aurelio Lopez	.04
368	Greg Brock	.06
369	Al Holland	.04
370	Vince Coleman (R)	2.50
371	Bill Stein	.04
372	Ben Ogilvie	.06
373	Urbano Lugo	.15
374	Terry Francona	.06
375	Rich Gedman	.06
376	Bill Dawley	.04
377	Joe Carter	.35
378	Bruce Bochte	.04
379	Bobby Meacham	.04
380	LaMarr Hoyt	.10
381	Ray Miller (Mgr.)	.08
	Twins Checklist	
382	Ivan Calderon (R)	.75
383	Chris Brown (R)	.20
384	Steve Trout	.04
385	Cecil Cooper	.15
386	Cecil Fielder (R)	7.00
387	Steve Kemp	.06
388	Dickie Noles	.04
389	Glenn Davis	3.00
390	Tom Seaver	.40
391	Julio Franco	.15
392	John Russell	.08
393	Chris Pittaro	.15
394	Checklist No. 3	.08
395	Scott Garrelts	.30
396	Red Sox Leaders:	.08
	Dwight Evans	
397	Steve Buechele (R)	.20
398	Earnie Riles (R)	.25
399	Bill Swift	.04
400	Rod Carew	.40
401	Turn Back the Clock:	.15
	F. Valenzuela (1981)	
402	Turn Back the Clock:	.15
	Tom Seaver (1976)	
403	Turn Back the Clock:	.15
	Willie Mays (1971)	
404	Turn Back the Clock:	.15
	Frank Robinson (1966)	
405	Turn Back the Clock:	.15
	Roger Maris (1961)	
406	Scott Sanderson	.04
407	Sal Butera	.04
408	Dave Smith	.04

NO.	PLAYER	MINT
409	Paul Runge (R)	.15
410	Dave Kingman	.10
411	Sparky Anderson (Mgr.)	.10
	Tigers Checklist	
412	Jim Clancy	.04
413	Tim Flannery	.04
414	Tom Gorman	.04
415	Hal McRae	.04
416	Denny Martinez	.04
417	R.J. Reynolds	.04
418	Alan Knicely	.04
419	Frank Wills	.15
420	Von Hayes	.15
421	Dave Palmer	.04
422	Mike Jorgensen	.04
423	Dan Spillner	.04
424	Rick Miller	.04
425	Larry McWilliams	.04
426	Brewers Leaders:	.04
	Charlie Moore	
427	Joe Cowley	.04
428	Max Venable	.04
429	Greg Booker	.04
430	Kent Hrbek	.25
431	George Frazier	.04
432	Mark Bailey	.04
433	Chirs Codiroli	.04
434	Curt Wilkerson	.04
435	Bill Caudill	.04
436	Doug Flynn	.04
437	Rick Mahler	.04
438	Clint Hurdle	.04
439	Rick Honeycutt	.04
440	Alvin Davis	.20
441	Whitey Herzog (Mgr.)	.10
	Cardinals Checklist	
442	Ron Robinson	.20
443	Bill Buckner	.08
444	Alex Trevino	.04
445	Bert Blyleven	.10
446	Lenn Sakata	.04
447	Jerry Don Gleaton	.04
448	Herm Winningham	.15
449	Rod Scurry	.04
450	Graig Nettles	.15
451	Mark Brown	.15
452	Bob Clark	.04
453	Steve Jeltz	.10
454	Burt Hooton	.04
455	Willie Randolph	.08
456	Braves Leaders:	.15
	Dale Murphy	
457	Mickey Tettleton	.35
458	Kevin Bass	.04
459	Luis Leal	.04
460	Leon Durham	.15
461	Walt Terrell	.04
462	Domingo Ramos	.04
463	Jim Gott	.04
464	Ruppert Jones	.04
465	Jesse Orosco	.04
466	Tom Foley	.04
467	Bob James	.04
468	Mike Scioscia	.04
469	Storm Davis	.08
470	Bill Madlock	.15
471	Bobby Cox (Mgr.)	.08
	Blue Jays Checklist	
472	Joe Hesketh	.10
473	Mark Brouhard	.04
474	John Tudor	.15
475	Juan Samuel	.15
476	Ron Mathis	.12
477	Mike Easler	.04
478	Andy Hawkins	.08
479	Bob Melvin	.12
480	Oddibe McDowell	.20
481	Scott Bradley	.10
482	Rick Lysander	.04
483	George Vukovich	.04
484	Donnie Hill	.04
485	Gary Matthews	.06
486	Angels Leaders:	.08
	Bob Grich	
487	Bret Saberhagen	.60

NO.	PLAYER	MINT
488	Lou Thornton	.12
489	Jim Winn	.04
490	Jeff Leonard	.04
491	Pascual Perez	.04
492	Kelvin Chapman	.04
493	Gene Nelson	.04
494	Garry Roenicke	.04
495	Mark Langston	.25
496	Jay Johnstone	.04
497	John Stuper	.04
498	Tito Landrum	.04
499	Bob Gibson	.04
500	Rickey Henderson	1.00
501	Dave Johnson (Mgr.)	.12
	Mets Checklist	
502	Glen Cook	.12
503	Mike Fitzgerald	.04
504	Denny Walling	.04
505	Jerry Koosman	.08
506	Bill Russell	.04
507	Steve Ontiveros (R)	.15
508	Alan Wiggins	.08
509	Ernie Camacho	.04
510	Wade Boggs	2.00
511	Ed Nuñez	.04
512	Thad Bosley	.04
513	Ron Washington	.04
514	Mike Jones	.04
515	Darrell Evans	.08
516	Giants Leaders:	.08
	Greg Minton	
517	Milt Thompson (R)	.30
518	Buck Martinez	.04
519	Danny Darwin	.04
520	Keith Hernandez	.25
521	Nate Snell	.12
522	Bob Bailor	.04
523	Joe Price	.04
524	Darrell Miller	.08
525	Marvel Wynne	.04
526	Charlie Lea	.04
527	Checklist No. 4	.08
528	Terry Pendleton	.08
529	Marc Sullivan	.12
530	Rich Gossage	.15
531	Tony LaRussa (Mgr.)	.08
	White Sox Checklist	
532	Don Carman (R)	.25
533	Billy Sample	.04
534	Jeff Calhoun	.12
535	Toby Harrah	.04
536	Rich Rijo	.04
537	Mark Salas	.15
538	Dennis Eckersley	.20
539	Glenn Hubbard	.04
540	Dan Petry	.15
541	Jorge Orta	.04
542	Don Schulze	.04
543	Jerry Narron	.04
544	Eddie Milner	.04
545	Jimmy Key	.12
546	Mariners Leaders:	.06
	Dave Henderson	
547	Roger McDowell (R)	.35
548	Mike Young	.20
549	Bob Welch	.06
550	Tom Herr	.10
551	Dave LaPoint	.04
552	Marc Hill	.04
553	Jim Morrison	.04
554	Paul Householder	.04
555	Hubie Brooks	.08
556	John Denny	.06
557	Gerald Perry	.15
558	Tim Stoddard	.04
559	Tommy Dunbar	.04
560	Dave Righetti	.10
561	Bob Lillis (Mgr.)	.06
	Astros Checklist	
562	Joe Beckwith	.04
563	Alejandro Sanchez	.08
564	Warren Brusstar	.04
565	Tom Brunansky	.12
566	Alfredo Griffin	.04
567	Jeff Barkley	.12

NO.	PLAYER	MINT
568	Donnie Scott	.04
569	Jim Acker	.04
570	Rusty Staub	.08
571	Mike Jeffcoat	.04
572	Paul Zuvella	.08
573	Tom Hume	.04
574	Ron Kittle	.10
575	Mike Boddicker	.10
576	Expos Leaders:	.12
	Andre Dawson	
577	Jerry Reuss	.06
578	Lee Mazzilli	.04
579	Jim Slaton	.04
580	Willie McGee	.20
581	Bruce Hurst	.04
582	Jim Gantner	.04
583	Al Bumbry	.04
584	Brian Fisher (R)	.20
585	Garry Maddox	.04
586	Greg Harris	.04
587	Rafael Santana	.04
588	Steve Lake	.04
589	Sid Bream	.04
590	Bob Knepper	.04
591	Jackie Moore (Mgr.)	.08
	A's Checklist	
592	Frank Tanana	.06
593	Jesse Barfield	.25
594	Chris Bando	.04
595	Dave Parker	.25
596	Onix Concepcion	.04
597	Sammy Stewart	.04
598	Jim Presley	.25
599	Rick Aguilera (R)	.35
600	Dale Murphy	.35
601	Gary Lucas	.04
602	Mariano Duncan (R)	.30
603	Bill Laskey	.04
604	Gary Pettis	.08
605	Dennis Boyd	.06
606	Royals Leaders:	.10
	Hal McRae	
607	Ken Dayley	.04
608	Bruce Bochy	.04
609	Barbaro Garbey	.04
610	Ron Guidry	.15
611	Gary Woods	.04
612	Richard Dotson	.06
613	Roy Smalley	.04
614	Rick Waits	.04
615	Johnny Ray	.08
616	Glenn Brummer	.04
617	Lonnie Smith	.08
618	Jim Pankovits	.06
619	Danny Heep	.04
620	Bruce Sutter	.15
621	John Felske (Mgr.)	.08
	Phillies Checklist	
622	Gary Lavelle	.04
623	Floyd Rayford	.04
624	Steve McCatty	.04
625	Bob Brenly	.04
626	Roy Thomas	.04
627	Ron Oester	.04
628	Kirk McCaskill (R)	.50
629	Mitch Webster (R)	.30
630	Fernando Valenzuela	.25
631	Steve Braun	.04
632	Dave Von Ohlen	.04
633	Jackie Gutierrez	.04
634	Roy Lee Jackson	.04
635	Jason Thompson	.06
636	Cubs Leaders:	.10
	Lee Smith	
637	Rudy Law	.04
638	John Butcher	.04
639	Bo Diaz	.04
640	Jose Cruz	.08
641	Wayne Tolleson	.04
642	Ray Searage	.04
643	Tom Brookens	.04
644	Mark Gubicza	.20
645	Dusty Baker	.06
646	Mike Moore	.04
647	Mel Hall	.06

NO.	PLAYER	MINT
648	Steve Bedrosian	.10
649	Ronn Reynolds	.10
650	Dave Stieb	.15
651	Billy Martin (Mgr.)	.10
	Yankees Checklist	
652	Tom Browning	.25
653	Jim Dwyer	.04
654	Ken Howell	.10
655	Manny Trillo	.04
656	Brian Harper	.08
657	Juan Agosto	.04
658	Rob Wilfong	.04
659	Checklist No. 5	.08
660	Steve Garvey	.30
661	Roger Clemens	2.00
662	Bill Schroeder	.04
663	Neil Allen	.04
664	Tim Corcoran	.04
665	Alejandro Pena	.06
666	Rangers Leaders:	.06
	Charlie Hough	
667	Tim Tuefel	.08
668	Cecilio Guante	.04
669	Ron Cey	.10
670	Willie Hernandez	.12
671	Lynn Jones	.04
672	Rob Picciolo	.04
673	Ernie Whitt	.04
674	Pat Tabler	.04
675	Claudell Washington	.06
676	Matt Young	.04
677	Nick Esasky	.06
678	Dan Gladden	.06
679	Britt Burns	.06
680	George Foster	.15
681	Dick Williams (Mgr.)	.08
	Padres Checklist	
682	Junior Ortiz	.04
683	Andy Van Slyke	.15
684	Bob McClure	.04
685	Tim Wallach	.08
686	Jeff Stone	.06
687	Mike Trujillo	.12
688	Larry Herndon	.04
689	Dave Stewart	.25
690	Ryne Sandberg	1.25
691	Mike Madden	.04
692	Dale Berra	.04
693	Tom Tellmann	.04
694	Garth Iorg	.04
695	Mike Smithson	.04
696	Dodgers Leaders:	.10
	Bill Russell	
697	Bud Black	.04
698	Brad Komminsk	.06
699	Pat Corrales (Mgr.)	.08
	Indians Checklist	
700	Reggie Jackson	.40
701	Keith Hernandez (AS)	.15
702	Tom Herr (AS)	.08
703	Tim Wallach (AS)	.08
704	Ozzie Smith (AS)	.08
705	Dale Murphy (AS)	.25
706	Pedro Guerrero (AS)	.20
707	Willie McGee (AS)	.20
708	Gary Carter (AS)	.20
709	Dwight Gooden (AS)	.35
710	John Tudor (AS)	.08
711	Jeff Reardon (AS)	.08
712	Don Mattingly (AS)	.70
713	Damaso Garcia (AS)	.08
714	George Brett (AS)	.35
715	Cal Ripken (AS)	.30
716	Rickey Henderson (AS)	.30
717	Dave Winfield (AS)	.25
718	Jorge Bell (AS)	.08
719	Carlton Fisk (AS)	.10
720	Bret Saberhagen (AS)	.25
721	Ron Guidry (AS)	.10
722	Dan Quisenberry (AS)	.10
723	Marty Bystrom	.04
724	Tim Hulett	.08
725	Mario Soto	.08
726	Orioles Leaders:	.08
	Rick Dempsey	

NO. PLAYER	MINT	NO. PLAYER	MINT	NO. PLAYER	MINT	NO. PLAYER	MINT
727 David Green	.04	748 Steve Henderson	.04	769 Harold Reynolds (R)	.50	789 Kurt Bevacqua	.04
728 Mike Marshall	.15	749 Ed Jurak	.04	770 Vida Blue	.08	790 Phil Niekro	.15
729 Jim Beattie	.04	750 Gorman Thomas	.08	771 John McNamara (Mgr.)	.08	791 Checklist No. 6	.08
730 Ozzie Smith	.20	751 Howard Johnson	.30	Red Sox Checklist		792 Charles Hudson	.06
731 Don Robinson	.04	752 Mike Krukow	.04	772 Brian Downing	.04		
732 Floyd Youmans (R)	.25	753 Dan Ford	.04	773 Greg Pryor	.04		
733 Ron Romanick	.06	754 Pat Clements (R)	.12	774 Terry Leach	.04		
734 Marty Barrett	.15	755 Harold Baines	.20	775 Al Oliver	.10		
735 Dave Dravecky	.04	756 Pirates Leaders:	.06	776 Gene Garber	.04		
736 Glenn Wilson	.08	Rick Rhoden		777 Wayne Krenchicki	.04		
737 Pete Vuckovich	.04	757 Darrell Porter	.04	778 Jerry Hairston	.04		
738 Andre Robertson	.04	758 Dave Anderson	.04	779 Rick Reuschel	.04		
739 Dave Rozema	.04	759 Moose Haas	.04	780 Robin Yount	.30		
740 Lance Parrish	.20	760 Andre Dawson	.40	781 Joe Nolan	.04		
741 Pete Rose (Mgr.)	.40	761 Don Slaught	.04	782 Ken Landreaux	.04		
Reds Checklist		762 Eric Show	.04	783 Ricky Horton	.04		
742 Frank Viola	.25	763 Terry Puhl	.04	784 Alan Bannister	.04		
743 Pat Sheridan	.04	764 Kevin Gross	.04	785 Bob Stanley	.04		
744 Lary Sorensen	.04	765 Don Baylor	.15	786 Twins Leaders:	.06		
745 Willie Upshaw	.08	766 Rick Langford	.04	Mickey Hatcher			
746 Denny Gonzalez	.08	767 Jody Davis	.08	787 Vance Law	.04		
747 Rick Cerone	.04	768 Vern Ruhle	.04	788 Marty Castillo	.04		

1986 Topps Traded.... Complete Set of 132 Cards—Value $35.00

Updates the main 1986 card set with players who changed teams during the season, and rookies. Features the first Topps card of Jose Canseco, Will Clark, Kevin Mitchell and Bo Jackson. The set was packaged in a printed box and distributed exclusively through card hobby dealers. A "Tiffany" version of the set was also issued.

JOSE CANSECO

WILL CLARK

KEVIN MITCHELL

BO JACKSON

WALLY JOYNER

NO. PLAYER	MINT	NO. PLAYER	MINT	NO. PLAYER	MINT	NO. PLAYER	MINT
1T Andy Allanson	.15	34T Mark Eichhorn	.15	67T Steve Lyons	.06	100T Ken Schrom	.06
2T Neil Allen	.06	35T Steve Farr	.06	68T Mickey Mahler	.06	101T Tom Seaver	.60
3T Joaquin Andujar	.06	36T Scott Fletcher	.06	69T Candy Maldonado	.15	102T Ted Simmons	.06
4T Paul Assenmacher	.15	37T Terry Forster	.06	70T Roger Mason	.10	103T Sammy Stewart	.06
5T Scott Bailes	.15	38T Terry Francona	.06	71T Bob McClure	.06	104T Kurt Stillwell	.40
6T Don Baylor	.10	39T Jim Fregosi	.06	72T Andy McGaffigan	.06	105T Franklin Stubbs	.30
7T Steve Bedrosian	.10	40T Andres Galarraga (RR)	.1.25	73T Gene Michael	.06	106T Dale Sveum	.20
8T Juan Beniquez	.06	41T Ken Griffey	.06	74T Kevin Mitchell (RR)	5.00	107T Chuck Tanner	.06
9T Juan Berenguer	.06	42T Bill Gullickson	.06	75T Omar Moreno	.06	108T Danny Tartabull	.60
10T Mike Bielecki	.35	43T Jose Guzman	.25	76T Jerry Mumphrey	.06	109T Tim Teufel	.06
11T Barry Bonds (RR)	3.00	44T Moose Haas	.06	77T Phil Niekro	.30	110T Bob Tewksbury	.15
12T Bobby Bonilla (RR)	2.50	45T Billy Hatcher	.20	78T Randy Nieman	.06	111T Andres Thomas	.20
13T Juan Bonilla	.06	46T Mike Heath	.06	79T Juan Nieves	.20	112T Milt Thomson	.06
14T Rich Bordi	.06	47T Tom Hume	.06	80T Otis Nixon	.15	113T Robby Thompson	.35
15T Steve Boros	.06	48T Pete Incaviglia (RR)	.75	81T Bob Ojeda	.08	114T Jay Tibbs	.06
16T Rick Burleson	.06	49T Dane Iorg	.06	82T Jose Oquendo	.10	115T Wayne Tolleson	.06
17T Bill Campbell	.06	50T Bo Jackson (RR)	10.00	83T Tom Paciorek	.06	116T Alex Trevino	.06
18T Tom Candiotti	.06	51T Wa. Joyner (RR)	2.00	84T Dave Palmer	.06	117T Manny Trillo	.06
19T John Cangelosi	.15	52T Charlie Kerfeld	.15	85T Frank Pastore	.06	118T Ed VandeBerg	.06
20T Jose Canseco (RR)	9.00	53T Eric King	.30	86T Lou Piniella	.08	119T Ozzie Virgil	.06
21T Carmen Castillo	.10	54T Bob Kipper	.06	87T Dan Plesac	.20	120T Bob Walk	.06
22T Rick Cerone	.06	55T Wayne Krenchicki	.06	88T Darrell Porter	.06	121T Gene Walter	.10
23T John Cerutti	.30	56T John Kruk (RR)	.40	89T Rey Quinones	.20	122T C. Washington	.06
24T Will Clark (RR)	9.00	57T Mike LaCoss	.06	90T Gary Redus	.06	123T Bill Wegman	.15
25T Mark Clear	.06	58T Pete Ladd	.06	91T Bip Roberts	.25	124T Dick Williams	.06
26T Darrell Coles	.08	59T Mike Laga	.06	92T Billy Jo Robidoux	.15	125T Mitch Williams	.35
27T Dave Collins	.06	60T Hal Lanier	.06	93T Jeff Robinson	.06	126T Bobby Witt (RR)	.50
28T Tim Conroy	.06	61T Dave LaPoint	.06	94T Gary Roenicke	.06	127T Todd Worrell (RR)	.45
29T Joe Cowley	.10	62T Rudy Law	.06	95T Ed Romero	.06	128T George Wright	.06
30T Joel Davis	.10	63T Rick Leach	.06	96T Argenis Salazar	.06	129T Ricky Wright	.12
31T Rob Deer	.30	64T Tim Leary	.06	97T Joe Sambito	.06	130T Steve Yeager	.06
32T John Denny	.06	65T Dennis Leonard	.06	98T Billy Sample	.06	131T Paul Zuvella	.06
33T Mike Easler	.06	66T Jim Leyland	.06	99T Dave Schmidt	.06	132T Checklist	.06

1987 Topps.... Complete Set of 792 Cards—Value $45.00

Features the rookie cards of Will Clark, Bo Jackson, Ruben Sierra and Mike Greenwell. A "Tiffany" version of the set was also issued.

NO.	PLAYER	MINT
1	'86 Record: Clemens	.45
2	'86 Record: Deshaies	.08
3	'86 Record: Evans	.10
4	'86 Record: Lopes	.10
5	'86 Record: Righetti	.08
6	'86 Record: Sierra	.20
7	'86 Record: Worrell	.10
8	Terry Pendleton	.04
9	Jay Tibbs	.04
10	Cecil Cooper	.08
11	Indians Leaders	.06
12	Jeff Sellers (R)	.15
13	Nick Esasky	.04
14	Dave Stewart	.20
15	Claudell Washington	.04
16	Pat Clements	.04
17	Pete O'Brien	.10
18	Dick Howser (Mgr.)	.04
19	Matt Young	.04
20	Gary Carter	.20
21	Mark Davis	.04
22	Doug DeCinces	.06
23	Lee Smith	.04
24	Tony Walker (R)	.15
25	Bert Blyleven	.08
26	C. Brock	.04
27	Joe Cowley	.04
28	Rick Dempsey	.04
29	Jimmy Key	.15
30	Tim Raines	.20
31	Braves Leaders	.06
32	Tim Leary	.04
33	Andy Van Slyke	.12
34	Jose Rijo	.04
35	Sid Bream	.04
36	Eric King (R)	.25
37	Marvell Wynne	.04
38	Dennis Leonard	.04
39	Marty Barrett	.06
40	Dave Righetti	.10
41	Bo Diaz	.04
42	Gary Redus	.04
43	Gene Michael (Mgr.)	.04
44	Greg Harris	.04
45	Jim Presley	.15
46	Danny Gladden	.04
47	Dennis Powell	.12
48	Wally Backman	.04
49	Terry Harper	.04
50	Dave Smith	.04
51	M. Hall	.04
52	Keith Atherton	.04
53	Ruppert Jones	.04
54	Bill Dawley	.04
55	Tim Wallach	.08
56	Brewers Leaders	.06
57	Scott Nielsen (R)	.15
58	Thad Bosley	.04
59	Ken Dayley	.04
60	Tony Pena	.10
61	Bobby Thigpen (R)	.75
62	Bobby Meacham	.04
63	Fred Tollver	.12
64	Harry Spilman	.04
65	Tom Browning	.10
66	Marc Sullivan	.04

NO.	PLAYER	MINT
67	Bill Swift	.04
68	Tony LaRussa (Mgr.)	.04
69	Lonnie Smith	.04
70	Charlie Hough	.04
71	Mike Aldrete (R)	.20
72	Walt Terrell	.04
73	Dave Anderson	.04
74	Dan Pasqua	.15
75	Ron Darling	.20
76	Rafael Ramirez	.04
77	Bryan Oelkers	.04
78	Tom Foley	.04
79	Juan Nieves	.15
80	Wally Joyner (R)	1.00
81	Padres Leaders	.06
82	Rob Murphy (R)	.20
83	Mike Davis	.04
84	Steve Lake	.04
85	Kevin Bass	.04
86	Nate Snell	.04
87	Mark Salas	.04
88	Ed Wojna	.04
89	Ozzie Guillen	.20
90	Dave Stieb	.10
91	Harold Reynolds	.08
92	U. Lugo	.05
92	U. Lugo (no t.m.)	.30
93	Jim Leyland (Mgr.)	.04
94	Calvin Schiraldi	.08
95	Oddibe McDowell	.10
96	Frank Williams	.04
97	Glenn Wilson	.08
98	Bill Scherrer	.04
99	Darryl Motley	.04
100	Steve Garvey	.25
101	Carl Willis (R)	.15
102	Paul Zuvella	.04
103	Rick Aguilera	.04
104	Billy Sample	.04
105	Floyd Youmans	.15
106	Blue Jays Leaders	.06
107	John Butcher	.04
108	Jim Gantner	.04
109	R. J. Reynolds	.04
110	John Tudor	.12
111	Alfredo Griffin	.04
112	Alan Ashby	.04
113	Neil Allen	.04
114	Billy Beane	.08
115	Donnie Moore	.04
116	Bill Russell	.04
117	Jim Beattie	.04
118	Bobby Valentine (Mgr.)	.04
119	Ron Robinson	.04
120	Eddie Murray	.30
121	Kevin Romine (R)	.15
122	Jim Clancy	.04
123	John Kruk (R)	.30
124	Ray Fontenot	.04
125	Bob Brenly	.04
126	Mike Loynd (R)	.15
127	Vance Law	.04
128	Checklist: 1-132	.06
129	Rick Cerone	.04
130	Dwight Gooden	.75
131	Pirates Leaders	.06
132	P. Assenmacher (R)	.15

NO.	PLAYER	MINT
133	Jose Oquendo	.04
134	Rich Yett (R)	.15
135	Mike Easler	.04
136	Ron Romanick	.04
137	Jerry Willard	.04
138	Roy Lee Jackson	.04
139	Devon White (R)	.50
140	Bret Saberhagen	.25
141	Herm Winningham	.04
142	Rick Sutcliffe	.12
143	Steve Boros (Mgr.)	.04
144	Mike Scioscia	.04
145	Charlie Kerfeld	.15
146	Tracy Jones	.20
147	Randy Niemann	.04
148	Dave Collins	.04
149	Ray Searage	.04
150	Wade Boggs	.75
151	Mike LaCoss	.04
152	Toby Harrah	.04
153	Duane Ward (R)	.20
154	Tom O'Malley	.04
155	Eddie Whitson	.04
156	Mariners Leaders	.06
157	Danny Darwin	.04
158	Tim Teufel	.04
159	Ed Olwine (R)	.15
160	Julio Franco	.10
161	Steve Ontiveros	.04
162	Mike LaValliere (R)	.20
163	Kevin Gross	.04
164	Sammy Khalifa	.04
165	Jeff Reardon	.08
166	Bob Boone	.04
167	Jim Deshaies (R)	.25
168	Lou Piniella (Mgr.)	.06
169	Ron Washington	.04
170	Bo Jackson (R)	4.00
171	Chuck Cary (R)	.15
172	Ron Oester	.04
173	Alex Trevino	.04
174	Henry Cotto	.04
175	Bob Stanley	.04
176	Steve Buechele	.04
177	Keith Moreland	.04
178	Cecil Fielder	1.75
179	Bill Wegman	.04
180	Chris Brown	.10
181	Cardinals Leaders	.06
182	Lee Lacy	.04
183	Andy Hawkins	.04
184	Bobby Bonilla (R)	1.50
185	Roger McDowell	.10
186	Bruce Benedict	.04
187	Mark Huismann	.04
188	Tony Phillips	.04
189	Joe Hesketh	.04
190	Jim Sundberg	.04
191	Charles Hudson	.04
192	Cory Snyder	.50
193	Roger Craig (Mgr.)	.04
194	Kirk McCaskill	.10
195	Mike Pagliarulo	.15
196	Randy O'Neal	.04
197	Mark Bailey	.04
198	Lee Mazzilli	.08

NO.	PLAYER	MINT
199	Mariano Duncan	.10
200	Pete Rose	.50
201	John Cangelosi (R)	.20
202	Ricky Wright	.04
203	Mike Kingery (R)	.20
204	Sammy Stewart	.04
205	Graig Nettles	.08
206	Twins Leaders	.06
207	George Frazier	.04
208	John Shelby	.04
209	Rick Schu	.04
210	Lloyd Moseby	.12
211	John Morris	.04
212	Mike Fitzgerald	.04
213	Randy Myers (R)	.50
214	Omar Moreno	.04
215	Mark Langston	.15
216	B.J. Surhoff (R)	.30
217	Chris Codiroli	.04
218	S. Anderson (Mgr.)	.04
219	Cecilio Guante	.04
220	Joe Carter	.25
221	Vern Ruhle	.04
222	Denny Walling	.04
223	Charlie Leibrandt	.04
224	Wayne Tolleson	.04
225	Mike Smithson	.04
226	Max Venable	.04
227	Jamie Moyer (R)	.20
228	Curt Wilkerson	.04
229	Mike Birkbeck (R)	.15
230	Don Baylor	.12
231	Giants Leaders	.06
232	Reggie Williams (R)	.12
233	Russ Morman (R)	.12
234	Pat Sheridan	.04
235	Alvin Davis	.12
236	Tommy John	.12
237	Jim Morrison	.04
238	Bill Krueger	.04
239	Juan Espino	.04
240	Steve Balboni	.08
241	Danny Heep	.04
242	Rick Mahler	.04
243	Whitey Herzog (Mgr.)	.04
244	Dickie Noles	.04
245	Willie Upshaw	.04
246	Jim Dwyer	.04
247	Jeff Reed	.04
248	Gene Walter	.10
249	Jim Pankovits	.04
250	Teddy Higuera	.15
251	Rob Wilfong	.04
252	Denny Martinez	.04
253	Eddie Milner	.04
254	Bob Tewksbury (R)	.15
255	Juan Samuel	.15
256	Royals Leaders	.06
257	Bob Forsch	.04
258	Steve Yeager	.04
259	Mike Greenwell (R)	2.00
260	Vida Blue	.06
261	Ruben Sierra (R)	2.50
262	Jim Winn	.04
263	Stan Javier	.08
264	Checklist: 133-264	.06

NO. PLAYER	MINT
265 Darrell Evans	.10
266 Jeff Hamilton (R)	.15
267 Howard Johnson	.20
268 Pat Corrales (Mgr.)	.04
269 Cliff Speck (R)	.15
270 Jody Davis	.04
271 Mike Brown	.04
272 Andres Galarraga	.50
273 Gene Nelson	.04
274 Jeff Hearron (R)	.15
275 LaMarr Hoyt	.04
276 Jackie Gutierrez	.04
277 Juan Agosto	.04
278 Gary Pettis	.04
279 Dan Plesac (R)	.25
280 Jeffrey Leonard	.04
281 Reds Leaders	.12
282 Jeff Calhoun	.04
283 Doug Drabek (R)	1.00
284 John Moses	.10
285 Dennis Boyd	.12
286 Mike Woodard	.10
287 Dave Von Ohlen	.04
288 Tito Landrum	.04
289 Bob Kipper	.04
290 Leon Durham	.10
291 Mitch Williams (R)	.30
292 Franklin Stubbs	.12
293 Bob Rodgers (Mgr.)	.04
294 Steve Jeltz	.04
295 Len Dykstra	.35
296 Andres Thomas (R)	.20
297 Don Schulze	.04
298 Larry Herndon	.04
299 Joel Davis	.10
300 Reggie Jackson	.30
301 Luis Aquino (R)	.15
302 Bill Schroeder	.04
303 Juan Berenguer	.04
304 Phil Garner	.04
305 John Franco	.10
306 Red Sox Leaders	.10
307 Lee Guetterman (R)	.15
308 Don Slaught	.04
309 Mike Young	.04
310 Frank Viola	.25
311 Turn Back—1982	.15
312 Turn Back-1977	.15
313 Turn Back—1972	.15
314 Turn Back—1967	.15
315 Turn Back—1962	.15
316 Brian Fisher	.04
317 Clint Hurdle	.04
318 Jim Fregosi (Mgr.)	.04
319 Greg Swindell (R)	.75
320 Barry Bonds (R)	2.50
321 Mike Laga	.04
322 Chris Bando	.04
323 Al Newman (R)	.15
324 Dave Palmer	.04
325 Garry Templeton	.04
326 Mark Gubicza	.04
327 Dale Sveum (R)	.25
328 Bob Welch	.04
329 Ron Roenicke	.04
330 Mike Scott	.25
331 Mets Leaders	.25
332 Joe Price	.04
333 Ken Phelps	.04
334 Ed Correa (R)	.20
335 Candy Maldonado	.06
336 Allan Anderson (R)	.30
337 Darrell Miller	.04
338 Tim Conroy	.04
339 Donnie Hill	.04
340 Roger Clemens	.75
341 Mike Brown	.04
342 Bob James	.04
343 Hal Lanier (Mgr.)	.04
344 Joe Niekro	.06
345 Andre Dawson	.25
346 Shawon Dunston	.15
347 Mickey Brantley	.15
348 Carmelo Martinez	.04
349 Storm Davis	.06

NO. PLAYER	MINT
350 Keith Hernandez	.25
351 Gene Garber	.04
352 Mike Felder	.12
353 Ernie Camacho	.04
354 Jamie Quick	.04
355 Don Carman	.04
356 White Sox Leaders	.06
357 Steve Fireovid (R)	.15
358 Sal Butera	.04
359 Doug Corbett	.04
360 Pedro Guerrero	.20
361 Mark Thurmond	.04
362 Luis Quinones (R)	.15
363 Jose Guzman	.15
364 Randy Bush	.04
365 Rick Rhoden	.04
366 Mark McGwire	2.50
367 Jeff Lahti	.04
368 J. McNamara (Mgr.)	.04
369 Brian Dayett	.04
370 Fred Lynn	.15
371 Mark Eichhorn (R)	.12
372 Jerry Mumphrey	.04
373 Jeff Dedmon	.04
374 Glenn Hoffman	.04
375 Ron Guidry	.15
376 Scott Bradley	.04
377 John Henry Johnson	.04
378 Rafael Santana	.04
379 John Russell	.04
380 Rich Gossage	.12
381 Expos Leaders	.06
382 Rudy Law	.04
383 Ron Davis	.04
384 Johnny Grubb	.04
385 Orel Hershiser	.25
386 Dickie Thon	.04
387 T. R. Bryden (R)	.20
388 Geno Petralli	.04
389 Jeff Robinson	.04
390 Gary Matthews	.04
391 Jay Howell	.04
392 Checklist: 265-396	.06
393 Pete Rose (Mgr.)	.40
394 Mike Bielecki	.12
395 Damaso Garcia	.04
396 Tim Lollar	.04
397 Greg Walker	.08
398 Brad Havens	.04
399 Curt Ford	.12
400 George Brett	.35
401 Billy Jo Robidoux	.15
402 Mike Trujillo	.04
403 Jerry Royster	.04
404 Doug Sisk	.04
405 Brook Jacoby	.10
406 Yankees Leaders	.25
407 Jim Acker	.04
408 John Mizerock	.04
409 Milt Thompson	.04
410 Fernando Valenzuela	.20
411 Darnell Coles	.04
412 Eric Davis	.75
413 Moose Haas	.04
414 Joe Orsulak	.04
415 Bobby Witt (R)	.50
416 Tom Nieto	.04
417 Pat Perry	.08
418 Dick Williams (Mgr.)	.04
419 Mark Portugal (R)	.15
420 Will Clark (R)	4.00
421 Jose DeLeon	.04
422 Jack Howell	.04
423 Jaime Cocanower	.04
424 Chris Speier	.04
425 Tom Seaver	.30
426 Floyd Rayford	.04
427 Ed Nunez	.04
428 Bruce Bochy	.04
429 Tim Pyznarski (R)	.15
430 Mike Schmidt	.40
431 Dodgers Leaders	.15
432 Jim Slaton	.04
433 Ed Hearn (R)	.12

NO. PLAYER	MINT
434 Mike Fischlin	.04
435 Bruce Sutter	.10
436 Andy Allanson (R)	.15
437 Ted Power	.04
438 Kelly Downs (R)	.20
439 Karl Best	.04
440 Dave McGee	.15
441 Dave Leiper (R)	.15
442 Mitch Webster	.04
443 John Felske (Mgr.)	.04
444 Jeff Russell	.04
445 Dave Lopes	.08
446 Chuck Finley (R)	.75
447 Bill Almon	.04
448 Chris Bosio (R)	.20
449 Pat Dodson (R)	.20
450 Kirby Puckett	.60
451 Joe Sambito	.04
452 Dave Henderson	.04
453 Scott Terry (R)	.20
454 Luis Salazar	.04
455 Mike Boddicker	.04
456 A's Leaders	.06
457 Len Matuszek	.04
458 Kelly Gruber	.75
459 Dennis Eckersley	.06
460 Darryl Strawberry	.50
461 Craig McMurtry	.04
462 Scott Fletcher	.04
463 Tom Candiotti	.04
464 Butch Wynegar	.04
465 Todd Worrell	.25
466 Kal Daniels	.75
467 Randy St. Claire	.04
468 G. Bamberger (Mgr.)	.04
469 Mike Diaz (R)	.20
470 Dave Dravecky	.04
471 Ronn Reynolds	.04
472 Bill Doran	.08
473 Steve Farr	.04
474 Jerry Narron	.04
475 Scott Garrelts	.04
476 Danny Tartabull	.50
477 Ken Howell	.04
478 Tim Laudner	.04
479 Bob Sebra (R)	.15
480 Jim Rice	.20
481 Phillies Leaders	.06
482 Daryl Boston	.04
483 Dwight Lowry (R)	.15
484 Jim Traber	.10
485 Tony Fernandez	.12
486 Otis Nixon	.08
487 Dave Gumpert	.04
488 Ray Knight	.04
489 Bill Gullickson	.04
490 Dale Murphy	.35
491 Ron Karkovice (R)	.15
492 Mike Heath	.04
493 Tom Lasorda (Mgr.)	.04
494 Barry Jones (R)	.20
495 Gorman Thomas	.10
496 Bruce Bochte	.04
497 Dale Mohorcic (R)	.15
498 Bob Kearney	.04
499 Bruce Ruffin (R)	.25
500 Don Mattingly	1.00
501 Craig Lefferts	.04
502 Dick Schofield	.04
503 Larry Andersen	.04
504 Mickey Hatcher	.04
505 Bryn Smith	.04
506 Orioles Leaders	.08
507 Dave Stapleton	.04
508 Scott Bankhead	.15
509 Enos Cabell	.04
510 Tom Henke	.10
511 Steve Lyons	.04
512 Dave Magadan (R)	1.00
513 Carmen Castillo	.04
514 Orlando Mercado	.04
515 Willie Hernandez	.10
516 Ted Simmons	.10
517 Mario Soto	.04
518 Gene Mauch (Mgr.)	.04

NO. PLAYER	MINT
519 Curt Young	.04
520 Jack Clark	.20
521 Rick Reuschel	.04
522 Checklist: 397-528	.06
523 Earnie Riles	.04
524 Bob Shirley	.04
525 Phil Bradley	.12
526 Roger Mason	.08
527 Jim Wohlford	.04
528 Ken Dixon	.04
529 Alvaro Espinoza (R)	.10
530 Tony Gwynn	.45
531 Astros Leaders	.06
532 Jeff Stone	.04
533 Argenis Salazar	.04
534 Scott Sanderson	.04
535 Tony Armas	.06
536 Terry Mulholland (R)	.15
537 Rance Mulliniks	.04
538 Tom Niedenfuer	.04
539 Reid Nichols	.04
540 Terry Kennedy	.04
541 Rafael Belliard (R)	.12
542 Ricky Horton	.04
543 Dave Johnson (Mgr.)	.04
544 Zane Smith	.06
545 Buddy Bell	.10
546 Mike Morgan	.04
547 Rob Deer	.20
548 Bill Mooneyham (R)	.15
549 Bob Melvin	.04
550 Pete Incaviglia (R)	.75
551 Frank Wills	.04
552 Larry Sheets	.15
553 Mike Maddux (R)	.15
554 Buddy Biancalana	.04
555 Dennis Rasmussen	.10
556 Angels Leaders	.06
557 John Cerutti (R)	.20
558 Greg Gagne	.04
559 Lance McCullers	.04
560 Glenn Davis	.30
561 Rey Quinones (R)	.20
562 B. Clutterbuck (R)	.15
563 John Stefero	.04
564 Larry McWilliams	.04
565 Dusty Baker	.04
566 Tim Hulett	.04
567 Greg Mathews (R)	.20
568 Earl Weaver (Mgr.)	.04
569 Wade Rowdon	.15
570 Sid Fernandez	.20
571 Ozzie Virgil	.04
572 Pete Ladd	.04
573 Hal McRae	.04
574 Manny Lee	.04
575 Pat Tabler	.04
576 Frank Pastore	.04
577 Dann Bilardello	.04
578 Billy Hatcher	.08
579 Rick Burleson	.04
580 Mike Krukow	.04
581 Cubs Leaders	.08
582 Bruce Berenyi	.04
583 Junior Ortiz	.04
584 Ron Kittle	.08
585 Scott Bailes (R)	.15
586 Ben Oglivie	.04
587 Eric Plunk	.10
588 Wallace Johnson	.04
589 Steve Crawford	.04
590 Vince Coleman	.30
591 Spike Owen	.04
592 Chris Welsh	.04
593 Chuck Tanner (Mgr.)	.08
594 Rick Anderson (R)	.15
595 Keith Hernandez (AS)	.15
596 Steve Sax (AS)	.10
597 Mike Schmidt (AS)	.25
598 Ozzie Smith (AS)	.10
599 Tony Gwynn (AS)	.25
600 Dave Parker (AS)	.15
601 Darryl Strawberry (AS)	.25
602 Gary Carter (AS)	.20
603 Dwight Gooden (AS)	.35
603 D. Gooden (no t.m.)	1.00

NO.	PLAYER	MINT
604	F. Valenzuela (AS)	.15
605	Todd Worrell (AS)	.15
606	Don Mattingly (AS)	.65
606	D. Matt (no t.m.)	2.00
607	Tony Bernazard (AS)	.08
608	Wade Boggs (AS)	.40
609	Cal Ripken (AS)	.15
610	Jim Rice (AS)	.15
611	Kirby Puckett (AS)	.25
612	George Bell (AS)	.15
613	Lance Parrish (AS)	.10
614	Roger Clemens (AS)	.25
615	Teddy Higuera (AS)	.10
616	Dave Righetti (AS)	.10
617	Al Nipper	.04
618	Tom Kelly (Mgr.)	.04
619	Jerry Reed	.04
620	Jose Canseco	4.00
621	Danny Cox	.08
622	Glenn Braggs (R)	.40
623	Kurt Stillwell (R)	.30
624	Tim Burke	.04
625	Mookie Wilson	.04
626	Joel Skinner	.04
627	Ken Oberkfell	.04
628	Bob Walk	.04
629	Larry Parrish	.04
630	John Candelaria	.04
631	Tigers Leaders	.15
632	Rob Woodward	.08
633	Jose Uribe	.04
634	Rafael Palmeiro (R)	1.00
635	Ken Schrom	.04
636	Darren Daulton	.04
637	Bip Roberts (R)	.35
638	Rich Bordi	.04
639	Gerald Perry	.20
640	Mark Clear	.04
641	Domino Ramos	.04
642	Al Pulido	.04
643	Ron Shepherd	.15
644	John Denny	.04
645	Dwight Evans	.12
646	Mike Mason	.04
647	Tom Lawless	.04
648	Barry Larkin (R)	2.00
649	Mickey Tettleton	.15
650	Hubie Brooks	.10
651	Benny Distefano	.04
652	Terry Forster	.04
653	Kevin Mitchell (R)	3.00

NO.	PLAYER	MINT
654	Checklist: 529-660	.06
655	Jesse Barfield	.20
656	Rangers Leaders	.06
657	Tom Waddell	.04
658	Robby Thompson (R)	.25
659	Aurelio Lopez	.04
660	Bob Horner	.10
661	Lou Whitaker	.10
662	Frank DiPino	.04
663	Cliff Johnson	.04
664	Mike Marshall	.12
665	Rod Scurry	.04
666	Von Hayes	.10
667	Ron Hassey	.04
668	Juan Bonilla	.04
669	Bud Black	.04
670	Jose Cruz	.08
671	Ray Soff (R)	.12
672	Chili Davis	.10
673	Don Sutton	.15
674	Bill Campbell	.04
675	Ed Romero	.04
676	Charlie Moore	.04
677	Bob Grich	.04
678	Carney Lansford	.10
679	Kent Hrbek	.15
680	Ryne Sandberg	.50
681	George Bell	.30
682	Jerry Reuss	.04
683	Gary Roenicke	.04
684	Kent Tekulve	.04
685	Jerry Hairston	.04
686	Doyle Alexander	.04
687	Alan Trammell	.12
688	Juan Beniquez	.04
689	Darrell Porter	.04
690	Dane Iorg	.04
691	Dave Parker	.20
692	Frank White	.04
693	Terry Puhl	.04
694	Phil Niekro	.15
695	Chico Walker (R)	.15
696	Gary Lucas	.04
697	Ed Lynch	.04
698	Ernie Whitt	.04
699	Ken Landreaux	.04
700	Dave Bergman	.04
701	Willie Randolph	.08
702	Greg Gross	.04
703	Dave Schmidt	.04

NO.	PLAYER	MINT
704	Jesse Orosco	.06
705	Bruce Hurst	.12
706	Rick Manning	.04
707	Bob McClure	.04
708	Scott McGregor	.04
709	Dave Kingman	.10
710	Gary Gaetti	.10
711	Ken Griffey	.08
712	Don Robinson	.04
713	Tom Brookens	.04
714	Don Quisenberry	.12
715	Bob Dernier	.04
716	Rick Leach	.04
717	Ed Vande Berg	.04
718	Steve Carlton	.25
719	Tom Hume	.04
720	Richard Dotson	.04
721	Tom Herr	.04
722	Bob Knepper	.08
723	Brett Butler	.04
724	Greg Minton	.04
725	George Hendrick	.04
726	Frank Tanana	.04
727	Mike Moore	.04
728	Tippy Martinez	.04
729	Tom Paciorek	.04
730	Eric Show	.06
731	Dave Concepcion	.08
732	Manny Trillo	.04
733	Bill Caudill	.04
734	Bill Madlock	.12
735	Rickey Henderson	.50
736	Steve Bedrosian	.10
737	Floyd Bannister	.04
738	Jorge Orta	.04
739	Chet Lemon	.06
740	Rich Gedman	.04
741	Paul Molitor	.15
742	Andy McGaffigan	.04
743	Dwayne Murphy	.04
744	Roy Smalley	.04
745	Glenn Hubbard	.04
746	Bob Ojeda	.12
747	Johnny Ray	.04
748	Mike Flanagan	.06
749	Ozzie Smith	.15
750	Steve Trout	.04
751	Garth Iorg	.04
752	Dan Petry	.04
753	Rick Honeycutt	.04

NO.	PLAYER	MINT
754	Dave LaPoint	.04
755	Luis Aguayo	.04
756	Carlton Fisk	.15
757	Nolan Ryan	.50
758	Tony Bernazard	.04
759	Joel Youngblood	.04
760	Mike Witt	.10
761	Greg Pryor	.04
762	Gary Ward	.04
763	Tim Flannery	.04
764	Bill Buckner	.04
765	Kirk Gibson	.20
766	Don Aase	.04
767	Ron Cey	.04
768	Dennis Lamp	.04
769	Steve Sax	.15
770	Dave Winfield	.25
771	Shane Rawley	.04
772	Harold Baines	.15
773	Robin Yount	.30
774	Wayne Krenchicki	.04
775	Joaquin Andujar	.04
776	Tom Brunansky	.12
777	Chris Chambliss	.04
778	Jack Morris	.15
779	Craig Reynolds	.04
780	Andre Thornton	.04
781	Atlee Hammaker	.04
782	Brian Downing	.04
783	Willie Wilson	.10
784	Cal Ripken	.25
785	Terry Francona	.04
786	Jimy Williams (Mgr.)	.04
787	Alejandro Pena	.04
788	Tim Stoddard	.04
789	Dan Schatzeder	.04
790	Julio Cruz	.04
791	Lance Parrish	.15
792	Checklist: 661-792	.06

1987 Topps Traded.... Complete Set of 132 Cards—Value $15.00

Updates the main 1987 card set with players who changed teams during the season and rookies who joined their teams early in the season. Features the first Topps card of Ellis Burks, David Cone, Fred McGriff and Matt Williams. The complete set was packaged in a printed box and primarily distributed through card hobby dealers. A "Tiffany" version of the set was also issued.

NO.	PLAYER	MINT
1T	Bill Almon	.06
2T	Scott Bankhead	.10
3T	Eric Bell	.10
4T	Juan Beniquez	.06
5T	Juan Berenguer	.06
6T	Greg Booker	.06
7T	Thad Bosley	.06

NO.	PLAYER	MINT
8T	Larry Bowa	.08
9T	Greg Brock	.10
10T	Bob Brower	.15
11T	Jerry Browne	.25
12T	Ralph Bryant	.15
13T	DeWayne Buice	.12
14T	Ellis Burks (RR)	2.00

NO.	PLAYER	MINT
15T	Ivan Calderon	.15
16T	Jeff Calhoun	.06
17T	Casey Candaele	.15
18T	John Cangelosi	.10
19T	Steve Carlton	.25
20T	Juan Castillo	.10
21T	Rick Cerone	.06

NO.	PLAYER	MINT
22T	Ron Cey	.12
23T	John Christensen	.06
24T	Dave Cone	1.25
25T	Chuck Grim	.15
26T	Storm Daviss	.06
27T	Andre Dawson	.45
28T	Rick Dempsey	.10

NO. PLAYER	MINT	NO. PLAYER	MINT	NO. PLAYER	MINT	NO. PLAYER	MINT
29T Doug Drabek	.35	55T Stan Jefferson	.20	81T Kevin Mitchell	1.00	107T Mark Salas	.06
30T Mike Dunne	.15	56T Joe Johnson	.10	82T Charlie Moore	.06	108T Luis Salazar	.06
31T Dennis Eckersley	.15	57T Terry Kennedy	.08	83T Jeff Musselman	.20	109T Benny Santiago (RR)	.75
32T Lee Ella	.06	58T Mike Kingery	.10	84T Gene Nelson	.06	110T Dave Schmidt	.06
33T Brian Fisher	.10	59T Ray Knight	.08	85T Graig Nettles	.15	111T Kevin Seitzer (RR)	1.00
34T Terry Francona	.06	60T Gene Larkin	.25	86T Al Newman	.06	112T John Shelby	.06
35T Willie Fraser	.12	61T Mike LaValliere	.10	87T Reid Nichols	.06	113T Steve Shields	.20
36T Billy Gardner	.06	62T Jack Lazorko	.06	88T Tom Niedenfuer	.06	114T John Smiley	.45
37T Ken Gerhart	.15	63T Terry Leach	.15	89T Joe Niekro	.15	115T Chris Speier	.06
38T Danny Gladden	.10	64T Tim Leary	.06	90T Tom Nieto	.06	116T Mike Stanley	.25
39T Jim Gott	.12	65T Jim Lindeman	.15	91T Matt Nokes (RR)	.50	117T Terry Steinbach (RR)	.40
40T Cecilio Guante	.06	66T Steve Lombardozzi	.15	92T Dickie Noles	.06	118T Les Straker	.15
41T Albert Hall	.08	67T Bill Long	.20	93T Pat Pacillo	.15	119T Jim Sundberg	.06
42T Terry Harper	.06	68T Barry Lyons	.25	94T Lance Parrish	.15	120T Danny Tartabull	.30
43T Mickey Hatcher	.06	69T Shane Mack	.20	95T Tony Pena	.15	121T Tom Trebelhorn	.06
44T Brad Havens	.06	70T Greg Maddux	.60	96T Luis Polonia	.20	122T Dave Valle	.10
45T Neal Heaton	.10	71T Bill Madlock	.15	97T Randy Ready	.08	123T Ed VandeBerg	.06
46T Mike Henneman	.40	72T Joe Magrane (RR)	1.00	98T Jeff Reardon	.12	124T Andy Van Slyke	.25
47T Donnie Hill	.06	73T Dave Martinez	.25	99T Gary Redus	.08	125T Gary Ward	.06
48T Guy Hoffman	.06	74T Fred McGriff (RR)	2.00	100T Jeff Reed	.06	126T Alan Wiggins	.06
49T Brian Holton	.15	75T Mark McLemore	.12	101T Rick Rhoden	.10	127T Bill Wilkinson	.10
50T Charles Hudson	.06	76T Kevin McReynolds	.25	102T Cal Ripken, Sr.	.06	128T Frank Williams	.06
51T Dany Jackson	.20	77T Dave Meads	.12	103T Wally Ritchie	.15	129T Matt Williams (RR)	3.00
52T Reggie Jackson	.60	78T Eddie Milner	.06	104T Jeff Robinson (RR)	.40	130T Jim Winn	.06
53T Chris James (RR)	.45	79T Greg Minton	.06	105T Gary Roenicke	.06	131T Matt Young	.06
54T Dion James	.12	80T John Mitchell	.15	106T Jerry Royster	.06	132T Checklist	.06

1988 Topps.... Complete Set of 792 Cards—Value $25.00

Features the rookie cards of Ellis Burks, Matt Williams, Sam Horn, and Al Leiter. A new feature of this year's set was "This Way to the Clubhouse" which explained how a player joined his current team. A "Tiffany" version of the set was also issued.

NO. PLAYER	MINT	NO. PLAYER	MINT	NO. PLAYER	MINT	NO. PLAYER	MINT
1 '87 Record: Coleman	.20	29 Argenis Salazar	.04	57 Tim Crews (R)	.15	85 Howard Johnson	.15
2 '87 Record: Mattingly	.40	30 Sid Fernandez	.10	58 Dave Magadan	.15	86 Ron Karkovice	.04
3 '87 Record: McGwire	.40	31 Bruce Bochy	.04	59 Danny Cox	.04	87 Mike Mason	.04
3 McGwire (error)	1.00	32 Mike Morgan	.04	60 Rickey Henderson	.30	88 Earnie Riles	.04
4 '87 Record: Murray	.25	33 Rob Deer	.15	61 Mark Knudson (R)	.15	89 Gary Thurman (R)	.15
4 Murray (error)	1.00	34 Rickey Horton	.04	62 Jeff Hamilton	.04	90 Dale Murphy	.25
5 '87 Record: Niekro Bros	.10	35 Harold Baines	.10	63 Jimmy Jones	.10	91 Joey Cora (R)	.15
6 '87 Record: Ryan	.30	36 Jamie Moyer	.04	64 Ken Caminiti (R)	.20	92 Len Matuszek	.04
7 '87 Record: Santiago	.10	37 Ed Romero	.04	65 Leon Durham	.06	93 Bob Sebra	.04
8 Jeff Elster	.15	38 Jeff Calhoun	.04	66 Shane Rawley	.04	94 Chuck Johnson (R)	.15
9 Andy Hawkins	.04	39 Gerald Perry	.08	67 Ken Oberkfell	.04	95 Lance Parrish	.08
10 Ryne Sandberg	.30	40 Orel Hershiser	.20	68 Dave Dravecky	.06	96 Todd Benzinger (R)	.25
11 Mike Young	.04	41 Bob Melvin	.04	69 Mike Hart (R)	.12	97 Scott Garrelts	.04
12 Bill Schroeder	.04	42 Bill Landrum (R)	.15	70 Roger Clemens	.40	98 Rene Gonzales (R)	.15
13 Andres Thomas	.04	43 Dick Schofield	.04	71 Gary Pettis	.04	99 Chuck Finley	.04
14 Sparky Anderson	.04	44 Lou Piniella	.06	72 Dennis Eckersley	.06	100 Jack Clark	.15
15 Chili Davis	.08	45 Kent Hrbek	.15	73 Randy Bush	.04	101 Allan Anderson	.04
16 Kirk McCaskill	.06	46 Darnell Coles	.04	74 Tom Lasorda (Mgr.)	.04	102 Barry Larkin	.30
17 Ron Oester	.04	47 Joaquin Andujar	.04	75 Joe Carter	.12	103 Curt Young	.04
18 Al Leiter (error-R)	.60	48 Alan Ashby	.04	76 Denny Martinez	.04	104 Dick Williams	.04
18 Al Leiter (correct-R)	.30	49 Dave Clark	.12	77 Tom O'Malley	.04	105 Jesse Orosco	.06
19 Mark Davidson (R)	.15	50 Hubie Brooks	.04	78 Dan Petry	.06	106 Jim Walewander (R)	.15
20 Kevin Gross	.04	51 Oriole Team	.10	79 Ernie Whitt	.04	107 Scott Bailes	.04
21 Red Sox Team	.08	52 Don Robinson	.04	80 Mark Langston	.10	108 Steve Lyons	.04
22 Greg Swindell	.12	53 Curt Wilkerson	.04	81 Reds Team	.06	109 Joel Skinner	.04
23 Ken Landreaux	.04	54 Jim Clancy	.04	82 Darrel Akerfelds (R)	.15	110 Teddy Higuera	.12
24 Jim Deshaies	.04	55 Phil Bradley	.10	83 Jose Oquendo	.06	111 Expos Team	.06
25 Andres Galarraga	.20	56 Ed Hearn	.04	84 Cecilio Guante	.04	112 Les Lancaster (R)	.15
26 Mitch William	.04						
27 R.J. Reynolds	.04						
28 Jose Nunez (R)	.15						

NO. PLAYER	MINT	NO. PLAYER	MINT	NO. PLAYER	MINT	NO. PLAYER	MINT
113 Kelly Gruber	.25	198 Franklin Stubbs	.06	283 Phil Lombardi	.08	368 Gerald Young (R)	.15
114 Jeff Russell	.04	199 Dave Meads (R)	.12	284 Larry Bowa	.04	369 Greg Harris	.04
115 Johnny Ray	.04	200 Wade Boggs	.50	285 Jim Presley	.08	370 Jose Canseco	1.25
116 J.D. Gleaton	.04	201 Rangers Team	.06	286 Chuck Grim (R)	.12	371 Joe Hesketh	.04
117 James Steels (R)	.10	202 Glenn Hoffman	.04	287 Manny Trillo	.04	372 Matt Williams (R)	1.50
118 Bob Welch	.04	203 Fred Toliver	.04	288 Pat Pacillo	.12	373 Checklist: 265-396	.06
119 Robbie Wine (R)	.15	204 Paul O'Neill	.15	289 Dave Bergman	.04	374 Doc Edwards	.04
120 Kirby Puckett	.40	205 Nelson Liriano (R)	.20	290 Tony Fernandez	.12	375 Tom Brunansky	.08
121 Checklist: 1-132	.06	206 Domingo Ramos	.04	291 Astros Team	.06	376 Bill Wilkinson (R)	.12
122 Tony Bernazard	.04	207 John Mitchell (R)	.15	292 Carney Lansford	.04	377 Sam Horn (R)	.20
123 Tom Candiotti	.06	208 Steve Lake	.04	293 Doug Jones (R)	.25	378 Todd Frohwirth (R)	.15
124 Ray Knight	.04	209 Richard Dotson	.04	294 Al Pedrique (R)	.12	379 Rafael Ramirez	.04
125 Bruce Hurst	.08	210 Willie Randolph	.10	295 Bert Blyleven	.06	380 Joe Magrane (R)	.30
126 Steve Jeltz	.04	211 Frank Dipino	.04	296 Floyd Rayford	.04	381 Angels Team	.06
127 Jim Gott	.04	212 Greg Brock	.04	297 Zane Smith	.04	382 Keith Miller (R)	.20
128 Johnny Grubb	.04	213 Albert Hall	.04	298 Milt Thompson	.04	383 Eric Bell (R)	.12
129 Greg Minton	.04	214 Dave Schmidt	.04	299 Steve Crawford	.04	384 Neil Allen	.04
130 Buddy Bell	.10	215 Von Hayes	.08	300 Don Mattingly	1.00	385 Carlton Fisk	.20
131 Don Schulze	.04	216 Jerry Ruess	.04	301 Bud Black	.06	386 Don Mattingly (AS)	.40
132 Donnie Hill	.04	217 Harry Spillman	.04	302 Jose Uribe	.04	387 Willie Randolph (AS)	.08
133 Greg Mathews	.04	218 Dan Schatzeder	.04	303 Eric Show	.06	388 Wade Boggs (AS)	.30
134 Chuck Tanner (mgr.)	.04	219 Mike Stanley	.12	304 George Hendrick	.06	389 Alan Trammell (AS)	.08
135 Dennis Rasmussen	.06	220 Tom Henke	.04	305 Steve Sax	.10	390 George Bell (AS)	.15
136 Brian Dayett	.04	221 Rafael Belliard	.04	306 Billy Hatcher	.10	391 Kirby Puckett (AS)	.20
137 Chris Bosio	.04	222 Steve Farr	.04	307 Mike Trujillo	.04	392 Dave Winfield (AS)	.12
138 Mitch Webster	.06	223 Stan Jefferson	.12	308 Lee Mazzilli	.06	393 Matt Nokes (AS)	.25
139 Jerry Browne	.12	224 Tom Trebelhorn (R)	.12	309 Bill Long (R)	.15	394 Roger Clemens (AS)	.20
140 Jesse Barfield	.15	225 Mike Scioscia	.04	310 Tom Herr	.04	395 Jimmy Key (AS)	.04
141 Royals Team	.10	226 Dave Lopes	.06	311 Scott Sanderson	.04	396 Tom Henke (AS)	.04
142 Andy Van Slyke	.12	227 Ed Correa	.04	312 Joey Meyer	.10	397 Jack Clark (AS)	.15
143 Mickey Tettleton	.04	228 Wallace Johnson	.04	313 Bob McClure	.04	398 Juan Samuel (AS)	.08
144 Don Gordon (R)	.10	229 Jeff Musselman	.12	314 Jimy Williams	.12	399 Tim Wallach (AS)	.06
145 Bill Madlock	.08	230 Pat Tabler	.04	315 Dave Parker	.15	400 Ozzie Smith (AS)	.08
146 Donnell Nixon (R)	.12	231 Pirates Team	.06	316 Jose Rijo	.04	401 Andre Dawson (AS)	.12
147 Bill Buckner	.04	232 Bob James	.04	317 Tom Nieto	.04	402 Tony Gwynn (AS)	.15
148 Carmelo Martinez	.04	233 Rafael Santana	.04	318 Mel Hall	.04	403 Tim Raines (AS)	.10
149 Ken Howell	.04	234 Ken Dayley	.04	319 Mike Loynd	.04	404 Benny Santiago (AS)	.15
150 Eric Davis	.40	235 Gary Ward	.04	320 Alan Trammell	.15	405 Dwight Gooden (AS)	.20
151 Bob Knepper	.04	236 Ted Power	.04	321 White Sox Team	.06	406 Shane Rawley (AS)	.06
152 Jody Reed (R)	.50	237 Mike Heath	.04	322 Vincente Palacios (R)	.15	407 Steve Bedrosian (AS)	.08
153 John Habyan	.08	238 Luis Polonia (R)	.20	323 Rick Leach	.04	408 Dion James	.04
154 Jeff Stone	.04	239 Roy Smalley	.04	324 Danny Jackson	.15	409 Joel McKeon	.04
155 Bruce Sutter	.08	240 Lee Smith	.08	325 Glenn Hubbard	.04	410 Tony Pena	.04
156 Gary Mathews	.04	241 Damaso Garcia	.06	326 Al Nipper	.04	411 Wayne Tolleson	.04
157 Atlee Hammaker	.04	242 Tom Niedenfuer	.04	327 Larry Sheets	.12	412 Randy Myers	.12
158 Tim Hulett	.04	243 Mark Ryal	.12	328 Greg Cadaret (R)	.15	413 John Christensen	.04
159 Brad Arnsberg (R)	.15	244 Jeff D. Robinson	.04	329 Chris Speier	.04	414 John McNamara	.04
160 Willie McGee	.10	245 Rich Gedman	.04	330 Eddie Whitson	.04	415 Don Carman	.04
161 Bryn Smith	.04	246 Mike Campbell (R)	.20	331 Brian Downing	.04	416 Keith Moreland	.04
162 Mark McLemore	.08	247 Thad Bosley	.04	332 Jerry Reed	.04	417 Mark Ciardi (R)	.12
163 Dale Mahorcic	.04	248 Storm Davis	.04	333 Wally Backman	.04	418 Joel Youngblood	.04
164 Dave Johnson	.04	249 Mike Marshall	.08	334 Dave LaPoint	.04	419 Scott McGregor	.04
165 Robin Yount	.25	250 Nolan Ryan	.50	335 C. Washington	.04	420 Wally Joyner	.25
166 Rick Rodriguez (R)	.12	251 Tom Foley	.04	336 Ed Lynch	.04	421 Ed VandeBerg	.04
167 Rance Mulliniks	.04	252 Bob Brower	.08	337 Jim Gantner	.04	422 Dave Concepcion	.04
168 Barry Jones	.04	253 Checklist: 133-264	.06	338 Brian Holton	.08	423 John Smiley (R)	.30
169 Ross Jones (R)	.15	254 Lee Elia	.04	339 Kurt Stillwell	.08	424 Dwayne Murphy	.04
170 Rich Gossage	.08	255 Mookie Wilson	.06	340 Jack Morris	.12	425 Jeff Reardon	.04
171 Cubs Team	.06	256 Ken Schrom	.04	341 Carmen Castillo	.04	426 Randy Ready	.04
172 Lloyd McClendon (R)	.15	257 Jerry Royster	.04	342 Larry Andersen	.04	427 Paul Kigus (R)	.12
173 Eric Plunk	.04	258 Ed Nunez	.04	343 Greg Gagne	.04	428 John Shelby	.04
174 Phil Garner	.04	259 Ron Kittle	.06	344 Tony LaRussa	.04	429 Tigers Team	.08
175 Kevin Bass	.10	260 Vince Coleman	.20	345 Scott Fletcher	.04	430 Glenn Davis	.12
176 Jeff Reed	.04	261 Giants Team	.06	346 Vance Law	.04	431 Casey Candaele	.08
177 Frank Tanana	.08	262 Drew Hall	.12	347 Joe Johnson	.06	432 Mike Moore	.04
178 Dwayne Henry	.08	263 Glenn Braggs	.12	348 Jim Eisenreich	.04	433 Bill Pecota (R)	.15
179 Charlie Puleo	.04	264 Les Straker (R)	.15	349 Bob Walk	.04	434 Rick Aguilera	.04
180 Terry Kennedy	.04	265 Bo Diaz	.04	350 Will Clark	1.00	435 Mike Pagliarulo	.06
181 Dave Cone	.60	266 Paul Assenmacher	.04	351 Cardinals Team	.06	436 Mike Bielecki	.04
182 Ken Phelps	.04	267 Billy Bean (R)	.15	352 Billy Ripken (R)	.25	437 Fred Manrique (R)	.15
183 Tom Lawless	.04	268 Bruce Ruffin	.04	353 Ed Olwine	.04	438 Rob Ducey (R)	.20
184 Ivan Calderon	.15	269 Ellis Burks (R)	1.00	354 Marc Sullivan	.04	439 Dave Martinez	.15
185 Rick Rhoden	.04	270 Mike Witt	.06	355 Roger McDowell	.04	440 Steve Bedrosian	.10
186 Rafael Palmeiro	.25	271 Ken Gerhart	.10	356 Luis Aguayo	.04	441 Rick Manning	.04
187 Steve Kiefer	.12	272 Steve Ontiveros	.04	357 Floyd Bannister	.04	442 Tom Bolton (R)	.25
188 John Russell	.04	273 Garth Iorg	.04	358 Rey Quinones	.04	443 Ken Griffey	.04
189 Wes Gardner (R)	.15	274 Junior Ortiz	.04	359 Tim Stoddard	.04	444 Cal Ripken, Sr.	.04
190 Candy Maldonado	.10	275 Kevin Seitzer	.50	360 Tony Gwynn	.35	445 Mike Krukow	.04
191 John Cerutti	.04	276 Luis Salazar	.04	361 Greg Maddux	.30	446 Doug DeCinces	.04
192 Devon White	.15	277 Alejandro Pena	.04	362 Juan Castillo	.10	447 Jeff Montgomery (R)	.25
193 Brian Fisher	.06	278 Jose Cruz	.04	363 Willie Fraser	.10	448 Mike Davis	.04
194 Tom Kelly	.04	279 Randy St. Claire	.04	364 Nick Esasky	.04	449 Jeff M. Robinson (R)	.20
195 Dan Quisenberry	.08	280 Pete Incaviglia	.15	365 Floyd Youmans	.04	450 Barry Bonds	.35
196 Dave Engle	.04	281 Jerry Hairston	.04	366 Chet Lemon	.04	451 Keith Atherton	.04
197 Lance McCullers	.04	282 Pat Perry	.04	367 Tim Leary	.04	452 Willie Wilson	.08

NO.	PLAYER	MINT
453	Dennis Powell	.04
454	Marvell Wynne	.04
455	Shawn Hillegas (R)	.15
456	Dave Anderson	.04
457	Terry Leach	.04
458	Ron Hassey	.04
459	Yankees Team	.08
460	Ozzie Smith	.12
461	Danny Darwin	.04
462	Don Slaught	.04
463	Fred McGriff	1.00
464	Jay Tibbs	.04
465	Paul Molitor	.15
466	Jerry Mumphrey	.04
467	Don Aase	.04
468	Darren Daulton	.04
469	Jeff Dedmon	.04
470	Dwight Evans	.08
471	Donnie Moore	.04
472	Robby Thompson	.04
473	Joe Niekro	.06
474	Tom Brookens	.04
475	Pete Rose (mgr.)	.30
476	Dave Stewart	.20
477	Jamie Quirk	.04
478	Sid Bream	.04
479	Brett Butler	.04
480	Dwight Gooden	.40
481	Mariano Duncan	.06
482	Mark Davis	.04
483	Rod Booker (R)	.15
484	Pat Clements	.04
485	Harold Reynolds	.04
486	Pat Keedy (R)	.12
487	Jim Pankovits	.04
488	Andy McGaffigan	.04
489	Dodgers Team	.10
490	Larry Parrish	.04
491	B.J. Surhoff	.15
492	Doyle Alexander	.04
493	Mike Greenwell	.50
494	Wally Ritchie (R)	.12
495	Eddie Murray	.25
496	Guy Hoffman	.04
497	Kevin Mitchell	.30
498	Bob Boone	.04
499	Eric King	.04
500	Andre Dawson	.20
501	Tim Birtsas	.04
502	Danny Gladden	.04
503	Junior Noboa (R)	.12
504	Bob Rodgers	.04
505	Willie Upshaw	.06
506	John Cangelosi	.04
507	Mark Gubicza	.04
508	Tim Teufel	.04
509	Bill Dawley	.04
510	Dave Winfield	.20
511	Joel Davis	.04
512	Alex Trevino	.04
513	Tim Flannery	.04
514	Pat Sheridan	.04
515	Juan Nieves	.04
516	Jim Sundberg	.04
517	Ron Robinson	.04
518	Greg Gross	.04
519	Mariners Team	.04
520	Dave Smith	.04
521	Jim Dwyer	.04
522	Bob Patterson (R)	.12
523	Gary Roenicke	.04
524	Gary Lucas	.04
525	Marty Barrett	.06
526	Juan Berenguer	.04
527	Steve Henderson	.04
528	CL: 397-528 (error)	.75
529	Tim Burke	.04
530	Gary Carter	.20
531	Rich Yett	.04
532	Mike Kingery	.04
533	John Farrell (R)	.20
534	John Wathan	.04
535	Ron Guidry	.10
536	John Morris	.04
537	Steve Buechele	.04
538	Bill Wegman	.04
539	Mike LaValliere	.04
540	Bret Saberhagen	.12
541	Juan Beniquez	.04
542	Paul Noce (R)	.12
543	Kent Tekulve	.04
544	Jim Traber	.04
545	Don Baylor	.08
546	John Candelaria	.06
547	Felix Fermin (R)	.10
548	Shane Mack	.15
549	Braves Team	.06
550	Pedro Guerrero	.20
551	Terry Steinbach	.25
552	Mark Thurmond	.04
553	Tracy Jones	.10
554	Mike Smithson	.04
555	Brook Jacoby	.08
556	Stan Clarke (R)	.10
557	Craig Reynolds	.04
558	Bob Ojeda	.04
559	Ken Williams (R)	.20
560	Tim Wallach	.08
561	Rick Cerone	.04
562	Jim Lindeman	.15
563	Jose Guzman	.04
564	Frank Lucchesi	.04
565	Lloyd Moseby	.15
566	Charlie O'Brien (R)	.10
567	Mike Diaz	.04
568	Chris Brown	.10
569	C. Liebrandt	.06
570	Jeffrey Leonard	.04
571	Mark Williamson (R)	.15
572	Chris James	.20
573	Bob Stanley	.04
574	Graig Nettles	.10
575	Don Sutton	.15
576	Tommy Hinzo (R)	.12
577	Tom Browning	.06
578	Gary Gaetti	.12
579	Mets Team	.15
580	Mark McGwire	.75
581	Tito Landrum	.04
582	Mike Henneman (R)	.15
583	Dave Valle	.08
584	Steve Trout	.04
585	Ozzie Guillen	.04
586	Bob Forsch	.04
587	Terry Puhl	.04
588	Jeff Parrett (R)	.15
589	Geno Petralli	.04
590	George Bell	.15
591	Doug Drabek	.15
592	Dale Sveum	.06
593	Bob Tewksbury	.04
594	Bobby Valentine	.04
595	Frank White	.04
596	John Kruk	.12
597	Gene Garber	.04
598	Lee Lacy	.04
599	Calvin Schiraldi	.04
600	Mike Schmidt	.35
601	Jack Lazorko	.04
602	Mike Aldrete	.04
603	Rob Murphy	.04
604	Chris Bando	.04
605	Kirk Gibson	.15
606	Moose Haas	.04
607	Mickey Hatcher	.04
608	Charlie Kerfeld	.06
609	Twins Team	.08
610	Keith Hernandez	.15
611	Tommy John	.08
612	Curt Ford	.04
613	Bobby Thigpen	.20
614	Herm Winningham	.04
615	Jody Davis	.04
616	Jay Aldrich (R)	.12
617	Oddibe McDowell	.10
618	Cecil Fielder	.50
619	Mike Dunne	.20
620	Cory Snyder	.15
621	Gene Nelson	.04
622	Kal Daniels	.20
623	Mike Flanagan	.04
624	Jim Leyland	.04
625	Frank Viola	.15
626	Glenn Wilson	.04
627	Joe Boever (R)	.12
628	Dave Henderson	.04
629	Kelly Downs	.04
630	Darrell Evans	.12
631	Jack Howell	.04
632	Steve Shields	.10
633	Barry Lyons (R)	.15
634	Jose DeLeon	.06
635	Terry Pendleton	.06
636	Charles Hudson	.04
637	Jay Bell (R)	.20
638	Steve Balboni	.04
639	Brewers Team	.06
640	Garry Templeton	.06
641	Bob Honeycutt	.06
642	Bob Dernier	.04
643	Rocky Childress (R)	.12
644	Terry McGriff	.15
645	Matt Nokes (R)	.30
646	Checklist: 529-660	.06
647	Pascual Perez	.04
648	Al Newman	.04
649	DeWayne Buice (R)	.15
650	Cal Ripken	.20
651	Mike Jackson	.15
652	Bruce Benedict	.04
653	Jeff Sellers	.04
654	Roger Craig	.04
655	Len Dykstra	.15
656	Lee Guetterman	.04
657	Gary Redus	.04
658	Tim Conroy	.04
659	Bobby Meacham	.04
660	Rick Reuschel	.04
661	Turn Back—1983	.08
662	Turn Back—1978	.08
663	Turn Back—1973	.08
664	Turn Back—1968	.08
665	Turn Back—1963	.10
666	Mario Soto	.04
667	Luis Quinones	.04
668	Walt Terrell	.04
669	Phillies Team	.06
670	Dan Plesac	.04
671	Tim Laudner	.04
672	John Davis (R)	.20
673	Tony Phillips	.04
674	Mike Fitzgerald	.04
675	Jim Rice	.15
676	Ken Dixon	.04
677	Eddie Milner	.04
678	Jim Acker	.04
679	Darrell Miller	.04
680	Charlie Hough	.06
681	Bobby Bonilla	.35
682	Jimmy Key	.08
683	Julio Franco	.12
684	Hal Lanier	.04
685	Ron Darling	.15
686	Terry Francona	.04
687	Mickey Brantley	.08
688	Jim Winn	.04
689	Tom Pagnozzi (R)	.15
690	Jay Howell	.04
691	Dan Pasqua	.10
692	Mike Birkbeck	.04
693	Benny Santiago	.45
694	Eric Nolte (R)	.12
695	Shawon Dunston	.12
696	Duane Ward	.04
697	S. Lombardozzi	.10
698	Brad Havens	.04
699	Padres Team	.15
700	George Brett	.25
701	Sammy Stewart	.04
702	Mike Gallego	.04
703	Bob Brenly	.04
704	Dennis Boyd	.04
705	Juan Samuel	.15
706	Rick Mahler	.04
707	Fred Lynn	.10
708	Gus Polidor	.08
709	George Frazier	.04
710	D. Strawberry	.40
711	Bill Gullickson	.04
712	John Moses	.04
713	Willie Hernandez	.08
714	Jim Fregosi	.04
715	Todd Worrell	.10
716	Lenn Sakata	.04
717	Jay Baller	.08
718	Mike Felder	.04
719	Denny Walling	.04
720	Tim Raines	.20
721	Pete O'Brien	.10
722	Manny Lee	.04
723	Bob Kipper	.04
724	Danny Tartabull	.15
725	Mike Boddicker	.04
726	Alfredo Griffin	.04
727	Greg Booker	.04
728	Andy Allanson	.04
729	Blue Jays Team	.06
730	John Franco	.06
731	Rick Schu	.04
732	Dave Palmer	.04
733	Spike Owen	.04
734	Craig Lefferts	.04
735	Kevin McReynolds	.15
736	Matt Young	.04
737	Butch Wynegar	.04
738	Scott Bankhead	.04
739	Daryl Boston	.04
740	Rick Sutcliffe	.15
741	Mike Easler	.04
742	Mark Clear	.04
743	Larry Herndon	.04
744	Whitey Herzog (mgr.)	.04
745	Bill Doran	.10
746	Gene Larkin (R)	.25
747	Bobby Witt	.10
748	Reid Nichols	.04
749	Mark Eichhorn	.04
750	Bo Jackson	1.00
751	Jim Morrison	.04
752	Mark Grant	.08
753	Danny Heep	.04
754	Mike LaCoss	.04
755	Ozzie Virgil	.06
756	Mike Maddux	.04
757	John Marzano	.15
758	Eddie Williams (R)	.15
759	A's Team	.30
760	Mike Scott	.15
761	Tony Armas	.06
762	Scott Bradley	.04
763	Doug Sisk	.04
764	Greg Walker	.08
765	Neal Heaton	.10
766	Henry Cotto	.04
767	Jose Lind (R)	.25
768	Dickie Noles	.04
769	Cecil Cooper	.06
770	Lou Whitaker	.15
771	Ruben Sierra	.30
772	Sal Butera	.04
773	Frank Williams	.04
774	Gene Mauch	.04
775	Dave Stieb	.06
776	Checklist: 661-792	.06
777	Lonnie Smith	.04
778	K. Comstock (R)(error)	5.00
778	K. Comstock (R)(correct)	.25
779	Tom Glavine (R)	.25
780	F. Valenzuela	.15
781	Keith Hughes (R)	.15
782	Jeff Ballard (R)	.25
783	Ron Roenicke	.04
784	Joe Sambito	.04
785	Alvin Davis	.08
786	Joe Price	.04
787	Bill Almon	.04
788	Ray Searage	.04
789	Indians Team	.08
790	Dave Righetti	.10
791	Ted Simmons	.08
792	John Tudor	.08

1988 Topps Traded.... Complete Set of 132 Cards—Value $25.00

Updates the main 1988 card set with players who changed teams during the season and rookies. Features the first Topps card for Mark Grace, Jim Abbott, Andy Benes and the USA Olympic Team. The complete set was packaged in a printed box and distributed primarily through card hobby dealers. A "Tiffany" version of the set was also issued.

NO. PLAYER	MINT	NO. PLAYER	MINT	NO. PLAYER	MINT	NO. PLAYER	MINT
1 T Jim Abbott (OLY)	5.00	34 T Jose DeLeon	.06	67 T Billy Masse (OLY)	.20	100 T Luis Salazar	.06
2 T Juan Agosto	.06	35 T Richard Dotson	.06	68 T Jack McDowell	.25	101 T Rafael Santana	.06
3 T Luis Alicea	.10	36 T Cecil Espy	.15	69 T Jack McKeon	.06	102 T Nelson Santovenia	.20
4 T Roberto Alomar (RR)	1.50	37 T Tom Filer	.06	70 T Larry McWilliams	.06	103 T Mackey Sasser	.30
5 T Brady Anderson	.35	38 T Mike Fiore (OLY)	.15	71 T M. Morandini (OLY)	.30	104 T Calvin Schiraldi	.06
6 T Jack Armstrong	.75	39 T Ron Gant (RR)	2.00	72 T Keith Moreland	.06	105 T Mike Schooler	.25
7 T Don August	.06	40 T Kirk Gibson	.20	73 T Mike Morgan	.06	106 T Scott Servais (OLY)	.15
8 T Floyd Bannister	.06	41 T Rich Gossage	.06	74 T Charles Nagy (OLY)	.50	107 T Dave Silvestri (OLY)	.15
9 T Bret Barberie (OLY)	.20	42 T Mark Grace (RR)	5.00	75 T Al Nipper	.06	108 T Don Slaught	.06
10 T Jose Bautista	.15	43 T Alfredo Griffin	.06	76 T Russ Nixon	.06	109 T Joe Slusarski (OLY)	.15
11 T Don Baylor	.06	44 T Ty Griffin (OLY)	1.00	77 T Jesse Orosco	.06	110 T Lee Smith	.06
12 T Tim Belcher	.10	45 T Bryan Harvey	.20	78 T Joe Orsulak	.06	111 T Pete Smith	.20
13 T Buddy Bell	.06	46 T Ron Hassey	.06	79 T Dave Palmer	.06	112 T Jim Snyder	.06
14 T Andy Benes (OLY)	2.00	47 T Ray Hayward	.10	80 T Mark Parent	.10	113 T Ed Sprague (OLY)	.25
15 T Damon Berryhill	.35	48 T Dave Henderson	.06	81 T Dave Parker	.15	114 T Pete Stanicek	.10
16 T Bud Black	.06	49 T Tom Herr	.06	82 T Dan Pasqua	.06	115 T Kurt Stillwell	.10
17 T Pat Borders	.25	50 T Bob Horner	.06	83 T Melido Perez	.25	116 T Todd Stottlemyre	.25
18 T Phil Bradley	.06	51 T Rickey Horton	.06	84 T Steve Peters	.10	117 T Bill Swift	.06
19 T Jeff Branson (OLY)	.20	52 T Jay Howell	.06	85 T Dan Petry	.06	118 T Pat Tabler	.06
20 T Tom Brunansky	.15	53 T Glenn Hubbard	.06	86 T Gary Pettis	.06	119 T Scott Terry	.06
21 T Jay Buhner	.40	54 T Jeff Innis	.20	87 T Jeff Pico	.15	120 T Mickey Tettleton	.06
22 T Brett Butler	.06	55 T Danny Jackson	.20	88 T Jim Poole (OLY)	.20	121 T Dickie Thon	.06
23 T Jim Campanis (OLY)	.20	56 T Darrin Jackson	.10	89 T Ted Power	.06	122 T Jeff Treadway	.25
24 T Sil Campusano	.20	57 T Roberto Kelly (RR)	.75	90 T Rafael Ramirez	.06	123 T Willie Upshaw	.06
25 T John Candelaria	.06	58 T Ron Kittle	.06	91 T Dennis Rasmussen	.06	124 T Robin Ventura (OLY)	2.00
26 T Jose Cecana	.08	59 T Ray Knight	.06	92 T Jose Rijo	.06	125 T Ron Washington	.06
27 T Rick Cerone	.06	60 T Vance Law	.06	93 T Ernie Riles	.06	126 T Walt Weiss (RR)	1.00
28 T Jack Clark	.15	61 T Jeffrey Leonard	.06	94 T Luis Rivera	.10	127 T Bob Welch	.06
29 T Kevin Coffman	.10	62 T Mike Macfarlane	.15	95 T Doug Robbins	.15	128 T David Wells	.15
30 T Pat Combs (OLY)	1.00	63 T Scott Madison	.10	96 T Frank Robinson	.15	129 T Glenn Wilson	.06
31 T Henry Cotto	.06	64 T Kirt Manwaring	.10	97 T Cookie Rojas	.06	130 T Ted Wood (OLY)	.30
32 T Chill Davis	.06	65 T Mark Marquess	.06	98 T Chris Sabo (RR)	2.00	131 T Don Zimmer	.06
33 T Mike Davis	.06	66 T Tino Martinez (OLY)	3.00	99 T Mark Salas	.06	132 T Checklist	.06

1989 Topps.... Complete Set of 792 Cards—Value $25.00

Features the rookie cards of Sandy Alomar, Jr., Ricky Jordan, Robin Ventura and Gary Sheffield. New features this year are "#1 Draft Picks" and 1988 "Monthly Scoreboard." A "Tiffany" version of the set was also issued.

NO. PLAYER	MINT	NO. PLAYER	MINT	NO. PLAYER	MINT	NO. PLAYER	MINT
1 '88 Record: G. Bell	.15	4 '88 Record: Dawson	.10	7 '88 Rec.: McReynolds	.10	10 Andre Dawson	.15
2 '88 Record: Boggs	.20	5 '88 Rec.: Hershiser	.10	8 Dave Eiland (R)	.15	11 Bruce Sutter	.08
3 '88 Record: G. Carter	.10	6 '88 Record: D. Jones	.05	9 Tim Teufel	.05	12 Dale Sveum	.08

NO.	PLAYER	MINT
13	Doug Sisk	.05
14	Tom Kelly	.05
15	Robby Thompson	.05
16	Ron Robinson	.08
17	Brian Downing	.08
18	Rick Rhoden	.05
19	Greg Gagne	.05
20	Steve Bedrosian	.08
21	Walker: *Bonus*	.05
22	Tim Crews	.05
23	Mike Fitzgerald	.05
24	Larry Andersen	.05
25	Frank White	.05
26	Dale Mohorcac	.05
27	Orestes Destrade (R)	.25
28	Mike Moore	.05
29	Kelly Gruber	.15
30	Doc Gooden	.30
31	Terry Francona	.10
32	Dennis Rasmussen	.05
33	B.J. Surhoff	.08
34	Ken Williams	.05
35	John Tudor	.05
36	Mitch Webster	.05
37	Bob Stanley	.05
38	Paul Runge	.05
39	Mike Maddux	.05
40	Steve Sax	.12
41	Terry Mulholland	.05
42	Jim Eppard	.10
43	Guillermo Hernandez	.05
44	Jim Snyder (R)	.10
45	Kal Daniels	.15
46	Mark Portugal	.05
47	Carney Lansford	.08
48	Tim Burke	.05
49	Craig Biggio (R)	.35
50	George Bell	.15
51	McLemore: *Bonus*	.05
52	Bob Brenly	.05
53	Ruben Sierra	.15
54	Steve Trout	.05
55	Julio Franco	.08
56	Pat Tabler	.08
57	Alejandro Pena	.08
58	Lee Mazzilli	.05
59	Mark Davis	.10
60	Tom Brunansky	.08
61	Neil Allen	.05
62	Alfredo Griffin	.05
63	Mark Clear	.05
64	Alex Trevino	.05
65	Rick Reuschel	.05
66	Manny Trillo	.05
67	Dave Palmer	.05
68	Darrell Miller	.05
69	Jeff Ballard	.05
70	Mark McGwire	.50
71	Mike Boddicker	.08
72	John Moses	.05
73	Pascual Perez	.05
74	Nick Leyva (R)	.05
75	Tom Henke	.05
76	Terry Blocker (R)	.15
77	Doyle Alexander	.05
78	Jim Sundberg	.05
79	Scott Bankhead	.05
80	Cory Snyder	.15
81	Raines: *Bonus*	.08
82	Dave Leiper	.05
83	Jeff Blauser	.10
84	Bill Bene (R)	.20
85	Kevin McReynolds	.15
86	Al Nipper	.05
87	Larry Owen	.05
88	Darryl Hamilton (R)	.15
89	Dave LaPoint	.05
90	Vince Coleman	.15
91	Floyd Youmans	.05
92	Jeff Kunkel	.05
93	Ken Howell	.05
94	Chris Speier	.05
95	Gerald Young	.08
96	Rick Cerone	.05
97	Greg Mathews	.05
98	Larry Sheets	.05
99	Sherman Corbett (R)	.15
100	Mike Schmidt	.25
101	Les Straker	.05
102	Mike Gallego	.05
103	Tim Birtsas	.05
104	Dallas Green	.05
105	Ron Darling	.10
106	Willie Upshaw	.05
107	Jose DeLeon	.05
108	Fred Manrique	.05
109	Hipolito Pena (R)	.15
110	Paul Molitor	.12
111	Davis: *Bonus*	.15
112	Jim Presley	.06
113	Lloyd Moseby	.12
114	Bob Kipper	.05
115	Jody Davis	.05
116	Jeff Montgomery	.05
117	Dave Anderson	.05
118	Checklist: 1-132	.08
119	Terry Puhl	.05
120	Frank Viola	.15
121	Garry Templeton	.05
122	Lance Johnson	.10
123	Spike Owen	.05
124	Jim Traber	.05
125	Mike Krukow	.08
126	Sid Bream	.05
127	Walt Terrell	.05
128	Milt Thompson	.05
129	Terry Clark (R)	.15
130	Gerald Perry	.10
131	Dave Otto	.15
132	Curt Ford	.05
133	Bill Long	.05
134	Don Zimmer	.05
135	Jose Rijo	.08
136	Joey Meyer	.05
137	Geno Petralli	.05
138	Wallace Johnson	.05
139	Mike Flanagan	.05
140	Shawon Dunston	.10
141	Jacoby: *Bonus*	.05
142	Mike Diaz	.05
143	Mike Campbell	.05
144	Jay Bell	.05
145	Dave Stewart	.15
146	Gary Pettis	.05
147	DeWayne Buice	.05
148	Bill Pecota	.05
149	Doug Dascenzo (R)	.15
150	Fernando Valenzuela	.10
151	Terry McGriff	.05
152	Mark Thurmond	.05
153	Jim Pankovits	.05
154	Don Carman	.05
155	Marty Barrett	.05
156	Dave Gallagher (R)	.15
157	Tom Glavine	.05
158	Mike Aldrete	.05
159	Pat Clements	.05
160	Jeffrey Leonard	.05
161	Gregg Olson (R)	.75
162	John Davis	.05
163	Bob Forsch	.05
164	Hal Lanier	.05
165	Mike Dunne	.05
166	Doug Jennings (R)	.15
167	Steve Searcy (R)	.15
168	Willie Wilson	.08
169	Mike Jackson	.05
170	Tony Fernandez	.10
171	Thomas: *Bonus*	.05
172	Frank Williams	.05
173	Mel Hall	.05
174	Todd Burns (R)	.20
175	John Shelby	.05
176	Jeff Parrett	.08
177	Monty Fariss (R)	.25
178	Mark Grant	.05
179	Ozzie Virgil	.05
180	Mike Scott	.15
181	Craig Worthington (R)	.25
182	Bob McClure	.05
183	Oddibe McDowell	.08
184	John Costello (R)	.15
185	Claudell Washington	.05
186	Pat Perry	.05
187	Darren Daulton	.05
188	Dennis Lamp	.05
189	Kevin Mitchell	.30
190	Mike Witt	.08
191	Sil Campusano (R)	.20
192	Paul Mirabella	.05
193	Sparky Anderson	.05
194	Greg Harris (R)	.20
195	Ozzie Guillen	.08
196	Denny Walling	.05
197	Neal Heaton	.05
198	Danny Heep	.05
199	Mike Schooler (R)	.25
200	George Brett	.25
201	Gruber: *Bonus*	.05
202	Brad Moore (R)	.15
203	Rob Ducey	.05
204	Brad Havens	.05
205	Dwight Evans	.15
206	Roberto Alomar	.50
207	Terry Leach	.05
208	Tom Pagnozzi	.05
209	Jeff Bittiger (R)	.15
210	Dale Murphy	.25
211	Mike Pagliarulo	.10
212	Scott Sanderson	.05
213	Rene Gonzales	.05
214	Charlie O'Brien	.05
215	Kevin Gross	.05
216	Jack Howell	.08
217	Joe Price	.05
218	Mike LaValliere	.05
219	Jim Clancy	.05
220	Gary Gaetti	.10
221	Cecil Espy	.10
222	Mark Lewis (R)	.40
223	Jay Buhner	.15
224	Tony LaRussa	.05
225	Ramon Martinez (R)	1.00
226	Bill Doran	.08
227	John Farrell	.10
228	Nelson Santovenia (R)	.15
229	Jimmy Key	.12
230	Ozzie Smith	.12
231	R. Alomar: *Bonus*	.10
232	Ricky Horton	.05
233	Gregg Jefferies	1.50
234	Tom Browning	.08
235	John Kruk	.15
236	Charles Hudson	.08
237	Glenn Hubbard	.05
238	Eric King	.05
239	Tim Laudner	.05
240	Greg Maddux	.15
241	Brett Butler	.05
242	Ed VandeBerg	.05
243	Bob Boone	.05
244	Jim Acker	.05
245	Jim Rice	.12
246	Rey Quinones	.05
247	Shawn Hillegas	.05
248	Tony Phillips	.05
249	Tim Leary	.10
250	Cal Ripken	.20
251	John Dopson (R)	.20
252	Billy Hatcher	.05
253	Jose Alvarez (R)	.15
254	Tom Lasorda	.05
255	Ron Guidry	.08
256	Benny Santiago	.10
257	Rick Aguilera	.05
258	Checklist: 133-264	.08
259	Larry McWilliams	.05
260	Dave Winfield	.15
261	Brunansky *Bonus*	.08
262	Jeff Pico (R)	.15
263	Mike Felder	.05
264	Rob Dibble (R)	.30
265	Kent Hrbek	.10
266	Luis Aquino	.05
267	Jeff Robinson	.05
268	Keith Miller (R)	.15
269	Tom Bolton	.05
270	Wally Joyner	.15
271	Jay Tibbs	.05
272	Ron Hassey	.05
273	Jose Lind	.05
274	Mark Eichhorn	.05
275	Danny Tartabull	.15
276	Paul Kilgus	.05
277	Mike Davis	.05
278	Andy McGaffigan	.05
279	Scott Bradley	.05
280	Bob Knepper	.05
281	Gary Redus	.05
282	Cris Carpenter (R)	.20
283	Andy Allanson	.05
284	Jim Leyland	.05
285	John Candelaria	.08
286	Darrin Jackson	.12
287	Juan Nieves	.05
288	Pat Sheridan	.05
289	Ernie Whitt	.05
290	John Franco	.08
291	Strawberry: *Bonus*	.20
292	Jim Corsi (R)	.15
293	Glenn Wilson	.05
294	Juan Berenguer	.05
295	Scott Fletcher	.05
296	Ron Gant	.30
297	Oswald Peraza (R)	.15
298	Chris James	.08
299	Steve Ellsworth (R)	.15
300	Darryl Strawberry	.35
301	Charlie Leibrandt	.08
302	Gary Ward	.05
303	Felix Fermin	.05
304	Joel Youngblood	.05
305	Dave Smith	.05
306	Tracy Woodson	.10
307	Lance McCullers	.08
308	Ron Karkovice	.05
309	Mario Diaz	.10
310	Rafael Palmeiro	.15
311	Chris Bosio	.05
312	Tom Lawless	.05
313	Denny Martinez	.05
314	Bobby Valentine	.05
315	Greg Swindell	.10
316	Walt Weiss	.25
317	Jack Armstrong (R)	.30
318	Gene Larkin	.05
319	Greg Booker	.05
320	Lou Whitaker	.08
321	Reed: *Bonus*	.10
322	John Smiley	.08
323	Gary Thurman	.05
324	Bob Milacki (R)	.20
325	Jesse Barfield	.12
326	Dennis Boyd	.08
327	Mark Lemke (R)	.15
328	Rick Honeycutt	.05
329	Bob Melvin	.05
330	Eric Davis	.25
331	Curt Wilkerson	.05
332	Tony Armas	.05
333	Bob Ojeda	.08
334	Steve Lyons	.05
335	Dave Righetti	.10
336	Steve Balboni	.05
337	Calvin Schiraldi	.05
338	Jim Adduci	.08
339	Scott Bailes	.05
340	Kirk Gibson	.15
341	Jim Deshaies	.05
342	Tom Brookens	.05
343	Gary Sheffield (R)	1.00
344	Tom Trebelhorn	.05
345	Charlie Hough	.08
346	Rex Hudler	.10
347	John Cerutti	.05
348	Ed Hearn	.05
349	Ron Jones (R)	.20
350	Andy Van Slyke	.15
351	Melvin: *Bonus*	.05
352	Rick Schu	.05

NO.	PLAYER	MINT
353	Marvell Wynne	.05
354	Larry Parrish	.05
355	Mark Langston	.10
356	Kevin Elster	.08
357	Jerry Reuss	.05
358	Ricky Jordan (R)	.60
359	Tommy John	.10
360	Ryne Sandberg	.20
361	Kelly Downs	.06
362	Jack Lazorko	.05
363	Rich Yett	.05
364	Rob Deer	.08
365	Mike Henneman	.05
366	Herm Winningham	.05
367	Johnny Paredes (R)	.15
368	Brian Holton	.05
369	Ken Caminiti	.05
370	Dennis Eckersley	.10
371	Manny Lee	.05
372	Craig Lefferts	.05
373	Tracy Jones	.05
374	John Wathan	.05
375	Terry Pendleton	.08
376	Steve Lombardozzi	.05
377	Mike Smithson	.05
378	Checklist: 265-396	.08
379	Tim Flannery	.05
380	Rickey Henderson	.25
381	Sheets: Bonus	.05
382	John Smoltz (R)	.50
383	Howard Johnson	.15
384	Mark Salas	.05
385	Von Hayes	.08
386	Andres Galarraga (AS)	.10
387	Ryne Sandberg (AS)	.10
388	Bobby Bonilla (AS)	.10
389	Ozzie Smith (AS)	.08
390	Darryl Strawberry (AS)	.20
391	Andre Dawson (AS)	.10
392	Andy Van Slyke (AS)	.10
393	Gary Carter (AS)	.10
394	Orel Hershiser (AS)	.10
395	Danny Jackson (AS)	.08
396	Kirk Gibson (AS)	.10
397	Don Mattingly (AS)	.35
398	Julio Franco (AS)	.08
399	Wade Boggs (AS)	.25
400	Alan Trammell (AS)	.08
401	Jose Canseco (AS)	.40
402	Mike Greenwell (AS)	.25
403	Kirby Puckett (AS)	.15
404	Bob Boone (AS)	.05
405	Roger Clemens (AS)	.20
406	Frank Viola (AS)	.10
407	Dave Winfield (AS)	.08
408	Greg Walker	.05
409	Ken Dayley	.05
410	Jack Clark	.10
411	Mitch Williams	.05
412	Barry Lyons	.05
413	Mike Kingery	.05
414	Jim Fregosi	.05
415	Rich Gossage	.08
416	Fred Lynn	.08
417	Mike LaCoss	.05
418	Bob Dernier	.05
419	Tom Filer	.05
420	Joe Carter	.15
421	Kirk McCaskill	.05
422	Bo Diaz	.05
423	Brian Fisher	.05
424	Luis Polonia	.05
425	Jay Howell	.08
426	Danny Gladden	.05
427	Eric Show	.05
428	Craig Reynolds	.05
429	Gagne: Bonus	.05
430	Mark Gubicza	.10
431	Luis Rivera	.15
432	Chad Kreuter (R)	.15
433	Albert Hall	.05
434	Ken Patterson (R)	.15
435	Len Dykstra	.15
436	Bobby Meacham	.05
437	Andy Benes (R)	.60
438	Greg Gross	.05
439	Frank Dipino	.05
440	Bobby Bonilla	.15
441	Jerry Reed	.05
442	Jose Oquendo	.05
443	Rod Nichols (R)	.15
444	Moose Stubing (R)	.05
445	Matt Nokes	.10
446	Rob Murphy	.05
447	Donell Nixon	.05
448	Eric Plunk	.05
449	Carmelo Martinez	.05
450	Roger Clemens	.25
451	Mark Davidson	.05
452	Israel Sanchez (R)	.15
453	Tom Prince	.10
454	Paul Assenmacher	.05
455	Johnny Ray	.10
456	Tim Belcher	.15
457	Mackey Sasser	.15
458	Donn Pall (R)	.15
459	Valle: Bonus	.05
460	Dave Stieb	.08
461	Buddy Bell	.08
462	Jose Guzman	.05
463	Steve Lake	.05
464	Bryn Smith	.05
465	Mark Grace	1.00
466	Chuck Crim	.05
467	Jim Walewander	.05
468	Henry Cotto	.05
469	Jose Bautista (R)	.15
470	Lance Parrish	.10
471	Steve Curry (R)	.15
472	Brian Harper	.05
473	Don Robinson	.05
474	Bob Rodgers	.05
475	Dave Parker	.10
476	Jon Perlman	.05
477	Dick Schofield	.05
478	Doug Drabek	.10
479	Mike Macfarlane	.15
480	Keith Hernandez	.15
481	Chris Brown	.08
482	Steve Peters (R)	.15
483	Mickey Hatcher	.05
484	Steve Shields	.05
485	Hubie Brooks	.05
486	Jack McDowell	.12
487	Scott Lusader	.10
488	Kevin Coffman	.10
489	Schmidt: Bonus	.15
490	Chris Sabo (R)	1.00
491	Mike Birkbeck	.05
492	Alan Ashby	.05
493	Todd Benzinger	.15
494	Shane Rawley	.05
495	Candy Maldonado	.10
496	Dwayne Henry	.05
497	Pete Stanicek	.08
498	Dave Valle	.05
499	Don Heinkel (R)	.15
500	Jose Canseco	.75
501	Vance Law	.05
502	Duane Ward	.05
503	Al Newman	.05
504	Bob Walk	.05
505	Pete Rose	.20
506	Kirt Manwaring	.15
507	Steve Farr	.05
508	Wally Backman	.05
509	Bud Black	.05
510	Bob Horner	.05
511	Richard Dotson	.08
512	Donnie Hill	.05
513	Jesse Orosco	.05
514	Chet Lemon	.05
515	Barry Larkin	.20
516	Eddie Whitson	.05
517	Greg Brock	.05
518	Bruce Ruffin	.05
519	Randolph: Bonus	.08
520	Rick Sutcliffe	.10
521	Mickey Tettleton	.05
522	Randy Kramer (R)	.15
523	Andres Thomas	.05
524	Checklist: 397-528	.08
525	Chili Davis	.08
526	Wes Gardner	.05
527	Dave Henderson	.05
528	Luis Medina (R)	.20
529	Tom Foley	.05
530	Nolan Ryan	.50
531	Dave Hengel	.10
532	Jerry Browne	.05
533	Andy Hawkins	.05
534	Doc Edwards	.05
535	Todd Worrell	.08
536	Joel Skinner	.05
537	Pete Smith	.12
538	Juan Castillo	.05
539	Barry Jones	.05
540	Bo Jackson	.60
541	Cecil Fielder	.30
542	Todd Frohwirth	.05
543	Damon Berryhill	.20
544	Jeff Sellers	.05
545	Mookie Wilson	.08
546	Mark Williamson	.05
547	Mark McLemore	.05
548	Bobby Witt	.05
549	Moyer: Bonus	.05
550	Orel Hershiser	.20
551	Randy Ready	.05
552	Greg Cadaret	.05
553	Luis Salazar	.05
554	Nick Esasky	.10
555	Bert Blyleven	.15
556	Bruce Fields	.10
557	Keith Miller	.05
558	Dan Pasqua	.08
559	Juan Agosto	.05
560	Tim Raines	.15
561	Luis Aguayo	.05
562	Danny Cox	.05
563	Bill Schroeder	.05
564	Russ Nixon	.05
565	Jeff Russell	.05
566	Al Pedrique	.05
567	David Wells	.10
568	Mickey Brantley	.08
569	German Jimenez (R)	.15
570	Tony Gwynn	.20
571	Billy Ripken	.05
572	Atlee Hammaker	.05
573	Jim Abbott (R)	1.25
574	Dave Clark	.05
575	Juan Samuel	.10
576	Greg Minton	.05
577	Randy Bush	.05
578	John Morris	.05
579	G. Davis: Bonus	.08
580	Harold Reynolds	.08
581	Gene Nelson	.05
582	Mike Marshall	.08
583	Paul Gibson (R)	.15
584	Randy Velarde	.15
585	Harold Baines	.10
586	Joe Boever	.05
587	Mike Stanley	.05
588	Luis Alicea (R)	.15
589	Dave Meads	.05
590	Andres Galarraga	.15
591	Jeff Musselman	.05
592	John Cangelosi	.05
593	Drew Hall	.05
594	Jimy Williams	.05
595	Teddy Higuera	.10
596	Kurt Stillwell	.05
597	Terry Taylor (R)	.15
598	Ken Gerhart	.05
599	Tom Candiotti	.08
600	Wade Boggs	.40
601	Dave Dravecky	.05
602	Devon White	.08
603	Frank Tanana	.08
604	Paul O'Neill	.10
605	Bob Welch (Correct)	.20
605	Bob Welch (error)	3.00
606	Rick Dempsey	.05
607	Willie Ansley (R)	.40
608	Phil Bradley	.08
609	Tanana: Bonus	.08
610	Randy Myers	.08
611	Don Slaught	.05
612	Dan Quisenberry	.08
613	Gary Varsho (R)	.15
614	Joe Hesketh	.05
615	Robin Yount	.25
616	Steve Rosenberg (R)	.15
617	Mark Parent (R)	.15
618	Rance Mulliniks	.05
619	Checklist: 529-660	.08
620	Barry Bonds	.25
621	Rick Mahler	.05
622	Stan Javier	.05
623	Fred Toliver	.05
624	Jack McKeon	.05
625	Eddie Murray	.20
626	Jeff Reed	.05
627	Greg Harris	.20
628	Matt Williams	.25
629	Pete O'Brien	.10
630	Mike Greenwell	.30
631	Dave Bergman	.05
632	Bryan Harvey (R)	.25
633	Daryl Boston	.05
634	Marvin Freeman	.10
635	Willie Randolph	.08
636	Bill Wilkinson	.05
637	Carmen Castillo	.05
638	Floyd Bannister	.05
639	Weiss: Bonus	.15
640	Willie McGee	.08
641	Curt Young	.05
642	Argenis Salazar	.05
643	Louie Meadows (R)	.15
644	Lloyd McClendon	.05
645	Jack Morris	.10
646	Kevin Bass	.08
647	Randy Johnson (R)	.30
648	Sandy Alomar (R)	1.00
649	Stewart Cliburn	.05
650	Kirby Puckett	.25
651	Tom Niedenfuer	.05
652	Rich Gedman	.05
653	Tommy Barrett (R)	.15
654	Whitey Herzog	.05
655	Dave Magadan	.10
656	Ivan Calderon	.10
657	Joe Magrane	.10
658	R.J. Reynolds	.05
659	Al Leiter	.10
660	Will Clark	.50
661	Turn Back—1984	.15
662	Turn Back—1979	.15
663	Turn Back—1974	.15
664	Turn Back—1969	.15
665	Turn Back—1964	.15
666	Randy St. Claire	.15
667	Dwayne Murphy	.05
668	Mike Bielecki	.05
669	Hershiser: Bonus	.15
670	Kevin Seitzer	.15
671	Jim Gantner	.05
672	Allan Anderson	.08
673	Don Baylor	.08
674	Otis Nixon	.05
675	Bruce Hurst	.15
676	Ernie Riles	.05
677	Dave Schmidt	.05
678	Dion James	.05
679	Willie Fraser	.05
680	Gary Carter	.15
681	Jeff Robinson	.15
682	Rick Leach	.05
683	Jose Cecena (R)	.15
684	Dave Johnson	.05
685	Jeff Treadway	.15
686	Scott Terry	.08
687	Alvin Davis	.08
688	Zane Smith	.05
689	Stan Jefferson	.08
690	Doug Jones	.05
691	Roberto Kelly	.25
692	Steve Ontiveros	.05

1989 Topps (Continued)

NO.	PLAYER	MINT
693	Pat Borders (R)	.30
694	Les Lancaster	.05
695	Carlton Fisk	.15
696	Don August	.10
697	Franklin Stubbs	.05
698	Keith Atherton	.05
699	Pedrique: Bonus	.05
700	Don Mattingly	.75
701	Storm Davis	.05
702	Jamie Quirk	.05
703	Scott Garrelts	.05
704	Carlos Quintana (R)	.35
705	Terry Kennedy	.05
706	Pete Incaviglia	.10
707	Steve Jeltz	.05
708	Chuck Finley	.12
709	Tom Herr	.05
710	Dave Cone	.15
711	Candy Sierra (R)	.15
712	Bill Swift	.05
713	Ty Griffin (R)	.75
714	Joe Morgan	.05
715	Tony Pena	.08
716	Wayne Tolleson	.05
717	Jamie Moyer	.05

NO.	PLAYER	MINT
718	Glenn Braggs	.05
719	Danny Darwin	.05
720	Tim Wallach	.08
721	Ron Tingley (R)	.10
722	Todd Stottlemyre	.12
723	Rafael Belliard	.05
724	Jerry Don Gleaton	.05
725	Terry Steinbach	.12
726	Dickie Thon	.05
727	Joe Orsulak	.05
728	Charlie Puleo	.05
729	Buechele: Bonus	.05
730	Danny Jackson	.10
731	Mike Young	.05
732	Steve Buechele	.05
733	Randy Bockus (R)	.15
734	Jody Reed	.15
735	Roger McDowell	.05
736	Jeff Hamilton	.05
737	Norm Charlton (R)	.20
738	Darnell Coles	.05
739	Brook Jacoby	.05
740	Dan Plesac	.05
741	Ken Phelps	.05
742	Mike Harkey (R)	.35

NO.	PLAYER	MINT
743	Mike Heath	.05
744	Roger Craig	.05
745	Fred McGriff	.25
746	German Gonzalez (R)	.15
747	Wil Tejada	.10
748	Jimmy Jones	.05
749	Rafael Ramirez	.05
750	Bret Saberhagen	.15
751	Ken Oberkfell	.05
752	Jim Gott	.05
753	Jose Uribe	.05
754	Bob Brower	.05
755	Mike Scioscia	.05
756	Scott Medvin (R)	.15
757	Brady Anderson (R)	.25
758	Gene Walter	.05
759	Deer: Bonus	.05
760	Lee Smith	.08
761	Dante Bichette (R)	.35
762	Bobby Thigpen	.05
763	Dave Martinez	.05
764	Robin Ventura (R)	1.00
765	Glenn Davis	.10
766	Cecilio Guante	.05
767	Mike Capel (R)	.15

NO.	PLAYER	MINT
768	Bill Wegman	.05
769	Junior Ortiz	.05
770	Alan Trammell	.10
771	Ron Kittle	.08
772	Ron Oester	.05
773	Keith Moreland	.05
774	Frank Robinson	.08
775	Jeff Reardon	.08
776	Nelson Liriano	.05
777	Ted Power	.05
778	Bruce Benedict	.05
779	Craig McMurtry	.05
780	Pedro Guerrero	.15
781	Greg Briley (R)	.40
782	Checklist: 681-792	.08
783	Trevor Wilson (R)	.20
784	Steve Avery (R)	.50
785	Ellis Burks	.25
786	Melido Perez	.15
787	Dave West (R)	.20
788	Mike Morgan	.05
789	Jackson: Bonus	.08
790	Sid Fernandez	.10
791	Jim Lindeman	.05
792	Rafael Santana	.05

1989 Topps Traded.... Complete Set of 132 Cards—Value $15.00

Updates the main 1989 card set with players who changed teams during the season and rookies who joined their teams early in the season. Features the first Topps Card of Ken Griffey, Jr., Jerome Walton, Tom Gordon, Junior Felix and Dwight Smith. The complete set was packaged in a printed box and distributed primarily through card hobby dealers.

NO.	PLAYER	MINT
1	Don Aase	.05
2	Jim Abbott	.75
3	Kent Anderson	.15
4	Keith Atherton	.05
5	Wally Backman	.05
6	Steve Balboni	.05
7	Jesse Barfield	.05
8	Steve Bedrosian	.05
9	Todd Benzinger	.05
10	Geronimo Berroa	.10
11	Bert Blyleven	.05
12	Bob Boone	.05
13	Phil Bradley	.05
14	Jeff Brantley	.25
15	Kevin Brown	.20
16	Jerry Browne	.05
17	Chuck Cary	.10
18	Carmen Castillo	.05
19	Jim Clancy	.05
20	Jack Clark	.10
21	Bryan Clutterbuck	.05
22	Jody Davis	.05
23	Mike Devereaux	.15
24	Frank DiPino	.05
25	Benny DiStefano	.05
26	John Dopson	.10
27	Len Dykstra	.20
28	Jim Eisenreich	.05
29	Nick Esasky	.10
30	Alvaro Espinoza	.10
31	Darrell Evans	.05
32	Junior Felix	.75
33	Felix Fermin	.05

NO.	PLAYER	MINT
34	Julio Franco	.15
35	Terry Francona	.05
36	Cito Gaston	.05
37	Bob Geren	.25
38	Tom Gordon	.50
39	Tommy Gregg	.15
40	Ken Griffey	.15
41	Ken Griffey, Jr.	5.00
42	Kevin Gross	.05
43	Lee Guetterman	.05
44	Mel Hall	.05
45	Erik Hanson	.20
46	Gene Harris	.25
47	Andy Hawkins	.05
48	Rickey Henderson	.50
49	Tom Herr	.05
50	Ken Hill	.20
51	Brian Holman	.25
52	Brian Holton	.05
53	Art Howe	.05
54	Ken Howell	.05
55	Bruce Hurst	.05
56	Chris James	.05
57	Randy Johnson	.10
58	Jimmy Jones	.05
59	Terry Kennedy	.05
60	Paul Kilgus	.05
61	Eric King	.05
62	Ron Kittle	.05
63	John Kruk	.05
64	Randy Kutcher	.10
65	Steve Lake	.05
66	Mark Langston	.15

NO.	PLAYER	MINT
67	Dave LaPoint	.05
68	Terry Leach	.05
69	Terry Leach	.05
70	Jim Levebvre	.05
71	Al Leiter	.05
72	Jeffrey Leonard	.05
73	Derek Lilliquist	.15
74	Rick Mahler	.05
75	Tom McCarthy	.15
76	Lloyd McClendon	.10
77	Lance McCullers	.05
78	Oddibe McDowell	.05
79	Roger McDowell	.05
80	Larry McWilliams	.05
81	Randy Milligan	.15
82	Mike Moore	.10
83	Keith Moreland	.05
84	Mike Morgan	.05
85	Jamie Moyer	.05
86	Rob Murphy	.05
87	Eddie Murray	.20
88	Pete O'Brien	.05
89	Gregg Olson	.60
90	Steve Ontiveros	.05
91	Jesse Orosco	.05
92	Spike Owen	.05
93	Rafael Palmeiro	.15
94	Clay Parker	.20
95	Jeff Parrett	.05
96	Lance Parrish	.05
97	Dennis Powell	.05
98	Rey Quinones	.05
99	Doug Rader	.05

NO.	PLAYER	MINT
100	Willie Randolph	.05
101	Shane Rawley	.05
102	Randy Ready	.05
103	Bip Roberts	.05
104	Kenny Rogers	.15
105	Ed Romero	.05
106	Nolan Ryan	1.00
107	Luis Salazar	.05
108	Juan Samuel	.05
109	Alex Sanchez	.20
110	Deion Sanders	.60
111	Steve Sax	.10
112	Rick Schu	.05
113	Dwight Smith	.50
114	Lonnie Smith	.05
115	Billy Spiers	.20
116	Kent Tekulve	.05
117	Walt Terrell	.05
118	Milt Thompson	.05
119	Dickie Thon	.05
120	Jeff Torborg	.05
121	Jeff Treadway	.05
122	Omar Vizquel	.15
123	Jerome Walton	1.25
124	Gary Ward	.05
125	Claudell Washington	.05
126	Curt Wilkerson	.05
127	Eddie Williams	.05
128	Frank Williams	.05
129	Ken Williams	.05
130	Mitch Williams	.15
131	Steve Wilson	.15
132	Checklist	.05

1990 Topps.... Complete Set of 792 Cards—Value $25.00

The front of the cards feature six different color schemes. A card was issued to honor deceased Commissioner Giamatti. Four special cards were issued to honor Nolan Ryan—each card showed him with a different team. In a revised checklist format, the cards were listed by team.

JUAN GONZALEZ

FRANK THOMAS

TODD ZEILE

ERIC ANTHONY

BEN McDONALD

NO.	PLAYER	MINT
1	Nolan Ryan	.50
2	Nolan Ryan	.20
	Mets (1965 to 1971)	
3	Nolan Ryan	.20
	Angels (1972 to 1979)	
4	Nolan Ryan	.20
	Astros (1980 to 1988)	
5	Nolan Ryan	.20
	Rangers (1989)	
6	'89 Record: V. Coleman	.08
7	'89 Record: R. Henderson	.10
8	'89 Record: C. Ripken	.08
9	Eric Plunk	.05
10	Barry Larkin	.10
11	Paul Gibson	.05
12	Joe Girardi	.15
13	Mark Williamson	.05
14	Mike Fetters	.15
15	Teddy Higuera	.05
16	Kent Anderson	.12
17	Kelly Downs	.08
18	Carlos Quintana	.15
19	Al Newman	.05
20	Mark Gubicza	.05
21	Jeff Torborg	.05
22	Bruce Ruffin	.05
23	Randy Velarde	.05
24	Joe Hesketh	.05
25	Willie Randolph	.08
26	Don Slaught	.05
27	Rick Leach	.05
28	Duane Ward	.05
29	John Cangelosi	.05
30	David Cone	.12
31	Henry Cotto	.05
32	John Farrell	.08
33	Greg Walker	.05
34	Tony Fossas (R)	.15
35	Benny Santiago	.10
36	John Costello	.05
37	Domingo Ramos	.05
38	Wes Gardner	.05
39	Curt Ford	.05
40	Jay Howell	.08
41	Matt Williams	.20
42	Jeff Robinson	.08
43	Dante Bichette	.05
44	R. Salkeld (#1 DP)(R)	.25
45	Dave Parker	.10
46	Rob Dibble	.10
47	Brian Harper	.08
48	Zane Smith	.05
49	Tom Lawless	.05
50	Glenn Davis	.10
51	Doug Rader	.05
52	Jack Daugherty (R)	.15
53	Mike LaCoss	.05
54	Joel Skinner	.05
55	Darrell Evans	.05
56	Franklin Stubbs	.05
57	Greg Vaughn	.50
58	Keith Miller	.05
59	Ted Power	.05
60	George Brett	.15
61	Deion Sanders	.35
62	Ramon Martinez	.25
63	Mike Pagliarulo	.08

NO.	PLAYER	MINT
64	Danny Darwin	.05
65	Devon White	.10
66	Greg Litton	.15
67	Scott Sanderson	.05
68	Dave Henderson	.05
69	Todd Frohwirth	.05
70	Mike Greenwell	.20
71	Allan Anderson	.08
72	Jeff Huson (R)	.15
73	Bob Milacki	.08
74	J. Jackson (#1 DP) (R)	.15
75	Doug Jones	.05
76	Dave Valle	.05
77	Dave Bergman	.05
78	Mike Flanagan	.05
79	Ron Kittle	.05
80	Jeff Russell	.05
81	Bob Rodgers	.05
82	Scott Terry	.05
83	Hensley Meulens	.25
84	Ray Searage	.05
85	Jaun Samuel	.08
86	Paul Kilgus	.05
87	Rick Luecken (R)	.15
88	Glenn Braggs	.05
89	Clint Zavaras (R)	.12
90	Jack Clark	.08
91	Steve Frey (R)	.15
92	Mike Stanley	.05
93	Shawn Hillegas	.05
94	Herm Winningham	.05
95	Todd Worrell	.08
96	Jody Reed	.05
97	Curt Schilling	.10
98	Jose Gonzalez	.05
99	Rich Monteleone	.10
100	Will Clark	.50
101	Shane Rawley	.05
102	Stan Javier	.05
103	Marvin Freeman	.05
104	Bob Knepper	.05
105	Randy Myers	.08
106	Charlie O'Brien	.05
107	Fred Lynn	.08
108	Rod Nichols	.05
109	Roberto Kelly	.08
110	Tommy Helms (Mgr.)	.05
111	Ed Whited (R)	.15
112	Glenn Wilson	.05
113	Manny Lee	.05
114	Mike Bielecki	.05
115	Tony Pena	.08
116	Floyd Bannister	.05
117	Mike Sharperson	.05
118	Eric Hanson	.08
119	Billy Hatcher	.05
120	John Franco	.08
121	Robin Ventura	.30
122	Shawn Abner	.05
123	Rich Gedman	.05
124	Dave Dravecky	.05
125	Kent Hrbek	.08
126	Randy Kramer	.05
127	Mike Deveraux	.08
128	Checklist No. 1	.05
129	Ron Jones	.05
130	Bert Blyleven	.08

NO.	PLAYER	MINT
131	Matt Nokes	.08
132	Lance Blankenship	.08
133	Ricky Horton	.05
134	Earl Cunningham (R)	.35
	(#1 DP)	
135	Dave Magadan	.08
136	Kevin Brown	.08
137	Marty Pevey (R)	.15
138	Al Leiter	.05
139	Greg Brock	.05
140	Andre Dawson	.12
141	John Hart (Mgr.)	.05
142	Jeff Wetherby (R)	.15
143	Rafael Belliard	.05
144	Bud Black	.05
145	Terry Steinbach	.10
146	Rob Richie	.15
147	Chuck Finley	.08
148	Edgar Martinez	.10
149	Steve Farr	.05
150	Kirk Gibson	.08
151	Rick Mahler	.05
152	Lonnie Smith	.05
153	Randy Milligan	.10
154	Mike Maddux	.05
155	Ellis Burks	.15
156	Ken Patterson	.05
157	Craig Biggio	.10
158	Craig Lefferts	.05
159	Mike Felder	.05
160	Dave Righetti	.10
161	Harold Reynolds	.05
162	Todd Zeile	.75
163	Phil Bradley	.08
164	Jeff Juden (# 1 DP) (R)	.30
165	Walt Weiss	.10
166	Bobby Witt	.05
167	Kevin Appier	.25
168	Jose Lind	.05
169	Richard Dotson	.05
170	George Bell	.10
171	Russ Nixon (Mgr.)	.05
172	Tom Lampkin	.05
173	Tim Belcher	.08
174	Jeff Kunkel	.05
175	Mike Moore	.08
176	Luis Quinones	.05
177	Mike Henneman	.05
178	Chris James	.05
179	Brian Holton	.05
180	Rock Raines	.12
181	Juan Agosto	.05
182	Mookie Wilson	.08
183	Steve Lake	.05
184	Danny Cox	.05
185	Ruben Sierra	.20
186	Dave LaPoint	.05
187	Rick Wrona	.10
188	Mike Smithson	.05
189	Dick Schofield	.05
190	Rick Reuschel	.08
191	Pat Borders	.05
192	Don August	.08
193	Andy Benes	.20
194	Glenallen Hill	.15
195	Tim Burke	.05
196	Gerard Young	.05
197	Doug Drabek	.05

NO.	PLAYER	MINT
198	Mike Marshall	.08
199	Sergio Valdez (R)	.15
200	Don Mattingly	.50
201	Cito Gaston (Mgr.)	.05
202	Mike MacFarlane	.05
203	Mike Roesler (R)	.15
204	Bob Dernier	.05
205	Mark Davis	.10
206	Nick Esasky	.05
207	Bob Ojeda	.05
208	Brook Jacoby	.05
209	Greg Mathews	.05
210	Ryne Sandberg	.15
211	John Cerutti	.05
212	Joe Orsulak	.05
213	Scott Bankhead	.05
214	Terry Francona	.05
215	Kirk McCaskill	.08
216	Ricky Jordan	.15
217	Don Robinson	.05
218	Wally Backman	.05
219	Donn Pall	.05
220	Barry Bonds	.20
221	Gary Mielke (R)	.15
222	Kurt Stillwell	.05
223	Tommy Gregg	.05
224	Delino DeShields (R)	.50
225	Jim Deshaies	.05
226	Mickey Hatcher	.05
227	Kevin Tapani (R)	.30
228	Dave Martinez	.05
229	David Wells	.05
230	Keith Hernandez	.08
231	Jack McKeon (Mgr.)	.05
232	Darnell Coles	.05
233	Ken Hill	.08
234	Mariano Duncan	.05
235	Jeff Reardon	.08
236	Hal Morris	.35
237	Kevin Ritz (R)	.15
238	Felix Jose	.10
239	Eric Show	.05
240	Mark Grace	.25
241	Mike Krukow	.08
242	Fred Manrique	.05
243	Barry Jones	.05
244	Bill Schroeder	.05
245	Roger Clemens	.25
246	Jim Eisenreich	.05
247	Jerry Reed	.05
248	Dave Anderson	.05
249	Mike Smith (R)	.15
250	Jose Canseco	.60
251	Jeff Blauser	.05
252	Otis Nixon	.05
253	Mark Portugal	.05
254	Francisco Cabrera (R)	.25
255	Bobby Thigpen	.05
256	Marvell Wynne	.05
257	Jose DeLeon	.05
258	Barry Lyons	.05
259	Lance McCullers	.05
260	Eric Davis	.20
261	Whitey Herzog (Mgr.)	.05
262	Checklist No. 2	.05
263	Mel Stottlemyre, Jr.	.15
264	Bryan Clutterbuck	.05

NO.	PLAYER	MINT
265	Pete O'Brien	.08
266	German Gonzalez	.05
267	Mark Davidson	.05
268	Rob Murphy	.05
269	Dickie Thon	.05
270	Dave Stewart	.10
271	Chet Lemon	.05
272	Bryan Harvey	.05
273	Bobby Bonilla	.15
274	Goose Gozzo (R)	.15
275	Mickey Tettleton	.05
276	Gary Thurman	.05
277	Lenny Harris	.05
278	Pascual Perez	.05
279	Steve Buechele	.05
280	Lou Whitaker	.08
281	Kevin Bass	.05
282	Derek Lilliquist	.08
283	Joey Belle	.25
284	Mark Gardner (R)	.15
285	Willie McGee	.08
286	Lee Guetterman	.05
287	Vance Law	.05
288	Greg Briley	.10
289	Norm Charlton	.05
290	Robin Yount	.20
291	Dave Johnson (Mgr.)	.05
292	Jim Gott	.05
293	Mike Gallego	.05
294	Craig McMurtry	.05
295	Fred McGriff	.15
296	Jeff Ballard	.08
297	Tom Herr	.08
298	Danny Gladden	.05
299	Adam Petterson	.08
300	Bo Jackson	.50
301	Don Aase	.05
302	Marcus Lawton (R)	.20
303	Rick Cerone	.05
304	Marty Clary	.05
305	Eddie Murray	.10
306	Tom Niedenfuer	.05
307	Bip Roberts	.05
308	Jose Guzman	.05
309	Eric Yelding	.25
310	Steve Bedrosian	.05
311	Dwight Smith	.20
312	Dan Quisenberry	.05
313	Gus Polidor	.05
314	D. Harris (# 1 DP) (R)	.20
315	Bruce Hurst	.05
316	Carney Lansford	.08
317	Mark Guthrie (R)	.15
318	Wallace Johnson	.05
319	Dion James	.05
320	Dave Stieb	.05
321	Joe Morgan (Mgr.)	.05
322	Junior Ortiz	.05
323	Willie Wilson	.08
324	Pete Harnisch	.05
325	Robby Thompson	.10
326	Tom McCarthy	.15
327	Ken Williams	.05
328	Curt Young	.05
329	Oddibe McDowell	.05
330	Ron Darling	.10
331	Juan Gonzalez (R)	1.00
332	Paul O'Neill	.15
333	Bill Wegman	.05
334	Johnny Ray	.05
335	Andy Hawkins	.05
336	Ken Griffey, Jr.	2.50
337	Lloyd McClendon	.05
338	Dannis Lamp	.05
339	Dave Clark	.05
340	Fernando Valenzuela	.10
341	Tom Foley	.05
342	Alex Trevino	.05
343	Frank Tanana	.05
344	George Canale (R)	.15
345	Harold Baines	.08
346	Jim Presley	.05
347	Junior Felix	.30
348	Gary Wayne	.10
349	Steve Finley	.12
350	Bret Saberhagen	.10
351	Craig Roger (Mgr.)	.05
352	Bryn Smith	.05
353	Sandy Alomar	.30
354	Stan Belinda (R)	.15
355	Marty Barrett	.05
356	Randy Ready	.05
357	Dave West	.10
358	Andres Thomas	.05
359	Jimmy Jones	.05
360	Paul Molitor	.10
361	Randy McCament (R)	.15
362	Damon Berryhill	.08
363	Dan Petry	.05
364	Rolando Roomes	.08
365	Ozzie Guillen	.08
366	Mike Heath	.05
367	Mike Morgan	.05
368	Bill Doran	.05
369	Todd Burns	.05
370	Tim Wallach	.05
371	Jimmy Key	.08
372	Terry Kennedy	.05
373	Alvin Davis	.08
374	Steve Cummings (R)	.15
375	Dwight Evans	.08
376	Checklist No. 3	.05
377	Mickey Weston (R)	.15
378	Luis Salazar	.05
379	Steve Rosenburg	.05
380	Dave Winfield	.12
381	Frank Robinson (Mgr.)	.10
382	Jeff Musselman	.05
383	John Morris	.05
384	Pat Combs	.20
385	Fred McGriff (AS)	.12
386	Franco Julio (AS)	.08
387	Wade Boggs (AS)	.15
388	Cal Ripken (AS)	.12
389	Robin Yount (AS)	.15
390	Ruben Sierra (AS)	.15
391	Kirby Puckett (AS)	.20
392	Carlton Fisk (AS)	.10
393	Bret Saberhagen (AS)	.05
394	Jeff Ballard (AS)	.08
395	Jeff Russell (AS)	.05
396	A. Bartlett Giamatti	.40
	Baseball Commissioner	
	(deceased)	
397	Will Clark (AS)	.20
398	Ryne Sandberg (AS)	.10
399	Howard Johnson (AS)	.10
400	Ozzie Smith (AS)	.08
401	Kevin Mitchell (AS)	.15
402	Eric Davis (AS)	.15
403	Tony Gwynn (AS)	.15
404	Craig Biggio (AS)	.10
405	Mike Scott (AS)	.10
406	Joe Magrane (AS)	.10
407	Mark Davis (AS)	.10
408	Trevor Wilson	.05
409	Tom Brunansky	.05
410	Jose Boever	.05
411	Ken Phelps	.05
412	Jamie Moyer	.05
413	Brian Dubois (R)	.15
414	F. Thomas (#1 DP) (R)	1.00
415	Shawon Dunston	.08
416	Dave Johnson (R)	.12
417	Jim Gantner	.05
418	Tom Browning	.05
419	Beau Allred (R)	.20
420	Carlton Fisk	.10
421	Greg Minton	.05
422	Pat Sheridan	.05
423	Fred Toliver	.05
424	Jerry Reuss	.05
425	Bill Landrum	.05
426	Jeff Hamilton	.05
427	Carmen Castillo	.05
428	Steve Davis (R)	.15
429	Tom Kelly (Mgr.)	.05
430	Pete Incaviglia	.10
431	Randy Johnson	.08
432	Damaso Garcia	.05
433	Steve Olin (R)	.15
434	Mark Carreon	.05
435	Kevin Seitzer	.10
436	Mel Hall	.05
437	Les Lancaster	.05
438	Greg Myers	.05
439	Jeff Parrett	.05
440	Alan Trammell	.08
441	Bob Kipper	.05
442	Jerry Browne	.08
443	Cris Carpenter	.05
444	Kyle Abbott (#1 DP) (R)	.20
445	Danny Jackson	.08
446	Dan Pasqua	.05
447	Atlee Hammaker	.05
448	Greg Gagne	.05
449	Dennis Rasmussen	.05
450	Rickey Henderson	.20
451	Mark Lemke	.05
452	Luis de los Santos	.10
453	Jody Davis	.05
454	Jeff King	.10
455	Jeffrey Leonard	.05
456	Chris Gwynn	.08
457	Gregg Jefferies	.25
458	Bob McClure	.05
459	Jim Lefebvre (Mgr.)	.05
460	Mike Scott	.08
461	Carlos Martinez	.15
462	Denny Walling	.05
463	Drew Hall	.05
464	Jerome Walton	.50
465	Kevin Gross	.05
466	Rance Mulliniks	.05
467	Juan Nieves	.05
468	Billy Ripken	.08
469	John Kruk	.05
470	Frank Viola	.10
471	Mike Brumley	.05
472	Jose Uribe	.05
473	Joe Price	.05
474	Rich Thompson	.08
475	Bob Welch	.05
476	Brad Komminsk	.05
477	Willie Fraser	.05
478	Mike LaValliere	.05
479	Frank White	.05
480	Sid Fernandez	.08
481	Garry Templeton	.05
482	Steve Carter	.15
483	Alejandro Pena	.05
484	Mike Fitzgerald	.05
485	John Candelaria	.05
486	Jeff Treadway	.05
487	Steve Searcy	.10
488	Ken Oberfell	.05
489	Nick Leyva (Mgr.)	.05
490	Dan Plesac	.05
491	Dave Cochrane (R)	.12
492	Ron Oester	.05
493	Jason Grimsley (R)	.15
494	Terry Puhl	.05
495	Lee Smith	.08
496	Cecil Espy	.05
497	Dave Schmidt	.08
498	Rick Schu	.05
499	Bill Long	.05
500	Kevin Mitchell	.25
501	Matt Young	.05
502	Mitch Webster	.05
503	Randy St. Claire	.05
504	Tom O'Malley	.05
505	Kelly Gruber	.15
506	Tom Glavine	.08
507	Gary Redus	.05
508	Terry Leach	.08
509	Tom Pagnozzi	.05
510	Doc Gooden	.20
511	Clay Parker	.05
512	Gary Pettis	.05
513	Mark Eichhorn	.05
514	Andy Allanson	.05
515	Lenny Dykstra	.10
516	Tim Leary	.08
517	Roberto Alomar	.15
518	Bill Krueger	.05
519	Bucky Dent (Mgr.)	.05
520	Mitch Williams	.08
521	Craig Worthington	.08
522	Mike Dunne	.05
523	Jay Bell	.05
524	Daryl Boston	.05
525	Wally Joyner	.10
526	Checklist No. 4	.05
527	Ron Hassey	.05
528	Kevin Wickander	.10
529	Greg Harris	.05
530	Mark Langston	.10
531	Ken Caminiti	.05
532	Cecilio Guante	.10
533	Tim Jones	.05
534	Louie Meadows	.05
535	John Smoltz	.10
536	Bob Geren	.15
537	Mark Grant	.05
538	Billy Spiers	.25
539	Neal Heaton	.05
540	Danny Tartabull	.10
541	Pat Perry	.05
542	Darren Daulton	.05
543	Nelson Liriano	.05
544	Dennis Boyd	.05
545	Kevin McReynolds	.10
546	Kevin Hickey	.15
547	Jack Howell	.05
548	Pat Clements	.05
549	Don Zimmer (Mgr.)	.05
550	Julio Franco	.10
551	Tim Crews	.05
552	Mike Smith (R)	.15
553	Scott Scudder	.10
554	Jay Buhner	.08
555	Jack Morris	.10
556	Gene Larkin	.05
557	Jeff Innis (R)	.10
558	Rafael Ramirez	.05
559	Andy McGaffigan	.05
560	Steve Sax	.08
561	Ken Dayley	.05
562	Chad Kreuter	.05
563	Alex Sanchez	.10
564	T. Houston (#1 DP) (R)	.25
565	Scott Fletcher	.05
566	Mark Knudson	.05
567	Ron Gant	.20
568	John Smiley	.08
569	Ivan Calderon	.05
570	Cal Ripken	.12
571	Brett Butler	.05
572	Greg Harris	.05
573	Danny Heep	.05
574	Bill Swift	.05
575	Lance Parrish	.08
576	Mike Dyer (R)	.15
577	Charlie Hayes	.05
578	Joe Magrane	.10
579	Art Howe (Mgr.)	.05
580	Joe Carter	.10
581	Ken Griffey	.05
582	Rick Honeycutt	.05
583	Bruce Benedict	.05
584	Phil Stephenson	.10
585	Kal Daniels	.10
586	Ed Nunez	.05
587	Lance Johnson	.05
588	Rick Rhoden	.05
589	Mike Aldrette	.05
590	Ozzie Smith	.10
591	Todd Stottlemyre	.10
592	R.J. Reynolds	.05
593	Scott Bradley	.05
594	Luis Sojo (R)	.15
595	Greg Swindell	.10
596	Jose DeJesus	.05
597	Chris Bosio	.05
598	Brady Anderson	.05
599	Frank Williams	.05
600	Darryl Strawberry	.25
601	Luis Rivera	
602	Scott Garrelts	
603	Tony Armas	
604	Ron Robinson	
605	Mike Scioscia	
606	Storm Davis	

NO.	PLAYER	MINT
607	Steve Jeltz	.05
608	Eric Anthony (R)	.75
609	Sparky Anderson (Mgr.)	.05
610	Pedro Guerrero	.10
611	Walt Terrell	.05
612	Dave Gallagher	.05
613	Jeff Pico	.05
614	Nelson Santovenia	.05
615	Rob Deer	.05
616	Brian Holman	.15
617	Geronimo Berroa	.05
618	Eddie Whitson	.05
619	Rob Ducey	.07
620	Tony Castillo	.10
621	Melido Perez	.05
622	Sid Bream	.05
623	Jim Corsi	.05
624	Darrin Jackson	.05
625	Roger McDowell	.05
626	Bob Melvin	.05
627	Jose Rojo	.05
628	Candy Maldonado	.05
629	Eric Hetzel	.05
630	Gary Gaetti	.10
631	John Wetteland	.15
632	Scott Lusader	.05
633	Dennis Cook	.10
634	Luis Polonia	.05
635	Brian Downing	.05
636	Jesse Orosco	.05
637	Craig Reynolds	.05
638	Jeff Montgomery	.08
639	Tony LaRussa (Mgr.)	.05
640	Rick Sutcliffe	.05
641	Doug Strange (R)	.15
642	Jack Armstrong	.05
643	Alfredo Griffin	.08
644	Paul Assenmacher	.05
645	Jose Oquendo	.05
646	Checklist No. 5	.05
647	Rex Hudler	.05
648	Jim Clancy	.05
649	Dan Murphy (R)	.12
650	Mike Witt	.08
651	Rafael Santana	.05
652	Mike Boddicker	.08
653	John Moses	.05
654	P. Coleman (#1 DP)(R)	.30

NO.	PLAYER	MINT
655	Gregg Olson	.20
656	Mackey Sasser	.05
657	Terry Mulholland	.05
658	Donell Nixon	.05
659	Greg Cadaret	.05
660	Vince Coleman	.08
661	Turn Back Clock—1985 Dick Howser	.08
662	Turn Back Clock—1980 Mike Schmidt	.12
663	Turn Back Clock—1975 Fred Lynn	.08
664	Turn Back Clock—1970 Johnny Bench	.08
665	Turn Back Clock—1965 Sandy Koufax	.08
666	Brian Fisher	.05
667	Curt Wilkerson	.05
668	Joe Oliver	.15
669	Tom Lasorda (Mgr.)	.05
670	Dennis Eckersley	.08
671	Bob Boone	.05
672	Roy Smith	.05
673	Joey Meyer	.05
674	Spike Owen	.05
675	Jim Abbott	.25
676	Randy Kutcher	.05
677	Jay Tibbs	.05
678	Kirt Manwaring	.05
679	Gary Ward	.05
680	Howard Johnson	.10
681	Mike Schooler	.10
682	Dann Bilardello	.05
683	Kenny Rogers	.15
684	Julio Machado (R)	.15
685	Tony Fernandez	.10
686	Carmelo Martinez	.05
687	Tim Birtsas	.05
688	Milt Thompson	.05
689	Rich Yett	.05
690	Mark McGwire	.30
691	Chuck Cary	.05
692	Sammy Sosa (R)	.40
693	Calvin Schiraldi	.05
694	Mike Stanton (R)	.15
695	Tom Henke	.05
696	B.J. Surhoff	.05
697	Mike Davis	.05

NO.	PLAYER	MINT
698	Omar Vizquel	.20
699	Jim Leyland (Mgr.)	.05
700	Kirby Puckett	.20
701	Bernie Williams (R)	.20
702	Tony Phillips	.05
703	Jeff Brantley	.15
704	Chip Hale (R)	.15
705	Claudell Washington	.05
706	Geno Petralli	.05
707	Luis Aquino	.05
708	Larry Sheets	.05
709	Juan Berenguer	.05
710	Von Hayes	.08
711	Rick Aguilera	.05
712	Todd Benzinger	.05
713	Tim Drummond (R)	.15
714	Marquis Grissom (R)	.35
715	Greg Maddux	.12
716	Steve Balboni	.05
717	Ron Karkovice	.05
718	Gary Sheffield	.25
719	Wally Whitehurst	.15
720	Andres Galarraga	.10
721	Lee Mazzilli	.05
722	Felix Fermin	.05
723	Jeff Robinson	.08
724	Jaun Bell	.15
725	Terry Pendleton	.05
726	Gene Nelson	.05
727	Pat Tabler	.05
728	Jim Acker	.05
729	Bobby Valentine (Mgr.)	.05
730	Tony Gwynn	.15
731	Don Carman	.05
732	Ernie Riles	.05
733	John Dobson	.08
734	Kevin Elster	.08
735	Charlie Hough	.05
736	Rick Dempsey	.05
737	Chris Sabo	.15
738	Gene Harris	.15
739	Dale Sveum	.05
740	Jesse Barfield	.05
741	Steve Wilson	.10
742	Ernie Whitt	.05
743	Tom Candiotti	.05
744	Kelly Mann (R)	.15
745	Hubie Brooks	.05

NO.	PLAYER	MINT
746	Dave Smith	.08
747	Randy Bush	.05
748	Doyle Alexander	.08
749	Mark Parent	.05
750	Dale Murphy	.12
751	Steve Lyons	.05
752	Tom Gordon	.25
753	Chris Speier	.05
754	Bob Walk	.05
755	Rafael Palmeiro	.10
756	Ken Howell	.05
757	Larry Walker (R)	.30
758	Mark Thurmond	.05
759	Tom Trebelhorn (Mgr.)	.05
760	Wade Boggs	.25
761	Mike Jackson	.05
762	Doug Dascenzo	.05
763	Denny Martinez	.05
764	Tim Teufel	.05
765	Chili Davis	.05
766	Brian Meyer	.10
767	Tracy Jones	.05
768	Chuck Crim	.05
769	Greg Hibbard (R)	.15
770	Cory Snyder	.10
771	Pete Smith	.05
772	Jeff Reed	.05
773	Dave Leiper	.05
774	Ben McDonald (R)	1.50
775	Andy Van Slyke	.10
776	Charlie Leibrandt	.08
777	Tim Laudner	.05
778	Mike Jeffcoat	.05
779	Lloyd Moseby	.08
780	Orel Hershiser	.12
781	Mario Diaz	.05
782	Jose Alvarez	.05
783	Checklist No. 6	.05
784	Scott Bailes	.05
785	Jim Rice	.10
786	Eric King	.05
787	Rene Gonzales	.05
788	Frank DiPino	.05
789	John Wathan (Mgr.)	.05
790	Gary Carter	.08
791	Alvaro Espinoza	.05
792	Gerald Perry	.05

1990 Topps Traded.... Complete Set of 132 Cards—Value $12.00

Updates the main 1990 card set with players who changed teams during the season and rookies who joined their teams early in the season. For the first time Topps traded cards were available in wax packs (gray backs). The complete set version was sold in a box (white backs). Features the first Topps card of Dave Justice, Kevin Maas and John Olerud.

KEVIN MAAS — TRAVIS FRYMAN — DAVE JUSTICE — CARLOS BAERGA — JOHN OLERUD

NO.	PLAYER	MINT
1T	Darrel Akerfelds	.05
2T	Sandy Alomar Jr.	.30
3T	Brad Arnsberg	.05
	Steve Avery	.25

NO.	PLAYER	MINT
5T	Wally Backman	.05
6T	Carlos Baerga	.50
7T	Kevin Bass	.05
8T	Willie Blair	.10

NO.	PLAYER	MINT
9T	Mike Blowers	.25
10T	Shawn Boskie	.15
11T	Daryl Boston	.08
12T	Dennis Boyd	.05

NO.	PLAYER	MINT
13T	Glenn Braggs	.05
14T	Hubie Brooks	.08
15T	Tom Brunansky	.05
16T	John Burkett	.25

NO.	PLAYER	MINT	NO.	PLAYER	MINT	NO.	PLAYER	MINT	NO.	PLAYER	MINT
17T	Casey Candaele	.05	46T	Chris James	.05	75T	Alan Mills	.05	104T	Ron Robinson	.05
18T	John Candelaria	.05	47T	Stan Javier	.05	76T	Hal Morris	.20	105T	Kevin Romine	.05
19T	Gary Carter	.10	48T	Dave Justice	3.00	77T	Lloyd Moseby	.05	106T	Scott Ruskin	.15
20T	Joe Carter	.10	49T	Jeff Kaiser	.10	78T	Randy Myers	.08	107T	John Russel	.05
21T	Rick Cerone	.05	50T	Dana Kiecker	.25	79T	Tim Naehring	.35	108T	Bill Sampen	.20
22T	Scott Coolbaugh	.15	51T	Joe Klink	.10	80T	Junior Noboa	.05	109T	Juan Samuel	.05
23T	Bobby Cox	.05	52T	Brent Knackert	.10	81T	Matt Nokes	.05	110T	Scott Sanderson	.05
24T	Mark Davis	.05	53T	Brad Komminsk	.05	82T	Pete O'Brien	.05	111T	Jack Savage	.05
25T	Storm Davis	.05	54T	Mark Langston	.05	83T	John Olerud	1.50	112T	Dave Schmidt	.05
26T	Edgar Diaz	.10	55T	Tim Layana	.15	84T	Greg Olson	.20	113T	Red Schoendienst	.05
27T	Wayne Edwards	.10	56T	Rick Leach	.05	85T	Junior Ortiz	.05	114T	Terry Shumpert	.15
28T	Mark Eichhorn	.05	57T	Terry Leach	.05	86T	Dave Parker	.10	115T	Matt Sinatro	.05
29T	Scott Erickson	.40	58T	Tim Leary	.05	87T	Rick Parker	.08	116T	Don Slaught	.05
30T	Nick Esasky	.05	59T	Craig Lefferts	.05	88T	Bob Patterson	.05	117T	Bryn Smith	.05
31T	Cecil Fielder	.60	60T	Charlie Leibrandt	.05	89T	Alejandro Pena	.05	118T	Lee Smith	.08
32T	John Franco	.05	61T	Jim Leyritz	.20	90T	Tony Pena	.05	119T	Paul Sorrento	.10
33T	Travis Fryman	.75	62T	Fred Lynn	.05	91T	Pascual Perez	.05	120T	Franklin Stubbs	.05
34T	Bill Guillickson	.05	63T	Kevin Maas	2.50	92T	Gerald Perry	.08	121T	Russ Swan	.20
35T	Darryl Hamilton	.08	64T	Shane Mack	.05	93T	Dan Petry	.05	122T	Bob Tewksbury	.05
36T	Mike Harkey	.15	65T	Candy Maldonado	.05	94T	Gary Pettis	.05	123T	Wayne Tolleson	.05
37T	Bud Harrelson	.05	66T	Fred Manrique	.05	95T	Tony Phillips	.05	124T	John Tudor	.05
38T	Billy Hatcher	.05	67T	Mike Marshall	.05	96T	Lou Piniella	.05	125T	Randy Veres	.15
39T	Keith Hernandez	.05	68T	Carmelo Martinez	.05	97T	Luis Polonia	.05	126T	Hector Villanueva	.20
40T	Joie Hesketh	.05	69T	John Marzana	.08	98T	Jim Presley	.05	127T	Mitch Webster	.05
41T	Dave Hollins	.20	70T	Ben McDonald	1.00	99T	Scott Radinsky	.15	128T	Ernie Whitt	.05
42T	Sam Horn	.05	71T	Jack McDowell	.05	100T	Willie Randolph	.05	129T	Frank Wills	.05
43T	Steve Howard	.10	72T	John McNamara	.05	101T	Jeff Reardon	.05	130T	Dave Winfield	.10
44T	Todd Hundley	.15	73T	Orlando Mercado	.05	102T	Greg Riddoch	.05	131T	Matt Young	.05
45T	Jeff Huson	.05	74T	Stump Merrill	.05	103T	Jeff Robinson	.05	132T	Checklist Card	.05

1991 Topps. . . . Complete Set of 792 Cards—Value $25.00

All players of the same team have cards with the same border colors. Subsets include Record Breakers, No. 1 Draft Picks, Future Stars and Rookie All-Star Team. For the first time since 1974 some cards feature horizontal photos. In a special promotion, over 300,000 original Topps cards issued from 1952 to 1990 or certificates were randomly inserted in packs.

NO.	PLAYER	MINT	NO.	PLAYER	MINT	NO.	PLAYER	MINT	NO.	PLAYER	MINT
1	Nolan Ryan	.30	29	Bob Walk	.05	57	Jack Howell	.05	85	Jesse Barfield	.05
2	'89 Record: G. Brett	.08	30	Gregg Jefferies	.15	58	Mel Stottlemyre	.05	86	Les Lancaster	.05
3	'89 Record: C. Fisk	.08	31	Colby Ward (R)	.12	59	Eric Yelding	.05	87	Tracy Jones	.05
4	'89 Record: K. Maas	.20	32	Mike Simms (R)	.12	60	Frank Viola	.10	88	Bob Tewksbury	.05
5	'89 Record: C. Ripken	.08	33	Barry Jones	.05	61	Stan Javier	.05	89	Darren Daulton	.05
6	'89 Record: N. Ryan	.20	34	Atlee Hammaker	.05	62	Lee Guetterman	.05	90	Danny Tartabull	.05
7	'89 Record: R. Sandberg	.10	35	Greg Maddux	.05	63	Milt Thompson	.05	91	Greg Colbrunn (R)	.12
8	'89 Record: B. Thigpen	.08	36	Donnie Hill	.05	64	Tom Herr	.05	92	Danny Jackson	.05
9	Darrin Fletcher	.10	37	Tom Bolton	.05	65	Bruce Hurst	.08	93	Ivan Calderon	.05
10	Gregg Olson	.10	38	Scott Bradley	.05	66	Terry Kennedy	.05	94	John Dopson	.05
11	Roberto Kelly	.05	39	Jim Neidlinger (R)	.15	67	Rick Honeycutt	.05	95	Paul Molitor	.10
12	Paul Assenmacher	.05	40	Kevin Mitchell	.15	68	Gary Sheffield	.10	96	Trevor Wilson	.05
13	Mariano Duncan	.05	41	Ken Dayley	.05	69	Steve Wilson	.05	97	Brady Anderson	.05
14	Dennis Lamp	.05	42	Chris Hoiles	.12	70	Ellis Burks	.10	98	Segio Valdez	.05
15	Von Hayes	.05	43	Roger McDowell	.05	71	Jim Acker	.05	99	Chris Gwynn	.05
16	Mike Heath	.05	44	Mike Felder	.05	72	Junior Ortiz	.05	100	Don Mattingly	.50
17	Jeff Brantley	.05	45	Chris Sabo	.12	73	Craig Worthington	.05	101	Rob Ducey	.05
18	Nelson Liriano	.05	46	Tim Drummond	.05	74	Shane Andrews (R)	.12	102	Gene Larkin	.05
19	Jeff Robinson	.05	47	Brook Jacoby	.05	75	Jack Morris	.08	103	Tim Costo (R)	.35
20	Pedro Guerrero	.10	48	Dennis Boyd	.05	76	Jerry Browne	.05	104	Don Robinson	.05
21	Joe Morgan	.08	49	Pat Borders	.05	77	Drew Hall	.05	105	Kevin McReynolds	.05
22	Storm Davis	.05	50	Bob Welch	.05	78	Geno Petralli	.05	106	Ed Nunez	.05
23	Jim Gantner	.05	51	Art Howe	.05	79	Frank Thomas	.35	107	Luis Polonia	.05
24	Dave Martinez	.05	52	Francisco Oliveras	.05	80	Fernando Valenzuela	.10	108	Matt Young	.05
25	Tim Belcher	.05	53	Mike Sharperson	.05	81	Cito Gaston	.05	109	Greg Riddoch	.05
26	Luis Sojo	.05	54	Gary Mielke	.05	82	Tom Glavine	.05	110	Tom Henke	.05
27	Bobby Witt	.05	55	Jeffrey Leonard	.05	83	Daryl Boston	.05	111	Andres Thomas	.05
28	Alvaro Espinoza	.05	56	Jeff Parrett	.05	84	Bob McClure	.05	112	Frank Dipino	.05

NO.	PLAYER	MINT
113	Carl Everett (R)	.25
114	Lance Dickson (R)	.25
115	Hubie Brooks	.05
116	Mark Davis	.05
117	Dion James	.05
118	Tom Edens (R)	.10
119	Carl Nichols	.05
120	Joe Carter	.05
121	Eric King	.05
122	Paul O'Neill	.05
123	Greg Harris	.05
124	Randy Bush	.05
125	Steve Bedrosian	.05
126	Bernard Gilkey	.20
127	Joe Price	.05
128	Travis Fryman	.35
129	Mark Eichhorn	.05
130	Ozzie Smith	.10
131	Checklist No. 1	.05
132	Jamie Quirk	.05
133	Gregg Briley	.05
134	Kevin Elster	.05
135	Jerome Walton	.25
136	Dave Schmidt	.05
137	Randy Ready	.05
138	Jamie Moyer	.05
139	Jeff Treadway	.05
140	Fred McGriff	.12
141	Nick Leyva	.05
142	Curt Wilkerson	.05
143	John Smiley	.05
144	Dave Henderson	.05
145	Lou Whitaker	.05
146	Dan Plesac	.05
147	Carlos Baerga	.15
148	Rey Palacios	.05
149	Al Osuna (R)	.12
150	Cal Ripken	.12
151	Tom Browning	.05
152	Mickey Hatcher	.05
153	Bryan Harvey	.05
154	Jay Buhner	.05
155	Dwight Evans	.08
156	Carlos Martinez	.05
157	John Smoltz	.05
158	Jose Uribe	.05
159	Joe Boever	.05
160	Vince Coleman	.10
161	Tim Leary	.05
162	Ozzie Canseco	.15
163	Dave Johnson	.05
164	Edgar Diaz	.05
165	Sandy Alomar	.15
166	Harold Baines	.05
167	Randy Tomlin (R)	.10
168	John Olerud	.35
169	Luis Aquino	.05
170	Carlton Fisk	.10
171	Tony LaRussa	.05
172	Pete Incaviglia	.05
173	Jason Grimsley	.05
174	Ken Caminiti	.05
175	Jack Armstrong	.05
176	John Orton	.05
177	Reggie Harris	.10
178	Dave Valle	.05
179	Pete Harnisch	.05
180	Tony Gwynn	.15
181	Duane Ward	.05
182	Junior Noboa	.05
183	Clay Parker	.05
184	Gary Green	.05
185	Joe Magrane	.05
186	Rod Booker	.05
187	Greg Cadaret	.05
188	Damon Berryhill	.05
189	Daryl Irvine (R)	.12
190	Matt Williams	.12
191	Willie Blair	.05
192	Rob Deer	.05
193	Felix Fermin	.05
194	Xavier Hernandez	.05
195	Wally Joyner	.10
196	Jim Vatcher (R)	.15
197	Chris Nabholz	.12
198	R.J. Reynolds	.05
199	Mike Hartley	.10
200	Darryl Strawberry	.20
201	Tom Kelly	.05
202	Jim Leyritz	.10
203	Gene Harris	.05
204	Herm Winningham	.05
205	Mike Perez (R)	.12
206	Carlos Quintana	.05
207	Gary Wayne	.05
208	Willie Wilson	.05
209	Ken Howell	.05
210	Lance Parrish	.05
211	Brian Barnes (R)	.12
212	Steve Finley	.05
213	Frank Wills	.05
214	Joe Girardi	.05
215	Dave Smith	.05
216	Greg Gagne	.05
217	Chris Bosio	.05
218	Rick Parker	.05
219	Jack McDowell	.05
220	Tim Wallach	.05
221	Don Slaught	.05
222	Brian McRae (R)	.50
223	Allan Anderson	.05
224	Juan Gonzalez	.20
225	Randy Johnson	.05
226	Alfredo Griffin	.05
227	Steve Avery	.12
228	Rex Hudler	.05
229	Rance Mulliniks	.05
230	Sid Fernandez	.05
231	Doug Rader	.05
232	Jose DeJesus	.10
233	Al Leiter	.05
234	Scott Erickson	.08
235	Dave Parker	.10
236	Frank Tanana	.05
237	Rick Cerone	.05
238	Mike Dunne	.05
238	Walt Terrell	.25
239	Darren Lewis	.05
240	Mike Scott	.08
241	Dave Clark	.05
242	Mike LaCoss	.05
243	Lance Johnson	.05
244	Mike Jeffcoat	.05
245	Kal Daniels	.08
246	Kevin Wickander	.05
247	Jody Reed	.05
248	Tom Gordon	.08
249	Bob Melvin	.05
250	Dennis Eckersley	.10
251	Mark Lemke	.05
252	Mel Rojas	.05
253	Garry Templeton	.05
254	Shawn Boskie	.05
255	Brian Downing	.05
256	Greg Hibbard	.05
257	Tom O'Malley	.05
258	Chris Hammond	.08
259	Hensley Meulens	.12
260	Harold Reynolds	.05
261	Bud Harrelson	.05
262	Tim Jones	.05
263	Checklist No. 2	.05
264	Dave Hollins	.05
265	Mark Gubicza	.05
266	Carmelo Castillo	.05
267	Mark Knudson	.05
268	Tom Brookens	.05
269	Joe Hesketh	.05
270	Mark McGwire	.25
271	Omar Olivares	.12
272	Jeff King	.05
273	Johnny Ray	.05
274	Ken Williams	.05
275	Alan Trammell	.10
276	Bill Swift	.05
277	Scott Coolbaugh	.05
278	Alex Fernandez	.75
279	Jose Gonzalez	.05
280	Bret Saberhagen	.10
281	Larry Sheets	.05
282	Don Carman	.05
283	Marquis Grissom	.15
284	Billy Spiers	.05
285	Jim Abbott	.15
286	Ken Oberkfell	.05
287	Mark Grant	.05
288	Derrick May	.30
289	Tim Birtsas	.05
290	Steve Sax	.08
291	John Wathan	.05
292	Bud Black	.05
293	Jay Bell	.05
294	Mike Moore	.05
295	Rafael Palmeiro	.05
296	Mark Williamson	.05
297	Manny Lee	.05
298	Omar Vizquel	.05
299	Scott Radinsky	.05
300	Kirby Puckett	.20
301	Steve Farr	.05
302	Tim Teufel	.05
303	Mike Boddicker	.08
304	Kevin Reimer	.05
305	Mike Scioscia	.05
306	Lonnie Smith	.05
307	Andy Benes	.10
308	Tom Pagnozzi	.05
309	Norm Charlton	.08
310	Gary Carter	.10
311	Jeff Pico	.05
312	Charlie Hayes	.05
313	Ron Robinson	.05
314	Gary Pettis	.05
315	Roberto Alomar	.10
316	Gene Nelson	.05
317	Mike Fitzgerald	.05
318	Rick Aguilera	.05
319	Jeff McKnight	.08
320	Tony Fernandez	.05
321	Bob Rodgers	.05
322	Terry Shumpert	.05
323	Cory Snyder	.08
324	Ron Kittle	.05
325	Brett Butler	.05
326	Ken Patterson	.05
327	Ron Hassey	.05
328	Walt Terrell	.05
329	Dave Justice	.60
330	Doc Gooden	.15
331	Eric Anthony	.15
332	Kenny Rogers	.05
333	Chipper Jones (R)	.60
334	Todd Benzinger	.08
335	Mitch Williams	.05
336	Matt Nokes	.05
337	Keith Comstock	.05
338	Luis Rivera	.05
339	Larry Walker	.10
340	Ramon Martinez	.12
341	John Moses	.05
342	Mickey Morandini	.15
343	Jose Oquendo	.05
344	Jeff Russell	.05
345	Len Dykstra	.05
346	Jesse Orosco	.05
347	Greg Vaughn	.10
348	Todd Stottlemyre	.05
349	Dave Gallagher	.05
350	Glenn Davis	.08
351	Joe Torre	.05
352	Frank White	.05
353	Tony Castillo	.05
354	Sid Bream	.05
355	Chili Davis	.05
356	Mike Marshall	.05
357	Jack Savage	.05
358	Mark Parent	.05
359	Chuck Cary	.05
360	Tim Raines	.10
361	Scott Garrelts	.05
362	Hector Villanueva	.08
363	Rick Mahler	.05
364	Dan Pasqua	.05
365	Mike Schooler	.05
366	Checklist No. 3	.05
367	Dave Walsh (R)	.12
368	Felix Jose	.05
369	Steve Searcy	.05
370	Kelly Gruber	.10
371	Jeff Montgomery	.05
372	Spike Owen	.05
373	Darrin Jackson	.05
374	Larry Casian (R)	.12
375	Tony Pena	.05
376	Mike Harkey	.05
377	Rene Gonzales	.05
378	Wilson Alvarez	.25
379	Randy Velarde	.05
380	Willie McGee	.10
381	Jim Leyland	.05
382	Mackey Sasser	.05
383	Pete Smith	.05
384	Gerald Perry	.05
385	Mickey Tettleton	.05
386	Cecil Fielder (AS)	.20
387	Julio Franco (AS)	.05
388	Kelly Gruber (AS)	.10
389	Alan Trammell (AS)	.10
390	Jose Canseco (AS)	.30
391	Rickey Henderson (AS)	.20
392	Ken Griffey Jr. (AS)	.30
393	Carlton Fisk (AS)	.05
394	Bob Welch (AS)	.05
395	Chuck Finley (AS)	.05
396	Bobby Thigpen (AS)	.08
397	Eddie Murray (AS)	.10
398	Ryne Sandberg (AS)	.15
399	Matt Williams (AS)	.12
400	Barry Larkin (AS)	.08
401	Barry Bonds (AS)	.12
402	Darryl Strawberry (AS)	.20
403	Bobby Bonilla (AS)	.10
404	Mike Scioscia (AS)	.05
405	Doug Drabek (AS)	.05
406	Frank Viola (AS)	.08
407	John Franco (AS)	.05
408	Ernie Riles	.05
409	Mike Stanley	.05
410	Dave Righetti	.05
411	Lance Blankenship	.05
412	Dave Bergman	.05
413	Terry Mulholland	.05
414	Sammy Sosa	.12
415	Rick Sutcliffe	.08
416	Randy Mulligan	.05
417	Bill Krueger	.05
418	Nick Esasky	.05
419	Jeff Reed	.05
420	Bobby Thigpen	.08
421	Alex Cole	.25
422	Rick Reuschel	.05
423	Rafael Ramirez	.05
424	Calvin Schiraldi	.05
425	Andy Van Slyke	.10
426	Joe Grahe (R)	.10
427	Rick Dempsey	.05
428	John Barfield (R)	.08
429	Stump Merrill	.05
430	Gary Gaetti	.05
431	Paul Gibson	.05
432	Delino DeShields	.20
433	Pat Tabler	.05
434	Julio Machado	.05
435	Kevin Maas	.35
436	Scott Bankhead	.05
437	Doug Dascenzo	.05
438	Vincente Palacios	.05
439	Dickie Thon	.05
440	George Bell	.10
441	Zane Smith	.05
442	Charlie O'Brien	.05
443	Jeff Innis	.05
444	Glenn Braggs	.05
445	Greg Swindell	.05
446	Craig Grebeck	.05
447	John Burkett	.05
448	Craig Lefferts	.05
449	Juan Berenguer	.05
450	Wade Boggs	.15
451	Neal Heaton	.05
452	Bill Schroeder	.05

NO.	PLAYER	MINT
453	Lenny Harris	.05
454	Kevin Appier	.05
455	Walt Weiss	.05
456	Charlie Liebrandt	.05
457	Todd Hundley	.10
458	Brian Holman	.05
459	Tom Trebelhorn	.05
460	Dave Stieb	.05
461	Robin Ventura	.15
462	Steve Frey	.05
463	Dwight Smith	.05
464	Steve Buechele	.05
465	Ken Griffey	.05
466	Charles Nagy	.10
467	Dennis Cook	.05
468	Tim Hulett	.05
469	Chet Lemon	.05
470	Howard Johnson	.08
471	Mike Lieberthal (R)	.20
472	Kirt Manwaring	.05
473	Curt Young	.05
474	Phil Plantier (R)	.50
475	Teddy Higuera	.05
476	Glenn Wilson	.05
477	Mike Fetters	.05
478	Kurt Stillwell	.05
479	Bob Patterson	.05
480	Dave Magadan	.10
481	Eddie Whitson	.05
482	Tino Martinez	.25
483	Mike Aldrete	.05
484	Dave LaPoint	.05
485	Terry Pendleton	.05
486	Tommy Greene	.05
487	Rafael Belliard	.05
488	Jeff Manto	.05
489	Bobby Valentine	.05
490	Kirk Gibson	.10
491	Kurt Miller (R)	.15
492	Ernie Whitt	.05
493	Jose Rijo	.05
494	Chris James	.05
495	Charlie Hough	.05
496	Marty Barrett	.05
497	Ben McDonald	.30
498	Mark Salas	.05
499	Melido Perez	.05
500	Will Clark	.35
501	Mike Bielecki	.05
502	Carney Lansford	.05
503	Roy Smith	.05
504	Julio Valera	.05
505	Chuck Finely	.05
506	Darnell Coles	.05
507	Steve Jeltz	.05
508	Mike York	.10
509	Glenallen Hill	.05
510	John Franco	.05
511	Steve Balboni	.05
512	Jose Mesa	.05
513	Jerald Clark	.05
514	Mike Stanton	.05
515	Alvin Davis	.05
516	Karl Rhodes	.05
517	Joe Oliver	.05
518	Cris Carpenter	.05
519	Sparky Anderson	.05
520	Mark Grace	.15
521	Joe Orsulak	.05
522	Stan Belinda	.05
523	Rodney McCray (R)	.12
524	Darrel Akerfelds	.05
525	Willie Randolph	.05
526	Moises Alou	.20
527	Checklist No. 4	.05
528	Denny Martinez	.05
529	Marc Newfield (R)	.20
530	Roger Clemens	.20
531	Dave Rohde	.05
532	Kirk McCaskill	.05
533	Oddibe McDowell	.05
534	Mike Jackson	.05
535	Ruben Sierra	.05
536	Mike Witt	.12
537	Jose Lind	.05
538	Bip Roberts	.05
539	Scott Terry	.05
540	George Brett	.12
541	Domingo Ramos	.05
542	Rob Murphy	.05
543	Junior Felix	.10
544	Alejandro Pena	.05
545	Dale Murphy	.15
546	Jeff Ballard	.05
547	Mike Pagliarulo	.05
548	Jaime Navarro	.05
549	John McNamara	.05
550	Eric Davis	.20
551	Bob Kipper	.05
552	Jeff Hamilton	.05
553	Joe Klink (R)	.12
554	Brian Harper	.05
555	Turner Ward (R)	.15
556	Gary Ward	.05
557	Wally Whitehurst	.05
558	Otis Nixon	.05
559	Adam Peterson	.05
560	Greg Smith	.05
561	Tim McIntosh	.05
562	Jeff Kunkel	.05
563	Brent Knackert	.05
564	Dante Bichette	.05
565	Craig Biggio	.05
566	Craig Wilson (R)	.12
567	Dwayne Henry	.05
568	Ron Karkovice	.05
569	Curt Schilling	.05
570	Barry Bonds	.15
571	Pat Combs	.05
572	Dave Anderson	.05
573	Rich Rodriguez	.05
574	John Marzano	.05
575	Robin Yount	.15
576	Jeff Kaiser	.05
577	Bill Doran	.05
578	Dave West	.05
579	Roger Craig	.05
580	Dave Stewart	.12
581	Luis Quinones	.05
582	Marty Clary	.05
583	Tony Phillips	.05
584	Kevin Brown	.05
585	Pete O'Brien	.05
586	Fred Lynn	.05
587	Jose Offerman	.30
588	Mark Whiten	.35
589	Scott Ruskin	.05
590	Eddie Murray	.10
591	Ken Hill	.05
592	B.J. Surhoff	.05
593	Mike Walker	.05
594	Rich Garces (R)	.12
595	Bill Landrum	.05
596	Ronnie Walden (R)	.12
597	Jerry Don Gleaton	.05
598	Sam Horn	.05
599	Greg Myers	.05
600	Bo Jackson	.40
601	Bob Ojeda	.05
602	Casey Candaele	.05
603	Wes Chamberlain (R)	.35
604	Billy Hatcher	.05
605	Jeff Reardon	.05
606	Jim Gott	.05
607	Edgar Martinez	.05
608	Todd Burns	.05
609	Jeff Torborg	.05
610	Andres Galarraga	.08
611	Dave Eiland	.05
612	Steve Lyons	.05
613	Eric Show	.05
614	Luis Salazar	.05
615	Bert Blyeven	.05
616	Todd Zeile	.15
617	Bill Wegman	.05
618	Sil Campusano	.05
619	David Wells	.05
620	Ozzie Guillen	.05
621	Ted Power	.05
622	Jack Daugherty	.05
623	Jeff Blauser	.05
624	Tom Candiotti	.05
625	Terry Steinbach	.05
626	Gerald Young	.05
627	Tim Layana	.05
628	Greg Litton	.05
629	Wes Gardner	.05
630	Dave Winfield	.15
631	Mike Morgan	.05
632	Lloyd Moseby	.08
633	Kevin Tapani	.05
634	Henry Cotto	.05
635	Andy Hawkins	.05
636	Geronimo Pena	.10
637	Bruce Ruffin	.05
638	Mike Macfarlane	.05
639	Frank Robinson	.05
640	Andre Dawson	.12
641	Mike Henneman	.05
642	Hal Morris	.12
643	Jim Presley	.05
644	Chuck Crim	.05
645	Juan Samuel	.05
646	Andujar Cedeno	.50
647	Mark Portugal	.05
648	Lee Stevens	.15
649	Bill Sampen	.05
650	Jack Clark	.12
651	Alan Mills	.05
652	Kevin Romine	.05
653	Anthony Telford (R)	.12
654	Paul Sorrento	.05
655	Erik Hanson	.05
656	Checklist No. 5	.05
657	Mike Kingery	.05
658	Scott Aldred	.10
659	Oscar Azocar	.15
660	Lee Smith	.05
661	Steve Lake	.05
662	Rob Dibble	.05
663	Greg Brock	.05
664	John Farrell	.05
665	Mike LaValliere	.05
666	Danny Darwin	.05
667	Kent Anderson	.05
668	Bill Long	.05
669	Lou Piniella	.05
670	Rickey Henderson	.25
671	Andy McGaffigan	.05
672	Shane Mack	.05
673	Greg Olson	.12
674	Kevin Gross	.05
675	Tom Brunansky	.05
676	Scott Chiamparino	.25
677	Billy Ripken	.05
678	Mark Davidson	.05
679	Bill Bathe	.05
680	David Cone	.05
681	Jeff Schaefer	.05
682	Ray Lankford	.35
683	Derek Lilliquist	.05
684	Milt Cuyler	.12
685	Doug Drabek	.05
686	Mike Gallego	.05
687	John Cerutti	.05
688	Rosario Rodriguez (R)	.12
689	John Kruk	.05
690	Orel Hershiser	.12
691	Mike Blowers	.05
692	Efrain Valdez (R)	.12
693	Francisco Cabrera	.05
694	Randy Veres	.05
695	Kevin Seitzer	.05
696	Steve Olin	.05
697	Shawn Abner	.05
698	Mark Guthrie	.05
699	Jim Lefebvre	.05
700	Jose Canseco	.40
701	Pascual Perez	.05
702	Tim Naehring	.15
703	Juan Agosto	.05
704	Devon White	.05
705	Robby Thompson	.05
706	Brad Arnsberg	.05
707	Jim Eisenreich	.05
708	John Mitchell	.05
709	Matt Sinatro	.05
710	Kent Hrbek	.12
711	Jose DeLeon	.05
712	Ricky Jordan	.05
713	Scott Scudder	.05
714	Marvell Wynne	.05
715	Tim Burke	.05
716	Bob Geren	.05
717	Phil Bradley	.05
718	Steve Crawford	.05
719	Keith Miller	.10
720	Cecil Fielder	.25
721	Mark Lee (R)	.12
722	Wally Backman	.05
723	Candy Maldonado	.05
724	David Segui	.25
725	Ron Gant	.10
726	Phil Stephenson	.05
727	Mookie Wilson	.05
728	Scott Sanderson	.05
729	Don Zimmer	.05
730	Barry Larkin	.10
731	Jeff Gray (R)	.12
732	Franklin Stubbs	.05
733	Kelly Downs	.05
734	John Russell	.05
735	Ron Darling	.05
736	Dick Schofield	.05
737	Tim Crews	.05
738	Mel Hall	.05
739	Russ Swan	.05
740	Ryne Sandberg	.15
741	Jimmy Key (R)	.12
742	Tommy Gregg	.05
743	Bryn Smith	.05
744	Nelson Santovenia	.05
745	Doug Jones	.05
746	John Shelby	.05
747	Tony Fossas	.05
748	Al Newman	.05
749	Greg Harris	.05
750	Bobby Bonilla	.05
751	Wayne Edwards	.05
752	Kevin Bass	.05
753	Paul Marak (R)	.12
754	Bill Pecota	.05
755	Mark Langston	.05
756	Jeff Huson	.05
757	Mark Gardner	.05
758	Mike Devereaux	.05
759	Bobby Cox	.05
760	Benny Santiago	.08
761	Larry Anderson	.05
762	Mitch Webster	.05
763	Dana Kiecker	.05
764	Mark Carreon	.05
765	Shawon Dunston	.05
766	Jeff Robinson	.05
767	Dán Wilson (R)	.15
768	Donn Pall	.05
769	Tim Sherrill (R)	.12
770	Jay Howell	.05
771	Gary Redus	.05
772	Kent Mercker	.05
773	Tom Foley	.05
774	Dennis Rasmussen	.05
775	Julio Franco	.05
776	Brent Mayne	.05
777	John Candelaria	.05
778	Danny Gladden	.05
779	Carmelo Martinez	.05
780	Randy Myers	.05
781	Darryl Hamilton	.05
782	Jim Deshaies	.05
783	Joel Skinner	.05
784	Willie Fraser	.05
785	Scott Fletcher	.05
786	Eric Plunk	.05
787	Checklist No. 6	.05
788	Bob Milacki	.05
789	Tom Lasorda	.05
790	Ken Griffey Jr.	.75
791	Mike Benjamin	.05
792	Mike Greenwell	.15

1989 BOWMAN.... Complete Set of 484 Cards (2½″ x 3¾″)—Value $25.00

This was the first Bowman card set since 1955 when Topps bought the Bowman Gum Co. The set which was released in July includes hot rookie stars from Spring training '89, traded players in their new uniforms, and all of the top stars of the game. The cards are the same size as the classic '53 Bowmans, 2½″ x 3¾″. Features the rookie cards of Ken Griffey, Jr., Jerome Walton, Gary Sheffield and Ricky Jordan.

NO.	PLAYER	MINT
1	Oswald Peraza (R)	.12
2	Briand Holton	.05
3	Jose Bautista (R)	.12
4	Pete Harnisch (R)	.15
5	Dave Schmidt	.05
6	Gregg Olson (R)	.75
7	Jeff Ballard	.15
8	Bob Melvin	.05
9	Cal Ripken	.15
10	Randy Milligan	.20
11	Juan Bell (R)	.20
12	Billy Ripken	.08
13	Jim Traber	.05
14	Pete Stanicek	.10
15	Steve Finley (R)	.25
16	Larry Sheets	.05
17	Phil Bradley	.08
18	Brady Anderson (R)	.20
19	Lee Smith	.08
20	Tom Fischer (R)	.12
21	Mike Boodicker	.05
22	Rob Murphy	.05
23	Wes Gardner	.05
24	John Dopson (R)	.20
25	Bob Stanley	.05
26	Roger Clemens	.35
27	Rich Gedman	.05
28	Marty Barrett	.05
29	Luis Rivera	.05
30	Jody Reed	.08
31	Nick Esasky	.08
32	Wade Boggs	.40
33	Jim Rice	.12
34	Mike Greenwell	.30
35	Dwight Evans	.10
36	Ellis Burks	.30
37	Chuck Finley	.12
38	Kirk McCaskill	.10
39	Jim Abbott (R)	1.00
40	Bryan Harvey (R)	.20
41	Bert Blyleven	.08
42	Mike Witt	.08
43	Bob McClure	.05
44	Bill Schroeder	.05
45	Lance Parrish	.10
46	Dick Schofield	.05
47	Wally Joyner	.20
48	Jack Howell	.05
49	Johnny Ray	.10
50	Chili Davis	.08
51	Tony Armas	.05
52	Claudell Washington	.05
53	Brian Downing	.08
54	Devon White	.10
55	Bobby Thigpen	.05
56	Bill Long	.05
57	Jerry Reuss	.05
58	Shawn Hillegas	.05
59	Melido Perez	.10
60	Jeff Bittiger (R)	.15
61	Jack McDowell	.12
62	Carlton Fisk	.10
63	Steve Lyons	.05
64	Ozzie Guillen	.08
65	Robin Ventura (R)	.75
66	Fred Manrique	.05

NO.	PLAYER	MINT
67	Dan Pasqua	.08
68	Ivan Calderon	.08
69	Ron Kittle	.05
70	Daryl Boston	.05
71	Dave Gallagher (R)	.20
72	Harold Baines	.08
73	Charles Nagy (R)	.20
74	John Farrell	.05
75	Kevin Wickander (R)	.12
76	Greg Swindell	.10
77	Mike Walker (R)	.15
78	Doug Jones	.05
79	Rich Yett	.05
80	Tom Candiotti	.05
81	Jesse Orosco	.05
82	Bud Black	.05
83	Andy Allanson	.05
84	Pete O'Brien	.10
85	Jerry Browne	.05
86	Brook Jacoby	.05
87	Mark Lewis (R)	.25
88	Luis Aguayo	.05
89	Cory Snyder	.10
90	Oddibe McDowell	.05
91	Joe Carter	.15
92	Frank Tanana	.05
93	Jack Morris	.10
94	Doyle Alexander	.05
95	Steve Searcy (R)	.15
96	Randy Bockus (R)	.10
97	Jeff Robinson	.08
98	Mike Henneman	.05
99	Paul Gibson (R)	.10
100	Frank Williams	.05
101	Matt Nokes	.10
102	Ricco Brogna (R)	.15
103	Lou Whitaker	.08
104	Al Pedrique	.05
105	Alan Trammell	.12
106	Chris Brown	.05
107	Pat Sheridan	.05
108	Chet Lemon	.05
109	Keith Moreland	.05
110	Mel Stottlemyre, Jr. (R)	.20
111	Bret Saberhagen	.12
112	Floyd Bannister	.05
113	Jeff Montgomery	.12
114	Steve Farr	.05
115	Tom Gordon (R)	.60
116	Charlie Leibrandt	.08
117	Mark Gubicza	.08
118	Mike Macfarlane (R)	.15
119	Bob Boone	.05
120	Kurt Stillwell	.05
121	George Brett	.20
122	Frank White	.05
123	Kevin Seitzer	.20
124	Willie Wilson	.08
125	Pat Tabler	.05
126	Bo Jackson	1.00
127	Hugh Walker (R)	.15
128	Danny Tartabull	.15
129	Teddy Higuera	.08
130	Don August	.08
131	Juan Nieves	.05
132	Mike Birkbeck	.05

NO.	PLAYER	MINT
133	Dan Plesac	.05
134	Chris Bosio	.05
135	Bill Wegman	.05
136	Chuck Crim	.05
137	B.J. Surhoff	.08
138	Joey Meyer	.05
139	Dale Sveum	.05
140	Paul Molitor	.12
141	Jim Gantner	.05
142	Gary Sheffield (R)	1.00
143	Greg Brock	.05
144	Robin Yount	.15
145	Glenn Braggs	.05
146	Rob Deer	.08
147	Fred Toliver	.05
148	Jeff Reardon	.08
149	Allan Anderson	.08
150	Frank Viola	.12
151	Shane Rawley	.05
152	Juan Berenguer	.05
153	Johnny Ard (R)	.15
154	Tim Laudner	.05
155	Brian Harper	.05
156	Al Newman	.05
157	Kent Hrbek	.12
158	Gary Gaetti	.12
159	Wally Backman	.05
160	Gene Larkin	.05
161	Greg Gagne	.05
162	Kirby Puckett	.35
163	Danny Gladden	.05
164	Randy Bush	.05
165	Dave LaPoint	.05
166	Andy Hawkins	.05
167	Dave Righetti	.08
168	Lance McCullers	.08
169	Jimmy Jones	.08
170	Al Leiter	.05
171	John Candelaria	.08
172	Don Slaught	.05
173	Jamie Quirk	.05
174	Rafael Santana	.05
175	Mike Pagliarulo	.05
176	Don Mattingly	.75
177	Ken Phelps	.08
178	Steve Sax	.10
179	Dave Winfield	.15
180	Stan Jefferson	.05
181	Rickey Henderson	.30
182	Bob Brower	.05
183	Roberto Kelly	.20
184	Curt Young	.05
185	Gene Nelson	.05
186	Bob Welch	.08
187	Rick Honeycutt	.05
188	Dave Stewart	.10
189	Mike Moore	.05
190	Dennis Eckersley	.05
191	Eric Plunk	.05
192	Storm Davis	.05
193	Terry Steinbach	.10
194	Ron Hassey	.05
195	Stan Royer (R)	.15
196	Walt Weiss	.20
197	Mark McGwire	.60
198	Carney Lansford	.08

NO.	PLAYER	MINT
199	Glenn Hubbard	.05
200	Dave Henderson	.05
201	Jose Canseco	.75
202	Dave Parker	.12
203	Scott Bankhead	.10
204	Tom Niedenfuer	.05
205	Mark Langston	.12
206	Erik Hanson (R)	.20
207	Mike Jackson	.05
208	Dave Valle	.05
209	Scott Bradley	.05
210	Harold Reynolds	.08
211	Tino Martinez (R)	.75
212	Rich Renteria (R)	.15
213	Rey Quinones	.05
214	Jim Presley	.08
215	Alvin Davis	.08
216	Edgar Martinez	.15
217	Darnell Coles	.05
218	Jeffrey Leonard	.05
219	Jay Buhner	.15
220	Ken Griffey, Jr. (R)	4.00
221	Drew Hall	.05
222	Bobby Witt	.08
223	Jamie Moyer	.05
224	Charlie Hough	.05
225	Nolan Ryan	.60
226	Jeff Russell	.05
227	Jim Sundberg	.05
228	Julio Franco	.08
229	Buddy Bell	.05
230	Scott Fletcher	.05
231	Jeff Kunkel	.05
232	Steve Buechele	.05
233	Monty Fariss ((R)	.15
234	Rick Leach	.05
235	Ruben Sierra	.20
236	Cecil Espy	.08
237	Rafael Palmeiro	.15
238	Pete Incaviglia	.08
239	Dave Stieb	.05
240	Jeff Musselman	.05
241	Mike Flanagan	.05
242	Todd Stottlemyre	.15
243	Jimmy Key	.08
244	Tony Castillo (R)	.15
245	Alex Sanchez (R)	.20
246	Tom Henke	.05
247	John Cerutti	.05
248	Ernie Whitt	.05
249	Bob Brenly	.05
250	Rance Mulliniks	.05
251	Kelly Gruber	.12
252	Ed Sprague	.15
253	Fred McGriff	.15
254	Tony Fernandez	.08
255	Tom Lawless	.05
256	George Bell	.10
257	Jesse Barfield	.08
258	S. Alomar, Jr./Sr.	.25
259	Griffey, Jr./Sr.	.75
260	Cal Ripken, Sr.,	.05
261	Mel Stottlemyre	.05
262	Zane Smith	.05
263	Charlie Puleo	.05
264	Derek Lilliquist (R)	.20

NO.	PLAYER	MINT
265	Paul Assenmacher	.05
266	John Smoltz (R)	.45
267	Tom Glavine	.10
268	Steve Avery (R)	.60
269	Pete Smith	.08
270	Jody Davis	.05
271	Bruce Benedict	.05
272	Andres Thomas	.05
273	Gerald Perry	.08
274	Ron Gant	.45
275	Darrell Evans	.05
276	Dale Murphy	.15
277	Dion James	.05
278	Lonnie Smith	.05
279	Geronimo Berroa	.10
280	Steve Wilson (R)	.15
281	Rick Sutcliffe	.08
282	Kevin Coffman	.08
283	Mitch Williams	.08
284	Greg Maddux	.08
285	Paul Kilgus	.05
286	Mike Harkey (R)	.25
287	Lloyd McClendon	.10
288	Damon Berryhill	.15
289	Ty Griffin (R)	.75
290	Ryne Sandberg	.20
291	Mark Grace	1.50
292	Curt Wilkerson	.05
293	Vance Law	.05
294	Shawon Dunston	.08
295	Jerome Walton (R)	2.00
296	Mitch Webster	.05
297	Dwight Smith (R)	.75
298	Andre Dawson	.15
299	Jeff Sellers	.05
300	Jose Rijo	.10
301	John Franco	.08
302	Rick Mahler	.05
303	Ron Robinson	.05
304	Danny Jackson	.08
305	Rob Dibble (R)	.25
306	Tom Browning	.05
307	Bo Diaz	.05
308	Manny Trillo	.05
309	Chris Sabo (R)	.50
310	Ron Oester	.05
311	Barry Larkin	.15
312	Todd Benzinger	.08
313	Paul O'Neill	.08
314	Kal Daniels	.12
315	Joel Youngblood	.05
316	Eric Davis	.25
317	Dave Smith	.05
318	Mark Portugal	.05
319	Brian Meyer (R)	.12
320	Jim Deshaies	.05
321	Juan Agosto	.05
322	Mike Scott	.08
323	Rick Rhoden	.05
324	Jim Clancy	.05
325	Larry Andersen	.05
326	Alex Trevino	.05
327	Alan Ashby	.05
328	Craig Reynolds	.05
329	Bill Doran	.05
330	Rafael Ramirez	.05
331	Glenn Davis	.12
332	Willie Ansley (R)	.25
333	Gerald Young	.05
334	Cameron Drew (R)	.10
335	Jay Howell	.05
336	Tim Belcher	.15
337	Fernando Valenzuela	.08
338	Ricky Horton	.05
339	Tim Leary	.05
340	Bill Bene (R)	.10
341	Orel Hershiser	.20
342	Mike Scioscia	.05
343	Rick Dempsey	.05
344	Willie Randolph	.08
345	Alfredo Griffin	.05
346	Eddie Murray	.12
347	Mickey Hatcher	.05
348	Mike Sharperson	.05
349	John Shelby	.05
350	Mike Marshall	.08
351	Kirk Gibson	.15
352	Mike Davis	.05
353	Bryn Smith	.05
354	Pascual Perez	.05
355	Kevin Gross	.05
356	Andy McGaffigan	.05
357	Brian Holman (R)	.12
358	Dave Wainhouse (R)	.12
359	Denny Martinez	.05
360	Tim Burke	.05
361	Nelson Santovenia (R)	.12
362	Tim Wallach	.08
363	Spike Owen	.05
364	Rex Hudler	.05
365	Andres Galarraga	.10
366	Otis Nixon	.05
367	Hubie Brooks	.05
368	Mike Aldrete	.05
369	Tim Raines	.15
370	Dave Martinez	.05
371	Bob Ojeda	.05
372	Ron Darling	.10
373	Wally Whitehurst (R)	.15
374	Randy Myers	.05
375	David Cone	.20
376	Doc Gooden	.30
377	Sid Fernandez	.05
378	Dave Proctor (R)	.15
379	Gary Carter	.08
380	Keith Miller	.05
381	Gregg Jefferies	1.00
382	Tim Teufel	.05
383	Kevin Elster	.05
384	Dave Magadan	.05
385	Keith Hernandez	.10
386	Mookie Wilson	.05
387	Darryl Strawberry	.40
388	Kevin McReynolds	.10
389	Mark Carreon	.10
390	Jeff Parrett	.05
391	Mike Maddux	.05
392	Don Carman	.05
393	Bruce Ruffin	.05
394	Ken Howell	.05
395	Steve Bedrosian	.10
396	Floyd Youmans	.05
397	Larry McWilliams	.05
398	Pat Combs (R)	.30
399	Steve Lake	.05
400	Dickie Thon	.05
401	Ricky Jordan (R)	.50
402	Mike Schmidt	.30
403	Tom Herr	.08
404	Chris James	.08
405	Juan Samuel	.05
406	Von Hayes	.08
407	Ron Jones (R)	.20
408	Curt Ford	.05
409	Bob Walk	.05
410	Jeff Robinson	.05
411	Jim Gott	.05
412	Scott Medvin	.08
413	John Smiley	.08
414	Bob Kipper	.05
415	Brian Fisher	.05
416	Doug Drabek	.08
417	Mike LaValliere	.05
418	Ken Oberkfell	.05
419	Sid Bream	.05
420	Austin Manahan (R)	.15
421	Jose Lino	.05
422	Bobby Bonilla	.15
423	Glenn Wilson	.05
424	Andy Van Slyke	.10
425	Gary Redus	.05
426	Barry Bonds	.20
427	Don Heinkel (R)	.15
428	Ken Dayley	.05
429	Todd Worrell	.05
430	Brad DuVall (R)	.15
431	Jose DeLeon	.05
432	Joe Magrane	.08
433	John Ericks (R)	.20
434	Frank DiPino	.05
435	Tony Pena	.08
436	Ozzie Smith	.15
437	Terry Pendleton	.05
438	Jose Oquendo	.05
439	Tim Jones (R)	.15
440	Pedro Guerrero	.10
441	Milt Thompson	.08
442	Willie McGee	.08
443	Vince Coleman	.15
444	Tom Brunansky	.05
445	Walt Terrell	.05
446	Eric Show	.05
447	Mark Davis	.08
448	Andy Benes (R)	.75
449	Eddie Whitson	.05
450	Dennis Rasmussen	.05
451	Bruce Hurst	.08
452	Pat Clements	.05
453	Benny Santiago	.10
454	Sandy Alomar, Jr. (R)	.75
455	Garry Templeton	.05
456	Jack Clark	.10
457	Tim Flannery	.05
458	Roberto Alomar	.40
459	Carmelo Martinez	.05
460	John Kruk	.08
461	Tony Gwynn	.25
462	Jerald Clark (R)	.15
463	Don Robinson	.05
464	Craig Lefferts	.05
465	Kelly Downs	.05
466	Rick Reuschel	.05
467	Scott Garrelts	.05
468	Wil Tejada	.05
469	Kirt Manwaring	.05
470	Terry Kennedy	.05
471	Jose Uribe	.05
472	Royce Clayton (R)	.15
473	Robby Thompson	.05
474	Kevin Mitchell	.30
475	Ernie Riles	.05
476	Will Clark	.75
477	Donell Nixon	.05
478	Candy Maldonado	.08
479	Tracy Jones	.05
480	Brett Butler	.08
481	Checklist	.08
482	Checklist	.08
483	Checklist	.08
484	Checklist	.08

1990 Bowman.... Complete Set of 528 Cards—Value $25.00

Card size was reduced to the standard 2½" x 3½". The set was increased to 528 cards and issued in July. Features the rookie cards of John Olerud, Kevin Maas, Frank Thomas and Ben McDonald.

NO.	PLAYER	MINT
1	Tommy Greene (R)	.20
2	Tom Glavine	.05
3	Andy Nezelek	.05
4	Mike Stanton (R)	.10
5	Rick Luecken (R)	.10
6	Kent Mercker (R)	.15
7	Derek Lilliquist	.05
8	Charlie Leibrandt	.05
9	Steve Avery	.25
10	John Smoltz	.10
11	Mark Lemke	.05
12	Lonnie Smith	.05
13	Oddibe McDowell	.05
14	Tyler Houston (R)	.20
15	Jeff Blauser	.05
16	Ernie Whitt	.05
17	Alexis Infante	.05
18	Jim Presley	.05
19	Dale Murphy	.10
20	Nick Esasky	.05
21	Rick Sutcliffe	.08
22	Mike Bielecki	.05
23	Steve Wilson	.05
24	Kevin Blankenship	.05
25	Mitch Williams	.05
26	Dean Wilkins (R)	.12
27	Greg Maddux	.05
28	Mike Harkey	.05
29	Mark Grace	.20
30	Ryne Sandberg	.20
31	Greg Smith (R)	.15
32	Dwight Smith	.10
33	Damon Berryhill	.05
34	Earl Cunningham (R)	.25
35	Jerome Walton	.40
36	Lloyd McClendon	.05
37	Ty Griffin	.12
38	Shawon Dunston	.10
39	Andre Dawson	.10
40	Luis Salazar	.05
41	Tim Layana (R)	.20
42	Rob Dibble	.05
43	Tom Browning	.05
44	Danny Jackson	.05
45	Jose Rijo	.05
46	Scott Scudder	.15
47	Randy Myers	.05
48	Brian Lane (R)	.12
49	Paul O'Neill	.05
50	Barry Larkin	.12
51	Reggie Jefferson (R)	.25
52	Jeff Branson (R)	.15
53	Chris Sabo	.15
54	Joe Oliver	.10
55	Todd Benzinger	.08
56	Rolando Roomes	.05
57	Hal Morris	.20
58	Eric Davis	.15
59	Scott Bryant (R)	.15
60	Ken Griffey	.08
61	Darryl Kile	.15
62	Dave Smith	.05
63	Mark Portugal	.05
64	Jeff Juden (R)	.25
65	Bill Gullickson	.05
66	Danny Darwin	.05
67	Larry Andersen	.05
68	Jose Cano	.08
69	Dan Schatzeder	.05
70	Jim Deshaies	.05
71	Mike Scott	.08
72	Gerald Young	.05
73	Ken Caminiti	.05
74	Ken Oberkfell	.05
75	Dave Rohde (R)	.15
76	Bill Doran	.05
77	Andujar Cedeno (R)	.15
78	Craig Biggio	.05
79	Karl Rhodes (R)	.15
80	Glenn Davis	.12
81	Eric Anthony (R)	.50
82	John Wetteland	.12
83	Jay Howell	.05
84	Orel Hershiser	.10
85	Tim Belcher	.05
86	Kiki Jones (R)	.25
87	Mike Hartley	.10
88	Ramon Martinez	.30
89	Mike Scioscia	.05
90	Willie Randolph	.05
91	Juan Samuel	.05
92	Jose Offerman (R)	.75
93	Dave Hansen (R)	.20
94	Jeff Hamilton	.05
95	Alfredo Griffin	.05
96	Tom Goodwin (R)	.30
97	Kirk Gibson	.10
98	Jose Vizcaino (R)	.15
99	Kal Daniels	.10
100	Hubie Brooks	.05
101	Eddie Murray	.15
102	Dennis Boyd	.05
103	Tim Burke	.05
104	Bill Sampen (R)	.20
105	Brett Gideon	.05
106	Mark Gardner (R)	.15
107	Howard Farmer (R)	.12
108	Mel Rojas (R)	.12
109	Kevin Gross	.05
110	Dave Schmidt	.05
111	Denny Martinez	.05
112	Jerry Goff	.10
113	Andres Galarraga	.08
114	Tim Welch	.05
115	Marquis Grissom (R)	.40
116	Spike Owen	.05
117	Larry Walker (R)	.25
118	Tim Raines	.08
119	Delino DeShields (R)	.50
120	Tom Foley	.05
121	Dave Martinez	.05
122	Frank Viola	.10
123	Julio Valera (R)	.15
124	Alejandro Pena	.05
125	David Cone	.08
126	Doc Gooden	.20
127	Kevin Brown (R)	.15
128	John Franco	.05
129	Terry Bross (R)	.12
130	Blaine Beatty (R)	.12
131	Sid Fernandez	.05
132	Mike Marshall	.05
133	Howard Johnson	.08
134	Jaime Roseboro (R)	.20
135	Alan Zinter (R)	.20
136	Keith Miller	.05
137	Kevin Elster	.05
138	Kevin McReynolds	.10
139	Barry Lyons	.05
140	Gregg Jefferies	.20
141	Darryl Strawberry	.20
142	Todd Hundley (R)	.25
143	Scott Service	.05
144	Chuck Malone (R)	.15
145	Steve Ontiveros	.05
146	Roger McDowell	.05
147	Ken Howell	.05
148	Pat Combs	.10
149	Jeff Parrett	.05
150	Chuck McElroy (R)	.15
151	Jason Grimsley	.12
152	Len Dykstra	.10
153	Mickey Morandini (R)	.15
154	John Kruk	.05
155	Dickie Thon	.05
156	Ricky Jordan	.12
157	Jeff Jackson (R)	.15
158	Darren Daulton	.05
159	Tom Herr	.05
160	Von Hayes	.08
161	Dave Hollins (R)	.25
162	Carmelo Martinez	.05
163	Bob Walk	.05
164	Doug Drabek	.05
165	Walt Terrell	.05
166	Bill Landrum	.05
167	Scott Ruskin (R)	.15
168	Bob Patterson	.05
169	Bobby Bonilla	.15
170	Jose Lind	.05
171	Andy Van Slyke	.10
172	Mike LaValliere	.05
173	Willie Greene (R)	.20
174	Jay Bell	.05
175	Sid Bream	.05
176	Tom Prince	.05
177	Wally Backman	.05
178	Moises Alou (R)	.20
179	Steve Carter	.05
180	Gary Redus	.05
181	Barry Bonds	.15
182	Don Slaught	.05
183	Joe Magrane	.05
184	Bryn Smith	.05
185	Todd Worrell	.05
186	Jose DeLeon	.05
187	Frank DiPino	.05
188	John Tudor	.05
189	Howard Hilton (R)	.15
190	John Ericks	.05
191	Ken Dayley	.05
192	Ray Lankford (R)	.75
193	Todd Zelle	.50
194	Willie McGee	.10
195	Ozzie Smith	.10
196	Milt Thompson	.05
197	Terry Pendleton	.05
198	Vince Coleman	.10
199	Paul Coleman (R)	.25
200	Jose Oquendo	.05
201	Pedro Guerrero	.12
202	Tom Brunansky	.05
203	Roger Smithberg (R)	.15
204	Eddie Whitson	.05
205	Dennis Rassmussen	.05
206	Craig Lefferts	.05
207	Andy Benes	.15
208	Bruce Hurst	.05
209	Eric Show	.05
210	Rafael Valdez (R)	.15
211	Joey Cora	.05
212	Thomas Howard	.15
213	Rob Nelson	.05
214	Jack Clark	.10
215	Garry Templeton	.05
216	Fred Lynn	.08
217	Tony Gwynn	.12
218	Benny Santiago	.10
219	Mike Pagliarulo	.05
220	Joe Carter	.08
221	Roberto Alomar	.10
222	Bip Roberts	.05
223	Rick Reuschel	.05
224	Russ Swan (R)	.15
225	Eric Gunderson (R)	.15
226	Steve Bedrosian	.05
227	Mike Remlinger (R)	.15
228	Scott Garrelts	.05
229	Ernie Camacho	.05
230	Andres Santana (R)	.20
231	Will Clark	.50
232	Kevin Mitchell	.20
233	Robby Thompson	.05
234	Bill Bathe	.05
235	Tony Perezchica	.05
236	Gary Carter	.10
237	Brett Butler	.05
238	Matt Williams	.15
239	Ernie Riles	.05
240	Kevin Bass	.05
241	Terry Kennedy	.05
242	Steve Hosey (R)	.25
243	Ben McDonald (R)	1.00
244	Jeff Ballard	.05
245	Joe Price	.05
246	Curt Schilling	.05
247	Pete Harnisch	.05
248	Mark Williamson	.05
249	Gregg Olson	.15
250	Chris Myers (R)	.15
251	David Segui (R)	.35
252	Joe Orsulak	.05
253	C. Worthington	.10
254	Mickey Tettleton	.05
255	Cal Ripken	.15
256	Billy Ripken	.05
257	Randy Milligan	.08
258	Brady Anderson	.05
259	Chris Holles (R)	.25
260	Mike Devereaux	.05
261	Phil Bradley	.05
262	Leo Gomez (R)	.40
263	Lee Smith	.05
264	Mike Rochford	.05
265	Jeff Reardon	.05
266	Wes Gardner	.05
267	Mike Boddicker	.08
268	Roger Clemens	.25
269	Rob Murphy	.05
270	Mickey Pina (R)	.30
271	Tony Pena	.05
272	Jody Reed	.05
273	Kevin Romine	.05
274	Mike Greenwell	.20
275	Maurice Vaughn (R)	.75
276	Danny Heep	.05
277	Scott Cooper (R)	.20
278	Greg Blosser (R)	.35
279	Dwight Evans	.08
280	Ellis Burks	.10
281	Wade Boggs	.20
282	Marty Barrett	.05
283	Kirk McCaskill	.05
284	Mark Langston	.10
285	Bert Blyleven	.05
286	Mike Fetters (R)	.10
287	Kyle Abbott (R)	.15
288	Jim Abbott	.15
289	Chuck Finley	.05
290	Gary DiSarcina (R)	.10
291	Dick Schofield	.05
292	Devon White	.05
293	Bobby Rose (R)	.20
294	Brian Downing	.05
295	Lance Parrish	.05
296	Jack Howell	.05
297	C. Washington	.05
298	John Orton	.08
299	Wally Joyner	.12
300	Lee Stevens	.20
301	Chili Davis	.08
302	Johnny Ray	.05
303	Greg Hibbard (R)	.15
304	Eric King	.05
305	Jack McDowell	.05
306	Bobby Thigpen	.10
307	Adam Peterson	.05
308	Scott Radinsky (R)	.20
309	Wayne Edwards (R)	.15
310	Melido Perez	.05
311	Robin Ventura	.20
312	Sammy Sosa (R)	.35
313	Dan Pasqua	.05
314	Carlton Fisk	.10
315	Ozzie Guillen	.05
316	Ivan Calderon	.05
317	Daryl Boston	.05
318	Craig Grebeck (R)	.10
319	Scott Fletcher	.05
320	Frank Thomas (R)	1.50
321	Steve Lyons	.05
322	Carlos Martinez	.10
323	Joe Skalski	.10
324	Tom Candiotti	.05
325	Greg Swindell	.05
326	Steve Olin (R)	.10
327	Kevin Wickander	.05
328	Doug Jones	.05
329	Jeff Shaw (R)	.10
330	Kevin Bearse (R)	.12
331	Dion James	.05
332	Jerry Browne	.05
333	Joey Bell	.20
334	Felix Fermin	.05
335	Candy Maldonado	.05
336	Cory Snyder	.08
337	Sandy Alomar	.25
338	Mark Lewis	.10
339	Carlos Baerga (R)	.30
340	Chris James	.05

NO.	PLAYER	MINT
341	Brook Jacoby	.05
342	Keith Hernandez	.05
343	Frank Tanana	.05
344	Scott Aldred (R)	.12
345	Mike Henneman	.05
346	Steve Wapnick (R)	.10
347	Greg Gohr (R)	.10
348	Eric Stone (R)	.15
349	Brian DuBois (R)	.10
350	Kevin Ritz (R)	.12
351	Rico Brogna	.05
352	Mike Heath	.05
353	Alan Trammell	.10
354	Chet Lemon	.05
355	Dave Bergman	.05
356	Lou Whitaker	.05
357	Cecil Fielder	.50
358	Milt Cuyler (R)	.25
359	Tony Phillips	.05
360	Travis Fryman (R)	.60
361	Ed Romero	.05
362	Lloyd Moseby	.05
363	Mark Gubicza	.05
364	Bret Saberhagen	.10
365	Tom Gordon	.12
366	Steve Farr	.05
367	Kevin Appier	.20
368	Storm Davis	.05
369	Mark Davis	.05
370	Jeff Montgomery	.05
371	Frank White	.05
372	Brent Mayne (R)	.15
373	Bob Boone	.05
374	Jim Eisenreich	.05
375	Danny Tartabull	.05
376	Kurt Stillwell	.05
377	Bill Pecota	.05
378	Bo Jackson	.50
379	Bob Hamelin (R)	.25
380	Kevin Seltzer	.05
381	Rey Palacios	.05
382	George Brett	.15
383	Gerald Perry	.05
384	Teddy Higuera	.05
385	Tom Filer	.05
386	Dan Plesac	.05
387	Cal Eldred (R)	.15
388	Jaime Navarro	.12
389	Chris Bosio	.05
390	Randy Veres	.10
391	Gary Sheffield	.20
392	George Canale (R)	.10
393	B.J. Surhoff	.05
394	Tim McIntosh (R)	.15
395	Greg Brock	.05
396	Greg Vaughn	.50
397	Darryl Hamilton	.10
398	Dave Parker	.12
399	Paul Molitor	.10
400	Jim Gantner	.05
401	Rob Deer	.05
402	Billy Spiers	.10
403	Glenn Braggs	.05
404	Robin Yount	.15
405	Rick Aguilera	.05
406	Johnny Ard	.05
407	Kevin Tapani (R)	.20
408	Park Pittman (R)	.15
409	Allan Anderson	.05
410	Juan Berenguer	.05
411	Willie Banks (R)	.25
412	Rich Yett	.05
413	Dave West	.05
414	Greg Gagne	.05
415	Chuck Knoblauch (R)	.15
416	Randy Bush	.05
417	Gary Gaetti	.05
418	Kent Hrbek	.10
419	Al Newman	.05
420	Danny Gladden	.05
421	Paul Sorrento (R)	.15
422	Derek Parks (R)	.20
423	Scott Lelus (R)	.15
424	Kirby Puckett	.15
425	Willie Smith (R)	.15
426	Dave Righetti	.05
427	Jeff Robinson	.05
428	Alan Mills (R)	.15
429	Tim Leary	.05
430	Pascual Perez	.05
431	Alvaro Espinoza	.05
432	Dave Winfield	.12
433	Jesse Barfield	.05
434	Randy Velarde	.05
435	Rick Cerone	.05
436	Steve Balboni	.05
437	Mel Hall	.05
438	Bob Geren	.05
439	Bernie Williams (R)	.25
440	Kevin Mass (R)	2.50
441	Mike Blowers (R)	.20
442	Steve Sax	.05
443	Don Mattingly	.40
444	Roberto Kelly	.08
445	Mike Moore	.05
446	Reggie Harris (R)	.15
447	Scott Sanderson	.05
448	Dave Otto	.05
449	Dave Stewart	.12
450	Rick Honeycutt	.05
451	Dennis Eckersley	.08
452	Carney Lansford	.05
453	Scott Hemond (R)	.20
454	Mark McGwire	.25
455	Felix Jose	.10
456	Terry Steinbach	.05
457	Rickey Henderson	.25
458	Dave Henderson	.05
459	Mike Gallego	.05
460	Jose Canseco	.50
461	Walt Weiss	.05
462	Ken Phelps	.05
463	Darren Lewis (R)	.50
464	Ron Hassey	.05
465	Roger Salkeld (R)	.15
466	Scott Bankhead	.05
467	Keith Comstock	.05
468	Randy Johnson	.10
469	Erik Hanson	.15
470	Mike Schooler	.08
471	Gary Eave (R)	.10
472	Jeffrey Leonard	.05
473	Dave Valle	.05
474	Omar Vizquel	.05
475	Pete O'Brien	.05
476	Henry Cotto	.05
477	Jay Buhner	.05
478	Harold Reynolds	.05
479	Alvin Davis	.05
480	Darnell Coles	.05
481	Ken Griffey, Jr.	1.75
482	Greg Briley	.10
483	Scott Bradley	.05
484	Tino Martinez	.30
485	Jeff Russell	.05
486	Nolan Ryan	.30
487	Robb Nen (R)	.12
488	Kevin Brown	.10
489	Brian Bohanon (R)	.12
490	Ruben Sierra	.15
491	Pete Incaviglia	.08
492	Juan Gonzalez (R)	1.00
493	Steve Buechele	.05
494	Scott Coolbaugh (R)	.12
495	Geno Petralli	.05
496	Rafael Palmeiro	.10
497	Julio Franco	.05
498	Gary Pettis	.05
499	Donald Harris (R)	.15
500	Monty Fariss	.05
501	Harold Baines	.05
502	Cecil Espy	.05
503	Jack Daugherty (R)	.12
504	Willie Blair (R)	.10
505	Dave Stieb	.05
506	Tom Henke	.05
507	John Cerutti	.05
508	Paul Kilgus	.05
509	Jimmy Key	.05
510	John Olerud (R)	2.00
511	Ed Sprague	.05
512	Manny Lee	.05
513	Fred McGriff	.12
514	Glenallen Hill	.10
515	George Bell	.12
516	Mookie Wilson	.05
517	Luis Sojo (R)	.12
518	Nelson Liriano	.05
519	Kelly Gruber	.08
520	Greg Myers	.05
521	Pat Borders	.05
522	Junior Felix	.25
523	Eddie Zosky (R)	.25
524	Tony Fernandez	.05
525	Checklist No. 1	.05
526	Checklist No. 2	.05
527	Checklist No. 3	.05
528	Checklist No. 4	.05

1981 Donruss.... Complete Set of 605 Cards—$50.00

This was Donruss' *first* baseball card set. Over 35 cards contained *errors;* they were corrected in the 2nd printing run. There is very little interest by collectors in the *variety* (error) cards; none are scarce or worth much more than ordinary cards. If a *variety* (error) is significant, it is listed and explained; if it is *minor,* it is noted by an *asterisk.* This set features the rookie cards of Tim Raines and Leon Durham. The 2½"x3½" cards were printed on thinner than usual paper stock. The checklist *cards* are *not* numbered.

MOOKIE WILSON SHORTSTOP   JEFF REARDON PITCHER   LEON DURHAM INFIELD-OF   JOHN TUDOR PITCHER   TIM RAINES SECOND BASE

NO.	PLAYER	MINT	NO.	PLAYER	MINT	NO.	PLAYER	MINT	NO.	PLAYER	MINT
1	Ozzie Smith	1.00	65	George Foster	.20	131	Pete Rose*	1.50	197	Rick Camp	.05
2	Rollie Fingers	.50	66	Jeff Burroughs	.05	132	Willie Stargell	.45	198	Andre Thornton	.10
3	Rick Wise	.05	67	Keith Hernandez	.40	133	Ed Ott	.05	199	Tom Veryzer	.05
4	Gene Richards	.05	68	Tommy Herr	.15	134	Jim Bibby	.05	200	Gary Alexander	.05
5	Alan Trammell	.40	69	Bob Forsch	.05	135	Bert Blyleven	.30	201	Rick Waits	.05
6	Tom Brookens	.05	70	John Fulgham	.05	136	Dave Parker	.40	202	Rick Manning	.05
7	Duffy Dyer*	.05	71	Bobby Bonds*	.12	137	Bill Robinson	.05	203	Paul Molitor	.40
8	Mark Fidrych	.08	72	Rennie Stennett*	.10	138	Enos Cabell	.05	204	Jim Gantner	.05
9	Dave Rozema	.05	73	Joe Strain	.05	139	Dave Bergman	.05	205	Paul Mitchell	.05
10	Ricky Peters	.05	74	Ed Whitson	.10	140	J.R. Richard	.05	206	Reggie Cleveland	.05
11	Mike Schmidt	2.00	75	Tom Griffin	.05	141	Ken Forsch	.05	207	Sixto Lezcano	.05
12	Willie Stargell	.40	76	Bill North	.05	142	Larry Bowa	.05	208	Bruce Benedict	.05
13	Tim Foli	.05	77	Gene Garber	.05	143	Frank LaCorte	.05	209	Rodney Scott	.05
14	Manny Sanguillen	.05	78	Mike Hargrove	.05	144	Dennis Walling	.05	210	John Tamargo	.05
15	Grant Jackson	.05	79	Dave Rosello	.05	145	Buddy Bell	.10	211	Bill Lee	.05
16	Eddie Solomon	.05	80	Ron Hassey	.05	146	Ferguson Jenkins	.10	212	Andre Dawson	.75
17	Omar Moreno	.05	81	Sid Monge	.05	147	Danny Darwin	.05	213	Rowland Office	.05
18	Joe Morgan	.50	82	Joe Charboneau*	.10	148	Johnny Grubb	.05	214	Carl Yastrzemski	1.00
19	Rafael Landestoy	.05	83	Cecil Cooper	.20	149	Alfredo Griffin	.05	215	Jerry Remy	.05
20	Bruce Bochy	.05	84	Sal Bando	.05	150	Jerry Garvin	.05	216	Mike Torrez	.05
21	Joe Sambito	.05	85	Moose Haas	.05	151	Paul Mirabella	.05	217	Skip Lockwood	.05
22	Manny Trillo	.05	86	Mike Caldwell	.05	152	Rick Bosetti	.05	218	Fred Lynn	.25
23	Dave Smith* (R)	.35	87	Larry Hisle*	.10	153	Dick Ruthven	.05	219	Chris Chambliss	.08
24	Terry Puhl	.05	88	Luis Gomez	.05	154	Frank Taveras	.05	220	Willie Aikens	.05
25	Bump Wills	.05	89	Larry Parrish	.10	155	Craig Swan	.05	221	John Wathan	.05
26	John Ellis (error)	.50	90	Gary Carter	.50	156	Jeff Reardon (R)	.75	222	Dan Quisenberry	.20
	(photo of Danny Walten)		91	Bill Gullickson (R)	.30	157	Steve Henderson	.05	223	Willie Wilson	.15
26	John Ellis (correct)	.10	92	Fred Norman	.05	158	Jim Morrison	.05	224	Clint Hurdle	.05
27	Jim Kern	.05	93	Tom Hutton	.05	159	Glenn Borgmann	.05	225	Bob Watson	.05
28	Richie Zisk	.05	94	Carl Yastrzemski	1.00	160	LaMarr Hoyt	.20	226	Jim Spencer	.05
29	John Mayberry	.05	95	Glenn Hoffman	.08	161	Rich Wortham	.05	227	Ron Guidry	.25
30	Bob Davis	.05	96	Dennis Eckersley	.50	162	Thad Bosley	.05	228	Reggie Jackson	1.50
31	Jackson Todd	.05	97	Tom Burgmeier*	.10	163	Julio Cruz	.05	229	Oscar Gamble	.05
32	Al Woods	.05	98	Win Remmerswaal	.05	164	Del Unser*	.05	230	Jeff Cox	.05
33	Steve Carlton	1.25	99	Bob Horner	.20	165	Jim Anderson	.05	231	Luis Tiant	.05
34	Lee Mazzilli	.05	100	George Brett	1.25	166	Jim Beattie	.05	232	Rich Dauer	.05
35	John Stearns	.05	101	Dave Chalk	.05	167	Shane Rawley	.05	233	Dan Graham	.05
36	Roy Jackson	.08	102	Dennis Leonard	.05	168	Joe Simpson	.05	234	Mike Flanagan	.05
37	Mike Scott	.75	103	Renie Martin	.05	169	Rod Carew	1.00	235	John Lowenstein	.05
38	Lamar Johnson	.05	104	Amos Otis	.05	170	Freddie Patek	.05	236	Benny Ayala	.05
39	Kevin Bell	.05	105	Graig Nettles	.15	171	Frank Tanana	.05	237	Wayne Gross	.05
40	Ed Farmer	.05	106	Eric Soderholm	.05	172	Alfredo Martinez	.05	238	Rick Langford	.05
41	Ross Baumgarten	.05	107	Tommy John	.20	173	Chris Knapp	.05	239	Tony Armas	.20
42	Leo Sutherland	.05	108	Tom Underwood	.05	174	Joe Rudi	.05	240	Bob Lacey*	.10
43	Danny Meyer	.05	109	Lou Piniella	.15	175	Greg Luzinski	.10	241	Gene Tenace	.05
44	Ron Reed	.05	110	Mickey Klutts	.05	176	Steve Garvey	.75	242	Bob Shirley	.05
45	Mario Mendoza	.05	111	Bobby Murcer	.10	177	Joe Ferguson	.05	243	Gary Lucas	.05
46	Rick Honeycutt	.05	112	Eddie Murray	1.00	178	Bob Welch	.40	244	Jerry Turner	.05
47	Glenn Abbott	.05	113	Rick Dempsey	.05	179	Dusty Baker	.10	245	John Wockenfuss	.05
48	Leon Roberts	.05	114	Scott McGregor	.05	180	Rudy Law	.05	246	Stan Papi	.05
49	Rod Carew	1.00	115	Ken Singleton	.05	181	Dave Concepcion	.15	247	Milt Wilcox	.05
50	Bert Campaneris	.05	116	Gary Roenicke	.05	182	Johnny Bench	1.25	248	Dan Schatzeder	.05
51	Tom Donohue*	.10	117	Dave Revering	.05	183	Mike LaCoss	.05	249	Steve Kemp	.08
52	Dave Frost	.05	118	Mike Norris	.05	184	Ken Griffey	.25	250	Jim Lentine	.05
53	Ed Halicki	.05	119	Rickey Henderson	.20	185	Dave Collins	.05	251	Pete Rose	1.25
54	Dan Ford	.05	120	Mike Heath	.05	186	Brian Asselstine	.05	252	Bill Madlock	.25
55	Garry Maddox	.05	121	Dave Cash	.05	187	Garry Templeton	.10	253	Dale Berra	.05
56	Steve Garvey*	.75	122	Randy Jones	.05	188	Mike Phillips	.05	254	Kent Tekulve	.05
57	Bill Russell	.05	123	Eric Rasmussen	.05	189	Pete Vuckovich	.08	255	Enrique Romo	.05
58	Don Sutton	.40	124	Jerry Mumphrey	.05	190	John Urrea	.05	256	Mike Easler	.05
59	Reggie Smith	.10	125	Richie Hebner	.05	191	Tony Scott	.05	257	Chuck Tanner (Mgr.)	.05
60	Rick Monday	.05	126	Mark Wagner	.05	192	Darrell Evans	.10	258	Art Howe	.05
61	Ray Knight	.05	127	Jack Morris	.30	193	Milt May	.05	259	Alan Ashby	.05
62	Johnny Bench	1.25	128	Dan Petry	.25	194	Bob Knepper	.05	260	Nolan Ryan	3.00
63	Mario Soto	.15	129	Bruce Robbins	.05	195	Randy Moffitt	.05	261	Vern Ruhle (error)	.50
64	Doug Bair	.05	130	Champ Summers	.05	196	Larry Herndon	.05		(Photo of Ken Forsch)	

NO.	PLAYER	MINT
261	Vern Ruhle (correct)	.10
262	Bob Boone	.08
263	Cesar Cedeno	.08
264	Jeff Leonard	.15
265	Pat Putnam	.05
266	John Matlack	.05
267	Dave Rajsich	.05
268	Billy Sample	.05
269	Damaso Garcia (R)	.15
270	Tom Buskey	.05
271	Joey McLaughlin	.05
272	Barry Bonnell	.05
273	Tug McGraw	.08
274	Mike Jorgensen	.05
275	Pat Zachry	.05
276	Neil Allen	.05
277	Joel Youngblood	.05
278	Greg Pryor	.05
279	Britt Burns (R)	.20
280	Rich Dotson (R)	.30
281	Chet Lemon	.10
282	Rusty Kuntz	.05
283	Ted Cox	.05
284	Sparky Lyle	.08
285	Larry Cox	.05
286	Floyd Bannister	.05
287	Byron McLaughlin	.05
288	Rodney Craig	.05
289	Bob Grich	.08
290	Dickie Thon	.10
291	Mark Clear	.05
292	Dave Lemanczyk	.05
293	Jason Thompson	.05
294	Rick Miller	.05
295	Lonnie Smith	.08
296	Ron Cey	.15
297	Steve Yeager	.05
298	Bobby Castillo	.05
299	Manny Mota	.05
300	Jay Johnstone	.05
301	Dan Driessen	.05
302	Joe Nolan	.05
303	Paul Householder	.15
304	Harry Spilman	.05
305	Cesar Geronimo	.05
306	Gary Matthews*	.10
307	Ken Reitz	.05
308	Ted Simmons	.10
309	John Littlefield	.05
310	George Frazier	.05
311	Dane Iorg	.05
312	Mike Ivie	.05
313	Dennis Littlejohn	.05
314	Gary LaVelle	.05
315	Jack Clark	.35
316	Jim Wohlford	.05
317	Rick Matula	.05
318	Toby Harrah	.05
319	Duane Kuiper*	.10
320	Len Barker	.05
321	Victor Cruz	.05
322	Dell Alston	.05
323	Robin Yount	1.50
324	Charlie Moore	.05
325	Lary Sorensen	.05
326	Gorman Thomas*	.15
327	Bob Rodgers	.05
328	Phil Niekro	.30
329	Chris Speier	.05
330	Steve Rogers*	.10
331	Woodie Fryman	.05
332	Warren Cromartie	.05
333	Jerry White	.05
334	Tony Perez	.20
335	Carlton Fisk	.75
336	Dick Drago	.05
337	Steve Renko	.05
338	Jim Rice	.40
339	Jerry Royster	.05
340	Frank White	.05
341	Jamie Quirk	.05
342	Paul Splittorff*	.10
343	Marty Pattin	.05
344	Pete LaCock	.05
345	Willie Randolph	.10
346	Rick Cerone	.05
347	Rich Gossage	.25
348	Reggie Jackson	1.50
349	Ruppert Jones	.05
350	Dave McKay	.05
351	Yogi Berra	.20
352	Doug DeCinces	.15
353	Jim Palmer	.75
354	Tippy Martinez	.05
355	Al Bumbry	.05
356	Earl Weaver (Mgr.)	.10
357	Rob Picciolo*	.10
358	Matt Keough	.05
359	Dwayne Murphy	.05
360	Brian Kingman	.05
361	Bill Fahey	.05
362	Steve Mura	.05
363	Dennis Kinney	.05
364	Dave Winfield	.60
365	Lou Whitaker	.30
366	Lance Parrish	.30
367	Tim Corcoran	.05
368	Pat Underwood	.05
369	Al Cowens	.05
370	Sparky Anderson (Mgr.)	.05
371	Pete Rose	1.25
372	Phil Garner	.05
373	Steve Nicosia	.05
374	John Candelaria	.05
375	Don Robinson	.05
376	Lee Lacy	.05
377	John Milner	.05
378	Craig Reynolds	.05
379	Luis Pujols*	.10
380	Joe Niekro	.10
381	Joaquin Andujar	.15
382	Keith Moreland (R)	.25
383	Jose Cruz	.15
384	Bill Virdon (Mgr.)	.05
385	Jim Sundberg	.05
386	Doc Medich	.05
387	Al Oliver	.15
388	Jim Norris	.05
389	Bob Bailor	.05
390	Ernie Whitt	.05
391	Otto Velez	.05
392	Roy Howell	.05
393	Bob Walk	.20
394	Doug Flynn	.05
395	Pete Falcone	.05
396	Tom Hausman	.05
397	Elliott Maddox	.05
398	Mike Squires	.05
399	Marvis Foley	.05
400	Steve Trout	.05
401	Wayne Nordhagen	.05
402	Tony LaRussa (Mgr.)	.05
403	Bruce Bochte	.05
404	Bake McBride	.05
405	Jerry Narron	.05
406	Rob Dressler	.05
407	Dave Heaverlo	.05
408	Tom Paciorek	.05
409	Carney Lansford	.20
410	Brian Downing	.05
411	Don Aase	.05
412	Jim Barr	.05
413	Don Baylor	.25
414	Jim Fregosi (Mgr.)	.05
415	Dallas Green (Mgr.)	.05
416	Dave Lopes	.10
417	Jerry Reuss	.05
418	Rick Sutcliffe	.35
419	Derrel Thomas	.05
420	Tommy Lasorda (Mgr.)	.15
421	Charlie Leibrandt (R)	.35
422	Tom Seaver	1.00
423	Ron Oester	.05
424	Junior Kennedy	.05
425	Tom Seaver	1.00
426	Bobby Cox (Mgr.)	.05
427	Leon Durham (R)	.30
428	Terry Kennedy	.10
429	Silvio Martinez	.05
430	George Hendrick	.05
431	R. Schoendienst (Mgr.)	.10
432	John LeMaster	.05
433	Vida Blue	.05
434	John Montefusco	.05
435	Terry Whitfield	.05
436	Dave Bristol (Mgr.)	.05
437	Dale Murphy	1.25
438	Jerry Dybzinski	.05
439	Jorge Orta	.05
440	Wayne Garland	.05
441	Miguel Dilone	.05
442	Dave Garcia (Mgr.)	.05
443	Don Money	.05
444	Buck Martinez*	.10
445	Jerry Augustine	.05
446	Ben Oglivie	.10
447	Jim Slaton	.05
448	Doyle Alexander	.05
449	Tony Bernazard	.05
450	Scott Sanderson	.05
451	Dave Palmer	.05
452	Stan Bahnsen	.05
453	Dick Williams (Mgr.)	.05
454	Rick Burleson	.05
455	Gary Allenson	.05
456	Bob Stanley	.05
457	John Tudor (R)	1.25
458	Dwight Evans	.40
459	Glenn Hubbard	.05
460	U.L. Washington	.05
461	Larry Gura	.05
462	Rich Gale	.05
463	Hal McRae	.05
464	Jim Frey (Mgr.)	.05
465	Bucky Dent	.05
466	Dennis Werth	.05
467	Ron Davis	.05
468	Reggie Jackson	1.50
469	Bobby Brown	.05
470	Mike Davis (R)	.20
471	Gaylord Perry	.30
472	Mark Belanger	.05
473	Jim Palmer	.75
474	Sammy Stewart	.05
475	Tim Stoddard	.05
476	Steve Stone	.05
477	Jeff Newman	.05
478	Steve McCatty	.05
479	Billy Martin (Mgr.)	.15
480	Mitchell Page	.05
481	S. Carlton (Cy Young)	.50
482	Bill Buckner	.15
483	Ivan DeJesus*	.10
484	Cliff Johnson	.05
485	Lenny Randle	.05
486	Larry Milbourne	.05
487	Roy Smalley	.05
488	John Castino	.05
489	Ron Jackson	.05
490	Dave Roberts*	.10
491	George Brett (MVP)	1.00
492	Mike Cubbage	.05
493	Rob Wilfong	.05
494	Danny Goodwin	.05
495	Jose Morales	.05
496	Mickey Rivers	.05
497	Mike Edwards	.05
498	Mike Sadek	.05
499	Lenn Sakata	.05
500	Gene Michael (Mgr.)	.05
501	Dave Roberts	.05
502	Steve Dillard	.05
503	Jim Essian	.05
504	Rance Mulliniks	.05
505	Darrell Porter	.10
506	Joe Torre (Mgr.)	.05
507	Terry Crowley	.05
508	Bill Travers	.05
509	Nelson Norman	.05
510	Bob McClure	.05
511	Steve Howe (R)	.15
512	Dave Rader	.05
513	Mick Kelleher	.05
514	Kiko Garcia	.05
515	Larry Biittner	.05
516	Willie Norwood*	.05
517	Bo Diaz	.10
518	Juan Beniquez	.05
519	Scot Thompson	.05
520	Jim Tracy	.05
521	Carlos Lezcano	.05
522	Joe Amalfitano	.05
523	Preston Hanna	.05
524	Ray Burris*	.10
525	Broderick Perkins	.05
526	Mickey Hatcher	.05
527	John Goryl (Mgr.)	.05
528	Dick Davis	.05
529	Butch Wynegar	.05
530	Sal Butera	.05
531	Jerry Koosman	.05
532	Jeff Zahn*	.10
533	Dennis Martinez	.05
534	Gary Thomasson	.05
535	Steve Macko	.05
536	Jim Kaat	.15
537	Best Hitters: George Brett, Rod Care	2.00
538	Tim Raines (R)	6.00
539	Keith Smith	.05
540	Ken Macha	.05
541	Burt Hooton	.05
542	Butch Hobson	.05
543	Bill Stein	.05
544	Dave Stapleton (R)	.15
545	Bob Pate	.05
546	Doug Corbett	.12
547	Darrell Jackson	.05
548	Pete Redfern	.05
549	Roger Erickson	.05
550	Al Hrabosky	.05
551	Dick Tidrow	.05
552	Dave Ford	.05
553	Dave Kingman	.15
554	Mike Vail*	.10
555	Jerry Martin*	.10
556	Jesus Figueroa*	.10
557	Don Stanhouse	.05
558	Barry Foote	.05
559	Tim Blackwell	.05
560	Bruce Sutter	.25
561	Rick Reuschel	.05
562	Lynn McGlothen	.05
563	Bob Owchinko*	.10
564	John Verhoeven	.05
565	Ken Landreaux	.05
566	Glenn Adams*	.10
567	Hosken Powell	.05
568	Dick Noles	.05
569	Danny Ainge (R)	.40
570	Bobby Mattick (Mgr.)	.05
571	Joe LeFebvre (R)	.15
572	Bobby Clark	.05
573	Dennis Lamp	.05
574	Randy Lerch	.05
575	Mookie Wilson (R)	.60
576	Ron LeFlore	.05
577	Jim Dwyer	.05
578	Bill Castro	.05
579	Greg Minton	.05
580	Mark Littell	.05
581	Andy Hassler	.05
582	Dave Stieb	.50
583	Ken Oberkfell	.05
584	Larry Bradford	.05
585	Fred Stanley	.05
586	Bill Caudill	.10
587	Doug Capilla	.05
588	George Riley	.05
589	Willie Hernandez	.05
590	Mike Schmidt (MVP)	1.00
591	Steve Stone (Cy Young)	.10
592	Rick Sofield	.05
593	Bombo Rivera	.05
594	Gary Ward	.05
595	Dave Edwards*	.10
596	Mike Proly	.05
597	Tommy Boggs	.05
598	Greg Gross	.05
599	Elias Sosa	.05
600	Pat Kelly	.05
—	Checklist No. 1*	.10
—	Checklist No. 2	.10
—	Checklist No. 3*	.10
—	Checklist No. 4*	.10
—	Checklist No. 5*	.10

1982 Donruss.... Complete Set of 660 Cards—Value $50.00

Features the rookie cards of Cal Ripken, George Bell and Dave Stewart. Several errors were corrected; none are scarce or worth much more than ordinary cards. If a *variety* (error) is significant, it is listed and explained; if it is minor, it is noted by an *asterisk*. The *checklist* cards are *not* numbered.

NO. PLAYER	MINT	NO. PLAYER	MINT	NO. PLAYER	MINT	NO. PLAYER	MINT
No. 1 to 26—Diamond Kings		66 Bruce Kison	.05	132 Gorman Thomas	.15	198 Duane Kuiper	.05
1 Pete Rose (DK)	1.50	67 Wayne Nordhagen	.05	133 Dan Petry	.15	199 Rick Cerone	.05
2 Gary Carter (DK)	.35	68 Woodie Fryman	.05	134 Bob Stanley	.05	200 Jim Rice	.30
3 Steve Garvey (DK)	.40	69 Billy Sample	.05	135 Lou Piniella	.10	201 Steve Yeager	.05
4 Vida Blue (DK)	.10	70 Amos Otis	.10	136 Pedro Guerrero	.50	202 Tom Brookens	.05
5 A. Trammell (DK)	.35	71 Matt Keough	.05	137 Len Barker	.05	203 Jose Morales	.05
(correct)		72 Toby Harrah	.05	138 Richard Gale	.05	204 Roy Howell	.05
5 A. Trammell (DK)	1.25	73 Dave Righetti (R)	1.50	139 Wayne Gross	.05	205 Tippy Martinez	.05
(error)		74 Carl Yastrzemski	1.00	140 Tim Wallach (R)	1.50	206 Moose Haas	.05
6 Len Barker (DK)	.10	75 Bob Welch	.35	141 Gene Mauch	.05	207 Al Cowens	.05
7 Dwight Evans (DK)	.15	76 A. Trammell (cor.)	.50	142 Doc Medich	.05	208 Dave Stapleton	.05
8 Rod Carew (DK)	.60	76 A. Trammell (error)	1.25	143 Tony Bernazard	.05	209 Bucky Dent	.05
9 George Hendrick (DK)	.10	77 Rick Dempsey	.05	144 Bill Virdon (Mgr.)	.05	210 Ron Cey	.15
10 Phil Niekro (DK)	.25	78 Paul Molitor	.30	145 John Littlefield	.05	211 Jorge Orta	.05
11 Richie Zisk (DK)	.10	79 Dennis Martinez	.05	146 Dave Bergman	.05	212 Jamie Quirk	.05
12 Dave Parker (DK)	.30	80 Jim Slaton	.05	147 Dick Davis	.05	213 Jeff Jones	.05
13 Nolan Ryan (DK)	1.50	81 Champ Summers	.05	148 Tom Seaver	.75	214 Tim Raines	1.00
14 Ivan DeJesus (DK)	.10	82 Carney Lansford	.20	149 Matt Sinatro	.07	215 Jon Matlack	.05
15 George Brett (DK)	1.00	83 Barry Foote	.05	150 Chuck Tanner (Mgr.)	.05	216 Rod Carew	.75
16 Tom Seaver (DK)	.75	84 Steve Garvey	.50	151 Leon Durham	.20	217 Jim Kaat	.10
17 Dave Kingman (DK)	.10	85 Rick Manning	.05	152 Gene Tenace	.05	218 Joe Pittman	.05
18 Dave Winfield (DK)	.50	86 John Wathan	.05	153 Al Bumbry	.05	219 Larry Christenson	.05
19 Mike Norris (DK)	.10	87 Brian Kingman	.05	154 Mark Brouhard	.05	220 Juan Bonilla	.07
20 Carlton Fisk (DK)	.40	88 Andre Dawson	.60	155 Rick Peters	.05	221 Mike Easler	.05
21 Ozzie Smith (DK)	.50	89 Jim Kern	.05	156 Jerry Remy	.05	222 Vida Blue	.05
22 Roy Smalley (DK)	.10	90 Bobby Grich	.05	157 Rick Reuschel	.10	223 Rick Camp	.05
23 Buddy Bell (DK)	.10	91 Bob Forsch	.05	158 Steve Howe	.05	224 Mike Jorgensen	.05
24 Ken Singleton (DK)	.10	92 Art Howe	.05	159 Alan Bannister	.05	225 Jody Davis (R)	.30
25 John Mayberry (DK)	.10	93 Marty Bystrom	.05	160 U.L. Wasington	.05	226 Mike Parrott	.05
26 Garmon Thomas (DK)	.10	94 Ozzie Smith	.60	161 Rick Langford	.05	227 Jim Clancy	.05
27 Earl Weaver (Mgr.)	.10	95 Dave Parker	.30	162 Bill Gullickson	.05	228 Hosken Powell	.05
28 Rollie Fingers	.30	96 Doyle Alexander	.05	163 Mark Wagner	.05	229 Tom Hume	.05
29 Sparky Anderson (Mgr.)	.10	97 Al Hrabosky	.05	164 Geoff Zahn	.05	230 Britt Burns	.05
30 Dennis Eckersley	.35	98 Frank Taveras	.05	165 Ron LeFlore	.05	231 Jim Palmer	.50
31 Dave Winfield	.50	99 Tim Blackwell	.05	166 Dane Iorg	.05	232 Bob Rodgers (Mgr.)	.05
32 Burt Hooton	.05	100 Floyd Bannister	.05	167 Joe Niekro	.10	233 Milt Wilcox	.05
33 Rick Waits	.05	101 Alfredo Griffin	.05	168 Pete Rose	1.00	234 Dave Revering	.05
34 George Brett	1.25	102 Dave Engle	.05	169 Dave Collins	.05	235 Mike Torrez	.05
35 Steve McCatty	.05	103 Mario Soto	.15	170 Rick Wise	.05	236 Bobby Castillo	.05
36 Steve Rogers	.05	104 Ross Baumgarten	.05	171 Jim Bibby	.05	237 Von Hayes (R)	1.00
37 Bill Stein	.05	105 Ken Singleton	.10	172 Larry Herndon	.05	238 Renie Martin	.05
38 Steve Renko	.05	106 Ted Simmons	.15	173 Bob Horner	.15	239 Dwayne Murphy	.05
39 Mike Squires	.05	107 Jack Morris	.25	174 Steve Dillard	.05	240 Rodney Scott	.05
40 George Hendrick	.08	108 Bob Watson	.05	175 Mookie Wilson	.10	241 Freddie Patek	.05
41 Bob Knepper	.12	109 Dwight Evans	.30	176 Danny Meyer	.05	242 Mickey Rivers	.05
42 Steve Carlton	1.00	110 Tommy LaSorda (Mgr.)	.10	177 Fernando Arroyo	.05	243 Steve Trout	.05
43 Larry Biittner	.05	111 Bert Blyleven	.25	178 Jackson Todd	.05	244 Jose Cruz	.10
44 Chris Welsh	.07	112 Dan Quisenberry	.25	179 Darrell Jackson	.05	245 Manny Trillo	.05
45 Steve Nicosia	.05	113 Rickey Henderson	.75	180 Al Woods	.05	246 Lary Sorensen	.05
46 Jack Clark	.30	114 Gary Carter	.50	181 Jim Anderson	.05	247 Dave Edwards	.05
47 Chris Chambliss	.05	115 Brian Downing	.05	182 Dave Kingman	.15	248 Dan Driessen	.05
48 Ivan DeJesus	.05	116 Al Oliver	.15	183 Steve Henderson	.05	249 Tommy Boggs	.05
49 Lee Mazzilli	.05	117 LaMarr Hoyt	.15	184 Brian Asselstine	.05	250 Dale Berra	.05
50 Julio Cruz	.05	118 Cesar Cedeno	.10	185 Rod Scurry	.05	251 Ed Whitson	.05
51 Pete Redfern	.05	119 Keith Moreland	.05	186 Fred Breining	.08	252 Lee Smith (R)	.75
52 Dave Stieb	.50	120 Bob Shirley	.05	187 Danny Boone	.05	253 Tom Paciorek	.05
53 Doug Corbett	.05	121 Terry Kennedy	.10	188 Junior Kennedy	.05	254 Pat Zachry	.05
54 Jorge Bell (R)	6.00	122 Frank Pastore	.05	189 Sparky Lyle	.05	255 Luis Leal	.05
55 Joe Simpson	.05	123 Gene Garber	.05	190 Whitey Herzog (Mgr.)	.05	256 John Castino	.05
56 Rusty Staub	.10	124 Tony Pena	.50	191 Dave Smith	.05	257 Rich Dauer	.05
57 Hector Cruz	.05	125 Allen Ripley	.05	192 Ed Ott	.05	258 Cecil Cooper	.20
58 Claudell Washington	.10	126 Randy Martz	.05	193 Greg Luzinski	.10	259 Dave Rozema	.05
59 Enrique Romo	.05	127 Richie Zisk	.05	194 Bill Lee	.05	260 John Tudor	.25
60 Gary Lavelle	.05	128 Mike Scott	.40	195 Don Zimmer (Mgr.)	.05	261 Jerry Mumphrey	.05
61 Tim Flannery	.05	129 Lloyd Moseby	.35	196 Hal McRae	.05	262 Jay Johnstone	.05
62 Joe Nolan	.05	130 Rob Wilfong	.05	197 Mike Norris	.05	263 Bo Diaz	.05
63 Larry Bowa	.05	131 Tim Stoddard	.05				
64 Sixto Lezcano	.05						
65 Joe Sambito	.05						

NO.	PLAYER	MINT
264	Dennis Leonard	.05
265	Jim Spencer	.05
266	John Milner	.05
267	Don Aase	.05
268	Jim Sundberg	.05
269	Lamar Johnson	.05
270	Frank LaCorte	.05
271	Barry Evans	.05
272	Enos Cabell	.05
273	Del Unser	.05
274	George Foster	.20
275	Brett Butler (R)	1.00
276	Lee Lacy	.05
277	Ken Reitz	.05
278	Keith Hernandez	.35
279	Doug DeCinces	.10
280	Charlie Moore	.05
281	Lance Parrish	.25
282	Ralph Houk (Mgr.)	.05
283	Rich Gossage	.20
284	Jerry Reuss	.05
285	Mike Stanton	.05
286	Frank White	.05
287	Bob Owchinko	.05
288	Scott Sanderson	.05
289	Bump Wills	.05
290	Dave Frost	.05
291	Chet Lemon	.05
292	Tito Landrum	.05
293	Vern Ruhle	.05
294	Mike Schmidt	1.25
295	San Mejias	.05
296	Gary Lucas	.05
297	John Candelaria	.05
298	Jerry Martin	.05
299	Dale Murphy	.75
300	Mike Lum	.05
301	Tom Hausman	.05
302	Glenn Abbott	.05
303	Roger Erickson	.05
304	Otto Velez	.05
305	Danny Goodwin	.05
306	John Mayberry	.05
307	Lenny Randle	.05
308	Bob Bailor	.05
309	Jerry Morales	.05
310	Rufino Linares	.05
311	Kent Tekulve	.05
312	Joe Morgan	.30
313	John Urrea	.05
314	Paul Householder	.05
315	Garry Maddox	.05
316	Mike Ramsey	.05
317	Alan Ashby	.05
318	Bob Clark	.05
319	Tony LaRussa (Mgr.)	.05
320	Charlie Lea	.05
321	Danny Darwin	.05
322	Cesar Geronimo	.05
323	Tom Underwood	.05
324	Andre Thornton	.10
325	Rudy May	.05
326	Frank Tanana	.05
327	Davey Lopes	.05
328	Richie Hebner	.05
329	Mike Flanagan	.08
330	Mike Caldwell	.05
331	Scott McGregor	.05
332	Jerry Augustine	.05
333	Stan Papi	.05
334	Rick Miller	.05
335	Graig Nettles	.15
336	Dusty Baker	.10
337	Dave Garcia (Mgr.)	.05
338	Larry Gura	.05
339	Cliff Johnson	.05
340	Warren Cromartie	.05
341	Steve Comer	.05
342	Rick Burleson	.05
343	John Martin	.05
344	Craig Reynolds	.05
345	Mike Proly	.05
346	Ruppert Jones	.05
347	Omar Moreno	.05
348	Greg Minton	.05
349	Rick Mahler (R)	.25
350	Alex Trevino	.05
351	Mike Krukow	.05
352	Shane Rawley	.75
	(photo of Jim Anderson)	
352	Shane Rawley (correct)	.10
353	Garth Iorg	.05
354	Pete Mackanin	.05
355	Paul Moskau	.05
356	Rich Dotson	.05
357	Steve Stone	.05
358	Larry Hisle	.05
359	Aurelio Lopez	.05
360	Oscar Gamble	.05
361	Tom Burgmeier	.05
362	Terry Forster	.08
363	Joe Charboneau	.05
364	Ken Brett	.05
365	Tony Armas	.15
366	Chris Speier	.05
367	Fred Lynn	.20
368	Buddy Bell	.10
369	Jim Essian	.05
370	Terry Puhl	.05
371	Greg Gross	.05
372	Bruce Sutter	.20
373	Joe LeFebvre	.05
374	Ray Knight	.05
375	Bruce Benedict	.05
376	Tim Foli	.05
377	Al Holland	.05
378	Ken Kravec	.05
379	Jeff Burroughs	.05
380	Pete Falcone	.05
381	Ernie Whitt	.05
382	Brad Havens	.05
383	Terry Crowley	.05
384	Don Money	.05
385	Dan Schatzeder	.05
386	Gary Allenson	.05
387	Yogi Berra	.25
388	Ken Landreaux	.05
389	Mike Hargrove	.05
390	Darryl Motley	.20
391	Dave McKay	.05
392	Stan Bahnsen	.05
393	Ken Forsch	.05
394	Mario Mendoza	.05
395	Jim Morrison	.05
396	Mike Ivie	.05
397	Broderick Perkins	.05
398	Darrell Evans	.10
399	Ron Reed	.05
400	Johnny Bench	1.00
401	Steve Bedrosian (R)	.75
402	Bill Robinson	.05
403	Bill Buckner	.15
404	Ken Oberkfell	.05
405	Cal Ripken Jr. (R)	15.00
406	Jim Gantner	.05
407	Kirk Gibson	1.50
408	Tony Perez	.15
409	Tommy John	.15
410	Dave Stewart (R)	8.00
411	Dan Spillner	.05
412	Willie Aikens	.05
413	Mike Heath	.05
414	Ray Burris	.05
415	Leon Roberts	.05
416	Mike Witt	.75
417	Bobby Molinaro	.05
418	Steve Braun	.05
419	Nolan Ryan	3.00
420	Tug McGraw	.05
421	Dave Concepcion	.10
422	Juan Eichelberger	.75
	(photo of Gary Lucas)	
422	J. Eichelberger (correct)	.05
423	Rick Rhoden	.05
424	Frank Robinson (Mgr.)	.15
425	Eddie Miller	.05
426	Bill Caudill	.05
427	Doug Flynn	.05
428	Larry Andersen	.05
429	Al Williams	.05
430	Jerry Garvin	.05
431	Glenn Adams	.05
432	Barry Bonnell	.05
433	Jerry Narron	.05
434	John Stearns	.05
435	Mike Tyson	.05
436	Glenn Hubbard	.05
437	Eddie Solomon	.05
438	Jeff Leonard	.15
439	Randy Bass	.05
440	Mike LaCoss	.05
441	Gary Matthews	.10
442	Mark Littell	.05
443	Don Sutton	.40
444	John Harris	.05
445	Vada Pinson	.05
446	Elias Sosa	.05
447	Charlie Hough	.05
448	Willie Wilson	.15
449	Fred Stanley	.05
450	Tommy Veryzer	.05
451	Ron Davis	.05
452	Mark Clear	.05
453	Bill Russell	.05
454	Lou Whitaker	.20
455	Dan Graham	.05
456	Reggie Cleveland	.05
457	Sammy Stewart	.05
458	Pete Vuckovich	.10
459	John Wockenfuss	.05
460	Glenn Hoffman	.05
461	Willie Randolph	.05
462	Fernando Valenzuela	1.00
463	Ron Hassey	.05
464	Paul Splittorff	.05
465	Rob Picciolo	.05
466	Larry Parrish	.05
467	John Grubb	.05
468	Dan Ford	.05
469	Silvio Martinez	.05
470	Kiko Garcia	.05
471	Bob Boone	.05
472	Luis Salazar	.15
473	Randy Niemann	.05
474	Tom Griffin	.05
475	Phil Niekro	.35
476	Hubie Brooks	.75
477	Dick Tidrow	.05
478	Jim Beattie	.05
479	Damaso Garcia	.10
480	Mickey Hatcher	.05
481	Joe Price	.05
482	Ed Farmer	.05
483	Eddie Murray	.75
484	Ben Oglivie	.10
485	Kevin Saucier	.05
486	Bobby Murcer	.10
487	Bill Campbell	.05
488	Reggie Smith	.10
489	Wayne Garland	.05
490	Jim Wright	.05
491	Billy Martin (Mgr.)	.20
492	Jim Fanning (Mgr.)	.05
493	Don Baylor	.15
494	Rick Honeycutt	.05
495	Carlton Fisk	.50
496	Denny Walling	.05
497	Bake McBride	.05
498	Darrell Porter	.05
499	Gene Richards	.05
500	Ron Oester	.05
501	Ken Dayley (R)	.15
502	Jason Thompson	.10
503	Milt May	.05
504	Doug Bird	.05
505	Bruce Bochte	.05
506	Neil Allen	.05
507	Joey McLaughlin	.05
508	Butch Wynegar	.06
509	Gary Roenicke	.05
510	Robin Yount	1.00
511	Dave Tobik	.05
512	Rich Gedman (R)	.35
513	Gene Nelson	.08
514	Rick Monday	.05
515	Miguel Dilone	.05
516	Clint Hurdle	.05
517	Jeff Newman	.05
518	Grant Jackson	.05
519	Andy Hassler	.05
520	Pat Putnam	.05
521	Greg Pryor	.05
522	Tony Scott	.05
523	Steve Mura	.05
524	John LeMaster	.05
525	Dick Ruthven	.05
526	John McNamara (Mgr.)	.05
527	Larry McWilliams	.05
528	Johnny Ray (R)	.75
529	Pat Tabler (R)	.40
530	Tom Herr	.10
531	San Diego Chicken*	.75
532	Sal Butera	.05
533	Mike Griffin	.05
534	Kelvin Moore	.05
535	Reggie Jackson	1.00
536	Ed Romero	.05
537	Derrel Thomas	.05
538	Mike O'Berry	.05
539	Jack O'Connor	.05
540	Bob Ojeda (R)	.50
541	Roy Lee Jackson	.05
542	Lynn Jones	.05
543	Gaylord Perry	.25
544	Phil Garner*	.10
545	Garry Templeton	.10
546	Rafael Ramirez	.05
547	Jeff Reardon	.20
548	Ron Guidry	.20
549	Tim Laudner	.15
550	John Henry Johnson	.05
551	Chris Bando	.05
552	Bobby Brown	.05
553	Larry Bradford	.05
554	Scott Fletcher (R)	.35
555	Jerry Royster	.05
556	Shooty Babbitt	.05
557	Kent Hrbek (R)	3.50
558	Yankee Winners:	.15
	Ron Guidry, Tommy John	
559	Mark Bomback	.05
560	Julio Valdez	.08
561	Buck Martinez	.05
562	Mike Marshall (R)	1.50
563	Rennie Stennett	.05
564	Steve Crawford	.07
565	Bob Babcock	.05
566	Johnny Podres	.05
567	Paul Serna	.07
568	Harold Baines	1.50
569	Dave LaRoche	.05
570	Lee May	.05
571	Gary Ward	.05
572	John Denny	.05
573	Roy Smalley	.05
574	Bob Brenly (R)	.25
575	Bronx Bombers:	.45
	R. Jackson, D. Winfield	
576	Luis Pujols	.05
577	Butch Hobson	.05
578	Harvey Kuenn (Mgr.)	.05
579	Cal Ripken, Sr.	.05
580	Juan Berenguer	.05
581	Benny Ayala	.05
582	Vance Law	.15
583	Rick Leach	.08
584	George Frazier	.05
585	Phillies Finest:	1.00
	Pete Rose, Mike Schmidt	
586	Joe Rudi	.05
587	Juan Beniquez	.05
588	Luis DeLeon (R)	.15
589	Craig Swan	.05
590	Dave Chalk	.05
591	Billy Gardner (Mgr.)	.05
592	Sal Bando	.05
593	Bert Campaneris	.05
594	Steve Kemp	.05
595	Randy Lerch' (Braves)	.75
595	Randy Lerch (Brewers)	.08

NO. PLAYER	MINT	NO. PLAYER	MINT	NO. PLAYER	MINT	NO. PLAYER	MINT
596 Bryan Clark	.08	613 Joel Youngblood	.05	629 Paul Mirabella	.05	646 Jesse Orosco	.10
597 Dave Ford	.05	614 Larry Milbourne	.05	630 Rance Mulliniks	.05	647 Jerry Dybzinski	.05
598 Mike Scioscia	.20	615 Phil Roof	.07	631 Kevin Hickey	.05	648 Tommy Davis	.05
599 John Lowenstein	.05	616 Keith Drumright	.05	632 Reid Nichols	.05	649 Ron Gardenhire	.10
600 Rene Lachmann (Mgr.)	.05	617 Dave Rosello	.05	633 Dave Geisel	.05	650 Felipe Alou	.05
601 Mick Kelleher	.05	618 Rickey Keeton	.05	634 Ken Griffey	.20	651 Harvey Haddix	.05
602 Ron Jackson	.05	619 Dennis Lamp	.05	635 Bob Lemon (Mgr.)	.10	652 Willie Upshaw	.10
603 Jerry Koosman	.15	620 Sid Monge	.05	636 Orlando Sanchez	.08	653 Bill Madlock	.15
604 Dave Goltz	.05	621 Jerry White	.05	637 Bill Almon	.05	DK Checklist*	.10
605 Ellis Valentine	.05	622 Luis Aguayo	.05	638 Danny Ainge	.05	— Checklist No. 1	.08
606 Lonnie Smith	.10	623 Jamie Easterly	.05	639 Willie Stargell	.40	— Checklist No. 2	.08
607 Joaquin Andujar	.15	624 Steve Sax (R)	3.00	640 Bob Sykes	.05	— Checklist No. 3	.08
608 Garry Hancock	.05	625 Dave Roberts	.05	641 Ed Lynch (R)	.10	— Checklist No. 4	.08
609 Jerry Turner	.05	626 Rick Bosetti	.05	642 John Ellis	.05	— Checklist No. 5	.08
610 Bob Bonner	.05	627 Terry Francona (R)	.15	643 Fergie Jenkins	.15	— Checklist No. 6	.08
611 Jim Dwyer	.05	628 Pride of Reds:	.60	644 Lenn Sakata	.05		
612 Terry Bulling	.05	Tom Seaver, Johnny Bench		645 Julio Gonzalez	.05		

1983 Donruss.... Complete Set of 660 Cards—Value $110.00 (Factory-Sealed set—Value $125.00)

Features the rookie cards of Wade Boggs, Howard Johnson, Ryne Sandberg and Tony Gwynn. The *checklist* cards are *not* numbered.

NO. PLAYER	MINT	NO. PLAYER	MINT	NO. PLAYER	MINT	NO. PLAYER	MINT
No. 1 to 26—Diamond Kings		41 Jose Cruz	.10	82 Rick Miller	.05	123 Chris Chambliss	.05
1 F. Valenzuela (DK)	.50	42 Pete Rose	1.00	83 Graig Nettles	.10	124 Chuck Tanner (Mgr.)	.05
2 Rollie Fingers (DK)	.20	43 Cesar Cedeno	.10	84 Ron Cey	.15	125 Johnnie LeMaster	.05
3 Reggie Jackson (DK)	.50	44 Floyd Chiffer	.07	85 Miguel Dilone	.05	126 Mel Hall (R)	.75
4 Jim Palmer (DK)	.30	45 Larry McWilliams	.05	86 John Wathan	.05	127 Bruce Bochte	.05
5 Jack Morris (DK)	.15	46 Alan Fowlkes	.07	87 Kelvin Moore	.05	128 Charlie Puleo	.07
6 George Foster (DK)	.15	47 Dale Murphy	.75	88 Bryn Smith	.35	129 Luis Leal	.05
7 Jim Sundberg (DK)	.15	48 Doug Bird	.05	89 Dave Hostetler	.08	130 John Pacella	.05
8 Willie Stargell (DK)	.35	49 Hubie Brooks	.30	90 Rod Carew	.50	131 Glenn Gulliver	.07
9 Dave Stieb (DK)	.30	50 Floyd Bannister	.05	91 Lonnie Smith	.07	132 Don Money	.05
10 Joe Niekro (DK)	.10	51 Joe O'Connor	.05	92 Bob Knepper	.05	133 Dave Rozema	.05
11 Rickey Henderson (DK)	1.50	52 Steve Senteney	.07	93 Marty Bystrom	.05	134 Bruce Hurst	.50
12 Dale Murphy (DK)	.50	53 Gary Gaetti (R)	3.00	94 Chris Welsh	.05	135 Rudy May	.05
13 Toby Harrah (DK)	.10	54 Damaso Garcia	.10	95 Jason Thompson	.07	136 Tom LaSorda (Mgr.)	.10
14 Bill Buckner (DK)	.15	55 Gene Nelson	.05	96 Tom O'Malley	.08	137 Dan Spillner	.10
15 Willie Wilson (DK)	.20	56 Mookie Wilson	.08	97 Phil Niekro	.20	(photo of Ed Whitson)	
16 Steve Carlton (DK)	.40	57 Allen Ripley	.05	98 Neil Allen	.05	138 Jerry Martin	.05
17 Ron Guidry (DK)	.25	58 Bob Horner	.20	99 Bill Buckner	.10	139 Mike Norris	.05
18 Steve Rogers (DK)	.10	59 Tony Pena	.15	100 Ed VandeBerg	.10	140 Al Oliver	.10
19 Kent Hrbek (DK)	.35	60 Gary Lavelle	.05	101 Jim Clancy	.05	141 Daryl Sconiers	.05
20 Keith Hernandez (DK)	.25	61 Tim Lollar	.05	102 Robert Castillo	.05	142 Lamar Johnson	.05
21 Floyd Bannister (DK)	.10	62 Frank Pastore	.05	103 Bruce Berenyi	.05	143 Harold Baines	.20
22 Johnny Bench (DK)	.60	63 Garry Maddox	.05	104 Carlton Fisk	.50	144 Alan Ashby	.05
23 Britt Burns (DK)	.10	64 Bob Forsch	.05	105 Mike Flanagan	.10	145 Garry Templeton	.10
24 Joe Morgan (DK)	.25	65 Harry Spilman	.05	106 Cecil Cooper	.15	146 Al Holland	.05
25 Carl Yastrzemski (DK)	.75	66 Geoff Zahn	.05	107 Jack Morris	.20	147 Bo Diaz	.05
26 Jerry Kennedy (DK)	.10	67 Salome Barojas	.07	108 Mike Morgan	.05	148 Dave Concepcion	.10
27 Gary Roenicke	.05	68 David Palmer	.05	109 Luis Aponte	.05	149 Rick Camp	.05
28 Dwight Bernard	.05	69 Charlie Hough	.05	110 Pedro Guerrero	.30	150 Jim Morrison	.05
29 Pat Underwood	.05	70 Dan Quisenberry	.20	111 Len Barker	.05	151 Randy Martz	.05
30 Gary Allenson	.05	71 Tony Armas	.15	112 Willie Wilson	.20	152 Keith Hernandez	.30
31 Ron Guidry	.20	72 Rick Sutcliffe	.20	113 Dave Beard	.05	153 John Lowenstein	.05
32 Burt Hooton	.05	73 Steve Balboni	.10	114 Mike Gates	.07	154 Mike Caldwell	.05
33 Chris Bando	.05	74 Jerry Remy	.05	115 Reggie Jackson	.50	155 Milt Wilcox	.05
34 Vida Blue	.10	75 Mike Scioscia	.05	116 George Wright	.15	156 Rich Gedman	.05
35 Rickey Henderson	3.00	76 John Wockenfuss	.05	117 Vance Law	.05	157 Rich Gossage	.20
36 Ray Burris	.05	77 Jim Palmer	.50	118 Nolan Ryan	2.00	158 Jerry Reuss	.05
37 John Butcher	.05	78 Rollie Fingers	.25	119 Mike Krukow	.05	159 Ron Hassey	.05
38 Don Aase	.05	79 Joe Nolan	.05	120 Ozzie Smith	.60	160 Larry Gura	.05
39 Jerry Koosman	.05	80 Pete Vuckovich	.05	121 Broderick Perkins	.05	161 Dwayne Murphy	.05
40 Bruce Sutter	.20	81 Rick Leach	.05	122 Tom Seaver	.50	162 Woodie Fryman	.05

NO.	PLAYER	MINT
163	Steve Comer	.05
164	Ken Forsch	.05
165	Dennis Lamp	.05
166	David Green (R)	.15
167	Terry Puhl	.05
168	Mike Schmidt	1.50
169	Eddie Milner (R)	.15
170	John Curtis	.05
171	Don Robinson	.05
172	Richard Gale	.05
173	Steve Bedrosian	.20
174	Willie Hernandez	.20
175	Ron Gardenhire	.05
176	Jim Beattie	.05
177	Tim Laudner	.05
178	Buck Martinez	.05
179	Kent Hrbek	.50
180	Alfredo Griffin	.05
181	Larry Andersen	.05
182	Pete Falcone	.05
183	Jody Davis	.10
184	Glenn Hubbard	.05
185	Dale Berra	.05
186	Greg Minton	.05
187	Gary Lucas	.05
188	Dave Van Gorder	.08
189	Bob Dernier	.05
190	Willie McGee (R)	3.00
191	Dickie Thon	.07
192	Bob Boone	.05
193	Britt Burns	.05
194	Jeff Reardon	.10
195	Jon Matlack	.05
196	Don Slaught (R)	.30
197	Fred Stanley	.05
198	Rick Manning	.05
199	Dave Righetti	.25
200	Dave Stapleton	.05
201	Steve Yeager	.05
202	Enos Cabell	.05
203	Sammy Stewart	.05
204	Moose Haas	.05
205	Lenn Sakata	.05
206	Charlie Moore	.05
207	Alan Trammell	.25
208	Jim Rice	.30
209	Roy Smalley	.05
210	Bill Russell	.05
211	Andre Thornton	.07
212	Willie Aikens	.05
213	Dave McKay	.05
214	Tim Blackwell	.05
215	Buddy Bell	.10
216	Doug DeCinces	.15
217	Tom Herr	.10
218	Frank LaCorte	.05
219	Steve Carlton	.50
220	Terry Kennedy	.10
221	Mike Easler	.05
222	Jack Clark	.25
223	Gene Garber	.05
224	Scott Holman	.07
225	Mike Proly	.05
226	Terry Bulling	.05
227	Jerry Garvin	.05
228	Ron Davis	.05
229	Tom Hume	.05
230	Marc Hill	.05
231	Dennis Martinez	.05
232	Jim Gantner	.05
233	Larry Pashnick	.07
234	Dave Collins	.05
235	Tom Burgmeier	.05
236	Ken Landreaux	.05
237	John Denny	.10
238	Hal McRae	.05
239	Matt Keough	.05
240	Doug Flynn	.05
241	Fred Lynn	.20
242	Billy Sample	.05
243	Tom Paciorek	.05
244	Joe Sambito	.05
245	Sid Monge	.05
246	Ken Oberkfell	.05
247	Joe Pittman	.10
	(photo of Juan Eichelberger)	
248	Mario Soto	.10
249	Claudell Washington	.10
250	Rick Rhoden	.05
251	Darrell Evans	.10
252	Steve Henderson	.05
253	Manny Castillo	.05
254	Craig Swan	.05
255	Joey McLaughlin	.05
256	Pete Redfern	.05
257	Ken Singleton	.08
258	Robin Yount	.75
259	Elias Sosa	.05
260	Bob Ojeda	.08
261	Bobby Murcer	.10
262	Candy Maldonado (R)	.75
263	Rick Waits	.05
264	Greg Pryor	.05
265	Bob Owchinko	.05
266	Chris Speier	.05
267	Bruce Kison	.05
268	Mark Wagner	.05
269	Steve Kemp	.05
270	Phil Garner	.05
271	Gene Richards	.05
272	Renie Martin	.05
273	Dave Roberts	.05
274	Dan Driessen	.05
275	Rufino Linares	.05
276	Lee Lacy	.05
277	Ryne Sandberg (R)	25.00
278	Darrell Porter	.05
279	Cal Ripken	3.00
280	Jamie Easterly	.05
281	Bill Fahey	.05
282	Glenn Hoffman	.05
283	Willie Randolph	.10
284	Fernando Valenzuela	.30
285	Alan Bannister	.05
286	Paul Splittorff	.05
287	Joe Rudi	.05
288	Bill Gullickson	.05
289	Danny Darwin	.05
290	Andy Hassler	.05
291	Ernesto Escarrega	.07
292	Steve Mura	.05
293	Tony Scott	.05
294	Manny Trillo	.05
295	Greg Harris	.05
296	Luis DeLeon	.05
297	Kent Tekulve	.05
298	Atlee Hammaker	.05
299	Bruce Benedict	.05
300	Fergie Jenkins	.15
301	Dave Kingman	.10
302	Bill Caudill	.05
303	John Castino	.05
304	Ernie Whitt	.05
305	Randy Johnson	.05
306	Garth Iorg	.05
307	Gaylord Perry	.20
308	Ed Lynch	.05
309	Keith Moreland	.10
310	Rafael Ramirez	.05
311	Bill Madlock	.15
312	Milt May	.05
313	John Montefusco	.05
314	Wayne Krenchicki	.05
315	George Vukovich	.05
316	Joaquin Andujar	.10
317	Craig Reynolds	.05
318	Rick Burleson	.05
319	Richard Dotson	.05
320	Steve Rogers	.05
321	Dave Schmidt	.10
322	Bud Black (R)	.30
323	Jeff Burroughs	.05
324	Von Hayes	.25
325	Butch Wynegar	.05
326	Carl Yastrzemski	1.00
327	Ron Roenicke	.05
328	Howard Johnson (R)	11.00
329	Rick Dempsey	.05
330	Jim Slaton	.50
331	Benny Ayala	.05
332	Ted Simmons	1.00
333	Lou Whitaker	.20
334	Chuck Rainey	.05
335	Lou Piniella	.10
336	Steve Sax	.30
337	Toby Harrah	.05
338	George Brett	1.00
339	Davey Lopes	.05
340	Gary Carter	.40
341	John Grubb	.05
342	Tim Foli	.05
343	Jim Kaat	.05
344	Mike LaCoss	.05
345	Larry Christenson	.05
346	Juan Bonilla	.05
347	Omar Moreno	.05
348	Chili Davis	.30
349	Tommy Boggs	.05
350	Rusty Staub	.10
351	Bump Wills	.05
352	Rick Sweet	.05
353	Jim Gott	.25
354	Terry Felton	.05
355	Jim Kern	.05
356	Bill Almon	.05
357	Tippy Martinez	.05
358	Roy Howell	.05
359	Dan Petry	.15
360	Jerry Mumphrey	.05
361	Mark Clear	.05
362	Mike Marshall	.30
363	Lary Sorensen	.05
364	Amos Otis	.08
365	Rick Langford	.05
366	Brad Mills	.05
367	Brian Downing	.05
368	Mike Richardt	.07
369	Aurelio Rodriguez	.05
370	Dave Smith	.05
371	Tug McGraw	.08
372	Doug Bair	.10
373	Ruppert Jones	.05
374	Alex Trevino	.05
375	Ken Dayley	.05
376	Rod Scurry	.05
377	Bob Brenly	.05
378	Scot Thompson	.05
379	Julio Cruz	.05
380	John Stearns	.05
381	Dale Murray	.05
382	Frank Viola (R)	8.00
383	Al Bumbry	.05
384	Ben Oglivie	.10
385	Dave Tobik	.05
386	Bob Stanley	.05
387	Andre Robertson	.05
388	Jorge Orta	.05
389	Ed Whitson	.05
390	Don Hood	.05
391	Tom Underwood	.05
392	Tim Wallach	.25
393	Steve Renko	.05
394	Mickey Rivers	.05
395	Greg Luzinski	.10
396	Art Howe	.05
397	Alan Wiggins	.15
398	Jim Barr	.05
399	Ivan DeJesus	.05
400	Tom Lawless	.08
401	Bob Walk	.05
402	Jimmy Smith	.07
403	Lee Smith	.10
404	George Hendrick	.10
405	Eddie Murray	.50
406	Marshall Edwards	.05
407	Lance Parrish	.20
408	Carney Lansford	.25
409	Dave Winfield	.40
410	Bob Welch	.30
411	Larry Milbourne	.05
412	Dennis Leonard	.05
413	Dan Meyer	.05
414	Charlie Lea	.05
415	Rick Honeycutt	.05
416	Mike Witt	.20
417	Steve Trout	.05
418	Glenn Brummer	.05
419	Denny Walling	.05
420	Gary Matthews	.10
421	Charlie Leibrandt	.05
422	Juan Eichelberger	.05
423	Matt Guante	.07
424	Bill Laskey (R)	.15
425	Jerry Royster	.05
426	Dickie Noles	.05
427	George Foster	.20
428	Mike Moore (R)	1.25
429	Gary Ward	.05
430	Barry Bonnell	.05
431	Ron Washington	.08
432	Rance Mulliniks	.05
433	Mike Stanton	.05
434	Jesse Orosco	.10
435	Larry Bowa	.08
436	Biff Pocoroba	.05
437	Johnny Ray	.12
438	Joe Morgan	.30
439	Eric Show (R)	.30
440	Larry Biittner	.05
441	Greg Gross	.05
442	Gene Tenace	.05
443	Danny Heep	.05
444	Bobby Clark	.05
445	Kevin Hickey	.05
446	Scott Sanderson	.05
447	Frank Tanana	.10
448	Cesar Geronimo	.05
449	Jimmy Sexton	.05
450	Mike Hargrove	.05
451	Doyle Alexander	.05
452	Dwight Evans	.20
453	Terry Forster	.05
454	Tom Brookens	.05
455	Rich Dauer	.05
456	Rob Picciolo	.05
457	Terry Crowley	.05
458	Ned Yost	.05
459	Kirk Gibson	.40
460	Reid Nichols	.05
461	Oscar Gamble	.05
462	Dusty Baker	.10
463	Jack Perconte	.05
464	Frank White	.05
465	Mickey Klutts	.05
466	Warren Cromartie	.05
467	Larry Parrish	.05
468	Bobby Grich	.08
469	Dane Iorg	.05
470	Joe Niekro	.10
471	Ed Farmer	.05
472	Tim Flannery	.05
473	Dave Parker	.30
474	Jeff Leonard	.05
475	Al Hrabosky	.05
476	Ron Hodges	.05
477	Leon Durham	.20
478	Jim Essian	.05
479	Roy Lee Jackson	.05
480	Brad Havens	.05
481	Joe Price	.05
482	Tony Bernazard	.05
483	Scott McGregor	.08
484	Paul Molitor	.20
485	Mike Ivie	.05
486	Ken Griffey	.20
487	Dennis Eckersley	.35
488	Steve Garvey	.40
489	Mike Fischlin	.05
490	U.L. Washington	.05
491	Steve McCatty	.05
492	Roy Johnson	.07
493	Don Baylor	.10
494	Bobby Johnson	.05
495	Mike Squires	.05
496	Bert Roberge	.05
497	Dick Ruthven	.05

NO. PLAYER	MINT	NO. PLAYER	MINT	NO. PLAYER	MINT	NO. PLAYER	MINT
498 Tito Landrum	.05	540 Tim Raines	.50	582 Bob McClure	.05	623 Gene Petralli	.07
499 Sixto Lezcano	.05	541 Paul Mirabella	.05	583 Jim Dwyer	.05	624 Duane Walker (R)	.15
500 Johnny Bench	.75	542 Luis Tiant	.10	584 Ed Romero	.05	625 Dick Williams (Mgr.)	.05
501 Larry Whisenton	.05	543 Ron LeFlore	.05	585 Larry Herndon	.05	626 Pat Corrales (Mgr.)	.05
502 Manny Sarmiento	.05	544 Dave LaPoint (R)	.35	586 Wade Boggs (R)	22.00	627 Vern Ruhle	.05
503 Fred Breining	.05	545 Randy Moffitt	.05	587 Jay Howell	.05	628 Joe Torre (Mgr.)	.05
504 Bill Campbell	.05	546 Luis Aguayo	.05	588 Dave Stewart	1.25	629 Anthony Johnson	.08
505 Todd Cruz	.05	547 Brad Lesley	.10	589 Bert Blyleven	.25	630 Steve Howe	.05
506 Bob Bailor	.05	548 Luis Salazar	.05	590 Dick Howser (Mgr.)	.08	631 Gary Woods	.05
507 Dave Stieb	.35	549 John Candelaria	.05	591 Wayne Gross	.05	632 LaMarr Hoyt	.15
508 Al Williams	.05	550 Dave Bergman	.05	592 Terry Francona	.08	633 Steve Swisher	.05
509 Dan Ford	.05	551 Bob Watson	.05	593 Don Werner	.05	634 Terry Leach	.15
510 Gorman Thomas	.10	552 Pat Tabler	.05	594 Bill Stein	.05	635 Jeff Newman	.05
511 Chet Lemon	.10	553 Brent Gaff	.08	595 Jesse Barfield	.75	636 Brett Butler	.20
512 Mike Torrez	.05	554 Al Cowens	.05	596 Bobby Molinaro	.05	637 Gary Gray	.05
513 Shane Rawley	.05	555 Tom Brunansky	1.00	597 Mike Vail	.05	638 Lee Mazzilli	.05
514 Mark Belanger	.05	556 Lloyd Moseby	.15	598 Tony Gwynn (R)	16.00	639 R. Jackson	.15
515 Rodney Craig	.05	557 Pascual Perez	.30	599 Gary Rajsich	.08	639 R. Jackson (error)	10.00
516 Onix Concepcion (R)	.10	558 Willie Upshaw	.10	600 Jerry Ujdur	.05	640 Juan Beniquez	.05
517 Mike Heath	.05	559 Richie Zisk	.05	601 Cliff Johnson	.05	641 Dave Rucker	.05
518 Andre Dawson	.50	560 Pat Zachry	.05	602 Jerry White	.05	642 Luis Pujols	.05
519 Luis Sanchez	.05	561 Jay Johnstone	.05	603 Bryan Clark	.05	643 Rick Monday	.05
520 Terry Bogener	.07	562 Carlos Diaz	.10	604 Joe Ferguson	.05	644 Hosken Powell	.05
521 Rudy Law	.05	563 John Tudor	.20	605 Guy Sularz	.07	645 The Chicken	.20
522 Ray Knight	.05	564 Frank Robinson (Mgr.)	.15	606 Ozzie Virgil	.10	646 Dave Engle	.05
523 Joe LeFebvre	.05	565 Dave Edwards	.05	607 Terry Harper	.05	647 Dick Davis	.05
524 Jim Wohlford	.05	566 Paul Householder	.05	608 Harvey Kuenn (Mgr.)	.05	648 MVP's: Frank Robinson, Vida Blue, Joe Morgan	.15
525 Julio Franco (R)	6.00	567 Ron Reed	.05	609 Jim Sundberg	.05	649 Al Chambers	.15
526 Ron Oester	.05	568 Mike Ramsey	.05	610 Willie Stargell	.30	650 Jesus Vega	.07
527 Rick Mahler	.05	569 Kiko Garcia	.05	611 Reggie Smith	.10	651 Jeff Jones	.05
528 Steve Nicosia	.05	570 Tommy John	.20	612 Rob Wilfong	.05	652 Marvis Foley	.05
529 Junior Kennedy	.05	571 Tony LaRussa (Mgr.)	.05	613 Niekro Brothers Joe and Phil	.15	653 Ty Cobb Puzzle	.20
530 Whitey Herzog (Mgr.)	.05	572 Joel Youngblood	.05	614 Lee Elia (Mgr.)	.05	— Checklist (DK)	.08
531 Don Sutton	.35	573 Wayne Tolleson	.15	615 Mickey Hatcher	.05	— Checklist No. 1	.08
532 Mark Brouhard	.05	574 Keith Creel	.07	616 Jerry Hairston	.05	— Checklist No. 2	.08
533 Sparky Anderson (Mgr.)	.05	575 Billy Martin (Mgr.)	.15	617 John Martin	.05	— Checklist No. 3	.08
534 Roger LaFrancois	.05	576 Jerry Dybzinski	.05	618 Wally Backman	.25	— Checklist No. 4	.08
535 George Frazier	.05	577 Rick Cerone	.05	619 Storm Davis (R)	.50	— Checklist No. 5	.08
536 Tom Niedenfuer	.07	578 Tony Perez	.15	620 Alan Knicely	.05	— Checklist No. 6	.08
537 Ed Glynn	.05	579 Greg Brock (R)	.35	621 John Stuper	.10		
538 Lee May	.05	580 Glen Wilson (R)	.30	622 Matt Sinatro	.05		
539 Bob Kearney	.10	581 Tim Stoddard	.05				

1984 Donruss.... Complete Set of 658 Cards—Value $325.00

(Factory-Sealed set which includes corrected cards no. 29 and 30—value $375.00)

Features the rookie cards of Don Mattingly, Darryl Strawberry, Ron Darling, Kevin McReynolds and Joe Carter. For the first time Donruss limited production of its main card set causing the price to rise substantially. *Living Legends* cards "A" and "B" were only issued in wax packs and were not part of the factory sealed set. The *checklist* cards are *not* numbered. Cards 29 and 30 exist with the card numbers deleted. Values for card no's. 1 to 26 are for the error cards (Perez "Steel") on the back. The corrected cards (Perez "Steele") are worth double the value.

NO. PLAYER	MINT	NO. PLAYER	MINT	NO. PLAYER	MINT	NO. PLAYER	MINT
No. 1 to 26—Diamond Kings		18 Ron Kittle (DK)	.25	31 Dion James (R)	.50	49 Lance Parrish	.40
1 Robin Yount (DK)	1.00	19 Jim Clancy (DK)	.15	32 Tony Fernandez (R)	7.50	50 Jim Rice	.50
2 Dave Concepcion (DK)	.20	20 Bill Madlock (DK)	.20	33 Angel Salazar (R)	.15	51 Dav Winfield	1.00
3 Dwayne Murphy (DK)	.15	21 Larry Parrish (DK)	.20	34 Kevin McReynolds (R)	.10.00	52 Fernando Valenzuela	.50
4 John Castino (DK)	.15	22 Eddie Murray (DK)	1.00	35 Dick Schofield (R)	.50	53 George Brett	3.00
5 Leon Durham (DK)	.30	23 Mike Schmidt (DK)	2.00	36 Brad Komminsk (R)	.30	54 Rickey Henderson	15.00
6 Rusty Staub (DK)	.15	24 Pedro Guerrero (DK)	.40	37 Tim Teufel (R)	.45	55 Gary Carter	.60
7 Jack Clark (DK)	.30	25 Andre Thornton (DK)	.15	38 Doug Frobel (R)	.15	56 Buddy Bell	.15
8 Dave Dravecky (DK)	.15	26 Wade Bogg (DK)	3.50	39 Greg Gagne (R)	.50	57 Reggie Jackson	2.50
9 Al Oliver (DK)	.20	**No. 27 to 46—(Rated Rookies)**		40 Mike Fuentes (R)	.15	58 Harold Baines	.35
10 Dave Righetti (DK)	.25	27 Joel Skinner (R)	.25	41 Joe Carter (R)	.12.00	59 Ozzie Smith	1.25
11 Hal McRae (DK)	.15	28 Tommy Dunbar (R)	.15	42 Mike Brown (R)	.25	60 Nolan Ryan	7.50
12 Ray Knight (DK)	.15	29 Mike Stenhouse (R)	.25	43 Mike Jeffcoat (R)	.15	61 Pete Rose	2.50
13 Bruce Sutter (DK)	.25	(no number on back)		44 Sid Fernandez (R)	6.00	62 Ron Oester	.10
14 Bob Horner (DK)	.25	29 Mike Stenhouse (R)	2.50	45 Brian Dayett (R)	.20	63 Steve Garvey	.75
15 Lance Parrish (DK)	.30	30 Ron Darling (R)	5.00	46 Chris Smith (R)	.15	64 Jason Thompson	.15
16 Matt Young (DK)	.15	(no number on back)		47 Eddie Murray	1.50	65 Jack Clark	.35
17 Fred Lynn (DK)	.25	30 Ron Darling (R)	15.00	48 Robin Yount	1.50	66 Dale Murphy	1.50

NO. PLAYER	MINT	NO. PLAYER	MINT	NO. PLAYER	MINT	NO. PLAYER	MINT
67 Leon Durham	.25	152 Don Baylor	.20	237 Mike Caldwell	.10	322 Jim Morrison	.10
68 Darryl Strawberry (R)	35.00	153 Bob Welch	.50	238 Keith Hernandez	.60	323 Max Venable	.10
69 Richie Zisk	.10	154 Alan Bannister	.10	239 Larry Bowa	.10	324 Tony Gwynn	7.00
70 Kent Hrbek	.75	155 Willie Aikens	.10	240 Tony Bernazard	.10	325 Duane Walker	.10
71 Dave Stieb	.60	156 Jeff Burroughs	.10	241 Damaso Garcia	.15	326 Ozzie Virgil	.10
72 Ken Schrom	.10	157 Bryan Little	.15	242 Tom Brunansky	.40	327 Jeff Lahti	.10
73 George Bell	2.00	158 Bob Boone	.10	243 Dan Driessen	.15	328 Bill Dawley	.20
74 Jon Moses	.15	159 Dave Hostetler	.10	244 Ron Kittle	.35	329 Rob Wilfong	.10
75 Ed Lynch	.10	160 Jerry Dybzinski	.10	245 Tim Stoddard	.10	330 Marc Hill	.10
76 Chuck Rainey	.10	161 Mike Madden	.15	246 Bob Gibson	.10	331 Ray Burris	.10
77 Biff Pocoroba	.10	162 Luis DeLeon	.10	247 Marty Castillo	.10	332 Allan Ramirez	.12
78 Cecilio Guante	.10	163 Willie Hernandez	.25	248 Don Mattingly (R)	75.00	333 Chuck Porter	.10
79 Jim Barr	.10	164 Frank Pastore	.10	249 Jeff Newman	.10	334 Wayne Krenchicki	.10
80 Kurt Bevacqua	.10	165 Rick Camp	.10	250 Alejandro Pena	.50	335 Gary Allenson	.10
81 Tom Foley	.15	166 Lee Mazzilli	.12	251 Toby Harrah	.12	336 Bob Meacham	.20
82 Joe LeFebvre	.10	167 Scot Thompson	.10	252 Cesar Geronimo	.10	337 Joe Beckwith	.10
83 Andy Van Slyke (R)	6.00	168 Bob Forsch	.12	253 Tom Underwood	.10	338 Rick Sutcliffe	.40
84 Bob Lillis (Mgr.)	.10	169 Mike Flanagan	.10	254 Doug Flynn	.10	339 Mark Huismann	.15
85 Rick Adams	.15	170 Rick Manning	.10	255 Andy Hassler	.10	340 Tim Conroy	.15
86 Jerry Hairston	.10	171 Chet Lemon	.15	256 Odell Jones	.10	341 Scott Sanderson	.10
87 Bob James	.20	172 Jerry Remy	.10	257 Rudy Law	.10	342 Larry Biittner	.10
88 Joe Altobelli (Mgr.)	.10	173 Ron Guidry	.30	258 Harry Spilman	.10	343 Dave Stewart	2.00
89 Ed Romero	.10	174 Pedro Guerrero	.50	259 Marty Bystrom	.10	344 Darryl Motley	.10
90 John Grubb	.10	175 Willie Wilson	.25	260 Dave Rucker	.10	345 Chris Codiroli	.12
91 John H. Johnson	.10	176 Carney Lansford	.30	261 Ruppert Jones	.10	346 Rich Behenna	.12
92 Juan Espino	.12	177 Al Oliver	.15	262 Jeff Jones	.15	347 Andre Robertson	.10
93 Candy Maldonado	.35	178 Jim Sundberg	.10	263 Gerald Perry	1.25	348 Mike Marshall	.25
94 Andre Thornton	.15	179 Bobby Grich	.10	264 Gene Tenace	.10	349 Larry Herndon	.10
95 Onix Concepcion	.10	180 Richard Dotson	.10	265 Brad Wellman	.12	350 Rich Dauer	.10
96 Don Hill	.12	181 Joaquin Andujar	.15	266 Dickie Noles	.10	351 Cecil Cooper	.15
97 Andre Dawson	1.25	182 Jose Cruz	.10	267 Jamie Allen	.12	352 Rod Carew	1.50
98 Frank Tanana	.15	183 Mike Schmidt	10.00	268 Jim Gott	.12	353 Willie McGee	.75
99 Curt Wilkerson	.15	184 Gary Redus (R)	.40	269 Ron Davis	.10	354 Phil Garner	.10
100 Larry Gura	.10	185 Garry Templeton	.15	270 Benny Ayala	.10	355 Joe Morgan	1.00
101 Dwayne Murphy	.15	186 Tony Pena	.25	271 Ned Yost	.10	356 Luis Salazar	.10
102 Tom Brennan	.10	187 Greg Minton	.10	272 Dave Rozema	.10	357 John Candelaria	.15
103 Dave Righetti	.30	188 Phil Niekro	.35	273 Dave Stapleton	.10	358 Bill Laskey	.10
104 Steve Sax	.50	189 Ferguson Jenkins	.25	274 Lou Piniella	.10	359 Bob McClure	.10
105 Dan Petry	.20	190 Mookie Wilson	.15	275 Jose Morales	.10	360 Dave Kingman	.15
106 Cal Ripken	4.00	191 Jim Beattie	.10	276 Brod Perkins	.10	361 Ron Cey	.15
107 Paul Molitor	.30	192 Gary Ward	.10	277 Butch Davis	.15	362 Matt Young (R)	.20
108 Fred Lynn	.25	193 Jesse Barfield	.40	278 Tony Phillips	.25	363 Lloyd Moseby	.15
109 Neil Allen	.15	194 Pete Filson	.15	279 Jeff Reardon	.15	364 Frank Viola	2.00
110 Joe Niekro	.15	195 Roy Lee Jackson	.10	280 Ken Forsch	.10	365 Eddie Milner	.10
111 Steve Carlton	2.00	196 Rick Sweet	.10	281 Pete O'Brien (R)	1.00	366 Floyd Bannister	.12
112 Terry Kennedy	.15	197 Jesse Orosco	.15	282 Tom Paciorek	.10	367 Dan Ford	.12
113 Bill Madlock	.20	198 Steve Lake	.12	283 Frank LaCorte	.10	368 Moose Haas	.10
114 Chili Davis	.15	199 Ken Dayley	.10	284 Tim Lollar	.10	369 Doug Bair	.10
115 Jim Gantner	.10	200 Manny Sarmiento	.10	285 Greg Gross	.10	370 Ray Fontenot (R)	.15
116 Tom Seaver	2.50	201 Mark Davis	1.00	286 Alex Trevino	.10	371 Luis Aponte	.10
117 Bill Buckner	.15	202 Tim Flannery	.10	287 Gene Garber	.10	372 Jack Fimple	.10
118 Bill Caudill	.10	203 Bill Scherrer	.12	288 Dave Parker	.60	373 Neal Heaton	.40
119 Jim Clancy	.10	204 Al Holland	.10	289 Lee Smith	.15	374 Greg Pryor	.10
120 John Castino	.10	205 Dave Von Ohlen	.15	290 Dave LaPoint	.10	375 Wayne Gross	.10
121 Dave Concepcion	.15	206 Mike LaCoss	.10	291 John Shelby	.60	376 Charlie Lea	.10
122 Greg Luzinski	.15	207 Juan Beniquez	.10	292 Charlie Moore	.10	377 Steve Lubratich	.12
123 Mike Boddicker	.15	208 Juan Agosto	.20	293 Alan Trammell	.75	378 Jon Matlack	.12
124 Pete Ladd	.10	209 Bobby Ramos	.10	294 Tony Armas	.15	379 Julio Cruz	.10
125 Juan Berenguer	.10	210 Al Bumbry	.10	295 Shane Rawley	.12	380 John Mizerock	.12
126 Juan Montefusco	.10	211 Mark Brouhard	.10	296 Greg Brock	.15	381 Kevin Gross (R)	.60
127 Ed Jurak	.12	212 Howard Bailey	.10	297 Hal McRae	.12	382 Mike Ramsey	.10
128 Tom Niedenfuer	.10	213 Bruce Hurst	.15	298 Mike Davis	.10	383 Doug Gwosdz	.10
129 Bert Blyleven	.35	214 Bob Shirley	.10	299 Tim Raines	.75	384 Kelly Paris	.15
130 Bud Black	.10	215 Pat Zachry	.10	300 Bucky Dent	.12	385 Pete Falcone	.10
131 Gorman Heimueller	.15	216 Julio Franco	1.50	301 Tommy John	.30	386 Milt May	.10
132 Dan Schatzeder	.10	217 Mike Armstrong	.10	302 Carlton Fisk	1.00	387 Fred Breining	.10
133 Ron Jackson	.10	218 Dave Beard	.10	303 Darrell Porter	.10	388 Craig Lefferts (R)	.75
134 Tom Henke (R)	1.00	219 Steve Rogers	.10	304 Dickie Thon	.10	389 Steve Henderson	.10
135 Kevin Hickey	.10	220 John Butcher	.10	305 Garry Maddox	.10	390 Randy Moffitt	.10
136 Mike Scott	.50	221 Mike Smithson	.15	306 Cesar Cedeno	.15	391 Ron Washington	.10
137 Bo Diaz	.10	222 Frank White	.12	307 Gary Lucas	.10	392 Gary Roenicke	.10
138 Glenn Brummer	.10	223 Mike Heath	.10	308 Johnny Ray	.20	393 Tom Candiotti (R)	1.00
139 Sid Monge	.10	224 Chris Bando	.10	309 Andy McGaffigan	.10	394 Larry Pashnick	.10
140 Rich Gale	.10	225 Roy Smalley	.10	310 Claudell Washington	.15	395 Dwight Evans	.50
141 Brett Butler	.30	226 Dusty Baker	.10	311 Ryne Sandberg	12.00	396 Goose Gossage	.25
142 Brian Harper (R)	1.00	227 Lou Whitaker	.40	312 George Foster	.20	397 Derrel Thomas	.10
143 John Rabb	.12	228 John Lowenstein	.10	313 Spike Owen (R)	.35	398 Juan Eichelberger	.10
144 Gary Woods	.10	229 Ben Ogilvie	.10	314 Gary Gaetti	1.00	399 Leon Roberts	.10
145 Pat Putnam	.10	230 Doug DeCinces	.15	315 Willie Upshaw	.15	400 Davey Lopes	.15
146 Jim Acker	.15	231 Lonnie Smith	.15	316 Al Williams	.10	401 Bill Gullickson	.12
147 Mickey Hatcher	.10	232 Ray Knight	.15	317 Jorge Orta	.10	402 Geoff Zahn	.10
148 Todd Cruz	.10	233 Gary Matthews	.15	318 Orlando Mercado	.12	403 Billy Sample	.10
149 Tom Tellmann	.10	234 Juan Bonilla	.10	319 Junior Ortiz	.12	404 Mike Squires	.10
150 John Wockenfuss	.10	235 Rod Scurry	.10	320 Mike Proly	.10	405 Craig Reynolds	.10
151 Wade Boggs	10.00	236 Atlee Hammaker	.10	321 Randy Johnson	.10	406 Eric Show	.10

NO.	PLAYER	MINT
407	John Denny	.20
408	Dann Bilardello	.12
409	Bruce Benedict	.10
410	Kent Tekulve	.12
411	Mel Hall	.15
412	John Stuper	.10
413	Rick Dempsey	.12
414	Don Sutton	.40
415	Jack Morris	.30
416	John Tudor	.30
417	Willie Randolph	.15
418	Jerry Reuss	.12
419	Don Slaught	.12
420	Steve McCatty	.10
421	Tim Wallach	.30
422	Larry Parrish	.15
423	Brian Downing	.15
424	Britt Burns	.15
425	David Green	.15
426	Jerry Mumphrey	.10
427	Ivn DeJesus	.10
428	Mario Soto	.12
429	Gene Richards	.10
430	Dale Berra	.10
431	Darrell Evans	.15
432	Glenn Hubbard	.10
433	Jody Davis	.12
434	Danny Heep	.10
435	Ed Nunez	.20
436	Bobby Castillo	.10
437	Ernie Whitt	.10
438	Scott Ullger	.15
439	Doyle Alexander	.15
440	Domingo Ramos	.12
441	Craig Swan	.10
442	Warren Brusstar	.10
443	Len Barker	.10
444	Mike Easler	.10
445	Renie Martin	.10
446	Dennis Rasmussen (R)	.75
447	Ted Power	.15
448	Charlie Hudson (R)	.20
449	Danny Cox (R)	.50
450	Kevin Bass	.25
451	Daryl Sconiers	.10
452	Scott Fletcher	.12
453	Bryn Smith	.12
454	Jim Dwyer	.10
455	Rob Picciolo	.10
456	Enos Cabell	.10
457	"Oil Can" Boyd (R)	.75
458	Butch Wynegar	.10
459	Burt Hooton	.10
460	Ron Hassey	.10
461	Danny Jackson (R)	2.50
462	Bob Kearney	.10
463	Terry Francona	.10
464	Wayne Tolleson	.10
465	Mickey Rivers	.15
466	John Wathan	.10
467	Bill Almon	.10
468	George Vukovich	.10
469	Steve Kemp	.12
470	Ken Landreaux	.10
471	Milt Wilcox	.10

NO.	PLAYER	MINT
472	Tippy Martinez	.10
473	Ted Simmons	.15
474	Tim Foli	.10
475	George Hendrick	.10
476	Terry Puhl	.15
477	Von Hayes	.30
478	Bobby Brown	.10
479	Lee Lacy	.10
480	Joel Youngblood	.10
481	Jim Slaton	.10
482	Mike Fitzgerald	.10
483	Keith Moreland	.10
484	Ron Roenicke	.10
485	Luis Leal	.10
486	Bryan Oelkers	.12
487	Bruce Berenyi	.10
488	LaMarr Hoyt	.15
489	Joe Nolan	.10
490	Marshall Edwards	.10
491	Mike Laga	.12
492	Rick Cerone	.10
493	Rick Miller	.10
494	Rick Honeycutt	.12
495	Mike Hargrove	.12
496	Joe Simpson	.10
497	Keith Atherton	.12
498	Chris Welsh	.10
499	Bruce Kison	.10
500	Bobby Johnson	.10
501	Jerry Koosman	.20
502	Frank DiPino	.10
503	Tony Perez	.35
504	Ken Oberkfell	.10
505	Mark Thurmond (R)	.20
506	Joe Price	.10
507	Pascual Perez	.25
508	Marvell Wynne	.20
509	Mike Krukow	.15
510	Dick Ruthven	.10
511	Al Cowens	.10
512	Cliff Johnson	.10
513	Randy Bush	.25
514	Sammy Stewart	.10
515	Bill Schroeder (R)	.20
516	Aurelio Lopez	.10
517	Mike Brown	.15
518	Graig Nettles	.20
519	Dave Sax	.12
520	Gerry Willard	.15
521	Paul Splittorff	.12
522	Tom Burgmeier	.10
523	Chris Speier	.10
524	Bobby Clark	.10
525	George Wright	.10
526	Dennis Lamp	.10
527	Tony Scott	.10
528	Ed Whitson	.12
529	Ron Reed	.10
530	Charlie Puleo	.10
531	Jerry Royster	.10
532	Don Robinson	.10
533	Steve Trout	.10
534	Bruce Sutter	.20
535	Bob Horner	.20
536	Pat Tabler	.15

NO.	PLAYER	MINT
537	Chris Chambliss	.15
538	Bob Ojeda	.20
539	Alan Ashby	.10
540	Jay Johnstone	.12
541	Bob Dernier	.10
542	Brook Jacoby (R)	2.50
543	U.L. Washington	.10
544	Danny Darwin	.10
545	Kiko Garcia	.10
546	Vance Law	.10
547	Tug McGraw	.15
548	Dave Smith	.10
549	Len Matuszek	.10
550	Tom Hume	.10
551	Dave Dravecky	.40
552	Rick Rhoden	.15
553	Duane Kuiper	.10
554	Rusty Staub	.15
555	Bill Campbell	.10
556	Mike Torrez	.10
557	Dave Henderson	.75
558	Len Whitehouse	.12
559	Barry Bonnell	.10
560	Rick Lysander	.12
561	Garth Iorg	.10
562	Bryan Clark	.10
563	Brian Giles	.10
564	Vern Ruhle	.10
565	Steve Bedrosian	.25
566	Larry McWilliams	.10
567	Jeff Leonard	.15
568	Alan Wiggins	.12
569	Jeff Russell	.45
570	Salome Barojas	.10
571	Dane Iorg	.10
572	Bob Knepper	.15
573	Gary Lavelle	.10
574	Gorman Thomas	.15
575	Manny Trillo	.10
576	Jim Palmer	1.25
577	Dale Murray	.10
578	Tom Brookens	.10
579	Rich Gedman	.12
580	Bill Doran (R)	1.50
581	Steve Yeager	.10
582	Dan Spillner	.10
583	Dan Quisenberry	.25
584	Rance Mulliniks	.10
585	Storm Davis	.15
586	Dave Schmidt	.10
587	Bill Russell	.10
588	Pat Sheridan	.30
589	Rafael Ramirez	.12
590	Bud Anderson	.10
591	George Frazier	.10
592	Lee Tunnell	.15
593	Kirk Gibson	.60
594	Scott McGregor	.10
595	Bob Bailor	.10
596	Tom Herr	.15
597	Luis Sanchez	.10
598	Dave Engle	.10
599	Craig McMurtry (R)	.15
600	Carlos Diaz	.10
601	Tom O'Malley	.10

NO.	PLAYER	MINT
602	Nick Esasky (R)	2.00
603	Ron Hodges	.10
604	Ed Vande Berg	.10
605	Alfredo Griffin	.15
606	Glenn Hoffman	.10
607	Hubie Brooks	.30
608	Richard Barnes	.12
609	Greg Walker (R)	.40
610	Ken Singleton	.15
611	Mark Clear	.10
612	Buck Martinez	.10
613	Ken Griffey	.15
614	Reid Nichols	.10
615	Doug Sisk (R)	.15
616	Bob Brenly	.10
617	Joey McLaughlin	.10
618	Glenn Wilson	.15
619	Bob Stoddard	.10
620	Len Sakata	.08
621	Mike Young (R)	.25
622	John Stefero	.12
623	Carmelo Martinez (R)	.50
624	Dave Bergman	.10
625	Runnin' Redbirds:	.25
	David Green, Willie McGee,	
	Lonnie Smith, Ozzie Smith	
626	Rudy May	.10
627	Matt Keough	.10
628	Jose DeLeon (R)	.50
629	Jim Essian	.10
630	Darnell Coles (R)	.35
631	Mike Warren	.15
632	Del Crandall (Mgr.)	.10
633	Dennis Martinez	.12
634	Mike Moore	.25
635	Lary Sorensen	.10
636	Ricky Nelson	.15
637	Omar Moreno	.10
638	Charlie Hough	.10
639	Dennis Eckersley	.75
640	Walt Terrell (R)	.35
641	Denny Walling	.10
642	Dave Anderson	.25
643	Jose Oquendo (R)	.75
644	Bob Stanley	.10
645	Dave Geisel	.10
646	Scott Garrelts (R)	1.00
647	Gary Pettis (R)	.40
648	Duke Snider Puzzle	.15
649	Johnnie LeMaster	.10
650	Dave Collins	.12
651	The Chicken	.25
—	Charlist (DK)	.18
—	Checklist No. 1	.15
—	Checklist No. 2	.15
—	Checklist No. 3	.15
—	Checklist No. 4	.15
—	Checklist No. 5	.15
—	Checklist No. 6	.15

Cards From Wax Packs

A	Living Legends:	3.00
	G. Perry, R. Fingers	
B	Living Legends:	6.00
	C. Yastrzemski, J. Bench	

1985 Donruss.... Complete Set of 660 Cards—Value $175.00

(Factory-Sealed set which includes corrected cards no. 424 and 534—Value $200.00)

Features the rookie cards of Dwight Gooden, Roger Clemens, Eric Davis, Orel Hershiser, Bret Saberhagen and Kirby Puckett. As in 1984, Donruss limited the quantity of cards printed. The *checklist* cards are *not* numbered.

NO. PLAYER	MINT	NO. PLAYER	MINT	NO. PLAYER	MINT	NO. PLAYER	MINT
No. 1 to 26 (Diamond Kings)		84 Bill Doran	.15	169 Cal Ripken, Jr.	.75	254 Pete Rose	1.25
1 Ryne Sandberg (DK)	1.00	85 Rod Carew	.50	170 Cecil Cooper	.15	255 Don Aase	.10
2 Doug DeCinces (DK)	.12	86 LaMarr Hoyt	.10	171 Alan Trammell	.25	256 George Wright	.08
3 Rich Dotson (DK)	.12	87 Tim Wallach	.12	172 Wade Boggs	4.00	257 Britt Burns	.08
4 Bert Blyleven (DK)	.12	88 Mike Flanagan	.08	173 Don Baylor	.15	258 Mike Scott	.35
5 Lou Whitaker (DK)	.20	89 Jim Sundberg	.08	174 Pedro Guerrero	.25	259 Len Matuszek	.08
6 Dan Quisenberry (DK)	.20	90 Chet Lemon	.08	175 Frank White	.08	260 Dave Rucker	.08
7 Don Mattingly (DK)	6.00	91 Bob Stanley	.08	176 Rickey Henderson	3.00	261 Craig Lefferts	.08
8 Carney Lansford (DK)	.12	92 Willie Randolph	.08	177 Charlie Lea	.08	262 Jay Tibbs	.20
9 Frank Tanana (DK)	.12	93 Bill Russell	.08	178 Pete O'Brien	.12	263 Bruce Benedict	.08
10 Willie Upshaw (DK)	.12	94 Julio Franco	.50	179 Doug DeCinces	.12	264 Don Robinson	.08
11 C. Washington (DK)	.12	95 Dan Quisenberry	.20	180 Ron Kittle	.15	265 Gary Lavelle	.08
12 Mike Marshall (DK)	.15	96 Bill Claudill	.08	181 George Hendrick	.08	266 Scott Sanderson	.08
13 Joaquin Andujar (DK)	.12	97 Bill Gullickson	.08	182 Joe Niekro	.12	267 Matt Young	.08
14 Cal Ripken (DK)	.75	98 Danny Darwin	.08	183 Juan Samuel	1.00	268 Ernie Whitt	.08
15 Jim Rice (DK)	.35	99 Curt Wilkerson	.08	184 Mario Soto	.12	269 Houston Jimenez	.08
16 Don Sutton (DK)	.10	100 Bud Black	.08	185 Goose Gossage	.15	270 Ken Dixon	.20
17 Frank Viola (DK)	.10	101 Tony Phillips	.08	186 Johnny Ray	.12	271 Peter Ladd	.08
18 Alvin Davis (DK)	.65	102 Tony Bernazard	.08	187 Bob Brenly	.08	272 Juan Berenguer	.08
19 Mario Soto (DK)	.10	103 Jay Howell	.08	188 Craig McMurtey	.08	273 Roger Clemens (R)	18.00
20 Jose Cruz (DK)	.10	104 Burt Hooton	.08	189 Leon Durham	.15	274 Rick Cerone	.08
21 Charlie Lea (DK)	.10	105 Milt Wilcox	.08	190 Dwight Gooden (R)	12.00	275 Dave Anderson	.08
22 Jesse Orosco (DK)	.10	106 Rich Dauer	.08	191 Barry Bonnell	.08	276 George Vukovich	.08
23 Juan Samuel (DK)	.30	107 Don Sutton	.20	192 Tim Teufel	.08	277 Greg Pryor	.08
24 Tony Pena (DK)	.10	108 Mike Witt	.12	193 Dave Stieb	.25	278 Mike Warren	.08
25 Tony Gwynn (DK)	.35	109 Bruce Sutter	.15	194 Mickey Hatcher	.08	279 Bob James	.08
26 Bob Brenly (DK)	.10	110 Enos Cabell	.08	195 Jesse Barfield	.30	280 Bobby Grich	.10
No. 27 to 46 (Rated Rookies)		111 John Denny	.12	196 Al Cowens	.08	281 Mike Mason	.15
27 Danny Tartabull (R)	4.00	112 Dave Dravecky	.15	197 Hubie Brooks	.15	282 Ron Reed	.08
28 Mike Bielecki (R)	.50	113 Marvell Wynne	.08	198 Steve Trout	.08	283 Alan Ashby	.08
29 Steve Lyons (R)	.20	114 John LeMaster	.08	199 Glenn Hubbard	.08	284 Mark Thurmond	.08
30 Jeff Reed (R)	.15	115 Chuck Porter	.08	200 Bill Madlock	.12	285 Joe Lefebvre	.08
31 Tony Brewer (R)	.15	116 John Gibbons	.15	201 Jeff Robinson (R)	.35	286 Ted Power	.08
32 John Morris (R)	.15	117 Keith Moreland	.08	202 Eric Show	.15	287 Chris Chambliss	.08
33 Daryl Boston (R)	.75	118 Darnell Coles	.08	203 Dave Concepcion	.12	288 Lee Tunnell	.08
34 Alfonso Pulido (R)	.15	119 Dennis Lamp	.08	204 Ivan DeJesus	.08	289 Rich Bordi	.08
35 Steve Kiefer (R)	.15	120 Ron Davis	.08	205 Neil Allen	.10	290 Glenn Brummer	.08
36 Larry Sheets (R)	.40	121 Nick Esasky	.25	206 Jerry Mumphrey	.08	291 Mike Boddicker	.10
37 Scott Bradley (R)	.35	122 Vance Law	.08	207 Mike Brown	.08	292 Rollie Fingers	.15
38 Calvin Schiraldi (R)	1.00	123 Gary Roenicke	.08	208 Carlton Fisk	.50	293 Lou Whitaker	.20
39 Shawon Dunston (R)	4.00	124 Bill Schroeder	.08	209 Bryn Smith	.08	294 Dwight Evans	.15
40 Charlie Mitchell (R)	.15	125 Dave Rozema	.08	210 Tippy Martinez	.08	295 Don Mattingly	15.00
41 Billy Hatcher (R)	1.50	126 Bobby Meacham	.08	211 Dion James	.08	296 Mike Marshall	.15
42 Russ Stephans (R)	.15	127 Marty Barrett	.25	212 Willie Hernandez	.15	297 Willie Wilson	.12
43 Alejandro Sanchez (R)	.15	128 R.J. Reynolds (R)	.35	213 Mike Easler	.08	298 Mike Heath	.08
44 Steve Jeltz (R)	.20	129 Ernie Camacho	.08	214 Ron Guidry	.20	299 Tim Raines	.40
45 Jim Traber (R)	.30	130 Jorge Orta	.08	215 Rick Honeycutt	.08	300 Larry Parrish	.08
46 Doug Loman (R)	.20	131 Lary Sorensen	.08	216 Brett Butler	.10	301 Geoff Zahn	.08
47 Eddie Murray	.50	132 Terry Francona	.08	217 Larry Gura	.08	302 Rich Dotson	.08
48 Robin Yount	.75	133 Fred Lynn	.20	218 Ray Burris	.08	303 David Green	.08
49 Lance Parrish	.20	134 Bobby Jones	.08	219 Steve Rogers	.08	304 Jose Cruz	.10
50 Jim Rice	.35	135 Jerry Hairston	.08	220 Frank Tanana	.08	305 Steve Carlton	.60
51 Dave Winfield	.35	136 Kevin Bass	.15	221 Ned Yost	.08	306 Gary Redus	.08
52 Fernando Valenzuela	.25	137 Garry Maddox	.08	222 Bret Saberhagen (R)	7.00	307 Steve Garvey	.35
53 George Brett	1.00	138 Jose LaPoint	.08	223 Mike Davis	.08	308 Jose DeLeon	.08
54 Dave Kingman	.10	139 Kevin McReynolds	1.00	224 Bert Blyleven	.15	309 Randy Lerch	.08
55 Gary Carter	.30	140 Wayne Krenchicki	.08	225 Steve Kemp	.08	310 Claudell Washington	.10
56 Buddy Bell	.10	141 Rafael Ramirez	.08	226 Jerry Reuss	.08	311 Lee Smith	.10
57 Reggie Jackson	.75	142 Rod Scurry	.08	227 Darrell Evans	.15	312 Darryl Strawberry	5.00
58 Harold Baines	.20	143 Greg Minton	.08	228 Wayne Gross	.08	313 Jim Beattie	.08
59 Ozzie Smith	.50	144 Tim Stoddard	.08	229 Jim Gantner	.08	314 John Butcher	.08
60 Nolan Ryan	3.00	145 Steve Henderson	.08	230 Bob Boone	.08	315 Damaso Garcia	.10
61 Mike Schmidt	2.00	146 George Bell	.75	231 Lonnie Smith	.08	316 Mike Smithson	.08
62 Dave Parker	.20	147 Dave Meier	.15	232 Frank DiPino	.08	317 Luis Leal	.08
63 Tony Gwynn	2.00	148 Sammy Stewart	.08	233 Jerry Koosman	.08	318 Ken Phelps	.35
64 Tony Pena	.15	149 Mark Brouhard	.08	234 Graig Nettles	.15	319 Wally Backman	.08
65 Jack Clark	.30	150 Larry Herndon	.08	235 John Tudor	.15	320 Ron Cey	.12
66 Dale Murphy	.75	151 Oil Can Boyd	.15	236 John Rabb	.08	321 Brad Komminsk	.12
67 Ryne Sandberg	3.00	152 Brian Dayett	.08	237 Rick Manning	.08	322 Jason Thompson	.10
68 Keith Hernandez	.30	153 Tom Niedenfuer	.08	238 Mike Fitzgerald	.08	323 Frank Williams	.12
69 Alvin Davis (R)	4.00	154 Brook Jacoby	.15	239 Gary Matthews	.08	324 Tim Lollar	.08
70 Kent Hrbek	.40	155 Onix Concepcion	.08	240 Jim Presley (R)	1.00	325 Eric Davis (R)	18.00
71 Willie Upshaw	.10	156 Tim Conroy	.08	241 Dave Collins	.08	326 Von Hayes	.20
72 Dave Engle	.08	157 Joe Hesketh (R)	.20	242 Gary Gaetti	.35	327 Andy Van Slyke	.75
73 Alfredo Griffin	.08	158 Brian Downing	.15	243 Dann Bilardello	.08	328 Craig Reynolds	.08
74 Jack Perconte	.08	159 Tom Dunbar	.08	244 Rudy Law	.08	329 Dick Schofield	.10
75 Jesse Orosco	.10	160 Marc Hill	.08	245 John Lowenstein	.08	330 Scott Fletcher	.10
76 Jody Davis	.10	161 Phil Garner	.08	246 Tom Tellman	.08	331 Jeff Reardon	.10
77 Bob Horner	.15	162 Jerry Davis	.12	247 Howard Johnson	2.00	332 Rick Dempsey	.10
78 Larry McWilliams	.08	163 Bill Campbell	.08	248 Ray Fontenot	.08	333 Ben Oglivie	.15
79 Joel Youngblood	.08	164 John Franco (R)	3.00	249 Tony Armas	.12	334 Dan Petry	.15
80 Alan Wiggins	.10	165 Len Barker	.08	250 Candy Maldonado	.15	335 Jackie Gutierrez	.15
81 Ron Oester	.08	166 Benny Distefano	.12	251 Mike Jeffcoat	.08	336 Dave Righetti	.15
82 Ozzie Virgil	.08	167 George Frazier	.08	252 Dane Iorg	.08	337 Alejandro Pena	.08
83 Ricky Horton (R)	.25	168 Tito Landrum	.08	253 Bruce Bochte	.08	338 Mel Hall	.08

NO.	PLAYER	MINT
339	Pat Sheridan	.08
340	Keith Atherton	.08
341	David Palmer	.08
342	Gary Ward	.08
343	Dave Stewart	.75
344	Mark Gubicza (R)	2.00
345	Carney Lansford	.12
346	Jerry Willard	.08
347	Ken Griffey	.08
348	Franklin Stubbs (R)	.75
349	Aurelio Lopez	.08
350	Al Bumbry	.08
351	Charlie Moore	.08
352	Luis Sanchez	.08
353	Darrell Porter	.08
354	Bill Dawley	.08
355	Charlie Hudson	.08
356	Garry Templeton	.12
357	Cecilio Guante	.08
358	Jeff Leonard	.12
359	Paul Molitor	.25
360	Ron Gardenhire	.08
361	Larry Bowa	.08
362	Bob Kearney	.08
363	Garth Iorg	.08
364	Tom Brunansky	.30
365	Brad Gulden	.08
366	Greg Walker	.12
367	Mike Young	.15
368	Rick Waits	.08
369	Doug Bair	.08
370	Bob Shirley	.08
371	Bob Ojeda	.08
372	Bob Welch	.30
373	Neal Heaton	.08
374	Dan Jackson	.50
375	Donnie Hill	.08
376	Mike Stenhouse	.08
377	Bruce Kison	.08
378	Wayne Tolleson	.08
379	Floyd Bannister	.08
380	Vern Ruhle	.08
381	Tim Corcoran	.08
382	Kurt Kepshire (R)	.15
383	Bobby Brown	.08
384	Dave Van Gorder	.08
385	Rick Mahler	.08
386	Lee Mazzilli	.08
387	Bill Laskey	.08
388	Thad Bosley	.08
389	Al Chambers	.08
390	Tony Fernandez	.75
391	Ron Washington	.08
392	Bill Swaggerty (R)	.15
393	Bob L. Gibson	.08
394	Marty Castillo	.08
395	Steve Crawford	.08
396	Clay Christiansen (R)	.15
397	Bob Bailor	.08
398	Mike Hargrove	.08
399	Charlie Leibrandt	.08
400	Tom Burgmeier	.08
401	Razor Shines (R)	.15
402	Rob Wilfong	.08
403	Tom Henke	.15
404	Al Jones (R)	.15
405	Mike LaCoss	.08
406	Luis DeLeon	.08
407	Greg Gross	.08
408	Tom Hume	.08
409	Rick Camp	.08
410	Milt May	.08
411	Henry Cotto (R)	.20
412	David Von Ohlen	.08
413	Scott McGregor	.10
414	Ted Simmons	.10
415	Jack Morris	.20
416	Bill Buckner	.10
417	Butch Wynegar	.08
418	Steve Sax	.25
419	Steve Balboni	.08
420	Dwayne Murphy	.08
421	Andre Dawson	.40
422	Charlie Hough	.08
423	Tommy John	.15
424	Tom Seaver	1.50
	(photo of Floyd Bannister)	
424	Tom Seaver	12.00
425	Tom Herr	.10
426	Terry Puhl	.08
427	Al Holland	.08
428	Eddie Milner	.08
429	Terry Kennedy	.08
430	John Candelaria	.08
431	Manny Trillo	.08
432	Ken Oberkfell	.08
433	Rick Sutcliffe	.15
434	Ron Darling	.75
435	Spike Owen	.08
436	Frank Viola	.75
437	Lloyd Moseby	.20
438	Kirby Puckett (R)	25.00
439	Jim Clancy	.08
440	Mike Moore	.08
441	Doug Sisk	.08
442	Dennis Eckersley	.30
443	Gerald Perry	.25
444	Dale Berra	.08
445	Dusty Baker	.08
446	Ed Whitson	.08
447	Cesar Cedeno	.10
448	Rick Schu (R)	.25
449	Joaquin Andujar	.10
450	Mark Bailey (R)	.15
451	Ron Romanick (R)	.20
452	Julio Cruz	.08
453	Miguel Dilone	.08
454	Storm Davis	.08
455	Jaime Cocanower (R)	.15
456	Barbaro Garbey (R)	.15
457	Rich Gedman	.08
458	Phil Niekro	.20
459	Mike Scioscia	.08
460	Pat Tabler	.12
461	Darryl Motley	.08
462	Chris Codorili	.08
463	Doug Flynn	.08
464	Billy Sample	.08
465	Mickey Rivers	.08
466	John Wathan	.08
467	Bill Krueger	.08
468	Andre Thornton	.12
469	Rex Hudler (R)	.35
470	Sid Bream (R)	.50
471	Kirk Gibson	.30
472	John Shelby	.08
473	Moose Haas	.08
474	Doug Corbett	.08
475	Willie McGee	.50
476	Bob Knepper	.12
477	Kevin Gross	.08
478	Carmelo Martinez	.12
479	Kent Tekulve	.08
480	Chili Davis	.12
481	Bobby Clark	.08
482	Mookie Wilson	.08
483	Dave Owen (R)	.15
484	Ed Nunez	.08
485	Rance Mulliniks	.08
486	Ken Schrom	.08
487	Jeff Russell	.08
488	Tom Paciorek	.08
489	Dan Ford	.08
490	Mike Caldwell	.08
491	Scottie Earl (R)	.15
492	Jose Rijo (R)	1.25
493	Bruce Hurst	.08
494	Ken Landreaux	.08
495	Mike Fischlin	.08
496	Don Slaught	.08
497	Steve McCatty	.08
498	Gary Lucas	.08
499	Gary Pettis	.10
500	Marvis Foley	.08
501	Mike Squires	.08
502	Jim Pankovitz	.12
503	Luis Aguayo	.08
504	Ralph Citarella	.12
505	Bruce Bochy	.08
506	Bob Owchinko	.08
507	Pascual Perez	.08
508	Lee Lacy	.08
509	Atlee Hammaker	.08
510	Bob Dernier	.08
511	Ed Vande Berg	.08
512	Cliff Johnson	.08
513	Len Whitehouse	.08
514	Dennis Martinez	.10
515	Ed Romero	.08
516	Rusty Kuntz	.08
517	Rick Miller	.08
518	Dennis Rasmussen	.10
519	Steve Yeager	.08
520	Chris Bando	.08
521	U.L. Washington	.08
522	Curt Young (R)	.35
523	Angel Salazar	.08
524	Curt Kaufman (R)	.15
525	Odell Jones	.08
526	Juan Agosto	.08
527	Denny Walling	.08
528	Andy Hawkins	.25
529	Sixto Lezcano	.08
530	Skeeter Barnes	.12
531	Randy Johnson	.08
532	Jim Morrison	.08
533	Warren Brusstar	.08
534	Jeff Pendleton	1.00
	(incorrect first name)	
534	Terry Pendleton	3.00
535	Vic Rodriguez (R)	.15
536	Bob McClure	.08
537	Dave Bergman	.08
538	Mark Clear	.08
539	Mike Pagliarulo (R)	1.00
540	Terry Whitfield	.08
541	Joe Beckwith	.08
542	Jeff Burroughs	.08
543	Dan Schatzeder	.08
544	Donnie Scott	.12
545	Jim Slaton	.08
546	Greg Luzinski	.10
547	Mark Salas (R)	.20
548	Dave Smith	.08
549	John Wockenfuss	.08
550	Frank Pastore	.08
551	Tim Flannery	.08
552	Rick Rhoden	.12
553	Mark Davis	.25
554	Jeff Dedmon (R)	.12
555	Gary Woods	.08
556	Danny Heep	.08
557	Mark Langston (R)	5.00
558	Darrell Brown	.08
559	Jimmy Key (R)	1.25
560	Rick Lysander	.08
561	Doyle Alexander	.08
562	Mike Stanton	.08
563	Sid Fernandez	.75
564	Richie Hebner	.08
565	Alex Trevino	.08
566	Brian Harper	.15
567	Dan Gladden (R)	.75
568	Luis Salazar	.08
569	Tom Foley	.08
570	Larry Andersen	.08
571	Danny Cox	.12
572	Joe Sambito	.08
573	Juan Beniquez	.08
574	Joel Skinner	.08
575	Randy St. Claire	.12
576	Floyd Rayford	.08
577	Roy Howell	.08
578	John Grubb	.08
579	Ed Jurak	.08
580	John Montefusco	.08
581	Orel Hershiser (R)	9.00
582	Tom Waddell (R)	.15
583	Mark Huismann	.08
584	Joe Morgan	.30
585	Jim Wohlford	.08
586	Dave Schmidt	.08
587	Jeff Kunkel	.15
588	Hal McRae	.08
589	Bill Almon	.08
590	Carmen Castillo	.08
591	Omar Moreno	.08
592	Ken Howell (R)	.20
593	Tom Brookens	.08
594	Joe Nolan	.08
595	Willie Lozado	.12
596	Tom Nieto	.15
597	Walt Terrell	.08
598	Al Oliver	.10
599	Shane Rawley	.08
600	Denny Gonzalez	.12
601	Mark Grant	.15
602	Mike Armstrong	.08
603	George Foster	.15
604	Davey Lopes	.12
605	Salome Barojas	.08
606	Roy Lee Jackson	.08
607	Pete Filson	.08
608	Duane Walker	.08
609	Glenn Wilson	.10
610	Rafael Santana (R)	.25
611	Roy Smith	.15
612	Ruppert Jones	.08
613	Joe Cowley	.08
614	Al Nipper (R)	.20
615	Gene Nelson	.08
616	Joe Carter	2.50
617	Ray Knight	.10
618	Chuck Rainey	.08
619	Dan Driessen	.08
620	Daryl Sconiers	.08
621	Bill Stein	.08
622	Roy Smalley	.08
623	Ed Lynch	.08
624	Jeff Stone (R)	.20
625	Bruce Berenyi	.08
626	Kelvin Chapman (R)	.15
627	Joe Price	.08
628	Steve Bedrosian	.12
629	Vic Mata	.15
630	Mike Krukow	.10
631	Phil Bradley (R)	1.00
632	Jim Gott	.08
633	Randy Bush	.08
634	Tom Browning (R)	2.00
635	Lou Gehrig Puzzle	.10
636	Reid Nichols	.08
637	Dan Pasqua (R)	.75
638	German Rivera	.12
639	Don Schulze	.10
640	Mike Jones	.10
641	Pete Rose (Mgr.)	1.00
642	Wade Rowdon	.10
643	Jerry Narron	.08
644	Darrell Miller	.15
645	Tim Hulett (R)	.15
646	Andy McGaffigan	.08
647	Kurt Bevacqua	.05
648	John Russell (R)	.15
649	Ron Robinson	.60
650	Donnie Moore	.08
651	Two For the Title:	5.00
	D. Winfield, D. Mattingly	
652	Tim Laudner	.08
653	Steve Farr	.50
—	Checklist (DK)	.10
—	Checklist No. 1	.08
—	Checklist No. 2	.08
—	Checklist No. 3	.08
—	Checklist No. 4	.08
—	Checklist No. 5	.08
—	Checklist No. 6	.08

Features the rookie cards of Jose Canseco and Fred McGriff. Donruss limited production. The *checklist* cards are *not* numbered.

NO. PLAYER	MINT	NO. PLAYER	MINT	NO. PLAYER	MINT	NO. PLAYER	MINT
No. 1 to 26—Diamond Kings		65 Chili Davis	.10	131 Carney Lansford	.10	197 Darryl Strawberry	3.00
1 Kirk Gibson (DK)	.35	66 Dale Murphy	.50	132 Vance Law	.07	198 Ron Cey	.10
2 Goose Gossage (DK)	.15	67 Ryne Sandberg	1.50	133 Dick Schofield	.07	199 Steve Bedrosian	.15
3 Willie McGee (DK)	.20	68 Gary Carter	.30	134 Wayne Tolleson	.07	200 Steve Kemp	.07
4 George Bell (DK)	.20	69 Alvin Davis	.25	135 Greg Walker	.10	201 Manny Trillo	.07
5 Tony Armas (DK)	.10	70 Kent Hrbek	.20	136 Denny Walling	.07	202 Garry Templeton	.07
6 Chili Davis (DK)	.10	71 George Bell	.30	137 Ozzie Virgil	.07	203 Dave Parker	.20
7 Cecil Cooper (DK)	.15	72 Kirby Puckett	4.00	138 Ricky Horton	.07	204 John Denny	.07
8 Mike Boddicker (DK)	.10	73 Lloyd Moseby	.10	139 LaMarr Hoyt	.10	205 Terry Pendleton	.07
9 Davey Lopes (DK)	.10	74 Bob Kearney	.07	140 Wayne Krenchicki	.07	206 Terry Puhl	.07
10 Bill Doran (DK)	.10	75 Dwight Gooden	2.00	141 Glenn Hubbard	.07	207 Bobby Grich	.07
11 Bret Saberhagen (DK)	.40	76 Gary Matthews	.07	142 Cecilio Guante	.07	208 Ozzie Guillen (R)	1.25
12 Brett Butler (DK)	.10	77 Rick Mahler	.07	143 Mike Krukow	.07	209 Jeff Reardon	.10
13 Harold Baines (DK)	.20	78 Benny Distefano	.07	144 Lee Smith	.07	210 Cal Ripken, Jr.	.60
14 Mike Davis (DK)	.10	79 Jeff Leonard	.07	145 Ed Nunez	.07	211 Bill Schroeder	.07
15 Tony Perez (DK)	.15	80 Kevin McReynolds	.40	146 Dave Stieb	.15	212 Dan Petry	.15
16 Willie Randolph (DK)	.10	81 Ron Oester	.07	147 Mike Smithson	.07	213 Jim Rice	.25
17 Bob Boone (DK)	.10	82 John Russell	.07	148 Ken Dixon	.07	214 Dave Righetti	.10
18 Orel Hershiser (DK)	.50	83 Tommy Herr	.10	149 Danny Darwin	.07	215 Fernando Valenzuela	.25
19 Johnny Ray (DK)	.10	84 Jerry Mumphrey	.07	150 Chris Pittaro	.15	216 Julio Franco	.30
20 Gary Ward (DK)	.10	85 Ron Romanick	.07	151 Bill Buckner	.10	217 Darryl Motley	.07
21 Rick Mahler (DK)	.10	86 Daryl Boston	.07	152 Mike Pagliarulo	.15	218 Dave Collins	.07
22 Phil Bradley (DK)	.20	87 Andre Dawson	.35	153 Bill Russell	.07	219 Tim Wallach	.10
23 Jerry Koosman (DK)	.10	88 Eddie Murray	.40	154 Brook Jacoby	.10	220 George Wright	.07
24 Tom Brunansky (DK)	.10	89 Dion James	.07	155 Pat Sheridan	.07	221 Tommy Dunbar	.07
25 Andre Dawson (DK)	.30	90 Chet Lemon	.07	156 Mike Gallego	.12	222 Steve Balboni	.07
26 Dwigt Gooden (DK)	1.00	91 Bob Stanley	.07	157 Jim Wohlford	.07	223 Jay Howell	.07
No. 27 to 46 (Rated Rookies)		92 Willie Randolph	.07	158 Gary Pettis	.10	224 Joe Carter	.50
27 Kal Daniels (R)	4.00	93 Mike Scioscia	.07	159 Toby Harrah	.07	225 Ed Whitson	.07
28 Fred McGriff (R)	15.00	94 Tom Waddell	.07	160 Rich Dotson	.07	226 Orel Hershiser	1.50
29 Cory Snyder (R)	2.00	95 Danny Jackson	.30	161 Bob Knepper	.07	227 Willie Hernandez	.15
30 Jose Guzman (R)	.25	96 Mike Davis	.07	162 Dave Dravecky	.07	228 Lee Lacy	.07
31 Ty Gainey (R)	.15	97 Mike Fitzgerald	.07	163 Greg Gross	.07	229 Rollie Fingers	.15
32 Johnny Abrego (R)	.15	98 Gary Ward	.07	164 Eric Davis	3.00	230 Bob Boone	.07
33 Andres Galarraga (R)	5.00	99 Pete O'Brien	.07	165 Gerald Perry	.20	231 Joaquin Andujar	.10
34 Dave Shipanoff (R)	.15	100 Bret Saberhagen	1.00	166 Rick Rhoden	.07	232 Craig Reynolds	.07
35 Mark McLemore (R)	.20	101 Alfredo Griffin	.07	167 Keith Moreland	.07	233 Shane Rawley	.07
36 Marty Clary (R)	.15	102 Brett Butler	.07	168 Jack Clark	.25	234 Eric Show	.07
37 Paul O'Neill (R)	3.00	103 Ron Guidry	.15	169 Storm Davis	.07	235 Jose DeLeon	.07
38 Danny Tartabull	1.00	104 Jerry Reuss	.07	170 Cecil Cooper	.15	236 Jose Uribe (R)	.30
39 Jose Canseco (R)	110.00	105 Jack Morris	.15	171 Alan Trammell	.25	237 Moose Haas	.07
40 Juan Nieves (R)	.30	106 Rick Dempsey	.07	172 Roger Clemens	5.00	238 Wally Backman	.07
41 Lance McCullers (R)	.35	107 Ray Burris	.07	173 Don Mattingly	5.00	239 Dennis Eckersley	.25
42 Rick Surhoff (R)	.15	108 Brian Downing	.07	174 Pedro Guerrero	.25	240 Mike Moore	.07
43 Todd Worrell (R)	.75	109 Willie McGee	.20	175 Willie Wilson	.15	241 Damaso Garcia	.07
44 Bob Kipper (R)	.20	110 Bill Doran	.07	176 Dwayne Murphy	.07	242 Tim Teufel	.07
45 John Habyan (R)	.15	111 Kent Tekulve	.07	177 Tim Raines	.30	243 Dave Concepcion	.07
46 Mike Woodard (R)	.15	112 Tony Gwynn	1.00	178 Larry Parrish	.07	244 Floyd Bannister	.07
47 Mike Boddicker	.10	113 Marvell Wynne	.07	179 Mike Witt	.10	245 Fred Lynn	.15
48 Robin Yount	.50	114 David Green	.07	180 Harold Baines	.20	246 Charlie Moore	.07
49 Lou Whitaker	.15	115 Jim Gantner	.07	181 Vince Coleman (R)	3.00	247 Walt Terrell	.07
50 Oil Can Boyd	.05	116 George Foster	.15	182 Jeff Heathcock (R)	.15	248 Dave Winfield	.30
51 Ricky Henderson	1.50	117 Steve Trout	.07	183 Steve Carlton	.50	249 Dwight Evans	.15
52 Mike Marshall	.10	118 Mark Langston	.50	184 Mario Soto	.10	250 Dennis Powell	.12
53 George Brett	.80	119 Tony Fernandez	.20	185 Goose Gossage	.15	251 Andre Thornton	.07
54 Dave Kingman	.10	120 John Butcher	.07	186 Johnny Ray	.10	252 Onix Concepcion	.07
55 Hubie Brooks	.10	121 Ron Robinson	.07	187 Dan Gladden	.07	253 Mike Heath	.07
56 Oddibe McDowell	.20	122 Dan Spillner	.07	188 Bob Horner	.15	254 David Palmer	.07
57 Doug DeCinces	.10	123 Mike Young	.15	189 Rick Sutcliffe	.15	255 Donnie Moore	.07
58 Britt Burns	.05	124 Paul Molitor	.20	190 Keith Hernandez	.25	256 Curtis Wilkerson	.07
59 Ozzie Smith	.35	125 Kirk Gibson	.30	191 Phil Bradley	.15	257 Julio Cruz	.07
60 Jose Cruz	.10	126 Ken Griffey	.07	192 Tom Brunansky	.20	258 Nolan Ryan	1.50
61 Mike Schmidt	1.50	127 Tony Armas	.10	193 Jesse Barfield	.25	259 Jeff Stone	.07
62 Pete Rose	.75	128 Mariano Duncan (R)	.50	194 Frank Viola	.50	260 John Tudor	.15
63 Steve Garvey	.35	129 Pat Tabler	.07	195 Willie Upshaw	.10	261 Mark Thurmond	.07
64 Tony Pena	.10	130 Frank White	.07	196 Jim Beattie	.07	262 Jay Tibbs	.07

NO.	PLAYER	MINT
263	Rafael Ramirez	.07
264	Larry McWilliams	.07
265	Mark Davis	.07
266	Bob Dernier	.07
267	Matt Young	.07
268	Jim Clancy	.07
269	Mickey Hatcher	.07
270	Sammy Stewart	.07
271	Bob Gibson	.07
272	Nelson Simmons (R)	.15
273	Rich Gedman	.07
274	Butch Wynegar	.07
275	Ken Howell	.07
276	Mel Hall	.07
277	Jim Sundberg	.07
278	Chris Codiroli	.07
279	H. Winningham (R)	.15
280	Rod Carew	.35
281	Don Slaught	.07
282	Scott Fletcher	.07
283	Bill Dawley	.07
284	Andy Hawkins	.07
285	Glenn Wilson	.10
286	Nick Esasky	.07
287	Claudell Washington	.07
288	Lee Mazzilli	.07
289	Jody Davis	.07
290	Darrell Porter	.07
291	Scott McGregor	.07
292	Ted Simmons	.10
293	Aurelio Lopez	.07
294	Marty Barrett	.07
295	Dale Berra	.07
296	Greg Brock	.07
297	Charlie Leibrandt	.07
298	Bill Krueger	.07
299	Bryn Smith	.07
300	Burt Hooton	.07
301	Stu Cliburn (R)	.15
302	Luis Salazar	.07
303	Ken Dayley	.07
304	Frank DiPino	.07
305	Von Hayes	.15
306	Gary Redus	.07
307	Craig Lefferts	.07
308	Sam Khalifa	.15
309	Scott Garrelts	.07
310	Rick Cerone	.07
311	Shawon Dunston	.75
312	Howard Johnson	.60
313	Jim Presley	.15
314	Gary Gaetti	.25
315	Luis Leal	.07
316	Mark Salas	.07
317	Bill Caudill	.07
318	Dave Henderson	.07
319	Rafael Santana	.07
320	Leon Durham	.15
321	Bruce Sutter	.15
322	Jason Thompson	.07
323	Bob Brenly	.07
324	Carmelo Martinez	.07
325	Eddie Milner	.07
326	Juan Samuel	.15
327	Tom Nieto	.07
328	Dave Smith	.07
329	Urbano Lugo (R)	.15
330	Joel Skinner	.07
331	Bill Gullickson	.07
332	Floyd Rayford	.07
333	Ben Oglivie	.07
334	Lance Parrish	.15
335	Jackie Gutierrez	.07
336	Dennis Rasmussen	.07
337	Terry Whitfield	.07
338	Neal Heaton	.07
339	Jorge Orta	.07
340	Donnie Hill	.07
341	Joe Hesketh	.10
342	Charlie Hough	.07
343	Dave Rozema	.07
344	Greg Pryor	.07
345	Mickey Tettleton (R)	.50
346	George Vukovich	.07
347	Don Baylor	.10
348	Carlos Diaz	.07
349	Barbaro Garbey	.07
350	Larry Sheets	.15
351	Teddy Higuera (R)	1.50
352	Juan Beniquez	.07
353	Bob Forsch	.07
354	Mark Bailey	.07
355	Larry Andersen	.07
356	Terry Kennedy	.07
357	Don Robinson	.07
358	Jim Gott	.07
359	Earnest Riles (R)	.15
360	John Christensen	.15
361	Ray Fontenot	.07
362	Spike Owen	.07
363	Jim Acker	.07
364	Ron Davis	.07
365	Tom Hume	.07
366	Carlton Fisk	.35
367	Nate Snell (R)	.15
368	Rick Manning	.07
369	Darrell Evans	.10
370	Ron Hassey	.07
371	Wade Boggs	2.50
372	Rick Honeycutt	.07
373	Chris Bando	.07
374	Bud Black	.07
375	Steve Henderson	.07
376	Charlie Lea	.07
377	Reggie Jackson	.60
378	Dave Schmidt	.07
379	Bob James	.07
380	Glenn Davis	4.00
381	Tim Corcoran	.07
382	Danny Cox	.10
383	Tim Flannery	.07
384	Tom Browning	.15
385	Rick Camp	.07
386	Jim Morrison	.07
387	Dave LaPoint	.07
388	Davey Lopes	.07
389	Al Cowens	.07
390	Doyle Alexander	.07
391	Tim Laudner	.07
392	Don Aase	.07
393	Jaime Cocanower	.07
394	Randy O'Neal	.07
395	Mike Easler	.07
396	Scott Bradley	.07
397	Tom Niedenfuer	.07
398	Jerry Willard	.07
399	Lonnie Smith	.10
400	Bruce Bochte	.07
401	Terry Francona	.07
402	Jim Slaton	.07
403	Bill Stein	.07
404	Timmy Hulett	.07
405	Alan Ashby	.07
406	Tim Stoddard	.07
407	Garry Maddox	.07
408	Ted Power	.07
409	Len Barker	.07
410	Denny Gonzalez	.07
411	George Frazier	.07
412	Andy Van Slyke	.30
413	Jim Dwyer	.07
414	Paul Householder	.07
415	Alejandro Sanchez	.07
416	Steve Crawford	.07
417	Dan Pasqua	.15
418	Enos Cabell	.07
419	Mike Jones	.07
420	Mike Kiefer	.07
421	Tim Burke (R)	.30
422	Mike Mason	.07
423	Ruppert Jones	.07
424	Jerry Hairston	.07
425	Tito Landrum	.07
426	Jeff Calhoun (R)	.12
427	Don Carman (R)	.25
428	Tony Perez	.15
429	Jerry Davis	.07
430	Bob Walk	.07
431	Brad Wellman	.07
432	Terry Forster	.07
433	Billy Hatcher	.15
434	Clint Hurdle	.07
435	Ivan Calderon (R)	1.00
436	Pete Filson	.07
437	Tom Henke	.10
438	Dave Engle	.07
439	Tom Filer	.07
440	Gorman Thomas	.10
441	Rick Aguilera (R)	.35
442	Scott Sanderson	.07
443	Jeff Dedmon	.07
444	Joe Orsulak (R)	.25
445	Atlee Hammaker	.07
446	Jerry Royster	.07
447	Buddy Bell	.10
448	Dave Rucker	.07
449	Ivan DeJesus	.07
450	Jim Pankovits	.07
451	Jerry Narron	.07
452	Bryan Little	.07
453	Gary Lucas	.07
454	Dennis Martinez	.07
455	Ed Romero	.07
456	Bob Melvin (R)	.12
457	Glenn Hoffman	.07
458	Bob Shirley	.07
459	Bob Welch	.07
460	Carmen Castillo	.07
461	Dave Leeper (R)	.12
462	Tim Birtsas (R)	.15
463	Randy St. Claire	.07
464	Chris Welsh	.07
465	Greg Harris	.07
466	Lynn Jones	.07
467	Dusty Baker	.07
468	Roy Smith	.07
469	Andre Robertson	.07
470	Ken Landreaux	.07
471	Dave Bergman	.07
472	Gary Roenicke	.07
473	Pete Vuckovich	.07
474	Kirk McCaskill (R)	.50
475	Jeff Lahti	.07
476	Mike Scott	.35
477	Darren Daulton (R)	.50
478	Graig Nettles	.10
479	Bill Almon	.07
480	Greg Minton	.07
481	Randy Ready	.07
482	Len Dykstra (R)	4.00
483	Thad Bosley	.07
484	Harold Reynolds (R)	.60
485	Al Oliver	.10
486	Roy Smalley	.07
487	John Franco	.25
488	Juan Agosto	.07
489	Al Pardo	.15
490	Bill Wegman (R)	.15
491	Frank Tanana	.07
492	Brian Fisher (R)	.20
493	Mark Clear	.07
494	Len Matuszek	.07
495	Ramon Romero (R)	.10
496	John Wathan	.07
497	Rob Picciolo	.07
498	U.L. Washington	.07
499	John Candelaria	.07
500	Duane Walker	.07
501	Gene Nelson	.07
502	John Mizerock	.07
503	Luis Aguayo	.07
504	Kurt Kepshire	.07
505	Ed Wojna (R)	.15
506	Joe Price	.07
507	Milt Thompson (R)	.30
508	Junior Ortiz	.07
509	Vida Blue	.07
510	Steve Engel (R)	.10
511	Karl Best (R)	.10
512	Cecil Fielder (R)	15.00
513	Frank Eufemia (R)	.15
514	Tippy Martinez	.07
515	Billy Robidoux (R)	.20
516	Bill Scherrer	.07
517	Bruce Hurst	.10
518	Rich Bordi	.07
519	Steve Yeager	.07
520	Tony Bernazard	.07
521	Hal McRae	.07
522	Jose Rijo	.07
523	Mitch Webster (R)	.25
524	Jack Howell (R)	.35
525	Alan Bannister	.07
526	Ron Kittle	.10
527	Phil Garner	.07
528	Kurt Bevacqua	.07
529	Kevin Gross	.07
530	Bo Diaz	.07
531	Ken Oberkfell	.07
532	Rick Reuschel	.07
533	Ron Meridith (R)	.15
534	Steve Braun	.07
535	Wayne Gross	.07
536	Ray Searage	.07
537	Tom Brookens	.07
538	Al Nipper	.07
539	Billy Sample	.07
540	Steve Sax	.20
541	Dan Quisenberry	.15
542	Tony Phillips	.07
543	Floyd Youmans (R)	.25
544	Steve Buechele (R)	.25
545	Craig Gerber (R)	.10
546	Joe DeSa (R)	.15
547	Brian Harper	.10
548	Kevin Bass	.07
549	Tom Foley	.07
550	Dave Van Gorder	.07
551	Bruce Bochy	.07
552	R.J. Reynolds	.07
553	Chris Brown (R)	.20
554	Bruce Benedict	.07
555	Warren Brusstar	.07
556	Danny Heep	.07
557	Darnell Coles	.07
558	Greg Gagne	.07
559	Ernie Whitt	.07
560	Ron Washington	.07
561	Jimmy Key	.15
562	Billy Swift	.07
563	Ron Darling	.25
564	Dick Ruthven	.07
565	Zane Smith	.40
566	Sid Bream	.07
567	Joel Youngblood	.07
568	Mario Ramirez	.07
569	Tom Runnells (R)	.10
570	Rick Schu	.07
571	Bill Campbell	.07
572	Dickie Thon	.07
573	Al Holland	.07
574	Reid Nichols	.07
575	Bert Roberge	.07
576	Mike Flanagan	.07
577	Tim Leary	.35
578	Mike Laga	.07
579	Steve Lyons	.07
580	Phil Niekro	.20
581	Gilberto Reyes (R)	.15
582	Jamie Easterly	.07
583	Mark Gubicza	.15
584	Stan Javier (R)	.40
585	Bill Laskey	.07
586	Jeff Russell	.07
587	Dickie Noles	.07
588	Steve Farr	.07
589	Steve Ontiveros (R)	.15
590	Mike Hargrove	.07
591	Marty Bystrom	.07
592	Franklin Stubbs	.10
593	Larry Herndon	.07
594	Bill Swaggerty	.07
595	Carlos Ponce (R)	.10
596	Pat Perry (R)	.10
597	Ray Knight	.15
598	Steve Lombardozzi (R)	.15
599	Brad Havens	.07
600	Pat Clements (R)	.20
601	Joe Niekro	.10
602	Hank Aaron Puzzle	.15

1986 Donruss (Continued)

NO. PLAYER	MINT
603 Dwayne Henry (R)	.10
604 Mookie Wilson	.07
605 Buddy Biancalana	.07
606 Rance Mulliniks	.07
607 Alan Wiggins	.07
608 Joe Cowley	.07
609 Tom Seaver	.50
610 Neil Allen	.07
611 Don Sutton	.20
612 Fred Toliver (R)	.15
613 Jay Baller (R)	.15
614 Marc Sullivan (R)	.10
615 John Grubb	.07
616 Bruce Kison	.07
617 Bill Madlock	.10
618 Chris Chambliss	.07
619 Dave Stewart	.50
620 Tim Lollar	.07
621 Gary Lavelle	.07

NO. PLAYER	MINT
622 Charles Hudson	.07
623 Joel Davis (R)	.15
624 Joe Johnson (R)	.15
625 Sid Fernandez	.15
626 Dennis Lamp	.07
627 Terry Harper	.07
628 Jack Lazorko	.07
629 Roger McDowell (R)	.50
630 Mark Funderburk (R)	.20
631 Ed Lynch	.07
632 Rudy Law	.07
633 Roger Mason (R)	.15
634 Mike Felder (R)	.15
635 Ken Schrom	.07
636 Bob Ojeda	.07
637 Ed Vande Berg	.07
638 Bobby Meacham	.07
639 Cliff Johnson	.07

NO. PLAYER	MINT
640 Garth Iorg	.07
641 Dan Driessen	.07
642 Mike Brown	.07
643 John Shelby	.07
644 Pete Rose Ty-Breaking Hit #4192:	.30
645 Knuckle Brothers: Phil and Joe Niekro	.10
646 Jesse Orosco	.07
647 Billy Beane (R)	.15
648 Cesar Cedeno	.07
649 Bert Blyleven	.10
650 Max Venable	.07
651 Fleet Feet: W. McGee, V. Coleman	.30
652 Calvin Schiraldi	.07
653 King of Kings: Pete Rose	.75

NO. PLAYER	MINT
— Checklist (DK)	.08
— Checklist No. 1	.08
— Checklist No. 2	.08
— Checklist No. 3	.08
— Checklist No. 4	.08
— Checklist No. 5	.08
— Checklist No. 6	.08

1986 Donruss Rookies. . . . Complete Set of 56 Cards—Value $50.00

Features the outstanding rookies of the 1986 season. The cards are coated with a glossy finish. The entire set was packaged in a printed box, and distributed exclusively through card hobby dealers.

NO. PLAYER	MINT
1 Wally Joyner (RR)	3.50
2 Tracy Jones	.30
3 Allan Anderson	.40
4 Ed Correa	.15
5 Reggie Williams	.15
6 Charlie Kerfeld	.15
7 Andres Galarraga	1.00
8 Bob Tewksbury	.20
9 Al Newman	.15
10 Andres Thomas	.15
11 Barry Bonds (RR)	5.00
12 Juan Nieves	.10
13 Mark Eichhorn	.15
14 Dan Plesac	.25

NO. PLAYER	MINT
15 Cory Snyder	1.00
16 Kelly Gruber	2.00
17 Kevin Mitchell (RR)	7.50
18 Steve Lombardozzi	.15
19 Mitch Williams	.50
20 John Cerutti	.25
21 Todd Worrell	.45
22 Jose Canseco	12.00
23 Pete Incaviglia (RR)	1.00
24 Jose Guzman	.15
25 Scott Bailes	.15
26 Greg Matthews	.25
27 Eric King	.35
28 Paul Assenmacher	.15

NO. PLAYER	MINT
29 Jeff Sellers	.20
30 Bobby Bonilla (RR)	5.00
31 Doug Drabek	2.00
32 Will Clark (RR)	10.00
33 Leon "Bip" Roberts	.50
34 Jim Deshaies	.35
35 Mike Lavalliere	.30
36 Scott Bankhead	.30
37 Dale Sveum	.20
38 Bo Jackson (RR)	13.00
39 Rob Thompson	.40
40 Eric Plunk	.15
41 Bill Bathe	.20
42 John Kruk	.50

NO. PLAYER	MINT
43 Andy Allanson	.15
44 Mark Portugal	.20
45 Danny Tartabull	.75
46 Bob Kpper	.15
47 Gene Walter	.15
48 Rey Quinonez	.15
49 Bobby Witt	1.25
50 Bill Mooneyham	.15
51 John Cangelos	.15
52 Ruben Sierra (RR)	6.00
53 Rob Woodward	.15
54 Ed Hearn	.15
55 Joel McKeon	.15
56 Checklist	.20

1987 Donruss.... Complete Set of 660 Cards—Value $75.00 (Factory-Sealed set—Value-$90.00)

Features the rookie cards of Bo Jackson, Wally Joyner, Kevin Mitchell, Will Clark, Ruben Sierra and Mike Greenwell. Donruss limited production. Cards 14, 22 and 25 exist with the "yellow" strip missing on back—worth triple the value of the corrected cards.

NO.	PLAYER	MINT
No. 1 to 26—Diamond Kings		
1	Wally Joyner (DK)	.75
2	Roger Clemens (DK)	.75
3	Dale Murphy (DK)	.40
4	Darryl Strawberry (DK)	.60
5	Ozzie Smith (DK)	.10
6	Jose Canseco (DK)	1.50
7	Charlie Hough (DK)	.10
8	Brook Jacoby (DK)	.10
9	Fred Lynn (DK)	.15
10	Rick Rhoden (DK)	.10
11	Chris Brown (DK)	.15
12	Von Hayes (DK)	.10
13	Jack Morris (DK)	.20
14	K. McReynolds (DK)	.35
14	McReynolds (error)	1.00
15	George Brett (DK)	.35
16	Ted Higuera (DK)	.20
17	Hubie Brooks (DK)	.10
18	Mike Scott (DK)	.20
19	Kirby Puckett (DK)	.45
20	Dave Winfield (DK)	.25
21	Lloyd Moseby (DK)	.10
22	Eric Davis (DK)	1.00
22	E. Davis (error)	2.50
23	Jim Presley (DK)	.15
24	Keith Moreland (DK)	.10
25	Greg Walker (DK)	.15
26	St. Sax (DK)	.20
27	Checklist	.10
No. 28 to 47—Rated Rookies		
28	B.J. Surhoff (R)	.50
29	Randy Myers (R)	.50
30	Ken Gerhart (R)	.20
31	Benito Santiago	2.00
32	Greg Swindell (R)	1.25
33	Mike Birkbeck (R)	.20
34	Terry Steinbach (R)	.75
35	Bo Jackson (R)	10.00
36	Greg Maddux (R)	1.25
37	Jim Lindeman (R)	.20
38	Devon White (R)	.75
39	Eric Bell (R)	.15
40	Will Fraser (R)	.20
41	Jerry Browne (R)	.40
42	Chris James (R)	.75
43	Rafael Palmeiro (R)	3.00
44	Pat Dodson (R)	.20
45	Duane Ward (R)	.25
46	Mark McGwire	8.00
47	Bruce Fields (R)	.15
48	Eddie Murray	.30
49	Ted Higuera	.20
50	Kirk Gibson	.25
51	Oil Can Boid	.10
52	Don Mattingly	2.00
53	Pedro Guerrero	.20
54	George Brett	.50
55	Jose Rijo	.05
56	Tim Raines	.25
57	Ed Correa (R)	.20
58	Mike Witt	.10
59	Greg Walker	.05
60	Ozzie Smith	.25
61	Glenn Davis	.35
62	Glenn Wilson	.10
63	Tom Browning	.05
64	Tony Gwynn	.50

NO.	PLAYER	MINT
65	R.J. Reynolds	.05
66	Will Clark (R)	10.00
67	Ozzie Virgil	.05
68	Rick Sutcliffe	.10
69	Gary Carter	.25
70	Mike Moore	.05
71	Bert Blyleven	.05
72	Tony Fernandez	.15
73	Kent Hrbek	.15
74	Lloyd Moseby	.10
75	Alvin Davis	.10
76	Keith Hernandez	.25
77	Ryne Sandberg	.60
78	Dale Murphy	.40
79	Sid Bream	.05
80	Chris Brown	.15
81	Steve Garvey	.30
82	Mario Soto	.05
83	Shane Rawley	.05
84	Willie McGee	.20
85	Jose Cruz	.12
86	Brian Downing	.05
87	Ozzie Guillen	.20
88	Hubie Brooks	.12
89	Cal Ripken	.30
90	Juan Nieves	.10
91	Lance Parrish	.20
92	Jim Rice	.25
93	Ron Guidry	.15
94	Fernando Valenzuela	.25
95	Andy Allanson (R)	.15
96	Willie Wilson	.15
97	Jose Canseco	10.00
98	Jeff Reardon	.05
99	Bobby Witt (R)	.60
100	Checklist: 28 to 133	.10
101	Jose Guzman	.20
102	Steve Balboni	.10
103	Tony Phillips	.05
104	Brook Jacoby	.10
105	Dave Winfield	.25
106	Orel Hershiser	.30
107	Lou Whitaker	.15
108	Fred Lynn	.15
109	Bill Wegman	.05
110	Donnie Moore	.05
111	Jack Clark	.20
112	Bob Knepper	.05
113	Von Hayes	.10
114	"Bip" Roberts (R)	.50
115	Tony Pena	.12
116	Scott Garrelts	.05
117	Paul Molitor	.15
118	Darryl Strawberry	.75
119	Shawon Dunston	.25
120	Jim Presley	.20
121	Jesse Barfield	.20
122	Gary Gaetti	.20
123	Kurt Stillwell (R)	.40
124	Joel Davis	.05
125	Mike Boddicker	.05
126	Robin Yount	.45
127	Alan Trammell	.20
128	Dave Righetti	.15
129	Dwight Evans	.15
130	Mike Scioscia	.05

NO.	PLAYER	MINT
131	Julio Franco	.12
132	Bret Saberhagen	.30
133	Mike Davis	.05
134	Joe Hesketh	.05
135	Wally Joyner (R)	1.50
136	Don Slaught	.05
137	Daryl Boston	.05
138	Nolan Ryan	1.00
139	Mike Schmidt	.75
140	Tommy Herr	.05
141	Garry Templeton	.05
142	Kal Daniels	.75
143	Billy Sample	.05
144	Johnny Ray	.12
145	Rob Thompson (R)	.30
146	Bob Dernier	.05
147	Danny Tartabull	.25
148	Ernie Whitt	.05
149	Kirby Puckett	1.25
150	Mike Young	.05
151	Ernest Riles	.15
152	Frank Tanana	.05
153	Rich Gedman	.05
154	Willie Randolph	.08
155	Bill Madlock	.15
156	Joe Carter	.25
157	Danny Jackson	.20
158	Carney Lansford	.05
159	Bryn Smith	.05
160	Gary Pettis	.05
161	Oddibe McDowell	.15
162	John Cangelosi (R)	.12
163	Mike Scott	.20
164	Eric Show	.05
165	Juan Samuel	.12
166	Nick Esasky	.05
167	Zane Smith	.05
168	Mike Brown	.05
169	Keith Moreland	.05
170	John Tudor	.10
171	Ken Dixon	.05
172	Jim Gantner	.05
173	Jack Morris	.15
174	Bruce Hurst	.10
175	Dennis Rasmussen	.12
176	Mike Marshall	.10
177	Dan Quisenberry	.12
178	Eric Plunk	.10
179	Tim Wallach	.05
180	Steve Buechele	.05
181	Don Sutton	.15
182	Dave Schmidt	.05
183	Terry Pendleton	.05
184	Jim Deshaies (R)	.25
185	Steve Bedrosian	.15
186	Pete Rose (Mgr.)	.50
187	Dave Dravecky	.05
188	Rick Reuschel	.05
189	Dan Gladden	.05
190	Rick Mahler	.05
191	Thad Bosley	.05
192	Ron Darling	.20
193	Matt Young	.05
194	Tom Brunansky	.20
195	Dave Stieb	.15
196	Frank Viola	.25

NO.	PLAYER	MINT
197	Tom Henke	.10
198	Karl Best	.05
199	Dwight Gooden	.75
200	Checklist: 134-209	.08
201	Steve Trout	.05
202	Rafael Ramirez	.05
203	Bob Walk	.05
204	Roger Mason	.05
205	Terry Kennedy	.05
206	Ron Oester	.05
207	John Russell	.05
208	Greg Mathews (R)	.20
209	Charlie Kerfeld	.10
210	Reggie Jackson	.50
211	Floyd Bannister	.05
212	Vance Law	.05
213	Rich Bordi	.05
214	Dan Plesac (R)	.20
215	Dave Collins	.05
216	Bob Stanley	.05
217	Joe Niekro	.10
218	Tom Niedenfuer	.05
219	Brett Butler	.05
220	Charlie Leibrandt	.05
221	Steve Ontiveros	.05
222	Tim Burke	.05
223	Curtis Wilkerson	.05
224	Pete Incaviglia (R)	.75
225	Lonnie Smith	.05
226	Chris Codiroli	.05
227	Scott Bailes (R)	.15
228	Rickey Henderson	.75
229	Ken Howell	.05
230	Darnell Coles	.08
231	Don Aase	.05
232	Tim Leary	.05
233	Bob Boone	.05
234	Ricky Horton	.05
235	Mark Bailey	.05
236	Kevin Gross	.05
237	Lance McCullers	.10
238	Cecilio Guante	.05
239	Bob Melvin	.05
240	Billy Jo Robidoux	.12
241	Roger McDowell	.15
242	Leon Durham	.10
243	Ed Nunez	.05
244	Jimmy Key	.10
245	Mike Smithson	.05
246	Bo Diaz	.05
247	Carlton Fisk	.25
248	Larry Sheets	.15
249	Juan Castillo	.12
250	Eric King (R)	.25
251	Doug Drabek (R)	1.50
252	Wade Boggs	1.00
253	Mariano Duncan	.10
254	Pat Tabler	.05
255	Frank White	.05
256	Alfredo Griffin	.05
257	Floyd Youmans	.15
258	Rob Wilfong	.05
259	Pete O'Brien	.08
260	Tim Hulett	.05
261	Dickie Thon	.05
262	Darren Daulton	.05

NO.	PLAYER	MINT
263	Vince Coleman	.40
264	Andy Hawkins	.05
265	Eric Davis	1.00
266	Andres Thomas (R)	.20
267	Mike Diaz (R)	.15
268	Chili Davis	.10
269	Jody Davis	.05
270	Phil Bradley	.10
271	George Bell	.25
272	Keith Atherton	.05
273	Storm Davis	.08
274	Rob Deer	.15
275	Walt Terrell	.05
276	Roger Clemens	1.25
277	Mike Easler	.05
278	Steve Sax	.15
279	Andre Thornton	.05
280	Jim Sundberg	.05
281	Bill Bathe (R)	.15
282	Jay Tibbs	.05
283	Dick Schofield	.05
284	Mike Mason	.05
285	Jerry Hairston	.05
286	Bill Doran	.05
287	Tim Flannery	.05
288	Gary Redus	.05
289	John Franco	.05
290	P. Assenmacher (R)	.15
291	Joe Orsulak	.05
292	Lee Smith	.05
293	Mike Laga	.05
294	Rick Dempsey	.05
295	Mike Felder	.05
296	Tom Brookens	.05
297	Al Nipper	.05
298	Mike Pagliarulo	.15
299	Franklin Stubbs	.15
300	Checklist: 240-345	.08
301	Steve Farr	.05
302	Bill Mooneyham (R)	.15
303	Andres Galarraga	.25
304	Scott Fletcher	.05
305	Jack Howell	.05
306	Russ Morman (R)	.15
307	Todd Worrell	.15
308	Dave Smith	.05
309	Jeff Stone	.05
310	Ron Robinson	.05
311	Bruce Bochy	.05
312	Jim Winn	.08
313	Mark Davis	.05
314	Jeff Dedmon	.05
315	Jamie Moyer (R)	.15
316	Wally Backman	.05
317	Ken Phelps	.05
318	Steve Lombardozzi	.12
319	Rance Mulliniks	.05
320	Tim Laudner	.05
321	Mark Eichhorn (R)	.15
322	Lee Guetterman (R)	.15
323	Sid Fernandez	.15
324	Jerry Mumphrey	.05
325	David Palmer	.05
326	Bill Almon	.05
327	Candy Maldonado	.10
328	John Kruk (R)	.30
329	John Denny	.05
330	Milt Thompson	.05
331	Mike LaValliere (R)	.25
332	Alan Ashby	.05
333	Doug Corbett	.05
334	Ron Karkovice (R)	.15
335	Mitch Webster	.05
336	Lee Lacy	.05
337	Glenn Braggs (R)	.50
338	Dwight Lowry (R)	.15
339	Don Baylor	.15
340	Brian Fisher	.05
341	Reggie Williams (R)	.15
342	Tom Candiotti	.05
343	Rudy Law	.05
344	Curt Young	.05
345	Mike Fitzgerald	.05
346	Ruben Sierra (R)	6.00
347	Mitch Williams (R)	.40
348	Jorge Orta	.05
349	Mickey Tettleton	.15
350	Ernie Camacho	.05
351	Ron Kittle	.10
352	Ken Landreaux	.05
353	Chet Lemon	.08
354	John Shelby	.05
355	Mark Clear	.05
356	Doug DeCinces	.08
357	Ken Kayley	.05
358	Phil Garner	.05
359	Steve Jeltz	.05
360	Ed Whitson	.05
361	Barry Bonds (R)	6.00
362	Vida Blue	.08
363	Cecil Cooper	.10
364	Bob Ojeda	.15
365	Dennis Eckersley	.08
366	Mike Morgan	.05
367	Willie Upshaw	.05
368	Allan Anderson (R)	.25
369	Bill Gullickson	.05
370	Bobby Thigpen (R)	1.25
371	Juan Beniquez	.05
372	Charlie Moore	.05
373	Dan Petry	.08
374	Rod Scurry	.05
375	Tom Seaver	.35
376	Ed Vande Berg	.05
377	Tony Bernazard	.05
378	Greg Pryor	.05
379	Dwayne Murphy	.05
380	Andy McGaffigan	.05
381	Kirk McCaskill	.10
382	Greg Harris	.05
383	Rich Dotson	.05
384	Craig Reynolds	.05
385	Greg Gross	.05
386	Tito Landrum	.05
387	Craig Lefferts	.05
388	Dave Parker	.20
389	Bob Horner	.15
390	Pat Clements	.05
391	Jeff Leonard	.10
392	Chris Speier	.05
393	John Moses	.15
394	Garth Iorg	.05
395	Greg Gagne	.05
396	Nate Snell	.05
397	Bryan Clutterbuck (R)	.15
398	Darrell Evans	.12
399	Steve Crawford	.05
400	Checklist: 346-451	.08
401	Phil Lombardi (R)	.15
402	Rick Honeycutt	.05
403	Ken Schrom	.05
404	Bud Black	.05
405	Donnie Hill	.05
406	Wayne Krenchicki	.05
407	Chuck Finley (R)	1.25
408	Toby Harrah	.05
409	Steve Lyons	.05
410	Kevin Bass	.10
411	Marvell Wynne	.05
412	Ron Roenicke	.05
413	Tracy Jones (R)	.20
414	Gene Garber	.05
415	Mike Bielecki	.05
416	Frank DiPino	.05
417	Andy Van Slyke	.15
418	Jim Dwyer	.05
419	Ben Oglivie	.05
420	Dave Bergman	.05
421	Joe Sambito	.05
422	Bob Tewksbury (R)	.20
423	Len Matuszek	.05
424	Mike Kingery (R)	.15
425	Dave Kingman	.10
426	Al Newman (R)	.15
427	Gary Ward	.05
428	Ruppert Jones	.05
429	Harold Baines	.12
430	Pat Perry	.05
431	Terry Puhl	.05
432	Don Carman	.05
433	Eddie Milner	.05
434	LaMarr Hoyt	.05
435	Rick Rhoden	.05
436	Jose Uribe	.05
437	Ken Oberkfell	.05
438	Ron Davis	.05
439	Jesse Orosco	.08
440	Scott Bradley	.05
441	Randy Bush	.05
442	John Cerutti (R)	.20
443	Roy Smalley	.05
444	Kelly Gruber	1.50
445	Bob Kearney	.05
446	Ed Hearn (R)	.15
447	Scott Sanderson	.05
448	Bruce Benedict	.05
449	Junior Ortiz	.05
450	Mike Aldrete (R)	.20
451	Kevin McReynolds	.25
452	Rob Murphy (R)	.20
453	Kent Tekulve	.05
454	Curt Ford	.12
455	Davey Lopes	.08
456	Bobby Grich	.05
457	Jose DeLeon	.05
458	Andre Dawson	.35
459	Mike Flanagan	.05
460	Joey Meyer (R)	.25
461	Chuck Cary (R)	.20
462	Bill Buckner	.08
463	Bob Shirley	.05
464	Jeff Hamilton (R)	.20
465	Phil Niekro	.20
466	Mark Gubicza	.05
467	Jerry Willard	.05
468	Bob Sebra (R)	.15
469	Larry Parrish	.05
470	Charlie Hough	.05
471	Hal McRae	.05
472	Dave Leiper	.12
473	Mel Hall	.05
474	Dan Pasqua	.15
475	Bob Welch	.05
476	Johnny Grubb	.05
477	Jim Traber	.12
478	Chris Bosio (R)	.30
479	Mark McLemore	.08
480	John Morris	.05
481	Billy Hatcher	.05
482	Dan Schatzeder	.05
483	Rich Gossage	.12
484	Jim Morrison	.05
485	Bob Brenly	.05
486	Bill Schroeder	.05
487	Mookie Wilson	.05
488	Dave Martinez	.25
489	Harold Reynolds	.05
490	Jeff Hearron	.15
491	Mickey Hatcher	.05
492	Barry Larkin (R)	5.00
493	Bob James	.05
494	John Habyan	.05
495	Jim Adduci (R)	.15
496	Mike Heath	.05
497	Tim Stoddard	.05
498	Tony Armas	.08
499	Dennis Powell	.05
500	Checklist: 452-557	.08
501	Chris Bando	.05
502	David Cone (R)	3.00
503	Jay Howell	.05
504	Tom Foley	.05
505	Ray Chadwick (R)	.15
506	Mike Loynd (R)	.15
507	Neil Allen	.05
508	Danny Darwin	.05
509	Rick Schu	.05
510	Jose Oquendo	.05
511	Gene Walter	.10
512	Terry McGriff (R)	.15
513	Ken Griffey	.08
514	Benny Distefano	.05
515	Terry Mulholland (R)	.25
516	Ed Lynch	.05
517	Bill Swift	.05
518	Manny Lee	.05
519	Andre David	.05
520	Scott McGregor	.05
521	Rick Manning	.05
522	Willie Hernandez	.05
523	Marty Barrett	.10
524	Wayne Tolleson	.05
525	Jose Gonzalez (R)	.20
526	Cory Snyder	.35
527	Buddy Biancalana	.05
528	Moose Haas	.05
529	Wilfredo Tejada (R)	.15
530	Stu Cliburn	.05
531	Dale Mohorcic (R)	.15
532	Ron Hassey	.05
533	Ty Gainey	.05
534	Jerry Royster	.05
535	Mike Maddux (R)	.20
536	Ted Power	.05
537	Ted Simmons	.08
538	Rafael Belliard (R)	.15
539	Chico Walker (R)	.15
540	Bob Forsch	.05
541	John Stefero	.05
542	Dale Sveum (R)	.20
543	Mark Thurmond	.05
544	Jeff Sellers (R)	.20
545	Joel Skinner	.05
546	Alex Trevino	.05
547	Randy Kutcher (R)	.15
548	Joaquin Andujar	.05
549	Casey Candaele (R)	.15
550	Jeff Russell	.05
551	John Candelaria	.08
552	Joe Cowley	.05
553	Danny Cox	.05
554	Denny Walling	.05
555	Bruce Ruffin (R)	.20
556	Buddy Bell	.10
557	Jimmy Jones (R)	.20
558	Bobby Bonilla (R)	6.00
559	Jeff Robinson	.05
560	Ed Olwine (R)	.15
561	Glenallen Hill (R)	.75
562	Lee Mazzilli	.08
563	Mike Brown	.05
564	George Frazier	.05
565	Mike Sharperson (R)	.15
566	Mark Portugal (R)	.20
567	Rick Leach	.05
568	Mark Langston	.20
569	Rafael Santana	.05
570	Manny Trillo	.05
571	Cliff Speck (R)	.15
572	Bob Kipper	.05
573	Kelly Downs (R)	.25
574	Randy Asadoor (R)	.15
575	Dave Magadan (R)	2.50
576	Marvin Freeman (R)	.15
577	Jeff Lahti	.05
578	Jeff Calhoun	.05
579	Gus Polidor	.08
580	Gene Nelson	.05
581	Tim Teufel	.05
582	Odell Jones	.05
583	Mark Ryal	.15
584	Randy O'Neal	.05
585	Mike Greenwell	6.00
586	Ray Knight	.10
587	Ralph Bryant (R)	.20
588	Carmen Castillo	.05
589	Ed Wojna	.05
590	Stan Javier	.05
591	Jeff Musselman (R)	.20
592	Mike Stanley (R)	.15
593	Darrell Porter	.05
594	Drew Hall (R)	.15
595	Rob Nelson (R)	.15
596	Bryan Oelkers	.05
597	Scott Nielsen (R)	.15
598	Brian Holton (R)	.20

1987 Donruss (Continued)

NO.	PLAYER	MINT
599	Kevin Mitchell (R)	5.00
600	Checklist: 558-660	.08
601	Jackie Gutierrez	.05
602	Barry Jones (R)	.30
603	Jerry Narron	.05
604	Steve Lake	.05
605	Jim Pankovits	.05
606	Ed Romero	.05
607	Dave LaPoint	.05
608	Don Robinson	.05
609	Mike Krukow	.05
610	Dave Valle	.12
611	Len Dykstra	.50
612	"Puzzle"—Clemente	.08
613	Mike Trujillo	.08
614	Damaso Garcia	.05
615	Neal Heaton	.05
616	Juan Berenguer	.05

NO.	PLAYER	MINT
617	Steve Carlton	.25
618	Gary Lucas	.05
619	Geno Petralli	.05
620	Rick Aguilera	.08
621	Fred McGriff	3.50
622	Dave Henderson	.05
623	Dave Clark (R)	.30
624	Angel Salazar	.05
625	Randy Hunt	.05
626	John Gibbons	.05
627	Kevin Brown (R)	1.00
628	Bill Dawley	.05
629	Aurelio Lopez	.05
630	Charlie Hudson	.05
631	Ray Soff (R)	.15
632	Ray Hayward (R)	.15
633	Spike Owen	.05
634	Glenn Hubbard	.05

NO.	PLAYER	MINT
635	Kevin Elster (R)	.50
636	Mike LaCoss	.05
637	Dwayne Henry	.05
638	Rey Quinones (R)	.20
639	Jim Clancy	.05
640	Larry Anderson	.05
641	Calvin Schiraldi	.08
642	Stan Jefferson (R)	.25
643	Marc Sullivan	.05
644	Mark Grant (R)	.15
645	Cliff Johnson	.05
646	Howard Johnson	.30
647	Dave Sax	.05
648	Dave Stewart	.35
649	Danny Heep	.05
650	Joe Johnson	.05
651	Bob Brower (R)	.20
652	Rob Woodward	.08

NO.	PLAYER	MINT
653	John Mizerock	.05
654	Tim Pyznarski (R)	.15
655	Luis Aquino	.12
656	Mickey Brantley	.20
657	Doyle Alexander	.05
658	Sammy Stewart	.05
659	Jim Acker	.05
660	Pete Ladd	.05

1987 Donruss Rookies. . . . Complete Set of 56 Cards—Value $20.00

Features the outstanding rookies of the 1987 season. The cards are coated with a glossy finish. The entire set was packaged in a printed box and distributed exclusively through card hobby dealers. Features Donruss' first card of Ellis Burks, Matt Williams and Matt Nokes.

NO.	PLAYER	MINT
1	Mark McGwire	3.00
2	Eric Bell	.08
3	Mark Williamson	.25
4	Mike Greenwell	2.50
5	Ellis Burks (RR)	2.50
6	DeWayne Buice	.12
7	Mark McLemore	.08
8	Devon White	.30
9	Willie Fraser	.08
10	Les Lancaster	.20
11	Ken Williams	.12
12	Matt Nokes	.50
13	Jeff Robinson	.40
14	Bo Jackson	4.00

NO.	PLAYER	MINT
15	Kevin Seitzer (RR)	1.00
16	Billy Ripken	.25
17	B.J. Surhoff	.20
18	Chuck Crim	.12
19	Mike Birkbeck	.08
20	Chris Bosio	.08
21	Les Straker	.12
22	Mark Davidson	.15
23	Gene Larkin	.40
24	Ken Gerhart	.12
25	Luis Polonia	.25
26	Jerry Steinbach	.25
27	Mickey Brantley	.15
28	Mike Stanley	.15

NO.	PLAYER	MINT
29	Jerry Browne	.08
30	Todd Benzinger (RR)	.75
31	Fred McGriff	2.50
32	Mike Henneman	.35
33	Casey Candaele	.08
34	Dave Magadan	.75
35	David Cone	1.00
36	Mike Jackson	.25
37	John Mitchell	.15
38	Mike Dunne	.15
39	John Smiley	.50
40	Joe Magrane (RR)	1.00
41	Jim Lindeman	.15
42	Shane Mack	.25

NO.	PLAYER	MINT
43	Stanley Jefferson	.15
44	Benito Santiago	.50
45	Matt Williams (RR)	7.00
46	Dave Meads	.15
47	Rafael Palmeiro	1.00
48	Bill Long	.15
49	Bob Brower	.08
50	James Steels	.15
51	Paul Noci	.15
52	Greg Maddux	.60
53	Jeff Musselman	.08
54	Brian Holton	.08
55	Chuck Jackson	.15
56	Checklist	.15

1988 Donruss. . . . Complete Set of 660 Cards—Value $30.00 (Factory-Sealed set—Value $40.00)

Features the rookie cards of Mark Grace, Matt Williams, Ellis Burks and Gregg Jefferies. Donruss limited production. 26 cards were issued in much smaller quantities than other cards in the set (see asterisk) and are worth a premium. Six checklist cards were issued two ways to indicate the inclusion of the Bonus MVP cards.

NO.	PLAYER	MINT
	No. 1 to 26—Diamond Kings	
1	Mark McGwire (DK)	.50
2	Tim Raines (DK)	.15
3	Benito Santiago (DK)	.20
4	Alan Trammell (DK)	.15
5	Danny Tartabull (DK)	.15
6	Ron Darling (DK)	.15
7	Paul Molitor (DK)	.15
8	Devon White (DK)	.15
9	Andre Dawson (DK)	.15
10	Julio Franco (DK)	.10
11	Scott Fletcher (DK)	.10
12	Tony Fernandez (DK)	.15
13	Shane Rawley (DK)	.10
14	Kal Daniels (DK)	.15
15	Jack Clark (DK)	.10
16	Dwight Evans (DK)	.10
17	Tommy John (DK)	.10
18	Andy Van Slyke (DK)	.10
19	Gary Gaetti (DK)	.10
20	Mark Langston (DK)	.10
21	Will Clark (DK)	.50
22	Glenn Hubbard (DK)	.10
23	Billy Hatcher (DK)	.15
24	Bob Welch (DK)	.10
25	Ivan Calderon (DK)	.10
26	Cal Ripkin, Jr., (DK)	.25
27	Checklist	.15
	No. 28 to 47—Rated Rookies	
28	Mackey Sasser (R)	.40
29	Jeff Treadway (R)	.20
30	Mike Campbell (R)	.15
31	Lance Johnson (R)	.20
32	Nelson Liriano (R)	.20
33	Shawn Abner	.25
34	Roberto Alomar (R)	1.50
35	Shawn Hillegas (R)	.15
36	Joey Meyer	.20
37	Kevin Elster	.15
38	Jose Lind (R)	.30
39	Kirt Manwaring (R)	.15
40	Mark Grace (R)	3.00
41	Jody Reed (R)	.60
42	John Farrell (R)	.20
43	Al Leiter (R)	.25
44	Gary Thurman (R)	.15
45	Vincente Palacios (R)	.15
46	Eddie Williams (R)	.15
47	Jack McDowell (R)	.50
48	Ken Dixon	.05
49	Mike Birkbeck	.05
50	Eric King	.05
51	Roger Clemen	.50
52	Pat Clements	.05
53	Fernando Valenzuela	.15
54	Mark Gubicza	.05
55	Jay Howell	.05
56	Floyd Youmans	.12
57	Ed Correa	.10
58	DeWayne Buice (R)	.15
59	Jose DeLeon	.05
60	Danny Cox	.08
61	Nolan Ryan	.60
62	Steve Bedrosian	.10
63	Tom Browning	.08
64	Mark Davis	.05
65	R.J. Reynolds	.08
66	Kevin Mitchell	.50
67	Ken Oberkfell	.05
68	Rick Sutcliffe	.12
69	Dwight Gooden	.40
70	Scott Bankhead	.12
71	Bert Blyleven	.15
72	Jimmy Key	.12
73	Les Straker (R)	.15
74	Jim Clancy	.08
75	Mike Moore	.08
76	Ron Darling	.15
77	Ed Lynch	.08
78	Dale Murphy	.30
79	Doug Drabek	.20
80	Scott Garrelts	.05
81	Ed Whitson	.05
82	Rob Murphy	.05
83	Shane Rawley	.05
84	Greg Mathews	.08
85	Jim Deshaies	.10
86	Mike Witt	.12
87	Donnie Hill	.08
88	Jeff Reed	.08
89	Mike Boddicker	.12
90	Ted Higuera	.15
91	Walt Terrell	.08
92	Bob Stanley	.05
93	Dave Righetti	.15
94	Orel Hershiser	.20
95	Chris Bando	.05
96	Bret Saberhagen	.15
97	Curt Young	.05
98	Tim Burke	.05
99	Charlie Hough	.05
100	Checklist	
101	Bobby Witt	.15
102	George Brett	.35
103	Mickey Tettleton	.05
104	Scott Bailes	.05
105	Mike Pagliarulo	.10
106	Mike Scioscia	.05
107	Tom Brookens	.05
108	Ray Knight	.10
109	Dan Plesac	.12
110	Wally Joyner	.25
111	Bob Forsch	.08
112	Mike Scott	.15
113	Kevin Gross	.08
114	Benito Santiago	.30
115	Bob Kipper	.05
116	Mike Krukow	.05
117	Chris Bosio	.05
118	Sid Fernandez	.12
119	Jody Davis	.05
120	Mike Morgan	.05
121	Mark Eichhorn	.05
122	Jeff Reardon	.10
123	John Franco	.08
124	Richard Dotson	.05
125	Eric Bell	.05
126	Juan Nieves	.10
127	Jack Morris	.15
128	Rick Rhoden	.08
129	Rich Gedman	.05
130	Ken Howell	.05
131	Brook Jacoby	.08
132	Danny Jackson	.10
133	Gene Nelson	.05
134	Neal Heaton	.05
135	Willie Fraser	.05
136	Jose Guzman	.05
137	Ozzie Guillen	.10
138	Bob Knepper	.08
139	Mike Jackson (R)	.15
140	Joe Magrane (R)	.50
141	Jimmy Jones	.05
142	Ted Power	.05
143	Ozzie Virgil	.05
144	Felix Fermin (R)	.15
145	Kelly Downs	.08
146	Shawon Dunston	.12
147	Scott Bradley	.05
148	Dave Stieb	.12
149	Frank Viola	.15
150	Terry Kennedy	.05
151	Bill Wegman	.05
152	Matt Nokes (R)	.30
153	Wade Boggs	.50
154	Wayne Tolleson	.05
155	Mariano Duncan	.05
156	Julio Franco	.12
157	Charlie Leibrandt	.08
158	Terry Steinbach	.12
159	Mike Fitzgerald	.05
160	Jack Lazorko	.05
161	Mitch Williams	.05
162	Greg Walker	.05
163	Alan Ashby	.05
164	Tony Gwynn	.30
165	Bruce Ruffin	.08
166	Ron Robinson	.05
167	Zane Smith	.08
168	Junior Ortiz	.05
169	Jamie Moyer	.05
170	Tony Pena	.08
171	Cal Ripken	.25
172	B.J. Surhoff	.15
173	Lou Whitaker	.15
174	Ellis Burks (R)	1.50
175	Ron Guidry	.15
176	Steve Sax	.15
177	Danny Tartabull	.20
178	Carney Lansford	.05
179	Casey Candaele	.05
180	Scott Fletcher	.05
181	Mark McLemore	.05
182	Ivan Calderon	.15
183	Jack Clark	.15
184	Glenn Davis	.15
185	Luis Aguayo	.05
186	Bo Diaz	.05
187	Stan Jefferson	.08
188	Sid Bream	.05
189	Bob Brenly	.05
190	Dion James	.05
191	Leon Durham	.10
192	Jesse Orosco	.05
193	Alvin Davis	.10
194	Gary Gaetti	.12
195	Fred McGriff	.45
196	Steve Lombardozzi	.08
197	Rance Mulliniks	.05
198	Rey Quinones	.05
199	Gary Carter	.20
200	Checklist	.08
201	Keith Moreland	.05
202	Ken Griffey	.05
203	Tommy Gregg (R)	.05
204	Will Clark	1.00
205	John Kruk	.15
206	Buddy Bell	.15
207	Von Hayes	.10
208	Tommy Herr	.05
209	Craig Reynolds	.05
210	Gary Pettis	.05
211	Harold Baines	.15
212	Vance Law	.05
213	Ken Gerhart	.08
214	Jim Gantner	.05
215	Chet Lemon	.08
216	Dwight Evans	.10
217	Don Mattingly	1.00
218	Franklin Stubbs	.08
219	Pat Tabler	.05
220	Bo Jackson	1.00
221	Tony Phillips	.05
222	Tim Wallach	.08
223	Ruben Sierra	.50
224	Steve Buechele	.05
225	Frank White	.05
226	Alfredo Griffin	.05
227	Greg Swindell	.15
228	Willie Randolph	.10
229	Mike Marshall	.10
230	Alan Trammell	.15
231	Eddie Murray	.25
232	Dale Sveum	.08
233	Dick Schofield	.05
234	Jose Oquendo	.05
235	Bill Doran	.05
236	Milt Thompson	.05
237	Marvell Wynne	.05
238	Bobby Bonilla	.35
239	Chris Speier	.05
240	Glenn Braggs	.10
241	Wally Backman	.05
242	Ryne Sandberg	.50
243	Phil Bradley	.12
244	Kelly Gruber	.30
245	Ron Brunansky	.10
246	Ron Oester	.05
247	Bobby Thigpen	.15
248	Fred Lynn	.15
249	Paul Molitor	.15
250	Darrell Evans	.10
251	Gary Ward	.08
252	Bruce Hurst	.08
253	Bob Welch	.05
254	Joe Carter	.12
255	Willie Wilson	.12
256	Mark McGwire	.75
257	Mitch Webster	.05
258	Brian Downing	.05
259	Mike Stanley	.05
260	Carlton Fisk	.15
261	Billy Hatcher	.10
262	Glenn Wilson	.05
263	Ozzie Smith	.15
264	Randy Ready	.05
265	Kurt Stillwell	.10
266	David Palmer	.05
267	Mike Diaz	.05
268	Rob Thompson	.08
269	Andre Dawson	.20
270	Lee Guetterman	.05
271	Willie Upshaw	.05
272	Randy Bush	.05
273	Larry Sheets	.12
274	Rob Deer	.10
275	Kirk Gibson	.20
276	Marty Barrett	.10
277	Rickey Henderson	.35
278	Pedro Guerrero	.15
279	Brett Butler	.05
280	Kevin Seitzer	.40
281	Mike Davis	.05
282	Andres Galarraga	.15
283	Devon White	.15
284	Pete O'Brien	.10
285	Jerry Hairston	.05
286	Kevin Bass	.08
287	Carmelo Martinez	.05
288	Juan Samuel	.10
289	Kal Daniels	.20
290	Albert Hall	.05
291	Andy Van Slyke	.12
292	Lee Smith	.10
293	Vince Coleman	.20
294	Tom Niedenfuer	.05
295	Robin Yount	.25
296	Jeff Robinson (R)	.25
297	Todd Benzinger (R)	.30
298	Dave Winfield	.15
299	Mickey Hatcher	.05
300	Checklist	.08
301	Bud Black	.05
302	Jose Canseco	1.50
303	Tom Foley	.05
304	Pete Incaviglia	.20
305	Bob Boone	.05
306	Bill Long (R)	.15
307	Willie McGee	.15
308	Ken Caminiti (R)	.20
309	Darren Daulton	.05
310	Tracy Jones	.10
311	Greg Booker	.05
312	Mike LaValliere	.05
313	Chili Davis	.10
314	Glenn Hubbard	.05
315	Paul Noce (R)	.15
316	Keith Hernandez	.15
317	Mark Langston	.10
318	Keith Atherton	.05
319	Tony Fernandez	.12
320	Kent Hrbek	.15
321	John Cerutti	.05
322	Mike Kingery	.05
323	Dave Magadan	.15
324	Rafael Palmeiro	.40
325	Jeff Dedmon	.05
326	Barry Bonds	.50
327	Jeffrey Leonard	.05
328	Tim Flannery	.05
329	Dave Concepcion	.05
330	Mike Schmidt	.50
331	Bill Dawley	.05
332	Larry Anderson	.05
333	Jack Howell	.05
334	Ken Williams (R)	.15
335	Bryn Smith	.05
336	Billy Ripken (R)	.20
337	Greg Brock	.05
338	Mike Heath	.05
339	Mike Greenwell	.75
340	Claudell Washington	.05
341	Jose Gonzalez	.05
342	Mel Hall	.05

NO. PLAYER	MINT	NO. PLAYER	MINT	NO. PLAYER	MINT	NO. PLAYER	MINT
343 Jim Eisenreich	.08	430 Ricky Horton	.05	516 Manny Trillo	.05	602 Don August	.20
344 Tony Bernazard	.05	431 Gerald Young (R)	.15	517 Jerry Reed	.05	*603 Terry Leach	.12
345 Tim Raines	.25	432 Rick Schu	.05	518 Rick Leach	.05	604 Tom Newell (R)	.15
346 Bob Brower	.05	433 Paul O'Neill	.15	519 Mark Davidson (R)	.15	*605 Randall Byers (R)	.20
347 Larry Parrish	.05	434 Rich Gossage	.15	520 Jeff Ballard (R)	.30	606 Jim Gott	.05
348 Thad Bosley	.05	435 John Cangelosi	.05	521 Dave Stapleton	.15	607 Harry Spilman	.05
349 Dennis Eckersley	.15	436 Mike LaCoss	.05	522 Pat Sheridan	.05	608 John Candelaria	.05
350 Cory Snyder	.15	437 Gerald Perry	.10	523 Al Nipper	.05	609 Mike Brumley (R)	.15
351 Rick Cerone	.05	438 Dave Martinez	.05	524 Steve Trout	.05	610 Mickey Brantley	.15
352 John Shelby	.05	439 Darryl Strawberry	.50	525 Jeff Hamilton	.05	*611 Jose Nunez (R)	.20
353 Larry Herndon	.05	440 John Moses	.05	526 Tommy Hinzo (R)	.15	612 Tom Nieto	.05
354 John Habyan	.05	441 Greg Gagne	.05	527 Lonnie Smith	.08	613 Rick Reuschel	.05
355 Chuck Crim (R)	.15	442 Jesse Barfield	.15	528 Greg Cadaret (R)	.20	*614 Lee Mazzilli	.12
356 Gus Polidor	.05	443 George Frazier	.05	529 Rob McClure	.05	615 Scott Lusader	.20
357 Ken Dayley	.05	444 Garth Iorg	.05	530 Chuck Finley	.15	616 Bobby Meacham	.05
358 Danny Darwin	.05	445 Ed Nunez	.05	531 Jeff Russell	.05	*617 Kevin McReynolds	.20
359 Lance Parrish	.15	446 Rick Aguilera	.05	532 Steve Lyons	.05	618 Gene Garber	.05
360 James Steels (R)	.15	447 Jerry Mumphrey	.05	533 Terry Puhl	.05	*619 Barry Lyons	.20
361 Al Pedrique (R)	.15	448 Rafael Ramirez	.05	534 Eric Nolte (R)	.20	620 Randy Myers	.15
362 Mike Aldrete	.05	449 John Smiley (R)	.30	535 Kent Tekulve	.05	621 Donnie Moore	.05
363 Juan Castillo	.05	450 Atlee Hammaker	.05	536 Pat Pacillo	.15	622 Domingo Ramos	.05
364 Len Dykstra	.25	451 Lance McCullers	.08	537 Charlie Puleo	.05	623 Ed Romero	.05
365 Luis Quinones	.05	452 Guy Hoffman	.05	538 Tom Prince (R)	.15	624 Greg Myers (R)	.15
366 Jim Presley	.10	453 Chris James	.10	539 Greg Maddux	.15	625 Ripken Family	.25
367 Lloyd Moseby	.10	454 Terry Pendleton	.05	540 Jim Lindeman	.10	626 Pat Perry	.15
368 Kirby Puckett	.40	455 Dave Meads (R)	.15	541 Pete Stanicek (R)	.15	*627 Andres Thomas	.15
369 Eric Davis	.35	456 Bill Buckner	.05	542 Steve Kiefer	.05	*628 Matt Williams (R)	3.00
370 Gary Redus	.05	457 John Pawlowski (R)	.15	543 Jim Morrison	.05	629 Dave Hengel (R)	.20
371 Dave Schmidt	.05	458 Bob Sebra	.05	544 Spike Owen	.05	*630 Jeff Musselman	.15
372 Mark Clear	.05	459 Jim Dwyer	.05	545 Jay Buhner (R)	.30	631 Tim Laudner	.05
373 Dave Bergman	.05	460 Jay Aldrich (R)	.15	546 Mike Devereaux (R)	.25	*632 Bob Ojeda	.12
374 Charles Hudson	.05	461 Frank Tanana	.05	547 Jerry Don Gleaton	.05	633 Rafael Santana	.05
375 Calvin Schiraldi	.05	462 Oil Can Boyd	.05	548 Jose Rijo	.05	634 Wes Gardner (R)	.15
376 Alex Trevino	.05	463 Dan Pasqua	.08	549 Dennis Martinez	.05	*635 Roberto Kelly (R)	1.00
377 Tom Candiotti	.05	464 Tim Crews (R)	.05	550 Mike Loynd	.05	*636 Mike Flanagan	.15
378 Steve Farr	.05	465 Andy Allanson	.05	551 Darrell Miller	.05	637 Jay Bell (R)	.25
379 Mike Gallego	.05	466 Bill Pecota (R)	.15	552 Dave LaPoint	.05	638 Bob Melvin	.05
380 Andy McGaffigan	.05	467 Steve Ontiveros	.05	553 John Tudor	.10	639 Damon Berryhill (R)	.25
381 Kirk McCaskill	.05	468 Hubie Brooks	.05	554 Rocky Childress (R)	.15	*640 David Wells (R)	.35
382 Oddibe McDowell	.08	469 Paul Kilgus (R)	.15	555 Wally Ritchie (R)	.15	641 Puzzle Card	.05
383 Floyd Bannister	.08	470 Dale Mohorcic	.05	556 Terry McGriff	.05	642 Doug Sisk	.05
384 Denny Walling	.05	471 Dan Quisenberry	.10	557 Dave Leiper	.05	643 Keith Hughes (R)	.20
385 Don Carman	.05	472 Dave Stewart	.20	558 Jeff Robinson	.05	644 Tom Glavine (R)	.30
386 Todd Worrell	.15	473 Dave Clark	.05	559 Jose Uribe	.05	645 Al Newman	.15
387 Eric Show	.05	474 Joel Skinner	.05	560 Ted Simmons	.05	646 Scott Sanderson	.05
388 Dave Parker	.20	475 Dave Anderson	.05	561 Lester Lancaster (R)	.15	647 Scott Terry	.15
389 Rick Mahler	.05	476 Dan Petry	.05	562 Keith Miller (R)	.20	*648 Tim Teufel	.15
390 Mike Dunne	.10	477 Carl Nichols (R)	.15	563 Harold Reynolds	.05	*649 Garry Templeton	.15
391 Candy Maldonado	.08	478 Ernest Riles	.05	564 Gene Larkin	.20	*650 Manny Lee	.15
392 Bob Dernier	.05	479 George Hendrick	.05	565 Cecil Fielder	.50	*651 Roger McDowell	.15
393 Dave Valle	.05	480 John Morris	.05	566 Roy Smalley	.05	*652 Mookie Wilson	.15
394 Ernie Whitt	.08	481 Manny Hernandez (R)	.15	567 Duane Ward	.05	*653 David Cone	.60
395 Juan Berenguer	.05	482 Jeff Stone	.05	568 Bill Wilkinson (R)	.15	*654 Ron Gant (R)	1.50
396 Mike Young	.08	483 Chris Brown	.10	569 Howard Johnson	.20	*655 Joe Price	.15
397 Mike Felder	.05	484 Mike Bielecki	.05	570 Frank DiPino	.05	*656 George Bell	.25
398 Willie Hernandez	.08	485 Dave Dravecky	.05	571 Pete Smith (R)	.15	*657 Gregg Jefferies (R)	4.00
399 Jim Rice	.20	486 Rick Manning	.05	572 Darnell Coles	.05	*658 Todd Stottlemyre (R)	.40
400 Checklist	.08	487 Bill Almon	.05	573 Don Robinson	.05	*659 Geronimo Berroa (R)	.35
401 Tommy John	.12	488 Jim Sundberg	.05	574 Rob Nelson	.05	*660 Jerry Royster	.15
402 Brian Holton	.05	489 Ken Phelps	.05	575 Dennis Rasmussen	.05		
403 Carmen Castillo	.05	490 Tom Henke	.05	576 Steve Jeltz	.05		
404 Jamie Quirk	.05	491 Dan Gladden	.05	577 Tom Pagnozzi (R)	.15		
405 Dwayne Murphy	.05	492 Barry Larkin	.40	578 Ty Gainey	.05		
406 Jeff Parrett (R)	.15	493 Fred Manrique (R)	.20	579 Gary Lucas	.05		
407 Don Sutton	.15	494 Mike Griffin	.05	580 Ron Hassey	.05		
408 Jerry Browne	.05	495 Mark Knudson (R)	.12	581 Herm Winningham	.05		
409 Jim Winn	.05	496 Bill Madlock	.12	582 Rene Gonzales (R)	.15		
410 Dave Smith	.05	497 Tim Stoddard	.05	583 Brad Komminsk	.05		
411 Shane Mack	.10	498 Sam Horn	.20	584 Doyle Alexander	.05		
412 Greg Gross	.05	499 Tracy Woodson (R)	.15	585 Jeff Sellers	.05		
413 Nick Esasky	.05	500 Checklist	.08	586 Bill Gullickson	.05		
414 Damaso Garcia	.05	501 Ken Schrom	.05	587 Tim Belcher	.40		
415 Brian Fisher	.05	502 Angel Salazar	.05	588 Doug Jones (R)	.35		
416 Brian Dayett	.05	503 Eric Plunk	.05	589 Melido Perez (R)	.25		
417 Curt Ford	.05	504 Joe Hesketh	.05	590 Rick Honeycutt	.05		
418 Mark Williamson (R)	.15	505 Greg Minton	.05	591 Pascual Perez	.05		
419 Bill Schroeder	.05	506 Geno Petralli	.05	592 Curt Wilkerson	.05		
420 Mike Henneman (R)	.20	507 Bob James	.05	593 Steve Howe	.05		
421 John Marzano	.20	508 Robbie Wine (R)	.15	594 John Davis (R)	.20		
422 Ron Kittle	.08	509 Jeff Calhoun	.05	595 Storm Davis	.05		
423 Matt Young	.05	510 Steve Lake	.05	596 Sammy Stewart	.05		
424 Steve Balboni	.05	511 Mark Grant	.05	597 Neil Allen	.05		
425 Luis Polonia (R)	.20	512 Frank Williams	.05	598 Alejandro Pena	.05		
426 Randy St. Claire	.05	513 Jeff Blauser (R)	.20	599 Mark Thurmond	.05		
427 Greg Harris	.05	514 Bob Walk	.05	600 Checklist	.08		
428 Johnny Ray	.05	515 Craig Lefferts	.05	601 Jose Mesa (R)	.15		
429 Ray Searage	.05						

1988 Donruss Rookies. . . . Complete Set of 56 Cards—Value $15.00

Features the outstanding rookies of the 1988 season. The cards are coated with a glossy finish. The entire set was packaged in a printed box and distributed primarily through card hobby dealers. Features Donruss' first card of Chris Sabo and Walt Weiss.

NO.	PLAYER	MINT	NO.	PLAYER	MINT	NO.	PLAYER	MINT	NO.	PLAYER	MINT
1	Mark Grace	4.00	15	Pete Stanicek	.10	29	Johnny Paredes	.15	43	John Dopson	.25
2	Mike Campbell	.08	16	Roberto Kelly	.40	30	Chris Sabo (RR)	2.50	44	Jody Reed	.20
3	Todd Frohwirth	.10	17	Jeff Treadway	.15	31	Dannon Berryhill	.25	45	Darrin Jackson	.15
4	Dave Stapleton	.08	18	Walt Weiss (RR)	1.00	32	Randy Miligan	.50	46	Mike Capel	.10
5	Shawn Abner	.08	19	Paul Gibson	.10	33	Gary Thurman	.15	47	Ron Gant	1.00
6	Jose Cecenazi	.10	20	Tim Crews	.10	34	Kevin Elster	.20	48	John Davis	.10
7	Dave Gallagher	.35	21	Melido Perez	.15	35	Roberto Alomar	.50	49	Kevin Coffman	.15
8	Mark Parent	.15	22	Steve Peters	.10	36	Edgar Martinez	.40	50	Cris Carpenter	.20
9	Cecil Espy	.20	23	Craig Worthington	.50	37	Todd Stottlemyre	.15	51	Mick Sasser	.15
10	Pete Smith	.08	24	John Trautwein	.10	38	Joey Meyer	.20	52	Luis Alicea	.15
11	Jay Buhner	.15	25	DeWayne Vaughn	.10	39	Carl Nichols	.10	53	Bryan Harvey	.25
12	Pat Borders	.25	26	David Well	.10	40	Jack McDowell	.15	54	Steve Ellsworth	.20
13	Doug Jennings	.20	27	Al Leiter	.15	41	Jose Bautista	.20	55	Mike Macfarlane	.20
14	Brady Anderson	.35	28	Tim Belcher	.25	42	Sil Campusano	.25	56	Checklist	.10

1989 Donruss. . . . Complete Set of 660 Cards—Value $25.00

Features the rookie cards of Sandy Alomar, Jr., Ken Griffey, Jr., Tom Gordon Gary Sheffield and Rickey Jordan.

NO.	PLAYER	MINT	NO.	PLAYER	MINT	NO.	PLAYER	MINT	NO.	PLAYER	MINT
	No. 1 to 26—Diamond Kings		7	Carlton Fisk (DK)	.15	14	Andres Galarraga (DK)	.10	21	Harold Reynolds (DK)	.10
1	Mike Greenwell (DK)	.30	8	Cory Snyder (DK)	.10	15	Kirk Gibson (DK)	.10	22	Gerald Perry (DK)	.10
2	Bobby Bonilla (DK)	.15	9	David Cone (DK)	.15	16	Fred McGriff (DK)	.20	23	Frank Viola (DK)	.20
3	Pete Incaviglia (DK)	.10	10	Kevin Seitzer (DK)	.10	17	Mark Grace (DK)	.50	24	Steve Bedrosian (DK)	.08
4	Chris Sabo (DK)	.15	11	Rick Rueschel (DK)	.08	18	Jeff Robinson (DK)	.10	25	Glenn Davis (DK)	.10
5	Robin Yount (DK)	.20	12	Johnny Ray (DK)	.08	19	Vince Coleman (DK)	.10	26	Don Mattingly (DK)	.50
6	Tony Gwynn (DK)	.20	13	Dave Schmidt (DK)	.08	20	Dave Henderson (DK)	.10	27	Diamond King Checklist	.08

NO.	PLAYER	MINT	NO.	PLAYER	MINT	NO.	PLAYER	MINT	NO.	PLAYER	MINT
No. 28 to 47—Rated Rookies			111	Keith Moreland	.08	195	John Tudor	.05	279	Denny Walling	.05
28	Sandy Alomar, Jr. (R)	2.00	112	Tom Brunansky	.08	196	Neil Allen	.05	280	Roger Clemens	.30
29	Steve Searcy (R)	.25	113	Kelly Gruber	.20	197	Orel Hershiser	.15	281	Greg Mathews	.05
30	Cameron Drew (R)	.15	114	Brook Jacoby	.05	198	Kal Daniels	.15	282	Tom Niedenfuer	.05
31	Gary Sheffield (R)	1.50	115	Keith Brown (R)	.15	199	Kent Hrbek	.10	283	Paul Kilgus	.05
32	Erik Hanson (R)	.40	116	Matt Nokes	.10	200	Checklist	.08	284	Jose Guzman	.05
33	Ken Griffey, Jr. (R)	7.00	117	Keith Hernandez	.15	201	Joe Magrane	.10	285	Calvin Schiraldi	.05
34	Greg Harris (R)	.20	118	Bob Forsch	.05	202	Scott Bailes	.05	286	Charlie Puleo	.05
35	Gregg Jefferies (R)	1.00	119	Bert Blyleven	.15	203	Tim Belcher	.15	287	Joe Orsulak	.05
36	Luis Medina (R)	.25	120	Willie Wilson	.08	204	George Brett	.25	288	Jack Howell	.08
37	Carlos Quintana (R)	.40	121	Tommy Gregg	.05	205	Benito Santiago	.10	289	Kevin Elster	.08
38	Felix Jose (R)	.30	122	Jim Rice	.12	206	Tony Fernandez	.10	290	Jose Lind	.05
39	Cris Carpenter (R)	.20	123	Bob Knepper	.05	207	Gerald Young	.08	291	Paul Molitor	.08
40	Ron Jones (R)	.20	124	Danny Jackson	.10	208	Bo Jackson	.75	292	Cecil Espy	.10
41	Dave West (R)	.25	125	Eric Plunk	.05	209	Chet Lemon	.05	293	Bill Wegman	.05
42	Randy Johnson (R)	.35	126	Brian Fisher	.05	210	Storm Davis	.05	294	Dan Pasqua	.08
43	Mike Harkey (R)	.40	127	Mike Pagliarulo	.10	211	Doug Drabek	.10	295	Scott Garrelts	.05
44	Pete Harnisch (R)	.15	128	Tony Gwynn	.25	212	Mickey Brantley	.08	296	Walt Terrell	.05
45	Tom Gordon (R)	.50	129	Lance McCullers	.08	213	Devon White	.08	297	Ed Hearn	.05
46	Gregg Olson (R)	.75	130	Andres Galarraga	.15	214	Dave Stewart	.15	298	Lou Whitaker	.08
47	Alex Sanchez (R)	.20	131	Jose Uribe	.05	215	Dave Schmidt	.05	299	Ken Dayley	.05
48	Ruben Sierra	.20	132	Kirk Gibson	.15	216	Bryn Smith	.05	300	Checklist	.08
49	Rafael Palmeiro	.15	133	David Palmer	.05	217	Brett Butler	.05	301	Tommy Herr	.05
50	Ron Gant	.25	134	R. J. Reynolds	.05	218	Bob Ojeda	.08	302	Mike Brumley	.05
51	Cal Ripken, Jr.	.20	135	Greg Walker	.05	219	Steve Rosenberg (R)	.15	303	Ellis Burks	.25
52	Wally Joyner	.15	136	Kirk McCaskill	.05	220	Hubie Brooks	.05	304	Curt Young	.05
53	Gary Carter	.15	137	Shawon Dunston	.12	221	B.J. Surhoff	.08	305	Jody Reed	.15
54	Andy Van Slyke	.15	138	Andy Allanson	.05	222	Rick Mahler	.05	306	Bill Doran	.08
55	Robin Yount	.20	139	Rob Murphy	.05	223	Rick Sutcliffe	.10	307	David Wells	.05
56	Pete Incaviglia	.10	140	Mike Aldrete	.05	224	Neal Heaton	.05	308	Ron Robinson	.08
57	Greg Brock	.05	141	Terry Kennedy	.05	225	Mitch Williams	.05	309	Rafael Santana	.05
58	Melido Perez	.10	142	Scott Fletcher	.05	226	Chuck Finley	.12	310	Julio Franco	.08
59	Craig Lefferts	.05	143	Steve Balboni	.05	227	Mark Langston	.10	311	Jack Clark	.10
60	Gary Pettis	.05	144	Bret Saberhagen	.15	228	Jesse Orosco	.05	312	Chris James	.08
61	Danny Tartabull	.15	145	Ozzie Virgil	.05	229	Ed Whitson	.05	313	Milt Thompson	.05
62	Guillermo Hernandez	.05	146	Dale Sveum	.08	230	Terry Pendelton	.08	314	John Shelby	.05
63	Ozzie Smith	.15	147	Darryl Strawberry	.45	231	Lloyd Moseby	.15	315	Al Leiter	.10
64	Gary Gaetti	.10	148	Harold Baines	.10	232	Greg Swindell	.10	316	Mike Davis	.05
65	Mark Davis	.10	149	George Bell	.15	233	John Franco	.08	317	Chris Sabo (R)	.75
66	Lee Smith	.08	150	Dave Parker	.10	234	Jack Morris	.10	318	Greg Gagne	.05
67	Dennis Eckersley	.10	151	Bobby Bonilla	.30	235	Howard Johnson	.15	319	Jose Oquendo	.05
68	Wade Boggs	.50	152	Mookie Wilson	.08	236	Glenn Davis	.15	320	John Farrell	.10
69	Mike Scott	.15	153	Tod Power	.05	237	Frank Viola	.15	321	Franklin Stubbs	.05
70	Fred McGriff	.20	154	Nolan Ryan	.50	238	Kevin Seitzer	.15	322	Kurt Stillwell	.05
71	Tom Browning	.08	155	Jeff Reardon	.08	239	Gerald Perry	.10	323	Shawn Abner	.05
72	Claudell Washington	.05	156	Tim Wallach	.08	240	Dwight Evans	.15	324	Mike Flanagan	.05
73	Mel Hall	.05	157	Jamie Moyer	.05	241	Jim Deshaies	.05	325	Kevin Bass	.08
74	Don Mattingly	.75	158	Rich Gossage	.08	242	Bo Diaz	.05	326	Pat Tabler	.08
75	Steve Bedrosian	.08	159	Dave Winfield	.15	243	Carney Lansford	.08	327	Mike Henneman	.05
76	Juan Samuel	.10	160	Von Hayes	.08	244	Mike Lavalliere	.05	328	Rick Honeycutt	.05
77	Mike Scioscia	.05	161	Willie McGee	.08	245	Rickey Henderson	.30	329	John Smiley	.08
78	Dave Righetti	.10	162	Rich Gedman	.05	246	Roberto Alomar	.25	330	Rey Quinones	.05
79	Alfredo Griffin	.05	163	Tony Pena	.08	247	Jimmy Jones	.05	331	Johnny Ray	.10
80	Eric Davis	.30	164	Mike Morgan	.05	248	Pascual Perez	.05	332	Bob Welch	.08
81	Juan Berenguer	.05	165	Charlie Hough	.08	249	Will Clark	.75	333	Larry Sheets	.05
82	Todd Worrell	.05	166	Mike Stanley	.05	250	Fernando Valenzuela	.10	334	Jeff Parrett	.08
83	Joe Carter	.15	167	Andre Dawson	.15	251	Shane Rawley	.05	335	Rick Rueschel	.05
84	Steve Sax	.12	168	Joe Boever	.05	252	Sid Bream	.05	336	Randy Myers	.08
85	Frank White	.05	169	Pete Stanicek	.05	253	Steve Lyons	.05	337	Ken Williams	.05
86	John Kruk	.15	170	Bob Boone	.05	254	Brian Downing	.08	338	Andy McGaffigan	.05
87	Rance Mulliniks	.05	171	Ron Darling	.10	255	Mark Grace	1.25	339	Joey Meyer	.05
88	Alan Ashby	.05	172	Bob Walk	.05	256	Tom Candiotti	.08	340	Dion James	.05
89	Charlie Leibrandt	.08	173	Rob Deer	.08	257	Barry Larkin	.25	341	Les Lancaster	.05
90	Frank Tanana	.08	174	Steve Buechele	.05	258	Mike Krukow	.08	342	Tom Foley	.05
91	Jose Canseco	1.00	175	Ted Higuera	.10	259	Billy Ripken	.05	343	Geno Petralli	.05
92	Barry Bonds	.35	176	Ozzie Guillen	.08	260	Cecilio Guante	.05	344	Dan Petry	.05
93	Harold Reynolds	.08	177	Candy Maldonado	.10	261	Scott Bradley	.05	345	Alvin Davis	.08
94	Mark McLemore	.05	178	Doyle Alexander	.05	262	Floyd Bannister	.05	346	Mickey Hatcher	.05
95	Mark McGwire	.50	179	Mark Gubicza	.10	263	Pete Smith	.08	347	Marvelle Wynn	.05
96	Eddie Murray	.20	180	Alan Trammell	.10	264	Jim Gantner	.05	348	Danny Cox	.05
97	Tim Raines	.15	181	Vince Coleman	.15	265	Roger McDowell	.05	349	Dave Stieb	.08
98	Rob Thompsomn	.05	182	Kirby Puckett	.25	266	Bobby Thigpen	.05	350	Jay Bell	.05
99	Kevin McReynolds	.15	183	Chris Brown	.08	267	Jim Clancy	.05	351	Jeff Treadway	.05
100	Checklist	.08	184	Marty Barrett	.05	268	Terry Steinbach	.12	352	Luis Salazar	.05
101	Carlton Fisk	.20	185	Stan Javier	.05	269	Mike Dunne	.05	353	Lenny Dykstra	.15
102	Dave Martinez	.05	186	Mike Greenwell	.35	270	Dwight Gooden	.30	354	Juan Agosto	.05
103	Glenn Braggs	.05	187	Billy Hatcher	.05	271	Mike Heath	.05	355	Gene Larkin	.05
104	Dale Murphy	.20	188	Jimmy Key	.12	272	Dave Smith	.05	356	Steve Farr	.05
105	Ryne Sandberg	.25	189	Nick Esasky	.10	273	Keith Atherton	.05	357	Paul Assenmacher	.05
106	Dennis Martinez	.05	190	Don Slaught	.05	274	Tim Burke	.05	358	Todd Benzinger	.15
107	Pete O'Brien	.10	191	Cory Snyder	.15	275	Damon Beryhill	.15	359	Larry Andersen	.05
108	Dick Schofield	.05	192	John Candelaria	.08	276	Vance Law	.05	360	Paul O'Neill	.12
109	Henry Cotto	.05	193	Mike Schmidt	.30	277	Rich Dotson	.08	361	Ron Hassey	.05
110	Mike Marshall	.08	194	Kevin Gross	.05	278	Lance Parrish	.10	362	Jim Gott	.05

NO. PLAYER	MINT	NO. PLAYER	MINT	NO. PLAYER	MINT	NO. PLAYER	MINT
363 Ken Phelps	.05	444 Jerry Don Gleaton	.05	525 Bryan Harvey (R)	.20	606 Lance Johnson	.05
364 Tim Flannery	.05	445 Paul Gibson (R)	.15	526 Rick Aguilera	.05	607 Terry Clark (R)	.15
365 Randy Ready	.05	446 Walt Weiss	.25	527 Tom Prince	.05	608 Manny Trillo	.05
366 Nelson Santovenia (R)	.15	447 Glenn Wilson	.05	528 Mark Clear	.05	609 Scott Jordan (R)	.15
367 Kelly Downs	.05	448 Mike Moore	.05	529 Jerry Browne	.05	610 Jay Howell	.08
368 Danny Heep	.05	449 Chili Davis	.08	530 Juan Castillo	.05	611 Francisco Melendez (R)	.15
369 Phil Bradley	.08	450 Dave Henderson	.05	531 Jack McDowell	.10	612 Mike Boddicker	.08
370 Jeff Robinson	.05	451 Jose Bautista (R)	.15	532 Chris Speier	.05	613 Kevin Brown	.20
371 Ivan Calderon	.10	452 Rex Hudler	.10	533 Darrell Evans	.05	614 Dave Valle	.05
372 Mike Witt	.08	453 Bob Brenly	.05	534 Luis Aquino	.05	615 Tim Laudner	.05
373 Greg Maddux	.15	454 Mackey Sasser	.08	535 Eric King	.05	616 Andy Nezelek (R)	.20
374 Carmen Castillo	.05	455 Daryl Boston	.05	536 Ken Hill (R)	.20	617 Chuck Crim	.05
375 Jose Rijo	.08	456 Mike Fitzgerald	.05	537 Randy Bush	.05	618 Jack Savage	.15
376 Joe Price	.05	457 Jeffery Leonard	.05	538 Shane Mack	.05	619 Adam Peterson	.12
377 R.C. Gonzalez	.05	458 Bruce Sutter	.08	539 Tom Bolton	.10	620 Todd Stottlemyre	.08
378 Oddibe McDowell	.08	459 Mitch Webster	.05	540 Gene Nelson	.05	621 Lance Blankenship (R)	.15
379 Jim Presley	.05	460 Joe Hesketh	.05	541 Wes Gardner	.05	622 Miquel Garcia (R)	.15
380 Brad Wellman	.05	461 Bobby Witt	.05	542 Ken Caminiti	.05	623 Keith Miller	.05
381 Tom Glavine	.05	462 Stew Cliburn	.05	543 Duane Ward	.05	624 Ricky Jordan (R)	.50
382 Dan Plesac	.05	463 Scott Bankhead	.05	544 Norm Charlton (R)	.20	625 Ernest Riles	.05
383 Wally Backman	.05	464 Ramon Martinez (R)	1.00	545 Hal Morris (R)	.60	626 John Moses	.05
384 Dave Gallagher (R)	.15	465 Dave Leiper	.05	546 Rich Yett	.05	627 Nelson Liriano	.05
385 Tom Henke	.05	466 Luis Alicea (R)	.15	547 Hensley Meulens (R)	.50	628 Mike Smithson	.05
386 Luis Polonia	.05	467 John Cerutti	.05	548 Greg Harris	.15	629 Scott Sanderson	.05
387 Junior Ortiz	.05	468 Ron Washington	.05	549 Darren Daulton	.05	630 Dale Mohorcic	.05
388 David Cone	.15	469 Jeff Reed	.05	550 Jeff Hamilton	.05	631 Marvin Freeman	.05
389 Dave Bergman	.05	470 Jeff Robinson	.10	551 Luis Aguayo	.05	632 Mike Young	.05
390 Danny Darwin	.05	471 Sid Fernandez	.10	552 Tim Leary	.10	633 Dennis Lamp	.05
391 Dan Gladden	.05	472 Terry Puhl	.05	553 Ron Oester	.05	634 Dante Bichette (R)	.25
392 John Dopson (R)	.20	473 Charlie Lea	.05	554 Steve Lombardozzi	.05	635 Curt Schilling (R)	.15
393 Frank DiPino	.05	474 Israel Sanchez (R)	.15	555 Tim Jones (R)	.15	636 Scott May (R)	.15
394 Al Nipper	.05	475 Bruce Benedict	.05	556 Bud Black	.05	637 Mike Schooler (R)	.35
395 Willie Randolph	.08	476 Oil Can Boyd	.08	557 Alejandro Pena	.08	638 Rick Leach	.05
396 Don Carmen	.05	477 Craig Reynolds	.05	558 Jose DeJesus (R)	.15	639 Tom Lampkin (R)	.15
397 Scott Terry	.05	478 Frank Williams	.05	559 Dennis Rasmussen	.05	640 Brian Meyer (R)	.15
398 Rick Cerone	.05	479 Greg Cadaret	.05	560 Pat Borders (R)	.15	641 Brian Harper	.05
399 Tom Pagnozzi	.05	480 Randy Kramer (R)	.15	561 Craig Biggio (R)	.35	642 John Smoltz (R)	.60
400 Checklist	.08	481 Dave Eiland (R)	.20	562 Luis de los Santos (R)	.20	643 Jose—40/40 Club	.60
401 Mickey Tettleton	.05	482 Eric Show	.05	563 Fred Lynn	.08	644 Bill Schroeder	.05
402 Curtis Wilkerson	.05	483 Garry Templeton	.05	564 Todd Burns (R)	.25	645 Edgar Martinez	.30
403 Jeff Russel	.05	484 Wallace Johnson	.05	565 Felix Fermin	.05	646 Dennis Cook (R)	.25
404 Pat Perry	.05	485 Kevin Mitchell	.35	566 Darnell Coles	.05	647 Barry Jones	.05
405 Jose Alvarez (R)	.15	486 Tim Crews	.05	567 Willie Fraser	.05	648 Orel—59 and Counting	.20
406 Rick Schu	.05	487 Mike Maddux	.05	568 Glenn Hubbard	.05	649 Rod Nichols (R)	.15
407 Sherman Corbett (R)	.15	488 Dave LaPoint	.05	569 Craig Worthington (R)	.20	650 Jody Davis	.05
408 Dave Magadan	.10	489 Fred Manrique	.05	570 Johnny Paredes (R)	.20	651 Bob Milacki (R)	.25
409 Bob Kipper	.05	490 Greg Minton	.05	571 Don Robinson	.05	652 Mike Jackson	.05
410 Don August	.10	491 Doug Dascenzo (R)	.25	572 Barry Lyons	.05	653 Derek Lilliquist (R)	.25
411 Bob Brower	.05	492 Willie Upshaw	.05	573 Bill Long	.05	654 Paul Mirabella	.05
412 Chris Bosio	.05	493 Jack Armstrong (R)	.40	574 Tracy Jones	.05	655 Mike Diaz	.05
413 Jerry Reuss	.05	494 Kirt Manwaring	.05	575 Juan Nieves	.05	656 Jeff Musselman	.05
414 Atlee Hammaker	.05	495 Jeff Ballard	.05	576 Andres Thomas	.05	657 Jerry Reed	.05
415 Jim Walewander	.10	496 Jeff Kunkel	.05	577 Rolando Roomes (R)	.20	658 Kevin Blankenship (R)	.15
416 Mike Macfarlane (R)	.20	497 Mike Campbell	.05	578 Luis Rivera	.15	659 Wayne Tolleson	.05
417 Pat Sheridan	.05	498 Gary Thurman	.05	579 Chad Kreuter (R)	.15	660 Eric Hetzel (R)	.15
418 Pedro Guerrero	.15	499 Zane Smith	.05	580 Tony Armas	.05		
419 Allan Anderson	.08	500 Checklist	.08	581 Jay Buhner	.15		
420 Mark Parent (R)	.15	501 Mike Birkbeck	.05	582 Ricky Horton	.05		
421 Bob Stanley	.05	502 Terry Leach	.05	583 Andy Hawkins	.05		
422 Mike Gallego	.05	503 Shawn Hillegas	.05	584 Sil Campusano (R)	.20		
423 Bruce Hurst	.15	504 Manny Lee	.05	585 Dave Cark	.05		
424 Dave Meads	.05	505 Doug Jennings (R)	.20	586 Van Snider (R)	.15		
425 Jesse Barfield	.12	506 Ken Oberkfell	.05	587 Todd Frohwirth	.05		
426 Rob Dibble (R)	.40	507 Tim Tuefel	.05	588 Puzzle Card	.08		
427 Joel Skinner	.05	508 Tom Brookens	.05	589 William Brennan (R)	.15		
428 Ron Kittle	.08	509 Rafael Ramirez	.05	590 German Gonzalez (R)	.15		
429 Rick Rhoden	.05	510 Fred Toliver	.05	591 Ernie Whitt	.05		
430 Bob Dernier	.05	511 Brian Holman (R)	.20	592 Jeff Blauser	.05		
431 Steve Jeltz	.05	512 Mike Bielecki	.05	593 Spike Owen	.05		
432 Rick Dempsey	.05	513 Jeff Pico (R)	.15	594 Matt Williams	.50		
433 Roberto Kelly	.15	514 Charles Hudson	.08	595 Lloyd McClendon	.10		
434 Dave Anderson	.05	515 Bruce Ruffin	.05	596 Steve Ontiveros	.05		
435 Herm Winningham	.05	516 Larry McWilliams	.05	597 Scott Medvin (R)	.15		
436 Al Newman	.05	517 Jeff Sellers	.05	598 Hipolito Pena (R)	.15		
437 Jose Deleon	.05	518 John Costello (R)	.15	599 Jerald Clark (R)	.20		
438 Doug Jones	.05	519 Brady Anderson (R)	.25	600 Checklist	.08		
439 Brian Holton	.05	520 Craig McMurtry	.05	601 Carmelo Martinez	.05		
440 Jeff Montgomery	.10	521 Ray Hayward	.05	602 Mike LaCoss	.05		
441 Dickie Thon	.05	522 Drew Hall	.10	603 Mike Devereaux	.05		
442 Cecil Fielder	.35	523 Mark Lemke (R)	.15	604 Alex Madrid (R)	.15		
443 John Fishel (R)	.15	524 Oswald Peraza (R)	.15	605 Gary Redus	.05		

1989 Donruss Rookies.... Complete Set of 56 Cards—Value $20.00

Features the outstanding rookies of the 1989 Season. The cards are coated with a glossy finish. The entire set was packaged in a printed box and distributed primarily through card hobby dealers. Features Donruss' first card of Jim Abbott, Jerome Walton and Dwight Smith.

NO.	PLAYER	MINT
1	Gary Sheffield	1.25
2	Gregg Jefferies	1.00
3	Ken Griffey, Jr.	6.00
4	Tom Gordon	.50
5	Billy Spiers	.35
6	Deion Sanders	1.00
7	Donn Pall	.15
8	Steve Carter	.20
9	Francisco Oliveras	.15
10	Steve Wilson	.12
11	Bob Geren	.20
12	Tony Castillo	.15
13	Kenny Rogers	.20
14	Carlos Martinez	.20
15	Edgar Martinez	.20
16	Jim Abbott	1.25
17	Torey Lovullo	.15
18	Mark Carreon	.15
19	Geronimo Berroa	.10
20	Luis Medina	.15
21	Sandy Alomar, Jr.	.75
22	Bob Milacki	.12
23	Joe Girardi	.30
24	German Gonzalez	.10
25	Craig Worthington	.20
26	Jerome Walton	2.00
27	Gary Wayne	.20
28	Tim Jones	.10
29	Dante Bichette	.10
30	Alexis Infante	.15
31	Ken Hill	.10
32	Dwight Smith	.75
33	Luis de los Santos	.15
34	Eric Yelding	.30
35	Gregg Olson	.75
36	Phil Stephenson	.15
37	Ken Patterson	.15
38	Rick Wrona	.20
39	Mike Brumley	.10
40	Cris Carpenter	.10
41	Jeff Brantley	.30
42	Ron Jones	.15
43	Randy Johnson	.10
44	Kevin Brown	.15
45	Ramon Martinez	1.00
46	Greg Harris	.15
47	Steve Finley	.25
48	Randy Kramer	.10
49	Erik Hanson	.30
50	Matt Merullo	.20
51	Mike Devereaux	.10
52	Clay Parker	.12
53	Omar Vizquel	.20
54	Derek Lilliquist	.15
55	Junior Felix	1.00
56	Checklist	.10

1990 Donruss.... Complete Set of 716 Cards—Value $30.00

The set was increased from 660 to 716 cards. Special cards honor Mike Schmidt's retirement and Nolan Ryan's strikeout record. Features the rookie cards of Todd Zeile, Eric Anthony, Andy Benes and Ben McDonald. Special Packaging is being introduced this year to help reduce tampering.

NO.	PLAYER	MINT
No. 1 to 26—Diamond Kings		
1	Bo Jackson (DK)	.60
2	Steve Sax (DK)	.10
3	R. Sierra (DK) (correct)	.15
3	R. Sierra (DK) (error)	1.25
4	Ken Griffey Jr. (DK)	.60
5	Mickey Tettleton (DK)	.10
6	Dave Stewart (DK)	.10
7	Jim DeShaies (DK)	.10
8	John Smoltz (DK)	.10
9	Mike Bielecki (DK)	.10
10	Brian Downing (DK)	.20
11	Kevin Mitchell (DK)	.15
12	Kelly Gruber (DK)	.10
13	Joe Magrane (DK)	.12
14	John Franco (DK)	.10
15	Ozzie Guillen (DK)	.10
16	Lou Whitaker (DK)	.10
17	John Smiley (DK)	.10
18	Howard Johnson (DK)	.15
19	Willie Randolph (DK)	.10
20	Chris Bosio (DK)	.10
21	Tommy Herr (DK)	.10
22	Dan Gladden (DK)	.10
23	Ellis Burks (DK)	.15
24	Pete O'Brien (DK)	.10
25	Bryn Smith (DK)	.10
26	Ed Whitson (DK)	.10
27	DK Checklist	.05
No. 28 to 47—Rated Rookies		
28	Robin Ventura	.35
29	Todd Zeile	.75
30	Sandy Alomar Jr.	.30
31	Kent Mercker (R)	.25
32	Ben McDonald (R)	1.50
33	J. Gonzalez (R) (correct)	2.00
33	J. Gonzalez (R) (error)	3.00
34	Eric Anthony (R)	1.00
35	Mike Fetters (R)	.15
36	Marquis Grissom (R)	.50
37	Greg Vaughn	.75
38	Brian Dubois (R)	.15
39	Steve Avery	.50
40	Mark Gardner (R)	.20
41	Andy Benes	.30
42	Delino Deshields (R)	.60
43	Scott Coolbaugh (R)	.25
44	Pat Combs	.15
45	Alex Sanchez	.15
46	Kelly Mann (R)	.15

1990 Donruss (Continued)

NO.	PLAYER	MINT
47	Julio Machado (R)	.15
48	Pete Incaviglia	.10
49	Shawon Dunston	.08
50	Jeff Treadway	.05
51	Jeff Ballard	.08
52	Claudell Washington	.08
53	Juan Samuel	.08
54	John Smiley	.10
55	Rob Deer	.05
56	Geno Petralli	.05
57	Chris Bosio	.05
58	Carlton Fisk	.12
59	Kirt Manwaring	.05
60	Chet Lemon	.05
61	Bo Jackson	.75
62	Doyle Alexander	.08
63	Pedro Guerrero	.12
64	Allan Anderson	.08
65	Greg Harris	.05
66	Mike Greenwell	.20
67	Walt Weiss	.10
68	Wade Boggs	.25
69	Jim Clancy	.05
70	Junior Felix	.35
71	Barry Larkin	.12
72	Dave LaPoint	.05
73	Joel Skinner	.05
74	Jesse Barfield	.05
75	Tommy Herr	.08
76	Ricky Jordan	.15
77	Eddie Murray	.12
78	Steve Sax	.10
79	Tim Belcher	.08
80	Danny Jackson	.10
81	Kent Hrbek	.10
82	Milt Thompson	.05
83	Brook Jacoby	.05
84	Mike Marshall	.08
85	Kevin Seitzer	.08
86	Tony Gwynn	.20
87	Dave Stieb	.05
88	Dave Smith	.08
89	Bret Saberhagen	.12
90	Alan Trammell	.10
91	Tony Phillips	.05
92	Doug Drabek	.10
93	Jeffrey Leonard	.05
94	Wally Joyner	.10
95	Carney Lansford	.08
96	Cal Ripken	.15
97	Andres Galarraga	.10
98	Kevin Mitchell	.20
99	Howard Johnson	.10
100	Checklist	.05
101	Melido Perez	.05
102	Spike Owen	.05
103	Paul Molitor	.10
104	Geronimo Berroa	.05
105	Ryne Sandberg	.15
106	Bryn Smith	.05
107	Steve Buechele	.05
108	Jim Abbott	.35
109	Alvin Davis	.10
110	Leo Smith	.25
111	Roberto Alomar	.10
112	Rick Reuschel	.08
113	Kelly Gruber	.12
114	Joe Carter	.12
115	Jose Rijo	.05
116	Greg Minton	.05
117	Bob Ojeda	.05
118	Glenn Davis	.12
119	Jeff Reardon	.08
120	Kurt Stillwell	.05
121	John Smoltz	.10
122	Dwight Evans	.08
123	Eric Yelding	.15
124	John Franco	.12
125	Jose Canseco	.60
126	Barry Bonds	.20
127	Lee Guetterman	.05
128	Jack Clark	.08
129	Dave Valle	.05
130	Hubie Brooks	.05
131	Ernest Riles	.05
132	Mike Morgan	.05
133	Steve Jeltz	.05
134	Jeff Robinson	.08
135	Ozzie Guillen	.08
136	Chili Davis	.05
137	Mitch Webster	.05
138	Jerry Browne	.08
139	Bo Diaz	.05
140	Robby Thompson	.10
141	Craig Worthington	.10
142	Julio Franco	.08
143	Brian Holman	.05
144	George Brett	.15
145	Tom Glavine	.10
146	Robin Yount	.20
147	Gary Carter	.10
148	Ron Kittle	.05
149	Tony Fernandez	.10
150	Dave Stewart	.10
151	Gary Gaetti	.10
152	Kevin Elster	.08
153	Gerald Perry	.05
154	Jesse Orosco	.05
155	Wally Backman	.05
156	Dennis Martinez	.05
157	Rick Sutcliffe	.05
158	Greg Maddux	.10
159	Andy Hawkins	.05
160	John Kruk	.05
161	Jose Oquendo	.05
162	John Dopson	.08
163	Joe Magrane	.10
164	Billy Ripken	.08
165	Fred Manrique	.05
166	Nolan Ryan	.50
167	Damon Berryhill	.08
168	Dale Murphy	.15
169	Mickey Tettleton	.05
170	Kirk McCaskill	.08
171	Dwight Gooden	.20
172	Jose Lind	.05
173	B.J. Surhoff	.05
174	Ruben Sierra	.20
175	Dan Plesac	.05
176	Dan Pasqua	.05
177	Kelly Downs	.08
178	Matt Nokes	.10
179	Luis Aquino	.05
180	Frank Tanana	.05
181	Tony Pena	.08
182	Dan Gladden	.05
183	Bruce Hurst	.05
184	Roger Clemens	.25
185	Mark McGwire	.25
186	Rob Murphy	.05
187	Jim Deshaies	.05
188	Fred McGriff	.15
189	Rob Dibble	.12
190	Don Mattingly	.50
191	Felix Fermin	.05
192	Roberto Kelly	.10
193	Dennis Cook	.05
194	Darren Daulton	.05
195	Alfredo Griffen	.08
196	Eric Plunk	.05
197	Orel Hershiser	.15
198	Paul O'Brien	.10
199	Randy Bush	.05
200	Checklist	.05
201	Ozzie Smith	.10
202	Pete O'Brien	.10
203	Jay Howell	.08
204	Mark Gubicza	.05
205	Ed Whitson	.05
206	George Bell	.10
207	Mike Scott	.08
208	Charlie Leibrandt	.05
209	Mike Heath	.05
210	Dennis Eckersley	.10
211	Mike LaValliere	.05
212	Darnell Coles	.05
213	Lance Parrish	.08
214	Mike Moore	.08
215	Steve Finley	.15
216	Tim Raines	.12
217	Scott Garrelts	.08
218	Kevin McReynolds	.10
219	Dave Gallagher	.05
220	Tim Wallach	.05
221	Chuck Crim	.05
222	Lonnie Smith	.05
223	Andre Dawson	.15
224	Nelson Santovenia	.05
225	Rafael Palmeiro	.10
226	Devon White	.12
227	Harold Reynolds	.05
228	Ellis Burks	.15
229	Mark Parent	.05
230	Will Clark	.60
231	Jimmy Key	.10
232	John Ferrell	.08
233	Eric Davis	.25
234	Johnny Ray	.08
235	Darryl Strawberry	.25
236	Bill Doran	.05
237	Greg Gagne	.05
238	Jim Eisenreich	.05
239	Tommy Gregg	.05
240	Marty Barrett	.05
241	Rafael Ramirez	.05
242	Chris Sabo	.20
243	Dave Henderson	.08
244	Andy Van Slyke	.10
245	Alvaro Espinoza	.05
246	Garry Templeton	.05
247	Gene Harris (R)	.15
248	Kevin Gross	.05
249	Brett Butler	.05
250	Willie Randolph	.10
251	Roger McDowell	.05
252	Rafael Belliard	.05
253	Steve Rosenberg	.05
254	Jack Howell	.05
255	Marvell Wynne	.05
256	Tom Candiotti	.05
257	Todd Benzinger	.08
258	Don Robinson	.05
259	Phil Bradley	.08
260	Cecil Espy	.05
261	Scott Bankhead	.05
262	Frank White	.05
263	Andres Thomas	.05
264	Glenn Braggs	.05
265	David Cone	.10
266	Bobby Thigpen	.05
267	Nelson Liriano	.05
268	Terry Steinbach	.12
269	Kirby Puckett	.30
270	Gregg Jefferies	.25
271	Jeff Blauser	.05
272	Cory Snyder	.10
273	Roy Smith	.05
274	Tom Foley	.05
275	Mitch Williams	.08
276	Paul Kilgus	.05
277	Don Slaught	.05
278	Von Hayes	.08
279	Vince Coleman	.10
280	Mike Boddicker	.08
281	Ken Dayley	.05
282	Mike Devereaux	.08
283	Kenny Rogers (R)	.15
284	Jeff Russell	.05
285	Jerome Walton	.50
286	Derek Lilliquist	.10
287	Joe Orsulak	.05
288	Dick Schofield	.05
289	Ron Darling	.10
290	Bobby Bonilla	.20
291	Jim Gantner	.05
292	Bobby Witt	.08
293	Greg Brock	.05
294	Ivan Calderon	.05
295	Steve Bedrosian	.05
296	Mike Henneman	.05
297	Tim Gordon	.20
298	Lou Whitaker	.08
299	Terry Pendleton	.05
300	Checklist No. 2	.05
301	Juan Berenguer	.05
302	Mark Davis	.10
303	Nick Esasky	.05
304	Rickey Henderson	.25
305	Rick Cerone	.05
306	Craig Biggio	.12
307	Duane Ward	.05
308	Tom Browning	.05
309	Walt Terrell	.05
310	Greg Swindell	.10
311	Dave Righetti	.10
312	Mike Maddux	.05
313	Lenny Dykstra	.08
314	Jose Gonzalez	.05
315	Steve Balboni	.05
316	Mike Scioscia	.08
317	Ron Oester	.05
318	Gary Wayne (R)	.15
319	Todd Worrell	.08
320	Doug Jones	.05
321	Jeff Hamilton	.05
322	Danny Tartabull	.10
323	Chris James	.05
324	Mike Flanagan	.05
325	Gerald Young	.05
326	Bob Boone	.05
327	Frank Williams	.05
328	Dave Parker	.12
329	Sid Bream	.05
330	Mike Schooler	.10
331	Bert Blyleven	.08
332	Bob Welch	.05
333	Bob Milacki	.08
334	Tim Burke	.05
335	Jose Uribe	.05
336	Randy Myers	.08
337	Eric King	.05
338	Mark Langston	.10
339	Ted Higuera	.05
340	Oddibe McDowell	.05
341	Lloyd McClendon	.05
342	Pascual Perez	.05
343	Kevin Brown	.05
344	Chuck Finley	.08
345	Erik Hanson	.08
346	Rich Gedman	.05
347	Bip Roberts	.05
348	Matt Williams	.15
349	Tom Henke	.05
350	Brad Komminsk	.05
351	Jeff Reed	.05
352	Brian Downing	.05
353	Frank Viola	.08
354	Terry Puhl	.05
355	Brian Harper	.05
356	Steve Farr	.05
357	Joe Boever	.05
358	Danny Heep	.05
359	Larry Anderson	.05
360	Rolando Roomes	.08
361	Mike Gallego	.05
362	Bob Kipper	.05
363	Clay Parker	.08
364	Mike Pagliarulo	.08
365	Ken Griffey Jr.	2.50
366	Rex Hudler	.05
367	Pat Sheridan	.05
368	Kirk Gibson	.10
369	Jeff Parrett	.05
370	Bob Walk	.05
371	Ken Patterson	.08
372	Bryan Harvey	.05
373	Mike Bielecki	.05
374	Tom Magrann (R)	.15
375	Rick Mahler	.05
376	Craig Lefferts	.05
377	Gregg Olson	.20
378	Jamie Moyer	.05
379	Randy Johnson	.08
380	Jeff Montgomery	.08
381	Marty Clary	.05
382	Bill Spiers	.20

NO.	PLAYER	MINT
383	Dave Magadan	.08
384	Greg Hibbard (R)	.20
385	Ernie Whitt	.05
386	Rick Honeycutt	.05
387	Dave West	.08
388	Keith Hernandez	.08
389	Jose Alvarez	.05
390	Joey Belle	.30
391	Rick Aguilera	.05
392	Mike Fitzgerald	.05
393	Dwight Smith	.25
394	Steve Wilson	.10
395	Bob Geren	.15
396	Randy Ready	.05
397	Ken Hill	.08
398	Jody Reed	.05
399	Tom Brunansky	.05
400	Checklist No. 3	.05
401	Rene Gonzales	.05
402	Harold Baines	.05
403	Cecilio Guante	.05
404	Joe Girardi	.10
405	Sergio Valdez (R)	.15
406	Mark Williamson	.05
407	Glenn Hoffman	.05
408	Jeff Innis	.10
409	Randy Kramer	.05
410	Charlie O'Brien	.05
411	Charlie Hough	.05
412	Gus Polidor	.05
413	Ron Karkovice	.05
414	Trevor Wilson	.10
415	Kevin Ritz (R)	.15
416	Gary Thurman	.05
417	Jeff Robinson	.08
418	Scott Terry	.05
419	Tim Laudner	.05
420	Dennis Rasmussen	.05
421	Luis Rivera	.05
422	Jim Corsi	.05
423	Dennis Lampl	.05
424	Ken Caminiti	.05
425	David Wells	.05
426	Norm Charlton	.05
427	Deion Sanders	.25
428	Dion James	.05
429	Chuck Cary	.05
430	Ken Howell	.05
431	Steve Lake	.05
432	Kal Daniels	.10
433	Lance McCullers	.05
434	Lenny Harris	.05
435	Scott Scudder	.15
436	Gene Larkin	.05
437	Dan Quisenberry	.05
438	Steve Olin (R)	.15
439	Mickey Hatcher	.05
440	Willie Wilson	.08
441	Mark Grant	.05
442	Mookie Wilson	.08
443	Alex Trevino	.05
444	Pat Tabler	.05
445	Dave Bergman	.05
446	Todd Burns	.05
447	R.J. Reynolds	.05
448	Jay Buhner	.08
449	Les Stevens	.30
450	Ron Hassey	.05
451	Bob Melvin	.05
452	Dave Martinez	.05
453	Greg Litton	.15
454	Mark Carreon	.05
455	Scott Fletcher	.05
456	Otis Nixon	.05
457	Tony Fossas (R)	.15
458	John Russel	.05
459	Paul Assenmacher	.05
460	Zane Smith	.05
461	Jack Daugherty (R)	.15
462	Rich Monteleone	.15
463	Greg Briley	.15
464	Mike Smithson	.05
465	Benito Santiago	.10
466	Jeff Brantley	.15
467	Jose Nunez	.05
468	Scott Bailes	.05
469	Ken Griffey	.05
470	Bob McClure	.05
471	Mackey Sasser	.05
472	Glenn Wilson	.05
473	Kevin Tapani (R)	.30
474	Bill Buckner	.05
475	Ron Gant	.15
476	Kevin Romine	.05
477	Juan Agosto	.05
478	Herm Winningham	.05
479	Storm Davis	.05
480	Jeff King	.10
481	Kevin Mmahat (R)	.15
482	Carmelo Martinez	.05
483	Omar Vizquel	.15
484	Jim Dwyer	.05
485	Bob Knepper	.05
486	Dave Anderson	.05
487	Ron Jones	.05
488	Jay Bell	.05
489	Sammy Sosa (R)	.50
490	Kent Anderson	.12
491	Domingo Ramos	.05
492	Dave Clark	.05
493	Tim Birtsas	.05
494	Ken Oberkfell	.05
495	Larry Sheets	.05
496	Jeff Kunkel	.05
497	Jim Presley	.05
498	Mike Macfarlane	.05
499	Pete Smith	.05
500	Checklist	.05
501	Gary Sheffield	.25
502	Terry Bross (R)	.15
503	Jerry Kutzler (R)	.15
504	Lloyd Moseby	.08
505	Curt Young	.05
506	Al Newman	.05
507	Keith Miller	.05
508	Mike Stanton (R)	.15
509	Rich Yett	.05
510	Tim Drummond (R)	.15
511	Joe Hesketh	.05
512	Rick Wrona	.15
513	Luis Salazar	.05
514	Hal Morns	.20
515	Terry Mulholland	.05
516	John Morris	.05
517	Carlos Quintana	.12
518	Frank DiPino	.10
519	Randy Milligan	.12
520	Chad Kreuter	.05
521	Mike Jeffcoat	.05
522	Mike Harkey	.10
523	Andy Nezalek	.05
524	Dave Schmidt	.08
525	Tony Armas	.05
526	Barry Lyons	.05
527	Rick Reed (R)	.15
528	Jerry Reuss	.05
529	Dean Palmer (R)	.20
530	Jeff Peterek (R)	.15
531	Carlos Martinez	.20
532	Atlee Hammaker	.05
533	Mike Brumley	.05
534	Terry Leach	.05
535	Doug Strange (R)	.15
536	Jose DeLeon	.05
537	Shane Rawley	.05
538	Joey Cora	.05
539	Eric Hetzel	.05
540	Gene Nelson	.05
541	Wes Gardner	.05
542	Mark Portugal	.05
543	Al Leiter	.05
544	Jack Armstrong	.05
545	Greg Cadaret	.05
546	Rod Nichols	.05
547	Luis Polonia	.05
548	Charles Hayes	.05
549	Dickie Thon	.05
550	Tim Crews	.05
551	Dave Winfield	.15
552	Mike Davis	.05
553	Ron Robinson	.05
554	Carmen Castillo	.05
555	John Costello	.05
556	Bud Black	.05
557	Rick Dempsey	.05
558	Jim Acker	.05
559	Eric Show	.05
560	Pat Borders	.05
561	Danny Darwin	.05
562	Rick Luecken (R)	.15
563	Edwin Nunez	.05
564	Felix Jose	.12
565	John Cangelosi	.05
566	Billy Swift	.05
567	Bill Schroeder	.05
568	Stan Javier	.05
569	Jim Traber	.05
570	Wallace Johnson	.05
571	Donnell Nixon	.05
572	Sid Fernandez	.08
573	Lance Johnson	.05
574	Andy McGaffigan	.05
575	Mark Knudson	.05
576	Tommy Greene (R)	.30
577	Mark Grace	.25
578	Larry Walker (R)	.35
579	Mike Stanley	.05
580	Mike Witt	.08
581	Scott Bradley	.05
582	Greg Harris	.05
583	Kevin Hickey	.10
584	Lee Mazzilli	.05
585	Jeff Pico	.05
586	Joe Oliver	.15
587	Willie Fraser	.05
588	Puzzle Card	.05
589	Kevin Bass	.05
590	John Moses	.05
591	Tom Pagnozzi	.05
592	Tony Castillo	.10
593	Jerald Clark	.05
594	Dan Schatzeder	.05
595	Luis Quinones	.05
596	Pete Harnisch	.08
597	Gary Redus	.05
598	Mel Hall	.08
599	Rick Schu	.05
600	Checklist	.05
601	Mike Kingery	.05
602	Terry Kennedy	.05
603	Mike Sharperson	.05
604	Don Carman	.05
605	Jim Gott	.05
606	Donn Pall	.05
607	Rance Mulliniks	.05
608	Curt Wilkerson	.05
609	Mike Felder	.05
610	Guillermo Hermandez	.05
611	Candy Maldonado	.05
612	Mark Thurmond	.05
613	Rick Leach	.05
614	Jerry Reed	.05
615	Franklin Stubbs	.05
616	Billy Hatcher	.05
617	Don August	.08
618	Tim Teufel	.05
619	Shawn Hillegas	.05
620	Manny Lee	.05
621	Gary Ward	.05
622	Mark Guthrie (R)	.15
623	Jeff Musselman	.05
624	Mark Lemke	.05
625	Fernando Valenzuela	.10
626	Paul Sorrento (R)	.15
627	Glenallen Hill	.10
628	Les Lancaster	.05
629	Vance Law	.05
630	Randy Velarde	.05
631	Todd Frohwirth	.05
632	Willie McGee	.08
633	Oil Can Boyd	.05
634	Cris Carpenter	.05
635	Brian Holton	.05
636	Tracy Jones	.05
637	Terry Steinbach (AS)	.08
638	Brady Anderson	.05
639	Jack Morris	.15
640	Jaime Navarro	.20
641	Darrin Jackson	.12
642	Mike Dyer (R)	.15
643	Mike Schmidt	.25
644	Henry Cotto	.05
645	John Cerutti	.05
646	Francisco Cabera	.20
647	Scott Sanderson	.05
648	Brian Meyer	.10
649	Ray Searage	.05
650	Bo Jackson (AS)	.50
651	Steve Lyons	.05
652	Mike LaCoss	.05
653	Ted Power	.05
654	Howard Johnson (AS)	.10
655	Mauro Gozzo (R)	.15
656	Mike Blowers (R)	.20
657	Paul Gibson	.05
658	Neal Heaton	.05
659	N. Ryan 5000 K (cor.)	1.00
659	N. Ryan 5000 K (error)	7.00
660	Harold Baines (AS)	.20
661	Steve Lyons	.05
662	Clint Zavaras (R)	.15
663	Rick Reuschel (AS)	.08
664	Alejandro Pena	.05
665	Nolan Ryan (correct)	1.00
665	Nolan Ryan (error)	7.00
666	Ricky Horton	.05
667	Curt Schilling	.05
668	Bill Landrum	.05
669	Todd Stottlemyre	.10
670	Tim Leary	.08
671	John Wetteland	.25
672	Calvin Schiraldi	.05
673	Ruben Sierra (AS)	.20
674	Pedro Guerrero (AS)	.12
675	Ken Phelps	.05
676	Cal Ripken (AS)	.15
677	Denny Walling	.05
678	Goose Gossage	.05
679	Gary Mielke (R)	.15
680	Bill Bathe	.05
681	Tom Lawless	.05
682	Xavier Hernandez (R)	.15
683	Kirby Puckett (AS)	.25
684	Mariano Duncan	.05
685	Ramon Martinez	.40
686	Tim Jones	.05
687	Tom Filer	.05
688	Steve Lombardozzi	.05
689	Bernie Williams (R)	.40
690	Chip Hale (R)	.15
691	Beau Allerd (R)	.15
692	Ryne Sandberg (AS)	.20
693	Jeff Huson (R)	.15
694	Curt Ford	.05
695	Eric Davis (AS)	.15
696	Scott Lusader	.05
697	Mark McGwire (AS)	.20
698	Steve Cummings (R)	.15
699	George Canale (R)	.15
700	Checklist	.05
701	Julio Franco (AS)	.12
702	Dave Johnson	.12
703	Dave Stewart (AS)	.12
704	Dave Justice (R)	3.50
705	Tony Gwynn (AS)	.20
706	Greg Myers	.05
707	Will Clark (AS)	.35
708	Benito Santiago (AS)	.12
709	Larry McWilliams	.05
710	Ozzie Smith (AS)	.10
711	John Olerud (R)	3.00
712	Wade Boggs (AS)	.20
713	Gary Eave (R)	.15
714	Bob Tewksbury	.05
715	Kevin Mitchell (AS)	.20
716	A. Bartlett Giamatti BB Commissioner	1.00

1990 Donruss Rookies. . . . Complete Set of 56 Cards—Value $12.00

Features the outstanding rookies of the 1989 season. The cards are coated with a glossy finish. The entire set was packaged in a printed box, and distributed through card hobby dealers.

NO.	PLAYER	MINT	NO.	PLAYER	MINT	NO.	PLAYER	MINT	NO.	PLAYER	MINT
1	Sandy Alomar	.25	15	Robin Ventura	.20	29	Willie Blair	.08	43	Mark Lemke	.05
2	John Olerud	1.25	16	Greg Vaughn	.40	30	Ben McDonald	1.00	44	Alan Mills	.15
3	Pat Combs	.08	17	Wayne Edwards	.15	31	Todd Zeile	.40	45	Marquis Grissom	.20
4	Brian DuBois	.05	18	Shawn Boskie	.15	32	Scott Coolbaugh	.10	46	Greg Olson	.25
5	Felix Jose	.10	19	Carlos Baerga	.45	33	Xavier Hernandez	.05	47	Dave Hollins	.30
6	Delino DeShields	.60	20	Mark Gardner	.15	34	Mike Hartley	.25	48	Jerald Clark	.10
7	Mike Stanton	.05	21	Kevin Appier	.25	35	Kevin Tapani	.15	49	Eric Anthony	.40
8	Mike Munoz	.10	22	Mike Harkey	.20	36	Kevin Wickander	.10	50	Tim Drummond	.05
9	Craig Grebeck	.10	23	Tim Layana	.15	37	Carlos Hernandez	.08	51	John Burkett	.25
10	Joe Kraemer	.10	24	Glenallen Hill	.10	38	Brian Traxler	.12	52	Brent Knackert	.15
11	Jeff Huson	.05	25	Jerry Kutzler	.05	39	Marty Brown	.12	53	Jeff Shaw	.10
12	Bill Sampen	.20	26	Mike Blowers	.10	40	Scott Radinsky	.15	54	John Orton	.10
13	Brian Bohanon	.15	27	Scott Ruskin	.15	41	Julio Machado	.05	55	Terry Shumpert	.15
14	Dave Justice	2.50	28	Dana Kiecker	.20	42	Steve Avery	.20	56	Checklist	.05

1991 Donruss. . . . Series One Set of 396 Cards—Value $12.50; Series Two Set of 396 Cards—Value $12.50

The set was increased from 716 to 792 cards. For the first time Donruss cards were issued in two series (396 cards each). Heavier card stock was used this year. Features 40 Rated Rookies cards—(twice as many as last year) and 22 Highlights cards.

NO.	PLAYER	MINT	NO.	PLAYER	MINT	NO.	PLAYER	MINT	NO.	PLAYER	MINT
SERIES NO. 1			17	Dave Magadan (DK)	.05	34	Terry Bross	.08	52	Cal Ripken (AS)	.10
No. 1 to 26—Diamond Kings			18	Matt Williams (DK)	.10	35	Leo Gomez	.35	53	Rickey Henderson (AS)	.20
1	Dave Stieb (DK)	.08	19	Rafael Palmeiro (DK)	.10	36	Derrick May	.30	54	Bob Welch (AS)	.05
2	Craig Biggio (DK)	.05	20	Bob Welch (DK)	.05	37	Kevin Morton (R)	.12	55	Wade Boggs (AS)	.12
3	Cecil Fielder (DK)	.15	21	Dave Righetti (DK)	.05	38	Moises Alou	.25	56	Mark McGwire (AS)	.15
4	Barry Bonds (DK)	.12	22	Brian Harper (DK)	.05	39	Julio Valera	.12	57	Jack McDowell	.05
5	Barry Larkin (DK)	.10	23	Gregg Olson (DK)	.05	40	Milt Cuyler	.15	58	Jose Lind	.05
6	Dave Parker (DK)	.08	24	Kurt Stillwell (DK)	.05	41	Phil Plantier (R)	.50	59	Alex Fernandez	1.00
7	Len Dykstra (DK)	.05	25	Pedro Guerrero (DK)	.08	42	Scott Chiamparino	.20	60	Pat Combs	.05
8	Bobby Thigpen (DK)	.05	26	Chuck Finley (DK)	.05	43	Ray Lankford	.35	61	Mike Walker	.05
9	Roger Clemens (DK)	.12	27	Diamond King Checklist	.05	44	Mickey Morandini	.15	62	Juan Samuel	.05
10	Ron Gant (DK)	.05	**No. 28 to 47—Rated Rookies**			45	Dave Hansen	.20	63	Mike Blowers	.05
11	Delino DeShields (DK)	.12	28	Tino Martinez	.30	46	Kevin Belcher (R)	.12	64	Mark Guthrie	.05
12	Roberto Alomar (DK)	.10	29	Mark Lewis	.15	47	Darrin Fletcher	.10	65	Mark Salas	.05
13	Sandy Alomar (DK)	.10	30	Bernard Gilkey	.25	48	Steve Sax (AS)	.08	66	Tim Jones	.05
14	Ryne Sandberg (DK)	.15	31	Hensley Meulens	.12	49	Ken Griffey, Jr. (AS)	.08	67	Tim Leary	.05
15	Ramon Martinez (DK)	.08	32	Derek Bell	.25	50	Jose Canseco (AS)	.30	68	Andres Galarraga	.08
16	Edgar Martinez (DK)	.05	33	Jose Offerman	.40	51	Sandy Alomar (AS)	.10	69	Bob Milacki	.05

NO.	PLAYER	MINT	NO.	PLAYER	MINT	NO.	PLAYER	MINT	NO.	PLAYER	MINT
70	Tim Belcher	.05	155	Todd Stottlemyre	.05	241	Shawn Boskie	.05	326	Dave Henderson	.05
71	Todd Zeile	.15	156	Glenn Wilson	.05	242	Tom Gordon	.10	327	Wayne Edwards	.05
72	Jerome Walton	.15	157	Bob Walk	.05	243	Tony Gwynn	.15	328	Mark Knudson	.05
73	Kevin Seltzer	.05	158	Mike Gallego	.05	244	Tommy Gregg	.05	329	Terry Steinbach	.05
74	Jerald Clark	.05	159	Greg Hibbard	.05	245	Jeff Robinson	.05	330	Colby Ward (R)	.12
75	John Smoltz	.05	160	Chris Bosio	.05	246	Keith Comstock	.05	331	Oscar Azocar	.20
76	Mike Henneman	.05	161	Mike Moore	.05	247	Jack Howell	.05	332	Scott Radinsky	.05
77	Ken Griffey, Jr.	.75	162	Jerry Browne	.05	248	Keith Miller	.05	333	Eric Anthony	.12
78	Jim Abbott	.15	163	Steve Sax	.05	249	Bobby Witt	.05	334	Steve Lake	.05
79	Gregg Jefferies	.15	164	Melido Perez	.05	250	Rob Murphy	.05	335	Bob Melvin	.05
80	Kevin Reimer	.05	165	Danny Darwin	.05	251	Spike Owen	.05	336	Kal Daniels	.10
81	Roger Clemens	.20	166	Roger McDowell	.05	252	Garry Templeton	.05	337	Tom Pagnozzi	.05
82	Mike Fitzgerald	.05	167	Billy Ripken	.05	253	Glenn Braggs	.05	338	Alan Mills	.05
83	Bruce Hurst	.05	168	Mike Sharperson	.05	254	Ron Robinson	.05	339	Steve Olin	.05
84	Eric Davis	.15	169	Lee Smith	.05	255	Kevin Mitchell	.20	340	Juan Berenguer	.05
85	Paul Molitor	.10	170	Matt Nokes	.05	256	Les Lancaster	.05	341	Francisco Cabrera	.05
86	Will Clark	.30	171	Jesse Orosco	.05	257	Mel Stottlemyre	.05	342	Dave Bergman	.05
87	Mike Bielecki	.05	172	Rick Aguiera	.05	258	Kenny Rogers	.05	343	Henry Cotto	.05
88	Bret Saberhagen	.10	173	Jim Presley	.05	259	Lance Johnson	.05	344	Sergio Valdez	.05
89	Nolan Ryan	.30	174	Lou Whitaker	.05	260	John Kruk	.05	345	Bob Patterson	.05
90	Bobby Thigpen	.08	175	Harold Reynolds	.05	261	Fred McGriff	.10	346	John Marzano	.05
91	Dickie Thon	.05	176	Brook Jacoby	.05	262	Dick Schofield	.05	347	Dana Kiecker	.05
92	Duane Ward	.05	177	Wally Backman	.05	263	Trevor Wilson	.05	348	Dion James	.05
93	Luis Polonia	.05	178	Wade Boggs	.20	264	David West	.05	349	Hubie Brooks	.05
94	Terry Kennedy	.05	179	Chuck Cary	.05	265	Scott Scudder	.05	350	Bill Landrum	.05
95	Kent Hrbek	.10	180	Tom Foley	.05	266	Dwight Gooden	.15	351	Bill Sampen	.05
96	Danny Jackson	.05	181	Peter Harnisch	.05	267	Willie Blair	.05	352	Greg Briley	.05
97	Sid Fernandez	.05	182	Mike Morgan	.05	268	Mark Portugal	.05	353	Paul Gibson	.05
98	Jimmy Key	.05	183	Bob Tewksbury	.05	269	Doug Drabek	.05	354	Dave Eiland	.05
99	Franklin Stubbs	.05	184	Joe Girardi	.05	270	Dennis Eckersley	.10	355	Steve Finley	.05
100	Checklist No. 1	.05	185	Storm Davis	.05	271	Eric King	.05	356	Bob Boone	.05
101	R. J. Reynolds	.05	186	Ed Whitson	.05	272	Robin Yount	.15	357	Steve Buechele	.05
102	Dave Stewart	.12	187	Steve Avery	.15	273	Carney Lansford	.05	358	Chris Hoiles	.10
103	Dan Pasqua	.05	188	Lloyd Moseby	.05	274	Carlos Baerga	.15	359	Larry Walker	.10
104	Dan Plesac	.05	189	Scott Bankhead	.05	275	Dave Righetti	.05	360	Frank DiPino	.05
105	Mark McGwire	.20	190	Mark Langston	.05	276	Scott Fletcher	.05	361	Mark Grant	.05
106	John Farrell	.05	191	Kevin McReynolds	.10	277	Eric Yelding	.05	362	Dave Magadan	.08
107	Don Mattingly	.30	192	Julio Franco	.05	278	Charles Hayes	.05	363	Robby Thompson	.05
108	Carlton Fisk	.10	193	John Dopson	.05	279	Jeff Ballard	.05	364	Lonnie Smith	.05
109	Ken Oberkfell	.05	194	Oil Can Boyd	.05	280	Orel Hershiser	.10	365	Steve Farr	.05
110	Darrel Akerfelds	.05	195	Bip Roberts	.05	281	Jose Oquendo	.05	366	Dave Valle	.05
111	Gregg Olson	.12	196	Billy Hatcher	.05	282	Mike Witt	.05	367	Tim Naehring	.25
112	Mike Scioscia	.05	197	Edgar Diaz	.05	283	Mitch Webster	.05	368	Jim Acker	.05
113	Bryn Smith	.05	198	Greg Litton	.05	284	Greg Gagne	.05	369	Jeff Reardon	.05
114	Bob Geren	.05	199	Mark Grace	.15	285	Greg Olson	.10	370	Tim Teufel	.05
115	Tom Candlotti	.05	200	Checklist No. 2	.05	286	Tony Phillips	.05	371	Juan Gonzalez	.25
116	Kevin Tapani	.05	201	George Brett	.15	287	Scott Bradley	.05	372	Luis Salazar	.05
117	Jeff Treadway	.05	202	Jeff Russell	.05	288	Cory Snyder	.08	373	Rick Honeycutt	.05
118	Alan Trammell	.08	203	Ivan Calderon	.05	289	Jay Bell	.05	374	Greg Maddux	.05
119	Pete O'Brien	.05	204	Ken Howell	.05	290	Kevin Romine	.05	375	Jose Uribe	.05
120	Joel Skinner	.05	205	Tom Henke	.05	291	Jeff Robinson	.05	376	Donnie Hill	.05
121	Mike LaValliere	.05	206	Bryan Harvey	.05	292	Steve Frey	.05	377	Don Carman	.05
122	Dwight Evans	.05	207	Steve Bedrosian	.05	293	Craig Worthington	.05	378	Craig Grebeck	.05
123	Jody Reed	.05	208	Al Newman	.05	294	Tim Crews	.05	379	Willie Fraser	.05
124	Lee Guetterman	.05	209	Randy Myers	.05	295	Joe Magrane	.05	380	Glenallen Hill	.05
125	Tim Burke	.05	210	Daryl Boston	.05	296	Hector Villanueva	.10	381	Joe Oliver	.05
126	Dave Johnson	.05	211	Manny Lee	.05	297	Terry Shumpert	.05	382	Randy Bush	.05
127	Fernando Valenzuela	.10	212	Dave Smith	.05	298	Joe Carter	.08	383	Alex Cole	.25
128	Jose DeLeon	.05	213	Don Slaught	.05	299	Kent Mercker	.05	384	Norm Charlton	.05
129	Andre Dawson	.12	214	Walt Weiss	.05	300	Checklist No. 3	.05	385	Gene Nelson	.05
130	Gerald Perry	.05	215	Donn Pall	.05	301	Chet Lemon	.05	386	Checklist No. 4	.05
131	Greg Harris	.05	216	Jamie Navarro	.05	302	Mike Schooler	.05			
132	Tom Glavine	.05	217	Willie Randolph	.05	303	Dante Bichette	.05			
133	Lance McCullers	.05	218	Rudy Seanez	.05	304	Kevin Elster	.05			
134	Randy Johnson	.05	219	Jim Leyritz	.08	305	Jeff Huson	.05			
135	Lance Parrish	.05	220	Ron Karkovice	.05	306	Greg Harris	.05			
136	Mackey Sasser	.05	221	Ken Caminiti	.05	307	Marquis Grissom	.10			
137	Geno Petralli	.05	222	Von Hayes	.05	308	Calvin Schiraldi	.05			
138	Dennis Lamp	.05	223	Cal Ripken	.15	309	Mariano Duncan	.05			
139	Dennis Martinez	.05	224	Lenny Harris	.05	310	Bill Spiers	.05			
140	Mike Pagliarulo	.05	225	Milt Thompson	.05	311	Scott Garrelts	.05			
141	Hal Morris	.05	226	Alvaro Espinoza	.05	312	Mitch Williams	.05			
142	Dave Parker	.10	227	Chris James	.05	313	Mike Macfarlane	.05			
143	Brett Butler	.05	228	Dan Gladden	.05	314	Kevin Brown	.05			
144	Paul Assenmacher	.05	229	Jeff Blauser	.05	315	Robin Ventura	.15			
145	Mark Gubicza	.05	230	Mike Heath	.05	316	Darren Daulton	.05			
146	Charlie Hough	.05	231	Omar Vizquel	.05	317	Pat Borders	.05			
147	Sammy Sosa	.12	232	Jeff King	.05	318	Mark Eichhorn	.05			
148	Randy Ready	.05	234	Luis Rivera	.05	319	Jeff Brantley	.05			
149	Kelly Gruber	.10	235	Ellis Burks	.10	320	Shane Mack	.05			
150	Devon White	.05	236	Greg Cadaret	.05	321	Rob Dibble	.05			
151	Gary Carter	.10	237	Dave Martinez	.05	322	John Franco	.05			
152	Gene Larkin	.05	238	Mark Williamson	.05	323	Junior Felix	.10			
153	Chris Sabo	.10	239	Stan Javier	.05	324	Casey Candaele	.05			
154	David Cone	.05	240	Ozzie Smith	.10	325	Bobby Bonilla	.15			

**SERIES TWO
NOT AVAILABLE
AT PRESS TIME**

1981 Fleer .... Complete Set of 660 Cards (1st printing, with corrected "Graig" Nettles)—Value $50.00; Complete Set of 660 Cards (1st printing, with error "Craig" Nettles)—Value $60.00; Complete Set of 660 Cards (2nd printing)—Value $50.00; Complete Set of 660 Cards (3rd printing)—Value $50.00

This was Fleer's first baseball card set since 1963. Over 30 cards contained errors; they were corrected in the 2nd and 3rd printing runs. The "Craig" Nettles error was corrected during the first printing. There is very little interest by collectors in the *variety* (error) cards; none are scarce or worth much more than ordinary cards, except card 87, "Craig" Nettles. If a *variety* (error) is significant, it is listed and explained; if it is *minor*, it is noted by an *asterisk*. This set features the rookie cards of Fernando Valenzuela, Kirk Gibson and Harold Baines.

  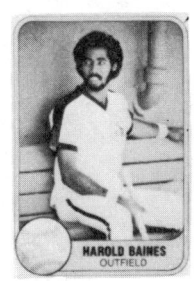  

NO. PLAYER	MINT
PHILADELPHIA PHILLIES	
1 Pete Rose	1.50
2 Larry Bowa	.12
3 Manny Trillo	.05
4 Bob Boone	.05
5 Mike Schmidt	1.50
(MVP) Third Base	
See No. 640	
6 Steve Carlton	.75
(Pitcher of Year)	
See No. 660	
Error—"1066"	
Cardinals" on Back	
6 Steve Carlton	2.00
Corrected "1966" Cardinals	
7 Tug McGraw	.07
See No. 657	
8 Larry Christenson	.05
9 Bake McBride	.05
10 Greg Luzinski	.10
11 Ron Reed	.05
12 Dickie Noles	.05
13 Keith Moreland (R)	.20
14 Bob Walk	.25
15 Lonnie Smith	.08
16 Dick Ruthven	.05
17 Sparky Lyle	.07
18 Greg Gross	.05
19 Garry Maddox	.05
20 Nino Espinosa	.05
21 George Vukovich	.05
22 John Vukovich	.05
23 Ramon Aviles	.05
24 Ken Saucier*	.08
25 Randy Lerch	.05
26 Del Uncer	.05
27 Tim McCarver	.08
KANSAS CITY ROYALS	
28 George Brett—MVP	1.50
See No. 655	
29 Willie Wilson	.20
See No. 653	
30 Paul Splittorff	.05
31 Dan Quisenberry	.15
32 Amos Otis*	.10
33 Steve Busby	.05
34 U.L. Washington	.05
35 Dave Chalk	.05
36 Darrell Porter	.08
37 Marty Pattin	.05
38 Larry Gura	.05
39 Renie Martin	.05
40 Rich Gale	.05
41 Hal McRae*	.25
42 Dennis Leonard	.05
43 Willie Aikens	.05
44 Frank White	.08
45 Clint Hurdle	.05
46 John Wathan	.05
47 Pete LaCock	.05
48 Rance Mulliniks	.05

NO. PLAYER	MINT
49 Jeff Twitty	.05
50 Jamie Quirk	.05
HOUSTON ASTROS	
51 Art How	.05
52 Ken Forsch	.05
53 Vern Ruhle	.05
54 Joe Niekro	.08
55 Frank LaCorte	.05
56 J.R. Richard	.08
57 Nolan Ryan	3.00
58 Enos Cabell	.05
59 Cesar Cedeno	.08
60 Jose Cruz	.15
61 Bill Virdon (Mgr.)	.05
62 Terry Puhl	.05
63 Joaquin Andujar	.10
64 Alan Ashby	.05
65 Joe Sambito	.05
66 Denny Walling	.05
67 Jeff Leonard	.15
68 Luis Pujols	.05
69 Bruce Bochy	.05
70 Rafael Landestoy	.05
71 Dave Smith (R)	.30
72 Danny Heep	.20
73 Julio Gonzalez	.05
74 Craig Reynolds	.05
75 Gary Woods	.05
76 Dave Bergman	.05
77 Randy Niemann	.05
78 Joe Morgan	.40
NEW YORK YANKEES	
79 Reggie Jackson	1.00
See No. 650	
80 Bucky Dent	.07
81 Tommy John	.15
82 Luis Tiant	.05
83 Rick Cerone	.05
84 Dick Howser (Mgr.)	.05
85 Lou Piniella	.10
86 Ron Davis	.05
87 Graig Nettles	11.00
Error—"Craig" on Back	
87 Graig Nettles	.30
Corrected—"Graig"	
88 Ron Guidry	.25
89 Rich Gossage	.20
90 Rudy May	.05
91 Gaylord Perry	.30
92 Eric Soderholm	.05
93 Bob Watson	.05
94 Bobby Murcer	.08
95 Bobby Brown	.05
96 Jim Spencer	.05
97 Tom Underwood	.05
98 Oscar Gamble	.05
99 Johnny Oates	.05
100 Fred Stanley	.05
101 Ruppert Jones	.05
102 Dennis Werth	.05
103 Joe LeFebvre	.12

NO. PLAYER	MINT
104 Brian Doyle	.05
105 Aurelio Rodriguez	.05
106 Doug Bird	.05
107 Mike Griffin	.05
108 Tim Lollar (R)	.20
109 Willie Randolph	.12
LOS ANGELES DODGERS	
110 Steve Garvey	.50
111 Reggie Smith	.08
112 Don Sutton	.30
113 Burt Hooton	.05
114 Dave Lopes*	.08
115 Dusty Baker	.10
116 Tom Lasorda (Mgr.)	.08
117 Bill Russell	.05
118 Jerry Reuss	.08
119 Terry Forster	.05
120 Robert Welch*	.50
121 Don Stanhouse	.05
122 Rick Monday	.08
123 Derrel Thomas	.05
124 Joe Ferguson	.05
125 Rick Sutcliffe	.30
126 Ron Cey*	.15
127 Dave Goltz	.05
128 Jay Johnstone	.05
129 Steve Yeager	.05
130 Gary Weiss	.05
131 Mike Scioscia (R)	.50
132 Vic Davalillo	.05
133 Doug Rau	.05
134 Pepe Frias	.05
135 Mickey Hatcher	.05
136 Steve Howe (R)	.15
137 Robert Castillo	.05
138 Gary Thomasson	.05
139 Rudy Law	.05
140 F. Valenzuela (R)	4.00
141 Manny Mota	.08
MONTREAL EXPOS	
142 Gary Carter	.40
143 Steve Rogers	.08
144 Warren Cromartie	.05
145 Andre Dawson	.75
146 Larry Parrish	.05
147 Rowland Office	.05
148 Ellis Valentine	.05
149 Dick Williams (Mgr.)	.05
150 Bill Gullickson (R)	.25
151 Elias Sosa	.05
152 John Tamargo	.05
153 Chris Speier	.05
154 Ron LeFlore	.05
155 Rodney Scott	.05
156 Stan Bahnsen	.05
157 Bill Lee	.05
158 Fred Norman	.05
159 Woodie Fryman	.05
160 Dave Palmer	.05
161 Jerry White	.05
162 Roberto Ramos	.05

NO. PLAYER	MINT
163 John D'Acquisto	.05
164 Tommy Hutton	.05
165 Charlie Lea (R)	.15
166 Scott Sanderson	.05
167 Ken Macha	.05
168 Tony Bernazard	.05
BALTIMORE ORIOLES	
169 Jim Palmer	.60
170 Steve Stone	.05
171 Mike Flanagan	.08
172 Al Bumbry	.05
173 Doug DeCinces	.12
174 Scott McGregor	.08
175 Mark Belanger	.05
176 Tim Stoddard	.05
177 Rick Dempsey*	.10
178 Earl Weaver (Mgr.)	.10
179 Tippy Martinez	.05
180 Dennis Martinez	.05
181 Sammy Stewart	.05
182 Rich Dauer	.05
183 Lee May	.05
184 Eddie Murray	.75
185 Benny Ayala	.05
186 John Lowenstein	.05
187 Gary Roenicke	.05
188 Ken Singleton	.08
189 Dan Graham	.05
190 Terry Crowley	.05
191 Kiko Garcia	.05
192 Dave Ford	.05
193 Mark Corey	.05
194 Lenn Sakata	.05
195 Doug DeCinces	.08
CINCINNATI REDS	
196 Johnny Bench	1.00
197 Dave Concepcion	.15
198 Ray Knight	.08
199 Ken Griffey	.15
200 Tom Seaver	.75
201 Dave Collins	.07
202 George Foster	.20
(Slugger) Error—No. 216	
202 George Foster	.20
(Slugger) Correct No. 202	
203 Junior Kennedy	.05
204 Frank Pastore	.05
205 Dan Driessen	.05
206 Hector Cruz	.05
207 Paul Moskau	.05
208 Charlie Leibrandt (R)	.25
209 Harry Spilman	.05
210 Joe Price	.05
211 Tom Hume	.05
212 Joe Nolan	.05
213 Doug Bair	.05
214 Mario Soto	.08
215 Bill Bonham*	.08
216 George Foster	.15
See No. 202	
217 Paul Householder	.10

NO. PLAYER	MINT
218 Ron Oester	.05
219 Sam Mejias	.05
220 Sheldon Burnside	.05
BOSTON RED SOX	
221 Carl Yastrzemski	1.00
222 Jim Rice	.30
223 Fred Lynn	.25
224 Carlton Fisk	.50
225 Rick Burleson	.05
226 Dennis Eckersley	.35
227 Butch Hobson	.05
228 Tom Burgmeier	.05
229 Garry Hancock	.05
230 Don Zimmer (Mgr.)	.05
231 Steve Renko	.05
232 Dwight Evans	.30
233 Mike Torrez	.05
234 Bob Stanley	.08
235 Jim Dwyer	.05
236 Dave Stapleton	.15
237 Glenn Hoffman	.12
238 Jerry Remy	.05
239 Dick Drago	.05
240 Bill Campbell	.05
241 Tony Perez	.15
ATLANTA BRAVES	
242 Phil Niekro	.25
243 Dale Murphy	1.00
244 Bob Horner	.20
245 Jeff Burroughs	.05
246 Rick Camp	.05
247 Bob Cox (Mgr.)	.05
248 Bruce Benedict	.05
249 Gene Garber	.05
250 Jerry Royster	.05
251 Gary Matthews*	.10
252 Chris Chambliss	.08
253 Luis Gomez	.05
254 Bill Nahorodny	.05
255 Doyle Alexander	.10
256 Brian Asselstine	.05
257 Biff Pocoroba	.05
258 Mike Lum	.05
259 Charlie Spikes	.05
260 Glenn Hubbard	.05
261 Tommy Boggs	.05
262 Al Hrabosky	.05
263 Rick Matula	.05
264 Preston Hanna	.05
265 Larry Bradford	.05
266 Rafael Ramirez	.20
267 Larry McWilliams	.05
CALIFORNIA ANGELS	
268 Rod Carew	.75
269 Bobby Grich	.08
270 Carney Lansford	.20
271 Don Baylor	.20
272 Joe Rudi	.05
273 Dan Ford	.05
274 Jim Fregosi	.05
275 Dave Frost	.05
276 Frank Tanana	.10
277 Dickie Thon	.07
278 Jason Thompson	.08
279 Rick Miller	.05
280 Bert Campaneris	.10
281 Tom Donohue	.05
282 Brian Downing	.05
283 Fred Patek	.05
284 Bruce Kison	.05
285 Dave LaRoche	.05
286 Don Aase	.05
287 Jim Barr	.05
288 Alfredo Martinez	.05
289 Larry Harlow	.05
290 Andy Hassler	.05
CHICAGO CUBS	
291 Dave Kingman	.12
292 Bill Buckner	.10
293 Rick Reuschel	.10
294 Bruce Sutter	.20
295 Jerry Martin	.05
296 Scot Thompson	.05
297 Ivan DeJesus	.05
298 Steve Dillard	.05

NO. PLAYER	MINT
299 Dick Tidrow	.05
300 Randy Martz	.05
301 Lenny Randle	.05
302 Lynn McGlothen	.05
303 Cliff Johnson	.05
304 Tim Blackwell	.05
305 Dennis Lamp	.05
306 Bill Caudill	.08
307 Carlos Lezcano	.05
308 Jim Tracy	.05
309 Doug Capilla	.05
310 Willie Hernandez	.20
311 Mike Vail	.05
312 Mike Krukow	.05
313 Barry Foote	.05
314 Larry Biittner	.05
315 Mike Tyson	.05
NEW YORK METS	
316 Lee Mazzilli	.05
317 John Stearns	.05
318 Alex Trevino	.05
319 Craig Swan	.05
320 Frank Taveras	.05
321 Steve Henderson	.05
322 Neil Allen	.05
323 Mark Bomback	.05
324 Mike Jorgensen	.05
325 Joe Torre	.07
326 Elliott Maddox	.05
327 Pete Falcone	.05
328 Ray Burris	.05
329 Claudell Washington	.08
330 Doug Flynn	.05
331 Joel Youngblood	.05
332 Bill Almon	.05
333 Tom Hausman	.05
334 Pat Zachry	.05
335 Jeff Reardon (R)	1.00
336 Wally Backman (R)	.40
337 Dan Norman	.05
338 Jerry Morales	.05
CHICAGO WHITE SOX (Except 351)	
339 Ed Farmer	.05
340 Bob Molinaro	.05
341 Todd Cruz	.05
342 Britt Burns*	.35
343 Kevin Bell	.05
344 Tony LaRussa (Mgr.)	.05
345 Steve Trout	.05
346 Harold Baines (R)	2.00
347 Richard Wortham	.05
348 Wayne Nordhagen	.05
349 Mike Squires	.05
350 Lamar Johnson	.05
351 Rickey Henderson	10.00
Most Stolen Bases, AL	
352 Francisco Barrios	.05
353 Thad Bosley	.05
354 Chet Lemon	.08
355 Bruce Kimm	.05
356 Richard Dotson (R)	.35
357 Jim Morrison	.05
358 Mike Proly	.07
359 Greg Pryor	.05
PITTSBURGH PIRATES	
360 Dave Parker	.30
361 Omar Moreno	.05
362 Kent Tekulve*	.10
363 Willie Stargell	.40
364 Phil Garner	.05
365 Ed Ott	.05
366 Don Robinson	.05
367 Chuck Tanner (Mgr.)	.05
368 Jim Rooker	.05
369 Dale Berra	.05
370 Jim Bibby	.05
371 Steve Nicosia	.05
372 Mike Easler	.10
373 Bill Robinson	.05
374 Lee Lacy	.05
375 John Candelaria	.10
376 Manny Sanguillen	.05
377 Rick Rhoden	.12
378 Grant Jackson	.05
379 Tim Foli	.05

NO. PLAYER	MINT
380 Rod Scurry	.05
381 Bill Madlock	.15
382 Kurt Bevacqua*	.08
383 Bert Blyleven	.20
384 Eddie Solomon	.05
385 Enrique Romo	.05
386 John Milner	.05
CLEVELAND INDIANS	
387 Mike Hargrove	.05
388 Jorge Orta	.05
389 Toby Harrah	.05
390 Tom Veryzer	.05
391 Miguel Dilone	.05
392 Dan Spillner	.05
393 Jack Brohamer	.05
394 Wayne Garland	.05
395 Sid Monge	.05
396 Rick Waits	.05
397 Joe Charboneau	.12
398 Gary Alexander	.05
399 Jerry Dybzinski	.05
400 Mike Stanton	.05
401 Mike Paxton	.05
402 Gary Gray	.05
403 Rick Manning	.05
404 Bo Diaz	.08
405 Ron Hassey	.05
406 Ross Grimsley	.05
407 Victor Cruz	.05
408 Len Barker	.08
TORONTO BLUE JAYS	
409 Bob Bailor	.05
410 Otto Velez	.05
411 Ernie Whitt	.05
412 Jim Clancy	.05
413 Barry Bonnell	.05
414 Dave Stieb	.50
415 Damaso Garcia (R)	.15
416 John Mayberry	.05
417 Roy Howell	.05
418 Dan Ainge	.35
419 Jesse Jefferson*	.08
420 Joey McLaughlin	.05
421 Lloyd Moseby (R)	.60
422 Al Woods	.05
423 Garth Iorg	.05
424 Doug Ault	.05
425 Ken Schrom	.15
426 Mike Willis	.05
427 Steve Braun	.05
428 Bob Davis	.05
429 Jerry Garvin	.05
430 Alfredo Griffin	.08
431 Bob Mattick (Mgr.)	.05
SAN FRANCISCO GIANTS	
432 Vida Blue	.08
433 Jack Clark	.30
434 Willie McCovey	.35
435 Mike Ivie	.05
436 Darrell Evans*	.15
437 Terry Whitfield	.05
438 Rennie Stennett	.05
439 John Montefusco	.05
440 Jim Wohlford	.05
441 Bill North	.05
442 Milt May	.05
443 Max Venable	.05
444 Ed Whitson	.05
445 Al Holland	.15
446 Randy Moffitt	.05
447 Bob Knepper	.05
448 Gary Lavelle	.05
449 Greg Minton	.05
450 Johnnie LeMaster	.05
451 Larry Herndon	.05
452 Rich Murray	.05
453 Joe Pettini	.05
454 Allen Ripley	.05
455 Dennis Littlejohn	.05
456 Tom Griffin	.05
457 Alan Hargesheimer	.05
458 Joe Strain	.05
DETROIT TIGERS	
459 Steve Kemp	.08
460 Sparky Anderson (Mgr.)	.08

NO. PLAYER	MINT
461 Alan Trammell	.40
462 Mark Fidrych	.08
463 Lou Whitaker	.25
464 Dave Rozema	.05
465 Milt Wilcox	.05
466 Champ Summers	.05
467 Lance Parrish	.30
468 Dan Petry	.15
469 Pat Underwood	.05
470 Rick Peters	.10
471 Al Cowens	.05
472 John Wockenfuss	.05
473 Tom Brookens	.05
474 Richie Hebner	.05
475 Jack Morris	.25
476 Jim Lentine	.05
477 Bruce Robbins	.05
478 Mark Wagner	.05
479 Tim Corcoran	.05
480 Stan Papi*	.08
481 Kirk Gibson (R)	3.00
482 Dan Schatzeder	.05
483 Amos Otis	.60
See card No. 32	
SAN DIEGO PADRES	
484 Dave Winfield	.50
485 Rollie Fingers	.40
486 Gene Richards	.05
487 Randy Jones	.05
488 Ozzie Smith	.75
489 Gene Tenace	.05
490 Bill Fahey	.05
491 John Curtis	.05
492 Dave Cash	.05
493 Tim Flannery*	.12
494 Jerry Mumphrey	.05
495 Bob Shirley	.05
496 Steve Mura	.05
497 Eric Rasmussen	.05
498 Broderick Perkins	.05
499 Barry Evans	.05
500 Chuck Baker	.05
501 Luis Salazar	.15
502 Gary Lucas	.10
503 Mike Armstrong	.05
504 Jerry Turner	.05
505 Dennis Kinney	.05
506 Willie Montanez	.05
MILWAUKEE BREWERS	
507 Gorman Thomas	.15
508 Ben Oglivie	.08
509 Larry Hisle	.05
510 Sal Bando	.50
511 Robin Yount	1.00
512 Mike Caldwell	.05
513 Sixto Lezcano	.05
514 Bill Travers	.15
Error—Jerry Augustine photo and back	
514 Bill Travers	.08
515 Paul Molitor	.30
516 Moose Haas	.05
517 Bill Castro	.05
518 Jim Slaton	.05
519 Lary Sorensen	.05
520 Bob McClure	.05
521 Charlie Moore	.05
522 Jim Gantner	.05
523 Reggie Cleveland	.05
524 Don Money	.05
525 Bill Travers	.05
526 Buck Martinez	.05
527 Dick Davis	.05
ST. LOUIS CARDINALS	
528 Ted Simmons	.12
529 Garry Templeton	.12
530 Ken Reitz	.05
531 Tony Scott	.05
532 Ken Oberkfell	.05
533 Bob Sykes	.05
534 Keith Smith	.05
535 John Littlefield	.05
536 Jim Kaat	.10
537 Bob Forsch	.05
538 Mike Phillips	.05

NO.	PLAYER	MINT
539	Terry Landrum	.08
540	Leon Durham (R)	.30
541	Terry Kennedy	.08
542	George Hendrick	.08
543	Dane Iorg	.05
544	Mark Littell	.05
545	Keith Hernandez	.30
546	Silvio Martinez	.05
547	Don Hood	.25
	Error—Pete Vuckovich	
	photo and back	
547	Don Hood	.10
548	Bobby Bonds	.08
549	Mike Ramsey	.05
550	Tom Herr	.15

MINNESOTA TWINS

NO.	PLAYER	MINT
551	Roy Smalley	.05
552	Jerry Koosman	.15
553	Ken Landreaux	.05
554	John Castino	.05
555	Doug Corbett	.12
556	Bombo Rivera	.05
557	Ron Jackson	.05
558	Butch Wynegar	.05
559	Hosken Powell	.05
560	Pete Redfern	.05
561	Roger Erickson	.05
562	Glenn Adams	.08
563	Rick Sofield	.05
564	Geoff Zahn	.05
565	Pete Mackanin	.05
566	Mike Cubbage	.05
567	Darrell Jackson	.05
568	Dave Edwards	.05
569	Rob Wilfong	.05
570	Sal Butera	.05
571	Jose Morales	.05

OAKLAND A'S

NO.	PLAYER	MINT
572	Rick Langford	.05
573	Mike Norris	.05
574	Rickey Henderson	15.00
575	Tony Armas	.15
576	Dave Revering	.05
577	Jeff Newman	.05
578	Bob Lacey	.05
579	Brian Kingman	.05
580	Mitchell Page	.05
581	Billy Martin (Mgr.)	.15
582	Rob Picciolo	.05
583	Mike Heath	.05
584	Mickey Klutts	.05
585	Orlando Gonzalez	.05
586	Mike Davis (R)	.20
587	Wayne Gross	.05
588	Matt Keough	.05
589	Steve McCatty	.05
590	Dwayne Murphy	.08
591	Mario Guerrero	.05
592	Dave McKay	.05
593	Jim Essian	.05
594	Dave Heaverlo	.05

SEATTLE MARINERS (Except 606)

NO.	PLAYER	MINT
595	Maury Wills (Mgr.)	.10
596	Juan Beniquez	.05
597	Rodney Craig	.05
598	Jim Anderson	.05
599	Floyd Bannister	.08
600	Bruce Bochte	.05
601	Julio Cruz	.05
602	Ted Cox	.05
603	Dan Meyer	.05
604	Larry Cox	.05
605	Bill Stein	.05
606	Steve Garvey	.50
	Most Hits, NL	
607	Dave Roberts	.05
608	Leon Roberts	.05
609	Reggie Walton	.05
610	Dave Edler	.05

NO.	PLAYER	MINT
611	Larry Milbourne	.05
612	Kim Allen	.05
613	Mario Mendoza	.05
614	Tom Paciorek	.05
615	Glenn Abbott	.05
616	Joe Simpson	.05

TEXAS RANGERS

NO.	PLAYER	MINT
317	Mickey Rivers	.08
618	Jim Kern	.05
619	Jim Sundberg	.05
620	Richie Zisk	.05
621	Jon Matlack	.05
622	Ferguson Jenkins	.12
623	Pat Corrales (Mgr.)	.05
624	Ed Figueroa	.05
625	Buddy Bell	.15
626	Al Oliver	.15
627	Doc Medich	.05
628	Bump Wills	.05
629	Rusty Staub	.12
630	Pat Putnam	.05
631	John Grubb	.05
632	Danny Darwin	.05
633	Ken Clay	.05
634	Jim Norris	.05
635	John Butcher	.15
636	Dave Roberts	.05
637	Billy Sample	.05

SPECIAL CARDS

NO.	PLAYER	MINT
638	Carl Yastrzemski	1.00
	400 Home Run Club	
639	Cecil Cooper	.20
640	Mike Schmidt	1.25
	(Third Base)	
	Error—No. 5	
640	Mike Schmidt	1.00
	(Home Run King)	
641	Checklist (1 to 50)*	.08
642	Checklist (51 to 109)	.08
643	Checklist (110 to 168)	.08

NO.	PLAYER	MINT
644	Checklist (169 to 220)*	.08
645	Triple Threat:*	1.75
	Schmidt, Rose, Bowa	
646	Checklist (221 to 267)	.08
647	Checklist (268 to 315)	.08
648	Checklist (316 to 359)	.08
649	Checklist (360 to 408)	.08
650	Reggie Jackson	1.00
	Mr. Baseball	
	Error—No. 79	
650	Reggie Jackson	.75
	Mr. Baseball	
651	Checklist (409 to 458)	.08
652	Checklist (459 to 506)*	.08
653	Willie Wilson	.15
	Most Hits, Most Runs	
	Error—No. 29	
653	Willie Wilson	.15
	Most Hits, Most Runs	
654	Checklist (507 to 550)*	.08
655	G. Brett (.390 Avg.)	1.25
	Error—No. 28*	
656	Checklist (551 to 593)	.08
657	Tug McGraw	.08
	Game Saver, Error—No. 7	
657	Tug McGraw	.08
	Game Saver	
658	Checklist (594 to 637)	.08
659	Checklist (Specials)*	.08
660	Steve Carlton	1.00
	"Lefty"—The Golden Arm	
	Errors—Card No.6	
	and "1066" Cardinals	
660	Steve Carlton	.75
	"Lefty"—The Golden Arm	
	Error—"1066" Cardinals	
660	Steve Carlton	2.00
	"Lefty"—The Golden Arm	
	Corrected—"1966"	
	Cardinals	

1982 Fleer.... Complete Set of 660 Cards—Value $50.00

Features the rookie cards of Cal Ripken, Dave Stewart and George Bell. Several errors were corrected; none are scarce or worth much more than ordinary cards, except cards 438 and 576. If a *variety* (error) is significant, it is listed and explained; if it is minor it is noted by an *asterisk*.

LOS ANGELES DODGERS

NO.	PLAYER	MINT
1	Dusty Baker	.10
2	Robert Castillo	.05
3	Roy Cey	.15
4	Terry Forster	.05
5	Steve Garvey	.40
6	Dave Goltz	.05
7	Pedro Guerrero	.60
8	Burt Hooton	.05
9	Steve Howe	.05
10	Jay Johnstone	.05
11	Ken Landreaux	.05
12	Davey Lopes	.05
13	Mike Marshall (R)	1.25
14	Bobby Mitchell	.09
15	Rick Monday	.10
16	Tom Niedenfuer (R)	.25
17	Ted Power (R)	.25

NO.	PLAYER	MINT
18	Jerry Reuss	.10
19	Ron Roenicke	.05
20	Bill Russell	.05
21	Steve Sax (R)	3.00
22	Mike Scioscia	.05
23	Reggie Smith	.10
24	Dave Stewart (R)	7.00
25	Rick Sutcliffe	.20
26	Darrell Thomas	.05
27	Fernando Valenzuela	.50
28	Bob Welch	.35
29	Steve Yeager	.05

NEW YORK YANKEES

NO.	PLAYER	MINT
30	Bobby Brown	.05
31	Rick Cerone	.05
32	Ron Davis	.05
33	Bucky Dent	.08
34	Barry Foote	.05

NO.	PLAYER	MINT
35	George Frazier	.05
36	Oscar Gamble	.05
37	Rich Gossage	.20
38	Ron Guidry	.20
39	Reggie Jackson	.75
40	Tommy John	.15
41	Rudy May	.05
42	Larry Milbourne	.05
43	Jerry Mumphrey	.05
44	Bobby Murcer	.10
45	Gene Nelson (R)	.15
46	Graig Nettles	.15
47	Johnny Oates	.05
48	Lou Piniella	.10
49	Willie Randolph	.12
50	Rick Reuschel	.12
51	Dave Reverink	.05
52	Dave Righetti (R)	1.25

NO.	PLAYER	MINT
53	Aurelio Rodriguez	.05
54	Bob Watson	.05
55	Dennis Werth	.05
56	Dave Winfield	.50

CINCINNATI REDS

NO.	PLAYER	MINT
57	Johnny Bench	.75
58	Bruce Berenyi	.05
59	Larry Biittner	.05
60	Scott Brown	.09
61	Dave Collins	.05
62	Geoff Combe	.05
63	Dave Concepcion	.10
64	Dan Driessen	.05
65	Joe Edelen	.05
66	George Foster	.20
67	Ken Griffey	.20
68	Paul Householder	.05
69	Tom Hume	.05

NO.	PLAYER	MINT
70	Junior Kennedy	.05
71	Ray Knight	.10
72	Mike LaCoss	.05
73	Rafael Landestoy	.05
74	Charlie Leibrandt	.05
75	Sam Mejias	.05
76	Paul Moskau	.05
77	Joe Nolan	.05
78	Mike O'Berry	.05
79	Ron Oester	.05
80	Frank Pastore	.05
81	Joe Price	.05
82	Tom Seaver	.75
83	Mario Soto	.10
84	Mike Vail	.05

OAKLAND A'S

NO.	PLAYER	MINT
85	Tony Armas	.10
86	Shooty Babitt	.05
87	Dave Beard	.05
88	Rick Bosetti	.05
89	Keith Drumright	.05
90	Wayne Gross	.05
91	Mike Heath	.05
92	Rickey Henderson	4.00
93	Cliff Johnson	.05
94	Jeff Jones	.05
95	Matt Keough	.05
96	Brian Kingman	.05
97	Mickey Klutts	.05
98	Rick Langford	.05
99	Steve McCatty	.05
100	Dave McKay	.05
101	Dwayne Murphy	.07
102	Jeff Newman	.05
103	Mike Norris	.05
104	Bob Owchinko	.05
105	Mitchell Page	.05
106	Rob Picciolo	.05
107	Jim Spencer	.05
108	Fred Stanley	.05
109	Tom Underwood	.05

ST. LOUIS CARDINALS

NO.	PLAYER	MINT
110	Joaquin Andujar	.15
111	Steve Braun	.05
112	Bob Forsch	.05
113	George Hendrick	.08
114	Keith Hernandez	.30
115	Tom Herr	.15
116	Dane Iorg	.05
117	Jim Kaat	.10
118	Tito Landrum	.05
119	Sixto Lezcano	.05
120	Mark Littell	.05
121	John Martin	.05
122	Silvio Martinez	.05
123	Ken Oberkfell	.05
124	Darrell Porter	.05
125	Mike Ramsey	.05
126	Orlando Sanchez	.08
127	Bob Shirley	.05
128	Lary Sorensen	.05
129	Bruce Sutter	.20
130	Bob Sykes	.05
131	Garry Templeton	.15
132	Gene Tenace	.05

MILWAUKEE BREWERS

NO.	PLAYER	MINT
133	Jerry Augustine	.05
134	Sal Brando	.05
135	Mark Brouhard	.08
136	Mike Caldwell	.05
137	Reggie Cleveland	.05
138	Cecil Cooper	.20
139	Jamie Easterly	.05
140	Marshall Edwards	.05
141	Rollie Fingers	.20
142	Jim Gantner	.05
143	Moose Haas	.05
144	Larry Hisle	.05
145	Roy Howell	.05
146	Rickey Keeton	.05
147	Randy Lerch	.05
148	Paul Molitor	.25
149	Don Money	.05
150	Charlie Moore	.05
151	Ben Oglivie	.10

NO.	PLAYER	MINT
152	Ted Simmons	.10
153	Jim Slaton	.05
154	Gorman Thomas	.10
155	Robin Yount	1.25
156	Pete Vuckovich	.10

BALTIMORE ORIOLES

NO.	PLAYER	MINT
157	Benny Ayala	.05
158	Mark Belanger	.05
159	Al Bumbry	.05
160	Terry Crowley	.05
161	Rich Dauer	.05
162	Doug DeCinces	.10
163	Rick Dempsey	.05
164	Jim Dwyer	.05
165	Mike Flanagan	.10
166	Dave Ford	.05
167	Dan Graham	.05
168	Wayne Krenchicki	.05
169	John Lowenstein	.05
170	Dennis Martinez	.05
171	Tippy Martinez	.05
172	Scott McGregor	.10
173	Jose Morales	.05
174	Eddie Murray	.60
175	Jim Palmer	.50
176	Cal Ripken, Jr. (R)	15.00
177	Gary Roenicke	.05
178	Lenn Sakata	.05
179	Ken Singleton	.10
180	Sammy Stewart	.05
181	Tim Stoddard	.05
182	Steve Stone	.05

MONTREAL EXPOS

NO.	PLAYER	MINT
183	Stan Bahnsen	.05
184	Ray Burris	.05
185	Gary Carter	.50
186	Warren Cromartie	.05
187	Andre Dawson	.50
188	Terry Francona (R)	.20
189	Woodie Fryman	.05
190	Bill Gullickson	.05
191	Grant Jackson	.05
192	Wallace Johnson	.05
193	Charlie Lea	.05
194	Bill Lee	.05
195	Jerry Manuel	.05
196	Brad Mills	.07
197	John Milner	.05
198	Rowland Office	.05
199	David Palmer	.05
200	Larry Parrish	.05
201	Mike Phillips	.05
202	Tim Raines	2.00
203	Bobby Ramos	.05
204	Jeff Reardon	.20
205	Steve Rogers	.10
206	Scott Sanderson	.05
207	Rodney Scott	.15
208	Elias Sosa	.05
209	Chris Speier	.05
210	Tim Wallach (R)	1.50
211	Jerry White	.05

HOUSTON ASTROS

NO.	PLAYER	MINT
212	Alan Ashby	.05
213	Cesar Cedeno	.10
214	Jose Cruz	.15
215	Kiko Garcia	.05
216	Phil Garner	.05
217	Danny Heep	.05
218	Art Howe	.05
219	Bob Knepper	.05
220	Frank LaCorte	.05
221	Joe Niekro	.10
222	Joe Pittman	.05
223	Terry Puhl	.05
224	Luis Pujols	.05
225	Craig Reynolds	.05
226	J.R. Richard	.10
227	Dave Roberts	.05
228	Vern Ruhle	.05
229	Nolan Ryan	3.00
230	Joe Sambito	.05
231	Tony Scott	.05
232	Dave Smith	.05
233	Harry Spilman	.05

NO.	PLAYER	MINT
234	Don Sutton	.25
235	Dickie Thon	.10
236	Denny Walling	.05
237	Gary Woods	.05

PHILADELPHIA PHILLIES

NO.	PLAYER	MINT
238	Luis Aguayo	.05
239	Ramon Aviles	.05
240	Bob Boone	.05
241	Larry Bowa	.10
242	Warren Brusstar	.05
243	Steve Carlton	.75
244	Larry Christenson	.05
245	Dick Davis	.05
246	Greg Gross	.05
247	Sparky Lyle	.08
248	Garry Maddox	.10
249	Gary Matthews	.10
250	Bake McBride	.05
251	Tug McGraw	.10
252	Keith Moreland	.08
253	Dickie Noles	.05
254	Mike Proly	.05
255	Ron Reed	.05
256	Pete Rose	1.00
257	Dick Ruthven	.05
258	Mike Schmidt	1.50
259	Lonnie Smith	.10
260	Manny Trillo	.05
261	Del Unser	.05
262	George Vukovich	.05

DETROIT TIGERS

NO.	PLAYER	MINT
263	Tom Brookens	.05
264	George Cappuzzello	.05
265	Marty Castillo	.05
266	Al Cowens	.05
267	Kirk Gibson	.75
268	Richie Hebner	.05
269	Ron Jackson	.05
270	Lynn Jones	.05
271	Steve Kemp	.10
272	Rick Leach	.08
273	Aurelio Lopez	.05
274	Jack Morris	.25
275	Kevin Saucier	.05
276	Lance Parrish	.25
277	Rick Peters	.05
278	Dan Petry	.15
279	David Rozema	.05
280	Stan Papi	.05
281	Dan Schatzeder	.05
282	Champ Summers	.05
283	Alan Trammell	.30
284	Lou Whitaker	.20
285	Milt Wilcox	.05
286	John Wockenfuss	.05

BOSTON RED SOX

NO.	PLAYER	MINT
287	Gary Allenson	.05
288	Tom Burgmeier	.05
289	Bill Campbell	.05
290	Mark Clear	.05
291	Steve Crawford	.05
292	Dennis Eckersley	.35
293	Dwight Evans	.20
294	Rich Gedman (R)	.30
295	Garry Hancock	.05
296	Glenn Hoffman	.05
297	Bruce Hurst	.50
298	Carney Lansford	.20
299	Rick Miller	.05
300	Reid Nichols	.05
301	Bob Ojeda (R)	.45
302	Tony Perez	.15
303	Chuck Rainey	.05
304	Jerry Remy	.05
305	Jim Rice	.35
306	Joe Rudi	.05
307	Bob Stanley	.05
308	Dave Stapleton	.05
309	Frank Tanana	.15
310	Mike Torrez	.05
311	John Tudor	.40
312	Carl Yastrzemski	1.00

TEXAS RANGERS

NO.	PLAYER	MINT
313	Buddy Bell	.15
314	Steve Comer	.05

NO.	PLAYER	MINT
315	Danny Darwin	.05
316	John Ellis	.05
317	John Grubb	.05
318	Rick Honeycutt	.05
319	Charlie Hough	.05
320	Ferguson Jenkins	.15
321	John Henry Johnson	.05
322	Jim Kern	.05
323	Jon Matlack	.05
324	Doc Medich	.05
325	Mario Mendoza	.05
326	Al Oliver	.15
327	Pat Putnam	.05
328	Mickey Rivers	.05
329	Leon Roberts	.05
330	Billy Sample	.05
331	Bill Stein	.05
332	Jim Sundberg	.05
333	Mark Wagner	.05
334	Bump Wills	.05

CHICAGO WHITE SOX

NO.	PLAYER	MINT
335	Bill Almon	.05
336	Harold Baines	.30
337	Ross Baumgarten	.05
338	Tony Bernazard	.05
339	Britt Burns	.10
340	Richard Dotson	.10
341	Jim Essian	.05
342	Ed Farmer	.05
343	Carlton Fisk	.50
344	Kevin Hickey	.05
345	LaMarr Hoyt	.10
346	Lamar Johnson	.05
347	Jerry Koosman	.05
348	Rusty Kuntz	.05
349	Dennis Lamp	.05
350	Ron LeFlore	.05
351	Chet Lemon	.08
352	Greg Luzinski	.10
353	Bob Molinaro	.05
354	Jim Morrison	.05
355	Wayne Nordhagen	.05
356	Greg Pryor	.05
357	Mike Squires	.05
358	Steve Trout	.05

CLEVELAND INDIANS

NO.	PLAYER	MINT
359	Alan Bannister	.05
360	Len Barker	.05
361	Bert Blyleven	.25
362	Joe Charboneau	.05
363	John Denny	.10
364	Bo Diaz	.05
365	Miguel Dilone	.05
366	Jerry Dybzinski	.05
367	Wayne Garland	.05
368	Mike Hargrove	.05
369	Toby Harrah	.05
370	Ron Hassey	.05
371	Von Hayes (R)	1.25
372	Pat Kelly	.05
373	Duane Kuiper	.05
374	Rick Manning	.05
375	Sid Monge	.05
376	Jorge Orta	.05
377	Dave Rosello	.05
378	Dan Spillner	.05
379	Mike Stanton	.05
380	Andre Thornton	.10
381	Tom Veryzer	.05
382	Rick Waits	.05

SAN FRANCISCO GIANTS

NO.	PLAYER	MINT
383	Doyle Alexander	.05
384	Vida Blue	.05
385	Fred Breining	.07
386	Enos Cabell	.05
387	Jack Clark	.25
388	Darrell Evans	.10
389	Tom Griffin	.05
390	Larry Herndon	.05
391	Al Holland	.05
392	Gary Lavelle	.05
393	Johnnie LeMaster	.05
394	Jerry Martin	.05
395	Milt May	.05
396	Greg Minton	.05

NO.	PLAYER	MINT
397	Joe Morgan	.30
398	Joe Pettini	.05
399	Alan Ripley	.05
400	Billy Smith	.05
401	Rennie Stennett	.05
402	Ed Whitson	.05
403	Jim Wohlford	.05
KANSAS CITY ROYALS		
404	Willie Aikens	.05
405	George Brett	1.00
406	Ken Brett	.05
407	Dave Chalk	.05
408	Rich Gale	.05
409	Cesar Geronimo	.05
410	Larry Gura	.05
411	Clint Hurdle	.05
412	Mike Jones	.05
413	Dennis Leonard	.05
414	Renie Martin	.05
415	Lee May	.05
416	Hal McRae	.05
417	Darryl Motley (R)	.15
418	Rance Mulliniks	.05
419	Amos Otis	.05
420	Ken Phelps (R)	.50
421	Jamie Quirk	.05
422	Dan Quisenberry	.20
423	Paul Splittorff	.05
424	U.L. Washington	.05
425	John Wathan	.05
426	Frank White	.05
427	Willie Wilson	.15
ATLANTA BRAVES		
428	Brian Asselstine	.05
429	Bruce Benedict	.05
430	Tom Boggs	.05
431	Larry Bradford	.05
432	Rick Camp	.05
433	Chris Chambliss	.05
434	Gene Garber	.05
435	Preston Hanna	.05
436	Bob Horner	.20
437	Glenn Hubbard	.05
438	"All" Hrabosky (error)	16.00
	"Al" misspelled	
438	Al Hrabosky	1.00
	(height 5'1"—error)	
438	Al Hrabosky	.12
	(height 5'10" correct)	
439	Rufino Linares	.05
440	Rick Mahler (R)	.25
441	Ed Miller	.05
442	John Montefusco	.05
443	Dale Murphy	1.00
444	Phil Niekro	.25
445	Gaylord Perry	.30
446	Biff Pocoroba	.05
447	Rafael Ramirez	.05
448	Jerry Royster	.05
449	Claudell Washington	.08
CALIFORNIA ANGELS		
450	Don Aase	.05
451	Don Baylor	.15
452	Juan Beniquez	.05
453	Rick Burleson	.05
454	Bert Campaneris	.05
455	Rod Carew	.60
456	Bob Clark	.05
457	Brian Downing	.05
458	Dan Ford	.05
459	Ken Forsch	.05
460	Dave Frost*	.05
461	Bobby Grich	.10
462	Larry Harlow	.05
463	John Harris	.05
464	Andy Hassler	.05

NO.	PLAYER	MINT
465	Butch Hobson	.05
466	Jesse Jefferson	.05
467	Bruce Kison	.05
468	Fred Lynn	.25
469	Angel Moreno	.05
470	Ed Ott	.05
471	Fred Patek	.05
472	Steve Renko	.05
473	Mike Witt (R)	.75
474	Geoff Zahn	.05
PITTSBURGH PIRATES		
475	Gary Alexander	.05
476	Dale Berra	.05
477	Kurt Bevacqua	.05
478	Jim Bibby	.05
479	John Candelaria	.05
480	Victor Cruz	.05
481	Mike Easler	.05
482	Tim Foli	.05
483	Lee Lacy	.05
484	Vance Law	.12
485	Bill Madlock	.15
486	Willie Montanez	.05
487	Omar Moreno	.05
488	Steve Nicosia	.05
489	Dave Parker	.25
490	Tony Pena	.50
491	Pascual Perez	.30
492	Johnny Ray (R)	.60
493	Rick Rhoden	.05
494	Bill Robinson	.05
495	Don Robinson	.05
496	Enrique Romo	.05
497	Rod Scurry	.05
498	Eddie Solomon	.05
499	Willie Stargell	.40
500	Kent Tekulve	.05
501	Jason Thompson	.05
SEATTLE MARINERS		
502	Glenn Abbott	.05
503	Jim Anderson	.05
504	Floyd Bannister	.05
505	Bruce Bochte	.05
506	Jeff Burroughs	.05
507	Bryan Clark	.07
508	Ken Clay	.05
509	Julio Cruz	.05
510	Dick Drago	.05
511	Gary Gray	.05
512	Dan Meyer	.05
513	Jerry Narron	.05
514	Tom Paciorek	.05
515	Casey Parsons	.05
516	Lenny Randle	.05
517	Shane Rawley	.05
518	Joe Simpson	.05
519	Richie Zisk	.05
NEW YORK METS		
520	Neil Allen	.05
521	Bob Bailor	.05
522	Hubie Brooks	.60
523	Mike Cubbage	.05
524	Pete Falcone	.05
525	Doug Flynn	.05
526	Tom Hausman	.05
527	Ron Hodges	.05
528	Randy Jones	.05
529	Mike Jorgensen	.05
530	Dave Kingman	.15
531	Ed Lynch	.10
532	Mike Marshall	.05
533	Lee Mazzilli	.05
534	Dyar Miller	.05
535	Mike Scott	.35
536	Rusty Staub	.10
537	John Stearns	.05

NO.	PLAYER	MINT
538	Craig Swan	.05
539	Frank Taveras	.05
540	Alex Trevino	.05
541	Ellis Valentine	.05
542	Mookie Wilson	.05
543	Joel Youngblood	.05
544	Pat Zachry	.05
MINNESOTA TWINS		
545	Glenn Adams	.05
546	Fernando Arroyo	.05
547	John Verhoeven	.05
548	Sal Butera	.05
549	John Castino	.05
550	Don Cooper	.05
551	Doug Corbett	.05
552	Dave Engle	.05
553	Roger Erickson	.05
554	Danny Goodwin	.05
555	Darrell Jackson	1.25
	(error—black hat)	
555	Darrell Jackson	.10
	(correct—red hat)	
556	Pete Mackanin	.05
557	Jack O'Connor	.05
558	Hosken Powell	.05
559	Pete Redfern	.05
560	Roy Smalley	.05
561	Chuck Baker	.05
562	Gary Ward	.05
563	Rob Wilfong	.05
564	Al Williams	.05
565	Butch Wynegar	.05
SAN DIEGO PADRES		
566	Randy Bass	.05
567	Juan Bonilla	.07
568	Danny Boone	.05
569	John Curtis	.05
570	Juan Eichelberger	.05
571	Barry Evans	.05
572	Tim Flannery	.05
573	Ruppert Jones	.05
574	Terry Kennedy	.10
575	Joe LeFebvre	.05
576	John Littlefield	125.00
	(left handed—error)	
576	John Littlefield	.10
	(right handed—corrected)	
577	Gary Lucas	.05
578	Steve Mura	.05
579	Broderick Perkins	.05
580	Gene Richards	.05
581	Luis Salazar	.05
582	Ozzie Smith	.50
583	John Urrea	.05
584	Chris Welsh	.07
585	Rick Wise	.05
CHICAGO CUBS		
586	Doug Bird	.05
587	Tim Blackwell	.05
588	Bobby Bonds	.10
589	Bill Buckner	.10
590	Bill Caudill	.05
591	Hector Cruz	.05
592	Jody Davis (R)	.30
593	Ivan DeJesus	.05
594	Steve Dillard	.05
595	Leon Durham	.15
596	Rawly Eastwick	.05
597	Steve Henderson	.05
598	Mike Krukow	.05
599	Mike Lum	.05
600	Randy Martz	.05
601	Jerry Morales	.05
602	Ken Reitz	.05
603	Lee Smith (R)*	.75
604	Dick Tidrow	.05

NO.	PLAYER	MINT
605	Jim Tracy	.05
606	Mike Tyson	.05
607	Ty Waller	.08
TORONTO BLUE JAYS		
608	Danny Ainge	.10
609	Jorge Bell (R)	7.00
610	Mark Bomback	.05
611	Barry Bonnell	.05
612	Jim Clancy	.05
613	Damaso Garcia	.10
614	Jerry Garvin	.05
615	Alfredo Griffin	.10
616	Garth Iorg	.05
617	Luis Leal	.05
618	Ken Macha	.05
619	John Mayberry	.05
620	Joey McLaughlin	.05
621	Lloyd Moseby	.15
622	Dave Stieb	.20
623	Jackson Todd	.05
624	Willie Upshaw	.15
625	Otto Velez	.05
626	Ernie Whitt	.05
627	Al Woods	.05
SPECIAL CARDS		
628	All-Star Game	.05
629	All-Star Infielders:	.05
	Frank White, Bucky Dent	
630	Big Red Machine:	.10
	Driessen, Concepcion,	
	Foster	
631	Bruce Sutter	.10
	"Top NL Relief Pitcher"	
632	"Steve and Carlton"	.20
	Steve Carlton, Carlton Fisk	
633	Carl Yastrzemski	.30
	"3000th Game"	
634	"Dynamic Duo"	.35
	Johnny Bench, Tom Seaver	
635	"West Meets East"	.25
	Valenzuela, Carter	
636	Fernando Valenzuela:*	.30
	"NL Strikeout King"	
637	Mike Schmidt	.50
	"Home Run King"	
638	"NL All Stars"	.20
	Gary Carter, Dave Parker	
639	"Perfect Game"	.10
	Len Barker, Bo Diaz	
640	"Pete & Re-Pete"	2.00
	Pete Rose and Son	
641	"Phillies' Finest"	.30
	Carlton, Smith, Schmidt	
642	"Red Sox Reunion"	.10
	Fred Lynn, Dwight Evans	
643	Rickey Henderson	1.50
	"Most Hits, Most Runs"	
644	Rollie Fingers	.10
	"Most 'Saves AL"	
645	Tom Seaver	.20
	"Most 1981 Wins"	
646	"Yankee Powerhouse"*	.50
	R. Jackson, D. Winfield	
647	Checklist No. 1	.08
648	Checklist No. 2	.08
649	Checklist No. 3	.08
650	Checklist No. 4	.08
651	Checklist No. 5	.08
652	Checklist No. 6	.08
653	Checklist No. 7	.08
654	Checklist No. 8	.08
655	Checklist No. 9	.08
656	Checklist No. 10	.08
657	Checklist No. 11	.08
658	Checklist No. 12	.08
659	Checklist No. 13	.08
660	Checklist No. 14	.08

1983 Fleer.... Complete Set of 660 Cards—Value $100.00

Features the rookie cards of Wade Boggs, Tony Gwynn, Howard Johnson and Ryne Sandberg. The back of the card is printed in two shades of brown.

Willie McGee
OUTFIELD

Howard Johnson
THIRD BASE

Wade Boggs

Tony Gwynn
OUTFIELD

Ryne Sandberg

NO. PLAYER	MINT
ST. LOUIS CARDINALS	
1 Joaquin Andujar	.10
2 Doug Bair	.05
3 Steve Braun	.05
4 Glenn Brummer	.05
5 Bob Forsch	.05
6 David Green (R)	.15
7 George Hendrick	.10
8 Keith Hernandez	.30
9 Tom Herr	.10
10 Dane Iorg	.05
11 Jim Kaat	.10
12 Jeff Lahti	.10
13 Tito Landrum	.05
14 Dave LaPoint (R)	.35
15 Willie McGee (R)	3.00
16 Steve Mura	.05
17 Ken Oberkfell	.05
18 Darrell Porter	.05
19 Mike Ramsey	.05
20 Gene Roof	.05
21 Lonnie Smith	.10
22 Ozzie Smith	.50
23 John Stuper	.12
24 Bruce Sutter	.15
25 Gene Tenace	.05
MILWAUKEE BREWERS	
26 Jerry Augustin	.05
27 Dwight Bernard	.05
28 Mark Brouhard	.05
29 Mike Caldwell	.05
30 Cecil Cooper	.15
31 Jamie Easterly	.05
32 Marshall Edwards	.05
33 Rollie Fingers	.20
34 Jim Gantner	.05
35 Moose Haas	.05
36 Roy Howell	.05
37 Peter Ladd	.05
38 Bob McClure	.05
39 Doc Medich	.05
40 Paul Molitor	.20
41 Don Money	.05
42 Charlie Moore	.05
43 Ben Oglivie	.07
44 Ed Romero	.05
45 Ted Simmons	.10
46 Jim Slaton	.05
47 Don Sutton	.25
48 Gorman Thomas	.10
49 Pete Vuckovich	.05
50 Ned Yost	.05
51 Robin Yount	.75
BALTIMORE ORIOLES	
52 Benny Ayala	.05
53 Bob Bonner	.05
54 Al Bumbry	.05
55 Terry Crowley	.05
56 Storm Davis (R)	.50
57 Rich Dauer	.05
58 Rick Dempsey	.05
59 Jim Dwyer	.05
60 Mike Flanagan	.10
61 Dan Ford	.05
62 Glenn Gulliver	.12
63 John Lowenstein	.05

NO. PLAYER	MINT
64 Dennis Martinez	.05
65 Tippy Martinez	.05
66 Scott McGregor	.10
67 Eddie Murray	.50
68 Joe Nolan	.05
69 Jim Palmer	.40
70 Cal Ripken Jr.	3.00
71 Gary Roenicke	.05
72 Lenn Sakata	.05
73 Ken Singleton	.05
74 Sammy Stewart	.05
75 Tim Stoddard	.05
CALIFORNIA ANGELS	
76 Don Aase	.05
77 Don Baylor	.10
78 Juan Beniquez	.05
79 Bob Boone	.05
80 Rick Burleson	.05
81 Rod Carew	.50
82 Bobby Clark	.05
83 Doug Corbett	.05
84 John Curtis	.05
85 Doug DeCinces	.10
86 Brian Downing	.05
87 Joe Ferguson	.05
88 Tim Foli	.05
89 Ken Forsch	.05
90 Dave Goltz	.05
91 Bobby Grich	.05
92 Andy Hassler	.05
93 Reggie Jackson	.50
94 Ron Jackson	.05
95 Tommy John	.15
96 Bruce Kison	.05
97 Fred Lynn	.20
98 Ed Ott	.05
99 Steve Renko	.05
100 Luis Sanchez	.05
101 Rob Wilfong	.05
102 Mike Witt	.15
103 Geoff Zahn	.05
KANSAS CITY ROYALS	
104 Willie Aikens	.05
105 Mike Armstrong	.05
106 Vida Blue	.10
107 Bud Black (R)	.35
108 George Brett	1.00
109 Bill Castro	.05
110 Onix Concepcion	.12
111 Dave Frost	.05
112 Cesar Geronimo	.05
113 Larry Gura	.05
114 Steve Hammond	.12
115 Don Hood	.05
116 Dennis Leonard	.05
117 Jerry Martin	.05
118 Lee May	.05
119 Hal McRae	.05
120 Amos Otis	.05
121 Greg Pryor	.05
122 Dan Quisenberry	.20
123 Don Slaught (R)	.25
124 Paul Splittorff	.05
125 U.L. Washington	.05
126 John Wathan	.05
127 Frank White	.07

NO. PLAYER	MINT
128 Willie Wilson	.20
ATLANTA BRAVES	
129 Steve Bedrosian	.30
130 Bruce Benedict	.05
131 Tommy Boggs	.05
132 Brett Butler	.30
133 Rick Camp	.05
134 Chris Chambliss	.05
135 Ken Dayley	.05
136 Gene Garber	.05
137 Terry Harper	.05
138 Bob Horner	.15
139 Glenn Hubbard	.05
140 Rufino Linares	.05
141 Rick Mahler	.05
142 Dale Murphy	.75
143 Phil Niekro	.20
144 Pascual Perez	.10
145 Biff Pocoroba	.05
146 Rafael Ramirez	.05
147 Jerry Royster	.05
148 Ken Smith	.12
149 Bob Walk	.05
150 Claudell Washington	.10
151 Bob Watson	.05
152 Larry Whisenton	.05
PHILADELPHIA PHILLIES	
153 Porfirio Altamirano	.12
154 Marty Bystrom	.05
155 Steve Carlton	.40
156 Larry Christenson	.05
157 Ivan DeJesus	.05
158 John Denny	.10
159 Bob Dernier	.05
160 Bo Diaz	.05
161 Ed Farmer	.05
162 Greg Gross	.05
163 Mike Krukow	.05
164 Garry Maddox	.05
165 Gary Matthews	.10
166 Tug McGraw	.08
167 Bob Molinaro	.05
168 Sid Monge	.05
169 Ron Reed	.05
170 Bill Robinson	.05
171 Pete Rose	1.00
172 Dick Ruthven	.05
173 Mike Schmidt	1.50
174 Manny Trillo	.05
175 Ozzie Virgil	.05
176 George Vuckovich	.05
BOSTON RED SOX	
177 Gary Allenson	.05
178 Luis Aponte	.12
179 Wade Boggs (R)	17.50
180 Tom Burgmeier	.05
181 Mark Clear	.05
182 Dennis Eckersley	.25
183 Dwight Evans	.20
184 Rich Gedman	.05
185 Glenn Hoffman	.05
186 Bruce Hurst	.10
187 Carney Lansford	.15
188 Rick Miller	.05
189 Reid Nichols	.05
190 Bob Ojeda	.10

NO. PLAYER	MINT
191 Tony Perez	.15
192 Chuck Rainey	.05
193 Jerry Remy	.05
194 Jim Rice	.35
195 Bob Stanley	.05
196 Dave Stapleton	.05
197 Mike Torrez	.05
198 John Tudor	.15
199 Julio Valdez	.05
200 Carl Yastrzemski	1.00
LOS ANGELES DODGERS	
201 Dusty Baker	.10
202 Joe Beckwith	.05
203 Greg Brock (R)	.30
204 Roy Cey	.15
205 Terry Forster	.05
206 Steve Garvey	.40
207 Pedro Guerrero	.30
208 Burt Hooton	.05
209 Steve Howe	.05
210 Ken Landreaux	.05
211 Mike Marshall	.25
212 Candy Maldonado (R)	1.00
213 Rick Monday	.05
214 Tom Niedenfuer	.05
215 Jorge Orta	.05
216 Jerry Reuss	.05
217 Ron Roenicke	.05
218 Vicente Romo	.05
219 Bill Russell	.05
220 Steve Sax	.50
221 Mike Scioscia	.05
222 Dave Stewart	1.25
223 Derrel Thomas	.05
224 Fernando Valenzuela	.30
225 Bob Welch	.25
226 Ricky Wright	.12
227 Steve Yeager	.05
CHICAGO WHITE SOX	
228 Bill Almon	.05
229 Harold Baines	.25
230 Salome Barojas	.12
231 Tony Bernazard	.05
232 Britt Burns	.05
233 Richard Dotson	.05
234 Ernesto Escarrega	.12
235 Carlton Fisk	.40
236 Jerry Hairston	.05
237 Kevin Hickey	.05
238 LaMarr Hoyt	.15
239 Steve Kemp	.05
240 Jim Kern	.05
241 Ron Kittle (R)	1.00
242 Jerry Koosman	.15
243 Dennis Lamp	.05
244 Rudy Law	.05
245 Vance Law	.05
246 Ron LeFlore	.05
247 Greg Luzinski	.10
248 Tom Paciorek	.05
249 Aurelio Rodriguez	.05
250 Mike Squires	.05
251 Steve Trout	.05
SAN FRANCISCO GIANTS	
252 Jim Barr	.05
253 Dave Bergman	.05

1983 Fleer (Continued)

NO.	PLAYER	MINT
254	Fred Breining	.05
255	Bob Brenly	.05
256	Jack Clark	.30
257	Chili Davis	.20
258	Darrell Evans	.10
259	Alan Fowlkes	.12
260	Rich Gale	.05
261	Atlee Hammaker	.05
262	Al Holland	.05
263	Duane Kuiper	.05
264	Bill Laskey (R)	.15
265	Gary Lavelle	.05
266	Johnnie LeMaster	.05
267	Renie Martin	.05
268	Milt May	.05
269	Greg Minton	.05
270	Joe Morgan	.30
271	Tom O'Malley	.12
272	Reggie Smith	.10
273	Guy Sularz	.12
274	Champ Summers	.05
275	Max Venable	.05
276	Jim Wohlford	.05

MONTREAL EXPOS

277	Ray Burris	.05
278	Gary Carter	.35
279	Warren Cromartie	.05
280	Andre Dawson	.40
281	Terry Francona	.05
282	Doug Flynn	.05
283	Woody Fryman	.05
284	Bill Gullickson	.05
285	Wallace Johnson	.05
286	Charlie Lea	.05
287	Randy Lerch	.05
288	Brad Mills	.05
289	Dan Norman	.05
290	Al Oliver	.20
291	David Palmer	.05
292	Tim Raines	.40
293	Jeff Reardon	.10
294	Steve Rogers	.10
295	Scott Sanderson	.05
296	Dan Schatzeder	.05
297	Bryn Smith	.40
298	Chris Speier	.05
299	Tim Wallach	.20
300	Jerry White	.05
301	Joel Youngblood	.05

PITTSBURGH PIRATES

302	Ross Baumgarten	.05
303	Dale Berra	.05
304	John Candelaria	.05
305	Dick Davis	.05
306	Mike Easler	.05
307	Richie Hebner	.05
308	Lee Lacy	.05
309	Bill Madlock	.15
310	Larry McWilliams	.05
311	John Milner	.05
312	Omar Moreno	.05
313	Jim Morrison	.05
314	Steve Nicosia	.05
315	Dave Parker	.25
316	Tony Pena	.15
317	Johnny Ray	.15
318	Rick Rhoden	.05
319	Don Robinson	.05
320	Enrique Romo	.05
321	Manny Sarmiento	.05
322	Rod Scurry	.05
323	Jim Smith	.12
324	Willie Stargell	.30
325	Jason Thompson	.10
326	Kent Tekulve	.05

DETROIT TIGERS

327	Tom Brookens	.05
328	Enos Cabell	.05
329	Kirk Gibson	.40
330	Larry Herndon	.05
331	Mike Ivie	.05
332	Howard Johnson (R)	8.00
333	Lynn Jones	.05
334	Rick Leach	.05
335	Chet Lemon	.07
336	Jack Morris	.20
337	Lance Parrish	.25
338	Larry Pashnick	.12
339	Dan Petry	.15
340	Dave Rozema	.05
341	Dave Rucker	.05
342	Elias Sosa	.05
343	Dave Tobik	.05
344	Alan Trammell	.25
345	Jerry Turner	.05
346	Jerry Ujdur	.05
347	Pat Underwood	.05
348	Lou Whitaker	.20
349	Milt Wilcox	.05
350	Glenn Wilson (R)	.40
351	John Wockenfuss	.05

SAN DIEGO PADRES

352	Kurt Bevacqua	.05
353	Juan Bonilla	.05
354	Floyd Chiffer	.12
355	Luis DeLeon	.05
356	Dave Dravecky (R)	.75
357	Dave Edwards	.05
358	Juan Eichelberger	.05
359	Tim Flannery	.05
360	Tony Gwynn (R)	15.00
361	Ruppert Jones	.05
362	Terry Kennedy	.10
363	Joe Lefebvre	.05
364	Sixto Lezcano	.05
365	Tim Lollar	.05
366	Gary Lucas	.05
367	John Montefusco	.05
368	Broderick Perkins	.05
369	Joe Pittman	.05
370	Gene Richards	.05
371	Luis Salazar	.05
372	Eric Show (R)	.30
373	Garry Templeton	.10
374	Chris Welsh	.05
375	Alan Wiggins (R)	.15

NEW YORK YANKEES

376	Rick Cerone	.05
377	Dave Collins	.05
378	Roger Erickson	.05
379	George Frazier	.05
380	Oscar Gamble	.05
381	Goose Gossage	.20
382	Ken Griffey	.15
383	Ron Guidry	.20
384	Dave LaRoche	.05
385	Rudy May	.05
386	John Mayberry	.05
387	Lee Mazzilli	.05
388	Mike Morgan	.05
389	Jerry Mumphrey	.05
390	Bobby Murcer	.10
391	Graig Nettles	.15
392	Lou Piniella	.10
393	Willie Randolph	.05
394	Shane Rawley	.05
395	Dave Righetti	.15
396	Andre Robertson	.05
397	Roy Smalley	.05
398	Dave Winfield	.40
399	Butch Wynegar	.05

CLEVELAND INDIANS

400	Chris Bando	.05
401	Alan Bannister	.05
402	Len Barker	.05
403	Tom Brennan	.05
404	Carmelo Castillo (R)	.10
405	Miguel Dilone	.05
406	Jerry Dybzinski	.05
407	Mike Fischlin	.05
408	Ed Glynn	.05
409	Mike Hargrove	.05
410	Toby Harrah	.05
411	Ron Hassey	.05
412	Von Hayes	.25
413	Rick Manning	.05
414	Bake McBride	.05
415	Larry Milbourne	.05
416	Bill Nahorodny	.05
417	Jack Perconte	.05
418	Lary Sorensen	.05
419	Dan Spillner	.05
420	Rick Sutcliffe	.20
421	Andre Thornton	.10
422	Rick Waits	.05
423	Eddie Whitson	.05

TORONTO BLUE JAYS

424	Jesse Barfield	.60
425	Barry Bonnell	.05
426	Jim Clancy	.05
427	Damaso Garcia	.10
428	Jerry Garvin	.05
429	Alfredo Griffin	.05
430	Garth Iorg	.05
431	Roy Lee Jackson	.05
432	Luis Leal	.05
433	Buck Martinez	.05
434	Joey McLaughlin	.05
435	Lloyd Moseby	.15
436	Rance Mulliniks	.05
437	Dale Murray	.05
438	Wayne Nordhagen	.05
439	Gene Petralli	.12
440	Hosken Powell	.05
441	Dave Stieb	.30
442	Willie Upshaw	.10
443	Ernie Whitt	.05
444	Al Woods	.05

HOUSTON ASTROS

445	Alan Ashby	.05
446	Jose Cruz	.15
447	Kiko Garcia	.05
448	Phil Garner	.05
449	Danny Heep	.05
450	Art Howe	.05
451	Bob Knepper	.05
452	Alan Knicely	.05
453	Ray Knight	.05
454	Frank LaCorte	.05
455	Mike LaCoss	.05
456	Randy Moffitt	.05
457	Joe Niekro	.05
458	Terry Puhl	.05
459	Luis Pujols	.05
460	Craig Reynolds	.05
461	Bert Roberge	.05
462	Vern Ruhle	.05
463	Nolan Ryan	2.00
464	Joe Sambito	.05
465	Tony Scott	.05
466	Dave Smith	.05
467	Harry Spilman	.05
468	Dickie Thon	.05
469	Denny Walling	.05

SEATTLE MARINERS

470	Larry Andersen	.05
471	Floyd Bannister	.08
472	Jim Beattie	.05
473	Bruce Bochte	.05
474	Manny Castillo	.05
475	Bill Caudill	.05
476	Bryan Clark	.05
477	Al Cowens	.05
478	Julio Cruz	.05
479	Todd Cruz	.05
480	Gary Gray	.05
481	Dave Henderson	.75
482	Mike Moore (R)	1.00
483	Gaylord Perry	.30
484	Dave Revering	.05
485	Joe Simpson	.05
486	Mike Stanton	.05
487	Rick Sweet	.05
488	Ed VandeBerg (R)	.15
489	Richie Zisk	.05

CHICAGO CUBS

490	Doug Bird	.05
491	Larry Bowa	.10
492	Bill Buckner	.10
493	Bill Campbell	.05
494	Jody Davis	.10
495	Leon Durham	.15
496	Steve Henderson	.05
497	Willie Hernandez	.20
498	Ferguson Jenkins	.15
499	Jay Johnstone	.05
500	Junior Kennedy	.05
501	Randy Martz	.05
502	Jerry Morales	.05
503	Keith Moreland	.05
504	Dickie Noles	.05
505	Mike Proly	.05
506	Allen Ripley	.05
507	Ryne Sandberg (R)	25.00
508	Lee Smith	.10
509	Pat Tabler	.30
510	Dick Tidrow	.05
511	Bump Wills	.05
512	Gary Woods	.05

OAKLAND A'S

513	Tony Armas	.15
514	Dave Beard	.05
515	Jeff Burroughs	.05
516	John D'Acquisto	.05
517	Wayne Gross	.05
518	Mike Heath	.05
519	Rickey Henderson	3.00
520	Cliff Johnson	.05
521	Matt Keough	.05
522	Brian Kingman	.05
523	Rick Langford	.05
524	Davey Lopes	.05
525	Steve McCatty	.05
526	Dave McKay	.05
527	Dan Meyer	.05
528	Dwayne Murphy	.05
529	Jeff Newman	.05
530	Mike Norris	.05
531	Bob Owchinko	.05
532	Joe Rudi	.05
533	Jimmy Sexton	.05
534	Fred Stanley	.05
535	Tom Underwood	.05

NEW YORK METS

536	Neil Allen	.05
537	Wally Backman	.05
538	Bob Bailor	.05
539	Hubie Brooks	.25
540	Carlos Diaz (R)	.15
541	Pete Falcone	.05
542	George Foster	.15
543	Ron Gardenhire	.05
544	Brian Giles	.12
545	Ron Hodges	.05
546	Randy Jones	.05
547	Mike Jorgensen	.05
548	Dave Kingman	.15
549	Ed Lynch	.05
550	Jesse Orosco	.10
551	Rick Ownbey	.12
552	Charlie Puleo	.05
553	Gary Rajsich	.12
554	Mike Scott	.30
555	Rusty Staub	.10
556	John Stearns	.05
557	Craig Swan	.05
558	Ellis Valentine	.05
559	Tom Veryzer	.05
560	Mookie Wilson	.10
561	Pat Zachry	.05

TEXAS RANGERS

562	Buddy Bell	.15
563	John Butcher	.05
564	Steve Comer	.05
565	Danny Darwin	.05
566	Bucky Dent	.05
567	John Grubb	.05
568	Rick Honeycutt	.05
569	Dave Hostetler	.12
570	Charlie Hough	.05
571	Lamar Johnson	.05
572	Jon Matlack	.05
573	Paul Mirabella	.05
574	Larry Parrish	.05
575	Mike Richardt	.12
576	Mickey Rivers	.05
577	Billy Sample	.05
578	Dave Schmidt	.10
579	Bill Stein	.05
580	Jim Sundberg	.05

NO.	PLAYER	MINT
581	Frank Tanana	.10
582	Mark Wagner	.05
583	George Wright (R)	.15
CINCINNATI REDS		
584	Johnny Bench	.50
585	Bruce Berenyi	.05
586	Larry Biittner	.05
587	Cesar Cedeno	.10
588	Dave Concepcion	.10
589	Dan Driessen	.05
590	Greg Harris	.05
591	Ben Hayes	.12
592	Paul Householder	.05
593	Tom Hume	.05
594	Wayne Krenchicki	.05
595	Rafael Landestoy	.05
596	Charlie Leibrandt	.05
597	Eddie Milner	.10
598	Ron Oester	.05
599	Frank Pastore	.05
600	Joe Price	.05
601	Tom Seaver	.50
602	Bob Shirley	.05
603	Mario Soto	.10
604	Alex Trevino	.05
605	Mike Vail	.05

NO.	PLAYER	MINT
606	Duane Walker (R)	.15
MINNESOTA TWINS		
607	Tom Brunansky	1.00
608	Bobby Castillo	.05
609	John Castino	.05
610	Ron Davis	.05
611	Lenny Gaetti	.05
612	Terry Felton	.12
613	Gary Gaetti (R)	3.00
614	Mickey Hatcher	.05
615	Brad Havens	.05
616	Kent Hrbek	1.50
617	Randy Johnson	.05
618	Tim Laudner	.05
619	Jeff Little	.12
620	Bob Mitchell	.05
621	Jack O'Connor	.05
622	John Pacella	.05
623	Pete Redfern	.05
624	Jesus Vega	.12
625	Frank Viola (R)	7.00
626	Ron Washington	.12
627	Gary Ward	.05
628	Al Williams	.05
SPECIAL CARDS		
629	Red Sox All-Stars:	.20
	Eckersley, Yaz, Clear	

NO.	PLAYER	MINT
630	"300 Career Wins"	.15
	Perry and Bulling	
631	Pride of Venezuela:	.10
	Concepcion, Trillo	
632	All-Star Infielders:	.15
	Yount and Bell	
633	Mr. Vet & Mr. Rookie:	.25
	Winfield, Hrbek	
634	Fountain of Youth:	.60
	Stargell, Rose	
635	Big Chiefs:	.10
	Harrah, Thornton	
636	Smith Brothers:	.10
	Ozzie and Lonnie	
637	Base Stealers' Threat:	.10
	Diaz and Carter	
638	All-Star Catchers:	.15
	Fisk, Carter	
639	The Silver Shoe:	.75
	Rickey Henderson	
640	Home Run Threats:	.15
	Oglivie, Jackson	
641	Two Teams on the	
	Same Day:	.08
	Joel Youngblood 8/4/82	

NO.	PLAYER	MINT
642	Last Perfect Game:	.08
	Hassey, Barker	
643	Black and Blue:	.08
	Vida Blue	
644	Black and Blue:	.08
	Bud Black	
645	Speed and Power:	.35
	Reggie Jackson	
646	Speed and Power:	.60
	Rickey Henderson	
647	Checklist No. 1	.08
648	Checklist No. 2	.08
649	Checklist No. 3	.08
650	Checklist No. 4	.08
651	Checklist No. 5	.08
652	Checklist No. 6	.08
653	Checklist No. 7	.08
654	Checklist No. 8	.08
655	Checklist No. 9	.08
656	Checklist No. 10	.08
657	Checklist No. 11	.08
658	Checklist No. 12	.08
659	Checklist No. 13	.08
660	Checklist No. 14	.08

1984 Fleer.... Complete Set of 660 Cards—Value $175.00

Features the rookie cards of Don Mattingly, Darryl Strawberry and Kevin McReynolds. For the first time a traded update set was issued.

NO.	PLAYER	MINT
BALTIMORE ORIOLES		
1	Mike Boddicker	.20
2	Al Bumbry	.05
3	Todd Cruz	.05
4	Rich Dauer	.05
5	Storm Davis	.10
6	Rick Dempsey	.05
7	Jim Dwyer	.05
8	Mike Flanagan	.10
9	Dan Ford	.05
10	John Lowenstein	.05
11	Dennis Martinez	.10
12	Tippy Martinez	.05
13	Scott McGregor	.10
14	Eddie Murray	.75
15	Joe Nolan	.05
16	Jim Palmer	1.00
17	Cal Ripken, Jr.	2.50
18	Gary Roenicke	.05
19	Lenn Sakata	.05
20	John Shelby (R)	.35
21	Ken Singleton	.10
22	Sammy Stewart	.05
23	Tim Stoddard	.05
PHILADELPHIA PHILLIES		
24	Marty Bystrom	.05
25	Steve Carlton	.75
26	Ivon DeJesus	.05
27	John Denny	.10
28	Bob Dernier	.05
29	Bo Diaz	.05
30	Kiko Garcia	.05
31	Greg Gross	.05
32	Kevin Gross (R)	.30

NO.	PLAYER	MINT
33	Von Hayes	.25
34	Willie Hernandez	.20
35	Al Holland	.05
36	Charles Hudson (R)	.20
37	Joe Lefebvre	.05
38	Sixto Lezcano	.05
39	Garry Maddox	.05
40	Gary Matthews	.10
41	Len Matuszek	.05
42	Tug McGraw	.10
43	Joe Morgan	.40
44	Tony Perez	.20
45	Ron Reed	.05
46	Pete Rose	1.25
47	Juan Samuel (R)	3.00
48	Mike Schmidt	5.00
49	Ozzie Virgil	.05
CHICAGO WHITE SOX		
50	Juan Agosto	.15
51	Howard Baines	.30
52	Floyd Bannister	.10
53	Salome Barojas	.05
54	Britt Burns	.05
55	Julio Cruz	.05
56	Richard Dotson	.10
57	Jerry Dybzinski	.05
58	Carlton Fisk	.75
59	Scott Fletcher	.20
60	Jerry Hairston	.05
61	Kevin Hickey	.05
62	Marc Hill	.05
63	LaMarr Hoyt	.10
64	Ron Kittle	.20
65	Jerry Koosman	.15

NO.	PLAYER	MINT
66	Dennis Lamp	.05
67	Rudy Law	.05
68	Vance Law	.05
69	Greg Luzinski	.10
70	Tom Paciorek	.05
71	Mike Squires	.05
72	Dick Tidrow	.05
73	Greg Walker (R)	.30
DETROIT TIGERS		
74	Glenn Abbott	.05
75	Howard Bailey	.05
76	Doug Bair	.05
77	Juan Berenguer	.05
78	Tom Brookens	.05
79	Enos Cabell	.05
80	Kirk Gibson	.35
81	John Grubb	.05
82	Larry Herndon	.05
83	Wayne Krenchicki	.05
84	Rick Leach	.05
85	Chet Lemon	.10
86	Aurelio Lopez	.05
87	Jack Morris	.25
88	Lance Parrish	.25
89	Dan Petry	.15
90	Dave Rozema	.05
91	Alan Trammell	.50
92	Lou Whitaker	.30
93	Milt Wilcox	.05
94	Glenn Wilson	.10
95	John Wockenfuss	.05
LOS ANGELES DODGERS		
96	Dusty Baker	.10
97	Joe Beckwith	.05

NO.	PLAYER	MINT
98	Greg Brock	.10
99	Jack Fimple	.12
100	Pedro Guerrero	.35
101	Rick Honeycutt	.05
102	Burt Hooton	.05
103	Steve Howe	.05
104	Ken Landreaux	.05
105	Mike Marshall	.20
106	Rick Monday	.05
107	Jose Morales	.05
108	Tom Niedenfuer	.05
109	Alejandro Pena (R)	.35
110	Jerry Reuss	.05
111	Bill Russell	.05
112	Steve Sax	.40
113	Mike Scioscia	.05
114	Derrel Thomas	.05
115	Fernando Valenzuela	.35
116	Bob Welch	.30
117	Steve Yeager	.05
118	Pat Zachry	.05
NEW YORK YANKEES		
119	Don Baylor	.10
120	Bert Campaneris	.05
121	Rick Cerone	.05
122	Ray Fontenot (R)	.15
123	George Frazier	.05
124	Oscar Gamble	.05
125	Goose Gossage	.15
126	Ken Griffey	.10
127	Ron Guidry	.25
128	Jay Howell	.30
129	Steve Kemp	.05
130	Matt Keough	.05

NO. PLAYER	MINT
131 Don Mattingly (R)	40.00
132 John Montefusco	.05
133 Omar Moreno	.05
134 Dale Murray	.05
135 Graig Nettles	.10
136 Lou Piniella	.10
137 Willie Randolph	.10
138 Shane Rawley	.05
139 Dave Righetti	.15
140 Andre Robertson	.05
141 Bob Shirley	.05
142 Roy Smalley	.05
143 Dave Winfield	.50
144 Butch Wynegar	.05
TORONTO BLUE JAYS	
145 Jim Acker (R)	.15
146 Doyle Alexander	.10
147 Jesse Barfield	.25
148 Jorge Bell	1.25
149 Barry Bonnell	.05
150 Jim Clancy	.05
151 Dave Collins	.05
152 Tony Fernandez (R)	3.75
153 Damaso Garcia	.10
154 Dave Geisel	.05
155 Jim Gott	.15
156 Alfredo Griffin	.05
157 Garth Iorg	.05
158 Roy Lee Jackson	.05
159 Cliff Johnson	.05
160 Luis Leal	.05
161 Buck Martinez	.05
162 Joey McLaughlin	.05
163 Randy Moffitt	.05
164 Lloyd Moseby	.15
165 Rance Mulliniks	.05
166 Jorge Orta	.05
167 Dave Stieb	.35
168 Willie Upshaw	.15
169 Ernie Whitt	.05
ATLANTA BRAVES	
170 Len Barker	.05
171 Steve Bedrosian	.15
172 Bruce Benedict	.05
173 Brett Butler	.10
174 Rick Camp	.05
175 Chris Chambliss	.05
176 Ken Dayley	.05
177 Pete Falcone	.05
178 Terry Forster	.05
179 Gene Garber	.05
180 Terry Harper	.05
181 Bob Horner	.15
182 Glenn Hubbard	.05
183 Randy Johnson	.05
184 Craig McMurtry	.10
185 Donnie Moore	.05
186 Dale Murphy	1.25
187 Phil Niekro	.25
188 Pascual Perez	.05
189 Biff Pocoroba	.05
190 Rafael Ramirez	.05
191 Jerry Royster	.05
192 Claudell Washington	.10
193 Bob Watson	.05
MILWAUKEE BREWERS	
194 Jerry Augustine	.05
195 Mark Brouhard	.05
196 Mike Caldwell	.05
197 Tom Candiotti (R)	.50
198 Cecil Cooper	.15
199 Rollie Fingers	.25
200 Jim Gantner	.05
201 Bob Gibson	.12
202 Moose Haas	.05
203 Roy Howell	.05
204 Pete Ladd	.05
205 Rick Manning	.05
206 Bob McClure	.05
207 Paul Molitor	.20
208 Don Money	.05
209 Charlie Moore	.05
210 Ben Oglivie	.10
211 Chuck Porter	.05
212 Ed Romero	.05

NO. PLAYER	MINT
213 Ted Simmons	.10
214 Jim Slaton	.05
215 Don Sutton	.25
216 Tom Tellmann	.05
217 Pete Vuckovich	.05
218 Ned Yost	.05
219 Robin Yount	1.25
HOUSTON ASTROS	
220 Alan Ashby	.05
221 Kevin Bass	.20
222 Jose Cruz	.10
223 Bill Dawley (R)	.20
224 Frank DiPino	.05
225 Bill Doran (R)	1.00
226 Phil Garner	.05
227 Art Howe	.05
228 Bob Knepper	.10
229 Ray Knight	.10
230 Frank LaCorte	.05
231 Mike LaCoss	.05
232 Mike Madden (R)	.15
233 Jerry Mumphrey	.05
234 Joe Niekro	.10
235 Terry Puhl	.05
236 Luis Pujols	.05
237 Craig Reynolds	.05
238 Vern Ruhle	.05
239 Nolan Ryan	4.00
240 Mike Scott	.35
241 Tony Scott	.05
242 Dave Smith	.05
243 Dickie Thon	.08
244 Denny Walling	.05
PITTSBURGH PIRATES	
245 Dale Berra	.05
246 Jim Bibby	.05
247 John Candelaria	.05
248 Jose DeLeon (R)	.35
249 Mike Easler	.08
250 Cecilio Guante	.05
251 Richie Hebner	.05
252 Lee Lacy	.05
253 Bill Madlock	.15
254 Milt May	.05
255 Lee Mazzilli	.05
256 Larry McWilliams	.05
257 Jim Morrison	.05
258 Dave Parker	.35
259 Tony Pena	.20
260 Johnny Ray	.15
261 Rick Rhoden	.05
262 Don Robinson	.05
263 Manny Sarmiento	.05
264 Rod Scurry	.05
265 Kent Tekulve	.05
266 Gene Tenace	.05
267 Jason Thompson	.10
268 Lee Tunnell (R)	.15
269 Marvell Wynne (R)	.15
MONTREAL EXPOS	
270 Ray Burris	.05
271 Gary Carter	.35
272 Warren Cromartie	.05
273 Andre Dawson	.60
274 Doug Flynn	.05
275 Terry Francona	.05
276 Bill Gullickson	.05
277 Bob James (R)	.20
278 Charlie Lea	.05
279 Bryan Little	.05
280 Al Oliver	.15
281 Tim Raines	.50
282 Bobby Ramos	.05
283 Jeff Reardon	.10
284 Steve Rogers	.05
285 Scott Sanderson	.05
286 Dan Schatzeder	.05
287 Bryn Smith	.05
288 Chris Speier	.05
289 Manny Trillo	.05
290 Mike Vail	.05
291 Tim Wallach	.25
292 Chris Welsh	.05
293 Jim Wohlford	.05

NO. PLAYER	MINT
SAN DIEGO PADRES	
294 Kurt Bevacqua	.05
295 Juan Bonilla	.05
296 Bobby Brown	.05
297 Luis DeLeon	.05
298 Dave Dravecky	.10
299 Tim Flannery	.05
300 Steve Garvey	.50
301 Tony Gwynn	4.00
302 Andy Hawkins (R)	.45
303 Ruppert Jones	.05
304 Terry Kennedy	.10
305 Tim Lollar	.05
306 Gary Lucas	.05
307 Kevin McReynolds (R)	6.00
308 Sid Monge	.05
309 Mario Ramirez	.05
310 Gene Richards	.12
311 Luis Salazar	.05
312 Eric Show	.05
313 Elias Sosa	.05
314 Garry Templeton	.10
315 Mark Thurmond (R)	.20
316 Ed Whitson	.05
317 Alan Wiggins	.10
ST. LOUIS CARDINALS	
318 Neil Allen	.05
319 Joaquin Andujar	.10
320 Steve Braun	.05
321 Glenn Brummer	.05
322 Bob Forsch	.10
323 David Green	.05
324 George Hendrick	.08
325 Tom Herr	.10
326 Dane Iorg	.05
327 Jeff Lahti	.05
328 Dave LaPoint	.05
329 Willie McGee	.60
330 Ken Oberkfell	.05
331 Darrell Porter	.05
332 Jamie Quirk	.05
333 Mike Ramsey	.05
334 Floyd Rayford	.05
335 Lonnie Smith	.10
336 Ozzie Smith	.60
337 John Stuper	.05
338 Bruce Sutter	.15
339 Andy Van Slyke (R)	3.50
340 Dave Von Ohlen	.12
KANSAS CITY ROYALS	
341 Willie Aikens	.05
342 Mike Armstrong	.05
343 Bud Black	.05
344 George Brett	1.50
345 Onix Concepcion	.05
346 Keith Creel	.05
347 Larry Gura	.05
348 Don Hood	.05
349 Dennis Leonard	.05
350 Hal McRae	.05
351 Amos Otis	.05
352 Gaylord Perry	.30
353 Greg Pryor	.05
354 Dan Quisenberry	.20
355 Steve Renko	.05
356 Leon Roberts	.05
357 Pat Sheridan (R)	.25
358 Joe Simpson	.05
359 Don Slaught	.05
360 Paul Splittorff	.05
361 U.L. Washington	.05
362 John Wathan	.05
363 Frank White	.05
364 Willie Wilson	.15
SAN FRANCISCO GIANTS	
365 Jim Barr	.05
366 Dave Bergman	.05
367 Fred Breining	.05
368 Bob Brenly	.05
369 Jack Clark	.30
370 Chili Davis	.15
371 Mark Davis	.35
372 Darrell Evans	.10
373 Atlee Hammaker	.05
374 Mike Krukow	.05

NO. PLAYER	MINT
375 Duane Kuiper	.05
376 Bill Laskey	.05
377 Gary Lavelle	.05
378 Johnnie LeMaster	.05
379 Jeff Leonard	.05
380 Randy Lerch	.05
381 Renie Martin	.05
382 Andy McGaffigan	.05
383 Greg Minton	.05
384 Tom O'Malley	.05
385 Max Venable	.05
386 Brad Wellman	.05
387 Joel Youngblood	.12
BOSTON RED SOX	
388 Gary Allenson	.05
389 Luis Aponte	.05
390 Tony Armas	.15
391 Doug Bird	.05
392 Wade Boggs	7.00
393 Dennis Boyd (R)	.75
394 Mike Brown	.12
395 Mark Clear	.05
396 Dennis Eckersley	.35
397 Dwight Evans	.20
398 Rich Gedman	.10
399 Glenn Hoffman	.05
400 Bruce Hurst	.15
401 John Henry Johnson	.05
402 Ed Jurak	.12
403 Rick Miller	.05
404 Jeff Newman	.05
405 Reid Nichols	.05
406 Bob Ojeda	.10
407 Jerry Remy	.05
408 Jim Rice	.30
409 Bob Stanley	.05
410 Dave Stapleton	.05
411 John Tudor	.20
412 Carl Yastrzemski	1.00
TEXAS RANGERS	
413 Buddy Bell	.15
414 Larry Biittner	.05
415 John Butcher	.05
416 Danny Darwin	.05
417 Bucky Dent	.05
418 Dave Hostetler	.05
419 Charlie Hough	.05
420 Bobby Johnson	.05
421 Odell Jones	.05
422 Jon Matlack	.05
423 Pete O'Brien (R)	1.00
424 Larry Parrish	.05
425 Mickey Rivers	.10
426 Billy Sample	.05
427 Dave Schmidt	.05
428 Mike Smithson (R)	.15
429 Bill Stein	.05
430 Dave Stewart	1.00
431 Jim Sundberg	.05
432 Frank Tanana	.10
433 Dave Tobik	.05
434 Wayne Tolleson	.15
435 George Wright	.05
OAKLAND A'S	
436 Bill Almon	.05
437 Keith Atherton	.12
438 Dave Beard	.05
439 Tom Burgmeier	.05
440 Jeff Burroughs	.05
441 Chris Codiroli	.10
442 Tim Conroy	.12
443 Mike Davis	.10
444 Wayne Gross	.05
445 Garry Hancock	.05
446 Mike Heath	.05
447 Rickey Henderson	5.00
448 Don Hill	.12
449 Bob Kearney	.05
450 Bill Krueger	.12
451 Rick Langford	.05
452 Carney Lansford	.15
453 Davey Lopes	.10
454 Steve McCatty	.05
455 Dan Meyer	.05
456 Dwayne Murphy	.05

NO.	PLAYER	MINT
457	Mike Norris	.05
458	Ricky Peters	.05
459	Tony Phillips	.25
460	Tom Underwood	.05
461	Mike Warren (R)	.15

CINCINNATI REDS

NO.	PLAYER	MINT
462	Johnny Bench	1.00
463	Bruce Berenyi	.05
464	Dann Bilardello	.05
465	Cesar Cedeno	.05
466	Dave Concepcion	.10
467	Dan Driessen	.05
468	Nick Esasky (R)	1.50
469	Rich Gale	.05
470	Ben Hayes	.05
471	Paul Householder	.05
472	Tom Hume	.05
473	Alan Knicely	.05
474	Eddie Milner	.05
475	Ron Oester	.05
476	Kelly Paris	.10
477	Frank Pastore	.05
478	Ted Power	.05
479	Joe Price	.05
480	Charlie Puleo	.05
481	Gary Redus (R)	.25
482	Bill Scherrer	.12
483	Mario Soto	.10
484	Alex Trevino	.05
485	Duane Walker	.05

CHICAGO CUBS

NO.	PLAYER	MINT
486	Larry Bowa	.05
487	Warren Brusstar	.05
488	Bill Buckner	.10
489	Bill Campbell	.05
490	Ron Cey	.15
491	Jody Davis	.05
492	Leon Durham	.15
493	Mel Hall	.25
494	Ferguson Jenkins	.15
495	Jay Johnstone	.05
496	Craig Lefferts (R)	.35
497	Carmelo Martinez (R)	.40
498	Jerry Morales	.05
499	Keith Moreland	.05
500	Dickie Noles	.05
501	Mike Proly	.05
502	Chuck Rainey	.05
503	Dick Ruthven	.05
504	Ryne Sandberg	8.00
505	Lee Smith	.12
506	Steve Trout	.05
507	Gary Woods	.05

CALIFORNIA ANGELS

NO.	PLAYER	MINT
508	Juan Beniquez	.05
509	Bob Boone	.05
510	Rick Burleson	.10
511	Rod Carew	.75
512	Bobby Clark	.05
513	John Curtis	.05
514	Doug DeCinces	.10
515	Brian Downing	.05
516	Tim Foli	.05
517	Ken Forsch	.05
518	Bobby Grich	.05
519	Andy Hassler	.05
520	Reggie Jackson	1.00
521	Ron Jackson	.05
522	Tommy John	.15
523	Bruce Kison	.05
524	Steve Lubratich	.12
525	Fred Lynn	.15
526	Gary Pettis (R)	.30
527	Luis Sanchez	.05
528	Daryl Sconiers	.10
529	Ellis Valentine	.05
530	Rob Wilfong	.05
531	Mike Witt	.10
532	Geoff Zahn	.05

CLEVELAND INDIANS

NO.	PLAYER	MINT
533	Bud Anderson	.05
534	Chris Bando	.05
535	Alan Bannister	.05
536	Bert Blyleven	.25
537	Tom Brennan	.05
538	Jamie Easterly	.05
539	Juan Eichelberger	.05
540	Jim Essian	.05
541	Mike Fischlin	.05
542	Julio Franco	2.50
543	Mike Hargrove	.05
544	Toby Harrah	.05
545	Ron Hassey	.05
546	Neal Heaton (R)	.50
547	Bake McBride	.05
548	Broderick Perkins	.12
549	Lary Sorensen	.05
550	Dan Spillner	.05
551	Rick Sutcliffe	.25
552	Pat Tabler	.10
553	Gorman Thomas	.10
554	Andre Thornton	.10
555	George Vukovich	.05

MINNESOTA TWINS

NO.	PLAYER	MINT
556	Darrell Brown	.05
557	Tom Brunansky	.35
558	Randy Bush	.25
559	Bobby Castillo	.05
560	John Castino	.05
561	Ron Davis	.05
562	Dave Engle	.05
563	Lenny Faedo	.05
564	Pete Filson	.12
565	Gary Gaetti	.75
566	Mickey Hatcher	.05
567	Kent Hrbek	.50
568	Rusty Kuntz	.05
569	Tim Laudner	.05
570	Rick Lysander	.12
571	Bobby Mitchell	.05
572	Ken Schrom	.05
573	Ray Smith	.12
574	Tim Teufel (R)	.30
575	Frank Viola	2.00
576	Gary Ward	.05
577	Ron Washington	.05
578	Len Whitehouse	.05
579	Al Williams	.05

NEW YORK METS

NO.	PLAYER	MINT
580	Bob Bailor	.05
581	Mark Bradley	.10
582	Hubie Brooks	.25
583	Carlos Diaz	.05
584	George Foster	.15
585	Brian Giles	.05
586	Danny Heep	.05
587	Keith Hernandez	.30
588	Ron Hodges	.05
589	Scott Holman	.05
590	Dave Kingman	.15
591	Ed Lynch	.05
592	Jose Oquendo	.50
593	Jesse Orosco	.10
594	Junior Ortiz	.12
595	Tom Seaver	1.50
596	Doug Sisk	.15
597	Rusty Staub	.10
598	John Stearns	.05
599	Darryl Strawberry (R)	25.00
600	Craig Swan	.05
601	Walt Terrell (R)	.35
602	Mike Torrez	.05
603	Mookie Wilson	.10

SEATTLE MARINERS

NO.	PLAYER	MINT
604	Jamie Allen	.12
605	Jim Beattie	.05
606	Tony Bernazard	.05
607	Manny Castillo	.05
608	Bill Caudill	.05
609	Bryan Clark	.05
610	Al Cowens	.05
611	Dave Henderson	.30
612	Steve Henderson	.05
613	Orlando Mercado	.12
614	Mike Moore	.25
615	Ricky Nelson	.12
616	Spike Owen (R)	.30
617	Pat Putnam	.05
618	Ron Roenicke	.05
619	Mike Stanton	.05
620	Bob Stoddard	.05
621	Rick Sweet	.05
622	Roy Thomas	.05
623	Ed Vande Berg	.05
624	Matt Young (R)	.15
625	Richie Zisk	.05

SPECIAL CARDS

NO.	PLAYER	MINT
626	Fred Lynn: "All-Star Record Breaker"	.15
627	Manny Trillo: "All-Star Record Breaker"	.05
628	Steve Garvey: "NL Iron Man"	.25
629	Rod Carew: "AL Batting Runner-Up"	.30
630	Wade Boggs: "AL Batting Champion"	.50
631	Tim Raines: "Letting Go Of The Raines"	.15
632	Al Oliver: "Double Trouble"	.15
633	Steve Sax: "All-Star Second Base"	.10
634	Dickie Thon: "All-Star Shortstop"	.10
635	Quisenberry & Martinez: "Ace Fireman"	.10
636	Perez, Rose, & Morgan: "Reds Reunited"	.40
637	Parrish & Boone: "Backstop Stars"	.10
638	Brett & Perry: "Pine Tar Incident"	.25
639	Forsch, Warren & Righetti: "1983 No-Hitters"	.10
640	Bench and Yaz: "Retiring Superstars"	1.00
641	Gaylord Perry: "Going Out In Style"	.15
642	Steve Carlton: 300 Club and Strikeout Record	.30
643	Altobelli and Owens: "World Series Managers"	.05
644	Rick Dempsey: "World Series MVP"	.05
645	Mike Boddicker: "Rookie Winner"	.10
646	Scott McGregor: "The Clincher"	.10
647	Checklist No. 1	.08
648	Checklist No. 2	.08
649	Checklist No. 3	.08
650	Checklist No. 4	.08
651	Checklist No. 5	.08
652	Checklist No. 6	.08
653	Checklist No. 7	.08
654	Checklist No. 8	.08
655	Checklist No. 9	.08
656	Checklist No. 10	.08
657	Checklist No. 11	.08
658	Checklist No. 12	.08
659	Checklist No 13	.08
660	Checklist No. 14	.08

1984 Fleer Traded Update.... Complete Set of 132 Cards—Value $500.00

This was Fleer's first traded update set. It updates the main 1984 card set with players who had changed teams during the season and rookies. This set features Fleer's first card of Dwight Gooden, Roger Clemens, Bret Saberhagen and Kirby Puckett. Production was extremely limited. The complete set was packaged in its own printed box and distributed exclusively through card hobby dealers.

Card values shown here fluctuate considerably.

NO. PLAYER	MINT	NO. PLAYER	MINT	NO. PLAYER	MINT	NO. PLAYER	MINT
U1 Willie Aikens	.25	U34 Dennis Eckersley	2.50	U67 Frank LaCorte	.20	U100 Jeff Robinson	.50
U2 Luis Aponte	.20	U35 Jim Essian	.20	U68 Dennis Lamp	.20	U101 R. Romanick	.40
U3 Mark Bailey	.30	U36 Darrell Evans	.40	U69 Tito Landrum	.20	U102 Pete Rose	15.00
U4 Bob Bailor	.20	U37 Mike Fitzgerald	.35	U70 Mark Langston (RR)	15.00	U103 B. Saberhagen (RR)	35.00
U5 Dusty Baker	.25	U38 Tim Foli	.20	U71 Rick Leach	.20	U104 Scott Sanderson	.25
U6 Steve Balboni	.25	U39 John Franco (RR)	11.00	U72 Craig Lefferts	.20	U105 Dick Schofield	.50
U7 Alan Bannister	.20	U40 George Frazier	.20	U73 Gary Lucas	.20	U106 Tom Seaver	11.00
U8 Marty Barrett (RR)	3.00	U41 Rich Gale	.20	U74 Jerry Martin	.20	U107 Jim Slaton	.20
U9 Dave Beard	.20	U42 Barbaro Garbey	.25	U75 Carmelo Martinez	.25	U108 Mike Smithson	.20
U10 Joe Beckwith	.20	U43 Dwight Gooden (RR)	90.00	U76 Mike Mason	.30	U109 Lary Sorensen	.20
U11 Dave Bergman	.20	U44 Goose Gossage	.50	U77 Gary Matthews	.20	U110 Tim Stoddard	.20
U12 Tony Bernazard	.20	U45 Wayne Gross	.20	U78 Andy McGaffigan	.20	U111 Jeff Stone	.40
U13 Bruce Bochte	.20	U46 Mark Gubicza (RR)	5.00	U79 Joey McLaughlin	.20	U112 Champ Summers	.20
U14 Barry Bonnell	.20	U47 Jackie Gutierrez	.40	U80 Joe Morgan	3.00	U113 Jim Sundberg	.20
U15 Phil Bradley (RR)	5.00	U48 Toby Harrah	.20	U81 Darryl Motley	.25	U114 Rick Sutcliffe	.75
U16 Fred Breining	.20	U49 Ron Hassey	.20	U82 Graig Nettles	.40	U115 Craig Swan	.20
U17 Mike Brown	.25	U50 Richie Hebner	.20	U83 Phil Niekro	3.00	U116 Derrel Thomas	.20
U18 Bill Buckner	.30	U51 Willie Hernandez	.60	U84 Ken Oberkfell	.20	U117 Gorman Thomas	.25
U19 Ray Burris	.20	U52 Ed Hodge	.35	U85 Al Oliver	.30	U118 Alex Trevino	.20
U20 John Butcher	.20	U53 Ricky Horton	.40	U86 Jorge Orta	.20	U119 Manny Trillo	.20
U21 Brett Butler	.40	U54 Art Howe	.35	U87 Amos Otis	.30	U120 John Tudor	.35
U22 Enos Cabell	.20	U55 Dane Iorg	.20	U88 Bob Owchinko	.20	U121 Tom Underwood	.20
U23 Bill Campbell	.20	U56 Brook Jacoby (RR)	3.00	U89 Dave Parker	3.00	U122 Mike Vail	.20
U24 Bill Caudill	.20	U57 Dion James	.50	U90 Jack Perconte	.20	U123 Tom Waddell	.30
U25 Bobby Clark	.20	U58 Mike Jeffcoat	.35	U91 Tony Perez	2.00	U124 Gary Ward	.20
U26 Brian Clark	.20	U59 Ruppert Jones	.20	U92 Gerald Perry	2.00	U125 Terry Whitfield	.20
U27 R. Clemens (RR)	125.00	U60 Bob Kearney	.20	U93 Kirby Puckett (RR)	160.00	U126 Curtis Wilkerson	.35
U28 Jaime Cocanower	.30	U61 Jimmy Key (RR)	4.50	U94 Shane Rawley	.30	U127 Frank Williams	.30
U29 Ron Darling (RR)	7.00	U62 Dave Kingman	.35	U95 Floyd Rayford	.20	U128 Glenn Wilson	.30
U30 Alvin Davis (RR)	14.00	U63 B. Komminsk	.35	U96 Ron Reed	.20	U129 John Wockenfuss	.20
U31 Bob Dernier	.25	U64 Jerry Koosman	.40	U97 R.J. Reynolds	1.25	U130 Ned Yost	.20
U32 Carlos Diaz	.20	U65 Wayne Krenchicki	.20	U98 Gene Richards	.20	U131 Mike Young	.35
U33 Mike Easler	.20	U66 Rusty Kuntz	.20	U99 Jose Rijo (RR)	4.00	U132 Checklist	.50

1985 Fleer.... Complete Set of 660 Cards—Value $150.00

Features the rookie cards of Dwight Gooden, Roger Clemens, Bret Saberhagen, Eric Davis, Orel Hershiser and Kirby Puckett. The frames on the front of the cards are color coded to the player's team. The back is printed in two shades of black and red ink. A new feature was "Major League Prospect" cards—each featuring two rookies.

NO. PLAYER	MINT	NO. PLAYER	MINT	NO. PLAYER	MINT	NO. PLAYER	MINT
DETROIT TIGERS		7 Barbaro Garbey (R)	.15	14 Rusty Kuntz	.05	21 Dave Rozema	.05
1 Doug Bair	.10	8 Kirk Gibson	.40	15 Chet Lemon	.05	22 Bill Scherrer	.05
2 Juan Berenguer	.05	9 John Grubb	.05	16 Aurelio Lopez	.05	23 Alan Trammell	.35
3 Dave Bergman	.05	10 Willie Hernandez	.15	17 Sid Monge	.05	24 Lou Whitaker	.20
4 Tom Brookens	.05	11 Larry Herndon	.05	18 Jack Morris	.20	25 Milt Wilcox	.05
5 Marty Castillo	.05	12 Howard Johnson	2.00	19 Lance Parrish	.20	**SAN DIEGO PADRES**	
6 Darrell Evans	.10	13 Ruppert Jones	.05	20 Dan Petry	.15	26 Curt Bevacqua	.05

NO. PLAYER	MINT
27 Greg Booker (R)	.10
28 Bobby Brown	.05
29 Luis DeLeon	.05
30 Dave Dravecky	.05
31 Tim Flannery	.05
32 Steve Garvey	.40
33 Goose Gossage	.15
34 Tony Gwynn	2.00
35 Greg Harris	.05
36 Andy Hawkins	.05
37 Terry Kennedy	.05
38 Craig Lefferts	.05
39 Tim Lollar	.05
40 Carmelo Martinez	.05
41 Kevin McReynolds	.75
42 Graig Nettles	.10
43 Luis Salazar	.05
44 Eric Show	.05
45 Garry Templeton	.12
46 Mark Thurmond	.05
47 Ed Whitson	.05
48 Alan Wiggins	.10

CHICAGO CUBS

NO. PLAYER	MINT
49 Rich Bordi	.05
50 Larry Bowa	.10
51 Warren Brusster	.05
52 Ron Cey	.15
53 Henry Cotto (R)	.15
54 Jody Davis	.10
55 Bob Dernier	.05
56 Leon Durham	.15
57 Dennis Eckersley	.30
58 George Frazier	.05
59 Richie Hebner	.05
60 Dave Lopes	.10
61 Gary Matthews	.10
62 Keith Moreland	.05
63 Rick Reuschel	.10
64 Dick Ruthven	.05
65 Ryne Sandberg	3.00
66 Scott Sanderson	.05
67 Lee Smith	.10
68 Tim Stoddard	.05
69 Rick Sutcliffe	.20
70 Steve Trout	.05
71 Gary Woods	.05

NEW YORK METS

NO. PLAYER	MINT
72 Wally Backman	.05
73 Bruce Berenyi	.05
74 Hubie Brooks	.10
75 Kelvin Chapman (R)	.15
76 Ron Darling	.75
77 Sid Fernandez	1.00
78 Mike Fitzgerald	.05
79 George Foster	.15
80 Brent Gaff	.05
81 Ron Gardenhire	.05
82 Dwight Gooden (R)	10.00
83 Tom Gorman	.05
84 Danny Heep	.05
85 Keith Hernandez	.30
86 Ray Knight	.10
87 Ed Lynch	.05
88 Jose Oquendo	.12
89 Jesse Orosco	.10
90 Rafael Santana (R)	.20
91 Doug Sisk	.05
92 Rusty Staub	.10
93 Darryl Strawberry	5.00
94 Walt Terrell	.05
95 Mookie Wilson	.05

TORONTO BLUE JAYS

NO. PLAYER	MINT
96 Jim Acker	.05
97 Willie Aikens	.05
98 Doyle Alexander	.05
99 Jesse Barfield	.30
100 George Bell	.50
101 Jim Clancy	.05
102 Dave Collins	.05
103 Tony Fernandez	.40
104 Damaso Garcia	.10
105 Jim Gott	.05
106 Alfredo Griffin	.05
107 Garth Iorg	.05
108 Roy Lee Jackson	.05
109 Cliff Johnson	.05

NO. PLAYER	MINT
110 Jimmy Key (R)	1.00
111 Dennis Lamp	.05
112 Rick Leach	.05
113 Luis Leal	.05
114 Buck Martinez	.05
115 Lloyd Moseby	.15
116 Rance Mulliniks	.05
117 Dave Stieb	.15
118 Willie Upshaw	.10
119 Ernie Whitt	.05

NEW YORK YANKEES

NO. PLAYER	MINT
120 Mike Armstrong	.05
121 Don Baylor	.10
122 Marty Bystrom	.05
123 Rick Cerone	.05
124 Joe Cowley	.05
125 Brian Dayett	.05
126 Tim Foli	.05
127 Ray Fontenot	.05
128 Ken Griffey	.10
129 Ron Guidry	.15
130 Toby Harrah	.05
131 Jay Howell	.05
132 Steve Kemp	.05
133 Don Mattingly	12.00
134 Bobby Meacham	.05
135 John Montefusco	.05
136 Omar Moreno	.05
137 Dale Murray	.05
138 Phil Niekro	.30
139 Mike Pagliarulo (R)	.80
140 Willie Randolph	.05
141 Dennis Rasmussen	.25
142 Dave Righetti	.15
143 Jose Rijo (R)	1.00
144 Andre Robertson	.05
145 Bob Shirley	.05
146 Dave Winfield	.35
147 Butch Wynegar	.05

BOSTON RED SOX

NO. PLAYER	MINT
148 Gary Allenson	.05
149 Tony Armas	.10
150 Marty Barrett	.25
151 Wade Boggs	3.50
152 Dennis Boyd	.10
153 Bill Buckner	.10
154 Mark Clear	.05
155 Roger Clemens (R)	15.00
156 Steve Crawford	.05
157 Mike Easler	.12
158 Dwight Evans	.20
159 Rich Gedman	.10
160 Jackie Gutierrez (R)	.15
161 Bruce Hurst	.15
162 John H. Johnson	.05
163 Rick Miller	.05
164 Reid Nichols	.05
165 Al Nipper (R)	.15
166 Bob Ojeda	.10
167 Jerry Remy	.05
168 Jim Rice	.30
169 Bob Stanley	.05

BALTIMORE ORIOLES

NO. PLAYER	MINT
170 Mike Boddicker	.10
171 Al Bumbry	.05
172 Todd Cruz	.05
173 Rich Dauer	.05
174 Storm Davis	.05
175 Rick Dempsey	.05
176 Jim Dwyer	.05
177 Mike Flanagan	.05
178 Dan Ford	.05
179 Wayne Gross	.05
180 John Lowenstein	.05
181 Dennis Martinez	.10
182 Tippy Martinez	.05
183 Scott McGregor	.05
184 Eddie Murray	.50
185 Joe Nolan	.05
186 Floyd Rayford	.05
187 Cal Ripken, Jr.	.75
188 Gary Roenicke	.05
189 Lenn Sakata	.05
190 John Shelby	.05
191 Ken Singleton	.05

NO. PLAYER	MINT
192 Sammy Stewart	.05
193 Bill Swaggerty (R)	.15
194 Tom Underwood	.05
195 Mike Young	.10

KANSAS CITY ROYALS

NO. PLAYER	MINT
196 Steve Balboni	.10
197 Joe Beckwith	.05
198 Bud Black	.05
199 George Brett	.75
200 Onix Concepcion	.05
201 Mark Gubicza (R)	2.25
202 Larry Gura	.05
203 Mark Huisman	.05
204 Dane Iorg	.05
205 Danny Jackson	.75
206 Charlie Leibrandt	.05
207 Hal McRae	.05
208 Darryl Motley	.05
209 Jorge Orta	.05
210 Greg Pryor	.05
211 Dan Quisenberry	.15
212 Bret Saberhagen (R)	6.00
213 Pat Sheridan	.05
214 Don Slaught	.05
215 U.L. Washington	.05
216 John Wathan	.05
217 Frank White	.05
218 Willie Wilson	.15

ST. LOUIS CARDINALS

NO. PLAYER	MINT
219 Neil Allen	.05
220 Joaquin Andujar	.10
221 Steve Braun	.05
222 Danny Cox	.05
223 Bob Forsch	.10
224 David Green	.05
225 George Hendrick	.08
226 Tom Herr	.10
227 Ricky Horton (R)	.25
228 Art Howe	.05
229 Mike Jorgensen	.05
230 Kurt Kepshire (R)	.15
231 Jeff Lahti	.05
232 Tito Landrum	.05
233 Dave LaPoint	.05
234 Willie McGee	.30
235 Tom Nieto (R)	.15
236 Terry Pendleton (R)	.50
237 Darrell Porter	.05
238 Dave Rucker	.05
239 Lonnie Smith	.12
240 Ozzie Smith	.45
241 Bruce Sutter	.15
242 Andy Van Slyke	.60
243 Dave Von Ohlen	.05

PHILADELPHIA PHILLIES

NO. PLAYER	MINT
244 Larry Andersen	.05
245 Bill Campbell	.05
246 Steve Carlton	.30
247 Tim Corcoran	.05
248 Ivan DeJesus	.05
249 John Denny	.05
250 Bo Diaz	.05
251 Greg Gross	.05
252 Kevin Gross	.05
253 Von Hayes	.15
254 Al Holland	.05
255 Charles Hudson	.05
256 Jerry Koosman	.10
257 Joe Lefebvre	.05
258 Sixto Lezcano	.05
259 Garry Maddox	.05
260 Len Matuszek	.05
261 Tug McGraw	.10
262 Al Oliver	.10
263 Shane Rawley	.05
264 Juan Samuel	.30
265 Mike Schmidt	1.50
266 Jeff Stone (R)	.20
267 Ozzie Virgil	.05
268 Glenn Wilson	.10
269 John Wockenfuss	.05

MINNESOTA TWINS

NO. PLAYER	MINT
270 Darrell Brown	.05
271 Tom Brunansky	.25
272 Randy Bush	.05

NO. PLAYER	MINT
273 John Butcher	.05
274 Bobby Castillo	.05
275 Ron Davis	.05
276 Dave Engle	.05
277 Pete Filson	.05
278 Gary Gaetti	.40
279 Mickey Hatcher	.05
280 Ed Hodge (R)	.15
281 Kent Hrbek	.35
282 Houston Jimenez	.05
283 Tim Laudner	.05
284 Rick Lysander	.05
285 Dave Meier (R)	.15
286 Kirby Puckett (R)	20.00
287 Pat Putnam	.05
288 Ken Schrom	.05
289 Mike Smithson	.05
290 Tim Teufel	.05
291 Frank Viola	.75
292 Ron Washington	.05

CALIFORNIA ANGELS

NO. PLAYER	MINT
293 Don Aase	.05
294 Juan Beniquez	.05
295 Bob Boone	.05
296 Mike Brown	.05
297 Rod Carew	.50
298 Doug Corbett	.05
299 Doug DeCinces	.05
300 Brian Downing	.10
301 Ken Forsch	.05
302 Bobby Grich	.05
303 Reggie Jackson	.50
304 Tommy John	.15
305 Curt Kaufman (R)	.15
306 Bruce Kison	.05
307 Fred Lynn	.15
308 Gary Pettis	.10
309 Ron Romanick (R)	.20
310 Luis Sanchez	.05
311 Dick Schofield	.10
312 Daryl Sconiers	.05
313 Jim Slaton	.05
314 Derrel Thomas	.05
315 Rob Wilfong	.05
316 Mike Witt	.10
317 Geoff Zahn	.05

ATLANTA BRAVES

NO. PLAYER	MINT
318 Len Barker	.05
319 Steve Bedrosian	.10
320 Bruce Benedict	.05
321 Rick Camp	.05
322 Chris Chambliss	.10
323 Jeff Dedmon (R)	.10
324 Terry Forster	.05
325 Gene Garber	.05
326 Albert Hall (R)	.15
327 Terry Harper	.05
328 Bob Horner	.15
329 Glenn Hubbard	.05
330 Randy Johnson	.05
331 Brad Komminsk	.05
332 Rick Mahler	.05
333 Craig McMurtry	.05
334 Donnie Moore	.05
335 Dale Murphy	.60
336 Ken Oberkfell	.05
337 Pascual Perez	.05
338 Gerald Perry	.40
339 Rafael Ramirez	.05
340 Jerry Royster	.05
341 Alex Trevino	.05
342 Claudell Washington	.08

HOUSTON ASTROS

NO. PLAYER	MINT
343 Alan Ashby	.05
344 Mark Bailey	.10
345 Kevin Bass	.10
346 Enos Cabell	.05
347 Jose Cruz	.10
348 Bill Dawley	.05
349 Frank DiPino	.05
350 Bill Doran	.05
351 Phil Garner	.05
352 Bob Knepper	.10
353 Mike LaCoss	.05
354 Jerry Mumphrey	.05
355 Joe Niekro	.10

NO.	PLAYER	MINT
356	Terry Puhl	.05
357	Craig Reynolds	.05
358	Vern Ruhle	.05
359	Nolan Ryan	3.00
360	Joe Sambito	.05
361	Mike Scott	.30
362	Dave Smith	.05
363	Julio Solano (R)	.10
364	Dickie Thon	.05
365	Denny Walling	.05

LOS ANGELES DODGERS

NO.	PLAYER	MINT
366	Dave Anderson	.05
367	Bob Bailor	.05
368	Greg Brock	.05
369	Carlos Diaz	.05
370	Pedro Guerrero	.25
371	Orel Hershiser (R)	7.50
372	Rick Honeycutt	.05
373	Burt Hooton	.05
374	Ken Howell (R)	.20
375	Ken Landreaux	.05
376	Candy Maldonado	.20
377	Mike Marshall	.10
378	Tom Niedenfuer	.05
379	Alejandro Pena	.05
380	Jerry Reuss	.10
381	R.J. Reynolds (R)	.30
382	German Rivera (R)	.15
383	Bill Russell	.05
384	Steve Sax	.30
385	Mike Scioscia	.05
386	Franklin Stubbs (R)	.60
387	Fernando Valenzuela	.30
388	Bob Welch	.20
389	Terry Whitfield	.05
390	Steve Yeager	.05
391	Pat Zachry	.05

MONTREAL EXPOS

NO.	PLAYER	MINT
392	Fred Breining	.05
393	Gary Carter	.30
394	Andre Dawson	.50
395	Miguel Dilone	.05
396	Dan Driessen	.05
397	Doug Flynn	.05
398	Terry Francona	.05
399	Bill Gullickson	.05
400	Bob James	.05
401	Chrlie Lea	.05
402	Bryan Little	.05
403	Gary Lucas	.05
404	David Palmer	.05
405	Tim Raines	.30
406	Mike Ramsey	.05
407	Jeff Reardon	.10
408	Steve Rogers	.05
409	Dan Schatzeder	.05
410	Bryn Smith	.05
411	Mike Stenhouse	.05
412	Tim Wallach	.12
413	Jim Wohlford	.05

OAKLAND A'S

NO.	PLAYER	MINT
414	Bill Almon	.05
415	Keith Atherton	.05
416	Bruce Bochte	.05
417	Tom Burgmeier	.05
418	Ray Burris	.05
419	Bill Caudill	.05
420	Chris Codiroli	.05
421	Tim Conroy	.05
422	Mike Davis	.05
423	Jim Essian	.05
424	Mike Heath	.05
425	Rickey Henderson	2.50
426	Donnie Hill	.05
427	Dave Kingman	.10
428	Bill Krueger	.05
429	Carney Lansford	.10
430	Steve McCatty	.05
431	Joe Morgan	.25
432	Dwayne Murphy	.05
433	Tony Phillips	.05
434	Lary Sorensen	.05
435	Mike Warren	.05
436	Curt Young (R)	.35

CLEVELAND INDIANS

NO.	PLAYER	MINT
437	Luis Aponte	.05
438	Chris Bando	.05
439	Tony Bernazard	.05
440	Bert Blyleven	.15
441	Brett Butler	.05
442	Ernie Camacho	.05
443	Joe Carter	3.00
444	Carmelo Castillo	.05
445	Jamie Easterly	.05
446	Steve Farr (R)	.40
447	Mike Fischlin	.05
448	Julio Franco	.40
449	Mel Hall	.10
450	Mike Hargrove	.05
451	Neal Heaton	.05
452	Brook Jacoby	.35
453	Mike Jeffcoat	.05
454	Don Schulze (R)	.15
455	Roy Smith (R)	.15
456	Pat Tabler	.05
457	Andre Thornton	.05
458	George Vukovich	.05
459	Tom Waddell (R)	.15
460	Jerry Willard	.05

PITTSBURGH PIRATES

NO.	PLAYER	MINT
461	Dale Berra	.05
462	John Candelaria	.10
463	Jose DeLeon	.05
464	Doug Frobel	.05
465	Cecilio Guante	.05
466	Brian Harper	.30
467	Lee Lacy	.05
468	Bill Madlock	.10
469	Lee Mazzilli	.05
470	Larry McWilliams	.05
471	Jim Morrison	.05
472	Tony Pena	.10
473	Johnny Ray	.10
474	Rick Rhoden	.10
475	Don Robinson	.05
476	Rod Scurry	.05
477	Kent Tekulve	.05
478	Jason Thompson	.05
479	John Tudor	.10
480	Lee Tunnell	.05
481	Marvell Wynne	.05

SEATTLE MARINERS

NO.	PLAYER	MINT
482	Salome Barojas	.05
483	Dave Beard	.05
484	Jim Beattie	.05
485	Barry Bonnell	.05
486	Phil Bradley (R)	1.00
487	Al Cowens	.05
488	Alvin Davis (R)	3.00
489	Dave Henderson	.15
490	Steve Henderson	.05
491	Bob Kearney	.05
492	Mark Langston (R)	3.00
493	Larry Milbourne	.05
494	Paul Mirabella	.05
495	Mike Moore	.05
496	Edwin Nunez	.05
497	Spike Owen	.05
498	Jack Perconte	.05
499	Ken Phelps	.05
500	Jim Presley (R)	.75
501	Mike Stanton	.05
502	Bob Stoddard	.05
503	Gorman Thomas	.10
504	Ed VandeBerg	.05
505	Matt Young	.05

CHICAGO WHITE SOX

NO.	PLAYER	MINT
506	Juan Agosto	.05
507	Harold Baines	.20
508	Floyd Bannister	.10
509	Britt Burns	.05
510	Julio Cruz	.05
511	Richard Dotson	.05
512	Jerry Dybzinski	.05
513	Carlton Fisk	.30
514	Scott Fletcher	.05
515	Jerry Hairston	.05
516	Marc Hill	.05
517	LaMarr Hoyt	.10
518	Ron Kittle	.15

NO.	PLAYER	MINT
519	Rudy Law	.05
520	Vance Law	.05
521	Greg Luzinski	.10
522	Gene Nelson	.05
523	Tom Paciorek	.05
524	Ron Reed	.05
525	Bert Roberge	.05
526	Tom Seaver	.50
527	Roy Smalley	.05
528	Dan Spillner	.05
529	Mike Squires	.05
530	Greg Walker	.10

CINCINNATI REDS

NO.	PLAYER	MINT
531	Cesar Cedeno	.10
532	Dave Concepcion	.10
533	Eric Davis (R)	16.00
534	Nick Esasky	20.00
535	Tom Foley	.05
536	John Franco (R)	2.00
537	Brad Guden	.05
538	Tom Hume	.05
539	Wayne Krenchicki	.05
540	Andy McGaffigan	.05
541	Eddie Milner	.05
542	Ron Oester	.05
543	Bob Owchinko	.05
544	Dave Parker	.20
545	Frank Pastore	.05
546	Tony Perez	.15
547	Ted Power	.05
548	Joe Price	.05
549	Gary Redus	.05
550	Pete Rose	.75
551	Jeff Russell	.25
552	Mario Soto	.10
553	Jay Tibbs (R)	.20
554	Duane Walker	.05

TEXAS RANGERS

NO.	PLAYER	MINT
555	Alan Bannister	.05
556	Buddy Bell	.10
557	Danny Darwin	.05
558	Charlie Hough	.05
559	Bobby Jones	.05
560	Odell Jones	.05
561	Jeff Kunkel (R)	.15
562	Mike Mason	.15
563	Pete O'Brien	.10
564	Larry Parrish	.05
565	Mickey Rivers	.10
566	Billy Sample	.05
567	Dave Schmidt	.05
568	Donnie Scott (R)	.15
569	Dave Stewart	.40
570	Frank Tanana	.10
571	Wayne Tolleson	.05
572	Gary Ward	.05
573	Curtis Wilkerson	.05
574	George Wright	.05
575	Ned Yost	.05

MILWAUKEE BREWERS

NO.	PLAYER	MINT
576	Mark Brouhard	.05
577	Mike Caldwell	.05
578	Bobby Clark	.05
579	Jaime Cocanower (R)	.15
580	Cecil Cooper	.10
581	Rollie Fingers	.15
582	Jim Gantner	.05
583	Moose Haas	.05
584	Dion James	.20
585	Pete Ladd	.05
586	Rick Manning	.05
587	Bob McClure	.05
588	Paul Molitor	.20
589	Charlie Moore	.05
590	Ben Oglivie	.05
591	Chuck Porter	.05
592	Randy Ready (R)	.25
593	Ed Romero	.05
594	Bill Schroeder	.05
595	Ray Searage	.05
596	Ted Simmons	.10
597	Jim Sundberg	.05
598	Don Sutton	.20
599	Tom Tellmann	.05
600	Rick Waits	.05

NO.	PLAYER	MINT
601	Robin Yount	.60

SAN FRANCISCO GIANTS

NO.	PLAYER	MINT
602	Dusty Baker	.05
603	Bob Brenly	.05
604	Jack Clark	.25
605	Chili Davis	.10
606	Mark Davis	.20
607	Dan Gladden (R)	.50
608	Atlee Hammaker	.05
609	Mike Krukow	.05
610	Duane Kuiper	.05
611	Bob Lacey	.05
612	Bill Laskey	.05
613	Gary Lavelle	.05
614	Johnnie LeMaster	.05
615	Jeff Leonard	.15
616	Randy Lerch	.05
617	Greg Minton	.05
618	Steve Nicosia	.05
619	Gene Richards	.05
620	Jeff Robinson (R)	.35
621	Scot Thompson	.05
622	Manny Trillo	.05
623	Brad Wellman	.05
624	Frank Williams (R)	.15
625	Joel Youngblood	.05

SPECIAL CARDS

NO.	PLAYER	MINT
626	Ripken-In-Action	.25
627	Schmidt-In-Action	.50
628	Giving The Signs: Sparky Anderson	.05
629	AL Pitcher's Nightmare: Henderson & Winfield	.35
630	NL Pitcher's Nightmare: Schmidt & Sandberg	.50
631	NL All-Stars: Strawberry, Carter, Garvey, Smith	.25
632	All-Star Game Winning Battery: Carter, Lea	.10
633	NL Pennant Clinchers: Garvey, Gossage	.15
634	NL Rookie Phenoms: Samuel, Gooden	.75
635	Toronto's Big Guns: Willie Upshaw	.10
636	Toronto's Big Guns: Lloyd Moseby	.25
637	Al Holland	
638	Lee Tunnell	
639	500th Homer: Reggie Jackson	.35
640	4,000th Hit: Pete Rose	.50
641	Father and Son: Cal Ripken & Cal, Jr.	.25
642	Cubs: Division Champs	.05
643	Two Perfect Games and One No-Hitter: Witt, Palmer, Morris	.10
644	Willie Lozado (R), Vic Mata (R)	.15
645	Kelly Gruber (R), Randy O'Neal (R)	6.00
646	Jose Roman (R), Joel Skinner (R)	.20
647	Steve Kiefer (R), Danny Tartabull (R)	4.00
648	Rob Deer (R), Alejandro Sanchez (R)	1.25
649	Bill Hatcher (R), Shawon Dunston (R)	6.00
650	Ron Robinson (R), Mike Bielecki (R)	.50
651	Zane Smith (R), Paul Zuvella (R)	1.00
652	Joe Hesketh (R), Glenn Davis (R)	10.00
653	John Russell (R), Steve Jeltz (R)	.20
654	Checklist No. 1	.08
655	Checklist No. 2	.08
656	Checklist No. 3	.08
657	Checklist No. 4	.08
658	Checklist No. 5	.08
659	Checklist No. 6	.08
660	Checklist No. 7	.08

1985 Fleer Traded Update.... Complete Set of 132 Cards— Value $20.00

This set updates the main 1985 card with players who had changed teams during the season, and rookies. This set features Fleer's first card of Vince Coleman, Tom Browning and Teddy Higuera. The set was packaged in a printed box and distributed exclusively through card hobby dealers.

NO.	PLAYER	MINT
U1	Don Aase	.15
U2	Bill Almon	.07
U3	Dusty Baker	.10
U4	Dale Berra	.07
U5	Karl Best	.15
U6	Tim Birtsas	.15
U7	Vida Blue	.07
U8	Rich Bordi	.07
U9	Daryl Boston	.30
U10	Hubie Brooks	.25
U11	Chris Brown	.15
U12	T. Browning	1.00
U13	Al Bumbry	.07
U14	Tim Burke	.50
U15	Ray Burris	.07
U16	Jeff Burroughs	.07
U17	Ivan Calderon (RR)	.50
U18	Jeff Calhoun	.15
U19	Bill Campbell	.07
U20	Don Carman	.30
U21	Gary Carter	.60
U22	Bobby Castillo	.07
U23	Bill Caudill	.07
U24	Rick Cerone	.07
U25	Jack Clark	.40
U26	Pat Clement	.15
U27	Stewart Cliburn	.15
U28	V. Coleman (RR)	7.00
U29	Dave Collins	.07
U30	Fritz Connally	.15
U31	Henry Cotto	.07
U32	Danny Darwin	.07
U33	Darren Daulton	.50

NO.	PLAYER	MINT
U34	Jerry Davis	.15
U35	Brian Dayett	.15
U36	Ken Dixon	.20
U37	Tommy Dunbar	.20
U38	M. Duncan	1.00
U39	Bob Fallon	.15
U40	Brian Fisher	.15
U41	Mike Fitzgerald	.07
U42	Ray Fontenot	.07
U43	Greg Gagne	.35
U44	Oscar Gamble	.07
U45	Jim Gott	.07
U46	David Green	.07
U47	Alfredo Griffin	.07
U48	Ozzie Guillen (RR)	2.00
U49	Toby Harrah	.07
U50	Ron Hassey	.07
U51	Rickey Henderson	4.00
U52	Steve Henderson	.07
U53	George Hendrick	.07
U54	Teddy Higuera (RR)	2.00
U55	Al Holland	.07
U56	Burt Hooton	.07
U57	Jay Howell	.15
U58	LaMarr Hoyt	.12
U59	Tim Hulett	.15
U60	Bob James	.07
U61	Cliff Johnson	.05
U62	Howard Johnson	2.00
U63	Ruppert Jones	.07
U64	Steve Kemp	.07
U65	Bruce Kison	.07
U66	Mike LaCoss	.07

NO.	PLAYER	MINT
U67	Lee Lacy	.07
U68	Dave LaPoint	.07
U69	Gary Lavelle	.07
U70	Vance Law	.07
U71	Manny Lee	.15
U72	Sixto Lezcano	.07
U73	Tim Lollar	.07
U74	Urbano Lugo	.12
U75	Fred Lynn	.20
U76	Steve Lyons	.25
U77	Mickey Mahler	.07
U78	Ron Mathis	.15
U79	Len Matuszek	.10
U80	O. McDowell (RR)	.60
U81	R. McDowell (RR)	.75
U82	Donnie Moore	.10
U83	Ron Musselman	.12
U84	Al Oliver	.15
U85	Joe Orsulak	.30
U86	Dan Pasqua	.45
U87	Chris Pittaro	.15
U88	Rick Reuschel	.12
U89	Earnie Riles	.20
U90	Jerry Royster	.07
U91	Dave Rozema	.07
U92	Dave Rucker	.07
U93	Vern Ruhle	.07
U94	Mark Salas	.15
U95	Luis Salazar	.07
U96	Joe Sambito	.07
U97	Billy Sample	.10
U98	Alex Sanchez	.07
U99	Calvin Schiraldi	.15

NO.	PLAYER	MINT
U100	Rick Schu	.15
U101	Larry Sheets	.35
U102	Ron Shephard	.15
U103	Nelson Simmons	.15
U104	Don Slaught	.10
U105	Roy Smalley	.10
U106	Lonnie Smith	.10
U107	Nate Snell	.10
U108	Lary Sorensen	.07
U109	Chris Speier	.07
U110	Mike Stenhouse	.07
U111	Tim Stoddard	.07
U112	John Stuper	.07
U113	Jim Sundberg	.07
U114	Bruce Sutter	.25
U115	Don Sutton	.50
U116	Bruce Tanner	.15
U117	Kent Tekulve	.10
U118	Walt Terrell	.10
U119	Mickey Tettleton	1.00
U120	Rich Thompson	.10
U121	Louis Thornton	.10
U122	Alex Trevino	.07
U123	John Tudor	.15
U124	Jose Uribe	.25
U125	Dave Valle	.12
U126	Dave Von Ohlen	.07
U127	Curt Wardle	.12
U128	U.L. Washington	.07
U129	Ed Whitson	.07
U130	Herm Winningham	.15
U131	Rich Yett	.12
U132	Update Checklist	.20

1986 Fleer.... Complete Set of 660 Cards—Value $135.00

Features the rookie cards of Vince Coleman, Jose Canseco, Andres Galarraga, Kal Daniels and Cory Snyder.

NO.	PLAYER	MINT
KANSAS CITY ROYALS		
1	Steve Balboni	.10
2	Joe Beckwith	.05
3	Buddy Biancalana	.05
4	Bud Black	.05
5	George Brett	.75
6	Onix Concepcion	.05
7	Steve Farr	.05

NO.	PLAYER	MINT
8	Mark Gubicza	.15
9	Dane Iorg	.05
10	Danny Jackson	.25
11	Lynn Jones	.05
12	Mike Jones	.05
13	Charlie Leibrandt	.05
14	Hal McRae	.05
15	Omar Moreno	.05

NO.	PLAYER	MINT
16	Darryl Motley	.05
17	Jorge Orta	.05
18	Dan Quisenberry	.15
19	Bret Saberhagen	1.00
20	Pat Sheridan	.05
21	Lonnie Smith	.05
22	Jim Sundberg	.05
23	John Wathan	.05

NO.	PLAYER	MINT
24	Frank White	.05
25	Willie Wilson	.15
ST. LOUIS CARDINALS		
26	Joaquin Andejar	.10
27	Steve Braun	.05
28	Bill Campbell	.05
29	Cesar Cedeno	.05
30	Jack Clark	.25

NO. PLAYER	MINT
31 Vince Coleman (R)	3.00
32 Danny Cox	.10
33 Ken Dayley	.05
34 Ivan DeJesus	.05
35 Bob Forsch	.05
36 Brian Harper	.10
37 Tom Herr	.10
38 Ricky Horton	.05
39 Kurt Kepshire	.05
40 Jeff Lahti	.05
41 Tito Landrum	.05
42 Willie McGee	.20
43 Tom Nieto	.05
44 Terry Pendleton	.05
45 Darrell Porter	.05
46 Ozzie Smith	.30
47 John Tudor	.15
48 Andy Van Slyke	.30
49 Todd Worrell (R)	.75

TORONTO BLUE JAYS

NO. PLAYER	MINT
50 Jim Acker	.05
51 Doyl Alexander	.05
52 Jesse Barfield	.20
53 George Bell	.25
54 Jeff Burroughs	.05
55 Bill Caudill	.05
56 Jim Clancy	.05
57 Tony Fernandez	.20
58 Tom Filer	.05
59 Damaso Garcia	.10
60 Tom Henke	.30
61 Garth Iorg	.05
62 Cliff Johnson	.05
63 Jimmy Key	.10
64 Dennis Lamp	.05
65 Gary Lavelle	.05
66 Buck Martinez	.05
67 Lloyd Moseby	.10
68 Rance Mulliniks	.05
69 Al Oliver	.10
70 Dave Stieb	.15
71 Louis Thornton	.15
72 Willie Upshaw	.10
73 Ernie Whitt	.05

NEW YORK METS

NO. PLAYER	MINT
74 Rick Aguilera (R)	.40
75 Wally Backman	.05
76 Gary Carter	.30
77 Ron Darling	.20
78 Len Dykstra (R)	4.00
79 Sid Fernandez	.15
80 George Foster	.15
81 Dwight Gooden	2.00
82 Tom Gorman	.05
83 Danny Heep	.05
84 Keith Hernandez	.25
85 Howard Johnson	.50
86 Ray Knight	.05
87 Terry Leach	.15
88 Ed Lynch	.05
89 Roger McDowell (R)	.45
90 Jesse Orosco	.05
91 Tom Paciorek	.05
92 Ronn Reynolds	.15
93 Rafael Santana	.05
94 Doug Sisk	.05
95 Rusty Staub	.10
96 Darryl Strawberry	2.50
97 Mookie Wilson	.05

NEW YORK YANKEES

NO. PLAYER	MINT
98 Neil Allen	.05
99 Don Baylor	.10
100 Dale Berra	.05
101 Rich Bordi	.05
102 Marty Bystrom	.05
103 Joe Cowley	.05
104 Brian Fisher (R)	.25
105 Ken Griffey	.05
106 Ron Guidry	.15
107 Ron Hassey	.05
108 Rickey Henderson	1.50
109 Dan Mattingly	4.00
110 Bobby Meacham	.06
111 John Montefusco	.05
112 Phil Niekro	.20
113 Mike Pagliarulo	.10

NO. PLAYER	MINT
114 Dan Pasqua	.20
115 Willie Randolph	.05
116 Dave Righetti	.10
117 Andre Robertson	.05
118 Billy Sample	.05
119 Bob Shirley	.05
120 Ed Whitson	.05
121 Dave Winfield	.30
122 Butch Wynegar	.05

LOS ANGELES DODGERS

NO. PLAYER	MINT
123 Dave Anderson	.05
124 Bob Bailor	.05
125 Greg Brock	.05
126 Enos Cabell	.05
127 Bobby Castillo	.05
128 Carlos Diaz	.05
129 Mariano Duncan (R)	.35
130 Pedro Guerrero	.25
131 Orel Hershiser	1.50
132 Rick Honeycutt	.05
133 Ken Howell	.05
134 Ken Landreaux	.05
135 Bill Madlock	.10
136 Candy Maldonado	.10
137 Mike Marshall	.10
138 Len Matuszek	.05
139 Tom Niedenfuer	.05
140 Alejandro Pena	.05
141 Jerry Reuss	.05
142 Bill Russell	.05
143 Steve Sax	.15
144 Mike Scioscia	.05
145 Fernando Valenzuela	.30
146 Bob Welch	.05
147 Terry Whitfield	.05

CALIFORNIA ANGELS

NO. PLAYER	MINT
148 Juan Beniquez	.05
149 Bob Boone	.05
150 John Candelaria	.05
151 Rod Carew	.40
152 Stewart Cliburn (R)	.20
153 Doug DeCinces	.10
154 Brian Downing	.05
155 Ken Forsch	.05
156 Craig Gerber (R)	.15
157 Bobby Grich	.10
158 George Hendrick	.05
159 Al Holland	.05
160 Reggie Jackson	.50
161 Ruppert Jones	.05
162 Urbano Lugo (R)	.15
163 Kirk McCaskill (R)	.50
164 Donnie Moore	.05
165 Gary Pettis	.05
166 Ron Romanick	.05
167 Dick Schofield	.05
168 Darly Sconiers	.05
169 Jim Slaton	.05
170 Don Sutton	.20
171 Mike Witt	.10

CINCINNATI REDS

NO. PLAYER	MINT
172 Buddy Bell	.10
173 Tom Browning	.30
174 Dave Concepcion	.10
175 Eric Davis	3.00
176 Bo Diaz	.05
177 Nick Esasky	.05
178 John Franco	.25
179 Tom Hume	.05
180 Wayne Krenchicki	.05
181 Andy McGaffigan	.05
182 Eddie Milner	.05
183 Ron Oester	.05
184 Dave Parker	.15
185 Frank Pastore	.05
186 Tony Perez	.10
187 Ted Power	.05
188 Joe Price	.05
189 Gary Redus	.05
190 Ron Robinson	.05
191 Pete Rose	.60
192 Mario Soto	.10
193 John Stuper	.05
194 Jay Tibbs	.05
195 Dave Van Gorder	.05
196 Max Venable	.05

CHICAGO WHITE SOX

NO. PLAYER	MINT
197 Juan Agosto	.05
198 Harold Baines	.15
199 Floyd Bannister	.05
200 Britt Burns	.05
201 Julio Cruz	.05
202 Joel Davis (R)	.20
203 Richard Dotson	.05
204 Carlton Fisk	.30
205 Scott Fletcher	.05
206 Ozzie Guillen (R)	1.25
207 Jerry Hairston	.05
208 Tim Hulett	.05
209 Bob James	.05
210 Ron Kittle	.10
211 Rudy Law	.05
212 Bryan Little	.05
213 Gene Nelson	.05
214 Reid Nichols	.05
215 Luis Salazar	.05
216 Tom Seaver	.35
217 Dan Spillner	.05
218 Bruce Tanner (R)	.15
219 Greg Walker	.10
220 Dave Wehrmeister	.05

DETROIT TIGERS

NO. PLAYER	MINT
221 Juan Berenguer	.05
222 Dave Bergman	.05
223 Tom Brookens	.05
224 Darrell Evans	.10
225 Barbaro Garbey	.05
226 Kirk Gibson	.30
227 John Grubb	.05
228 Willie Hernandez	.15
229 Larry Herndon	.05
230 Chet Lemon	.05
231 Aurelio Lopez	.05
232 Jack Morris	.20
233 Randy O'Neal	.05
234 Lance Parrish	.15
235 Dan Petry	.15
236 Alex Sanchez	.05
237 Bill Scherrer	.05
238 Nelson Simmons (R)	.10
239 Frank Tanana	.05
240 Walt Terrell	.05
241 Alan Trammell	.20
242 Lou Whitaker	.15
243 Milt Wilcox	.05

MONTREAL EXPOS

NO. PLAYER	MINT
244 Hubie Brooks	.10
245 Tim Burke (R)	.40
246 Andre Dawson	.35
247 Mike Fitzgerald	.08
248 Terry Francona	.05
249 Bill Gullickson	.05
250 Joe Hesketh	.10
251 Bill Laskey	.05
252 Vance Law	.05
253 Charlie Lea	.05
254 Gary Lucas	.05
255 David Palmer	.05
256 Tim Raines	.25
257 Jeff Reardon	.10
258 Bert Roberge	.05
259 Dan Schatzeder	.05
260 Bryn Smith	.05
261 Randy St. Claire	.05
262 Scot Thompson	.05
263 Tim Wallach	.10
264 U.L. Washington	.05
265 Mitch Webster (R)	.35
266 Herm Winningham (R)	.15
267 Floyd Youmans (R)	.30

BALTIMORE ORIOLES

NO. PLAYER	MINT
268 Don Aase	.05
269 Mike Boddicker	.10
270 Rich Dauer	.05
271 Storm Davis	.05
272 Rick Dempsey	.05
273 Ken Dixon	.05
274 Jim Dwyer	.05
275 Mike Flanagan	.05
276 Wayne Gross	.05
277 Lee Lacy	.05
278 Fred Lynn	.15

NO. PLAYER	MINT
279 Tippy Martinez	.05
280 Dennis Martinez	.05
281 Scott McGregor	.05
282 Eddie Murray	.30
283 Floyd Rayford	.05
284 Cal Ripken, Jr.	.60
285 Gary Roenicke	.05
286 Larry Sheets	.25
287 John Shelby	.05
288 Nate Snell (R)	.15
289 Sammy Stewart	.05
290 Alan Wiggins	.05
291 Mike Young	.10

HOUSTON ASTROS

NO. PLAYER	MINT
292 Alan Ashby	.05
293 Mark Bailey	.05
294 Kevin Bass	.05
295 Jeff Calhoun (R)	.15
296 Jose Cruz	.10
297 Glenn Davis	1.50
298 Bill Dawley	.05
299 Frank DiPino	.05
300 Bill Doran	.05
301 Phil Garner	.05
302 Jeff Heathcock (R)	.15
303 Charlie Kerfeld (R)	.20
304 Bob Knepper	.05
305 Ron Mathis (R)	.15
306 Jerry Mumphrey	.05
307 Jim Pankovits	.05
308 Terry Puhl	.05
309 Craig Reynolds	.05
310 Nolan Ryan	1.50
311 Mike Scott	.25
312 Dave Smith	.05
313 Dickie Thon	.05
314 Denny Walling	.05

SAN DIEGO PADRES

NO. PLAYER	MINT
315 Kurt Bevacqua	.05
316 Al Bumbry	.05
317 Jerry Davis	.05
318 Luis DeLeon	.05
319 Dave Dravecky	.05
320 Tim Flannery	.05
321 Steve Garvey	.35
322 Goose Gossage	.15
323 Tony Gwynn	.75
324 Andy Hawkins	.05
325 LaMarr Hoyt	.05
326 Roy Lee Jackson	.05
327 Terry Kennedy	.05
328 Craig Lefferts	.05
329 Carmelo Martinez	.05
330 Lance McCullers (R)	.30
331 Kevin McReynolds	.25
332 Graig Nettles	.10
333 Jerry Royster	.05
334 Eric Show	.05
335 Tim Stoddard	.05
336 Garry Templeton	.08
337 Mark Thurmond	.05
338 Ed Wojna (R)	.15

BOSTON RED SOX

NO. PLAYER	MINT
339 Tony Armas	.10
340 Marty Barrett	.05
341 Wade Boggs	2.00
342 Dennis Boyd	.10
343 Bill Buckner	.10
344 Mark Clear	.05
345 Roger Clemens	3.00
346 Steve Crawford	.05
347 Mike Easler	.05
348 Dwight Evans	.12
349 Rich Gedman	.08
350 Jackie Gutierrez	.05
351 Glenn Hoffman	.05
352 Bruce Hurst	.10
353 Bruce Kison	.05
354 Tim Lollar	.05
355 Steve Lyons	.05
356 Al Nipper	.05
357 Bob Ojeda	.05
358 Jim Rice	.25
359 Bob Stanley	.05
360 Mike Trujillo (R)	.10

NO.	PLAYER	MINT

CHICAGO CUBS
- 361 Thad Bosley 05
- 362 Warren Brusstar 05
- 363 Ron Cey 10
- 364 Jody Davis 07
- 365 Bob Dernier 05
- 366 Shawon Dunston 75
- 367 Leon Durham 15
- 368 Dennis Eckersley 30
- 369 Ray Fontenot..........05
- 370 George Frazier 05
- 371 Bill Hatcher 20
- 372 Dave Lopes 05
- 373 Gary Matthews 05
- 374 Ron Meredith (R) 15
- 375 Keith Moreland 05
- 376 Reggie Patterson 05
- 377 Dick Ruthven 05
- 378 Ryne Sandberg.......1.50
- 379 Scott Sanderson 05
- 380 Lee Smith 10
- 381 Lary Sorensen..........05
- 382 Chris Speier 05
- 383 Rick Sutcliffe 15
- 384 Steve Trout 05
- 385 Gary Woods 05

MINNESOTA TWINS
- 386 Bert Blyleven 10
- 387 Tom Brunansky 15
- 388 Randy Bush 05
- 389 John Butcher 05
- 390 Ron Davis 05
- 391 Dave Engle 05
- 392 Frank Eufemia 15
- 393 Pete Filson 05
- 394 Gary Gaetti 20
- 395 Greg Gagne 10
- 396 Mickey Hatcher 05
- 397 Kent Hrbek 20
- 398 Tim Laudner 05
- 399 Rick Lysander 05
- 400 Dave Meier 05
- 401 Kirby Puckett 4.00
- 402 Mark Salas 05
- 403 Ken Schrom 05
- 404 Roy Smalley 05
- 405 Mike Smithson 05
- 406 Mike Stenhouse 05
- 407 Tim Teufel 05
- 408 Frank Viola............50
- 409 Ron Washington........05

OAKLAND A'S
- 410 Keith Atherton 05
- 411 Dusty Baker............05
- 412 Tim Birtsas (R) 15
- 413 Bruce Bochte 05
- 414 Chris Codiroli 05
- 415 Dave Collins 05
- 416 Mike Davis 05
- 417 Alfredo Griffin 05
- 418 Mike Heath..........05
- 419 Steve Henderson 05
- 420 Donnie Hill 05
- 421 Jay Howell 10
- 422 Tommy John 10
- 423 Dave Kingman 10
- 424 Bill Krueger 05
- 425 Rick Langford 05
- 426 Carney Lansford 10
- 427 Steve McCatty 05
- 428 Dwayne Murphy 05
- 429 Steve Ontiveros (R).....15
- 430 Tony Phillips 05
- 431 Jose Rijo..............05
- 432 Mickey Tettleton (R) ...50

PHILADELPHIA PHILLIES
- 433 Luis Aguayo 05
- 434 Larry Andersen.........05
- 435 Steve Carlton 30
- 436 Don Carman (R)........25
- 437 Tim Corcoran 05
- 438 Darren Daulton (R) 40
- 439 John Denny 08
- 440 Tom Foley 05
- 441 Greg Gross 05
- 442 Kevin Gross 05
- 443 Von Hayes 15
- 444 Charles Hudson 05
- 445 Garry Maddox..........05
- 446 Shane Rawley 05
- 447 Dave Rucker 05
- 448 John Russell 05
- 449 Juan Samuel 15
- 450 Mike Schmidt 1.00
- 451 Rick Schu............05
- 452 Dave Shipanoff (R) 15
- 453 Dave Stewart 40
- 454 Jeff Stone 05
- 455 Kent Tekulve 05
- 456 Ozzie Virgil 05
- 457 Glenn Wilson 10

SEATTLE MARINERS
- 458 Jim Beattie............05
- 459 Karl Best 10
- 460 Barry Bonnell 05
- 461 Phil Bradley 20
- 462 Ivan Calderon (R) 1.00
- 463 Al Cowens 05
- 464 Alvin Davis 20
- 465 Dave Henderson 05
- 466 Bob Kearney 05
- 467 Mark Langston 35
- 468 Bob Long 05
- 469 Mike Moore 05
- 470 Edwin Nunez 05
- 471 Spike Owen 05
- 472 Jack Perconte 05
- 473 Jim Presley 20
- 474 Donnie Scott 05
- 475 Bill Swift 05
- 476 Danny Tartabull (R) 65
- 477 Gorman Thomas 10
- 478 Roy Thomas 05
- 479 Ed VandeBerg 05
- 480 Frank Wills (R) 15
- 481 Matt Young 05

MILWAUKEE BREWERS
- 482 Ray Burris 05
- 483 Jaime Cocanower 05
- 484 Cecil Cooper 15
- 485 Danny Darwin 05
- 486 Rollie Fingers 15
- 487 Jim Gantner 05
- 488 Bob Gibson 05
- 489 Moose Haas 05
- 490 Teddy Higuera (R) 1.25
- 491 Paul Householder 05
- 492 Pete Ladd 05
- 493 Rick Manning 05
- 494 Bob McClure 05
- 495 Paul Molitor 20
- 496 Charlie Moore 05
- 497 Ben Oglivie 05
- 498 Randy Ready 05
- 499 Earnie Riles (R) 20
- 500 Ed Romero 05
- 501 Bill Schroeder 05
- 502 Ray Searage 05
- 503 Ted Simmons 10
- 504 Pete Vuckovich 05
- 505 Rick Waits 05
- 506 Robin Yount 40

ATLANTA BRAVES
- 507 Len Barker..............05
- 508 Steve Bedrosian 15
- 509 Bruce Benedict 05
- 510 Rick Camp 05
- 511 Rick Cerone 05
- 512 Chris Chambliss 05
- 513 Jeff Dedmon 05
- 514 Terry Forster 05
- 515 Gene Garber 05
- 516 Terry Harper 05
- 517 Bob Horner 15
- 518 Glenn Hubbard 05
- 519 Joe Johnson (R) 15
- 520 Brad Komminsk 05
- 521 Rick Mahler 05
- 522 Dale Murphy 50
- 523 Ken Oberkfell 05
- 524 Pascual Perez 05
- 525 Gerald Perry 20
- 526 Rafael Ramirez 05

S.F. GIANTS
- 527 Steve Shields (R) 15
- 528 Zane Smith 10
- 529 Bruce Sutter 15
- 530 Milt Thompson (R) 35
- 531 Claudell Washington 05
- 532 Paul Zuvella 05

S.F. GIANTS
- 533 Vida Blue 05
- 534 Bob Brenly 05
- 535 Chris Brown (R) 20
- 536 Chili Davis 10
- 537 Mark Davis 10
- 538 Rob Deer 30
- 539 Dan Driessen 05
- 540 Scott Garrelts 30
- 541 Dan Gladden 05
- 542 Jim Gott 05
- 543 David Green 05
- 544 Atlee Hammaker 05
- 545 Mike Jeffcoat 05
- 546 Mike Krukow 05
- 547 Dave LaPoint 05
- 548 Jeff Leonard 05
- 549 Greg Minton 05
- 550 Alex Trevino 05
- 551 Manny Trillo 05
- 552 Jose Uribe (R) 35
- 553 Brad Wellman 05
- 554 Frank Williams 05
- 555 Joel Youngblood 05

TEXAS RANGERS
- 556 Alan Bannister 05
- 557 Glenn Brummer 05
- 558 Steve Buechele (R) 25
- 559 Jose Guzman (R) 25
- 560 Toby Harrah 05
- 561 Greg Harris 05
- 562 Dwayne Henry (R) 15
- 563 Burt Hooton 05
- 564 Charlie Hough 05
- 565 Mike Mason 05
- 566 Oddibe McDowell 15
- 567 Dickie Noles 05
- 568 Pete O'Brien 15
- 569 Larry Parrish 05
- 570 Dave Rozema 05
- 571 Dave Schmidt 05
- 572 Don Slaught 05
- 573 Wayne Tolleson 05
- 574 Duane Walker 05
- 575 Gary Ward 05
- 576 Chris Welsh 05
- 577 Curtis Wilkerson 05
- 578 George Wright 05

CLEVELAND INDIANS
- 579 Chris Bando 05
- 580 Tony Bernazard 05
- 581 Brett Butler 10
- 582 Ernie Camacho 05
- 583 Joe Carter 50
- 584 Carmello Castillo 05
- 585 Jamie Easterly 05
- 586 Julio Franco 20
- 587 Mel Hall 05
- 588 Mike Hargrove 05
- 589 Neal Heaton 05
- 590 Brook Jacoby 10
- 591 Otis Nixon (R) 20
- 592 Jerry Reed (R) 15
- 593 Vern Ruhle 05
- 594 Pat Tabler 05
- 595 Rich Thompson (R) 15
- 596 Andre Thornton 05
- 597 Dave Von Ohlen 05
- 598 George Vuckovich 05
- 599 Tom Waddell 05
- 600 Curt Wardle (R) 15
- 601 Jerry Willard 05

PITTSBURGH PIRATES
- 609 Cecilio Guante 05
- 610 Steve Kemp 05
- 611 Sam Khalifa (R) 15
- 612 Lee Mazzilli 05
- 613 Larry McWilliams 05
- 614 Jim Morrison 05
- 615 Joe Orsulak (R) 25
- 616 Tony Pena 10
- 617 Johnny Ray 10
- 618 Rick Reuschel 05
- 619 R.J. Reynolds 05
- 620 Rick Rhoden 05
- 621 Don Robinson 05
- 622 Jason Thompson 05
- 623 Lee Tunnell 05
- 624 Jim Winn 05
- 625 Marvell Wynne 05

SPECIAL CARDS
- 626 Gooden in Action 35
- 627 Mattingly in Action 1.25
- 628 Pete Rose—4,192........50
- 629 3,000 Career Hits: 25
  Rod Carew
- 630 300 Career Wins: 20
  Tom Seaver, Phil Niekro
- 631 Ouch:
  Don Baylor 15
- 632 Instant Offense: 30
  Raines and Strawberry
- 633 Shortshops Supreme:......25
  Trammell & Ripken
- 634 Boggs and "Hero" 50
  Wade Boggs, George Brett
- 635 Braves Dynamic Duo:.....30
  Horner and Murphy
- 636 Cardinal Ignitors: 35
  Coleman & McGee
- 637 Terror on Basepaths: 35
  Vince Coleman
- 638 Charlie Hustle and 75
  Dr. K: Rose and Gooden
- 639 1984 and 1985 AL 1.50
  Batting Champs:
  Mattingly and Boggs
- 640 NL West Sluggers:........30
  Murphy, Garvey, Parker
- 641 Staff Aces: 35
  Valenzuela & Gooden
- 642 Blue Jay Stoppers: 10
  Key and Stieb
- 643 AL All-Star Backstops 10
  Fisk & Gedman
- 644 Benito Santiago (R) 6.00
  and Gene Walter (R)
- 645 Mike Woodard (R) and .. .15
  Colin Ward (R)
- 646 Kal Daniels (R) and..... 5.00
  Paul O'Neill (R)
- 647 Fred Toliver (R) and ... 3.00
  Andres Galarraga (R)
- 648 Bob Kipper (R) and .... .20
  Curt Ford (R)
- 649 Eric Plunk (R) and.... 50.00
  Jose Canseco (R)
- 650 Gus Polidor (R) and ... .20
  Mark McLemore (R)
- 651 Rob Woodward (R) and . .20
  Mickey Brantley (R)
- 652 Billy Joe Robidoux (R) . .20
  and Mark Funderburk (R)
- 653 Cecil Fielder (R) and ...15.00
  Cory Snyder
- 654 Checklist No. 1 08
- 655 Checklist No. 2 08
- 656 Checklist No. 3 08
- 657 Checklist No. 4 08
- 658 Checklist No. 5 08
- 659 Checklist No. 6 08
- 660 Checklist No. 7 08

1986 Fleer Traded Update.... Complete Set of 132 Cards—Value $35.00

This set updates the main 1986 card set with players who had changed teams during the season, and rookies. This set features Fleer's first card of Jose Canseco, Ruben Sierra, Kevin Mitchell and Will Clark. The set was packaged in a printed box and distributed exclusively through card dealers.

NO.	PLAYER	MINT
U1	Mike Aldrete	.15
U2	Andy Allanson	.20
U3	Nell Allen	.07
U4	Joaquin Andujar	.07
U5	Paul Assenmacher	.20
U6	Scott Bailes	.15
U7	Jay Baller	.15
U8	Scott Bankhead	.30
U9	Bill Bathe	.15
U10	Don Baylor	.12
U11	Billy Beane	.15
U12	Steve Bedrosian	.15
U13	Juan Beniquez	.10
U14	Barry Bonds (RR)	6.00
U15	Bobby Bonilla (RR)	4.00
U16	Rich Bordi	.07
U17	Bill Campbell	.07
U18	Tom Candiotti	.10
U19	John Cangelosi	.20
U20	Jose Canseco (RR)	12.00
U21	Chuck Cary	.20
U22	Juan Castillo	.15
U23	Rick Cerone	.07
U24	John Cerutti	.25
U25	Will Clark (RR)	13.00
U26	Marc Clear	.07
U27	Darnell Coles	.15
U28	Dave Collins	.07
U29	Tim Conroy	.07
U30	Ed Correa	.15
U31	Joe Cowley	.07
U32	Bill Dawley	.07
U33	Rob Deer	.25

NO.	PLAYER	MINT
U34	John Denny	.07
U35	Jim DeShaies	.20
U36	Doug Drabek	1.00
U37	Mike Easler	.07
U38	Mark Eichhorn	.20
U39	Dave Engle	.07
U40	Mike Fischlin	.07
U41	Scott Fletcher	.07
U42	Terry Forster	.07
U43	Terry Francona	.07
U44	Andres Galarraga	1.00
U45	Lee Guetterman	.25
U46	Bill Gullickson	.07
U47	Jackie Gutierrez	.07
U48	Moose Haas	.07
U49	Bily Hatcher	.20
U50	Mike Heath	.10
U51	Guy Hofman	.07
U52	Tom Hume	.07
U53	Pete Incaviglia (RR)	.75
U54	Dane Iorg	.07
U55	Chris James (RR)	1.00
U56	Stan Javier	.40
U57	Tommy John	.15
U58	Tracy Jones	.20
U59	Wally Joyner (RR)	2.25
U60	Wayne Krenchicki	.07
U61	John Kruk	.50
U62	Mike LaCoss	.07
U63	Pete Ladd	.07
U64	Dave LaPoint	.07
U65	Mike LaValliere	.25
U66	Rudy Law	.07

NO.	PLAYER	MINT
U67	Dennis Leonard	.07
U68	Steve Lombardozzi	.20
U69	Aurelio Lopez	.07
U70	Miceky Mahler	.07
U71	Candy Maldonado	.20
U72	Roger Mason	.15
U73	Greg Mathews	.20
U74	Andy McGaffigan	.10
U75	Joel McKeon	.15
U76	Kevin Mitchell (RR)	7.00
U77	Bill Mooneyham	.12
U78	Omar Moreno	.07
U79	Jerry Mumphrey	.07
U80	Al Newman	.12
U81	Phil Niekro	.35
U82	Randy Niemann	.07
U83	Juan Nieves	.20
U84	Bob Ojeda	.20
U85	Rick Ownbey	.07
U86	Tom Paciorek	.07
U87	David Palmer	.07
U88	Jeff Parrett	.15
U89	Pat Perry	.20
U90	Dan Plesac	.20
U91	Darrell Porter	.07
U92	Luis Quinones	.15
U93	Rey Quinonez	.20
U94	Gary Redus	.12
U95	Jeff Reed	.12
U96	Bip Roberts	.40
U97	Billy Joe Robidoux	.20
U98	Gary Roenicke	.07
U99	Ron Roenicke	.07

NO.	PLAYER	MINT
U100	Angel Salazar	.12
U101	Joe Sambito	.07
U102	Billy Sample	.07
U103	Dave Schmidt	.07
U104	Ken Schrom	.07
U105	Ruben Sierra (RR)	7.00
U106	Ted Simmons	.10
U107	Sammy Stewart	.07
U108	Kurt Stillwell	.50
U109	Dale Sveum	.20
U110	Tim Teufel	.07
U111	Bob Tewksbury	.20
U112	Andres Thomas	.20
U113	Jason Thompson	.12
U114	Milt Thompson	.07
U115	Rob Thompson	.40
U116	Jay Tibbs	.07
U117	Fred Toliver	.07
U118	Wayne Tolleson	.07
U119	Alex Trevino	.07
U120	Manny Trillo	.07
U121	Ed Vande Berg	.07
U122	Ozzie Virgil	.07
U123	Tony Walker	.20
U124	Gene Walter	.15
U125	Duane Ward	.25
U126	Jerry Willard	.07
U127	Mitch Williams	.50
U128	Reggie Williams	.20
U129	Bobby Witt (RR)	.60
U130	Marvell Wynne	.07
U131	Steve Yeager	.10
U132	Checklist	.15

1987 Fleer.... Complete Set of 660 Cards—Value $120.00

Features the rookie cards of Kevin Mitchell, Will Clark, Bo Jackson and Ruben Sierra. The back of each card features a *Scouting Report*. A high gloss version of the set was issued in a tin box.

NO.	PLAYER	MINT
NEW YORK METS		
1	Rick Aguilera	.15
2	R. Anderson (R)	.15
3	Wally Backman	.07
4	Gary Carter	.25
5	Ron Darling	.20
6	Len Dykstra	.75
7	Kevin Elster (R)	.50
8	Sid Fernandez	.20
9	Dwight Gooden	1.00

NO.	PLAYER	MINT
10	Ed Hearn (R)	.15
11	Danny Heep	.05
12	Keith Hernandez	.25
13	Howard Johnson	.35
14	Ray Knight	.07
15	Lee Mazzilli	.07
16	Roger McDowell	.15
17	Kevin Mitchell (R)	7.50
18	Randy Niemann	.05
19	Bob Ojeda	.15

NO.	PLAYER	MINT
20	Jesse Orosco	.07
21	Rafael Santana	.07
22	Doug Sisk	.07
23	Darryl Strawberry	1.00
24	Tim Teufel	.07
25	Mookie Wilson	.07
BOSTON RED SOX		
26	Toni Armas	.07
27	Marty Barrett	.12
28	Don Baylor	.12

NO.	PLAYER	MINT
29	Wade Boggs	.150
30	Oil Can Boyd	.12
31	Bill Buckner	.08
32	Roger Clemens	2.00
33	Steve Crawford	.07
34	Dwight Evans	.15
35	Rich Gedman	.07
36	Dave Henderson	.07
37	Bruce Hurst	.10
38	Tim Lollar	.07

NO.	PLAYER	MINT
39	Al Nipper	.07
40	Spike Owen	.07
41	Jim Rice	.20
42	Ed Romero	.07
43	Joe Sambito	.07
44	Calvin Schiraldi	.15
45	Tom Seaver	.50
46	Jeff Sellers (R)	.15
47	Bob Stanley	.07
48	Sammy Stewart	.07

HOUSTON ASTROS

NO.	PLAYER	MINT
49	Larry Andersen	.05
50	Alan Ashby	.05
51	Keven Bass	.05
52	Jeff Calhoun	.05
53	Jose Cruz	.10
54	Danny Darwin	.05
55	Glenn Davis	.35
56	Jim Deshaies (R)	.25
57	Bill Doran	.05
58	Phil Garner	.05
59	Billy Hatcher	.10
60	Charlie Kerfeld	.12
61	Bob Knepper	.08
62	Dave Lopes	.08
63	Aurelio Lopez	.05
64	Jim Pankovits	.05
65	Terry Puhl	.08
66	Craig Reynolds	.08
67	Nolan Ryan	1.50
68	Mike Scott	.20
69	Dave Smith	.05
70	Dickie Thon	.05
71	Tony Walker (R)	.15
72	Denny Walling	.05

CALIFORNIA ANGELS

NO.	PLAYER	MINT
73	Bob Boone	.05
74	Rick Burleson	.05
75	John Candelaria	.08
76	Doug Corbett	.05
77	Doug DeCinces	.08
78	Brian Downing	.05
79	Chuck Finley (R)	2.00
80	Terry Forster	.05
81	Bobby Grich	.05
82	George Hendrick	.05
83	Jack Howell	.10
84	Reggie Jackson	.50
85	Ruppert Jones	.05
86	Wally Joyner (R)	2.00
87	Gary Lucas	.05
88	Kirk McCaskill	.12
89	Donnie Moore	.05
90	Gary Pettis	.05
91	Vern Ruhle	.05
92	Dick Schofield	.05
93	Don Sutton	.12
94	Rob Wilfong	.05
95	Mike Witt	.12

NEW YORK YANKEES

NO.	PLAYER	MINT
96	Doug Drabek (R)	3.00
97	Mike Easler	.07
98	Mike Fischlin	.07
99	Brian Fisher	.07
100	Ron Guidry	.15
101	Rickey Henderson	1.25
102	Tommy John	.15
103	Ron Kittle	.10
104	Don Mattingly	2.25
105	Bobby Meacham	.07
106	Joe Niekro	.12
107	Mike Pagliarulo	.15
108	Dan Pasqua	.15
109	Willie Randolph	.10
110	Dennis Rasmussen	.10
111	Dave Righetti	.15
112	Gary Roenicke	.07
113	Rod Scurry	.07
114	Bob Shirley	.07
115	Joel Skinner	.07
116	Tim Stoddard	.07
117	Bob Tewksbury (R)	.15
118	Wayne Tolleson	.07
119	C. Washington	.07
120	Dave Winfield	.30

TEXAS RANGERS

NO.	PLAYER	MINT
121	Steve Buechele	.05
122	Ed Correa (R)	.20
123	Scott Fletcher	.05
124	Joe Guzman	.15
125	Toby Harrah	.05
126	Greg Harris	.05
127	Charlie Hough	.05
128	Pete Incaviglia (R)	1.00
129	Mike Mason	.05
130	Oddibe McDowell	.15
131	Dale Mohorcic (R)	.15
132	Pete O'Brien	.10
133	Tom Paciorek	.05
134	Larry Parrish	.05
135	Geno Petralli	.05
136	Darrell Porter	.05
137	Jeff Russell	.05
138	Ruben Sierra (R)	10.00
139	Don Slaught	.05
140	Gary Ward	.05
141	Curtis Wilkerson	.05
142	Mitch Williams (R)	.50
143	Bobby Witt (R)	1.00

DETROIT TIGERS

NO.	PLAYER	MINT
144	Dave Bergman	.05
145	Tom Brookens	.05
146	Bill Campbell	.05
147	Chuck Cary (R)	.20
148	Darnell Coles	.05
149	Dave Collins	.05
150	Darrell Evans	.12
151	Kirk Gibson	.30
152	John Grubb	.05
153	Willie Hernandez	.05
154	Larry Herndon	.05
155	Eric King (R)	.50
156	Chet Lemon	.07
157	Dwight Lowry (R)	.15
158	Jack Morris	.15
159	Randy O'Neal	.05
160	Lance Parrish	.15
161	Dan Petry	.10
162	Pat Sheridan	.05
163	Jim Slaton	.05
164	Frank Tanana	.05
165	Walt Terrell	.05
166	Mark Thurmond	.05
167	Alan Trammell	.20
168	Lou Whitaker	.12

PHILADELPHIA PHILLIES

NO.	PLAYER	MINT
169	Luis Aguayo	.05
170	Steve Bedrosian	.15
171	Don Carman	.05
172	Darren Daulton	.05
173	Greg Gross	.05
175	Von Hayes	.12
176	Charles Hudson	.05
177	Tom Hume	.05
178	Steve Jeltz	.05
179	Mike Maddux (R)	.20
180	Shane Rawley	.05
181	Gary Redus	.05
182	Ron Roenicke	.05
183	Bruce Ruffin (R)	.20
184	John Russell	.05
185	Juan Samuel	.15
186	Dan Schatzeder	.05
187	Mike Schmidt	1.00
188	Rick Schu	.08
189	Jeff Stone	.05
190	Kent Tekulve	.05
191	Milt Thompson	.05
192	Glenn Wilson	.05

CINCINNATI REDS

NO.	PLAYER	MINT
193	Buddy Bell	.10
194	Tom Browning	.07
195	Sal Butera	.05
196	Dave Concepcion	.07
197	Kal Daniels	.75
198	Eric Davis	1.50
199	John Denny	.05
200	Bo Diaz	.05
201	Nick Esasky	.05
202	John Franco	.10
203	Bill Gullickson	.05
204	Barry Larkin (R)	6.00
205	Eddie Milner	.05
206	Rob Murphy (R)	.20
207	Ron Oester	.05
208	Dave Parker	.15
209	Tony Perez	.12
210	Ted Power	.05
211	Joe Price	.05
212	Ron Robinson	.05
213	Pete Rose (Mgr.)	.50
214	Mario Soto	.05
215	Kurt Stillwell (R)	.75
216	Max Venable	.05
217	Chris Welsh	.05
218	Carl Willis (R)	.15

TORONTO BLUE JAYS

NO.	PLAYER	MINT
219	Jesse Barfield	.15
220	George Bell	.30
221	Bill Caudill	.05
222	John Cerutti (R)	.30
223	Jim Clancy	.05
224	Mark Eichhorn (R)	.20
225	Tony Fernandez	.15
226	Damaso Garcia	.07
227	Kelly Gruber (R)	.75
228	Tom Henke	.10
229	Garth Iorg	.05
230	Joe Johnson	.07
231	Cliff Johnson	.05
232	Jimmy Key	.10
233	Dennis Lamp	.05
234	Rick Leach	.05
235	Buck Martinez	.05
236	Lloyd Moseby	.07
237	Rance Mulliniks	.05
238	Dave Stieb	.10
239	Willie Upshaw	.05
240	Ernie Whitt	.05

CLEVELAND INDIANS

NO.	PLAYER	MINT
241	Andy Allanson (R)	.15
242	Scott Bailes (R)	.15
243	Chris Bando	.05
244	Tony Bernazard	.05
245	John Butcher	.05
246	Brett Butler	.05
247	Ernie Camacho	.05
248	Tom Candiotti	.05
249	Joe Carter	.35
250	Carmen Castillo	.05
251	Julio Franco	.15
252	Mel Hall	.05
253	Brook Jacoby	.05
254	Phil Niekro	.15
255	Otis Nixon	.05
256	Dickie Noles	.05
257	Bryan Oelkers	.05
258	Ken Schrom	.05
259	Don Schulze	.05
260	Cory Snyder	.50
261	Pat Tabler	.10
262	Andre Thornton	.05
263	Rich Yett (R)	.10

SAN FRANCISCO GIANTS

NO.	PLAYER	MINT
264	Mike Aldrete (R)	.25
265	Juan Berenguer	.05
266	Vida Blue	.05
267	Bob Brenly	.05
268	Chris Brown	.15
269	Will Clark (R)	30.00
270	Chili Davis	.10
271	Mark Davis	.05
272	Kelly Downs (R)	.30
273	Scott Garrelts	.05
274	Dan Gladden	.05
275	Mike Krukow	.05
276	Randy Kutcher (R)	.15
277	Mike LaCoss	.05
278	Jeff Leonard	.05
279	Candy Maldonado	.15
280	Roger Mason	.05
281	Bob Melvin	.05
282	Greg Minton	.05
283	Jeff Robinson	.05
284	Harry Spilman	.05
285	Rob Thompson (R)	.35
286	Jose Uribe	.05
287	Frank Williams	.05
288	Joel Youngblood	.05

ST. LOUIS CARDINALS

NO.	PLAYER	MINT
289	Jack Clark	.20
290	Vince Coleman	.40
291	Tim Conroy	.05
292	Danny Cox	.05
293	Ken Dayley	.05
294	Curt Ford	.08
295	Bob Forsch	.05
296	Tom Herr	.05
297	Ricky Horton	.05
298	Clint Hurdle	.05
299	Jeff Lahti	.05
300	Steve Lake	.05
301	Tito Landrum	.05
302	Mike LaValliere (R)	.25
303	Greg Mathews (R)	.25
304	Willie McGee	.15
305	Jose Oquendo	.05
306	Terry Pendleton	.05
307	Pat Perry	.10
308	Ozzie Smith	.25
309	Ray Soff (R)	.15
310	John Tudor	.10
311	Andy Van Slyke	.20
312	Todd Worrell	.15

MONTREAL EXPOS

NO.	PLAYER	MINT
313	Dann Bilardello	.05
314	Hubie Brooks	.10
315	Tim Burke	.05
316	Andre Dawson	.35
317	Mike Fitzgerald	.05
318	Tom Foley	.05
319	Andres Galarraga	.30
320	Joe Hesketh	.05
321	Wallace Johnson	.05
322	Wayne Krenchicki	.05
323	Vance Law	.05
324	Dennis Martinez	.05
325	Bob McClure	.05
326	Andy McGaffigan	.05
327	Al Newman (R)	.15
328	Tim Raines	.25
329	Jeff Reardon	.10
330	Luis Rivera (R)	.15
331	Bob Sebra (R)	.15
332	Bryn Smith	.05
333	Jay Tibbs	.05
334	Tim Wallach	.05
335	Mitch Webster	.12
336	John Wohlford	.05
337	Floyd Youmans	.15

MILWAUKEE BREWERS

NO.	PLAYER	MINT
338	Chris Bosio (R)	.40
339	Glenn Braggs (R)	.75
340	Rick Cerone	.05
341	Mark Clear	.05
342	B. Clutterbuck (R)	.15
343	Cecil Cooper	.15
344	Rob Deer	.20
345	Jim Gantner	.05
346	Ted Higuera	.20
347	J.H. Johnson	.05
348	Tim Leary	.25
349	Rick Manning	.05
350	Paul Molitor	.15
351	Charlie Moore	.05
352	Juan Nieves	.15
353	Ben Oglivie	.05
354	Dan Plesac (R)	.30
355	Ernest Riles	.05
356	Billy Joe Robidoux	.10
357	Bill Schroeder	.05
358	Dale Sveum (R)	.20
359	Gorman Thomas	.10
360	Bill Wegman	.05
361	Robin Yount	.50

KC ROYALS

NO.	PLAYER	MINT
362	Steve Balboni	.07
363	Scott Bankhead	.20
364	Buddy Biancalana	.05
365	Bud Black	.05
366	George Brett	.75
367	Steve Farr	.05
368	Mark Gubicza	.05
369	Bo Jackson (R)	18.00
370	Danny Jackson	.20
371	Mike Kingery (R)	.15
372	Rudy Law	.05
373	Charlie Leibrandt	.05

NO. PLAYER	MINT
374 Dennis Leonard	.05
375 Hal McRae	.05
376 Jorge Orta	.05
377 Jamie Quirk	.05
378 Dan Quisenberry	.10
379 Bret Saberhagen	.30
380 Angel Salazar	.05
381 Lonnie Smith	.05
382 Jim Sundberg	.05
383 Frank White	.05
384 Willie Wilson	.12
OAKLAND A's	
385 Joaquin Andujar	.05
386 Doug Bair	.05
387 Dusty Baker	.05
388 Bruce Bochte	.05
389 Jose Canseco	10.00
390 Chris Codiroli	.05
391 Mike Davis	.05
392 Alfredo Griffin	.05
393 Moose Haas	.05
394 Donnie Hill	.05
395 Jay Howell	.05
396 Dave Kingman	.12
397 Carney Lansford	.05
398 David Leiper	.12
399 B. Mooneyham (R)	.15
400 Dwayne Murphy	.05
401 Steve Ontiveros	.05
402 Tony Phillips	.05
403 Eric Plunk	.05
404 Jose Rijo	.05
405 Terry Steinbach (R)	1.00
406 Dave Stewart	.50
407 Mickey Tettleton	.20
408 Dave Von Ohlen	.05
409 Jerry Willard	.05
410 Curt Young	.05
SAN DIEGO PADRES	
411 Bruce Bochy	.05
412 Dave Dravecky	.05
413 Tim Flannery	.05
414 Steve Garvey	.30
415 Goose Gossage	.12
416 Tony Gwynn	.50
417 Andy Hawkins	.05
418 LaMarr Hoyt	.05
419 Terry Kennedy	.05
420 John Kruk (R)	.50
421 Dave LaPoint	.05
422 Craig Letters	.05
423 Carmelo Martinez	.05
424 Lance McCullers	.12
425 Kevin McReynolds	.30
426 Graig Nettles	.10
427 Bip Roberts (R)	.50
428 Jerry Royster	.05
429 Benito Santiago	1.00
430 Eric Show	.07
431 Bob Stoddard	.05
432 Garry Templeton	.05
433 Gene Walter	.10
434 Ed Whitson	.05
435 Marvell Wynne	.05
LA DODGERS	
436 Dave Anderson	.05
437 Greg Brock	.05
438 Enos Cabell	.05
439 Mariano Duncan	.12
440 Pedro Guerrero	.20
441 Orel Hershiser	.30
442 Rick Honeycutt	.05
443 Ken Howell	.05
444 Ken Landreaux	.05
445 Bill Madlock	.08
446 Mike Marshall	.08
447 Len Matuszek	.05
448 Tom Niedenfuer	.05
449 Alejandro Pena	.05
450 Dennis Powell	.05
451 Jerry Reuss	.05
452 Bill Russell	.05
453 Steve Sax	.15
454 Mike Scioscia	.05
455 Franklin Stubbs	.05
456 Alex Trevino	.05
457 F. Valenzuela	.25
458 Ed Vande Berg	.05

NO. PLAYER	MINT
459 Bob Welch	.05
460 Reggie Williams (R)	.15
BALTIMORE ORIOLES	
461 Don Aase	.05
462 Juan Beniquez	.05
463 Mike Boddicker	.05
464 Juan Bonilla	.05
465 Rich Bordi	.05
466 Storm Davis	.05
467 Rick Dempsey	.05
468 Ken Dixon	.05
469 Jim Dwyer	.05
470 Mike Flanagan	.05
471 Jackie Gutierrez	.05
472 Brad Havens	.05
473 Lee Lacy	.05
474 Fred Lynn	.15
475 Scott McGregor	.08
476 Eddie Murray	.30
477 Tom O'Malley	.05
478 Cal Ripken, Jr.	.30
479 Larry Sheets	.10
480 John Shelby	.05
481 Nate Snell	.05
482 Jim Traber	.10
483 Mike Young	.05
CHICAGO WHITE SOX	
484 Neil Allen	.05
485 Harold Baines	.15
486 Floyd Bannister	.05
487 Daryl Boston	.05
488 Ivan Calderon	.20
489 John Cangelosi (R)	.20
490 Steve Carlton	.35
491 Joe Cowley	.05
492 Julio Cruz	.05
493 Bill Dawley	.05
494 Jose DeLeon	.05
495 Richard Dotson	.05
496 Carlton Fisk	.30
497 Ozzie Guillen	.25
498 Jerry Hairston	.05
499 Ron Hassey	.05
500 Tim Hulett	.05
501 Bob James	.05
502 Steve Lyons	.05
503 Joel McKeon (R)	.15
504 Gene Nelson	.05
505 Dave Schmidt	.05
506 Ray Searage	.05
507 Bobby Thigpen (R)	3.00
508 Greg Walker	.05
ATLANTA BRAVES	
509 Jim Acker	.05
510 Doyle Alexander	.05
511 P. Assenmacher (R)	.15
512 Bruce Benedict	.05
513 Chris Chambliss	.08
514 Jeff Dedmon	.05
515 Gene Garber	.05
516 Ken Griffey	.08
517 Terry Harper	.05
518 Bob Horner	.15
519 Glenn Hubbard	.05
520 Rick Mahler	.05
521 Omar Moreno	.05
522 Dale Murphy	.40
523 Ken Oberkfell	.05
524 Ed Olwine (R)	.15
525 David Palmer	.05
526 Rafael Ramirez	.05
527 Billy Sample	.05
528 Ted Simmons	.05
529 Zane Smith	.05
530 Bruce Sutter	.12
531 Andres Thomas (R)	.25
532 Ozzie Virgil	.05
MINNESOTA TWINS	
533 A. Anderson (R)	.35
534 Keith Atherton	.05
535 Billy Beane	.05
536 Bert Blyleven	.05
537 Tom Brunansky	.20
538 Randy Bush	.05
539 George Frazier	.05
540 Gary Gaetti	.20
541 Greg Gagne	.05
542 Mickey Hatcher	.05

NO. PLAYER	MINT
543 Neal Heaton	.05
544 Kent Hrbek	.15
545 Roy Lee Jackson	.05
546 Tim Laudner	.05
547 Steve Lombardozzi	.05
548 Mark Portugal (R)	.25
549 Kirby Puckett	2.00
550 Jeff Reed	.05
551 Mark Salas	.05
552 Roy Smalley	.05
553 Mike Smithson	.05
554 Frank Viola	.30
CHICAGO CUBS	
555 Thad Bosley	.05
556 Ron Cey	.05
557 Jody Davis	.10
558 Ron Davis	.05
559 Bob Dernier	.05
560 Frank DiPino	.05
561 Shawon Dunston	.30
562 Leon Durham	.10
563 Dennis Eckersley	.05
564 Terry Francona	.05
565 Dave Gumpert	.05
566 Guy Hoffman	.05
567 Ed Lynch	.05
568 Gary Matthews	.05
569 Keith Moreland	.05
570 Jamie Moyer (R)	.20
571 Jerry Mumphrey	.05
572 Ryne Sandberg	1.00
573 Scott Sanderson	.05
574 Lee Smith	.05
575 Chris Speier	.05
576 Rick Sutcliffe	.07
577 Manny Trillo	.05
578 Steve Trout	.05
SEATTLE MARINERS	
579 Karl Best	.05
580 Scott Bradley	.10
581 Phil Bradley	.05
582 Mickey Brantley	.05
583 Mike Brown	.05
584 Alvin Davis	.15
585 L. Guetterman (R)	.20
586 Mark Huismann	.05
587 Bob Kearney	.05
588 Pete Ladd	.05
589 Mark Langston	.25
590 Mike Moore	.05
591 Mike Morgan	.05
592 John Moses	.05
593 Ken Phelps	.05
594 Jim Presley	.20
595 Rey Quinonez (R)	.20
596 Harold Reynolds	.15
597 Billy Swift	.05
598 Danny Tartabull	.30
599 Steve Yeager	.05
600 Matt Young	.05
PITTSBURGH PIRATES	
601 Bill Almon	.05
602 Rafael Belliard (R)	.15
603 Mike Bielecki	.05
604 Barry Bonds (R)	10.00
605 Bobby Bonilla (R)	8.00
606 Sid Bream	.05
607 Mike Brown	.05
608 Pat Clements	.05
609 Mike Diaz (R)	.15
610 Cecilio Guante	.05
611 Barry Jones (R)	.30
612 Bob Kipper	.05
613 Larry McWilliams	.05
614 Jim Morrison	.05
615 Joe Orsulak	.05
616 Junior Ortiz	.05
617 Tony Pena	.05
618 Johnny Ray	.05
619 Rick Reuschel	.05
620 R.J. Reynolds	.05
621 Rick Rhoden	.05
622 Don Robinson	.05
623 Bob Walk	.05
624 Jim Winn	.05
SPECIAL CARDS	
625 Youthful Power:	.60
P. Incaviglia, J. Canseco	

NO. PLAYER	
626 300 Game Winners:	.15
D. Sutton, P. Niekro	
627 A.L. Firemen:	.15
D. Righetti, D. Asse	
628 Rookie All-Stars:	1.25
W. Joyner, J. Canseco	
629 Magic Mets:	.50
G. Carter, S. Fernandez,	
D. Gooden, K. Hernandez,	
D. Strawberry	
630 N.L. Best Righties:	.15
M. Scott, M. Krukow	
631 Sensational Southpaws:	.15
F. Venezuela, J. Franco	
632 4 HR's in Game:	.15
Bob Horner	
633 Pitcher's Nightmare:	.60
J. Canseco, J. Rice,	
K. Puckett	
634 All-Star Battery:	.30
G. Carter, R. Clemens	
635 4,000 Strikeouts:	.20
S. Carlton	
636 Big Bats at First Sack:	.20
G. Davis, E. Murray	
637 On Base:	.25
W. Boggs, K. Hernandez	
638 Sluggers from Left Side:	1.00
D. Mattingly,	
D. Strawberry	
639 Former MVP's:	.20
D. Parker, R. Sandberg	
640 Dr. K. & Super K:	.50
D. Gooden, R. Clemens	
641 A.L. West Stoppers:	.15
M. Witt, C. Hough	
642 Doubles & Triples:	.15
J. Samuel, T. Raines	
643 Outfielders with Punch:	.15
H. Baines, J. Barfield	
No. 644 to 653—Major League Prospects	
644 D. Clark (R) and	
G. Swindell (R)	1.25
645 Ron Karkovice (R) and	
Russ Morman (R)	.20
646 Devon White (R) and	
Willie Fraser (R)	.75
647 Mike Stanley (R) and	
Jerry Browne (R)	.30
648 Dave Magadan (R) and	
Phil Lombardi (R)	3.00
649 Jose Gonzalez (R) and	
Ralph Bryant (R)	.20
650 Jimmy Jones (R) and	
Randy Asadoor (R)	.25
651 Tracy Jones (R) and	
Marvin Freeman (R)	.25
652 John Stefero (R) and	
Kevin Seitzer (R)	5.00
653 Rob Nelson (R) and	
Steve Fireovid (R)	.25
654 Checklist No. 1	.08
655 Checklist No. 2	.08
656 Checklist No. 3	.08
657 Checklist No. 4	.08
658 Checklist No. 5	.08
659 Checklist No. 6	.08
660 Checklist No. 7	.08

1987 Fleer Traded Update.... Complete Set of 132 Cards—Value $20.00

This set updates the main 1987 card set with players who had changed teams during the season, and rookies. This set features Fleer's first card of Ellis Burks, Mike Greenwell, Mark McGwire, and Matt Williams. The set was packaged in a printed box and distributed exclusively through card dealers. A high gloss version of the set was issued in a tin box.

NO. PLAYER	MINT	NO. PLAYER	MINT	NO. PLAYER	MINT	NO. PLAYER	MINT
U1 Scott Bankhead	.07	U34 Ken Gerhart	.15	U67 Mike Loynd	.15	J100 Randy Ready	.07
U2 Eric Bell	.15	U35 Jim Gott	.07	U68 Greg Maddux (RR)	.75	U101 Jeff Reardon	.15
U3 Juan Beniquez	.07	U36 Dan Gladden	.07	U69 Bill Madlock	.07	U102 Gary Redus	.07
U4 Juan Berenguer	.07	U37 Mike Greenwell (RR)	3.00	U70 Dave Magadan	.50	U103 Rick Rhoden	.15
U5 Mike Birkbeck	.20	U38 Cecilio Guante	.07	U71 Joe Magrane (RR)	1.00	U104 Wally Ritchie	.12
U6 Randy Bockus	.12	U39 Albert Hall	.07	U72 Fred Manrique	.15	U105 Jeff Robinson (RR)	.25
U7 Rod Booker	.07	U40 Atlee Hammaker	.07	U73 Mike Mason	.07	U106 Mark Salas	.07
U8 Thad Bosley	.07	U41 Mickey Hatcher	.07	U74 Lloyd McClendon	.20	U107 Dave Schmidt	.07
U9 Greg Brock	.10	U42 Mike Heath	.07	U75 Fred McGriff (RR)	2.50	U108 Kevin Seitzer	1.00
U10 Bob Brower	.15	U43 Neal Heaton	.07	U76 Mark McGwire (RR)	2.50	U109 John Shelby	.07
U11 Chris Brown	.10	U44 Mike Henneman	.30	U77 Mark McLemore	.07	U110 John Smiley (RR)	.40
U12 Jerry Browne	.07	U45 Guy Hoffman	.07	U78 Kevin McReynolds	.30	U111 Lary Sorensen	.07
U13 Ralph Bryant	.07	U46 Charlie Hudson	.07	U79 Dave Meads	.15	U112 Chris Speier	.07
U14 De Wayne Buice	.10	U47 Chuck Jackson	.15	U80 Greg Minton	.12	U113 Randy St. Claire	.07
U15 Ellis Burks (RR)	3.00	U48 Mike Jackson	.20	U81 John Mitchell	.12	U114 Jim Sundberg	.07
U16 Casey Candaele	.15	U49 Reggie Jackson	.60	U82 Kevin Mitchell	2.00	U115 B.J. Surhoff (RR)	.30
U17 Steve Carlton	.30	U50 Chris James	.30	U83 John Morris	.10	U116 Greg Swindell	.40
U18 Juan Castillo	.07	U51 Dian James	.15	U84 Jeff Musselman	.20	U117 Danny Tartabull	.25
U19 Chuck Crim	.15	U52 Stan Javier	.07	U85 Randy Myers (RR)	.50	U118 Dorn Taylor	.10
U20 Mark Davidson	.15	U53 Stan Jefferson	.20	U86 Gene Nelson	.07	U119 Lee Tunnell	.07
U21 Mark Davis	.15	U54 Jimmy Jones	.10	U87 Joe Niekro	.15	U120 Ed Vande Berg	.07
U22 Storm Davis	.15	U55 Tracy Jones	.20	U88 Tom Nieto	.07	U121 Andy Van Slyke	.25
U23 Bill Dawley	.07	U56 Terry Kennedy	.07	U89 Reid Nichols	.07	U122 Gary Ward	.07
U24 Andre Dawson	.35	U57 Mike Kingery	.07	U90 Matt Nokes (RR)	.50	U123 Devon White	.25
U25 Brian Dayett	.07	U58 Ray Knight	.07	U91 Dickie Noles	.07	U124 Alan Wiggins	.07
U26 Rick Dempsay	.07	U59 Gene Larkin	.30	U92 Edwin Nunez	.07	U125 Bill Wilkinson	.12
U27 Ken Dowell	.12	U60 Mike La Valliere	.07	U93 Jose Nunez	.15	U126 Jim Winn	.07
U28 Dave Dravecky	.07	U61 Jack Lazorko	.12	U94 Paul O'Neill	.30	U127 Frank Williams	.07
U29 Mike Dunne (RR)	.20	U62 Terry Leach	.12	U95 Jim Paciorek	.15	U128 Kenny Williams (RR)	.20
U30 Dennis Eckersley	.15	U63 Rick Leach	.07	U96 Lance Parrish	.20	U129 Matt Williams (RR)	5.00
U31 Cecil Fielder	2.50	U64 Craig Lefferts	.07	U97 Bill Pecota	.15	U130 Herm Winningham	.07
U32 Brian Fisher	.07	U65 Jim Lindeman (RR)	.15	U98 Tony Pena	.07	U131 Matt Young	.07
U33 Willie Fraser	.07	U66 Bill Long	.20	U99 Luis Polonia	.25	U132 Checklist	.08

1988 Fleer.... Complete Set of 660 Cards—Value $50.00

Features the rookie cards of Mark Grace, Gregg Jefferies, Ellis Burks and Matt Williams. A new feature on the back of the card is "At Their Best." It reveals the player's record regarding day/night and home/road games.

NO. PLAYER	MINT	NO. PLAYER	MINT	NO. PLAYER	MINT	NO. PLAYER	MINT
MINNESOTA TWINS		8 Mark Davidson (R)	.15	16 Steve Lombardozzi	.05	24 Les Straker (R)	.15
1 Keith Atherton	.05	9 George Frazier	.05	17 Al Newman	.05	25 Frank Viola	.25
2 Don Baylor	.08	10 Gary Gaetti	.15	18 Joe Niekro	.08	**ST. LOUIS CARDINALS**	
3 Juan Berenguer	.05	11 Greg Gagne	.05	19 Kirby Puckett	.50	26 Jk. Clark	.15
4 Bert Blyleven	.10	12 Dan Gladden	.05	20 Jeff Reardon	.05	27 Vince Coleman	.20
5 Tom Brunansky	.15	13 Kent Hrbek	.15	21 Dan Schatzader	.05	28 Danny Cox	.05
6 Randy Bush	.05	14 Gene Larkin (R)	.30	22 Roy Smalley	.05	29 Bill Dawley	.05
7 Steve Carlton	.20	15 Tim Laudner	.05	23 Mike Smithson	.05	30 Ken Dayley	.05

NO.	PLAYER	MINT
31	Doug DeCinces	.05
32	Curt Ford	.05
33	Bob Forsch	.05
34	David Green	.05
35	Tom Herr	.05
36	Ricky Horton	.05
37	Lance Johnson (R)	.25
38	Steve Lake	.05
39	Jim Lindeman	.12
40	Joe Magrane (R)	.75
41	Greg Mathews	.05
42	Willie McGee	.15
43	John Morris	.12
44	Jose Oquendo	.05
45	Tony Pena	.05
46	Terry Pendleton	.05
47	Ozzie Smith	.15
48	John Tudor	.10
49	Lee Tunnell	.05
50	Todd Worrell	.10

DETROIT TIGERS

NO.	PLAYER	MINT
51	Doyle Alexander	.05
52	Dave Bergman	.05
53	Tom Brookens	.05
54	Darrell Evans	.05
55	Kirk Gibson	.20
56	Mike Heath	.05
57	Mike Henneman (R)	.25
58	Willie Hernandez	.10
59	Larry Herndon	.05
60	Eric King	.05
61	Chet Lemon	.05
62	Scott Lusader (R)	.20
63	Bill Madlock	.15
64	Jack Morris	.15
65	Jim Morrison	.05
66	Matt Nokes (R)	.50
67	Dan Petry	.05
68	Jeff Robinson	.30
68	J. Robinson (error)	.60
69	Pat Sheridan	.05
70	Nate Snell	.05
71	Frank Tanana	.05
72	Walt Terrell	.05
73	Mark Thurmond	.05
74	Alan Trammell	.15
75	Lou Whitaker	.20

SAN FRANCISCO GIANTS

NO.	PLAYER	MINT
76	Mike Aldrete	.05
77	Bob Brenly	.05
78	Will Clark	3.50
79	Chili Davis	.10
80	Kelly Downs	.05
81	Dave Dravecky	.05
82	Scott Garrelts	.05
83	Atlee Hammaker	.05
84	Dave Henderson	.05
85	Mike Krukow	.05
86	Mike LaCoss	.05
87	Craig Lefferts	.05
88	Jeff Leonard	.10
89	Candy Maldonado	.10
90	Bob Melvin	.05
91	Ed Milner	.05
92	Kevin Mitchell	1.00
93	Jon Perlman (R)	.12
94	Rick Reuschel	.05
95	Don Robinson	.05
96	Chris Speier	.05
97	Harry Spilman	.05
98	Robbie Thompson	.05
99	Jose Uribe	.05
100	Mark Wasinger (R)	.15
101	Matt Williams (R)	5.00

TORONTO BLUE JAYS

NO.	PLAYER	MINT
102	Jesse Barfield	.15
103	George Bell	.20
104	Juan Beniquez	.05
105	John Cerutti	.05
106	Jim Clancy	.05
107	Rob Ducey (R)	.20
108	Mark Eichhorn	.05
109	Tony Fernandez	.12
110	Cecil Fielder	1.00
111	Kelly Gruber	.50
112	Tom Henke	.05
113	Garth Iorg	.05
114	Jimmy Key	.10
115	Rick Leach	.05
116	Manny Lee	.08
117	Nelson Liriano (R)	.25
118	Fred McGriff	2.00
119	Lloyd Moseby	.10
120	Rance Mulliniks	.05
121	Jeff Musselman	.12
122	Jose Nunez	.15
123	Dave Stieb	.05
124	Willie Upshaw	.05
125	Duane Ward	.08
126	Ernie Whitt	.05

NEW YORK METS

NO.	PLAYER	MINT
127	Rick Aguilera	.05
128	Wally Backman	.05
129	Mark Carreon (R)	.40
130	Gary Carter	.20
131	David Cone	1.00
132	Ron Darling	.15
133	Len Dykstra	.35
134	Sid Fernandez	.08
135	Dwight Gooden	.60
136	Keith Hernandez	.20
137	Gregg Jefferies (R)	6.00
138	Howard Johnson	.35
139	Terry Leach	.05
140	Barry Lyons (R)	.25
141	Dave Magadan	.35
142	Roger McDowell	.05
143	Kevin McReynolds	.15
144	Keith Miller (R)	.20
145	John Mitchell (R)	.15
146	Randy Myers	.40
147	Bob Ojeda	.10
148	Jesse Orosco	.05
149	Rafael Santana	.05
150	Doug Sisk	.05
151	Darryl Strawberry	.60
152	Tim Teufel	.05
153	Gene Walter	.05
154	Mookie Wilson	.08

MILWAUKEE BREWERS

NO.	PLAYER	MINT
155	Jay Aldrich (R)	.15
156	Chris Bosio	.05
157	Glenn Braggs	.10
158	Greg Brock	.05
159	Juan Castillo	.08
160	Mark Clear	.05
161	Cecil Cooper	.08
162	Chuck Crim (R)	.15
163	Rob Deer	.10
164	Mike Felder	.05
165	Jim Gantner	.05
166	Ted Higuera	.12
167	Steve Kiefer	.05
168	Rick Manning	.05
169	Paul Molitor	.15
170	Juan Nieves	.10
171	Dan Plesac	.05
172	Earnest Riles	.05
173	Bill Schroeder	.05
174	Steve Stanicek (R)	.20
175	B.J. Surhoff	.20
176	Dale Sveum	.08
177	Bill Wegman	.05
178	Robin Yount	.25

MONTREAL EXPOS

NO.	PLAYER	MINT
179	Hubie Brooks	.10
180	Tim Burke	.05
181	Casey Candaele	.10
182	Mike Fitzgerald	.05
183	Tom Foley	.05
184	Andres Galarraga	.20
185	Neal Heaton	.05
186	Wallace Johnson	.05
187	Vance Law	.05
188	Dennis Martinez	.08
189	Bob McClure	.05
190	Andy McGaffigan	.05
191	Reid Nichols	.05
192	Pascual Perez	.05
193	Tim Raines	.20
194	Jeff Reed	.05
195	Bob Sebra	.05
196	Bryn Smith	.05
197	Randy St. Claire	.05
198	Tim Wallach	.10
199	Mitch Webster	.05
200	Herm Winningham	.05
201	Floyd Youmans	.08

N.Y. YANKEES

NO.	PLAYER	MINT
202	Brad Arnsberg (R)	.35
203	Rick Cerone	.05
204	Pat Clements	.05
205	Henry Cotto	.05
206	Mike Easler	.05
207	Ron Guidry	.10
208	Bill Gullickson	.05
209	Rickey Henderson	.50
210	Charles Hudson	.05
211	Tommy John	.10
212	Roberto Kelly (R)	1.25
213	Ron Kittle	.08
214	Don Mattingly	1.50
215	Bobby Meacham	.05
216	Mike Pagliarulo	.15
217	Dan Pasqua	.10
218	Willie Randolph	.12
219	Rick Rhoden	.05
220	Dave Righetti	.10
221	Jerry Royster	.05
222	Tim Stoddard	.05
223	Wayne Tolleson	.05
224	Gary Ward	.05
225	Claudell Washington	.05
226	Dave Winfield	.20

CINCINNATI REDS

NO.	PLAYER	MINT
227	Buddy Bell	.15
228	Tom Browning	.05
229	Dave Concepcion	.05
230	Kal Daniels	.25
231	Eric Davis	.75
232	Bo Diaz	.05
233	Nick Esasky	.05
234	John Franco	.08
235	Guy Hoffman	.05
236	Tom Hume	.05
237	Tracy Jones	.10
238	Bill Landrum (R)	.20
239	Barry Larkin	1.00
240	Terry McGriff	.12
241	Rob Murphy	.05
242	Ron Oester	.05
243	Dave Parker	.15
244	Pat Perry	.05
245	Ted Power	.05
246	Dennis Rasmussen	.05
247	Ron Robinson	.05
248	Kurt Stillwell	.08
249	Jeff Treadway (R)	.40
250	Frank Williams	.05

K.C. ROYALS

NO.	PLAYER	MINT
251	Steve Balboni	.05
252	Bud Black	.05
253	Thad Bosley	.05
254	George Brett	.35
255	John Davis (R)	.15
256	Steve Farr	.05
257	Gene Garber	.05
258	Jerry Gleaton	.05
259	Mark Gubicza	.05
260	Bo Jackson	3.00
261	Danny Jackson	.10
262	Ross Jones (R)	.12
263	Charlie Leibrandt	.05
264	Bill Pecota (R)	.15
265	Melido Perez (R)	.25
266	Jamie Quirk	.05
267	Dan Quisenberry	.10
268	Bret Saberhagen	.25
269	Angel Salazar	.05
270	Kevin Seitzer	.30
271	Danny Tartabull	.20
272	Gary Thurman (R)	.20
273	Frank White	.05
274	Willie Wilson	.10

OAKLAND A'S

NO.	PLAYER	MINT
275	Tony Bernazard	.05
276	Jose Canseco	3.00
277	Mike Davis	.05
278	Storm Davis	.05
279	Dennis Eckersley	.05
280	Alfredo Griffin	.05
281	Rick Honeycutt	.05
282	Jay Howell	.05
283	Reggie Jackson	.30
284	Dennis Lamp	.05
285	Carney Lansford	.05
286	Mark McGwire	3.00
287	Dwayne Murphy	.05
288	Gene Nelson	.05
289	Steve Ontiveros	.05
290	Tony Philips	.05
291	Eric Plunk	.05
292	Luis Polonia (R)	.25
293	Rick Rodriguez (R)	.15
294	Terry Steinbach	.15
295	Dave Stewart	.25
296	Curt Young	.05

PHILADELPHIA PHILLIES

NO.	PLAYER	MINT
297	Luis Aguayo	.05
298	Steve Bedrosian	.05
299	Jeff Calhoun	.05
300	Don Carman	.05
301	Todd Frohwirth (R)	.20
302	Greg Gross	.05
303	Kevin Gross	.05
304	Von Hayes	.05
305	Keith Hughes (R)	.20
306	Mike Jackson (R)	.15
307	Chris James	.25
308	Steve Jeltz	.05
309	Mike Maddux	.05
310	Lance Parrish	.12
311	Shane Rawley	.05
312	Wally Ritchie (R)	.15
313	Bruce Ruffin	.05
314	Juan Samuel	.10
315	Mike Schmidt	.50
316	Rick Schu	.05
317	Jeff Stone	.05
318	Kent Tekulve	.05
319	Milt Thompson	.05
320	Glenn Wilson	.08

PITTSBURGH PIRATES

NO.	PLAYER	MINT
321	Rafael Belliard	.05
322	Barry Bonds	1.50
323	Bobby Bonilla	1.00
324	Sid Bream	.05
325	John Cangelosi	.05
326	Mike Diaz	.05
327	Doug Drabek	.30
328	Mike Dunne	.20
329	Brian Fisher	.05
330	Brett Gideon (R)	.15
331	Terry Harper	.05
332	Bob Kipper	.05
333	Mike LaValliere	.05
334	Jose Lind (R)	.50
335	Junior Ortiz	.05
336	Vincente Palacios (R)	.15
337	Bob Patterson (R)	.15
338	Al Pedrique (R)	.15
339	R.J. Reynolds	.05
340	John Smiley (R)	.35
341	Andy Van Slyke	.15
342	Bob Walk	.05

BOSTON RED SOX

NO.	PLAYER	MINT
343	Marty Barrett	.10
344	Todd Benzinger (R)	.40
345	Wade Boggs	.75
346	Tom Bolton (R)	.30
347	Oil Can Boyd	.05
348	Ellis Burks (R)	2.50
349	Roger Clemens	.75
350	Steve Crawford	.15
351	Dwight Evans	.10
352	Wes Gardner (R)	.20
353	Rich Gedman	.05
354	Mike Greenwell	2.00
355	Sam Horn (R)	.30
356	Bruce Hurst	.10
357	John Marzano	.20
358	Al Nipper	.05
359	Spike Owen	.05
360	Jody Reed (R)	1.00
361	Jim Rice	.20
362	Ed Romero	.05
363	Kevin Romine	.10
364	Joe Sambito	.05
365	Calvin Schiraldi	.05

NO. PLAYER	MINT
366 Jeff Sellers	.05
367 Bob Stanley	.05
SEATTLE MARINERS	
368 Scott Bankhead	.05
369 Phil Bradley	.08
370 Scott Bradley	.05
371 Mickey Brantley	.10
372 Mike Campbell (R)	.15
373 Alvin Davis	.15
374 Lee Guetterman	.05
375 Dave Hengel (R)	.15
376 Mike Kingery	.05
377 Mark Langston	.15
378 Edgar Martinez (R)	1.00
379 Mike Moore	.05
380 Mike Morgan	.05
381 John Moses	.05
382 Donnell Nixon (R)	.15
383 Edwin Nunez	.05
384 Ken Phelps	.05
385 Jim Presley	.05
386 Rey Quinones	.05
387 Jerry Reed	.05
388 Harold Reynolds	.05
389 Dave Valle	.08
390 Bill Wilkinson (R)	.15
CHICAGO WHITE SOX	
391 Harold Baines	.10
392 Floyd Bannister	.05
393 Daryl Boston	.05
394 Ivan Calderon	.05
395 Jose DeLeon	.05
396 Richard Dotson	.05
397 Carlton Fisk	.20
398 Ozzie Guillen	.05
399 Ron Hassey	.05
400 Donnie Hill	.05
401 Bob James	.05
402 Dave LaPoint	.05
403 Bill Lindsey (R)	.15
404 Bill Long (R)	.15
405 Steve Lyons	.05
406 Fred Manrique (R)	.15
407 Jack McDowell (R)	.50
408 Gary Redus	.05
409 Ray Searage	.05
410 Bobby Thigpen	.15
411 Greg Walker	.05
412 Kenny Williams (R)	.20
413 Jim Winn	.05
CHICAGO CUBS	
414 Jody Davis	.05
415 Andre Dawson	.35
416 Brian Dayett	.05
417 Bob Dernier	.05
418 Frank DiPino	.05
419 Shawon Dunston	.25
420 Leon Durham	.10
421 Les Lancaster (R)	.20
422 Ed Lynch	.05
423 Greg Maddux	.60
424 Dave Martinez	.15
425 K. Moreland (error)	3.50
(photo of Jody Davis)	
425 K. Moreland (correct)	.25
426 Jamie Moyer	.05
427 Jerry Mumphrey	.05
428 Paul Noce (R)	.15
429 Rafael Palmeiro	1.50
430 Wade Rowdon	.10
431 Ryne Sandberg	.60
432 Scott Sanderson	.05
433 Lee Smith	.10
434 Jim Sundberg	.05
435 Rick Sutcliffe	.10
436 Manny Trillo	.05
HOUSTON ASTROS	
437 Juan Agosto	.05
438 Larry Andersen	.05
439 Alan Ashby	.05
440 Kevin Bass	.05
441 Ken Caminiti (R)	.30
442 Rocky Childress (R)	.15
443 Jose Cruz	.05
444 Danny Darwin	.05
445 Glenn Davis	.15
446 Jim Deshaies	.05

NO. PLAYER	MINT
447 Bill Doran	.05
448 Ty Gainey	.05
449 Billy Hatcher	.10
450 Jeff Heathcock	.05
451 Bob Knepper	.05
452 Rob Mallicoat (R)	.15
453 Dave Meads (R)	.15
454 Craig Reynolds	.05
455 Nolan Ryan	.75
456 Mike Scott	.15
457 Dave Smith	.05
458 Denny Walling	.05
459 Robbie Wine (R)	.15
460 Gerald Young (R)	.25
TEXAS RANGERS	
461 Bob Brower	.10
462 J. Browne (error)	3.50
(photo of Bob Brower)	
462 J. Browne (correct)	.25
463 Steve Buechele	.05
464 Edwin Correa	.05
465 Cecil Espy (R)	.20
466 Scott Fletcher	.05
467 Jose Guzman	.05
468 Greg Harris	.05
469 Charlie Hough	.05
470 Pete Incaviglia	.15
471 Paul Kilgus (R)	.15
472 Mike Loynd	.08
473 Oddibe McDowell	.10
474 Dale Mohorcic	.05
475 Pete O'Brien	.10
476 Larry Parrish	.05
477 Geno Petralli	.05
478 Jeff Russell	.05
479 Ruben Sierra	1.25
480 Mike Stanley	.05
481 Curtis Wilkerson	.05
482 Mitch Williams	.05
483 Bobby Witt	.15
CALIFORNIA ANGELS	
484 Tony Armas	.05
485 Bob Boone	.05
486 Bill Buckner	.05
487 DeWayne Buice (R)	.15
488 Brian Downing	.05
489 Chuck Finley	.20
490 Willie Fraser	.05
491 Jack Howell	.05
492 Ruppert Jones	.05
493 Wally Joyner	.30
494 Jack Lazorko	.10
495 Gary Lucas	.05
496 Kirk McCaskill	.05
497 Mark McLemore	.05
498 Darrell Miller	.05
499 Greg Minton	.05
500 Donnie Moore	.05
501 Gus Polidor	.05
502 Johnny Ray	.05
503 Mark Ryal	.05
504 Dick Schofield	.05
505 Don Sutton	.15
506 Devon White	.15
507 Mike Witt	.10
LOS ANGELES DODGERS	
508 Dave Anderson	.05
509 Tim Belcher	.50
510 Ralph Bryant	.05
511 Tim Crews (R)	.15
512 Mike Devereaux (R)	.25
513 Mariano Duncan	.05
514 Pedro Guerrero	.15
515 Jeff Hamilton	.15
516 Mickey Hatcher	.05
517 Brad Havens	.05
518 Orel Hershiser	.20
519 Shawn Hillegas (R)	.20
520 Ken Howell	.05
521 Tim Leary	.05
522 Mike Marshall	.10
523 Steve Sax	.15
524 Mike Scioscia	.05
525 Mike Sharperson	.05
526 John Shelby	.05
527 Franklin Stubbs	.05

NO. PLAYER	MINT
528 Fernando Valenzuela	.15
529 Bob Welch	.05
530 Matt Young	.05
ATLANTA BRAVES	
531 Jim Acker	.05
532 Paul Assenmacher	.05
533 Jeff Blauser (R)	.30
534 Joe Boever (R)	.15
535 Martin Clary	.05
536 Kevin Coffman	.15
537 Jeff Dedmon	.05
538 Ron Gant (R)	2.50
539 Tom Glavine (R)	.35
540 Ken Griffey	.05
541 Al Hall	.05
542 Glenn Hubbard	.05
543 Dion James	.05
544 Dale Murphy	.35
545 Ken Oberkfell	.05
546 David Palmer	.05
547 Gerald Perry	.15
548 Charlie Puleo	.05
549 Ted Simmons	.05
550 Zane Smith	.05
551 Andres Thomas	.05
552 Ozzie Virgil	.05
BALTIMORE ORIOLES	
553 Don Aase	.05
554 Jeff Ballard (R)	.35
555 Eric Bell	.05
556 Mike Boddicker	.05
557 Ken Dixon	.05
558 Jim Dwyer	.05
559 Ken Gehart	.05
560 Rene Gonzales (R)	.15
561 Mike Griffin	.05
562 John Hayban	.10
563 Terry Kennedy	.05
564 Ray Knight	.05
565 Lee Lacy	.05
566 Fred Lynn	.15
567 Eddie Murray	.25
568 Tom Niedenfuer	.05
569 Bill Ripken (R)	.20
570 Cal Ripken, Jr.	.25
571 Dave Schmidt	.05
572 Larry Sheets	.10
573 Pete Stanicek (R)	.15
574 Mark Williamson (R)	.15
575 Mike Young	.05
SAN DIEGO PADRES	
576 Shawn Abner	.20
577 Greg Booker	.05
578 Chris Brown	.10
579 Keith Comstock (R)	.15
580 Joey Cora (R)	.15
581 Mark Davis	.10
582 Tim Flannery	.05
583 Goose Gossage	.10
584 Mark Grant	.05
585 Tony Gwynn	.30
586 Andy Hawkins	.05
587 Stan Jefferson	.15
588 Jimmy Jones	.05
589 John Kruk	.10
590 Shane Mack	.20
591 Carmelo Martinez	.05
592 Lance McCullers	.05
593 Eric Nolte (R)	.15
594 Randy Ready	.05
595 Luis Salazar	.05
596 Benito Santiago	.40
597 Eric Show	.05
598 Garry Templeton	.05
599 Ed Whitson	.05
CLEVELAND INDIANS	
600 Scott Bailes	.05
601 Chris Bando	.05
602 Jay Bell (R)	.40
603 Brett Butler	.05
604 Tom Candiotti	.10
605 Joe Carter	.20
606 Carmen Castillo	.05
607 Brian Dorsett (R)	.15
608 John Farrell (R)	.25
609 Julio Franco	.15

NO. PLAYER	MINT
610 Mel Hall	.05
611 Tommy Hinzo (R)	.15
612 Brook Jacoby	.10
613 Doug Jones (R)	.40
614 Ken Schrom	.05
615 Cory Snyder	.20
616 Sammy Stewart	.05
617 Greg Swindell	.15
618 Pat Tabler	.05
619 Ed Vande Berg	.05
620 Eddie Williams (R)	.20
621 Rich Yett	.05
SPECIAL CARDS	
622 Slugging Sophomores	.20
623 Dominican Dynamite	.10
624 Oakland's Power Team	.75
625 Classic Relief	.10
626 All Star Righties	.10
627 Game Closers	.10
628 Masters of Double Play	.10
629 Rookie Record Setter	.35
630 Changing the Guard	.60
631 N.L. Batting Champs	.25
632 Pitching Magic	.10
633 Big Bats At First	.25
634 Hitting King and Thief	.20
635 Slugging Shortstop	.10
636 Tried and True Sluggers	.20
637 Crunch Time	.30
638 A.L. All Stars	.15
639 N.L. All-Stars	.15
640 The "O's" Brothers	.10
No. 641 to 653—	
Major League Prospects	
641 Mark Grace (R) and Darrin Jackson (R)	8.00
642 Damon Berryhill (R) and Jeff Montgomery (R)	.75
643 Felix Fermin (R) and Jessie Reid (R)	.20
644 Greg Myers (R) and Greg Tabor (R)	.20
645 Joey Meyer and Jim Eppard (R)	.25
646 Adam Peterson (R) and Randy Velarde (R)	.25
647 Peter Smith (R) and Chris Gwynn (R)	.40
648 Tom Newell (R) and Greg Jelks (R)	.25
649 Mario Diaz (R) and Clay Parker (R)	.30
650 Jack Savage (R) and Todd Simmons (R)	.25
651 John Burkett (R) and Kirt Manwaring (R)	1.00
652 Dave Otto (R) and Walt Weiss (R)	1.25
653 Jeff King (R) and Randell Byers (R)	.30
654 Checklist No. 1	.08
655 Checklist No. 2	.08
656 Checklist No. 3	.08
657 Checklist No. 4	.08
658 Checklist No. 5	.08
659 Checklist No. 6	.08
660 Checklist No. 7	.08

1988 Fleer Traded Update.... Complete Set of 132 Cards—Value $15.00

This set updates the main 1988 card set with players who had changed teams during the season, and rookies. This set features Fleer's first card of Chris Sabo and Ricky Jordan. This set was packaged in a printed box and distributed primarily through card dealers. For the first time Fleer arranged the cards of its update set in alphabetical order, by team.

NO.	PLAYER	MINT	NO.	PLAYER	MINT	NO.	PLAYER	MINT	NO.	PLAYER	MINT
U1	Jose Bautista	.12	U34	Israel Sanchez	.12	U67	Mike Flanagan	.07	U100	Brian Holman	.30
U2	Jose Orsulak	.10	U35	Kurt Stillwelll	.15	U68	Todd Stottlemyre	.25	U101	Rex Hudler	.15
U3	Doug Sisk	.07	U36	Pat Tabler	.07	U69	David Wells	.15	U102	Jeff Parrett	.07
U4	Craig Worthington	.40	U37	Don August	.15	U70	Jose Alvarez	.15	U103	Nelson Santovenia	.30
U5	Mike Boddiker	.07	U38	Darryl Hamilton	.20	U71	Paul Runge	.07	U104	Kevin Elster	.15
U6	Rick Cerone	.07	U39	Jeff Leonard	.07	U72	Cesar Jimenez	.15	U105	Jeff Innis	.20
U7	Larry Parrish	.07	U40	Joey Meyer	.12	U73	Pete Smith	.15	U106	Mackey Sasser	.25
U8	Lee Smith	.07	U41	Allan Anderson	.07	U74	John Smoltz	1.25	U107	Phil Bradley	.07
U9	Mike Smithson	.07	U42	Brian Harper	.07	U75	Damon Berryhill	.25	U108	Danny Clay	.12
U10	John Trautwein	.12	U43	Tom Herr	.07	U76	Goose Gossage	.07	U109	Greg Harris	.07
U11	Sherman Corbett	.15	U44	Charlie Lea	.07	U77	Mark Grace	3.00	U110	Ricky Jordan (RR)	1.00
U12	Chili Davis	.10	U45	John Moses	.07	U78	Darrin Jackson	.15	U111	David Palmer	.07
U13	Jim Eppard	.15	U46	John Candelaria	.10	U79	Vance Law	.07	U112	Jim Gott	.07
U14	Bryan Harvey	.25	U47	Jack Clark	.12	U80	Jeff Pico	.15	U113	Tommy Gregg	.15
U15	John Davis	.07	U48	Richard Dotson	.07	U81	Gary Varsho	.20	U114	Barry Jones	.07
U16	Dave Gallagher	.30	U49	Al Leiter	.15	U82	Tim Birtsas	.07	U115	Randy Miligan	.50
U17	Ricky Horton	.07	U50	Rafael Santana	.07	U83	Rob Dibble	.75	U116	Luis Alicea	.15
U18	Dan Pasqua	.07	U51	Dons Slaught	.07	U84	Danny Jackson	.20	U117	Tom Brunansky	.15
U19	Melido Perez	.07	U52	Todd Burns	.20	U85	Paul O'Neill	.12	U118	John Costello	.15
U20	Jose Segura	.12	U53	Dave Henderson	.07	U86	Jose Rijo	.07	U119	Jose DeLeon	.07
U21	Andy Allanson	.07	U54	Doug Jennings	.20	U87	Chris Sabo (RR)	2.00	U120	Bob Horner	.07
U22	John Perlman	.07	U55	Dave Parker	.20	U88	John Fishel	.20	U121	Scott Terry	.15
U23	Domingo Ramos	.07	U56	Walt Weiss	.60	U89	Craig Biggio	.12	U122	Roberto Alomar (RR)	1.50
U24	Rick Rodriquez	.07	U57	Bob Welch	.07	U90	Terry Puhl	.07	U123	Dave Leiper	.07
U25	Willie Upshaw	.10	U58	Henry Cotto	.07	U91	Rafael Ramirez	.07	U124	Keith Moreland	.07
U26	Phil Gibson	.12	U59	Mario Diaz	.07	U92	Louie Meadows	.15	U125	Mark Parent	.15
U27	Don Heinkel	.15	U60	Mike Jackson	.07	U93	Kirk Gibson	.25	U126	Dennis Rasmussen	.07
U28	Ray Knight	.07	U61	Bill Swift	.07	U94	Alfredo Griffin	.07	U127	Randy Bockus	.07
U29	Gary Pettis	.07	U62	Jose Cecena	.12	U95	Jay Howell	.12	U128	Brett Butler	.07
U30	Luis Salazar	.07	U63	Ray Haywad	.15	U96	Jesse Orosco	.07	U129	Donnell Nixon	.07
U31	Mike MacFarlane	.15	U64	Jim Steels	.12	U97	Alejandro Pena	.07	U130	Ernest Riles	.07
U32	Jeff Montgomery	.15	U65	Pat Borders	.30	U98	Tracy Woodson	.15	U131	Roger Samuels	.15
U33	Ted Power	.07	U66	Sil Campusano	.15	U99	John Dopson	.25	U132	Checklist	.07

1989 Fleer.... Complete Set of 660 Cards—Value $35.00

Features the rookie cards of Gary Sheffield, Tom Gordon, Sandy Alomar, Jr. and Ken Griffey, Jr. A new feature on the back is a comparison of each player's statistics before and after the All-Star break.

NO.	PLAYER	MINT	NO.	PLAYER	MINT	NO.	PLAYER	MINT	NO.	PLAYER	MINT
OAKLAND A'S			8	Mike Gallego	.05	16	Carney Lansford	.08	24	Walt Weiss	.20
1	Don Baylor	.08	9	Ron Hassey	.05	17	Mark McGwire	.60	25	Bob Welch	.08
2	Lance Blankenship (R)	.25	10	Dave Henderson	.05	18	Gene Nelson	.05	26	Curt Young	.05
3	Todd Burns (R)	.30	11	Rick Honeycutt	.05	19	Dave Parker	.10	**NEW YORK METS**		
4	Greg Cadaret	.10	12	Glenn Hubbard	.05	20	Eric Plunk	.05	27	Rick Aguilera	.05
5	Jose Canseco	1.25	13	Stan Javier	.05	21	Luis Polonia	.05	28	Wally Backman	.05
6	Storm Davis	.05	14	Doug Jennings (R)	.20	22	Terry Steinbach	.15	29	Mark Carreon	.05
7	Dennis Eckersley	.12	15	Felix Jose (R)	.40	23	Dave Stewart	.15	30	Gary Carter	.15

NO.	PLAYER	MINT
31	Dave Cone	.20
32	Ron Darling	.10
33	Len Dykstra	.20
34	Kevin Elster	.08
35	Sid Fernandez	.10
36	Dwight Gooden	.30
37	Keith Hernandez	.15
38	Gregg Jefferies	1.50
39	Howard Johnson	.20
40	Terry Leach	.05
41	Dave Magadan	.10
42	Bob McClure	.05
43	Roger McDowell	.05
44	Kevin McReynolds	.15
45	Keith Miller	.05
46	Randy Myers	.08
47	Bob Ojeda	.08
48	Mackey Sasser	.15
49	Darryl Strawberry	.50
50	Tim Teufel	.05
51	Dave West (R)	.20
52	Mookie Wilson	.08

LOS ANGELES DODGERS

NO.	PLAYER	MINT
53	Dave Anderson	.05
54	Tim Belcher	.15
55	Mike Davis	.05
56	Mike Devereaux	.05
57	Kirk Gibson	.15
58	Alfredo Griffin	.05
59	Chris Gwynn	.10
60	Jeff Hamilton	.05
61	Danny Heep	.15
62	Orel Hershiser	.20
63	Brian Holton	.05
64	Jay Howell	.08
65	Tim Leary	.10
66	Mike Marshall	.08
67	Ramon Martinez (R)	2.00
68	Jess Orosco	.05
69	Alejandro Pena	.08
70	Steve Sax	.12
71	Mike Scioscia	.05
72	Mike Sharperson	.05
73	John Shelby	.05
74	Fanklin Stubbs	.05
75	John Tudor	.05
76	Fernando Velenzuela	.12
77	Tracy Woodson	.10

BOSTON RED SOX

NO.	PLAYER	MINT
78	Marty Barrett	.05
79	Todd Benzinger	.15
80	Mike Boddicker	.08
81	Wade Boggs	.50
82	"Oil Can" Boyd	.08
83	Ellis Burks	.30
84	Rick Cerone	.05
85	Roger Clemens	.35
86	Steve Curry (R)	.15
87	Dwight Evans	.15
88	Wes Gardner	.05
89	Rich Gedman	.05
90	Mike Greenwell	.30
91	Bruce Hurst	.15
92	Dennis Lamp	.05
93	Spike Owen	.05
94	Larry Parrish	.10
95	Carlos Quintana (R)	.50
96	Jody Reed	.15
97	Jim Rice	.15
98	Kevin Romine	.25
98	K. Romine (error)	.50
99	Lee Smith	.08
100	Mike Smithson	.05
101	Bob Stanley	.05

MINNESOTA TWINS

NO.	PLAYER	MINT
102	Allan Anderson	.08
103	Keith Atherton	.05
104	Juan Berenguer	.05
105	Bert Blyleven	.15
106	Eric Bullock	.15
107	Randy Bush	.05
108	John Christensen	.05
109	Mark Davidson	.05
110	Gary Gaetti	.10
111	Greg Gagne	.05
112	Dan Gladden	.05
113	German Gonzalez (R)	.15
114	Brian Harper	.05
115	Tom Herr	.05

NO.	PLAYER	MINT
116	Kent Hrbek	.15
117	Gene Larken	.05
118	Tim Laudner	.05
119	Charlie Lea	.05
120	Steve Lombardozzi	.05
121	J. Moses (Phoenix)	.20
121	J. Moses (Tempe)	.75
122	Al Newman	.05
123	Mark Portugal	.05
124	Kirby Puckett	.30
125	Jeff Reardon	.08
126	Fred Toliver	.05
127	Frank Viola	.15

DETROIT TIGERS

NO.	PLAYER	MINT
128	Doyle Alexander	.05
129	Dave Bergman	.05
130	Tom Brookens	.15
130	T. Brookens (error)	1.50
131	Paul Gibson (R)	.15
132	Mike Heath	.20
132	M. Heath (error)	1.50
133	Don Heinkel (R)	.15
134	Mike Henneman	.05
135	Guillermo Hernandez	.05
136	Eric King	.05
137	Chet Lemon	.05
138	Fred Lynn	.08
139	Jack Morris	.10
140	Matt Nokes	.10
141	Gary Pettis	.05
142	Ted Power	.05
143	Jeff M. Robinson	.15
144	Luis Salazar	.05
145	Steve Searcy (R)	.20
146	Pat Sheridan	.05
147	Frank Tanana	.08
148	Alan Trammell	.12
149	Walt Terrell	.08
150	Jim Walewander	.10
151	Lou Whitaker	.08

CINCINNATI REDS

NO.	PLAYER	MINT
152	Tim Birtsas	.05
153	Tom Browning	.08
154	Keith Brown (R)	.15
155	Norm Charlton (R)	.35
156	Dave Concepcion	.05
157	Kal Daniels	.15
158	Eric Davis	.30
159	Bo Diaz	.05
160	Rob Dibble	.50
161	Nick Esasky	.10
162	John Franco	.08
163	Danny Jackson	.12
164	Barry Larkin	.20
165	Rob Murphy	.05
166	Paul O'Neil	.10
167	Jeff Reed	.10
168	Jose Rijo	.08
169	Ron Robinson	.05
170	Chris Sabo (R)	1.25
171	Candy Sierra (R)	.15
172	Van Snider (R)	.25
173	Jeff Treadway	.08
174	Frank Williams	.05
175	Herm Winningham	.05

MILWAUKEE BREWERS

NO.	PLAYER	MINT
176	Jim Adduci	.08
177	Don August	.10
178	Mike Birkbeck	.05
179	Chris Bosio	.05
180	Glenn Braggs	.05
181	Greg Brock	.05
182	Mark Clear	.05
183	Chuck Crim	.05
184	Rob Deer	.08
185	Tom Filer	.05
186	Jim Gantner	.05
187	Darryl Hamilton (R)	.20
188	Ted Higuera	.10
189	Odell Jones	.05
190	Jeffrey Leonard	.05
191	Joey Meyer	.05
192	Paul Mirabella	.05
193	Paul Molitor	.08
194	Charlie O'Brien	.08
195	Dan Plesac	.08
196	Gary Sheffield (R)	2.00
197	B.J. Surhoff	.08
198	Dale Sveum	.08

NO.	PLAYER	MINT
199	Bill Wegman	.05
200	Robin Yount	.15

PITTSBURGH PIRATES

NO.	PLAYER	MINT
201	Rafael Belliard	.05
202	Barry Bonds	.30
203	Bobby Bonilla	.25
204	Sid Bream	.05
205	Benny Distefano	.10
206	Doug Drabek	.10
207	Mike Dunne	.05
208	Felix Fermin	.05
209	Brian Fisher	.05
210	Jim Gott	.05
211	Bob Kipper	.05
212	Dave LaPoint	.05
213	Mike LaValliere	.05
214	Jose Lind	.05
215	Junior Ortiz	.05
216	Vincente Palacios	.05
217	Tom Prince	.10
218	Gary Redus	.05
219	R.J. Reynolds	.05
220	Jeff Robinson	.05
221	John Smiley	.08
222	Andy Van Slyke	.15
223	Bob Walk	.05
224	Glenn Wilson	.05

TORONTO BLUE JAYS

NO.	PLAYER	MINT
225	Jesse Barfield	.12
226	George Bell	.15
227	Pat Borders (R)	.25
228	John Cerutti	.05
229	Jim Clancy	.05
230	Mark Eichhorn	.05
231	Tony Fernandez	.10
232	Cecil Fielder	.40
233	Mike Flanagan	.05
234	Kelly Gruber	.20
235	Tom Henke	.05
236	Jimmy Key	.15
237	Rick Leach	.05
238	Manny Lee	.05
239	Nelson Liriano	.05
240	Fred McGriff	.25
241	Lloyd Moseby	.12
242	Rance Mulliniks	.05
243	Jeff Musselman	.05
244	Dave Stieb	.08
245	Todd Stottlemyre	.25
246	Duane Ward	.05
247	David Wells	.10
248	Ernie Whitt	.05

NEW YORK YANKEES

NO.	PLAYER	MINT
249	Luis Aguayo	.05
250	Neil Allen (N.Y.)	.20
250	Neil Allen (Fla.)	1.50
251	John Candelaria	.08
252	Jack Clark	.10
253	Richard Dotson	.08
254	Rickey Henderson	.40
255	Tommy John	.10
256	Roberto Kelly	.15
257	Al Leiter	.10
258	Don Mattingly	1.00
259	Dale Mohorcic	.05
260	Hal Morris (R)	1.00
261	Scott Nielsen	.05
262	Mike Pagliarulo	.10
263	Hipolito Peno (R)	.15
264	Ken Phelps	.05
265	Willie Randolph	.08
266	Rick Rhoden	.05
267	Dave Righetti	.10
268	Rafael Santana	.05
269	Steve Shields	.05
270	Joel Skinner	.05
271	Don Slaught	.05
272	Claudell Washington	.05
273	Gary Ward	.05
274	Dave Winfield	.15

KC ROYALS

NO.	PLAYER	MINT
275	Luis Aquino	.05
276	Floyd Bannister	.05
277	George Brett	.30
278	Bill Buckner	.08
279	Nick Capra (R)	.15
280	Jose DeJesus (R)	.20
281	Steve Farr	.05

NO.	PLAYER	MINT
282	Jerry Don Gleaton	.05
283	Mark Gubicza	.10
284	Tom Gordon (R)	.75
285	Bo Jackson	1.00
286	Charlie Leibrandt	.08
287	Mike MacFarlane (R)	.15
288	Jeff Montgomery	.05
289	Bill Pecota	.05
290	Jamie Quirk	.05
291	Bret Saberhagen	.12
292	Kevin Seitzer	.15
293	Kurt Stillwell	.05
294	Pat Tabler	.08
295	Danny Tartabull	.15
296	Gary Thurman	.05
297	Frank White	.05
298	Willie Wilson	.08

SAN DIEGO PADRES

NO.	PLAYER	MINT
299	Roberto Alomar	.75
300	Sandy Alomar Jr. (R)	2.00
301	Chris Brown	.08
302	Mike Brumley	.10
303	Mark Davis	.10
304	Mark Grant	.05
305	Tony Gwynn	.25
306	Greg W. Harris (R)	.20
307	Andy Hawkins	.05
308	Jimmy Jones	.05
309	John Kruk	.10
310	Dave Leiper	.05
311	Carmelo Martinez	.05
312	Lance McCullers	.08
313	Keith Moreland	.05
314	Dennis Rasmussen	.05
315	Randy Ready	.05
316	Benito Santiago	.20
317	Eric Show	.05
318	Todd Simmons	.05
319	Garry Templeton	.05
320	Dickie Thon	.05
321	Ed Whitson	.05
322	Marvell Wynne	.05

SF GIANTS

NO.	PLAYER	MINT
323	Mike Aldrete	.05
324	Bret Butler	.05
325	Will Clark	1.00
326	Kelly Downs	.05
327	Dave Dravecky	.05
328	Scott Garrelts	.05
329	Atlee Hammaker	.05
330	Charlie Hayes (R)	.30
331	Mike Krukow	.08
332	Craig Lefferts	.05
333	Candy Maldonado	.10
334	Kirt Manwaring	.05
335	Bob Melvin	.05
336	Kevin Mitchell	.45
337	Donell Nixon	.05
338	Tony Perezchica (R)	.15
339	Joe Price	.05
340	Rick Reuschel	.05
341	Ernest Riles	.05
342	Don Robinson	.05
343	Chris Speier	.05
344	Robby Thompson	.05
345	Jose Uribe	.08
346	Matt Williams	.50
347	Trevor Wilson (R)	.30

HOUSTON ASTROS

NO.	PLAYER	MINT
348	Juan Agosto	.05
349	Larry Anderson	.10
350	Alan Ashby	.05
351	Kevin Bass	.08
352	Buddy Bell	.08
353	Craig Biggio (R)	.75
354	Danny Darwin	.05
355	Glenn Davis	.15
356	Jim Deshaies	.05
357	Bill Doran	.08
358	John Fisher (R)	.20
359	Billy Hatcher	.05
360	Bob Knepper	.05
361	Louie Meadows (R)	.15
362	Dave Meads	.05
363	Jim Pankovits	.05
364	Terry Puhl	.05
365	Rafael Ramirez	.05

NO.	PLAYER	MINT
366	Craig Reynolds	.05
367	Mike Scott	.15
368	Nolan Ryan	.60
369	Dave Smith	.05
370	Gerald Young	.08

MONTREAL EXPOS

NO.	PLAYER	MINT
371	Hubie Brooks	.05
372	Tim Burke	.05
373	John Dopson (R)	.20
374	Mike Fitzgerald	.05
375	Tom Foley	.05
376	Andres Galarraga	.15
377	Neal Heaton	.05
378	Joe Hesketh	.05
379	Brian Holman (R)	.20
380	Rex Hudler	.10
381	Randy Johnson (R)	.50
382	Wallace Johnson	.05
383	Tracy Jones	.05
384	Dave Martinez	.05
385	Dennis Martinez	.05
386	Andy McGaffigan	.05
387	Otis Nixon	.05
388	Johnny Padres (R)	.15
389	Jeff Parrett	.08
390	Pascual Perez	.05
391	Tim Raines	.15
392	Luis Rivera	.05
393	Nelson Santovenia (R)	.20
394	Bryn Smith	.05
395	Tim Wallach	.08

CLEVELAND INDIANS

NO.	PLAYER	MINT
396	Andy Allanson	.05
397	Rod Allen (R)	.15
398	Scott Bailes	.05
399	Tom Candiotti	.08
400	Joe Carter	.15
401	Carmen Castillo	.05
402	Dave Clark	.10
403	John Farrell	.10
404	Julio Franco	.08
405	Don Gordon	.10
406	Mel Hall	.05
407	Brad Havens	.05
408	Brook Jacoby	.05
409	Doug Jones	.05
410	Jeff Kaiser (R)	.15
411	Luis Medina (R)	.30
412	Cory Snyder	.15
413	Greg Swindell	.10
414	Ron Tingley	.15
415	Willie Upshaw	.05
416	Ron Washington	.05
417	Rich Yett	.05

CHICAGO CUBS

NO.	PLAYER	MINT
418	Damon Berryhill	.10
419	Mike Bielecki	.05
420	Doug Dascenzo (R)	.25
421	Jody Davis	.05
422	Andre Dawson	.20
423	Frank Dipino	.05
424	Shawon Dunston	.15
425	"Goose" Gossage	.08
426	Mark Grace	1.50
427	Mike Harkey (R)	.40
428	Darrin Jackson	.08
429	Les Lancaster	.05
430	Vance Law	.05
431	Greg Maddux	.15
432	Jamie Moyer	.05
433	Al Nipper	.05
434	Rafael Palmeiro	.15
435	Pat Perry	.05
436	Jeff Pico (R)	.15
437	Ryne Sandberg	.30
438	Calvin Schiraldi	.05
439	Rick Sutcliffe	.10
440	Manny Trillo	.05
441	Gary Varsho	.20
442	Mitch Webster	.05

ST. LOUIS CARDINALS

NO.	PLAYER	MINT
443	Luis Alicea (R)	.15
444	Tom Brunansky	.08
445	Vince Coleman	.15
446	John Costello (R)	.15
447	Danny Cox	.05
448	Ken Dayley	.05
449	Jose Deleon	.05
450	Curt Ford	.05
451	Pedro Guerrero	.15
452	Bob Horner	.05
453	Tim Jones (R)	.15
454	Steve Lake	.05
455	Joe Magrane	.10
456	Greg Mathews	.05
457	Willie McGee	.08
458	Larry McWilliams	.05
459	Jose Oquendo	.05
460	Tony Pena	.08
461	Terry Pendleton	.08
462	Steve Peters (R)	.15
463	Ozzie Smith	.15
464	Scott Terry	.05
465	Denny Walling	.05
466	Todd Worrell	.08

CALIFORNIA ANGELS

NO.	PLAYER	MINT
467	Tony Armas	.05
468	Dante Bichette (R)	.35
469	Bob Boone	.05
470	Terry Clark (R)	.15
471	Stew Cliburn	.05
472	Mike Cook (R)	.15
473	Sherman Corbett (R)	.15
474	Chili Davis	.08
475	Brian Downing	.08
476	Jim Eppard	.05
477	Chuck Finley	.15
478	Willie Fraser	.05
479	Bryan Harvey (R)	.20
480	Jack Howell	.08
481	Wally Joyner	.15
482	Jack Lazorko	.05
483	Kirk McCaskill	.05
484	Mark McLemore	.05
485	Greg Minton	.05
486	Dan Petry	.05
487	Johnny Ray	.10
488	Dick Schofield	.05
489	Devon White	.10
490	Mike Witt	.08

CHICAGO WHITE SOX

NO.	PLAYER	MINT
491	Harold Baines	.10
492	Daryl Boston	.05
493	Ivan Calderon	.10
494	Mike Diaz	.05
495	Carlton Fisk	.15
496	Dave Gallagher (R)	.20
497	Ozzie Guillen	.08
498	Shawn Hillegas	.05
499	Lance Johnson	.05
500	Barry Jones	.05
501	Bill Long	.05
502	Steve Lyons	.05
503	Fred Manrique	.05
504	Jack McDowell	.10
505	Donn Pall	.15
506	Kelly Paris	.05
507	Dan Pasqua	.08
508	Ken Patterson (R)	.15
509	Melido Perez	.10
510	Jerry Reuss	.05
511	Mark Salas	.05
512	Bobby Thigpen	.05
513	Mike Woodard	.05

TEXAS RANGERS

NO.	PLAYER	MINT
514	Bob Brower	.05
515	Steve Buechele	.05
516	Jose Cecena (R)	.15
517	Cecil Espy	.05
518	Scott Fletcher	.05
519	Cecilio Guante	.05
520	Jose Guzman	.05
521	Ray Hayward	.05
522	Charlie Hough	.08
523	Pete Incaviglia	.10
524	Mike Jeffcoat	.05
525	Paul Kilgus	.05
526	Chad Kreuter (R)	.15
527	Jeff Kunkel	.05
528	Oddibe McDowell	.08
529	Pete O'Brien	.10
530	Geno Petralli	.05
531	Jeff Russell	.05
532	Ruben Sierra	.25
533	Mike Stanley	.05
534	Ed VandeBerg	.05
535	Curtis Wilkerson	.05
536	Mitch Williams	.05
537	Bobby Witt	.05

SEATTLE MARINERS

NO.	PLAYER	MINT
538	Steve Balboni	.05
539	Scott Bankhead	.05
540	Scott Bradley	.05
541	Mickey Brantley	.08
542	Jay Buhner	.20
543	Mike Campbell	.05
544	Darnell Coles	.05
545	Henry Cotto	.05
546	Alvin Davis	.08
547	Mario Diaz	.05
548	Ken Griffey Jr. (R)	10.00
549	Erik Hanson (R)	.60
550	Mike Jackson	.05
551	Mark Langston	.12
552	Edgar Martinez	.15
553	Bill McGuire (R)	.15
554	Mike Moore	.05
555	Jim Presley	.05
556	Rey Quinones	.05
557	Jerry Reed	.05
558	Harold Reynolds	.08
559	Mike Schooler (R)	.35
560	Bill Swift	.05
561	Dave Valle	.05

PHILADELPHIA PHILLIES

NO.	PLAYER	MINT
562	Steve Bedrosian	.08
563	Phil Bradley	.08
564	Don Carman	.05
565	Bob Dernier	.05
566	Marvin Freeman	.05
567	Todd Frohwirth	.05
568	Greg Gross	.05
569	Kevin Gross	.05
570	Greg Harris	.12
571	Von Hayes	.08
572	Chris James	.08
573	Steve Jeltz	.05
574	Ron Jones (R)	.25
575	Ricky Jordan (R)	.75
576	Mike Maddux	.05
577	David Palmer	.05
578	Lance Parrish	.10
579	Shane Rawley	.05
580	Bruce Ruffin	.05
581	Juan Samuel	.10
582	Mike Schmidt	.35
583	Kent Tekulve	.05
584	Milt Thompson	.05

ATLANTA BRAVES

NO.	PLAYER	MINT
585	Jose Alvarez (R)	.15
586	Paul Assenmacher	.05
587	Bruce Benedict	.05
588	Jeff Blauser	.05
589	Terry Blocker (R)	.15
590	Ron Gant	.30
591	Tom Glavine	.05
592	Tommy Gregg	.15
593	Albert Hall	.05
594	Dion James	.05
595	Rich Mahler	.05
596	Dale Murphy	.25
597	Gerald Perry	.12
598	Charlie Puleo	.05
599	Ted Simmons	.05
600	Pete Smith	.08
601	Zane Smith	.05
602	John Smoltz (R)	.50
603	Bruce Sutter	.08
604	Andres Thomas	.05
605	Ozzie Virgil	.05

BALTIMORE ORIOLES

NO.	PLAYER	MINT
606	Brady Anderson (R)	.25
607	Jeff Ballard	.05
608	Jose Bautista (R)	.15
609	Ken Gerhart	.05
610	Terry Kennedy	.05
611	Eddie Murray	.20
612	Carl Nichols	.10
613	Tom Niedenfuer	.05
614	Joe Orsulak	.05
615	Oswaldo Perraza (R)	.15
616	Billy Ripken obscenity blocked out in black	.75
616	Billy Ripken obscenity on bat	15.00
616	Billy Ripken obscenity blocked out in white	36.00
617	Cal Ripken Jr.	.15
618	Dave Schmidt	.35
619	Rich Schu	.05
620	Larry Sheets	.05
621	Doug Sisk	.05
622	Pete Stanicek	.05
623	Mickey Tettleton	.05
624	Jay Tibbs	.05
625	Jim Traber	.05
626	Mark Williamson	.05
627	Craig Worthington (R)	.40

SPECIAL CARDS

NO.	PLAYER	MINT
628	Speed/Power	.50
629	Pitcher Perfect	.08
630	Like Father-Like Son	.25
631	N.L. All Stars	.20
632	Homeruns-Coast to Coast	.25
633	Hot Corners-Hot Hitters	.20
634	Triple A's	.35
635	Dual Heat	.15
636	N.L. Pitching Power	.15
637	Cannon Arms	.15
638	Double Trouble	.15
639	Power Center	.20

No. 640 to 653—
Major League Prospects

NO.	PLAYER	MINT
640	S. Wilson (R)/C. Drew (R)	.15
641	K.Brown (R)/K. Reimer (R)	.35
642	B.Pounders (R)/J.Clark (R)	.15
643	M. Capel (R)/D. Hall	.15
644	J.Girardi (R)/R. Roomes (R)	.35
645	L. Harris (R)/M. Brown (R)	.50
646	L.Santos (R)/J.Campbell (R)	.25
647	R.Kramer (R)/M.Garcia (R)	.15
648	T.Lovullo (R)/R.Palacios (R)	.15
649	J. Corsi (R)/B. Milacki (R)	.25
650	G.Hall (R)/M.Rochford (R)	.15
651	T.Taylor (R)/V.Lovelace (R)	.15
652	K. Hill (R)/D. Cook (R)	.50
653	S. Service (R)/S.Turner (R)	.20
654	Checklist No. 1	.08
655	Checklist No. 2	.08
656	Checklist No. 3	.08
657	Checklist No. 4	.08
658	Checklist No. 5	.08
659	Checklist No. 6	.08
660	Checklist No. 7	.08

1989 Fleer Traded Update.... Complete Set of 132 Cards—Value $20.00

This set updates the main 1989 card set with players who had changed teams during the season, and rookies. This set features the first card of Jim Abbott, Greg Vaughn, Jerome Walton and Todd Zeile. The set was packaged in a printed box and distributed primarily through card hobby dealers.

NO.	PLAYER	MINT	NO.	PLAYER	MINT	NO.	PLAYER	MINT	NO.	PLAYER	MINT
U1	Phil Bradley	.06	U34	Frank Williams	.06	U67	Nolan Ryan	1.50	U100	Don Aase	.06
U2	Mike Devereaux	.08	U35	Kevin Appier	.35	U68	Francisco Cabrera	.40	U101	Barry Lyons	.06
U3	Steve Finley	.30	U36	Bob Boone	.06	U69	Junior Felix	1.00	U102	Juan Samuel	.06
U4	Kevin Hickey	.06	U37	Luis del los Santos	.15	U70	Al Leiter	.06	U103	Wally Whitehurst	.30
U5	Brian Holton	.10	U38	Jim Eisenreich	.10	U71	Alex Sanchez	.25	U104	Dennis Cook	.20
U6	Bob Milacki	.20	U39	Jaime Navarro	.30	U72	Geronimo Berroa	.08	U105	Lenny Dykstra	.25
U7	Randy Milligan	.15	U40	Bill Spiers	.35	U73	Derek Lilliquist	.20	U106	Charlie Hayes	.10
U8	John Dopson	.10	U41	Greg Vaughn	2.00	U74	Lonnie Smith	.08	U107	Tommy Herr	.06
U9	Nick Esasky	.15	U42	Randy Veres	.25	U75	Jeff Treadway	.06	U108	Ken Howell	.06
U10	Rob Murphy	.06	U43	Wally Backman	.06	U76	Paul Kilgus	.06	U109	John Kruk	.06
U11	Jim Abbott	1.50	U44	Shane Rawley	.06	U77	Lloyd McClendon	.10	U110	Roger McDowell	.06
U12	Bert Blyleven	.06	U45	Steve Balboni	.06	U78	Scott Sanderson	.06	U111	Terry Mulholland	.10
U13	Jeff Manto	.30	U46	Jesse Barfield	.06	U79	Dwight Smith	1.00	U112	Jeff Parrett	.06
U14	Bob McClure	.06	U47	Alvaro Espinosa	.25	U80	Jerome Walton	2.00	U113	Neal Heaton	.06
U15	Lance Parrish	.06	U48	Bob Geren	.25	U81	Mitch Williams	.25	U114	Jeff King	.12
U16	Lee Stevens	.75	U49	Mel Hall	.06	U82	Steve Wilson	.15	U115	Randy Kramer	.06
U17	Claudell Washington	.06	U50	Andy Hawkins	.06	U83	Todd Benzinger	.06	U116	Bill Landrum	.06
U18	Mark Davis	.06	U51	Hensley Muelens	.50	U84	Ken Griffey	.15	U117	Cris Carpenter	.10
U19	Eric King	.06	U52	Steve Sax	.20	U85	Rick Mahler	.06	U118	Frank DiPino	.06
U20	Ron Kittle	.06	U53	Deion Sanders	1.00	U86	Rolando Roomes	.15	U119	Ken Hill	.10
U21	Matt Murullo	.20	U54	Rickey Henderson	.60	U87	Scott Scudder	.25	U120	Dan Quisenberry	.06
U22	Steve Rosenberg	.10	U55	Mike Moore	.06	U88	Jim Clancy	.06	U121	Milt Thompson	.06
U23	Robin Ventura	1.00	U56	Tony Phillips	.06	U89	Rick Rhoden	.06	U122	Todd Zeile	2.00
U24	Keith Atherton	.06	U57	Greg Briley	.50	U90	Dan Schatzeder	.06	U123	Jack Clark	.12
U25	Joey Belle	.50	U58	Gene Harris	.25	U91	Mike Morgan	.06	U124	Bruce Hurst	.06
U26	Jerry Browne	.06	U59	Randy Johnson	.06	U92	Eddie Murray	.15	U125	Mark Parent	.06
U27	Felix Fermin	.06	U60	Jeffrey Leonard	.06	U93	Willie Randolph	.06	U126	Bip Roberts	.06
U28	Brad Komminsk	.06	U61	Dennis Powell	.06	U94	Ray Searage	.06	U127	Jeff Brantley	.25
U29	Pete O'Brien	.06	U62	Omar Vizquel	.25	U95	Mike Aldrete	.06	U128	Terry Kennedy	.06
U30	Mike Brumley	.06	U63	Kevin Brown	.20	U96	Kevin Gross	.06	U129	Mike LaCoss	.06
U31	Tracy Jones	.06	U64	Julio Franco	.10	U97	Mark Langston	.20	U130	Greg Litton	.25
U32	Mike Schwabe	.20	U65	Jamie Moyer	.06	U98	Spike Owen	.06	U131	Mike Schmidt	1.50
U33	Gary Ward	.06	U66	Rafael Palmeiro	.10	U99	Zane Smith	.06	U132	Checklist	.06

1990 Fleer.... Complete Set of 660 Cards—Value $30.00

A new feature is a 10 card subset "Players of the Decade." New features on the back are "Vital Signs" and some cards feature "Did You Know."

NO.	PLAYER	MINT	NO.	PLAYER	MINT	NO.	PLAYER	MINT	NO.	PLAYER	MINT
	OAKLAND A'S		8	Ron Hassey	.06	16	Mike Moore	.08	24	Curt Young	.06
1	Lance Blankenship	.08	9	Dave Burns	.08	17	Gene Nelson	.06		**CHICAGO CUBS**	
2	Todd Burns	.05	10	Rickey Henderson	.25	18	Dave Parker	.10	25	Paul Assenmacher	.06
3	Jose Canseco	.60	11	Rick Honeycutt	.06	19	Tony Phillips	.06	26	Damon Beryhill	.08
4	Jim Corsi	.06	12	Stan Javier	.06	20	Terry Steinbach	.15	27	Mike Bielecki	.06
5	Storm Davis	.06	13	Felix Jose	.10	21	Dave Stewart	.10	28	Kevin Blankenship	.08
6	Dennis Eckersley	.10	14	Carney Lansford	.08	22	Walt Weiss	.10	29	Andre Dawson	.12
7	Mike Gallego	.06	15	Mark McGwire	.25	23	Bob Welch	.06	30	Shawon Dunston	.08

168

NO.	PLAYER	MINT
31	Joe Girardi	.10
32	Mark Grace	.25
33	Mike Harkey	.10
34	Paul Kilgus	.06
35	Les Lancaster	.06
36	Vance Law	.06
37	Greg Maddux	.12
38	Lloyd McClendon	.06
39	Jeff Pico	.06
40	Ryne Sandberg	.25
41	Scott Sanderson	.06
42	Dwight Smith	.20
43	Rick Sutcliffe	.06
44	Jerome Walton	.50
45	Mitch Webster	.06
46	Curt Wilkerson	.06
47	Dean Wilkins (R)	.15
48	Mitch Williams	.08
49	Steve Wilson	.06

SAN FRANCISCO GIANTS

50	Steve Bedrosian	.06
51	Mike Benjamin (R)	.25
52	Jeff Brantley	.25
53	Brett Butler	.06
54	Will Clark	.50
55	Kelly Downs	.08
56	Scott Garrelts	.08
57	Atlee Hammaker	.06
58	Terry Kennedy	.06
59	Mike LaCoss	.06
60	Craig Lefferts	.06
61	Greg Litton	.20
62	Candy Maldonado	.06
63	Kirt Manwaring	.08
64	Randy McCament (R)	.15
65	Kevin Mitchell	.25
66	Donell Nixon	.06
67	Ken Okberkfell	.06
68	Rick Reuschel	.08
69	Ernest Riles	.06
70	Don Robinson	.06
71	Pat Sheridan	.06
72	Chris Speler	.06
73	Robby Thompson	.10
74	Jose Uribe	.06
75	Matt Williams	.20

TORONTO BLUE JAYS

76	George Bell	.10
77	Pat Borders	.06
78	John Cerutti	.06
79	Junior Felix	.40
80	Tony Fernandez	.10
81	Mike Flanagan	.06
82	Mauro Gozzo (R)	.20
83	Kelly Gruber	.15
84	Tom Henke	.06
85	Jimmy Key	.08
86	Manny Lee	.06
87	Nelson Liriano	.06
88	Lee Mazzilli	.06
89	Fred McGriff	.15
90	Lloyd Moseby	.08
91	Rance Mulliniks	.06
92	Alex Sanchez	.15
93	Dave Stieb	.06
94	Todd Stottlemyre	.10
95	Duane Ward	.06
96	David Wells	.06
97	Ernie Whitt	.06
98	Frank Wills	.06
99	Mookie Wilson	.08

KANSAS CITY ROYALS

100	Kevin Appier	.25
101	Luis Aquino	.06
102	Bob Boone	.06
103	George Brett	.15
104	Jose DeJesus	.06
105	Luis de los Santos	.06
106	Jim Eisenreich	.06
107	Steve Farr	.06
108	Tom Gordon	.20
109	Mark Gubicza	.06
110	Bo Jackson	.60
111	Terry Leach	.06

112	Charlie Leibrandt	.06
113	Rich Luecken (R)	.15
114	Mike Macfarlane	.06
115	Jeff Montgomery	.08
116	Bret Saberhagen	.12
117	Kevin Seitzer	.08
118	Kurt Stillwell	.06
119	Pat Tabler	.06
120	Danny Tartabull	.06
121	Gary Thurman	.06
122	Frank White	.06
123	Willie Wilson	.08
124	Matt Winters (R)	.15

CALIFORNIA ANGELS

125	Jim Abbott	.35
126	Tony Armas	.06
127	Dante Bichette	.08
128	Bert Blyleven	.08
129	Chill Davis	.06
130	Brian Downing	.06
131	Mike Fetters (R)	.15
132	Chuck Finley	.08
133	Willie Fraser	.06
134	Bryan Harvey	.06
135	Jack Howell	.06
136	Wally Joyner	.10
137	Jeff Manto	.20
138	Kirk McCaskill	.08
139	Bob McClure	.06
140	Greg Minton	.06
141	Lance Parrish	.08
142	Dan Petry	.06
143	Johnny Ray	.08
144	Dick Schofield	.06
145	Lee Stevens	.30
146	Claudell Washington	.06
147	Devon White	.10
148	Mike Witt	.08

SAN DIEGO PADRES

149	Roberto Alomar	.15
150	Sandy Alomar, Jr.	.30
151	Andy Benes	.35
152	Jack Clark	.08
153	Pat Clements	.06
154	Joey Cora	.06
155	Mark Davis	.08
156	Mark Grant	.06
157	Tony Gwynn	.15
158	Greg Harris	.06
159	Bruce Hurst	.06
160	Darrin Jackson	.06
161	Chris James	.06
162	Carmelo Martinez	.06
163	Mike Pagliarulo	.08
164	Mark Parent	.06
165	Dennis Rasmussen	.06
166	Bip Roberts	.06
167	Benito Santiago	.15
168	Calvin Schiraldi	.06
169	Eric Show	.06
170	Garry Templeton	.06
171	Ed Whitson	.06

BALTIMORE ORIOLES

172	Brady Anderson	.06
173	Jeff Ballard	.08
174	Phil Bradley	.06
175	Mike Devereaux	.08
176	Steve Finley	.15
177	Pete Harnisch	.08
178	Kevin Hickey	.10
179	Brian Holton	.06
180	Ben McDonald (R)	1.50
181	Bob Melvin	.06
182	Bob Milacki	.15
183	Randy Milligan	.10
184	Gregg Olson	.25
185	Joe Orsulak	.06
186	Bill Ripken	.08
187	Cal Ripken, Jr.	.15
188	Dave Schmidt	.06
189	Larry Sheets	.06
190	Mickey Tettleton	.06
191	Mark Thurmond	.06
192	Jay Tibbs	.06

193	Jim Traber	.06
194	Mark Williamson	.06
195	Craig Worthington	.10

NEW YORK METS

196	Don Aase	.06
197	Blaine Beatty (R)	.15
198	Mark Carreon	.06
199	Gary Carter	.10
200	David Cone	.10
201	Ron Darling	.10
202	Kevin Elster	.08
203	Sid Fernandez	.08
204	Dwight Gooden	.20
205	Keith Hernandez	.10
206	Jeff Innis	.10
207	Gregg Jefferies	.30
208	Howard Johnson	.10
209	Barry Lyons	.06
210	Dave Magadan	.06
211	Kevin McReynolds	.10
212	Jeff Musselman	.06
213	Randy Myers	.10
214	Bob Ojeda	.06
215	Juan Samuel	.08
216	Mackey Sasser	.06
217	Darryl Strawberry	.25
218	Tim Teufel	.06
219	Frank Viola	.10

HOUSTON ASTROS

220	Juan Agosto	.06
221	Larry Andersen	.06
222	Eric Anthony (R)	1.00
223	Kevin Bass	.06
224	Craig Biggio	.15
225	Ken Caminiti	.06
226	Jim Clancy	.06
227	Danny Darwin	.06
228	Glenn Davis	.10
229	Jim Deshaies	.06
230	Bill Doran	.06
231	Bob Forsch	.10
232	Brian Meyer	.08
233	Terry Puhl	.06
234	Rafael Ramirez	.06
235	Rick Rhoden	.06
236	Dan Schatzeder	.06
237	Mike Scott	.08
238	Dave Smith	.08
239	Alex Trevino	.06
240	Glenn Wilson	.06
241	Gerald Young	.06

ST. LOUIS CARDINALS

242	Tom Brunansky	.06
243	Cris Carpenter	.06
244	Alex Cole (R)	.06
245	Vince Coleman	1.00
246	John Costello	.12
247	Ken Dayley	.06
248	Jose DeLeon	.06
249	Frank Depino	.06
250	Pedro Guerrero	.06
251	Ken Hill	.10
252	Joe Magrane	.15
253	Willie McGee	.08
254	John Morris	.06
255	Jose Oquendo	.06
256	Tony Pena	.08
257	Terry Pendleton	.06
258	Ted Power	.06
259	Dan Quisenberry	.06
260	Ozzie Smith	.10
261	Scott Terry	.06
262	Milt Thompson	.06
263	Denny Walling	.06
264	Todd Worrell	.08
265	Todd Zeile	.75

BOSTON RED SOX

266	Marty Barrett	.06
267	Mike Boddicker	.08
268	Wade Boggs	.25
269	Ellis Burks	.15
270	Rick Cerone	.06
271	Roger Clemens	.25
272	John Dopson	.08

273	Nick Esasky	.08
274	Dwight Evans	.10
275	Wes Gardner	.08
276	Rich Gedman	.06
277	Mike Greenwell	.20
278	Danny Heep	.06
279	Eric Hetzel	.08
280	Dennis Lamp	.06
281	Rob Murphy	.06
282	Joe Price	.06
283	Carlos Quintana	.12
284	Jody Reed	.06
285	Luis Rivera	.06
286	Kevin Romine	.06
287	Lee Smith	.08
288	Mike Smithson	.06
289	Bob Stanley	.06

TEXAS RANGERS

290	Harold Baines	.08
291	Kevin Brown	.08
292	Steve Buechele	.06
293	Scott Coolbaugh (R)	.25
294	Jack Daugherty (R)	.15
295	Cecil Espy	.06
296	Julio Franco	.12
297	Juan Gonalez (R)	1.50
298	Cecilio Guante	.05
299	Drew Hall	.06
300	Charlie Hough	.06
301	Pete Incaviglia	.12
302	Mike Jeffcoat	.06
303	Chad Kreuter	.06
304	Jeff Kunkel	.06
305	Rich Leach	.06
306	Fred Manrique	.06
307	Jamie Moyer	.06
308	Rafael Palmeiro	.10
309	Geno Petralli	.06
310	Kevin Reimer	.08
311	Kenny Rogers	.15
312	Jeff Russell	.06
313	Nolan Ryan	.35
314	Ruben Sierra	.15
315	Bobby Witt	.08

MILWAUKEE BREWERS

316	Chris Bosio	.06
317	Glenn Braggs	.06
318	Greg Brock	.06
319	Chuck Crim	.06
320	Rob Deer	.06
321	Mike Felder	.06
322	Tom Filer	.06
323	Tony Fossas (R)	.15
324	Jim Gantner	.06
325	Darryl Hamilton	.06
326	Ted Higuera	.06
327	Mark Knudson	.10
328	Bill Krueger	.06
329	Tim McIntosh (R)	.20
330	Paul Molitor	.12
331	Jamie Navarro	.20
332	Charlie O'Brien	.06
333	Jeff Peterek (R)	.15
334	Dan Plesac	.06
335	Jerry Reuss	.06
336	Gary Sheffield	.30
337	Billy Spiers	.20
338	B.J. Surhoff	.06
339	Greg Vaughn	.75
340	Robin Yount	.15

MONTREAL EXPOS

341	Hubie Brooks	.06
342	Tim Burke	.06
343	Mike Fitzgerald	.06
344	Tom Foley	.06
345	Andres Galarraga	.15
346	Damaso Garcia	.06
347	Marquis Grissom (R)	.50
348	Kevin Gross	.06
349	Joe Hesketh	.06
350	Jeff Huson (R)	.15
351	Wallace Johnson	.06
352	Mark Langston	.10
353	Dave Martinez	.06

NO.	PLAYER	MINT
354	Dennis Martinez	.06
355	Andy McGaffigan	.06
356	Otis Nixon	.06
357	Spike Owen	.06
358	Pascual Perez	.06
359	Tim Raines	.15
360	Nelson Santovenia	.08
361	Bryn Smith	.06
362	Zane Smith	.06
363	Larry Walker (R)	.35
364	Tim Wallach	.06

MINNESOTA TWINS

NO.	PLAYER	MINT
365	Rick Aguilera	.06
366	Allan Anderson	.08
367	Wally Backman	.06
368	Doug Baker	.06
369	Juan Berenguer	.06
370	Randy Bush	.06
371	Carmen Castillo	.06
372	Mike Dyer (R)	.15
373	Gary Gaetti	.10
374	Greg Gagne	.06
375	Dan Gladden	.06
376	German Gonzalez	.06
377	Brian Harper	.06
378	Kent Hrbek	.10
379	Gene Larkin	.06
380	Tim Laudner	.06
381	John Moses	.06
382	Al Newman	.06
383	Kirby Puckett	.30
384	Shane Rawley	.06
385	Jeff Reardon	.08
386	Roy Smith	.06
387	Gary Wayne	.15
388	Dave West	.08

LOS ANGELES DODGERS

NO.	PLAYER	MINT
389	Tim Belcher	.08
390	Tim Crews	.06
391	Mike Davis	.06
392	Rick Dempsey	.06
393	Kirk Gibson	.10
394	Jose Gonzalez	.06
395	Alfredo Griffin	.08
396	Jeff Hamilton	.06
397	Lenny Harris	.06
398	Mickey Hatcher	.06
399	Orel Hershiser	.10
400	Jay Howell	.08
401	Mike Marshall	.08
402	Ramon Martinez	.35
403	Mike Morgan	.06
404	Eddie Murray	.15
405	Alejandro Pena	.08
406	Willie Randolph	.12
407	Mike Scioscia	.08
408	Ray Searage	.06
409	Fernando Valenzuela	.12
410	Jose Vizcaino (R)	.15
411	John Wetteland	.20

CINCINNATI REDS

NO.	PLAYER	MINT
412	Jack Armstrong	.15
413	Todd Benzinger	.08
414	Tim Birtsas	.06
415	Tom Browning	.06
416	Norm Charlton	.06
417	Eric Davis	.20
418	Rob Dibble	.12
419	John Franco	.08
420	Ken Griffey, Sr.	.20
421	Chris Hammond (R)	.30
422	Danny Jackson	.10
423	Barry Larkin	.15
424	Tim Leary	.08
425	Rick Mahler	.06
426	Joe Oliver	.15
427	Paul O'Neill	.06
428	Luis Quinones	.06
429	Jeff Reed	.06
430	Jose Rijo	.06
431	Ron Robinson	.06
432	Rolando Roomes	.08
433	Chris Sabo	.12
434	Scott Scudder	.20

NO.	PLAYER	MINT
435	Herm Winningham	.06

NEW YORK YANKEES

NO.	PLAYER	MINT
436	Steve Balboni	.06
437	Jesse Barfield	.06
438	Mike Blowers (R)	.20
439	Tom Brookens	.06
440	Greg Cadaret	.06
441	Alvaro Espinoza	.06
442	Bob Geren	.15
443	Lee Guetterman	.06
444	Mel Hall	.06
445	Andy Hawkins	.06
446	Roberto Kelly	.12
447	Don Mattingly	.50
448	Lance McCullers	.06
449	Hensley Meulens	.35
450	Dale Mohorcic	.06
451	Clay Parker	.06
452	Eric Plunk	.06
453	Dave Righetti	.12
454	Deion Sanders	.35
455	Steve Sax	.12
456	Don Slaught	.06
457	Walt Terrell	.06
458	Dave Winfield	.15

PITTSBURGH PIRATES

NO.	PLAYER	MINT
459	Jay Bell	.06
460	Rafael Belliard	.06
461	Barry Bonds	.25
462	Bobby Bonilla	.20
463	Sid Bream	.06
464	Benny Distefano	.06
465	Doug Drabek	.06
466	Jim Gott	.06
467	Billy Hatcher	.06
468	Neal Heaton	.06
469	Jeff King	.08
470	Bob Kipper	.06
471	Randy Kramer	.06
472	Bill Landrum	.06
473	Mike LaVailliere	.06
474	Jose Lind	.06
475	Junior Ortiz	.06
476	Gary Redus	.06
477	Rick Reed (R)	.15
478	R.J. Reynolds	.06
479	Jeff Robinson	.10
480	John Smiley	.08
481	Andy Van Slyke	.08
482	Bob Walk	.06

CLEVELAND INDIANS

NO.	PLAYER	MINT
483	Andy Allanson	.06
484	Scott Bailes	.06
485	Joey Belle	.25
486	Bud Black	.06
487	Jerry Browne	.06
488	Tom Candiotti	.06
489	Joe Carter	.12
490	David Clark	.06
491	John Farrell	.08
492	Felix Fermin	.06
493	Brook Jacoby	.06
494	Dion James	.06
495	Doug Jones	.06
496	Brad Komminsk	.06
497	Rod Nichols	.10
498	Pete O'Brien	.12
499	Steven Ofin (R)	.15
500	Jesse Orosco	.06
501	Joel Skinner	.06
502	Cory Snyder	.10
503	Greg Swindell	.12
504	Rich Yett	.06

SEATTLE MARINERS

NO.	PLAYER	MINT
505	Scott Bankhead	.06
506	Scott Bradley	.06
507	Greg Briley	.20
508	Jay Buhner	.08
509	Darnell Coles	.06
510	Keith Comstock	.06
511	Henry Cotto	.06
512	Alvin Davis	.12
513	Ken Griffey, Jr.	2.00
514	Erik Hanson	.08

NO.	PLAYER	MINT
515	Gene Harris	.15
516	Brian Holman	.06
517	Mike Jackson	.06
518	Randy Johnson	.10
519	Jeffrey Leonard	.06
520	Edgar Martinez	.08
521	Dennis Powell	.06
522	Jim Presley	.06
523	Jerry Reed	.06
524	Harold Reynolds	.06
525	Mike Schooler	.10
526	Bill Swift	.06
527	David Valle	.06
528	Omar Vizquel	.15

CHICAGO WHITE SOX

NO.	PLAYER	MINT
529	Ivan Calderon	.06
530	Carlton Fisk	.12
531	Scott Fletcher	.06
532	Dave Gallagher	.06
533	Ozzie Guillen	.08
534	Greg Hibbard (R)	.20
535	Shawn Hillegas	.06
536	Lance Johnson	.06
537	Eric King	.06
538	Ron Kittle	.06
539	Steve Lyons	.06
540	Carlos Martinez	.20
541	Tom McCarthy	.15
542	Matt Merullo	.15
543	Donn Pall	.06
544	Dan Pasqua	.06
545	Ken Patterson	.06
546	Melido Perez	.06
547	Steve Rosenberg	.06
548	Sammy Sosa (R)	.50
549	Bobby Thigpen	.06
550	Robin Ventura	.35
551	Greg Walker	.06

PHILADELPHIA PHILLIES

NO.	PLAYER	MINT
552	Don Carman	.06
553	Pat Combs	.15
554	Dennis Cook	.06
555	Darren Daulton	.06
556	Lenny Dykstra	.10
557	Curt Ford	.06
558	Charlie Hayes	.06
559	Von Hayes	.08
560	Tom Herr	.08
561	Ken Howell	.06
562	Steve Jeltz	.06
563	Ron Jones	.06
564	Ricky Jordan	.15
565	John Kruk	.06
566	Steve Lake	.06
567	Roger McDowell	.06
568	Terry Mulholland	.06
569	Dwayne Murphy	.06
570	Jeff Parrett	.06
571	Randy Ready	.06
572	Bruce Ruffin	.06
573	Dickie Thon	.06

ATLANTA BRAVES

NO.	PLAYER	MINT
574	Jose Alvarez	.06
575	Geronimo Berroa	.10
576	Jeff Blauser	.06
577	Joe Boever	.06
578	Marty Clary	.06
579	Jody Davis	.06
580	Mark Eichhorn	.06
581	Darrell Evans	.06
582	Ron Gant	.15
583	Tom Glavine	.12
584	Tommy Greene (R)	.25
585	Tommy Gregg	.06
586	David Justice (R)	3.00
587	Mark Lemke	.08
588	Derek Lilliquist	.10
589	Oddibe McDowell	.06
590	Ken Mercker (R)	.20
591	Dale Murphy	.15
592	Gerald Perry	.06
593	Lonnie Smith	.06
594	Pete Smith	.06
595	John Smoltz	.10

NO.	PLAYER	MINT
596	Mike Stanton (R)	.15
597	Andres Thomas	.06
598	Jeff Treadway	.06

DETROIT TIGERS

NO.	PLAYER	MINT
599	Doyle Alexander	.08
600	Dave Bergman	.06
601	Brian Dubois	.15
602	Paul Gibson	.06
603	Mike Heath	.06
604	Mike Henneman	.06
605	Guillermo Hernandez	.06
606	Shawn Holman (R)	.15
607	Tracy Jones	.06
608	Chet Lemon	.06
609	Fred Lynn	.08
610	Jack Morris	.08
611	Matt Nokes	.10
612	Gary Pettis	.06
613	Kevin Ritz (R)	.15
614	Jeff Robinson	.08
615	Steve Searcy	.08
616	Frank Tanana	.06
617	Alan Trammell	.15
618	Gary Ward	.06
619	Lou Whitaker	.08
620	Frank Williams	.06

PLAYERS OF THE DECADE

NO.	PLAYER	MINT
621	1980—G. Brett (correct)	.20
621	1980—G. Brett (error)	2.50
622	1981—F. Valenzuela	.10
623	1982—Dale Murphy	.15
624	1983—Cal Ripken, Jr.	.35
625	1984—Ryne Sandberg	.15
626	1985—Don Mattingly	.35
627	1986—Roger Clemens	.15
628	1987—George Bell	.10
629	1988—Jose Canseco	.50
630	1989—Will Clark	.35

SPECIAL CARDS

NO.	PLAYER	MINT
631	Game Savers	.15
632	Boston Igniters	.20
633	Starter & Stopper	.15
634	League's Best Shortstops	.15
635	Human Dynamos	.25
636	300 Strikeout Club	.20
637	Dynamic Duo	.25
638	A.L. All-Stars	.20
639	N.L. East Rivals	.25

No. 640 to 653—
Major League Prospects

NO.	PLAYER	MINT
640	R. Seanez (R) and C. Charland (R)	.15
641	G. Canale (R) and K. Mass (R)	3.00
642	K. Mann (R) and D. Hansen (R)	.25
643	G. Smith (R) and S. Tate (R)	.20
644	T. Drees (R) and D. Howitt (R)	.20
645	M. Roesler (R) and D. May (R)	.75
646	S. Hemond (R) and M. Gardner (R)	.35
647	J. Orlan (R) and S. Leuis (R)	.20
648	R. Monteleone (R) and D. Williams (R)	.20
649	M. Huff (R) and S. Frey (R)	.20
650	C. McElroy (R) and M. Alou (R)	.35
651	B. Rose (R) and M. Hartley (R)	.20
652	M. Kinzer (R) and W. Edwards (R)	.25
653	D. Deshields (R) and J. Grimsley (R)	.75
654	Checklist No. 1	.10
655	Checklist No. 2	.10
656	Checklist No. 3	.10
657	Checklist No. 4	.10
658	Checklist No. 5	.10
659	Checklist No. 6	.10
660	Checklist No. 7	.10

1990 Fleer Traded Update. . . . Complete Set of 132 Cards—Value $12.00

This set updates the main 1990 card set with players who had changed teams during the season, and rookies. The set features the first card of Alex Fernandez, Frank Thomas and John Olerud.

NO.	PLAYER	MINT	NO.	PLAYER	MINT	NO.	PLAYER	MINT	NO.	PLAYER	MINT
1	Steve Avery	.25	34	Chuck Carr	.10	67	Dave Johnson	.10	100	Larry Sheets	.05
2	Francisco Cabrera	.20	35	John Franco	.05	68	Curt Schilling	.10	101	Mark Davis	.05
3	Nick Esasky	.05	36	Todd Hundley	.20	69	David Segui	.40	102	Storm Davis	.05
4	Jim Kremers	.20	37	Julio Machado	.10	70	Tom Brunansky	.05	103	Gerald Perry	.05
5	Greg Olson	.20	38	Alejandro Pena	.05	71	Greg Harris	.05	104	Terry Shumpert	.20
6	Jim Presley	.05	39	Darren Reed	.15	72	Dana Kiecker	.25	105	Edgar Diaz	.15
7	Shawn Boskie	.15	40	Kelvin Torve	.15	73	Tim Naehring	.35	106	Dave Parker	.10
8	Joe Kraemer	.10	41	Darrel Akerfelds	.10	74	Tony Pena	.05	107	Tim Drummond	.10
9	Luis Salazar	.05	42	Jose DeJesus	.15	75	Jeff Reardon	.05	108	Junior Ortiz	.05
10	Hector Villanueva	.30	43	Dave Hollins	.20	76	Jerry Reed	.05	109	Park Pittman	.15
11	Glenn Braggs	.05	44	Carmelo Martinez	.05	77	Mark Eichhorn	.05	110	Kevin Tapani	.15
12	Mariano Duncan	.05	45	Brad Moore	.10	78	Mark Langston	.10	111	Oscar Azocar	.30
13	Billy Hatcher	.05	46	Dale Murphy	.12	79	John Orton	.05	112	Jim Leyritz	.20
14	Tim Layana	.15	47	Wally Backman	.05	80	Luis Polonia	.05	113	Kevin Maas	2.50
15	Hal Morris	.20	48	Stan Belinda	.10	81	Dave Winfield	.15	114	Alan Mills	.15
16	Javier Ortiz	.10	49	Bob Patterson	.05	82	Cliff Young	.15	115	Matt Nokes	.15
17	Dave Rohde	.15	50	Ted Power	.05	83	Wayne Edwards	.15	116	Pascual Perez	.05
18	Eric Yelding	.20	51	Don Slaught	.05	84	Alex Fernandez	1.25	117	Ozzie Canseco	.60
19	Hubie Brooks	.05	52	Geronimo Pena	.15	85	Craig Grebeck	.12	118	Scott Sanderson	.05
20	Kal Daniels	.05	53	Lee Smith	.05	86	Scott Radinsky	.15	119	Tino Martinez	.60
21	Dave Hansen	.05	54	John Tudor	.05	87	Frank Thomas	1.50	120	Jeff Schaefer	.10
22	Mike Hartley	.05	55	Joe Carter	.15	88	Beau Allred	.15	121	Matt Young	.05
23	Stan Javier	.05	56	Tom Howard	.25	89	Sandy Alomar, Jr.	.35	122	Brian Bohanon	.12
24	Jose Offerman	1.00	57	Craig Lefferts	.05	90	Carlos Baerga	.35	123	Jeff Huson	.05
25	Juan Samuel	.05	58	Rafael Valdez	.15	91	Kevin Bearse	.15	124	Ramon Manon	.10
26	Dennis Boyd	.05	59	Dave Anderson	.05	92	Chris James	.05	125	Gary Mielke	.10
27	Delino DeShields	.60	60	Kevin Bass	.05	93	Candy Maldonado	.05	126	Willie Blair	.15
28	Steve Frey	.05	61	John Burkett	.20	94	Jeff Manto	.05	127	Glenallen Hill	.10
29	Mark Gardner	.05	62	Gary Carter	.10	95	Cecil Fielder	.60	128	John Olerud	1.75
30	Chris Nabholz	.25	63	Rick Parker	.15	96	Travis Fryman	.50	129	Luis Sojo	.15
31	Bill Sampen	.30	64	Trevor Wilson	.10	97	Lloyd Moseby	.05	130	Mark Whiten	.40
32	Dave Schmidt	.05	65	Chris Hoiles	.35	98	Edwin Nunez	.05	131	Nolan Ryan	1.00
33	Daryl Boston	.05	66	Tim Hulett	.05	99	Tony Phillips	.05	132	CHECKLIST	.05

1991 Fleer. . . . Complete Set of 720 Cards—Value $25.00

The set was increased from 660 to 720 cards. Fleer introduced two new subsets—12 Pro-Vision sports art cards are in rack and wax packs, and 10 All Star cards are in cello packs. Fleer announced a new policy of not creating variations by reprinting minor errors.

NO.	PLAYER	MINT	NO.	PLAYER	MINT	NO.	PLAYER	MINT	NO.	PLAYER	MINT
OAKLAND A's			7	Mike Gallego	.05	14	Carney Lansford	.05	21	Jamie Quirk	.05
1	Tony Afenir (R)	.12	8	Ron Hassey	.05	15	Darren Lewis	.35	22	Willie Randolph	.05
2	Harold Baines	.05	9	Dave Henderson	.05	16	Willie McGee	.10	23	Scott Sanderson	.05
3	Lance Blankenship	.05	10	Rickey Henderson	.25	17	Mark McGwire	.25	24	Terry Steinbach	.05
4	Todd Burns	.05	11	Rick Honeycutt	.05	18	Mike Moore	.05	25	Dave Stewart	.15
5	Jose Canseco	.35	12	Doug Jennings	.05	19	Gene Nelson	.05	26	Walt Weiss	.05
6	Dennis Eckersley	.10	13	Joe Klink	.08	20	Dave Otto	.05	27	Bob Welch	.05

NO.	PLAYER	MINT
28	Curt Young	.05
PITTSBURGH PIRATES		
29	Wally Backman	.05
30	Stan Belinda	.05
31	Jay Bell	.05
32	Rafael Belliard	.05
33	Barry Bonds	.15
34	Bobby Bonilla	.15
35	Sid Bream	.05
36	Doug Drabek	.08
37	Carlos Garcia (R)	.12
38	Neal Heaton	.05
39	Jeff King	.05
40	Bob Kipper	.05
41	Bill Landrum	.05
42	Mike LaValliere	.05
43	Jose Lind	.05
44	Carmelo Martinez	.05
45	Bob Patterson	.05
46	Ted Power	.05
47	Gary Redus	.05
48	R. J. Reynolds	.05
49	Don Slaught	.05
50	John Smiley	.05
51	Zane Smith	.05
52	Randy Tomlin (R)	.12
53	Andy Van Slyke	.08
54	Bob Walk	.05
CINCINNATI REDS		
55	Jack Armstrong	.08
56	Todd Benzinger	.08
57	Glenn Braggs	.05
58	Keith Brown	.05
59	Tom Browning	.05
60	Norm Charlton	.05
61	Eric Davis	.15
62	Rob Dibble	.05
63	Bill Doran	.05
64	Mariano Duncan	.05
65	Chris Hammond	.05
66	Billy Hatcher	.05
67	Danny Jackson	.05
68	Barry Larkin	.10
69	Tim Layana	.05
70	Terry Lee (R)	.15
71	Rick Mahler	.05
72	Hal Morris	.12
73	Randy Myers	.05
74	Ron Oester	.05
75	Joe Oliver	.05
76	Paul O'Neill	.05
77	Luis Quinones	.05
78	Jeff Reed	.05
79	Jose Rijo	.05
80	Chris Sabo	.12
81	Scott Scudder	.05
82	Herm Winningham	.05
BOSTON RED SOX		
83	Larry Anderson	.05
84	Marty Barrett	.05
85	Mike Boddicker	.08
86	Wade Boggs	.20
87	Tom Bolton	.05
88	Tom Brunansky	.08
89	Ellis Burks	.10
90	Roger Clemens	.20
91	Scott Cooper	.15
92	John Dopson	.05
93	Dwight Evans	.05
94	Wes Gardner	.05
95	Jeff Gray (R)	.12
96	Mike Greenwell	.15
97	Greg Harris	.05
98	Daryl Irvine (R)	.12
99	Dana Klecker	.05
100	Randy Kutcher	.05
101	Dennis Lamp	.05
102	Mike Marshall	.05
103	John Marzano	.05
104	Rob Murphy	.05
105	Tim Naehring	.20
106	Tony Pena	.05
107	Phil Plantier (R)	.60

NO.	PLAYER	MINT
108	Carlos Quintana	.08
109	Jeff Reardon	.05
110	Jerry Reed	.05
111	Jody Reed	.05
112	Luis Rivera	.05
113	Kevin Romina	.05
CHICAGO WHITE SOX		
114	Phil Bradley	.05
115	Ivan Calderon	.05
116	Wayne Edwards	.05
117	Alex Fernandez	.75
118	Carlton Fisk	.10
119	Scott Fletcher	.05
120	Craig Grebeck	.05
121	Ozzie Guilen	.05
122	Greg Hibbard	.05
123	Lance Johnson	.05
124	Barry Jones	.05
125	Ron Karkovice	.05
126	Eric King	.05
127	Steve Lyons	.05
128	Carlos Martinez	.05
129	Jack McDowell	.05
130	Donn Pall	.05
131	Dan Pasqua	.05
132	Ken Patterson	.05
133	Melido Perez	.05
134	Adam Peterson	.05
135	Scott Radinsky	.05
136	Sammy Sosa	.15
137	Bobby Thigpen	.08
138	Frank Thomas	.75
139	Robin Ventura	.15
NEW YORK METS		
140	Daryl Boston	.05
141	Chuck Carr	.05
142	Mark Carreon	.05
143	David Cone	.08
144	Ron Darling	.05
145	Kevin Elster	.05
146	Sid Fernandez	.05
147	John Franco	.05
148	Dwight Gooden	.15
149	Tom Herr	.05
150	Todd Hundley	.10
151	Gregg Jefferies	.20
152	Howard Johnson	.08
153	Dave Madagan	.05
154	Kevin McReynolds	.08
155	Keith Miller	.05
156	Bob Ojeda	.05
157	Tom O'Malley	.05
158	Alejandro Pena	.05
159	Darren Reed	.05
160	Mackey Sasser	.05
161	Darryl Strawberry	.20
162	Tim Teufel	.05
163	Kelvin Torve	.05
164	Julio Valera	.10
165	Frank Viola	.10
166	Wally Whitehurst	.05
TORONTO BLUE JAYS		
167	Jim Acker	.05
168	Derek Bell	.25
169	George Bell	.08
170	Willie Blair	.05
171	Pat Borders	.05
172	John Cerutti	.05
173	Junior Felix	.10
174	Tony Fernandez	.05
175	Kelly Gruber	.08
176	Tom Henke	.05
177	Glenallen Hill	.05
178	Jimmy Key	.05
179	Manny Lee	.05
180	Fred McGriff	.10
181	Rance Mulliniks	.05
182	Greg Myers	.05
183	John Olerud	.30
184	Luis Solo	.05
185	Dave Stieb	.08
186	Todd Stottlemyre	.05
187	Duane Ward	.05
188	David Wells	.05

NO.	PLAYER	MINT
189	Mark Whiten	.30
190	Ken Williams	.05
191	Frank Wills	.05
192	Mookie Wilson	.05
LOS ANGELES DODGERS		
193	Don Aase	.05
194	Tim Belcher	.05
195	Hubie Brooks	.05
196	Dennis Cook	.05
197	Tim Crews	.05
198	Kal Daniels	.08
199	Kirk Gibson	.10
200	Jim Gott	.05
201	Alfredo Griffin	.05
202	Chris Gwynn	.05
203	Dave Hansen	.05
204	Lenny Harris	.05
205	Mike Hartley	.05
206	Mickey Hatcher	.05
207	Carlos Hernandez	.08
208	Orel Hershiser	.10
209	Jay Howell	.05
210	Mike Huff	.05
211	Stan Javier	.05
212	Ramon Martinez	.15
213	Mike Morgan	.05
214	Eddie Murray	.12
215	Jim Niediinger (R)	.15
216	Jose Offerman	.30
217	Jim Poole	.10
218	Juan Samuel	.05
219	Mike Scioscia	.05
220	Ray Searage	.05
221	Mike Sharperson	.05
222	Fernando Valenzuela	.10
223	Jose Vizcalno	.05
MONTREAL EXPOS		
224	Mike Aldrete	.05
225	Scott Anderson (R)	.12
226	Dennis Boyd	.05
227	Tim Burke	.05
228	Delino DeShields	.20
229	Mike Fitzgerald	.05
230	Tom Foley	.05
231	Steve Frey	.05
232	Andres Galarraga	.08
233	Mark Gardner	.05
234	Marquis Grissom	.12
235	Kevin Gross	.05
236	Drew Hall	.05
237	Dave Martinez	.05
238	Dennis Martinez	.05
239	Dale Mohorcic	.05
240	Chris Nabholz	.05
241	Otis Nixon	.05
242	Junior Noboa	.05
243	Spike Owen	.05
244	Tim Raines	.08
245	Mal Rojas	.05
246	Scott Ruskin	.08
247	Bill Sampen	.05
248	Nelson Santovenia	.05
249	Dave Schmidt	.05
250	Larry Walker	.08
251	Tim Wallach	.05
SAN FRANCISCO GIANTS		
252	Dave Anderson	.05
253	Kevin Bass	.05
254	Steve Bedrosian	.05
255	Jeff Brantley	.05
256	John Burkett	.05
257	Brett Butler	.05
258	Cary Carter	.10
259	Will Clark	.30
260	Steve Decker (R)	.35
261	Kelly Downs	.05
262	Scott Garreits	.05
263	Terry Kennedy	.05
264	Mike LaCoss	.05
265	Mark Leonard (R)	.25
266	Greg Litton	.05
267	Kevin Mitchell	.15
268	Randy O'Neal	.05
269	Rick Parker	.05

NO.	PLAYER	MINT
270	Rick Reuschel	.05
271	Ernest Riles	.05
272	Don Robinson	.05
273	Robby Thompson	.05
274	Mark Thurmond	.05
275	Jose Uribe	.05
276	Matt Williams	.10
277	Trevor Wilson	.05
TEXAS RANGERS		
278	Gerald Alexander (R)	.10
279	Brad Arnsberg	.05
280	Kevin Belcher (R)	.15
281	Joe Bitker (R)	.12
282	Kevin Brown	.05
283	Steve Buechele	.05
284	Jack Daugherty	.05
285	Julio Franco	.05
286	Juan Gonzalez	.20
287	Bill Haselman (R)	.12
288	Charlie Hough	.05
289	Jeff Huson	.05
290	Peter Incaviglia	.05
291	Mike Jeffcoat	.05
292	Jeff Kunkel	.05
293	Gary Mielke	.05
294	Jamie Moyer	.05
295	Rafael Palmeiro	.08
296	Geno Petralli	.05
297	Gary Pettis	.05
298	Kevin Reimer	.08
299	Kenny Rogers	.05
300	Jeff Russell	.05
301	John Russell	.05
302	Nolan Ryan	.25
303	Ruben Sierra	.10
304	Bobby Witt	.05
CALIFORNIA ANGELS		
305	Jim Abbott	.10
306	Kent Anderson	.05
307	Dante Bichette	.05
308	Bert Blyleven	.05
309	Chili Davis	.05
310	Brian Downing	.05
311	Mark Eichhorn	.05
312	Mike Fetters	.05
313	Chuck Finley	.05
314	Willie Fraser	.05
315	Bryan Harvey	.05
316	Donnie Hill	.05
317	Wally Joyner	.10
318	Mark Langston	.10
319	Kirk McCaskill	.05
320	John Orton	.05
321	Lance Parrish	.05
322	Luis Polonia	.05
323	Johnny Ray	.05
324	Bobby Rose	.05
325	Dick Schofield	.05
326	Rick Schu	.05
327	Lee Stevens	.12
328	Devon White	.05
329	Dave Winfield	.15
330	Cliff Young	.05
DETROIT TIGERS		
331	Dave Bergman	.05
332	Phil Clark (R)	.20
333	Darnell Coles	.05
334	Milt Cuyler	.15
335	Cecil Fielder	.25
336	Travis Fryman	.35
337	Paul Gibson	.05
338	Jerry Don Gleaton	.05
339	Mike Heath	.05
340	Mike Henneman	.05
341	Chet Lemon	.05
342	Lance McCullers	.05
343	Jack Morris	.08
344	Lloyd Moseby	.05
345	Edwin Nunez	.05
346	Clay Parker	.05
347	Dan Petry	.05
348	Tony Phillips	.05
349	Jeff Robinson	.05
350	Mark Salas	.05

NO.	PLAYER	MINT
351	Mike Schwabe	.05
352	Larry Sheets	.05
353	John Shelby	.05
354	Frank Tanana	.05
355	Alan Trammell	.08
356	Gary Ward	.05
357	Lou Whitaker	.05

CLEVELAND INDIANS

NO.	PLAYER	MINT
358	Beau Allred	.05
359	Sandy Alomar, Jr.	.15
360	Carlos Baerga	.15
361	Kevin Bearse	.05
362	Tom Brookens	.05
363	Jerry Browne	.05
364	Tom Candiotti	.05
365	Alex Cole	.15
366	John Farrell	.05
367	Felix Fermin	.05
368	Keith Hernandez	.05
369	Brook Jacoby	.05
370	Chris James	.05
371	Dion James	.05
372	Doug Jones	.05
373	Candy Maldonado	.05
374	Steve Olin	.05
375	Jesse Orosco	.05
376	Rudy Seanez	.05
377	Joel Skinner	.05
378	Cory Snyder	.05
379	Greg Swindell	.05
380	Sergio Valdez	.05
381	Mike Walker	.08
382	Colby Ward (R)	.12
383	Turner Ward (R)	.20
384	Mitch Webster	.05
385	Kevin Wickander	.05

PHILADELPHIA PHILLIES

NO.	PLAYER	MINT
386	Darrel Akerfelds	.05
387	Joe Boever	.05
388	Rod Booker	.05
389	Sid Campusano	.05
390	Don Carman	.05
391	Wes Chamberlain (R)	.25
392	Pat Combs	.05
393	Darren Daulton	.05
394	Jose DeJesus	.05
395	Len Dykstra	.10
396	Jason Grimsley	.05
397	Charlie Hayes	.05
398	Von Hayes	.05
399	David Hollins	.10
400	Ken Howell	.05
401	Ricky Jordan	.05
402	John Kruk	.05
403	Steve Lake	.05
404	Chuck Malone	.05
405	Roger McDowell	.05
406	Chuck McElroy	.05
407	Mickey Morandini	.15
408	Terry Mulholland	.05
409	Dale Murphy	.10
410	Randy Ready	.05
411	Bruce Ruffin	.05

CHICAGO CUBS

NO.	PLAYER	MINT
412	Dickie Thon	.05
413	Paul Assenmacher	.05
414	Damon Berryhill	.05
415	Mike Bielecki	.05
416	Shawn Boskie	.05
417	Dave Clark	.05
418	Doug Dascenzo	.05
419	Andre Dawson	.12
420	Shawon Dunston	.10
421	Joe Girardi	.05
422	Mark Grace	.15
423	Mike Harkey	.05
424	Les Lancaster	.05
425	Bill Long	.05
426	Greg Maddux	.05
427	Derrick May	.25
428	Jeff Pico	.05
429	Domingo Ramos	.05
430	Luis Salazar	.05
431	Ryne Sandberg	.15

NO.	PLAYER	MINT
432	Dwight Smith	.05
433	Greg Smith	.05
434	Rick Sutcliffe	.05
435	Gary Varsho	.05
436	Hector Villanueva	.10
437	Jerome Walton	.20
438	Curtis Wilkerson	.05
439	Mitch Williams	.05
440	Steve Wilson	.05
441	Marvell Wynne	.05

SEATTLE MARINERS

NO.	PLAYER	MINT
442	Scott Bankhead	.05
443	Scott Bradley	.05
444	Greg Briley	.05
445	Mike Brumley	.05
446	Jay Buhner	.05
447	Dave Burba (R)	.12
448	Henry Cotto	.05
449	Alvin Davis	.05
450	Ken Griffey Jr.	.75
451	Erik Hanson	.05
452	Gene Harris	.05
453	Brian Holman	.05
454	Mike Jackson	.05
455	Randy Johnson	.05
456	Jeffrey Leonard	.05
457	Edgar Martinez	.05
458	Tino Martinez	.25
459	Pete O'Brien	.05
460	Harold Reynolds	.05
461	Mike Schooler	.05
462	Bill Swift	.05
463	David Valle	.05
464	Omar Vizquel	.05
465	Matt Young	.05

BALTIMORE ORIOLES

NO.	PLAYER	MINT
466	Brady Anderson	.05
467	Jeff Ballard	.05
468	Juan Bell	.05
469	Mike Deveraux	.05
470	Steve Finley	.05
471	Dave Gallagher	.05
472	Leo Gomez	.35
473	Rene Gonzales	.05
474	Peter Harnisch	.05
475	Kevin Hickey	.05
476	Chris Holles	.10
477	Sam Horn	.05
478	Tim Hulett	.05
479	Dave Johnson	.05
480	Ron Kittle	.05
481	Ben McDonald	.30
482	Bob Melvin	.05
483	Bob Milacki	.05
484	Randy Milligan	.05
485	John Mitchell	.05
486	Gregg Olson	.10
487	Joe Orsulak	.05
488	Joe Price	.05
489	Bill Ripken	.05
490	Cal Ripken Jr.	.15
491	Curt Schilling	.05
492	David Segui	.20
493	Anthony Telford (R)	.12
494	Mickey Tettleton	.05
495	Mark Williamson	.05
496	Craig Worthington	.05

HOUSTON ASTROS

NO.	PLAYER	MINT
497	Juan Agosto	.05
498	Eric Anthony	.15
499	Craig Biggio	.05
500	Ken Caminiti	.05
501	Casey Candaele	.05
502	Andujar Cedeno	.40
503	Danny Darwin	.05
504	Mark Davidson	.05
505	Glenn Davis	.10
506	Jim Deshales	.05
507	Luis Gonzalez (R)	.12
508	Bill Gullickson	.05
509	Xavier Hernandez	.08
510	Brian Meyer	.05
511	Ken Oberkfell	.05
512	Mark Portugal	.05

NO.	PLAYER	MINT
513	Rafael Ramirez	.05
514	Karl Rhodes	.10
515	Mike Scott	.05
516	Mike Simms (R)	.10
517	Dave Smith	.05
518	Franklin Stubbs	.05
519	Glenn Wilson	.05
520	Eric Yelding	.05
521	Gerald Young	.05

SAN DIEGO PADRES

NO.	PLAYER	MINT
522	Shawn Abner	.05
523	Roberto Alomar	.08
524	Andy Benes	.10
525	Joe Carter	.08
526	Jack Clark	.10
527	Joey Cora	.05
528	Paul Farles (R)	.10
529	Tony Gwynn	.15
530	Atles Hammaker	.05
531	Greg Harris	.05
532	Thomas Howard	.05
533	Bruce Hurst	.05
534	Craig Lefferts	.05
535	Derek Lilliquist	.05
536	Fred Lynn	.05
537	Mike Pagliarulo	.05
538	Mark Parent	.05
539	Dennis Rasmussen	.05
540	Bip Roberts	.05
541	Richard Rodriguez	.05
542	Benito Santiago	.10
543	Calvin Schiraldi	.05
544	Eric Show	.05
545	Phil Stephenson	.05
546	Garry Templeton	.05
547	Ed Whitson	.05
548	Eddie Williams	.05

KANSAS CITY ROYALS

NO.	PLAYER	MINT
549	Kevin Appier	.05
550	Luis Aquino	.05
551	Bob Boone	.05
552	George Brett	.15
553	Jeff Conine (R)	.50
554	Steve Crawford	.05
555	Mark Davis	.05
556	Storm Davis	.05
557	Jim Elsenreich	.05
558	Steve Farr	.05
559	Tom Gordon	.10
560	Mark Gubicza	.05
561	Bo Jackson	.35
562	Mike Macfarlane	.05
563	Brian McRae (R)	.50
564	Jeff Montgomery	.05
565	Bill Pecota	.05
566	Gerald Perry	.05
567	Bret Saberhagen	.10
568	Jeff Schultz (R)	.12
569	Kevin Seltzer	.05
570	Terry Shumpert	.05
571	Kurt Stillwell	.05
572	Danny Tartabull	.05
573	Gary Thurman	.05
574	Frank White	.05
575	Willie Wilson	.05

MILWAUKEE BREWERS

NO.	PLAYER	MINT
576	Chris Boslo	.05
577	Greg Brock	.05
578	George Canale	.05
579	Chuck Crim	.05
580	Rob Deer	.05
581	Edgar Diaz	.05
582	Tom Edens (R)	.12
583	Mike Felder	.05
584	Jim Gantner	.05
585	Darryl Hamilton	.05
586	Ted Higuera	.05
587	Mark Knudson	.05
588	Bill Krueger	.05
589	Tim McIntosh	.08
590	Paul Mirabella	.05
591	Paul Molitor	.10
592	Jaime Navarro	.05
593	Dave Parker	.12

NO.	PLAYER	MINT
594	Dan Plesac	.05
595	Ron Robinson	.05
596	Gary Sheffield	.10
597	Bill Spiers	.05
598	B.J. Surhoff	.05
599	Greg Vaughn	.10
600	Randy Veres	.05
601	Robin Yount	.15

MINNESOTA TWINS

NO.	PLAYER	MINT
602	Rick Aguilera	.05
603	Allan Anderson	.05
604	Juan Berenguer	.05
605	Randy Bush	.05
606	Carmen Castillo	.05
607	Tim Drummond	.05
608	Scott Erickson	.15
609	Gary Gaetti	.05
610	Greg Gagne	.05
611	Dan Gladden	.05
612	Mark Guthrie	.10
613	Brian Harper	.05
614	Kent Hrbek	.10
615	Gene Larkin	.05
616	Terry Leach	.05
617	Nelson Liriano	.05
618	Shane Mack	.05
619	John Moses	.05
620	Pedro Munoz (R)	.15
621	Al Newman	.05
622	Junior Ortiz	.05
623	Kirby Puckett	.15
624	Roy Smith	.05
625	Kevin Tapani	.05
626	Gary Wayne	.05
627	David West	.05

ST. LOUIS CARDINALS

NO.	PLAYER	MINT
628	Cris Carpenter	.05
629	Vince Coleman	.10
630	Ken Dayley	.05
631	Jose DeLeon	.05
632	Frank DiPino	.05
633	Bernard Gilkey	.25
634	Pedro Guerrero	.10
635	Ken Hill	.05
636	Felix Jose	.05
637	Ray Lankford	.35
638	Joe Magrane	.05
639	Tom Niedenfuer	.05
640	Jose Oquendo	.05
641	Tom Pagnozzi	.05
642	Terry Pendleton	.05
643	Mike Perez (R)	.10
644	Bryn Smith	.05
645	Lee Smith	.05
646	Ozzie Smith	.10
647	Scott Terry	.05
648	Bob Tewksbury	.05
649	Milt Thompson	.05
650	John Tudor	.05
651	Denny Walling	.05
652	Craig Wilson (R)	.12
653	Todd Worrell	.05
654	Todd Zelle	.15

NEW YORK YANKEES

NO.	PLAYER	MINT
655	Oscar Azocar	.20
656	Steve Balboni	.05
657	Jesse Barfield	.05
658	Greg Cadaret	.05
659	Chuck Cary	.05
660	Rick Cerone	.05
661	David Elland	.05
662	Alvaro Espinoza	.05
663	Bob Geren	.05
664	Lee Guetterman	.05
665	Mel Hall	.05
666	Andy Hawkins	.05
667	Jimmy Jones	.05
668	Roberto Kelly	.10
669	Dave LaPoint	.05
670	Tim Leary	.05
671	Jim Leyritz	.10
672	Kevin Maas	.40
673	Don Mattingly	.30
674	Matt Nokes	.05

NO.	PLAYER	MINT
675	Pascual Perez	.05
676	Eric Plunk	.05
677	Dave Righetti	.05
678	Jeff Robinson	.05
679	Steve Sax	.05
680	Mike Witt	.05

ATLANTA BRAVES

NO.	PLAYER	MINT
681	Steve Avery	.15
682	Mike Bell (R)	.12
683	Jeff Blauser	.05
684	Francisco Cabrera	.05
685	Tony Castillo	.05
686	Marty Clary	.05
687	Nick Esasky	.05
688	Ron Gant	.12
689	Tom Glavine	.05

NO.	PLAYER	MINT
690	Mark Grant	.05
691	Tommy Gregg	.05
692	Dwayne Henry	.05
693	Dave Justice	.60
694	Jimmy Kremers	.05
695	Charlie Leibrandt	.05
696	Mark Lemke	.05
697	Oddible McMcDowell	.05
698	Greg Olson	.08
699	Jeff Parrett	.05
700	Jim Presley	.05
701	Victor Rosario (R)	.12
702	Lonnie Smith	.05
703	Pete Smith	.05
704	John Smoltz	.05

NO.	PLAYER	MINT
705	Mike Stanton	.05
706	Andres Thomas	.05
707	Jeff Treadway	.05
708	Jim Vatcher (R)	.15

SPECIAL CARDS

NO.	PLAYER	MINT
709	Home Run Kings— Sandberg, Fielder	.15
710	Second Generation Stars—Bonds, Griffey Jr.	.30
711	NLCS Team Leaders— Bonilla, Larkin	.08
712	Top Games Savers— Thigpen, Franco	.10
713	Chicago's 100 Club— Dawson, Sandberg	.10

NO.	PLAYER	MINT
714	Checklists—Athletics, Pirates, Reds, Red Sox	.07
715	Checklists—White Sox, Mets, Blue Jays, Dodgers	.07
716	Checklists—Giants, Rangers, Angels, Expos	.07
717	Checklists—Tigers, Indians, Phillies, Cubs	.07
718	Checklists—Mariners, Orioles, Astros, Padres	.07
719	Checklists—Royals, Brewers, Twins, Cardinals	.07
720	Checklists—Yankees, Braves, Super Stars	.07

1990 Leaf. . . . Series One Set of 264 Cards—Value $45.00;
Series Two Set of 264 Cards—Value $40.00

Leaf, the parent company of Donruss produced this limited printing, upscale baseball card set. There was an ultra gloss finish on front and back with 5-color photo clarity. The cards were issued late in the year—July (series one) and September (series two). Leaf previously issued baseball cards in 1948 and 1960. From 1985 to 1988 Leaf issued a set for the Canadian market. Features the rookie cards of Dave Justice, John Olerud, Frank Thomas and Kevin Maas.

JOHN ALFRED

BEN McDONALD

DAVE JUSTICE

FRANK THOMAS

KEVIN MAAS

NO.	PLAYER	MINT
	SERIES NO. 1	
1	The Leaf Set	.05
2	Mike Henneman	.05
3	Steve Bedrosian	.05
4	Mike Scott	.08
5	Allan Anderson	.05
6	Rick Sutcliffe	.08
7	Gregg Olson	.35
8	Kevin Elster	.05
9	Pete O'Brien	.05
10	Carlton Fisk	.20
11	Joe Magrane	.05
12	Roger Clemens	.35
13	Tom Glavine	.05
14	Tom Gordon	.30
15	Todd Benzinger	.05
16	Hubie Brooks	.08
17	Roberto Kelly	.20
18	Barry Larkin	.20
19	Mike Boddicker	.08
20	Roger McDowell	.05
21	Nolan Ryan	1.50
22	John Farrell	.05
23	Bruce Hurst	.05
24	Wally Joyner	.12
25	Greg Maddux	.05
26	Chris Bosio	.05
27	John Cerutti	.05
28	Tim Burke	.05
29	Dennis Eckersley	.08
30	Glenn Davis	.12
31	Jim Abbott	.40
32	Mike LaValliere	.05
33	Andres Thomas	.05
34	Lou Whitaker	.05
35	Alvin Davis	.05
36	Melido Perez	.05
37	Craig Biggio	.12
38	Rick Aguilera	.05
39	Pete Harnisch	.15
40	David Cone	.15
41	Scott Garrelts	.05
42	Jay Howell	.05
43	Eric King	.05
44	Pedro Guerrero	.15
45	Mike Bielecki	.05
46	Bob Boone	.05
47	Kevin Brown	.12
48	Jerry Browne	.05
49	Mike Scioscia	.05
50	Chuck Cary	.05
51	Wade Boggs	.30
52	Von Hayes	.05
53	Tony Fernandez	.05
54	Dennis Martinez	.05
55	Tom Candiotti	.05
56	Andy Benes	.40
57	Rob Dibble	.08
58	Chuck Crim	.05
59	John Smoltz	.15
60	Mike Heath	.05
61	Kevin Gross	.05

NO.	PLAYER	MINT
62	Mark McGwire	.50
63	Bert Blyleven	.05
64	Bob Walk	.05
65	Mickey Tettleton	.05
66	Sid Fernandez	.05
67	Terry Kennedy	.05
68	Fernando Valenzuela	.15
69	Don Mattingly	.60
70	Paul O'Neill	.05
71	Robin Yount	.30
72	Bret Saberhagen	.15
73	Geno Petralli	.05
74	Brook Jacoby	.05
75	Roberto Alomar	.15
76	Devon White	.05
77	Jose Lind	.05
78	Pat Combs	.12
79	Dave Stieb	.08
80	Tim Wallach	.05
81	Dave Stewart	.15
82	Eric Anthony (R)	.75
83	Randy Bush	.05
84	Checklist No. 1	.10
85	Jaime Navarro	.20
86	Tommy Gregg	.05
87	Frank Tanana	.05
88	Omar Vizquel	.15
89	Ivan Calderon	.05
90	Vince Coleman	.15
91	Barry Bonds	.35
92	Randy Milligan	.12
93	Frank Viola	.15
94	Matt Williams	.30
95	Alfredo Griffin	.05
96	Steve Sax	.05
97	Gary Gaetti	.05
98	Ryne Sandberg	.50
99	Danny Tartabull	.05
100	Rafael Palmeiro	.20
101	Jesse Orosco	.05
102	Garry Templeton	.05
103	Frank DiPino	.05
104	Tony Pena	.05
105	Dickie Thon	.05
106	Kelly Gruber	.15
107	Marquis Grissom (R)	.50
108	Jose Canseco	1.00
109	Mike Blowers (R)	.25
110	Tom Browning	.05
111	Greg Vaughn	.75
112	Oddibe McDowell	.05
113	Gary Ward	.05
114	Jay Buhner	.05
115	Eric Show	.05
116	Bryan Harvey	.05
117	Andy Van Slyke	.05
118	Jeff Ballard	.05
119	Barry Lyons	.05
120	Kevin Mitchell	.30
121	Mike Gallego	.05
122	Dave Smith	.05
123	Kirby Puckett	.30

NO.	PLAYER	MINT
124	Jerome Walton	.60
125	Bo Jackson	1.50
126	Harold Baines	.08
127	Scott Bankhead	.05
128	Ozzie Guillen	.05
129	Jose Oquendo	.05
130	John Dopson	.05
131	Charlie Hayes	.15
132	Fred McGriff	.15
133	Chet Lemon	.05
134	Gary Carter	.12
135	Rafael Ramirez	.05
136	Shane Mack	.05
137	Mark Grace	.50
138	Phil Bradley	.05
139	Dwight Gooden	.25
140	Harold Reynolds	.05
141	Scott Fletcher	.05
142	Ozzie Smith	.15
143	Mike Greenwell	.25
144	Pete Smith	.05
145	Mark Gubicza	.05
146	Chris Sabo	.25
147	Ramon Martinez	1.25
148	Tim Leary	.05
149	Randy Myers	.08
150	Jody Reed	.05
151	Bruce Ruffin	.05
152	Jeff Russell	.05
153	Doug Jones	.05
154	Tony Gwynn	.25
155	Mark Langston	.15
156	Mitch Williams	.05
157	Gary Sheffield	.35
158	Tom Henke	.05
159	Oil Can Boyd	.05
160	Rickey Henderson	.50
161	Bill Doran	.05
162	Chuck Finley	.05
163	Jeff King	.10
164	Nick Esasky	.05
165	Cecil Fielder	1.00
166	Dave Valle	.05
167	Robin Ventura	.40
168	Jim Deshaies	.05
169	Juan Berenguer	.05
170	Craig Worthington	.12
171	Gregg Jefferies	.35
172	Will Clark	.75
173	Kirk Gibson	.12
174	Checklist No. 2	.10
175	Bobby Thigpen	.08
176	John Tudor	.05
177	Andre Dawson	.25
178	George Brett	.30
179	Steve Buechele	.05
180	Joey Belle	.20
181	Eddie Murray	.20
182	Bob Geren	.15
183	Rob Murphy	.05
184	Tom Herr	.05
185	George Bell	.15

NO.	PLAYER	MINT
186	Spike Owen	.05
187	Cory Snyder	.05
188	Fred Lynn	.08
189	Eric Davis	.25
190	Dave Parker	.15
191	Jeff Blauser	.05
192	Matt Nokes	.05
193	Delino DeShields (R)	1.50
194	Scott Sanderson	.05
195	Lance Parrish	.25
196	Bobby Bonilla	.35
197	Cal Ripken, Jr.	.25
198	Kevin McReynolds	.15
199	Robby Thompson	.05
200	Tim Belcher	.05
201	Jesse Barfield	.08
202	Mariano Duncan	.05
203	Bill Spiers	.20
204	Frank White	.05
205	Julio Franco	.05
206	Greg Swindell	.05
207	Benito Santiago	.15
208	Johnny Ray	.05
209	Gary Redus	.05
210	Jeff Parrett	.05
211	Jimmy Key	.05
212	Tim Raines	.15
213	Carney Lansford	.05
214	Gerald Young	.05
215	Gene Larkin	.05
216	Dan Plesac	.05
217	Lonnie Smith	.05
218	Alan Trammell	.15
219	Jeffrey Leonard	.05
220	Sammy Sosa (R)	1.00
221	Todd Zeile	.75
222	Bill Landrum	.05
223	Mike Devereaux	.05
224	Mike Marshall	.05
225	Jose Uribe	.05
226	Juan Samuel	.05
227	Mel Hall	.05
228	Kent Hrbek	.15
229	Shawon Dunston	.15
230	Kevin Seitzer	.05
231	Pete Incaviglia	.08
232	Sandy Alomar	.50
233	Rip Roberts	.05
234	Scott Terry	.05
235	Dwight Evans	.08
236	Ricky Jordan	.15
237	John Olerud (R)	3.50
238	Zane Smith	.05
239	Walt Weiss	.05
240	Alvaro Espinoza	.05
241	Billy Hatcher	.05
242	Paul Molitor	.15
243	Dale Murphy	.15
244	Dave Bergman	.05
245	Ken Griffey, Jr.	5.00
246	Ed Whitson	.05
247	Kirk McCaskill	.05

NO. PLAYER	MINT
248 Jay Bell	.05
249 Ben McDonald (R)	4.00
250 Darryl Strawberry	.50
251 Brett Butler	.05
252 Terry Steinbach	.05
253 Ken Caminiti	.05
254 Dan Gladden	.05
255 Dwight Smith	.20
256 Kurt Stillwell	.05
257 Ruben Sierra	.20
258 Mike Schooler	.12
259 Lance Johnson	.05
260 Terry Pendleton	.05
261 Ellis Burks	.20
262 Len Dykstra	.15
263 Mookie Wilson	.08
264 Checklist No. 3	.20
SERIES NO. 2	
265 Ryan "No Hit King"	2.00
266 Brian DuBois (R)	.15
267 Don Robinson	.05
268 Glenn Wilson	.05
269 Kevin Tapani (R)	.60
270 Marvell Wynne	.05
271 Billy Ripken	.05
272 Howard Johnson	.15
273 Brian Holman	.12
274 Dan Pasqua	.05
275 Ken Dayley	.05
276 Jeff Reardon	.05
277 Jim Presley	.05
278 Jim Eisenreich	.05
279 Danny Jackson	.05
280 Orel Hershiser	.20
281 Andy Hawkins	.05
282 Jose Rijo	.05
283 Luis Rivera	.05
284 John Kruk	.08
285 Jeff Huson (R)	.15
286 Joel Skinner	.05
287 Jack Clark	.20
288 Chili Davis	.05
289 Joe Girardi	.15
290 B.J. Surhoff	.05
291 Luis Sojo (R)	.20
292 Tom Foley	.05
293 Mike Moore	.05
294 Ken Oberkfell	.05
295 Luis Polonia	.05
296 Doug Drabek	.12
297 Dave Justice (R)	7.50
298 Paul Gibson	.05
299 Edgar Martinez	.05
300 Frank Thomas (R)	5.00
301 Eric Yelding	.25
302 Greg Gagne	.05
303 Brad Komminsk	.05
304 Ron Darling	.08
305 Kevin Bass	.05
306 Jeff Hamilton	.05
307 Ron Karkovice	.05
308 Milt Thompson	.05
309 Mike Harkey	.40
310 Mel Stottlemyre	.15
311 Kenny Rogers	.15
312 Mitch Webster	.05
313 Kal Daniels	.15
314 Matt Nokes	.05
315 Dennis Lamp	.05
316 Ken Howell	.05

NO. PLAYER	MINT
317 Glenallen Hill	.15
318 Dave Martinez	.05
319 Chris James	.05
320 Mike Pagliarulo	.05
321 Hal Morris	.75
322 Rob Deer	.05
323 Greg Olson (R)	.25
324 Tony Phillips	.05
325 Larry Walker (R)	.75
326 Ron Hassey	.05
327 Jack Howell	.05
328 John Smiley	.05
329 Steve Finley	.25
330 Dave Magadan	.05
331 Greg Litton	.15
332 Mickey Hatcher	.05
333 Lee Guetterman	.05
334 Norm Charlton	.25
335 Edgar Diaz	.12
336 Willie Wilson	.05
337 Bobby Witt	.05
338 Candy Maldonado	.05
339 Craig Lefferts	.05
340 Dante Bichette	.15
341 Wally Backman	.05
342 Dennis Cook	.10
343 Pat Borders	.20
344 Wallace Johnson	.05
345 Willie Randolph	.08
346 Danny Darwin	.05
347 Al Newman	.05
348 Mark Knudson	.05
349 Joe Boever	.05
350 Larry Sheets	.05
351 Mike Jackson	.05
352 Wayne Edwards (R)	.25
353 Bernard Gilkey (R)	.50
354 Don Slaught	.05
355 Joe Orsulak	.05
356 John Franco	.05
357 Jeff Brantley	.25
358 Mike Morgan	.05
359 Deion Sanders	.50
360 Terry Leach	.05
361 Les Lancaster	.05
362 Storm Davis	.05
363 Scott Coolbaugh (R)	.25
364 Checklist No. 4	.10
365 Cecilio Guante	.05
366 Joey Cora	.05
367 Willie McGee	.15
368 Jerry Reed	.05
369 Darren Daulton	.05
370 Manny Lee	.05
371 Mark Gardner (R)	.25
372 Rick Honeycutt	.05
373 Steve Balboni	.05
374 Jack Armstrong	.20
375 Charlie O'Brien	.05
376 Ron Gant	.50
377 Lloyd Moseby	.05
378 Gene Harris	.12
379 Joe Carter	.15
380 Scott Bailes	.05
381 R.J. Reynolds	.05
382 Bob Melvin	.05
383 Tim Teufel	.05
384 John Burkett	.30
385 Felix Jose	.15
386 Larry Andersen	.05

NO. PLAYER	MINT
387 David West	.05
388 Luis Salazar	.05
389 Mike Macfarlane	.05
390 Charlie Hough	.08
391 Greg Briley	.15
392 Donn Pall	.05
393 Bryn Smith	.05
394 Carlos Quintana	.20
395 Steve Lake	.05
396 Mark Whiten (R)	.75
397 Edwin Nunez	.05
398 Rick Parker (R)	.12
399 Mark Portugal	.05
400 Roy Smith	.05
401 Hector Villanueva (R)	.30
402 Bob Milacki	.12
403 Alejandro Pena	.05
404 Scott Bradley	.05
405 Ron Kittle	.05
406 Bob Tewksbury	.05
407 Wes Gardner	.05
408 Ernie Whitt	.05
409 Terry Shumpert (R)	.20
410 Tim Layana (R)	.30
411 Chris Gwynn	.05
412 Jeff Robinson	.05
413 Scott Scudder	.25
414 Kevin Romine	.05
415 Jose DeJesus	.15
416 Mike Jeffcoat	.05
417 Rudy Seanez (R)	.15
418 Mike Dunne	.05
419 Dick Schofield	.05
420 Steve Wilson	.10
421 Bill Krueger	.05
422 Junior Felix	.50
423 Drew Hall	.05
424 Curt Young	.05
425 Franklin Stubbs	.05
426 Dave Winfield	.20
427 Rick Reed (R)	.15
428 Charlie Leibrandt	.05
429 Jeff Robinson	.05
430 Erik Hanson	.35
431 Barry Jones	.05
432 Alex Trevino	.05
433 John Moses	.05
434 Dave Johnson (R)	.15
435 Mackey Sasser	.05
436 Rick Leach	.05
437 Lenny Harris	.20
438 Carlos Martinez	.05
439 Rex Hudler	.05
440 Domingo Ramos	.05
441 Gerald Perry	.05
442 Jeff Russell	.05
443 Carlos Baerga (R)	.75
444 Checklist No. 5	.05
445 Stan Javier	.05
446 Kevin Maas (R)	4.00
447 Tom Brunansky	.08
448 Carmelo Martinez	.05
449 Willie Blair	.10
450 Andres Galarraga	.08
451 Bud Black	.05
452 Greg Harris	.15
453 Joe Oliver	.25
454 Greg Brock	.05
455 Jeff Treadway	.05
456 Lance McCullers	.05
457 Dave Schmidt	.05

NO. PLAYER	MINT
458 Todd Burns	.05
459 Max Venable	.05
460 Neal Heaton	.05
461 Mark Williamson	.05
462 Keith Miller	.05
463 Mike LaCoss	.05
464 Jose Offerman (R)	1.50
465 Jim Leyritz (R)	.30
466 Glenn Braggs	.05
467 Ron Robinson	.05
468 Mark Davis	.05
469 Gary Pettis	.05
470 Keith Hernandez	.05
471 Dennis Rasmussen	.05
472 Mark Eichhorn	.05
473 Ted Power	.05
474 Terry Mulholland	.05
475 Todd Stottlemyre	.05
476 Jerry Goff	.10
477 Gene Nelson	.05
478 Rich Gedman	.05
479 Brian Harper	.05
480 Mike Felder	.05
481 Steve Avery	.50
482 Jack Morris	.08
483 Randy Johnson	.15
484 Scott Radinsky (R)	.25
485 Jose DeLeon	.05
486 Stan Belinda (R)	.20
487 Brian Holton	.05
488 Mark Carreon	.05
489 Trevor Wilson	.20
490 Mike Sharperson	.05
491 Alan Mills (R)	.25
492 John Candelaria	.05
493 Paul Assenmacher	.05
494 Steve Crawford	.05
495 Brad Arnsberg (R)	.05
496 Sergio Valdez (R)	.15
497 Mark Parent	.05
498 Tom Pagnozzi	.05
499 Greg Harris	.05
500 Randy Ready	.05
501 Duane Ward	.05
502 Nelson Santovenia	.05
503 Joe Klink (R)	.12
504 Eric Plunk	.05
505 Jeff Reed	.05
506 Ted Higuera	.05
507 Joe Hesketh	.05
508 Dan Petry	.05
509 Matt Young	.05
510 Jerald Clark	.12
511 John Orton	.20
512 Scott Ruskin (R)	.30
513 Chris Hoiles (R)	.30
514 Daryl Boston	.05
515 Francisco Oliveras	.10
516 Ozzie Canseco	.75
517 Xavier Hernandez (R)	.15
518 Fred Manrique	.05
519 Shawn Boskie (R)	.35
520 Jeff Montgomery	.05
521 Jack Daugherty (R)	.15
522 Keith Comstock	.05
523 Greg Hibbard (R)	.25
524 Lee Smith	.05
525 Dana Kiecker (R)	.25
526 Darrel Akerfelds	.05
527 Greg Myers	.05
528 Checklist No. 6	.10

This was Score's *first* baseball card set. It was issued by the same company that produced the Sportsflic card sets. Features the rookie cards of Gregg Jefferies, Ellis Burks and Matt Williams.

NO.	PLAYER	MINT
1	Don Mattingly	1.25
2	Wade Boggs	.50
3	Tim Raines	.20
4	Andre Dawson	.20
5	Mark McGwire	1.00
6	Kevin Seitzer	.50
7	Wally Joyner	.30
8	Jesse Barfield	.20
9	Pedro Guerrero	.15
10	Eric Davis	.35
11	George Brett	.30
12	Ozzie Smith	.20
13	Rickey Henderson	.40
14	Jim Rice	.20
15	Matt Nokes (R)	.30
16	Mike Schmidt	.40
17	Dave Parker	.15
18	Eddie Murray	.20
19	Andres Galarraga	.15
20	Tony Fernandez	.08
21	Kevin McReynolds	.12
22	B.J. Surhoff	.15
23	Pat Tabler	.05
24	Kirby Puckett	.35
25	Benito Santiago	.40
26	Ryn Sandberg	.35
27	Kelly Downs	.05
28	Jose Cruz	.05
29	Pete O'Brien	.08
30	Mark Langston	.08
31	Lee Smith	.08
32	Juan Samuel	.10
33	Kevin Bass	.08
34	R.J. Reynolds	.08
35	Steve Sax	.15
36	John Kruk	.10
37	Alan Trammell	.15
38	Chris Bosio	.05
39	Brook Jacoby	.08
40	Willie McGee	.10
41	Dave Magadan	.15
42	Fred Lynn	.10
43	Kent Hrbek	.15
44	Brian Downing	.05
45	Jose Canseco	1.25
46	Jim Presley	.05
47	Mike Stanley	.10
48	Tony Pena	.05
49	David Cone	.50
50	Rick Sutcliffe	.10
51	Doug Drabeck	.15
52	Bill Doran	.05
53	Mike Scioscia	.05
54	Candy Maldonado	.08
55	Dave Winfield	.20
56	Lou Whitaker	.10
57	Tom Henke	.05
58	Ken Gerhardt	.08
59	Glenn Braggs	.08
60	Julio Franco	.08
61	Charlie Leibrandt	.05
62	Gary Gaetti	.15
63	Bob Boone	.05
64	Luis Polonia (R)	.20
65	Dwight Evans	.10
66	Phil Bradley	.08
67	Mike Boddicker	.05

NO.	PLAYER	MINT
68	Vince Coleman	.20
69	Howard Johnson	.15
70	Tim Wallach	.08
71	Keith Moreland	.05
72	Barry Larkin	.35
73	Alan Ashby	.05
74	Rick Rhoden	.05
75	Darrell Evans	.08
76	Dave Stieb	.08
77	Dan Plesac	.08
78	Will Clark	1.25
79	Frank White	.05
80	Joe Carter	.15
81	Mike Witt	.08
82	Terry Steinbach	.25
83	Alvin Davis	.08
84	Tom Herr	.05
85	Vance Law	.05
86	Kal Daniels	.20
87	Rick Honeycutt	.05
88	Alfredo Griffin	.05
89	Bret Saberhagen	.15
90	Bert Blyleven	.08
91	Jeff Reardon	.05
92	Cory Snyder	.15
93	Greg Walker	.08
94	Joe Magrane (R)	.35
95	Rob Deer	.10
96	Ray Knight	.05
97	Casey Candaele	.05
98	John Cerutti	.05
99	Buddy Bell	.10
100	Jack Clark	.20
101	Eric Bell (R)	.05
102	Willie Wilson	.10
103	Dave Schmidt	.05
104	Dennis Eckersley	.10
105	Don Sutton	.10
106	Danny Tartabull	.15
107	Fred McGriff	1.00
108	Les Straker (R)	.15
109	Lloyd Moseby	.15
110	Roger Clemens	.50
111	Glenn Hubbard	.05
112	Ken Williams (R)	.15
113	Ruben Sierra	.35
114	Stan Jefferson	.15
115	Milt Thompson	.05
116	Bobby Bonilla	.40
117	Wayne Tolleson	.05
118	Matt Williams (R)	2.50
119	Chet Lemon	.05
120	Dale Sveum	.05
121	Dennis Boyd	.05
122	Brett Butler	.05
123	Terry Kennedy	.05
124	Jack Howell	.05
125	Curt Young	.05
126	Dale Valle (error)	.30
126	Dave Valle (correct)	.12
127	Curt Wilkerson	.05
128	Tim Teufel	.05
129	Ozzie Virgil	.05
130	Brian Fisher	.05
131	Lance Parrish	.10
132	Tom Browning	.05
133	L. Anderson (error)	.25
133	L. Anderson (correct)	.05

NO.	PLAYER	MINT
134	B. Brenley (error)	.25
134	B. Brenley (correct)	.05
135	Mike Marshall	.10
136	Gerald Perry	.10
137	Bobby Meacham	.05
138	Larry Herndon	.05
139	Fred Manrique (R)	.15
140	Charlie Hough	.05
141	Ron Darling	.10
142	Herm Winningham	.05
143	Mike Diaz	.05
144	Mike Jackson (R)	.10
145	Denny Walling	.05
146	Rob Thompson	.05
147	Franklin Stubbs	.05
148	Albert Hall	.05
149	Bobby Witt	.10
150	Lance McCullers	.08
151	Scott Bradley	.05
152	Mark McLemore	.08
153	Tim Laudner	.05
154	Greg Swindell	.10
155	Marty Barrett	.10
156	Mike Heath	.05
157	Gary Ward	.05
158	Lee Mazilli (error)	.25
158	Lee Mazilli (correct)	.05
159	Tom Foley	.05
160	Robin Yount	.20
161	Steve Bedrosian	.08
162	Bob Walk	.05
163	Nick Esasky	.05
164	Ken Caminiti (R)	.15
165	Jose Uribe	.05
166	Dave Anderson	.05
167	Ed Whitson	.05
168	Ernie Whitt	.05
169	Cecil Cooper	.10
170	Mike Pagliarulo	.10
171	Pat Sheridan	.05
172	Chris Bando	.05
173	Lee Lacy	.05
174	Steve Lombardozzi	.05
175	Mike Greenwell	1.00
176	Greg Minton	.05
177	Moose Haas	.05
178	Mike Kingery	.05
179	Greg Harris	.05
180	Bo Jackson	1.50
181	Carmelo Martinez	.05
182	Alex Trevino	.05
183	Ron Oester	.05
184	Danny Darwin	.05
185	Mike Krukow	.05
186	Rafael Palmeiro	.75
187	Tim Burke	.05
188	Roger McDowell	.05
189	Garry Templeton	.05
190	Terry Pendleton	.05
191	Larry Parrish	.05
192	Rey Quinones	.05
193	Joaquin Andujar	.05
194	Tom Brunansky	.10
195	Donnie Moore	.05
196	Dan Pasqual	.10
197	Jim Gantner	.05
198	Mark Eichhorn	.05

NO.	PLAYER	MINT
199	John Grubb	.05
200	Bill Ripken (R)	.20
201	Sam Horn (R)	.20
202	Todd Worrell	.10
203	Terry Leach	.05
204	Garth Iorg	.05
205	Brian Dayett	.05
206	Bo Diaz	.05
207	Craig Reynolds	.05
208	Brian Holton	.10
209	Marvelle Wynne	.05
210	Dave Concepcion	.10
211	Mike Davis	.05
212	Devon White	.15
213	Mickey Brantley	.08
214	Greg Gagne	.05
215	Oddibe McDowell	.08
216	Jimmy Key	.10
217	Dave Bergman	.05
218	Calvin Schiraldi	.05
219	Larry Sheets	.10
220	Mike Easler	.05
221	Kurt Stillwell	.10
222	Chuck Jackson (R)	.15
223	Dave Martinez	.05
224	Tim Leary	.05
225	Steve Garvey	.20
226	Greg Mathews	.05
227	Doug Sisk	.05
228	Dave Henderson	.05
229	Jimmy Dwyer	.05
230	Larry Owen	.05
231	Andre Thornton	.05
232	Mark Salas	.05
233	Tom Brookens	.05
234	Greg Brock	.05
235	Rance Mulliniks	.05
236	Bob Brower	.08
237	Joe Niekro	.10
238	Scott Bankhead	.05
239	Doug DeCinces	.05
240	Tommy John	.10
241	Rich Gedman	.05
242	Ted Power	.05
243	Dave Meads (R)	.15
244	Jim Sundberg	.05
245	Ken Oberkfell	.05
246	Jimmy Jones	.10
247	Ken Landreaux	.05
248	Jose Oquendo	.05
249	John Mitchell (R)	.15
250	Don Baylor	.05
251	Scott Fletcher	.05
252	Al Newman	.05
253	Carney Lansford	.05
254	Johnny Ray	.08
255	Gary Pettis	.05
256	Ken Phelps	.05
257	Rick Leach	.05
258	Tim Stoddard	.05
259	Ed Romero	.05
260	Sid Bream	.05
261	T. Niedenfuer (error)	.25
261	T. Niedenfuer (cor.)	.05
262	Rick Dempsey	.05
263	Lonnie Smith	.05
264	Bob Forsch	.05

NO.	PLAYER	MINT
265	Barry Bonds	.40
266	Willie Randolph	.10
267	Mike Ramsey	.10
268	Don Slaught	.05
269	Mickey Tettleton	.05
270	Jerry Reuss	.05
271	Marc Sullivan	.05
272	Jim Morrison	.05
273	Steve Balboni	.05
274	Dick Schofield	.05
275	John Tudor	.10
276	Gene Larkin (R)	.20
277	Harold Reynolds	.05
278	Jerry Browne	.05
279	Willie Upshaw	.05
280	Ted Higuera	.15
281	Terry McGriff	.10
282	Terry Puhl	.05
283	Mark Wasinger (R)	.15
284	Luis Salazar	.05
285	Ted Simmons	.08
286	John Shelby	.05
287	John Smiley (R)	.25
288	Curt Ford	.05
289	Steve Crawford	.05
290	Dan Quisenberry	.08
291	Alan Wiggins	.05
292	Randy Bush	.05
293	John Candelaria	.08
294	Tony Phillips	.05
295	Mike Morgan	.05
296	Bill Wegman	.05
297	T. Francona (error)	.25
297	T. Francona (correct)	.05
298	Mickey Hatcher	.05
299	Andres Thomas	.05
300	Bob Stanley	.05
301	Alfredo Pedrique (R)	.12
302	Jim Lindeman	.10
303	Wally Backman	.05
304	Paul O'Neill	.15
305	Hubie Brooks	.08
306	Steve Buechele	.05
307	Bobby Thigpen	.15
308	George Hendrick	.05
309	John Moses	.05
310	Ron Guidry	.08
311	Bill Schroeder	.05
312	Jose Nunez (R)	.15
313	Bud Black	.05
314	Joe Sambito	.05
315	Scott McGregor	.05
316	Rafael Santana	.05
317	Frank Williams	.05
318	Mike Fitzgerald	.05
319	Rick Mahler	.05
320	Jim Gott	.05
321	Mariano Duncan	.05
322	Jose Guzman	.05
323	Lee Guetterman	.05
324	Dan Gladden	.05
325	Gary Carter	.15
326	Tracy Jones	.08
327	Floyd Youmans	.05
328	Bill Dawley	.05
329	Paul Noce (R)	.15
330	Angel Salazar	.05
331	Goose Gossage	.10
332	George Frazier	.05
333	Ruppert Jones	.05
334	Billy Jo Robidoux	.05
335	Mike Scott	.10
336	Randy Myers	.20
337	Bob Sebra	.05
338	Eric Show	.05
339	Mitch Williams	.05
340	Paul Molitor	.15
341	Gus Polidor	.05
342	Steve Trout	.05
343	Jerry Don Gleaton	.05
344	Bob Knepper	.05
345	Mitch Webster	.05
346	John Morris	.05
347	Andy Hawkins	.05
348	Dave Leiper	.05
349	Ernest Riles	.05
350	Dwight Gooden	.50
351	Dave Righetti	.10
352	Pat Dodson	.12
353	John Habyan	.08
354	Jim Deshaies	.05
355	Butch Wynegar	.05
356	Bryn Smith	.05
357	Matt Young	.05
358	Tom Pagnozzi (R)	.15
359	Floyd Rayford	.05
360	Darryl Strawberry	.40
361	Sal Butera	.05
362	Domingo Ramos	.05
363	Chris Brown	.10
364	Jose Gonzalez	.10
365	Dave Smith	.05
366	Andy McGaffigan	.05
367	Stan Javier	.05
368	Henry Cotto	.05
369	Mike Birkbeck	.05
370	Len Dykstra	.20
371	Dave Collins	.05
372	Spike Owen	.05
373	Geno Petralli	.05
374	Ron Karkovice	.05
375	Shane Rawley	.05
376	Dewayne Buice (R)	.15
377	Bill Pecota (R)	.15
378	Leon Durham	.05
379	Ed Olwine	.05
380	Bruce Hurst	.10
381	Bob McClure	.05
382	Mark Thurmond	.05
383	Buddy Biancalana	.05
384	Tim Conroy	.05
385	Tony Gwynn	.30
386	Greg Gross	.05
387	Barry Lyons (R)	.15
388	Mike Felder	.05
389	Pat Clements	.05
390	Ken Griffey	.08
391	Mark Davis	.05
392	Jose Rijo	.05
393	Mike Young	.05
394	Willie Fraser	.10
395	Dion James	.05
396	Steve Shields	.12
397	Randy St. Claire	.05
398	Danny Jackson	.10
399	Cecil Fielder	.35
400	Keith Hernandez	.15
401	Don Carman	.05
402	Chuck Crim (R)	.15
403	Rob Woodward	.05
404	Junior Ortiz	.05
405	Glenn Wilson	.05
406	Ken Howell	.05
407	Jeff Kunkel	.05
408	Jeff Reed	.05
409	Chris James	.15
410	Zane Smith	.05
411	Ken Dixon	.05
412	Rickey Horton	.05
413	Frank Dipino	.05
414	Shane Mack	.15
415	Danny Cox	.05
416	Andy Van Slyke	.12
417	Danny Heep	.05
418	John Cangelosi	.05
419	J. Christensen (err.)	.25
419	J. Christensen (cor.)	.05
420	Joey Cora (R)	.15
421	Mike Lavalliere	.05
422	Kelly Gruber	.25
423	Bruce Benedict	.05
424	Len Matuszek	.05
425	Kent Tekulve	.05
426	Rafael Ramirez	.05
427	Mike Flanagan	.05
428	Mike Gallego	.05
429	Juan Castillo	.05
430	Neal Heaton	.05
431	Phil Garner	.05
432	Mike Dunne	.10
433	Wallace Johnson	.05
434	Jack O'Connor	.05
435	Steve Jeltz	.05
436	Donnell Nixon (R)	.15
437	Jack Lazorko	.05
438	Keith Comstock (R)	.12
439	Jeff Robinson	.05
440	Graig Nettles	.10
441	Mel Hall	.05
442	Gerald Young (R)	.15
443	Gary Redus	.05
444	Charlie Moore	.05
445	Bill Madlock	.08
446	Mark Clear	.05
447	Greg Booker	.05
448	Rick Schu	.05
449	Ron Kittle	.10
450	Dale Murphy	.20
451	Bob Dernier	.05
452	Dale Mohorcic	.05
453	Rafael Belliard	.05
454	Charlie Puleo	.05
455	Dwayne Murphy	.05
456	Jim Eisenreich	.05
457	David Palmer	.05
458	Dave Stewart	.15
459	Pasqual Perez	.05
460	Glenn Davis	.15
461	Dan Petry	.08
462	Jim Winn	.05
463	Darrell Miller	.05
464	Mike Moore	.05
465	Mike LaCoss	.05
466	Steve Farr	.05
467	Jerry Mumphrey	.05
468	Kevin Gross	.05
469	Bruce Bochy	.05
470	Orel Hershiser	.20
471	Eric King	.05
472	Ellis Burks (R)	1.00
473	Darren Daulton	.05
474	Mookie Wilson	.05
475	Frank Viola	.15
476	Ron Robinson	.05
477	Bob Melvin	.05
478	Jeff Musselman	.12
479	Charlie Kerfeld	.05
480	Richard Dotson	.05
481	Kevin Mitchell	.35
482	Gary Roenicke	.05
483	Tim Flannery	.05
484	Rich Yett	.05
485	Pete Incaviglia	.15
486	Rick Cerone	.05
487	Tony Armas	.05
488	Jerry Reed	.05
489	Davey Lopes	.05
490	Frank Tanana	.05
491	Mike Loynd	.10
492	Bruce Ruffin	.05
493	Chris Speier	.05
494	Tom Hume	.05
495	Jesse Orosco	.05
496	Robbie Wine, Jr. (R)	.15
497	Jeff Montgomery (R)	.30
498	Jeff Dedmon	.05
499	Luis Aguayo	.05
500	Reggie Jackson #1	.20
501	Reggie Jackson #2	.20
502	Reggie Jackson #3	.20
503	Reggie Jackson #4	.20
504	Reggie Jackson #5	.20
505	Billy Hatcher	.10
506	Ed Lynch	.05
507	Willie Hernandez	.05
508	Jose DeLeon	.05
509	Joel Youngblood	.05
510	Bob Welch	.05
511	Steve Ontiveros	.05
512	Randy Ready	.05
513	Juan Nieves	.05
514	Jeff Russell	.05
515	Von Hayes	.10
516	Mark Gubicza	.05
517	Ken Dayley	.05
518	Don Aase	.05
519	Rick Reuschel	.05
520	Mike Henneman (R)	.20
521	Rick Aguilera	.05
522	Jay Howell	.05
523	Ed Correa	.05
524	Manny Trillo	.05
525	Kirk Gibson	.20
526	Wally Ritchie (R)	.15
527	Al Nipper	.05
528	Atlee Hammaker	.05
529	Shawon Dunston	.12
530	Jim Clancy	.05
531	Tom Paciorek	.05
532	Joel Skinner	.05
533	Scott Garrelts	.05
534	Tom O'Malley	.05
535	John Franco	.10
536	Paul Kilgus (R)	.15
537	Darrell Porter	.05
538	Walt Terrell	.05
539	Bill Long (R)	.12
540	George Bell	.15
541	Jeff Sellers	.05
542	Joe Boever (R)	.15
543	Steve Howe	.05
544	Scott Sanderson	.05
545	Jack Morris	.10
546	Todd Benzinger (R)	.30
547	Steve Henderson	.05
548	Eddie Milner	.05
549	Jeff Robinson (R)	.25
550	Cal Ripken, Jr.	.20
551	Jody Davis	.08
552	Kirk McCaskill	.05
553	Craig Lefferts	.05
554	Darnell Coles	.05
555	Phil Niekro	.15
556	Mike Aldrete	.05
557	Pat Perry	.05
558	Juan Agosto	.05
559	Rob Murphy	.05
560	Dennis Rasmussen	.05
561	Manny Lee	.05
562	Jeff Blauser (R)	.20
563	Bob Ojeda	.05
564	Dave Dravecky	.05
565	Gene Garber	.05
566	Ron Roenicke	.05
567	Tommy Hinzo (R)	.15
568	Eric Nolte (R)	.12
569	Ed Hearn	.05
570	Mark Davidson (R)	.15
571	Jim Walewander (R)	.15
572	Donnie Hill	.05
573	Jamie Moyer	.05
574	Ken Schrom	.05
575	Nolan Ryan	.50
576	Jim Acker	.05
577	Jamie Quirk	.05
578	Jay Alrich (R)	.12
579	Claudell Washington	.05
580	Jeff Leonard	.08
581	Carmen Castillo	.05
582	Darryl Boston	.05
583	Jeff DeWillis (R)	.12
584	John Marzano (R)	.10
585	Bill Gullickson	.05
586	Andy Allanson	.05
587	Lee Tunnell	.05
588	Gene Nelson	.05
589	Dave LaPoint	.05
590	Harold Baines	.10
591	Bill Buckner	.05
592	Carlton Fisk	.15
593	Rick Manning	.05
594	Doug Jones (R)	.25
595	Tom Candiotti	.08
596	Steve Lake	.05
597	Jose Lind (R)	.30
598	Ross Jones (R)	.15
599	Gary Matthews	.05
600	Fernando Valenzuela	.15

NO.	PLAYER	MINT
601	Dennis Martinez	.05
602	Les Lancaster (R)	.12
603	Ozzie Guillen	.05
604	Tony Bernazard	.05
605	Chili Davis	.05
606	Roy Smalley	.05
607	Ivan Calderon	.10
608	Jay Tibbs	.05
609	Guy Hoffman	.05
610	Doyle Alexander	.05
611	Mike Bielecki	.05
612	Shawn Hillegas (R)	.15
613	Keith Atherton	.05
614	Eric Plunk	.05
615	Sid Fernandez	.10
616	Dennis Lamp	.05
617	Dave Engle	.05
618	Harry Spilman	.05

NO.	PLAYER	MINT
619	Don Robinson	.05
620	John Farrell (R)	.20
621	Nelson Liriano (R)	.15
622	Floyd Bannister	.05
623	Randy Milligan (R)	.75
624	Kevin Elster	.15
625	Jody Reed (R)	.60
626	Shawn Abner	.15
627	Kurt Manwaring (R)	.15
628	Pete Stanicek (R)	.15
629	Rob Ducey (R)	.15
630	Steve Kiefer	.10
631	Gary Thurman (R)	.20
632	Darrel Akerfelds (R)	.15
633	Dave Clark	.15
634	Roberto Kelly (R)	.75
635	Keith Hughes (R)	.15

NO.	PLAYER	MINT
636	John Davis (R)	.15
637	Mike Devereaux (R)	.25
638	Tom Glavine (R)	.25
639	Keith Miller (R)	.20
640	Chris Gwynn (R)	.25
641	Tim Crews (R)	.15
642	Mackey Sasser (R)	.50
643	Vincente Palacios (R)	.15
644	Kevin Romine (R)	.15
645	Gregg Jefferies (R)	2.50
646	Jeff Treadway (R)	.25
647	Ronnie Gant (R)	1.50
648	M. McGwire/M. Nokes	.20
649	E. Davis/T. Raines	.15
650	D. Mattingly/J. Clark	.30
651	A. Trammell/T. Fernandez/ C. Ripken	.15

NO.	PLAYER	MINT
652	Highlights: Coleman 100 SB	.15
653	Highlights: Puckett 10 Hits	.20
654	Highlights: Santiago Hit Streak	.15
655	Highlights: Nieves No-Hitter	.10
656	Highlights: Bedrosian Saves	.10
657	Highlights: Schmidt 500 HR's	.20
658	Highlights: Mattingly HR's	.30
659	Highlights: McGwire HR's	.30
660	Highlights: Molitor Hit Streak	.35

1988 Score Traded & Rookie.... Complete Set of 110 Cards—Value $75.00

Updates the main 1988 card set with players who changed teams during the season, and rookies. Features the first Score card of Mark Grace, Chris Sabo, Ricky Jordan and Craig Biggio. The set was packaged in a printed box and distributed primarily through card hobby dealers.

NO.	PLAYER	MINT
1	Jack Clark	.25
2	Danny Jackson	.12
3	Brett Butler	.06
4	Kurt Stillwell	.20
5	Tom Brunansky	.10
6	Dennis Lamp	.06
7	Jose DeLeon	.06
8	Tom Herr	.06
9	Keith Moreland	.06
10	Kirk Gibson	.20
11	Bud Black	.06
12	Rafael Ramirez	.06
13	Luis Salazar	.06
14	Goose Gossage	.06
15	Bob Welch	.06
16	Vance Law	.06
17	Ray Knight	.06
18	Dan Quisenberry	.06
19	Don Slaught	.06
20	Lee Smith	.06
21	Rick Cerone	.06
22	Pat Tabler	.06
23	Larry McWilliams	.06
24	Rick Horton	.06
25	Graig Nettles	.06
26	Dan Petry	.06
27	Jose Rijo	.06
28	Chili Davis	.06

NO.	PLAYER	MINT
29	Dickie Thon	.06
30	Mackey Sasser	.50
31	Mickey Tettleton	.06
32	Rick Dempsey	.06
33	Ron Hassey	.06
34	Phil Bradley	.06
35	Jay Howell	.06
36	Bill Buckner	.06
37	Alfredo Griffin	.06
38	Gary Pettis	.06
39	Calvin Schiraldi	.06
40	John Candelaria	.06
41	Joe Orsulak	.06
42	Willie Upshaw	.06
43	Herm Winningham	.06
44	Ron Kittle	.06
45	Bob Dernier	.06
46	Steve Balboni	.06
47	Steve Shields	.06
48	Henry Cotto	.06
49	Dave Henderson	.06
50	Dave Parker	.25
51	Mike Young	.06
52	Mark Salas	.06
53	Mike Davis	.06
54	Rafael Santana	.06
55	Don Baylor	.06

NO.	PLAYER	MINT
56	Dan Pasqua	.06
57	Ernest Riles	.06
58	Glenn Hubbard	.06
59	Mike Smithson	.06
60	Richard Dotson	.06
61	Jerry Reuss	.06
62	Mike Jackson	.06
63	Floyd Bannister	.06
64	Jesse Orosco	.06
65	Larry Parrish	.06
66	Jeff Bittiger	.15
67	Ray Hayward	.10
68	Ricky Jordan (RR)	2.00
69	Tommy Gregg	.25
70	Brady Anderson	.75
71	Jeff Montgomery	.06
72	Darryl Hamilton	.40
73	Cecil Espy	.25
74	Greg Briley (RR)	2.00
75	Joey Meyer	.15
76	Mike Macfarlane	.35
77	Oswald Peraze	.15
78	Jack Armstrong (RR)	1.50
79	Don Heinkel	.15
80	Mark Grace (RR)	24.00
81	Steve Curry	.20
82	Damon Barryhill (RR)	.75

NO.	PLAYER	MINT
83	Steve Ellsworth	.15
84	Pete Smith	.20
85	Jack McDowell	.75
86	Rob Dibble (RR)	2.00
87	Bryan Harvey (RR)	.60
88	John Dopson	.40
89	Dave Gallagher	.50
90	Todd Stottlemyre	.50
91	Mike Schooler	1.00
92	Don Gordon	.15
93	Sil Campusano	.40
94	Jeff Pico	.15
95	Jay Buhner (RR)	1.50
96	Nelson Santovenia	.30
97	Al Leiter	.25
98	Luis Alicea	.20
99	Pat Borders	.75
100	Chris Sabo (RR)	7.50
101	Tim Belcher	.50
102	Walt Weiss (RR)	2.50
103	Craig Biggio (RR)	3.00
104	Don August	.20
105	Roberto Alomar (RR)	6.00
106	Todd Burns	.50
107	John Costello	.15
108	Melodo Perez	.35
109	Darrin Jackson	.20
110	Orestes Destrade	.25

1989 Score. . . . Complete Set of 660 Cards—Value $25.00

Features the rookie cards of Sandy Alomar, Jr., Ricky Jordan, Tom Gordon and Gary Sheffield. The set includes 9 Highlight cards and 32 Rookie Prospect cards.

NO. PLAYER	MINT
1 Jose Canseco	1.00
2 Andre Dawson	.15
3 Mark McGwire	.30
4 Benny Santiago	.10
5 Rick Reuschel	.05
6 Fred McGriff	.20
7 Kal Daniels	.15
8 Gary Gaetti	.10
9 Ellis Burks	.20
10 Darryl Strawberry	.30
11 Julio Franco	.08
12 Lloyd Moseby	.12
13 Jeff Pico (R)	.15
14 Johnny Ray	.10
15 Cal Ripken, Jr.	.20
16 Dick Schofield	.05
17 Mel Hall	.05
18 Bill Ripken	.05
19 Brook Jacoby	.05
20 Kirby Puckett	.25
21 Bill Doran	.08
22 Pete O'Brien	.10
23 Matt Nokes	.10
24 Brian Fisher	.05
25 Jack Clark	.10
26 Gary Petis	.05
27 Dave Valle	.05
28 Willie Wilson	.08
29 Curt Young	.05
30 Dale Murphy	.20
31 Barry Larkin	.15
32 Dave Stewart	.15
33 Mike LaValliere	.05
34 Glen Hubbard	.05
35 Ryne Sandberg	.20
36 Tony Pena	.08
37 Greg Walker	.05
38 Von Hayes	.08
39 Kevin Mitchell	.25
40 Tim Raines	.15
41 Keith Hernandez	.15
42 Keith Moreland	.05
43 Ruben Sierra	.15
44 Chet Lemon	.05
45 Willie Randolph	.08
46 Andy Allanson	.05
47 Candy Maldonado	.10
48 Sid Bream	.05
49 Denny Walling	.05
50 Dave Winfield	.15
51 Alvin Davis	.08
52 Cory Snyder	.10
53 Hubie Brooks	.05
54 Chili Davis	.08
55 Kevin Seitzer	.10
56 Jose Uribe	.05
57 Tony Fernandez	.10
58 Tim Teufel	.05
59 Oddibe McDowell	.08
60 Les Lancaster	.05
61 Billy Hatcher	.05
62 Dan Gladden	.05
63 Marty Barrett	.05
64 Nick Esasky	.10
65 Wally Joyner	.15
66 Mike Greenwell	.25
67 Ken Williams	.05
68 Bob Horner	.05

NO. PLAYER	MINT
69 Steve Sax	.12
70 Rickey Henderson	.30
71 Mitch Webster	.05
72 Rob Deer	.08
73 Jim Presley	.05
74 Albert Hall	.05
75 G. Brett (correct)	.35
75 G. Brett (error)	1.00
76 Brian Downing	.08
77 Dave Martinez	.05
78 Scott Fletcher	.05
79 Phil Bradley	.08
80 Ozzie Smith	.15
81 Larry Sheets	.05
82 Mike Aldrete	.05
83 Darnell Coles	.05
84 Len Dykstra	.15
85 Jim Rice	.12
86 Jeff Treadway	.05
87 Jose Lind	.05
88 Willie McGee	.08
89 Mickey Brantley	.08
90 Tony Gwynn	.20
91 R.J. Reynolds	.05
92 Milt Thompson	.05
93 Kevin McReynolds	.15
94 Eddie Murray	.15
95 Lance Parrish	.10
96 Ron Kittle	.08
97 Gerald Young	.08
98 Ernie Whitt	.05
99 Jeff Reed	.05
100 Don Mattingly	.75
101 Gerald Perry	.10
102 Vance Law	.05
103 John Shelby	.05
104 Chris Sabo (R)	1.00
105 Danny Tartabull	.15
106 Glenn Wilson	.05
107 Mark Davidson	.05
108 Dave Parker	.10
109 Eric Davis	.30
110 Alan Trammell	.10
111 Ozzie Virgil	.05
112 Frank Tanana	.08
113 Rafael Ramirez	.05
114 Dennis Martinez	.05
115 Jose DeLeon	.05
116 Bob Ojeda	.08
117 Doug Drabek	.10
118 Andy Hawkins	.05
119 Greg Maddux	.15
120 Cecil Fielder	.35
121 Mike Scioscia	.05
122 Dan Petry	.05
123 Terry Kennedy	.05
124 Kelly Downs	.05
125 Greg Gross	.05
126 Fred Lynn	.08
127 Barry Bonds	.30
128 Harold Baines	.10
129 Doyle Alexander	.05
130 Kevin Elster	.08
131 Mike Heath	.05
132 Teddy Higuera	.10
133 Charlie Leibrandt	.08
134 Tim Laudner	.05
135 Ray Knight (correct)	.15
135 Ray Knight (error)	.75

NO. PLAYER	MINT
136 Howard Johnson	.20
137 Terry Pendleton	.08
138 Andy McGaffigan	.05
139 Ken Oberkfell	.05
140 Butch Wynegar	.05
141 Rob Murphy	.05
142 Rich Renteria	.10
143 Jose Guzman	.05
144 Andres Galarraga	.15
145 Rick Horton	.05
146 Frank DiPino	.05
147 Glenn Braggs	.05
148 John Kruk	.15
149 Mike Schmidt	.30
150 Lee Smith	.08
151 Robin Yount	.15
152 Mark Eichhorn	.05
153 DeWayne Buice	.05
154 B.J. Surhoff	.08
155 Vince Coleman	.15
156 Tony Phillips	.05
157 Willie Fraser	.05
158 Lance McCullers	.08
159 Greg Gagne	.05
160 Jesse Barfield	.12
161 Mark Langston	.10
162 Kurt Stillwell	.05
163 Dion James	.05
164 Glenn Davis	.10
165 Walt Weiss	.20
166 Dave Concepcion	.05
167 Alfredo Griffin	.05
168 Don Heinkel (R)	.15
169 Luis Rivera	.10
170 Shane Rawley	.05
171 Darrell Evans	.05
172 Robby Thompson	.05
173 Jody Davis	.05
174 Andy Van Slyke	.12
175 Wade Boggs	.40
176 Garry Templeton	.05
177 Gary Redus	.05
178 Craig Lefferts	.05
179 Carney Lansford	.08
180 Ron Darling	.10
181 Kirk McCaskill	.05
182 Tony Armas	.05
183 Steve Farr	.05
184 Tom Brunansky	.08
185 Bryan Harvey (R)	.15
186 Mike Marshall	.08
187 Bo Diaz	.05
188 Willie Upshaw	.05
189 Mike Pagliarulo	.10
190 Mike Krukow	.08
191 Tommy Herr	.05
192 Jim Pankovits	.05
193 Dwight Evans	.15
194 Kelly Gruber	.15
195 Bobby Bonilla	.20
196 Wallace Johnson	.05
197 Dave Stieb	.08
198 Pat Borders (R)	.20
199 Rafael Palmeiro	.12
200 Doc Gooden	.30
201 Pete Incaviglia	.10
202 Chris James	.08
203 Marvell Wynne	.05

NO. PLAYER	MINT
204 Pat Sheridan	.05
205 Don Baylor	.08
206 Paul O'Neill	.10
207 Pete Smith	.12
208 Mark McLemore	.05
209 Henry Cotto	.05
210 Kirk Gibson	.15
211 Claudell Washington	.05
212 Randy Bush	.05
213 Joe Carter	.15
214 Bill Buckner	.08
215 Bert Blyleven	.15
216 Brett Butler	.05
217 Lee Mazzilli	.05
218 Spike Owen	.05
219 Bill Swift	.05
220 Tim Wallach	.08
221 David Cone	.15
222 Don Carman	.05
223 Rich Gossage	.08
224 Bob Walk	.05
225 Dave Righetti	.10
226 Kevin Bass	.08
227 Kevin Gross	.05
228 Tim Burke	.05
229 Rick Mahler	.05
230 Lou Whitaker	.08
231 Luis Alicea (R)	.15
232 Roberto Alomar	.50
233 Bob Boone	.05
234 Dickie Thon	.05
235 Shawon Dunston	.10
236 Pete Stanicek	.05
237 Craig Biggio (R)	.25
238 Dennis Boyd	.08
239 Tom Candiotti	.08
240 Gary Carter	.15
241 Mike Stanley	.05
242 Ken Phelps	.05
243 Chris Bosio	.05
244 Les Straker	.05
245 Dave Smith	.05
246 John Candelaria	.05
247 Joe Orsulak	.05
248 Storm Davis	.05
249 Floyd Bannister	.05
250 Jack Morris	.10
251 Bret Saberhagen	.15
252 Tom Niedenfuer	.05
253 Neal Heaton	.05
254 Eric Show	.05
255 Juan Samuel	.10
256 Dale Sveum	.08
257 Jim Gott	.05
258 Scott Garrelts	.05
259 Larry McWilliams	.05
260 Steve Bedrosian	.08
261 Jack Howell	.08
262 Jay Tibbs	.05
263 Jamie Moyer	.05
264 Doug Sisk	.05
265 Todd Worrell	.08
266 John Farrell	.10
267 Dave Collins	.05
268 Sid Fernandez	.10
269 Tom Brookens	.05
270 Shane Mack	.05
271 Paul Kilgus	.05

NO.	PLAYER	MINT
272	Chuck Crim	.05
273	Bob Knepper	.05
274	Mike Moore	.05
275	Guillermo Hernandez	.05
276	Dennis Eckersley	.10
277	Craig Nettles	.10
278	Rich Dotson	.08
279	Larry Herndon	.05
280	Gene Larkin	.05
281	Roger McDowell	.05
282	Greg Swindell	.10
283	Juan Agosto	.05
284	Jeff Robinson	.15
285	Mike Dunne	.05
286	Greg Mathews	.05
287	Kent Tekulve	.05
288	Jerry Mumphrey	.05
289	Jack McDowell	.15
290	Frank Viola	.15
291	Mark Gubicza	.10
292	Dave Schmidt	.05
293	Mike Henneman	.05
294	Jimmy Jones	.05
295	Charlie Hough	.08
296	Rafael Santana	.05
297	Chris Speier	.05
298	Mike Witt	.08
299	Pascual Perez	.05
300	Nolan Ryan	.50
301	Mitch Williams	.05
302	Mookie Wilson	.08
303	Mackey Sasser	.08
304	John Cerutti	.05
305	Jeff Reardon	.08
306	Randy Myers	.08
307	Greg Brock	.05
308	Bob Welch	.08
309	Jeff Robinson	.05
310	Harold Reynolds	.08
311	Jim Walewander	.05
312	Dave Magadan	.10
313	Jim Gantner	.05
314	Walt Terrell	.05
315	Wally Backman	.05
316	Luis Salazar	.05
317	Rick Rhoden	.05
318	Tom Henke	.05
319	Mike Macfarlane (R)	.15
320	Dan Plesac	.05
321	Calvin Schiraldi	.05
322	Stan Javier	.05
323	Devon White	.10
324	Scott Bradley	.05
325	Bruce Hurst	.15
326	Manny Lee	.05
327	Rick Aguilera	.05
328	Bruce Ruffin	.05
329	Ed Whitson	.05
330	Bo Jackson	.75
331	Ivan Calderon	.10
332	Mickey Hatcher	.05
333	Barry Jones	.05
334	Ron Hassey	.05
335	Bill Wegman	.05
336	Damon Berryhill	.15
337	Steve Ontiveros	.05
338	Dan Pasqua	.08
339	Bill Pecota	.05
340	Greg Cadaret	.08
341	Scott Bankhead	.05
342	Ron Guidry	.08
343	Danny Heep	.05
344	Bob Brower	.05
345	Rich Gedman	.05
346	Nelson Santovenia (R)	.15
347	George Bell	.15
348	Ted Power	.05
349	Mark Grant	.05
350	R. Clemens (correct)	.50
350	R. Clemens (error)	3.50
351	Bill Long	.05
352	Jay Bell	.10
353	Steve Balboni	.05

NO.	PLAYER	MINT
354	Bob Kipper	.05
355	Steve Jeltz	.05
356	Jesse Orosco	.05
357	Bob Dernier	.05
358	Mickey Tettleton	.05
359	Duane Ward	.05
360	Darrin Jackson	.12
361	Rey Quinones	.05
362	Mark Grace	1.00
363	Steve Lake	.05
364	Pat Perry	.05
365	Terry Steinbach	.12
366	Alan Ashby	.05
367	Jeff Montgomery	.05
368	Steve Buechele	.05
369	Chris Brown	.08
370	Orel Hershiser	.15
371	Todd Benzinger	.10
372	Ron Gant	.20
373	Paul Assenmacher	.05
374	Joey Meyer	.10
375	Neil Allen	.05
376	Mike Davis	.05
377	Jeff Parrett	.08
378	Jay Howell	.08
379	Rafael Belliard	.05
380	Luis Polonia	.05
381	Keith Atherton	.05
382	Kent Hrbek	.10
383	Bob Stanley	.05
384	Dave LaPoint	.05
385	Rance Mulliniks	.05
386	Melido Perez	.10
387	Doug Jones	.05
388	Steve Lyons	.05
389	Alejandro Pena	.08
390	Frank White	.05
391	Pat Tabler	.08
392	Eric Plunk	.05
393	Mike Maddux	.05
394	Allan Anderson	.08
395	Bob Brenly	.05
396	Rick Cerone	.05
397	Scott Terry	.05
398	Mike Jackson	.05
399	Bobby Thigpen	.05
400	Don Sutton	.10
401	Cecil Espy	.10
402	Junior Ortiz	.05
403	Mike Smithson	.05
404	Bud Black	.05
405	Tom Foley	.05
406	Andres Thomas	.05
407	Rick Sutcliffe	.10
408	Brian Harper	.05
409	John Smiley	.08
410	Juan Nieves	.05
411	Shawn Abner	.05
412	Wes Gardner	.05
413	Darren Daulton	.05
414	Juan Berenguer	.05
415	Charles Hudson	.08
416	Rick Honeycutt	.05
417	Greg Booker	.05
418	Tim Belcher	.20
419	Don August	.15
420	Dale Monorcic	.05
421	Steve Lombardozzi	.05
422	Atlee Hammaker	.05
423	Jerry Don Gleaton	.05
424	Scott Bailes	.05
425	Bruce Sutter	.08
426	Randy Ready	.05
427	Jerry Reed	.05
428	Bryn Smith	.05
429	Tim Leary	.10
430	Mark Clear	.05
431	Terry Leach	.05
432	John Moses	.05
433	Ozzie Guillen	.08
434	Gene Nelson	.05
435	Gary Ward	.05
436	Luis Aguayo	.05

NO.	PLAYER	MINT
437	Fernando Valenzuela	.10
438	Jeff Russell	.05
439	Cecilio Guante	.05
440	Don Robinson	.05
441	Rick Anderson	.05
442	Tom Glavine	.05
443	Daryl Boston	.05
444	Joe Price	.05
445	Stewart Cliburn	.05
446	Manny Trillo	.05
447	Joel Skinner	.05
448	Charlie Puleo	.05
449	Carlton Fisk	.10
450	Will Clark	.50
451	Otis Nixon	.05
452	Rick Schu	.05
453	Todd Stottlemyre	.15
454	Tim Birtsas	.05
455	Dave Gallagher (R)	.15
456	Barry Lyons	.05
457	Fred Manrique	.05
458	Ernest Riles	.05
459	Doug Jennings (R)	.20
460	Joe Magrane	.10
461	Jamie Quirk	.05
462	Jack Armstrong (R)	.20
463	Bobby Witt	.05
464	Keith Miller	.05
465	Todd Burns (R)	.20
466	John Dopson (R)	.15
467	Rich Yett	.05
468	Craig Reynolds	.05
469	Dave Bergman	.05
470	Rex Hudler	.10
471	Eric King	.05
472	Joaquin Andujar	.05
473	Sil Campusano (R)	.20
474	Terry Mulholland	.05
475	Mike Flanagan	.05
476	Greg Harris	.15
477	Tommy John	.10
478	Dave Anderson	.05
479	Fred Toliver	.05
480	Jimmy Key	.12
481	Donell Nixon	.05
482	Mark Portugal	.05
483	Tom Pagnozzi	.05
484	Jeff Kunkel	.05
485	Frank Williams	.05
486	Jody Reed	.10
487	Roberto Kelly	.15
488	Shawn Hillegas	.05
489	Jerry Reuss	.05
490	Mark Davis	.05
491	Jeff Sellers	.05
492	Zane Smith	.05
493	Al Newman	.05
494	Mike Young	.05
495	Larry Parrish	.05
496	Herm Winningham	.05
497	Carmen Castillo	.05
498	Joe Hesketh	.05
499	Darrell Miller	.05
500	Mike LaCoss	.05
501	Charlie Lea	.05
502	Bruce Benedict	.05
503	Chuck Finley	.10
504	Brad Wellman	.05
505	Tim Crews	.05
506	Ken Gerhart	.05
507	Brian Holton	.05
508	Dennis Lamp	.05
509	Bobby Meacham	.05
510	Tracy Jones	.05
511	Mike Fitzgerald	.05
512	Jeff Bittiger (R)	.15
513	Tim Flannery	.05
514	Ray Hayward	.05
515	Dave Leiper	.05
516	Rod Scurry	.05
517	Carmelo Martinez	.05
518	Curtis Wilkerson	.05
519	Stan Jefferson	.08

NO.	PLAYER	MINT
520	Dan Quisenberry	.08
521	Lloyd McClendon	.08
522	Steve Trout	.05
523	Larry Andersen	.05
524	Don Aase	.05
525	Bob Forsch	.05
526	Geno Petralli	.05
527	Angel Salazar	.05
528	Mike Schooler (R)	.25
529	Jose Oquendo	.05
530	Jay Buhner	.15
531	Tom Bolton	.10
532	Al Nipper	.05
533	Dave Henderson	.05
534	John Costello (R)	.15
535	Donnie Moore	.05
536	Mike Laga	.05
537	Mike Gallego	.05
538	Jim Clancy	.05
539	Joel Youngblood	.05
540	Rick Leach	.05
541	Kevin Romine	.05
542	Mark Salas	.05
543	Greg Minton	.05
544	Dave Palmer	.05
545	Dwayne Murphy	.05
546	Jim Deshaies	.05
547	Don Gordon	.10
548	Ricky Jordan (R)	.40
549	Mike Boddicker	.08
550	Mike Scott	.15
551	Jeff Ballard	.12
552	Jose Rijo	.15
552	Jose Rijo (error)	.75
553	Danny Darwin	.05
554	Tom Browning	.08
555	Danny Jackson	.10
556	Rick Dempsey	.05
557	Jeffrey Leonard	.05
558	Jeff Musselman	.05
559	Ron Robinson	.08
560	John Tudor	.05
561	Don Slaught	.05
562	Dennis Rasmussen	.05
563	Brady Anderson (R)	.20
564	Pedro Guerrero	.15
565	Paul Molitor	.08
566	Terry Clark (R)	.15
567	Terry Puhl	.05
568	Mike Campbell	.05
569	Paul Mirabella	.05
570	Jeff Hamilton	.05
571	Oswald Peraza (R)	.15
572	Bob McClure	.05
573	Jose Bautista (R)	.15
574	Alex Trevino	.05
575	John Franco	.08
576	Mark Parent (R)	.15
577	Nelson Liriano	.05
578	Steve Shields	.05
579	Odell Jones	.05
580	Al Leiter	.10
581	Dave Stapleton	.05
582	'88 World Series	.20
583	Donnie Hill	.05
584	Chuck Jackson	.05
585	Rene Gonzales	.05
586	Tracy Woodson	.10
587	Jim Adduci	.08
588	Mario Soto	.05
589	Jeff Blauser	.05
590	Jim Traber	.05
591	Jon Perlman	.05
592	Mark Williamson	.10
593	Dave Meads	.05
594	Jim Eisenreich	.05
595	P. Gibson (err.) (R)	1.00
595	P. Gibson (cor.) (R)	.15
596	Mike Birkbeck	.05
597	Terry Francona	.05
598	Paul Zuvella	.05
599	Franklin Stubbs	.05
600	Gregg Jefferies	.75
601	John Cangelosi	.05

NO.	PLAYER	MINT
602	Mike Sharperson	.05
603	Mike Diaz	.05
604	Gary Varsho (R)	.15
605	Terry Blocker (R)	.15
606	Charlie O'Brien	.05
607	Jim Eppard	.10
608	John Davis	.05
609	Ken Griffey, Sr.	.10
610	Buddy Bell	.05
611	Ted Simmons	.05
612	Matt Williams	.30
613	Danny Cox	.05
614	Al Pedrique	.05
615	Ron Oester	.05
616	John Smoltz (R)	.35
617	Bob Melvin	.05
618	Rob Dibble (R)	.40

NO.	PLAYER	MINT
619	Kirt Manwaring	.05
No. 620 to 651 (Rookie Prospects)		
620	Felix Fermin	.10
621	Doug Dascenzo (R)	.15
622	Bill Brennan (R)	.15
623	Carlos Quintana (R)	.35
624	Mike Harkey (R)	.35
625	Gary Sheffield (R)	1.00
626	Tom Prince	.10
627	Steve Searcy (R)	.15
628	Charlie Hayes (R)	.20
629	Felix Jose (R)	.25
630	Sandy Alomar (R)	1.00
631	Derek Lilliquist (R)	.20
632	Geronimo Berroa	.15
633	Luis Medina (R)	.20
634	Tom Gordon (R)	.50

NO.	PLAYER	MINT
635	Ramon Martinez (R)	1.00
636	Craig Worthington (R)	.25
637	Edgar Martinez (R)	.25
638	Chad Krueter (R)	.15
639	Ron Jones (R)	.25
640	Van Snider (R)	.15
641	Lance Blankenship (R)	.15
642	Dwight Smith (R)	1.00
643	Cameron Drew (R)	.15
644	Jerald Clark (R)	.15
645	Randy Johnson (R)	.35
646	Norm Charlton (R)	.20
647	Todd Frohwirth	.12
648	Luis De los Santos (R)	.15
649	Tim Jones (R)	.15
650	Dave West (R)	.20
651	Bob Milacki (R)	.20

NO.	PLAYER	MINT
652	Highlight—Wrigley Field– night opener	.15
653	Highlight—Hershiser– scoreless inning record	.20
654	Highlight—Boggs—6 yrs. consecutive 200 hits	.40
654	HL Boggs (error)	3.00
655	Highlight—Canseco 40 hr's, 40 stolen bases	.50
656	Highlight—Jones—saves	.05
657	Highlight—Henderson– lead off homers	.25
658	Highlight—Browning– perfect game	.10
659	Highlight—Greenwell—A.L. game-winning record	.15
660	Highlight—Red Sox—24 home game-winning streak	15

1989 Score Traded & Rookie. . . . Complete Set of 110 Cards—Value $15.00

Updates the main 1989 card set with players who changed teams during the season, and rookies. Features the first Score card of Jerome Walton, Jim Abbott and Ken Griffey, Jr.

NO.	PLAYER	MINT
1	Rafael Palmeiro	.15
2	Nolan Ryan	1.25
3	Jack Clark	.15
4	Dave LaPoint	.05
5	Mike Moore	.05
6	Pete O'Brien	.05
7	Jeffrey Leonard	.05
8	Rob Murphy	.05
9	Tom Herr	.05
10	Claudell Washington	.05
11	Mike Pagliarulo	.05
12	Steve Lake	.05
13	Spike Owen	.05
14	Andy Hawkins	.05
15	Todd Benzinger	.05
16	Mookie Wilson	.05
17	Bert Blyleven	.10
18	Jeff Treadway	.05
19	Bruce Hurst	.05
20	Steve Sax	.15
21	Juan Samuel	.05
22	Jesse Barfield	.05
23	Carmelo Castillo	.05
24	Terry Leach	.05
25	Mark Langston	.15
26	Eric King	.05
27	Steve Balboni	.05
28	Len Dykstra	.05

NO.	PLAYER	MINT
29	Keith Moreland	.05
30	Terry Kennedy	.05
31	Eddie Murray	.12
32	Mitch Williams	.15
33	Jeff Parrett	.05
34	Wally Backman	.05
35	Julio Franco	.10
36	Lance Parrish	.05
37	Nick Esasky	.10
38	Luis Polonia	.05
39	Kevin Gross	.05
40	John Dopson	.05
41	Willie Randolph	.05
42	Jim Clancy	.05
43	Tracy Jones	.05
44	Phil Bradley	.05
45	Milt Thompson	.05
46	Chris James	.05
47	Scott Fletcher	.05
48	Kal Daniels	.10
49	Steve Bedrosian	.05
50	Rickey Henderson	.60
51	Dion James	.05
52	Tim Leary	.05
53	Roger Mcdowell	.05
54	Mel Hall	.05
55	Dickie Thon	.05

NO.	PLAYER	MINT
56	Zane Smith	.05
57	Danny Heep	.05
58	Bob McClure	.05
59	Brian Holton	.05
60	Randy Ready	.05
61	Bob Melvin	.05
62	Harold Baines	.05
63	Lance McCullers	.05
64	Jody Davis	.05
65	Darrell Evans	.05
66	Joel Youngblood	.05
67	Frank Viola	.15
68	Mike Aldrete	.05
69	Greg Cadaret	.05
70	John Kruk	.05
71	Pat Sheridan	.05
72	Oddibe McDowell	.05
73	Tom Brookens	.05
74	Bob Boone	.05
75	Walt Terrell	.05
76	Joel Skinner	.05
77	Randy Johnson	.05
78	Felix Fermin	.05
79	Rick Mahler	.05
80	Rich Dotson	.05
81	Cris Carpenter	.20
82	Bill Spiers	.30

NO.	PLAYER	MINT
83	Junior Felix	1.00
84	Joe Girardi	.30
85	Jerome Walton	1.50
86	Greg Litton	.25
87	Greg Harris	.20
88	Jim Abbott	1.00
89	Kevin Brown	.20
90	John Wetteland	.40
91	Gary Wayne	.20
92	Rich Monteleone	.15
93	Bob Geren	.15
94	Clay Parker	*.15
95	Steve Finley	.30
96	Gregg Olson	1.00
97	Ken Patterson	.12
98	Ken Hill	.12
99	Scott Scudder	.30
100	Ken Griffey, Jr.	6.00
101	Jeff Brantley	.20
102	Donn Pall	.15
103	Carlos Martinez	.20
104	Joe Oliver	.30
105	Omar Vizquel	.20
106	Joey Belle	.50
107	Kenny Rogers	.20
108	Mark Carreon	.15
109	Rolando Roomes	.15
110	Pete Harnisch	.20

1990 Score. . . . Complete Set of 704 Cards—Value $30.00

The set was increased from 660 to 704 cards. New features this year include 22 First Round Draft Pick cards, 13 Dream Team cards (styled after the 1911 T-206 cards), 4 World Series cards and 5 Highlight cards.

NO.	PLAYER	MINT
1	Don Mattingly	.40
2	Cal Ripken, Jr.	.12
3	Dwight Evans	.08
4	Barry Bonds	.20
5	Kevin McReynolds	.10
6	Ozzie Guillen	.08
7	Terry Kennedy	.05
8	Bryan Harvey	.05
9	Alan Trammell	.08
10	Cory Snyder	.10
11	Jody Reed	.05
12	Roberto Alomar	.10
13	Pedro Guerrero	.10
14	Gary Redus	.05
15	Marty Barrett	.05
16	Ricky Jordan	.10
17	Joe Magrane	.10
18	Sid Fernandez	.08
19	Rich Dotson	.05
20	Jack Clark	.08
21	Bob Walk	.05
22	Ron Karkovice	.05
23	Lenny Harris	.10
24	Phil Bradley	.08
25	Andres Galarraga	.12
26	Brian Downing	.05
27	Dave Martinez	.05
28	Eric King	.05
29	Barry Lyons	.05
30	Dave Schmidt	.08
31	Mike Boddicker	.08
32	Tom Foley	.05
33	Brady Anderson	.05
34	Jim Presley	.05
35	Lance Parrish	.08
36	Von Hayes	.08
37	Lee Smith	.08
38	Herm Winningham	.05
39	Alejandro Pena	.05
40	Mike Scott	.08
41	Joe Orsulak	.05
42	Rafael Ramirez	.05
43	Gerald Young	.10
44	Dick Schofield	.05
45	Dve Smith	.08
46	Dave Magadan	.08
47	Dennis Martinez	.05
48	Greg Minton	.05
49	Milt Thompson	.05
50	Orel Hershiser	.12
51	Bip Roberts	.05
52	Jerry Browne	.08
53	Bob Ojeda	.05
54	Fernando Valenzuela	.10
55	Matt Nokes	.08
56	Brook Jacoby	.05
57	Frank Tanana	.05
58	Scott Fletcher	.05
59	Ron Oester	.05
60	Bob Boone	.05
61	Dan Gladden	.05
62	Darnell Coles	.05
63	Gregg Olson	.25
64	Todd Burns	.05

NO.	PLAYER	MINT
65	Todd Benzinger	.08
66	Dale Murphy	.12
67	Mike Flanagan	.05
68	Jose Oquendo	.05
69	Cecil Espy	.05
70	Chris Sabo	.20
71	Shane Rawley	.05
72	Tom Brunansky	.05
73	Vance Law	.05
74	B.J. Surhoff	.05
75	Lou Whitaker	.08
76	Ken Caminiti	.05
77	Nelson Liriano	.05
78	Tommy Gregg	.05
79	Don Slaught	.05
80	Eddie Murray	.10
81	Joe Boever	.05
82	Charlie Leibrandt	.05
83	Jose Lind	.05
84	Tony Phillips	.05
85	Mitch Webster	.05
86	Dan Plesac	.05
87	Rick Mahler	.05
88	Steve Lyons	.05
89	Tony Fernandez	.10
90	Ryne Sandberg	.15
91	Nick Esasky	.05
92	Luis Salazar	.05
93	Pete Incaviglia	.10
94	Ivan Calderon	.05
95	Jeff Treadway	.05
96	Kurt Stillwell	.05
97	Gary Sheffield	.25
98	Jeffrey Leonard	.05
99	Andres Thomas	.05
100	Roberto Kelly	.12
101	Alvaro Espinoza	.05
102	Greg Gagne	.05
103	John Farrell	.08
104	Willie Wilson	.08
105	Glenn Braggs	.05
106	Chet Lemon	.05
107	J. Moyer (error)	.10
107	J. Moyer (correct)	.35
108	Chuck Crim	.05
109	Dave Valle	.05
110	Walt Weiss	.10
111	Larry Sheets	.05
112	Don Robinson	.05
113	Danny Heep	.05
114	Carmelo Martinez	.05
115	Dave Gallagher	.05
116	Mike LaValliere	.05
117	Bob McClure	.05
118	Rene Gonzales	.05
119	Mark Parent	.05
120	Wally Joyner	.10
121	Mark Gubicza	.05
122	Tony Pena	.08
123	Carmelo Castillo	.05
124	Howard Johnson	.10
125	Steve Sax	.08
126	Tim Belcher	.08
127	Tim Burke	.05
128	Al Newman	.05

NO.	PLAYER	MINT
129	Dennis Rasmussen	.05
130	Doug Jones	.05
131	Fred Lynn	.08
132	Jeff Hamilton	.05
133	German Gonzalez	.05
134	John Morris	.05
135	Dave Parker	.10
136	Gary Pettis	.05
137	Dennis Boyd	.05
138	Candy Maldonado	.05
139	Rick Cerone	.05
140	George Brett	.15
141	Dave Clark	.05
142	Dickie Thon	.05
143	Junior Ortiz	.05
144	Don August	.08
145	Gary Gaetti	.10
146	Kirt Manwaring	.05
147	Jeff Reed	.05
148	Jose Alvarez	.05
149	Mike Schooler	.10
150	Mark Grace	.30
151	Geronimo Berroa	.07
152	Barry Jones	.05
153	Geno Petralli	.05
154	Jim Deshaies	.05
155	Barry Larkin	.12
156	Alfredo Griffin	.08
157	Tom Henke	.05
158	Mike Jeffcoat	.05
159	Bob Welch	.05
160	Julio Franco	.10
161	Henry Cotto	.05
162	Terry Steinbach	.10
163	Damon Berryhill	.08
164	Tim Crews	.05
165	Tom Browning	.05
166	Fred Manrique	.05
167	Harold Reynolds	.05
168	R. Hassey (error)	.10
168	R. Hassey (correct)	1.00
169	Shawon Dunston	.08
170	Bobby Bonilla	.15
171	Tom Herr	.05
172	Mike Heath	.05
173	Rich Gedman	.05
174	Bill Ripken	.08
175	Pete O'Brien	.08
176	L. McClendon (err.)	1.00
176	L. McClendon (cor.)	.10
177	Brian Holton	.05
178	Jeff Blauser	.05
179	Jim Eisenreich	.05
180	Bert Blyleven	.08
181	Rob Murphy	.05
182	Bill Doran	.05
183	Curt Ford	.05
184	Mike Henneman	.05
185	Eric Davis	.20
186	Lance McCullers	.05
187	Steve Davis (R)	.15
188	Bill Wegman	.05
189	Brian Harper	.05
190	Mike Moore	.08
191	Dale Mohorcic	.05
192	Tim Wallach	.05

NO.	PLAYER	MINT
193	Keith Hernandez	.08
194	Dave Righetti	.10
195	Bret Saberhagen	.15
196	Paul Kilgus	.05
197	Bud Black	.05
198	Juan Samuel	.08
199	Kevin Seitzer	.10
200	Darryl Strawberry	.25
201	Dave Stieb	.05
202	Charlie Hough	.05
203	Jack Morris	.10
204	Rance Mulliniks	.05
205	Alvin Davis	.08
206	Jack Howell	.05
207	Ken Patterson	.05
208	Terry Pendleton	.05
209	Craig Lefferts	.05
210	Kevin Brown	.05
211	Dan Petry	.05
212	Dave Leiper	.05
213	Daryl Boston	.05
214	Kevin Hickey	.08
215	Mike Krukow	.08
216	Terry Francona	.05
217	Mirk McCaskill	.08
218	Scott Bailes	.05
219	Bob Forsch	.05
220	M. Aldrete (err.)	.10
220	M. Aldrete (cor.)	.35
221	Steve Buechele	.05
222	Jesse Barfield	.05
223	Juan Berenguer	.05
224	Andy McGaffigan	.05
225	Pete Smith	.05
226	Mike Witt	.08
227	Jay Howell	.08
228	Scott Bradley	.05
229	Jerome Walton	.50
230	Greg Swindell	.10
231	Atlee Hammaker	.05
232	M. Devereaux (err.)	.10
232	M. Devereaux (cor.)	1.00
233	Ken Hill	.08
234	Craig Worthington	.08
235	Scott Terry	.05
236	Brett Butler	.05
237	Doyle Alexander	.08
238	Dave Anderson	.05
239	Bob Milacki	.08
240	Dwight Smith	.15
241	Otis Nixon	.05
242	Pat Tabler	.05
243	Derek Lilliquist	.08
244	Danny Tartabull	.10
245	Wade Boggs	.20
246	Scott Garrelts	.08
247	Spike Owen	.05
248	Norm Charlton	.05
249	Gerald Perry	.05
250	Nolan Ryan	.35
251	Kevin Gross	.05
252	Randy Milligan	.05
253	Mike LaCoss	.05
254	Dave Bergman	.05
255	Tony Gwynn	.15
256	Felix Fermin	.05

NO.	PLAYER	MINT
257	Greg Harris	.10
258	Junior Felix	.30
259	Mark Davis	.08
260	Vince Coleman	.08
261	Paul Gibson	.05
262	Mitch Williams	.08
263	Jeff Russell	.05
264	Omar Vizquel	.15
265	Andre Dawson	.12
266	Storm Davis	.05
267	Guillermo Hernandez	.05
268	Mike Felder	.05
269	Tom Candiotti	.05
270	Bruce Hurst	.05
271	Fred McGriff	.15
272	Glenn Davis	.10
273	John Franco	.08
274	Rich Yett	.08
275	Craig Biggio	.10
276	Gene Larkin	.05
277	Rob Dibble	.10
278	Randy Bush	.05
279	Kevin Bass	.05
280	Bo Jackson (error)	.75
280	Bo Jackson (correct)	1.50
281	Wally Backman	.05
282	Larry Andersen	.05
283	Chris Bosio	.05
284	Juan Agosto	.05
285	Ozzie Smith	.08
286	George Bell	.08
287	Rex Hudler	.05
288	Pat Borders	.05
289	Danny Jackson	.10
290	Carlton Fisk	.10
291	Tracy Jones	.05
292	Allan Anderson	.08
293	Johnny Ray	.08
294	Lee Guetterman	.05
295	Paul O'Neill	.08
296	Carney Lansford	.08
297	Tom Brookens	.05
298	Claudell Washington	.05
299	Hubie Brooks	.05
300	Will Clark	.50
301	Kenny Rogers	.10
302	Darrell Evans	.05
303	Greg Briley	.15
304	Donn Pall	.08
305	Teddy Higuera	.05
306	Dan Pasqua	.05
307	Dave Winfield	.12
308	Dennis Powell	.05
309	Jose DeLeon	.05
310	Roger Clemens	.20
311	Melido Perez	.05
312	Devon White	.10
313	Doc Gooden	.20
314	Carlos Martinez	.10
315	Dennis Eckersley	.08
316	Clay Parker	.10
317	Rick Honeycutt	.05
318	Tim Laudner	.05
319	Joe Carter	.10
320	Robin Yount	.20
321	Felix Jose	.05
322	Mickey Tettleton	.05
323	Mike Gallego	.05
324	Edgar Martinez	.10
325	Dave Henderson	.08
326	Chili Davis	.05
327	Steve Balboni	.05
328	Jody Davis	.05
329	Shawn Hillegas	.05
330	Jim Abbott	.25
331	John Dopson	.08
332	Mark Williamson	.05
333	Jeff Robinson	.08
334	John Smiley	.08
335	Bobby Thigpen	.05
336	Garry Templeton	.05
337	Marvell Wynne	.05
338	Ken Griffey, Sr. (cor.)	3.00
338	Ken Griffey, Sr. (error)	.15
339	Steve Finley	.15
340	Ellis Burks	.15
341	Frank Williams	.05
342	Mike Morgan	.05
343	Kevin Mitchell	.20
344	Joel Youngblood	.05
345	Mike Greenwell	.15
346	Glenn Wilson	.05
347	John Costello	.05
348	Wes Gardner	.05
349	Jeff Ballard	.08
350	Mark Thurmond	.05
351	Randy Myers	.08
352	Shawn Abner	.05
353	Jesse Orosco	.05
354	Greg Walker	.05
355	Pete Harnisch	.08
356	Steve Farr	.05
357	Dave LaPoint	.05
358	Willie Fraser	.05
359	Mickey Hatcher	.08
360	Rickey Henderson	.25
361	Mike Fitzgerald	.05
362	Bill Schroeder	.05
363	Mark Carreon	.05
364	Ron Jones	.05
365	Jeff Montgomery	.08
366	Bill Krueger	.05
367	John Cangelosi	.05
368	Jose Gonzalez	.05
369	Greg Hibbard (R)	.15
370	John Smoltz	.10
371	Jeff Brantley	.15
372	Frank White	.05
373	Ed Whitson	.05
374	Willie McGee	.08
375	Jose Canseco	.50
376	Randy Ready	.05
377	Don Aase	.05
378	Tony Armas	.05
379	Steve Bedrosian	.05
380	Chuck Finley	.08
381	Kent Hrbek	.08
382	Jim Gantner	.05
383	Mel Hall	.05
384	Mike Marshall	.08
385	Mark McGwire	.25
386	Wayne Tolleson	.05
387	Brian Holman	.10
388	John Wetteland	.15
389	Darren Daulton	.05
390	Rob Deer	.05
391	John Moses	.05
392	Todd Worrell	.08
393	Chuck Cary	.05
394	Stan Javier	.05
395	Willie Randolph	.08
396	Bill Buckner	.05
397	Robby Thompson	.10
398	Mike Scioscia	.08
399	Lonnie Smith	.05
400	Kirby Puckett	.25
401	Mark Langston	.10
402	Danny Darwin	.05
403	Greg Maddux	.08
404	Lloyd Moseby	.08
405	Rafael Palmeiro	.10
406	Chad Kreuter	.05
407	Jimmy Key	.08
408	Tim Birtsas	.05
409	Tim Raines	.12
410	Dave Stewart	.10
411	Eric Yelding	.15
412	Kent Anderson	.10
413	Les Lancaster	.05
414	Rick Dempsey	.05
415	Randy Johnson	.08
416	Gary Carter	.08
417	Rolando Roomes	.08
418	Dan Schatzeder	.05
419	Bryn Smith	.05
420	Ruben Sierra	.15
421	Steve Jeltz	.08
422	Ken Oberkfell	.05
423	Sid Bream	.05
424	Jim Clancy	.05
425	Kelly Gruber	.10
426	Rick Leach	.05
427	Lenny Dykstra	.10
428	Jeff Pico	.05
429	John Cerutti	.05
430	David Cone	.10
431	Jeff Kunkel	.05
432	Luis Aquino	.05
433	Ernie Whitt	.05
434	Bo Diaz	.05
435	Steve Lake	.05
436	Pat Perry	.05
437	Mike Davis	.05
438	Cecilio Guante	.05
439	Duane Ward	.05
440	Andy Van Slyke	.10
441	Gene Nelson	.05
442	Luis Polonia	.05
443	Kevin Elster	.08
444	Keith Moreland	.05
445	Roger McDowell	.05
446	Ron Darling	.10
447	Ernest Riles	.05
448	Mookie Wilson	.08
449	B. Spiers (correct)	.25
449	B. Spiers (error)	1.00
450	Rick Sutcliffe	.05
451	Nelson Santovenia	.05
452	Andy Allanson	.05
453	Bob Melvin	.05
454	Benny Santiago	.10
455	Jose Uribe	.05
456	Bill Landrum	.05
457	Bobby Witt	.08
458	Kevin Romine	.05
459	Lee Mazzilli	.05
460	Paul Molitor	.10
461	Ramon Martinez	.30
462	Frank DiPino	.05
463	Walt Terrell	.05
464	Bob Geren	.15
465	Rick Reuschel	.08
466	Mark Grant	.05
467	John Kruk	.05
468	Gregg Jefferies	.30
469	R.J. Reynolds	.05
470	Harold Baines	.08
471	Dennis Lamp	.05
472	Tom Gordon	.15
473	Terry Puhl	.05
474	Curtis Wilkerson	.05
475	Dan Quisenberry	.05
476	Oddibe McDowell	.05
477	Zane Smith	.05
478	Franklin Stubbs	.05
479	Wallace Johnson	.05
480	Jay Tibbs	.05
481	Tom Glavine	.08
482	Manny Lee	.05
483	Joe Hesketh	.05
484	Mike Bielecki	.05
485	Greg Brock	.05
486	Pascual Perez	.05
487	Kirk Gibson	.08
488	Scott Sanderson	.05
489	Domingo Ramos	.05
490	Kal Daniels	.10
491	David Wells (correct)	.10
491	David Wells (error)	2.00
492	Jerry Reed	.05
493	Eric Show	.05
494	Mike Pagliarulo	.08
495	Ron Robinson	.05
496	Brad Komminsk	.05
497	Greg Litton	.10
498	Chris James	.05
499	Luis Quinones	.05
500	Frank Viola	.10
501	Tim Teufel	.05
502	Terry Leach	.05
503	Matt Williams	.20
504	Tim Leary	.08
505	Doug Drabek	.05
506	Mariano Duncan	.05
507	Charlie Hayes	.05
508	Joey Belle	.20
509	Pat Sheridan	.05
510	Mackey Sasser	.05
511	Jose Rijo	.05
512	Mike Smithson	.05
513	Gary Ward	.05
514	Dion James	.05
515	Jim Gott	.05
516	Drew Hall	.05
517	Doug Bair	.05
518	Scott Scudder	.15
519	Rick Aguilera	.05
520	Rafael Belliard	.05
521	Jay Buhner	.08
522	Jeff Reardon	.08
523	Steve Rosenberg	.05
524	Randy Verlarde	.05
525	Jeff Musselman	.05
526	Bill Long	.05
527	Gary Wayne	.10
528	Dave Johnson (R)	.10
529	Ron Kittle	.05
530	Erik Hanson	.15
531	Steve Wilson	.10
532	Joey Meyer	.05
533	Curt Young	.05
534	Kelly Downs	.08
535	Joe Girardi	.10
536	Lance Blankenship	.05
537	Greg Mathews	.05
538	Donell Nixon	.05
539	Mark Knudson	.08
540	Jeff Wetherby (R)	.15
541	Darrin Jackson	.05
542	Terry Mulholland	.05
543	Eric Hetzel	.05
544	Rick Reed (R)	.15
545	Dennis Cook	.10
546	Mike Jackson	.05
547	Brian Fisher	.05
548	Gene Harris	.15
549	Jeff King	.12
550	Dave Dravecky	.05
551	Randy Kutcher	.05
552	Mark Portugal	.05
553	Jim Corsi	.08
554	Todd Stottlemyre	.08
555	Scott Bankhead	.05
556	Ken Dayley	.05
557	Rick Wrona	.15
558	Sammy Sosa (R)	.45
559	Keith Miller	.05
560	Ken Griffey, Jr.	2.00
561	HL: R. Sandberg (cor.)	.30
561	HL: R. Sandberg (error)	8.00
562	Billy Hatcher	.05
563	Jay Bell	.05
564	Jack Daugherty (R)	.15
565	Rich Monteleone	.10
566	Bo Jackson (MVP)	.60
567	Tony Fossas (R)	.15
568	Roy Smith	.05
569	Jaime Navarro	.15
570	Lance Johnson	.05
571	Mike Dyer (R)	.15
572	Kevin Ritz (R)	.15
573	Dave West	.10
574	Gary Mielke (R)	.15
575	Scott Lusader	.05
576	Joe Oliver	.15
577	Sandy Alomar, Jr.	.30
578	Andy Benes	.25
579	Tim Jones	.05
580	Randy McCament (R)	.15
581	Curt Schilling	.10
582	John Orton (R)	.15
583	M. Cuyler (error)	1.00
583	M. Cuyler (correct)	.25
584	Eric Anthony (R)	.75
585	Greg Vaughn	.50
586	Deion Sanders	.50
587	Jose DeJesus	.05
588	Chip Hale (R)	.15
589	John Olerud (R)	2.50
590	Steve Olin (R)	.15
591	Marquis Grissom (R)	.75
592	Moises Alou (R)	.30

NO. PLAYER	MINT
593 Mark Lemke	.05
594 Dean Palmer (R)	.20
595 Robin Ventura	.30
596 Tino Martinez	.60
597 Mike Huff (R)	.20
598 Scott Hemond (R)	.25
599 Wally Whitehurst	.10
600 Todd Zeile	.60
601 Hill Glenallen	.10
602 Hal Morris	.35
603 Juan Bell	.10
604 Bobby Rose (R)	.20
605 Matt Merullo	.10
606 Kevin Maas (R)	3.00
607 Randy Nosek (R)	.15
608 Billy Bates (R)	.15
609 Mike Stanton (R)	.15
610 Goose Gozzo (R)	.15
611 Charles Nagy	.20
612 Scott Coolbaugh (R)	.15
613 Jose Vizcaino (R)	.15
614 Greg Smith (R)	.15
615 Jeff Huson (R)	.15
616 Mickey Weston (R)	.15
617 John Pawlowski	.10
618 Joe Skalski (error)	.10
618 Joe Skalski (correct)	1.25
619 Bernie Williams (R)	.35
620 Shawn Holman (R)	.15

NO. PLAYER	MINT
621 Gary Eave (R)	.15
622 Darrin Fletcher (R)	.30
623 Pat Combs	.15
624 Mike Blowers (R)	.20
625 Kevin Appier	.25
626 Pat Austin (R)	.15
627 Kelly Mann (R)	.15
628 Matt Kinzer (R)	.15
629 Chris Hammond (R)	.20
630 Dean Wilkins (R)	.15
631 Larry Walker (R)	.35
632 Blaine Beatty (R)	.15
633 T. Barrett (error)	.10
633 T. Barrett (correct)	2.50
634 Stan Belinda (R)	.15
635 Mike Smith (Tex) (R)	.15
636 Hensley Meulens (R)	.30
637 Juan Gonzalez (R)	1.50
638 Lenny Webster (R)	.15
639 Mark Gardner (R)	.15
640 Tommy Greene (R)	.25
641 Mike Hartley (R)	.15
642 Phil Stephenson	.10
643 Kevin Mmahat (R)	.15
644 Ed Whited (R)	.15
645 Delino DeShields (R)	.75
646 Kevin Blankenship	.08
647 Paul Sorrento (R)	.15
648 Mike Roesler (R)	.15

NO. PLAYER	MINT
649 Jason Brimsely (R)	.15
650 Dave Justice (R)	3.00
651 Scott Cooper (R)	.30
652 Dave Eiland	.10
653 Mike Munoz (R)	.12
654 Jeff Fischer (R)	.15
655 Terry Jorgenson (R)	.15
656 George Canale (R)	.15
657 Brian Dubois (R)	.15
658 Carlos Quintana	.08
659 Luis De Los Santos	.05
660 Jerald Clark	.05
No. 661 to 682—No. 1 Draft Picks	
661 Donald Harris (R)	.20
662 Paul Coleman (R)	.30
663 Frank Thomas (R)	2.50
664 Brent Mayne (R)	.15
665 Eddie Zosky (R)	.20
666 Steve Hosey (R)	.30
667 Scott Bryant (R)	.25
668 Tom Goodwin (R)	.35
669 Cal Eldred (R)	.20
670 Earl Cunningham (R)	.25
671 Alan Zinter (R)	.20
672 Chuck Knoblauch (R)	.20
673 Kyle Abbott (R)	.25
674 Roger Salkeld (R)	.30
675 Maurice Vaughn (R)	1.00
676 Keith Jones (Kiki) (R)	.50

NO. PLAYER	MINT
677 Tyler Houston (R)	.35
678 Jeff Jackson (R)	.15
679 Greg Gohr (R)	.20
680 Ben McDonald (R)	1.25
681 Greg Blosser (R)	.40
682 Willie Green (R)	.25
No. 683 to 695—Dream Team	
683 Wade Boggs	.20
684 Will Clark	.30
685 Tony Gwynn	.15
686 Rickey Henderson	.30
687 Bo Jackson	.65
688 Mark Langston	.12
689 Barry Larkin	.12
690 Kirby Puckett	.25
691 Ryne Sandberg	.20
692 Mike Scott	.08
693 T. Steinbach (err.)	.10
693 T. Steinbach (cor.)	.35
694 Bobby Thigpen	.10
695 Mitch Williams	.08
Special Cards	
696 Nolan Ryan	.40
697 Bo Jackson FB/BB	8.00
698 Rickey Henderson	.20
699 Will Clark	.30
No. 700 to 703—World Series	
700 WS Games 1,2	.10
701 Candlestick Park	.15
702 WS Game 3	.10
703 WS Wrap-up	.10
704 HL: Wade Boggs	.20

1990 Score Traded & Rookie. . . . Complete Set of 110 Cards—Value $12.00

Updates the main 1990 card set with players who changed teams during the season, and rookies. Features the first Score card of Eric Lindros.

NO. PLAYER	MINT
1T Dave Winfield	.10
2T Kevin Bass	.05
3T Nick Esasky	.05
4T Mitch Webster	.05
5T Pascual Perez	.05
6T Gary Pettis	.05
7T Tony Pena	.05
8T Candy Maldonado	.05
9T Cecil Fielder	.60
10T Carmelo Martinez	.05
11T Mark Langston	.05
12T Dave Parker	.10
13T Don Slaught	.05
14T Tony Phillips	.05
15T John Franco	.05
16T Randy Myers	.05
17T Jeff Reardon	.05
18T Sandy Alomar Jr.	.25
19T Joe Carter	.10
20T Fred Lynn	.08
21T Storm Davis	.05
22T Craig Lefferts	.05
23T Pete O'Brien	.05
24T Dennis Boyd	.05
25T Lloyd Moseby	.05
26T Mark Davis	.05
27T Tim Leary	.05
28T Gerald Perry	.05

NO. PLAYER	MINT
29T Don Aase	.05
30T Ernie Whitt	.05
31T Dale Murphy	.08
32T Alejandro Pena	.05
33T Juan Samuel	.05
34T Hubie Brooks	.05
35T Gary Carter	.05
36T Jim Presley	.05
37T Wally Backman	.05
38T Matt Nokes	.08
39T Dan Petry	.05
40T Franklin Stubbs	.05
41T Jeff Huson	.05
42T Billy Hatcher	.05
43T Terry Leach	.05
44T Phil Bradley	.05
45T Claudell Washington	.05
46T Luis Polonia	.05
47T Daryl Boston	.05
48T Lee Smith	.08
49T Tom Brunansky	.08
50T Mike Witt	.05
51T Willie Randolph	.05
52T Stan Javier	.05
53T Brad Komminsk	.05
54T John Candelaria	.05
55T Bryn Smith	.05

NO. PLAYER	MINT
56T Glenn Braggs	.05
57T Keith Hernandez	.05
58T Ken Oberkfell	.05
59T Steve Jeltz	.05
60T Chris James	.05
61T Scott Sanderson	.05
62T Bill Long	.05
63T Rick Cerone	.05
64T Scott Bailes	.05
65T Larry Sheets	.05
66T Junior Ortiz	.05
67T Francisco Cabrera	.15
68T Gary Disarcina	.15
69T Greg Olson	.15
70T Beau Allred	.10
71T Oscar Azocar	.15
72T Kent Mercker	.10
73T John Burkett	.25
74T Carlos Baerga	.35
75T Dave Hollins	.20
76T Todd Hundley	.15
77T Rick Parker	.10
78T Steve Cummings	.10
79T Bill Sampen	.25
80T Jerry Kutzler	.10
81T Derek Bell	.30
82T Kevin Tapani	.25

NO. PLAYER	MINT
83T Jim Leyritz	.20
84T Ray Lankford	.75
85T Wayne Edwards	.10
86T Frank Thomas	1.25
87T Tim Naehring	.25
88T Willie Blair	.10
89T Alan Mills	.15
90T Scott Randinsky	.15
91T Howard Farmer	.20
92T Julio Machado	.10
93T Rafael Valdez	.10
94T Shawn Boskie	.20
95T David Sequi	.30
96T Chris Hoiles	.20
97T D.J. Dozier	.40
98T Hector Villanueva	.20
99T Eric Gunderson	.10
100T Eric Lindros	2.00
101T Dave Otto	.10
102T Dana Kiecker	.20
103T Tim Drummond	.10
104T Mickey Pina	.30
105T Craig Grebeck	.10
106T Bernard Gilkey	.35
107T Tim Layana	.15
108T Scott Chiamparino	.35
109T Steve Avery	.30
110T Terry Schumpert	.15

The set was increased from 704 to 893 cards—the largest baseball card set ever issued. For the first time Score cards were issued in two series—series one contains 441 cards; series two has 452 cards. There are several new subsets for 1991—the Franchise, No-Hit Club, Master Blasters. K-Man and Rifleman. Factory sets include seven bonus cards.

NO.	PLAYER	MINT
	SERIES ONE	
1	Jose Canseco	.35
2	Ken Griffey, Jr.	.75
3	Ryne Sandberg	.20
4	Nolan Ryan	.30
5	Bo Jackson	.35
6	Bret Saberhagen	.10
7	Will Clark	.30
8	Ellis Burks	.08
9	Joe Carter	.08
10	Rickey Henderson	.25
11	Ozzie Guillen	.05
12	Wade Boggs	.20
13	Jerome Walton	.15
14	John Franco	.05
15	Ricky Jordan	.05
16	Wally Backman	.05
17	Rob Dibble	.05
18	Glenn Braggs	.05
19	Cory Snyder	.08
20	Kal Daniels	.08
21	Mark Langston	.08
22	Kevin Gross	.05
23	Don Mattingly	.30
24	Dave Righetti	.05
25	Roberto Alomar	.08
26	Robby Thompson	.05
27	Jack McDowell	.05
28	Bip Roberts	.05
29	Jay Howell	.05
30	Dave Stieb	.08
31	Johnny Ray	.05
32	Steve Sax	.05
33	Terry Mulholland	.05
34	Lee Guetterman	.05
35	Tim Raines	.08
36	Scott Fletcher	.05
37	Lance Parrish	.05
38	Tony Phillips	.05
39	Todd Stottlemyre	.05
40	Alan Trammell	.08
41	Todd Burns	.05
42	Mookie Wilson	.05
43	Chris Bosio	.05
44	Jeffrey Leonard	.05
45	Doug Jones	.05
46	Mike Scott	.05
47	Andy Hawkins	.05
48	Harold Reynolds	.05
49	Paul Molitor	.08
50	John Farrell	.05
51	Danny Darwin	.05
52	Jeff Blauser	.05
53	John Tudor	.05
54	Milt Thompson	.05
55	Dave Justice	.60
56	Greg Olson	.08
57	Willie Blair	.05
58	Rick Parker	.05
59	Shawn Boskie	.05
60	Kevin Tapani	.05
61	Dave Hollins	.10
62	Scott Radinsky	.05
63	Francisco Cabrera	.05
64	Tim Layana	.05
65	Jim Leyritz	.08
66	Wayne Edwards	.05
67	Lee Stevens	.12
68	Bill Sampen	.05
69	Craig Grebeck	.05
70	John Burkett	.05
71	Hector Villanueva	.10
72	Oscar Azocar	.10
73	Alan Mills	.05
74	Carlos Baerga	.15
75	Charles Nagy	.10
76	Tim Drummond	.05
77	Dana Kiecker	.05
78	Tom Edens (R)	.10
79	Kent Mercker	.05
80	Steve Avery	.12
81	Lee Smith	.05
82	Dave Martinez	.05
83	Dave Winfield	.08
84	Bill Spiers	.05
85	Dan Pasqua	.05
86	Randy Milligan	.05
87	Tracy Jones	.05
88	Greg Myers	.05
89	Keith Hernandez	.05
90	Todd Benzinger	.08
91	Mike Jackson	.05
92	Mike Stanley	.05
93	Candy Maldonado	.05
94	John Kruk	.05
95	Cal Ripken, Jr.	.12
96	Willie Fraser	.05
97	Mike Felder	.05
98	Bill Landrum	.05
99	Chuck Crim	.05
100	Chuck Finley	.05
101	Kirt Manwaring	.05
102	Jaime Navarro	.05
103	Dickie Thon	.05
104	Brian Downing	.05
105	Jim Abbott	.10
106	Tom Brookens	.05
107	Darryl Hamilton	.05
108	Bryan Harvey	.05
109	Greg Harris	.05
110	Greg Swindell	.05
111	Juan Berenguer	.05
112	Mike Heath	.05
113	Scott Bracley	.05
114	Jack Morris	.08
115	Barry Jones	.05
116	Kevin Romine	.05
117	Garry Templeton	.05
118	Scott Sanderson	.05
119	Roberto Kelly	.05
120	George Brett	.15
121	Oddibe McDowell	.05
122	Jim Acker	.05
123	Bill Swift	.05
124	Eric King	.05
125	Jay Buhner	.05
126	Matt Young	.05
127	Alvaro Espinoza	.05
128	Greg Hibbard	.05
129	Jeff Robinson	.05
130	Mike Greenwell	.15
131	Dion James	.05
132	Donn Pall	.05
133	Lloyd Moseby	.05
134	Randy Velarde	.05
135	Allan Anderson	.05
136	Mark Davis	.05
137	Eric Davis	.15
138	Phil Stephenson	.05
139	Felix Fermin	.05
140	Pedro Guerrero	.10
141	Charlie Hough	.05
142	Mike Henneman	.05
143	Jeff Montgomery	.05
144	Lenny Harris	.05
145	Bruce Hurst	.05
146	Eric Anthony	.15
147	Paul Assenmacher	.05
148	Jesse Barfield	.08
149	Carlos Quintana	.08
150	Dave Stewart	.12
151	Roy Smith	.05
152	Paul Gibson	.05
153	Mickey Hatcher	.05
154	Jim Eisenreich	.05
155	Kenny Rogers	.05
156	Dave Schmidt	.05
157	Lance Johnson	.05
158	Dave West	.05
159	Steve Balboni	.05
160	Jeff Brantley	.05
161	Craig Biggio	.05
162	Brook Jacoby	.05
163	Dan Gladden	.05
164	Jeff Reardon	.05
165	Mark Carreon	.05
166	Mel Hall	.05
167	Gary Mielke	.05
168	Cecil Fielder	.25
169	Darrin Jackson	.05
170	Rick Aguilera	.05
171	Walt Weiss	.05
172	Steve Farr	.05
173	Jody Reed	.05
174	Mike Jeffcoat	.05
175	Mark Grace	.15
176	Larry Sheets	.05
177	Bill Gullickson	.05
178	Chris Gwynn	.05
179	Melido Perez	.05
180	Sid Fernandez	.05
181	Tim Burke	.05
182	Gary Pettis	.05
183	Rob Murphy	.05
184	Craig Lefferts	.05
185	Howard Johnson	.10
186	Ken Caminiti	.05
187	Tim Belcher	.05
188	Greg Cadaret	.05
189	Matt Williams	.15
190	Dave Magadan	.08
191	Geno Petralli	.05
192	Jeff Robinson	.05
193	Jim Deshaies	.05
194	Willie Randolph	.05
195	George Bell	.08
196	Hubie Brooks	.05
197	Tom Gordon	.10
198	Mike Fitzgerald	.05
199	Mike Pagliarulo	.05
200	Kirby Puckett	.20
201	Shawon Dunston	.08
202	Dennis Boyd	.05
203	Junior Felix	.08
204	Alejandro Pena	.05
205	Pete Smith	.05
206	Tom Glavine	.05
207	Luis Salazar	.05
208	John Smoltz	.05
209	Doug Dascenzo	.05
210	Tim Wallach	.05
211	Greg Gagne	.05
212	Mark Gubicza	.05
213	Mark Parent	.05
214	Ken Oberkfell	.05
215	Gary Carter	.10
216	Rafael Palmeiro	.05
217	Tom Niedenfuer	.05
218	Dave LaPoint	.05
219	Jeff Treadway	.05
220	Mitch Williams	.05
221	Jose DeLeon	.05
222	Mike LaValliere	.05
223	Darrel Akerfelds	.05
224	Kent Anderson	.05
225	Dwight Evans	.05
226	Gary Redus	.05
227	Paul O'Neill	.05
228	Marty Barrett	.05
229	Tom Browning	.05
230	Terry Pendleton	.05
231	Jack Armstrong	.05
232	Mike Boddicker	.05
233	Neal Heaton	.05
234	Marquis Grissom	.10
235	Bert Blyleven	.05
236	Curt Young	.05
237	Don Carman	.05
238	Charlies Hayes	.05
239	Mark Knudson	.05
240	Todd Zeile	.15
241	Larry Walker	.08
242	Jerald Clark	.05
243	Jeff Ballard	.05
244	Jeff King	.05
245	Tom Brunansky	.08
246	Darren Daulton	.05
247	Scott Terry	.05
248	Rob Deer	.05

NO.	PLAYER	MINT
249	Brady Anderson	.05
250	Lenny Dykstra	.10
251	Gerg Harris	.05
252	Mike Hartley	.05
253	Joey Cora	.05
254	Ivan Calderon	.05
255	Ted Power	.05
256	Sammy Sosa	.12
257	Steve Buechele	.05
258	Mike Devereaux	.05
259	Brad Komminsk	.05
260	Teddy Higuera	.05
261	Shawn Abner	.05
262	Dave Valle	.05
263	Jeff Huson	.05
264	Edgar Martinez	.05
265	Carlton Fisk	.05
266	Steve Finley	.05
267	John Wetteland	.05
268	Kevin Appier	.05
269	Steve Lyons	.05
270	Mickey Tettleton	.05
271	Luis Rivera	.05
272	Steve Jeltz	.05
273	R.J. Reynolds	.05
274	Carlos Martinez	.05
275	Dan Plesac	.05
276	Mike Morgan	.05
277	Jeff Russell	.05
278	Pete Incaviglia	.05
279	Kevin Seitzer	.05
280	Bobby Thigpen	.08
281	Stan Javier	.05
282	Henry Cotto	.05
283	Gary Wayne	.05
284	Shane Mack	.05
285	Brian Holman	.05
286	Gerald Perry	.05
287	Steve Crawford	.05
288	Nelson Liriano	.05
289	Don Aase	.05
290	Randy Johnson	.05
291	Harold Baines	.05
292	Kent Hrbek	.12
293	Les Lancaster	.05
294	Jeff Musselman	.05
295	Kurt Stillwell	.05
296	Stan Belinda	.05
297	Lou Whitaker	.05
298	Glenn Wilson	.05
299	Omar Vizquel	.05
300	Ramon Martinez	.12
301	Dwight Smith	.05
302	Tim Crews	.05
303	Lance Blankenship	.05
304	Sid Bream	.05
305	Rafael Ramirez	.05
306	Steve Wilson	.05
307	Mackey Sasser	.05
308	Franklin Stubbs	.05
309	Jack Daugherty	.05
310	Eddie Murray	.15
311	Bob Welch	.05
312	Brian Harper	.05
313	Lance McCullers	.05
314	Dave Smith	.05
315	Bobby Bonilla	.15
316	Jerry Don Gleaton	.05
317	Greg Maddux	.05
318	Keith Miller	.05
319	Mark Portugal	.05
320	Robin Ventura	.15
321	Bob Ojeda	.05
322	Mike Harkey	.05
323	Jay Bell	.05
324	Mark McGwire	.25
325	Gary Gaetti	.05
326	Jeff Pico	.05
327	Kevin McReynolds	.08
328	Frank Tanana	.05
329	Eric Yelding	.05
330	Barry Bonds	.15

No. 331 to 379—Rookie Prospects

NO.	PLAYER	MINT
331	Brian McRae (R)	.65
332	Pedro Munoz (R)	.20
333	Daryl Irvine (R)	.12
334	Chris Hoiles	.12
335	Thomas Howard	.12
336	Jeff Schulz (R)	.12
337	Jeff Manto	.07
338	Beau Allred	.07
339	Mike Brodick (R)	.12
340	Todd Hundley	.12
341	Jim Vatcher (R)	.20
342	Luis Sojo	.07
343	Jose Offerman	.30
344	Pete Coachman (R)	.30
345	Mike Benjamin	.08
346	Ozzie Canseco	.15
347	Tim McIntosh	.08
348	Phil Plantier (R)	.40
349	Terry Shumpert	.05
350	Darren Lewis	.35
351	David Walsh (R)	.12
352	Scott Chiamparino	.30
353	Julio Valera	.08
354	Anthony Telford (R)	.12
355	Kevin Wickander	.07
356	Tim Naehring	.20
357	Jim Poole (R)	.12
358	Mark Whiten	.35
359	Terry Wells (R)	.12
360	Rafael Valdez	.07
361	Mel Stottlemyre, Jr.	.07
362	David Segui	.25
363	Paul Abbott (R)	.15
364	Steve Howard	.08
365	Karl Rhodes	.12
366	Rafael Novoa (R)	.12
367	Joe Grahe (R)	.12
368	Darren Reed	.07
369	Jeff McKnight	.08
370	Scott Leius	.07
371	Mark Dewey (R)	.12
372	Mark Lee (R)	.12
373	Rosario Rodriguez (R)	.12
374	Chuck McElroy	.07
375	Mike Bell (R)	.12
376	Mickey Morandini	.12
377	Bill Haselman (R)	.12
378	Dave Pavlas (R)	.12
379	Derrick May	.30

No. 380 to 391—
1st Round Draft Pick

NO.	PLAYER	MINT
380	Jeromy Burnitz (R)	.40
381	Donald Peters (R)	.15
382	Alex Fernandez (R)	1.00
383	Mike Mussina (R)	.30
384	Daniel Smith (R)	.15
385	Lance Dickson (R)	.20
386	Carl Everett (R)	.35
387	Tom Nevers (R)	.15
388	Adam Hyzdu (R)	.25
389	Todd Van Poppel (R)	1.25
390	Rondell White (R)	.35
391	Marc Newfield (R)	.20

No. 392 to 401—Score All Star Team

NO.	PLAYER	MINT
392	Julio Franco	.07
393	Wade Boggs	.15
394	Ozzie Guillen	.07
395	Cecil Fielder	.15
396	Ken Griffey, Jr.	.30
397	Rickey Henderson	.15
398	Jose Canseco	.30
399	Roger Clemens	.10
400	Sandy Alomar, Jr.	.10
401	Bobby Thigpen	.07

No. 402 to 406—Master Blaster

NO.	PLAYER	MINT
402	Bobby Bonilla	.10
403	Eric Davis	.10
404	Fred McGriff	.10
405	Glenn Davis	.10
406	Kevin Mitchell	.15

No. 407 to 411—K-Man

NO.	PLAYER	MINT
407	Rob Dibble	.07
408	Ramon Martinez	.10
409	David Cone	.07
410	Bobby Witt	.07
411	Mark Langston	.07

No. 412 to 416—Rifleman

NO.	PLAYER	MINT
412	Bo Jackson	.30
413	Shawon Dunston	.07
414	Jesse Barfield	.07
415	Ken Caminiti	.07
416	Benny Santiago	.07

No. 417 to 421—1990 Highlights's

NO.	PLAYER	MINT
417	Nolan Ryan	.30
418	Bobby Thigpen	.05
419	Ramon Martinez	.15
420	Bo Jackson	.30
421	Carlton Fisk	.05
422	Jimmy Key	.05
423	Junior Noboa	.05
424	Al Newman	.05
425	Pat Borders	.05
426	Von Hayes	.05
427	Tim Teufel	.05
428	Eric Plunk	.05
429	John Moses	.05
430	Mike Witt	.05
431	Otis Nixon	.05
432	Tony Fernandez	.05
433	Rance Mulliniks	.05
434	Dan Petry	.05
435	Bob Geren	.05
436	Steve Frey	.05
437	Jamie Moyer	.05
438	Junior Ortiz	.05
439	Tom O'Malley	.05
440	Pat Combs	.05
441	Jose Canseco	1.25

SERIES TWO NOT AVAILABLE AT PRESS TIME

1986 Sportflics. . . . Complete Set of 200 Cards—Value $40.00

Sportflics entered the baseball card market in 1986. Each card can be tilted to show three different photos. The set includes 139 cards, each featuring three poses of the same player; 50 "Tri-Stars"—each card featuring three players; 10 "Big Six" cards—each featuring six players; 1 World Series card—featuring 12 players.

Dwight Gooden—Phase 1

Dwight Gooden—Phase 2

Dwight Gooden—Phase 3

NO. PLAYER	MINT
1 George Brett	1.00
2 Don Mattingly	4.00
3 Wade Boggs	2.00
4 Eddie Murray	.50
5 Dale Murphy	.50
6 Rickey Henderson	1.00
7 Harold Baines	.25
8 Cal Ripken, Jr.	.60
9 Orel Hershiser	.50
10 Bret Saberhagen	.40
11 Tim Raines	.35
12 Fernando Valenzuela	.30
13 Tony Gwynn	.75
14 Pedro Guerrero	.30
15 Keith Hernandez	.30
16 Ernest Riles	.20
17 Jim Rice	.35
18 Ron Guidry	.30
19 Willie McGee	.25
20 Ryne Sandberg	1.00
21 Kirk Gibson	.40
22 Ozzie Guillen	.50
23 Dave Parker	.30
24 Vince Coleman	1.75
25 Tom Seaver	.60
26 Bret Butler	.15
27 Steve Carlton	.50
28 Gary Carter	.35
29 Cecil Cooper	.25
30 Jose Cruz	.20
31 Alvin Davis	.20
32 Dwight Evans	.25
33 Julio Franco	.15
34 Damaso Garcia	.15
35 Steve Garvey	.60
36 Kent Hrbek	.50
37 Reggie Jackson	.75
38 Fred Lynn	.25
39 Paul Molitor	.25
40 Jim Presley	.20
41 Dave Righetti	.20
42 Robin Yount	.75
43 Nolan Ryan	1.50
44 Mike Schmidt	1.50
45 Lee Smith	.20
46 Rick Sutcliffe	.20
47 Bruce Sutter	.20
48 Lou Whitaker	.20
49 Dave Winfield	.50
50 Pete Rose	1.25

No. 51 to 75—TRI-STARS

NO. PLAYER	MINT
51 Nat'l. League MVPs: Ryn Sandberg, Steve Garvey, Pete Rose	.75
52 Slugging Stars: Harold Baines, George Brett, Jim Rice	.30
53 No-Hitters: Mike Witt, Phil Niekro, Jerry Reuss	.25
54 Big Hitters: Robin Yount, Don Mattingly, Cal Ripken, Jr.	1.00
55 Bullpen Aces: Dan Quisenberry, Lee Smith, Goose Gossage	.20
56 Rookies of The Year: Pete Rose, Steve Sax, Darryl Strawberry	.75
57 Am. League MVP's: Cal Ripken, Jr., Don Baylor, Reggie Jackson	.40
58 Batting Champs: Bill Madlock, Pete Rose, Dave Parker	.40
59 Cy Young Winners: LaMarr Hoyt, Mike Flanagan, Ron Guidry	.20
60 Double Award Winners: Fernando Valenzuela, Rick Sutcliffe, Tom Seaver	.30
61 Home Run Champs: Tony Armas, Reggie Jackson, Jim Rice	.40
62 Nat'l League MVP's: Keith Hernandez, Mike Schmidt, Dale Murphy	.50
63 Am. League MVP's: George Brett, Robin Yount, Fred Lynn	.40
64 Comeback Players: Bert Blyleven, Jerry Koosman, John Denny	.15
65 Cy Young Relievers: Willie Hernandez, Rollie Fingers, Bruce Sutter	.20
66 Rookies of The Year: Bob Horner, Andre Dawson, G. Matthews	.20
67 Rookies of The Year: Ron Kittle, Carlton Fisk, Tom Seaver	.35
68 Home Run Champs: Dave Kingman, Mike Schmidt, George Foster	.30
69 Dbl. Award Winners: Cal Ripken, Jr., Pete Rose, Rod Carew	.75
70 Cy Young Winners: Rick Sutcliffe, Steve Carlton, Tom Seaver	.30
71 Top Sluggers: Reggie Jackson, Fred Lynn, Robin Yount	.35
72 Rookies of The Year: Rick Sutcliffe, Dave Righetti, F. Valenzuela	.25
73 Rookies of The Year: Fred Lynn, Eddie Murray, Cal Ripken, Jr.	.35
74 Rookies of The Year: Alvin Davis, Lou Whitaker, Rod Carew	.25
75 Batting Champs: Don Mattingly, Carney Lansford, Wade Boggs	1.00

NO. PLAYER	MINT
76 Jesse Barfield	.20
77 Phil Bradley	.20
78 Chris Brown	.25
79 Tom Browning	.25
80 Tom Brunansky	.25
81 Bill Buckner	.15
82 Chili Davis	.15
83 Mike Davis	.15
84 Rich Gedman	.15
85 Willie Hernandez	.15
86 Ron Kittle	.15
87 Lee Lacy	.15
88 Bill Madlock	.15
89 Mike Marshall	.15
90 Keith Moreland	.15
91 Graig Nettles	.15
92 Lance Parrish	.25
93 Kirby Puckett	2.00
94 Juan Samuel	.20
95 Steve Sax	.20
96 Dave Stieb	.25
97 Darryl Strawberry	1.00
98 Willie Upshaw	.15
99 Frank Viola	.35
100 Dwight Gooden	1.25
101 Joaquin Andujar	.15
102 George Bell	.30
103 Bert Blyleven	.20
104 Mike Boddicker	.15
105 Britt Burns	.15
106 Rod Carew	.50
107 Jack Clark	.30
108 Danny Cox	.15
109 Ron Darling	.20
110 Andre Dawson	.40
111 Leon Durham	.15
112 Tony Fernandez	.20
113 Tom Herr	.15
114 Teddy Higuera	.30
115 Bob Horner	.20
116 Dave Kingman	.15
117 Jack Morris	.20
118 Dan Quisenberry	.20
119 Jeff Reardon	.20
120 Bryn Smith	.15
121 Ozzie Smith	.35
122 John Tudor	.15
123 Tim Wallach	.15
124 Willie Wilson	.15
125 Carlton Fisk	.30

No. 126 to 150—TRI-STARS

NO. PLAYER	MINT
126 RBI Sluggers: George Foster, Gary Carter, Al Oliver	.20
127 Run Scorers: Keith Hernandez, Tim Raines, Ryne Sandberg	.35
128 Run Scorers: Willie Wilson, Paul Molitor, Cal Ripken, Jr.	.35
129 No-Hitters: J. Candelaria, B. Forsch, D. Eckersley	.20

NO. PLAYER	MINT
130 World Series MVP's: Rollie Fingers, Pete Rose, Ron Cey	.35
131 All-Star Game MVP's: George Foster, Dave Concepcion, Bill Madlock	.20
132 Cy Young Winners: Vida Blue, John Denny, Fernando Valenzuela	.20
133 Comeback Players: Richard Dotson, Joaquin Andujar, Doyle Alexander	.20
134 Big Winners: Rick Sutcliffe, Tom Seaver, John Denny	.30
135 Veteran Pitchers: Tom Seaver, Phil Niekro, Don Sutton	.35
136 Rookies of The Year: Dwight Gooden, Vince Coleman, Alfredo Griffin	.75
137 All-Star Game MVP's: Steve Garvey, Gary Carter, Fred Lynn	.35
138 Veteran Hitters: Tony Perez, Pete Rose, Rusty Staub	.50
139 Power Hitters: Mike Schmidt, Jim Rice, George Foster	.50
140 Batting Champs: Tony Gwynn, Al Oliver, Bill Buckner	.35
141 No-Hitters: Jack Morris, Dave Righetti, Nolan Ryan	1.00
142 No-Hitters: Tom Seaver, Bert Blyleven, Vida Blue	.30
143 Strikeout Kings: Nolan Ryan, Fernando Valenzuela, Dwight Gooden	1.00
144 Base Stealers: Willie Wilson, Tim Raines, Davey Lopes	.25
145 RBI Sluggers: Tony Armas, Cecil Cooper, Eddie Murray	.35
146 Am. League MVP's: Rod Carew, Jim Rice, Rollie Fingers	.25
147 World Series MVP's: Alan Trammell, Rick Dempsey, Reggie Jackson	.30
148 World Series MVP's: Darrell Porter, Mike Schmidt, Pedro Guerrero	.35
149 ERA Leaders: Mike Boddicker, Rick Sutcliffe, Ron Guidry	.20
150 Comeback Players: Reggie Jackson, Dave Kingman, Fred Lynn	.40

NO. PLAYER	MINT
151 Buddy Bell	.15
152 Dennis Boyd	.15
153 Dave Concepcion	.15
154 Brian Downing	.15
155 Shawon Dunston	.35
156 John Franco	.25
157 Scott Garrelts	.15
158 Bob James	.15
159 Charlie Leibrandt	.15
160 Oddibe McDowell	.20
161 Roger McDowell	.35
162 Mike Moore	.15
163 Phil Niekro	.35
164 Al Oliver	.15
165 Tony Pena	.20
166 Ted Power	.15
167 Mike Scioscia	.15
168 Mario Soto	.15
169 Bob Stanley	.15
170 Gary Templeton	.15
171 Andre Thornton	.15
172 Alan Trammell	.35
173 Doug DeCinces	.20
174 Greg Walker	.20
175 Don Sutton	.35

NO. PLAYER	MINT
No. 176 to 185—THE BIG SIX	
176 1985 Award Winners:	1.00
Vince Coleman, Ozzie	
Guillen, Bret Saberhagen,	
Don Mattingly, Dwight	
Gooden, Willie McGee	
177 1985 Hot Rookies:	.40
Mark Salas, Stew Cliburn,	
Brian Fisher, Joe Hesketh,	
Joe Orsulak, Larry Sheets	
178 Future Stars:	10.00
Steve Lombardozzi, Jose	
Canseco, Mark Funderburk,	
Mike Greenwell, Billy Joe	
Robidoux, Dan Tartabull	
179 1985 Gold Glovers:	.75
George Brett, Don	
Mattingly, Ron Guidry,	
Keith Hernandez, Willie	
McGee, Dale Murphy	
180 Active .300 Hitters	.75
Wade Boggs, George Brett,	
Rod Carew, Cecil Cooper,	
Don Mattingly, W. Wilson	

NO. PLAYER	MINT
181 Active .300 Hitters	.75
Tony Gwynn, Bill Madlock,	
Pedro Guerrero,	
Dave Parker, Pete Rose,	
Keith Hernandez	
182 1985 Milestones:	.75
Rod Carew, Phil Niekro,	
Pete Rose, Tom Seaver,	
Nolan Ryan, Matt Tallman	
183 1985 Triple Crown:	.75
Willie McGee, Dave Parker,	
Wade Boggs, Darrell Evans,	
D. Mattingly, D. Murphy	
184 1985 Highlights:	.75
Wade Boggs, Rickey	
Henderson, Don Mattingly,	
Willie McGee, Dwight	
Gooden, John Tudor	
185 20 Game Winners:	.75
Dwight Gooden,	
Ron Guidry, John Tudor,	
Joaquin Andujar,	
Bret Saberhagen,	
Tom Browning	

NO. PLAYER	MINT
186 W. Series Champions:	.40
D. Iorg, W. Wilson,	
C. Leibrandt, L. Smith,	
G. Brett, B. Saberhagen,	
D. Motley, D. Quisenberry,	
J. Sundberg, S. Balboni,	
F. White, D. Jackson	
187 Hubie Brooks	.20
188 Glenn Davis	.75
189 Darrell Evans	.15
190 Rich Gossage	.15
191 Andy Hawkins	.15
192 Jay Howell	.15
193 LaMarr Hoyt	.15
194 Davey Lopes	.15
195 Mike Scott	.35
196 Ted Simmons	.20
197 Gary Ward	.15
198 Bob Welch	.15
199 Mike Young	.15
200 Buddy Blancalana	.15

1987 Sportflics. . . . Complete Set of 200 Cards—Value $35.00

Each card can be tilted to show three different photos. The set included 165 individual players, 20 "Tri-Star" cards and 15 other cards. There are three different copyright on the back—1986, 1987 and no copyright.

NO. PLAYER	MINT
1 Don Mattingly	2.00
2 Wade Boggs	1.00
3 Dale Murphy	.35
4 Rickey Henderson	1.00
5 George Brett	.60
6 Eddie Murray	.50
7 Kirby Puckett	1.00
8 Ryne Sandberg	.75
9 Cal Ripken Jr.	.40
10 Roger Clemens	1.00
11 Teddy Higuera	.25
12 Steve Sax	.25
13 Chris Brown	.15
14 Jesse Barfield	.20
15 Kent Hrbek	.25
16 Robin Yount	.50
17 Glenn Davis	.35
18 Hubie Brooks	.15
19 Mike Scott	.25
20 Darryl Strawberry	.75
21 Alvin Davis	.20
22 Eric Davis	.75
23 Danny Tartabull	.35
24 Cory Snyder (correct)	1.50
24 C. Snyder (error)	1.50
(photo of Pat Tabler)	
25 Pete Rose	1.00
26 Wally Joiner	1.00
27 Pedro Guerrero	.25
28 Tom Seaver	.50
29 Bob Knepper	.15
30 Mike Schmidt	1.00
31 Tony Gwynn	.75
32 Don Slaught	.15
33 Todd Worrell	.25
34 Tim Raines	.30
35 Dave Parker	.25
36 Bob Ojeda	.15
37 Pete Incaviglia	.50
38 Bruce Hurst	.20
39 Bobby Witt (R)	.40
40 Steve Garvey	.50
41 Dave Winfield	.40
42 Jose Cruz	.15
43 Orel Hershiser	.35
44 Reggie Jackson	.60
45 Chili Davis	.20

NO. PLAYER	MINT
46 Robby Thompson	.20
47 Dennis Boyd	.15
48 Kirk Gibson	.30
49 Fred Lynn	.25
50 Gary Carter	.25
51 George Bell	.35
52 Pete O'Brien	.15
53 Ron Darling	.20
54 Paul Molitor	.15
55 Mike Pagliarulo	.15
56 Mike Boddicker	.15
57 Dave Righetti	.20
58 Len Dykstra	.50
59 Mike Witt	.15
60 Tony Bernazard	.15
61 John Kruk	.15
62 Mike Krukow	.15
63 Sid Fernandez	.20
64 Gary Gaetti	.15
65 Vince Coleman	.50
66 Pat Tabler	.15
67 Mike Scioscia	.15
68 Scott Garrelts	.15
69 Brett Butler	.15
70 Bill Buckner	.15
71 Dennis Rasmussen	.15
72 Tim Wallach	.15
73 Bob Horner	.15
74 Willie McGee	.20
75 Tri-Stars:	1.00
Mattingly, Joyner, Murray	
76 Jesse Orosco	.15
77 Tri-Stars:	.15
Worrell, Reardon, Smith	
78 Candy Maldonado	.15
79 Tri-Stars:	.20
Smith, Brooks, Dunston	
80 Tri-Stars:	1.00
Bell, Canseco, Rice	
81 Bert Blyleven	.15
82 Mike Marshall	.15
83 Ron Guidry	.15
84 Julio Franco	.15
85 Willie Wilson	.15
86 Lee Lacy	.15

NO. PLAYER	MINT
87 Jack Morris	.20
88 Ray Knight	.15
89 Phil Bradley	.20
90 Jose Canseco	3.00
91 Gary Ward	.15
92 Mike Easler	.15
93 Tony Pena	.15
94 Dave Smith	.15
95 Will Clark	4.00
96 Lloyd Moseby	.15
97 Jim Rice	.25
98 Shawon Dunston	.20
99 Don Sutton	.25
100 Dwight Gooden	.75
101 Lance Parrish	.15
102 Mark Langston	.25
103 Floyd Youmans	.15
104 Lee Smith	.20
105 Willie Hernandez	.15
106 Doug DeCinces	.15
107 Ken Schrom	.15
108 Don Carman	.15
109 Brook Jacoby	.15
110 Steve Bedrosian	.25
111 Tri-Stars:	.50
Clemens, Morris, Higuer	
112 Tri-Stars:	.20
Barrett, Bernazard, Whitaker	
113 Tri-Stars:	.25
Ripken, Fletcher, Fernandez	
114 Tri-Stars:	.75
Boggs, Brett, Gaetti	
115 Tri-Stars:	.40
Schmidt, Brown, Wallach	
116 Tri-Stars:	.25
Sandberg, Ray, Doran	
117 Tri-Stars:	.25
Parker, Gwynn, Bass	
118 Big 6 Rookies:	1.00
Ty Gainey, Terry Steinbach,	
David Clark, Pat Dodson,	
Phil Lombardi, B. Santiago	
119 Hi-Lite Tri-Stars:	.25
Righetti, Valenzuela, Scott	

NO. PLAYER	MINT
120 Tri-Stars:	.50
Valenzuela, Scott, Gooden	
121 Johnny Ray	.15
122 Keith Moreland	.15
123 Juan Samuel	.15
124 Wally Backman	.15
125 Nolan Ryan	1.00
126 Greg Harris	.15
127 Kirk McCaskill	.15
128 Dwight Evans	.25
129 Rick Rhoden	.15
130 Bill Madlock	.15
131 Oddibe McDowell	.15
132 Darrell Evans	.15
133 Keith Hernandez	.25
134 Tom Brunansky	.20
135 Kevin McReynolds	.30
136 Scott Fletcher	.15
137 Lou Whitaker	.15
138 Carney Lansford	.15
139 Andre Dawson	.35
140 Carlton Fisk	.30
141 Buddy Bell	.15
142 Ozzie Smith	.35
143 Dan Pasqua	.15
144 Kevin Mitchell	1.00
145 Bret Saberhagen	.30
146 Charlie Kerfeld	.15
147 Phil Niekro	.25
148 John Candelaria	.15
149 Rich Gedman	.15
150 Fernando Valenzuela	.25
151 Tri-Stars:	.20
Carter, Scioscia, Pena	
152 Tri-Stars:	.25
Raines, Cruz, Coleman	
153 Tri-Stars:	.25
Barfield, Baines, Winfield	
154 Tri-Stars:	.20
Parrish, Slaught, Gedman	
155 Tri-Stars:	.60
Murphy, McReynolds, Davis	
156 Hi-Lite Tri-Stars:	.40
Sutton, Schmidt, Deshaies	

NO.	PLAYER	MINT	NO.	PLAYER	MINT	NO.	PLAYER	MINT	NO.	PLAYER	MINT
157	Speedburners: Henderson, Cangelosi, Pettis	.35	165	Don Aase	.15	179	Jim Presley	.20	193	Von Hayes	.15
158	Big 6 Rookies: Randy Asadoor, C. Candaele, K. Seitzer, Rafael Palmeiro, Tim Pyznarski, D. Cochrane	1.00	166	Glenn Wilson	.15	180	Mel Hall	.15	194	Tri-Stars: Aase, Righetti, Eichhorn	.15
			167	Dan Quisenberry	.20	181	Shane Rawley	.15			
			168	Frank White	.15	182	Marty Barrett	.20	195	Tri-Stars: Hernandez, Clark, Davis	.50
			169	Cecil Cooper	.15	183	Damaso Garcia	.15			
159	Big 6: Mattingly, Henderson, Clemens, Murphy, Murray, Gooden	1.50	170	Jody Davis	.15	184	Bobby Grich	.15	196	Hi-Lite Tri-Stars: Clemens, Cowley, Horner	.40
			171	Harold Baines	.25	185	Leon Durham	.15	197	Big 6: Brett, Brooks, Gwynn, Sandberg, Raines, Boggs	.75
			172	Rob Deer	.20	186	Ozzie Guillen	.15			
160	Roger McDowell	.15	173	John Tudor	.20	187	Tony Fernandez	.25			
161	Brian Downing	.15	174	Larry Parrish	.15	188	Alan Trammell	.25			
162	Bill Doran	.15	175	Kevin Bass	.15	189	Jim Clancy	.15	198	Tri-Stars: Puckett, Henderson, Lynn	.40
163	Don Baylor	.20	176	Joe Carter	.35	190	Bo Jackson	3.00	199	Speedburners: Raines, Coleman, Davis	.50
164	Alfredo Griffin	.15	177	Mitch Webster	.15	191	Bob Forsch	.15			
			178	Dave Kingman	.20	192	John Franco	.25	200	Steve Carlton	.35

1988 Sportflics.... Complete Set of 255 Cards—Value $35.00

Each card can be tilted to show three different photos. The set includes 219 individual players, 3 Highlights and 3 Rookie Prospects.

NO.	PLAYER	MINT	NO.	PLAYER	MINT	NO.	PLAYER	MINT	NO.	PLAYER	MINT
1	Don Mattingly	1.25	60	Jody Davis	.12	119	Barry Bonds	.60	178	Ken Griffey	.15
2	Tim Raines	.25	61	Todd Worrell	.10	120	Reggie Jackson	.75	179	Lee Smith	.15
3	Andre Dawson	.30	62	Von Hayes	.15	121	Mike Pagliarulo	.15	180	Hi-Lite Tri-Stars: Puckett, Nieves, Schmidt	.40
4	George Bell	.25	63	Billy Hatcher	.15	122	Tommy John	.25			
5	Joe Carter	.25	64	John Kruk	.10	123	Bill Madlock	.20	181	Brian Downing	.15
6	Matt Nokes	.25	65	Tom Henke	.12	124	Ken Caminiti	.20	182	Andres Galarraga	.20
7	Dave Winfield	.35	66	Mike Scott	.20	125	Gary Ward	.15	183	Rob Deer	.15
8	Kirby Puckett	.60	67	Vince Coleman	.25	126	Candy Maldonado	.15	184	Greg Brock	.12
9	Will Clark	1.50	68	Ozzie Smith	.30	127	Harold Reynolds	.15	185	Doug DeCinces	.12
10	Eric Davis	.75	69	Ken Williams	.15	128	Joe Magrane	.30	186	Johnny Ray	.12
11	Rickey Henderson	.60	70	Steve Bedrosian	.15	129	Mike Henneman	.20	187	Hubie Brooks	.12
12	Ryne Sandberg	.40	71	Luis Polonia	.20	130	Jim Gantner	.12	188	Darrell Evans	.20
13	Jesse Barfield	.20	72	Brook Jacoby	.15	131	Bobby Bonilla	.50	189	Mel Hall	.15
14	Ozzie Guillen	.15	73	Ron Darling	.25	132	John Farrell	.20	190	Jim Deshaies	.12
15	Bret Saberhagen	.20	74	Lloyd Moseby	.20	133	Frank Tanana	.15	191	Dan Plesac	.15
16	Tony Gwynn	.50	75	Wally Joyner	.25	134	Zane Smith	.20	192	Willie Wilson	.12
17	Kevin Seitzer	.40	76	Dan Quisenberry	.15	135	Dave Righetti	.20	193	Mike LaValliere	.12
18	Jack Clark	.15	77	Scott Fletcher	.12	136	Rick Reuschel	.20	194	Tom Brunansky	.20
19	Danny Tartabull	.20	78	Kirk McKaskill	.12	137	Dwight Evans	.25	195	John Franco	.20
20	Ted Higuera	.20	79	Paul Molitor	.25	138	Howard Johnson	.30	196	Frank Viola	.30
21	Charlie Liebrandt, Jr.	.10	80	Mike Aldrete	.15	139	Terry Leach	.15	197	Bruce Hurst	.20
22	Benny Santiago	.50	81	Neal Heaton	.12	140	Casey Candaele	.12	198	John Tudor	.15
23	Fred Lynn	.20	82	Jeffrey Leonard	.12	141	Tom Herr	.15	199	Bob Forsch	.15
24	Rob Thompson	.10	83	Dave Magadan	.20	142	Tony Pena	.15	200	Dwight Gooden	.60
25	Alan Trammell	.20	84	Danny Cox	.15	143	Lance Parrish	.20	201	Jose Canseco	2.00
26	T. Fernandez	.20	85	Lance McCullers	.12	144	Ellis Burks	1.00	202	Carney Lansford	.15
27	Rick Sutcliffe	.20	86	Jay Howell	.12	145	Pete O'Brien	.20	203	Kelly Downs	.15
28	Gary Carter	.20	87	Charlie Hough	.12	146	Mike Boddicker	.15	204	Glenn Wilson	.15
29	Cory Snyder	.15	88	Gene Garber	.12	147	Buddy Bell	.15	205	Pat Tabler	.15
30	Lou Whitaker	.15	89	Jesse Orosco	.12	148	Bo Jackson	1.50	206	Mike Davis	.15
31	Keith Hernandez	.20	90	Don Robinson	.12	149	Frank White	.15	207	Roger Clemens	.75
32	Mike Witt	.15	91	Willie McGee	.20	150	George Brett	.50	208	Dave Smith	.15
33	Harold Baines	.15	92	Bert Blyleven	.15	151	Tim Wallach	.15	209	Curt Young	.15
34	Robin Yount	.40	93	Phil Bradley	.15	152	Cal Ripken, Jr.	.30	210	Mark Eichhorn	.15
35	Mike Schmidt	.75	94	Terry Kennedy	.12	153	Brett Butler	.20	211	Juan Nieves	.15
36	Dion James	.10	95	Kent Hrbek	.20	154	Gary Gaetti	.20	212	Bob Boone	.15
37	Tom Candiotti	.10	96	Juan Samuel	.15	155	Darryl Strawberry	.75	213	Don Sutton	.20
38	Tracy Jones	.10	97	Pedro Guerrero	.15	156	Alfredo Griffin	.15	214	Cecil Upshaw	.15
39	Nolan Ryan	.75	98	Sid Bream	.12	157	Marty Barrett	.15	215	Jim Clancy	.10
40	Fernando Valenzuela	.25	99	Devon White	.15	158	Jim Rice	.25	216	Bill Ripken	.20
41	Vance Law	.10	100	Mark McGwire	.75	159	Terry Pendleton	.15	217	Ozzie Virgil	.15
42	Roger McDowell	.15	101	Dave Parker	.20	160	Orel Hershiser	.30	218	Dave Concepcion	.10
43	Carlton Fisk	.25	102	Glen Davis	.20	161	Larry Sheets	.15	219	Alan Ashby	.15
44	Scott Garrelts	.10	103	Greg Walker	.15	162	Dave Stewart	.30	220	Mike Marshall	.20
45	Lee Guetterman	.10	104	Rick Rhoden	.15	163	Shawon Dunston	.20	221	Hi-Lite Tri-Stars: McGwire, Molitor, Coleman	.50
46	Mark Langston	.15	105	Mitch Webster	.15	164	Keith Moreland	.15			
47	Willie Randolph	.20	106	Lenny Dykstra	.25	165	Ken Oberkfell	.15	222	Hi-Lite Tri-Stars: Santiago, Bedrosian, Mattingly	.75
48	Bill Doran	.10	107	Gene Larkin	.15	166	Ivan Calderon	.20			
49	Larry Parrish	.10	108	Floyd Youmans	.15	167	Bob Welch	.20			
50	Wade Boggs	.75	109	Andy Van Slyke	.20	168	Fred McGriff	.40	223	Rookies: Shawn Abner, Jay Buhner, Gary Thurman	.25
51	Shan Rawley	.10	110	Mike Scioscia	.12	169	Pete Incaviglia	.20			
52	Alvin Davis	.15	111	Kirk Gibson	.25	170	Dale Murphy	.30			
53	Jeff Reardon	.10	112	Kal Daniels	.25	171	Mike Dunne	.15	224	Rookies: Tim Crews, Vincente Palacios, John Davis	.20
54	Jim Presley	.15	113	Ruben Sierra	.75	172	Chili Davis	.20			
55	Kevin Bass	.15	114	Sam Horn	.20	173	Milt Thompson	.15			
56	Kevin McReynolds	.20	115	Ray Knight	.12	174	Terry Steinbach	.25	225	Rookies: Jody Reed, Jeff Treadway, Keith Miller	.50
57	B.J. Surhoff	.15	116	Jimmy Key	.15	175	Oddibe McDowell	.15			
58	Julio Franco	.15	117	Bo Diaz	.12	176	Jack Morris	.15			
59	Eddie Murray	.35	118	Mike Greenwell	.75	177	Sid Fernandez	.20			

1989 Sportflics. . . . Complete Set of 225 Cards—Value $35.00

Each card can be tilted to show three different photos. The set includes 219 individual players, 2 Highlights and 3 Rookie Prospects.

NO.	PLAYER	MINT	NO.	PLAYER	MINT	NO.	PLAYER	MINT	NO.	PLAYER	MINT
1	Jose Canseco	1.50	58	Steve Sax	.15	114	Tim Wallach	.15	170	Will Clark	1.25
2	Wally Joyner	.25	59	Lance Parrish	.15	115	Nolan Ryan	1.00	171	Chet Lemon	.12
3	Roger Clemens	.50	60	Keith Hernandez	.15	116	Walt Weiss	.20	172	Pat Tabler	.12
4	Greg Swindell	.15	61	Jose Uribe	.12	117	Brian Downing	.12	173	Jim Rice	.15
5	Jack Morris	.15	62	Jose Lind	.12	118	Melido Perez	.15	174	Billy Hatcher	.12
6	Mickey Brantley	.12	63	Steve Bedrosian	.12	119	Terry Steinbach	.15	175	Bruce Hurst	.15
7	Jim Presley	.12	64	George Brett	.30	120	Mike Scott	.15	176	John Franco	.15
8	Pete O'Brien	.15	65	Kirk Gibson	.20	121	Tim Belcher	.15	177	Van Snider	.15
9	Jesse Barfield	.15	66	Cal Ripken Jr.	.25	122	Mike Boddicker	.15	178	Ron Jones	.15
10	Frank Viola	.20	67	Mitch Webster	.12	123	Len Dykstra	.20	179	Jerald Clark	.15
11	Kevin Bass	.12	68	Fred Lynn	.15	124	Fernando Valenzuela	.20	180	Tom Browning	.15
12	Glenn Wilson	.12	69	Eric Davis	.35	125	Gerald Young	.15	181	Von Hayes	.12
13	Chris Sabo	.30	70	Bo Jackson	1.50	126	Tom Henke	.12	182	Bobby Bonilla	.25
14	Fred McGriff	.25	71	Kevin Elster	.15	127	Dave Henderson	.15	183	Todd Worrell	.12
15	Mark Grace	1.50	72	Rick Reuschel	.12	128	Dan Plesac	.12	184	John Kruk	.12
16	Devon White	.15	73	Tim Burke	.12	129	Chili Davis	.12	185	Scott Fletcher	.12
17	Juan Samuel	.15	74	Mark Davis	.12	130	Bryan Harvey	.15	186	Willie Wilson	.15
18	Lou Whitaker	.15	75	Claudell Washington	.15	131	Don August	.15	187	Jody Davis	.12
19	Greg Walker	.12	76	Lance McCullers	.15	132	Mike Harkey	.30	188	Kent Hrbek	.15
20	Roberto Alomar	.40	77	Mike Moore	.12	133	Luis Polonia	.12	189	Ruben Sierra	.30
21	Mike Schmidt	.60	78	Robby Thompson	.12	134	Craig Worthington	.20	190	Shawon Dunston	.15
22	Benny Santiago	.30	79	Roger McDowell	.15	135	Joey Meyer	.12	191	Ellis Burks	.40
23	Dave Stewart	.20	80	Danny Jackson	.15	136	Barry Larkin	.25	192	Brook Jacoby	.12
24	Dave Winfield	.20	81	Tim Leary	.15	137	Glenn Davis	.20	193	Jeff Robinson	.15
25	George Bell	.15	82	Bobby Witt	.15	138	Mike Scioscia	.12	194	Rich Dotson	.15
26	J. Clark	.20	83	Jim Gott	.12	139	Andres Galarraga	.20	195	Johnny Ray	.15
27	Doug Drabek	.15	84	Andy Hawkins	.12	140	Dwight Gooden	.35	196	Cory Snyder	.15
28	Ron Gant	.35	85	Ozzie Guillen	.15	141	Keith Moreland	.12	197	Mike Witt	.12
29	Glenn Braggs	.12	86	John Tudor	.12	142	Kevin Mitchell	.50	198	Marty Barrett	.12
30	Rafael Palmeiro	.25	87	Todd Burns	.15	143	Mike Greenwell	.35	199	Robin Yount	.35
31	Brett Butler	.12	88	Dave Gallagher	.15	144	Mel Hall	.15	200	Mark McGwire	.75
32	Ron Darling	.15	89	Jay Buhner	.15	145	Rickey Henderson	.50	201	Ryne Sandberg	.40
33	Alvin Davis	.15	90	Gregg Jefferies	1.00	146	Barry Bonds	.40	202	John Candelaria	.15
34	Bob Walk	.12	91	Bob Welch	.15	147	Eddie Murray	.25	203	Matt Nokes	.15
35	Dave Stieb	.15	92	Charlie Hough	.15	148	Lee Smith	.15	204	Dwight Evans	.20
36	Orel Hershiser	.35	93	Tony Fernandez	.15	149	Julio Franco	.15	205	Darryl Strawberry	.50
37	John Farrell	.15	94	Ozzie Virgil	.12	150	Tim Raines	.20	206	Willie McGee	.15
38	Doug Jones	.12	95	Andre Dawson	.25	151	Mitch Williams	.15	207	Bobby Thigpen	.12
39	Kelly Downs	.12	96	Hubie Brooks	.12	152	Tim Laudner	.12	208	B.J. Surhoff	.12
40	Bob Boone	.12	97	Kevin McReynolds	.15	153	Mike Pagliarulo	.15	209	Paul Molitor	.15
41	Gary Sheffield	1.00	98	Mike LaValliere	.12	154	Floyd Bannister	.12	210	Jody Reed	.15
42	Doug Dascenzo	.15	99	Terry Pendleton	.12	155	Gary Carter	.20	211	Doyle Alexander	.15
43	Chad Krueter	.15	100	Wade Boggs	.50	156	Kirby Puckett	.50	212	Dennis Rasmussen	.12
44	Ricky Jordan	.35	101	Dennis Eckersley	.15	157	Harold Baines	.15	213	Kevin Gross	.12
45	Dave West	.15	102	Mark Gubicza	.15	158	Dave Righetti	.15	214	Kirk McCaskill	.12
46	Danny Tartabull	.15	103	Frank Tanana	.15	159	Mark Langston	.15	215	Alan Trammell	.15
47	Teddy Higuera	.15	104	Joe Carter	.25	160	Tony Gwynn	.35	216	Damon Berryhill	.15
48	Gary Gaetti	.15	105	Ozzie Smith	.25	161	Tom Brunansky	.15	217	Rick Sutcliffe	.15
49	Dave Parker	.20	106	Dennis Martinez	.15	162	Vance Law	.12	218	Don Slaught	.12
50	Don Mattingly	1.00	107	Jeff Treadway	.15	163	Kelly Gruber	.25	219	Carlton Fisk	.20
51	David Cone	.20	108	Greg Maddux	.20	164	Gerald Perry	.15	220	Allan Anderson	.20
52	Kal Daniels	.15	109	Bret Saberhagen	.20	165	Harold Reynolds	.12	221	Boggs, Canseco, Greenwell	1.00
53	Carney Lansford	.15	110	Dale Murphy	.35	166	Andy Van Slyke	.15	222	Hershiser, Eckersley, Browning	.35
54	Mike Marshall	.15	111	Rob Deer	.15	167	Jimmy Key	.15	223	Sheffield, Jefferies, Alomar	2.00
55	Kevin Seitzer	.15	112	Pete Incaviglia	.15	168	Jeff Reardon	.15	224	Milacki, Johnson, Martinez	.25
56	Mike Henneman	.15	113	Vince Coleman	.20	169	Milt Thompson	.12	225	Drew, Berroa, Jones	.15
57	Bill Doran	.12									

1990 Sportflics. . . . Complete Set of 225 Cards—Value $35.00

Each card can be tilted to show three different photos.

NO.	PLAYER	MINT	NO.	PLAYER	MINT	NO.	PLAYER	MINT	NO.	PLAYER	MINT
1	Kevin Mitchell	.30	16	Ozzie Smith	.20	31	Bryan Harvey	.15	46	Kevin Seitzer	.15
2	Wade Boggs	.35	17	George Bell	.20	32	Jim Deshaies	.15	47	Bruce Hurst	.15
3	Cory Snyder	.15	18	Robin Yount	.25	33	Terry Steinbach	.15	48	Ozzie Guillen	.15
4	Paul O'Neill	.15	19	Glenn Davis	.20	34	Tom Glavine	.15	49	Wally Joyner	.20
5	Will Clark	.75	20	Jeffrey Leonard	.15	35	Bob Welch	.15	50	Mike Greenwell	.30
6	Tony Fernandez	.15	21	Chili Davis	.15	36	Charlie Hayes	.15	51	Gary Gaetti	.20
7	Ken Griffey, Jr.	2.00	22	Craig Biggio	.15	37	Jeff Reardon	.15	52	Gary Sheffield	.35
8	Nolan Ryan	1.00	23	Jose Canseco	1.00	38	Joe Orsulak	.15	53	Dennis Martinez	.15
9	Rafael Palmeiro	.20	24	Derek Lilliquist	.15	39	Scott Garrelts	.15	54	Ryne Sandberg	.50
10	Jesse Barfield	.15	25	Chris Bosio	.10	40	Bob Boone	.15	55	Mike Scott	.15
11	Kirby Puckett	.35	26	Dave Stieb	.15	41	Scott Bankhead	.15	56	Todd Benzinger	.15
12	Steve Sax	.20	27	Bobby Thigpen	.15	42	Tom Henke	.15	57	Kelly Gruber	.15
13	Fred McGriff	.20	28	Jack Clark	.15	43	Greg Briley	.15	58	Jose Lind	.15
14	Gregg Jefferies	.35	29	Kevin Ritz	.35	44	Teddy Higuera	.15	59	Allan Anderson	.15
15	Mark Grace	.40	30	Tom Gordon	.60	45	Pat Borders	.15	60	Robby Thompson	.15

NO.	PLAYER	MINT
61	John Smoltz	.15
62	Mark Davis	.10
63	Tom Herr	.10
64	Randy Johnson	.15
65	Lonnie Smith	.15
66	Pedro Guerrero	.15
67	Jerome Walton	.75
68	Ramon Martinez	.35
69	Tim Raines	.20
70	Matt Williams	.35
71	Joe Oliver	.20
72	Nick Esasky	.15
73	Kevin Brown	.15
74	Walt Weiss	.10
75	Roger McDowell	.10
76	Jose DeLeon	.10
77	Brian Downing	.10
78	Jay Howell	.10
79	Jose Uribe	.10
80	Ellis Burks	.20
81	Sammy Sosa	.40
82	Johnny Ray	.15
83	Danny Darwin	.15
84	Carney Lansford	.15
85	Jose Oquendo	.15
86	John Cerutti	.15
87	Dave Winfield	.20
88	Dave Righetti	.15
89	Danny Jackson	.15
90	Andy Benes	.30
91	Tom Browning	.15
92	Pete O'Brien	.15
93	Roberto Alomar	.20
94	Bret Saberhagen	.20
95	Phil Bradley	.15
96	Doug Jones	.15
97	Eric Davis	.25
98	Tony Gwynn	.30
99	Jim Abbott	.50
100	Cal Ripken, Jr.	.20
101	Andy Van Slyke	.15
102	Dan Plesac	.15

NO.	PLAYER	MINT
103	Lou Whitaker	.15
104	Steve Bedrosian	.15
105	Dave Gallagher	.15
106	Keith Hernandez	.15
107	Duane Ward	.15
108	Andre Dawson	.20
109	Howard Johnson	.20
110	Mark Langston	.15
111	Jerry Browne	.15
112	Alvin Davis	.15
113	Sid Fernandez	.15
114	Mike Devereaux	.15
115	Benny Santiago	.20
116	Bip Roberts	.15
117	Craig Worthington	.15
118	Kevin Elster	.15
119	Harold Reynolds	.15
120	Joe Carter	.20
121	Brian Harper	.15
122	Frank Viola	.15
123	Jeff Ballard	.15
124	John Kruk	.15
125	Harold Baines	.15
126	Tom Candiotti	.15
127	Kevin McReynolds	.15
128	Mookie Wilson	.15
129	Danny Tartabull	.15
130	Craig Lefferts	.15
131	Jose DeJesus	.15
132	John Orton	.20
133	Curt Schilling	.15
134	Marquis Grissom	.40
135	Greg Vaughn	.60
136	Brett Butler	.15
137	Rob Deer	.15
138	John Franco	.20
139	Keith Moreland	.15
140	Dave Smith	.15
141	Mark McGwire	.35
142	Vince Coleman	.20
143	Barry Bonds	.30

NO.	PLAYER	MINT
144	Mike Henneman	.15
145	Doc Gooden	.25
146	Darryl Strawberry	.30
147	Von Hayes	.15
148	Andres Galarraga	.15
149	Roger Clemens	.40
150	Don Mattingly	.75
151	Joe Magrane	.15
152	Dwight Smith	.20
153	Ricky Jordan	.15
154	Alan Trammell	.15
155	Lenny Dykstra	.15
156	Lenny Dykstra	.15
157	Mike LaValliere	.15
158	Julio Franco	.20
159	Joey Belle	.15
160	Barry Larkin	.20
161	Rick Reuschel	.15
162	Nelson Santovenia	.15
163	Mike Scioscia	.15
164	Damon Berryhill	.15
165	Todd Worrell	.15
166	Jim Eisenreich	.15
167	Ivan Calderon	.15
168	Goose Gozzo	.20
169	Kirk McCaskill	.15
170	Dennis Eckersley	.15
171	Mickey Tettleton	.15
172	Chuck Finley	.15
173	Dave Magadan	.15
174	Terry Pendleton	.15
175	Willie Randolph	.15
176	Jeff Huson	.15
177	Todd Zeile	.70
178	Steve Olin	.15
179	Eric Anthony	.75
180	Scott Coolbaugh	.25
181	Rick Sutcliffe	.15
182	Tim Wallach	.15
183	Paul Molitor	.15
184	Roberto Kelly	.15

NO.	PLAYER	MINT
185	Mike Moore	.15
186	Junior Felix	.30
187	Mike Schooler	.15
188	Ruben Sierra	.20
189	Dale Murphy	.20
190	Dan Gladden	.15
191	John Smiley	.15
192	Jeff Russell	.15
193	Burt Blyleven	.15
194	Dave Stewart	.20
195	Bobby Bonilla	.25
196	Mitch Williams	.15
197	Orel Hershiser	.20
198	Kevin Bass	.15
199	Tim Burke	.15
200	Bo Jackson	1.00
201	David Cone	.10
202	Gary Pettis	.15
203	Kent Hrbek	.15
204	Carlton Fisk	.20
205	Bob Geren	.15
206	Bill Spiers	.20
207	Oddibe McDowell	.15
208	Rickey Henderson	.50
209	Ken Caminiti	.15
210	Devon White	.15
211	Greg Maddux	.15
212	Ed Whitson	.15
213	Carlos Martinez	.15
214	George Brett	.35
215	Gregg Olson	.30
216	Kenny Rogers	.15
217	Dwight Evans	.20
218	Pat Tabler	.15
219	Jeff Treadway	.15
220	Scott Fletcher	.15
221	Deion Sanders	.40
222	Robin Ventura	.35
223	Chip Hale	.15
224	Tommy Greene	.25
225	Dean Palmer	.25

1989 Upper Deck. . . . Complete Set of 700 Cards—Value $70.00

This was the premier issue of Upper Deck—the sixth major card manufacturer. Features the rookie cards of Gary Sheffield and Ken Griffey, Jr. A special feature is a small hologram on the card's back to discourage counterfeiting. The first 26 cards feature Upper Deck's selection of star rookies. Each team checklist features a drawing of a player on the team.

Ricky Jordan

Craig Biggio

Gary Sheffield

Sandy Alomar Jr.

Ken Griffey Jr.

NO.	PLAYER	MINT
1	Ken Griffey Jr. (R)	25.00
2	Luis Medina (R)	.25
3	Tony Chance (R)	.15
4	Dave Otto	.15
5	Sandy Alomar, Jr. (R)	4.00
6	Rolando Roomes (R)	.20
7	David West (R)	.25
8	Cris Carpenter (R)	.25
9	Gregg Jefferies	3.00
10	Doug Dascenzo (R)	.25
11	Ron Jones (R)	.25
12	Luis De Los Santos (R)	.20
13	Gary Sheffield (R)	3.00
13	Gary Sheffield (error)	4.00
14	Mike Harkey (R)	.75
15	Lance Blanckenship (R)	.20
16	William Brennan (R)	.15
17	John Smoltz (R)	.75
18	Ramon Martinez (R)	4.00
19	Mark Lemke (R)	.15
20	Juan Bell (R)	.25
21	Rey Palacios (R)	.15
22	Felix Jose (R)	.40
23	Van Snider (R)	.25
24	Dante Bichete (R)	.35
25	Randy Johnson (R)	.60
26	Carlos Quintana (R)	.75
27	Star Rookie Checklist	.10
28	Mike Schooler (R)	.35
29	Randy St. Claire	.12
30	Gerald Clark (R)	.20
31	Kevin Gross	.08
32	Dan Firova (R)	.15
33	Jeff Calhoun	.08
34	Tommy Hinze	.08
35	Ricky Jordan (R)	.75
36	Larry Parrish	.10
37	Bret Saberhagen	.25
38	Mike Smithson	.08
39	Dave Dravecky	.08
40	Ed Romero	.08
41	Jeff Musselman	.08
42	Ed Hearn	.08
43	Rance Mulliniks	.08
44	Jim Eisenreich	.08
45	Sil Campusano (R)	.25
46	Mike Krukow	.10
47	Paul Gibson (R)	.15
48	Mike LaCoss	.08
49	Larry Herndon	.08
50	Scott Garreits	.08
51	Duane Henry	.08
52	Jim Acker	.08
53	Steve Sax	.12
54	Pete O'Brien	.08
55	Paul Runge	.08
56	Rick Rhoden	.08
57	John Dopson (R)	.25
58	Casey Candaele	.08
59	Dave Righetti	.08
60	Joe Hesketh	.08
61	Frank DiPino	.08
62	Tim Laudner	.08
63	Jamie Moyer	.08
64	Fred Toliver	.08
65	Mitch Webster	.08
66	John Tudor	.12
67	John Cangelosi	.08

NO.	PLAYER	MINT
68	Mike Devereaux	.12
69	Brian Fisher	.08
70	Mike Marshall	.10
71	Zane Smith	.08
72	B. Holton (error)	1.00
72	B. Holton (correct)	.25
73	Jose Guzman	.08
74	Rick Mahler	.10
75	John Shelby	.08
76	Jim Deshaies	.08
77	Bobby Meacham	.08
78	Bryn Smith	.08
79	Joaquin Andujar	.08
80	Richard Dotson	.08
81	Charlie Lea	.08
82	Calvin Schiraldi	.08
83	Les Straker	.08
84	Les Lancaster	.08
85	Allan Anderson	.08
86	Junior Oritz	.08
87	Jesse Orosco	.08
88	Felix Fermin	.08
89	Dave Anderson	.08
90	Rafael Belliard	.08
91	Franklin Stubbs	.08
92	Cecil Espy	.08
93	Albert Hall	.08
94	Tim Leary	.08
95	Mitch Williams	.08
96	Tracy Jones	.08
97	Danny Darwin	.08
98	Gary Ward	.08
99	Neal Heaton	.08
100	Jim Pankovits	.08
101	Bill Doran	.08
102	Tim Wallach	.08
103	Joe Magrane	.08
104	Ozzie Virgil	.08
105	Alvin Davis	.08
106	Tom Brookens	.08
107	Shawon Dunston	.10
108	Tracy Woodson	.08
109	Nelson Liriano	.08
110	Devon White	.12
111	Steve Balboni	.10
112	Buddy Bell	.08
113	German Jimenez (R)	.15
114	Ken Dayley	.08
115	Andres Galarraga	.15
116	Mike Scioscia	.08
117	Gary Pettis	.08
118	Ernie Whitt	.08
119	Bob Boone	.08
120	Ryne Sandberg	.40
121	Bruce Benedict	.08
122	Hubie Brooks	.08
123	Mike Moore	.08
124	Wallace Johnson	.08
125	Bob Horner	.08
126	Chili Davis	.08
127	Manny Trillo	.08
128	Chet Lemon	.10
129	John Cerutti	.08
130	Orel Hershiser	.25
131	Terry Pendleton	.08
132	Jeff Blauser	.08
133	Mike Fitzgerald	.08
134	Henry Cotto	.08

NO.	PLAYER	MINT
135	Gerald Young	.08
136	Luis Salazar	.08
137	Alejandro Pena	.08
138	Jack Howell	.08
139	Tony Fernandez	.08
140	Mark Grace	2.00
141	Ken Caminiti	.08
142	Mike Jackson	.08
143	Larry McWilliams	.08
144	Andres Thomas	.08
145	Nolan Ryan	2.00
146	Mike Davis	.08
147	DeWayne Buice	.08
148	Jody Davis	.08
149	Jesse Barfield	.12
150	Matte Nokes	.10
151	Jerry Reuss	.08
152	Rick Cerone	.08
153	Storm Davis	.08
154	Marvell Wynee	.08
155	Will Clark	1.50
156	Luis Aguayo	.08
157	Willie Upshaw	.08
158	Randy Bush	.08
159	Ron Darling	.12
160	Kal Daniels	.15
161	Spike Owen	.08
162	Luis Polonia	.08
163	Kevin Mitchell	.50
164	Dave Gallagher (R)	.20
165	Benito Santiago	.20
166	Greg Gagne	.08
167	Ken Phelps	.08
168	Sid Fernandez	.08
169	Bo Diaz	.08
170	Cory Snyder	.20
171	Eric Show	.10
172	Ron Thompson	.08
173	Marty Barrett	.10
174	Dave Henderson	.08
175	Ozzie Guillen	.08
176	Barry Lyons	.08
177	Kelvin Torve (R)	.15
178	Don Slaught	.08
179	Steve Lombardozzi	.08
180	Chris Sabo	2.00
181	Jose Uribe	.08
182	Shane Mack	.08
183	Ron Karkovice	.08
184	Todd Benzinger	.10
185	Dave Stewart	.20
186	Julio Franco	.08
187	Ron Robinson	.08
188	Wally Backman	.08
189	Randy Velarde	.08
190	Joe Carter	.10
191	Bob Welch	.08
192	Kelly Paris	.08
193	Chris Brown	.08
194	Rick Reuschel	.10
195	Roger Clemens	.50
196	Dave Concepcion	.08
197	Al Newman	.08
198	Brook Jacoby	.08
199	Mookie Wilson	.08
200	Don Mattingly	1.00
201	Dick Schofield	.08
202	Mark Gubicza	.08

NO.	PLAYER	MINT
203	Gary Gaetti	.12
204	Dan Pasqua	.08
205	Andre Dawson	.15
206	Chris Speier	.08
207	Kent Tekulve	.08
208	Rod Scurry	.08
209	Scott Bailes	.08
210	Rickey Henderson	.50
211	Harold Baines	.08
212	Tony Armas	.08
213	Kent Hrbek	.10
214	Darrin Jackson	.10
215	George Brett	.30
216	Rafael Santana	.08
217	Andy Allanson	.08
218	Brett Butler	.08
219	Steve Jeltz	.08
220	Jay Buhner	.20
221	Bo Jackson	2.00
222	Angel Salazar	.08
223	Kirk McCaskill	.08
224	Steve Lyons	.08
225	Bert Blyleven	.08
226	Scott Bradley	.08
227	Bob Melvin	.08
228	Ron Kittle	.08
229	Phil Bradley	.08
230	Tommy John	.08
231	Greg Walker	.08
232	Juan Berenguer	.08
233	Pat Tabler	.08
234	Terry Clark (R)	.15
235	Rafael Palmeiro	.20
236	Paul Zuvella	.08
237	Willie Randolph	.10
238	Bruce Fields	.08
239	Mike Aldrete	.08
240	Lance Parrish	.10
241	Gregg Maddux	.20
242	John Moses	.08
243	Melido Perez	.15
244	Willie Wilson	.08
245	Mark McLemore	.08
246	Von Hayes	.10
247	Matt Williams	.50
248	John Candelaria	.12
249	Harold Reynolds	.08
250	Greg Swindell	.08
251	Juan Agosto	.08
252	Mike Felder	.08
253	Vince Coleman	.15
254	Larry Sheets	.08
255	George Bell	.15
256	Terry Steinbach	.08
257	Jack Armstrong (R)	.40
258	Dickie Thon	.08
259	Ray Knight	.08
260	Darryl Strawberry	.50
261	Doug Sisk	.08
262	Alex Trevino	.08
263	Jeff Leonard	.08
264	Tom Henke	.08
265	Ozzie Smith	.20
266	Dave Bergman	.08
267	Tony Phillips	.08
268	Mark Davis	.08
269	Kevin Elster	.08
270	Barry Larkin	.25

NO.	PLAYER	MINT
271	Manny Lee	.08
272	Tom Brunansky	.10
273	Craig Biggio (R)	.75
274	Jim Gantner	.08
275	Eddie Murray	.15
276	Jeff Reed	.08
277	Tim Teufel	.08
278	Rick Honeycutt	.08
279	Guillermo Hernandez	.08
280	John Kruk	.08
281	Luis Alice (R)	.15
282	Jim Clancy	.08
283	Billy Ripken	.10
284	Craig Reynolds	.08
285	Robin Yount	.25
286	Jimmy Jones	.08
287	Ron Oester	.08
288	Terry Leach	.08
289	Dennis Eckersley	.08
290	Alan Trammel	.15
291	Jimmy Key	.08
292	Chris Bosio	.08
293	Jose DeLeon	.08
294	Jim Traber	.08
295	Mike Scott	.15
296	Roger McDowell	.08
297	Gary Templeton	.08
298	Doyle Alexander	.08
299	Nick Esasky	.08
300	Mark McGwire	.75
301	Darryl Hamilton (R)	.20
302	Dave Smith	.08
303	Rick Sutcliffe	.08
304	Dave Stapleton	.10
305	Alan Ashby	.08
306	Pedro Guererro	.12
307	Ron Guidry	.08
308	Steve Farr	.08
309	Curt Ford	.08
310	Claudell Washington	.08
311	Tom Prince	.08
312	Chad Kreuter (R)	.15
313	Ken Oberkfell	.08
314	Jerry Browne	.08
315	R.J. Reynolds	.08
316	Scott Bankhead	.08
317	Milt Thompson	.08
318	Mario Diaz	.08
319	Bruce Ruffin	.08
320	Dave Valle	.08
321	Gary Varsho (R)	.25
321	Gary Varsho (error)	2.00
322	Paul Mirabella	.08
323	Chuck Jackson	.08
324	Drew Hall	.08
325	Don August	.08
326	Israel Sanchez (R)	.15
327	Denny Walling	.08
328	Joel Skinner	.08
329	Danny Tartabull	.12
330	Tony Pena	.08
331	Jim Sundberg	.08
332	Jeff Robinson	.08
333	Odibbe McDowell	.08
334	Jose Lind	.08
335	Paul Kilgus	.08
336	Juan Samuel	.08
337	Mike Campbell	.10
338	Mike Maddux	.08
339	Darnell Coles	.08
340	Bob Dernier	.08
341	Rafael Ramirez	.08
342	Scott Sanderson	.08
343	B.J. Surhoff	.08
344	Billy Hatcher	.08
345	Pat Perry	.08
346	Jack Clark	.12
347	Gary Thurman	.08
348	Timmy Jones (R)	.15
349	Dave Winfield	.15
350	Frank White	.08
351	Dave Collins	.08
352	Jack Morris	.08
353	Eric Plunk	.08
354	Leon Durham	.08
355	Ivan DeJesus	.15
356	Brian Holman (R)	.30

NO.	PLAYER	MINT
357	Dale Murphy (cor.)	.75
357	Dale Murphy (err.) reversed negative	80.00
358	Mark Portugal	.08
359	Andy McGaffigan	.08
360	Tom Glavine	.08
361	Keith Moreland	.08
362	Todd Stottlemyre	.12
363	Dave Leiper	.08
364	Cecil Fielder	.75
365	Carmelo Martinez	.08
366	Dwight Evans	.08
367	Kevin McReynolds	.15
368	Rich Gedman	.08
369	Len Dykstra	.08
370	Jody Reed	.10
371	Jose Canseco	1.50
372	Rob Murphy	.08
373	Mike Henneman	.08
374	Walt Weiss	.50
375	Bob Dibble (R)	.60
376	Kirby Puckett	.50
377	Denny Martinez	.08
378	Ron Gant	1.00
379	Brian Harper	.08
380	Nelson Santovenia (R)	.20
381	Lloyd Moseby	.10
382	Lance McCullers	.08
383	Dave Stieb	.10
384	Tony Gwynn	.30
385	Mike Flanagan	.08
386	Bob Ojeda	.08
387	Bruce Hurst	.08
388	Dave Magadan	.15
389	Wade Boggs	.60
390	Gary Carter	.15
391	Frank Tanana	.08
392	Curt Young	.08
393	Jeff Treadway	.15
394	Darrell Evans	.08
395	Glenn Hubbard	.08
396	Chuck Cary	.08
397	Frank Viola	.12
398	Jeff Parrett	.10
399	Terry Blocker (R)	.15
400	Dan Gladden	.08
401	Louis Meadows (R)	.15
402	Tim Raines	.15
403	Joey Meyer	.10
404	Larry Anderson	.08
405	Rex Hudler	.08
406	Mike Schmidt	.75
407	John Franco	.08
408	Brady Anderson (R)	.30
409	Don Carmen	.08
410	Eric Davis	.30
411	Bob Stanley	.08
412	Pete Smith	.12
413	Jim Rice	.12
414	Bruce Sutter	.10
415	Oil Can Boyd	.08
416	Ruben Sierra	.35
417	Mike LaValiere	.08
418	Steve Buechele	.08
419	Gary Redus	.08
420	Scott Fletcher	.08
421	Dale Sveum	.08
422	Bob Knepper	.08
423	Luis Rivera	.08
424	Ted Higuera	.08
425	Kevin Bass	.08
426	Ken Gerhart	.08
427	Shane Rawley	.08
428	Paul O'Neill	.12
429	Joe Orsulak	.08
430	Jack Gutierrez	.08
431	Gerald Perry	.08
432	Mike Greenwell	.40
433	Jerry Royster	.08
434	Ellis Burks	.40
435	Ed Olwine	.08
436	Dave Rucker	.08
437	Charlie Hough	.08
438	Bob Walk	.08
439	Bob Brower	.08
440	Bobby Bonds	.35
441	Tom Foley	.08

NO.	PLAYER	MINT
442	Rob Deer	.08
443	Glenn Davis	.15
444	Dave Martinez	.08
445	Bill Wegman	.08
446	Loyd McClendon	.12
447	Dave Schmidt	.08
448	Darren Daulton	.08
449	Frank Williams	.08
450	Dan Aase	.08
451	Lou Whitaker	.08
452	Goose Gossage	.08
453	Ed Whitson	.08
454	Jim Walewander	.08
455	Damon Berryhill	.20
456	Tim Burke	.08
457	Barry Jones	.08
458	Joel Youngblood	.08
459	Floyd Youmans	.08
460	Mark Salas	.08
461	Jeff Russell	.08
462	Darrell Miller	.08
463	Jeff Kunkel	.08
464	Sherman Corbett	.10
465	Curtis Wilkerson	.08
466	Bud Black	.08
467	Cal Ripken Jr.	.15
468	John Farrell	.08
469	Terry Kennedy	.08
470	Tom Candiotti	.08
471	Roberto Alomar	.40
472	Jeff Robinson	.08
473	Vance Law	.08
474	Randy Ready	.08
475	Walt Terrell	.08
476	Kelly Downs	.08
477	Johnny Paredes	.10
478	Shawn Hillegas	.08
479	Bob Brenly	.08
480	Otis Nixon	.08
481	Johnny Ray	.08
482	Geno Petralli	.08
483	Stu Cliburn	.08
484	Pete Incaviglia	.12
485	Bria Downing	.08
486	Jeff Stone	.08
487	Carmen Castillo	.08
488	Tom Niedenfeuer	.08
489	Jay Bell	.10
490	Rick Schu	.10
491	Jeff Pico (R)	.15
492	Mark Parent (R)	.15
493	Eric King	.08
494	Al Nipper	.08
495	Andy Hawkins	.08
496	Daryl Boston	.08
497	Ernie Riles	.08
498	Pascual Perez	.08
499	Bill Long	.08
500	Kirt Manwaring	.08
501	Chuck Crim	.08
502	Candy Maldonado	.08
503	Dennis Lamp	.08
504	Glenn Braggs	.08
505	Joe Price	.08
506	Ken Williams	.08
507	Bill Pecota	.08
508	Rey Quinones	.08
509	Jeff Bittiger (R)	.15
510	Kevin Seitzer	.15
511	Steve Bedrosian	.08
512	Todd Worrell	.10
513	Chris James	.08
514	Jose Oquendo	.08
515	David Palmer	.08
516	John Smiley	.08
517	Dave Clark	.08
518	Mike Dunne	.08
519	Ron Washington	.08
520	Bob Kipper	.08
521	Lee Smith	.08
522	Juan Castillo	.08
523	Don Robinson	.08
524	Kevin Romine	.08
525	Paul Molitor	.12
526	Mark Langston	.10
527	Donnie Hill	.08
528	Larry Owen	.08

NO.	PLAYER	MINT
529	Jerry Reed	.08
530	Jack McDowell	.25
531	Greg Mathews	.08
532	John Russell	.08
533	Dan Quisenberry	.08
534	Greg Gross	.08
535	Danny Cox	.08
536	Terry Francona	.08
537	Andy Van Slyke	.12
538	Mel Hall	.08
539	Jim Gott	.08
540	Doug Jones	.08
541	Craig Lefferts	.08
542	Mike Boddicker	.08
543	Greg Brock	.08
544	Atlee Hammaker	.08
545	Tom Bolton	.08
546	Mike MacFarlane (R)	.15
547	Rich Rentiera	.15
548	John Davis	.08
549	Floyd Bannister	.08
550	Mickey Tettleton	.08
551	Duane Ward	.08
552	Dan Petry	.08
553	Mickey Tettleton	.08
554	Rick Leach	.08
555	Mike Witt	.08
556	Sid Bream	.08
557	Bobby Witt	.08
558	Tommy Herr	.08
559	Randy Milligan	.40
560	Jose Cecena	.12
561	Mackey Sasser	.20
562	Carney Lansford	.08
563	Rick Aguilera	.08
564	Ron Hassey	.08
565	Dwight Gooden	.40
566	Paul Assenmacher	.08
567	Neil Allen	.08
568	Jim Morrison	.08
569	Mike Pagliarulo	.10
570	Tedd Simmons	.08
571	Mark Thurmond	.08
572	Fred McGriff	.25
573	Wally Joyner	.20
574	Jose Bautista (R)	.15
575	Kelly Gruber	.20
576	Cecilo Guante	.08
577	Mark Davidson	.08
578	Bobby Bonilla	.30
579	Mike Stanley	.08
580	Gene Larkin	.08
581	Stan Javier	.08
582	Howard Johnson	.20
583	Mike Gallego	.30
583	M. Gallego (error)	1.50
584	David Cone	.20
585	Doug Jennings (R)	.20
586	Charlie Hudson	.25
587	Dion James	.08
588	Al Leiter	.10
589	Charlie Puleo	.08
590	Roberto Kelly	.40
591	Thad Bosley	.08
592	Pete Stanicek	.08
593	Pat Borders (R)	.35
594	Bryan Harvey (R)	.20
595	Jeff Ballard	.15
596	Jeff Reardon	.08
597	Doug Drabek	.08
598	Edwin Correa	.08
599	Keith Atherton	.08
600	Dave LaPoint	.08
601	Don Baylor	.08
602	Tom Pagnozzi	.08
603	Tim Flannery	.08
604	Gene Walter	.08
605	Dave Parker	.12
606	Mike Diaz	.08
607	Chris Gwynn	.12
608	Odell Jones	.08
609	Carlton Fisk	.12
610	Jay Howell	.08
611	Tim Crews	.08
612	Keith Hernandez	.15
613	Willie Fraser	.08
614	Jim Eppard	.08

NO.	PLAYER	MINT
615	Jeff Hamilton	.08
616	Kurt Stilwell	.08
617	Tom Browning	.08
618	Jeff Montgomery	.25
619	Jose Rijo	.08
620	Jamie Quirk	.08
621	Willie McGee	.15
622	Mark Grant	.08
623	Bill Swift	.08
624	Orlando Mercado	.08
625	John Costello	.15
626	Jose Gonzalez	.08
627	Bill Schroeder	.30
627	B. Schroeder (error)	1.50
628	Fred Manrique	.12
628	F. Manrique (error)	.50
629	Ricky Horton	.08
630	Dan Plesac	.08
631	Alfredo Griffin	.08
632	Chuck Finley	.15
633	Kirk Gibson	.20
634	Randy Myers	.08
635	Greg Minton	.08

NO.	PLAYER	MINT
636	H. Winningham (err.)	.32
636	H. Winningham (cor.)	.12
637	Charlie Leibrandt	.08
638	Tim Birtsas	.08
639	Bill Buckner	.08
640	Danny Jackson	.10
641	Greg Booker	.08
642	Jim Presley	.08
643	Gene Nelson	.08
644	Rod Booker	.08
645	Dennis Rasmussen	.08
646	Juan Nieves	.08
647	Bobby Thigpen	.08
648	Tim Belcher	.25
649	Mike Young	.08
650	Ivan Calderon	.08
651	Oswaldo Peraza (R)	.15
652	Pat Sheridan (cor.)	.20
652	Pat Sheridan (err.)	25.00
653	Mike Morgan	.08
654	Mike Heath	.08
655	Jay Tibbs	.08

NO.	PLAYER	MINT
656	Fernando Valenzuela	.15
657	Lee Mazzilli	.10
658	AL Cy Young	.12
659	AL MVP	.50
660	AL Rookie of the Year	.15
661	NL Cy Young	.15
662	NL MVP	.15
663	NL Rookie of the Year	.20
664	ALCS MVP	.15
665	NLCS MVP	.20
666	World Series Moment	.15
667	World Series MVP	.20
668	Angels Checklist	.15
669	Astros Checklist	.50
670	Athletics Checklist	.50
671	Blue Jays Checklist	.08
672	Braves Checklist	.15
673	Brewers Checklist	.08
674	Cardinals Checklist	.08
675	Cubs Checklist	.15
676	Dodgers Checklist	.15
677	Expos Checklist	.08
678	Giants Checklist	.40

NO.	PLAYER	MINT
679	Indians Checklist	.08
680	Mariners Checklist	.08
681	Mets Checklist	.50
682	Orioles Checklist	.15
683	Padres Checklist	.15
684	Phillies Checklist	.30
685	Pirates Checklist	.08
686	Rangers Checklist	.15
687	Red Sox Checklist	.25
688	Reds Checklist	.25
689	Royals Checklist	.20
690	Tigers Checklist	.12
691	Twins Checklist	.08
692	White Sox Checklist	.08
693	Yankees Checklist	.40
694	Checklist 1-100	.08
695	Checklist 101-200	.08
696	Checklist 201-300	.08
697	Checklist 301-400	.08
698	Checklist 401-500	.08
699	Checklist 501-600	.08
700	Checklist 601-700	.08

1989 Upper Deck Extended.... Complete Set of 100 Cards—Value $25.00

This set updates the main 1989 card set with players who had changed teams during the season, and rookies. The set was packaged in a printed box and also included with the factory sets. Features the first Upper Deck card of Gregg Olson, Tom Gordon, Todd Zeile, Jim Abbott and Jerome Walton.

Gregg Olson

Todd Zeile

Dwight Smith

Jim Abbott

Tom Gordon

NO.	PLAYER	MINT
701	Checklist 701-800	.15
702	Jesse Barfield	.20
703	Walt Terrell	.15
704	Dickie Thon	.15
705	Al Leiter	.15
706	Dave LaPoint	.15
707	Charlie Hayes	.30
708	Andy Hawkins	.15
709	Mickey Hatcher	.15
710	Lance McCullers	.15
711	Ron Kittle	.15
712	Bert Blyleven	.20
713	Rick Dempsey	.15
714	Ken Williams	.15
715	Steve Rosenberg	.25
716	Joe Skalski	.15
717	Spike Owen	.15
718	Todd Burns	.25
719	Kevin Gross	.15
720	Tommy Herr	.15
721	Rob Ducey	.20
722	Gary Green	.20
723	Gregg Olson	2.00
724	Greg W. Harris	.25
725	Craig Worthinton	.40

NO.	PLAYER	MINT
726	Tom Howard	.25
727	Dale Mohorcic	.15
728	Rich Yett	.15
729	Mel Hall	.15
730	Floyd Youmans	.20
731	Lonnie Smith	.15
732	Wally Backman	.15
733	Trevor Wilson	.30
734	Jose Alvarez	.20
735	Bob Milacki	.15
736	Tom Gordon	2.00
737	Wally Whitehurst	.30
738	Mike Aldrete	.15
739	Keith Miller	.20
740	Randy Milligan	.20
741	Jeff Parrett	.15
742	Steve Finley	.30
743	Junior Felix	1.50
744	Pate Harnisch	.15
745	Bill Spiers	.30
746	Hensley Meulens	1.50
747	Juan Bell	.15
748	Steve Sax	.20
749	Phil Bradley	.15
750	Rey Quinones	.15

NO.	PLAYER	MINT
751	Tommy Gregg	.15
752	Kevin Brown	.50
753	Derek Lilliquist	.25
754	Todd Zeile	4.00
755	Jim Abbott	4.00
756	Ozzie Canseco	1.00
757	Nick Esasky	.25
758	Mike Moore	.15
759	Rob Murphy	.15
760	Rick Mahler	.15
761	Fred Lynn	.15
762	Kevin Blankenship	.20
763	Eddie Murray	.25
764	Steve Searcy	.20
765	Jerome Walton	4.00
766	Erik Hanson	.75
767	Bob Boone	.15
768	Edgar Martinez	.75
769	Jose DeJesus	.15
770	Greg Briley	1.00
771	Steve Peters	.25
772	Rafael Palmeiro	.20
773	Jack Clark	.25
774	Nolan Ryan	3.00
775	Lance Parrish	.15

NO.	PLAYER	MINT
776	Joe Girardi	.40
777	Willie Randolph	.20
778	Mitch Williams	.15
779	Dennis Cook	.35
780	Dwight Smith	1.50
781	Lenny Harris	.50
782	Torey Lovullo	.20
783	Norm Charlton	.35
784	Chris Brown	.15
785	Todd Benzinger	.15
786	Shane Rawley	.15
787	Omar Vizquel	.30
788	LaVel Freeman	.30
789	Jeffrey Leonard	.20
790	Eddie Williams	.15
791	Jamie Moyer	.15
792	Bruce Hurst	.15
793	Julio Franco	.20
794	Claudell Washington	.15
795	Jody Davis	.15
796	Odibbe McDowell	.15
797	Paul Kilgus	.15
798	Tracy Jones	.15
799	Steve Wilson	.20
800	Pete O'Brien	.15

1990 Upper Deck.... Complete Set of 700 Cards—Value $40.00

Features the rookie cards of Greg Vaughn, Eric Anthony, Ben McDonald, John Olerud and Todd Zeile.

Jose Offerman

Juan Gonzalez

John Olerud

Kevin Maas

Ben McDonald

NO.	PLAYER	MINT
1	Star Rookie checklist	.10
2	Randy Nosek (R)	.15
3	Tom Dress (R)	.25
4	Curt Young	.08
5	Angels checklist	.08
6	Luis Salazar	.08
7	Phillies checklist	.08
8	Jose Bautista	.08
9	Marquis Grissom (R)	.60
10	Dodgers checklist	.08
11	Rick Aguilera	.08
12	Padres checklist	.08
13	Deion Sanders	.35
14	Marvell Wynne	.08
15	David West	.10
16	Pirates checklist	.08
17	Sammy Sosa (R)	.60
18	Yankees checklist	.08
19	Jack Howell	.08
20	Special card-Schmidt	.75
21	Robin Ventura	.50
22	Brian Meyer	.15
23	Blaine Beatty (R)	.20
24	Mariners checklist	.60
25	Greg Vaughn	.50
26	Xavier Hernandez (R)	.15
27	Jason Grimsley (R)	.15
28	Eric Anthony (R)	1.00
29	Expos checklist	.08
30	David Wells	.08
31	Hal Morris	.75
32	Royals checklist	.50
33	Kelly Mann (R)	.15
34	Special card-Ryan	1.00
35	Scott Service	.15
36	Athletics checklist	.30
37	Tino Martinez (R)	1.25
38	Chili Davis	.08
39	Scott Sanderson	.08
40	Giants checklist	.20
41	Tigers checklist	.08
42	Scott Coolbaugh (R)	.25
43	Jose Cano (R)	.25
44	Jose Vizcaino (R)	.25
45	Bob Hamelin (R)	.50
46	Jose Offerman (R)	1.25
47	Kevin Blankenship	.12
48	Twins checklist	.25
49	Tommy Greene (R)	.35
50	Special card-Clark	.50
51	Rob Nelson	.08
52	Chris Hammond (R)	.30
53	Indians checklist	.08
54	Ben McDonald (R)	3.00
54	B. McDonald (error)	25.00
55	Andy Benes	.40
56	John Olerud (R)	3.00
57	Red Sox checklist	.15
58	Tony Armas	.08
59	George Canale (R)	.15
60	Orioles CL (error)	3.00
60	Orioles CL (correct)	.15
61	Mike Stanton (R)	.15
62	Mets checklist	.15
63	Kent Mercker (R)	.30
64	Francisco Cabrera	.25
65	Steve Avery	.60
66	Jose Canseco	.75

NO.	PLAYER	MINT
67	Matt Merullo	.15
68	Cardinals checklist	.08
69	Ron Karkovice	.08
70	Kevin Mass (R)	3.50
71	Dennis Cook	.12
72	Juan Gonzalez (R)	2.50
73	Cubs checklist	.08
74	Dean Palmer (R)	.35
75	Special card-Jackson	1.00
76	Rob Richie	.15
77	Bobby Rose (R)	.30
78	Brian DuBois (R)	.15
79	White Sox checklist	.08
80	Gene Nelson	.08
81	Bob McClure	.08
82	Rangers checklist	.08
83	Greg Minton	.08
84	Braves checklist	.08
85	Willie Fraser	.08
86	Neal Heaton	.08
87	Kevin Tapani (R)	.40
88	Astros checklist	.08
89	Jim Gott (correct)	.15
89	Jim Gott (error)	6.00
90	Lance Johnson	.12
91	Brewers checklist	.15
92	Jeff Parrett	.08
93	Julio Machado (R)	.15
94	Ron Jones	.08
95	Blue Jays checklist	.08
96	Jerry Reuss	.08
97	Brian Fisher	.08
98	Kevin Ritz (R)	.15
99	Reds checklist	.08
100	Checklist 1-100	.08
101	Gerald Perry	.08
102	Kevin Appier	.40
103	Julio Franco	.10
104	Craig Biggio	.10
105	Bo Jackson	1.00
106	Junior Felix	.40
107	Mike Markey	.35
108	Fred McGriff	.15
109	Rick Sutcliffe	.08
110	Pete O'Brien	.10
111	Kelly Gruber	.20
112	Pat Borders	.08
113	Dwight Evans	.12
114	Dwight Gooden	.30
115	Kevin Batiste (R)	.20
116	Eric Davis	.25
117	Kevin Mitchell	.25
118	Ron Oester	.08
119	Brett Butler	.08
120	Danny Jackson	.12
121	Tommy Gregg	.08
122	Ken Caminiti	.08
123	Kevin Brown	.15
124	George Brett	.20
125	Mike Scott	.12
126	Cory Snyder	.10
127	George Bell	.10
128	Mark Grace	.30
129	Devon White	.10
130	Tony Fernandez	.10
131	Don Aase	.08
132	Rance Mulliniks	.08

NO.	PLAYER	MINT
133	Marty Barrett	.08
134	Nelson Liriano	.08
135	Mark Carreon	.08
136	Candy Maldonado	.08
137	Tim Birtsas	.08
138	Tom Brookens	.08
139	John Franco	.10
140	Mike LaCoss	.08
141	Jeff Treadway	.08
142	Pat Tabler	.08
143	Darrell Evans	.08
144	Rafael Ramirez	.08
145	Odibbe McDowell	.08
146	Brian Downing	.08
147	Curtis Wilkerson	.08
148	Ernie Whitt	.08
149	Bill Schroeder	.08
150	Domingo Ramos	.08
151	Rick Honeycutt	.08
152	Don Slaught	.08
153	Mitch Webster	.10
154	Tony Phillips	.08
155	Paul Kilgus	.08
156	Ken Griffey, Jr.	3.00
157	Gary Sheffield	.30
158	Wally Backman	.08
159	B.J. Surhoff	.08
160	Louie Meadows	.08
161	Paul O'Neill	.08
162	Jeff McKnight (R)	.20
163	Alvaro Espinoza	.25
164	Scott Scudder	.15
165	Jeff Reed	.08
166	Gregg Jefferies	.50
167	Barry Larkin	.15
168	Gary Carter	.15
169	Robby Thompson	.10
170	Rolando Roomes	.10
171	Mark McGwire	.30
172	Steve Sax	.15
173	Mark Williamson	.08
174	Mitch Williams	.08
175	Brian Holton	.08
176	Rob Deer	.08
177	Tim Raines	.15
178	Mike Felder	.08
179	Harold Reynolds	.08
180	Terry Francona	.08
181	Chris Sabo	.15
182	Darryl Strawberry	.35
183	Willie Randolph	.15
184	Billy Ripken	.10
185	Mackey Sasser	.08
186	Todd Benzinger	.08
187	Kevin Elster	.08
188	Jose Uribe	.08
189	Tom Browning	.08
190	Keith Miller	.08
191	Don Mattingly	.50
192	Dave Parker	.15
193	Roberto Kelly	.12
194	Phil Bradley	.08
195	Ron Hassey	.08
196	Gerald Young	.08
197	Hubie Brooks	.08
198	Bill Doran	.08
199	Al Newman	.08

NO.	PLAYER	MINT
200	Checklist 101-200	.08
201	Terry Puhl	.08
202	Frank DiPino	.08
203	Jim Clancy	.08
204	Bob Ojeda	.08
205	Alex Trevino	.08
206	Dave Henderson	.10
207	Henry Cotto	.08
208	Rafael Belliard	.08
209	Stan Javier	.08
210	Jerry Reed	.08
211	Doug Dascenzo	.08
212	Andres Thomas	.08
213	Greg Maddux	.10
214	Mike Schooler	.10
215	Lonnie Smith	.08
216	Jose Rijo	.08
217	Greg Gagne	.08
218	Jim Gantner	.08
219	Allan Anderson	.08
220	Rick Mahler	.08
221	Jim Deshaies	.08
222	Keith Hernandez	.12
223	Vince Colman	.15
224	David Cone	.10
225	Ozzie Smith	.12
226	Matt Nokes	.10
227	Barry Bonds	.30
228	Felix Jose	.12
229	Dennis Powell	.08
230	Mike Gallego	.08
231	Shawon Dunston	.10
232	Ron Gant	.20
233	Omar Vizquel	.10
234	Derek Lilliquist	.12
235	Erik Hanson	.20
236	Kirby Puckett	.35
237	Bill Spiers	.15
238	Dan Gladden	.08
239	Bryan Clutterbuck	.08
240	John Moses	.08
241	Ron Darling	.12
242	Joe Magrane	.10
243	Dave Magadan	.10
244	Pedro Guererro	.12
245	Glenn Davis	.12
246	Terry Steinbach	.10
247	Fred Lynn	.10
248	Gary Redus	.08
249	Kenny Williams	.08
250	Sid Bream	.08
251	Bob Welch	.08
252	Bill Buckner	.08
253	Carney Lansford	.08
254	Paul Molitor	.12
255	Jose DeJesus	.08
256	Orel Hershiser	.15
257	Tom Brunansky	.08
258	Mike Davis	.08
259	Jeff Ballard	.08
260	Scott Terry	.08
261	Sid Fernandez	.08
262	Mike Marshall	.08
263	Howard Johnson	.15
264	Kirk Gibson	.12

NO.	PLAYER	MINT
265	Kevin McReynolds	.10
266	Cal Ripken, Jr.	.15
267	Ozzie Guillen	.08
268	Jim Traber	.08
269	Bobby Thigpen	.08
270	Joe Orsulak	.08
271	Bob Boone	.08
272	Dave Stewart	.12
273	Tim Wallach	.08
274	Luis Aquino	.08
275	Mike Moore	.08
276	Tony Pena	.08
277	Eddie Murray	.15
278	Milt Thompson	.08
279	Alejandro Pena	.08
280	Ken Dayley	.08
281	Carmen Castillo	.08
282	Tom Henke	.08
283	Mickey Hatcher	.08
284	Roy Smith	.08
285	Manny Lee	.08
286	Dan Pasqua	.08
287	Larry Sheets	.08
288	Garry Templeton	.08
289	Eddie Williams	.10
290	Brady Anderson	.08
291	Spike Owen	.08
292	Storm Davis	.08
293	Chris Bosio	.08
294	Jim Eisenreich	.08
295	Don August	.10
296	Jeff Hamilton	.08
297	Mickey Tettleton	.08
298	Mike Scioscia	.10
299	Kevin Hickey	.10
300	Checklist 201-300	.08
301	Shawn Abner	.08
302	Kevin Bass	.08
303	Bip Roberts	.08
304	Joe Girardi	.15
305	Danny Darwin	.08
306	Mike Heath	.08
307	Mike MacFarlane	.08
308	Ed Whitson	.08
309	Tracy Jones	.08
310	Scott Fletcher	.08
311	Darnell Coles	.08
312	Mike Brumley	.08
313	Bill Swift	.08
314	Charlie Hough	.08
315	Jim Presley	.08
316	Luis Polonia	.08
317	Mike Morgan	.08
318	Lee Guetterman	.08
319	Jose Oquendo	.08
320	Wayne Tolleson	.08
321	Jody Reed	.08
322	Damon Berryhill	.12
323	Roger Clemens	.25
324	Ryne Sandberg	.25
325	Benito Santiago	.10
326	Bret Saberhagen	.10
327	Lou Whitaker	.08
328	Dave Gallagher	.08
329	Mike Pagliarulo	.08
330	Doyle Alexander	.08
331	Jeffrey Leonard	.08
332	Torey Lovullo	.10
333	Pete Incaviglia	.10
334	Rickey Henderson	.35
335	Rafael Palmeiro	.15
336	Ken Hill	.12
337	Dave Winfield	.15
338	Alfredo Griffin	.08
339	Andy Hawkins	.08
340	Ted Power	.08
341	Steve Wilson	.10
342	Jack Clark	.12
343	Ellis Burks	.20
344	Tony Gwynn	.20
345	Jerome Walton	.60
346	Roberto Alomar	.15
347	Carlos Martinez	.25
348	Chet Lemon	.08

NO.	PLAYER	MINT
349	Willie Wilson	.08
350	Greg Walker	.08
351	Tom Bolton	.08
352	German Gonzalez	.08
353	Harold Baines	.08
354	Mike Greenwell	.20
355	Ruben Sierra	.20
356	Andres Galarraga	.10
357	Andre Dawson	.15
358	Jeff Brantley	.20
359	Mike Bielecki	.08
360	Ken Oberkfell	.08
361	Kurt Stillwell	.08
362	Brian Homan	.08
363	Kevin Seitzer	.12
364	Alvin Davis	.10
365	Tom Gordon	.30
366	Bobby Bonilla	.25
367	Carlton Fisk	.12
368	Steve Carter	.10
369	Joel Skinner	.08
370	John Cangelosi	.08
371	Cecil Espy	.08
372	Gary Wayne	.10
373	Jim Rice	.15
374	Mike Dyer (R)	.15
375	Joe Carter	.15
376	Dwight Smith	.20
377	John Wetteland	.15
378	Ernie Riles	.08
379	Otis Nixon	
380	Vance Law	.15
381	Dave Bergman	.08
382	Frank White	.15
383	Scott Bradley	.12
427	Eric Yelding	.20
385	Gary Pettis	.08
386	Donn Pall	.08
387	John Smiley	.08
388	Tom Candiotti	.10
389	Junior Ortiz	.08
390	Steve Lyons	.08
391	Brian Harper	.08
392	Fred Manrique	.10
393	Lee Smith	.08
394	Jeff Kunkel	.08
395	Claudell Washington	.08
396	John Tudor	.08
397	Terry Kennedy	.08
398	Lloyd McClendon	.08
399	Craig Lefferts	.08
400	Checklist 301-400	.08
401	Keith Moreland	.08
402	Rich Gedman	.08
403	Jeff Robinson	.12
404	Randy Ready	.08
405	Rick Cerone	.08
406	Jeff Blauser	.08
407	Larry Andersen	.08
408	Joe Boever	.08
409	Felix Fermin	.08
410	Glenn Wilson	.08
411	Rex Hudler	.08
412	Mark Grant	.08
413	Dennis Martinez	.08
414	Darrin Jackson	.08
415	Mike Aldrete	.08
416	Roger McDowell	.08
417	Jeff Reardon	.08
418	Darren Daulton	.08
419	Tim Laudner	.08
420	Don Carman	.08
421	Lloyd Moseby	.08
422	Doug Drabek	.08
423	Lenny Harris	.10
424	Jose Lind	.08
425	Dave Johnson	.12
426	Jerry Browne	.12
427	Eric Yelding	.15
428	Brad Komminsk	.08
429	Jody Davis	.08
430	Mariano Duncan	.08
431	Mark Davis	.10
432	Nelson Santovenia	.08

NO.	PLAYER	MINT
433	Bruce Hurst	.08
434	Jeff Huson (R)	.15
435	Chris James	.08
436	Mark Guthrie (R)	.15
437	Charlie Hayes	.10
438	Shane Rawley	.08
439	Dickie Thon	.08
440	Juan Berenguer	.08
441	Kevin Romine	.08
442	Bill Landrum	.08
443	Todd Frohwirth	.08
444	Craig Worthington	.10
445	Fernando Valenzuela	.15
446	Joey Belle	.20
447	Ed Whited (R)	.20
448	Dave Smith	.08
449	Dave Clark	.08
450	Juan Agosta	.08
451	Dave Valle	.08
452	Kent Hrbek	.10
453	Von Hayes	.08
454	Gary Gaetti	.12
455	Greg Briley	.20
456	Glenn Braggs	.08
457	Kirt Manwaring	.08
458	Mel Hall	.08
459	Brook Jacoby	.08
460	Pat Sheridan	.08
461	Rob Murphy	.08
462	Jimmy Key	.08
463	Nick Esasky	.08
464	Rob Ducey	.08
465	Carlos Quintana	.15
466	Larry Walker (R)	.50
467	Todd Worrell	.08
468	Kevin Gross	.08
469	Terry Pendleton	.08
470	Dave Martinez	.08
471	Gene Larkin	.08
472	Len Dykstra	.15
473	Barry Lyons	.08
474	Terry Mulholland	.08
475	Chip Hale (R)	.15
476	Jesse Barfield	.08
477	Dan Plesac	.08
478	Scott Garrelts	.10
479	Dave Righetti	.10
480	Gus Polidor	.08
481	Mookie Wilson	.10
482	Luis Rivera	.08
483	Mike Falangan	.08
484	Dennis "Oil Can" Boyd	.08
485	John Cerutti	.08
486	John Costello	.08
487	Pascual Perez	.08
488	Tommy Herr	.10
489	Tom Foley	.08
490	Curt Ford	.08
491	Steve Lake	.08
492	Tim Teufel	.08
493	Randy Bush	.08
494	Mike Jackson	.08
495	Steve Jeitz	.08
496	Paul Gibson	.08
497	Steve Balboni	.08
498	Bud Black	.08
499	Dale Sveum	.08
500	Checklist 401-500	.08
501	Timmy Jones	.08
502	Mark Portugal	.08
503	Ivan Calderon	.08
504	Rick Rhoden	.08
505	Willie McGee	.15
506	Kirk McCaskill	.10
507	Dave LaPoint	.08
508	Jay Howell	.08
509	Johnny Ray	.08
510	Dave Anderson	.08
511	Chuck Crim	.08
512	Joe Hesketh	.08
513	Dennis Eckersley	.12
514	Greg Brock	.08
515	Tim Burke	.08
516	Frank Tanana	.08

NO.	PLAYER	MINT
517	Jay Bell	.08
518	Guillermo Hernandez	.08
519	Randy Kramer	.08
520	Charles Hudson	.08
521	Jim Corsi	.08
522	Steve Rosenberg	.08
523	Cris Carpeter	.08
524	Matt Winters (R)	.15
525	Melido Perez	.08
526	Chris Gwynn	.12
527	Bert Blyleven	.12
528	Chuck Cary	.08
529	Daryl Boston	.08
530	Dale Mohorcic	.08
531	Geronomi Berroa	.10
532	Edgar Martinez	.12
533	Dale Murphy	.20
534	Jay Buhner	.12
535	John Smoltz	.15
536	Andy Van Slyke	.12
537	Mike Henneman	.08
538	Miguel Garcia	.08
539	Frank Williams	.08
540	R.J. Reynolds	.08
541	Shawn Hillegas	.08
542	Walt Weiss	.12
543	Greg Hibbard (R)	.35
544	Nolan Ryan	1.00
545	Todd Zeile	.75
546	Hensley Meulens	.30
547	Tim Belcher	.08
548	Mike Witt	.10
549	Greg Cadaret	.08
550	Franklin Stubbs	.08
551	Tony Castillo	.08
552	Jeff Robinson	.10
553	Steve Olin (R)	.15
554	Alan Trammell	.10
555	Wade Boggs	.50
556	Will Clark	.60
557	Jeff King	.15
558	Mike Fitzgerald	.08
559	Ken Howell	.08
560	Bob Kipper	.08
561	Scott Bankhead	.08
562	Jeff Innis (error)	2.50
562	Jeff Innis (correct)	.10
563	Randy Johnson	.10
564	Wally Whitehurst	.20
565	Gene Harris	.15
566	Norm Charlton	.30
567	Robin Yount	.30
568	Joe Oliver	.20
569	Mark Parent	.08
570	John Farrell	.10
571	Tom Glavine	.12
572	Rod Nichols	.10
573	Jack Morris	.10
574	Greg Swindell	.10
575	Steve Searcy	.15
576	Ricky Jordan	.15
577	Matt Williams	.30
578	Mike LaValliere	.12
579	Bryn Smith	.08
580	Bruce Ruffin	.08
581	Randy Myers	.12
582	Rick Wrona	.15
583	Juan Samuel	.10
584	Les Lancaster	.08
585	Jeff Musselman	.08
586	Rob Dibble	.12
587	Eric Show	.08
588	Jesse Orosco	.08
589	Herm Winningham	.08
590	Andy Allanson	.08
591	Dion James	.08
592	Carmelo Martinez	.08
593	Luis Quinones	.08
594	Dennis Rasmussen	.08
595	Rich Yett	.08
596	Bob Walk	.08
597	A. McGaffigan (err.)	.50
597	A. McGaffigan (cor.)	.20
598	Billy Hatcher	.08
599	Bob Knepper	.08
600	Checklist 501-600	.08

NO.	PLAYER	MINT
601	Joey Cora	.12
602	Steve Finley	.15
603	Kal Daniels	.10
604	Gregg Olson	.25
605	Dave Stieb	.08
606	Kenny Rogers	.15
607	Zane Smith	.08
608	Bob Geren	.15
609	Chad Kreuter	.08
610	Mike Smithson	.08
611	Jeff Wetherby (R)	.20
612	Gary Mielke (R)	.15
613	Pete Smith	.08
614	Jack Daugherty (R)	.15
615	Lance McCullers	.08
616	Don Robinson	.08
617	Jose Guzman	.08
618	Steve Bedrosian	.08
619	Jamie Moyer	.08
620	Atlee Hammaker	.08
621	Rick Luecken (R)	.15
622	Greg W. Harris	.10
623	Pete Harnisch	.10
624	Jerald Clark	.08
625	Jack McDowell	.10

NO.	PLAYER	MINT
626	Frank Viola	.12
627	Ted Higuera	.08
628	Marty Pevey (R)	.15
629	Bill Wegman	.08
630	Eric Plunk	.08
631	Drew Hall	.08
632	Doug Jones	.08
633	Geno Petralli	.08
634	Jose Alvarez	.08
635	Bob Milacki	.12
636	Bobby Witt	.12
637	Trevor Wilson	.15
638	Jeff Russell	.08
639	Mike Krukow	.08
640	Rick Leach	.08
641	Dave Schmidt	.08
642	Terry Leach	.08
643	Calvin Schiraldi	.08
644	Bob Melvin	.08
645	Jim Abbott	.40
646	Jaime Navarro	.15
647	Mark Langston	.15
648	Juan Nieves	.08
649	Damasco Garcia	.08
650	Charlie O'Brien	.08

NO.	PLAYER	MINT
651	Eric King	.08
652	Mike Boddicker	.08
653	Duane Ward	.08
654	Bob Stanley	.08
655	Sandy Alomar, Jr.	.40
656	Danny Tartabull	.12
657	Rick McCament (R)	.15
658	Charlie Leibrandt	.08
659	Dan Quisenberry	.08
660	Paul Assenmacher	.08
661	Walt Terrell	.08
662	Tim Leary	.08
663	Randy Milligan	.10
664	Bo Diaz	.08
665	Mark Lemke	.08
666	Jose Gonzalez	.08
667	Chuck Finley	.10
668	John Kruk	.08
669	Dick Schofield	.08
670	Tim Crews	.08
671	John Dopson	.08
672	John Orton (R)	.15
673	Eric Hetzel	.08
674	Lance Parrish	.08
675	Ramon Martinez	.75

NO.	PLAYER	MINT
676	Mark Gubicza	.08
677	Greg Litton	.15
678	Greg Mathews	.08
679	Dave Dravecky	.08
680	Steve Farr	.08
681	Miek Devereaux	.08
682	Ken Griffey, Sr.	.08
683	J. Weston (R) (correct)	.15
683	J. Weston (error)	5.00
684	Jack Armstrong	.08
685	Steve Buechele	.08
686	Bryan Harvey	.08
687	Lance Blandenship	.08
688	Dante Bichette	.08
689	Todd Burns	.10
690	Dan Petry	.08
691	Kent Anderson	.10
692	Todd Stottlemyre	.10
693	Wally Joyner	.15
694	Mike Rochford	.10
695	Floyd Bannister	.08
696	Rick Reuschel	.12
697	Jose DeLeon	.08
698	Jeff Montgomery	.10
699	Kelly Downs	.10
700	CL: 601-700 (error)	2.50
700	CL: 601-700 (correct)	.10

1990 Upper Deck Extended. . . . Complete Set of 100 Cards—Value $15.00

This set updates the main 1990 card set with players who had changed teams during the season, and rookies.
Features the first Upper Deck card of Dave Justice.

Alex Cole

Ray Lankford

Nolan Ryan

Delino DeShields

Dave Justice

NO.	PLAYER	MINT
701	Jim Gott	.06
702	"Rookie Threats"	.75
703	Alejandro Pena	.06
704	Willie Randolph	.06
705	Tim Leary	.06
706	Chuck McElroy	.12
707	Gerald Perry	.06
708	Tom Brunansky	.06
709	John Franco	.06
710	Mark Davis	.06
711	Dave Justice	6.00
712	Storm Davis	.05
713	Scott Ruskin	.25
714	Glenn Braggs	.05
715	Kevin Bearse	.15
716	Jose Nunez	.06
717	Tim Layana	.20
718	Greg Myers	.05
719	Pete O'Brien	.05
720	John Candelaria	.06
721	Craig Grebeck	.15
722	Shawn Boskie	.25
723	Jim Leyritz	.30
724	Bill Sampen	.25
725	Scott Radinsky	.30

NO.	PLAYER	MINT
726	Todd Hundley	.35
727	Scott Hemond	.20
728	Lenny Webster	.15
729	Jeff Reardon	.05
730	Mitch Webster	.05
731	Brian Bohanon	.15
732	Rick Parker	.15
733	Terry Shumpert	.20
734	Ryan's No Hitter	15.00
734	Ryans 6th/300	2.00
735	John Burkett	.25
736	Derrick May	1.00
737	Carlos Baerga	.50
738	Greg Smith	.15
739	Scott Sanderson	.05
740	Joe Kraemer	.10
741	Hector Villanueva	.25
742	Mike Fetters	.15
743	Mark Gardner	.20
744	Matt Nokes	.05
745	Dave Winfield	.15
746	Delino DeShields	1.00
747	Dann Howitt	.20
748	Tony Pena	.05
749	Oil Can Boyd	.05
750	Mike Benjamin	.25

NO.	PLAYER	MINT
751	Alex Cole	1.00
752	Eric Gunderson	.15
753	Howard Farmer	.20
754	Joe Carter	.15
755	Ray Lankford	1.50
756	Sandy Alomar Jr.	.50
757	Alex Sanchez	.05
758	Nick Esasky	.05
759	Stan Belinda	.20
760	Jim Presley	.05
761	Gary DiSarcina	.15
762	Wayne Edwards	.25
763	Pat Combs	.15
764	Mickey Pina	.35
765	Wilson Alvarez	.40
766	Dave Parker	.10
767	Mike Blowers	.25
768	Tony Phillips	.05
769	Pascual Perez	.05
770	Gary Pettis	.05
771	Fred Lynn	.05
772	Mel Rojas	.20
773	David Segui	.50
774	Cary Carter	.10
775	Rafael Valdez	.12

NO.	PLAYER	MINT
776	Glenallen Hill	.15
777	Keith Hernandez	.08
778	Billy Hatcher	.05
779	Marty Clary	.05
780	Candy Maldonado	.05
781	Mike Marshall	.05
782	Billy Jo Robidoux	.05
783	Mark Langston	.10
784	Paul Sorrento	.12
785	Dave Hollins	.30
786	Cecil Fielder	.75
787	Matt Young	.06
788	Jeff Huson	.06
789	Lloyd Moseby	.06
790	Ron Kittle	.06
791	Hubie Brooks	.06
792	Craig Lefferts	.06
793	Kevin Bass	.06
794	Bryn Smith	.06
795	Juan Samuel	.06
796	Sam Horn	.08
797	Randy Myers	.08
798	Chris James	.06
799	Bill Gullickson	.06
800	Checklist 701-800	

1991 Upper Deck. . . . Complete Set of of 700 Cards—Value $35.00

A new subset is Top Prospects (26 cards). 2,500 signed Baseball Heroes Ryan cards will be randomly sorted into foil packs. As in past years, a hologram to deter counterfeiting appears on the reverse side.

NO.	PLAYER	MINT
	No. 1 to 27—	
	Star Rookies	
1	Star Rookie Checklist	.05
2	Phil Plantier (R)	.50
3	D.J. Dozier	.35
4	Dave Hansen	.35
5	Maurice Vaughn	.75
6	Leo Gomez	.50
7	Scott Aldred	.15
8	Scott Chiamparino	.40
9	Lance Dickson (R)	.25
10	Sean Berry (R)	.25
11	Bernie Williams	.25
12	Brian Barnes (R)	.15
13	Narciso Elvira (R)	.15
14	Mike Gardiner (R)	.15
15	Greg Colbrunn (R)	.15
16	Bernard Gilkey	.35
17	Mark Lewis	.25
18	Mickey Morandini	.20
19	Charles Nagy	.15
20	Geronimo Pena	.15
21	Henry Rodriguez (R)	.60
22	Scott Copper	.15
23	Andujar Cedeno (R)	.50
24	Eric Karros (R)	.50
25	Steve Decker (R)	.35
26	Kevin Belcher (R)	.15
27	Jeff Conine	.75
28	Athletics Checklist	.15
29	White Sox Checklist	.07
30	Rangers Checklist	.07
31	Angels Checklist	.07
32	Mariners Checklist	.07
33	Royals Checklist	.07
34	Twins Checklist	.07
35	Scott Leius	.10
36	Neal Heaton	.05
37	Terry Lee (R)	.15
38	Gary Redus	.05
39	Barry Jones	.05
40	Chuck Knoblauch	.15
41	Larry Andersen	.05
42	Darryl Hamilton	.05
43	Red Sox Checklist	.12
44	Blue Jays Checklist	.07
45	Tigers Checklist	.07
46	Indians Checklist	.10
47	Orioles Checklist	.07
48	Brewers Checklist	.10
49	Yankees Checklist	.08
	No. 50 to 76—	
	Top Prospects	
50	Top Prospect CL	.08
51	Kyle Abbott	.15
52	Juff Juden	.30
53	Todd Van Poppel (R)	1.50
54	Steve Karsay (R)	.50
55	Chipper Jones (R)	.75
56	Chris Johnson (R)	.15
57	John Ericks	.15
58	Gary Scott (R)	.15
59	Kiki Jones	.50
60	Wilfredo Cordero (R)	.25
61	Royce Clayton	.15
62	Tim Costo (R)	.50
63	Roger Salkeld	.40
64	Brook Fordyce (R)	.15
65	Mike Mussina (R)	.50
66	Dave Staton (R)	.15
67	Mike Lieberthal (R)	.35
68	Kurt Miller (R)	.20
69	Dan Peltier (R)	.25
70	Greg Blosser	.30
71	Reggie Sanders (R)	.30
72	Brent Mayne	.15
73	Rico Brogna	.25
74	Willie Banks	.20
75	Len Brutcher (R)	.15
76	Pat Kelly (R)	.15
77	Reds Checklist	.10
78	Dodgers Checklist	.10
79	Giants Checklist	.07
80	Padres Checklist	.07
81	Astros Checklist	.07
82	Braves Checklist	.07
83	"Fielder's Feat"	.30
84	Orlando Merced (R)	.15
85	Domingo Ramos	.05
86	Tom Bolton	.05
87	Andres Santana	.12
88	John Dopson	.05
89	Kenny Williams	.05
90	Marty Barrett	.05
91	Tom Pagnozzi	.05
92	Carmelo Martinez	.05
93	"Save Master"	.05
94	Pirates Checklist	.10
95	Mets Checklist	.10
96	Expos Checklist	.07
97	Phillies Checklist	.08
98	Cardinals Checklist	.07
99	Cubs Checklist	.10
100	Checklist 1-100	.05
101	Kevin Elster	.05
102	Tom Brookens	.05
103	Mackey Sasser	.05
104	Felix Fermin	.05
105	Kevin McReynolds	.10
106	Dave Stieb	.08
107	Jeffrey Leonard	.05
108	Dave Henderson	.05
109	Sid Bream	.05
110	Henry Cotto	.05
111	Shawon Dunston	.10
112	Mariano Duncan	.05
113	Joe Girardi	.05
114	Billy Hatcher	.05
115	Greg Maddux	.05
116	Jerry Browne	.05
117	Juan Samuel	.05
118	Steve Olin	.05
119	Alfredo Griffin	.05
120	Mitch Webster	.05
121	Joel Skipper	.05
122	Frank Viola	.10
123	Cory Snyder	.05
124	Howard Johnson	.08
125	Carlos Baerga	.25
126	Tony Fernandez	.05
127	Dave Stewart	.15
128	Jay Buhner	.05
129	Mike LaValliere	.05
130	Scott Bradley	.05
131	Tony Phillips	.05
132	Ryne Sandberg	.20
133	Paul O'Neill	.05
134	Mark Grace	.20
135	Chris Sabo	.15
136	Ramon Martinez	.25
137	Brook Jacoby	.05
138	Candy Maldonado	.05
139	Mike Scioscia	.05
140	Chris James	.05
141	Craig Worthington	.05
142	Manny Lee	.05
143	Tim Raines	.10
144	Sandy Alomar Jr.	.20
145	John Olerud	.35
146	Ozzie Canseco	.25
147	Pat Borders	.05
148	Harold Reynolds	.05
149	Tom Henker	.05
150	R.J. Reynolds	.05
151	Mike Gallego	.05
152	Bobby Bonilla	.15
153	Terry Steinbach	.05
154	Barry Bonds	.25
155	Jose Canseco	.50
156	Gregg Jefferies	.20
157	Matt Williams	.15
158	Craig Biggio	.05
159	Daryl Boston	.05
160	Ricky Jordan	.05
161	Stan Belinda	.05
162	Ozzie Smith	.10
163	Tom Brunansky	.08
164	Todd Zeile	.15
165	Mike Greenwell	.15
166	Kal Daniels	.10
167	Kent Hrbek	.12
168	Franklin Stubbs	.05
169	Dick Schofield	.05
170	Junior Ortiz	.05
171	Hector Villanueva	.15
172	Dennis Eckersley	.12
173	Mitch Williams	.05
174	Mark McGwire	.30
175	Fernando Valenzuela	.10
176	Gary Carter	.10
177	Dave Magadan	.08
178	Robby Thompson	.05
179	Bob Ojeda	.05
180	Ken Caminiti	.05
181	Don Slaught	.05
182	Luis Rivera	.05
183	Jay Bell	.05
184	Jody Reed	.05
185	Wally Backman	.05
186	Dave Martinez	.05
187	Luis Polonia	.05
188	Shane Mack	.05
189	Spike Owen	.05
190	Scott Bailes	.05
191	John Russell	.05
192	Walt Weiss	.05
193	Jose Oquendo	.05
194	Carney Lansford	.05
195	Jeff Huson	.05
196	Keith Miller	.05
197	Eric Yelding	.05
198	Ron Darling	.05
199	John Kruk	.05
200	Checklist 101-200	.05
201	John Shelby	.05
202	Bob Geren	.05
203	Lance McCullers	.05
204	Alvaro Espinoza	.05
205	Mark Salas	.05
206	Mike Pagliarulo	.05
207	Jose Uribe	.05
208	Jim DeShales	.05
209	Ron Karkovice	.05
210	Rafael Ramirez	.05
211	Donnie Hill	.05
212	Brian Harper	.05
213	Jack Howell	.05
214	Wes Gardner	.05
215	Tim Burke	.05
216	Doug Jones	.05
217	Hubie Brooks	.05
218	Tom Candiotti	.05
219	Gerald Perry	.05
220	Jose DeLeon	.05
221	Wally Whitehurst	.05
222	Alan Mills	.10
223	Alan Trammell	.10
224	Dwight Gooden	.20
225	Travis Fryman	.60
226	Joe Carter	.10
227	Julio Franco	.05
228	Craig Lefferts	.05
229	Gary Pettis	.05
230	Dennis Rasmussen	.05
231	Brian Downing	.05
232	Carlos Quintana	.10
233	Gary Gaetti	.05
234	Mark Langston	.05
235	Tim Wallach	.05
236	Greg Swindell	.05
237	Eddie Murray	.15
238	Jeff Manto	.05
239	Lenny Harris	.05
240	Jesse Orosco	.05
241	Scott Lusader	.05
242	Sid Fernandez	.05
243	Jim Leyritz	.15
244	Cecil Fielder	.30
245	Darryl Strawberry	.25
246	Frank Thomas	1.25
247	Kevin Mitchell	.20
248	Lance Johnson	.05
249	Rick Reuschel	.05
250	Mark Portugal	.05
251	Derek Lilliquist	.05
252	Brian Holman	.05
253	Rafael Valdez	.05
254	B.J. Surhoff	.05
255	Tony Gwynn	.20
256	Andy Van Slyke	.12

NO.	PLAYER	MINT
257	Todd Stottlemyre	.05
258	Jose Lind	.05
259	Greg Myers	.05
260	Jeff Ballard	.05
261	Bobby Thigpen	.08
262	Jimmy Kremers	.05
263	Robin Ventura	.20
264	John Smoltz	.05
265	Sammy Sosa	.20
266	Gary Sheffield	.15
267	Lenny Dykstra	.10
268	Bill Spiers	.05
269	Charlie Hayes	.05
270	Brett Butler	.05
271	Bip Roberts	.05
272	Rob Deer	.05
273	Fred Lynn	.05
274	Dave Parker	.12
275	Andy Benes	.12
276	Glenallen Hill	.05
277	Steve Howard	.08
278	Doug Drabek	.05
279	Joe Oliver	.05
280	Todd Benzinger	.08
281	Eric King	.05
282	Jim Presley	.05
283	Ken Patterson	.05
284	Jack Daugherty	.05
285	Ivan Calderon	.05
286	Edgar Diaz	.08
287	Kevin Bass	.05
288	Don Carman	.05
289	Greg Brock	.05
290	John Franco	.05
291	Joey Cora	.05
292	Bill Wegman	.05
293	Eric Show	.05
294	Scott Bankhead	.05
295	Garry Templeton	.05
296	Mickey Tettleton	.05
297	Luis Sojo	.05
298	Jose Rijo	.05
299	Dave Johnson	.05
300	Checklist 201-300	.05
301	Mark Grant	.05
302	Pete Harnisch	.05
303	Greg Olson	.15
304	Anthony Telford (R)	.15
305	Lonnie Smith	.05
306	Chris Hoiles	.15
307	Bryn Smith	.05
308	Mike Devereaux	.05
309	Milt Thompson	.05
310	Bob Melvin	.05
311	Luis Salazar	.05
312	Ed Whitson	.05
313	Charlie Hough	.05
314	Dave Clark	.05
315	Eric Gunderson	.05
316	Dan Petry	.05
317	Dante Bichette	.05
318	Mike Heath	.05
319	Damon Berryhill	.05
320	Walt Terrell	.05
321	Scott Fletcher	.05
322	Dan Plesac	.05
323	Jack McDowell	.05
324	Paul Molitor	.12
325	Ozzie Guillen	.05
326	Gregg Olson	.12
327	Pedro Guerrero	.10
328	Bob Milacki	.05
329	John Tudor	.05
330	Steve Finley	.05
331	Jack Clark	.15
332	Jerome Walton	.25
333	Andy Hawkins	.05
334	Derrick May	.30
335	Roberto Alomar	.10
336	Jack Morris	.08
337	Dave Winfield	.15
338	Steve Searcy	.05
339	Chilli Davis	.05
340	Larry Sheets	.05
341	Ted Higuera	.05
342	David Segui	.30
343	Greg Cadaret	.05
344	Robin Yount	.15
345	Nolan Ryan	.25
346	Ray Lankford	.50
347	Cal Ripken Jr.	.15
348	Lee Smith	.05
349	Brady Anderson	.05
350	Frank DiPino	.05
351	Hal Morris	.15
352	Deion Sanders	.15
353	Barry Larkin	.10
354	Don Mattingly	.35
355	Eric Davis	.15
356	Jose Offerman	.35
357	Mel Rojas	.08
358	Rudy Seanez	.10
359	Oil Can Boyd	.05
360	Nelson Liriano	.05
361	Ron Gant	.10
362	Howard Farmer	.10
363	David Justice	1.00
364	Delino DeShields	.20
365	Steve Avery	.20
366	David Cone	.10
367	Lou Whitaker	.05
368	Von Hayes	.05
369	Frank Tanana	.05
370	Tim Teufel	.05
371	Randy Myers	.05
372	Roberto Kelly	.08
373	Jack Armstrong	.05
374	Kelly Gruber	.15
375	Kevin Maas	.75
376	Randy Johnson	.05
377	David West	.05
378	Brent Knackert	.15
379	Rick Honeycutt	.05
380	Kevin Gross	.05
381	Tom Foley	.05
382	Jeff Blauser	.05
383	Scott Ruskin	.10
384	Andres Thomas	.05
385	Dennis Martinez	.05
386	Mike Henneman	.05
387	Felix Jose	.05
388	Alejandro Pena	.05
389	Chet Lemon	.05
390	Craig Wilson	.15
391	Chuck Crim (R)	.05
392	Mel Hall	.05
393	Mark Knudson	.05
394	Norm Charlton	.08
395	Mike Felder	.05
396	Tim Layana	.05
397	Steve Frey	.05
398	Bill Doran	.05
399	Dion James	.05
400	Checklist 301-400	.05
401	Ron Hassey	.05
402	Don Robinson	.05
403	Gene Nelson	.05
404	Terry Kennedy	.05
405	Todd Burns	.05
406	Roger McDowell	.05
407	Bob Kipper	.05
408	Darren Daulton	.05
409	Chuck Cary	.05
410	Bruce Ruffin	.05
411	Juan Berenguer	.05
412	Gary Ward	.05
413	Al Newman	.05
414	Danny Jackson	.05
415	Greg Gagne	.05
416	Tom Herr	.05
417	Jeff Parrett	.05
418	Jeff Reardon	.05
419	Mark Lemke	.05
420	Charlie O'Brien	.05
421	Willie Randolph	.05
422	Steve Bedrosian	.05
423	Mike Moore	.05
424	Jeff Brantley	.05
425	Bob Welch	.05
426	Terry Mulholland	.05
427	Willie Blair	.08
428	Darrin Fletcher	.15
429	Mike Witt	.05
430	Joe Boever	.05
431	Tom Gordon	.10
432	Pedro Munoz (R)	.25
433	Kevin Seitzer	.05
434	Kevin Tapani	.05
435	Bret Saberhagen	.10
436	Ellis Burks	.12
437	Chuck Finley	.05
438	Mike Boddicker	.05
439	Francisco Cabrera	.05
440	Todd Hundley	.10
441	Kelly Downs	.05
442	Dann Howitt	.10
443	Scott Garrelts	.05
444	Rickey Henderson	.35
445	Will Clark	.35
446	Ben McDonald	.35
447	Dale Murphy	.15
448	Dave Righetti	.05
449	Dickie Thon	.05
450	Ted Power	.05
451	Scott Coolbaugh	.05
452	Dwight Smith	.05
453	Pete Incaviglia	.05
454	Andre Dawson	.15
455	Ruben Sierra	.15
456	Andres Galarraga	.05
457	Alvin Davis	.05
458	Tony Castillo	.05
459	Pete O'Brien	.05
460	Charlie Leibrandt	.05
461	Vince Coleman	.12
462	Steve Sax	.05
463	Omar Olivares	.10
464	Oscar Azocar	.25
465	Joe Magrane	.05
466	Karl Rhodes	.12
467	Benito Santiago	.10
468	Joe Klink	.08
469	Sil Campusano	.05
470	Mark Parent	.05
471	Shawn Boskie	.05
472	Kevin Brown	.05
473	Rick Sutcliffe	.05
474	Rafael Palmeiro	.10
475	Mike Harkey	.05
476	Jaime Navarro	.05
477	Marquis Grissom	.15
478	Marty Clary	.05
479	Greg Briley	.05
480	Tom Glavine	.05
481	Lee Guetterman	.05
482	Rex Hudler	.05
483	Dave LaPoint	.05
484	Terry Pendleton	.05
485	Jesse Barfield	.05
486	Jose DeJesus	.05
487	Paul Abbott (R)	.15
488	Ken Howell	.05
489	Greg W. Harris	.05
490	Roy Smith	.05
491	Paul Assenmacher	.05
492	Geno Petralli	.05
493	Steve Wilson	.05
494	Kevin Reimer	.08
495	Bill Long	.05
496	Mike Jackson	.05
497	Oddibe McDowell	.05
498	Bill Swift	.05
499	Jeff Treadway	.05
500	Checklist 401-500	.05
501	Gene Larkin	.05
502	Bob Boone	.05
503	Allan Anderson	.05
504	Luis Aquino	.05
505	Mark Guthrie	.05
506	Joe Orsulak	.05
507	Dana Kiecker	.15
508	Dave Gallagher	.05
509	Greg A. Harris	.05
510	Mark Williamson	.05
511	Casey Candaele	.05
512	Mookie Wilson	.05
513	Dave Smith	.05
514	Chuck Carr	.12
515	Glenn Wilson	.05
516	Mike Fitzgerald	.05
517	Devon White	.05
518	Dave Hollins	.15
519	Mark Eichhorn	.05
520	Otis Nixon	.05
521	Terry Shumpert	.05
522	Scott Erickson	.15
523	Danny Tartabull	.05
524	Orel Hershiser	.10
525	George Brett	.15
526	Greg Vaughn	.15
527	Tim Naehring	.35
528	Curt Schilling	.05
529	Chris Bosio	.05
530	Sam Horn	.05
531	Mike Scott	.05
532	George Bell	.10
533	Eric Anthony	.25
534	Julio Valera	.10
535	Glenn Davis	.12
536	Larry Walker	.08
537	Pat Combs	.05
538	Chris Nabholz	.25
539	Kirk McCaskill	.05
540	Randy Ready	.05
541	Mark Gubicza	.05
542	Rick Aguilera	.05
543	Brian McRae (R)	.75
544	Kirby Puckett	.20
545	Bo Jackson	.50
546	Wade Boggs	.20
547	Tim McIntosh	.05
548	Randy Milligan	.05
549	Dwight Evans	.05
550	Billy Ripken	.05
551	Erik Hanson	.05
552	Lance Parrish	.05
553	Tino Martinez	.30
554	Jim Abbott	.15
555	Ken Griffey, Jr.	1.00
556	Milt Cuyler	.20
557	Mark Leonard (R)	.25
558	Jay Howell	.05
559	Lloyd Moseby	.05
560	Chris Gwynn	.05
561	Mark Whiten	.35
562	Harold Baines	.05
563	Junior Felix	.10
564	Darren Lewis	.50
565	Fred McGriff	.15
566	Kevin Appier	.05
567	Luis Gonzalez (R)	.15
568	Frank White	.05
569	Juan Agosto	.05
570	Mike Macfarlane	.05
571	Bert Blyleven	.05
572	Ken Griffey Sr.	.05
573	Lee Stevens	.25
574	Edgar Martinez	.05
575	Wally Joyner	.12
576	Tim Belcher	.05
577	John Burkett	.05
578	Mike Morgan	.05
579	Paul Gibson	.05
580	Jose Vizcaino	.05
581	Duane Ward	.05
582	Scott Sanderson	.05
583	David Wells	.05
584	Willie McGee	.15
585	John Cerutti	.05
586	Danny Darwin	.05
587	Kurt Stillwell	.05
588	Rich Gedman	.05
589	Mark Davis	.05
590	Bill Gullickson	.05
591	Matt Young	.05
592	Bryan Harvey	.05

NO.	PLAYER	MINT	NO.	PLAYER	MINT	NO.	PLAYER	MINT	NO.	PLAYER	MINT
593	Omar Vizquel	.05	620	Ron Robinson	.05	647	Ken Hill	.05	674	Rafael Novoa (R)	.15
594	Scott Lewis (R)	.15	621	Scott Radinsky	.05	648	Jeff Russell	.05	675	Hensley Muelens	.20
595	Dave Valle	.05	622	Pete Smith	.05	649	Chuck Malone	.05	676	Jeff M. Robinson	.05
596	Tim Crews	.05	623	Melido Perez	.05	650	Steve Buechele	.05	677	"Ground Breaking"	.05
597	Mike Bielecki	.05	624	Jerald Clark	.05	651	Mike Bejamin	.15	678	Johnny Ray	.05
598	Mike Sharperson	.05	625	Carlos Martinez	.05	652	Tony Pena	.05	679	Greg Hibbard	.05
599	Dave Bergman	.05	626	Wes Chamberlain (R)	.40	653	Trevor Wilson	.05	680	Paul Sorrento	.05
600	Checklist 501-600	.05	627	Bobby Witt	.05	654	Alex Cole	.30	681	Mike Marshall	.05
601	Steve Lyons	.05	628	Ken Dayley	.05	655	Roger Clemens	.20	682	Jim Clancy	.05
602	Bruce Hurst	.05	629	John Barfield (R)	.15	656	"The Bashing Years"	.30	683	Rob Murphy	.05
603	Donn Pall	.05	630	Bob Tewksbury	.05	657	Joe Grahe (R)	.15	684	Dave Schmidt	.05
604	Jim Vatcher (R)	.25	631	Glenn Braggs	.05	658	Jim Eisenreich	.05	685	Jeff Gray (R)	.15
605	Dan Pasqua	.05	632	Jim Neidlinger (R)	.25	659	Dan Gladden	.05	686	Mike Hartley	.15
606	Kenny Rogers	.05	633	Tom Browning	.05	660	Steve Farr	.05	687	Jeff King	.05
607	Jeff Schulz (R)	.15	634	Kirk Gibson	.12	661	Bill Sampen	.05	688	Stan Javier	.05
608	Brad Arnsberg	.05	635	Rob Dibble	.05	662	Dave Rohde	.05	689	Bob Walk	.05
609	Willie Wilson	.05	636	"Stolen Base Leaders"	.30	663	Mark Gardner	.05	690	Jim Gott	.05
610	Jamie Moyer	.05	637	Jeff Montgomery	.05	664	Mike Simms (R)	.15	691	Mike LaCoss	.05
611	Ron Oester	.05	638	Mike Schooler	.05	665	Moises Alou	.25	692	John Farrell	.05
612	Dennis Cook	.05	639	Storm Davis	.05	666	Mickey Hatcher	.05	693	Tim Leary	.05
613	Rick Mahler	.05	640	Rich Rodriguez (R)	.15	667	Jimmy Key	.05	694	Mike Walker	.05
614	Bill Landrum	.05	641	Phil Bradley	.05	668	John Wetteland	.05	695	Eric Plunk	.05
615	Scott Scudder	.05	642	Kent Mercker	.15	669	John Smiley	.05	696	Mike Fetters	.05
616	Tom Edens (R)	.15	643	Carlton Fisk	.10	670	Jim Acker	.05	697	Wayne Edwards	.05
617	"1917 Revisited"	.05	644	Mike Bell (R)	.15	671	Pascual Perez	.05	698	Tim Drummond	.05
618	Jim Gantner	.05	645	Alex Fernandez	1.50	672	Reggie Harris	.20	699	Willie Fraser	.05
619	Darrell Akerfelds	.05	646	Juan Gonzalez	.35	673	Matt Nokes	.05	700	Checklist 601-700	.05

RARE & FAMOUS BASEBALL CARDS

1910 Honus Wagner

1933 Goudey Gum

1933 Goudey Gum

1911 Sherry "Magie"

Year	Manufacturer	Player	Value Near Mint
1910	T-206 Tobacco	Honus Wagner (Pitt)	$150,000.00
1910	T-206 Tobacco	Eddie Plank (Phil)	20,000.00
1910	T-206 Tobacco	Ray Demmitt (St. L)	6,500.00
1911	T-206 Tobacco	Sherry "Magie" (misspelled)	9,000.00
1911	T-206 Tobacco	Joy Doyle	15,000.00
1911	T-3 Tobacco	Ty Cobb	6,000.00
1911	T-3 Tobacco	Walter Johnson	3,000.00
1911	T-3 Tobacco	Christy Mathewson	3,000.00
1911	T-205 Tobacco	Ty Cobb	3,500.00
1912	T-207 Tobacco	Duffy Lewis (Boston N.)	6,000.00
1914	Cracker Jack	Ty Cobb	7,000.00
1933	Goudey Gum	Napoleon Lajoie	25,000.00
1933	Goudey Gum	Babe Ruth (4 diff. cards)	5,000.00 each
1933	De Long Gum	Lou Gehrig	3,000.00
1934	Goudey Gum	Lou Gehrig (2 diff. cards)	3,000.00 each
1938	Goudey Gum	Joe DiMaggio (2 diff. cards)	3,000.00 each
1940	Play Ball (Gum, Inc.)	Joe DiMaggio	2,000.00
1941	Play Ball (Gum, Inc.)	Joe DiMaggio	2,400.00
1948	Leaf Gum	Satchel Paige	2,000.00
1951	Topps All-Stars	Jim Konstanty	7,500.00
1951	Topps All-Stars	Robin Roberts	8,000.00
1951	Topps All-Stars	Eddie Stanky	7,500.00
1951	Bowman Gum	Mickey Mantle	5,000.00
1951	Bowman Gum	Willie Mays	1,750.00
1952	Topps	Mickey Mantle	7,000.00
1954	Bowman Gum	Ted Williams	2,500.00
1968	Topps 3-D	Roberto Clemente	2,500.00

1910 Eddie Plank

1934 Goudey Gum

1912 Duffy Lewis

BASEBALL CARDS & SUPPLIES CATALOG & ORDER FORM

GEORGE BRETT   ROD CAREW   RICKEY HENDERSON   BOB CLEMENTE   JOHNNY BENCH   NOLAN RYAN   OUTFIELD   NETTLES   STEVE CARLTON

Enjoy the convenience of shopping by mail from one of America's largest dealers—Hygrade Sports Card Co. You're backed by our guarantee that you must be satisfied with your purchase or return it within 10 days for a re-fund. We sell *genuine*, original Topps, Donruss, Fleer, etc. cards in complete sets and assortments at *big* savings over individual card prices. Most orders shipped within one week by UPS. Select what you need and order today!

New! 1991 Baseball Complete Card Sets...Super Special Offer!

Each card set has its own beautiful design and features all of your favorite players—Bo Jackson, Nolan Ryan, Jose Canseco, Darryl Strawberry, Rickey Henderson . . . and more! You can buy each complete card set at a much lower price than you would pay if you bought the cards indi-vidually. And each card set is shipped in its own storage box.

1991 TOPPS Complete Set 792 Cards

$35.95

1991 DONRUSS Complete Set 772 Cards

FREE BONUS!
Hall of Fame Puzzle

$35.95

1991 FLEER Complete Set 720 Cards

FREE BONUS!
Team Logo Stickers

$35.95

ORDER ALL 3 1991 BASEBALL CARD SETS ABOVE AND SAVE $7.90

Special Price!

- Complete 1991 Set of 792 Topps Baseball Cards
- Complete 1991 Set of 772 Donruss Baseball Cards
- Complete 1991 Set of 720 Fleer Baseball Cards

$99.95

ASSORTMENTS OF "ROOKIE" CARDS

A rookie card is the player's *first* card from the main card set—and usually becomes the most popular and valuable card of his career. All cards are *genuine* originals—no duplicates!

50 Topps Rookies (1975-up) $12.95
100 Topps Rookies (1969-up) $24.95
200 Topps Rookies (1965-up) $49.95

ASSORTMENTS OF "STAR" CARDS

Each assortment saves you money over indi-vidual card prices. Includes: Jose Canseco, Rickey Henderson, Bo Jackson, Nolan Ryan.

50 Topps (1978-up) $14.95
100 Topps (1976-up) $29.95
200 Topps (1973-up) $59.95
50 Donruss, Fleer, Score, U.D. $12.95
100 Donruss, Fleer, Score, U.D. $25.95

HYGRADE SPORTS CARD CO.
5 East 17th Street, New York, N.Y. 10003

Credit Card
Phone Orders
(212) 807-7935